Gleim Publications, Inc., offers five university-level study systems:

Auditing & Systems Exam Questions and Explanations with Test Prep Software
Business Law/Legal Studies Exam Questions and Explanations with Test Prep Software
Federal Tax Exam Questions and Explanations with Test Prep Software
Financial Accounting Exam Questions and Explanations with Test Prep Software
Cost/Managerial Accounting Exam Questions and Explanations with Test Prep Software

The following is a list of Gleim examination review systems:

CIA Review: Part 1, The Internal Audit Activity's Role in Governance, Risk, and Control
CIA Review: Part 2, Conducting the Internal Audit Engagement
CIA Review: Part 3, Business Analysis and Information Technology
CIA Review: Part 4, Business Management Skills
CIA Review: A System for Success

CMA Review: Part 1, Financial Planning, Performance, and Control
CMA Review: Part 2, Financial Decision Making
CMA Review: A System for Success

CPA Review: Financial
CPA Review: Auditing
CPA Review: Business
CPA Review: Regulation
CPA Review: A System for Success

EA Review: Part 1, Individuals
EA Review: Part 2, Businesses
EA Review: Part 3, Representation, Practices, and Procedures
EA Review: A System for Success

An order form is provided at the back of this book or contact us at www.gleim.com or (800) 874-5346.

Visit www.gleim.com for the latest updates and information on all of our products.

REVIEWERS AND CONTRIBUTORS

Garrett Gleim, B.S., CPA (not in public practice), is a graduate of the Wharton School at the University of Pennsylvania and is one of our vice presidents. Mr. Gleim coordinated the production staff, reviewed the manuscript, and provided production assistance throughout the project.

Grady M. Irwin, J.D., is a graduate of the University of Florida College of Law, and he has taught in the University of Florida College of Business. Mr. Irwin provided substantial editorial assistance throughout the project.

Michael Kustanovich, M.A., CPA, Israeli CPA, is a graduate of Ben-Gurion University of the Negev, Israel. He has worked in the audit department of KPMG, Israel, and as a financial accounting lecturer in the department of Economics of Ben-Gurion University of the Negev.

John F. Rebstock, B.S.A., is a graduate of the Fisher School of Accounting at the University of Florida and has passed the CIA and CPA exams. He specializes in ensuring that our answer explanations and Knowledge Transfer Outlines are user-friendly. Mr. Rebstock reviewed portions of the manuscript.

Stewart B. White, B.M., *Cum Laude*, University of Richmond, B.S., Virginia Commonwealth University, has passed the CPA and CISA exams and has worked in the fields of retail management, financial audit, IT audit, COBOL programming, and data warehouse management. Mr. White provided editorial assistance throughout the project.

A PERSONAL THANKS

This manual would not have been possible without the extraordinary effort and dedication of Jacob Brunny, Julie Cutlip, Kate Devine, Eileen Nickl, Teresa Soard, Joanne Strong, and Candace Van Doren, who typed the entire manuscript and all revisions and drafted and laid out the diagrams and illustrations in this book.

The authors appreciate the production and editorial assistance of Melissa Del Valle, Alexander Karnazes, Katherine Larson, Cary Marcous, Shane Rapp, Drew Sheppard, Katie Wassink, and Martha Willis.

The authors also appreciate the critical reading assistance of Brett Babir, Ellen Buhl, Lauren Bull, Reed Daines, and Kristina Schoen.

Finally, we appreciate the encouragement, support, and tolerance of our families throughout this project.

IF YOU HAVE QUESTIONS

Content-specific questions about our materials will be answered most rapidly if they are sent to us via email to accounting@gleim.com. Our team of accounting experts will give your correspondence thorough consideration and a prompt response.

Questions regarding the information in this Introduction (study suggestions, studying plans, exam specifics) should be emailed to personalcounselor@gleim.com.

Questions concerning orders, prices, shipments, or payments should be sent via email to customerservice@gleim.com and will be promptly handled by our competent and courteous customer service staff.

For technical support, you may use our automated technical support service at www.gleim.com/support, email us at support@gleim.com, or call us at (800) 874-5346.

Seventeenth Edition

FINANCIAL ACCOUNTING

Exam Questions and Explanations

by

Irvin N. Gleim, Ph.D., CPA, CIA, CMA, CFM

with the assistance of
Grady M. Irwin, J.D.

ABOUT THE AUTHOR

Irvin N. Gleim is a Professor Emeritus in the Fisher School of Accounting at the University of Florida and is a member of the American Accounting Association, Academy of Legal Studies in Business, American Institute of Certified Public Accountants, Association of Government Accountants, Florida Institute of Certified Public Accountants, The Institute of Internal Auditors, and the Institute of Management Accountants. He has had articles published in the *Journal of Accountancy*, *The Accounting Review*, and *The American Business Law Journal* and is author/coauthor of numerous accounting and aviation books and CPE courses.

Gleim Publications, Inc.
P.O. Box 12848
University Station
Gainesville, Florida 32604
(800) 87-GLEIM or (800) 874-5346
(352) 375-0772
Fax: (352) 375-6940
Internet: www.gleim.com
Email: admin@gleim.com

For updates to the first printing of the seventeenth edition of *Financial Accounting Exam Questions and Explanations*

Go To: www.gleim.com/updates

Or: Email update@gleim.com with **FIN EQE 17-1** in the subject line. You will receive our current update as a reply.

Updates are available until the next edition is published.

ISSN: 1091-451X
ISBN: 978-1-58194-176-0

First Printing: August 2012

ACKNOWLEDGMENTS

Material from Uniform Certified Public Accountant Examination questions and unofficial answers, Copyright © 1972-2008 by the American Institute of Certified Public Accountants, Inc., is reprinted and/or adapted with permission.

The authors also appreciate and thank The Institute of Internal Auditors, Inc., for permission to use The Institute's Certified Internal Auditor Examination questions, Copyright © 1978-1996 by The Institute of Internal Auditors, Inc.

The authors also appreciate and thank the Institute of Certified Management Accountants for permission to use questions from past CMA examinations, Copyright © 1979-1996 by the Institute of Management Accountants.

The authors also acknowledge the Florida State Board of Accountancy and its written professional examination as a source of questions.

The authors appreciate questions contributed by the following individuals: Ken M. Boze, O. Whitfield Broome, Jr., H. Francis Bush, John Cerepak, Robert P. Derstine, James M. Emig, D.L. Flesher, C. Hall, J.O. Hall, Alene G. Helling, Wayne M. Higley, Judith A. Hora, Donald G. Kame, LaVern E. Krueger, Pete Lockett, J.W. Mantooth, Phil McBrayer, E. Milacek, Tim Miller, Alfonso R. Oddo, Ruth R. O'Keefe, T.J. Phillips, Jr., Roderick B. Posey, Karl Putnam, Sally Schultz, C.J. Skender, Edward C. Spede, John B. Sperry, James P. Trebby, and Sankaran Venkateswar. Each question submitted by these individuals can be noted by viewing the question source, which appears in the first line of its answer explanation in the column to the right of the question.

TABLE OF CONTENTS

PREFACE FOR ACCOUNTING STUDENTS

The purpose of this study manual is to help you understand financial accounting principles and procedures and their applications. In turn, these skills will enable you to perform better on your undergraduate examinations, as well as look ahead to (and prepare for) professional examinations.

One of the major benefits of this study manual is comprehensive coverage of financial accounting topics. Accordingly, when you use this study manual to help prepare for financial accounting courses and examinations, you are assured of covering virtually all topics that could reasonably be expected to be studied in typical college or university intermediate and advanced financial accounting courses. See Appendix A for a comprehensive list of cross-references.

The question-and-answer format is designed and presented to facilitate effective study. Students should be careful not to misuse this text by referring to the answers, which appear to the immediate right of each question, before independently answering each question. One way to overcome the temptation is to use our EQE Test Prep Software Download, which is packed with features and priced with a student's budget in mind.

The majority of the questions are from past CIA, CMA, and CPA examinations. Although a citation for the source of each question is provided, a substantial number have been modified to accommodate changes in professional pronouncements, to clarify questions, and/or to emphasize a financial accounting concept or its application. In addition, hundreds of publisher-written questions test areas covered in current textbooks but not directly tested on accounting certification examinations. Finally, we are pleased to use questions submitted by accounting professors.

Note that this study manual should not be relied upon to prepare for the professional examinations. You should use review manuals specifically developed for each examination. Gleim *CIA Review*, *CMA Review*, *CPA Review*, and *EA Review* are up-to-date manuals that comprehensively cover all material necessary for successful completion of each examination. Further descriptions of these examinations and our review materials are provided in the Introduction. To obtain any of these materials, order online at www.gleim.com, call us at (800) 874-5346, or use the order form provided at the back of this book.

Thank you for your interest in this book. We deeply appreciate the many letters and suggestions received from accounting students and educators during the past years, as well as from CIA, CMA, and CPA candidates. Please go to www.gleim.com/feedbackFIN to share your suggestions on how we can improve this edition.

Please read the Introduction carefully. It is very short but very important.

Good Luck on Your Exams,

Irvin N. Gleim

August 2012

INTRODUCTION

The format and content of this study manual are innovative in the accounting text market. The purpose is to provide accounting students with a well-organized, comprehensive collection of objective questions covering the topics taught in typical financial accounting undergraduate courses.

The Gleim exam question and explanation books and Test Prep Software really work! You can pretest yourself before class to see if you are strong or weak in the assigned area. You can retest after class to see if you really understand the material. The questions in these books cover **all** topics in your related courses, so you will encounter few questions on your exams for which you will not be well prepared.

The titles and organization of Study Units 1 through 28 are based on the current financial accounting textbooks listed in Appendix A. Appendix A contains the table of contents of each listed book with cross-references to Gleim study units and subunits. If you are using a textbook that is not included in our list or if you have any suggestions on how we can improve these cross-references to make them more relevant/useful, please submit your request/feedback at www.gleim.com/crossreferences/FIN or email them to FINcrossreferences@gleim.com.

OUR USE OF SUBUNITS

Each study unit of this book is divided into subunits to assist your study program. Subunits permit broad and perhaps overwhelming topics to be divided into more manageable study components.

Choosing subunits and arranging questions within them was challenging. Thus, topics and questions may overlap somewhat. The number of questions offers comprehensive coverage but does not present an insurmountable task. We define each subunit narrowly enough to cover a single topic but broadly enough to prevent questions from being repetitious.

SOURCES OF OBJECTIVE QUESTIONS

Past CIA, CMA, and CPA examinations and sample questions are the primary sources of questions included in this study manual.

Gleim Publications will continue to prepare questions (coded in this text as *Publisher, adapted*) based upon the content of financial accounting textbooks, pronouncements, etc. These *Publisher* questions review topics not adequately covered by questions from the other sources. Also, professionals and professors from schools around the country have contributed questions. See page iv for a list of their names.

If you, your professor, or your classmates wish to submit questions, we will consider using them in future editions. Please email questions you develop, complete with answers and explanations, to accounting@gleim.com. Alternatively, you can mail questions to

> Gleim Publications, Inc.
> EQE Question Bank
> P.O. Box 12848, University Station
> Gainesville, FL 32604

Writing and analyzing multiple-choice questions is an excellent way to prepare yourself for your exams. We will make every effort to consider, edit, and use questions you submit. However, we ask that you send us only serious, complete, carefully considered efforts.

IDENTIFICATION OF THE SOURCE OF EACH QUESTION

The source of each question appears in the first line of its answer explanation in the column to the right of the question. Summary of source codes:

CIA	Certified Internal Auditor Examination
CMA	Certified Management Accountant Examination
CPA	Uniform Certified Public Accountant Examination
Publisher	EQE FIN author
Individual's name	Name of professional or professor who contributed the question

UNIQUENESS OF OBJECTIVE QUESTIONS

The major advantage of objective questions is their ability to cover a large number of topics with little time and effort when compared to essay questions and/or computational problems.

A multiple-choice question is actually a series of statements of which all but one are incorrect given the facts of the question. The advantage of multiple-choice questions over true/false questions is that they require more analysis and result in a lower score for those with little or no knowledge. Random guessing on questions with four answer choices results in an expected grade of 25%. Random guessing on a true/false test results in an expected grade of 50%.

Students and professors both like multiple-choice questions. Because they present alternative answers from which only one needs to be selected, students find them relatively easy to answer. Professors like objective questions because they are easy to grade and because much more material can be tested in the same period of time. Most professors will also ask students to complete essay or computational questions.

ANSWER EXPLANATIONS ALONGSIDE THE QUESTIONS

The format of our book presents objective questions and their answer explanations side by side. The answer explanations are to the right of each question. The example below is from the CPA exam.

According to the FASB's conceptual framework, the objective of general-purpose financial reporting is most likely based on

A. Generally accepted accounting principles.

B. Reporting on how well management has discharged its responsibilities.

C. The need for conservatism.

D. The needs of the users of the information.

Answer (D) is correct. *(CPA, adapted)*

REQUIRED: The objective of general-purpose financial reporting.

DISCUSSION: The objective of general-purpose financial reporting is to provide information that is useful to existing and potential investors, lenders, and other creditors in making decisions about providing resources to the entity.

Answer (A) is incorrect. GAAP govern how to account for items in the financial statements. Answer (B) is incorrect. Financial reporting provides information that is helpful, among other things, in evaluating how well management has discharged its responsibilities to make effective and efficient use of entity resources. But it is the basis for general-purpose financial reporting. Answer (C) is incorrect. Conservatism is a constraint on recognition in the statements. It is a response uncertainty.

The format of this study manual is designed to facilitate your study of objective questions, their answers, and the answer explanations. The intent is to save you time and effort by eliminating the need to turn pages back and forth from questions to answers.

Be careful, however. Do not misuse this format by consulting the answers before you have answered the questions. Misuse of the readily available answers will give you a false sense of security and result in poor performance on examinations and decreased benefit from your studies. The best way to use this study manual is to cover the answer explanations with a sheet of paper as you read and answer each question. Alternatively, our EQE Test Prep Software automates this function as one of its many features. As a crucial part of the learning process, you must honestly commit yourself to an answer before looking at the answer explanation. Whether you are right or wrong, your memory of the correct answer will be reinforced by this process.

STUDY SUGGESTIONS

The emphasis in the next few pages is on developing strategies, approaches, and procedures to help you learn and understand better, in less time.

Using Tests as Study/Learning Devices

Tests, especially quizzes and midterms, provide feedback on your study and test-taking procedures. It is extremely important to diagnose your mistakes on quizzes and tests at the beginning of the term so you can take corrective action on subsequent tests, including your final exam.

When your test is returned, determine how you did relative to the rest of your class and your professor's grading standards. Next, analyze your relative performance between types of questions (essay vs. multiple-choice) and types of subject matter (topics or study units). The objective is to identify the areas where you should take corrective action.

Using Objective Questions to Study

Experts on testing continue to favor multiple-choice questions as a valid means of examining various levels of knowledge. Using objective questions to study for undergraduate examinations is an important tool not only for obtaining good grades, but also for long-range preparation for certification and other examinations. The following suggestions will help you study in conjunction with each Gleim *Exam Questions and Explanations* book and EQE Test Prep Software (visit www.gleim.com or see our order form at the back of this book):

1. Locate the study unit that contains questions on the topic you are currently studying. Each *Exam Questions and Explanations* book and EQE Test Prep contains cross-references to the tables of contents of most textbooks.

2. Work through a series of questions, selecting the answers you think are correct.

3. **If you are using the Gleim book, do not consult the answer or answer explanations on the right side of the page until after you have chosen and written down an answer.**

   a. It is crucial that you cover the answer explanations and intellectually commit yourself to an answer. This method will help you understand the concept much better, even if you answered the question incorrectly. EQE Test Prep Software automates this process for you.

4. Study the explanations to each question you answered incorrectly. In addition to learning and understanding the concept tested, analyze **why** you missed the question.

    - Did you misread the question?
    - Did you make a math error?
    - Did you not know the concept tested?

    Studying the important concepts that we provide in our answer explanations will help you understand the principles to the point that you can answer that question (or any other like it) successfully.

5. Identify your weaknesses in answering multiple-choice questions and take corrective action (before you take a test). Prepare a summary analysis of your work on each subunit (topic). With EQE Test Prep Software, simply view your performance analysis information. Some sample column headings could be

Date	Subunit	Time to Complete	Questions Answered	Avg. Time per Question	Questions Correct	Percent Correct

The analysis will show your weaknesses (areas needing more study) and also your strengths (areas of confidence). You can improve your performance on objective questions both by increasing your percentage of correct answers and by decreasing the time spent per question.

Multiple-Choice Question-Answering Technique

You need a personalized control system **(technique)** for answering multiple-choice questions, essay questions, and computational problems. The objective is to obtain complete, correct, and well-presented answers.

The following series of steps is suggested for answering multiple-choice questions. The important point is that you need to devote attention to and develop **the technique that works for you**. Personalize and practice your multiple-choice question-answering technique on questions in this study manual. Begin now, and develop **your** control system.

1. **Budget your time.**

    a. We make this point with emphasis. Just as you would fill up your gas tank prior to reaching empty, so too should you finish your exam before time expires.

    b. Calculate the time allowed for each multiple-choice question after you have allocated time to the other questions (e.g., essays) on the exam. If 20 multiple-choice questions are allocated 40 minutes on your exam, you should spend a little under 2 minutes per question (always budget extra time for transferring answers to answer sheets, interruptions, etc.).

    c. Before beginning a series of multiple-choice questions, write the starting time on the exam near the first question.

    d. As you work through the questions, check your time. Assuming a time allocation of 120 minutes for 60 questions, you are fine if you worked 5 questions in 9 minutes. If you spent 11 minutes on 5 questions, you need to speed up. Remember that your goal is to answer all questions and achieve the maximum score possible.

2. **Answer the items in consecutive order.**

    a. Do **not** agonize over any one item. Stay within your time budget.

    b. Mark any questions you are unsure of and return to them later as time allows.

    c. Never leave a question unanswered if you will not be penalized for incorrect answers. Make your best guess in the time allowed.

3. **For each multiple-choice question,**

    a. **Try to ignore the answer choices.** Do not allow the answer choices to affect your reading of the question.

        1) If four answer choices are presented, three of them are incorrect. These incorrect choices are called **distractors** for good reason. Often, distractors are written to appear correct at first glance until further analysis.

        2) In computational items, distractors are carefully calculated so they are the result of making common mistakes. Be careful, and double-check your computations if time permits.

    b. **Read the question** carefully to determine the precise requirement.

        1) Focusing on what is required enables you to ignore extraneous information and to proceed directly to determining the correct answer. You may wish to underline or circle key language or data.

            a) Be especially careful to note when the requirement is an **exception**; e.g., "Which of the following payments is **not** an investing cash flow?"

    c. **Determine the correct answer** before looking at the answer choices.

    d. **Read the answer choices carefully.**

        1) Even if the first answer appears to be the correct choice, do **not** skip the remaining answer choices. Questions often ask for the "best" of the choices provided. Thus, each choice requires your consideration.

        2) Treat each answer choice as a true/false question as you analyze it.

    e. **Select the best answer.**

        1) If you are uncertain, guess intelligently (see "If You Don't Know the Answer" below). Improve on your 25% chance of getting the correct answer with blind guessing.

        2) For many multiple-choice questions, two answer choices can be eliminated with minimal effort, thereby increasing your educated guess to a 50-50 proposition.

4. After you have answered all of the questions, **transfer your answers to the objective answer sheet**, if one is provided.

    a. Make sure you are within your time budget so you will be able to perform this vital step in an unhurried manner.

    b. Do not wait to transfer answers until the very end of the exam session because you may run out of time.

    c. Double-check that you have transferred the answers correctly; e.g., recheck every 5th or 10th answer from your test paper to your answer sheet to ensure that you have not fallen out of sequence.

If You Don't Know the Answer

If the exam you are taking does not penalize incorrect answers, you should guess. Make it an educated guess, which means select the best answer. First, rule out answers that you think are incorrect. Second, speculate on what the examiner is looking for and/or the rationale behind the question. Third, select the best answer or guess between equally appealing answers. Mark the question with a "?" in case you have time to return to it for further analysis.

If you cannot make an educated guess, read the stem and each answer, and pick the best or most intuitive answer. It's just a guess! Do **not** look at the previous answer to try to detect an answer. Answers are usually random, and it is possible to have four or more consecutive questions with the same answer letter, e.g., answer (B).

NOTE: Do not waste time beyond the amount you budgeted for each question. Move forward and stay on or ahead of schedule.

EXAM QUESTIONS AND EXPLANATIONS SERIES
IMPROVES GRADES AND INCREASES COMPETITIVENESS

Use the Gleim exam questions and explanations series to ensure your understanding of each topic you study in your accounting and business law courses. Access the largest bank of exam questions (including thousands from past certification exams) that is widely used by professors. Get immediate feedback on your study effort while you take your "practice" tests.

- Each book or Test Prep Software contains over 1,000 multiple-choice questions with correct and incorrect answer explanations and can be used in two or more classes.
- Exhaustive cross-references are presented for all related textbooks so that you can easily determine which group of questions pertains to a given chapter in your textbook.
- You absorb important information more efficiently, more quickly, and more permanently through *"programmed learning."*
- Questions taken directly from professional certification exams demonstrate the standards to which you will be held as a professional accountant and help prepare you for certification exams later.

The Gleim Series works! Each book is a comprehensive source of questions with thorough explanations of each correct and incorrect answer. You learn from our explanations regardless of your answers to the questions. Pretest before class to see if you are strong or weak in the assigned area. Retest after class and before each exam or quiz to be certain you really understand the material. The questions in these books cover virtually all topics in your courses. Rarely will you encounter questions for which you are not well prepared.

After graduation, you will compete with graduates from schools across the country in the accounting job market. Make sure you measure up to standards that are as demanding as the standards of your counterparts at other schools. These standards will be tested on professional certification exams.

AUDITING & SYSTEMS EXAM QUESTIONS AND EXPLANATIONS (Seventeenth Edition)

1. Engagement Responsibilities
2. Professional Responsibilities
3. Risk Assessment
4. Strategic Planning Issues
5. Internal Control Concepts and Information Technology
6. Internal Control – Sales-Receivables-Cash Receipts Cycle
7. Internal Control – Purchases, Payroll, and Other Cycles
8. Responses to Assessed Risks
9. Internal Control Communications and Reports
10. Evidence – Objectives and Nature
11. Evidence – The Sales-Receivables-Cash Cycle
12. Evidence – The Purchases-Payables-Inventory Cycle
13. Evidence – Other Assets, Liabilities, and Equities
14. Evidence – Key Considerations
15. Evidence – Sampling
16. Reports – Opinions and Disclaimers
17. Reports – Other Modifications
18. Review, Compilation, and Special Reports
19. Related Reporting Topics
20. Governmental Audits
21. Internal Auditing
22. Information Systems

COST/MANAGERIAL ACCOUNTING EXAM QUESTIONS AND EXPLANATIONS (Tenth Edition)

1. Overview and Terminology
2. Absorption vs. Variable Costing
3. Job-Order Costing
4. Process Costing
5. Activity-Based Costing
6. Cost Allocation: Support Costs and Joint Costs
7. Standard Costs and Variances
8. Inventory Management: Traditional and Modern Approaches
9. Responsibility Accounting, Performance Measurement, and Transfer Pricing
10. Quality
11. Cost-Volume-Profit Analysis
12. Budgeting
13. Nonroutine Decisions
14. Capital Budgeting
15. Probability and Statistics
16. Regression Analysis
17. Linear Programming
18. Other Quantitative Approaches

FINANCIAL ACCOUNTING EXAM QUESTIONS AND EXPLANATIONS (Seventeenth Edition)

1. The Financial Reporting Environment
2. The Accounting Process
3. Reporting Income
4. The Time Value of Money
5. Current Assets, Cash, Accounts Receivable, and Notes Receivable
6. Inventories
7. Property, Plant, and Equipment
8. Depreciation and Depletion
9. Intangible Assets and Research and Development Costs
10. Investments
11. Current Liabilities, Compensated Absences, and Contingencies
12. Noncurrent Liabilities
13. Pensions and Other Postretirement Benefits
14. Leases
15. Corporate Equity
16. EPS and Share-Based Payment
17. Accounting for Income Taxes
18. Accounting Changes and Error Corrections
19. Statement of Cash Flows
20. Financial Statement Disclosures
21. Long-Term Construction-Type Contracts, Installment Sales, and Consignments
22. Financial Statement Analysis
23. GAAP Accounting for Partnerships
24. Business Combinations and Consolidated Financial Reporting
25. Interim Financial Reporting
26. Foreign Currency Translation and Transactions
27. State and Local Governments
28. Not-for-Profit Entities

FEDERAL TAX EXAM QUESTIONS AND EXPLANATIONS (Twenty-Second Edition)

1. Gross Income
2. Exclusions from Gross Income
3. Business Expenses and Losses
4. Limitations on Losses
5. Other Deductions for Adjusted Gross Income
6. Deductions from AGI
7. Individual Tax Computations
8. Credits
9. Basis
10. Depreciation, Amortization, and Depletion
11. Capital Gains and Losses
12. Sale of Business Property
13. Nontaxable Property Transactions
14. Partnerships: Formation and Operation
15. Partnerships: Distributions, Sales, and Exchanges
16. Corporate Formations and Operations
17. Advanced Corporate Topics
18. Income Taxation of Estates, Trusts, and Tax-Exempt Organizations
19. Accounting Methods
20. Employment Taxes and Withholding
21. Wealth Transfer Taxes
22. Preparer Rules
23. Federal Tax Process and Procedure

BUSINESS LAW/LEGAL STUDIES EXAM QUESTIONS AND EXPLANATIONS (Ninth Edition)

1. The American Legal System
2. The American Court System
3. Civil Litigation and Procedure
4. Constitutional Law and Business
5. Administrative Law
6. Criminal Law and Procedure
7. Tort Law
8. Contracts: The Agreement
9. Contracts: Consideration
10. Contracts: Capacity, Legality, Mutuality, and Statute of Frauds
11. Contracts: Interpretation, Conditions, Discharge, and Remedies
12. Contracts: Third-Party Rights and Duties
13. Sale of Goods: The Sales Contract, Interpretation, and Risk of Loss
14. Sale of Goods: Performance, Remedies, and Warranties
15. Negotiable Instruments: Types, Negotiation, and Holder in Due Course
16. Negotiable Instruments: Liability, Bank Transactions, and Electronic Fund Transfers
17. Documents of Title and Letters of Credit
18. Secured Transactions
19. Suretyship
20. Bankruptcy
21. Personal Property and Bailments
22. Computers and the Law
23. Real Property: Interests and Rights
24. Real Property: Transactions
25. Mortgages
26. Creditor Law and Liens
27. Landlord and Tenant
28. Wills, Estate Administration, and Trusts
29. Agency
30. Partnerships and Other Entities
31. Corporations: Nature, Formation, and Financing
32. Corporations: Operations and Management
33. Federal Securities Regulation
34. Insurance
35. Environmental Law
36. Antitrust
37. Consumer Protection
38. Employment Regulation
39. International Business Law
40. Accountants' Legal Responsibilities

ACCOUNTING CERTIFICATION PROGRAMS--OVERVIEW

The CPA (Certified Public Accountant) exam is the grandparent of all the professional accounting examinations. Its origin was in the 1896 public accounting legislation of New York. In 1917, the American Institute of CPAs (AICPA) began to prepare and grade a uniform CPA exam. It is currently used to measure the technical competence of those applying to be licensed as CPAs in all 50 states, Guam, Puerto Rico, the Virgin Islands, and the District of Columbia.

The CIA (Certified Internal Auditor), CMA (Certified Management Accountant), and EA (IRS Enrolled Agent) examinations are relatively new certification programs compared with the CPA exam. The CMA exam was first administered in 1972 and the first CIA exam in 1974. The EA exam dates back to 1959. Why were these certification programs begun? Generally, the requirements of the CPA designation instituted by the boards of accountancy, especially the necessity for public accounting experience, led to the development of the CIA and CMA programs. The EA certification is available for persons specializing in tax.

ACCOUNTING CERTIFICATION PROGRAMS--PURPOSE

The primary purpose of professional exams is to measure the technical competence of candidates. Competence includes technical knowledge, ability to apply such knowledge with good judgment, comprehension of professional responsibility, and ethical considerations. Additionally, the nature of these exams (low pass rate, broad and rigorous coverage, etc.) has several very important effects:

1. Candidates are forced to learn all of the material that should have been presented and learned in a good accounting educational program.

2. Relatedly, candidates must integrate the topics and concepts that are presented in individual courses in accounting education programs.

3. The content of each exam provides direction to accounting education programs; i.e., what is tested on the exams will be taught to accounting students.

Certification is important to professional accountants because it provides

1. Participation in a recognized professional group
2. An improved professional training program arising out of the certification program
3. Recognition among peers for attaining the professional designation
4. An extra credential for the employment market/career ladder
5. The personal satisfaction of attaining a recognized degree of competency

These reasons hold true in the accounting field due to wide recognition of the CPA designation. Accountants and accounting students are often asked whether they are CPAs when people learn they are accountants. Thus, there is considerable pressure for accountants to become *certified*.

A new development is multiple certifications, which is important for the same reasons as initial certification. Accounting students and recent graduates should look ahead and obtain multiple certifications to broaden their career opportunities. The table of selected CIA, CMA, CPA, and EA examination data on the following page provides an overview of these accounting examinations.

Examination Content

The content of certification examinations is specified by the respective governing boards with lists of topics to be tested. In the Gleim review manuals – *CIA Review*, *CMA Review*, *CPA Review*, and *EA Review* – the material tested is divided into subtopics we call study units. A study unit is a more manageable undertaking than an overall part of each exam. The listings of study units on pages 10 through 14 provide an overview of the scope and content of these exams.

Examination Summary

	CIA (Certified Internal Auditor)	CMA (Certified Management Accountant)	EA (IRS Enrolled Agent)	CPA (Certified Public Accountant) (New CBT-e version)
Sponsoring Organization	Institute of Internal Auditors	Institute of Management Accountants	Internal Revenue Service	American Institute of Certified Public Accountants
Contact Information	www.globaliia.org (407) 937-1111	www.imanet.org (201) 573-9000	www.irs.gov (313) 234-1280	www.aicpa.org (201) 938-3750
Cost for Entire Exam	$675	$1,150	$303	$784.50 plus State Board fee
Student Discount	about 30%	50%	None	None
Exam Parts	1 – The Internal Audit Activity's Role in Governance, Risk, and Control (3 hrs.) 2 – Conducting the Internal Audit Engagement (3 hrs.) 3 – Business Analysis and Information Technology (3 hrs.) 4 – Business Management Skills (3 hrs.)	1 – Financial Planning, Performance, and Control (4 hrs.) 2 – Financial Decision Making (4 hrs.)	1 – Individuals (3.5 hrs.) 2 – Businesses (3.5 hrs.) 3 – Representation, Practices, and Procedures (3.5 hrs.)	Auditing and Attestation (4 hrs.) Business Environment and Concepts (3 hrs.) Financial Accounting and Reporting (4 hrs.) Regulation (3 hrs.)
Exam Format	Parts 1, 2, 3, and 4: 90 multiple-choice questions	Parts 1 and 2: 100 multiple-choice questions 2 essays	Parts 1, 2, and 3: 100 multiple-choice questions	AUD: 90 multiple-choice questions 7 TBS BEC: 72 multiple-choice questions 3 written communications FAR: 90 multiple-choice questions 7 TBS REG: 72 multiple-choice questions 6 TBS
Avg. Pass Rate	1 – 48% 2 – 60% 3 – 52% 4 – 59%	1 – 33% 2 – 46%	1 – 76% 2 – 69% 3 – 80%	AUD – 46% BEC – 47% FAR – 46% REG – 44%
Testing Windows	On demand throughout the year	January-February May-June September-October	May – February (e.g., 5/01/2012 - 2/28/2013)	January-February April-May July-August October-November

---

LISTING OF *CIA REVIEW* STUDY UNITS

Part 1: The Internal Audit Activity's Role in Governance, Risk, and Control

1. Overview of Internal Auditing
2. Internal Audit Proficiency, Due Care, and Quality Assurance
3. Internal Audit Ethics
4. Managing the Internal Audit Activity
5. Nature of Internal Audit Work
6. Control Knowledge Elements
7. Specific Controls
8. Control Aspects of Management
9. Planning and Supervising the Engagement
10. Internal Audit Responsibilities for Fraud

Part 2: Conducting the Internal Audit Engagement

1. Engagement Information
2. Procedures and Working Papers
3. Internal Audit Ethics
4. Communicating Results
5. Fraud Investigation
6. Conducting Assurance Engagements
7. Compliance, Consulting, and Other Engagements
8. Information Technology
9. Engagement Tools -- Statistical
10. Engagement Tools -- Others

Part 3: Business Analysis and Information Technology

1. Business Processes
2. Managing Business Resources
3. Financial Accounting -- Basic
4. Financial Accounting -- Advanced
5. Finance
6. Managerial Accounting
7. Regulatory, Legal, and Economic Issues
8. IT Controls, Networks, and Business Applications
9. IT Roles, Software, and Application Development
10. IT Contingency Planning, Systems Security, and Databases

Part 4: Business Management Skills*

1. Structural Analysis and Strategies
2. Industry and Market Analysis
3. Industry Environments
4. Strategic Decisions
5. Global Business Issues
6. Motivation and Communications
7. Organizational Structure and Effectiveness
8. Managing Groups
9. Influence and Leadership
10. Time Management, Conflict, and Negotiation

*Persons who have passed the CPA or CMA exams (and many other professional exams) are not required to take Part 4 of the CIA exam.

According to The IIA, the CIA is a "globally accepted certification for internal auditors" through which "individuals demonstrate their competency and professionalism in the internal auditing field." Successful candidates will have gained "educational experience, information, and business tools that can be applied immediately in any organization or business environment."

Passing this exam validates and confirms your professional work experience and requires your complete dedication and determination. The benefits include higher salary, increased confidence and competence, and recognition as a member of an elite group of professionals.

The CIA exam is computerized to facilitate testing. Each of the four parts consists of 90 multiple-choice questions and lasts about 2.5 hours (2 hours and 25 minutes for exam, 5 minutes for survey).

The first two parts of the CIA exam focus on the theory and practice of internal auditing. The body of knowledge of internal auditing and the auditing skills to be tested consist of

1. The typical undergraduate auditing class as represented by auditing texts

2. Internal auditing textbooks (e.g., *Sawyer's Internal Auditing* and Cascarino and van Esch's *Internal Auditing: An Integrated Approach*)

3. Various IIA (Institute of Internal Auditors) pronouncements (e.g., IIA *Code of Ethics, International Standards for the Professional Practice of Internal Auditing*, and Statement of Responsibilities of Internal Auditing)

4. Reasoning ability, communications and problem-solving skills, and dealing with auditees in an audit context (i.e., the questions will cover audit topics but test audit skills)

The remaining 50% of the exam, Parts 3 and 4, ensures that internal auditors are conversant with topics, methodologies, and techniques ranging from individual and organizational behavior to economics.

LISTING OF *CMA REVIEW* STUDY UNITS

Part 1: Financial Planning, Performance, and Control

1. Ethics for Management Accountants and Cost Management Concepts
2. Cost Accumulation Systems
3. Cost Allocation Techniques
4. Operational Efficiency and Business Process Performance
5. Budgeting Concepts and Forecasting Techniques
6. Budget Methodologies and Budget Preparation
7. Cost and Variance Measures
8. Responsibility Accounting and Performance Measures
9. Internal Controls -- Risk and Procedures for Control
10. Internal Controls -- Internal Auditing and Systems Controls

Part 2: Financial Decision Making

1. Ethics for the Organization and Basic Financial Statements
2. Ratio Analysis
3. Profitability Analysis and Analytical Issues
4. Investment Risk and Portfolio Management
5. Financial Instruments and Cost of Capital
6. Managing Current Assets
7. Raising Capital, Corporate Restructuring, and International Finance
8. CVP Analysis and Marginal Analysis
9. Decision Analysis and Risk Management
10. Investment Decisions

The CMA exam consists of two parts: (1) Financial Planning, Performance, and Control and (2) Financial Decision Making. Both parts consist of 100 multiple-choice questions and two 30-minute essay questions. Four hours is allowed for the completion of a part (3 hours for the multiple-choice, 1 hour for the essays).

According to the IMA, the "CMA is the advanced professional certification specifically designed to measure the accounting and financial management skills that drive business performance."

In their Resource Guide, the ICMA explains that through the certification test, "the requirements of the CMA Program . . . recognize those who can demonstrate that they possess a sufficient degree of knowledge and skills in the areas of management accounting and financial management. In this way, the ICMA helps identify practitioners who have met certain predetermined professional standards."

We have arranged the subject matter tested on the CMA examination into 10 study units for each part. Each part is presented in a separate book. Both of these books contain review outlines; prior CMA exam questions, answers, and answer explanations; and essay questions.

The CMA exam has broader coverage than the CPA exam in several areas. For example,

1. CMA topics like risk management, finance, management, and marketing are covered lightly, if at all, on the CPA exam.

2. The CMA exam focuses very heavily on internal decision making, such as special orders and capital budgeting, whereas the CPA exam is concerned with external reporting.

3. The CMA exam tests business ethics but not business law.

CMA questions are generally more analysis-oriented than CPA questions. On the CPA exam, the typical requirement is the solution of an accounting problem, e.g., consolidated worksheet, funds statement, etc.

LISTING OF *CPA REVIEW* STUDY UNITS

Business Environment and Concepts

1. Corporate Governance
2. Microeconomics
3. Macroeconomics
4. Globalization
5. Financial Risk Management
6. Forecasting Analysis
7. Corporate Capital Structure
8. Working Capital
9. Short-Term Financing and Capital Budgeting I
10. Capital Budgeting II and Corporate Performance
11. IT Roles, Systems, and Processing
12. IT Software and Data Organization
13. IT Networks and Electronic Commerce
14. IT Security
15. Strategic Planning and Budgeting Concepts
16. Budget Components
17. Quality Considerations and Benchmarking
18. Responsibility Accounting and Other Topics
19. Costing Fundamentals
20. Costing Systems and Variance Analysis

Financial Accounting and Reporting

1. The Financial Reporting Environment
2. Financial Statements
3. Statement of Cash Flows
4. Income Statement Items
5. Financial Statement Disclosure
6. Cash and Investments
7. Receivables
8. Inventories
9. Property, Plant, Equipment, and Depletable Resources
10. Intangible Assets and Other Capitalization Issues
11. Payables and Taxes
12. Employee Benefits
13. Noncurrent Liabilities
14. Leases and Contingencies
15. Equity
16. Business Combinations and Consolidated Financial Reporting
17. Derivatives, Hedging, and Other Topics
18. Governmental Accounting
19. Governmental Reporting
20. Not-for-Profit Concepts

Regulation

1. Ethics and Professional Responsibilities
2. CPAs and the Law
3. Agency
4. Contracts
5. Sales and Secured Transactions
6. Negotiable Instruments and Related Topics
7. Debtor-Creditor Relationships
8. Regulation and Certain Business Entities
9. Corporations
10. Federal Tax Legislation, Procedures, and Planning
11. Gross Income
12. Deductions
13. Tax Computations
14. Property Transactions
15. Corporate Taxable Income
16. Corporate Tax Computations
17. Corporate Tax Special Topics
18. S Corporations
19. Partnerships and Exempt Organizations
20. Estates, Trusts, and Wealth Transfer Taxes

Auditing and Attestation

1. Engagement Responsibilities
2. Professional Responsibilities
3. Risk Assessment
4. Strategic Planning Issues
5. Internal Control Concepts and Information Technology
6. Internal Control -- Sales-Receivables-Cash Receipts Cycle
7. Internal Control -- Purchases, Payroll, and Other Cycles
8. Responses to Assessed Risks
9. Internal Control Communications and Reports
10. Evidence -- Objectives and Nature
11. Evidence -- The Sales-Receivables-Cash Cycle
12. Evidence -- The Purchases-Payables-Inventory Cycle
13. Evidence -- Other Assets, Liabilities, and Equities
14. Evidence -- Key Considerations
15. Evidence -- Sampling
16. Reports -- Opinions and Disclaimers
17. Reports -- Other Modifications
18. Review, Compilation, and Special Reports
19. Related Reporting Topics
20. Governmental Audits

The CPA examination is designed to measure professional competence in auditing, business law, taxation, accounting, and related business topics, including

1. The command of adequate technical knowledge
2. The ability to apply such knowledge skillfully and with good judgment
3. An understanding of professional responsibilities

Passing this exam validates and confirms your professional accounting education and requires your complete dedication and determination. The benefits include higher salary, increased confidence and competence, and recognition as a member of an elite group of professionals.

The CPA exam is administered the first 2 months of every calendar quarter (i.e., January/February, April/May, and July/August, October/November) at Prometric testing centers throughout the U.S. and at select international locations. The exam is divided into four sections: Auditing and Attestation (AUD), Business Environment and Concepts (BEC), Financial Accounting and Reporting (FAR), and Regulation (REG). Each section consists of a series of testlets.

You will have three multiple-choice testlets followed by one task-based simulation testlet in Auditing, Financial, and Regulation. For Business, you will have three testlets of multiple choice and one testlet with written communication essays.

1. Multiple-choice testlets: There will be three groups of 30 multiple-choice questions given as testlets on Auditing and Financial. On Business and Regulation, there will be 24 instead of 30 multiple-choice questions.

2. Task-based simulation testlets: Auditing, Financial, and Regulation will each have six or seven task-based simulations. These simulations will account for 40% of the grade in each exam section.

3. Written communication testlets: Business will have one written communication testlet with three essay questions (two graded, one pretest). These questions will account for 15% of the total grade on this section.

LISTING OF *EA REVIEW* STUDY UNITS

Part 1: Individuals

1. Filing Requirements
2. Gross Income
3. Business Deductions
4. Above-the-Line Deductions and Losses
5. Itemized Deductions
6. Tax Credits, Other Taxes, and Payments
7. Basis
8. Adjustments to Asset Basis and Capital Gains and Losses
9. Business Property, Related Parties, and Installment Sales
10. Nonrecognition Property Transactions
11. Individual Retirement Accounts
12. Gift Tax
13. Estate Tax

Part 3: Representation, Practices, and Procedures

1. Practice before the IRS
2. Tax Preparers and Penalties
3. Representation
4. The Collection Process
5. Examination of Returns and the Appeals Process
6. Tax Authority
7. Record Keeping and Electronic Filing

Part 2: Businesses

1. Accounting Methods and Periods
2. Income and Property Transactions
3. Business Expenses
4. Other Deductions
5. Basis
6. Depreciation
7. Credits, Losses, and Additional Taxes
8. Contributions to a Partnership
9. Partnership Operations
10. Disposition of a Partner's Interest
11. Corporations
12. Corporate Formation
13. Corporate Income and Losses
14. Corporate Deductions
15. Distributions
16. Corporate Liquidations and Redemptions
17. S Corporations
18. Decedent, Estate, and Trust Income Tax Returns
19. Retirement Plans for Small Businesses
20. Exempt Organizations

Enrolled agents are individuals who have demonstrated special competence in tax matters and professional ethics and have been enrolled to practice before the IRS as taxpayers' agents or legal representatives. Practice before the IRS includes all matters connected with presentations to the IRS relating to a client's rights, privileges, and liabilities under laws or regulations administered by the IRS. Such presentations include

1. Preparing and filing documents;
2. Communicating with the IRS; and
3. Representing a client at conferences, hearings, and meetings.

The examination covers federal taxation and tax accounting and the use of tax return forms for individuals, partnerships, corporations, trusts, estates, and gifts. It also covers ethical considerations and procedural requirements.

The exam consists of three parts, with 3.5 hours for each part (4 hours total seat time to include tutorial and survey). The questions on the examination are directed toward the tasks that enrolled agents must perform to complete and file forms and tax returns and to represent taxpayers before the Internal Revenue Service. Each part of the examination consists of approximately 100 multiple-choice questions and covers the following tax topics:

Part 1 - Individuals
Part 2 - Businesses
Part 3 - Representation, Practices, and Procedures

Steps to Passing Certification Exams

1. Become knowledgeable about the exam you will be taking, and determine which part you will take first.

2. Purchase the complete Gleim Review System (including books, Test Prep Software, Audio Review, Gleim Online with your Personal Counselor, etc.) to thoroughly prepare yourself. Commit to systematic preparation for the exam as described in our review materials.

3. Communicate with your Personal Counselor to design a study plan that meets your needs. Call (888) 874-5346 or email personalcounselor@gleim.com.

4. Apply for membership in the exam's governing body and/or in the certification program as required.

5. Register online to take the desired part of the exam.

6. Schedule your test with the testing center in the location of your choice.

7. Work systematically through each study unit in the Gleim Review System.

8. Sit for and PASS the exam while you are in control. Gleim guarantees success!

9. Email or call Gleim with your comments on our study materials and how well they prepared you for the exam.

10. Enjoy your career, pursue multiple certifications (CIA, CPA, EA, CMA, etc.), and recommend Gleim to others who are also taking these exams. Stay up-to-date on your Continuing Professional Education requirements with Gleim CPE.

When to Sit for the Certification Exams

Sit for all examinations as soon as you can. While all of the certification programs except the EA have education requirements, candidates are allowed to sit for the exam and then complete the requirements within a certain time period. The CIA program allows full-time students in their senior year to sit for the exam, and the CMA program offers a 7-year window for submission of educational credentials. The CIA and CMA exams are offered at a reduced fee for students. The requirements for the CPA vary by jurisdiction, but many state boards allow candidates to sit for the exam before they have completed the required hours.

It would be difficult if not impossible to complete all four exams in 1 year. But it is a smart move to take full advantage of the knowledge and study habits you are gaining in your classes. Register for and schedule yourself to take the parts of each exam that best match up to the courses you are currently taking. For example, if you are taking a Business Law course and a Federal Tax course this semester, schedule your CPA Regulation date for the week after classes end. And, soon after you finish your Cost and Managerial Accounting class, schedule yourself for and take both parts of the CMA exam on the same day – doing so will save you over $300 in membership and exam fees!

Examination Pass Rates

The pass rates on the CPA, CIA, CMA, and EA exams are presented in the tables below. See also page 9.

Many schools and review courses advertise the quality of their programs by reporting pass rates. Obviously, the best rates are emphasized. Thus, the reported percentage may be that for first-time candidates, all candidates, candidates passing a specific section of the examination, candidates completing the examination, or even candidates successfully completing the exam after a specified number of sittings.

Pass Rates

CPA Exam	2009	2010	2011
AUD	49.8	48.9	45.6
BEC	48.3	47.8	47.1
FAR	48.5	46.7	45.6
REG	49.8	50.6	44.2

The passing percentages for the CPA exam have been in the high-forties when only one section is taken per exam window. We expect the per-section passing percentages to continue to be 40-50%. The pass rate on passing all four sections the first time in one exam window is about 7%.

CIA Exam	2009	2010	2011
Part 1	51.1	50.9	47.7
Part 2	58.6	62.2	59.9
Part 3	50.2	52.8	51.9
Part 4	58.7	56.6	58.5

CMA Exam	2009*	2010	2011
Part 1	49	40	33
Part 2	50	36	46
Part 3	52	N/A	N/A
Part 4	57	N/A	N/A

EA Exam**	2007-2008	2008-2009	2009-2010
Part 1	38	49	76
Part 2	45	67	69
Part 3	68	79	80

*These pass rates are for the four-part exam.
**The IRS had not posted passing rates for 2010-2011 or 2011-2012 at time of print.

Reasons for the Low Pass Rates

Although a very high percentage of serious candidates successfully complete each of the examinations, the 40%-60% CPA, CIA, and CMA pass rates warrant an explanation. First, the pass rates are low (relative to bar and medical exams) because these examinations reflect the high standards of the accounting profession, which contribute greatly to the profession's reputation and also attract persons with both competence and aspiration.

Second, the pass rates are low because most accounting educational programs are at the undergraduate rather than graduate level. Undergraduate students are generally less career-oriented than graduate students. Undergraduates may look on their program as a number of individual courses required for graduation rather than as an integrated program to prepare them for professional practice.

Third, the pass rates are low because accounting programs and curricula at most colleges and universities are not given the budgetary priority they deserve. Accounting faculties are often understaffed for the number of accounting majors, the number and nature of accounting courses (problem-oriented vs. descriptive), etc., relative to other faculties. However, you cannot use this as an excuse or reason for not achieving your personal goals. You must do your best to improve your control systems and study resources.

Cost to Maintain Professional Certification*

The cost to take the CIA exam for members of The Institute of Internal Auditors (The IIA) is a one-time $75 Exam Application fee plus a $150-per-part Registration fee, which totals $675 (assuming you pass all parts the first time you take them). Full-time students save $45 per part and $25 on the Exam Application fee. Membership in The IIA is not required. Nonmembers pay a $100 Exam Application fee plus a $200-per-part Registration fee. Nonmembers must also include a $100 processing fee when they submit their CPE report every 2 years. Annual membership dues vary from $70 to $235. See The IIA website at www.globaliia.org for more information.

The cost to take the new two-part CMA exam is $350 for each part and a $225 Certification Entrance fee plus Institute of Management Accountants (IMA) membership dues, which vary from $39 for students to $210 for regular members. Membership in the IMA is required, and all new members (except Students and Young Professionals) must pay a one-time registration fee of $15. Students may take each part of the examination once at a reduced fee of $175 per part, with a $75 Certification Entrance fee. See the IMA website at www.imanet.org for more information.

The cost of the entire CPA exam is $784.50 plus a varying State Board fee per section. See the NASBA website at www.nasba.org for links to each state board. Most states require an annual fee to maintain the CPA certificate and/or license. See www.aicpa.org for more information.

For the EA exam, the $105 testing fee for each of the three parts is due at the time the examination is scheduled. Once you have passed the exam, there is a $30 fee to apply for your enrollment to practice before the IRS. You must renew your enrollment every 3 years. See the test administrator's website at www.prometric.com/irs for more information.

*These rates have been verified to be correct at time of print but are subject to change at any time. Check with the governing board of the exam you're taking for the most current rates.

CITATIONS TO AUTHORITATIVE PRONOUNCEMENTS

Throughout the book and software, we refer to certain authoritative accounting pronouncements by the following abbreviations:

GAAP – The sources of authoritative U.S. generally accepted accounting principles (GAAP) recognized by the FASB as applicable by nongovernmental entities are (1) the FASB's Accounting Standards Codification™ and (2) (for SEC registrants only) pronouncements of the SEC. All guidance in the codification is equally authoritative. SEC pronouncements must be followed by registrants regardless of whether they are reflected in the codification.

IFRS and IASs – International Financial Reporting Standards (IFRS) are issued by the current standard-setter, the International Accounting Standards Board (IASB). International Accounting Standards (IASs), related Interpretations, and the framework for the preparation and presentation of financial statements were issued by the predecessor entity. IFRS also is the collective term for IFRS and IASs.

GASBS – The Governmental Accounting Standards Board issues Statements of Governmental Accounting Standards and other pronouncements. They apply to state and local governments.

SFAC – FASB Statements of Financial Accounting Concepts establish financial accounting and reporting objectives and concepts. SFACs are other accounting literature. They are considered only in the absence of applicable authoritative guidance (the FASB Accounting Standards Codification™ or SEC pronouncements). They were designed for use by the FASB in developing their other authoritative pronouncements.

STUDY UNIT ONE
THE FINANCIAL REPORTING ENVIRONMENT

Introduction to the Conceptual Framework

The conceptual framework is a coherent set of interrelated objectives and fundamental concepts. This framework is contained in the **Statements of Financial Accounting Concepts (SFACs)** issued by the **Financial Accounting Standards Board (FASB)**. These Statements do not themselves establish the accounting and reporting standards for particular transactions, events, and circumstances. Instead, their purpose is to describe concepts and relationships as a basis for developing a consistent set of standards defining accounting and reporting requirements. Thus, they are reflected in **U.S. generally accepted accounting principles (GAAP)**.

Certain **assumptions** underlie the environment in which the reporting entity operates but are **not** found in official pronouncements. They have developed over time and are generally recognized by the accounting profession. The **economic-entity assumption** is that every business is a separate entity. The economic affairs of the business are separate from the economic affairs of the owners. Also, the legal entity and the economic entity are not always the same, as in the case of a parent and its subsidiary, which are consolidated for reporting purposes. The **going-concern (business continuity) assumption** is that, unless stated otherwise, every business will continue operating indefinitely. As a result, liquidation values are not important because it is assumed that the business is not going to be liquidated in the near future. The **monetary-unit (unit-of-money) assumption** is that accounting records are kept in terms of money. Using money as the unit of measure is the best way of providing economic information to users of financial statements. Also, the changing purchasing power of the monetary unit is assumed not to be significant. The **periodicity (time period) assumption** is that financial statements are prepared periodically throughout the life of a business to ensure the **timeliness** of information. The periodicity assumption requires using **estimates** in the financial statements. This assumption sacrifices some degree of faithful representation for increased relevance.

Certain **principles** provide guidelines that the accountant follows when recording financial information. The **revenue recognition** and **expense recognition principles** were formally adopted by the FASB as recognition and measurement concepts and are discussed later in this summary. Under the **historical cost principle**, transactions are recorded at cost because that is the most objective measure of value. Under the **full-disclosure principle**, users should be able to assume that financial information that could influence their judgments about the entity is reported in the financial statements or disclosed in the **notes**. However, full disclosure is not a substitute for reporting in accordance with GAAP.

Certain doctrines limit the process of recognition in the financial statements. The **cost constraint** compares costs and benefits, and **materiality** relates to the significance of information. The cost constraint and materiality are discussed later in this summary. Two additional doctrines are presented here. Under the **industry practices constraint**, GAAP might not be followed in an industry if conformity would generate misleading or unnecessary information. For example, banks and insurance companies typically measured marketable equity securities at fair value before such reporting was required for all GAAP-based statements. Fair value and liquidity are most important to these industries. Under the **conservatism constraint**, when alternative accounting methods are appropriate, the one having the less favorable effect on net income and total assets is preferable. However, conservatism does not permit a deliberate understatement of total assets and net income. Furthermore, SFAC 5, *Recognition and Measurement in Financial Statements of Business Enterprises*, describes "a general tendency to emphasize purchase and sale transactions and to apply conservative procedures in accounting recognition."

Objective of Financial Reporting

According to **SFAC 8**, Chapter 1, *The Objective of General Purpose Financial Reporting*, and Chapter 3, *Qualitative Characteristics of Useful Financial Information*, the objective is to report financial information that is **useful** in making decisions about providing resources to the reporting entity. **Primary users** of financial information are current or prospective investors and creditors who cannot obtain it directly. Because their decisions depend on expected returns, primary users need information that helps them to assess the entity's potential for future net cash inflows. However, primary users cannot obtain all necessary information solely from general-purpose financial reports. These reports (1) are insufficient to determine the value of the entity and (2) are significantly based on estimates, judgments, and models.

The information in general-purpose financial reports relates to the entity's **economic resources and claims** to them (financial position) and to **changes** in those resources and claims. Information about economic resources and claims helps to evaluate liquidity, solvency, financing needs, and the probability of obtaining financing.

Changes in economic resources and claims result from either (1) the entity's performance or (2) other events and transactions (e.g., issuing debt and equity). Information about financial performance is useful for (1) understanding the return on economic resources, its variability, and its components; (2) evaluating management; and (3) predicting future returns.

The **accrual basis of accounting** is preferable to the cash basis for evaluating past performance and predicting future performance. It reports the effects of transactions and other events and circumstances when the effects occur, not when cash flows occur.

An entity should be able to increase its economic resources other than by obtaining resources from investors and creditors. Information about this performance is useful in evaluating the potential for net operating cash inflows. Information about financial performance also is useful in determining how external factors (e.g., interest rate changes) affected economic resources and claims.

Information about **cash flows** is helpful in

- Understanding operations;
- Evaluating financing and investing activities, liquidity, and solvency;
- Interpreting other financial information; and
- Assessing the potential for net cash inflows.

Qualitative Characteristics

SFAC 8 also identifies the qualitative characteristics of useful financial information. The **fundamental** qualitative characteristics are relevance and faithful representation.

Relevant information is able to make a difference in user decisions. To do so, it must have predictive value, confirmatory value, or both. Something has **predictive value** if it can be used as an input in a predictive process. Something has **confirmatory value** with respect to prior evaluations if it provides feedback that confirms or changes (corrects) them. Predictive value and confirmatory value are interrelated. For example, current revenue may confirm a prior prediction and also be used to predict the next period's revenue.

Information is **material** if its omission or misstatement can influence user decisions based on a specific entity's financial information. Thus, it is an **entity-specific** aspect of relevance.

Useful information **faithfully represents** economic phenomena. A representation is perfectly faithful if it is **complete** (containing what is needed for user understanding), **neutral** (unbiased in its selection and presentation), and **free from error**. A representation is free from error if it has no errors or omissions in (1) the descriptions of the phenomena and (2) the selection and application of the reporting process. However, freedom from error does not mean perfectly accurate. For example, the description of an estimate may be accurate, the limits of the process may be explained, and the selection and application of the process may be error-free. But the accuracy of the estimate may not be determinable.

The concept of **substance over form** guides accountants to present the financial reality of a transaction over its legal form. An example is the consolidation of a legally separate subsidiary by a parent. Presenting a parent and a separate entity that it controls as one reporting entity is faithfully representational.

Information is useful if it is relevant and faithfully represented. The process for applying these characteristics is to

- Identify what may be useful to users of the financial reports,
- Identify the relevant information, and
- Determine whether the information is available and can be faithfully represented.

The **enhancing qualitative characteristics** are comparability, verifiability, timeliness, and understandability. They enhance the usefulness of relevant and faithfully represented information.

Information should be **comparable** with similar information for (1) other entities and (2) the same entity for another period or date. Thus, comparability allows users to understand similarities and differences. **Consistency** is a means of achieving comparability. It is the use of the same methods, for example, accounting principles, for the same items.

Information is **verifiable** (directly or indirectly) if knowledgeable and independent observers can reach a consensus (but not necessarily unanimity) that it is faithfully represented.

Information is **timely** when it is available in time to influence decisions.

Information is **understandable** if it is clearly and concisely classified, characterized, and presented. Information should be readily understandable by reasonably knowledgeable and diligent users, but information should not be excluded because of its complexity.

The **cost constraint** affects all financial reporting. It states that the costs of reporting should be justified by its benefits. Provider reporting costs (collection, processing, verification, and distribution) ultimately are incurred by users as reduced returns. Other user costs include those to analyze and interpret the information provided or to obtain or estimate information not provided.

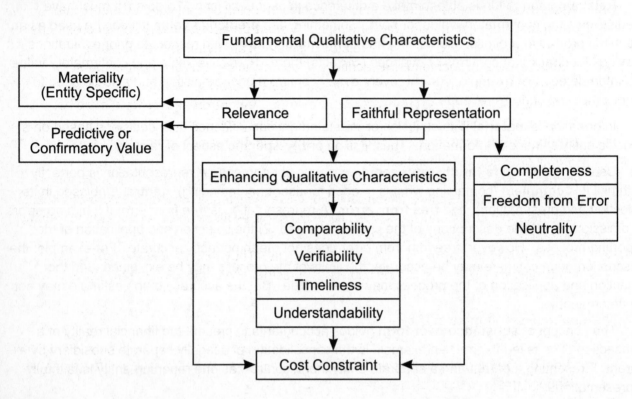

Elements

According to **SFAC 6**, *Elements of Financial Statements*, **financial statements** are the principal means of communicating financial information to users. A full set reports (1) financial position, (2) earnings (net income), (3) comprehensive income, (4) cash flows, and (5) investments by and distributions to owners. Notes to the statement and supplementary information provide disclosures essential to understanding the statements.

Elements of financial statements are broad classes of items. For business enterprises, they include (1) assets, (2) liabilities, (3) equity or net assets, (4) revenues, (5) expenses, (6) gains, (7) losses, (8) investments by owners, (9) distributions to owners, and (10) comprehensive income. (The last three do not apply to not-for-profit entities.) The traditional financial statements use a financial (not physical) **capital maintenance concept** to distinguish a return **on** capital from a return **of** capital. Under this concept, the effects of any recognized price changes on assets and liabilities are holding gains and losses. These are included in return on capital.

The following elements are distributed among the **financial statements** other than the statement of cash flows:

Statement of Financial Position (Balance Sheet)

- **Assets** are "probable future economic benefits obtained or controlled by a particular entity as a result of past transactions or events." **Valuation allowances**, such as premiums on notes receivable, are part of the related assets and are not assets or liabilities.
- **Liabilities** are "probable future sacrifices of economic benefits arising from present obligations of a particular entity to transfer assets or provide services to other entities in the future as a result of past transactions or events." **Valuation allowances**, such as discounts on bonds payable, are part of the related liability and are not liabilities or assets.
- **Equity (or net assets of a not-for-profit entity)** is the residual interest in the assets of an entity after subtracting liabilities.
- **Investments by owners** are increases in equity of a business entity. They result from transfers by other entities of something of value to increase ownership interests. Assets are the most commonly transferred item, but services also can be exchanged for equity interests (not applicable to NFPs).
- **Distributions to owners** are decreases in equity. They result from transferring assets, providing services, or incurring liabilities. A distribution to owners decreases the ownership interest (not applicable to NFPs).

Statement of Earnings (Net Income)

- **Revenues** are inflows or other enhancements of assets or settlements of liabilities (or both) from delivering or producing goods, providing services, or other activities that qualify as ongoing major or central operations.
- **Gains** are increases in equity (or net assets) other than from revenues or investments by owners.
- **Expenses** are outflows or other using up of assets or incurrences of liabilities (or both) from delivering or producing goods, providing services, or other activities that qualify as ongoing major or central operations.
- **Losses** are decreases in equity (or net assets) other than from expenses or distributions to owners.

Statement of Comprehensive Income

- **Comprehensive income** is the periodic change in equity of a business entity from nonowner sources. It excludes the effects of investments by owners and distributions to owners (not applicable to NFPs).

Statement of Investments by and Distributions to Owners

- **Investments by owners** (see above)
- **Distributions to owners** (see above)

The **statement of financial position** (balance sheet) provides information about assets, liabilities, and equity (the resource and financing structures of an entity) and their relationships at a moment in time. It does not indicate the value of a business enterprise.

Transactions and Other Events and Circumstances Affecting a Business Entity

Changes in Assets and Liabilities with No Change in Equity

- Asset exchanges
- Liability exchanges
- Receipt of goods or services with incurrence of payables
- Settlement of payables with assets

Changes in Assets and Liabilities with Change in Equity

- Comprehensive income

  - Revenues
  - Expenses
  - Gains
  - Losses

- Transfers between entity and owners

  - Investments by owners
  - Distributions to owners

Changes in Equity with No Change in Assets or Liabilities

- Declaration and distribution of stock dividends
- Conversion of preferred stock

Statements of earnings (net income) and comprehensive income together show the nonowner changes in equity during a period. The statement of earnings emphasizes what an entity receives or expects to receive (revenues) and what it sacrifices (expenses) in its ongoing major or central operations. But it also includes results of incidental or peripheral activities and the effects of certain environmental events (gains and losses).

Comprehensive income includes earnings. However, it also includes certain nonowner changes in equity (e.g., the changes in fair value of available-for-sale securities) not included in earnings.

A **statement of cash flows** reports, directly or indirectly, the major sources of cash flows associated with operating, investing, and financing (both debt and equity) activities. The purpose is to provide information for assessing liquidity, financial flexibility, profitability, and risk. It also provides information about the differences between earnings or comprehensive income and cash flows.

A **statement of investments by and distributions to owners** summarizes all the changes in equity during the period not arising from transactions with nonowners. The relevant transactions are those that **change ownership interests**, such as declarations of cash dividends, treasury stock purchases, distributions in kind, and increases in ownership interests through payments to the enterprise. **Statements of retained earnings and changes in equity**, which may be combined with other statements, convey this information.

Recognition and Measurement

SFAC 5, *Recognition and Measurement in Financial Statements of Business Enterprises*, defines **recognition** as the formal recording of an item in the financial statements. The item is recorded as a numerical effect on a particular account when the four fundamental recognition criteria are met: (1) The item must meet the definition of an element (see pages 22 and 23 for the definitions), (2) it must have a relevant attribute that can be quantified in monetary units with sufficient reliability, (3) the information about it must be relevant, and (4) the information must be reliable.

NOTE: SFAC 5 defines reliable information as representationally faithful, verifiable, and neutral.

An **attribute** is a trait or an aspect of what is to be measured. Assets and liabilities are measured by different attributes, depending on the nature of the item and the relevance and reliability of the attribute measured. The attributes currently used include the following:

1. **Historical cost** is the amount of cash paid to acquire an asset. It is commonly adjusted after acquisition for depreciation or other allocations.

2. **Historical proceeds** is the amount of cash received when an obligation was incurred. It may be adjusted for amortization or other allocations.

3. **Current (replacement) cost** is the amount of cash that would have to be paid for a current acquisition of the same or an equivalent asset.

4. **Current market value (exit value)** is the amount of cash that could be obtained by selling an asset in an orderly liquidation.

5. **Net realizable value** is the nondiscounted amount of cash expected to be received for an asset in the due course of business, minus the costs of completion and sale.

6. **Settlement value** is the nondiscounted amount of cash expected to be paid to liquidate an obligation in the due course of business, plus any necessary direct costs.

7. **Present (or discounted) value of future cash flows** is the net present value of future cash flows related to the disposal of an asset or the settlement of a liability in the due course of business.

Revenues and gains ordinarily are **measured** by the exchange value of the assets or liabilities involved. According to the **revenue recognition principle**, recognition of revenues depends on whether (1) they are realized or realizable and (2) an **earning process** is substantially complete. **Realized** means that products (goods or services) or other assets are exchanged for cash or claims to cash (receivables). **Realizable** means that the related assets held are readily convertible to known amounts of cash or claims to cash. **Earned** means that the earning process has been substantially completed and the entity is entitled to the resulting benefits or revenues. However, **gains** ordinarily do not flow from an earning process. Thus, for gain recognition, being realized or realizable is more important than being earned.

Depending on the primary operations of an entity, **revenues and gains** may be **recognized** at different times in the operating cycle:

1.   Revenues from manufacturing and selling activities and gains and losses from sales of other assets are most commonly recognized at the **time of delivery**.

2.   When services are rendered or rights to use assets extend continuously over time and reliable contractual prices exist, revenues are commonly recognized based on the **passage of time**.

3.   If a product is contracted for prior to production and reasonable estimates of total profit and percentage of completion exist, revenues may be recognized as production takes place on a **percentage-of-completion basis**.

4.   If products are readily realizable because they are salable at reliably determinable prices without significant effort, revenues and some gains or losses may be recognized at **completion of production**.

5.   If collectibility of receivables is doubtful, revenues and gains may be recognized on the basis of **cash received** (e.g., the cost recovery method or the installment method).

6.   Exchanges in which nonmonetary assets are received that are not readily convertible to cash may result in revenues or gains or losses because they have been **earned** and the transactions are **complete**.

7.   Gains and losses may result when nonmonetary assets are received or distributed in **nonreciprocal exchanges**.

According to the **expense recognition principle**, expenses generally are matched with revenues. This principle is consistent with the definition of expenses (see page 23). **Matching** also is known as **associating cause and effect**. When causal relations are generally but not specifically identified (e.g., depreciation), the basis of expense recognition is **systematic and rational allocation**. The basis of expense recognition in other cases is **immediate recognition** (SFAC 6).

SFAC 5 states, "Expenses and losses are generally recognized when an entity's economic benefits are used up in delivering or producing goods, rendering services, or other activities that constitute its ongoing major or central operations or when previously recognized assets are expected to provide reduced or no further benefits." A **consumption of benefit** is recognized (1) upon recognition of revenues that result directly and jointly from the same transaction or other event as related expenses (associating cause and effect); (2) based on a systematic and rational allocation to the periods in which the related assets are expected to provide benefits (systematic and rational allocation); or (3) during the period in which cash is spent or liabilities are incurred for goods and services that are used up simultaneously with acquisition or soon thereafter (immediate recognition). A **loss of future benefit** is recognized when (1) a recognized asset's future economic benefits have been reduced or eliminated, or (2) a liability has been incurred or increased without a corresponding increase in related economic benefits.

The following table summarizes the conceptual framework underlying financial accounting:

Objective of Financial Reporting
Provide information • Useful in investment and credit decisions • Useful in assessing cash-flow prospects • About entity resources, claims to those resources, and changes in them

Qualitative Characteristics	Elements of Financial Statements

Fundamental
   Relevance
      Materiality (entity specific)
      Predictive or confirmatory value
   Faithful representation
      Completeness
      Freedom from error
      Neutrality
Enhancing
   Comparability
   Verifiability
   Timeliness
   Understandability
Cost constraint
	Assets
	Liabilities
	Equity or net assets
	Investments by owners
	Distributions to owners
	Comprehensive income
	Revenues
	Expenses
	Gains
	Losses

Recognition and Measurement Concepts	
Financial statements	Expense recognition
Revenue recognition	Measurement attributes

Assumptions	Principles	Constraints
Economic entity	Historical cost	Industry practice
Going concern	Revenue recognition	Conservatism
Monetary unit	Expense recognition	
Periodicity	Full disclosure	

Fair Value

GAAP establish a **framework for fair value measurements (FVMs)**, define fair value, and expand required disclosures. "**Fair value** is the price that would be received to sell an asset or paid to transfer a liability in an orderly transaction between market participants at the measurement date."

- The FVM is for a **particular asset or liability** that may stand alone (e.g., a financial instrument) or be part of a group (e.g., a business).
- The FVM considers **attributes** specific to the asset or liability, e.g., restrictions on sale or use, condition, and location.
- The price is an **exit price** paid or received in a hypothetical transaction considered from the perspective of a market participant.
- The **transaction** is not forced, and time is assumed to be sufficient to allow for customary marketing activities.
- The transaction is assumed to occur in the **principal market** for the asset or liability. Absent such a market, it is assumed to occur in the most advantageous market.
- **Market participants** are not related parties. They are independent of the reporting entity. They also are knowledgeable and willing and able (but not compelled) to engage in transactions involving the asset or liability. The FVM is market-based, not entity-specific. Thus, it is based on pricing **assumptions of market participants**. However, these participants need not be specifically identified. For an **asset**, the FVM is based on the **highest and best use (HBU) by market participants**. This use maximizes the value of the asset. For a **liability**, the FVM assumes transfer, not settlement. Accordingly, **nonperformance risk** is unaffected. It is included in the FVM.

Valuation techniques should be consistently applied, appropriate in the circumstances, and based on sufficient data. All or any of the following should be used to measure fair value: (1) the market approach, (2) the income approach, and (3) the cost approach. The **market approach** is based on information, such as prices, from market transactions involving identical or comparable items. The **income approach** is based on current market expectations about future amounts, such as earnings or cash flows. It converts those amounts to a discounted current amount. Examples are present value methods (see **SFAC 7** in Study Unit 4) and option-pricing models. The **cost approach** is based on **current replacement cost**. It is the cost to a market participant to buy or build an asset of comparable utility adjusted for obsolescence.

The **fair value hierarchy** establishes priorities among inputs to valuation techniques. The level of the FVM depends on the lowest level input significant to the entire FVM. **Level 1 inputs** are unadjusted **quoted prices** in active markets for identical assets (liabilities) that the entity can access at the measurement date. **Level 2 inputs** are **observable** (excluding Level 1 quoted prices). Examples are quoted prices for similar items in active markets, quoted prices in markets that are not active, and observable inputs that are not quoted prices. **Level 3 inputs** are **unobservable**. They are used in the absence of observable inputs and should be based on the best available information in the circumstances. However, the entity need not exhaust every effort to gain information about the assumptions of market participants.

The availability of the fair value option for most financial assets and financial liabilities expands FVM. It gives entities the option to use FVMs for most financial assets and liabilities (and certain other items) for which the fair value attribute is not required.

Standards

The **FASB** is the body designated to establish **GAAP** for use in the general-purpose financial statements of **nongovernmental entities**.

The sources of **authoritative** GAAP recognized by the FASB as applicable by **nongovernmental** entities are (1) the FASB's **Accounting Standards Codification™** and (2) (for **SEC registrants** only) pronouncements of the SEC. All guidance in the codification is **equally authoritative**. **SEC pronouncements** must be followed by registrants regardless of whether they are reflected in the codification.

No source of authoritative GAAP for **nongovernmental** entities may exist for a transaction or an event. In these circumstances, the entity must consider applying the authoritative guidance for a **similar transaction and event**. The entity then considers **nonauthoritative guidance**. Examples are (1) widely recognized and prevalent practices; (2) FASB Concepts Statements; (3) AICPA Issues Papers; (4) International Financial Reporting Standards (IFRS); (5) pronouncements of other professional associations or regulatory agencies; (6) AICPA Technical Practice Aids; and (7) accounting textbooks, handbooks, and articles.

The FASB issues **Accounting Standards Updates (ASUs)** to revise the codification. However, ASUs are **not** authoritative. Only the codification provides authoritative FASB guidance.

The **International Accounting Standards Board (IASB)** has the following mission:

> *The IASB is committed to developing, in the public interest, a single set of high quality, understandable and enforceable global accounting standards that require transparent and comparable information in general purpose financial statements.*

The IASB issues authoritative pronouncements in the form of International Financial Reporting Standards (IFRS). The IASB's approach to standard setting recognizes a need to publish standards that will have worldwide acceptance. Accordingly, IFRS are principles-based and tend to be less detailed than U.S. GAAP, with few exceptions and less interpretive and implementation guidance. Thus, they require a greater exercise of professional judgment regarding their application to the economic substance of transactions. Moreover, the IASB has issued **IFRS for Small and Medium-Sized Entities**, a comprehensive, self-contained pronouncement separate from full IFRS. It is based on the same principles and framework but is a modification and simplification of full IFRS. IFRS for SMES is intended to meet the needs of users of private company reports.

SEC Reporting

The **U.S. Securities and Exchange Commission (SEC)** has been empowered by Congress to establish principles for financial reporting by publicly traded companies (called issuers) in the United States. The SEC delegated this authority to the FASB. The SEC enforces those principles by ensuring that issuers meet certain periodic reporting requirements.

SEC Regulation S-X governs the reporting of financial statements, including notes and schedules. Under the SEC's **integrated disclosure system**, financial statements are standardized, and a basic information package (BIP) common to most of the filings may be used.

Form 10-K is the annual report to the SEC. Annual statements must be audited and include (1) balance sheets for the 2 most recent fiscal year ends and (2) statements of income, cash flows, and changes in equity for the 3 most recent fiscal years. They are required in the annual shareholders' report as well as in forms filed with the SEC. The accountant certifying the financial statements must be independent of the management of the filer.

Form 10-Q is the quarterly report to the SEC. Interim financial information must be reviewed (not audited) by an independent accountant.

Form 8-K is a current report to the SEC to disclose certain material events, for example, a change in control of the entity or a change in auditors. It must be filed within 4 business days after the event occurs.

Differences between GAAP and IFRS

Under IFRS:

- The **elements** of financial statements are (1) assets, (2) liabilities, (3) equity, (4) income (including revenues and gains), and (5) expenses (including losses).

- For a **sale of goods**, revenue is recognized when **five conditions** are met: (1) The entity has transferred the significant **risks and rewards** of ownership, (2) the entity has neither the continuing **managerial involvement** associated with ownership nor effective **control** over the goods, (3) the revenue (measured at the fair value of the consideration received or receivable) can be **reliably measured**, (4) it is probable that the **economic benefits** will flow to the entity, and (5) **transaction costs** can be reliably measured.

- For the **rendering of a service**, if the outcome can be reliably estimated, revenue (measured as described above) is recognized based on the stage of completion (the **percentage-of-completion** method). The outcome can be reliably estimated when (1) revenue can be **reliably measured**, (2) it is probable that the **economic benefits** will flow to the entity, (3) the **stage of completion** can be reliably measured, and (4) the **costs incurred** and the **costs to complete** can be reliably measured.

- Revenue from interest, royalties, and dividends must meet the economic benefits and reliability criteria described above. The bases of recognition are (1) the effective interest method, (2) the accrual basis in accordance with an agreement, and (3) establishment of the right to receive, respectively.

- IAS 1, *Presentation of Financial Statements*, establishes minimum required line items for the statements of financial position and comprehensive income.

- An entity must disclose comparative information for the previous period for all amounts reported in the current statements.

QUESTIONS

1.1 Introduction to the Conceptual Framework

1. What are the Statements of Financial Accounting Concepts (SFAC) intended to establish?

A. Generally accepted accounting principles in financial reporting by businesses.

B. Generally accepted accounting principles for businesses, not-for-profit entities, and state and local governments.

C. The objectives and concepts for use in developing standards of financial accounting and reporting.

D. The hierarchy of sources of generally accepted accounting principles.

Answer (C) is correct. *(CPA, adapted)*
REQUIRED: The purpose of the SFACs.
DISCUSSION: SFACs define the objectives, qualitative characteristics, and other concepts that guide the Financial Accounting Standards Board (FASB) in developing sound accounting principles. They do not establish accounting and reporting requirements. Thus, they are not authoritative and are not included in the FASB Accounting Standards Codification.
Answer (A) is incorrect. SFACs are intended to guide the development of GAAP. Answer (B) is incorrect. The FASB establishes GAAP for businesses and NFPs. The Governmental Accounting Standards Board establishes GAAP for state and local governments. Answer (D) is incorrect. FASB Accounting Standards Codification establishes GAAP for nongovernmental entities.

2. During the lifetime of a business, accountants produce financial statements at arbitrary moments in time in accordance with which basic accounting concept?

A. Verifiability.

B. Periodicity.

C. Conservatism.

D. Matching.

Answer (B) is correct. *(CPA, adapted)*
REQUIRED: The basic accounting concept requiring financial statements to be issued at arbitrary moments in time.
DISCUSSION: A basic feature of the financial accounting process is that information about the economic activities of the business should be issued at regular intervals. These time periods should be of equal length to facilitate comparability. They should also be of relatively short duration, e.g., 1 year, to provide business information useful for decision making.
Answer (A) is incorrect. Verifiability is an enhancing qualitative characteristic, not a concept related to the timing of financial statements. Answer (C) is incorrect. Under the conservatism constraint, when alternative accounting methods are appropriate, the one having the less favorable effect is preferable. Answer (D) is incorrect. Matching (another term for the expense recognition principle) requires costs to be recognized as expenses on the basis of their direct association with specific revenues to the extent possible.

3. Continuation of an accounting entity in the absence of evidence to the contrary is an example of the basic concept of

A. Accounting entity.

B. Consistency.

C. Going concern.

D. Substance over form.

Answer (C) is correct. *(CPA, adapted)*
REQUIRED: The concept regarding the continuation of a business entity.
DISCUSSION: A basic feature of financial accounting is that a business is assumed to be a going concern in the absence of evidence to the contrary. The going-concern concept is based on the empirical observation that many entities have an indefinite life.
Answer (A) is incorrect. The accounting entity concept refers to the business entity, which may or may not be synonymous with the legal entity. The emphasis is also on the separation of the entity from its ownership. Answer (B) is incorrect. The consistency principle requires that similar events be accounted for similarly in succeeding accounting periods to facilitate comparability between periods. Answer (D) is incorrect. The concept of substance over form requires accounting treatment to be based upon the economic substance of events rather than upon the legal form.

4. Reporting inventory at the lower of cost or market (LCM) is a departure from the accounting principle of

A. Historical cost.

B. Consistency.

C. Conservatism.

D. Full disclosure.

Answer (A) is correct.   *(CPA, adapted)*
REQUIRED: The principle from which reporting inventory at the lower of cost or market is a departure.
DISCUSSION: Historical cost is the amount of cash, or its equivalent, paid to acquire an asset. Thus, the LCM rule departs from the historical cost principle when the utility of the inventory is judged no longer to be as great as its cost.
Answer (B) is incorrect. LCM does not violate the consistency principle as long as it is consistently applied. Answer (C) is incorrect. LCM yields a conservative inventory valuation. Answer (D) is incorrect. As long as the basis of stating inventories is disclosed, LCM does not violate the full disclosure principle.

1.2 Objective of Financial Reporting (SFAC 8)

5. According to the FASB's conceptual framework, the objective of general-purpose financial reporting is most likely based on

A. Generally accepted accounting principles.

B. Reporting on how well management has discharged its responsibilities.

C. The need for conservatism.

D. The needs of the users of the information.

Answer (D) is correct.   *(CPA, adapted)*
REQUIRED: The objective of general-purpose financial reporting.
DISCUSSION: The objective of general-purpose financial reporting is to provide information that is useful to existing and potential investors, lenders, and other creditors in making decisions about providing resources to the entity.
Answer (A) is incorrect. GAAP govern how to account for items in the financial statements. Answer (B) is incorrect. Financial reporting provides information that is helpful, among other things, in evaluating how well management has discharged its responsibilities to make effective and efficient use of entity resources. But it is the basis for general-purpose financial reporting. Answer (C) is incorrect. Conservatism is a constraint on recognition in the statements. It is a response uncertainty.

6. Which of the following best reflects the objective of general-purpose financial reporting?

A. The primary focus of financial reporting is information about an entity's resources.

B. The best indication of an entity's ability to generate favorable cash flows is information based on previous cash flows.

C. Financial accounting is expressly designed to accurately measure the value of a business.

D. Investment and credit decisions often are based, at least in part, on evaluations of the past performance of an entity.

Answer (D) is correct.   *(Publisher, adapted)*
REQUIRED: The true statement about the objective of general-purpose financial reporting.
DISCUSSION: Although investment and credit decisions reflect investors' and creditors' expectations about future performance, those expectations are commonly based, at least in part, on evaluations of past performance. Information about financial performance helps users to understand the return on the entity's economic resources and how well management has discharged its responsibilities.
Answer (A) is incorrect. General-purpose financial reporting provides information about (1) the entity's economic resources and claims to them (financial position) and (2) changes in those resources and claims. Answer (B) is incorrect. Accrual accounting is preferable to cash basis accounting for predicting future performance. Answer (C) is incorrect. General-purpose financial reports do not suffice to measure the value of the entity. But the information provided may be helpful to those who wish to estimate its value.

7. Which of the following is least likely to be accomplished by providing general-purpose financial information useful for making decisions about providing resources to an entity?

A. To provide information about an entity's performance through measures of earnings and its components.

B. To provide information to help investors, creditors, and others assess the amounts, timing, and uncertainty of prospective net cash inflows to the entity.

C. To provide sufficient information to determine the value of the entity.

D. To provide information about management's performance.

Answer (C) is correct. *(Publisher, adapted)*
REQUIRED: The least likely benefit of general-purpose financial information.
DISCUSSION: General-purpose financial reports are significantly based on estimates and do not suffice to determine the value of the entity.
Answer (A) is incorrect. Such reporting includes information useful for differentiating between changes in economic resources and claims arising from (1) the entity's performance and (2) transactions and other events and circumstances. Answer (B) is incorrect. Such reporting includes information to help investors, creditors, and others to assess cash flows. Answer (D) is incorrect. Such reporting includes information useful for evaluating management's performance.

8. Which of the following is a true statement about the objective of general-purpose financial reporting?

A. Financial reporting is ordinarily focused on industries rather than individual entities.

B. The objective applies only to information that is useful for investment professionals.

C. Financial reporting directly measures management performance.

D. The information provided relates to the entity's economic resources and claims.

Answer (D) is correct. *(Publisher, adapted)*
REQUIRED: The true statement about the objective of general-purpose financial reporting.
DISCUSSION: The information reported relates to the entity's economic resources and claims to them (financial position) and to changes in those resources and claims.
Answer (A) is incorrect. Financial reporting is focused on individual entities. Answer (B) is incorrect. The objectives apply to information that is useful for current and potential investors, creditors, and other users in making rational investment, credit, and other decisions. Answer (C) is incorrect. Entity performance is affected by many factors other than management.

9. Determining periodic earnings and financial position depends on measuring economic resources and obligations and changes in them as these changes occur. This explanation pertains to

A. Disclosure.

B. Accrual accounting.

C. Materiality.

D. The matching concept.

Answer (B) is correct. *(CPA, adapted)*
REQUIRED: The accounting concept described.
DISCUSSION: A basic feature of financial accounting is that it is an accrual system under which the determination of periodic earnings and financial position is dependent upon the measurement of all economic resources and obligations (e.g., receivables and payables) and changes in them as the changes occur.
Answer (A) is incorrect. Disclosure pertains to the requirement that the user of financial statements be provided with sufficient information to avoid being misled. Answer (C) is incorrect. Accounting data are material if they are sufficiently significant to be included in the accounting system. Answer (D) is incorrect. The matching concept concerns the association of cause and effect, that is, of costs with revenues.

1.3 Qualitative Characteristics (SFAC 8)

10. According to the FASB's conceptual framework, the two fundamental qualitative characteristics that make accounting information useful for decision making are

A. Neutrality and completeness.

B. Fairness and precision.

C. Relevance and faithful representation.

D. Consistency and comparability.

Answer (C) is correct. *(J. Cerepak)*
REQUIRED: The two fundamental qualities that make accounting information useful.
DISCUSSION: Relevance and faithful representation are the fundamental qualities that make accounting information useful for decision making. Relevance is the capacity of information to make a difference in the user's decision. A representation is perfectly faithful if it is complete, neutral, and free from error.
Answer (A) is incorrect. Neutrality and completeness are aspects of faithful representation. Answer (B) is incorrect. Accounting information should be fairly presented, but precision (perfect accuracy) is not always possible when estimates are necessary. Answer (D) is incorrect. Comparability is a qualitative characteristic that enhances the usefulness of relevant and faithfully represented information. Consistency helps achieve comparability.

11. According to the FASB's conceptual framework, which of the following correctly pairs a fundamental qualitative characteristic of useful financial information with one of its aspects?

A. Relevance and materiality.

B. Relevance and neutrality.

C. Faithful representation and predictive value.

D. Faithful representation and confirmatory value.

Answer (A) is correct. *(CPA, adapted)*
REQUIRED: The pairing of a fundamental qualitative characteristic with one of its aspects.
DISCUSSION: Relevance is a fundamental qualitative characteristic, and materiality is an entity-specific aspect of relevance. Relevant information is able to make a difference in user decisions. To do so, it must have predictive value, confirmatory value, or both. Information is material if its omission or misstatement can influence user decisions based on a specific entity's financial information.
Answer (B) is incorrect. Relevance and faithful representation are the fundamental qualitative characteristics. A representation is perfectly faithful if it is complete, neutral, and free from error. Answer (C) is incorrect. Relevant information has predictive value, confirmatory value, or both. Answer (D) is incorrect. Relevant information has predictive value, confirmatory value, or both.

12. According to the FASB's conceptual framework, neutrality relates to which qualitative characteristic(s), if any?

	Faithful Representation	Relevance
A.	Yes	Yes
B.	Yes	No
C.	No	Yes
D.	No	No

Answer (B) is correct. *(CPA, adapted)*
REQUIRED: The items, if any, to which neutrality relates.
DISCUSSION: Useful information faithfully represents the economic phenomena that it purports to represent. A representation is perfectly faithful if it is complete (containing what is needed for user understanding), neutral (unbiased in its selection or presentation), and free from error (but not necessarily perfectly accurate). Relevant information is able to make a difference in user decisions. To do so, it must have predictive value, confirmatory value, or both.

13. Which of the following is considered a pervasive constraint by the FASB's conceptual framework?

A. Cost.

B. Conservatism.

C. Timeliness.

D. Verifiability.

Answer (A) is correct. *(CPA, adapted)*
REQUIRED: The pervasive constraint.
DISCUSSION: Cost is a pervasive constraint on the information provided by financial reporting. The benefits of financial information should exceed the costs of reporting.
Answer (B) is incorrect. Under the conservatism constraint, when alternative accounting methods are appropriate, the one having the least favorable effect is preferable. Answer (C) is incorrect. Timeliness is an enhancing qualitative characteristic of relevant and faithfully represented financial information. Answer (D) is incorrect. Verifiability is an enhancing qualitative characteristic of relevant and faithfully represented financial information.

14. According to *Statements of Financial Accounting Concepts*, predictive value relates to

	Relevance	Faithful Representation
A.	No	No
B.	Yes	Yes
C.	No	Yes
D.	Yes	No

Answer (D) is correct. *(CPA, adapted)*
REQUIRED: The primary quality of which predictive value is an ingredient.
DISCUSSION: Relevance is a fundamental qualitative characteristic of useful financial information. It is the capacity of information to make a difference in a decision. It must have (1) predictive value, (2) confirmatory value, or both. Moreover, materiality is an entity-specific aspect of relevance. Information has predictive value if it can be used in a predictive process. Something has confirmatory value with respect to prior evaluations if it provides feedback that confirms or changes (corrects) them.

15. According to the FASB's conceptual framework, what does the concept of faithful representation in financial reporting include?

    A. Predictive value.

    B. Certainty.

    C. Perfectly accurate.

    D. Neutrality.

Answer (D) is correct. *(CPA, adapted)*
    REQUIRED: The item included in the concept of faithful representation.
    DISCUSSION: Faithful representation and relevance are the fundamental qualitative characteristics of accounting information. A perfectly faithful representation is complete, neutral, and free from error. Faithfully represented information is neutral if it is unbiased in its selection or presentation of information.
    Answer (A) is incorrect. Relevant information has predictive value, confirmatory value, or both. Faithfully represented information is not necessarily relevant. Answer (B) is incorrect. Certainty and perfect accuracy are not implied by faithful representation. The financial statements are a model of the reporting entity. This model may be representationally faithful for its intended purposes without corresponding precisely to the real-world original. Thus, uncertainty that does not reach the materiality threshold does not impair faithful representation. Answer (C) is incorrect. Information may be represented faithfully, that is, complete, neutral, and free from error, without being perfectly accurate.

16. According to the FASB's conceptual framework, the usefulness of providing information in financial statements is subject to the constraint of

    A. Consistency.

    B. Cost.

    C. Relevance.

    D. Representational faithfulness.

Answer (B) is correct. *(CPA, adapted)*
    REQUIRED: The constraint on financial reporting.
    DISCUSSION: Cost is a pervasive constraint on the information provided by financial reporting. The benefits of financial information should exceed the costs of reporting.
    Answer (A) is incorrect. Consistency is a means of achieving comparability, an enhancing qualitative characteristic. It is the use of the same methods, for example, accounting principles, for the same items. Answer (C) is incorrect. Relevance is a fundamental qualitative characteristic of useful information, not a constraint. Answer (D) is incorrect. Representational faithfulness is a fundamental qualitative characteristic of useful information, not a constraint.

17. According to the FASB's conceptual framework, which of the following most likely does not violate the concept of faithful representation?

    A. Financial statements were issued 9 months late.

    B. Report data on segments having the same expected risks and growth rates to analysts estimating future profits.

    C. Financial statements included property with a carrying amount increased to management's estimate of market value.

    D. Management reports to shareholders regularly refer to new projects undertaken, but the financial statements never report project results.

Answer (B) is correct. *(CPA, adapted)*
    REQUIRED: The violation of the concept of faithful representation.
    DISCUSSION: Useful information faithfully represents the economic phenomena that it purports to represent. A representation is perfectly faithful if it is complete (containing what is needed for user understanding), neutral (unbiased in its selection or presentation), and free from error (but not necessarily perfectly accurate). The faithful representation of any given information is logically unrelated to whether the segments have the same expected risks and growth rates (assuming freedom from error) or the identity of the users.
    Answer (A) is incorrect. Late issuance is a matter of timeliness. Timeliness is a qualitative characteristic that enhances relevance and faithful representation. Information is timely when it is available in time to influence decisions. Answer (C) is incorrect. Management's estimate of market value may not be verifiable. Verifiability is a qualitative characteristic that enhances relevance and faithful representation. Information is verifiable (directly or indirectly) if knowledgeable and independent observers can reach a consensus (but not necessarily unanimity) that it is faithfully represented. Answer (D) is incorrect. Failure to report results is a matter of timeliness. Timeliness is a qualitative characteristic that enhances relevance and faithful representation. Information is timely when it is available in time to influence decisions.

18. Under SFAC 8, the ability, through consensus among measurers, to ensure that information represents what it purports to represent is an example of the concept of

    A. Relevance.

    B. Verifiability.

    C. Comparability.

    D. Predictive value.

Answer (B) is correct. *(CPA, adapted)*
    REQUIRED: The term that describes the ability to ensure that information represents what it purports to represent.
    DISCUSSION: Verifiability is a qualitative characteristic that enhances relevance and faithful representation. Information is verifiable (directly or indirectly) if knowledgeable and independent observers can reach a consensus (but not necessarily unanimity) that it is faithfully represented.
    Answer (A) is incorrect. Relevance (a fundamental qualitative characteristic) is the capacity of information to make a difference in a decision. Answer (C) is incorrect. Comparability (an enhancing qualitative characteristic) is the quality of information that enables users to identify similarities in and differences among items. Answer (D) is incorrect. Relevant information is able to make a difference in user decisions. To do so, it must have predictive value, confirmatory value, or both. Something has predictive value if it can be used as an input in a predictive process.

19. According to the FASB's conceptual framework, which of the following enhances information that is relevant and faithfully represented?

    A. Comparability.

    B. Confirmatory value.

    C. Neutrality.

    D. Materiality.

Answer (A) is correct. *(CPA, adapted)*
    REQUIRED: The item that enhances information that is relevant and faithfully represented.
    DISCUSSION: Comparability is a qualitative characteristic that enhances the usefulness of relevant and faithfully represented information. It enables users to identify similarities in and differences among items.
    Answer (B) is incorrect. Relevance is a fundamental qualitative characteristic. Relevant information is able to make a difference in user decisions. To do so, it must have predictive value, confirmatory value, or both. Something has confirmatory value with respect to prior evaluations if it provides feedback that confirms or changes (corrects) them. Answer (C) is incorrect. Faithful representation and relevance are the fundamental qualitative characteristics of accounting information. A perfectly faithful representation is complete, neutral, and free from error. Faithfully represented information is neutral if it is unbiased in its selection or presentation of information. Answer (D) is incorrect. Information is material if its omission or misstatement can influence user decisions based on a specific entity's financial information. Thus, it is an entity-specific aspect of relevance.

20. Which of the following accounting concepts states that an accounting transaction should be supported by sufficient evidence to allow two or more qualified individuals to arrive at essentially similar measures and conclusions?

    A. Matching.

    B. Verifiability.

    C. Periodicity.

    D. Stable monetary unit.

Answer (B) is correct. *(CPA, adapted)*
    REQUIRED: The accounting concept described.
    DISCUSSION: Verifiability is a qualitative characteristic that enhances relevance and faithful representation. Information is verifiable (directly or indirectly) if knowledgeable and independent observers can reach a consensus (but not necessarily unanimity) that it is faithfully represented.
    Answer (A) is incorrect. Matching associates cause and effect, for example, recognition in the same period of revenues and the expenses incurred to produce them. Answer (C) is incorrect. Periodicity is the assumption that accounting information is reported at regular intervals to provide comparability and at relatively short intervals to provide useful information. Answer (D) is incorrect. The stable monetary unit assumption is that the purchasing power of the unit of measure (e.g., the U.S. dollar) does not fluctuate.

21. Financial information is most likely to be verifiable when an accounting transaction occurs that

    A. Involves an arm's-length transaction between two independent interests.

    B. Furthers the objectives of the entity.

    C. Is promptly recorded in a fixed amount of monetary units.

    D. Allocates revenues or expense items in a rational and systematic manner.

Answer (A) is correct. *(CPA, adapted)*
    REQUIRED: The accounting transaction that most likely results in verifiable information.
    DISCUSSION: Verifiability is an enhancing qualitative characteristic of relevant and faithfully represented financial information. Information is verifiable (directly or indirectly) if knowledgeable and independent observers can reach a consensus (but not necessarily unanimity) that it is faithfully represented. The existence of an arm's-length transaction between independent interests suggests that the transaction is verifiable.
    Answer (B) is incorrect. Verifiability relates to the enhancement of relevant and faithfully represented accounting measurement, not to the objectives of any entity. Answer (C) is incorrect. Recording at a fixed amount of monetary units does not ensure that the measurement is faithfully represented. Answer (D) is incorrect. Rational and systematic allocation is a specific means of expense recognition. Systematic and rational allocation of expenses is undertaken when a direct means of associating cause and effect (expense and revenue) is lacking.

22. The concept of consistency is sacrificed in the accounting for which of the following income statement items?

    A. Discontinued operations.

    B. Loss on disposal of a component of an entity.

    C. Extraordinary items.

    D. Change in accounting principle when the cumulative effect on any prior period is not known.

Answer (D) is correct. *(CPA, adapted)*
    REQUIRED: The income statement item that sacrifices consistency.
    DISCUSSION: Information should be comparable with similar information for (1) other entities and (2) the same entity for another period or date. Thus, comparability allows users to understand similarities and differences. Consistency is a means of achieving comparability. It is the use of the same methods, for example, accounting principles, for the same items. Changes in accounting principles ordinarily are accounted for by retrospective application. However, if it is impracticable to determine the cumulative effect of applying the change to any prior period, the change is applied prospectively. Thus, similar events are not accounted for in the same way in succeeding accounting periods.
    Answer (A) is incorrect. Principles may be consistently observed in the current period in relation to the preceding period even though operations have been discontinued. Substantially different transactions or events do not result in lack of consistency. Answer (B) is incorrect. Principles may be consistently observed in the current period in relation to the preceding period even though a component of an entity has been disposed of. Substantially different transactions or events do not result in lack of consistency. Answer (C) is incorrect. Principles may be consistently observed in the current period in relation to the preceding period even though an extraordinary item has been recognized. Substantially different transactions or events do not result in lack of consistency.

23. According to the FASB's conceptual framework, the quality of information that enables users to identify similarities in and differences between two sets of economic phenomena is

    A. Conservatism.

    B. Neutrality.

    C. Matching.

    D. Comparability.

Answer (D) is correct. *(Publisher, adapted)*
    REQUIRED: The quality of information that enables users to identify similarities in and differences between two sets of economic phenomena.
    DISCUSSION: Comparability is an enhancing qualitative characteristic. Information should be comparable with similar information for (1) other entities and (2) the same entity for another period or date. Thus, comparability allows users to understand similarities and differences.
    Answer (A) is incorrect. Under the conservatism constraint, when alternative accounting methods are appropriate, the one having the less favorable effect on net income and total assets is preferable. Answer (B) is incorrect. Useful information faithfully represents the economic phenomena that it purports to represent. A representation is perfectly faithful if it is complete (containing what is needed for user understanding), neutral (unbiased in its selection or presentation), and free from error (but not necessarily perfectly accurate). Answer (C) is incorrect. Matching associates cause and effect, for example, recognition in the same period of revenues and the expenses incurred to produce them.

24. According to the FASB's conceptual framework, the quality of information that helps users increase the likelihood of correctly forecasting the outcome of past or present events is called

    A. Confirmatory value.

    B. Predictive value.

    C. Representational faithfulness.

    D. Comparability.

Answer (B) is correct. *(CPA, adapted)*
    REQUIRED: The quality of information that helps increase the likelihood of correctly forecasting the outcome of past or present events.
    DISCUSSION: Relevant information is able to make a difference in user decisions. To do so, it must have predictive value, confirmatory value, or both. Financial information has predictive value if it can be used as an input in a predictive process.
    Answer (A) is incorrect. Relevance is a fundamental qualitative characteristic. Relevant information is able to make a difference in user decisions. To do so, it must have predictive value, confirmatory value, or both. Something has confirmatory value with respect to prior evaluations if it provides feedback that confirms or changes (corrects) them. Answer (C) is incorrect. Faithful representation is a fundamental qualitative characteristic. A perfectly faithful representation is complete, neutral, and free from error. Answer (D) is incorrect. Comparability is an enhancing qualitative characteristic. Information should be comparable with similar information for (1) other entities and (2) the same entity for another period or date. Thus, comparability allows users to understand similarities and differences.

25. To be relevant, financial information should have which of the following?

    A. Neutrality.

    B. Confirmatory value.

    C. Understandability.

    D. Costs and benefits.

Answer (B) is correct. *(CPA, adapted)*
    REQUIRED: The characteristic of relevant financial information.
    DISCUSSION: Relevance is a fundamental qualitative characteristic. Relevant information is able to make a difference in user decisions. To do so, it must have predictive value, confirmatory value, or both. Something has confirmatory value with respect to prior evaluations if it provides feedback that confirms or changes (corrects) them.
    Answer (A) is incorrect. Neutrality is an aspect of faithful representation. Answer (C) is incorrect. Understandability is an enhancing qualitative characteristic. Understandable information is clearly and concisely classified, characterized, and presented. Information should be readily understandable by reasonably knowledgeable and diligent users, but information should not be excluded because of its complexity. Answer (D) is incorrect. Cost is the pervasive constraint in the hierarchy of accounting qualities.

26. Which of the following characteristics relates to both accounting relevance and faithful representation?

    A. Verifiability.

    B. Timeliness.

    C. Comparability.

    D. All of the answers are correct.

Answer (D) is correct. *(CPA, adapted)*
    REQUIRED: The characteristic(s) relating to relevance and faithful representation.
    DISCUSSION: Verifiability, timeliness, comparability, and understandability are qualitative characteristics that enhance the relevance and faithful representation of accounting information.
    Answer (A) is incorrect. Verifiability is an enhancing qualitative characteristic of relevant and faithfully represented financial information. Information is verifiable (directly or indirectly) if knowledgeable and independent observers can reach a consensus (but not necessarily unanimity) that it is faithfully represented. Answer (B) is incorrect. Timeliness is an enhancing qualitative characteristic of relevant and faithfully represented financial information. Information is timely when it is available in time to influence decisions. Answer (C) is incorrect. Comparability enhances the relevance and faithful representation of information. It is the quality of information that enables users to identify similarities in and differences among items.

1.4 Elements (SFAC 6)

27. According to the FASB's conceptual framework, which of the following is an essential characteristic of an asset?

A. The claims to an asset's benefits are legally enforceable.

B. An asset is tangible.

C. An asset is obtained at a cost.

D. An asset provides future benefits.

Answer (D) is correct. *(CPA, adapted)*
REQUIRED: The essential characteristic of an asset.
DISCUSSION: One of the three essential characteristics of an asset is that the transaction or event giving rise to the entity's right to or control of its assets has already occurred. It is not expected to occur in the future. A second essential characteristic of an asset is that an entities can obtain the benefits of, and control others' access to, the asset. The third essential characteristic is that an asset must embody a probable future benefit that involves a capacity to contribute to future net cash inflows (SFAC 6, *Elements of Financial Statements*).
Answer (A) is incorrect. Claims to an asset's benefits may not be legally enforceable, for example, in the case of goodwill. Answer (B) is incorrect. Some assets are intangible. Answer (C) is incorrect. Assets may be obtained through donations or investments by owners.

28. Under SFAC 6, *Elements of Financial Statements*, interrelated elements of financial statements that are directly related to measuring the performance and status of an entity include

	Distribution to Owners	Notes to Financial Statements
A.	Yes	Yes
B.	Yes	No
C.	No	Yes
D.	No	No

Answer (B) is correct. *(CPA, adapted)*
REQUIRED: The financial statement element(s) directly related to measuring status and performance of an entity.
DISCUSSION: The elements of financial statements directly related to measuring the performance and status of both businesses and not-for-profit entities are (1) assets, (2) liabilities, (3) equity of a business or net assets of a not-for-profit entity, (4) revenues, (5) expenses, (6) gains, and (7) losses. The elements of investments by owners, distributions to owners, and comprehensive income relate only to businesses. Information disclosed in notes or parenthetically on the face of financial statements amplifies or explains information recognized in the financial statements.
Answer (A) is incorrect. The notes to the financial statements, while considered an integral part of the statements, are not among the "interrelated elements that are directly related to measuring performance and status of an entity" (SFAC 6). Answer (C) is incorrect. The interrelated elements of financial statements referred to in SFAC 6 include distributions to owners, as well as such items assets, liabilities, equity. The notes to the financial statements are not among the elements. Answer (D) is incorrect. Distributions to owners is one of the "10 interrelated elements that are directly related to measuring performance and status of an entity" defined in SFAC 6.

29. An essential characteristic of a liability is that

A. The obligated entity must pay cash to a recipient entity.

B. It must be legally enforceable.

C. The identity of the recipient entity must be known to the obligated entity before the time of settlement.

D. The obligation must have arisen as the result of a previous transaction.

Answer (D) is correct. *(Publisher, adapted)*
REQUIRED: The characteristic that is essential to the existence of a liability.
DISCUSSION: SFAC 6, *Elements of Financial Statements*, defines three essential characteristics of a liability: (1) It represents an obligation that requires settlement by probable future transfer or use of assets, (2) the entity has little or no discretion to avoid the obligation, and (3) the transaction or other event giving rise to the obligation has already occurred.
Answer (A) is incorrect. Liabilities often require the payment of cash, but they could also be satisfied through the use of other assets or the provision of services. Answer (B) is incorrect. Liabilities are usually but not always legally enforceable. Answer (C) is incorrect. The identity of the recipient must be known only by the time of settlement, not before.

30. According to the FASB's conceptual framework, asset valuation accounts are

A. Assets.

B. Neither assets nor liabilities.

C. Part of equity.

D. Liabilities.

Answer (B) is correct. *(CPA, adapted)*
REQUIRED: The conceptual framework's definition of asset valuation accounts.
DISCUSSION: Asset valuation accounts are separate items sometimes found in financial statements that reduce or increase the carrying amount of an asset. The conceptual framework considers asset valuation accounts (e.g., an allowance for bad debts) to be part of the related asset account. They are not considered to be assets or liabilities in their own right (SFAC 6, *Elements of Financial Statements*).
Answer (A) is incorrect. An asset valuation account adjusts the measurement of an asset but is not a separate asset. Answer (C) is incorrect. Asset valuation accounts are part of the related assets. They therefore cannot be part of equity. Answer (D) is incorrect. An asset valuation account is a separate item that reduces or increases the carrying amount of an asset. It therefore cannot be a liability.

31. A stated purpose of SFAC 6, *Elements of Financial Statements*, is to

A. Define three classes of net assets for businesses.

B. Define the elements necessary for presentation of financial statements of both business and not-for-profit entities.

C. Apply the comprehensive income concept to not-for-profit entities.

D. Apply its principles to reporting by state and local governmental units.

Answer (B) is correct. *(Publisher, adapted)*
REQUIRED: The stated purpose of SFAC 6.
DISCUSSION: SFAC 6 defines 10 interrelated elements of financial statements that are directly related to measuring the performance and status of an entity. Of these, seven are found in statements of both business and not-for-profit entities: (1) assets, (2) liabilities, (3) equity or net assets, (4) revenues, (5) expenses, (6) gains, and (7) losses. Investments by owners, distributions to owners, and comprehensive income are elements of financial statements of businesses only.
Answer (A) is incorrect. SFAC 6 defines three classes of net assets of not-for-profit entities and the changes therein during the period. Answer (C) is incorrect. The comprehensive income concept is not applicable to not-for-profit entities. Answer (D) is incorrect. SFAC 6 does not apply its principles to reporting by state and local governmental units. GASB Concepts Statements apply to such entities.

32. Which of the following statements about accrual accounting is false?

A. Accrual accounting is concerned with the process by which cash expended on resources and activities is returned as more (or perhaps less) cash to the entity, not just with the beginning and end of that process.

B. Accrual accounting recognizes that buying, producing, selling, and other operations of an entity during a period often do not coincide with the cash receipts and payments of the period.

C. Accrual accounting attempts to record the financial effects on an entity of transactions and other events and circumstances that have cash consequences for an entity.

D. Accrual accounting is primarily concerned with the cash receipts and cash payments of an entity.

Answer (D) is correct. *(Publisher, adapted)*
REQUIRED: The false statement about accrual accounting.
DISCUSSION: Accrual accounting attempts to record the financial effects on an entity of transactions and other events and circumstances that have cash consequences in the periods in which those transactions, events, and circumstances occur, rather than only in the periods in which cash is received or paid by the entity. Thus, the focus of accrual accounting is not primarily on the actual cash receipts and cash payments. It is concerned with the process by which cash expended on resources is returned as more (or perhaps less) cash to the entity, not just with the beginning and end of the process.
Answer (A) is incorrect. Accrual accounting is concerned with the process by which cash expended on resources and activities is returned as more (or perhaps less) cash to the entity, not just with the beginning and end of that process. Answer (B) is incorrect. Accrual accounting recognizes that buying, producing, selling, and other operations of an entity during a period often do not coincide with the cash receipts and payments of the period. Answer (C) is incorrect. Accrual accounting attempts to record the financial effects on an entity of transactions and other events and circumstances that have cash consequences for an entity.

33. According to the FASB's conceptual framework, an entity's revenue may result from

A. A decrease in an asset from primary operations.

B. An increase in an asset from incidental transactions.

C. An increase in a liability from incidental transactions.

D. A decrease in a liability from primary operations.

Answer (D) is correct. *(CPA, adapted)*
REQUIRED: The possible source of revenue.
DISCUSSION: According to SFAC 6, *Elements of Financial Statements*, revenues are inflows or other enhancements of assets or settlements of liabilities from activities that constitute the entity's ongoing major or central operations. Thus, a revenue may result from a decrease in a liability from primary operations, for example, by delivering goods that were paid for in advance.
Answer (A) is incorrect. A decrease in an asset from primary operations results in an expense. Answer (B) is incorrect. An increase in an asset from incidental transactions results in a gain. Answer (C) is incorrect. An increase in a liability from incidental transactions results in a loss.

34. Which of the following best describes the distinction between expenses and losses?

A. Losses are reported net of related tax effect, but expenses are not reported net of tax.

B. Losses are extraordinary charges, but expenses are ordinary charges.

C. Losses are material items, but expenses are immaterial items.

D. Losses result from peripheral or incidental transactions, but expenses result from ongoing major or central operations of the entity.

Answer (D) is correct. *(CIA, adapted)*
REQUIRED: The distinction between expenses and losses.
DISCUSSION: SFAC 6, *Elements of Financial Statements*, defines expenses as "outflows or other using up of assets or incurrences of liabilities (or a combination of both) from delivering or producing goods, rendering services, or carrying out other activities that constitute the entity's ongoing major or central operations." Losses are defined as "decreases in equity (net assets) from peripheral or incidental transactions of an entity and from all other transactions and other events and circumstances affecting the entity except those that result from expenses or distributions to owners."
Answer (A) is incorrect. Although some losses (e.g., losses from discontinued operations) are reported net of tax, most are not. Answer (B) is incorrect. Extraordinary gains or losses are items that are unusual and infrequent in the environment in which the entity operates. Thus, most losses are ordinary. Answer (C) is incorrect. The primary distinction is that expenses result from ongoing operations, and losses result from peripheral or incidental transactions.

35. The FASB's conceptual framework explains both financial and physical capital maintenance concepts. Which capital maintenance concept is applied to currently reported net income, and which is applied to comprehensive income?

	Currently Reported Net Income	Comprehensive Income
A.	Financial capital	Physical capital
B.	Physical capital	Physical capital
C.	Financial capital	Financial capital
D.	Physical capital	Financial capital

Answer (C) is correct. *(CPA, adapted)*
REQUIRED: The capital maintenance concept(s) applicable to currently reported net income and comprehensive income.
DISCUSSION: The financial capital maintenance concept is the traditional basis of financial statements, including comprehensive income (a return on financial capital). Under this concept, a return on investment (defined in terms of money) results only if the financial amount of net assets at the end of the period exceeds the amount at the beginning after excluding transactions with owners. Under a physical capital concept, a return on investment (in terms of physical capital) results only if the physical productive capacity (or the resources to achieve that capacity) at the end of the period exceeds the capacity at the beginning after excluding transactions with owners. The latter concept requires many assets to be measured at current (replacement) cost. Under the financial capital concept, price changes, if recognized, are holding gains and losses included in return on capital. Under the physical capital concept, those changes are recognized directly in equity.

36. The primary purpose of the statement of financial position of a business is to reflect

    A. The fair value of the entity's assets at some moment in time.

    B. The status of the entity's assets in case of forced liquidation.

    C. The entity's potential for growth in stock values in the stock market.

    D. Items of value, debts, and net worth.

Answer (D) is correct. *(CMA, adapted)*
    REQUIRED: The primary purpose of the statement of financial position (balance sheet).
    DISCUSSION: In conformity with GAAP, the statement of financial position or balance sheet of a business presents three major financial accounting elements: assets (items of value), liabilities (debts), and equity (net worth). According to SFAC 6, *Elements of Financial Statements*, "Assets are probable future economic benefits obtained or controlled by a particular entity as a result of past transactions or events." SFAC 6 defines liabilities as "probable future sacrifices of economic benefits arising from present obligations of a particular entity to transfer assets or provide services to other entities in the future as a result of past transactions or events." SFAC 6 defines the equity of a business as "the residual interest in the assets of an entity that remains after deducting its liabilities."
    Answer (A) is incorrect. Assets are reported in the balance sheet using various measurement attributes, including but not limited to fair values. Answer (B) is incorrect. The balance sheet usually does not report forced liquidation values. Answer (C) is incorrect. The future value of an entity's stock is more dependent upon future operations and investors' expectations than on the data found in the balance sheet.

37. Consolidated financial statements are prepared when a parent-subsidiary relationship exists in recognition of the accounting concept of

    A. Materiality.

    B. Entity.

    C. Verifiability.

    D. Going concern.

Answer (B) is correct. *(CPA, adapted)*
    REQUIRED: The accounting concept recognized in consolidated financial statements.
    DISCUSSION: According to SFAC 6, *Elements of Financial Statements*, the elements are defined in terms of a specific entity. For example, consolidated financial statements should reflect the economic activities of a business measured without regard to the boundaries of the legal entity. Accounting information pertains to a business, the boundaries of which are not necessarily those of the legal entity. Thus, a parent and subsidiary are legally separate but are treated as a single business in consolidated statements. A business also may be required to consolidate certain entities that are not subsidiaries (see Study Unit 24).
    Answer (A) is incorrect. Materiality requires reporting of information that has a value significant enough to affect decisions of those using the financial statements. Answer (C) is incorrect. Verifiability means having an existence independent of the observer. Answer (D) is incorrect. The going-concern concept assumes that the business will continue to operate in the absence of evidence to the contrary, but it is not a reason for preparing consolidated statements.

1.5 Recognition and Measurement (SFAC 5)

38. Recognition is the process of formally incorporating an item into the financial statements of an entity as an asset, liability, revenue, expense, or the like. Recognition criteria include all of the following except

    A. Measurability with sufficient reliability.

    B. Definitions of elements of financial statements.

    C. Decision usefulness.

    D. Relevance.

Answer (C) is correct. *(CMA, adapted)*
    REQUIRED: The item not included in the recognition criteria.
    DISCUSSION: SFAC 5, *Recognition and Measurement in Financial Statements of Business Enterprises*, states that an item and information about the item should be recognized when the following four fundamental recognition criteria are met: (1) The item meets the definition of an element of financial statements; (2) it has a relevant attribute measurable with sufficient reliability (measurability); (3) the information about the item is capable of making a difference in user decisions (relevance); and (4) the information is representationally faithful, verifiable, and neutral (reliability). Decision usefulness is the objective of general-purpose financial reporting stated in SFAC 8, not a specific recognition criterion.
    Answer (A) is incorrect. Measurability with sufficient reliability is among the recognition criteria. Answer (B) is incorrect. An item must meet the definition of an element of financial statements. Answer (D) is incorrect. Relevance is among the recognition criteria.

39. According to the FASB conceptual framework, which of the following statements conforms to the realization concept?

- A. Equipment depreciation was assigned to a production department and then to product unit costs.

- B. Depreciated equipment was sold in exchange for a note receivable.

- C. Cash was collected on accounts receivable.

- D. Product unit costs were assigned to cost of goods sold when the units were sold.

Answer (B) is correct. *(CPA, adapted)*
REQUIRED: The statement that conforms to the realization concept.
DISCUSSION: The term "realization" is used most precisely in accounting and financial reporting with regard to sales of assets for cash or claims to cash. According to SFACs 5 and 6, the terms "realized" and "unrealized" identify revenues or gains and losses on assets sold and unsold, respectively. Thus, the sale of depreciated equipment for a claim to cash meets the definition of realization.
Answer (A) is incorrect. Assigning costs to products is allocation, not realization. Answer (C) is incorrect. Realization occurred when the accounts receivable (claims to cash) were recognized. Answer (D) is incorrect. Assigning costs to products is allocation, not realization.

40. Revenues of an entity are usually measured by the exchange values of the assets or liabilities involved. Recognition of revenue does not occur until

- A. The revenue is realizable.

- B. The revenue is realized and earned.

- C. Products or services are exchanged for cash or claims to cash.

- D. The entity has substantially accomplished what it agreed to do.

Answer (B) is correct. *(CMA, adapted)*
REQUIRED: The appropriate timing of the recognition of revenue.
DISCUSSION: In accordance with SFAC 5, revenues should be recognized when they are realized or realizable and earned. Revenues are realized when products, merchandise, or other assets are exchanged for cash or claims to cash. Revenues are realizable when related assets received or held are readily convertible to known amounts of cash or claims to cash. Revenues are earned when the entity has substantially accomplished what it must do to be entitled to the benefits represented by the revenues.
Answer (A) is incorrect. Revenue is recognized when it is (1) realizable (or realized) and (2) earned. Answer (C) is incorrect. Revenues are realized when products or services are exchanged for cash or claims to cash. However, they also must be earned to be recognized. Answer (D) is incorrect. Substantial accomplishment is a business matter between the two parties. It may indicate that revenue has been earned, but not that it is realized or realizable.

41. The Star Company is a service entity that requires customers to place their orders 2 weeks in advance. Star bills its customers on the 15th day of the month following the date of service and requires that payment be made within 30 days of the billing date. Conceptually, Star should recognize revenue from its services at the date when

- A. A customer places an order.

- B. The service is provided.

- C. A billing is mailed.

- D. A customer's payment is received.

Answer (B) is correct. *(CIA, adapted)*
REQUIRED: The date at which a catering service should recognize revenue.
DISCUSSION: According to SFAC 5, revenues should be recognized when they are realized or realizable and earned. The most common time at which these two conditions are met is when the product or merchandise is delivered or services are rendered to customers.
Answer (A) is incorrect. When a customer places an order, Star has not met any of the recognition criteria. Answer (C) is incorrect. Mailing a bill is not necessary for the recognition of revenue. Star should recognize revenue from performing services when the revenue is realized or realizable and earned, that is, as soon as the service has been performed. Answer (D) is incorrect. Star need not wait for payment to be received from the customer. Revenue is recognized once Star has substantially completed the earning process, i.e., performed its service for the customer, and exchanged its service for a claim to cash (e.g., a receivable).

42. For a monthly fee, Roach Co. visits its customers' premises and performs pest control services. If customers experience problems between regularly scheduled visits, Roach makes service calls at no additional charge. Instead of paying monthly, customers may pay an annual fee in advance. For a customer who pays the annual fee in advance, Roach should recognize the related revenue

A. When the cash is collected.

B. At the end of the fiscal year.

C. At the end of the contract year after all of the services have been performed.

D. Evenly over the contract year as the services are performed.

Answer (D) is correct. *(CPA, adapted)*
REQUIRED: The timing of recognition of revenue.
DISCUSSION: Accrual-based revenue should be recognized when realized or realizable and earned. When the earning process involves service, these conditions are usually met when the services are rendered. Because these services involve monthly visits, the annual payment should be recognized evenly over the period in which the services are performed.
Answer (A) is incorrect. Recognition when cash is collected is appropriate when the cash basis is used. Answer (B) is incorrect. The matching principle requires revenues to be matched with the time periods in which the revenue is earned. Roach will perform services throughout the period covered by the contract. Thus, revenue should be matched with the interim fiscal period in which it is earned. Answer (C) is incorrect. Revenue should be recognized when it is (1) earned and (2) realized or realizable. The second criterion is fulfilled because Roach has already received payment. The first criterion is partially fulfilled each time Roach performs a service. Thus, revenue should be recognized throughout the contract period. Roach should not wait until the contract period is finished.

43. The selling price for a product is reasonably assured, the units are interchangeable, and the costs of selling and distributing the product are insignificant. To recognize revenue from the product as early in the revenue cycle as is permitted by GAAP, the revenue recognition method that should be used is the

A. Cash method.

B. Completion-of-production method.

C. Percentage-of-completion method.

D. Cost recovery method.

Answer (B) is correct. *(CMA, adapted)*
REQUIRED: The revenue recognition method allowing proper recognition of revenue prior to the sale of the merchandise.
DISCUSSION: Revenue is to be recognized when it is realized or realizable and earned. Some products or other assets, such as precious metals or certain agricultural products, are readily realizable (convertible) because they are salable at reliably determinable prices without significant effort. For such products, revenues and some gains or losses may be recognized when production is completed or when prices of the assets change. Readily realizable assets have (1) interchangeable units and (2) quoted prices in an active market.
Answer (A) is incorrect. When a product is readily realizable, revenue recognition need not be delayed until cash is received. Answer (C) is incorrect. The percentage-of-completion method would unnecessarily delay the recognition of revenue. Answer (D) is incorrect. The cost recovery method is appropriate when cash collection is in doubt.

44. Under a royalty agreement with another entity, a company will receive royalties from the assignment of a patent for 2 years. The royalties received should be reported as revenue

A. At the date of the royalty agreement.

B. In the period earned.

C. In the period received.

D. Evenly over the life of the royalty agreement.

Answer (B) is correct. *(CPA, adapted)*
REQUIRED: The timing of recognition of royalty revenue.
DISCUSSION: In accordance with SFAC 5, revenues should be recognized when they are realized or realizable and earned. Revenues are realized when products, merchandise, or other assets are exchanged for cash or claims to cash. Revenues are realizable when related assets received or held are readily convertible to known amounts of cash or claims to cash. Revenues are earned when the entity has substantially accomplished what it must do to be entitled to the benefits represented by the revenues. Earning embraces the activities that give rise to revenue, for example, allowing other entities to use assets (such as patents) or the occurrence of an event specified in a contract (such as production using the patented technology).
Answer (A) is incorrect. No earning process has yet taken place on the date of the royalty agreement. Answer (C) is incorrect. Revenue recognition under accrual accounting does not depend on the receipt of cash. Revenue is recognized when it is (1) earned and (2) realized or realizable. Answer (D) is incorrect. The life of the royalty agreement may not match the period in which the revenue from the agreement is actually earned.

45. Which of the following is not a theoretical basis for the allocation of expenses?

    A. Systematic allocation.

    B. Cause and effect.

    C. Profit maximization.

    D. Immediate recognition.

Answer (C) is correct. *(CPA, adapted)*
    REQUIRED: The accounting concept that is not a theoretical basis for allocation of expenses.
    DISCUSSION: Profit maximization is not a theoretical basis for the allocation of expense. The allocation of expenses on such a basis would subvert the purpose of GAAP to present fairly the results of operations and financial position because expenses would not be reported.
    Answer (A) is incorrect. Expenses are to be recognized by a systematic and rational allocation if causal relations are generally identifiable but particular amounts cannot be related directly to specific revenues or periods. Answer (B) is incorrect. Expenses should be recognized in a particular period if they have a direct association with that period or with specific revenues recognized in that period. Answer (D) is incorrect. Immediate recognition is appropriate when costs have no discernible future benefits or there is no other theoretically sound basis for allocation of the expenses.

46. Costs that can be reasonably associated with specific revenues but not with specific products should be

    A. Charged to expense in the period incurred.

    B. Allocated to specific products based on the best estimate of the production processing time.

    C. Expensed in the period in which the related revenue is recognized.

    D. Capitalized and then amortized over a period not to exceed 60 months.

Answer (C) is correct. *(CPA, adapted)*
    REQUIRED: The time to recognize costs that can be reasonably associated with specific revenues but not with specific products.
    DISCUSSION: The expense recognition principle of associating cause and effect (often called matching) applies when a direct cause-and-effect relationship can be demonstrated between costs and particular revenues. A typical example of expenses recognized by the association of cause and effect is cost of goods sold. Association of costs with revenues can also be applied to services. Association of costs with specific products is not necessary.
    Answer (A) is incorrect. Immediate recognition is permitted only if no cause-and-effect relationship can be demonstrated and there is no other basis on which to expense the costs. Answer (B) is incorrect. A systematic and rational allocation of costs (based on processing time or length of asset service) is made if only a general (not direct) cause-and-effect relationship exists between costs and revenues. Answer (D) is incorrect. A systematic and rational allocation of costs (based on processing time or length of asset service) is made if only a general (not direct) cause-and-effect relationship exists between costs and revenues.

47. Some costs cannot be directly related to particular revenues but are incurred to obtain benefits that are exhausted in the period in which the costs are incurred. An example of such a cost is

    A. Salespersons' monthly salaries.

    B. Salespersons' commissions.

    C. Transportation to customers.

    D. Prepaid insurance.

Answer (A) is correct. *(CPA, adapted)*
    REQUIRED: The costs not directly related to particular revenues but incurred to obtain benefits exhausted in the same period in which they are incurred.
    DISCUSSION: Expenses should be recognized when benefits have been consumed. The consumption of benefit may occur when (1) the expenses are matched with the revenues, (2) they are allocated on a systematic and rational basis to the periods in which the related assets are expected to provide benefits, or (3) the cash is spent or liabilities are incurred for goods and services that are used up either simultaneously with the acquisition or soon after. Salespersons' monthly salaries is an example of a cost that cannot be directly related to particular revenues but is incurred to obtain benefits that are exhausted in the period in which the cost is incurred.
    Answer (B) is incorrect. Salespersons' commissions are directly related to particular revenues. Answer (C) is incorrect. Transportation to specific customers can be linked to goods or services sold to those customers. Answer (D) is incorrect. Prepaid insurance benefits a number of accounting periods. Its cost should thus be allocated on a systematic and rational basis to the accounting periods benefited.

48. Ande Co. estimates uncollectible accounts expense using the ratio of past actual losses from uncollectible accounts to past net credit sales, adjusted for anticipated conditions. The practice follows the accounting concept of

    A. Consistency.

    B. Going-concern.

    C. Matching.

    D. Substance over form.

Answer (C) is correct. *(CPA, adapted)*
REQUIRED: The concept applied to estimate uncollectible accounts expense based on a ratio of past net credit sales.
DISCUSSION: Matching bad debt expense with related revenues is an application of the matching principle. Matching is synonymous with associating cause and effect. It is based on a direct relationship between the expense and the revenue.
Answer (A) is incorrect. Consistency is a means of achieving comparability, an enhancing qualitative characteristic of useful financial information. Consistency is the use of the same methods, e.g., accounting principles, for the same items. Answer (B) is incorrect. Going-concern is an assumption underlying the environment in which the reporting entity operates. It is the assumption that the entity will continue operating indefinitely. Answer (D) is incorrect. The concept of substance over form guides accountants to present the financial reality of a transaction over its legal form. An example is the consolidation of a legally separate subsidiary by a parent. Presenting a parent and a separate entity that it controls as one reporting entity is faithfully representational. Thus, substance over form is more closely related to a fundamental qualitative characteristic than to an expense recognition principle.

49. Why are certain costs of doing business capitalized when incurred and then depreciated or amortized over subsequent accounting cycles?

    A. To reduce the federal income tax liability.

    B. To aid management in the decision-making process.

    C. To match the costs of production with revenues as earned.

    D. To adhere to the accounting concept of conservatism.

Answer (C) is correct. *(CPA, adapted)*
REQUIRED: The reason certain costs are capitalized and then depreciated or amortized.
DISCUSSION: If costs benefit more than one accounting period, they should be systematically and rationally allocated to all periods benefited. This is done by capitalizing the costs and depreciating or amortizing them over the periods in which the asset helps generate revenue. Matching is most narrowly defined as the expense recognition principle of associating cause and effect, but it is sometimes used more broadly (as here) to apply to the entire process of expense recognition or even of income determination.
Answer (A) is incorrect. Capitalization and depreciation of costs on the financial statements have no effect on federal income tax liability. Answer (B) is incorrect. Expense recognition principles are applied to benefit all users of financial statements, not merely management. Answer (D) is incorrect. The accounting concept of conservatism requires a prudent approach to uncertainty but without the introduction of bias into financial reporting. Thus, the more conservative approach might be to recognize all costs immediately.

50. Which of the following is an example of the expense recognition principle of associating cause and effect?

    A. Allocation of insurance cost.

    B. Sales commissions.

    C. Depreciation of fixed assets.

    D. Officers' salaries.

Answer (B) is correct. *(CPA, adapted)*
REQUIRED: The example of associating cause and effect for expense recognition.
DISCUSSION: If a direct cause-and-effect relationship can be established between costs and revenues, the costs should be recognized as expenses when the related revenue is recognized. Costs of products sold or services provided and sales commissions are examples of costs that can be associated with specific revenues.
Answer (A) is incorrect. Allocation of insurance cost is an example of allocating costs among several periods on a systematic and rational basis. Answer (C) is incorrect. Depreciation is an example of allocating costs among several periods on a systematic and rational basis. Answer (D) is incorrect. Officers' salaries are expenses that are recognized immediately. They provide no discernible future benefits, and there is no other more useful basis of allocation.

51. Which of the following is an application of the principle of systematic and rational allocation?

    A. Amortization of intangible assets.

    B. Sales commissions.

    C. Research and development costs.

    D. Officers' salaries.

Answer (A) is correct. *(CPA, adapted)*
    REQUIRED: The application of the concept of systematic and rational allocation.
    DISCUSSION: The expense recognition principle of systematic and rational allocation is applied to the amortization of intangible assets because of the absence of a direct means of associating cause and effect. The costs benefit a number of periods (they generate revenue in those periods) and should be systematically and rationally allocated.
    Answer (B) is incorrect. Sales commissions directly relate to particular revenues and should be recognized as an expense when the related revenues are recognized. Answer (C) is incorrect. Research and development costs are expensed in the period incurred. Answer (D) is incorrect. Officers' salaries are expensed in the period incurred.

52. A patent, purchased in Year 1 and amortized over a 15-year life, was determined to be worthless in Year 6. The write-off of the asset in Year 6 is an application of which of the following principles?

    A. Associating cause and effect.

    B. Immediate recognition.

    C. Systematic and rational allocation.

    D. Objectivity.

Answer (B) is correct. *(CPA, adapted)*
    REQUIRED: The accounting principle of which the write-off of a patent is an example.
    DISCUSSION: The patent was being amortized in a systematic and rational manner. When it was determined that the costs associated with the patent (recorded as an asset) no longer provided discernible benefits, the remaining unamortized costs were written off; that is, the loss was recognized immediately.
    Answer (A) is incorrect. Associating cause and effect is a method of deferring costs to future periods that is not appropriate when a cost has no discernible future benefit. Answer (C) is incorrect. Systematic and rational allocation is a method of amortizing the patent. Answer (D) is incorrect. Objectivity is neither a quality of accounting information nor an accounting principle.

53. Items reported in financial statements must have a relevant attribute that can be measured in monetary units. According to the conceptual framework,

    A. The unit of measure should have constant general purchasing power.

    B. One attribute should be used for measuring all assets and one for all liabilities.

    C. Different measurement attributes are used for different items depending on the nature of the item.

    D. The unit of measure should be current cost.

Answer (C) is correct. *(Publisher, adapted)*
    REQUIRED: The approach to measurement.
    DISCUSSION: Current accounting practice is based on (1) nominal units of money (unadjusted for changes in purchasing power) and (2) quantifiable attributes. Attributes used in practice include (1) historical cost (historical proceeds), (2) current cost, (3) current market value, (4) net realizable (settlement) value, and (5) present (or discounted) value of future cash flows. The use of different attributes will continue.
    Answer (A) is incorrect. Unless inflation increases to an intolerable level, measurement will continue to be in nominal units of money. Answer (B) is incorrect. Use of different attributes will continue. Answer (D) is incorrect. Current cost is an attribute, not a unit of measure.

54. Which of the following is not a basis for the immediate recognition of a cost during a period?

    A. The cost provides no discernible future benefit.

    B. The cost recorded in a prior period no longer produces discernible benefits.

    C. The federal income tax savings using the immediate write-off method exceed the savings obtained by allocating the cost to several periods.

    D. Allocation of the cost on the basis of association with revenue or among several accounting periods is considered to serve no useful purpose.

Answer (C) is correct. *(CPA, adapted)*
    REQUIRED: The item that should not be immediately recognized as an expense.
    DISCUSSION: In applying the principles of expense recognition, costs are analyzed to determine whether they can be associated with revenue on a cause-and-effect basis, e.g., cost of goods sold. If not, a systematic and rational allocation should be attempted, e.g., depreciation. If neither principle is applicable, only then are costs recognized as expenses in the period incurred or in which a loss is discerned. Accordingly, even though federal income tax savings could be obtained by the immediate write-off method, GAAP might require another treatment of the expense.
    Answer (A) is incorrect. A cost with no discernible future benefit is not capitalized. It does not meet the definition of an asset. Answer (B) is incorrect. The matching principle requires costs to be matched with their associated revenues. If a particular cost will no longer produce benefits, it does not meet the definition of an asset and must be expensed. Answer (D) is incorrect. Allocation of a cost for the sake of allocation does not provide the user of financial statements with useful information. In this case, the cost should be expensed immediately.

55. Items currently reported in financial statements are measured by different attributes. The amount of cash or its equivalent that would have to be paid if the same or an equivalent asset were acquired currently defines the attribute of

A. Historical cost.

B. Current cost.

C. Current market value.

D. Net realizable value.

Answer (B) is correct. *(Publisher, adapted)*
REQUIRED: The measurement attribute defined by SFAC 5.
DISCUSSION: The amount of cash or its equivalent that would have to be paid if the same or an equivalent asset were acquired currently is the definition of the measurement attribute of current (replacement) cost. Some inventories are reported in accordance with this attribute.
Answer (A) is incorrect. Historical cost is the amount of cash or its equivalent paid to acquire an asset. Answer (C) is incorrect. Current market value is the amount of cash or its equivalent that could be obtained by selling an asset in orderly liquidation. Answer (D) is incorrect. Net realizable value is the nondiscounted amount of cash or its equivalent into which an asset is expected to be converted in due course of business minus any direct cost necessary to make that conversion.

56. The appropriate attribute for measuring noncurrent payables is

A. Historical cost.

B. Current cost.

C. Net realizable value.

D. Present value of future cash flows.

Answer (D) is correct. *(CMA, adapted)*
REQUIRED: The appropriate attribute to use when measuring noncurrent payables.
DISCUSSION: According to SFAC 5, the appropriate measurement attribute for noncurrent liabilities is "the present or discounted value of future cash outflows expected to be required to satisfy the liability in due course of business."
Answer (A) is incorrect. Historical cost is an attribute of assets, not liabilities. Assets are generally purchased in a marketplace or in a transaction in which "cost" is quantifiable. Liabilities are not "purchased" in the same way assets are. The attribute of a liability to provide goods or services is historical proceeds. Answer (B) is incorrect. Current cost is a concept used in assessing the outlays that would be required to replace assets. It is not a concept related to liabilities, such as noncurrent payables. Answer (C) is incorrect. Net realizable value is a valuation concept applied to current receivables and some inventories, not payables.

57. What is the purpose of information presented in notes to the financial statements?

A. To provide disclosures required by generally accepted accounting principles.

B. To correct improper presentation in the financial statements.

C. To provide recognition of amounts not included in the totals of the financial statements.

D. To present management's response to auditor comments.

Answer (A) is correct. *(CPA, adapted)*
REQUIRED: The purpose of information presented in notes to the financial statements.
DISCUSSION: Notes are an integral part of the basic financial statements. Notes provide information essential to understanding the financial statements, including disclosures required by GAAP (SFAC 5).
Answer (B) is incorrect. Notes may not be used to rectify an improper presentation. Answer (C) is incorrect. Disclosure in notes is not a substitute for recognition in financial statements for items that meet recognition criteria. Answer (D) is incorrect. Management's response to auditor comments is not an appropriate subject of financial reporting.

1.6 Fair Value

58. According to GAAP, fair value is

A. An entry price.

B. An exit price.

C. Based on an actual transaction.

D. An entity-specific measurement.

Answer (B) is correct. *(Publisher, adapted)*
REQUIRED: The nature of fair value.
DISCUSSION: "Fair value is the price that would be received to sell an asset or paid to transfer a liability in an orderly transaction between market participants at the measurement date." Thus, fair value is an exit price.
Answer (A) is incorrect. An entry price is what is paid or received in an orderly exchange to acquire an asset or assume a liability, respectively. Answer (C) is incorrect. Fair value is an exit price paid or received in a hypothetical transaction considered from the perspective of a market participant. Answer (D) is incorrect. Fair value is market-based. It is based on pricing assumptions of market participants.

59. For the purpose of a fair value measurement (FVM) of an asset or liability, a transaction is assumed to occur in the

  A. Principal market if one exists.

  B. Most advantageous market.

  C. Market in which the result is optimized.

  D. Principal market or most advantageous market at the election of the reporting entity.

Answer (A) is correct. *(Publisher, adapted)*
  REQUIRED: The market in which a transaction is assumed to occur.
  DISCUSSION: For FVM purposes, a transaction is assumed to occur in the principal market for an asset or liability if one exists. The principal market has the greatest volume or level of activity. If no such market exists, the transaction is assumed to occur in the most advantageous market.
  Answer (B) is incorrect. If no principal market exists, the transaction is assumed to occur in the most advantageous market. Answer (C) is incorrect. The principal market is not necessarily the most advantageous market. Answer (D) is incorrect. No election is allowed.

60. Fair value measurements (FVMs) of assets and liabilities are based on transactions between market participants at the measurement date. Market participants

  A. Must be specifically identified.

  B. May be related parties if they are knowledgeable about the asset or liability.

  C. Include parties who are forced to engage in the transactions if they are independent of the entity.

  D. Are willing and able to engage in transactions involving the asset or liability.

Answer (D) is correct. *(Publisher, adapted)*
  REQUIRED: The characteristic of market participants.
  DISCUSSION: Market participants are not related parties. They are independent of the reporting entity. They also are knowledgeable and willing and able (but not compelled) to engage in transactions involving the asset or liability.
  Answer (A) is incorrect. Market participants need not be specifically identified. Instead, the entity must identify their general characteristics, with consideration of factors specific to (1) the asset or liability, (2) the market, and (3) parties with whom the entity would deal. Answer (B) is incorrect. Market participants must be independent of the entity. Answer (C) is incorrect. Market participants do not include parties who engage in forced or liquidation sales or are otherwise compelled to act.

61. The fair value measurement (FVM) of an asset

  A. Assumes transfer, not a settlement.

  B. Is based on the expected use by the reporting entity.

  C. Reflects the highest and best use by market participants.

  D. Includes the entity's own credit risk.

Answer (C) is correct. *(Publisher, adapted)*
  REQUIRED: The true statement about the FVM of an asset.
  DISCUSSION: The FVM is based on the highest and best use (HBU) by market participants. This use maximizes the value of the asset. The HBU is in-use if the value-maximizing use is in combination with other assets in a group. An example is machinery. The HBU is in-exchange if the value-maximizing use is as a standalone asset. An example is a financial asset.
  Answer (A) is incorrect. The FVM of a liability, not an asset, assumes transfer without settlement. Answer (B) is incorrect. The FVM assumes use by market participants. Answer (D) is incorrect. The FVM of a liability includes nonperformance risk. An element of nonperformance risk is the entity's own credit risk (credit standing).

62. Valuation techniques for fair value measurement (FVM) must use

  A. The market approach or income approach but not the cost approach.

  B. The pricing assumptions of market participants.

  C. Only observable inputs.

  D. Current replacement cost to approximate fair value.

Answer (B) is correct. *(Publisher, adapted)*
  REQUIRED: The element used in valuation techniques for FVM.
  DISCUSSION: Inputs to valuation techniques are the pricing assumptions of market participants. The assumptions include those about the risk of a given technique or its inputs.
  Answer (A) is incorrect. The entity may use all or any of the following: (1) the market approach (based on information, such as prices, from market transactions involving identical or comparable items), (2) the income approach (based on current market expectations about future amounts, such as earnings or cash flows converted to a discounted current amount), and (3) the cost approach (based on current replacement cost, which is the cost to a market participant to buy or build an asset of comparable utility adjusted for obsolescence). Answer (C) is incorrect. Unobservable inputs are based on the entity's own assumptions about the assumptions of market participants that reflect the best available information in the circumstances. They should be minimized but are allowable in proper circumstances. Answer (D) is incorrect. The market and income approaches also may be used.

63. Which of the following items would best enable Driver Co. to determine whether the fair value of its investment in Favre Corp. is properly stated in the balance sheet?

    A. Discounted cash flow of Favre's operations.

    B. Quoted market prices available from a business broker for a similar asset.

    C. Quoted market prices on a stock exchange for an identical asset.

    D. Historical performance and return on Driver's investment in Favre.

Answer (C) is correct. *(CPA, adapted)*
    REQUIRED: The best measure of the fair value of an investment.
    DISCUSSION: In the fair value hierarchy, Level 1 inputs are the most reliable. They are unadjusted quoted prices in active markets for identical assets or liabilities that the entity can access at the measurement date.
    Answer (A) is incorrect. Discounted cash flow is consistent with the income approach to valuation. It is based on current market expectations, e.g., about earnings or cash flows. Discounted cash flow is a Level 2 input, so it is observable, that is, based on market data from independent sources. But it is less reliable than a Level 1 input. Answer (B) is incorrect. Quoted market prices available from a business broker for a similar asset are Level 2 inputs, that is, observable but less reliable than Level 1 inputs. Answer (D) is incorrect. Historical performance and return on Driver's investment in Favre are Level 3 inputs (unobservable). They are based on the entity's own assumptions about the assumptions of market participants that reflect the best available information. The use of Level 3 inputs should be minimized.

1.7 Standards

64. The primary current source of generally accepted accounting principles for nongovernmental U.S. entities is the

    A. Securities and Exchange Commission.

    B. Financial Accounting Foundation.

    C. Financial Accounting Standards Board.

    D. American Institute of Certified Public Accountants.

Answer (C) is correct. *(Publisher, adapted)*
    REQUIRED: The institution primarily responsible for the establishment of generally accepted accounting principles.
    DISCUSSION: The FASB is a full-time autonomous board with the responsibility of establishing financial accounting standards. It is charged to be responsive to the needs and views of the entire economic community, not just the public accounting profession, and it operates in public through a due process system. After the evaluation required by the Sarbanes-Oxley Act of 2002, the SEC reaffirmed the FASB as the U.S. standard-setting body for nongovernmental entities. All authoritative GAAP established by the FASB are contained in its Accounting Standards Codification™.
    Answer (A) is incorrect. The SEC has the authority to establish accounting rules for publicly held U.S. corporations, but it has effectively delegated that authority to the FASB. Answer (B) is incorrect. GAAP are issued by the FASB. The Financial Accounting Foundation is the body that oversees the FASB. Answer (D) is incorrect. The AICPA established the Financial Accounting Foundation, which in turn created the FASB for the purpose of issuing generally accepted accounting principles.

65. Arpco, Inc., a for-profit provider of healthcare services, recently purchased two smaller companies and is researching accounting issues arising from the two business combinations. Which of the following accounting pronouncements are the most authoritative?

    A. FASB Accounting Standards Updates.

    B. FASB Statements of Financial Accounting Concepts.

    C. FASB Statements of Financial Accounting Standards.

    D. The Accounting Standards Codification™.

Answer (D) is correct. *(CPA, adapted)*
    REQUIRED: The most authoritative pronouncements.
    DISCUSSION: The FASB's Accounting Standards Codification™ is the only source of authoritative guidance for nongovernmental entities that are not SEC registrants. SEC registrants also must follow SEC pronouncements. Everything else is nonauthoritative.
    Answer (A) is incorrect. The FASB Accounting Standards Updates are authoritative only to the extent they have been incorporated in the Accounting Standards Codification™. Answer (B) is incorrect. The FASB Statements of Financial Accounting Concepts are nonauthoritative. Answer (C) is incorrect. FASB Statements of Financial Accounting Standards are no longer issued. Existing SFASs are authoritative only to the extent they have been incorporated in the Accounting Standards Codification™.

1.8 SEC Reporting

66. Which of the following statements is correct concerning corporations subject to the reporting requirements of the Securities Exchange Act of 1934?

    A. The annual report (Form 10-K) need not include audited financial statements.

    B. The annual report (Form 10-K) must be filed with the SEC within 20 days of the end of the corporation's fiscal year.

    C. A quarterly report (Form 10-Q) need only be filed with the SEC by those corporations that are also subject to the registration requirements of the Securities Act of 1933.

    D. A report (Form 8-K) must be filed with the SEC after a material important event occurs.

Answer (D) is correct. *(CPA, adapted)*
    REQUIRED: The reporting required under the Securities Exchange Act of 1934.
    DISCUSSION: Current reports must be filed on Form 8-K describing specified material events: (1) changes in control of the registrant, (2) the acquisition or disposition of a significant amount of assets other than in the ordinary course of business, (3) bankruptcy or receivership, (4) resignation of a director, and (5) a change in the registrant's certifying accountant.
    Answer (A) is incorrect. Form 10-K must include audited financial statements: comparative balance sheets and statements of income, cash flows, and changes in equity. Answer (B) is incorrect. Form 10-K is due at least 60 days after the entity's fiscal year-end. Answer (C) is incorrect. An entity required to file Form 10-K must also file Form 10-Q for each of the first three quarters.

67. Integral Corp. is subject to the reporting provisions of the Securities Exchange Act of 1934. For its current fiscal year, Integral filed the following with the SEC: quarterly reports, an annual report, and a periodic report listing newly appointed officers of the corporation. Integral did not notify the SEC of shareholder "short-swing" profits, did not report that a competitor made a tender offer to Integral's shareholders, and did not report changes in the price of its stock as sold on the New York Stock Exchange. Under the SEC reporting requirements, which of the following was Integral required to do?

    A. Report the tender offer to the SEC.

    B. Notify the SEC of shareholder "short-swing" profits.

    C. File the periodic report listing newly appointed officers.

    D. Report the changes in the market price of its stock.

Answer (C) is correct. *(CPA, adapted)*
    REQUIRED: The reporting required of a covered corporation under the 1934 act.
    DISCUSSION: A covered corporation is required to file annual (10-K), quarterly (10-Q), and current events (8-K) reports with the SEC. Similar reports are sent to shareholders. The 10-K report contains information about the entity's business activities, securities, management, related parties, disagreements about accounting principles and disclosure, audited financial statements, etc. It is intended to bring the information in the registration statement up to date. Thus, newly appointed officers will be listed.
    Answer (A) is incorrect. The target need only file a statement with the SEC if the tender offer is hostile (unsolicited). Answer (B) is incorrect. Insiders are liable to the corporation for short-swing profits. Insiders include directors, officers, and persons owning more than 10% of the corporation's stock. Answer (D) is incorrect. Although the annual report (Form 10-K) requires disclosure of the market price of the common stock of the registrant (including the high and low sales prices) for each quarter of the last 2 fiscal years and any subsequent interim periods, not every change in the market price of its stock need be reported.

1.9 IFRS

68. On July 1, Year 2, a company decided to adopt IFRS. The company's first IFRS reporting period is as of and for the year ended December 31, Year 2. The company will present 1 year of comparative information. What is the company's date of transition to IFRS?

    A. January 1, Year 1.

    B. January 1, Year 2.

    C. July 1, Year 2.

    D. December 31, Year 2.

Answer (A) is correct. *(CPA, adapted)*
    REQUIRED: The date of transition to IFRS.
    DISCUSSION: The date of transition is "the beginning of the earliest period for which an entity presents full comparative information under IFRS in its first IFRS financial statements" (IFRS 1). Thus, the date of transition is January 1, Year 1. In the entity's first IFRS financial statements, it must present at least (1) three statements of financial position, (2) two statements of comprehensive income, (3) two separate income statements (if presented), (4) two statements of cash flows, and (5) two statements of changes in equity and related notes.
    Answer (B) is incorrect. January 1, Year 2, does not consider the requirement to present at least 1 year of comparative information. Answer (C) is incorrect. July 1, Year 2, is the date the entity decided to adopt IFRS. Answer (D) is incorrect. December 31, Year 2, is the reporting date.

69. Under IFRS, which of the following is the first step within the hierarchy of guidance to which management refers, and whose applicability it considers, when selecting accounting policies?

A. Consider the most recent pronouncements of other standard-setting bodies to the extent that do not conflict with the IFRS or the IASB Framework.

B. Apply a standard from IFRS if it specifically relates to the transaction, other event, or condition.

C. Consider the applicability of the definitions, recognition criteria, and measurement concepts in the IASB Framework.

D. Apply the requirements in IFRS dealing with similar and related issues.

Answer (B) is correct.   *(CPA, adapted)*
REQUIRED: The first step in the IFRS hierarchy.
DISCUSSION: When an IASB Standard or Interpretation specifically applies to a transaction, other event, or condition, it must be selected if the effect is material. Any Implementation Guidance also must be considered. Absent such a standard or Interpretation, management considers (1) guidance for similar and related issues in other IASB Standards and Interpretations and (2) the content of the Framework for the Preparation and Presentation of Financial Statements.
Answer (A) is incorrect. The IFRS hierarchy does not refer to pronouncements of other standard setters. Answer (C) is incorrect. The content of the Framework is considered only when a specific IASB Standard or Interpretation does not apply. Answer (D) is incorrect. An entity may apply the requirements in IFRS dealing with similar and related issues only when a specific IASB Standard or Interpretation does not apply.

70. Which of the following may be accounted for retrospectively by first-time adopters of IFRS?

A. Hedges.

B. Estimates.

C. Employee benefit plans.

D. Noncontrolling interests.

Answer (C) is correct.   *(Publisher, adapted)*
REQUIRED: The item for which retrospective application is allowed to first-time adopters of IFRS.
DISCUSSION: With certain exceptions, the six items for which retrospective application is prohibited for first-time adopters of IFRS are (1) derecognition of financial assets and financial liabilities, (2) hedges, (3) estimates, (4) noncontrolling interests, (5) classification and measurement of financial assets, and (6) embedded derivatives.
Answer (A) is incorrect. Retrospective application for hedge accounting is prohibited for first-time adopters of IFRS. Answer (B) is incorrect. Retrospective application for estimates is prohibited for first-time adopters of IFRS. Answer (D) is incorrect. Retrospective application for noncontrolling interests is prohibited for first-time adopters of IFRS.

Use Gleim **EQE Test Prep** Software Download for interactive study and performance analysis.

STUDY UNIT TWO
THE ACCOUNTING PROCESS

The Accounting System

An accounting system consists of a set of **accounts**, recorded in a **journal** and posted to a **ledger**. It records the effects of the **transactions and other events and circumstances** that must be recognized by the entity. The accounting system classifies the items, summarizes their effects, and reports the results in the form of **financial statements**. The accounting system is based on the **debit-credit** and **double-entry** convention. In accordance with the convention, a debit is an increase (decrease) in one type of account, and a credit is a decrease (increase) in the same account. For each account, the balance equals the sum of the amounts debited and credited. Moreover, the monetary amount of the total debits must be equal to the total credits. The result of applying the convention is that the effects both of individual recorded items and of total recorded items are reported in accordance with the **balance sheet equation**.

$$Assets = Liabilities + Equity\ (Net\ Assets)$$

This equation reports resources on one side and the claims to those resources on the other side. The equation may be restated as follows:

$$Assets - Liabilities = Net\ Assets$$

This equation presents **equity (net assets)** as the residual interest remaining after subtracting creditor claims. These two equations depict the resources and financing of an entity **at a moment in time**. The results of operations **over a period of time** are reported based on this equation:

$$Net\ income\ (Change\ in\ Net\ Assets) = Revenues - Expenses + Gains - Losses$$

Assets, liabilities, and equity (net assets) are recorded in **permanent (real) accounts**. Their balances at the end of one accounting period (the balance sheet date) are carried forward as the beginning balances of the next accounting period. Revenues, expenses, gains, losses, and dividends are recorded in **temporary (nominal) accounts** because they record the transactions, events, and other circumstances during a period of time. These accounts are closed (zeroed) at the end of each accounting period, and their balances are transferred to real accounts. An entity's **chart of accounts** names the accounts used in that entity's accounting system. The following table summarizes the application of the debit-credit convention:

	Permanent (Real) Accounts			Temporary (Nominal) Accounts	
	Balance Sheet			Income Statement	
	Assets	Liabilities	Equity (Net Assets)	Revenues & Gains	Expenses & Losses
Increase	Debit	Credit	Credit	Credit	Debit
Decrease	Credit	Debit	Debit	Debit	Credit

Accruals and Deferrals

To comply with GAAP, the **accrual basis of accounting** must be used. Accrual accounting involves recording the financial effects of transactions and other events and circumstances when they occur rather than when their direct cash consequences occur. Thus, accrual accounting provides information about assets, liabilities, and changes in them not provided by the cash method. Accrual accounting involves accruals and deferrals, including allocations and amortizations. **Accruals** anticipate future cash flows. They recognize noncash assets or liabilities and the related liabilities, assets, revenues, expenses, gains, or losses. Sales or purchases on account, interest, and taxes are common accruals. **Deferrals** reflect past cash flows. They recognize liabilities (for cash receipts) and assets (for cash payments), with deferral of the related revenues, expenses, gains, and losses. The deferral ends when the obligation is satisfied or the future economic benefit is used up. Prepaid insurance is a typical deferral. **Allocation** is the assignment or distribution of an amount according to a plan or formula. Examples are the apportionment of a lump-sum purchase price among the assets acquired and the assignment of manufacturing costs to products. **Amortization** is a form of allocation. It decreases an amount by periodic payments or write-downs. More specifically, it is an allocation process for deferrals. It involves reducing a liability (asset) recorded as a result of a cash receipt (payment) by recognizing revenues (expenses). Examples are depreciation and depletion expenses and the recognition of earned subscriptions revenue.

Journal Entries

Journal entries record the financial effects of transactions, events, and other circumstances in the accounting system. For every journal entry, the total debited must equal the total credited. Every journal entry therefore must affect at least two accounts, and the effects (debit and credit) must be posted to specific accounts. Journal entries are recorded in **books of original entry (journals)**. Account balances are maintained in the **general ledger**. Every entity maintains a general journal and a general ledger. Many entities also maintain special journals and subsidiary ledgers. During an accounting period, a series of journal entries and postings are made to record and classify the financial effects of transactions, events, and other circumstances in accordance with GAAP. **Adjusting entries** are made as of the balance sheet date to record the effects on periodic revenue and expense of prepayments (prepaid expenses and unearned revenues) and accruals (revenues earned but not yet realized in cash and expenses incurred but not yet paid in cash). Other adjustments also may be necessary, e.g., recognition of unrealized gains or losses on available-for-sale and trading securities. **Closing entries** transfer (close) temporary account balances to retained earnings. **Reversing entries** reverse the effects of adjusting entries to simplify the future recording of revenue and expense transactions related to the adjusting entries. Adjusting, closing, and reversing entries must affect at least one temporary account and at least one real account.

At the end of each accounting period, a process is undertaken known as **closing the books**. No more entries can be made for that accounting period, and reports can be produced. At various stages during this process, trial balances are prepared. A **trial balance** is a report of the balances of every account in the general ledger, providing proof that total debits continue to equal total credits. All of the recording, posting, and closing activities are parts of the **accounting cycle**, summarized as follows:

1. **Journalize** the entries
2. **Post** the entries to the ledger(s)
3. Prepare an **unadjusted** trial balance
4. Post the **adjusting** entries
5. Prepare an **adjusted** trial balance

6. Produce the **financial statements**
7. Post the **closing** entries
8. Prepare a **post-closing** trial balance
9. Post the **reversing** entries

The following is a memory aid: **J**ane **P**ost **U**pdated **A**n **A**nalysis of **F**ixed **C**osts, **P**roperty, and **R**evenues.

Other Comprehensive Basis of Accounting (OCBOA)

Financial statements based on a reporting system other than GAAP are prepared using an OCBOA. Examples are (1) a tax basis; (2) a basis required by a regulator; (3) the cash basis or modifications of it having substantial support; and (4) a definite set of criteria having substantial support that is applied to all material items, for example, the price-level basis. Statements prepared using an OCBOA should include a summary of significant accounting policies, including discussion of the basis used and how it differs from GAAP.

For individuals and very small businesses, the cash basis of accounting is sufficient. This system has the advantage of simplicity, but it is not acceptable for general-purpose external financial reporting by nongovernmental entities. Under the strict **cash basis** of accounting, revenues and expenses are recognized when cash is received or paid, respectively, regardless of when goods are delivered or received or when services are rendered. The cash basis ignores the revenue and expense recognition principles that are fundamental to the accrual basis. This method may be appropriate for small businesses operated as sole proprietorships. The **modified cash basis** uses the cash basis for typical operating activities with modifications having substantial support, for example, reporting inventory, accruing income taxes, or capitalizing and depreciating fixed assets. This method often is used by professional services firms, such as physicians, realtors, and architects. The **income tax basis** must be applied to calculate income tax liability. Certain doctrines underlying the federal tax code differ significantly from those in the conceptual framework. For example, the code requires the modified accelerated cost recovery system (MACRS), a depreciation method not recognized under GAAP.

Personal Financial Statements

Personal financial statements of individuals or families are prepared to plan their financial affairs in general or for a specific purpose, e.g., tax or retirement planning. **Assets** should be presented at their estimated current values. The **estimated current value** is the amount at which an item can be exchanged between a buyer and seller, each of whom is well informed and willing, and neither of whom is compelled to buy or sell. **Liabilities**, including payables, are presented at their estimated current amounts at the date of the statement. The **estimated current amount** is the lower of (1) the discounted amount of cash to be paid or (2) the amount at which the debt can currently be discharged. The discount rate is the rate implicit in the transaction in which the debt was incurred. Estimated current values (amounts) may be based on **recent transactions** involving similar assets (liabilities) in similar circumstances. Absent such transactions, other valuation bases, such as **discounted cash flow** or **appraisal value**, may be used if they are consistently applied.

A **statement of financial condition** must be prepared. It presents assets, liabilities, estimated income taxes, and net worth (total assets – total liabilities – estimated income tax) at a given date. **Estimated income taxes** are calculated as if the assets had been realized or the liabilities liquidated. Estimated income taxes are based on the differences between assets and liabilities and their tax bases. **Taxes payable**, including estimated taxes, are reported between liabilities and net worth.

A **statement of changes in net worth** and comparative financial statements may be presented. Assets and liabilities and changes in them are recognized on the **accrual basis**. **Noncancelable commitments to pay future sums** (e.g., fixed amounts of alimony for a definite future period) are presented at their discounted amounts as liabilities if they (1) are for fixed or determinable amounts, (2) are not contingent, and (3) do not require the future performance of service by another. **Nonforfeitable rights to receive future sums** (e.g., annuities) are presented as assets at their discounted amounts if they meet the same criteria. The assets and liabilities of an investment in a **limited business activity** not conducted in a separate business entity (such as an investment in real estate and a related mortgage) are separately presented. A **business interest** that is a large part of an individual's total assets is presented separately as a single amount equal to the estimated current value of the business interest.

Difference between GAAP and IFRS

Under IFRS:

- Personal financial statements are not specifically addressed.

QUESTIONS
2.1 The Accounting System

1. A chart of accounts is

A. A flowchart of all transactions.

B. An accounting procedures manual.

C. A journal.

D. A list of names of all account titles.

Answer (D) is correct. *(Publisher, adapted)*
REQUIRED: The definition of a chart of accounts.
DISCUSSION: A chart of accounts is a listing of all account titles used within an accounting system. Business transactions affecting these accounts are initially recorded by journal entries and then posted to the individual accounts maintained in the ledger.
Answer (A) is incorrect. Actual transactions are not flowcharted. Flowcharts of accounting procedures are developed by auditors and systems analysts (but are not called charts of accounts). Answer (B) is incorrect. An accounting procedures manual explains how to use the chart of accounts, e.g., whether to make adjusting entries, reversing entries, etc. Answer (C) is incorrect. A journal contains the initial recording of the transactions that affect the accounts contained in the chart of accounts.

2. As commonly used, the term "net assets" of a business enterprise represents

A. Retained earnings of a corporation.

B. Current assets minus current liabilities.

C. Total paid-in (contributed) capital of a corporation.

D. Total assets minus total liabilities.

Answer (D) is correct. *(CPA, adapted)*
REQUIRED: The definition of net assets.
DISCUSSION: Net assets of a business enterprise is equal to total assets minus total liabilities. It is synonymous with the net worth of an entity as expressed in the balance sheet equation: assets – liabilities = equity.
Answer (A) is incorrect. Retained earnings is the cumulative income earned by a corporation minus amounts declared as dividends. Answer (B) is incorrect. Current assets minus current liabilities is working capital. Answer (C) is incorrect. Total paid-in (contributed) capital of a corporation is the sum of all money and property received from investors. In addition to total paid-in (contributed) capital, net assets includes retained earnings and accumulated other comprehensive income.

3. What are real accounts?

A. Nonfictitious accounts.

B. Accounts in existence.

C. Balance sheet accounts.

D. Income statement accounts.

Answer (C) is correct. *(Publisher, adapted)*
REQUIRED: The definition of real accounts.
DISCUSSION: Real accounts are not closed at the end of the year and can carry forward nonzero balances from one accounting period to the next. Real accounts are typically balance sheet accounts and are also called permanent accounts.
Answer (A) is incorrect. The term "nonfictitious accounts" has no accounting meaning. Answer (B) is incorrect. Nominal accounts can also exist. Answer (D) is incorrect. Income statement accounts are nominal accounts.

4. What is the purpose of nominal accounts?

A. To provide temporary accumulations of certain account balances for a meaningful period of time.

B. To facilitate accounting for small amounts.

C. To correct errors as they are detected.

D. To record all transactions initially.

Answer (A) is correct. *(Publisher, adapted)*
REQUIRED: The purpose of nominal accounts.
DISCUSSION: The primary focus of financial reporting is to account for earnings. To facilitate the calculation of earnings, nominal revenue and expense accounts are created to accumulate temporarily the components of earnings during an accounting period. At the end of the period, they are usually aggregated to determine net income. Each nominal account is reduced to a zero balance by closing it to retained earnings, a balance sheet account.
Answer (B) is incorrect. Small amounts are recorded in real as well as nominal accounts. Answer (C) is incorrect. Errors are corrected wherever they are found, e.g., in real accounts, nominal accounts, ledgers, or journals. Answer (D) is incorrect. All transactions are initially recorded in the books of original entry called journals.

5. In the equation, assets + expenses + losses = liabilities + revenues + gains + equity, the expenses and revenues are

A. Contra asset and contra liability accounts, respectively, that assist analysis of the financial progress of the firm.

B. Incorrectly stated because their signs are reversed. Both are contra items that should have negative signs in the formula.

C. Adjustments to equity that are postponed until the end of a specific accounting period to determine their net effect on equity for that period.

D. Incorrectly included in the formula because assets = liabilities + equity.

Answer (C) is correct. *(Publisher, adapted)*
REQUIRED: The status of expenses and revenues in the basic accounting equation.
DISCUSSION: Expenses and revenues are adjustments to retained earnings (an equity account of a business) that are not made immediately upon their occurrence. Instead, they are postponed until the end of a specific accounting period to determine their net effect on equity for that period, i.e., at the time of computation of net income (revenues + gains – expenses – losses). They are initially recorded in nominal accounts.
Answer (A) is incorrect. Contra asset and contra liability accounts reduce the related accounts. For example, accumulated depreciation offsets the related asset. Answer (B) is incorrect. Expenses are debits (positive) on the left-hand side of the equation. Revenues are credits (positive) on the right-hand side of the equation. Answer (D) is incorrect. The debits to assets equal the sum of the credits to liabilities and equity accounts, but the given equation is also correct.

6. The basic accounting equation (assets – liabilities = equity) for a business reflects the

A. Entity point of view.

B. Fund theory.

C. Proprietary point of view.

D. Enterprise theory.

Answer (C) is correct. *(Publisher, adapted)*
REQUIRED: The concept reflected by the basic accounting equation.
DISCUSSION: The equation is based on the proprietary theory: The owners' interest (residual equity) is what remains after the economic obligations of the entity are subtracted from its economic resources.
Answer (A) is incorrect. The entity concept limits accounting information to that related to a specific entity (possibly not the same as the legal entity). Answer (B) is incorrect. Fund theory stresses that assets equal obligations (equity and liabilities are sources of assets). Answer (D) is incorrect. The enterprise concept stresses ownership of the assets. The emphasis is on the credit side of the balance sheet.

7. A subsidiary ledger is

A. A listing of the components of account balances.

B. A backup system to protect against record destruction.

C. A listing of account balances just before closing entries are prepared.

D. All accounts of a subsidiary.

Answer (A) is correct. *(Publisher, adapted)*
REQUIRED: The definition of a subsidiary ledger.
DISCUSSION: A general or controlling ledger contains the balance for each asset, liability, and equity account. A subsidiary ledger consists of the detail of a general ledger account, e.g., the individual receivables making up accounts receivable in the aggregate.
Answer (B) is incorrect. A subsidiary ledger is not a supplementary accounting system. Answer (C) is incorrect. A listing of account balances just before closing entries are prepared is a trial balance. Answer (D) is incorrect. The term "subsidiary ledger" relates to a specific general ledger account, not the accounting systems of a subsidiary company.

8. An example of a nominal account of a business enterprise is

    A. Customer deposits.

    B. Capital stock.

    C. Petty cash.

    D. Sales returns.

Answer (D) is correct. *(Publisher, adapted)*
    REQUIRED: The example of a nominal account.
    DISCUSSION: Sales returns is a nominal account because it is used to accumulate the amount of sales returns for a given period. At the end of the period, the balance of sales returns is zero because it is closed at the end of the period. Nominal accounts usually are closed to retained earnings. They exist for an accounting period for the purpose of determining the effect on equity of net income. (An exception is cash dividends payable, a nominal account sometimes debited when cash dividends are declared. It does not affect net income.)
    Answer (A) is incorrect. Customer deposits are a real account (balance sheet account) and is not closed at the end of an accounting period. The nonzero balances in real accounts at the end of one accounting period become the beginning balances of the next period. Answer (B) is incorrect. Capital stock is a real account (balance sheet account) and is not closed at the end of an accounting period. The nonzero balances in real accounts at the end of one accounting period become the beginning balances of the next period. Answer (C) is incorrect. Petty cash is a real account (balance sheet account) and is not closed at the end of an accounting period. The nonzero balances in real accounts at the end of one accounting period become the beginning balances of the next period.

9. Which of the following statements is a true description of reversing entries?

    A. The recording of reversing entries is a mandatory step in the accounting cycle.

    B. Reversing entries are made at the end of the next accounting period, after recording regular transactions of the period.

    C. Reversing entries are identical to the adjusting entries made in the previous period.

    D. Reversing entries are the exact opposite of the adjustments made in the previous period.

Answer (D) is correct. *(CIA, adapted)*
    REQUIRED: The true description of reversing entries.
    DISCUSSION: Reversing entries are made at the beginning of a period to reverse the effects of adjusting entries made at the end of the preceding period. They are optional entries made for the sake of convenience in recording the transactions of the period. In order for reversing entries to reverse the prior adjustments, they must be the exact opposite of the adjustments made in the previous period.
    Answer (A) is incorrect. Reversing entries are optional. Answer (B) is incorrect. Reversing entries are made at the beginning of the next accounting period. Answer (C) is incorrect. Reversing entries are the exact opposite of the adjustments made in the previous period.

10. The business reason usually given for a business to select a fiscal year different from the calendar year is that

    A. The firm's owners may have a personal preference.

    B. Tax laws favor firms that employ a fiscal year other than the calendar year.

    C. The fiscal year end is selected to coincide with the low points in sales, production, and inventories, which may occur at some period other than the calendar year end.

    D. Public accounting firms might not be able to handle the workload if all their clients were to report on a calendar-year basis.

Answer (C) is correct. *(CMA, adapted)*
    REQUIRED: The most common reason for selecting a fiscal year different from the calendar year.
    DISCUSSION: A fiscal year is a 12-month period that ends at a date other than December 31. The businesses' natural business year is normally chosen. A natural year runs from one low point in a firm's business activity to the same low point 12 months later.
    Answer (A) is incorrect. Personal preference is a less compelling reason than matching the period chosen with the entity's normal business cycle. Answer (B) is incorrect. In the long term, choice of a fiscal year provides no tax advantage. Answer (D) is incorrect. An entity should choose a reporting period based on its normal business cycle, not the convenience of accounting firms.

2.2 Accruals and Deferrals

11. An accrued expense can best be described as an amount

    A. Paid and currently matched with earnings.

    B. Paid and not currently matched with earnings.

    C. Not paid and not currently matched with earnings.

    D. Not paid and currently matched with earnings.

Answer (D) is correct. *(CPA, adapted)*
    REQUIRED: The best description of an accrued expense.
    DISCUSSION: An accrued expense is one that has been incurred but not paid. Thus, it should be charged (matched) against revenue in the current period and recorded as a liability.
    Answer (A) is incorrect. An expense paid in the same period in which it is incurred is not accrued and does not require an adjusting entry. Answer (B) is incorrect. An amount paid and not currently matched with earnings is a deferral of expense. Answer (C) is incorrect. An expense neither paid nor incurred requires no original entry and no adjusting entry.

12. How would the proceeds received from the advance sale of nonrefundable tickets for a theatrical performance be reported in the seller's financial statements before the performance?

    A. Revenue for the entire proceeds.

    B. Revenue to the extent of related costs expended.

    C. Unearned revenue to the extent of related costs expended.

    D. Unearned revenue for the entire proceeds.

Answer (D) is correct. *(CPA, adapted)*
    REQUIRED: The reporting of the proceeds received from the advance sale of nonrefundable tickets.
    DISCUSSION: Revenue is recognized when it is realized or realizable and earned. The entire proceeds should be reported as unearned revenue. The earning process is not complete until the performance has been given even though the tickets are not refundable. "Revenues are considered to have been earned when the entity has substantially accomplished what it must do to be entitled to the benefits represented by the revenues" (SFAC 5).
    Answer (A) is incorrect. Revenue cannot be recognized until two criteria have been satisfied: It must be both earned and realized or realizable. The tickets may be nonrefundable, but no revenue-generating activity has taken place until the performance on stage is underway. Answer (B) is incorrect. Costs incurred do not necessarily match the revenue earned. The revenues have been realized (payment has already been received), but they have not yet been earned. Thus, revenue recognition is inappropriate. Answer (C) is incorrect. The entire proceeds should be credited to unearned revenue.

13. An adjusting entry that records the earned portion of unearned revenue previously recorded always includes a

    A. Debit to an account in the asset category.

    B. Credit to an account in the asset category.

    C. Credit to an account in the equity category.

    D. Credit to an account in the liability category.

Answer (C) is correct. *(CMA, adapted)*
    REQUIRED: The effect of an adjusting entry that records the earned portion of unearned revenue previously recorded.
    DISCUSSION: When cash from customers is collected in advance, a credit is made to the unearned revenue account. When the revenue is earned, usually on the basis of production and delivery, the unearned revenue account must then be debited, with a corresponding credit to a revenue account (an equity account).
    Answer (A) is incorrect. The debit in any entry to reclassify unearned revenue to earned revenue is to unearned revenue. Answer (B) is incorrect. When unearned revenue is reclassified to earned revenue, the credit must be to earned revenue. Answer (D) is incorrect. The liability is unearned revenue, and it must be decreased (debited) when a portion of it is reclassified to earned revenue.

14. On February 12, Gleem Publishing, Inc., purchased the copyright to a book for $15,000 and agreed to pay royalties equal to 10% of book sales, with a guaranteed minimum royalty of $60,000. Gleem had book sales of $750,000 during the year. In its income statement, what amount should Gleem report as royalty expense for the year?

    A. $60,000

    B. $75,000

    C. $76,500

    D. $90,000

Answer (B) is correct. *(CPA, adapted)*
    REQUIRED: The royalty expense for the year.
    DISCUSSION: The royalty expense is equal to 10% of book sales, with a guaranteed minimum royalty of $60,000. Thus, royalty expense is $75,000 ($750,000 book sales × 10%).
    Answer (A) is incorrect. The guaranteed minimum royalty is $60,000, which is less than 10% of book sales. Answer (C) is incorrect. The amount of $76,500 includes 10% of the purchase price of the copyright. Answer (D) is incorrect. The copyright purchase price is not included in royalty expense.

15. A company that sprays chemicals in residences to eliminate or prevent infestation of insects requires that customers prepay for 3 months' service at the beginning of each new quarter. Which term appropriately describes the prepayment from the perspective of the service provider?

   A. Unearned revenue.

   B. Earned revenue.

   C. Accrued revenue.

   D. Prepaid expense.

Answer (A) is correct. *(CIA, adapted)*
   REQUIRED: The classification of collected fees that pertain to a future period.
   DISCUSSION: Under the revenue recognition principle, revenue is recognized (reported as revenue) in the period in which it is earned. Thus, when it is received in advance of its being earned, the amount applicable to future periods is deferred. The amount unearned (received in advance) is considered a liability because it represents an obligation to perform a service in the future arising from a past transaction. Unearned revenue is revenue that has been received but not earned.
   Answer (B) is incorrect. The revenue is not earned. The company has not performed the related services for the customer. Answer (C) is incorrect. Accrued revenue is revenue that has been earned but not received. The company reports revenue that has been received but not earned. Answer (D) is incorrect. The customer reports a prepaid expense (expense paid but not incurred). The company reports unearned revenue (revenue received but not earned).

16. On November 1, Fitz Co. paid $3,600 to renew its insurance policy for 3 years. On December 31, Fitz's unadjusted trial balance showed a balance of $90 for prepaid insurance and $4,410 for insurance expense. What amounts should be reported for prepaid insurance and insurance expense in Fitz's December 31 financial statements?

	Prepaid Expense	Insurance Expense
A.	$3,300	$1,200
B.	$3,400	$1,200
C.	$3,400	$1,100
D.	$3,490	$1,010

Answer (C) is correct. *(CPA, adapted)*
   REQUIRED: The amounts reported for prepaid insurance and insurance expense.
   DISCUSSION: At year end, the expense and prepaid insurance accounts should be adjusted to reflect the expired amounts. The entry to record the insurance renewal included a debit to insurance expense for $3,600. The balance in prepaid insurance has expired. The 3-year prepayment is amortized at $100 per month ($3,600 ÷ 36 months), or $200 for the first calendar year. Consequently, insurance expense for the year should be $1,100 [$90 prepaid insurance balance + ($4,410 – $3,400 unexpired amount of the November 1 prepayment)]. The $3,400 unexpired amount should be reported as prepaid insurance.
   Answer (A) is incorrect. An asset balance of $3,300 and an expense of $1,200 assume the renewed policy has been in effect for 3 months. Answer (B) is incorrect. An expense of $1,200 assumes the renewed policy has been in effect for 3 months. Answer (D) is incorrect. The unadjusted prepaid insurance balance ($90) is an expired amount.

17. An analysis of Patrick Corp.'s unadjusted prepaid expense account at December 31, Year 2, revealed the following:

- An opening balance at $1,500 for Patrick's comprehensive insurance policy. Patrick had paid an annual premium of $3,000 on July 1, Year 1.
- A $3,200 annual insurance premium payment made July 1, Year 2.
- A $2,000 advance rental payment for a warehouse Thrift leased for 1 year beginning January 1, Year 3.

In its December 31, Year 2, balance sheet, what amount should Patrick report as prepaid expenses?

   A. $5,200

   B. $3,600

   C. $2,000

   D. $1,600

Answer (B) is correct. *(CPA, adapted)*
   REQUIRED: The amount reported for prepaid expenses.
   DISCUSSION: The $1,500 beginning balance of prepaid insurance expired on June 30, Year 2, leaving a $0 balance. The $3,200 annual insurance premium paid on July 1, Year 2, should be allocated equally to Year 2 and Year 3, leaving a $1,600 prepaid insurance balance. The $2,000 advance rental payment is an expense that is wholly deferred until Year 3. Consequently, the total of prepaid expenses at year-end is $3,600 ($1,600 + $2,000).
   Answer (A) is incorrect. Half of the $3,200 of prepaid insurance should be expensed in Year 2. Answer (C) is incorrect. Half of the $3,200 of prepaid insurance should not be expensed in Year 2. Answer (D) is incorrect. The prepaid rent is deferred until Year 3.

18. Cathay Co. owns a royalty interest in an oil well. The contract stipulates that Cathay will receive royalty payments semiannually on January 31 and July 31. The January 31 payment will be for 20% of the oil sold to jobbers between the previous June 1 and November 30, and the July 31 payment will be for oil sold between the previous December 1 and May 31. Royalty receipts for Year 2 amounted to $80,000 and $100,000 on January 31 and July 31, respectively. On December 31, Year 1, accrued royalty revenue receivable amounted to $15,000. Production reports show the following oil sales:

June 1, Year 1 – November 30, Year 1	$400,000
December 1, Year 1 – May 31, Year 2	500,000
June 1, Year 2 – November 30, Year 2	425,000
December 1, Year 2 – December 31, Year 2	70,000

What amount should Cathay report as royalty revenue for Year 2?

A. $179,000

B. $180,000

C. $184,000

D. $194,000

Answer (C) is correct. *(CPA, adapted)*
REQUIRED: The royalty revenue for Year 2.
DISCUSSION: The royalty revenue for Year 2 is 20% of Year 2 oil sales. Given that 12/1/Year 1 – 5/31/Year 2 oil sales equaled $500,000 and that the accrued royalty for December Year 1 was $15,000, oil sales for that month must have been $75,000 ($15,000 accrued ÷ 20%). Hence, oil sales for Year 2 are $920,000 [($500,000 – $75,000) + $425,000 + $70,000]. Thus, royalty revenue for Year 2 is $184,000 ($920,000 × 20%).
Answer (A) is incorrect. The amount of $179,000 incorrectly computes part of the revenue with the sales from 6/1/Year 1 – 11/30/Year 1 instead of 1/1/Year 1 – 5/31/Year 2. Answer (B) is incorrect. The royalty payments received in Year 2 are $180,000. Answer (D) is incorrect. The amount of $194,000 is the royalty payments received in Year 2, plus 20% of December Year 2's sales.

19. Windy Co. must determine the December 31, Year 2, year-end accruals for advertising and rent expenses. A $500 advertising bill was received January 7, Year 3. It related to costs of $375 for advertisements in December Year 2 issues and $125 for advertisements in January Year 3 issues of the newspaper. A store lease, effective December 16, Year 1, calls for fixed rent of $1,200 per month, payable 1 month from the effective date and monthly thereafter. In addition, rent equal to 5% of net sales over $300,000 per calendar year is payable on January 31 of the following year. Net sales for Year 2 were $550,000. In its December 31, Year 2, balance sheet, Windy should report accrued liabilities of

A. $12,500

B. $12,875

C. $13,100

D. $13,475

Answer (D) is correct. *(CPA, adapted)*
REQUIRED: The accrued liabilities reported at year-end.
DISCUSSION: The $375 of advertising expense should be accrued in Year 2 because this amount can be directly related to events in that period. The $125 amount is related to events in Year 3 and should not be accrued in Year 2. The fixed rental is due at mid-month. Thus, the fixed rental for the last half month of Year 2 ($1,200 ÷ 2 = $600) and the rental based on annual sales [($550,000 – $300,000) × 5% = $12,500] should also be accrued, for a total of $13,475 ($375 + $600 + $12,500).
Answer (A) is incorrect. The amount of $12,500 omits the half-month of the fixed rental and the advertising bill for December. Answer (B) is incorrect. The amount of $12,875 omits the half-month of the fixed rental. Answer (C) is incorrect. The amount of $13,100 excludes the advertising bill for December.

20. Larsen Corp. pays commissions to its sales staff at the rate of 3% of net sales. Sales staff are not paid salaries but are given monthly advances of $15,000. Advances are charged to commission expense, and reconciliations against commissions are prepared quarterly. Net sales for the year ended March 31 were $15 million. The unadjusted balance in the commissions expense account on March 31 was $400,000. March advances were paid on April 3. In its income statement for the year ended March 31, what amount should Larsen report as commission expense?

A. $465,000

B. $450,000

C. $415,000

D. $400,000

Answer (B) is correct. *(CPA, adapted)*
REQUIRED: The commission expense for the year.
DISCUSSION: Sales commissions should be recognized as an expense when the related revenues are earned. Given that the entity pays commissions at a rate of 3% of net sales, commission expense is $450,000 ($15,000,000 net sales × 3%).
Answer (A) is incorrect. The sum of commission expense and one monthly advance is $465,000. Answer (C) is incorrect. The unadjusted balance in commissions expense plus one monthly advance is $415,000. Answer (D) is incorrect. The unadjusted balance in commissions expense is $400,000.

21. Jay Corp.'s trademark was licensed to John Co. for royalties of 15% of sales of the trademarked items. Royalties are payable semiannually on March 15 for sales in July through December of the prior year, and on September 15 for sales in January through June of the same year. Jay received the following royalties from John:

	March 15	September 15
Year 1	$10,000	$15,000
Year 2	12,000	18,000

John estimated that sales of the trademarked items would total $90,000 for July through December Year 2. In Jay's Year 2 income statement, the royalty revenue should be

A. $31,500

B. $30,000

C. $43,500

D. $46,500

Answer (A) is correct. *(CPA, adapted)*
REQUIRED: The amount of royalty revenue to be reported.
DISCUSSION: The royalty revenue for Year 2 is $31,500 [$18,000 received in September Year 2 + ($90,000 × 15%) to be received in March Year 3 for sales in Year 2].
Answer (B) is incorrect. The amount of $30,000 includes $12,000 that was received in March Year 2 but was applicable to Year 1 sales and omits the $13,500 ($90,000 × 15%) attributable to sales for July through December Year 2. Answer (C) is incorrect. The amount of $43,500 includes $12,000 that was received in March Year 2 but was applicable to Year 1 sales. Answer (D) is incorrect. The amount of $46,500 includes $15,000 that was received in September Year 1 and was applicable to Year 1 sales.

22. Seri Co.'s professional fees expense account had a balance of $92,000 at December 31, Year 1, before considering year-end adjustments relating to the following:

- Consultants were hired for a special project at a total fee not to exceed $65,000. Seri has recorded $55,000 of this fee based on billings for work performed in Year 1.
- The attorney's letter requested by the auditors, dated January 28, Year 2, indicated that legal fees of $6,000 were billed on January 15, Year 2, for work performed in November Year 1 and that unbilled fees for December Year 1 were $9,000.

What amount should Seri report for professional fees expense for the year ended December 31, Year 1?

A. $117,000

B. $107,000

C. $98,000

D. $92,000

Answer (B) is correct. *(CPA, adapted)*
REQUIRED: The professional fees expense for the year.
DISCUSSION: The entity should recognize an expense only for the work done by the consultants and attorneys in Year 1. Thus, no adjustment is necessary for the consulting fees, but the legal fees, billed and unbilled, for November and December Year 1 should be debited to the account. The professional fees expense for the year is therefore $107,000 ($92,000 + $6,000 + $9,000).
Answer (A) is incorrect. The amount of $117,000 includes the maximum fee that may be payable to the consultants. Answer (C) is incorrect. The amount of $98,000 excludes the attorneys' fees for December. Answer (D) is incorrect. The amount of $92,000 excludes the attorneys' fees for November and December.

23. Dix Company sells subscriptions to a specialized directory that is published semiannually and shipped to subscribers on April 15 and October 15. Subscriptions received after the March 31 and September 30 cutoff dates are held for the next publication. Cash from subscribers is received evenly during the year and is credited to deferred revenues from subscriptions. Data relating to Year 2 are as follows:

Deferred revenues from subscriptions, balance 12/31/Year 1	$1,500,000
Cash receipts from subscribers	7,200,000

In its December 31, Year 2, balance sheet, Dix should report deferred revenues from subscriptions of

A. $1,800,000

B. $3,300,000

C. $3,600,000

D. $5,400,000

Answer (A) is correct. *(CPA, adapted)*
REQUIRED: The balance to be reported as deferred revenues from subscriptions at year end.
DISCUSSION: The deferred revenues from subscriptions account records subscription fees received that have not been earned. The balance in this account in the December 31, Year 2, balance sheet should reflect the subscription fees received after the September 30 cutoff date. Because cash from subscribers is received evenly during the year, $1,800,000 [$7,200,000 × (3 months ÷ 12 months)] should be reported as deferred revenues from subscriptions.
Answer (B) is incorrect. The amount of $3,300,000 is the sum of the existing deferred revenues balance and the fees received after the September 30 cutoff. Answer (C) is incorrect. Six months of fees equals $3,600,000. Answer (D) is incorrect. Nine months of fees equals $5,400,000.

24. Based on current year sales of music recorded by an artist under a contract with Cyber Music, the artist earned $200,000 after an adjustment of $16,000 for anticipated returns. In addition, Cyber paid the artist $150,000 in the current year as a reasonable estimate of the amount recoverable from future royalties to be earned by the artist. What amount should Cyber report in its current year income statement for royalty expense?

A. $200,000

B. $216,000

C. $350,000

D. $366,000

Answer (A) is correct. *(CPA, adapted)*
REQUIRED: The royalty expense.
DISCUSSION: Income is earned by the artist and an expense is incurred by Cyber based on net sales (sales – returns). Amounts paid in advance and recoverable from future royalties are classified as prepaid expenses. Thus, Cyber should report royalty expense of $200,000.
Answer (B) is incorrect. The amount of $216,000 includes the adjustment of $16,000 for anticipated returns. Answer (C) is incorrect. The amount of $350,000 includes the prepayment. Answer (D) is incorrect. The amount of $366,000 includes the prepayment and the adjustment of $16,000 for anticipated returns.

25. Amy.com sells 1- and 2-year subscriptions for its electronic book-of-the-month download business. Subscriptions are collected in advance and credited to sales. An analysis of the recorded sales activity revealed the following:

	Year 1	Year 2
Sales	$420,000	$500,000
Minus cancelations	20,000	30,000
Net sales	$400,000	$470,000
Subscriptions expirations:		
Year 1	$120,000	
Year 2	155,000	$130,000
Year 3	125,000	200,000
Year 4		140,000
	$400,000	$470,000

In Amy.com's December 31, Year 2, balance sheet, the balance for unearned subscription revenue should be

A. $470,000

B. $465,000

C. $400,000

D. $340,000

Answer (B) is correct. *(CPA, adapted)*
REQUIRED: The balance for unearned subscription revenue.
DISCUSSION: The earning process for subscription revenue is complete upon production and delivery. The balance for unearned subscription revenue should reflect the advance collections for which production and delivery have not yet occurred. Thus, the unexpired subscriptions as of December 31, Year 2, total $465,000 ($125,000 + $200,000 + $140,000), which is the balance for unearned subscription revenue.
Answer (A) is incorrect. Net sales for Year 2 equal $470,000. Answer (C) is incorrect. Net sales for Year 1 equal $400,000. Answer (D) is incorrect. The amount of $340,000 omits the Year 1 sales of subscriptions that will expire in Year 3.

26. In its Year 2 financial statements, Cris Co. reported interest expense of $85,000 in its income statement and cash paid for interest of $70,000 in its cash flow statement. There was no prepaid interest or interest capitalization at either the beginning or the end of Year 2. Accrued interest at December 31, Year 1, was $20,000. What amount should Cris report as accrued interest payable in its December 31, Year 2, balance sheet?

A. $5,000

B. $20,000

C. $15,000

D. $35,000

Answer (D) is correct. *(CPA, adapted)*
REQUIRED: The accrued interest payable at year end.
DISCUSSION: The cash paid for interest was $70,000, including $20,000 of interest paid for Year 1. Consequently, $50,000 ($70,000 – $20,000) of the cash paid for interest related to Year 2. Interest payable is therefore $35,000 ($85,000 – $50,000).
Answer (A) is incorrect. The amount of $5,000 results from adding the $20,000 to $70,000 and subtracting the $85,000 interest expense. Answer (B) is incorrect. The interest paid in Year 2 that related to Year 1 is $20,000. Answer (C) is incorrect. The difference between the interest expense and cash paid is $15,000.

27. Qwik Co.'s officers' compensation expense account had a balance of $490,000 at December 31, Year 1, before any appropriate year-end adjustment relating to the following:

● No salary accrual was made for the week of December 25-31, Year 1. Officers' salaries for this period totaled $18,000 and were paid on January 5, Year 2.

● Bonuses to officers for Year 1 were paid on January 31, Year 2, in the total amount of $175,000.

The adjusted balance for officers' compensation expense for the year ended December 31, Year 1, should be

A. $683,000

B. $665,000

C. $508,000

D. $490,000

Answer (A) is correct. *(CPA, adapted)*
REQUIRED: The adjusted balance of officers' compensation expense.
DISCUSSION: The officers' compensation expense account should include the entire compensation expense incurred in Year 1. Accordingly, it should include the $490,000 previously recorded in the account, the $18,000 of accrued salaries, and the $175,000 of accrued bonuses. The adjusted balance should therefore be $683,000 ($490,000 + $18,000 + $175,000).
Answer (B) is incorrect. The amount of $665,000 does not include salaries accrued at year end. Answer (C) is incorrect. The amount of $508,000 does not include the bonuses. Answer (D) is incorrect. The amount of $490,000 does not include the bonuses and the accrued salaries.

28. Kiddie Kare Co. offers three payment plans on its 12-month contracts. Information on the three plans and the number of children enrolled in each plan for the June 1, Year 1, through May 31, Year 2, contract year follows:

Plan	Initial Payment per Child	Monthly Fees per Child	Number of Children
#1	$500	$ --	15
#2	200	30	12
#3	--	50	9
			36

Kiddie received $9,900 of initial payments on June 1, Year 1, and $5,670 of monthly fees during the period June 1 through December 31, Year 1. In its December 31, Year 1, balance sheet, what amount should Kiddie report as deferred revenues?

A. $5,670

B. $5,775

C. $4,125

D. $9,900

Answer (C) is correct. *(CPA, adapted)*
REQUIRED: The amount reported as deferred revenues.
DISCUSSION: Unearned (deferred) revenues relate to the portion of the contracts for which services have not been performed (the earning process has not been completed). At December 31, Year 1, deferred revenues should equal $4,125 [9,900 prepayments received × (5 months ÷ 12 months)].
Answer (A) is incorrect. The total of monthly fees collected in Year 1 is $5,670. Answer (B) is incorrect. The portion of prepayments earned in Year 1 is $5,775. Answer (D) is incorrect. The total prepayments equal $9,900.

29. O'Hara Co. owns an office building and leases the offices under a variety of rental agreements involving rent paid in advance monthly or annually. Not all tenants make timely payments of their rent. O'Hara's balance sheets contained the following data:

	Year 1	Year 2
Rentals receivable	$19,200	$24,800
Unearned rentals	64,000	48,000

During Year 2, O'Hara received $160,000 cash from tenants. What amount of rental revenue should O'Hara record for Year 2?

A. $181,600

B. $170,800

C. $144,000

D. $133,200

Answer (A) is correct. *(CPA, adapted)*
REQUIRED: The rental revenue for the current year.
DISCUSSION: The ending balance in the rental receivable was $5,600 higher than the beginning balance ($24,800 – $19,200). Thus, revenues exceeded cash receipts. The ending balance in unearned rent was $16,000 less than the beginning balance ($64,000 – $48,000), again indicating that revenues exceeded cash receipts. Rental revenue is $181,600 ($160,000 + $5,600 + $16,000).
Answer (B) is incorrect. The amount of $170,800 equals the cash received plus 50% of the sum of the increase in rentals receivable and the decrease in unearned rentals. Answer (C) is incorrect. The amount of $144,000 equals the cash received minus the decrease in unearned rentals. Answer (D) is incorrect. The amount of $133,200 equals the cash received, minus the decrease in unearned rentals, minus 50% of the sum of the increase in rentals receivable and the decrease in unearned rentals.

30. Under Best Co.'s accounting system, all insurance premiums paid are debited to prepaid insurance. For interim financial reports, Best makes monthly estimated charges to insurance expense with credits to prepaid insurance. Additional information for the year ended December 31, Year 2, is as follows:

Prepaid insurance at December 31, Year 1 $110,000
Charges to insurance expense during
  Year 2 (including a year-end adjustment
  of $10,500)   437,500
Prepaid insurance at December 31, Year 2 120,500

What was the total amount of insurance premiums paid by Best during Year 2?

A. $327,500

B. $427,000

C. $437,500

D. $448,000

Answer (D) is correct. *(CPA, adapted)*
REQUIRED: The total amount of insurance premiums paid.
DISCUSSION: The company debits prepaid insurance for all insurance premiums paid and credits the account when it charges insurance expense. Thus, total debits equal insurance premiums paid. The asset account had total credits (charges to expense) of $437,500 and increased by $10,500 ($120,500 ending balance – $110,000 beginning balance). Consequently, total debits (premiums paid) must have been $448,000 ($437,500 total charges to insurance expense + $10,500 increase in the asset account).
Answer (A) is incorrect. Total credits minus the beginning balance is $327,500. Answer (B) is incorrect. The amount of $427,000 results from subtracting, not adding, the difference between the beginning and ending balances. Answer (C) is incorrect. Total credits to the account equal $437,500.

31. A company provides the following information:

Cash Receipts from Customers:	Year 1	Year 2	Year 3
From Year 1 sales	$95,000	$120,000	
From Year 2 sales		200,000	$ 75,000
From Year 3 sales		50,000	225,000

What is the accrual-based revenue for Year 2?

A. $200,000

B. $275,000

C. $320,000

D. $370,000

Answer (B) is correct. *(CPA, adapted)*
REQUIRED: The accrual-based revenue for Year 2.
DISCUSSION: Under the accrual method, revenues and gains are realized when goods or services have been exchanged for cash or claims to cash, not when that cash is collected. Consequently, given that total cash collected for Year 2 sales is $275,000 ($200,000 Year 2 + $75,000 Year 3), revenue for Year 2 is $275,000.
Answer (A) is incorrect. The amount of $200,000 equals cash collected in Year 2 for sales from Year 2. Answer (C) is incorrect. The amount of $320,000 equals cash collected in Year 2 for sales from Year 1 and Year 2. Answer (D) is incorrect. The amount of $370,000 equals cash collected in Year 2.

32. Vanel Co. sells equipment service contracts that cover a 2-year period. The sales price of each contract is $600. Vanel's past experience is that, of the total dollars spent for repairs on service contracts, 40% is incurred evenly during the first contract year and 60% evenly during the second contract year. Vanel sold 1,000 contracts evenly throughout the year. In its December 31 balance sheet, what amount should Vanel report as deferred service contract revenue?

A. $540,000

B. $480,000

C. $360,000

D. $300,000

Answer (B) is correct. *(CPA, adapted)*
REQUIRED: The deferred service contract revenue.
DISCUSSION: Revenue should be recognized when it is realized or realizable and earned. Service contract revenue should be recognized as the services are provided. Assuming that services are provided in proportion to the incurrence of expenses, 40% of revenue should be recognized in the first year of a service contract. Given that expenses are incurred evenly throughout the year, revenue will also be recognized evenly. Moreover, given that Vanel sold 1,000 contracts evenly throughout the year, total revenue will be $600,000 (1,000 contracts × $600), and the average contract must have been sold at mid-year. Thus, the elapsed time of the average contract must be half a year, and revenue earned during the year must equal $120,000 ($600,000 total revenue × 40% × .5 year). Deferred revenue at year-end will equal $480,000 ($600,000 – $120,000).
Answer (A) is incorrect. The amount of $540,000 assumes the average contract has been outstanding for 3 months. Answer (C) is incorrect. The second year's revenue for all contracts is $360,000. Answer (D) is incorrect. This is the amount deferred if 50% of expenses are expected to be incurred each year and the average contract has been outstanding for 1 year.

33. Delect Co. provides repair services for the AZ195 TV set. Customers prepay the fee on the standard 1-year service contract. The Year 1 and Year 2 contracts were identical, and the number of contracts outstanding was substantially the same at the end of each year. However, Delect's December 31, Year 2, deferred revenue balance on unperformed service contracts was significantly less than the balance at December 31, Year 1. Which of the following situations might account for this reduction in the deferred revenue balance?

A. Most Year 2 contracts were signed later in the calendar year than were the Year 1 contracts.

B. Most Year 2 contracts were signed earlier in the calendar year than were the Year 1 contracts.

C. The Year 2 contract contribution margin was greater than the Year 1 contract contribution margin.

D. The Year 2 contribution margin was less than the Year 1 contract contribution margin.

Answer (B) is correct. *(CPA, adapted)*
REQUIRED: The situation that might explain the reduction in deferred revenue.
DISCUSSION: Revenue should be recognized when it is realized or realizable and earned. Service contract fees are not earned until the services are provided. Thus, the fees collected in advance should be reported as unearned (deferred) revenue in the liability section of the balance sheet until the services are provided. The earlier a service contract is signed, the longer the time to provide the service and earn the revenue. Completion of the earning process reduces the deferred revenue balance. Thus, if most contracts outstanding on December 31, Year 2, were signed earlier in the period than those outstanding a year earlier, the deferred revenue balance should have decreased.
Answer (A) is incorrect. If most Year 2 contracts were signed later in the calendar year than were the Year 1 contracts, the deferred revenue balance would have increased. Answer (C) is incorrect. The contribution margin relates to profit, not revenue. Answer (D) is incorrect. The contribution margin relates to profit, not revenue.

2.3 Journal Entries

34. In reviewing a set of journal entries, an auditor encounters an entry composed of a debit to interest expense and a credit to interest payable. The purpose of this journal entry is to record

A. An accrued expense.

B. A deferred expense.

C. A contingent liability.

D. An unexpired cost.

Answer (A) is correct. *(CIA, adapted)*
REQUIRED: The purpose of a journal entry that debits an expense and credits a payable.
DISCUSSION: An accrued expense is one that has been incurred in the current period but has not yet been paid. The journal entry to record an accrued expense requires a debit to an expense account and a credit to a payable account.
Answer (B) is incorrect. A deferred expense is a prepayment and is recorded as an asset. Answer (C) is incorrect. Interest expense is not a contingent liability. Answer (D) is incorrect. An unexpired cost is an asset.

35. In performing an audit, an auditor encounters an adjusting journal entry recorded at year end that contains a debit to rental revenue and a credit to unearned rental revenue. The purpose of this journal entry is to record

A. An accrued revenue.

B. An unexpired cost.

C. An expired cost.

D. A deferred revenue.

Answer (D) is correct. *(CIA, adapted)*
REQUIRED: The purpose of a journal entry that debits rental revenue and credits unearned rental revenue.
DISCUSSION: Revenues should be recognized when realized or realizable and earned. If rental fees are collected before the revenue is earned and a credit is made to rental revenue, an adjusting entry may be necessary at year end. The purpose of the journal entry is to adjust both rental revenue and unearned rental revenue to reflect the rental fees collected that had not been earned during this accounting period.
Answer (A) is incorrect. An accrued revenue is reflected as a receivable. Answer (B) is incorrect. An unexpired cost is recorded as an asset. Answer (C) is incorrect. An expired cost is charged to expense.

36. Closing entries

A. Transfer the balances in all of the nominal accounts to equity.

B. Must be made after the reversing entries but before the adjusting entries.

C. Close out all of the accounts in the general ledger.

D. Must be followed by reversing entries.

Answer (A) is correct. *(Publisher, adapted)*
REQUIRED: The true statement about closing entries.
DISCUSSION: Closing entries transfer the balances in all the nominal accounts to the retained earnings account. This process usually involves closing amounts to the income summary account and then to retained earnings.
Answer (B) is incorrect. Closing entries are made after adjusting entries and before reversing entries. Answer (C) is incorrect. Closing entries close only nominal accounts. Answer (D) is incorrect. Reversing entries are not required. They merely facilitate accounting for certain transactions in the next accounting period.

37. The correct order of the following steps of the accounting cycle is

A. Posting, closing, adjusting, reversing.

B. Posting, adjusting, closing, reversing.

C. Posting, reversing, adjusting, closing.

D. Adjusting, posting, closing, reversing.

Answer (B) is correct. *(CIA, adapted)*
REQUIRED: The proper sequence of steps in the accounting cycle.
DISCUSSION: The order of the steps in the accounting cycle is (1) journalization of transactions, events, and other circumstances required to be recognized; (2) posting from the journals to the ledgers; (3) the development of an unadjusted trial balance; (4) adjustments to produce an adjusted trial balance; (5) statement preparation; (6) closing; (7) taking a postclosing trial balance (optional); and (8) making reversing entries (optional).
Answer (A) is incorrect. Adjusting entries are made prior to closing. Answer (C) is incorrect. Reversing entries are made after adjustments and closing entries. Answer (D) is incorrect. Posting is done prior to adjusting.

38. Why are adjusting entries necessary?

A. To record revenues and expenses.

B. To make debits equal credits.

C. To close nominal accounts at year end.

D. To correct erroneous balances in accounts.

Answer (A) is correct. *(Publisher, adapted)*
REQUIRED: The reason for adjusting entries.
DISCUSSION: Adjusting entries are used to adjust expenses (and the related asset or liability accounts) or revenues (and the related asset or liability accounts) to year-end amounts. Adjusting entries are needed to properly reflect revenues recognized when they are realized or realizable and earned and expenses recognized in accordance with the expense recognition principles. Accrual adjusting entries are made when the expense or revenue is recognized prior to the payment or receipt of cash. Deferral adjusting entries are necessary when the expense or revenue is recognized after the payment or receipt of cash.
Answer (B) is incorrect. All transactions result in equal debits and credits, and the cumulative balances of debits and credits are always equal. Answer (C) is incorrect. Closing nominal accounts at year end is the function of closing entries, not adjusting entries. Answer (D) is incorrect. Correcting erroneous account balances is the function of correcting entries, not adjusting entries.

39. On October 1, Year 1, a company sold services to a customer and accepted a note in exchange with a $120,000 face amount and an interest rate of 10%. The note requires that both the principal and interest be paid at the maturity date, December 1, Year 2. The company's accounting period is the calendar year. What adjusting entry (related to this note) will be required at December 31, Year 1, on the company's books?

A. Deferred interest income $3,000
   Interest receivable $3,000

B. Interest income $3,000
   Interest receivable $3,000

C. Interest receivable $3,000
   Deferred interest income $3,000

D. Interest receivable $3,000
   Interest income $3,000

Answer (D) is correct. *(CIA, adapted)*
REQUIRED: The adjusting entry related to a note receivable.
DISCUSSION: Interest receivable should be debited and interest income credited for the interest on the note accrued (earned but not paid) at year end [$120,000 × 10% × (3 months ÷ 12 months) = $3,000].
Answer (A) is incorrect. The entry on December 31, Year 1, should reflect the interest earned by the passage of 3 months since the issuance of the note. The entry is to debit interest receivable (an asset) and credit interest income (a revenue). Answer (B) is incorrect. A debit to interest income and a credit to interest receivable is a reversing entry. Answer (C) is incorrect. Interest of $3,000 is not deferred. It has been earned by the passage of 3 months since the issuance of the note.

40. What is the purpose of the following entry?

| Supplies | $XXX | |
| Supplies expense | | $XXX |

   A. To recognize supplies used, if purchases of supplies are recorded in supplies.

   B. To recognize supplies on hand, if purchases of supplies are recorded in supplies expense.

   C. To record the purchase of supplies during or at the end of the period.

   D. To close the expense account for supplies at the end of the period.

Answer (B) is correct. *(CIA, adapted)*
   REQUIRED: The purpose of the given entry.
   DISCUSSION: The debit to supplies and credit to supplies expense is an end-of-period adjusting entry. Assuming the acquisition of supplies was debited to expense, an adjusting entry is needed to record the supplies on hand and to recognize the correct amount of expense.
   Answer (A) is incorrect. If purchases are initially recorded in a real account, the entry to record use of supplies is

| Supplies expense | $XXX | |
| Supplies | | $XXX |

Answer (C) is incorrect. The correct entry to record the purchase of supplies is

| Supplies or Supplies expense | $XXX | |
| Cash or Accounts payable | | $XXX |

Answer (D) is incorrect. The entry to close supplies expense is

| Income summary | $XXX | |
| Supplies expense | | $XXX |

41. On December 31, earned but unpaid wages amounted to $15,000. What reversing entry could be made on January 1?

| A. Wages expense | $15,000 | |
| Wages payable | | $15,000 |

| B. Prepaid wages | $15,000 | |
| Wages expense | | $15,000 |

| C. Wages expense | $15,000 | |
| Prepaid wages | | $15,000 |

| D. Wages payable | $15,000 | |
| Wages expense | | $15,000 |

Answer (D) is correct. *(Publisher, adapted)*
   REQUIRED: The reversing entry for an accrual of wages expense.
   DISCUSSION: The accrual of an expense requires a debit to expense and a credit to a liability. Accordingly, the reversing entry is to debit the liability and credit expense. The purpose of reversing this accrual of expense is to avoid having to apportion the first cash disbursement in the next period between the liability and expense accounts.
   Answer (A) is incorrect. A debit to wages expense and a credit to wages payable is the adjusting entry. Answer (B) is incorrect. A debit to prepaid wages and a credit to wages expense is an adjusting entry when wages have been prepaid and the original debit was to an expense (a method not frequently found in practice). Answer (C) is incorrect. A debit to wages expense and a credit to prepaid wages is the reversing entry for an adjusting entry made when wages have been prepaid and the original debit was to an expense account.

42. A consulting firm started and completed a project for a client in December of Year 1. The project has not been recorded on the consulting firm's books, and the firm will not receive payment from the client until February Year 2. The adjusting entry that should be made on the books of the consulting firm on December 31, Year 1, the last day of the firm's fiscal year, is

| A. Cash in transit | $XXX | |
| Consulting revenue | | $XXX |

| B. Consulting revenue receivable | $XXX | |
| Consulting revenue | | $XXX |

| C. Unearned consulting revenue | $XXX | |
| Consulting revenue | | $XXX |

| D. Consulting revenue receivable | $XXX | |
| Unearned consulting revenue | | $XXX |

Answer (B) is correct. *(CMA, adapted)*
   REQUIRED: The adjusting entry necessary to record consulting revenue.
   DISCUSSION: Revenues should be recognized when they are realized or realizable and earned. Consulting revenue is realized and earned when the consulting service has been performed. Thus, for a consulting project that was started and completed during Year 1, an adjusting entry should be made at year end to record both a receivable and the revenue. The journal entry is a debit to consulting revenue receivable and a credit to consulting revenue.
   Answer (A) is incorrect. Cash in transit is not an account. Answer (C) is incorrect. The unearned revenue account is used only if the client prepays. Answer (D) is incorrect. The revenue was earned during the period.

43. A 3-year insurance policy was purchased on October 1 for $6,000, and prepaid insurance was debited. Assuming a December 31 year end, what is the reversing entry at the beginning of the next period?

A. None is required.

B. Cash	$6,000	
Prepaid insurance		$6,000

C. Prepaid insurance	$5,500	
Insurance expense		$5,500

D. Insurance expense	$500	
Prepaid insurance		$500

Answer (A) is correct. *(Publisher, adapted)*
REQUIRED: The reversing entry when a prepaid expense was debited to an asset account.
DISCUSSION: Given that the original entry recorded the prepaid insurance as an asset, the adjusting entry will debit expense and credit the asset for the amount of insurance that has expired. Accordingly, at the beginning of the year, the unexpired insurance will be in an asset account. Thus, no reversing entry is required.
Answer (B) is incorrect. Debit cash and credit prepaid insurance is the opposite (not a reversing entry) of the entry made to record the purchase of the 3-year insurance policy. Answer (C) is incorrect. Debit prepaid insurance and credit expense is the correct adjusting entry if the original entry had debited insurance expense rather than prepaid insurance. Answer (D) is incorrect. Debit expense and credit prepaid insurance is the correct adjusting entry (which requires no reversing entry).

Questions 44 and 45 are based on the following information. Louviere Co. prepares monthly financial statements. The clerical staff is paid every 2 weeks on the Monday following the end of the 2-week (10 working days) pay period ending on the prior Friday. The last pay period ended on Friday, November 19. The next payday is Monday, December 6 for the pay period ending December 3. The total clerical payroll for a 2-week period is $30,000, income tax withholding averages 15%, and Social Security taxes amount to 7.65%. None of the clerical staff's earnings will exceed the maximum limit for Social Security taxes.

44. The adjusting entry required to accrue Louviere's payroll as of November 30 is to

A. Debit wage expense for $21,000 and credit wages payable for $21,000.

B. Debit wage expense for $30,000, credit payroll tax expense for $1,950, and credit wages payable for $28,050.

C. Debit wage expense for $21,000, credit income tax withholding payable for $3,150, credit payroll taxes payable for $1,606.50, and credit wages payable for $16,243.50.

D. Debit wage expense for $30,000, credit income tax withholding payable for $4,500, credit payroll taxes payable for $1,950, and credit wages payable for $23,550.

Answer (C) is correct. *(CMA, adapted)*
REQUIRED: The adjusting entry necessary to accrue the payroll.
DISCUSSION: The 7 days included in the period from November 20 through November 30 represents 70% of the 10 working days in a 2-week pay period. Thus, $21,000 in wages expense should be accrued ($30,000 × 70%). Of this amount, $3,150 ($21,000 × 15%) must be credited to income tax withholding payable, $1,606.50 ($21,000 × 7.65%) to payroll tax payable, and the remainder, $16,243.50, to wages payable.
Answer (A) is incorrect. Wages payable must be reduced by income tax withholding and Social Security. Answer (B) is incorrect. The period from November 20 through November 30 includes only 7 working days, not the full 2-week period. Answer (D) is incorrect. The period from November 20 through November 30 includes only 7 working days, not the full 2-week period.

45. Louviere also is required to record an accrual for its obligation for payroll tax expenses. This adjusting entry should be to

A. Debit payroll tax expense for $4,756.50 and credit payroll taxes payable for $4,756.50.

B. Debit payroll tax expense for $1,606.50 and credit payroll taxes payable for $1,606.50.

C. Debit payroll tax expense for $2,295 and credit payroll taxes payable for $2,295.

D. Debit payroll tax expense for $4,515 and credit payroll taxes payable for $4,515.

Answer (B) is correct. *(CMA, adapted)*
REQUIRED: The adjusting entry necessary to accrue the company's obligation for Social Security taxes.
DISCUSSION: In addition to the Social Security taxes that must be withheld from employees' wages and remitted to the tax collection agency, the employer also must accrue and remit an equivalent amount as the employer's share. Thus, an additional expense of $1,606.50 ($21,000 × 7.65%) must be accrued.
Answer (A) is incorrect. The amount of $4,756.50 includes the employee withholding tax. Answer (C) is incorrect. The amount of $2,295 ($30,000 × 7.65%) mistakenly accrues payroll taxes for the entire 2-week (10-day) period instead of just the 7 working days from November 20 to November 30. Answer (D) is incorrect. Only the employer's share of Social Security ($21,000 × 7.65% = $1,606.50) is an expense of the employer.

46. Dunlap Company sublet a portion of its warehouse for 5 years at an annual rental of $15,000, beginning on March 1. The tenant paid 1 year's rent in advance, which Dunlap recorded as a credit to unearned rental income. Dunlap reports on a calendar-year basis. The adjustment on December 31 of the first year should be

A. No entry.

B. Unearned rental income　$2,500
　　Rental income　　　　　　　　　$2,500

C. Rental income　$2,500
　　Unearned rental income　　　　$2,500

D. Unearned rental income　$12,500
　　Rental income　　　　　　　　　$12,500

Answer (D) is correct. *(CPA, adapted)*
　　REQUIRED: The adjusting entry at year end for unearned rental income.
　　DISCUSSION: Given that the sublessor originally recorded the $15,000 received as a credit to a liability account, the adjusting entry is to debit the liability account and credit revenue for the revenue earned, which equals $1,250 a month ($12,500) for 10 months.
　　Answer (A) is incorrect. An adjusting entry is needed for all deferrals and accruals. Answer (B) is incorrect. The rental income to be recognized is for 10 months at $1,250 a month, not for 2 months. Answer (C) is incorrect. The debit and credit entries are switched, and the rental income to be recognized should be for 10 months, not 2 months.

47. Hurlburt Corporation renewed an insurance policy for 3 years beginning July 1 and recorded the $81,000 premium in the prepaid insurance account. The $81,000 premium represents an increase of $23,400 from the $57,600 premium charged 3 years ago. Assuming Hurlburt's records its insurance adjustments only at the end of the calendar year, the adjusting entry required to reflect the proper balances in the insurance accounts at December 31 Hurlburt's year end is to

A. Debit insurance expense for $13,500 and credit prepaid insurance for $13,500.

B. Debit prepaid insurance for $13,500 and credit insurance expense for $13,500.

C. Debit insurance expense for $67,500 and credit prepaid insurance for $67,500.

D. Debit insurance expense for $23,100 and credit prepaid insurance for $23,100.

Answer (D) is correct. *(CMA, adapted)*
　　REQUIRED: The entry to adjust the prepaid insurance account assuming annual adjustments.
　　DISCUSSION: The $57,600 premium paid 3 years ago was equivalent to a rate of $1,600 per month ($57,600 ÷ 36 months). On January 1, the prepaid insurance account would have had a balance of $9,600 ($1,600 × 6 months). On July 1, the prepaid insurance account would have been debited for an additional $81,000 covering the next 36 months at a monthly rate of $2,250 ($81,000 ÷ 36 months). The expense is therefore $23,100 [$9,600 + ($2,250 × 6 months)]. The adjusting entry is to debit insurance expense and credit prepaid insurance for $23,100.
　　Answer (A) is incorrect. The expense for the last 6 months of the year is $13,500. Answer (B) is incorrect. If the initial payment is debited to a real account, the adjustment requires a debit to a nominal account and a credit to the real account. Answer (C) is incorrect. The ending balance in prepaid insurance is $67,500.

48. After a successful drive aimed at members of a specific national association, Online Publishing Company received a total of $180,000 for 3-year subscriptions beginning April 1 and recorded this amount in the unearned revenue account. Assuming Online records adjustments only at the end of the calendar year, the adjusting entry required to reflect the proper balances in the accounts at December 31 is to

A. Debit subscription revenue for $135,000 and credit unearned revenue for $135,000.

B. Debit unearned revenue for $135,000 and credit subscription revenue for $135,000.

C. Debit subscription revenue for $45,000 and credit unearned revenue for $45,000.

D. Debit unearned revenue for $45,000 and credit subscription revenue for $45,000.

Answer (D) is correct. *(CMA, adapted)*
　　REQUIRED: The year-end adjusting entry.
　　DISCUSSION: The company initially debited cash and credited unearned revenue, a liability account, for $180,000. Subscriptions revenue should be recognized when it is realized or realizable and the earning process is substantially complete. Because 25% (9 months ÷ 36 months) of the subscription period has expired, 25% of the realized but unearned revenue should be recognized. Thus, the adjusting entry is to debit unearned revenue and credit subscription revenue for $45,000.
　　Answer (A) is incorrect. The amount of $135,000 would be the debit to the revenue account if it had been credited initially. Answer (B) is incorrect. A $135,000 debit to the unearned revenue account would be appropriate if 75% of the subscription period had elapsed. Answer (C) is incorrect. The amount of $45,000 would be the debit to the revenue account if it had been credited initially and if 75% of the subscription period had elapsed.

49. A machine costing $27,000 with a residual value of $2,000 is to be depreciated on a straight-line basis over 5 years. What is the adjusting entry for a full year of depreciation?

A. Depreciation expense $5,000
    Machine $5,000

B. Depreciation expense $5,000
    Cash $5,000

C. Machine $27,000
    Cash $20,000
    Depreciation expense   5,000
    Residual value   2,000

D. Depreciation expense $5,000
    Accumulated depreciation $5,000

Answer (D) is correct. *(Publisher, adapted)*
REQUIRED: The year-end adjusting entry to depreciate a machine.
DISCUSSION: At year end, depreciation expense is debited, and accumulated depreciation (a contra asset) is credited. The amount of depreciation is 20% (1 year ÷ 5 years) of the depreciation base of $25,000 ($27,000 machine cost − $2,000 residual value).
Answer (A) is incorrect. The credit is not made directly to the asset but to the contra account, accumulated depreciation. Answer (B) is incorrect. Cash is paid when the machine is purchased, not each year when depreciation is recorded. Answer (C) is incorrect. The machine's cost was $27,000, depreciation expense is a debit rather than a credit, and residual value is not separately recorded.

2.4 Other Comprehensive Basis of Accounting (OCBOA)

50. Which of the following is not a comprehensive basis of accounting other than generally accepted accounting principles?

A. Cash receipts and disbursements basis of accounting.

B. Basis of accounting used by an entity to file its income tax returns.

C. Basis of accounting used by an entity to comply with the financial reporting requirements of a government regulatory agency.

D. Basis of accounting used by an entity to comply with the financial reporting requirements of a lending institution.

Answer (D) is correct. *(CPA, adapted)*
REQUIRED: The item not a comprehensive basis of accounting other than GAAP.
DISCUSSION: A comprehensive basis of accounting other than GAAP (OCBOA) may be (1) a basis that the reporting entity uses to comply with the requirements or financial reporting provisions of a regulatory agency; (2) a basis used for tax purposes; (3) the cash basis, and modifications of the cash basis having substantial support, such as recording depreciation on fixed assets or accruing income taxes; or (4) a definite set of criteria having substantial support that is applied to all material items, for example, the price-level basis. However, a basis of accounting used by an entity to comply with the financial reporting requirements of a lending institution does not qualify as governmentally mandated or as having substantial support.
Answer (A) is incorrect. The cash receipts and disbursements basis of accounting is an OCBOA. Answer (B) is incorrect. The basis of accounting used by an entity to file its income tax returns is an OCBOA. Answer (C) is incorrect. A basis of accounting used by an entity to comply with the financial reporting requirements of a government regulatory agency is an OCBOA.

51. Compared with the accrual basis of accounting, the cash basis of accounting understates income by the net decrease during the accounting period of

	Accounts Receivable	Accrued Expenses
A.	Yes	Yes
B.	Yes	No
C.	No	No
D.	No	Yes

Answer (D) is correct. *(CPA, adapted)*
REQUIRED: The cash-basis item(s), if any, the net decrease of which understates income compared with accrual-basis accounting.
DISCUSSION: A net decrease in accounts receivable indicates that cash collected exceeded accrual-basis revenue from receivables in the current period. A net decrease in accrued expenses indicates that cash paid for expenses exceeded the current period's accrual-basis expenses. Thus, a net decrease in receivables results in an overstatement of cash-basis income compared with accrual-basis income, and a net decrease in accrued expenses results in an understatement.
Answer (A) is incorrect. A net decrease in receivables results in an overstatement of cash-basis income compared with accrual-basis income. Answer (B) is incorrect. The net decrease in accrued expenses understates cash-basis compared with accrual-basis income, but accounts receivable does not. Answer (C) is incorrect. A net decrease in accrued expenses results in an understatement.

52. On April 1, Julie began operating a service proprietorship with an initial cash investment of $1,000. The proprietorship provided $3,200 of services in April and received a payment of $2,500 in May. The proprietorship incurred expenses of $1,500 in April that were paid in June. During May, Julie drew $500 from her capital account. What was the proprietorship's income for the 2 months ended May 31 under the following methods of accounting?

	Cash-Basis	Accrual-Basis
A.	$500	$1,200
B.	$1,000	$1,700
C.	$2,000	$1,200
D.	$2,500	$1,700

Answer (D) is correct. *(CPA, adapted)*
REQUIRED: The income for a proprietorship under the cash basis and accrual basis.
DISCUSSION: Under the cash basis, $2,500 of income is recognized for the payments received in May for the services rendered in April. The $1,500 of expenses is not recognized until June. Under the accrual basis, the $3,200 of income and the $1,500 of expenses incurred in April but not paid until June are recognized. The net income is $1,700 under the accrual basis. The cash investment and capital withdrawal are ignored because they do not affect net income.
Answer (A) is incorrect. The $500 withdrawal should not be recognized in the computation of net income under either method, and the $1,500 of expenses should not be recognized under the cash basis. Answer (B) is incorrect. The cash basis does not recognize the $1,500 in expenses until June. Answer (C) is incorrect. The $500 withdrawal should not be recognized in the computation of net income under either method.

53. Hahn Co. prepared financial statements on the cash basis of accounting. The cash basis was modified so that an accrual of income taxes was reported. Are these financial statements in accordance with the modified cash basis of accounting?

A. Yes.

B. No, because the modifications are illogical.

C. No, because there is no substantial support for recording income taxes.

D. No, because the modifications result in financial statements equivalent to those prepared under the accrual basis of accounting.

Answer (A) is correct. *(CPA, adapted)*
REQUIRED: The true statement about whether cash-basis statements may be modified for accrual of income taxes.
DISCUSSION: A comprehensive basis of accounting other than GAAP includes the cash basis. Modifications of the cash basis having substantial support, such as accruing income taxes or recording depreciation on fixed assets, may be made when preparing financial statements on the cash basis.
Answer (B) is incorrect. Accrual of quarterly income taxes is a logical modification of the cash basis of accounting. Answer (C) is incorrect. Substantial support exists for accrual of a reasonably estimable expense such as income taxes. Answer (D) is incorrect. A modification of the cash basis that accrues income taxes, but incorporates no other accruals or deferrals, will not result in financial statements equivalent to those prepared under the accrual basis.

54. Income tax-basis financial statements differ from those prepared under GAAP in that income tax-basis financial statements

A. Do not include nontaxable revenues and nondeductible expenses in determining income.

B. Include detailed information about current and deferred income tax liabilities.

C. Contain no disclosures about capital and operating lease transactions.

D. Recognize certain revenues and expenses in different reporting periods.

Answer (D) is correct. *(CPA, adapted)*
REQUIRED: The difference between income tax-basis financial statements and those prepared under GAAP.
DISCUSSION: Income tax-basis financial statements and those prepared under GAAP differ when the tax basis of an asset or a liability and its reported amount in the GAAP-based financial statements are not the same. The result will be taxable or deductible amounts in future years when the reported amount of the asset is recovered or the liability is settled. Thus, certain revenues and expenses are recognized in different periods. An example is subscriptions revenue received in advance, which is recognized in taxable income when received and in financial income when earned in a later period. Another example is a warranty liability, which is recognized as an expense in financial income when a product is sold and in taxable income when the expenditures are made in a later period.
Answer (A) is incorrect. Even if financial statements are prepared on the income tax basis, permanent difference items, e.g., nondeductible expenses, are included as revenues or expenses in the income statement. They do not have to be presented in a special category of the income statement. Answer (B) is incorrect. Detailed information about current and deferred income tax liabilities is necessary whether financial statements are prepared on the income-tax basis or in conformity with GAAP. Temporary differences, which result in deferred tax amounts, arise under either basis of accounting. Answer (C) is incorrect. Lease disclosures are the same under either basis of accounting.

55. To calculate net sales, <List A> must be <List B> cash receipts from customers.

List A	List B
A. An increase in net accounts receivable	Added to
B. An increase in net accounts receivable	Subtracted from
C. An increase in net accounts payable	Added to
D. A decrease in net accounts receivable	Neither added to nor subtracted from

Answer (A) is correct. *(CIA, adapted)*
REQUIRED: The calculation of net sales.
DISCUSSION: To convert from the cash basis (cash receipts) to the accrual basis (net sales), the increase in net accounts receivable must be added to cash receipts from customers.
Answer (B) is incorrect. An increase in net accounts receivable is added to cash receipts. Answer (C) is incorrect. Changes in accounts payable are not included in the conversion of cash receipts to net sales. Answer (D) is incorrect. A decrease in net accounts receivable is subtracted from cash receipts.

56. Young & Jamison's modified cash-basis financial statements indicate cash paid for operating expenses of $150,000, end-of-year prepaid expenses of $15,000, and accrued liabilities of $25,000. At the beginning of the year, Young & Jamison had prepaid expenses of $10,000, while accrued liabilities were $5,000. If cash paid for operating expenses is converted to accrual-basis operating expenses, what would be the amount of operating expenses?

A. $125,000

B. $135,000

C. $165,000

D. $175,000

Answer (C) is correct. *(CPA, adapted)*
REQUIRED: The amount of accrual-basis operating expenses.
DISCUSSION: During the year, prepaid expenses increased by $5,000 ($15,000 – $10,000), and accrued liabilities increased by $20,000 ($25,000 – $5,000). The increase in prepaid expenses is a cash outflow without accrual of an expense. It indicates that accrual-basis expenses were $5,000 lower than cash-basis expenses. The increase in accrued liabilities results in accrual of an expense without a cash outflow. It indicates that accrual-basis expenses were $20,000 higher than cash-basis expenses. Thus, the adjustments of cash-basis operating expenses are a $5,000 decrease and a $20,000 increase, respectively.

Cash-basis operating expenses	$150,000
Increase in prepaid expenses	(5,000)
Increase in accrued liabilities	20,000
Accrual-basis operating expenses	$165,000

Answer (A) is incorrect. The amount of $125,000 results from subtracting the $20,000 increase in accrued liabilities. Answer (B) is incorrect. The amount of $135,000 results from adding the $5,000 increase in prepaid expenses and subtracting the $20,000 increase in accrued liabilities. Answer (D) is incorrect. The amount of $175,000 results from adding the $5,000 in prepaid expenses.

57. The following information pertains to Falcon Co.'s current year sales:

Cash sales

Gross	$160,000
Returns and allowances	7,000

Credit sales

Gross	$240,000
Discounts	11,000

On January 1, customers owed Falcon $70,000.
On December 31, customers owed Falcon $60,000.
Falcon uses the direct write-off method for bad debts.
No bad debts were recorded in the current year.
Under the cash basis of accounting, what amount of net revenue should Falcon report for the current year?

A. $153,000

B. $340,000

C. $382,000

D. $392,000

Answer (D) is correct. *(CPA, adapted)*
REQUIRED: The revenue under the cash basis of accounting.
DISCUSSION: Under the cash basis of accounting, revenue is recognized when cash is received. Falcon had $153,000 ($160,000 – $7,000) in net cash sales and $229,000 ($240,000 – $11,000) in net credit sales. Given that accounts receivable decreased, cash collections thereon must have exceeded net credit sales by $10,000 ($70,000 – $60,000). No adjustment for bad debts is needed because no bad debts were recorded. Accordingly, net revenue is $392,000 ($153,000 + $229,000 + $10,000).
Answer (A) is incorrect. Net cash sales equals $153,000. Answer (B) is incorrect. Total gross sales minus ending accounts receivable is $340,000. Answer (C) is incorrect. The amount of $382,000 does not reflect an adjustment for the change in receivables.

58. A company records items on the cash basis throughout the year and converts to an accrual basis for year-end reporting. Its cash-basis net income for the year is $70,000. The company has gathered the following comparative balance sheet information:

	Beginning of Year	End of Year
Accounts payable	$3,000	$1,000
Unearned revenue	300	500
Wages payable	300	400
Prepaid rent	1,200	1,500
Accounts receivable	1,400	600

What amount should the company report as its accrual-based net income for the current year?

A. $68,800

B. $70,200

C. $71,200

D. $73,200

Answer (C) is correct. *(CPA, adapted)*
REQUIRED: The accrual-based net income.
DISCUSSION: The decrease in accounts payable implies that cash paid to suppliers exceeded purchases. The decrease ($3,000 – $1,000 = $2,000) is included in the calculation of cash-basis net income but not accrual-basis net income. The increase in the liability for unearned revenue ($500 – $300 = $200) implies a cash inflow that increased cash-basis net income but not accrual-basis net income. The increase in wages payable ($400 – $300 = $100) implies an accrual-basis expense not recognized in cash-basis net income. The increase in prepaid rent ($1,500 – $1,300 = $200) implies reduced cash-basis net income with no effect on accrual-basis net income. The decrease in accounts receivable ($1,400 – $600 = $800) implies that cash collections exceeded accrual-basis revenue. Accrual-basis net income based on these adjustments is therefore $71,200.

Cash-basis net income	$70,000
A/P decrease	2,000
Unearned revenue increase	(200)
Wages payable increase	(100)
Prepaid rent increase	300
A/R decrease	(800)
	$71,200

Answer (A) is incorrect. The amount of $68,800 equals cash-basis net income, minus the decrease in accounts payable, plus the decrease in accounts receivable. Answer (B) is incorrect. The amount of $70,200 equals cash-basis net income, plus the increase in unearned revenue. Answer (D) is incorrect. The amount of $73,200 equals cash-basis net income, plus the decrease in accounts payable, plus the decrease in accounts receivable, plus the increase in wages payable, plus the increase in prepaid rent.

2.5 Personal Financial Statements

59. Personal financial statements usually consist of

A. A statement of net worth and a statement of changes in net worth.

B. A statement of net worth, an income statement, and a statement of changes in net worth.

C. A statement of financial condition and a statement of changes in net worth.

D. A statement of financial condition, a statement of changes in net worth, and a statement of cash flows.

Answer (C) is correct. *(CPA, adapted)*
REQUIRED: The basic financial statements that should be included in personal financial statements.
DISCUSSION: According to GAAP, personal financial statements include at least a statement of financial condition. A statement of changes in net worth and comparative financial statements are recommended but not required. A personal statement of cash flows is neither required nor recommended.

60. Mrs. Taft owns a $150,000 insurance policy on her husband's life. The cash value of the policy is $125,000, and a $50,000 loan is secured by the policy. In the Tafts' personal statement of financial condition at December 31, what amount should be shown as an investment in life insurance?

A. $150,000

B. $125,000

C. $100,000

D. $75,000

Answer (D) is correct. *(CPA, adapted)*
REQUIRED: The amount at which an investment in life insurance should be presented in a personal statement of financial condition.
DISCUSSION: Assets are presented at their estimated current values in a personal statement of financial condition. Furthermore, investments in life insurance must be reported at their cash values minus the amount of any outstanding loans. Thus, the amount that should be reported in Mrs. Taft's personal financial statement is $75,000 ($125,000 cash value – $50,000 loan).
Answer (A) is incorrect. The amount of the policy is $150,000. Answer (B) is incorrect. The cash value is $125,000. Answer (C) is incorrect. The amount of the policy minus the loan is $100,000.

61. Green, a calendar-year taxpayer, is preparing a personal statement of financial condition as of April 30, Year 4. Green's Year 3 income tax liability was paid in full on April 15, Year 4. Green's tax on income earned between January and April Year 4 is estimated at $20,000. In addition, $40,000 is estimated for income tax on the differences between the estimated current values and current amounts of Green's assets and liabilities and their tax bases at April 30, Year 4. No withholdings or payments have been made towards the Year 4 income tax liability. In Green's April 30, Year 4, statement of financial condition, what amount should be reported, between liabilities and net worth, as estimated income taxes?

A. $0

B. $20,000

C. $40,000

D. $60,000

Answer (D) is correct. *(CPA, adapted)*
REQUIRED: The reported amount of estimated income taxes.
DISCUSSION: No amount should be reported for Year 3 taxes because the Year 3 liability was paid in full. Thus, Green will report estimated income taxes for amounts earned through April Year 4 and for the differences between the estimated current values of assets and the estimated current amounts of liabilities and their tax bases, a sum of $60,000 ($20,000 + $40,000).
Answer (A) is incorrect. Green must report estimated income taxes. Answer (B) is incorrect. This amount excludes estimated income taxes for the differences between the estimated current values of assets and the estimated current amounts of liabilities and their tax bases. Answer (C) is incorrect. This amount excludes the estimated income taxes on Year 4 income earned to date.

62. On December 31, Year 4, Shane is a fully vested participant in a company-sponsored pension plan. According to the plan's administrator, Shane has at that date the nonforfeitable right to receive a lump sum of $100,000 on December 28, Year 5. The discounted amount of $100,000 is $90,000 at December 31, Year 4. The right is not contingent on Shane's life expectancy and requires no future performance on Shane's part. In Shane's December 31, Year 4, personal statement of financial condition, the vested interest in the pension plan should be reported at

A. $0

B. $90,000

C. $95,000

D. $100,000

Answer (B) is correct. *(CPA, adapted)*
REQUIRED: The amount at which the vested interest in a pension plan should be reported in a personal statement of financial condition.
DISCUSSION: Noncancelable rights to receive future sums be presented at their estimated current value as assets in personal financial statements if they (1) are for fixed or determinable amounts; (2) are not contingent on the holder's life expectancy or the occurrence of a particular event, such as disability or death; and (3) do not require the future performance of service by the holder. The fully vested rights in the company-sponsored pension plan therefore should be reported at their current value, which is equal to the $90,000 discounted amount.
Answer (A) is incorrect. The current value of the right should be reported. Answer (C) is incorrect. It is a nonsense amount. Answer (D) is incorrect. The undiscounted amount is $100,000.

63. Quinn is preparing a personal statement of financial condition as of April 30. Included in Quinn's assets are the following:

● 50% of the voting stock of Ink Corp. A shareholders' agreement restricts the sale of the stock and, under certain circumstances, requires Ink to repurchase the stock. Quinn's tax basis for the stock is $430,000, and at April 30, the buyout value is $675,000.

● Jewelry with a fair value aggregating $70,000 based on an independent appraisal on April 30 for insurance purposes. This jewelry was acquired by purchase and gift over a 10-year period and has a total tax basis of $40,000.

What is the total amount at which the Ink stock and jewelry should be reported in Quinn's April 30 personal statement of financial condition?

A. $470,000

B. $500,000

C. $715,000

D. $745,000

Answer (D) is correct. *(CPA, adapted)*
REQUIRED: The amount at which stock and jewelry should be reported in a personal statement of financial condition.
DISCUSSION: Assets are reported at estimated current value. An interest in a closely held business is an asset and should be shown at its estimated current value. The buyout value is a better representation of the current value of the Ink stock than the tax basis. The appraisal value is the appropriate basis for reporting the jewelry. Thus, the stock and jewelry should be reported at $745,000 ($675,000 + $70,000).
Answer (A) is incorrect. The amount of $470,000 reports both assets at their tax basis. Answer (B) is incorrect. The amount of $500,000 includes the stock at its tax basis. Answer (C) is incorrect. The amount of $715,000 includes the jewelry's tax basis rather than its fair value.

64. On December 31, Year 5, Mr. and Mrs. Blake owned a parcel of land held as an investment. The land was purchased for $95,000 in Year 1, and was encumbered by a mortgage with a principal balance of $60,000 at December 31, Year 5. On this date, the fair value of the land was $150,000. In the Blakes' December 31, Year 5, personal statement of financial condition, at what amount should the land investment and mortgage payable be reported?

	Land Investment	Mortgage Payable
A.	$150,000	$60,000
B.	$95,000	$60,000
C.	$90,000	$0
D.	$35,000	$0

Answer (A) is correct. *(CPA, adapted)*
REQUIRED: The amounts at which the land investment and mortgage payable should be reported.
DISCUSSION: For an investment in a limited business activity not conducted in a separate business entity (such as an investment in real estate and a related mortgage), the assets and liabilities must not be presented as a net amount. Instead, they should be presented as separate assets at their estimated current values and separate liabilities at their estimated current amounts. This presentation is particularly important if a large portion of the liabilities may be satisfied with funds from sources unrelated to the investments. Thus, the land should be reported at its $150,000 fair value and the mortgage principal at $60,000 (the amount at which the debt could currently be discharged).
Answer (B) is incorrect. The cost of the land was $95,000. Answer (C) is incorrect. The asset and liability should be presented separately and not as a net amount. Answer (D) is incorrect. The cost minus the mortgage balance equals $35,000.

65. A business interest that constitutes a large part of an individual's total assets should be presented in a personal statement of financial condition as

A. A separate listing of the individual assets and liabilities at cost.

B. Separate line items of both total assets and total liabilities at cost.

C. A single amount equal to the proprietorship equity.

D. A single amount equal to the estimated current value of the business interest.

Answer (D) is correct. *(CPA, adapted)*
REQUIRED: The amount at which a business interest constituting a large part of an individual's total assets should be presented in a personal financial statement.
DISCUSSION: A business interest constituting a large part of an individual's total assets be presented in a personal statement of financial condition as a single amount equal to the estimated current value of the business interest. This investment should be disclosed separately from other investments if the entity is marketable as a going concern.
Answer (A) is incorrect. The business interest should be reported as a net amount. Answer (B) is incorrect. The business interest should be reported as a net amount. Answer (C) is incorrect. The business interest should be reported at its estimated current value.

Use Gleim **EQE Test Prep** Software Download for interactive study and performance analysis.

STUDY UNIT THREE
REPORTING INCOME

To increase the usefulness of the **statement of income**, different classifications of income are used. The major classifications are (1) income from continuing operations (or other proper title), (2) discontinued operations, and (3) extraordinary items.

The components of **net income** may be presented as follows in an income statement using the multiple-step format:

Gross sales revenue			$ xxx,xxx
Sales returns and discounts			(x,xxx)
Net sales revenue			$ xxx,xxx
Cost of goods sold			(xxx,xxx)
Gross profit			$ xx,xxx
Operating expenses			(x,xxx)
Operating income			$ xx,xxx
Other revenues and gains			x,xxx
Other expenses and losses			(x,xxx)
Income from continuing operations before income taxes			$ xx,xxx
Income taxes			(x,xxx)
Income from continuing operations*			$ xx,xxx
Discontinued operations:			
Income from operations of discontinued component unit (net of loss on disposal of $xxx)		$x,xxx	
Income tax expense		(xxx)	x,xxx
Income before extraordinary item			$ x,xxx
Extraordinary item:			
Loss from volcanic eruption (net of income tax benefit of $xxx)			(x,xxx)
Net Income			$ xx,xxx

	Basic	Diluted
Basic and diluted EPS (complex capital structure):		
Income from continuing operations before discontinued operation and extraordinary item	$y.yy	$y.yy
Income from operations of discontinued component unit, net of tax	y.yy	y.yy
Income before extraordinary item	$y.yy	$y.yy
Extraordinary loss, net of tax	(y.yy)	(y.yy)
Net income	$y.yy	$y.yy

*NOTE: This title is used when the entity reports a discontinued operation. If it does not report a discontinued operation, the title is modified. For example, if an extraordinary loss is reported, the line item may be income before extraordinary loss. For the sake of convenience, this text will use the term "income from continuing operations" unless the context requires a different title.

Income from Continuing Operations

Income (loss) from continuing operations includes the income effects of all transactions and events not included in discontinued operations or extraordinary items. The primary focus is on the income effects (revenues and expenses) directly related to the principal business activities of the entity. It also includes the income effects (gains and losses) of the entity's peripheral activities.

Income (loss) from continuing operations may be presented in a single-step or a multiple-step format (or some mixture). In the **single-step format**, revenues and gains are grouped separately from expenses and losses. Income from continuing operations is then calculated in a single step as the difference between the subtotals of the two groups. In the **multiple-step format**, certain revenues and expenses are assigned to an operating section. The most common subtotals are gross profit (margin) or loss (net sales revenue – cost of sales) and operating income or loss (gross profit or loss – operating expenses). The nonoperating section presents the income effects of significant recurring transactions not directly related to primary operations and gains and losses not assignable elsewhere. The common subtotals are other revenues and gains and other expenses and losses. The net of these other items is added to, or subtracted from, operating income (loss) to determine the subtotal, income (loss) from continuing operations before taxes. Subtracting (adding) the total applicable tax effect results in income (loss) from continuing operations.

Discontinued Operations

The operating results of a discontinued operation are reported separately in the income statement (or statement of activities of a not-for-profit entity) if three conditions are met: (1) A component of the entity has been **disposed of** or is **classified as held for sale**, (2) its operations and cash flows are or will be eliminated from the entity's operations, and (3) the entity will have no significant continuing involvement after disposal. A **component of an entity** has operations and cash flows that are clearly distinguishable for operating and financial reporting purposes. A component may be (1) a reportable segment, (2) an operating segment, (3) a reporting unit, (4) a subsidiary, or (5) an asset disposal group. If a long-lived asset or disposal group is not a component, a gain or loss on its sale is included in income from continuing operations.

Operating results (including the gain or loss on disposal) are reported in discontinued operations in the period(s) in which they occur. Operating results include any loss for a writedown to **fair value minus cost to sell** of a long-lived asset held for sale or a gain from an increase in fair value minus cost to sell (but limited to the losses previously recognized). The results of discontinued operations, minus (plus) income tax (benefit), are reported separately before extraordinary items (if any). The **gain or loss on disposal** must be disclosed on the face of the financial statements or in the notes.

Amounts previously reported in discontinued operations in a prior period may require adjustment in the current period. If such an adjustment is **directly related** to a prior-period disposal of a component, it is reported currently in discontinued operations as a separate item, and its nature and amount are disclosed.

Extraordinary Items

Extraordinary items are material gains or losses reported net of tax after income from continuing operations and discontinued operations. The event or transaction must be both unusual in nature and infrequent in occurrence in the environment in which the entity operates. If an item meets only one of these criteria, it must be presented separately as a component of income from continuing operations.

Comprehensive Income

Comprehensive income includes all changes in equity of a business enterprise except those changes resulting from investments by owners and distributions to owners. Comprehensive income includes two major categories, net income and other comprehensive income. Components of comprehensive income not included in net income are included in **other comprehensive income (OCI)** in annual and interim statements. Each such component must be presented either (1) net of tax or (2) before tax with one amount shown for the tax effect on total OCI. But the **tax effect** on each component must be disclosed if not presented in the statements.

An entity must report comprehensive income only when it has items of OCI in any period presented.

A **single continuous statement of comprehensive income** may be used that consists of (1) a total of net income with its components, (2) a total of OCI with its components, and (3) a total of comprehensive income. The only permitted alternative is to present **separate but consecutive statements** of net income and OCI. The first statement (the income statement) presents the components of net income and total net income. The second statement (the statement of OCI) is presented immediately after the first. It presents (1) the components of OCI, (2) the total of OCI, and (3) a total for comprehensive income. Also, the entity may begin the second statement with net income.

The total OCI for the period is recorded in a nominal account. It must be transferred to **accumulated OCI**, a real account presented in a separate component of equity in the balance sheet. The changes in the accumulated balances of each component of OCI must be disclosed in the notes or as a reconciliation in a statement of changes in equity.

Under existing standards, items of OCI include, among others,

- Unrealized gains and losses on available-for-sale securities, except those that are hedged items in a fair value hedge (see Study Unit 10)
- Gains and losses on derivatives designated, qualifying, and effective as cash flow hedges (see Study Unit 10)
- Certain amounts associated with recognition of the funded status of postretirement defined benefit plans (see Study Unit 13)
- Certain foreign currency items (see Study Unit 26)

To avoid double counting, **reclassification adjustments** are made when an item included in net income was included in OCI for the same or a prior period. For example, if a gain or loss on available-for-sale securities is realized in the current period, the prior-period recognition of an unrealized holding gain or loss must be eliminated from accumulated OCI.

The following is an example of the **single-statement format** for reporting comprehensive income of an entity with no noncontrolling interest:

CI Company
Consolidated Statement of
Comprehensive Income
Year Ended December 31, Year 1

Statement of Income		
Revenues		$XXX,XXX
Expenses	$(XX,XXX)	
Amortized prior service cost reclassified from OCI	(XXX)	(XX,XXX)
Gain – sale of available-for-sale securities	XXX	
Gains reclassified from OCI	X,XXX	X,XXX
Pre-tax operating income		XXX,XXX
Income tax expense		(XX,XXX)
Net income		XX,XXX
Statement of OCI		
OCI, net of tax:		
Foreign currency translation		X,XXX
Unrealized holding gains	XX,XXX	
Minus: reclassification of gains included in net income	(X,XXX)	XX,XXX
Defined benefit pension plan:		
Prior service cost	(X,XXX)	
Net loss	(X,XXX)	
Minus: reclassified prior service cost	XXX	(X,XXX)
OCI		XX,XXX
Comprehensive income		$ XX,XXX

A **two-statement** presentation is easily derived from the example above. The final component of the **statement of income** is net income. The first component of the **statement of OCI** is net income, and the final component is comprehensive income.

If a **noncontrolling interest** exists, amounts for net income and comprehensive income attributable to the parent and to the subsidiary must be reported in the appropriate statements.

Statement of Changes in Equity

Disclosures of changes in equity (including accumulated OCI) and in the number of shares of equity securities are required whenever financial position and results of operations are reported. Most entities report either a statement of retained earnings or a statement of changes in equity. The retained earnings statement (or section in a statement of changes in equity) consists of (1) the beginning and ending balances of retained earnings; (2) any error corrections (net of tax); (3) net income (loss); (4) dividends paid or declared; and (5) certain other rare items, e.g., quasi-reorganizations. Furthermore, the retained earnings balance is sometimes divided into **appropriated and unappropriated** amounts. However, transfers into and out of appropriated retained earnings (for example, general purpose contingency reserves or provisions for replacement costs of property, plant, and equipment) always are excluded from net income.

The following is a format for a statement of changes in equity of an entity with no noncontrolling interest:

CI Company
Consolidated Statement of
Changes in Equity
Year Ended December 31, Year 1

Retained earnings	
January 1	$ XXX,XXX
Net income	XXX,XXX
Dividends declared	(XX,XXX)
December 31	$ XXX,XXX
Accumulated OCI	
January 1	$ XX,XXX
OCI	XX,XXX
December 31	XX,XXX
Common stock	
January 1	$ XX,XXX
Shares issued	XX,XXX
December 31	$ XX,XXX
Additional paid-in capital	
January 1	$ XXX,XXX
Common shares issued	XXX,XXX
December 31	$ XXX,XXX
Total equity	$X,XXX,XXX

Differences between GAAP and IFRS

Under IFRS:

- Net cash flows from operating, investing, and financing activities of a discontinued operation must be disclosed in the notes or the statements.
- No items are classified as extraordinary, either on the statement of comprehensive income or in the notes.
- Expenses may be classified by the nature-of-expense method or the function-of-expense method.
- Items of OCI include changes in revaluation surplus for (1) property, plant, and equipment or (2) intangible assets.
- An entity must group items of OCI as follows: (1) those that will not be reclassified to profit or loss (e.g., actuarial gains and losses on defined benefit pension plans) and (2) those that may be (e.g., exchange differences arising from foreign operations).
- All recognized income and expense items are included in profit or loss unless a pronouncement requires otherwise. The minimum presentation on the face of the statement of comprehensive income includes the following line items: (1) revenue, (2) gains (losses) on (a) derecognition of financial assets measured at amortized cost and (b) reclassification of financial assets to fair value, (3) finance costs, (4) share of profits and losses of associates and joint ventures accounted for under the equity method, (5) tax expense, (6) one amount for the sum of (a) after-tax profit (loss) on discontinued operations and (b) after-tax gain (loss) on the measurement at fair value minus cost to sell or on disposal of the assets or disposal groups, (7) profit or loss, (8) each component of OCI classified by nature, (9) share of OCI of associates and joint ventures accounted for under the equity method, and (10) total comprehensive income.

QUESTIONS

3.1 Income from Continuing Operations

1. The all-inclusive income statement concept

A. Is synonymous with the current operating concept, and both are acceptable under GAAP.

B. Is generally more appropriate than the current operating concept.

C. Is not appropriate. The current operating concept is a generally accepted accounting principle.

D. Produces an interactive income statement that avoids the problems associated with the changing value of currencies.

Answer (B) is correct. *(Publisher, adapted)*
REQUIRED: The true statement about the all-inclusive income statement concept.
DISCUSSION: In the calculation of net income, the all-inclusive approach includes all transactions that affect equity during the current period except (1) transactions with owners, (2) prior-period adjustments, and (3) certain items that are reported initially in other comprehensive income. The current operating concept includes only the ordinary, normal, recurring operations in the net income of the current period. Other items are direct adjustments to retained earnings. GAAP adopt the all-inclusive approach. The all-inclusive concept was strengthened by the limitation of prior-period adjustments to corrections of errors. As a result, most revenue, expense, gain, and loss items are included in continuing operations in the income statement.
Answer (A) is incorrect. GAAP reject the current operating concept. Answer (C) is incorrect. GAAP reject the current operating concept. Answer (D) is incorrect. An "interactive income statement" does not exist in financial accounting.

2. Under GAAP, comparative financial statements are

A. Required for at least the current and the prior year.

B. Required for at least the current and the prior 2 years.

C. Recommended for at least the current and the prior year.

D. Neither required nor recommended.

Answer (C) is correct. *(S. Rubin)*
REQUIRED: The position of GAAP concerning comparative financial statements.
DISCUSSION: Presenting financial statements of two or more periods is ordinarily desirable. This position is commonly understood to be a recommendation rather than a requirement. However, public companies must file comparative statements with the SEC.
Answer (A) is incorrect. Although not required, comparative financial statements ordinarily should be presented. Answer (B) is incorrect. Comparative financial statements are not required. Answer (D) is incorrect. Comparative financial statements are recommended.

3. Select the best order for the following items appearing in income statements:

1. Extraordinary items
2. Income from continuing operations
3. Discontinued operations
4. Prior-period adjustments
5. Taxes on income from continuing operations
6. Dividends
7. Net income
8. Revenues
9. Expenses
10. Income from continuing operations before income tax

A. 9 - 10 - 8 - 7 - 6 - 2 - 4

B. 8 - 6 - 7 - 1 - 2 - 5

C. 9 - 10 - 8 - 6 - 3 - 2 - 1 - 4

D. 8 - 9 - 10 - 5 - 2 - 3 - 1 - 7

Answer (D) is correct. *(Publisher, adapted)*
REQUIRED: The order of items appearing in income statements.
DISCUSSION: The order of appearance in income statements of the items is

8. Revenues
9. Expenses
10. Income from continuing operations before income tax
5. Taxes on income from continuing operations
2. Income from continuing operations
3. Discontinued operations
1. Extraordinary items
7. Net income

Prior-period adjustments (4) and dividends (6) appear only in retained earnings statements.
Answer (A) is incorrect. The list begins with expenses, which cannot be the first item on a GAAP-based income statement. Answer (B) is incorrect. Although the first item (revenues) is correct, the other items are not in the right order. Answer (C) is incorrect. Among other things, prior-period adjustments and dividends affect retained earnings directly. They are not components of net income.

4. On December 31, Salo Corp.'s balance sheet accounts increased by the following amounts compared with those at the end of the prior year:

Assets	$178,000
Liabilities	62,000
Capital stock	125,000
Additional paid-in capital	17,000

Salo had no accumulated other comprehensive income (OCI), and the only charge to retained earnings during the year was for a dividend payment of $34,000. Net income for the year was

    A. $60,000

    B. $34,000

    C. $8,000

    D. $26,000

Answer (C) is correct. *(CPA, adapted)*
REQUIRED: The net income for the year given the increases in assets, liabilities, and paid-in capital.
DISCUSSION: Assets equal the sum of liabilities and equity (contributed capital, retained earnings, and accumulated other comprehensive income). To calculate net income, the first step is to add the dividend payment ($34,000) to the increase in assets ($178,000). The excess of this sum ($212,000) over the increase in liabilities ($62,000) gives the total increase in equity ($150,000). Given no accumulated OCI, the excess of this amount over the combined increases in the capital accounts ($142,000) equals the increase in retained earnings ($8,000) arising from net income.
Answer (A) is incorrect. The amount of $60,000 equals the dividend payment plus the excess of the sum of the increases in liabilities, capital stock, and additional paid-in capital over the increase in assets. Answer (B) is incorrect. The dividend payment is $34,000. Answer (D) is incorrect. The amount of $26,000 is the excess of the sum of the increases in liabilities, capital stock, and additional paid-in capital over the increase in assets.

5. The major distinction made between the multiple-step and single-step income statement formats is the separation of

    A. Operating and nonoperating data.

    B. Income tax expense and administrative expenses.

    C. Cost of goods sold expense and administrative expenses.

    D. The effect on income taxes due to extraordinary items and the effect on income taxes due to income before extraordinary items.

Answer (A) is correct. *(CIA, adapted)*
REQUIRED: The major distinction between the multiple-step and single-step income statement formats.
DISCUSSION: Within the income from continuing operations classification, the single-step income statement provides one grouping for revenue items and one for expense items. The single-step is the one subtraction necessary to arrive at income from continuing operations prior to the effect of income taxes. In contrast, the multiple-step income statement matches operating revenues and expenses separately from nonoperating items. This format emphasizes subtotals, such as gross profit or loss and operating income or loss, within the presentation of income from continuing operations.
Answer (B) is incorrect. Either format separates income tax expense and administrative expenses. Answer (C) is incorrect. Cost of goods sold and administrative expenses cannot be combined under GAAP reporting. Answer (D) is incorrect. GAAP require extraordinary items to be reported net of income tax effect, regardless of the report format.

6. On January 1 of the current year, Bricks and Mortar Co. (B&M) installed cabinets to display its merchandise in customers' stores. B&M expects to use these cabinets for 5 years. Its current-year multi-step income statement should include

    A. One-fifth of the cabinet costs in cost of goods sold.

    B. One-fifth of the cabinet costs in selling expenses.

    C. All of the cabinet costs in cost of goods sold.

    D. All of the cabinet costs in selling expenses.

Answer (B) is correct. *(CPA, adapted)*
REQUIRED: The costs included in the determination of current net income.
DISCUSSION: The cost of the cabinets is a selling expense. However, because the cabinets will provide benefits over a 5-year period, their cost should be allocated systematically and rationally over that period, for example, by the straight-line method. In effect, periodic depreciation of the cabinets should be recognized as a selling expense.
Answer (A) is incorrect. Under GAAP, no portion of selling costs can be included in cost of goods sold. Answer (C) is incorrect. The cabinets are purely for product display, and they play no role in the manufacture or acquisition of the merchandise. Thus, they cannot be a part of product cost included in cost of goods sold. Answer (D) is incorrect. The cost should be allocated to the periods benefited.

7. In Baer Food Co.'s single-step income statement, the section titled *Revenues* consisted of the following:

Net sales revenue	$187,000
Discontinued operations:	
Income from operations of component unit	
(including gain on disposal of $21,600)	18,000
Income tax	(6,000)
Interest revenue	10,200
Gain on sale of equipment	4,700
Total revenues	$213,900

In the revenues section of the income statement, Baer Food should have reported total revenues of

A. $213,900

B. $209,200

C. $203,700

D. $201,900

Answer (D) is correct. *(CPA, adapted)*
   REQUIRED: The total revenues.
   DISCUSSION: This single-step income statement classifies the items included in income from continuing operations as either revenues or expenses. Discontinued operations is a classification in the income statement separate from continuing operations. Hence, total revenues (including interest and the gain) were $201,900 ($213,900 – $12,000 results from discontinued operations).
   Answer (A) is incorrect. Reported total revenues equal $213,900. Answer (B) is incorrect. The amount of $209,200 excludes the gain. Answer (C) is incorrect. The amount of $203,700 excludes the interest.

8. A company has a 40% gross margin, general and administrative expenses of $50, interest expense of $20, and net income of $70 for the year just ended. If the corporate tax rate is 30%, the level of sales revenue for the year just ended was

A. $170

B. $255

C. $350

D. $425

Answer (D) is correct. *(CIA, adapted)*
   REQUIRED: The sales revenue for the year.
   DISCUSSION: Net income before taxes is $100 [$70 NI ÷ (1.0 – .3 tax rate)]. Hence, the gross margin (sales – cost of sales) is $170 ($100 NI before taxes + $20 interest + $50 G&A expenses). Sales must then be $425 ($170 gross margin ÷ 40% gross margin ratio).
   Answer (A) is incorrect. The gross margin is $170. Answer (B) is incorrect. The cost of goods sold is $255. Answer (C) is incorrect. The amount of $350 assumes pre-tax net income was $70.

9. Henderson Corp. reports operating expenses in two categories: (1) selling and (2) general and administrative. The adjusted trial balance on December 31 included the following expense and loss accounts:

Accounting and legal fees	$120,000
Advertising	150,000
Freight out	80,000
Interest	70,000
Loss on sale of long-term investment	30,000
Officers' salaries	225,000
Rent for office space	220,000
Sales salaries and commissions	140,000

One-half of the rented premises is occupied by the sales department. Henderson's total selling expenses for the year are

A. $480,000

B. $400,000

C. $370,000

D. $360,000

Answer (A) is correct. *(CPA, adapted)*
   REQUIRED: The total selling expenses.
   DISCUSSION: Within the categories of expenses presented, the $150,000 of advertising, the $80,000 of freight out, 50% of the $220,000 rent for office space, and the $140,000 of sales salaries and commissions should be classified as selling expenses. Total selling expenses are therefore $480,000. The costs of accounting and legal fees, officers' salaries, and 50% of rent for office space are general and administrative expenses. Interest and the loss on sale of the long-term investment are nonoperating items.
   Answer (B) is incorrect. The amount of $400,000 excludes the freight-out expense. Answer (C) is incorrect. The amount of $370,000 excludes 50% of the rent for office space. Answer (D) is incorrect. The amount of $360,000 excludes the advertising and freight-out expenses and includes the entire rent for the office.

10. The effect of a material transaction that is infrequent in occurrence but not unusual in nature should be presented separately as a component of income from continuing operations when the transaction results in a

	Gain	Loss
A.	Yes	Yes
B.	Yes	No
C.	No	No
D.	No	Yes

Answer (A) is correct. *(CPA, adapted)*
REQUIRED: The circumstances in which an infrequent but not unusual transaction is shown as a separate component of income from continuing operations.
DISCUSSION: To be classified as an extraordinary item, a transaction must be both unusual in nature and infrequent in occurrence within the environment in which the business operates. If an item meets one but not both of these criteria, it should be presented separately as a component of income from continuing operations. Whether the transaction results in a gain or a loss does not affect this presentation.
Answer (B) is incorrect. A loss from an infrequent but not unusual transaction does not qualify for treatment as an extraordinary item. It should be separately presented as a component of income from continuing operations. Answer (C) is incorrect. A gain or loss from an infrequent but not unusual transaction should be presented as a component of income from continuing operations. Answer (D) is incorrect. A gain from an infrequent but not unusual transaction is not extraordinary. Thus, it should be presented as a component of income from continuing operations.

11. A company's activities for Year 2 included the following:

Gross sales	$3,600,000
Cost of goods sold	1,200,000
Selling and administrative expense	500,000
Adjustment for a prior-year understatement of amortization expense	59,000
Sales returns	34,000
Gain on sale of available-for-sale securities	8,000
Gain on disposal of a discontinued business segment	4,000
Unrealized gain on available-for-sale securities	2,000

The company has a 30% effective income tax rate. What is the company's net income for Year 2?

A. $1,267,700

B. $1,273,300

C. $1,314,600

D. $1,316,000

Answer (C) is correct. *(CPA, adapted)*
REQUIRED: The net income.
DISCUSSION: Net sales equal $3,566,000 ($3,600,000 gross sales – $34,000 sales returns). The adjustment for a prior-year understatement of amortization expense is the basis for restatement of a prior-year income statement (if comparative statements are presented) or is made to beginning retained earnings (if single-year statements are presented). It has no effect on the current income statement. The unrealized gain on available-for-sale securities is recognized in other comprehensive income (OCI). Net income for Year 2 is calculated as follows:

Net sales		$3,566,000
Cost of goods sold		(1,200,000)
Gross profit		$2,366,000
Operating expenses:		
Selling and administrative		(500,000)
Income from operations		$1,866,000
Other revenues and gains:		
Gain on sale of available-for-sale securities		8,000
Income from continuing operations before taxes		$1,874,000
Income taxes ($1,874,000 × 30%)		(562,200)
Income from continuing operations		$1,311,800
Discontinued operations:		
Gain on disposal	$4,000	
Income taxes ($4,000 × 30%)	(1,200)	
Gain on discontinued operations		2,800
Net income		$1,314,600

Answer (A) is incorrect. The amount of $1,267,700 results from recognizing the adjustment for a prior-year understatement of amortization expense as an expense in the calculation of current-year net income and omitting the gain on sale of available-for-sale securities. Answer (B) is incorrect. The amount of $1,273,300 results from recognizing the adjustment for a prior-year understatement of amortization expense as an expense in the calculation of current-year net income. Answer (D) is incorrect. The amount of $1,316,000 results from including the unrealized gain on available-for-sale securities in the calculation of net income.

3.2 Discontinued Operations

12. Which of the following transactions qualifies as a discontinued operation?

A. Disposal of part of a line of business.

B. Planned and approved sale of a segment.

C. Phasing out of a production line.

D. Changes related to technological improvements.

Answer (B) is correct. *(CPA, adapted)*
REQUIRED: The discontinued operation.
DISCUSSION: The operating results of a discontinued operation are reported separately if three conditions are met: (1) a component of the entity has been disposed of or is classified as held for sale, (2) its operations and cash flows are or will be eliminated from the entity's operations, and (3) the entity will have no significant continuing involvement after disposal. A component of an entity has operations and cash flows that are clearly distinguishable for operating and financial reporting purposes. A component may be a(n) (1) reporting segment, (2) operating segment, (3) reporting unit, (4) subsidiary, or (5) asset group (a disposal group if it is to be disposed of). A long-lived asset is classified as held for sale when (1) management has committed to a plan to sell, (2) sale within 1 year is probable, (3) significant change in or withdrawal of the plan is unlikely, (4) the asset is available for immediate sale, (5) actions have begun to complete the plan, and (6) active marketing has begun at a reasonable price. Accordingly, a transaction qualifies as a discontinued operation if (1) the sale is of a segment (a component of the entity) and (2) the planning and approval of the sale satisfy the requirements for classifying the asset as held for sale. However, the sale need not actually have been completed.
    Answer (A) is incorrect. Part of a line of business is most likely below the lowest level at which operations and cash flows can be clearly distinguished from the rest of the entity. Answer (C) is incorrect. Phasing out of a production line is not a disposal or a classification of a component of an entity as held for sale. A gradual reduction in use is not a discontinuance of an operation. Answer (D) is incorrect. Changes related to technological improvements do not meet any of the criteria for reporting a discontinued operation.

13. Newt Co. sold a warehouse and used the proceeds to acquire a new warehouse. The excess of the proceeds over the carrying amount of the warehouse sold should be reported as a(n):

A. Reduction of the cost of the new warehouse.

B. Gain from discontinued operations, net of income taxes.

C. Part of continuing operations.

D. Extraordinary gain, net of taxes.

Answer (C) is correct. *(CPA, adapted)*
REQUIRED: The reporting of an excess of the proceeds over the carrying amount of a long-lived asset sold.
DISCUSSION: When property, plant, or equipment is disposed of other than by an exchange, the gain or loss is usually included in the results of continuing operations as an ordinary item unless the disposal is reported in discontinued operations. Discontinued operations and extraordinary items are presented in separate components of the income statement following continuing operations. The operating results of a discontinued operation are reported separately in the income statement if (1) a component of the entity has been disposed of or is classified as held for sale, (2) its operations will be eliminated from the entity's operations, and (3) the entity will have no significant continuing involvement after disposal. But the warehouse is not a component of the entity. The facts do not indicate that its operations and cash flows are clearly distinguishable for operating and financial reporting purposes. Thus, the gain on the sale is not from a discontinued operation. Moreover, the facts do not indicate that the transaction is unusual and infrequent in the environment in which the entity operates. It therefore does not qualify for separate presentation as an extraordinary item.
    Answer (A) is incorrect. The excess proceeds do not reduce the cost of the new warehouse. This transaction was not a nonmonetary exchange accounted for based on the carrying amount of the assets given up. The new warehouse is recorded at its initial cost. Answer (B) is incorrect. The criteria for reporting a discontinued operation, e.g., disposal of a component of the entity, have not been met. Answer (D) is incorrect. This transaction is not unusual in nature and infrequent in occurrence, so the gain is not extraordinary.

14. On April 30, Deer Corp. committed to a plan to sell a component of the entity. As a result, the component's operations and cash flows will be eliminated from the entity's operations, and the entity will have no significant continuing post-disposal involvement in the component's operations. For the period January 1 through April 30, the component had revenues of $500,000 and expenses of $800,000. The assets of the component were sold on October 15 at a loss for which no tax benefit is available. In its income statement for the year ended December 31, how should Deer report the component's operations from January 1 to April 30?

A. $500,000 and $800,000 should be included with revenues and expenses, respectively, as part of continuing operations.

B. $300,000 should be reported as part of the loss on disposal of a component.

C. $300,000 should be reported as an extraordinary loss.

D. $300,000 should be included in the determination of income or loss from operations of a discontinued component.

Answer (D) is correct. *(CPA, adapted)*
REQUIRED: The proper reporting of a loss related to operations of a discontinued component.
DISCUSSION: The results of operations of a component that has been disposed of or is classified as held for sale, together with any loss on a writedown to fair value minus cost to sell (or a gain from recoupment of such a loss), minus applicable income tax expense (benefit), should be reported separately as a component of income (discontinued operations) before extraordinary items (if any). These results should be reported in the period(s) when they occur. Thus, the operating results of the component from January 1 through October 15 and the loss on disposal are included in the determination of income or loss from operations of the discontinued component.
Answer (A) is incorrect. Discontinued operations should not be reported as part of continuing operations. Answer (B) is incorrect. Discontinued operations should be presented in two categories: income or loss from operations of the discontinued component and the applicable income tax expense (benefit). The loss on disposal is included in the determination of income or loss from the discontinued component. Answer (C) is incorrect. Income or loss from discontinued operations should be reported separately as a component of income before extraordinary items (if any).

15. On January 1, Year 2, Dart, Inc., entered into an agreement to sell the assets and product line of its Jay Division, which met the criteria for classification as an operating segment. The sale was consummated on December 31, Year 2, and resulted in a gain on disposal of $400,000. The division's operations resulted in losses before income tax of $225,000 in Year 2 and $125,000 in Year 1. Dart's income tax rate is 30% for both years, and the criteria for reporting a discontinued operation have been met. In a comparative statement of income for Year 2 and Year 1, under the caption discontinued operations, Dart should report a gain (loss) of

	Year 2	Year 1
A.	$122,500	$(87,500)
B.	$122,500	$0
C.	$(157,500)	$(87,500)
D.	$(157,500)	$0

Answer (A) is correct. *(CPA, adapted)*
REQUIRED: The amounts reported for discontinued operations in comparative statements.
DISCUSSION: When a component (e.g., an operating segment) has been disposed of or is classified as held for sale, and the criteria for reporting a discontinued operation have been met, the income statement of a business entity for current and prior periods must report its operating results in discontinued operations. The gain from operations of the component for Year 2 equals the $225,000 operating loss for Year 2, plus the $400,000 gain on disposal. The pretax gain is therefore $175,000 ($400,000 – $225,000). The after-tax amount is $122,500 [$175,000 × (1.0 – .30)]. Because Year 1 was prior to the time that the component was classified as held for sale, the $125,000 of operating losses would have been reported under income from continuing operations in the Year 1 income statement as originally issued. This loss is now attributable to discontinued operations, and the Year 1 financial statements presented for comparative purposes must be reclassified. In the reclassified Year 1 income statement, the $125,000 pretax loss should be reported as an $87,500 [$125,000 × (1.0 – .30)] loss from discontinued operations.
Answer (B) is incorrect. The comparative statement of income for Year 2 and Year 1 should report a loss on discontinued operations for Year 1. Answer (C) is incorrect. The after-tax amount for Year 2 is $122,500. It includes the gain on disposal. Answer (D) is incorrect. The comparative statement of income for Year 2 and Year 1 should report a loss on discontinued operations for Year 1. Furthermore, an after-tax loss of $157,500 for Year 2 does not consider the gain on disposal.

16. A company decided to sell an unprofitable division of its business. The company can sell the entire operation for $800,000, and the buyer will assume all assets and liabilities of the operations. The tax rate is 30%. The assets and liabilities of the discontinued operation are as follows:

Buildings	$5,000,000
Accumulated depreciation	3,000,000
Mortgage on buildings	1,100,000
Inventory	500,000
Accounts payable	600,000
Accounts receivable	200,000

What is the after-tax net loss on the disposal of the division?

A. $140,000

B. $200,000

C. $1,540,000

D. $2,200,000

Answer (A) is correct. *(CPA, adapted)*
REQUIRED: The after-tax net loss on disposal.
DISCUSSION: None of the items is measured at fair value under U.S. GAAP, assuming that the fair value option was not elected for the mortgage. Thus, the after-tax loss is calculated as follows based on the carrying amounts given:

Sale price		$800,000
Buildings, net ($5,000,000 –		
$3,000,000 acc. dep.)	$2,000,000	
Inventory	500,000	
Accounts receivable	200,000	
Mortgage	(1,100,000)	
Accounts payable	(600,000)	
Net carrying amount		1,000,000
Pre-tax loss		$(200,000)
Tax benefit ($200,000 × 30%)		60,000
After-tax loss		$(140,000)

Answer (B) is incorrect. The amount of $200,000 is the pre-tax loss. Answer (C) is incorrect. The amount of $1,540,000 equals the sum of the net carrying amount of the building, minus accounts payable, plus the after-tax loss. Answer (D) is incorrect. The amount of $2,200,000 equals the sum of the net carrying amount of the building and accounts receivable.

17. During January Year 4, Doe Corp. agreed to sell the assets and product line of its Hart division. The sale was completed on January 15, Year 5, and resulted in a gain on disposal of $900,000. Hart's operating losses were $600,000 for Year 4 and $50,000 for the period January 4 through January 15, Year 5. Disregarding income taxes, and assuming that the criteria for reporting a discontinued operation are met, what amount of net gain (loss) should be reported in Doe's comparative Year 5 and Year 4 income statements?

	Year 5	Year 4
A.	$0	$250,000
B.	$250,000	$0
C.	$850,000	$(600,000)
D.	$900,000	$(650,000)

Answer (C) is correct. *(CPA, adapted)*
REQUIRED: The amounts reported in comparative statements for discontinued operations.
DISCUSSION: The results of operations of a component classified as held for sale are reported separately in the income statement under discontinued operations in the periods when they occur. Thus, in its Year 4 income statement, Doe should recognize a $600,000 loss. For Year 5, a gain of $850,000 should be recognized ($900,000 – $50,000).

Answer (A) is incorrect. The net gain for Year 4 and Year 5 is $250,000. The results of discontinued operations should be reported in the periods when they occurred. Answer (B) is incorrect. The operating loss for Year 4 should not be deferred. Furthermore, the $900,000 gain on disposal of the discontinued component should be included in income from discontinued operations in Year 5. Answer (D) is incorrect. The operating loss ($50,000) for January Year 5 should be recognized in Year 5.

3.3 Extraordinary Items

18. A transaction that is unusual in nature and infrequent in occurrence should be reported separately

A. After income from continuing operations and before discontinued operations.

B. As part of income from continuing operations.

C. In the notes but not in the income statement.

D. After discontinued operations and before net income.

Answer (D) is correct. *(CPA, adapted)*
REQUIRED: The reporting of a transaction that is unusual in nature and infrequent in occurrence.
DISCUSSION: A material transaction that is unusual in nature and infrequent in occurrence in the environment in which the entity operates is classified as an extraordinary item. The following is the order of items to be reported separately in the income statement: (1) income from continuing operations, (2) discontinued operations, (3) extraordinary items, and (4) net income.

Answer (A) is incorrect. No items may be reported between income from continuing operations and discontinued operations. Answer (B) is incorrect. Material transactions that are both unusual in nature and infrequent in occurrence in the environment in which the reporting entity operates are extraordinary items. They are reported after income from continuing operations and discontinued operations (if any). Answer (C) is incorrect. Extraordinary items must be reported on the face of the income statement.

19. An extraordinary item should be reported separately on the income statement as a component of income

	Net of Income Taxes	Before Discontinued Operations
A.	Yes	Yes
B.	Yes	No
C.	No	No
D.	No	Yes

Answer (B) is correct. *(CPA, adapted)*
REQUIRED: The presentation of an extraordinary item.
DISCUSSION: Extraordinary items should be reported separately in the income statement, net of tax, after discontinued operations but before net income.
Answer (A) is incorrect. An extraordinary item is presented after discontinued operations. Answer (C) is incorrect. An extraordinary item is presented net of tax. Answer (D) is incorrect. An extraordinary item is presented net of tax after discontinued operations.

20. During the current year, both Raim Co. and Cane Co. suffered material losses due to the flooding of the Mississippi River. Raim is located 2 miles from the river and sustains flood losses every 2 to 3 years. Cane, which has been located 50 miles from the river for the past 20 years, has never before had flood losses. How should the flood losses be reported in each company's current-year income statement?

	Raim	Cane
A.	As a component of income from continuing operations	As an extraordinary item
B.	As a component of income from continuing operations	As a component of income from continuing operations
C.	As an extraordinary item	As a component of income from continuing operations
D.	As an extraordinary item	As an extraordinary item

Answer (A) is correct. *(CPA, adapted)*
REQUIRED: The reporting of flood losses in the income statement.
DISCUSSION: For Raim, flood losses are neither unusual nor infrequent in the environment in which it operates. Thus, these material losses should be classified as a separate component of income from continuing operations, not net of tax as an extraordinary item. For Cane, the flood losses meet the criteria of an extraordinary item because they are unusual and infrequent: Cane had never before suffered flood losses.
Answer (B) is incorrect. Cane, located 50 miles from the river, regards a flood as both unusual in nature and infrequent in occurrence. This requires treatment as an extraordinary item, which must be reported after income from continuing operations and discontinued operations (if any). Answer (C) is incorrect. Raim, who experiences such floods every 2 to 3 years, cannot reasonably consider this event an extraordinary item. But a flood is extraordinary to Cane, making reporting as a component of income from continuing operations inappropriate. Answer (D) is incorrect. Although extraordinary item treatment is proper for Cane, it is not proper for Raim.

21. In the year just ended, hail damaged several of Toncan Co.'s vans. Hailstorms had frequently inflicted similar damage to Toncan's vans. Over the years, Toncan had saved money by not buying hail insurance and either paying for repairs, or selling damaged vans and then replacing them. During the year, the damaged vans were sold for less than their carrying amount. How should the hail damage cost be reported in Toncan's financial statements?

A. The actual hail damage loss as an extraordinary loss, net of income taxes.

B. The actual hail damage loss in continuing operations, with no separate disclosure.

C. The expected average hail damage loss in continuing operations, with no separate disclosure.

D. The expected average hail damage loss in continuing operations, with separate disclosure.

Answer (B) is correct. *(CPA, adapted)*
REQUIRED: The reporting of hail damage costs when a company is uninsured and sells the damaged item for a loss.
DISCUSSION: Because Toncan sold its damaged vans for less than their carrying amount, the company suffered a loss. Because this occurrence is not unusual or infrequent, the actual loss should be included in continuing operations with no separate disclosure.
Answer (A) is incorrect. A frequent occurrence does not meet the definition of an extraordinary item. Answer (C) is incorrect. Toncan should report the actual loss incurred. Answer (D) is incorrect. Toncan should report the actual loss, and a separate disclosure is not needed.

22. In the current year, Teller Co. incurred material losses arising from its guilty plea in its first antitrust action and from a substantial increase in production costs caused when a major supplier's workers went on strike. Which of these losses should be reported as an extraordinary item?

	Antitrust Action	Production Costs
A.	No	No
B.	No	Yes
C.	Yes	No
D.	Yes	Yes

Answer (C) is correct. *(CPA, adapted)*
REQUIRED: The loss(es), if any, reported as an extraordinary item.
DISCUSSION: GAAP specify that the effects of a strike are not extraordinary. However, a material loss from the company's first antitrust action is clearly infrequent and most likely unusual, that is, abnormal and of a type unrelated to the typical activities of the entity in the environment in which it operates.
Answer (A) is incorrect. The litigation loss is extraordinary. Answer (B) is incorrect. The litigation loss is extraordinary, but the effects of the strike are not. Answer (D) is incorrect. The effects of the strike are not extraordinary.

23. Which one of the following material events is most likely to be classified as an extraordinary item on an income statement?

A. A write-down of obsolete inventories.

B. A loss from disposal of a component of an entity as a result of a newly enacted law.

C. A loss from sale of property, plant, or equipment used in a business that results from an expropriation.

D. A gain or loss from the exchange of foreign currency due to a major devaluation.

Answer (C) is correct. *(CMA, adapted)*
REQUIRED: The item that is classified as extraordinary.
DISCUSSION: Examples of transactions that are not extraordinary items include (1) write-down of receivables, inventories, equipment leased to others, deferred R&D costs, or other intangible assets; (2) gains or losses from exchange or translation of foreign currencies; (3) gains or losses on disposal of a component of an entity; (4) other gains or losses on sale or abandonment of property, plant, or equipment used in the business; (5) effects of strikes, including those against competitors and suppliers; and (6) adjustment of accruals on long-term contracts. However, gains and losses, such as those in (1) and (4) that (a) result from a major casualty, an expropriation, or a prohibition under a newly enacted law or regulation and (b) clearly meet the criteria for extraordinary treatment, are classified as extraordinary items.
Answer (A) is incorrect. A write-down of inventories as a result of obsolescence is unlikely to meet the criteria for extraordinary treatment. Answer (B) is incorrect. Disposal of a component of an entity is accounted for and presented in the income statement as a discontinued operation. This treatment applies even if the gain or loss (1) results from a major casualty, an expropriation, or a prohibition under a newly enacted law or regulation and (2) clearly meets the criteria for extraordinary treatment. Answer (D) is incorrect. Foreign currency transaction gains and losses are unlikely to meet the criteria for extraordinary treatment.

24. In open market transactions, Gold Corp. simultaneously sold its long-term investment in Iron Corp. bonds and purchased its own outstanding bonds. The broker remitted the net cash from the two transactions. Gold's gain on the purchase of its own bonds exceeded its loss on the sale of the Iron bonds. Gold should report the

A. Two transactions as extraordinary gains.

B. Two transactions in income before extraordinary items.

C. Effect of its own bond transaction gain in income before extraordinary items and report the Iron bond transaction as an extraordinary loss.

D. Effect of its own bond transaction as an extraordinary gain and report the Iron bond transaction loss in income before extraordinary items.

Answer (B) is correct. *(CPA, adapted)*
REQUIRED: The reporting of the sale of a long-term investment in bonds and an extinguishment of debt.
DISCUSSION: Differences between the reacquisition prices and the net carrying amounts of extinguished debt must be recognized currently as gains or losses in income of the period of extinguishment. Transactions are presumed to be ordinary and usual unless a pronouncement specifically states otherwise or the evidence clearly supports classification as extraordinary. No currently effective pronouncement classifies these transactions as extraordinary. No evidence indicates that the sale of securities and the extinguishment of debt are clearly infrequent and unusual in the environment in which the entity operates. Thus, the gain on the bond purchase and the loss on the sale of bonds should be reported in income before extraordinary items.
Answer (A) is incorrect. Retirement of one's own debt most likely is not an extraordinary item. Furthermore, the sale of the investment produced an ordinary loss, not an extraordinary gain. Answer (C) is incorrect. Investing in the debt securities of other entities is a part of any entity's ongoing operations. A loss on the sale of such securities is reported under other expenses and losses, which is a component of net income. Answer (D) is incorrect. The debt extinguishment is deemed not to be extraordinary, absent evidence to the contrary.

25. Kent Co. incurred the following infrequent losses during the current year:

● A $300,000 loss was incurred on disposal of one of four dissimilar factories.

● A major currency devaluation caused a $120,000 foreign currency transaction loss on an amount remitted by a customer.

● Inventory valued at $190,000 was made worthless by a competitor's unexpected product innovation.

In its current-year income statement, what amount should Kent report as losses that are not considered extraordinary?

    A. $610,000

    B. $490,000

    C. $420,000

    D. $310,000

Answer (A) is correct. *(CPA, adapted)*
    REQUIRED: The amount of losses not considered extraordinary.
    DISCUSSION: To be classified as an extraordinary item, a transaction must be both unusual in nature and infrequent in occurrence in the environment in which the business operates. Certain items are not usually considered extraordinary. These items include (1) gains and losses on disposal of a component of an entity; (2) gains and losses from exchange or translation of foreign currencies, including those resulting from major devaluations and revaluations; and (3) write-downs of receivables and inventories. Hence, the amount of ordinary losses is $610,000 ($300,000 + $120,000 + $190,000).
    Answer (B) is incorrect. The amount of $490,000 omits the foreign currency transaction loss. Answer (C) is incorrect. The amount of $420,000 omits the inventory write-off. Answer (D) is incorrect. The amount of $310,000 omits the loss on disposal of the factory. A gain or loss on disposal of a component of an entity is reported in discontinued operations.

26. Nikoto Steel Co. had the following unusual financial events occur during the current year:

● Bonds payable were retired 5 years before their scheduled maturity, resulting in a $260,000 gain. Nikoto has frequently retired bonds early when interest rates declined significantly.

● A steel forming plant suffered $255,000 in losses from hurricane damage. This was the fourth similar loss sustained in a 5-year period at that location.

● Nikoto's steel transportation operating segment was sold at a net loss of $350,000. This transaction was Nikoto's first divestiture of one of its component units.

Before income taxes, what amount should be reported as the gain (loss) from extraordinary items in the current year?

    A. $0

    B. $5,000

    C. $(90,000)

    D. $(350,000)

Answer (A) is correct. *(CPA, adapted)*
    REQUIRED: The amount disclosed as the gain (loss) from extraordinary items.
    DISCUSSION: Differences between the reacquisition prices and the net carrying amounts of extinguished debt must be recognized currently as gains or losses in income of the period of extinguishment. Transactions are presumed to be ordinary and usual unless a pronouncement specifically states otherwise or the evidence clearly supports classification as extraordinary. No currently effective pronouncement classifies this transaction as extraordinary, and no evidence clearly supports that classification. The extinguishment of debt is not clearly infrequent and unusual in the environment in which the entity operates. Thus, the gain on the bond purchase should be reported in income before extraordinary items. The divestiture of a component unit is reported as a discontinued operation. The hurricane damage, which is unusual but not infrequent, is reported separately as a component of income from continuing operations. Hence, no extraordinary item is reported.
    Answer (B) is incorrect. The amount of $5,000 is the net of the extinguishment gain and the $255,000 hurricane loss reported in continuing operations. Answer (C) is incorrect. The net of the loss from discontinued operations and the extinguishment gain is $(90,000). Answer (D) is incorrect. The loss from discontinued operations is $(350,000).

3.4 Comprehensive Income

27. When a business entity provides a full set of general-purpose financial statements reporting financial position, results of operations, and cash flows, comprehensive income must

A. Appear as a part of discontinued operations and extraordinary items.

B. Be reported net of related income tax effects, in total and individually.

C. Be reported in the statement of changes in equity.

D. Be reported only when the entity has items of other comprehensive income.

Answer (D) is correct. *(CPA, adapted)*
REQUIRED: The presentation of comprehensive income.
DISCUSSION: If an entity that reports a full set of financial statements has items of other comprehensive income (OCI) in any period presented, it must report comprehensive income either in (1) one continuous statement of comprehensive income with two sections (net income and other comprehensive income) or (2) two separate but consecutive statements (an income statement and a statement of other comprehensive income).
Answer (A) is incorrect. Discontinued operations and extraordinary items are components of net income, which is itself a component of comprehensive income. Answer (B) is incorrect. The components of OCI are displayed either (1) net of related tax effects or (2) before the related tax effects with one amount shown for the tax effect on total OCI. No amount is displayed for the tax effect related to total comprehensive income. Answer (C) is incorrect. Comprehensive income no longer may be reported in the statement of changes in equity. It must be reported in (1) one continuous statement of comprehensive income with two sections (net income and other comprehensive income) or (2) two separate but consecutive statements (an income statement and a statement of other comprehensive income).

28. What is the purpose of reporting comprehensive income?

A. To summarize all changes in equity from nonowner sources.

B. To reconcile the difference between net income and cash flows provided from operating activities.

C. To provide a consolidation of the income of the firm's segments.

D. To provide information for each segment of the business.

Answer (A) is correct. *(CPA, adapted)*
REQUIRED: The purpose of reporting comprehensive income.
DISCUSSION: Comprehensive income includes all changes in equity of a business during a period except those from investments by and distributions to owners. It includes all components of (1) net income and (2) other comprehensive income (OCI).
Answer (B) is incorrect. A statement of cash flows (direct or indirect method) includes a reconciliation of net income to net operating cash flow. Answer (C) is incorrect. The income statement presents aggregated information about revenues, gains, expenses, and losses. Answer (D) is incorrect. Information about specific segments is presented in the notes.

29. Which of the following is a component of other comprehensive income?

A. Minimum accrual of vacation pay.

B. Cumulative currency-translation adjustments.

C. Changes in market value of inventory.

D. Unrealized gain or loss on trading securities.

Answer (B) is correct. *(CPA, adapted)*
REQUIRED: The component of other comprehensive income.
DISCUSSION: Foreign currency translation adjustments for a foreign operation that is relatively self-contained and integrated within its environment do not affect cash flows of the reporting entity. They should be excluded from earnings. Accordingly, translation adjustments are reported in other comprehensive income (OCI).
Answer (A) is incorrect. Accrual of vacation pay affects earnings directly. Answer (C) is incorrect. A write-down to lower of cost or market affects earnings directly. Answer (D) is incorrect. Unrealized gain or loss on trading securities affects earnings directly.

30. On December 31, Year 1, the last day of its fiscal year, Smart Company purchased 2,000 shares of available-for-sale securities at a price of $10 per share. These securities had a fair value of $24,000 and $30,000 on December 31, Year 2, and December 31, Year 3, respectively. No dividends were paid, and all of the securities were sold on December 31, Year 3. Smart recognizes all holding gains and losses on available-for-sale securities before recognizing realized gain. If Smart's tax rate is 25%, the total after-tax effect on comprehensive income in Year 3 of the foregoing transactions was

- A. $10,000
- B. $7,500
- C. $4,500
- D. $3,000

Answer (C) is correct. *(Publisher, adapted)*
REQUIRED: The total after-tax effect on comprehensive income of a sale of available-for-sale securities in Year 3.
DISCUSSION: Comprehensive income includes all changes in equity (net assets) except from investments by and distributions to owners. The changes for the period in the fair value of available-for-sale securities are recognized in other comprehensive income. Unrealized holding gain (loss) is recognized in OCI and reclassified to income when the investment is disposed of. In Year 3, the net increase in the company's net assets from the investment in available-for-sale securities is $4,500 [($30,000 – $24,000 carrying amount at the end of Year 2) × (1.0 – 0.25)].
Answer (A) is incorrect. The pre-tax realized gain recognized in net income in Year 3 is $10,000. Answer (B) is incorrect. The amount of the reclassification adjustment and the realized after-tax gain is $7,500. Answer (D) is incorrect. The after-tax holding gain in Year 2 is $3,000.

31. Rock Co.'s financial statements had the following balances for the year ended on December 31:

Extraordinary gain	$ 50,000
Foreign currency translation gain	100,000
Net income	400,000
Unrealized gain on available-for-sale equity securities	20,000

What amount should Rock report as comprehensive income for the year ended December 31?

- A. $400,000
- B. $420,000
- C. $520,000
- D. $570,000

Answer (C) is correct. *(Publisher, adapted)*
REQUIRED: The comprehensive income to be reported on December 31.
DISCUSSION: Comprehensive income includes all changes in equity of a business entity except those changes resulting from investments by owners and distributions to owners. Comprehensive income includes two major categories: net income and other comprehensive income (OCI). Net income includes the results of continuing and discontinued operations and extraordinary items. Components of comprehensive income not included in net income are included in OCI, for example, unrealized gains and losses on available-for-sale securities (except those that are hedged items in a fair value hedge) and certain foreign currency items, such as a translation adjustment. Thus, Rock's comprehensive income equals $520,000 ($400,000 net income + $100,000 translation gain + $20,000 unrealized gain on available-for-sale securities).
Answer (A) is incorrect. Certain foreign currency items and unrealized gains on available-for-sale equity securities are components of OCI. Answer (B) is incorrect. A foreign currency translation gain is a component of OCI. Answer (D) is incorrect. The extraordinary gain is already included in the net income amount of $400,000.

3.5 Statement of Changes in Equity

32. The major segments of the statement of retained earnings for a period are

- A. Dividends declared, prior-period adjustments, and changes due to treasury stock transactions.
- B. Prior-period adjustments, before tax income or loss, income tax, and dividends paid.
- C. Net income or loss from operations, dividends paid, and extraordinary gains and losses.
- D. Net income or loss, error corrections, and dividends paid or declared.

Answer (D) is correct. *(CMA, adapted)*
REQUIRED: The major segments of the statement of retained earnings.
DISCUSSION: The statement of retained earnings consists of (1) the beginning and ending balances of retained earnings; (2) any error corrections (net of tax); (3) net income (loss); (4) dividends paid or declared; and (5) certain other rare adjustments, e.g., quasi-reorganizations and certain treasury stock transactions. The final amount is ending retained earnings.
Answer (A) is incorrect. Net income (loss) is a major segment of the retained earnings statement. Treasury stock transactions result in changes in retained earnings only in limited circumstances. Answer (B) is incorrect. After-tax net income is reflected in the statement of retained earnings. Answer (C) is incorrect. Operating income and extraordinary gains and losses are included in after-tax net income.

33. Which of the following should be reflected, net of applicable income taxes, in the statement of equity as an adjustment of the opening balance in retained earnings?

A. Correction of an error in previously issued financial statements.

B. Cumulative effect of a change in depreciation method.

C. Loss on disposal of a component of an entity.

D. Extraordinary item.

Answer (A) is correct.   *(CPA, adapted)*
REQUIRED: The item treated as an adjustment of beginning retained earnings.
DISCUSSION: The correction of an error occurring in a prior period must be accounted for by restatement. It must be charged or credited net of tax to retained earnings and reported as an adjustment in the statement of equity. It is not included in net income for the current period.
Answer (B) is incorrect. A change in depreciation method is a change in estimate that is accounted for prospectively.
Answer (C) is incorrect. A discontinued operation is reported under a separate caption in the income statement. Answer (D) is incorrect. An extraordinary item is reported under a separate caption in the income statement.

3.6 IFRS

34. During the current year, both Raim Co. and Cane Co. suffered material losses due to the flooding of the Mississippi River. Raim is located 2 miles from the river and sustains flood losses every 2 to 3 years. Cane, which has been located 50 miles from the river for the past 20 years, has never before had flood losses. In accordance with IFRS, how should the flood losses be reported in each company's current-year income statement?

	Raim	Cane
A.	As a component of income from continuing operations	As an extraordinary item
B.	As a component of income from continuing operations	As a component of income from continuing operations
C.	As an extraordinary item	As a component of income from continuing operations
D.	As an extraordinary item	As an extraordinary item

Answer (B) is correct.   *(Publisher, adapted)*
REQUIRED: The reporting of flood losses in the income statement under IFRS.
DISCUSSION: The flood losses should be classified as a separate component of income from continuing operations by Raim and Cane. IFRS do not permit recognition of extraordinary items.
Answer (A) is incorrect. Cane should recognize the flood loss in continuing operations. Answer (C) is incorrect. Raim should recognize the flood loss in continuing operations. Answer (D) is incorrect. Neither Raim nor Cane should recognize the flood loss as an extraordinary item.

35. A company that operates in Vermont incurred hurricane damage of $10 million. How is this loss reported in the financial statements prepared under IFRS and U.S. GAAP?

A. Under IFRS and U.S. GAAP as an extraordinary item.

B. Under IFRS and U.S. GAAP as a loss from continuing operations.

C. Under IFRS and U.S. GAAP as an item of other comprehensive income (OCI).

D. Under U.S. GAAP as an extraordinary item and under IFRS as an other expense in the continuing operations section.

Answer (D) is correct.   *(Publisher, adapted)*
REQUIRED: The reporting of a natural disaster loss under IFRS and U.S. GAAP.
DISCUSSION: The $10 million loss as a result of a hurricane is a material transaction that is (1) unusual in nature and (2) infrequent in occurrence in the environment in which the entity operates. Thus, under U.S. GAAP, this loss is reported as an extraordinary item in the income statement. Under IFRS, no items are classified as extraordinary. Accordingly, this loss is reported as an other expense in the continuing operations section of the income statement.
Answer (A) is incorrect. Under IFRS, no items are classified as extraordinary. Answer (B) is incorrect. Under U.S. GAAP, this loss is reported as an extraordinary item. It is unusual in nature and infrequent in occurrence in the environment in which the company operates. Answer (C) is incorrect. A loss as a result of a hurricane must not be classified as an item of OCI. Instead, it must be recognized in the income statement as an extraordinary item under U.S. GAAP or as a loss from continuing operations under IFRS.

STUDY UNIT FOUR
THE TIME VALUE OF MONEY

A quantity of money to be received or paid in the future is worth less than the same amount now. This effect is the **time value of money**. The difference, in nominal terms, between the two values is **interest**. Interest is the amount a borrower pays to a lender for the use of money for a given period. Simple interest is the amount lent (the principal) times the stated rate of interest times the number of periods the loan is outstanding. For example, the interest on $500 for 4 years at 6% simple interest is calculated as follows:

$$\$500 \times .06 \times 4 = \$120$$

Compound interest is calculated, not on the original principal, but on the current balance, which changes each period. However, accountants need not memorize formulas because standard tables have been developed to facilitate these calculations. Each entry in one of these tables is the factor by which any monetary amount can be modified to obtain its present or future value.

Present Value and Future Value

The following table contains the present value factors for a single sum for 10 different time periods at three different **discount rates**:

Factors for Present Value of 1 (Single Sum)
Number of Periods:

		0	1	2	3	4	5	6	7	8	9	10
Discount Rate	6%:	1.000	0.943	0.890	0.840	0.792	0.747	0.705	0.665	0.627	0.592	0.558
	8%:	1.000	0.926	0.857	0.794	0.735	0.681	0.630	0.583	0.540	0.500	0.463
	10%:	1.000	0.909	0.826	0.751	0.683	0.621	0.564	0.513	0.467	0.424	0.386

The appropriate factor is multiplied by an amount to be paid or received in the future to determine the amount's present value. For example, $500 received today is worth $500, but $500 received in 4 years discounted at 6% is worth $396 today ($500 × 0.792). The table below illustrates how the present value of an amount decreases the longer the discount period and the higher the discount rate. As an exercise, the reader may want to construct similar tables using the other sets of interest factors given in this summary.

Present Value of a Single Sum of $500
Number of Periods:

		Today	1	2	3	4	5	6	7	8	9	10
Discount Rate	6%:	$500	$472	$445	$420	$396	$374	$353	$333	$314	$296	$279
	8%:	$500	$463	$429	$397	$368	$341	$315	$292	$270	$250	$232
	10%:	$500	$455	$413	$376	$342	$311	$282	$257	$234	$212	$193

The future value of a single sum invested today is calculated using similar factors. All such factors are greater than 1 to reflect interest earned. In contrast, all present value of 1 factors are less than 1.

Factors for Future Value of 1 (Single Sum)
Number of Periods:

		0	1	2	3	4	5	6	7	8	9	10
Discount Rate	6%:	1.000	1.060	1.124	1.191	1.262	1.338	1.419	1.504	1.594	1.689	1.791
	8%:	1.000	1.080	1.166	1.260	1.360	1.469	1.587	1.714	1.851	1.999	2.159
	10%:	1.000	1.100	1.210	1.331	1.464	1.611	1.772	1.949	2.144	2.358	2.594

The tables on the previous page are used to measure a single sum. Another set of tables is available for **annuities**. An annuity is a stream of payments, a constant amount paid at predictable intervals. In an **ordinary annuity** (annuity in arrears), the payments are made at the **end** of each period. In an **annuity due** (annuity in advance), the payments are made at the **beginning** of each period. These tables have a relationship. Each factor for the **present value of an annuity due** equals the ordinary annuity factor for (n − 1) periods plus 1.000. Each factor for the **future value of an annuity due** equals the ordinary annuity factor for (n + 1) periods minus 1.000. These relationships reflect that a payment of 1 at the beginning of a period has a present value of 1 and a future value of $(1 + i)^n$ (i is the interest rate, and n the number of periods).

Factors for Present Value of an Ordinary Annuity of 1
Number of Periods:

Discount Rate		1	2	3	4	5	6	7	8	9	10
	6%:	0.943	1.833	2.673	3.465	4.212	4.917	5.582	6.210	6.802	7.360
	8%:	0.926	1.783	2.577	3.312	3.993	4.623	5.206	5.745	6.247	6.710
	10%:	0.909	1.736	2.487	3.170	3.791	4.355	4.868	5.335	5.759	6.145

Factors for Present Value of an Annuity Due of 1
Number of Periods:

Discount Rate		1	2	3	4	5	6	7	8	9	10
	6%:	1.000	1.943	2.833	3.673	4.465	5.212	5.917	6.582	7.210	7.802
	8%:	1.000	1.926	2.783	3.577	4.312	4.993	5.623	6.206	6.745	7.247
	10%:	1.000	1.909	2.736	3.487	4.170	4.791	5.355	5.868	6.335	6.759

Factors for Future Value of an Ordinary Annuity of 1
Number of Periods:

Discount Rate		1	2	3	4	5	6	7	8	9	10
	6%:	1.000	2.060	3.184	4.375	5.637	6.975	8.394	9.897	11.491	13.181
	8%:	1.000	2.080	3.246	4.506	5.867	7.336	8.923	10.637	12.488	14.487
	10%:	1.000	2.100	3.310	4.641	6.105	7.716	9.487	11.436	13.579	15.937

Factors for Future Value of an Annuity Due of 1
Number of Periods:

Discount Rate		1	2	3	4	5	6	7	8	9	10
	6%:	1.060	2.184	3.375	4.637	5.975	7.394	8.897	10.491	12.181	13.972
	8%:	1.080	2.246	3.506	4.867	6.336	7.923	9.637	11.488	13.487	15.645
	10%:	1.100	2.310	3.641	5.105	6.716	8.487	10.436	12.579	14.937	17.531

Cash Flow Information and Present Value

SFAC 7, *Using Cash Flow Information and Present Value in Accounting Measurements*, provides a conceptual framework for the use of present value. With regard to accounting measurements for **initial recognition** or **fresh-start purposes**, this framework states that present value should attempt to reflect **fair value**. The framework also describes the conditions under which an **interest method** of amortization should be considered. According to SFAC 7, **present value** should **reflect uncertainty** so that **variations in risks** are incorporated.

Elements of a PV Measurement
Estimates of future cash flows
Expected variability of their amount and timing
The time value of money based on the risk-free interest rate
The price of uncertainty inherent in an asset or liability
Other factors, such as lack of liquidity or market imperfections

The **traditional approach** to calculating present value uses one set of estimated cash flows and one interest rate. Uncertainty is reflected solely in the choice of an interest rate. This approach is expected to continue to be used in many cases, for example, when contractual cash flows are involved. The **expected cash flow (ECF)** approach applies in more complex circumstances, such as when no market or no comparable item exists for an asset or liability. The ECF results from multiplying each possible estimated amount by its **probability** and adding the products. This approach requires **explicit assumptions** about cash flows and their probabilities. Thus, the ECF approach permits the use of expected present value when the timing of cash flows is uncertain. **Expected present value** is the sum of the present values of estimated cash flows discounted using the same interest rate and weighted according to their respective probabilities.

QUESTIONS

4.1 Present Value

1. On July 1, Dichter Company obtained a $2,000,000, 180-day bank loan at an annual rate of 12%. The loan agreement requires Dichter to maintain a $400,000 compensating balance in its checking account at the lending bank. Dichter would otherwise maintain a balance of only $200,000 in this account. The checking account earns interest at an annual rate of 6%. Based on a 360-day year, the effective interest rate on the borrowing is

   A. 6%

   B. 12%

   C. 12.67%

   D. 13.33%

Answer (C) is correct. *(CPA, adapted)*
REQUIRED: The annual effective interest rate on a loan requiring a compensating balance.
DISCUSSION: The effective interest rate on the 180-day borrowing is equal to the net interest cost divided by the net available proceeds of $1,800,000 ($2,000,000 loan – $200,000 increase in the compensating balance). The net interest cost is equal to the gross interest cost minus the incremental interest revenue. The gross interest cost is $120,000 [$2,000,000 × 12% × (6 months ÷ 12 months)]. Because the incremental interest revenue is $6,000 [$200,000 × 6% × (6 months ÷ 12 months)], the net interest cost is $114,000 ($120,000 – $6,000). The 6-month effective interest rate is therefore 6.33% ($114,000 ÷ $1,800,000). The annual effective interest rate is 12.67% (6.33% × 2).
Answer (A) is incorrect. The checking account earns interest at an annual rate of 6%. Answer (B) is incorrect. Twelve percent is the annual rate. Answer (D) is incorrect. The interest revenue from the checking account must be included in the calculations.

2. The relationship between the present value of a future sum and the future value of a present sum can be expressed in terms of their respective interest factors. If the present value of $200,000 due at the end of 8 years, at 10%, is $93,300, what is the approximate future value of $200,000 invested for the same length of time and at the same rate?

   A. $93,300

   B. $200,000

   C. $293,300

   D. $428,724

Answer (D) is correct. *(CIA, adapted)*
REQUIRED: The approximate future value of an amount.
DISCUSSION: The interest factor for the future value of a present sum is equal to the reciprocal of the interest factor for the present value of a future sum. Thus, the future value is $428,724 [($200,000 ÷ $93,300) × $200,000].
Answer (A) is incorrect. The amount of $93,300 is the present value of $200,000 to be received in 8 years. Answer (B) is incorrect. The amount of $200,000 is the present value, not the future value, of $200,000 invested today. Answer (C) is incorrect. The addition of the present and future values has no accounting meaning.

3. A company purchased some large machinery on a deferred payment plan. The contract calls for $40,000 down on January 1 and $40,000 at the beginning of each of the next 4 years. There is no stated interest rate in the contract, and there is no established exchange price for the machinery. What should be recorded as the cost of the machinery?

A. $200,000.

B. $200,000 plus the added implicit interest.

C. Future value of an annuity due for 5 years at an imputed interest rate.

D. Present value of an annuity due for 5 years at an imputed interest rate.

Answer (D) is correct. *(CIA, adapted)*
REQUIRED: The cost of machinery acquired under a deferred payment plan.
DISCUSSION: The contract calls for an annuity due because the first annuity payment is due immediately. In an ordinary annuity (annuity in arrears), each payment is due at the end of the period. According to GAAP, an interest rate must be imputed in the given circumstances to arrive at the present value of the machinery.
Answer (A) is incorrect. The undiscounted sum of the payments is $200,000. Answer (B) is incorrect. The implicit interest should be subtracted from the $200,000 in total payments. Answer (C) is incorrect. The present value, not the future value, is the appropriate concept.

4. On September 1, Year 1, a company purchased a new machine that it does not have to pay for until September 1, Year 3. The total payment on September 1, Year 3, will include both principal and interest. Assuming interest at a 10% rate, the cost of the machine will be the total payment multiplied by what time value of money factor?

A. Present value of annuity of $1.

B. Present value of $1.

C. Future amount of annuity of $1.

D. Future amount of $1.

Answer (B) is correct. *(CPA, adapted)*
REQUIRED: The time value of money factor to compute current cost when payment is to be made in a lump sum at a future date.
DISCUSSION: The cost of the machine to the entity on 9/1/Year 1 is the present value of the payment to be made on 9/1/Year 3. To obtain the present value, i.e., today's price, the future payment is multiplied by the present value of $1 for two periods at 10%.
Answer (A) is incorrect. The present value of an annuity determines the value today of a series of future payments (not merely one payment). Answer (C) is incorrect. The future value of an annuity determines the amount available at a specified time in the future after a series of deposits (investments). Answer (D) is incorrect. The future value of a dollar determines how much will be available at a specified time in the future based on the single investment (deposit) today.

5. The computation of the current value of an asset using the present value of future cash flows method does not include the

A. Cost of alternate uses of funds given up.

B. Productive life of the asset.

C. Applicable interest rate.

D. Future amounts of cash receipts or cash savings.

Answer (A) is correct. *(CPA, adapted)*
REQUIRED: The information not used in computing current value using the present value of future cash flows method.
DISCUSSION: The calculation of the current value of an asset using the present value method requires (1) the discount period (the productive life of the asset), (2) the discount rate (the applicable interest rate), and (3) the future values (the future amounts of cash receipts or cash savings). This method does not consider opportunity costs (benefits of the best alternative use of funds).
Answer (B) is incorrect. The productive life of the asset is the number of periods used in calculating the asset's present value. Answer (C) is incorrect. The applicable interest rate is the discount rate in the present value computation. Answer (D) is incorrect. The future amounts of cash receipts or cash savings are the cash flows to be discounted.

6. In the determination of a present value, which of the following relationships is true?

A. The lower the discount rate and the shorter the discount period, the lower the present value.

B. The lower the future cash flow and the shorter the discount period, the lower the present value.

C. The higher the discount rate and the longer the discount period, the lower the present value.

D. The higher the future cash flow and the longer the discount period, the lower the present value.

Answer (C) is correct. *(Publisher, adapted)*
REQUIRED: The true relationship between the discount period, discount rate, and present value.
DISCUSSION: As the discount rate increases, the present value decreases. Also, as the discount period increases, the present value decreases.
Answer (A) is incorrect. Both conditions are untrue. As the discount rate decreases, present value increases. Also, as the discount period gets shorter, the present value increases. Answer (B) is incorrect. As the discount period gets shorter, the present value increases. Answer (D) is incorrect. Increased future cash flows increase the present value.

7. On July 1, Goblette Company sold some machinery to another company. The two companies entered into an installment sales contract at a predetermined interest rate. The contract required five equal annual payments with the first payment due on July 1, the date of sale. What present value concept is appropriate for this situation?

A. Present value of an annuity due of $1 for five periods.

B. Present value of an ordinary annuity of $1 for five periods.

C. Future amount of an annuity due of $1 for five periods.

D. Future amount of $1 for five periods.

Answer (A) is correct. *(CPA, adapted)*
REQUIRED: The present value concept appropriate for an installment sale with the first payment due immediately.
DISCUSSION: The contract calls for five equal annual payments with the first due immediately. Ordinary annuity tables assume the first payment occurs at the end of the first time period. An annuity in which the first payment occurs at the beginning of the first period is an annuity due (annuity in advance). The number of payments earning interest in an annuity due is one less than the number earning interest in an ordinary annuity because there is no interest on the first payment. Accordingly, the present value of an annuity due of $1 for five periods can be calculated by taking the present value of an ordinary annuity of $1 for four periods and adding $1. Hence, a special table for an annuity due or the method described above can be used in this situation.
Answer (B) is incorrect. The question describes an annuity due (not an ordinary annuity) for five periods. Answer (C) is incorrect. Although the question involves an annuity due, the present value, not the future amount, is required. Answer (D) is incorrect. The present value of an annuity due, not the future amount of a single sum, will provide the correct answer.

8. For which of the following transactions would the use of the present value of an annuity due concept be appropriate in calculating the present value of the asset obtained or liability owed at the date of incurrence?

A. A capital lease is entered into with the initial lease payment due 1 month subsequent to the signing of the lease agreement.

B. A capital lease is entered into with the initial lease payment due upon the signing of the lease agreement.

C. A 10-year 8% bond is issued on January 2 with interest payable semiannually on July 1 and January 1 yielding 7%.

D. A 10-year 8% bond is issued on January 2 with interest payable semiannually on July 1 and January 1 yielding 9%.

Answer (B) is correct. *(CPA, adapted)*
REQUIRED: The transaction for which the present value of an annuity due concept would be appropriate.
DISCUSSION: In an annuity due, the first payment is made at the beginning of the first period and is therefore not discounted. In an ordinary annuity, the first payment is made at the end of the first period and therefore is discounted. For annuities due, the first payment is included in the computation at its face value.
Answer (A) is incorrect. Given that the first payment is due 1 month from signing and not on the day of signing, an ordinary annuity, not an annuity due, is the relevant model. Answer (C) is incorrect. The bonds have just passed an interest payment (coupon) date. The next one is not for another 6 months. Given no immediate payment, the annuity is ordinary. Furthermore, the yield percentage is irrelevant to annuity. Answer (D) is incorrect. The initial payment is not due immediately.

9. Chambers Company bought Machine 1 on March 5, Year 1, for $5,000 cash. The estimated salvage was $200 and the estimated life was 11 years. On March 5, Year 2, the company learned that it could purchase a different machine for $8,000 cash. It would save the company an estimated $250 per year. The new machine would have no estimated salvage and an estimated life of 10 years. The company could sell Machine 1 for $3,000 on March 5, Year 2. Ignoring income taxes, which of the following calculations would best assist the company in deciding whether to purchase the new machine?

A. (Present value of an annuity of $250) + $3,000 – $8,000.

B. (Present value of an annuity of $250) – $8,000.

C. (Present value of an annuity of $250) + $3,000 – $8,000 – $5,000.

D. (Present value of an annuity of $250) + $3,000 – $8,000 – $4,800.

Answer (A) is correct. *(CPA, adapted)*
REQUIRED: The calculation that would best assist the company in deciding whether to purchase the new machine.
DISCUSSION: The sale of the first machine for $3,000 and the purchase of the new machine for $8,000 on 3/5/Year 2 results in an incremental cost of $5,000. If the present value of the future savings from the second machine (present value of an annuity of $250) exceeds $5,000, the company should purchase the new machine. Note that the remaining estimated useful life of the first machine is the same as that of the second. Also, the cost of Machine 1 should be ignored because it is a sunk cost.
Answer (B) is incorrect. The calculation (present value of an annuity of $250) – $8,000 fails to consider the resale value of Machine 1 on 3/5/Year 2. Answer (C) is incorrect. The calculation (present value of an annuity of $250) + $3,000 – $8,000 – $5,000 improperly considers the sunk cost of Machine 1 ($5,000). Answer (D) is incorrect. The calculation (present value of an annuity of $250) + $3,000 – $8,000 – $4,800 improperly considers the sunk cost of Machine 1 and its salvage value [$4,800 ($5,000 – $200)].

10. Stone Co. is considering the acquisition of equipment. To buy the equipment, the cost is $15,192. To lease the equipment, Stone must sign a noncancelable lease and make five payments of $4,000 each. The first payment will be paid on the first day of the lease. At the time of the last payment, Stone will receive title to the equipment. The present value of an ordinary annuity of $1 is as follows:

No. of Periods	Present Value		
	10%	12%	16%
1	0.909	0.893	0.862
2	1.736	1.690	1.605
3	2.487	2.402	2.246
4	3.170	3.037	2.798
5	3.791	3.605	3.274

The interest rate implicit in this lease is approximately

A. 10%

B. 12%

C. Between 10% and 12%.

D. 16%

Answer (D) is correct. *(CPA, adapted)*
REQUIRED: The interest rate implicit in a lease.
DISCUSSION: To perform this computation, a present value factor must be derived and compared with those in the table. The factor can be calculated by dividing the relevant present value by the periodic payment.

Full cost of equipment (present value)	$15,192
Minus: first payment, due immediately	(4,000)
Amount financed (present value of an ordinary annuity of four $4,000 payments)	$11,192
Divided by: periodic payment	÷ 4,000
Present value factor	2.798

Consulting the table reveals that the factor inherent in this calculation for a four-period annuity is 16%.

Answer (A) is incorrect. A 10% discount rate does not yield the appropriate cash flows. The amount financed is $11,192 ($15,192 – $4,000). The table reveals that the 10% factor for four periods is 3.17. The result of multiplying $4,000 by 3.170 is $12,680, not $11,192. Answer (B) is incorrect. A 12% discount rate does not yield the appropriate cash flows. The amount financed is $11,192 ($15,192 – $4,000). The table reveals that the 12% factor for four periods is 3.037. The result of multiplying $4,000 by 3.037 is $12,148, not $11,192. Answer (C) is incorrect. A discount rate between 10% and 12% does not yield the appropriate cash flows. The table reveals that the 12% factor for four periods is 3.037. The result of multiplying $4,000 by 3.037 is $12,148, not $11,192. Accordingly, a discount rate higher than 12% must be used because 12% gives an amount greater than $11,192.

11. On July 1, Year 4, Ahmed signed an agreement to operate as a franchisee of Teacake Pastries, Inc., for an initial franchise fee of $240,000. On the same date, Ahmed paid $80,000 and agreed to pay the balance in four equal annual payments of $40,000 beginning July 1, Year 5. The down payment is not refundable and no future services are required of the franchiser. Ahmed can borrow at 14% for a loan of this type.

Present value of $1 at 14% for 4 periods	0.59
Future amount of $1 at 14% for 4 periods	1.69
Present value of an ordinary annuity of $1 at 14% for 4 periods	2.91

Ahmed should record the acquisition cost of the franchise on July 1, Year 4, at

A. $270,400

B. $240,000

C. $196,400

D. $174,400

Answer (C) is correct. *(CPA, adapted)*
REQUIRED: The acquisition cost of a franchise to be paid for in installments.
DISCUSSION: The acquisition cost would have been recorded at $240,000 if this amount of cash had been paid immediately. Given that the $240,000 is to be paid in installments, the acquisition cost is equal to the down payment of $80,000 plus the present value of the series of four annuity payments beginning 1 year after the date of purchase. The proper interest factor to be employed is the present value of an ordinary annuity of $1 at 14% for four periods, or 2.91.

Periodic payment	$ 40,000
Times: PV factor	× 2.91
PV of periodic payments	$116,400
Plus: down payment	+ 80,000
PV of franchise fee	$196,400

Answer (A) is incorrect. The figure of $270,400 results from using the factor for the future amount, rather than an ordinary annuity, of $1 at 14% for four periods. Answer (B) is incorrect. The amount of $240,000 results from failing to account for the time value of money. Answer (D) is incorrect. The figure of $174,000 results from using the factor for a single amount, rather than an ordinary annuity, of $1 at 14% for four periods.

12. Harry Rawlings wants to withdraw $10,000 (including principal) from an investment fund at the end of each year for 5 years. How should he compute his required initial investment at the beginning of the first year if the fund earns 6% compounded annually?

A. $10,000 times the amount of an annuity of $1 at 6% at the end of each year for 5 years.

B. $10,000 divided by the amount of an annuity of $1 at 6% at the end of each year for 5 years.

C. $10,000 times the present value of an annuity of $1 at 6% at the end of each year for 5 years.

D. $10,000 divided by the present value of an annuity of $1 at 6% at the end of each year for 5 years.

Answer (C) is correct. *(CPA, adapted)*
REQUIRED: The computation for the initial investment required at a given rate to permit withdrawal of a fixed amount at the end of each of a series of years.
DISCUSSION: The question requires a present value rather than a future value, i.e., today's equivalent of $10,000 at the end of each of the next 5 years. The table used is for the present value of an ordinary annuity. The interest factor corresponding to 6% for five periods is multiplied by $10,000 to provide the answer.
Answer (A) is incorrect. The question requires a present value rather than a future value calculation. "Amount of an annuity" is synonymous with future value of an annuity. Answer (B) is incorrect. A present value computation is required. Moreover, the payment should be multiplied by the relevant interest factor. Answer (D) is incorrect. The amount of $10,000 must be multiplied (rather than divided) by the present value of an ordinary annuity of $1 for 6% and five periods.

13. On January 1, Year 3, Saucerer Company bought a building with an assessed value of $220,000 on the date of purchase. Saucerer gave as consideration a $400,000 noninterest-bearing note due on January 1, Year 6. There was no established exchange price for the building, and the note had no ready market. The prevailing rate of interest for a note of this type at January 1, Year 3, was 10%. The present value of $1 at 10% for three periods is 0.75. What amount of interest expense should be included in Saucerer's Year 3 income statement?

A. $22,000

B. $30,000

C. $33,333

D. $40,000

Answer (B) is correct. *(CPA, adapted)*
REQUIRED: The interest expense on a noninterest-bearing note.
DISCUSSION: The purchase of a building without an established exchange price should be recorded at the fair value of the consideration given. A noninterest-bearing note should be recorded at the present value of the future cash flows discounted at the prevailing rate of interest. The note and building should therefore be recorded at $300,000 ($400,000 × 0.75). The difference between the face amount and the present value is recorded as a discount and amortized to interest expense over the life of the note using the effective interest method. The amount of interest expense for the first year is $30,000 ($300,000 fair value of the note at the beginning of Year 3 × 10% effective rate).
Answer (A) is incorrect. The amount of $22,000 results from applying the interest rate to the assessment value of the building. Answer (C) is incorrect. The amount of $33,333 results from applying the straight-line method of amortizing the discount. Answer (D) is incorrect. The amount of $40,000 fails to consider the present value of the note.

14. Risoner Company plans to purchase a machine with the following conditions:

- Purchase price = $300,000.
- The down payment = 10% of purchase price with remainder financed at an annual interest rate of 16%.
- The financing period is 8 years with equal annual payments made every year.
- The present value of an annuity of $1 per year for 8 years at 16% is 4.3436.
- The present value of $1 due at the end of 8 years at 16% is .3050.

The annual payment (rounded to the nearest dollar) is

A. $39,150

B. $43,200

C. $62,160

D. $82,350

Answer (C) is correct. *(CIA, adapted)*
REQUIRED: The annual payment (rounded to the nearest dollar).
DISCUSSION: The periodic payment is found by dividing the amount to be accumulated ($300,000 price – $30,000 down payment = $270,000) by the interest factor for the present value of an ordinary annuity for 8 years at 16%. Consequently, the payment is $62,160 ($270,000 ÷ 4.3436).
Answer (A) is incorrect. The amount of $39,150 is based on dividing ($270,000 × 1.16) by 8 (years). Answer (B) is incorrect. The amount of $43,200 is 16% of $270,000. Answer (D) is incorrect. The amount of $82,350 reflects multiplication by the present value of a sum due (.305) instead of dividing by the present value of an annuity (4.3436).

15. On December 30 of the current year, Azrael, Inc., purchased a machine from Abiss Corp. in exchange for a noninterest-bearing note requiring eight payments of $20,000. The first payment was made on December 30, and the others are due annually on December 30. At date of issuance, the prevailing rate of interest for this type of note was 11%. Present value factors are as follows:

Period	Present Value of Ordinary Annuity of $1 at 11%	Present Value of Annuity in Advance of $1 at 11%
7	4.712	5.231
8	5.146	5.712

On Azrael's current year December 31 balance sheet, the note payable to Abiss was

  A. $94,240

  B. $102,920

  C. $104,620

  D. $114,240

Answer (A) is correct. *(CPA, adapted)*
  REQUIRED: The carrying amount of a noninterest-bearing note payable at the date of issuance.
  DISCUSSION: The payment terms of this purchase agreement provide for a $20,000 initial payment and seven equal payments of $20,000 to be received at the end of each of the next 7 years. The note payable, however, should reflect only the present value of the seven future payments. The present value factor to be used is the present value of an ordinary annuity for seven periods at 11%, or 4.712. The note payable should be recorded at $94,240 ($20,000 × 4.712).
  Answer (B) is incorrect. The amount of $102,920 uses the factor for eight periods rather than seven. Answer (C) is incorrect. The factor for an ordinary annuity should be used. Answer (D) is incorrect. The factor used should be for an ordinary annuity of seven periods, not an annuity in advance for eight periods.

16. Based on 8% interest compounded annually from day of deposit to day of withdrawal, what is the present value today of $4,000 to be received 6 years from today?

Periods	Present Value of $1 Discounted at 8% per Period
1	.926
2	.857
3	.794
4	.735
5	.681

  A. $4,000 × 0.926 × 6.

  B. $4,000 × 0.794 × 2.

  C. $4,000 × 0.681 × 0.926.

  D. Cannot be determined from the information given.

Answer (C) is correct. *(CPA, adapted)*
  REQUIRED: The present value today of an amount to be received at a given future date.
  DISCUSSION: To calculate the present value of an amount to be received 6 years from today when present value factors for only five periods are available, multiply $4,000 by the present value of $1 factor for five periods ($4,000 × .681 = $2,724). This discounts the $4,000 back 5 years. This new product should then be discounted back 1 additional year, i.e., multiplied by the present value factor for one period ($2,724 × .926 = $2,522.24).
  Answer (A) is incorrect. The $4,000 should first be discounted for 5 years. Then that amount should be discounted for 1 additional year. Answer (B) is incorrect. Discounting $4,000 for three periods twice overstates the present value. Answer (D) is incorrect. The present value can be determined from the information given.

17. Potter Corporation is contemplating the purchase of a new piece of equipment with a purchase price of $500,000. It plans to make a 10% down payment and will receive a loan for 25 years at 10% interest. The present value interest factor for an annuity of $1 per year for 25 years at 10% is 9.0770. The annual payment required on the loan will be

  A. $18,000

  B. $49,576

  C. $45,000

  D. $55,084

Answer (B) is correct. *(CIA, adapted)*
  REQUIRED: The annual payment required on the loan.
  DISCUSSION: The corporation plans a 10% down payment on equipment with a purchase price of $500,000. The amount of the loan will therefore equal $450,000. Because the loan will be financed at 10% for 25 years, the annual payments can be calculated by dividing the amount of the initial loan by the present value interest factor for an annuity of $1 per year for 25 years at 10%. The annual payment required is equal to $49,576 ($450,000 ÷ 9.0770).
  Answer (A) is incorrect. This amount results from allocating the $450,000 equally over 25 years. Answer (C) is incorrect. This amount results from multiplying $450,000 by the 10% interest. Answer (D) is incorrect. This amount results if the $50,000 down payment is not removed before the annual payment is calculated.

18. Murray is planning a project that will cost $22,000. The annual cash inflow, net of income taxes, will be $5,000 a year for 7 years. The present value of $1 at 12% is as follows:

Period	Present Value of $1 at 12%
1	.893
2	.797
3	.712
4	.636
5	.567
6	.507
7	.452

Using a rate of return of 12%, what is the present value of the cash flow generated by this project?

A. $22,600

B. $22,820

C. $34,180

D. $35,000

Answer (B) is correct. *(CPA, adapted)*
REQUIRED: The present value of the cash flow generated by the project.
DISCUSSION: If the cash inflow, net of taxes, at the end of each of 7 years is $5,000, and if the discount rate is 12%, the present value of this series of cash flows will be equal to the present value of an ordinary annuity of $5,000 for 7 years at 12%. The interest factor for the present value of an ordinary annuity is equal to the sum of the interest factors for the present value of $1 for the same period. The interest factor for an ordinary annuity of $5,000 for seven periods is 4.564. The present value is $22,820 ($5,000 × 4.564).

The alternative is to calculate the present value of each $5,000 cash flow using the interest factor for the present value of $1 at 12% for each of the periods one through seven. The sum of these products is equal to the present value of an ordinary annuity of $5,000 for seven periods at 12%.

$5,000	×	.893	=	$ 4,465
5,000	×	.797	=	3,985
5,000	×	.712	=	3,560
5,000	×	.636	=	3,180
5,000	×	.567	=	2,835
5,000	×	.507	=	2,535
5,000	×	.452	=	2,260
5,000	×	4.564	=	$22,820

Answer (A) is incorrect. This amount results from adding 12% of $5,000 to the project cost of $22,000. Answer (C) is incorrect. This amount results from subtracting the difference between the present value of the cash flows and the project cost ($22,820 – $22,000 = $820) from the $35,000 ($5,000 × 7 years) undiscounted total cash flows ($35,000 – $820 = $34,180). Answer (D) is incorrect. This amount fails to consider the time value of money.

19. A loan is to be repaid in eight annual installments of $1,875. The interest rate is 10%. The present value of an ordinary annuity for eight periods at 10% is 5.33. Identify the computation that approximates the outstanding loan balance at the end of the first year.

A. $1,875 × 5.33 = $9,994.

B. $1,875 × 5.33 = $9,994;
$9,994 – $1,875 = $8,119.

C. $1,875 × 5.33 = $9,994;
$1,875 – $999 = $876;
$9,994 – $876 = $9,118.

D. $1,875 × 8 = $15,000;
$15,000 – ($1,875 – $1,500) = $14,625.

Answer (C) is correct. *(CIA, adapted)*
REQUIRED: The computation approximating the outstanding loan balance at the end of Year 1.
DISCUSSION: The present value of an ordinary annuity of $1 for eight periods at 10% is 5.33. Thus, the present value of an ordinary annuity of $1,875 is $9,994 (5.33 × $1,875), the original balance of the loan. If the interest rate is 10%, the interest on the principal for Year 1 will be approximately $999. Accordingly, the first installment has an interest component of $999 and a principal component of $876 ($1,875 – $999 interest). The first payment therefore reduces the principal balance of $9,994 by $876 to $9,118.

Answer (A) is incorrect. This computation ($1,875 × 5.33 = $9,994) determines the present value of the annuity at the beginning of Year 1, not the loan balance at the end of Year 1. Answer (B) is incorrect. These computations ($1,875 × 5.33 = $9,994; $9,994 – $1,875 = $8,119) improperly subtract both principal and interest for Year 1 in arriving at the principal balance. Answer (D) is incorrect. These computations [$1,875 × 8 = $15,000; $15,000 – ($1,875 – $1,500) = $14,625] do not consider the time value of money.

4.2 Future Value

Questions 20 and 21 are based on the following information. Present value, amount of $1, and ordinary annuity information are presented below. All values are for four periods with an interest rate of 8%.

Amount of $1	1.36
Present value of $1	0.74
Amount of an ordinary annuity of $1	4.51
Present value of an ordinary annuity of $1	3.31

20. Cara Galadon decides to create a fund to earn 8% compounded annually that will enable her to withdraw $5,000 per year each June 30, beginning in Year 4 and continuing through Year 7. Cara wishes to make equal contributions on June 30 of each year from Year 0 through Year 3. Which equation would be used to compute the balance that must be in the fund on June 30, Year 3, for Cara to meet her objective?

   A. $X = $5,000 × 3.31.

   B. $X = $5,000 × (3.31 + 1.00).

   C. $X = $5,000 × 1.36.

   D. $X = $5,000 × 4.51.

Answer (A) is correct. *(CIA, adapted)*
   REQUIRED: The equation to compute the balance in the fund on a given date to permit withdrawals at equal intervals over a stated period.
   DISCUSSION: The fund balance on 6/30/Year 3 should be equal to the present value of four equal annual payments of $5,000 each discounted at a rate of 8%. If the factor for the present value of an ordinary annuity of $1 for four periods at 8% is 3.31, the present value of an ordinary annuity of $5,000 for four periods discounted at 8% is $5,000 × 3.31.
   Answer (B) is incorrect. The equation $X = $5,000 × (3.31 + 1.00) gives the present value of an annuity due for five periods. Answer (C) is incorrect. The equation $X = $5,000 × 1.36 gives the future value in four periods of $5,000 invested today. Answer (D) is incorrect. The equation $X = $5,000 × 4.51 is the future value of an annuity of four annual deposits of $5,000.

21. Pippen wants to accumulate $50,000 by making equal contributions at the end of each of 4 succeeding years. Which equation would be used to compute Pippen's annual contribution to achieve the $50,000 goal at the end of the fourth year?

   A. $X = $50,000 ÷ 4.51.

   B. $X = $50,000 ÷ 4.00.

   C. $X = $12,500 ÷ 1.36.

   D. $X = $50,000 ÷ 3.31.

Answer (A) is correct. *(CIA, adapted)*
   REQUIRED: The equation to compute the annual year-end payment necessary to accumulate a stated amount at the end of a stated period.
   DISCUSSION: The factor for the amount of an ordinary annuity of $1 for four periods at 8% (4.51) is used. If an investment of $1 at 8% at the end of each of four periods would generate a future amount of 4.51, an investment of $X per period for four periods at 8% would generate the necessary $50,000. The required annual payment is equal to $50,000 ÷ 4.51.
   Answer (B) is incorrect. The equation $X = $50,000 ÷ 4.00 does not take into account interest to be earned. Answer (C) is incorrect. The equation $X = $12,500 ÷ 1.36 gives the present value of $12,500 to be received four periods hence. Answer (D) is incorrect. The equation $X = $50,000 ÷ 3.31 gives the amount of the periodic payment needed to produce an ordinary annuity with a present value of $50,000.

22. Jarvis wants to invest equal semiannual payments in order to have $10,000 at the end of 20 years. Assuming that Jarvis will earn interest at an annual rate of 6% compounded semiannually, how would the periodic payment be calculated?

A. $10,000 divided by the future amount of an ordinary annuity of 40 payments of $1 each at an interest rate of 3% per period.

B. $10,000 divided by the present value of an ordinary annuity of 40 payments of $1 each at an interest rate of 3% per period.

C. The future amount of an ordinary annuity of 20 payments of $1 each at an interest rate of 6% per period divided into $10,000.

D. The present value of an ordinary annuity of 40 payments of $1 each at an interest rate of 3% per period divided by $10,000.

Answer (A) is correct. *(CPA, adapted)*
REQUIRED: The method of calculating the periodic payment to accumulate a known future amount.
DISCUSSION: The question involves future value because it requires computation of the periodic amount of an annuity that must be invested to produce a given future amount. Accordingly, the appropriate factor reflecting the compound interest effect will be derived from the formula for the future value of an ordinary annuity of $1. This factor multiplied by the periodic payment is equal to the desired future amount. If the payment is unknown, it may be calculated by dividing the known future amount ($10,000) by the appropriate factor derived from the future value of an ordinary annuity formula. If the payments are to be made semiannually for 20 years, 40 compounding periods are involved. If the interest rate is 6% per annum, the semiannual interest rate is 3%.
Answer (B) is incorrect. The question calls for a future value computation. Answer (C) is incorrect. Forty semiannual payments are to be made at an interest rate of 3% per period (not 20 payments at 6%). Answer (D) is incorrect. The future amount should be divided by the relevant interest factor for the future amount of an ordinary annuity.

23. On March 15, Year 1, Kathleen Corp. adopted a plan to accumulate $1,000,000 by September 1, Year 5. Kathleen plans to make four equal annual deposits to a fund that will earn interest at 10% compounded annually. Kathleen made the first deposit on September 1, Year 1. Future value and future amount factors are as follows:

Future value of $1 at 10% for four periods   1.46

Future amount of ordinary annuity of $1 at 10% for four periods   4.64

Future amount of annuity in advance of $1 at 10% for four periods   5.11

Kathleen should make four annual deposits (rounded) of

A. $250,000

B. $215,500

C. $195,700

D. $684,930

Answer (C) is correct. *(CPA, adapted)*
REQUIRED: The amount of an annuity in advance that would generate a future sum.
DISCUSSION: The depositor wishes to have $1,000,000 at the end of a 4-year period (from 9/1/Year 1 to 9/1/Year 5). The amount will be generated from four equal annual payments (an annuity) to be made starting at the beginning of the 4-year period. The annual payment for this annuity is calculated in advance by dividing the desired future amount of $1,000,000 by the factor for the future value of an annuity in advance of $1 at 10% for four periods. Each annual deposit should therefore equal $195,700 ($1,000,000 ÷ 5.11).
Answer (A) is incorrect. The amount of $250,000 does not take into account the interest. Answer (B) is incorrect. The amount of $215,500 is computed using the future value factor of an ordinary annuity instead of an annuity in advance (annuity due). Answer (D) is incorrect. The amount of $684,930 is computed using the future value factor of $1 instead of the future value factor of an annuity in advance.

24. If the amount to be received in 4 years is $137,350, and given the correct factor from the 10% time-value-of-money table below, what is the current investment?

Interest Factors for 10%			
Periods	FV	PV	FV of Ordinary Annuity	PV of Ordinary Annuity
1	1.1000	.9091	1.0000	.9091
2	1.2100	.8264	2.1000	1.7355
3	1.3310	.7513	3.3100	2.4869
4	1.4641	.6830	4.6410	3.1699
5	1.6105	.6029	6.1051	3.7908

A. $30,034.33

B. $43,329.44

C. $93,810.05

D. $201,094.14

Answer (C) is correct. *(CIA, adapted)*
REQUIRED: The current investment required to receive a future amount of money at a given interest rate.
DISCUSSION: The current investment is the present value of the given future amount. It equals the future amount multiplied by the factor for the present value of $1 for four periods at 10%. Accordingly, the current investment is $93,810.05 ($137,350 × .6830).
Answer (A) is incorrect. This amount cannot be derived from any of the time value factors given. Answer (B) is incorrect. The amount of $43,329.44 results from incorrectly dividing by the factor for the present value of an ordinary annuity for four periods. Answer (D) is incorrect. The amount of $201,094.14 results from incorrectly using the factor for the future value of $1 for four periods.

25. A pension fund is projecting the amount necessary today to fund a retiree's pension benefits. The retiree's first annual pension check will be in 10 years. Payments are expected to last for a total of 20 annual payments. Which of the following best describes the computation of the amount needed today to fund the retiree's annuity?

A. Present value of $1 for 10 periods, times the present value of an ordinary annuity of 20 payments, times the annual annuity payment.

B. Present value of $1 for nine periods, times the present value of an ordinary annuity of 20 payments, times the annual annuity payment.

C. Future value of $1 for 10 periods, times the present value of an ordinary annuity of 20 payments, times the annual annuity payment.

D. Future value of $1 for nine periods, times the present value of an ordinary annuity of 20 payments, times the annual annuity payment.

Answer (B) is correct. *(CIA, adapted)*
REQUIRED: The formula to compute the amount needed today to fund a pension that will begin in the future.
DISCUSSION: Multiplying the annual annuity pension payment times the present value of an ordinary annuity of 20 payments factor results in a present value determination 1 year prior to the start of the payments, or 9 years hence. Multiplying the present value of ordinary annuity pension payments by a present value of $1 factor for 9 years results in the amount needed today to fund the retiree's annuity.
Answer (A) is incorrect. The present value factor for nine periods should be used to determine the amount needed to fund the pension plan. Answer (C) is incorrect. A future value fact is not used to determine the amount needed to fund the pension plan. Answer (D) is incorrect. A present value factor should be used.

26. An actuary has determined that Jaykay Company should have $90,000,000 accumulated in a fund 20 years from now to be able to meet its pension obligations. An interest rate of 8% is considered appropriate for all pension fund calculations involving an interest component. Jaykay wishes to calculate how much it should contribute at the end of each of the next 20 years for the pension fund to have its required balance in 20 years. Which set of instructions correctly describes the procedures necessary to compute the annual amount the company should contribute to the fund?

A. Divide $90,000,000 by the interest factor for the present value of an ordinary annuity for n=20, i=8%.

B. Multiply $90,000,000 by the interest factor for the present value of an ordinary annuity for n=20, i=8%.

C. Divide $90,000,000 by the interest factor for the future value of an ordinary annuity for n=20, i=8%.

D. Multiply $90,000,000 by the interest factor for the future value of an ordinary annuity for n=20, i=8%.

Answer (C) is correct. *(CIA, adapted)*
REQUIRED: The set of instructions that correctly describes the procedures necessary to compute the annual amount the company should contribute to the fund.
DISCUSSION: The future value of an annuity equals the appropriate interest factor (for n periods at an interest rate of i), which is derived from standard tables, times the periodic payment. The $90,000,000 amount is the future value of the funding payments. The amount of each funding payment can be calculated by dividing the future value of the funding payments by the interest factor for future value of an ordinary annuity for n equals 20 and i equals 8%.
Answer (A) is incorrect. The $90,000,000 is a future value figure. The interest factor to be used for the division process should be a future value factor, not a present value factor. Answer (B) is incorrect. The $90,000,000 is a future value figure. The factor to be used should be a future value factor. That factor should be used in a division, rather than a multiplication, process. Answer (D) is incorrect. The $90,000,000 should be divided by the appropriate interest factor.

4.3 Cash Flow Information and Present Value (SFAC 7)

27. According to SFAC 7, *Using Cash Flow Information and Present Value in Accounting Measurements*, the objective of present value is to estimate fair value when used to determine accounting measurements for

	Initial-Recognition Purposes	Fresh-Start Purposes
A.	No	No
B.	Yes	Yes
C.	Yes	No
D.	No	Yes

Answer (B) is correct. *(Publisher, adapted)*

REQUIRED: The objective of present value in initial-recognition and fresh-start measurements.

DISCUSSION: SFAC 7 states that the objective of present value in initial-recognition or fresh-start measurements is to estimate fair value. "Present value should attempt to capture the elements that, taken together, would comprise a market price if one existed, that is, fair value." A present value measurement includes five elements: estimates of cash flows, expectations about their variability, the time value of money (the risk-free interest rate), the price of uncertainty inherent in an asset or liability, and other factors (e.g., illiquidity or market imperfections). Fair value encompasses all these elements using the estimates and expectations of participants in the market.

Answer (A) is incorrect. The objective of present value in both initial-recognition and fresh-start measurements is to estimate fair value. Answer (C) is incorrect. The objective of present value in fresh-start measurements is to estimate fair value. Answer (D) is incorrect. The objective of present value for initial-recognition purposes is to estimate fair value.

28. The expected cash flow approach to measuring present value described in SFAC 7, *Using Cash Flow Information and Present Value in Accounting Measurements*,

A. Uses a single set of estimated cash flows.

B. Is limited to assets and liabilities with contractual cash flows.

C. Focuses on explicit assumptions about the range of expected cash flows and their respective probabilities.

D. Focuses on the single most likely amount or best estimate.

Answer (C) is correct. *(Publisher, adapted)*

REQUIRED: The nature of the expected cash flow approach.

DISCUSSION: The traditional approach to calculating present value employs one set of estimated cash flows and one interest rate. This approach is expected to continue to be used in many cases, for example, when contractual cash flows are involved. However, SFAC 7 describes the expected cash flow approach, which is applicable in more complex circumstances, such as when no market or no comparable item exists for an asset or liability. The expected cash flow results from multiplying each possible estimated amount by its probability and adding the products. The expected cash flow approach emphasizes explicit assumptions about the possible estimated cash flows and their probabilities. The traditional method merely includes those uncertainties in the choice of interest rate. Moreover, by allowing for a range of possibilities, the expected cash flow method permits the use of present value when the timing of cash flows is uncertain.

Answer (A) is incorrect. The traditional present value measurement approach uses a single set of estimated cash flows and a single interest rate. Answer (B) is incorrect. The expected cash flow approach may also apply when the timing of cash flows is uncertain or when nonfinancial assets and liabilities are to be measured and no market or comparable item exists for them. Answer (D) is incorrect. Some current accounting applications use the estimated mode (single most likely amount or best estimate), but the expected cash flow approach arrives at an estimated mean by probabilistically weighting a range of possible estimated amounts.

Use Gleim **EQE Test Prep** Software Download for interactive study and performance analysis.

Visit the **GLEIM®** website for free updates,

which are available until the next edition is published.

gleim.com/updates

STUDY UNIT FIVE
CURRENT ASSETS, CASH,
ACCOUNTS RECEIVABLE, AND NOTES RECEIVABLE

Current Assets and Working Capital

In its balance sheet, an entity displays its assets, liabilities, and equity at a moment in time. If the balance sheet is classified, assets and liabilities are presented as current and noncurrent. **Current assets** include cash and other assets that are reasonably expected to be realized in cash or sold or consumed within 1 year from the balance sheet date or the normal **operating cycle**, whichever is longer. Current assets commonly include (1) cash; (2) cash equivalents; (3) short-term receivables; (4) prepaid expenses; and (5) certain individual trading, available-for-sale, and held-to-maturity securities. **Current liabilities** include those obligations that are expected to be satisfied by the (1) payment of cash; (2) use of current assets other than cash; or (3) creation of new current liabilities within 1 year from the balance sheet date or the normal operating cycle, whichever is longer. **Working capital** equals the difference between current assets and current liabilities. Assets and liabilities that are not current are **noncurrent**.

Some variation of the following classifications is used by most entities:

Assets	Liabilities
Current assets:	Current liabilities:
Cash	Accounts payable
Accounts and notes receivable	Current notes payable
Inventories	Current maturities of noncurrent liabilities
Prepaid expenses	Noncurrent liabilities:
Certain investments	Noncurrent notes payable
Noncurrent assets:	Bonds payable
Certain investments and funds	
Property, plant, and equipment (PPE)	Equity
Intangible assets	Investments by owners
Other noncurrent assets	Retained earnings (income reinvested)
	Accumulated other comprehensive income
	Noncontrolling interest in a consolidated entity

Cash

All **cash** balances on hand and on deposit that are readily available for current operating purposes are reported as cash. Restricted cash is reported under a separate caption. Because cash is the most liquid asset, it is usually the first asset listed on the balance sheet. However, cash and cash equivalents may be reported as a combined amount. **Cash equivalents** are short-term, highly liquid investments that are bought and sold for cash management purposes. Investments with original maturities of 3 months or less ordinarily are classified as cash equivalents.

A **bank reconciliation** is a schedule comparing the cash balance per books with the balance per bank statement (usually received monthly). The common approach is to reconcile from the bank balance and the book balance to the true balance. The bank and book balances usually vary. Thus, the reconciliation permits the entity to determine whether the difference is attributable to normal conditions, errors, or fraud. It is also a basis for entries to adjust the books to reflect unrecorded items. **Items known to the entity but not to the bank** are (1) outstanding checks, (2) deposits in transit, and (3) errors made by the bank. **Items known to the bank but not to the entity** are amounts added (collections and interest) or subtracted (or not added) by the bank (insufficient funds checks and service charges).

Common Reconciliation Items

	To Book Balance	To Bank Balance
Additions	Interest earned Deposits collected Errors	Deposits in transit Errors
Subtractions	Service charges NSF checks Errors	Outstanding checks Errors

A **petty cash** system sets aside a specific amount in the care of a custodian to pay office expenses that are too small to pay by check or to record in the accounting system as they occur. The entry to establish the fund is to debit petty cash and credit cash for the specified amount. The fund is reimbursed periodically for all payments based on expense receipts, and journal entries reflect the transactions. However, entries are made to petty cash only to (1) establish the fund, (2) change its amount, or (3) adjust the balance if it has not been reimbursed at year end.

Cash over and short is a nominal account for errors in petty cash. It is used when the total of the expense receipts and the cash remaining does not equal the amount that should be in the petty cash fund. An overage is a credit, and a shortage is a debit. The amount is classified on the income statement as a miscellaneous revenue or expense, respectively.

Accounts Receivable

Current receivables are amounts owed to an entity that are expected to be collected within 1 year or the operating cycle, whichever is longer. Receivables may be classified as trade or nontrade. Trade receivables arise when an entity sells goods or services on credit. Nontrade receivables primarily arise when an entity lends money on a short-term basis. Receivables also may be classified as accounts or notes receivable. **Accounts receivable** ordinarily consist of unwritten promises by credit customers. They normally do not include an interest component unless they become overdue.

Accounts Receivable – Measurement

Most current receivables are trade accounts receivable. GAAP require that they be reported at their **net realizable value** (gross accounts receivable – allowance for uncollectible accounts). The allowance is credited (increased) when bad debt expense is recognized. The allowance is debited (decreased) when a specific account is recognized as being uncollectible. GAAP also require that **bad debt expense** be recognized. For most credit-granting entities, it is probable that (1) gross accounts receivable are overstated and (2) the amounts can be reasonably estimated. GAAP allow two methods for estimating bad debt expense. The **income statement approach** calculates bad debt expense as a percentage of credit sales reported on the income statement. An equal amount is credited to the allowance. The **balance sheet approach** estimates the balance that should be recorded in the allowance based on the collectibility of ending gross accounts receivable. Bad debt expense is the amount necessary to adjust the allowance.

An entity rarely has a single rate of uncollectibility for all accounts. Thus, an entity using the balance-sheet approach generally prepares an **aging schedule** for accounts receivable. The entity stratifies the receivables according to how long they have been overdue (less than 30 days, 31-60 days, etc.). It then applies an appropriate rate to each stratum. If an account **previously written off** is collected, the entity reestablishes the account (debit accounts receivable, credit the allowance) and records the cash receipt (debit cash, credit accounts receivable). The net effect is to return the amount written off to the allowance to absorb future write-offs.

Notes Receivable

Notes receivable customarily are formal written agreements that may include an interest component. The basic measurement principle for noncurrent notes receivable and noncurrent notes payable is that they are recorded at the **present value of the consideration given or received**. When a note is exchanged for property, goods, or services, the interest rate determined by parties at arm's length is assumed to be fair. Exceptions occur when (1) no interest is stated, (2) the stated rate is unreasonable, or (3) the face amount of the note materially differs from the cash price of the item or the fair value of the note. In these cases, the transaction should be recorded at the more clearly determinable of (1) the fair value of the property, goods, or services; (2) the fair value of the note; or (3) the future payments discounted at an imputed rate. The prevailing rate for similar instruments of issuers with similar credit helps determine the **imputed** rate.

The stated rate may be less than the effective rate because the lender has received **other stated (or unstated) rights and privileges**. The difference between the present value of the note at the stated rate and the effective rate is the cost of the rights or privileges obtained. Periodic interest is recognized at a constant rate using the **effective-interest method**.

Transfers of Financial Assets

The accounting for **transfers of financial assets** is based on a **financial-components approach** and the concept of **control**. The objective is for each party to the transaction to (1) recognize the assets it controls and the liabilities it has incurred, (2) derecognize assets when control has been given up, and (3) derecognize liabilities when they have been extinguished. Whether control exists depends, among other things, on the transferor's continuing involvement. **Continuing involvement** means the right to receive benefits from the assets or an obligation to provide additional assets to a party related to the transfer. Examples are (1) servicing agreements, (2) options written or held, (3) recourse provisions, (4) a beneficial interest in a trust that holds the assets, or (5) a pledge of collateral. **Transfers of financial assets** include transfers of (1) an entire financial asset, (2) a group of entire financial assets, and (3) a participating interest in an entire financial asset. A **participating interest** exists if (1) it is a proportionate ownership interest, (2) receipts of cash flows are proportionate to shares of ownership, (3) each holder has the same priority, and (4) the entire asset cannot be pledged or exchanged without the agreement of all holders.

A transfer of financial assets is a **sale** when the transferor relinquishes control. The transferor relinquishes **control** only if certain conditions are met: (1) The transferred assets are beyond the reach of the transferor and its creditors; (2) transferees may pledge or exchange the assets or interests received; and (3) the transferor does not maintain effective control through, for example, (a) an agreement to reacquire the assets before maturity, (b) the unilateral ability to benefit from causing the holder to return specific assets, or (c) an agreement making it probable that the transferee will require repurchase.

If the transfer of a **participating interest** qualifies as a **sale**, the **carrying amount** of the entire financial asset is allocated **based on relative fair values** between the interests sold and retained, and the financial components approach is applied. Measurement of assets obtained and liabilities incurred is at **fair value**. If the sale of an **entire financial asset (or a group)** qualifies as a **sale**, the transferor's accounting is the same (but without allocation of the carrying amount).

If the transfer is not a sale, the parties treat the transferor as a debtor and the transferee as a creditor in possession of collateral. The transaction is then accounted for as a **secured borrowing**. If the transferee **may sell or repledge** the collateral, the transferor **reclassifies** and **separately reports** that asset. If the transferee **sells** the collateral, it recognizes the proceeds (debits assets) and credits a **liability** to return the collateral (now in the form of proceeds). This sale itself is a transfer.

Asset $XXX
Liability -- collateral (proceeds) $XXX

If the transferor **defaults** and no longer has the right of redemption, it derecognizes (credits) the pledged asset. The transferee initially recognizes (debits) an asset at fair value or derecognizes (debits) the liability to return the collateral. Thus, absent default, the collateral is an **asset of the transferor**.

A **servicing asset** is a contract under which future revenues from servicing fees, late charges, etc., are expected to more than adequately compensate the servicer. A **servicing liability** arises when such compensation is inadequate. Agreements by transferors to service transferred mortgage loans, credit card receivables, and other financial assets are common. **Servicing assets and liabilities** always are measured initially at **fair value**. **Subsequent measurement** of each class of separately recognized servicing assets or liabilities may be based on (1) the amortization method or (2) the fair value method.

When the conditions for surrender of control are met, a **transfer of receivables with recourse** is accounted for as a sale, with the proceeds reduced by the fair value of the recourse obligation. If the transfer does not meet the criteria for a sale, the parties account for the transfer as a **secured borrowing with a pledge** of noncash collateral.

Factoring is a transfer of receivables to a third party (a factor) who assumes the responsibility of collection. Factoring discounts receivables on a **nonrecourse, notification basis**. Thus, payments by the debtors on the transferred assets are made to the factor. A factor usually receives a high financing fee, plus a fee for collection. Furthermore, the factor often operates more efficiently than its clients because of the specialized nature of its services.

A **pledge** (a general assignment) is the use of receivables as collateral for a loan. The borrower agrees to use collections of receivables to repay the loan. Upon default, the lender can sell the receivables to recover the loan proceeds. Because a pledge is a relatively informal arrangement, it is not reflected in the accounts, although disclosure should be made in the financial statements.

The following summarizes **transferor accounting**:

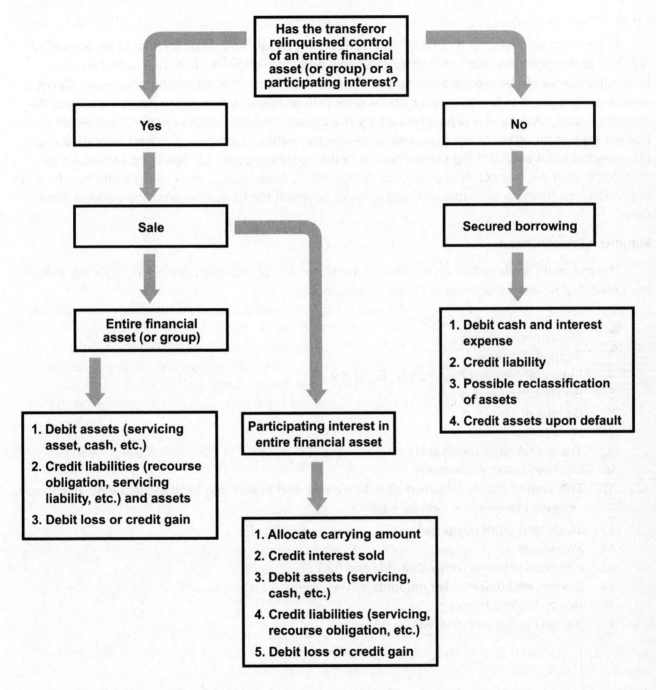

Differences between GAAP and IFRS

Under IFRS:

Separate classifications of **current and noncurrent** assets and liabilities should be presented unless a presentation by order of liquidity is reliable and more relevant. In either case, however, amounts expected to be recovered or settled in more than 12 months should be disclosed. **Current assets** are expected to be realized, or are held for sale or consumption, in the normal course of the operating cycle. Assets also are current if they are unrestricted cash items or cash equivalents or are held for trading purposes or are expected to be realized within 12 months. **Current liabilities** are (1) expected to be settled in the normal course of the operating cycle, (2) due to be settled within 12 months after the balance sheet date, (3) held primarily to be traded, or (4) obligations for which the entity does not have an unconditional right to defer payment for 12 months after the balance sheet date.

Minimum Presentation

The minimum presentation on the face of the statement of financial position includes the following line items (but no particular order or format is prescribed):

1. Property, plant, and equipment
2. Investment property
3. Intangible assets
4. Financial assets (other than 5., 8., and 9.)
5. Equity-based investments
6. Biological assets
7. Inventories
8. Trade and other receivables
9. Cash and cash equivalents
10. The total of assets classified as held for sale and assets and liabilities included in disposal groups classified as held for sale
11. Trade and other payables
12. Provisions
13. Financial liabilities (other than 11. and 12.)
14. Current and deferred tax amounts
15. Noncontrolling interests
16. Issued capital and reserves

QUESTIONS

5.1 Current Assets and Working Capital

1. On Geo's April 30, Year 3, balance sheet, a note receivable was reported as a noncurrent asset, and its accrued interest for 10 months was reported as a current asset. Which of the following terms would fit Geo's note receivable?

    A. Both principal and interest amounts are payable on June 30, Year 3 and Year 4.

    B. Principal and interest are due December 31, Year 3.

    C. Both principal and interest amounts are payable on December 31, Year 3 and Year 4.

    D. Principal is due June 30, Year 4, and interest is due June 30, Year 3 and Year 4.

Answer (D) is correct. *(CPA, adapted)*
    REQUIRED: The terms explaining classification of a note receivable as a noncurrent asset and its accrued interest as a current asset.
    DISCUSSION: A noncurrent note receivable is not expected to be converted into cash within 1 year or one operating cycle, whichever is longer. Because the principal is due more than 1 year from the balance sheet date, it must be regarded as noncurrent. However, the accrued interest is a current asset because it is due in 2 months.
    Answer (A) is incorrect. The portion of principal due in 2 months would be considered current. Answer (B) is incorrect. Principal amounts due in less than 1 year are current assets. Answer (C) is incorrect. Only the principal due at the end of Year 4 is noncurrent.

2. The operating cycle of a business is the span of time that

    A. Coincides with the economy's business cycle, which runs from one trough of the economy's business activity to the next.

    B. Corresponds with its natural business year, which runs from one trough of the particular entity's business activity to the next.

    C. Is set by the industry's trade association, usually on an average length of time for all entities that are members of the association.

    D. Runs from cash disbursement for items of inventory through their sale to the realization of cash from sale.

Answer (D) is correct. *(CPA, adapted)*
    REQUIRED: The operating cycle of a business.
    DISCUSSION: Operations usually follow a cycle that begins with cash payments and ends with cash receipts. The average amount of time from cash payment to the realization of cash from the sale is the operating cycle of the entity.
    Answer (A) is incorrect. Financial reporting is based on an entity's business cycle, not the economy's. Answer (B) is incorrect. An entity's fiscal year is not normally its operating cycle. One operating cycle may last 12 months or more, although usually the fiscal year of the entity includes a number of operating cycles. Answer (C) is incorrect. The operating cycle is determined by an entity's transactions, not by an industry trade association estimate.

3. At October 31, Dingo, Inc., had cash accounts at three different banks. One account balance is segregated solely for a November 15 payment into a bond sinking fund. A second account, used for branch operations, is overdrawn. The third account, used for regular corporate operations, has a positive balance. How should these accounts be reported in Dingo's October 31 classified balance sheet?

    A. The segregated account should be reported as a noncurrent asset, the regular account should be reported as a current asset, and the overdraft should be reported as a current liability.

    B. The segregated and regular accounts should be reported as current assets, and the overdraft should be reported as a current liability.

    C. The segregated account should be reported as a noncurrent asset, and the regular account should be reported as a current asset net of the overdraft.

    D. The segregated and regular accounts should be reported as current assets net of the overdraft.

Answer (A) is correct. *(CPA, adapted)*
    REQUIRED: The proper reporting of three cash accounts.
    DISCUSSION: Current assets include cash available for current operations and items that are the equivalent of cash. Hence, the account used for regular operations is current. Cash is noncurrent if it is (1) restricted to use for other than current operations, (2) designated for the acquisition or construction of noncurrent assets, or (3) segregated for the liquidation of long-term debts. Cash may be noncurrent even if it is not actually set aside in special accounts. Thus, cash that is clearly to be used in the near future for (1) the liquidation of long-term debts, (2) payments to sinking funds, or (3) other similar purposes is classified as noncurrent. The overdraft should be treated as a current liability and not netted against the other cash balances. If the company had another account in the same bank with a positive balance, netting would be appropriate because the bank would have a right of offset.
    Answer (B) is incorrect. The segregated account is noncurrent. Answer (C) is incorrect. The overdraft should not be netted. Answer (D) is incorrect. The segregated account is noncurrent and the overdraft should not be netted.

4. The following is Azzura Corp.'s June 30, Year 1, trial balance:

Cash overdraft		$ 10,000
Accounts receivable, net	$ 35,000	
Inventory	58,000	
Prepaid expenses	12,000	
Land held for resale	100,000	
Property, plant, and equipment, net	95,000	
Accounts payable and accrued expenses		32,000
Common stock		25,000
Additional paid-in capital		150,000
Retained earnings		83,000
	$300,000	$300,000

Additional information:

- Checks amounting to $30,000 were written to vendors and recorded on June 29, Year 1, resulting in a cash overdraft of $10,000. The checks were mailed on July 9, Year 1.
- Land held for resale was sold for cash on July 15, Year 1.
- Azzura issued its financial statements on July 31, Year 1.

In its June 30, Year 1, balance sheet, what amount should Azzura report as current assets?

A. $225,000

B. $205,000

C. $195,000

D. $125,000

Answer (A) is correct. *(CPA, adapted)*
REQUIRED: The amount reported for current assets on the balance sheet.
DISCUSSION: Current assets include cash; inventory; receivables; certain individual trading, held-to-maturity, and available-for-sale securities; and prepaid expenses. Examples of prepaid expenses are insurance, interest, rent, and taxes that are reasonably expected to be realized in cash, sold, or consumed within 1 year, or the normal operating cycle of the business, whichever is longer. Thus, Azzura's current assets include $20,000 of cash ($30,000 of checks mailed in the next period but prematurely recorded – $10,000 overdraft), net accounts receivable ($35,000), inventory ($58,000), prepaid expenses ($12,000), and the land held for resale (treated as a current asset because it was held for immediate sale). The total is $225,000.
Answer (B) is incorrect. The amount of $205,000 does not include the $20,000 in cash. Answer (C) is incorrect. The amount of $195,000 reflects the $30,000 of checks not mailed at 6/30/Year 1. Answer (D) is incorrect. The amount of $125,000 does not include the land held for resale, which was realized in cash after the balance sheet date.

5. A characteristic of all assets and liabilities included in working capital is that they are

A. Cash equivalents.

B. Current.

C. Monetary.

D. Marketable.

Answer (B) is correct. *(CPA, adapted)*
REQUIRED: The characteristic of all assets and liabilities included in working capital.
DISCUSSION: Working capital is the excess of current assets over current liabilities. Working capital identifies the relatively liquid portion of the capital of the entity available for meeting obligations within the operating cycle of the firm.
Answer (A) is incorrect. The assets and liabilities included in working capital are not limited to cash equivalents. Answer (C) is incorrect. Although assets and liabilities may be any combination of monetary, marketable, or cash equivalents in addition to cash, they must be current to be part of working capital. Answer (D) is incorrect. Assets need not be marketable to be current.

6. Griffin Corp. declared a $50,000 cash dividend on May 19, Year 1, to shareholders of record on May 30, Year 1, payable on June 9, Year 1. As a result of this cash dividend, working capital

A. Was not affected.

B. Decreased on June 9.

C. Decreased on May 30.

D. Decreased on May 19.

Answer (D) is correct. *(CPA, adapted)*
REQUIRED: The effect of a cash dividend on working capital.
DISCUSSION: On May 19, the date of declaration, retained earnings is debited and dividends payable credited. The declaration decreases working capital because a current liability is increased.
Answer (A) is incorrect. Working capital was decreased on May 19. Answer (B) is incorrect. When payment is made, both a current liability (dividends payable) and a current asset (cash) are decreased, which has no net effect on working capital. Answer (C) is incorrect. No entry is made on the record date.

7. The following transactions occurred during a company's first year of operations:

I. Purchased a delivery van for cash
II. Borrowed money by issuance of short-term debt
III. Purchased treasury stock

Which of the items above caused a change in the amount of working capital?

A. I only.

B. II and III only.

C. I and III only.

D. I, II, and III.

Answer (C) is correct. *(CIA, adapted)*
REQUIRED: The items that caused a change in the amount of working capital.
DISCUSSION: Working capital is computed by deducting total current liabilities from total current assets. The purchase of a delivery van for cash reduces current assets and has no effect on current liabilities. The borrowing of cash by incurring short-term debt increases current assets by the same amount as it increases current liabilities; hence, it will have no effect on working capital. The purchase of treasury stock decreases current assets but has no effect on current liabilities. Thus, the purchases of the van and treasury stock affect working capital.
Answer (A) is incorrect. The purchase of the treasury stock also affects working capital. Answer (B) is incorrect. The purchase of the van affects working capital, but not the issuance of short-term debt. Answer (D) is incorrect. The issuance of short-term debt does not affect working capital.

8. Current liabilities are best defined as those obligations

A. The liquidation of which will require the use of resources properly classifiable as current assets within the next operating cycle or 1 year, whichever is longer.

B. The liquidation of which will require the use of cash or increase current liabilities within the next operating cycle or 1 year, whichever is longer.

C. The liquidation of which is reasonably expected to require the use of current assets or the creation of other current liabilities within the next operating cycle or 1 year, whichever is longer.

D. Involving commitments made within the next operating cycle or 1 year, whichever is longer.

Answer (C) is correct. *(Publisher, adapted)*
REQUIRED: The correct description of current liabilities.
DISCUSSION: Current liabilities are obligations the liquidation of which is reasonably expected to require the use of existing resources properly classifiable as current assets or the creation of other current liabilities during the next operating cycle or year, whichever is longer. Current liabilities also include (1) obligations that by their terms are or will be due on demand within 1 year (or the operating cycle, if longer) and (2) obligations that are or will be callable by the creditor because of a violation of a debt covenant at the balance sheet date.
Answer (A) is incorrect. Liabilities also are current if their liquidation requires creation of other current liabilities. Answer (B) is incorrect. Liabilities are current if they are settled with any current assets, not just cash. Answer (D) is incorrect. Commitments made during the longer of the next year or the operating cycle may not even be liabilities at the balance sheet date.

9. Which of the following items enter into the determination of working capital?

A. Inventory of finished products that as of the balance sheet date has been held by a manufacturer for 1 year of a 3-year aging cycle.

B. Cash value of life insurance policies pledged as collateral against 90-day bank notes.

C. Cash held by an investment banker to be used to acquire in the open market an additional 25% of a 55%-owned subsidiary.

D. U.S. Treasury bills maturing 60 days after the balance sheet date, the proceeds of which, by direction of the board of directors, will be used to retire long-term debts.

Answer (A) is correct. *(Publisher, adapted)*
REQUIRED: The item that is considered part of working capital.
DISCUSSION: Working capital is the excess of current assets over current liabilities. An asset is current if it is reasonably expected to be realized in cash, sold, or consumed during the longer of 1 year or the normal operating cycle of the business. The operating cycle is the average time elapsing between the acquisition of materials or services entering into the earning process and the final cash realization. If a manufacturer's inventory must undergo a 3-year aging process before it can be sold, the inventory should be classified as a current asset because it will be sold during the current operating cycle.
Answer (B) is incorrect. The cash surrender value of life insurance policies is a long-term investment. Answer (C) is incorrect. Cash is not a current asset if it is restricted to purchase noncurrent assets. Answer (D) is incorrect. Treasury bills are not current assets if they are restricted to pay long-term debts.

10. A service company's working capital at the beginning of May of the current year was $70,000. The following transactions occurred during May:

Performed services on account	$30,000
Purchased supplies on account	5,000
Consumed supplies	4,000
Purchased office equipment for cash	2,000
Paid short-term bank loan	6,500
Paid salaries	10,000
Accrued salaries	3,500

What is the amount of working capital at the end of May?

A. $80,500

B. $78,500

C. $50,500

D. $47,500

Answer (A) is correct. *(CIA, adapted)*
REQUIRED: The amount of working capital.
DISCUSSION: Working capital is the excess of total current assets (CA) over total current liabilities (CL). Thus, working capital at the end of May equals $80,500 computed as follows:

		CA*	CL*
Beginning working capital	$70,000		
Performed services on account	30,000	I	N
Purchased supplies on account	--	I	I
Consumed supplies	(4,000)	D	N
Purchased office equipment	(2,000)	D	N
Paid short-term bank loan	--	D	D
Paid salaries	(10,000)	D	N
Accrued salaries	(3,500)	N	I
Working capital, end of January	$80,500		

* N = no effect; I = increase; D = decrease

Answer (B) is incorrect. This amount does not include the consumed supplies, the cash purchase of office equipment, and the accrued salaries, and it includes the supplies purchased on account and the repayment of the short-term bank loan. Answer (C) is incorrect. This amount does not include the services performed on account. Answer (D) is incorrect. This amount does not include the services performed on account and accrued salaries and includes the repayment of short-term loan.

11. Comparative balance sheets for a company are presented below:

Assets	12/31/Yr 2	12/31/Yr 1
Cash	$ 35,000	$ 30,000
Accounts receivable	80,000	75,000
Inventory	230,000	240,000
Equipment	620,000	600,000
Accumulated depreciation	(220,000)	(200,000)
Intangibles	150,000	140,000
Total assets	$895,000	$885,000

Liabilities and equity		
Accounts payable	$ 50,000	$ 60,000
Taxes payable	30,000	25,000
Salaries payable	55,000	70,000
Bonds payable (due Year 5)	400,000	400,000
Discount on bonds payable	(4,000)	(5,000)
Common stock	270,000	250,000
Retained earnings	94,000	85,000
Total liabilities and equity	$895,000	$885,000

What is the increase in working capital for the year ended December 31, Year 2?

A. $5,000

B. $10,000

C. $20,000

D. $29,000

Answer (C) is correct. *(CIA, adapted)*
REQUIRED: The increase in working capital for the current year.
DISCUSSION: Working capital is the excess of current assets over current liabilities. The change in working capital is equal to the aggregate change in those accounts classified as current assets and current liabilities. Increases in current assets and decreases in current liabilities increase (are sources of) working capital. Decreases in current assets and increases in current liabilities decrease (are uses of) working capital. The change in working capital for the year is presented below:

Working Capital Accounts	Increase (Decrease)
Cash	$ 5,000
Accounts receivable	5,000
Inventory	(10,000)
Accounts payable	10,000
Taxes payable	(5,000)
Salaries payable	15,000
Increase in working capital	$20,000

Answer (A) is incorrect. This amount does not include the change in salaries payable. Answer (B) is incorrect. This amount is the increase in total assets. Answer (D) is incorrect. This amount is the increase in working capital plus the increase in retained earnings.

5.2 Cash

12. The objective of a petty cash system is to

A. Facilitate office payment of small, miscellaneous items.

B. Cash checks for employees.

C. Account for cash sales.

D. Account for all cash receipts and disbursements.

Answer (A) is correct. *(Publisher, adapted)*
REQUIRED: The objective of a petty cash system.
DISCUSSION: In a petty cash system, a specific amount of money, e.g., $1,000, is set aside in the care of a petty cash custodian to pay office expenses that are too small to pay by check or to record in the accounting system as they occur. The entry is to debit petty cash and to credit cash. Periodically, the fund is reimbursed for all expenditures based on expense receipts, and journal entries are made to reflect the transactions. However, entries are made to the petty cash account only to establish the fund, to change its amount, or to adjust the balance if it has not been reimbursed at year end.
Answer (B) is incorrect. If necessary, a separate check-cashing fund should be established with daily bank deposits of checks cashed. Answer (C) is incorrect. Petty cash systems are for cash disbursements, not cash sales. Answer (D) is incorrect. Petty cash systems are for cash disbursements, not cash receipts.

13. Usually, if the petty cash fund is not reimbursed just prior to year end and an appropriate adjusting entry is not made,

A. A complete audit is necessary.

B. The petty cash account should be returned to the company cashier.

C. Expenses will be overstated and cash will be understated.

D. Cash will be overstated and expenses understated.

Answer (D) is correct. *(Publisher, adapted)*
REQUIRED: The effect of not reimbursing the petty cash fund prior to year end and not making the appropriate adjusting entry.
DISCUSSION: When the petty cash fund is established, petty cash is debited and cash credited. As monies are expended, expense receipts are obtained. The petty cash fund consists of the cash and expense receipts. Upon reimbursement of the petty cash fund, the various expenses are debited, and cash is credited. If the petty cash fund is not reimbursed at year end and an adjusting entry debiting expenses and crediting cash is not made, the cash account will be overstated and expenses understated because petty cash is a component of the cash account.
Answer (A) is incorrect. Complete audits are usually undertaken only if fraud is suspected. Petty cash is ordinarily not material. Answer (B) is incorrect. The petty cash cannot be returned to the cashier. At least some of the cash will usually have been expended. Answer (C) is incorrect. Expenses will be understated and cash overstated.

14. On January 1, a company establishes a petty cash account and designates one employee as petty cash custodian. The original amount included in the petty cash fund is $500, and it will be used to make small cash disbursements. The fund will be replenished on the first of each month, after the petty cash custodian presents receipts for disbursements to the general cashier. The following disbursements are made in January:

Office supplies	$127
Postage	83
Entertainment	84

The balance in the petty cash box at the end of January is $196.

The entry required at the end of January is

A.
Office supplies expense	$127
Postage expense	83
Entertainment expense	84
Cash	$294

B.
Office supplies expense	$127
Postage expense	83
Entertainment expense	84
Petty cash	$294

C.
Office supplies expense	$127
Postage expense	83
Entertainment expense	84
Cash over and short	10
Cash	$304

D.
Office supplies expense	$127
Postage expense	83
Entertainment expense	84
Cash	$284
Cash over and short	10

Answer (C) is correct. *(CIA, adapted)*
REQUIRED: The entry for petty cash fund disbursements.
DISCUSSION: Each expense item is recognized, cash is credited for the total expenditures plus the cash shortage ($127 + $83 + $84 + $10 = $304), and the discrepancy is debited to the cash over and short account. The discrepancy is the original balance of the fund, minus total documented expenditures, minus the ending balance of the fund ($500 – $294 – $196 = $10).
Answer (A) is incorrect. This entry does not recognize that $10 is missing from the petty cash fund. Answer (B) is incorrect. This entry credits petty cash rather than cash and does not recognize that $10 is missing from the petty cash fund. Answer (D) is incorrect. This entry credits the cash account for the wrong amount ($284 rather than $304) and credits the cash over and short account rather than debiting it.

15. Nefertiti Corporation had the following transactions in its first year of operations:

Sales (90% collected in first year)	$1,500,000
Bad debt write-offs	60,000
Disbursements for costs and expenses	1,200,000
Disbursements for income taxes	90,000
Purchases of fixed assets	400,000
Depreciation on fixed assets	80,000
Proceeds from issuance of common stock	500,000
Proceeds from short-term borrowings	100,000
Payments on short-term borrowings	50,000

What is the cash balance at the end of the first year?

A. $150,000

B. $170,000

C. $210,000

D. $280,000

Answer (C) is correct. *(CPA, adapted)*
REQUIRED: The cash balance at year end.
DISCUSSION: The cash balance may be determined by setting up a T account and appropriately debiting or crediting the account for each of the transactions listed. The beginning balance is $0 for the first year of operations. The sales collections result in a debit of $1,350,000 ($1,500,000 × 90%). The bad debt write-offs and depreciation on fixed assets are not cash transactions. The disbursements for costs and expenses, taxes, fixed assets, and debt service are credits. The proceeds from stock and short-term borrowings are debits. Thus, the account has a year-end debit balance of $210,000.

Cash (in 000s)

Sales	$1,350	$1,200	Disbursements
Stock	500	90	Taxes
Loan	100	400	FA
		50	Loan
	$ 210		

Answer (A) is incorrect. This amount results from a credit to the cash account for the bad debt write-offs. Answer (B) is incorrect. This amount results from debiting bad debt write-offs and not debiting proceeds from short-term borrowings to cash. Answer (D) is incorrect. This amount incorrectly debits cash for 100% of sales for the year and credits cash for depreciation on fixed assets.

16. Bank reconciliations are usually prepared on a monthly basis upon receipt of the bank statement to identify either bank errors or items that need to be adjusted on the depositor's books. The adjustments should be made for

A. Deposits in transit and outstanding checks.

B. All items except deposits in transit, outstanding checks, and bank errors.

C. Deposits in transit, outstanding checks, and bank errors.

D. All items except bank errors, NSF checks, outstanding checks, and deposits in transit.

Answer (B) is correct. *(Publisher, adapted)*
REQUIRED: The adjustments made as a result of a bank reconciliation.
DISCUSSION: Deposits in transit and outstanding checks are reconciling items that have no effect on the correctness of either the depositor's or the bank's accounting records. They reflect a timing difference between the two sets of books as to when cash receipts and disbursements are recognized. Thus, they require no adjustment by the bank or the depositor. Bank errors must be corrected by the bank, not the depositor. All other items must be adjusted on the depositor's books.
Answer (A) is incorrect. Deposits in transit and outstanding checks do not require adjustment on either the bank's or depositor's books. Answer (C) is incorrect. Deposits in transit and outstanding checks do not require adjustment on either the bank's or depositor's books. Answer (D) is incorrect. NSF checks require a debit to a receivable and a credit to cash on the depositor's books.

17. Hilltop Co.'s monthly bank statement shows a balance of $54,200. Reconciliation of the statement with company books reveals the following information:

Bank service charge	$ 10
Insufficient funds check	650
Checks outstanding	1,500
Deposits in transit	350
Check deposited by Hilltop and cleared by the bank for $125, but improperly recorded by Hilltop as $152	

What is the net cash balance after the reconciliation?

A. $52,363

B. $53,023

C. $53,050

D. $53,077

Answer (C) is correct. *(CPA, adapted)*
REQUIRED: The net cash balance after the reconciliation.
DISCUSSION: The bank balance is given ($54,200). The procedure is to adjust this amount for reconciling items. The bank balance includes the effects of the NSF check and the service charge. Thus, the reconciling adjustments are for the checks that have not yet cleared the bank and deposits in transit.

Bank balance	$54,200
Checks outstanding	(1,500)
Deposits in transit	350
True balance	$53,050

The error by Hilltop affects only the reconciliation from its book balance to the true balance.
Answer (A) is incorrect. The amount of $52,363 results from subtracting the service charge, NSF check, and recording error. Answer (B) is incorrect. The amount of $53,023 results from subtracting the recording error. Answer (D) is incorrect. The amount of $53,077 results from adding the recording error.

18. Piquet Corp.'s checkbook balance on December 31, Year 1, was $5,000. In addition, Piquet held the following items in its safe on that date:

Check payable to Piquet Corp., dated January 2, Year 2, in payment of a sale made in December Year 1, not included in December 31 checkbook balance.	$1,000
Check payable to Piquet Corp., deposited December 15 and included in December 31 checkbook balance, but returned by Bank on December 30 stamped "NSF." The check was redeposited on January 2, Year 2, and cleared on January 9.	600
Check drawn on Piquet Corp.'s account, payable to a vendor, dated and recorded in Piquet's books on December 31 but not mailed until January 10, Year 2.	700

The proper amount to be shown as cash on Piquet's balance sheet at December 31, Year 1, is

A. $5,100

B. $5,700

C. $5,400

D. $6,100

Answer (A) is correct. *(CPA, adapted)*
REQUIRED: The amount to be recorded as cash on the year-end balance sheet.
DISCUSSION: The December 31 checkbook balance is $5,000. The $1,000 check dated 1/2/Year 2 is properly not included in this balance because it is not negotiable at year end. The $600 NSF check should not be included in cash because it is a receivable. The $700 check that was not mailed until January 10 should be added to the balance. This predated check is still within the control of the company and should not decrease the cash account. Consequently, the cash balance to be reported on the 12/31/Year 1 balance sheet is $5,100.

Balance per checkbook	$5,000
Add: Predated check	700
Deduct: NSF check	(600)
Cash balance 12/31/Year 1	$5,100

Answer (B) is incorrect. The amount of $5,700 does not include the deduction for the NSF check. Answer (C) is incorrect. The amount of $5,400 includes the postdated check but not the predated check. Answer (D) is incorrect. The amount of $6,100 includes the postdated check.

19. Puddie Company maintains two checking accounts. A special account is used for the weekly payroll only, and the general account is used for all other disbursements. Every week, a check in the amount of the net payroll is drawn on the general account and deposited in the payroll account. The company maintains a $10,000 minimum balance in the payroll account. On a monthly bank reconciliation, the payroll account should

A. Show a zero balance per the bank statement.

B. Show a $10,000 balance per the bank statement.

C. Reconcile to $10,000.

D. Be reconciled jointly with the general account in a single reconciliation.

Answer (C) is correct. *(CPA, adapted)*
REQUIRED: The true statement concerning the monthly bank reconciliation of the payroll account.
DISCUSSION: Because a minimum balance of $10,000 is maintained, the check drawn on the general account is deposited to the special account before any payroll checks are written. The balance in the special account recorded by the bank, minus any outstanding checks, plus any bank charges not yet recorded on the company's books should equal $10,000.
Answer (A) is incorrect. The balance per bank statement should be equal to at least $10,000, less any bank charges.
Answer (B) is incorrect. The balance per bank statement should be equal to $10,000, plus the amount of any outstanding checks, minus any bank charges not recorded in the company's books.
Answer (D) is incorrect. Each checking account reflected in the formal accounting system should be separately reconciled with the related bank statement.

20. The following information is shown in the accounting records of a company:

Balances as of January 1, Year 1

Cash	$62,000
Merchandise inventory	86,000
Accounts receivable	67,000
Accounts payable	53,000

Balances as of December 31, Year 1

Merchandise inventory	$78,000
Accounts receivable	91,000
Accounts payable	48,000

Total sales and cost of goods sold for Year 1 were $798,000 and $583,000, respectively. All sales and all merchandise purchases were made on credit. Various operating expenses of $107,000 were paid in cash. Assume that there were no other pertinent transactions. The cash balance on December 31, Year 1, is

A. $108,000

B. $149,000

C. $256,000

D. $305,000

Answer (B) is correct. *(CIA, adapted)*
REQUIRED: The cash balance at year end.
DISCUSSION: Cash collected from customers equals $774,000 ($798,000 credit sales – $24,000 increase in A/R). The amount of credit purchases is $575,000 ($583,000 COGS – $8,000 decrease in inventory). Disbursements to suppliers totaled $580,000 ($575,000 Pur. + $5,000 decrease in A/P). The cash collected is added to the beginning balance in the cash account. The disbursements to suppliers and for operating expenses are subtracted to arrive at an ending cash balance of $149,000.

Accounts Receivable			
Beg. Bal.	$ 67,000		
Sales	798,000	$774,000	Collections
End. Bal.	$ 91,000		

Merchandise Inventory			
Beg. Bal.	$ 86,000		
Purchases	575,000	$583,000	COGS
End. Bal.	$ 78,000		

Accounts Payable			
		$ 53,000	Beg. Bal.
Disburse.	$580,000	575,000	Purchases
		$ 48,000	End. Bal.

Cash			
Beg. Bal.	$ 62,000		
Collections	774,000	$580,000	Disb.–Merchandise
		107,000	Disb.–Operating Exps.
End. Bal.	$149,000		

Answer (A) is incorrect. This amount is the excess of total sales over cost of goods sold and operating expenses.
Answer (C) is incorrect. This amount does not include a credit to cash for the operating expenses. Answer (D) is incorrect. This amount appears to be a random number.

21. An entity is reconciling its bank statement with internal records. The cash balance per the bank statement is $20,000, while the cash balance per the entity's books is $18,000. There are $2,000 of bank charges not yet recorded, $3,000 of outstanding checks, $5,000 of deposits in transit, and $6,000 of bank credits and collections not yet recorded in the entity's books. If there are no bank or book errors, what is the entity's actual cash balance?

A. $20,000

B. $22,000

C. $24,000

D. $29,000

Answer (B) is correct. *(CIA, adapted)*
REQUIRED: The cash balance given no bank or book errors.
DISCUSSION: The balance per bank is $20,000, which includes the bank charges, credits, and collections not recorded on the books. Adding deposits in transit and subtracting outstanding checks results in an actual cash balance of $22,000 ($20,000 + $5,000 – $3,000). This amount equals the adjusted balance per the entity's books ($18,000 + $6,000 of bank credits and collections not recorded in the books – $2,000 of bank charges).
Answer (A) is incorrect. The amount of $20,000 is the balance per bank before the reconciliation. Answer (C) is incorrect. The amount of $24,000 equals the balance per the entity's books, plus bank credits and collections. Answer (D) is incorrect. The amount of $29,000 results from adding outstanding checks, outstanding bank credits, and collections to the balance per bank.

22. A company shows a cash balance of $35,000 on its bank statement dated November 1. As of November 1, there are $11,000 of outstanding checks and $7,500 of deposits in transit. The cash balance on the company books as of November 1 is

A. $24,000

B. $31,500

C. $42,500

D. $53,500

Answer (B) is correct. *(CIA, adapted)*
REQUIRED: The cash balance on the company books.
DISCUSSION: The $35,000 cash balance on the November 1 bank statement does not reflect either the $11,000 of outstanding checks or the $7,500 of deposits in transit. Adding the deposits in transit and subtracting the outstanding checks result in a cash balance per books of $31,500 ($35,000 + $7,500 – $11,000).
Answer (A) is incorrect. The amount of $24,000 does not include the $7,500 of deposits in transit. Answer (C) is incorrect. The amount of $42,500 does not include the $11,000 of outstanding checks. Answer (D) is incorrect. The amount of $53,500 results from adding the $11,000 of outstanding checks and the $7,500 of deposits in transit.

23. In preparing its bank reconciliation at December 31, Year 1, Rhein Company has available the following data:

Balance per bank statement, 12/31/Year 1	$38,075
Deposit in transit, 12/31/Year 1	5,200
Outstanding checks, 12/31/Year 1	6,750
Amount erroneously credited by bank to Rhein's account, 12/28/Year 1	400
Bank service charges for December	75

Rhein's adjusted cash in bank balance at December 31, Year 1, is

A. $36,525

B. $36,450

C. $36,125

D. $36,050

Answer (C) is correct. *(CPA, adapted)*
REQUIRED: The adjusted cash in bank balance.
DISCUSSION: The balance per bank statement at December 31 is $38,075. As indicated below, the $5,200 deposit in transit should be added to this amount. The $6,750 in outstanding checks and the $400 that was erroneously credited by the bank to Rhein's account should be deducted. The $75 bank service charges are already included in the December 31 bank statement balance. The adjusted cash in bank balance at December 31 is $36,125.

Balance per statement	$38,075
Add: Deposit in transit	5,200
Deduct: Outstanding checks	(6,750)
Bank error	(400)
Adjusted cash in bank	$36,125

Answer (A) is incorrect. The amount of $36,525 does not include the deduction for the bank error. Answer (B) is incorrect. The amount of $36,450 does not include the deduction for the bank error and incorrectly includes the bank service charges. Answer (D) is incorrect. The amount of $36,050 incorrectly includes the deduction for bank service charges.

5.3 Accounts Receivable

Questions 24 and 25 are based on the following
information. ECG Company recorded two sales on
March 1 of $20,000 and $30,000 under credit terms
of 3/10, n/30. Payment for the $20,000 sale was
received March 10. Payment for the $30,000 sale
was received on March 25.

24. Under the gross method and the net method, net
sales in the March income statement should appear
as which of the following amounts?

	Gross Method	Net Method
A.	$48,500	$48,500
B.	$48,500	$49,400
C.	$49,400	$48,500
D.	$49,400	$49,400

Answer (C) is correct. *(Publisher, adapted)*
REQUIRED: The net sales under the gross and the net
methods.
DISCUSSION: The gross method accounts for credit sales
and receivables at their face amount. If a discount is taken, a
sales discount is recorded and classified as an offset to sales in
the income statement to yield net sales. The expression "3/10,
n/30" means that a 3% discount may be taken if payment is
made within 10 days of the invoice. The $20,000 payment was
received during this period. The $30,000 payment was not.
Under the gross method, a $600 sales discount offsets the
$50,000 of gross sales to give net sales of $49,400. The net
method records credit sales and receivables net of the applicable
discount. If the payment is not received during the discount
period, an other revenue account, such as sales discounts
forfeited, is credited at the end of the discount period or when the
payment is received. Consequently, both sales would be
recorded net of discount ($48,500), and $900 (3% of $30,000)
would be recorded as an interest income item. The gross and
net methods have the same income effect. The difference is in
how they present items in the income statement.
Answer (A) is incorrect. The gross method net sales of
$48,500 includes the $900 discount lost. Answer (B) is
incorrect. The net sales amounts should be reversed.
Answer (D) is incorrect. The net method records sales and
receivables net of all applicable discounts.

25. What are gross sales for the month of March?

	Gross Method	Net Method
A.	$50,000	$50,000
B.	$50,000	$48,500
C.	$49,400	$48,500
D.	$48,500	$50,000

Answer (B) is correct. *(Publisher, adapted)*
REQUIRED: The gross sales under the gross and the net
methods.
DISCUSSION: The gross method records March sales at
the gross amount ($50,000). Because the $20,000 receivable
was paid within the discount period, sales discount is debited for
$600 at the payment date. The net method records March sales
at the net amount ($48,500, or $50,000 minus 3% of $50,000).
The $30,000 receivable was not paid within the discount period,
and the following entry must also be made:

Accounts receivable $900
    Sales discounts forfeited $900

Answer (A) is incorrect. The net method records sales net of
all applicable discounts. Answer (C) is incorrect. The gross
method records sales at the gross amount. Answer (D) is
incorrect. The gross sales amounts should be reversed.

26. Which of the following statements is not valid in determining balance sheet disclosure of accounts receivable?

    A. Accounts receivable should be identified on the balance sheet as pledged if they are used as security for a loan even though the loan is shown on the same balance sheet as a liability.

    B. That portion of installment accounts receivable from customers coming due more than 12 months from the balance sheet date usually would be excluded from current assets.

    C. Allowances may be deducted from the accounts receivable for discounts, returns, and adjustments to be made in the future on accounts shown in the current balance sheet.

    D. Trade receivables are best shown separately from nontrade receivables when amounts of each are material.

Answer (B) is correct. *(CPA, adapted)*
    REQUIRED: The invalid statement about balance sheet disclosure of accounts receivable.
    DISCUSSION: Current assets are reasonably expected to be realized in cash or to be sold or consumed within 12 months or the operating cycle of the business, whichever is longer. If the ordinary trade receivables of the business fall due more than 12 months from the balance sheet date, the operating cycle is clearly longer than 12 months, and the trade receivables should be included in current assets.
    Answer (A) is incorrect. Accounts receivable pledged or used as security for a loan should be presented with relevant information disclosed in a note or in a parenthetical explanation. Answer (C) is incorrect. Various allowance or valuation accounts may be set up as contra accounts to receivables to arrive at the net realizable value of receivables in the balance sheet. Allowances may be made for discounts granted to customers, returned merchandise, collection expenses, and uncollectible accounts. Answer (D) is incorrect. If the different categories of receivables are material in amount, they should be segregated in the balance sheet.

27. On a balance sheet, what is the preferable presentation of notes receivable or accounts receivable from officers, employees, or affiliated companies?

    A. As trade notes and accounts receivable if they otherwise qualify as current assets.

    B. As assets but separately from other receivables.

    C. As offsets to capital.

    D. By means of disclosure in the notes.

Answer (B) is correct. *(CPA, adapted)*
    REQUIRED: The preferable balance sheet presentation of receivables from officers, employees, or affiliated companies.
    DISCUSSION: The basic principle is that, if the different categories of receivables are material in amount, they should be presented separately in the balance sheet. Receivables from officers, employees, or affiliated companies are assets and should be presented in the balance sheet as such. If these receivables are material, they should be segregated from other classifications of receivables.
    Answer (A) is incorrect. Such receivables, if material, should be separately classified even though they qualify as current assets. Answer (C) is incorrect. Such receivables are assets and should not be presented in the equity section. Answer (D) is incorrect. Such receivables are assets that should be included in the body of the balance sheet. Presentation by note disclosure would understate financial position.

28. Henry Stores, Inc., had sales of $2,000,000 during December. Experience has shown that merchandise equaling 7% of sales will be returned within 30 days and an additional 3% will be returned within 90 days. Returned merchandise is readily resalable. In addition, merchandise equaling 15% of sales will be exchanged for merchandise of equal or greater value. What amount should Henry report for net sales in its income statement for the month of December?

    A. $1,800,000

    B. $1,700,000

    C. $1,560,000

    D. $1,500,000

Answer (A) is correct. *(CPA, adapted)*
    REQUIRED: The amount of net sales.
    DISCUSSION: Net sales equal gross sales minus net returns and allowances. No adjustments are made for anticipated exchanges for merchandise of equal or greater value. Hence, net sales equal $1,800,000 [$2,000,000 – ($2,000,000 × 10%)].
    Answer (B) is incorrect. This amount equals sales minus 15% of sales. Answer (C) is incorrect. This amount equals sales, minus 15% of sales, minus 7% of sales. Answer (D) is incorrect. This amount equals net sales minus 15% of sales.

29. Clarion, Inc., sells to wholesalers on terms of 2/15, net 30. Clarion has no cash sales, but 50% of Clarion's customers take advantage of the discount. Clarion uses the gross method of recording sales and trade receivables. An analysis of Clarion's trade receivables balances at December 31 revealed the following:

Age	Amount	Collectible
0-15 days	$200,000	100%
16-30 days	120,000	95%
31-60 days	10,000	90%
Over 60 days	5,000	$500
	$335,000	

In its December 31 balance sheet, what amount should Clarion report for allowance for discounts?

A. $2,000

B. $3,240

C. $3,350

D. $4,000

Answer (A) is correct. *(CPA, adapted)*
REQUIRED: The amount to be reported as an allowance for discounts.
DISCUSSION: The allowance for discounts should include an estimate of the expected discount based on the eligible receivables. According to the analysis, receivables equal to $200,000 are still eligible. Based on past experience, 50% of the customers take advantage of the discount. Thus, the allowance should be $2,000 [$200,000 × 50% × 2% (the discount percentage)].
Answer (B) is incorrect. An allowance for discounts of $3,240 is based on two assumptions: (1) 50% of all collectible amounts not over 60 days of age are eligible, and (2) 100% of collectible amounts over 60 days of age are eligible. Answer (C) is incorrect. The amount of $3,350 assumes that 50% of the total gross receivables are eligible for the discount. Answer (D) is incorrect. The amount of $4,000 assumes 100% of eligible customers will take the discount.

30. Monte Company's usual sales terms are net 60 days, FOB shipping point. Sales, net of returns and allowances, totaled $2,300,000 for the year ended December 31, Year 1, before year-end adjustment. Additional data are as follows:

- On December 27, Year 1, Monte authorized a customer to return, for full credit, goods shipped and billed at $50,000 on December 15, Year 1. The returned goods were received by Monte on January 4, Year 2, and a $50,000 credit memo was issued on the same date.

- Goods with an invoice amount of $80,000 were billed to a customer on January 3, Year 2. The goods were shipped on December 31, Year 1.

- On January 5, Year 2, a customer notified Monte that goods billed and shipped on December 23, Year 1, were lost in transit. The invoice amount was $100,000.

Monte's adjusted net sales for Year 1 should be

A. $2,330,000

B. $2,280,000

C. $2,250,000

D. $2,230,000

Answer (A) is correct. *(CPA, adapted)*
REQUIRED: The adjusted net sales for the year.
DISCUSSION: Prior to adjustment, sales net of returns and allowances were $2,300,000. The goods returned ($50,000) should be recorded in the year in which the return was authorized (Year 1) rather than the year in which the credit memo was issued (Year 2). The $80,000 item billed in January should be added to the December sales because the shipment occurred in December. The company's terms are FOB shipping point, which means title and risk of loss normally pass to the buyer at the time and place of shipment. For this reason, the goods lost in transit are not an adjustment to sales because the buyer held title and bore the risk of loss at the point of shipment. Thus, Monte's adjusted net sales for Year 1 should be $2,330,000 ($2,300,000 – $50,000 + $80,000).
Answer (B) is incorrect. The amount of $2,280,000 incorrectly deducts the $100,000 of goods lost in transit and does not include the deduction for the returned goods. Answer (C) is incorrect. The amount of $2,250,000 does not include the $80,000 item shipped in December. Answer (D) is incorrect. The amount of $2,230,000 results from improperly subtracting the $100,000 of goods lost in transit.

5.4 Accounts Receivable – Measurement

31. When may an asset valuation allowance, such as the allowance for uncollectible accounts, be shown on the credit side of the balance sheet?

A. Never.

B. When they have to be repaid.

C. In the airline industry.

D. When it exceeds 10% of the accounts receivable balance.

Answer (A) is correct. *(Publisher, adapted)*
REQUIRED: The circumstances in which an asset valuation allowance may be shown on the credit side of the balance sheet.
DISCUSSION: All allowance accounts must be displayed contra to the related asset accounts. Thus, they are never reported as liabilities or elsewhere on the credit side of the balance sheet. They are subtracted from the related assets (or asset groups), with proper disclosure.
Answer (B) is incorrect. Valuation accounts are not repaid. Answer (C) is incorrect. There are no industry exceptions for presentation of asset valuation accounts. Answer (D) is incorrect. The materiality of the account does not affect its classification as a contra asset.

32. When the allowance method of recognizing uncollectible accounts is used, the entries at the time of collection of a small account previously written off

A. Increase the allowance for uncollectible accounts.

B. Increase net income.

C. Decrease the allowance for uncollectible accounts.

D. Have no effect on the allowance for uncollectible accounts.

Answer (A) is correct. *(CPA, adapted)*
REQUIRED: The effect of the collection of an account previously written off.
DISCUSSION: When an account receivable is written off, both accounts receivable and the allowance for uncollectible accounts are decreased. When an account previously written off is collected, the account must be reinstated by increasing both accounts receivable and the allowance. Accounts receivable is then decreased by the amount of cash collected.
Answer (B) is incorrect. Neither write-off nor reinstatement and collection affects bad debt expense or net income. Answer (C) is incorrect. The allowance is increased when a previously written-off account is collected. Answer (D) is incorrect. There is an effect on the allowance.

33. When the allowance method of recognizing uncollectible accounts is used, the entry to record the write-off of a specific account

A. Decreases both accounts receivable and the allowance for uncollectible accounts.

B. Decreases accounts receivable and increases the allowance for uncollectible accounts.

C. Increases the allowance for uncollectible accounts and decreases net income.

D. Decreases both accounts receivable and net income.

Answer (A) is correct. *(CPA, adapted)*
REQUIRED: The effect of the write-off of a specific uncollectible account.
DISCUSSION: The entry to record bad debt expense under the allowance method is to debit bad debt expense and credit the allowance account. When a specific account is then written off, the allowance is debited and accounts receivable credited. Net income is affected when bad debt expense is recognized, not at the time of the write-off. Because accounts receivable and the allowance account are decreased by the same amount, a write-off of an account also has no effect on the net amount of accounts receivable.
Answer (B) is incorrect. The allowance for uncollectible accounts decreases. Answer (C) is incorrect. The allowance for uncollectible accounts decreases, and net income is not affected. Answer (D) is incorrect. Net income is not affected.

34. A method of estimating uncollectible accounts that emphasizes asset valuation rather than income measurement is the allowance method based on

A. Aging the receivables.

B. Direct write-offs.

C. Gross sales.

D. Credit sales minus returns and allowances.

Answer (A) is correct. *(CPA, adapted)*
REQUIRED: The method of estimating uncollectible accounts that emphasizes asset valuation.
DISCUSSION: Under the allowance method, accounts are estimated in two ways. One method emphasizes asset valuation. The other emphasizes income measurement. The method that emphasizes asset valuation is based on an aging of the receivables to determine the balance in the allowance for uncollectible accounts. Bad debt expense is the amount necessary to adjust the allowance account to this estimated balance. The method emphasizing the income statement recognizes bad debt expense as a percentage of credit sales. The corresponding credit is to the allowance for uncollectible accounts. Both methods are acceptable under GAAP.
Answer (B) is incorrect. The direct write-off method is not a means of estimation. Answer (C) is incorrect. An estimate based on gross sales focuses on the income measurement. Answer (D) is incorrect. An estimate based on credit sales focuses on the income measurement.

35. Which method of recording uncollectible accounts expense is consistent with accrual accounting?

	Allowance	Direct Write-Off
A.	Yes	Yes
B.	Yes	No
C.	No	Yes
D.	No	No

Answer (B) is correct. *(CPA, adapted)*
REQUIRED: The method(s) of recording uncollectible accounts expense consistent with accrual accounting.
DISCUSSION: Accrual accounting records the financial effects of transactions and other events and circumstances when they occur, not when their cash effects occur. Thus, the allowance method is consistent with accrual accounting because it recognizes bad debt expense when sales transactions occur, not when a final determination about their cash effects (the extent of uncollectibility) is made. The direct write-off method is not consistent with accrual accounting because recognition of bad debt expense is deferred until a final determination is made about the cash collectible from a particular receivable.
Answer (A) is incorrect. The direct write-off method is not consistent with accrual accounting. Answer (C) is incorrect. The allowance method is consistent with accrual accounting. The direct write-off method is not. Answer (D) is incorrect. The allowance method is consistent with accrual accounting.

36. William Co. determined that the net realizable value (NRV) of its accounts receivable at December 31, based on an aging of the receivables, was $650,000. Additional information is as follows:

Allowance for uncollectible accounts -- 1/1	$ 60,000
Uncollectible accounts written off during the year	36,000
Uncollectible accounts recovered during the year	4,000
Accounts receivable at 12/31	700,000

What is William's bad debt expense for the year?

A. $10,000

B. $22,000

C. $30,000

D. $42,000

Answer (B) is correct. *(CPA, adapted)*
REQUIRED: The bad debt expense.
DISCUSSION: The allowance for uncollectible accounts before year-end adjustment is $28,000 ($60,000 beginning balance – $36,000 write-offs + $4,000 recovered). The balance should be $50,000 ($700,000 year-end A/R – $650,000 NRV based on aging). Thus, the allowance account should be credited and bad debt expense debited for $22,000 ($50,000 desired balance – $28,000).
Answer (A) is incorrect. The amount of $10,000 is the difference between gross and net accounts receivable ($50,000) and the balance in the allowance account at the beginning of the year ($60,000). Answer (C) is incorrect. The amount of $30,000 equals $50,000 minus the difference between the $60,000 allowance and the $36,000 written off, reduced by the $4,000 recovered. Answer (D) is incorrect. The amount of $42,000 equals the $60,000 allowance, plus $36,000 written off, reduced by $4,000 recovered, minus $50,000.

37. The following information relates to Soward Co.'s accounts receivable for the year just ended:

Accounts receivable, 1/1	$1,300,000
Credit sales for the year	2,700,000
Sales returns for the year	75,000
Accounts written off during the year	40,000
Collections from customers during the year	2,150,000
Estimated future sales returns at 12/31	50,000
Estimated uncollectible accounts at 12/31	220,000

What amount should Soward report for gross accounts receivable, before allowances for sales returns and uncollectible accounts, at December 31?

A. $1,850,000

B. $1,775,000

C. $1,735,000

D. $1,465,000

Answer (C) is correct. *(CPA, adapted)*
REQUIRED: The year-end balance in gross accounts receivable.
DISCUSSION: The $1,735,000 ending balance in accounts receivable is equal to the $1,300,000 beginning debit balance, plus debits for $2,700,000 of credit sales, minus credits for $2,150,000 of collections, $40,000 of accounts written off, and $75,000 of sales returns. The $220,000 of estimated uncollectible receivables and the $50,000 of estimated sales returns are not relevant because they affect the allowance accounts but not gross accounts receivable.

Gross Accounts Receivable (in 000s)		
1/1	$1,300	$ 75 Sales returns
Credit sales	2,700	2,150 Collections
		40 Write-off
	$1,735	

Answer (A) is incorrect. The amount of $1,850,000 does not subtract write-offs and sales returns from accounts receivable. Answer (B) is incorrect. The amount of $1,775,000 does not subtract write-offs from accounts receivable. Answer (D) is incorrect. Estimated future sales returns and uncollectible accounts affect their respective allowance accounts, not gross accounts receivable.

38. Turner Co. estimates its uncollectible accounts expense to be 2% of credit sales. Turner's credit sales for the year were $1,000,000. During the year, Turner wrote off $18,000 of uncollectible accounts. Turner's allowance for uncollectible accounts had a $15,000 balance on January 1. In its December 31 income statement, what amount should Turner report as bad debt expense?

A. $23,000

B. $20,000

C. $18,000

D. $17,000

Answer (B) is correct. *(CPA, adapted)*
REQUIRED: The uncollectible accounts expense as a percentage of sales.
DISCUSSION: When bad debt expense is estimated on the basis of net credit sales, a cost (bad debt expense) is being directly associated with a revenue of the period (net credit sales). Thus, uncollectible accounts expense is $20,000 ($1,000,000 credit sales × 2%).
Answer (A) is incorrect. The amount of $23,000 assumes that $20,000 is the required ending balance in the allowance account (expense = write-offs + the change in the allowance). Answer (C) is incorrect. The amount of $18,000 equals the write-offs for the year. Answer (D) is incorrect. The amount of $17,000 is the ending balance in the allowance account.

39. The following information pertains to Eire Co.'s accounts receivable at December 31, Year 2:

Days Outstanding	Amount	Estimated % Uncollectible
0 - 60	$240,000	1%
61 - 20	180,000	2%
Over 120	200,000	6%
	$620,000	

During Year 2, Eire wrote off $14,000 in receivables and recovered $8,000 that was written off in prior years. Its December 31, Year 1, allowance for uncollectible accounts was $44,000. Under the aging method, what amount of allowance for uncollectible accounts should Eire report at December 31, Year 2?

A. $18,000

B. $20,000

C. $26,000

D. $38,000

Answer (A) is correct. *(CPA, adapted)*
REQUIRED: The allowance for uncollectible accounts under the aging method.
DISCUSSION: The aging schedule determines the allowance for uncollectible accounts based on year-end accounts receivable, their age, and their estimated collectibility. This year-end amount is $18,000 [($240,000 × 1%) + ($180,000 × 2%) + ($200,000 × 6%)].
Answer (B) is incorrect. The amount of $20,000 equals the beginning balance, plus the recovery, minus write-offs, minus the amount determined by the aging schedule ($44,000 + $8,000 – $14,000 – $18,000). Answer (C) is incorrect. The amount of $26,000 equals the beginning balance minus the amount determined by the aging schedule ($44,000 – $18,000). Answer (D) is incorrect. The amount of $38,000 equals the beginning balance, plus the recovery, minus write-offs ($44,000 + $8,000 – $14,000).

40. The following accounts were abstracted from Pika Co.'s unadjusted trial balance at December 31:

	Debit	Credit
Accounts receivable	$2,000,000	
Allowance for uncollectible accounts	16,000	
Net credit sales		$6,000,000

Pika estimates that 3% of the gross accounts receivable will become uncollectible. After adjustment at December 31, the allowance for uncollectible accounts should have a credit balance of

A. $180,000

B. $164,000

C. $44,000

D. $60,000

Answer (D) is correct. *(CPA, adapted)*
REQUIRED: The ending balance in the allowance for uncollectible accounts.
DISCUSSION: The allowance for uncollectible accounts at year end should have a credit balance of $60,000. This amount is equal to the $2,000,000 of accounts receivable multiplied by the 3% that is estimated to become uncollectible.
Answer (A) is incorrect. The amount of $180,000 is equal to 3% of net credit sales. Answer (B) is incorrect. The amount of $164,000 equals 3% of net credit sales minus the unadjusted balance in the allowance account. Answer (C) is incorrect. The amount of $44,000 equals 3% of accounts receivable minus the unadjusted balance in the allowance account.

41. An analysis and aging of Hom Company's accounts receivable at December 31 disclosed the following:

Accounts receivable	$850,000
Allowance for uncollectible accounts per books	50,000
Amounts deemed uncollectible	64,000

The net realizable value (NRV) of the accounts receivable at December 31 should be

A. $836,000

B. $800,000

C. $786,000

D. $736,000

Answer (C) is correct. *(CPA, adapted)*
REQUIRED: The NRV of accounts receivable.
DISCUSSION: The NRV of accounts receivable is equal to the $850,000 gross accounts receivable minus the $64,000 estimate of the accounts estimated to be uncollectible. The $50,000 balance in the allowance account is not used because it is an unadjusted balance.
Answer (A) is incorrect. This amount is the gross accounts receivable account, minus the amount deemed uncollectible, plus the allowance for uncollectible accounts. Answer (B) is incorrect. This amount is the gross accounts receivable account minus the allowance for uncollectible accounts. Answer (D) is incorrect. This amount is the gross accounts receivable account minus the allowance for uncollectible accounts and the amount deemed uncollectible.

5.5 Notes Receivable

42. How should unearned discounts, finance charges, and unearned interest included in the face amount of notes receivable be presented in the balance sheet?

A. As a deferred credit.

B. As deductions from the related receivables.

C. In the notes to the financial statements.

D. As a current liability.

Answer (B) is correct. *(Publisher, adapted)*
REQUIRED: The proper presentation of unearned discounts, finance charges, and unearned interest.
DISCUSSION: Unearned discounts (except for cash discounts, quantity discounts, etc.), finance charges, and unearned interest included in the face amount of notes receivable should be displayed contra to the face amounts of the related receivables in the balance sheet. Thus, a note receivable should be recorded at its net amount, that is, as a debit for the face amount and a credit for the unearned discount, finance charge, or unearned interest.
Answer (A) is incorrect. Unearned discounts, finance charges, and unearned interest are displayed as deductions from the related receivables, not as a deferred credit. Answer (C) is incorrect. Unearned discounts, finance charges, and unearned interest are displayed as deductions from the related receivables, not in the notes. Answer (D) is incorrect. Unearned discounts, finance charges, and unearned interest are displayed as deductions from the related receivables, not as a current liability.

43. On August 15, Benet Co. sold goods for which it received a note bearing the market rate of interest on that date. The 4-month note was dated July 15. Note principal, together with all interest, is due November 15. When the note was recorded on August 15, which of the following accounts increased?

A. Unearned discount.

B. Interest receivable.

C. Prepaid interest.

D. Interest revenue.

Answer (B) is correct. *(CPA, adapted)*
REQUIRED: The account that increased when the note was recorded.
DISCUSSION: Because the note bears interest at a market rate, its present value at the date of issuance is the face amount. Hence, the note should be recorded at its face amount, and interest receivable should be debited.
Answer (A) is incorrect. The note bears interest at the market rate. Thus, no discount from its face value is recorded. Answer (C) is incorrect. No prepayment of interest has been made. Answer (D) is incorrect. Interest revenue has not yet been earned.

44. United Refinery Company, a refiner of peanut oil, lent $500,000 to James Barter, a peanut farmer, interest free for 5 years. The day after the loan agreement, Barter guaranteed that United Refinery could purchase up to 1 million pounds of shucked peanuts per year for the next 6 years at a price 5¢ less per pound than the prevailing market price. Barter asked for nothing in return for this price concession. United should record the loan at

A. Its face amount with no recognition of interest income over the 5-year period.

B. A discount using the average cost of capital as the rate for imputing interest.

C. Its face amount with interest income recognized each year in the amount of the price concession realized during that year.

D. A discount equal to the expected value of the price concession granted.

Answer (D) is correct. *(Publisher, adapted)*
REQUIRED: The accounting for an interest-free loan related to an unstated right or privilege.
DISCUSSION: Even though the price concession was not explicitly part of the loan agreement, the economic reality is that the noninterest-bearing loan is partial consideration for the purchase of products at less than the prevailing market price. The expected value of the price concession should be the measure of the loan discount. It is the difference between the amount of the loan and the present value of the note. The discount should be recorded as a debit to prepaid purchases and a credit to discount on notes receivable. The prepaid asset will be written off proportionally to the purchases made (debit purchases, credit prepaid purchases) during the contract term. The discount should be amortized using the interest method as interest income over the 5-year life of the loan.
Answer (A) is incorrect. The economic substance of the transaction must be explicitly recognized in the accounts by recognizing the unstated right as an asset and a discount to the note receivable. Answer (B) is incorrect. The present value of the price concession should be used to discount the note. Answer (C) is incorrect. The discount on the note should be recognized as a direct deduction from the note receivable.

45. The Brown Company received a 2-year, $190,000 note on January 1, Year 1, in exchange for property it sold to Gray Company. According to the terms of the note, interest of 5% is payable annually on January 1, Year 2, and January 1, Year 3, when the face amount is also due. There was no established exchange price for the property. The prevailing rate of interest for a note of this type was 12% at the beginning of Year 1 and 14% at the beginning of Year 2. What interest rates should be used to calculate the amount of interest revenue from this transaction for the years ended December 31, Year 1 and Year 2, respectively?

A. 0% and 5%.

B. 5% and 5%.

C. 12% and 12%.

D. 12% and 14%.

Answer (C) is correct. *(CIA, adapted)*
REQUIRED: The interest rates used to calculate interest revenue for successive years if the prevailing rate changes.
DISCUSSION: When the nominal interest rate on a note is not equal to the prevailing market rate for this type of note, the face amount of the note is not equal to its fair value or present value. In this case, the present value of the note should be determined by discounting the $190,000 maturity amount and the $9,500 annual interest payments using an appropriately imputed rate of interest. Given that 12% was the prevailing rate of interest for a note of that type at the issuance date, 12% should be used to determine both the fair market value and the interest revenue during the life of the note, regardless of fluctuations in prevailing interest rates.
Answer (A) is incorrect. Five percent is the nominal rate. Zero percent is not appropriate given that the note states a rate and that a rate may be imputed. Answer (B) is incorrect. The market rate of interest at the issuance date (12%) should be used to calculate the amount of interest revenue. Answer (D) is incorrect. Fourteen percent was not the prevailing rate at the issuance date.

46. Holder Co. has an 8% note receivable dated June 30, Year 1, in the original amount of $300,000. Payments of $100,000 in principal plus accrued interest are due annually on July 1, Year 2, Year 3, and Year 4. In its June 30, Year 3, balance sheet, what amount should Holder report as a current asset for interest on the note receivable?

A. $0

B. $8,000

C. $16,000

D. $24,000

Answer (C) is correct. *(CPA, adapted)*
REQUIRED: The amount reported as a current asset for interest on a note receivable.
DISCUSSION: Current assets are those reasonably expected to be realized in cash, sold, or consumed during the longer of the operating cycle of a business or 1 year. Given that the date of the balance sheet is 6/30/Year 3, the interest to be paid on the next day, 7/1/Year 3, of $16,000 ($200,000 principal × 8% stated interest rate) should be classified as a current asset.
Answer (A) is incorrect. An interest amount of $16,000 is reported as a current asset. Answer (B) is incorrect. This amount is the interest to be earned in Year 4. Answer (D) is incorrect. This amount is the interest earned in Year 2.

47. On January 1, the Fulmar Company sold personal property to the Austin Company. The personal property had cost Fulmar $40,000. Fulmar frequently sells similar items of property for $44,000. Austin gave Fulmar a noninterest-bearing note payable in six equal annual installments of $10,000 with the first payment due beginning this December 31. Collection of the note is reasonably assured. A reasonable rate of interest for a note of this type is 10%. The present value of an annuity of $1 in arrears at 10% for six periods is 4.355. What amount of sales revenue from this transaction should be reported in Fulmar's income statement for the year of sale ended December 31?

A. $10,000

B. $40,000

C. $43,550

D. $44,000

Answer (D) is correct. *(CPA, adapted)*
REQUIRED: The amount of sales revenue to be reported in the income statement of the recipient of a noninterest-bearing note.
DISCUSSION: When a noninterest-bearing note is exchanged for property, the note, the sales price, and the cost of the property exchanged for the note should be recorded at the fair value of the property or at the market value of the note, whichever is more clearly determinable. Here, the $44,000 fair value of the property is clearly determinable because Fulmar frequently sells similar items for that amount. Consequently, $44,000 is the proper amount to be recorded as sales revenue from this transaction.
Answer (A) is incorrect. The amount of $10,000 is the annual installment. Answer (B) is incorrect. The amount of $40,000 is the original cost of the property. Answer (C) is incorrect. The amount of $43,550 is the present value of the note, but the fair value of the property is more clearly determinable.

48. A 90-day, 15% interest-bearing note receivable is sold to a bank after being held for 30 days. The proceeds are calculated using an 18% interest rate. The note receivable has been

	Discounted	Pledged
A.	No	Yes
B.	No	No
C.	Yes	No
D.	Yes	Yes

Answer (C) is correct. *(CPA, adapted)*
REQUIRED: The proper description of the sale of a note receivable.
DISCUSSION: A note receivable sold before maturity has been discounted. A pledge is a security transaction in which the collateral to secure a debt is held by the secured party. No security has been given in this case.

49. On November 1, Year 1, Love Co. discounted with recourse at 10% a 1-year, noninterest-bearing, $20,500 note receivable maturing on January 31, Year 2. What amount of contingent liability for this note must Love disclose in its financial statements for the year ended December 31, Year 1?

A. $0

B. $20,000

C. $20,333

D. $20,500

Answer (D) is correct. *(CPA, adapted)*
REQUIRED: The amount to be disclosed in the financial statements for a contingent liability.
DISCUSSION: When a note receivable is discounted with recourse, the discounting firm is responsible for its full amount ($20,500) if it is not paid. Consequently, this amount should be disclosed as a contingent liability in the notes to the financial statements.
Answer (A) is incorrect. A note receivable should disclose the full potential liability. Answer (B) is incorrect. Love may be responsible for the full amount of the note receivable ($20,500). Answer (C) is incorrect. Full amounts are due when discounted with recourse.

50. Jayne Corp. discounted its own $50,000, 1-year note at a bank, at a discount rate of 12%, when the prime rate was 10%. In reporting the note on Jayne's balance sheet prior to the note's maturity, what rate should Jayne use for the accrual of interest?

A. 10.0%

B. 10.7%

C. 12.0%

D. 13.6%

Answer (D) is correct. *(CPA, adapted)*
REQUIRED: The effective rate of interest on a discounted note.
DISCUSSION: The note had a face amount of $50,000. The proceeds from discounting the note were $44,000 [$50,000 – ($50,000 × 12% × 1 year)]. Thus, Jayne paid $6,000 interest ($50,000 – $44,000) on $44,000 for 1 year. The effective interest rate was thus 13.6% ($6,000 ÷ $44,000).
Answer (A) is incorrect. The prime rate is not used for accruals. Answer (B) is incorrect. The rate used for the accrual of interest is the effective interest rate. Answer (C) is incorrect. The discount rate is not used for accruals.

51. Ayn, Inc., accepted from a customer an $80,000, 90-day, 12% interest-bearing note dated August 31. On September 30, Ayn discounted the note at the Nadir State Bank at 15%. However, the proceeds were not received until October 1. In Ayn's September 30 balance sheet, the amount receivable from the bank, based on a 360-day year, includes accrued interest revenue of

A. $340

B. $400

C. $600

D. $800

Answer (A) is correct. *(CPA, adapted)*
REQUIRED: The accrued interest revenue recognized when a note is discounted.
DISCUSSION: As determined below, the interest received by Ayn if it had held the 90-day note to maturity would have been $2,400. The discount fee charged on a note with a maturity amount of $82,400 ($80,000 face amount + $2,400 interest) discounted at 15% for 60 days is $2,060. The difference of $340 ($2,400 interest – $2,060 discount fee) should be reflected as accrued interest revenue at the balance sheet date because the cash proceeds were not received until the next period.

$80,000 × 12% × (90 days ÷ 360 days) = $2,400 interest
$82,400 × 15% × (60 days ÷ 360 days) = (2,060) discount fee
Accrued interest revenue $ 340

Answer (B) is incorrect. Incorrectly calculating the discount fee based on the $80,000 face amount rather than the $82,400 maturity amount results in $400. Answer (C) is incorrect. The accrued interest revenue is the difference between the interest on the note if held to maturity minus the discounted amount of the note. Answer (D) is incorrect. This amount incorrectly assumes no discount fee.

52. Halen, Inc., received from a customer a 1-year, $500,000 note bearing annual interest of 8%. After holding the note for 4 months, Halen discounted the note at Regional Bank at an effective interest rate of 10%. What amount of cash did Halen receive from the bank?

A. $540,000

B. $520,667

C. $504,000

D. $486,000

Answer (C) is correct. *(CPA, adapted)*
REQUIRED: The amount of cash received when a note is discounted.
DISCUSSION: The maturity amount of the note is $540,000 [$500,000 face amount + ($500,000 × 8%)]. The discount fee is $36,000 [$540,000 × 10% × (8 months ÷12 months)]. Consequently, the proceeds equal $504,000 ($540,000 – $36,000).
Answer (A) is incorrect. The amount of $540,000 is the maturity value. Answer (B) is incorrect. The amount of $520,667 assumes a nominal rate of 10% and a discount rate of 8%. Answer (D) is incorrect. The amount of $486,000 results from discounting the note for 1 year.

53. On August 1, Year 1, Beethoven Corp.'s $500,000 1-year, noninterest-bearing note due July 31, Year 2, was discounted at Gray Bank at 10.8%. Beethoven uses the straight-line method of amortizing bond discount. What carrying amount should Beethoven report for notes payable in its December 31, Year 1, balance sheet?

A. $500,000

B. $477,500

C. $468,500

D. $446,000

Answer (C) is correct. *(CPA, adapted)*
REQUIRED: The carrying amount reported for notes payable.
DISCUSSION: The discount is $54,000 ($500,000 × 10.8%). Hence, the carrying amount on August 1 was $446,000. Given straight-line amortization of the discount, the carrying amount at year end is $468,500 {$446,000 + [$54,000 × (5 months ÷ 12 months)]}.
Answer (A) is incorrect. This figure is the face amount of the note payable. Answer (B) is incorrect. This figure will be the carrying amount after 7 months. Answer (D) is incorrect. This figure was the carrying amount on August 1.

54. Sap Co. purchased from Azalea Co. a $20,000, 8%, 5-year note that required five equal annual year-end payments of $5,009. The note was discounted to yield a 9% rate to Sap. At the date of purchase, Sap recorded the note at its present value of $19,485. What should be the total interest revenue earned by Sap over the life of this note?

A. $5,045

B. $5,560

C. $8,000

D. $9,000

Answer (B) is correct. *(CPA, adapted)*
REQUIRED: The total interest revenue earned on a discounted note receivable.
DISCUSSION: Sap Co. will receive cash of $25,045 ($5,009 × 5 years). Hence, interest revenue is $5,560 ($25,045 – $19,485 present value).
Answer (A) is incorrect. The amount of $5,045 does not include the discount amortization. Answer (C) is incorrect. The amount of $8,000 equals $20,000 times 8% nominal interest for 5 years. Answer (D) is incorrect. The amount of $9,000 equals $20,000 times the 9% yield rate for 5 years.

55. Punn Co. has been forced into bankruptcy and liquidated. Unsecured claims will be paid at the rate of $.30 on the dollar. Mega Co. holds a noninterest-bearing note receivable from Punn in the amount of $50,000, collateralized by machinery with a liquidation value of $10,000. The total amount to be realized by Mega on this note receivable is

A. $25,000

B. $22,000

C. $15,000

D. $10,000

Answer (B) is correct. *(CPA, adapted)*
REQUIRED: The amount to be realized from a liquidation claim.
DISCUSSION: The $50,000 note receivable is secured to the extent of $10,000. The remaining $40,000 is unsecured, and Mega will be paid on this claim at the rate of $.30 on the dollar.

Secured claim	$10,000
Unsecured ($40,000 × .3)	12,000
	$22,000

Answer (A) is incorrect. The amount of $25,000 equals 30% of the note receivable plus the liquidation value of the collateral [($50,000 × .3) + $10,000]. Answer (C) is incorrect. The amount of $15,000 is what would be realized if no collateral had been pledged ($50,000 × 3%). Answer (D) is incorrect. The amount of $10,000 is the liquidation value of the collateral.

5.6 Transfers of Financial Assets

56. Which of the following is a method to generate cash from accounts receivable?

	Assignment	Factoring
A.	Yes	No
B.	Yes	Yes
C.	No	Yes
D.	No	No

Answer (B) is correct. *(CPA, adapted)*
REQUIRED: The method(s) of generating cash from accounts receivable.
DISCUSSION: Methods of generating cash from accounts receivable include both assignment and factoring. Assignment occurs when specifically named accounts receivable are pledged as collateral for a loan. The accounts receivable remain those of the assignor. However, when cash is collected from these accounts receivable, the cash must be remitted to the assignee. Accounts receivable are factored when they are sold outright to a third party. This sale may be with or without recourse.
Answer (A) is incorrect. Factoring is a way to generate cash from accounts receivable. Answer (C) is incorrect. Assignment is a way to generate cash from accounts receivable. Answer (D) is incorrect. Both assignment and factoring are ways to generate cash from accounts receivable.

57. On April 1, Aloe, Inc., factored $80,000 of its accounts receivable without recourse. The factor retained 10% of the accounts receivable as an allowance for sales returns and charged a 5% commission on the gross amount of the factored receivables. What amount of cash did Aloe receive from the factored receivables?

A. $68,000

B. $68,400

C. $72,000

D. $76,000

Answer (A) is correct. *(CPA, adapted)*
REQUIRED: The cash received from factoring receivables without recourse.
DISCUSSION: Factoring is a transfer of receivables to a third party (a factor) who assumes the responsibility of collection. Factoring discounts receivables on a nonrecourse, notification basis. If a sale is without recourse, the transferee (the factor) assumes the risks and rewards of collection. The factor retained 10% of the receivables ($80,000 × 10% = $8,000) as a reserve (an allowance for returns) and charged a 5% commission on the gross receivables ($80,000 × 5% = $4,000). Accordingly, the transferor received $68,000 ($800,000 – $8,000 – $4,000).
Answer (B) is incorrect. The amount of $68,400 equals the commission rate times the excess of the receivables factored over the receivables retained. Answer (C) is incorrect. The amount of $72,000 does not include the 5% commission. Answer (D) is incorrect. The amount of $76,000 does not include the allowance for the 10% of accounts receivable retained as an allowance for sales returns.

58. Milton Co. pledged some of its accounts receivable to Good Neighbor Financing Corporation in return for a loan. Which of the following statements is correct?

A. Good Neighbor Financing cannot take title to the receivables if Milton does not repay the loan. Title can only be taken if the receivables are factored.

B. Good Neighbor Financing will assume the responsibility of collecting the receivables.

C. Milton will retain control of the receivables.

D. Good Neighbor Financing will take title to the receivables and will return title to Milton after the loan is paid.

Answer (C) is correct. *(CPA, adapted)*
REQUIRED: The true statement about a pledge of accounts receivable.
DISCUSSION: A pledge (a general assignment) is the use of receivables as collateral (security) for a loan. The borrower agrees to use collections of receivables to repay the loan. Upon default, the lender can sell the receivables to recover the loan proceeds. Because a pledge is a relatively informal arrangement, it is not reflected in the accounts. A transfer of financial assets is a sale only when the transferor relinquishes control. If the transfer (e.g., a pledge) of accounts receivable is not a sale, the transaction is a secured borrowing. The transferor becomes a debtor, and the transferee, a creditor in possession of collateral. However, absent default, the collateral remains an asset of the transferor.
Answer (A) is incorrect. If the transferor defaults, the transferor loses its right of redemption, and the title remains with the transferee. Title to receivables can therefore be taken by means other than factoring. Answer (B) is incorrect. The risks and rewards of collection are passed to the transferee when the sale of receivables is without recourse. In this case, because the pledge is not a sale, the debtor retains the responsibility of collecting the receivables. Answer (D) is incorrect. The transfer of receivables is not a sale. The debtor retains title unless it defaults.

59. On January 1, Davis College assigned $500,000 of accounts receivable to the Scholastic Finance Company. Davis gave a 14% note for $450,000 representing 90% of the assigned accounts and received proceeds of $432,000 after payment of a 4% finance charge. On February 1, Davis remitted $80,000 of collections on the assigned receivables to Scholastic, including interest for 1 month on the unpaid balance. Davis does not amortize the finance charge because the note is expected to be repaid by the end of the fiscal year. As a result of the $80,000 remittance, accounts receivable assigned and notes payable will be decreased by what amounts?

	A/R Assigned	Notes Payable
A.	$80,000	$74,750
B.	$80,000	$80,000
C.	$72,000	$74,750
D.	$74,750	$80,000

Answer (A) is correct. *(A.G. Helling)*
REQUIRED: The decrease in assigned accounts receivable and notes payable when cash is collected and remitted to the assignor.
DISCUSSION: When assigned accounts receivable are collected, the cash should be remitted to the assignee. The accounts receivable assigned account should be decreased for the amount collected ($80,000), and the note should be decreased by the amount remitted ($80,000) minus interest [$450,000 × 14% × (1 month ÷ 12 months) = $5,250]. Davis made the following entries:

January 1

Cash	$432,000	
Finance charge ($450,000 × 4%)	18,000	
Notes payable		$450,000
Accounts receivable assigned	$500,000	
Accounts receivable		$500,000

February 1

Cash	$80,000	
Accounts receivable assigned		$80,000
Notes payable	$74,750	
Interest expense	5,250	
Cash		$80,000

Answer (B) is incorrect. Notes payable should be decreased by the amount remitted. Answer (C) is incorrect. Accounts receivable should be decreased by the amount collected. Answer (D) is incorrect. Notes payable should be decreased by the amount remitted, and the accounts receivable should be decreased by the amount collected.

60. In accounting for the transfer of financial assets, which of the following is the approach underlying the accounting prescribed by GAAP?

A. Financial-components approach.

B. The risks-and-rewards approach.

C. Inseparable-unit approach.

D. Linked-presentation approach.

Answer (A) is correct. *(Publisher, adapted)*
REQUIRED: The approach underlying the accounting for transfers of financial assets.
DISCUSSION: The accounting for the transfer of financial assets follows a financial-components approach based on control. The objective is for each party to the transaction to (1) recognize the assets it controls and the liabilities it has incurred, (2) derecognize assets when control has been given up, and (3) derecognize liabilities when they have been extinguished. Thus, it must be determined whether the transferor has given up control of the transferred financial assets.
Answer (B) is incorrect. The risks-and-rewards approach was rejected by the FASB. It is consistent with viewing each financial asset as an indivisible unit. Answer (C) is incorrect. The inseparable-unit approach was rejected by the FASB. It is consistent with viewing each financial asset as an indivisible unit. Answer (D) is incorrect. The linked-presentation approach was rejected by the FASB. It is consistent with viewing each financial asset as an indivisible unit.

61. A transfer of financial assets may be treated as a sale if the transferor surrenders control of the assets. Which of the following is one of the criteria that must be met before control is deemed to be surrendered?

A. The transferred assets are isolated from the transferor and its creditors except in bankruptcy.

B. The transferee cannot pledge or exchange the transferred assets.

C. The transferor is not a party to an agreement that both entitles and obligates it to repurchase or redeem the securities prior to maturity.

D. The transferor will benefit from the unilateral ability to require the holder to return specific assets.

Answer (C) is correct. *(Publisher, adapted)*
REQUIRED: The criterion that must be met before control over transferred financial assets is deemed to be surrendered.
DISCUSSION: A transfer of financial assets over which the transferor relinquishes control is a sale. The transferor relinquishes control only if certain conditions are met: (1) The transferred assets are beyond the reach of the transferor and its creditors; (2) transferees may pledge or exchange the assets or interests received; and (3) the transferor does not maintain effective control through, for example, (a) an agreement to repurchase or redeem the assets before maturity, (b) the unilateral ability to (i) cause the holder to return specific assets and (ii) benefit from that ability, or (c) an agreement making it probable that the transferee will require repurchase.
Answer (A) is incorrect. Control is not surrendered if the transferor's creditors can reach the assets in bankruptcy. Answer (B) is incorrect. The transferee is able to pledge or exchange the assets if control is surrendered. Answer (D) is incorrect. The transfer is accounted for as a sale only if the transferor will not benefit from the unilateral ability to require the holder to return specific assets.

62. Seller Co. transferred entire loans to Buyer Co. in a sale transaction. It did not retain a servicing interest. The loans had a fair value of $1,650 and a carrying amount of $1,500. Seller also undertook to repurchase delinquent loans. Furthermore, the loans had a fixed rate, but Seller agreed to provide Buyer a return at a variable rate. Thus, the transaction effectively included an interest rate swap. The following are the relevant fair values:

Cash received $1,575
Interest rate swap asset   60
Recourse obligation   90

Seller should recognize a gain of

A. $45

B. $90

C. $150

D. $225

Answer (A) is correct. *(Publisher, adapted)*
REQUIRED: The gain on a sale of financial assets.
DISCUSSION: The gain equals the net proceeds (cash or other assets obtained in a transfer of financial assets, minus liabilities incurred) minus the carrying amount of the assets derecognized. Any asset obtained that is not an interest in the transferred assets is included in the proceeds. Thus, the cash received and the fair value of the interest rate swap asset are debited as part of the proceeds. Any liability incurred, even if related to the assets transferred, reduces the proceeds, so the recourse obligation should be credited. After crediting the carrying amount of the loans sold and measuring assets and liabilities at fair value, Seller should recognize a gain on sale (a credit) of $45 ($1,575 cash + $60 interest rate swap – $90 recourse obligation – $1,500 carrying amount).
Answer (B) is incorrect. The fair value of the recourse obligation is $90. Answer (C) is incorrect. The sum of the recourse obligation and the interest rate swap asset is $150. Answer (D) is incorrect. The recourse obligation is a liability.

63. Lender Bank made a large loan to a major borrower and then transferred a participating interest in this loan to Student Union Bank. The transfer was on a nonrecourse basis, and Lender continued to service the loan. Student Union is not a major competitor of Lender. Lender should account for this transfer as a secured borrowing if the agreement

A. Allows Student Union Bank to pledge its participating interest.

B. Does not grant Lender the right of first refusal on the sale of Student Union's participating interest.

C. Does not allow Student Union to sell its participating interest.

D. Prohibits Student Union from selling its participating interest to banks that are direct, major competitors of Lender.

Answer (C) is correct. *(Publisher, adapted)*
REQUIRED: The condition under which a participating interest in a loan should be accounted for as a secured borrowing.
DISCUSSION: A transfer of financial assets, such as a participating interest in a loan, should be accounted for as a sale if the transferor surrenders control over the participating interest transferred to the transferee. If control is not surrendered, the transfer should be accounted for as a secured borrowing. Control is not surrendered if the agreement prevents the transferee from pledging or exchanging its participating interest.
Answer (A) is incorrect. The right to exchange or pledge participating interests is consistent with the relinquishment of control. Answer (B) is incorrect. Failing to grant Lender the right of first refusal on the sale of Student Union's participating interest is not a constraint on the transferee that permits the transferor to retain control. Indeed, a right of first refusal is not such a constraint. Answer (D) is incorrect. A prohibition on sale to the transferor's competitors is not a constraint on the transferee if other willing buyers exist.

64. On the last day of its fiscal year, Originator Co. transferred noncurrent loans to Transferee Co. in a transaction appropriately accounted for as a sale and retained a servicing asset. These loans have a 10% yield, a fair value of $220,000 (including servicing), and a carrying amount of $200,000. Originator sold the entire principal and the right to receive interest income at 8% for $198,000. The fee for continuing to service the loans is a portion of the interest income not transferred. This fee is not subordinate to any other interest and is equal to fair compensation for a substitute service provider. The remainder of the interest income not transferred is an interest-only strip receivable. The following are the relevant fair values:

Cash	$198,000
Interest-only strip receivable	13,200
Servicing asset	8,800
	$220,000

The gain on the sale is

A. $800

B. $1,200

C. $18,000

D. $20,000

Answer (D) is correct. *(Publisher, adapted)*
REQUIRED: The gain on the sale of noncurrent loans given retention of an interest-only strip receivable and a servicing asset.
DISCUSSION: The interests retained by the transferor do not qualify as participating interests. Thus, the interest-only strip receivable does not satisfy the requirement that all cash flows be divided in proportion to shares of ownership. The reason is that the transferor does not share in principal payments. Moreover, the servicing asset does not qualify because cash flows received as compensation for services ordinarily are excluded from proportionate cash flows. Accordingly, the carrying amount of the entire asset is not allocated among participating interests by the transferor. The entry based on fair values is

Cash	$198,000	
Interest-only strip receivable	13,200	
Servicing asset	8,800	
Loans		$200,000
Gain on sale		20,000

Answer (A) is incorrect. This amount equals the $8,800 fair value of the servicing asset minus an $8,000 allocation of the carrying amount. Answer (B) is incorrect. This amount equals the $13,200 fair value of the interest-only strip receivable minus a $12,000 allocation of the carrying amount. Answer (C) is incorrect. This amount equals the cash received ($198,000) minus a $180,000 allocation of the carrying amount to the loans.

65. Athens Corporation sold an 80% pro rata interest in a $2,000,000 note receivable to Sparta Company for $1,920,000. The note was originally issued at its face amount. Future benefits and costs of servicing the note are immaterial. If GAAP are followed, the amount of gain or loss Athens should recognize on the transfer of this participating interest is

A. $(80,000)

B. $0

C. $320,000

D. $400,000

Answer (C) is correct. *(Publisher, adapted)*
REQUIRED: The amount of gain or loss to be recognized on a transfer of a partial interest in a loan.
DISCUSSION: The fair value of the note is $2,400,000 ($1,920,000 ÷ 80%). The carrying amount is $2,000,000. Given no servicing asset or liability, Athens should debit cash for $1,920,000, reduce the carrying amount of the note receivable by $1,600,000 ($2,000,000 × 80%), and recognize a gain of $320,000 ($1,920,000 – $1,600,000).
Answer (A) is incorrect. A loss of $80,000 is equal to the $1,920,000 cash received minus the $2,000,000 carrying amount of the note. Answer (B) is incorrect. A gain should be recognized equal to the pro rata (80%) difference between the fair value and the carrying amount of the note. Answer (D) is incorrect. One hundred percent of the difference between the fair value and the carrying amount of the note is $400,000.

66. If a transfer of an entire financial asset meets the criteria for recognition as a sale, the transferor should

A. Account for any gain or loss in other comprehensive income.

B. Initially measure at fair value any assets obtained and liabilities incurred.

C. Allocate the previous carrying amount to the assets obtained and liabilities incurred.

D. Recognize liabilities in accordance with the accounting for contingencies.

Answer (B) is correct. *(Publisher, adapted)*
REQUIRED: The accounting for a transfer of an entire financial asset that meets the criteria for recognition as a sale.
DISCUSSION: The transferor should (1) derecognize assets when control has been relinquished, (2) recognize assets controlled and liabilities incurred, (3) derecognize liabilities when they have been extinguished, and (4) recognize gain or loss in earnings.
Answer (A) is incorrect. The transferor should recognize any gain or loss in earnings. Answer (C) is incorrect. Fair value accounting should be used. Answer (D) is incorrect. Under prior guidance that has been superseded, if fair value measurement of liabilities is not practicable, no gain is recognized, and the liabilities are recorded at the greater of (1) the excess, if any, of (a) the fair value of assets obtained minus the fair value of other liabilities incurred over (b) the sum of the carrying amounts of the assets transferred or (2) the amount determined under GAAP for contingencies.

Use Gleim **EQE Test Prep** Software Download for interactive study and performance analysis.

STUDY UNIT SIX
INVENTORIES

Inventory Fundamentals

Inventory is tangible personal property that is (1) held for sale in the ordinary course of business **(finished goods)**, (2) in the process of production for such sale **(work-in-process)**, or (3) to be consumed in the production of goods or services available for sale (materials and supplies). The major objective of inventory accounting is to determine income by matching costs and revenues.

For both manufacturers and retailers, **ending inventory** relates the balance sheet to the income statement. It is a current asset on the balance sheet and is part of the calculation of cost of goods sold on the income statement.

Cost of Goods Sold for a Retailer:

Beginning inventory		$ XXX,XXX
Purchases	$X,XXX,XXX	
Purchase returns and discounts	(XX,XXX)	
Freight-in	XX,XXX	
Net purchases	X,XXX,XXX	X,XXX,XXX
Goods available for sale		X,XXX,XXX
Ending inventory		**(XXX,XXX)**
Cost of goods sold		$X,XXX,XXX

A retailer has one class of inventory: the goods purchased from suppliers for resale. A manufacturer has three classes of inventory: materials, work-in-process, and finished goods.

Cost of Goods Sold for a Manufacturer:

Beginning materials inventory		$ XXX, XXX
Purchases	$X,XXX,XXX	
Purchase returns and discounts	(XX,XXX)	
Freight-in	XX,XXX	
Net purchases		X,XXX,XXX
Materials available for use		X,XXX,XXX
Ending materials inventory		**(XXX,XXX)**
Direct materials used in production		$X,XXX,XXX
Direct labor costs		X,XXX,XXX
Manufacturing overhead costs		XXX,XXX
Total manufacturing costs for the period		X,XXX,XXX
Beginning work-in-process inventory		XXX,XXX
Ending work-in-process inventory		**(XXX,XXX)**
Cost of goods manufactured		X,XXX,XXX
Beginning finished goods inventory		XXX,XXX
Goods available for sale		X,XXX,XXX
Ending finished goods inventory		**(XXX,XXX)**
Cost of goods sold		$X,XXX,XXX

Accounting for inventory is primarily based on **cost**, that is, the costs incurred directly or indirectly to bring it to its existing condition and location. Cost includes the price and such other items as freight-in, other delivery charges, normal spoilage, and handling costs. Returns, allowances, and discounts are subtracted from the cost of inventory. **Purchase discounts** are offered by the vendor to induce early payment and improve its cash flow. Two methods of accounting for them are in general use. The **net method** is used when the purchaser expects to pay soon enough to take the discount. The purchaser records the transaction at the discounted price at the time of sale. If the discount date is missed, purchase discounts lost, an expense, is debited for the difference. The **gross method** ignores cash discounts, assuming that the discount will not be taken. The purchaser records the transaction at the full, undiscounted price at the time of sale. If the discount is then taken, purchase discounts, a contra-inventory account, is credited for the difference.

Many factors determine inventory cost, especially with regard to measuring work-in-process and finished goods. For example, **variable overheads** incurred by a manufacturer are allocated based on actual use of facilities, and **fixed overheads** are allocated based on **normal capacity** (production expected over multiple periods under normal circumstances). When production is abnormally high, the per-unit allocation of fixed overhead must be reduced to avoid overstating inventory cost. But if production is abnormally low, the allocation to inventoriable cost is not increased. Unallocated overheads and abnormal freight, handling costs, spoilage, and similar items are expensed as incurred. **General and administrative expenses** are usually expensed as incurred, and **selling costs** are never inventoried. **Product (inventoriable) costs** are incurred to produce or acquire units of inventory. They are expensed in the period the product is sold. **Period costs** cannot be feasibly associated with the production or acquisition of inventory. They are expensed as incurred.

Inventory accounting systems are perpetual or periodic. In a **perpetual system**, purchases, purchase returns and allowances, purchase discounts, and freight-in (transportation in) are charged directly to inventory. Cost of goods sold is debited and inventory is credited at the time of each sale. The balance in inventory is (theoretically) accurate at all times. **Inventory over-and-short** is debited (credited) when the physical count is less (greater) than the balance in the perpetual records. This account is either closed to cost of goods sold or reported separately under other revenues and gains or other expenses and losses.

In a **periodic system**, beginning inventory is unchanged during the accounting period. Goods bought from suppliers and adjustments usually are tracked in separate temporary accounts (purchases, freight-in, etc.). The adjustments are added to or subtracted from purchases to determine net purchases. Cost of goods sold is not debited until the end of each accounting period. Ending inventory is determined by a period-end physical count (or statistical sampling). In a perpetual system, the physical count is needed to detect material misstatements in the perpetual records.

Periodic			Perpetual		
Purchases	$X,XXX		Inventory	$X,XXX	
Accounts payable		$X,XXX	Accounts payable		$X,XXX
Freight-in	$XXX				
Cash		$XXX			
Accounts payable	$XXX				
Purchase returns		$XXX			

(Acquisition and Returns)

Accounts receivable	$X,XXX		Accounts receivable	$X,XXX	
Sales		$X,XXX	Sales		$X,XXX
No entry			Cost of goods sold	$X,XXX	
			Inventory		$X,XXX

(Sale)

Inventory (physical count)	$X,XXX		Inventory over-and-short (Dr, Cr)	$XX	
Cost of goods sold	X,XXX		Inventory (correction) (Cr, Dr)		$XX
Purchase returns	XXX				
Purchases (total for period)		$X,XXX			
Inventory (beginning balance)		X,XXX			
Freight-in		XXX			

(Closing)

Inventory errors may have a material effect on current assets, working capital (current assets – current liabilities), cost of sales, net income, and equity. A common error is inappropriate timing of the recognition of transactions. The diagram below illustrates the effects of an overstatement of ending inventory on the financial statements of the year of the error.

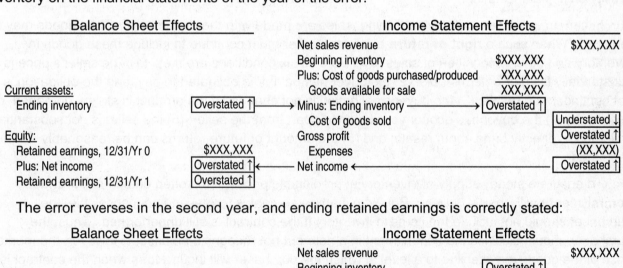

The error reverses in the second year, and ending retained earnings is correctly stated:

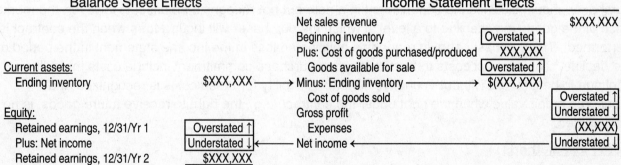

Items Counted in Inventory

Not all inventory is on hand. Most sales are recorded by the seller at the time of shipment and the buyer at the time of receipt. But this procedure may misstate inventory, receivables, payables, and earnings. Proper cut-off is observed by determining when legal title has passed under the FOB (free on board) terms of the contract. If goods are shipped **FOB shipping point**, title and risk of loss pass to the purchaser once the goods are in possession of the carrier. The purchaser then includes them in inventory. **FOB destination** means the seller retains title and risk of loss until the goods arrive at the place designated in the contract. The seller should therefore include them in inventory until that time.

Because of the greater risk of loss in installment sale transactions, the seller often retains title to the goods until full payment has been made. Nevertheless, these items should not be counted in the seller's inventory if uncollectible accounts expense can be reasonably estimated. Despite retention of title by the seller, the substance of the transaction is that control of the goods has passed to the buyer, assuming a reasonable expectation of payment in the ordinary course of business.

In a **consignment**, goods are not sold but are transferred to an agent for possible sale. The consignor continues to recognize an asset (inventory) for the goods until the consignee sells them. (They may be reclassified to a separate inventory account such as consigned goods out.) In a **sale with a buyback agreement** (a product financing arrangement), one party transfers inventory to another party for cash and agrees to buy back the inventory at a stated time. This transaction (sometimes called parking) is a borrowing with inventory as collateral. If the first party is required to repurchase the inventory at a specified price that is not adjusted except for fluctuations due to finance and holding costs, no sale is recognized. The first party must include the inventory and a related liability on its balance sheet.

In certain industries, notably publishing, sales are made with the understanding that goods may be returned. When such a **right of return** exists, the seller must continue to include these goods in inventory and defer recognition of sales revenue until six conditions are met: (1) The seller's price is substantially fixed or determinable; (2) the buyer has paid or is obligated to pay, and the obligation is not contingent on resale; (3) the buyer's obligation is not changed if the product is stolen, damaged, or destroyed; (4) the buyer has economic substance apart from the seller; (5) the seller is not substantially obligated to directly bring about resale; and (6) the amount of future returns can be reasonably estimated.

To ensure a steady supply of inventory at predictable prices, firms often enter into **purchase commitments** with their suppliers. But even if an agreement is formal and noncancelable, the purchaser should not include the items in inventory if the contract is still unperformed. Thus, the purchaser should disclose the commitment in a note but not recognize an asset. However, the market price of the goods may decline to a level at which the purchaser will incur a **loss** when the contract is performed. The purchaser should report this anticipated loss in the income statement in the period of the decline. The contract costs to terminate a firm purchase commitment include costs that will continue to be incurred without economic benefit. A liability for these costs is recognized and measured at fair value when the right under the contract, e.g., the right to receive future goods, is no longer used.

Cost Flow Methods

The **specific identification** method determines the specific items sold (the actual physical flow). One problem is that it permits income manipulation. For example, profit could be increased if less costly inventory is identified. Another problem is the need for detailed records. Accordingly, most entities select a cost-flow assumption.

Weighted-average is the simplest. It calculates one per-unit price at the end of each period and is suitable for a periodic system. The total of beginning inventory and purchases for the period is divided by the total units available to arrive at the weighted-average cost for the period.

Moving-average is more sophisticated. It calculates a new per-unit price after every purchase. Because this method requires recordkeeping for all purchases and sales, it can be used only with a perpetual system.

The **first-in, first-out (FIFO)** method assumes that the first goods purchased are the first sold and that ending inventory consists of the latest purchases. The measurement is the same regardless of whether it occurs at the end of the period (a periodic system) or on a perpetual basis. One advantage of FIFO is that ending inventory approximates current replacement cost. A disadvantage is that current revenues are matched with older costs.

The **last-in, first-out (LIFO)** method expenses the latest purchases first. In a time of inflation, this method results in the highest cost of goods sold. LIFO reduces income, defers income tax, and improves cash flow. LIFO may be used with a periodic or perpetual system. The accumulation of inventory over time results in the creation of LIFO layers. Whenever sales exceed purchases, however, the entity must reduce older layers **(LIFO liquidation)**. Distortions in net income can result from matching current revenues against the older (generally lower) costs.

The **dollar-value LIFO** method avoids such distortions. It determines changes in inventory in terms of dollars of constant purchasing power rather than units of physical inventory. This calculation uses a specific price index for each year. The ending inventory is stated at current (year-end acquisition) cost. It is then deflated to base-year cost using the current-year index. This amount is compared with the beginning inventory stated at base-year cost to determine what layers are to be in the ending inventory based on a LIFO flow assumption. Each layer is then inflated (weighted) by the price index applicable to the year in which the layer was added. The result is the total ending inventory.

Lower of Cost or Market (LCM)

Inventory must be measured subsequent to acquisition at the LCM. It is written down when the utility of the goods is impaired by (1) damage, (2) deterioration, (3) obsolescence, (4) changes in price levels, (5) changes in demand, (6) style changes, or (7) other causes. The impairment is recognized as a nonreversible loss of the current period. The LCM rule applies only to goods to be sold in the ordinary course of business. **Market (M)** is the **current replacement cost (CRC)** of the inventory, subject to certain limitations. Market should not exceed a **ceiling** equal to **net realizable value (NRV)**. This is the estimated selling price in the ordinary course of business minus reasonably predictable costs of completion and disposal. Reporting inventory above NRV overstates its utility and will result in a loss at the time of sale. Market should not be less than a **floor** equal to NRV minus a **normal profit margin (P)**. Depending on the nature of the inventory, the LCM rule may be applied either directly to **each item** or to the **total** of the inventory (or, in some cases, to the total of each major category). The choice should be the one that most clearly reflects periodic income.

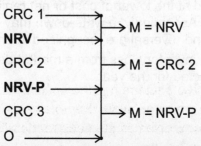

Inventory Estimation

The **gross profit method** (the gross margin method) estimates ending inventory. Because it is imprecise, GAAP and federal tax law do not permit its use at year end, but other applications are possible. If inventory is destroyed, the method may be used to estimate the loss. Also, external auditors apply the gross profit method as an analytical procedure to determine the fairness of the ending inventory. Moreover, it may be used internally to estimate inventory throughout the year, e.g., as a verification of perpetual records.

Beginning inventory (known)		$XX,XXX
Add: Purchases (known)		XX,XXX
Goods available for sale		$XX,XXX
Sales (at selling price)	$XX,XXX	
Minus: Gross profit (sales × known GP%)	(XX,XXX)	
Sales (at cost)		(XX,XXX)
Ending inventory (estimate)		$XX,XXX

Entities that have many transactions in relatively low-cost goods often use an easier and less expensive method of estimating ending inventory and cost of goods sold. The **retail inventory method** prices goods soon after acquisition without recording the cost for each transaction. Under this method, records of the beginning inventory and purchases (net of freight-in, purchase returns and allowances, and purchase discounts) are kept at both **cost and retail**. Sales at retail and any other appropriate items are subtracted from goods available for sale at retail (the sum of beginning inventory and net purchases at retail) to calculate ending inventory at retail. This amount is adjusted to estimated cost using a cost-to-retail ratio.

	Cost	Retail
Beginning inventory (known)	$XX,XXX	$XX,XXX
Add: Net purchases (known)	XX,XXX	XX,XXX
Goods available for sale (GAS)	$XX,XXX	$XX,XXX
Sales (at selling price)		(XX,XXX)
Ending inventory at retail		$XX,XXX

Cost-to-retail ratio = GAS at cost ÷ GAS at retail
Ending inventory at cost = Ending inventory at retail × Cost-to-retail ratio

The retail method requires that adjustments be made for purchase discounts, purchase returns and allowances, freight-in, etc., to determine the ending inventory. Variations of the retail method are FIFO cost, FIFO LCM, average cost, lower of average cost or market (the conventional retail inventory method), LIFO retail, and dollar-value LIFO retail.

Differences between GAAP and IFRS

Under IFRS:

- LIFO is not permitted.
- Inventories are measured at the lower of cost or net realizable value (NRV). NRV is assessed each period. Accordingly, a write-down may be reversed but not above original cost. The write-down and reversal are recognized in profit or loss.
- For an interim period, an inventory loss from a market decline must be recognized even if no loss is reasonably expected for the year.

QUESTIONS

6.1 Inventory Fundamentals

1. The following information pertains to Hague Corp.'s Year 2 cost of goods sold:

Inventory, 12/31/Year 1	$180,000
Year 2 purchases	248,000
Year 2 write-off of obsolete inventory	68,000
Inventory, 12/31/Year 2	60,000

The inventory written off became obsolete because of an unexpected and unusual technological advance by a competitor. In its Year 2 income statement, what amount should Hague report as cost of goods sold?

A. $436,000

B. $368,000

C. $300,000

D. $248,000

Answer (C) is correct. *(CPA, adapted)*
REQUIRED: The cost of goods sold for the year.
DISCUSSION: As indicated in the T-account analysis below, cost of goods sold equals purchases plus any decrease in inventory or minus any increase in inventory (purchases minus the change in inventory). The write-off of obsolete inventory is a loss, not a component of COGS. Thus, cost of goods sold is $300,000.

Inventory			
12/31/Year 1	$180,000	$ 68,000	Obsolescence
Purchases	248,000	300,000	COGS
	$ 60,000		

Answer (A) is incorrect. The amount of $436,000 results from adding obsolete inventory to, not subtracting it from, beginning inventory. Answer (B) is incorrect. The amount of $368,000 includes the obsolete inventory in COGS. Answer (D) is incorrect. The amount of $248,000 equals purchases.

2. Application rates for fixed production overheads best reflect anticipated fluctuations in production over a cycle of years when they are computed under the concept of

A. Maximum capacity.

B. Normal capacity.

C. Practical capacity.

D. Expected actual capacity.

Answer (B) is correct. *(CPA, adapted)*
REQUIRED: The concept of capacity for best applying overheads over a cycle of years.
DISCUSSION: Normal capacity is the production level that will approximate demand over a period of years that includes seasonal, cyclical, and trend variations. Deviations in one year will be offset in other years. Moreover, normal capacity is expected to be achieved under normal circumstances, including loss of capacity because of planned maintenance. Consequently, GAAP require allocation of fixed production overheads to conversion cost based on normal capacity.
Answer (A) is incorrect. Maximum (theoretical or ideal) capacity is the level at which output is maximized assuming perfectly efficient operations at all times. This level is impossible to maintain and results in underapplied overheads. Answer (C) is incorrect. Practical capacity is the maximum level at which output is produced efficiently. It usually also results in underapplied overheads. Answer (D) is incorrect. Expected actual capacity is a short-run output level. It minimizes under- or overapplied overheads but does not provide a consistent basis for assigning overhead cost. Per-unit overheads will fluctuate because of short-term changes in the expected production level.

3. In a retailer's periodic inventory system that uses the weighted-average cost flow method, the beginning inventory is the

A. Net purchases minus the ending inventory.

B. Net purchases minus the cost of goods sold.

C. Total goods available for sale minus the net purchases.

D. Total goods available for sale minus the cost of goods sold.

Answer (C) is correct. *(CPA, adapted)*
REQUIRED: The beginning inventory in a periodic system using weighted average cost.
DISCUSSION: In a retailer's periodic inventory system, goods available for sale is the sum of beginning inventory and net purchases. Thus, the beginning inventory equals the total goods available for sale minus the net purchases, regardless of the cost flow method used.
Answer (A) is incorrect. It states the difference between the beginning inventory and the cost of goods sold. Answer (B) is incorrect. This difference is the change in inventory valuation during the period. Answer (D) is incorrect. Goods available minus cost of sales equals ending inventory.

4. During December of Year 1, Nile Co. incurred special insurance costs but did not record these costs until payment was made during the following year. These insurance costs related to inventory that had been sold by December 31, Year 1. What is the effect of the omission on Nile's accrued liabilities and retained earnings at December 31, Year 1?

	Accrued Liabilities	Retained Earnings
A.	No effect	No effect
B.	No effect	Overstated
C.	Understated	Overstated
D.	Understated	No effect

Answer (C) is correct. *(CPA, adapted)*
REQUIRED: The effect on accrued liabilities and retained earnings of omitting insurance costs of inventory.
DISCUSSION: A liability must be recognized when (1) an item meets the definition of a liability (probable future sacrifice of economic benefits arising from a current obligation of the entity as a result of a past event or transaction), (2) it is measurable, and (3) the information about it is relevant and reliable. These criteria were met in Year 1 with respect to the insurance obligation. The insurance is a cost of inventory and theoretically should be accounted for as a product cost. Thus, the entry in Year 1 should have been to debit inventory and credit a liability. The omission of this entry understated accrued liabilities. Given that the related inventory was sold in Year 1, it also overstated net income and retained earnings by understating cost of goods sold. Moreover, the same effects would occur if the insurance costs were chargeable to expense as a period cost.

5. The following information applied to Atlas Co. for the current year:

Merchandise purchased for resale	$800,000
Freight-in	20,000
Freight-out	10,000
Purchase returns	4,000

The company's current-year inventoriable cost was

A. $800,000

B. $806,000

C. $816,000

D. $826,000

Answer (C) is correct. *(CPA, adapted)*
REQUIRED: The amount of inventoriable cost.
DISCUSSION: Inventoriable cost is the sum of the applicable expenditures and charges directly or indirectly incurred in bringing all items of inventory to their existing condition and location. Thus, inventoriable cost includes the $800,000 cost of the merchandise purchased, plus the $20,000 of freight-in, minus the $4,000 of purchase returns. Freight-out is not a cost incurred in bringing the inventory to a salable condition. The inventoriable cost for Atlas during the current year is $816,000 ($800,000 + $20,000 – $4,000).
Answer (A) is incorrect. The amount of $800,000 is gross purchases. Answer (B) is incorrect. The amount of $806,000 incorrectly includes freight-out as a cost instead of freight-in. Answer (D) is incorrect. The amount of $826,000 incorrectly includes freight-out.

6. If ending inventory is underestimated due to an error in the physical count of items on hand, cost of goods sold for the period will be <List A> and net earnings will be <List B>.

	List A	List B
A.	Underestimated	Underestimated
B.	Underestimated	Overestimated
C.	Overestimated	Underestimated
D.	Overestimated	Overestimated

Answer (C) is correct. *(CIA, adapted)*
REQUIRED: The effect on cost of goods sold and net earnings of an error in counting inventory.
DISCUSSION: Cost of goods sold equals beginning inventory, plus purchases, minus ending inventory. If the ending inventory is underestimated, the cost of goods sold will be overestimated. If cost of goods sold is overestimated, net earnings will be underestimated.
Answer (A) is incorrect. The cost of goods sold will be overestimated. Answer (B) is incorrect. The cost of goods sold will be overestimated and net earnings will be underestimated. Answer (D) is incorrect. Net earnings will be underestimated.

7. Heidelberg Co.'s beginning inventory at January 1 was understated by $52,000, and its ending inventory was overstated by $104,000. As a result, Heidelberg's cost of goods sold for the year was

A. Understated by $52,000.

B. Overstated by $52,000.

C. Understated by $156,000.

D. Overstated by $156,000.

Answer (C) is correct. *(CPA, adapted)*
REQUIRED: The misstatement of cost of goods sold.
DISCUSSION: When beginning inventory is understated, cost of goods sold will be understated. When ending inventory is overstated, cost of goods sold will be understated. Thus, Heidelberg Co.'s inventory is understated by $156,000 ($52,000 + $104,000).
Answer (A) is incorrect. The overstatement of ending inventory also understates cost of goods sold. Answer (B) is incorrect. The error understates cost of goods sold. Answer (D) is incorrect. The error understates cost of goods sold.

8. The following inventory errors have been discovered for Lithuania Corporation:

- The Year 1 year-end inventory was overstated by $23,000.
- The Year 2 year-end inventory was understated by $61,000.
- The Year 3 year-end inventory was understated by $17,000.

The reported income before taxes for Lithuania was

Year	Income before Taxes
Year 1	$138,000
Year 2	254,000
Year 3	168,000

Reported income before taxes for Year 1, Year 2, and Year 3, respectively, should have been

- A. $161,000, $170,000, and $212,000.
- B. $115,000, $338,000, and $124,000.
- C. $161,000, $338,000, and $90,000.
- D. $115,000, $338,000, and $212,000.

Answer (B) is correct. *(CMA, adapted)*
REQUIRED: The reported income after correction of inventory errors.
DISCUSSION: Cost of sales equals beginning inventory, plus purchases or cost of goods manufactured, minus ending inventory. Hence, over (under) statement of inventory affects cost of sales and income. The Year 1 pretax income was affected by the $23,000 Year 1 overstatement of year-end inventory. This error understated Year 1 cost of sales and overstated pretax income. The corrected income is $115,000 ($138,000 – $23,000). The same $23,000 error caused Year 2 income to be understated by overstating beginning inventory. In addition, the $61,000 understatement of Year 2 year-end inventory also caused Year 2 income to be understated. Thus, the corrected Year 2 pretax income is $338,000 ($254,000 + $23,000 + $61,000). The $61,000 understatement at the end of Year 2 caused Year 3 income to be overstated by understating beginning inventory. Income for Year 3 is understated by the $17,000 of year-end inventory understatement. Accordingly, the corrected income is $124,000 ($168,000 – $61,000 + $17,000).
Answer (A) is incorrect. Year 1 income of $161,000 results from adding, not subtracting, the $23,000 overstatement of ending inventory. Similarly, Year 2 income of $170,000 results from subtracting, not adding, the $23,000 overstatement of beginning inventory and the $61,000 understatement of ending inventory. Finally, Year 3 income of $212,000 results from adding, not subtracting, the $61,000 understatement of beginning inventory and subtracting, not adding, the understatement of ending inventory. Answer (C) is incorrect. Year 3 income of $90,000 results from subtracting, not adding, the $17,000 understatement of ending inventory. Answer (D) is incorrect. Year 3 pre-tax income should be $124,000.

9. According to the net method, which of the following items should be included in the cost of inventory?

	Freight Costs	Purchase Discounts Not Taken
A.	Yes	No
B.	Yes	Yes
C.	No	Yes
D.	No	No

Answer (A) is correct. *(CPA, adapted)*
REQUIRED: The items that should be included as inventoriable cost.
DISCUSSION: Cost is the sum of the relevant expenditures directly or indirectly incurred in bringing an item to its existing condition and location. Freight costs (but not abnormal amounts) are therefore an inventoriable cost. Under the net method, purchase discounts are treated as reductions in the invoice prices of specific purchases. Accordingly, goods available for sale reflect the purchase price net of the discount, and a purchase discount not taken is recognized as an item of interest expense.
Answer (B) is incorrect. Under the net method, purchase discounts not taken are an interest expense. Answer (C) is incorrect. Freight costs are part of inventory costs, but purchase discounts not taken under the net method are not inventory costs. Answer (D) is incorrect. Freight costs are included in the cost of inventory.

10. On July 1, Clio Company recorded purchases of inventory of $40,000 and $50,000 under credit terms of 2/15, net 30. The payment due on the $40,000 purchase was remitted on July 14. The payment due on the $50,000 purchase was remitted on July 25. Under the net method and the gross method, these purchases should be included at what respective net amounts in the determination of cost of goods available for sale?

	Net Method	Gross Method
A.	$90,000	$90,000
B.	$89,200	$88,200
C.	$88,200	$89,200
D.	$88,200	$88,200

Answer (C) is correct. *(Publisher, adapted)*
REQUIRED: The amounts at which net purchases should be measured under the net and gross methods.
DISCUSSION: The 2/15, net 30 credit term indicates that a 2% discount may be taken if payment is made within 15 days of the invoice date and that payment is overdue if not made within 30 days. The net method records purchases net of any discount. It is used when the purchaser expects to pay soon enough to take advantage of the discount provision. Accordingly, these two purchases should be recorded under the net method at $88,200 [($40,000 + $50,000) × 98%]. When the July 25 payment is made after the discount period, the purchases account is unaffected. The gross method records purchases at their gross amount. It is used when the purchaser does not expect to pay within the discount period. In this case, the July 14 payment was made within the discount period, but the July 25 payment was not. Accordingly, these two purchases should be recorded under the gross method at $89,200 [($40,000 × 98%) + $50,000]. This amount is net of the purchase discount taken, an item subtracted from purchases on the income statement.
Answer (A) is incorrect. The amount of $90,000 does not reflect the discount taken (gross method) or the discounts expected to be taken (net method). Answer (B) is incorrect. The net method and gross method amounts are $88,200 and $89,200, respectively. Answer (D) is incorrect. The two purchases should be recorded under the gross method at $89,200 [($40,000 × 98%) + $50,000].

11. The following costs were incurred by Parthos Co., a manufacturer, during the current year:

Accounting and legal fees	$ 50,000
Freight-in	350,000
Freight-out	320,000
Officers' salaries	300,000
Insurance	170,000
Sales representatives' salaries	430,000

What amount of these costs should be reported as general and administrative expenses for the current year?

A. $520,000

B. $1,100,000

C. $1,270,000

D. $1,620,000

Answer (A) is correct. *(CPA, adapted)*
REQUIRED: The amount to be reported as general and administrative expenses for the year.
DISCUSSION: General and administrative expenses are incurred for the direction of the entity as a whole and are not related wholly to a specific function, e.g., selling or manufacturing. They include (1) accounting, legal, and other fees for professional services; (2) officers' salaries; (3) insurance; (4) wages of office staff; (5) miscellaneous supplies; (6) utilities' costs; and (7) office occupancy costs. Thus, the general and administrative expenses for Parthos equaled $520,000 ($50,000 + $300,000 + $170,000).
Answer (B) is incorrect. The amount of $1,100,000 does not include insurance and incorrectly includes the sales representatives' salaries and freight-out (selling costs). Answer (C) is incorrect. Freight-out costs and sales representatives' salaries are included. Answer (D) is incorrect. Freight costs and sales representatives' salaries are not considered general and administrative costs.

12. In theory, the cash discounts allowed on purchased merchandise (purchase discounts) in a periodic inventory system should be

A. Deducted from purchases in determination of goods available for sale.

B. Deducted from cost of goods sold in the income statement.

C. Shown as other income in the income statement.

D. Deducted from inventory on the balance sheet at year end.

Answer (A) is correct. *(D.G. Kame)*
REQUIRED: The theoretically correct treatment of cash discounts earned on the purchase of merchandise.
DISCUSSION: In theory, cash discounts on purchases should be treated as reductions in the invoiced prices of specific purchases so that goods available for sale reflects the purchase price net of the discounts. It is consistent with this approach to record any purchase discounts not taken as a financial expense in the income statement.
Answer (B) is incorrect. Purchase discounts should be matched with the purchases with which they were associated, i.e., shown as a contra-account to purchases. Deducting them from cost of goods sold is therefore inappropriate. Answer (C) is incorrect. Under the net method, purchase discounts taken are not recognized. Under the gross method, they reduce purchases. Answer (D) is incorrect. Purchase discounts should be matched with the purchases with which they were associated, i.e., shown as a contra-account to purchases. They cannot be assigned in full to ending inventory.

13. Le Sud Retailers purchased merchandise with a list price of $20,000, subject to trade discounts of 20% and 10%, with no cash discounts allowable. Le Sud should record the cost of this merchandise as

A. $14,000

B. $14,400

C. $15,600

D. $20,000

Answer (B) is correct. *(CPA, adapted)*

REQUIRED: The amount to be recorded as a cost of inventory subject to trade discounts.

DISCUSSION: When inventory is subject to cash discounts, the purchases may be reflected either net of these discounts or at the gross prices. However, purchases always should be recorded net of trade discounts. A chain discount is the application of more than one trade discount to a list price. Chain discounts should be applied in steps as indicated below.

List price	$20,000
20% discount	(4,000)
	$16,000
10% discount	(1,600)
Cost of merchandise	$14,400

Answer (A) is incorrect. The amount of $14,000 applies both discounts to the retail price. Answer (C) is incorrect. The amount of $15,600 assumes the 10% discount is applied to the 20% discount. Answer (D) is incorrect. The amount of $20,000 is the list price, and it fails to reflect the discounts.

14. Madrid Corp.'s trial balance for the year ended December 31, Year 1, included the following:

	Debit	Credit
Sales		$600,000
Cost of sales	$240,000	
Administrative expenses	60,000	
Loss on sale of equipment	36,000	
Sales commissions	40,000	
Interest revenue		20,000
Freight-out	12,000	
Loss on early retirement of long-term debt	40,000	
Bad debt expense	12,000	
Totals	$440,000	$620,000

Other information:

Finished goods inventory:

January 1, Year 1	$400,000
December 31, Year 1	360,000

In Madrid's Year 1 multiple-step income statement, the cost of goods manufactured was

A. $200,000

B. $212,000

C. $280,000

D. $292,000

Answer (A) is correct. *(CPA, adapted)*

REQUIRED: The cost of goods manufactured.

DISCUSSION: Cost of goods sold equals beginning finished goods inventory, plus cost of goods manufactured, minus ending finished goods inventory. Hence, cost of goods manufactured equals cost of goods sold, plus ending finished goods inventory, minus beginning finished goods inventory, or $200,000 ($240,000 cost of goods sold + $360,000 ending finished goods inventory – $400,000 beginning finished goods inventory).

Answer (B) is incorrect. The amount of $212,000 includes the freight-out. Answer (C) is incorrect. The amount of $280,000 subtracts ending finished goods and adds beginning finished goods. Answer (D) is incorrect. The amount of $292,000 subtracts ending finished goods inventory and adds beginning finished goods. It also includes the freight-out.

15. On December 28, Nord Manufacturing Co. purchased goods costing $50,000. The terms were FOB destination. Some costs incurred in connection with the sale and delivery of the goods were

Packaging for shipment	$1,000
Shipping	1,500
Special handling charges	2,000

These goods were received on December 31. In Nord's December 31 balance sheet, what amount of cost should be included in inventory?

A. $54,500

B. $53,500

C. $52,000

D. $50,000

Answer (D) is correct. *(CPA, adapted)*

REQUIRED: The amount of cost for goods included in inventory.

DISCUSSION: FOB destination means that title passes upon delivery at the destination, the seller bears the risk of loss, and the seller is responsible for the expense of delivering the goods to the designated point. Consequently, the costs incurred for sale and delivery (packaging, shipping, and handling costs) other than to make the inventory salable are not included in the inventory. The amount that should be included is therefore the purchase price of $50,000.

Answer (A) is incorrect. The packaging, shipping, and handling costs should not be included. Answer (B) is incorrect. The shipping and handling costs should not be included. Answer (C) is incorrect. The handling costs should not be included.

6.2 Items Counted in Inventory

16. Guinea Corp. produced 1,000 units of its product that it sold for cash to Moresby Corp. In a related transaction, Guinea agreed to repurchase the 1,000 units at a specified price at a future date. The price specified in the agreement is not subject to change based on future market fluctuations except for fluctuations resulting from finance and holding costs incurred by Moresby. Guinea should account for these transactions by

A. Recording the sale in an ordinary manner and removing the inventory from the balance sheet.

B. Recording the sale, removing the inventory from the balance sheet, and disclosing the purchase commitment in the notes to the financial statements.

C. Continuing to recognize the inventory and recording a valuation account to be reported as a reduction of the inventory on the balance sheet, rather than recording a sale.

D. Recording a liability and continuing to recognize the inventory rather than recording a sale.

Answer (D) is correct. *(Publisher, adapted)*
REQUIRED: The proper accounting treatment of a sale of inventory coupled with a repurchase agreement.
DISCUSSION: The transaction is, in substance, a financing arrangement. In essence, the future reacquisition of the inventory is a return of collateral upon payment of a debt. Guinea should account for the transaction as if it were a financing arrangement, not record a sale.
Answer (A) is incorrect. Recording the sale in an ordinary manner and removing the inventory from the balance sheet is appropriate for a sale. Answer (B) is incorrect. The sale and repurchase transactions are, in substance, a financing arrangement. Answer (C) is incorrect. The transaction must be accounted for by recording a liability and finance charges rather than by reducing inventory.

17. Naples Company bought a product on behalf of Rome Corporation. In a related transaction, Rome agreed to buy the product from Naples at a specified price at a specified date in the future. Rome should record an asset and a related obligation at the date that

A. The agreement is signed.

B. Naples acquires the product.

C. Naples ships the product to Rome.

D. Rome receives the product.

Answer (B) is correct. *(Publisher, adapted)*
REQUIRED: The date on which a product financing arrangement should be recorded.
DISCUSSION: The transaction is essentially a financing arrangement because Rome has acquired rights in the product without an immediate expenditure. Rome should record the asset and the related liability when Naples acquires the product. Naples is acting for Rome, and Rome should treat the goods received by Naples as if Rome itself had received them.
Answer (A) is incorrect. Purchases are not ordinarily recorded until title to the goods passes. Answer (C) is incorrect. Rome should record the inventory and liability when Naples acquires the product, not later. Answer (D) is incorrect. Recognition should not be deferred until Rome receives the product.

18. Aramis Co.'s inventory at December 31, Year 1, was $1,500,000 based on a physical count priced at cost and before any necessary adjustment for the following:

● Merchandise costing $90,000, shipped FOB shipping point from a vendor on December 30, Year 1, was received and recorded on January 5, Year 2.

● Goods in the shipping area were excluded from inventory although shipment was not made until January 4, Year 2. The goods, billed to the customer FOB shipping point on December 30, Year 1, had a cost of $120,000.

What amount should Aramis report as inventory in its December 31, Year 1, balance sheet?

A. $1,500,000

B. $1,590,000

C. $1,620,000

D. $1,710,000

Answer (D) is correct. *(CPA, adapted)*
REQUIRED: The year-end inventory.
DISCUSSION: The inventory balance prior to adjustments was $1,500,000. The merchandise shipped FOB shipping point to Aramis should be included because title passed when the goods were shipped. The goods in the shipping area should be included because title did not pass until the goods were shipped on January 4, Year 2, even though the customer was billed in Year 1. Thus, the inventory should be $1,710,000 ($1,500,000 + $90,000 + $120,000).
Answer (A) is incorrect. The amount of $1,500,000 excludes the $90,000 of goods shipped by a vendor and the $120,000 of goods not shipped until January 4. Answer (B) is incorrect. The amount of $1,590,000 results from failing to include the $120,000 of goods not shipped until January 4. Answer (C) is incorrect. The amount of $1,620,000 does not include the $90,000 of goods shipped by a vendor FOB shipping point.

19. A sponsoring entity enters into an agreement by which it sells a product to another entity and agrees to repurchase that product at specified prices at later dates. If the specified prices fluctuate solely because of changes in purchasing, financing, and holding costs, the transaction should be treated as which of the following?

    A. A borrowing.

    B. A consignment.

    C. A sale and repurchase.

    D. Not recorded.

Answer (A) is correct. *(Publisher, adapted)*
REQUIRED: The correct accounting treatment of a product financing arrangement.
DISCUSSION: This arrangement is a transaction in which an entity sells and agrees to repurchase inventory, with the repurchase price equal to the original price plus carrying and financing costs. It should be treated as a borrowing if the specified prices do not fluctuate except to cover changes in purchasing, financing, and holding costs.
Answer (B) is incorrect. A consignment is the consignor's inventory physically located at the consignee's place of operations. Answer (C) is incorrect. A sale and repurchase describes the form of the transaction, not the substance. Answer (D) is incorrect. Liabilities must be recorded.

20. On December 30, Year 3, Exmoor Corp. sold merchandise for $75,000 to Frinia Co. The terms of the sale were net 30, FOB shipping point. The merchandise was shipped on December 31, Year 3, and arrived at Frinia on January 5, Year 4. Because of a clerical error, the sale was not recorded until January Year 4, and the merchandise, sold at a 25% markup, was included in Exmoor's inventory at December 31, Year 3. As a result, Exmoor's cost of goods sold for the year ended December 31, Year 3, was

    A. Understated by $75,000.

    B. Understated by $60,000.

    C. Understated by $15,000.

    D. Correctly stated.

Answer (B) is correct. *(CPA, adapted)*
REQUIRED: The cost of goods sold given delayed recording of a sale.
DISCUSSION: Under the shipping terms, the sale should have been recognized on December 31, Year 3, because title and risk of loss passed to the buyer on that date; that is, an earning process was complete. Exmoor should have debited a receivable and credited sales for $75,000, the net amount, on the date of shipment. Exmoor should also have debited cost of sales and credited inventory at cost on the same date. The error therefore understated cost of goods sold by $60,000 ($75,000 sales price ÷ 125% of cost).
Answer (A) is incorrect. The selling price is $75,000. Answer (C) is incorrect. The amount of the markup is $15,000. Answer (D) is incorrect. Cost of goods sold was understated.

21. Seller Co. is a calendar-year retailer. Its year-end physical count of inventory on hand did not consider the effects of the following transactions:

● Goods with a cost of $50,000 were shipped by Seller FOB shipping point on December 30 and were tendered to and accepted by the buyer on January 4.

● Goods with a cost of $40,000 were shipped FOB destination by a vendor on December 30 and were tendered to and accepted by Seller on January 4.

● Goods were sold on the installment basis by Seller. Installment receivables representing sales of goods with a cost of $30,000 were reported at year-end. Seller retains title to such goods until full payment is made.

● Goods with a cost of $20,000 were held on consignment for vendor. These goods were excluded from the count although they were sold in January.

If inventory based solely on the physical count of items on hand equaled $1 million, Seller should report inventory at year-end of

    A. $1,000,000

    B. $1,090,000

    C. $1,120,000

    D. $1,140,000

Answer (A) is correct. *(Publisher, adapted)*
REQUIRED: The year-end inventory.
DISCUSSION: Goods shipped FOB shipping point become the property of the buyer when shipped. Thus, they were properly excluded from inventory. Goods shipped FOB destination become the property of the buyer (Seller Co.) when tender of delivery is made, so these goods were also properly excluded. Although title is retained to goods sold on the installment basis, the goods are excluded from inventory because control over the goods has passed to the buyer, assuming a reasonable expectation of payment in the ordinary course of business. Finally, in a consignment, the consignor ships merchandise to the consignee, who acts as an agent for the consignor in selling the goods. The goods are held by the consignee but remain the property of the consignor and are included in the consignor's inventory at cost. Accordingly, the physical count requires no adjustment for any of the listed transactions. Ending inventory is $1 million.
Answer (B) is incorrect. The amount of $1,090,000 reflects the goods Seller shipped FOB shipping point and the goods Seller received that were shipped FOB destination. Answer (C) is incorrect. The amount of $1,120,000 reflects all the listed transactions except the consignment. Answer (D) is incorrect. The amount of $1,140,000 reflects all the listed transactions.

22. On June 1, Halle Corp. sold merchandise with a list price of $5,000 to Bonn on account. Halle allowed trade discounts of 30% and 20%. Credit terms were 2/15, n/40, and the sale was made FOB shipping point. Halle prepaid $200 of delivery costs for Bonn as an accommodation. On June 12, Halle received from Bonn a remittance in full payment amounting to

A. $2,744

B. $2,940

C. $2,944

D. $3,140

Answer (C) is correct.   *(CPA, adapted)*
REQUIRED: The amount received as a remittance in full payment.
DISCUSSION: Inventory sold always should be invoiced net of trade discounts. Remittances paid during the cash or purchase discount period should be net of these discounts. When goods are shipped FOB shipping point, they become the purchaser's inventory at the time of shipment. Thus, the purchaser is responsible for the payment of delivery costs. As indicated below, the remittance received by Halle should amount to $2,944.

List price	$5,000
30% trade discount	(1,500)
	$3,500
20% trade discount	(700)
	$2,800
2% cash discount	(56)
	$2,744
Delivery costs	200
	$2,944

Answer (A) is incorrect. The amount of $2,744 excludes the delivery costs. Answer (B) is incorrect. The amount of $2,940 includes a 2% cash discount on the delivery costs. Answer (D) is incorrect. The amount of $3,140 includes a 2% discount on the delivery costs and double counts the delivery costs.

23. Lew Co. sold 200,000 corrugated boxes for $2 each. Lew's cost was $1 per unit. The sales agreement gave the customer the right to return up to 60% of the boxes within the first 6 months, provided an appropriate reason was given. It was reasonably estimated that 5% of the boxes would be returned. Lew absorbed an additional $10,000 to process the returns and expects to resell the boxes. What amount should Lew report as operating profit from this transaction?

A. $170,000

B. $179,500

C. $180,000

D. $200,000

Answer (C) is correct.   *(CPA, adapted)*
REQUIRED: The amount reported as operating profit.
DISCUSSION: The sale may be recognized at the time of sale if all of the following conditions are met:

1.   The seller's price is substantially fixed or determinable.

2.   The buyer has paid the seller, or the buyer is obligated to pay, and the obligation is not contingent on resale.

3.   The buyer's obligation to the seller is unchanged by damage to, or theft or destruction of, the product.

4.   The buyer has economic substance apart from the seller.

5.   The seller does not have any significant obligations regarding resale of the product by the buyer.

6.   The amount of future returns can be reasonably estimated.

Assuming that these six conditions are met, Lew Co.'s revenues were $400,000 (200,000 boxes × $2), cost of goods sold was $200,000 (200,000 boxes × $1), and gross profit was $200,000 ($400,000 – $200,000). Cost of goods sold equals cost of goods manufactured (or purchases for a retailer) adjusted for the change in finished goods inventory. Because a reasonable estimate of returns could be made, Lew subtracts a 5% allowance ($200,000 × 5%) to arrive at operating profit. Lew will also incur an additional $10,000 to process the returns. Thus, operating profit is $180,000 ($200,000 gross profit – $10,000 additional processing cost – $10,000 allowance for returns).
Answer (A) is incorrect. The amount of $170,000 results from subtracting the cost of the returned boxes twice.
Answer (B) is incorrect. The amount of $179,500 results from an additional subtraction for 5% of the $10,000 processing cost.
Answer (D) is incorrect. The amount of $200,000 is the gross profit.

24. Lin Co., a distributor of machinery, bought a machine from the manufacturer in November for $10,000. On December 30, Lin sold this machine to Zee Hardware for $15,000 under the following terms: 2% discount if paid within 30 days, 1% discount if paid after 30 days but within 60 days, or payable in full within 90 days if not paid within the discount periods. However, Zee has the right to return this machine to Lin if Zee is unable to resell the machine before expiration of the 90-day payment period, in which case Zee's obligation to Lin is canceled. In Lin's net sales for the year ended December 31, how much should be included for the sale of this machine to Zee?

A. $0
B. $14,700
C. $14,850
D. $15,000

25. When a company sells its products and gives the buyer the right to return the product, revenue from the sale should be recognized at the time of sale only if certain criteria are met. Which one of the following is not a criterion?

A. The seller does not have significant obligations for future performance to directly bring about the resale of the product by the buyer.

B. The buyer acquiring the product for resale has economic substance apart from that provided by the seller.

C. The buyer's obligation to the seller would not be changed in the event of physical destruction of the product.

D. The seller's price to the buyer is contingent upon the ultimate selling price received when the product is resold.

Answer (A) is correct. *(CPA, adapted)*
REQUIRED: The sales revenue to be recognized when a right of return exists.
DISCUSSION: The sale may be recognized at the time of sale if all of the following conditions are met:

1. The seller's price is substantially fixed or determinable.
2. The buyer has paid the seller, or the buyer is obligated to pay, and the obligation is not contingent on resale.
3. The buyer's obligation to the seller is unchanged by damage to or theft of or destruction of the product.
4. The buyer has economic substance apart from the seller.
5. The seller does not have any significant obligations regarding resale of the product by the buyer.
6. The amount of future returns can be reasonably estimated.

The buyer has the right to return the machine to the seller, and the obligation to pay is contingent on resale. Thus, the second condition is not met, and no recognition of sales revenue and cost of sales is allowable.
Answer (B) is incorrect. The sale, net of the 2% discount, is not recorded on Lin's books. Answer (C) is incorrect. The net sale is not recorded on Lin's books. Answer (D) is incorrect. The gross sale is not recorded on Lin's books.

Answer (D) is correct. *(CMA, adapted)*
REQUIRED: The item not a criterion for the recognition of a sale when the right of return exists.
DISCUSSION: Revenue may be recognized at the time of sale if all of the following conditions are met:

1. The seller's price is substantially fixed or determinable.
2. The buyer has paid the seller, or the buyer is obligated to pay, and the obligation is not contingent on resale.
3. The buyer's obligation to the seller is unchanged by damage to, or theft of or destruction of, the product.
4. The buyer has economic substance apart from the seller.
5. The seller does not have any significant obligations regarding resale of the product by the buyer.
6. The amount of future returns can be reasonably estimated.

Thus, the seller's price must not be contingent on the resale price; the seller's price must be substantially fixed or determinable.
Answer (A) is incorrect. The seller may not have significant future obligations. Answer (B) is incorrect. The buyer must have economic substance apart from the seller. Answer (C) is incorrect. Risk of loss must reside with the buyer.

26. Net losses on firm purchase commitments for goods for inventory result from a contract price that exceeds the current market price. If a firm expects that losses will occur when the purchase is effected, expected losses, if material,

A. Should be recognized in the accounts and separately disclosed as losses on the income statement of the period during which the decline in price takes place.

B. Should be recognized in the accounts and separately disclosed as net unrealized losses on the balance sheet at the end of the period during which the decline in price takes place.

C. Should be recognized in the accounts and separately disclosed as net unrealized losses on the balance sheet at the end of the period during which the contract is executed.

D. Should not be recognized in the accounts until the contract is executed and need not be separately disclosed in the financial statements.

Answer (A) is correct. *(CMA, adapted)*
REQUIRED: The accounting treatment of losses arising from a firm (noncancelable) purchase commitment not yet exercised.
DISCUSSION: GAAP require the accrual of a loss in the current year's income statement on a firm purchase commitment to purchase goods for inventory if the market price of these goods declines below the commitment price. This loss should be measured in the same manner as inventory losses. Disclosure of the loss is also required. The entry is to debit an estimated loss and to credit an estimated liability. However, a gain on a noncancelable, unhedged firm commitment is not recognized. Furthermore, GAAP do not currently require recognition of an asset and liability when the firm commitment to purchase goods is made.
When a previously unrecognized firm commitment is designated as a hedged item, an asset or liability is recognized related to a gain or loss, respectively, recognized on the firm commitment.
Answer (B) is incorrect. The losses should be recognized in net income. Answer (C) is incorrect. The losses should be recognized in net income for the period during which they occurred. Answer (D) is incorrect. If a loss arises out of a firm, noncancelable, and unhedged commitment, it should be recognized in the current year.

27. At the beginning of its fiscal year, Ankara Corp. signed a 3-year, noncancelable purchase contract, which allows it to purchase up to 500,000 units of a component annually from Cairo Company at $.10 per unit and guarantees a minimum annual purchase of 100,000 units. During the year, the component unexpectedly became obsolete. Ankara had 250,000 units of this inventory at year end and believes they can be sold as scrap for $.02 per unit. What amount of probable loss from the purchase commitment should Ankara report in its income statement?

A. $24,000

B. $20,000

C. $16,000

D. $8,000

Answer (C) is correct. *(CPA, adapted)*
REQUIRED: The amount of probable loss from the purchase commitment.
DISCUSSION: GAAP require the accrual of a loss in the current year's income statement on a firm purchase commitment to purchase goods for inventory if the market price of these goods declines below the commitment price. This loss should be measured in the same manner as inventory losses. Disclosure of the loss is also required. Consequently, given that 200,000 units must be purchased over the next 2 years for $20,000 (200,000 × $.10) and the parts can be sold as scrap for $4,000 (200,000 × $.02), the amount of probable loss from the purchase commitment is $16,000 ($20,000 – $4,000).
Answer (A) is incorrect. The amount of $24,000 includes the purchase commitment for the current year. Answer (B) is incorrect. The amount of $20,000 excludes the net realizable value of the parts from the calculation. Answer (D) is incorrect. The amount of $8,000 excludes the probable loss expected in the last year of the purchase commitment.

28. During Year 4, R Corp., a manufacturer of chocolate candies, contracted to purchase 100,000 pounds of cocoa beans at $1.00 per pound, delivery to be made in the spring of Year 5. Because a record harvest is predicted for Year 5, the price per pound for cocoa beans had fallen to $.80 by December 31, Year 4. Of the following journal entries, the one that would properly reflect in Year 4 the effect of the commitment of R Corp. to purchase the 100,000 pounds of cocoa is

A. Cocoa inventory	$100,000	
Accounts payable		$100,000

B. Cocoa inventory	$80,000	
Loss on purchase commitments	$20,000	
Accounts payable		$100,000

C. Loss on purchase commitments	$20,000	
Accrued loss on purchase commitments		$20,000

D. No entry is necessary in Year 4.

Answer (C) is correct. *(CPA, adapted)*
REQUIRED: The journal entries to reflect the purchase commitment.
DISCUSSION: Recognition of the loss in the income statement and accrual of a liability in Year 4 are required (assuming the purchase commitment is noncancelable). The loss on purchase commitments is an expense. Accrued loss on purchase commitments is a liability.
Answer (A) is incorrect. The entry does not recognize a loss and improperly records an asset. Answer (B) is incorrect. The entry prematurely records the cocoa as an asset prior to acquisition. The loss on purchase commitments is an expense account. Answer (D) is incorrect. An entry is needed to recognize the loss.

6.3 Cost Flow Methods: FIFO, LIFO, Weighted Average

29. The weighted average for the year inventory cost flow method is applicable to which of the following inventory systems?

	Periodic	Perpetual
A.	Yes	Yes
B.	Yes	No
C.	No	Yes
D.	No	No

Answer (B) is correct. *(CPA, adapted)*
REQUIRED: The applicability of the weighted-average cost flow method to periodic and perpetual inventory systems.
DISCUSSION: The weighted-average method determines an average cost only once (at the end of the period) and is therefore applicable only to a periodic system. In contrast, the moving-average method requires determination of a new weighted-average cost after each purchase and thus applies only to a perpetual system.
Answer (A) is incorrect. The weighted-average method does not apply to the perpetual inventory system. Answer (C) is incorrect. The weighted-average method applies to the periodic inventory system. The moving-average method applies to a perpetual system. Answer (D) is incorrect. The weighted average applies to the periodic inventory system.

30. Assuming constant inventory quantities, which of the following inventory-costing methods will produce a lower inventory turnover ratio in an inflationary economy?

A. FIFO (first-in, first-out).

B. LIFO (last-in, first-out).

C. Moving average.

D. Weighted average.

Answer (A) is correct. *(CPA, adapted)*
REQUIRED: The inventory-costing method producing a lower inventory turnover ratio in an inflationary economy.
DISCUSSION: The inventory turnover ratio equals cost of goods sold divided by the average of beginning and ending inventory. Under FIFO, ending inventory is assumed to contain the most recently purchased items, and cost of goods sold is assumed to contain the costs of the earliest purchased items. Under LIFO, the opposite assumptions are made. In an inflationary economy, costs are increasing. Thus, FIFO cost of goods sold is lower, and FIFO ending or average inventory is higher than under LIFO. The inventory methods based on average costs produce results that lie between those of FIFO and LIFO. Accordingly, inventory turnover is lowest under FIFO because the numerator is lower and the denominator is higher than under other methods.
Answer (B) is incorrect. Use of LIFO results in the highest inventory turnover (highest COGS, lowest inventory). Answer (C) is incorrect. The moving average inventory costing method results in an inventory turnover ratio between those calculated using FIFO and LIFO. Answer (D) is incorrect. The weighted average inventory costing method results in an inventory turnover ratio between those calculated using FIFO and LIFO.

31. Sackett Corporation had a beginning inventory of 10,000 units, which were purchased in the prior year as follows:

	Units	Unit Price
September	4,000	$2.00
October	4,000	$2.10
December	2,000	$2.30

In the current year, Sackett purchases an additional 12,000 units (7,000 in June at $2.50 and 5,000 in November at $2.70) and sells 16,000 units. Using the FIFO method, what is Sackett's ending inventory?

A. $12,200 (4,000 @ $2.00 and 2,000 @ $2.10)

B. $13,000 (4,000 @ $2.10 and 2,000 @ $2.30)

C. $15,600 (6,000 @ $2.60 – average of $2.50 and $2.70)

D. $16,000 (5,000 @ $2.70 and 1,000 @ $2.50)

Answer (D) is correct. *(CPA, adapted)*
REQUIRED: The ending inventory based on FIFO.
DISCUSSION: Under FIFO, the first goods purchased are assumed to be the first sold. Using FIFO, all of the 10,000 units of inventory in beginning inventory were sold, and 6,000 (16,000 sold – 10,000 beginning inventory) of the units purchased in June were sold for $2.50 per unit. Ending inventory therefore is assumed to contain 1,000 units purchased in June for $2.50 per unit and all 5,000 units purchased in November for $2.70 per unit.
Answer (A) is incorrect. The amount of $12,200 is Sackett's ending inventory based on LIFO. Answer (B) is incorrect. The amount of $13,000 is based on two assumptions: All inventory purchased in the current year is sold before beginning inventory, and FIFO is applied to the units in beginning inventory. Answer (C) is incorrect. The amount of $15,600 is based on the assumption that the average price paid for the last two purchases is averaged and applied to the remaining units in inventory.

Questions 32 through 36 are based on the following information. Toulouse Co. began the month of November with 150 baubles on hand at a cost of $4.00 each. These baubles sell for $7.00 each. The following schedule presents the sales and purchases of this item during the month of November.

Date of Transaction	Purchases Quantity Received	Unit Cost	Units Sold
November 5			100
November 7	200	$4.20	
November 9			150
November 11	200	4.40	
November 17			220
November 22	250	4.80	
November 29			100

32. If Toulouse uses FIFO inventory pricing, the inventory on November 30 will be

A. $936

B. $1,012

C. $1,046

D. $1,104

Answer (D) is correct. *(CMA, adapted)*
REQUIRED: The value of the ending inventory using the FIFO method of inventory costing.
DISCUSSION: Under FIFO, the ending inventory consists of the most recent inventory purchased. The beginning inventory included 150 units and purchases totaled 650 units, a total of 800 units. Sales equaled 570 units (100 + 150 + 220 + 100). Thus, ending inventory was 230 units (800 – 570). Under FIFO, these units are valued at the cost of the most recent 230 units purchased, or $4.80. Ending inventory is therefore $1,104 (230 × $4.80).
Answer (A) is incorrect. The amount of $936 is based on periodic LIFO. Answer (B) is incorrect. The amount of $1,012 is based on the weighted-average unit cost of $4.40, not $4.80. Answer (C) is incorrect. The amount of $1,046 is the ending inventory under perpetual LIFO.

33. If Toulouse uses perpetual moving-average inventory pricing, the sale of 220 items on November 17 will be recorded at a unit cost of

A. $4.00

B. $4.16

C. $4.20

D. $4.32

Answer (D) is correct. *(CMA, adapted)*
REQUIRED: The unit cost of the items sold on November 17 under the perpetual moving-average method.
DISCUSSION: The beginning inventory consisted of 150 units at $4.00 each. Following the November 5 sale, the inventory valuation was $200 (50 units × $4). The November 7 purchase added 200 units at $4.20, after which the moving average unit cost was $4.16 {[$200 + (200 units × $4.20)] ÷ (50 units + 200 units)}. The November 9 sale of 150 units left 100 units at $4.16. Adding $416 (100 units × $4.16) to the $880 purchase on November 11 brought the total inventory to 300 units with a total cost of $1,296, or $4.32 each. Thus, $4.32 was the unit cost of items sold on November 17.
Answer (A) is incorrect. The amount of $4.00 was the cost of the beginning inventory. Answer (B) is incorrect. The amount of $4.16 was the unit cost of the items sold on November 9. Answer (C) is incorrect. The amount of $4.20 would have been the cost if the perpetual LIFO method had been used for the November 9 sale.

34. If Toulouse uses weighted-average inventory pricing, the gross profit for November will be

A. $1,046

B. $1,482

C. $1,516

D. $1,528

Answer (B) is correct. *(CMA, adapted)*

REQUIRED: The gross profit if the weighted-average method is used.

DISCUSSION: The total goods available for sale is determined as follows:

Beginning inventory	150	× $4.00	=	$ 600.00
Nov. 7 purchase	200	× $4.20	=	840.00
Nov. 11 purchase	200	× $4.40	=	880.00
Nov. 22 purchase	250	× $4.80	=	1,200.00
Total available	800			$3,520.00

The weighted-average unit cost is $4.40 ($3,520 ÷ 800 units available). The cost of goods sold and total sales are therefore $2,508 (570 units sold × $4.40) and $3,990 (570 units × $7), respectively. Consequently, gross profit is $1,482 ($3,990 – $2,508).

Answer (A) is incorrect. The amount of $1,046 is the ending inventory under perpetual LIFO. Answer (C) is incorrect. The amount of $1,516 is based on perpetual LIFO. Answer (D) is incorrect. The amount of $1,528 is based on the moving-average method.

35. If Toulouse uses periodic LIFO inventory pricing, the cost of goods sold for November will be

A. $2,416

B. $2,444

C. $2,474

D. $2,584

Answer (D) is correct. *(CMA, adapted)*

REQUIRED: The cost of goods sold using periodic LIFO.

DISCUSSION: The goods available for sale is as follows:

Beginning inventory	150	× $4.00	=	$ 600.00
Nov. 7 purchase	200	× $4.20	=	840.00
Nov. 11 purchase	200	× $4.40	=	880.00
Nov. 22 purchase	250	× $4.80	=	1,200.00
Total available	800			$3,520.00

The ending inventory consists of 230 units. Under periodic LIFO, these are costed at the prices paid for the earliest 230 units purchased, or 150 units at $4.00 and 80 units at $4.20, a total of $936. Hence, cost of goods sold is $2,584 ($3,520 goods available – $936 EI).

Answer (A) is incorrect. The amount of $2,416 is based on the FIFO method. Answer (B) is incorrect. The amount of $2,444 is based on the moving-average method. Answer (C) is incorrect. The amount of $2,474 is based on perpetual LIFO.

36. If Toulouse uses perpetual LIFO inventory pricing, the inventory at November 30 will be

A. $936

B. $1,012

C. $1,046

D. $1,076

Answer (C) is correct. *(CMA, adapted)*

REQUIRED: The value of the inventory.

DISCUSSION: Under perpetual LIFO, the inventory valuation is recalculated as follows after every purchase and sale. The 230 units in ending inventory consist of 150 units at $4.80 each, 30 units at $4.20 each, and 50 units from the beginning inventory at $4.00 each.

Date	Receipts	Sales	Ending Inventory
11-1	150 × $4.00 = $600		$ 600.00
11-5		100 × $4.00 = $400	200.00
11-7	200 × $4.20 = $840		1,040.00
11-9		150 × $4.20 = $630	410.00
11-11	200 × $4.40 = $880		1,290.00
11-17		200 × $4.40 = $880	
		20 × $4.20 = $84	326.00
11-22	250 × $4.80 = $1,200		1,526.00
11-29		100 × $4.80 = $480	1,046.00

Answer (A) is incorrect. The amount of $936 is based on periodic LIFO. Answer (B) is incorrect. The amount of $1,012 is based on the weighted-average method. Answer (D) is incorrect. The amount of $1,076 is based on the moving-average method.

37. The LIFO inventory cost flow method may be applied to which of the following inventory systems?

	Periodic	Perpetual
A.	No	No
B.	No	Yes
C.	Yes	Yes
D.	Yes	No

Answer (C) is correct. *(CPA, adapted)*
REQUIRED: The applicability of LIFO to periodic and perpetual inventory systems.
DISCUSSION: In a periodic system, a purchases account is used, and the beginning inventory remains unchanged during the accounting period. Cost of goods sold is determined at year end. It is the difference between the goods available for sale (beginning inventory + purchases) and ending inventory. In a perpetual system, purchases are directly recorded in the inventory account. Cost of goods sold is determined as the goods are sold. LIFO may be applied to both a periodic and a perpetual system, but the amount of cost of goods sold may vary with the system chosen.
Answer (A) is incorrect. LIFO may be used under both a periodic and a perpetual inventory system. Answer (B) is incorrect. LIFO may be used under a periodic inventory system. Answer (D) is incorrect. LIFO may be used under a perpetual inventory system.

38. The operations of a firm may be viewed as a continual series of transactions or as a series of separate ventures. The inventory cost flow method that views a firm as a series of separate ventures is

A. First-in, first-out.

B. Last-in, first-out.

C. Weighted average.

D. Specific identification.

Answer (D) is correct. *(CMA, adapted)*
REQUIRED: The inventory cost flow assumption that views a firm as a series of separate ventures.
DISCUSSION: When specific inventory is clearly identified from the time of purchase through the time of sale and is costed on that basis, the firm's operations may be viewed as a series of separate ventures or transactions. Much business activity, however, involves goods whose identity is lost between the time of acquisition and the time of sale. Moreover, if items of inventory are interchangeable, the use of specific identification may not result in the most useful financial information. For these reasons, other inventory cost flow assumptions essentially view the firm as a continual series of transactions.
Answer (A) is incorrect. FIFO views the firm's activities as a continual series of transactions. Answer (B) is incorrect. LIFO views the firm's activities as a continual series of transactions. Answer (C) is incorrect. Weighted average views the firm's activities as a continual series of transactions.

39. During periods of inflation, a perpetual inventory system will result in the same dollar amount of ending inventory as a periodic inventory system under which of the following inventory cost-flow assumptions?

	FIFO	LIFO
A.	Yes	No
B.	Yes	Yes
C.	No	Yes
D.	No	No

Answer (A) is correct. *(CPA, adapted)*
REQUIRED: The effect of perpetual and periodic inventory systems on the dollar amount of ending inventory.
DISCUSSION: In periods of inflation, a perpetual inventory system will result in the same dollar amount of ending inventory as a periodic inventory system assuming a FIFO cost flow. Under both perpetual and periodic systems, the same units are deemed to be in ending inventory. During periods of inflation, a perpetual inventory system will generate a dollar amount different from that of a periodic inventory system assuming a LIFO inventory cost flow. These two methods assume that different units are in the LIFO ending inventory. The periodic system determines the cost of sales only at year end, but the perpetual system determines cost of sales as the sales take place. Thus, the perpetual system assumes that layers of inventory may be liquidated during a year even though inventory quantities are restored by later purchases. The periodic system does not make this assumption.
Answer (B) is incorrect. LIFO periodic and LIFO perpetual inventory cost-flow assumptions result in different ending inventory amounts. They assume that different units are in ending inventory. Answer (C) is incorrect. LIFO periodic and LIFO perpetual inventory cost-flow assumptions result in different ending inventory amounts. They assume that different units are in ending inventory. FIFO perpetual and FIFO periodic methods assume that the same units are in ending inventory. Answer (D) is incorrect. FIFO periodic and FIFO perpetual inventory cost-flow assumptions assume that the same units are in ending inventory, resulting in the same ending inventory amount.

40. A company had 2,000 units of opening inventory that cost $20 per unit. On May 1, 2,000 units were purchased at a cost of $22 each, and on September 1, another 2,000 units were purchased at a cost of $24 each. If 4,000 units were sold during the year, the company will report cost of goods sold of <List A> if the <List B> method of inventory valuation is used.

	List A	List B
A.	$88,000	LIFO
B.	$92,000	Weighted average
C.	$84,000	FIFO
D.	$88,000	FIFO

41. Ordinarily, which inventory costing method approximates most closely the current cost for each of the following?

	Cost of Goods Sold	Ending Inventory
A.	LIFO	FIFO
B.	LIFO	LIFO
C.	FIFO	FIFO
D.	FIFO	LIFO

42. In a periodic inventory system that uses the weighted-average cost flow method, the beginning inventory is the

A. Net purchases minus the ending inventory.

B. Net purchases minus the cost of goods sold.

C. Total goods available for sale minus the net purchases.

D. Total goods available for sale minus the cost of goods sold.

Answer (C) is correct. *(CIA, adapted)*
REQUIRED: The proper match of cost of goods sold and inventory cost flow assumption.
DISCUSSION: Under FIFO, the first items purchased are presumed to be the first sold. Furthermore, under FIFO, perpetual and periodic systems produce the same ending inventory and cost of goods sold. If 6,000 units were available and 4,000 units were sold, FIFO cost of goods sold equals $84,000 [(2,000 × $20) BI + (2,000 × $22) May 1 purchase].
Answer (A) is incorrect. Cost of goods sold is $88,000 under the weighted-average method. Under LIFO (assuming a periodic system), cost of goods sold is $92,000 ($48,000 + $44,000). The 2,000 most recently purchased units are presumed to have been sold. Answer (B) is incorrect. The weighted-average unit cost of all items available for sale is $22 [($40,000 + $44,000 + $48,000) ÷ 6,000]. Given that 4,000 units were sold, cost of goods sold is $88,000 (4,000 × $22) under this method. Answer (D) is incorrect. FIFO cost of goods sold is $84,000. Under the weighted-average method, cost of goods sold is $88,000.

Answer (A) is correct. *(CPA, adapted)*
REQUIRED: The appropriate inventory costing method.
DISCUSSION: The LIFO basis assumes that the most recently purchased items are the first to be sold. Thus, LIFO is a better approximation of current cost of goods sold than FIFO. Assuming that turnover is rapid and material amounts of depreciation are not allocated to inventory, LIFO cost of goods sold may be an acceptable alternative to cost of goods sold measured at current cost. However, the effect of any LIFO inventory liquidations (decreases in earlier years' LIFO layers) must be excluded. Nevertheless, the FIFO basis more closely approximates the current cost of ending inventory because it assumes the most recent purchases are the last to be sold.
Answer (B) is incorrect. Current cost of ending inventory is most closely approximated by FIFO. Answer (C) is incorrect. Current cost of goods sold is most closely approximated by LIFO. Answer (D) is incorrect. Current cost of goods sold and current cost of ending inventory are most closely approximated by LIFO and FIFO, respectively.

Answer (C) is correct. *(CPA, adapted)*
REQUIRED: The beginning inventory in a periodic system using weighted-average cost.
DISCUSSION: In a periodic system, beginning inventory is equal to the total goods available for sale minus net purchases, regardless of the cost flow method used.
Answer (A) is incorrect. Net purchases minus the ending inventory is the difference between the beginning inventory and the cost of goods sold. Answer (B) is incorrect. Net purchases minus the cost of goods sold is the change in inventory valuation during the period. Answer (D) is incorrect. Goods available minus cost of sales equals ending inventory.

43. The acquisition cost of a heavily used raw material changes frequently. The carrying amount of the inventory of this material at year end will be the same if perpetual records are kept as it would be under a periodic inventory method only if the carrying amount is computed under the

A. Weighted-average method.

B. First-in, first-out method.

C. Last-in, first-out method.

D. Base-stock method.

Answer (B) is correct. *(CPA, adapted)*
REQUIRED: The cost flow assumption giving the same year-end carrying amount under both perpetual and periodic inventory systems.
DISCUSSION: Under FIFO, the oldest goods are assumed to have been sold first, and it would not matter whether the cost of goods sold was determined at the point of sale (perpetual) or at year end (periodic).
Answer (A) is incorrect. Under the weighted-average method, different goods are assumed to be sold if the determination is made at the time of sale (perpetual) rather than at year end (periodic). Answer (C) is incorrect. Under the last-in, first-out method, different goods are assumed to be sold if the determination is made at the time of sale (perpetual) rather than at year end (periodic). Answer (D) is incorrect. The base-stock method is not acceptable under GAAP or for tax purposes. The base-stock method assumes that a minimum amount of inventory is always required. Accordingly, the inventory base or minimum amount is considered a long-term investment to be recorded at its original cost. Last-in, first-out (LIFO) has the same effect if base levels of inventory are not sold.

44. Munich Co. uses the average-cost inventory method for internal reporting purposes and LIFO for financial statement and income tax reporting. At December 31, the inventory was $750,000 using average cost and $640,000 using LIFO. The unadjusted credit balance in the LIFO reserve account on the same date was $70,000. What adjusting entry should Munich record to adjust from average cost to LIFO at December 31?

	Cost of Goods Sold	Debit	Credit
A.	Cost of goods sold	$110,000	
	Inventory		$110,000
B.	Cost of goods sold	$110,000	
	LIFO reserve		$110,000
C.	Cost of goods sold	$40,000	
	Inventory		$40,000
D.	Cost of goods sold	$40,000	
	LIFO reserve		$40,000

Answer (D) is correct. *(CPA, adapted)*
REQUIRED: The journal entry to adjust from average cost to LIFO.
DISCUSSION: The LIFO reserve account is an allowance that adjusts the inventory balance stated according to the method used for internal reporting purposes to the LIFO amount appropriate for external reporting. If the LIFO effect is $110,000 ($750,000 average cost – $640,000 LIFO cost) and the account has a $70,000 credit balance, it must be credited for $40,000, with a corresponding debit to cost of goods sold.
Answer (A) is incorrect. The balance in the reserve account should equal $110,000, and inventory should not be adjusted. Answer (B) is incorrect. The balance in the reserve account should be $110,000. Answer (C) is incorrect. Inventory should not be adjusted.

45. Which of the following is not valid as it applies to inventory costing methods?

A. If inventory quantities are to be maintained, part of the earnings must be invested (plowed back) in inventories when FIFO is used during a period of rising prices.

B. LIFO tends to smooth out the net income pattern because it matches current cost of goods sold with current revenue, if inventories remain at constant quantities.

C. When a firm using the LIFO method fails to maintain its usual inventory position (reduces stock on hand below customary levels), there may be a matching of old costs with current revenue.

D. FIFO, but not LIFO, permits some control by management over the amount of net income for a period through controlled purchases.

Answer (D) is correct. *(CPA, adapted)*
REQUIRED: The invalid statement concerning inventory valuation.
DISCUSSION: Under LIFO, the most recent purchases are included in cost of goods sold. Management could affect net income with an end-of-period purchase that would immediately alter cost of goods sold. A last-minute FIFO purchase included in the ending inventory would have no such effect.
Answer (A) is incorrect. Maintenance of inventory quantities results in an increased dollar investment in inventory when FIFO is used during inflationary times. Answer (B) is incorrect. LIFO smooths income in a period of rising prices. The inflated current costs are matched with current sales prices. Answer (C) is incorrect. LIFO results in matching old, lower costs with current revenues when inventory is liquidated. If sales exceed purchases, a firm liquidates earlier, lower-priced LIFO layers.

46. The Poirot Company began operations on January 1 of the year before last and uses the FIFO method in costing its raw material inventory. Management is contemplating a change to the LIFO method and is interested in determining what effect such a change will have on net income. Accordingly, the following information has been developed:

Final Inventory	Year 1	Year 2
FIFO	$240,000	$270,000
LIFO	200,000	210,000
Net Income (per FIFO)	$120,000	$170,000

Based upon the above information, a change to the LIFO method in Year 2 results in net income for Year 2 of

A. $110,000

B. $150,000

C. $170,000

D. $230,000

Answer (B) is correct. *(CPA, adapted)*
REQUIRED: The second-year net income after a change from FIFO to LIFO in the second year of operations.
DISCUSSION: A change in accounting principle requires retrospective application. All periods reported must be individually adjusted for the period-specific effects of applying the new principle. The difference in income in the second year is equal to the $20,000 difference between the $30,000 FIFO inventory change ($270,000 – $240,000) and the $10,000 LIFO inventory change ($210,000 – $200,000). The $170,000 FIFO net income will decrease by $20,000. Net LIFO income will therefore be $150,000 ($170,000 – $20,000).
Answer (A) is incorrect. The amount of $110,000 incorrectly subtracts the difference from Year 1 from the net income under LIFO for Year 2. Answer (C) is incorrect. The amount of $170,000 is the income for Year 2 under FIFO. Answer (D) is incorrect. The amount of $230,000 incorrectly adds the cumulative difference between LIFO and FIFO to FIFO net income instead of subtracting the difference from FIFO net income.

6.4 Cost Flow Methods: Dollar-Value LIFO

47. Estimates of price-level changes for specific inventories are required for which of the following inventory methods?

A. Conventional retail.

B. Dollar-value LIFO.

C. Weighted-average cost.

D. Average cost retail.

Answer (B) is correct. *(CPA, adapted)*
REQUIRED: The inventory method for which estimates of price-level changes for specific inventories are required.
DISCUSSION: Dollar-value LIFO accumulates inventoriable costs of similar (not identical) items. These items should be similar in the sense of being interchangeable, having similar uses, belonging to the same product line, or constituting the raw materials for a given product. Dollar-value LIFO determines changes in ending inventory in terms of dollars of constant purchasing power rather than units of physical inventory. This calculation uses a specific price index for each year. The ending inventory is deflated by the current-year index to arrive at base-year cost. This amount is then compared with the beginning inventory stated at base-year cost to determine what layers are to be in the ending inventory. Each layer is then inflated by the relevant price index for the year it was created to determine the aggregate ending inventory measurement.
Answer (A) is incorrect. The lower-of-average-cost-or-market retail method includes net markups but not net markdowns in the determination of goods available for sale. The approximate LACM (conventional) retail method is a weighted-average method. Answer (C) is incorrect. The weighted-average cost method computes ending inventory based on an average cost determined at year end. Answer (D) is incorrect. Retail inventory methods calculate ending inventory at retail and then adjust it to cost by applying a cost-retail ratio. Average cost retail methods calculate the ratio based on goods available for sale.

48. The double-extension method and the link-chain method are two variations of which of the following inventory cost flow methods?

A. Moving average.

B. FIFO.

C. Dollar-value LIFO.

D. Conventional (lower-of-cost-or-market) retail.

Answer (C) is correct. *(CPA, adapted)*
REQUIRED: The inventory cost flow method of which the double-extension method and the link-chain method are variations.
DISCUSSION: The double-extension method and the link-chain method are variations of dollar-value LIFO. In dollar-value LIFO, similar (rather than identical) dollar-value pools of inventory are accumulated. Each layer of inventory is stated in dollar-value terms based on the price index for the relevant year. The link-chain version uses beginning-of-the-year costs as the denominator of the index for each year after the base year. Each successive year's index is multiplied by the cumulative index. The double-extension version uses the base-year prices in the annual index. The two methods are mutually exclusive.
Answer (A) is incorrect. The moving-average method calculates a new weighted-average unit inventory cost after each purchase. Answer (B) is incorrect. First-in, first-out (FIFO) is a basic inventory flow assumption. Answer (D) is incorrect. The lower-of-average-cost-or-market retail method includes net markups but not net markdowns in the determination of goods available for sale. The approximate LACM (conventional) retail method is a weighted-average method.

49. Which of the following inventory cost flow methods could use dollar-value pools?

A. Conventional (lower-of-cost-or-market) retail.

B. Weighted average.

C. FIFO.

D. LIFO.

Answer (D) is correct. *(CPA, adapted)*
REQUIRED: The cost flow assumption using dollar-value pools.
DISCUSSION: A modification of LIFO may be employed to account for dollar-value pools of similar items rather than identical items. This method overcomes a difficulty with traditional LIFO: Some items may be liquidated below the LIFO base while the value of similar items may increase. Dollar-value LIFO prevents the loss of the advantages of LIFO when the mixture of similar items changes.
Answer (A) is incorrect. The lower-of-average-cost-or-market retail method includes net markups but not net markdowns in the determination of goods available for sale. The approximate LACM (conventional) retail method is a weighted-average method. The dollar-value pool approach has been used only with LIFO. Answer (B) is incorrect. The weighted-average method determines an average unit inventory cost only at period end. The dollar-value pool approach has been used only with LIFO. Answer (C) is incorrect. First-in, first-out (FIFO) is a basic inventory flow assumption. The dollar-value pool approach has been used only with LIFO.

50. When the double-extension approach to the dollar-value LIFO inventory method is used, the inventory layer added in the current year is multiplied by an index number. Which of the following correctly states how components are used in the calculation of this index number?

A. In the numerator, the average of the ending inventory at base-year cost and at current-year cost.

B. In the numerator, the ending inventory at current-year cost, and, in the denominator, the ending inventory at base-year cost.

C. In the numerator, the ending inventory at base-year cost, and, in the denominator, the ending inventory at current-year cost.

D. In the denominator, the average of the ending inventory at base-year cost and at current-year cost.

Answer (B) is correct. *(CPA, adapted)*
REQUIRED: The true statement of how components are used in the calculation of an index number under the double-extension method.
DISCUSSION: An entity applying dollar-value LIFO may calculate price indexes rather than use externally determined numbers. The double-extension approach states ending inventory at current-year cost and then divides that amount by the base-year cost to determine the index for the current year. Hence, this method extends the quantity of the inventory at both current-year and base-year unit cost. The indexes determined in this way are then multiplied by the appropriate inventory layers stated at base-year cost.
Answer (A) is incorrect. The numerator is the current-year cost. Answer (C) is incorrect. The numerator is the current-year cost, and the denominator is the base-year cost. Answer (D) is incorrect. The denominator is the base-year cost.

51. The dollar-value LIFO inventory cost flow method involves computations based on

	Inventory Pools of Similar Items	A Specific Price Index for Each Year
A.	No	Yes
B.	No	No
C.	Yes	No
D.	Yes	Yes

Answer (D) is correct. *(CPA, adapted)*
    REQUIRED: The computations required for dollar-value LIFO inventory.
    DISCUSSION: Dollar-value LIFO accumulates inventoriable costs of similar (not identical) items. These items should be similar in the sense of being interchangeable, having similar uses, belonging to the same product line, or constituting the raw materials for a given product. Dollar-value LIFO determines changes in ending inventory in terms of dollars of constant purchasing power rather than units of physical inventory. This calculation uses a specific price index for each year. The ending inventory is deflated by the current-year index to arrive at base-year cost. This amount is then compared to the beginning inventory stated at base-year cost to determine what layers are to be in the ending inventory. Each layer is then inflated by the relevant price index for the year it was created to determine the aggregate ending inventory valuation.
    Answer (A) is incorrect. Dollar-value LIFO uses inventory pools of similar items. Answer (B) is incorrect. Dollar-value LIFO uses inventory pools and a price index. Answer (C) is incorrect. Dollar-value LIFO uses a price index for each year.

52. In January, Stitch, Inc., adopted the dollar-value LIFO method of inventory valuation. At adoption, inventory was valued at $50,000. During the year, inventory increased $30,000 using base-year prices, and prices increased 10%. The designated market value of Stitch's inventory exceeded its cost at year end. What amount of inventory should Stitch report in its year-end balance sheet?

A. $80,000

B. $83,000

C. $85,000

D. $88,000

Answer (B) is correct. *(CPA, adapted)*
    REQUIRED: The year-end inventory measured using dollar-value LIFO.
    DISCUSSION: Dollar-value LIFO determines changes in inventory in terms of dollars of constant purchasing power, not units of physical inventory. The first step is to determine the inventory layers at base-year prices by dividing current-year (year-end) cost amounts by the relevant respective annual price indexes. These layers are calculated using a LIFO assumption. The second step is to restate the layers by multiplying by the relevant indexes. In this case, the layers stated at base-year prices ($50,000 and $30,000) are given, and the relevant indexes are 1.0 for the base year and 1.1 (1 + .10) for the second year. The dollar-value LIFO measurement is $83,000.

Base layer	$50,000 × 1.0 =	$50,000
Second layer	30,000 × 1.1 =	33,000
	$80,000	$83,000

    Answer (A) is incorrect. The amount of $80,000 does not include an adjustment for the price change. Answer (C) is incorrect. The amount of $85,000 results from multiplying the base layer but not the second layer by the current-year price index. Answer (D) is incorrect. The amount of $88,000 results from multiplying both layers by the current-year price index.

Questions 53 and 54 are based on the following information. Minsk Company adopted the dollar-value last-in, first-out (LIFO) method of inventory valuation at December 31, Year 1. Inventory balances and price indices are shown below.

December 31	Ending Inventory at End-of-Year Prices	Price Index at December 31
Year 1	$240,000	100
Year 2	275,000	110
Year 3	300,000	120

53. Minsk Company's ending inventory as of December 31, Year 2, computed by the dollar-value LIFO method was

A. $240,000

B. $250,000

C. $251,000

D. $275,000

Answer (C) is correct. *(CMA, adapted)*
REQUIRED: The dollar-value LIFO inventory for Year 2.
DISCUSSION: The first step is to convert the Year 2 ending inventory into base-year prices. Dividing by the price index for Year 2 results in an inventory value of $250,000 ($275,000 ÷ 1.1). This amount consists of two layers: $240,000 purchased during the base year (Year 1) and $10,000 acquired in the current year (Year 2). The latter amount must be converted back into year-end prices because this merchandise was not purchased during the base year. The Year 2 increment therefore has a dollar-value LIFO valuation of $11,000 (1.1 × $10,000). Total inventory is $251,000 ($240,000 + $11,000).
Answer (A) is incorrect. The amount of $240,000 does not include the Year 2 layer. Answer (B) is incorrect. The amount of $250,000 includes the Year 2 layer at base-year prices. Answer (D) is incorrect. The amount of $275,000 is the ending inventory at end-of-year prices.

54. Minsk Company ending inventory as of December 31, Year 3, computed by the dollar-value LIFO method would be

A. $240,000

B. $250,000

C. $251,000

D. $300,000

Answer (C) is correct. *(CMA, adapted)*
REQUIRED: The dollar-value LIFO inventory for Year 3.
DISCUSSION: The first step is to convert the Year 3 ending inventory at year end prices into base-year prices. Dividing by the price index for Year 3 results in an inventory value at base-year prices of $250,000 ($300,000 ÷ 1.2). This figure is exactly the same as that for Year 2. Thus, no increment was added during Year 3, and the dollar-value LIFO ending inventory for Year 3 is the same as at the end of Year 2 ($251,000). This amount consists of a $240,000 layer purchased in Year 1 and an $11,000 layer purchased in Year 2. Under LIFO, the assumption is that nothing is still on hand from Year 3 purchases because the inventory stated in base-year prices is the same as at the end of the preceding year.
Answer (A) is incorrect. The amount of $240,000 does not include the Year 2 layer. Answer (B) is incorrect. The amount of $250,000 includes the Year 2 layer at base-year prices. Answer (D) is incorrect. The amount of $300,000 is the ending inventory at end-of-year prices.

55. Which of the following is an advantage of the dollar-value LIFO method over the specific-goods LIFO method?

A. The dollar-value LIFO method may be used only for identical inventory items.

B. Under dollar-value LIFO, new inventory items are entered into the inventory pool at their entry year cost.

C. Under dollar-value LIFO, a given inventory item may experience a unit count decrease, but no liquidation need be recorded.

D. Under dollar-value LIFO, updating of the cost basis of old inventory items is facilitated.

Answer (C) is correct. *(D.L. Flesher)*
REQUIRED: The advantage of the dollar-value LIFO method.
DISCUSSION: The dollar-value LIFO method is applicable to pools of similar but not identical inventory items. The method deals with layers of inventory, not with individual inventory items. Thus, when a given inventory item experiences a unit count decrease, but the overall pool of inventory does not decrease, no liquidation is recorded.
Answer (A) is incorrect. Dollar-value LIFO is used for inventory pools composed of similar but not identical items. Answer (B) is incorrect. New inventory items are placed in the pool at the substituted item's base-year price. Answer (D) is incorrect. No LIFO method permits an updating of old inventory items.

6.5 Lower of Cost or Market (LCM)

56. Metz Co. is selecting its inventory system in preparation for its first year of operations. The company intends to use either the periodic weighted-average method or the perpetual moving-average method and to apply the lower-of-cost-or-market (LCM) rule either to individual items or to the total inventory. Inventory prices are expected to increase throughout the year, although a few individual prices will decrease. What inventory system should Metz select if it wants to maximize the inventory carrying amount at the balance sheet date?

	Inventory Method	Cost or Market Application
A.	Perpetual	Total inventory
B.	Perpetual	Individual item
C.	Periodic	Total inventory
D.	Periodic	Individual item

Answer (A) is correct. *(CPA, adapted)*
REQUIRED: The inventory system that maximizes the inventory carrying amount at year end.
DISCUSSION: The weighted-average inventory pricing system is applicable to a periodic inventory system. The weighted-average unit cost is equal to the total cost of goods available for sale divided by the number of units available for sale. The moving-average system is applicable only to perpetual inventories. It requires that a new weighted average be computed after every purchase. This moving average is based on remaining inventory held and the new inventory purchased. In a period of rising prices, the moving-average method results in a higher unit and total ending inventory because the most recent purchases are given greater weight in the calculation. An entity may apply the LCM rule to (1) each item in the inventory, (2) the inventory as a whole, or (3) the total of the components of each major category. Applying the LCM rule to the total inventory will maximize the carrying amount because the reduction in the inventory will equal only the excess of aggregate cost over aggregate market. LCM applied on an individual item basis recognizes all of the inventory declines but none of the gains.
Answer (B) is incorrect. Applying the LCM rule to the total inventory results in a higher ending inventory. Answer (C) is incorrect. The perpetual moving-average method results in a higher ending inventory. Answer (D) is incorrect. Applying the perpetual moving-average method and the LCM rule to the total inventory result in a higher ending inventory.

57. Inventory may properly be stated above cost

A. When its market value or its net realizable value exceeds its cost.

B. When cost is determined under the first-in, first-out method.

C. When cost is determined under the last-in, first-out method.

D. Only in exceptional cases.

Answer (D) is correct. *(CMA, adapted)*
REQUIRED: The justification for stating inventory above cost.
DISCUSSION: Only in exceptional cases may inventories be stated above cost. Examples are (1) precious metals that have a fixed monetary value with no additional cost of marketing and (2) fungible (interchangeable) agricultural, mineral, and other products that have an immediate marketability at quoted prices and for which it may be difficult to obtain appropriate costs.
Answer (A) is incorrect. Inventory may be stated at market value or net realizable value (sales price – costs of completion and disposal) when these amounts are less (not more) than cost in accordance with the lower of cost or market rule. Answer (B) is incorrect. FIFO is an assumption about the flow of physical units. It does not determine the utility of those units. Answer (C) is incorrect. Last-in, first-out (LIFO) costing is a method for conveniently calculating the actual cost of inventory by making an assumption about the flow of physical units. It does not establish the utility of individual units.

58. The lower-of-cost-or-market (LCM) rule for inventories may be applied to total inventory, to major categories of inventory, or to each item. Which application usually results in the lowest inventory amount?

A. All applications result in the same amount.

B. Total inventory.

C. Groups of similar items.

D. Separately to each item.

Answer (D) is correct. *(CPA, adapted)*
REQUIRED: The application of the LCM rule that usually results in the lowest amount.
DISCUSSION: Applying the LCM rule to each item of inventory produces the lowest valuation for each item and therefore the lowest and most conservative valuation for the total inventory. The reason is that aggregating items results in the inclusion of some items at amounts greater than LCM. For example, if item A (cost $2, market $1) and item B (cost $3, market $4) are aggregated for LCM purposes, the inventory valuation is $5. If the rule is applied separately to A and B, the LCM valuation is $4.
Answer (A) is incorrect. Each application results in a different amount. Answer (B) is incorrect. Grouping all items results in a higher valuation than applying the LCM rule to individual items. Answer (C) is incorrect. Grouping some items results in a higher valuation than applying the LCM rule to individual items.

59. The replacement cost of an inventory item is below the net realizable value and above the net realizable value minus the normal profit margin. The original cost of the inventory item is below the net realizable value minus the normal profit margin. Under the lower-of-cost-or-market (LCM) method, the inventory item should be measured at

  A. Net realizable value.

  B. Net realizable value minus the normal profit margin.

  C. Original cost.

  D. Replacement cost.

Answer (C) is correct.   *(CPA, adapted)*
  REQUIRED: The measurement of an inventory item under the lower-of-cost-or-market method.
  DISCUSSION: When replacement cost is below the NRV and above the NRV minus the normal profit margin, market equals replacement cost. Given that the original cost of the inventory item is below market, the original cost should be used to measure the inventory item under the LCM method.
  Answer (A) is incorrect. The replacement cost, given the circumstances, is designated as market. Answer (B) is incorrect. The replacement cost is above net realizable value minus the normal profit margin and cost but below net realizable value. Answer (D) is incorrect. Cost is below market.

60. The original cost of an inventory item is below both replacement cost and net realizable value. The net realizable value minus normal profit margin is below the original cost. Under the lower-of-cost-or-market (LCM) method, the inventory item should be measured at

  A. Replacement cost.

  B. Net realizable value.

  C. Net realizable value minus normal profit margin.

  D. Original cost.

Answer (D) is correct.   *(CPA, adapted)*
  REQUIRED: The measurement of inventory under the LCM method.
  DISCUSSION: Market is current replacement cost subject to a ceiling and a floor. The maximum is net realizable value, and the minimum is net realizable value minus normal profit. When replacement cost is within this range, it is used as market. The original cost is above the NRV minus normal profit margin but below the NRV and the replacement cost. Thus, market must be the NRV (if it is less than replacement cost) or the replacement cost (which is greater than NRV minus normal profit), and LCM is equal to original cost.
  Answer (A) is incorrect. Replacement cost is greater than original cost. Answer (B) is incorrect. The NRV is greater than original cost. Answer (C) is incorrect. Net realizable value minus a normal profit margin is the LCM measure of inventory only if it is (1) below original cost and (2) equal to or greater than replacement cost.

61. Lorraine Co. has determined its fiscal year-end inventory on a FIFO basis to be $400,000. Information pertaining to that inventory follows:

Estimated selling price	$408,000
Estimated cost of disposal	20,000
Normal profit margin	60,000
Current replacement cost	360,000

Lorraine records losses that result from applying the lower-of-cost-or-market (LCM) rule. At its year end, what should be the net carrying amount of Lorraine's inventory?

  A. $400,000

  B. $388,000

  C. $360,000

  D. $328,000

Answer (C) is correct.   *(CPA, adapted)*
  REQUIRED: The net carrying amount of the ending inventory.
  DISCUSSION: Under the LCM method, market is current replacement cost subject to a maximum (ceiling) equal to net realizable value and a minimum (floor) equal to net realizable value minus a normal profit. NRV equals selling price minus costs of completion and disposal. Here, original cost is $400,000 and replacement cost is $360,000. The LCM method uses the lower of the two, $360,000, to measure inventory. However, the inventory measure cannot exceed the NRV of $388,000 ($408,000 selling price – $20,000 cost of disposal). Furthermore, the inventory carrying amount cannot be lower than NRV minus normal profit, or $328,000 ($388,000 NRV – $60,000 normal profit). Because the lower of cost or market ($360,000) is between $388,000 (ceiling) and $328,000 (floor), the net carrying amount is $360,000.
  Answer (A) is incorrect. The amount of $400,000 is the original cost. Answer (B) is incorrect. The amount of $388,000 is the NRV (ceiling). Answer (D) is incorrect. The amount of $328,000 is the NRV minus normal profit (floor).

Questions 62 through 64 are based on the following information. The data below concern items in Stockholm Co.'s inventory.

Per Unit	Gear	Stuff	Wickets
Historical cost	$190.00	$106.00	$53.00
Selling price	217.00	145.00	73.75
Cost to complete and sell	19.00	8.00	2.50
Current replacement cost	203.00	105.00	51.00
Normal profit margin	32.00	29.00	21.25

62. The limits to the market measurement (i.e., the ceiling and the floor) that Stockholm Co. should use in the lower-of-cost-or-market (LCM) comparison of gear are

A. $217 and $198.

B. $217 and $185.

C. $198 and $166.

D. $185 and $166.

Answer (C) is correct. *(CMA, adapted)*
REQUIRED: The limits of the market measurement for gear.
DISCUSSION: Market is current replacement cost subject to a maximum equal to net realizable value and a minimum equal to net realizable value minus a normal profit. Net realizable value is equal to selling price minus costs of completion and disposal. For gear, the net realizable value is $198 ($217 selling price – $19 distribution cost). Net realizable value minus normal profit is $166 ($198 net realizable value – $32 normal profit).
Answer (A) is incorrect. The amount of $217 is the selling price, and $198 is the NRV. Answer (B) is incorrect. The amount of $217 is the selling price, and $185 is the selling price minus normal profit. Answer (D) is incorrect. The ceiling equals the net realizable value, not selling price minus normal profit.

63. The cost amount that Stockholm Co. should use in the lower-of-cost-or-market (LCM) comparison of stuff is

A. $105

B. $106

C. $108

D. $137

Answer (B) is correct. *(CMA, adapted)*
REQUIRED: The cost amount for stuff.
DISCUSSION: The cost amount used in the LCM comparison is the historical cost of an item. Thus, for stuff, the historical cost of $106 is compared with market.
Answer (A) is incorrect. The amount of $105 is the current replacement cost, not the historical cost. Answer (C) is incorrect. The amount of $108 is the net realizable value minus the normal profit margin, not the historical cost. Answer (D) is incorrect. Net realizable value ($137) is not used in the calculation of historical cost.

64. The market amount that Stockholm Co. should use to measure the wickets on the basis of the lower-of-cost-or-market (LCM) rule is

A. $51.00

B. $53.00

C. $50.00

D. $71.25

Answer (A) is correct. *(CMA, adapted)*
REQUIRED: The market amount for wickets.
DISCUSSION: Net realizable value for wickets is $71.25 ($73.75 selling price – $2.50 distribution cost). The net realizable value minus normal profit is $50 ($71.25 net realizable value – $21.25 normal profit margin). The $51 replacement cost falls between the $71.25 ceiling and the $50 floor and is the appropriate market value. Because the $51 market value is lower than the $53 historical cost, it should be the basis of valuation for the wickets.
Answer (B) is incorrect. The amount of $53 is the historical cost. Answer (C) is incorrect. The amount of $50 is the floor. It is used only if replacement cost is lower. Answer (D) is incorrect. The amount of $71.25 is the net realizable value. It is used as the market amount only if replacement cost is greater.

65. Based on a physical inventory taken at year end, Brussels Co. determined its raw materials inventory on a FIFO basis at $26,000 with a replacement cost of $20,000. Brussels estimated that, after further processing costs of $12,000, the raw materials could be sold as finished goods for $40,000. The company's normal profit margin is 10% of sales. Under the lower-of-cost-or-market (LCM) rule, what amount should Brussels report as raw materials inventory at the balance sheet date?

A. $28,000

B. $26,000

C. $24,000

D. $20,000

Answer (C) is correct.   (CPA, adapted)
REQUIRED: The amount reported for inventory under the LCM rule.
DISCUSSION: Market is current replacement cost subject to a ceiling and a floor. The maximum is net realizable value, and the minimum is net realizable value minus normal profit. When replacement cost is within this range, it is used as market. Cost is given as $26,000. Net realizable value is $28,000 ($40,000 selling price – $12,000 additional processing costs), and net realizable amount minus a normal profit equals $24,000 [$28,000 – ($40,000 × 10%)]. Because the lowest amount in the range ($24,000) exceeds replacement cost ($20,000), it is used as market. Because market ($24,000) is less than cost ($26,000), it is also the inventory measurement.
Answer (A) is incorrect. The amount of $28,000 is the NRV. Answer (B) is incorrect. The amount of $26,000 is the cost. Answer (D) is incorrect. The amount of $20,000 is the replacement cost.

6.6 Inventory Estimation: Gross Profit Method

66. Which of the following methods of inventory measurement is allowable at interim dates but not at year end?

A. Weighted average.

B. Estimated gross profit rates.

C. Retail method.

D. Specific identification.

Answer (B) is correct.   (CPA, adapted)
REQUIRED: The inventory valuation method permitted at interim dates but not at year end.
DISCUSSION: The estimated gross profit method may be used to measure inventory for interim statements provided that adequate disclosure is made of reconciliations with the annual physical inventory at year end. Any method allowable at year end is also allowable at an interim date.
Answer (A) is incorrect. The weighted-average method is allowable at year end. Answer (C) is incorrect. The retail method is allowable at year end. Answer (D) is incorrect. The specific identification method is allowable at year end.

67. Norway Co. maintains a markup of 60% based on cost. The company's selling and administrative expenses average 30% of sales. Annual sales amounted to $960,000. Norway's cost of goods sold and operating profit for the year are

	Cost of Goods Sold	Operating Profit
A.	$576,000	$96,000
B.	$576,000	$288,000
C.	$600,000	$72,000
D.	$600,000	$288,000

Answer (C) is correct.   (CPA, adapted)
REQUIRED: The estimated cost of goods sold and operating profit.
DISCUSSION: A markup of 60% based on cost means that sales equal 160% of cost. Thus, cost of goods sold must be $600,000 ($960,000 sales ÷ 1.6). Selling and administrative expenses average 30% of sales and are estimated to be $288,000 ($960,000 sales × 30%). Accordingly, operating profit is $72,000 ($960,000 sales – $600,000 COGS – $288,000 S&A expenses).
Answer (A) is incorrect. Cost of goods sold is based on a 60% markup from cost, not sales, and the $96,000 operating profit is based on the incorrect cost of goods sold. Answer (B) is incorrect. Cost of goods sold is based on a 60% markup from cost, not sales, and the $288,000 is the selling and administrative expenses. Answer (D) is incorrect. The amount of $288,000 is the selling and administrative expenses.

68. The following information is available for Sweden Company for its most recent year:

Net sales	$3,600,000
Freight-in	90,000
Purchase discounts	50,000
Ending inventory	240,000

The gross margin is 40% of net sales. What is the cost of goods available for sale?

   A. $1,680,000

   B. $1,920,000

   C. $2,400,000

   D. $2,440,000

Answer (C) is correct. *(CPA, adapted)*
REQUIRED: The cost of goods available for sale.
DISCUSSION: Because the gross margin equals 40% of net sales, cost of goods sold equals 60% of net sales, or $2,160,000. Cost of goods available for sale equals the cost of goods sold plus the cost of the goods in ending inventory. Hence, cost of goods available for sale equals $2,160,000 plus $240,000, or $2,400,000 (BI + PUR = GAFS* = COGS + EI). Freight-in and purchase discounts are not used to estimate COGS or GAFS in the gross margin approach.

Ending inventory	$ 240,000
Cost of goods sold	2,160,000
Goods available for sale*	$2,400,000

   Answer (A) is incorrect. The amount of $1,680,000 is gross margin plus ending inventory. Answer (B) is incorrect. The amount of $1,920,000 is cost of goods sold minus ending inventory. Answer (D) is incorrect. The amount of $2,440,000 is cost of goods available for sale plus freight-in and minus purchase discounts.

69. The following information is available for the Sibelius Company for the 3 months ended March 31 of this year:

Merchandise inventory, January 1 of this year	$ 900,000
Purchases	3,400,000
Freight-in	200,000
Sales	4,800,000

The gross margin recorded was 25% of sales. What should be the merchandise inventory at March 31?

   A. $700,000

   B. $900,000

   C. $1,125,000

   D. $1,200,000

Answer (B) is correct. *(CPA, adapted)*
REQUIRED: The estimated ending inventory using the gross profit method.
DISCUSSION: If the gross profit margin is 25% of sales, cost of goods sold equals 75% of sales. Ending inventory is equal to goods available for sale minus cost of goods sold.

Beginning inventory	$ 900,000
Purchases	3,400,000
Freight-in	200,000
Goods available for sale	$4,500,000
COGS ($4,800,000) × (1.0 – .25)	(3,600,000)
Ending inventory	$ 900,000

   Answer (A) is incorrect. The amount of $700,000 excludes freight-in. Answer (C) is incorrect. Ending inventory is goods available for sale minus cost of goods sold. Answer (D) is incorrect. The amount of $1,200,000 is the gross margin.

70. A store uses the gross profit method to estimate inventory and cost of goods sold for interim reporting purposes. Past experience indicates that the average gross profit rate is 25% of sales. The following data relate to the month of March:

Inventory cost, March 1	$25,000
Purchases during the month at cost	67,000
Sales	84,000
Sales returns	3,000

Using the data above, what is the estimated ending inventory at March 31?

   A. $20,250

   B. $21,000

   C. $29,000

   D. $31,250

Answer (D) is correct. *(CIA, adapted)*
REQUIRED: The estimated ending inventory value based on a 25% gross margin ratio.
DISCUSSION: The gross profit rate is 25% of sales. Thus, estimated cost of goods sold is 75% (1.0 – .25) of sales. Subtracting estimated cost of goods sold from total goods available for sale leaves an estimated ending inventory figure of $31,250.

Beginning inventory	$25,000
Purchases	67,000
Goods available for sale	$92,000
Estimated COGS ($84,000 – $3,000) × (1.0 – .25)	(60,750)
Estimated ending inventory	$31,250

   Answer (A) is incorrect. The amount of $20,250 is the gross margin. Answer (B) is incorrect. The amount of $21,000 is the gross margin without considering sales returns. Answer (C) is incorrect. The amount of $29,000 fails to consider sales returns.

71. Finland Co. prepares monthly income statements. A physical inventory is taken only at year end; hence, month-end inventories must be estimated. All sales are made on account. The rate of markup on cost is 50%. The following information relates to the month of June:

Accounts receivable, June 1	$20,000
Accounts receivable, June 30	30,000
Collection of accounts receivable during June	50,000
Inventory, June 1	36,000
Purchases of inventory during June	32,000

The estimated cost of the June 30 inventory is

A. $24,000

B. $28,000

C. $38,000

D. $44,000

Answer (B) is correct. *(CPA, adapted)*
REQUIRED: The estimated cost of ending inventory assuming a 50% markup on cost.
DISCUSSION: To determine inventory cost, cost of sales must be determined. Sales can be derived from a T-account analysis of accounts receivable; that is, the beginning balance ($20,000) plus credit sales equals the collections ($50,000) plus the ending balance ($30,000). Thus, sales equal $60,000 ($50,000 + $30,000 – $20,000). Because sales equal cost of sales plus the 50% markup on cost, sales equal 150% of cost. Cost of sales therefore equals $40,000 ($60,000 sales ÷ 1.5). Cost of sales deducted from the cost of goods available for sale equals the ending inventory.

Beginning inventory	$36,000
Purchases	32,000
Goods available for sale	$68,000
Cost of goods sold	(40,000)
Ending inventory	$28,000

Answer (A) is incorrect. Sales are incorrectly computed. Answer (C) is incorrect. The amount of $38,000 results from a markup based on sales instead of cost. Answer (D) is incorrect. Sales are incorrectly computed.

72. Dart Company's accounting records indicated the following information:

Beginning inventory	$ 500,000
Purchases during the year	2,500,000
Sales during the year	3,200,000

A physical inventory taken on at year end resulted in an ending inventory of $575,000. Dart's gross profit on sales has remained constant at 25% in recent years. Dart suspects some inventory may have been taken by a new employee. At the balance sheet date, what is the estimated cost of missing inventory?

A. $25,000

B. $100,000

C. $175,000

D. $225,000

Answer (A) is correct. *(CPA, adapted)*
REQUIRED: The missing inventory estimated based on a gross margin ratio.
DISCUSSION: To estimate the missing inventory, the estimated cost of goods sold is subtracted from the cost of goods available for sale to estimate the amount of inventory that should be on hand. Given that the gross margin is 25% of sales, 75% of sales, or $2,400,000, is the estimated cost of goods sold.

Beginning balance	$ 500,000
Purchases	2,500,000
Cost of goods available	$3,000,000
Estimated cost of goods sold [$3,200,000 sales × (1.0 – .25)]	(2,400,000)
Estimated year-end balance	$ 600,000
Physical inventory year-end	(575,000)
Estimated theft loss	$ 25,000

Answer (B) is incorrect. The amount of $100,000 is the difference between estimated ending inventory and actual beginning inventory. Answer (C) is incorrect. The amount of $175,000 is the ending physical inventory minus beginning inventory, plus purchases, minus estimated cost of goods sold. Answer (D) is incorrect. The amount of $225,000 is the gross margin minus actual ending inventory.

73. A firm experienced a flood loss in the current year that destroyed all but $6,000 of inventory (at cost). Data available are below:

	Prior Year	Current (to Date of Flood)
Sales	$100,000	$40,000
Purchases	70,000	35,000
Cost of goods sold	60,000	
Ending inventory	10,000	

What is the approximate inventory lost?

    A. $10,000

    B. $15,000

    C. $16,000

    D. $21,000

Answer (B) is correct. *(CIA, adapted)*
    REQUIRED: The approximate inventory lost to flood.
    DISCUSSION: Based on the prior-year figures, the ratio of cost of goods sold to sales is 60% ($60,000 ÷ $100,000). This ratio can be used to approximate current-year cost of goods sold ($40,000 current-year sales × 60% = $24,000). As indicated below, this estimate is subtracted from goods available for sale to the date of the flood to determine estimated inventory at the time of the flood ($21,000). Given actual remaining inventory of $6,000, the inventory lost to flood is $15,000.

Beginning inventory	$10,000
Purchases	35,000
Cost of goods available	$45,000
Estimated cost of goods sold	(24,000)
Estimated inventory	$21,000
Actual inventory	(6,000)
Approximate inventory destroyed	$15,000

    Answer (A) is incorrect. The amount of $10,000 is the ending inventory for the prior year and the beginning inventory in the current year. Answer (C) is incorrect. The amount of $16,000 is the current year beginning inventory plus the actual ending inventory of $6,000. Answer (D) is incorrect. The amount of $21,000 is the estimated ending inventory.

6.7 Inventory Estimation: Retail Inventory Method

74. With regard to the retail inventory method, which of the following is the most accurate statement?

    A. Accountants usually ignore net markups and net markdowns in computing the cost-price percentage.

    B. Accountants usually include both net markups and net markdowns in computing the cost-price percentage.

    C. This method results in a lower ending inventory cost if net markups are included but net markdowns are excluded in computing the cost-price percentage.

    D. It is not adaptable to LIFO costing.

Answer (C) is correct. *(CPA, adapted)*
    REQUIRED: The most accurate statement concerning the retail inventory method.
    DISCUSSION: The cost-retail ratio is lower if retail (the denominator) is increased. Excluding markdowns increases the denominator, thus decreasing the ratio applied to ending inventory stated at retail and also decreasing ending inventory stated at cost. Excluding markdowns approximates lower of cost or market and is characteristic of the conventional retail method.
    Answer (A) is incorrect. Accountants usually include net markups but not net markdowns in the denominator of the cost-retail ratio. Answer (B) is incorrect. The LIFO version includes net markups and markdowns in the denominator of the cost-retail ratio, but it is not the most widely used method. Answer (D) is incorrect. Among the variations of the retail method are (1) LIFO retail, (2) dollar-value LIFO retail, (3) lower-of-average-cost-or-market, (4) FIFO cost, (5) FIFO LCM, and (6) average cost.

75. Under the retail inventory method, freight-in is included in the calculation of the goods available for sale for which of the following?

	Cost	Retail
A.	No	No
B.	No	Yes
C.	Yes	No
D.	Yes	Yes

Answer (C) is correct. *(CPA, adapted)*
    REQUIRED: The calculation that includes freight-in when determining goods available for sale.
    DISCUSSION: In the retail inventory method, records of the components of net purchases (purchases, freight-in, and purchase returns and allowances) are kept at cost and are included with beginning inventory in the calculation of the goods available for sale at cost. Records are kept at retail only for net purchases, not its components, because retail prices are usually set to cover a variety of costs, such as freight-in. Consequently, freight-in, a component of net purchases, is explicitly and directly included only in the calculation of goods available for sale at cost.
    Answer (A) is incorrect. Freight-in is used in the calculation of cost. Answer (B) is incorrect. Freight-in is used in the calculation of cost, and it is not used in the calculation of retail. Answer (D) is incorrect. Freight-in is not used in the calculation of retail.

76. The retail inventory method includes which of the following in the calculation of both cost and retail amounts of goods available for sale?

A. Purchase returns.

B. Sales returns.

C. Net markups.

D. Freight-in.

Answer (A) is correct. *(CPA, adapted)*

REQUIRED: The element common to calculation of goods available for sale at cost and at retail.

DISCUSSION: In the retail inventory method, records are kept of beginning inventory and net purchases at both cost and retail. Purchase returns are deducted in the calculation of net purchases at both cost and retail because the return of goods reduces both total cost and the total sales price of the purchased goods.

Answer (B) is incorrect. Sales returns is an element of retail only. Answer (C) is incorrect. Markups and markdowns affect only retail. Answer (D) is incorrect. Freight-in is an element of cost; there is no retail counterpart.

77. If the retail method is used to approximate a lower-of-average-cost-or-market (LACM) measurement, which of the following describes the proper treatment of net additional markups and markdowns in the cost-retail ratio calculation?

A. Net markups should be included, and net markdowns should be excluded.

B. Net markups should be excluded, and net markdowns should be included.

C. Net markups and markdowns should be included.

D. Net markups and markdowns should be excluded.

Answer (A) is correct. *(S. Venkateswar)*

REQUIRED: The treatment of markups and markdowns in computing the cost-retail ratio under a lower-of-average-cost-or-market approach.

DISCUSSION: The cost-retail ratio based on a lower-of-average-cost-or-market measurement approach should include net markups but not net markdowns. Including net markups and excluding net markdowns approximates lower of cost or market. The reason is that increasing the denominator of the ratio (BI at retail + Pur at retail + Markups) while holding the numerator (BI at cost + Pur at cost) constant gives a more conservative (a lower) measurement.

Answer (B) is incorrect. Under the LACM retail method, net markups are included in the cost-retail ratio. Net markdowns are excluded. Answer (C) is incorrect. Net markdowns are excluded. Answer (D) is incorrect. Net markups are included.

78. In the retail inventory method, when computing the cost-retail ratio, under what flow assumption(s) is beginning inventory excluded from both cost and retail?

A. FIFO only.

B. LIFO only.

C. Weighted-average cost or weighted-average lower of cost or market.

D. Both FIFO and LIFO.

Answer (D) is correct. *(Publisher, adapted)*

REQUIRED: The flow assumption(s) requiring that beginning inventory be excluded in determining the cost-retail ratio.

DISCUSSION: Under both FIFO and LIFO, the cost-retail ratio must be computed for purchases, not goods available for sale. For FIFO, beginning inventory is excluded because ending inventory includes only goods from current purchases. For LIFO, the layers of goods from the purchases of separate accounting periods must be considered separately.

Answer (A) is incorrect. FIFO excludes beginning inventory in determining the cost-retail ratio. Answer (B) is incorrect. LIFO excludes beginning inventory in determining the cost-retail ratio. Answer (C) is incorrect. Weighted average includes beginning inventory as well as purchases.

79. Using the retail inventory method, when is the cost-retail ratio based only on the cost and retail amounts in beginning inventory?

A. When FIFO is used and sales exceed purchases at retail.

B. When FIFO is used and sales are less than purchases at retail.

C. When LIFO is used and sales exceed purchases at retail.

D. When LIFO is used and sales are less than purchases at retail.

Answer (C) is correct. *(Publisher, adapted)*

REQUIRED: The circumstances in which the cost-retail ratio is based only upon beginning inventory cost and retail values.

DISCUSSION: If LIFO is used and sales exceed purchases at retail, the ending inventory will be less than beginning inventory. Ending inventory will be assumed to consist entirely of units from beginning inventory. Thus, it should be converted from retail to cost using the cost-retail ratio that existed in the beginning inventory.

Answer (A) is incorrect. Ending inventory includes goods purchased during the period when FIFO is used and sales exceed purchases at retail. Answer (B) is incorrect. Ending inventory includes goods purchased during the period when FIFO is used and sales are less than purchases at retail. Answer (D) is incorrect. Under LIFO, when sales are less than purchases at retail, the ending inventory will include beginning inventory plus a layer of goods purchased during the period.

80. The accounting records of Seraphina Co. contain the following amounts on November 30, the end of its fiscal year:

	Cost	Retail
Beginning inventory	$ 68,000	$100,000
Purchases	262,000	400,000
Net markups		50,000
Net markdowns		110,000
Sales		360,000

Seraphina's ending inventory as of November 30, computed by the conventional retail method, is

A. $80,000

B. $60,000

C. $54,400

D. $48,000

Answer (D) is correct. *(CMA, adapted)*
REQUIRED: The ending inventory under the conventional retail method.
DISCUSSION: The lower-of-average-cost-or-market retail method includes net markups but not net markdowns in the determination of goods available for sale. The approximate LACM (conventional) retail method is a weighted-average method. Accordingly, the numerator of the cost-retail ratio is the sum of the beginning inventory at cost plus purchases at cost, and the denominator is the sum of beginning inventory at retail, purchases at retail, and net markups.

	Cost	Retail
Beginning inventory	$ 68,000	$100,000
Purchases	262,000	400,000
Markups, net		50,000
Goods available	$330,000	$550,000
Sales		(360,000)
Markdowns, net		(110,000)
Ending inventory -- retail		$ 80,000
Cost-retail ratio ($330 ÷ $550 = 60%)		× .6
Ending inventory at cost		$ 48,000

Answer (A) is incorrect. The amount of $80,000 is ending inventory at retail. Answer (B) is incorrect. The amount of $60,000 incorrectly uses a 75% cost-retail ratio. Answer (C) is incorrect. The amount of $54,400 incorrectly uses a 68% cost-retail ratio.

81. Dublin Co. uses the conventional retail inventory method to account for inventory. The following information relates to current-year operations:

	Average	
	Cost	Retail
Beginning inventory and purchases	$600,000	$920,000
Net markups		40,000
Net markdowns		60,000
Sales		780,000

What amount should be reported as cost of sales for the year?

A. $480,000

B. $487,500

C. $520,000

D. $525,000

Answer (D) is correct. *(CPA, adapted)*
REQUIRED: The cost of sales based on the conventional retail inventory method.
DISCUSSION: The lower-of-average-cost-or-market retail method includes net markups but not net markdowns in the determination of goods available for sale. The approximate LACM (conventional) retail method is a weighted-average method. Accordingly, the numerator of the cost-retail ratio is the sum of the beginning inventory at cost plus purchases at cost, and the denominator is the sum of beginning inventory at retail, purchases at retail, and net markups. The numerator of the ratio (goods available at cost) is given as $600,000, and the denominator (goods available at retail) is $960,000 ($920,000 BI and purchases + $40,000 net markups). Ending inventory at retail is $120,000 ($960,000 goods available at retail – $60,000 net markdowns – $780,000 sales). Hence, ending inventory at cost is $75,000 [$120,000 EI at retail × ($600,000 ÷ $960,000) cost-retail ratio], and cost of sales must be $525,000 ($600,000 BI and purchases at cost – $75,000 EI at cost).
Answer (A) is incorrect. The amount of $480,000 results from subtracting ending inventory at retail from the sum of beginning inventory and purchases at cost. Answer (B) is incorrect. The amount of $487,500 omits net markdowns from the computation. Answer (C) is incorrect. The amount of $520,000 assumes net markdowns are deducted in determining the cost-retail ratio.

82. Londinium Ltd. values its inventory by using the retail method (FIFO basis, lower of cost or market). The following information is available for the year just ended:

	Cost	Retail
Beginning inventory	$ 80,000	$140,000
Purchases	297,000	420,000
Freight-in	4,000	
Shortages		8,000
Markups (net)		10,000
Markdowns (net)		2,000
Sales		400,000

At what amount would Londinium report its ending inventory?

A. $112,000

B. $113,400

C. $117,600

D. $119,000

Answer (A) is correct. (CPA, adapted)
REQUIRED: The ending inventory at cost using the retail method (FIFO basis, LCM).
DISCUSSION: Under FIFO, ending inventory is composed of the latest purchases. Thus, in calculating the cost-retail ratio, only current purchases are included. To approximate the lower of cost or market, the denominator of the ratio includes net markups but not net markdowns.

	Cost	Retail
Purchases	$297,000	$420,000
Freight-in	4,000	
Markups, net		10,000
Adjusted purchases	$301,000	$430,000
Beginning inventory	80,000	140,000
Goods available	$381,000	$570,000
Net markdowns		(2,000)
Shortages		(8,000)
Sales		(400,000)
Ending inventory -- retail		$160,000
Cost-retail ratio ($301,000 ÷ $430,000 = 70%)		× .7
Ending inventory		$112,000

Answer (B) is incorrect. The amount of $113,400 fails to consider net markdowns in retail ending inventory. Answer (C) is incorrect. The amount of $117,600 ignores the effects of shortages in retail ending inventory. Answer (D) is incorrect. The amount of $119,000 incorrectly includes net markups in retail ending inventory.

83. Riga PLC uses a calendar year and the LIFO retail inventory method (assuming stable prices). Information relating to the computation of the inventory at December 31 is as follows:

	Cost	Retail
Beginning inventory	$ 150	$ 300
Purchases (net)	1,650	4,860
Net markups		830
Net markdowns		970
Sales		4,180

What should be the ending inventory at cost at December 31 using the LIFO retail inventory method?

A. $252

B. $333

C. $339

D. $840

Answer (C) is correct. (K. Boze)
REQUIRED: The ending inventory at cost using the LIFO retail inventory method.
DISCUSSION: Under the LIFO retail method (assuming stable prices), markups and markdowns are included in the calculation of the cost-retail ratio because the lower of cost or market is not being approximated. The markups and markdowns are usually assumed to apply only to purchases, and the ratio applies only to the LIFO layer added from the current purchases. Hence, the cost-retail ratio excludes beginning inventory and includes only purchases, markups, and markdowns. As indicated below, this ratio is 35%. The ending inventory will consist of a layer at 35% and a layer at the previous year's ratio.

	Cost	Retail
Purchases	$1,650	$4,860
Markups		830
Markdowns		(970)
Adjusted purchases	$1,650	$4,720
Beginning inventory	150	300
Goods available	$1,800	$5,020
Sales		(4,180)
Ending inventory -- retail		$ 840

Current cost-retail ratio ($1,650 ÷ $4,720 = 35%)

BI layer at cost	$ 150
Current layer at cost = ($840 – $300) × 35%	189
Ending inventory at cost	$ 339

Answer (A) is incorrect. The amount of $252 is the ending inventory based on the conventional retail method. Answer (B) is incorrect. The amount of $333 results from using a cost-retail ratio equal to purchases at cost divided by purchases at retail. Answer (D) is incorrect. The amount of $840 is the retail ending inventory.

84. Tirana Co. uses the first-in, first-out retail method of inventory measurement. The following information is available:

	Cost	Retail
Beginning inventory	$12,000	$ 30,000
Purchases	60,000	110,000
Net additional markups		10,000
Net markdowns		20,000
Sales revenue		90,000

If the lower-of-cost-or-market (LCM) rule is disregarded, what would be the estimated cost of the ending inventory?

- A. $24,000
- B. $20,800
- C. $20,000
- D. $19,200

Answer (A) is correct. *(CPA, adapted)*
REQUIRED: The ending inventory using the FIFO version of the retail inventory method.
DISCUSSION: Under FIFO, ending inventory consists of purchases because beginning inventory is assumed to be sold first. Both markdowns and markups are used to calculate the cost-retail ratio because LCM is not being approximated.

	Cost	Retail
Purchases	$60,000	$110,000
Markups		10,000
Markdowns		(20,000)
Adjusted purchases	$60,000	$100,000
Beg. inv. 1/1	12,000	30,000
Goods available	$72,000	$130,000
Sales		(90,000)
Ending inventory -- retail		$ 40,000
Cost-retail ratio ($60,000 ÷ $100,000)		× .6
Ending inventory -- FIFO		$ 24,000

Answer (B) is incorrect. The amount of $20,800 incorrectly uses a 52% cost-retail ratio. Answer (C) is incorrect. The amount of $20,000 incorrectly uses a 50% cost-retail ratio. Answer (D) is incorrect. The amount of $19,200 incorrectly uses a 48% cost-retail ratio.

6.8 IFRS

85. A company determined the following values for its inventory as of the end of the fiscal year:

Historical cost	$100,000
Current replacement cost	70,000
Net realizable value	90,000
Net realizable value minus a normal profit margin	85,000
Fair value	95,000

Under IFRS, what amount should the company report as inventory on its balance sheet?

- A. $70,000
- B. $85,000
- C. $90,000
- D. $95,000

Answer (C) is correct. *(CPA, adapted)*
REQUIRED: The year-end inventory.
DISCUSSION: Inventory is measured at the lower of cost or NRV (estimated selling price in the ordinary course of business – estimated costs of completion and sale). Given cost of $100,000 and NRV of $90,000, inventory should be reported at $90,000.
Answer (A) is incorrect. Current replacement cost ($70,000) is neither cost nor NRV. Answer (B) is incorrect. The lower of cost or market ($85,000) is the appropriate measure under GAAP. Answer (D) is incorrect. Fair value is greater than NRV.

86. According to IFRS, inventory is measured at the <List A> of cost and <List B>.

	List A	List B
A.	Lower	Net realizable value
B.	Higher	Market
C.	Lower	Net realizable value minus normal profit margin
D.	Lower	Fair value

Answer (A) is correct. *(Publisher, adapted)*
REQUIRED: The measurement of inventory under IFRS.
DISCUSSION: Under IFRS, inventory is measured at the lower of cost and net realizable value. Under U.S. GAAP, inventory is measured at the lower of cost or market.
Answer (B) is incorrect. According to IFRS, inventory is not measured at market. Under U.S. GAAP, market is current replacement cost subject to certain limits. Answer (C) is incorrect. According to IFRS, normal profit margin is not considered in the measurement of inventory. According to U.S. GAAP, net realizable value minus normal profit margin is the minimum of the range of possible amounts of current replacement cost (market). Answer (D) is incorrect. According to IFRS, inventories are not measured at fair value but at the lower of cost and NRV.

87. According to IFRS, a write-down of inventory is recognized in <List A>, and it <List B> reversed in subsequent periods.

	List A	List B
A.	Profit or loss	May be
B.	Other comprehensive income	Must not be
C.	Directly in equity	May be
D.	Profit or loss	Must not be

Answer (A) is correct. *(Publisher, adapted)*
   REQUIRED: The accounting for a write-down of inventory under IFRS.
   DISCUSSION: Under IFRS, a write-down of inventory may be reversed in subsequent periods but not above the original cost. The write-down and reversal of inventory are recognized in profit or loss.
   Answer (B) is incorrect. A write-down of inventory is recognized in profit or loss, not in OCI, and it may be reversed in subsequent periods. Answer (C) is incorrect. The write-down of inventory is recognized as a loss in profit or loss and therefore ultimately decreases retained earnings (an equity amount). Answer (D) is incorrect. Under IFRS, a write-down of inventory may be reversed in subsequent periods.

88. A company determined the following amounts for its inventory at the end of the fiscal year:

Historical cost	$100,000
Selling price	140,000
Cost of disposal	10,000
Cost of completion	5,000
Normal profit margin	17,000

What is the net realizable value (NRV) of the inventory at year end?

- A. $125,000
- B. $108,000
- C. $130,000
- D. $135,000

Answer (A) is correct. *(Publisher, adapted)*
   REQUIRED: The NRV of inventory.
   DISCUSSION: NRV is the estimated selling price in the ordinary course of business ($140,000), minus reasonably predictable costs of completion ($5,000) and disposal ($10,000). NRV is $125,000 ($140,000 – $10,000 – $5,000).
   Answer (B) is incorrect. The normal profit margin should not be considered in calculating NRV. Answer (C) is incorrect. The cost of disposal of inventory must be considered in calculating its NRV. Answer (D) is incorrect. The cost of completion of inventory must be considered in calculating its NRV.

89. Which of the following cost flow methods of accounting for inventories is prohibited by IFRS?

- A. First-in, first-out (FIFO) method.
- B. Specific-identification method.
- C. Average-cost method.
- D. Last-in, first-out (LIFO) method.

Answer (D) is correct. *(Publisher, adapted)*
   REQUIRED: The cost flow method prohibited by IFRS.
   DISCUSSION: The last-in, first-out (LIFO) method is prohibited by IFRS but not U.S. GAAP.
   Answer (A) is incorrect. The first-in, first-out method is permitted by IFRS. Answer (B) is incorrect. The specific-identification method is permitted by IFRS. Answer (C) is incorrect. The average-cost method is permitted by IFRS.

Use Gleim **EQE Test Prep** Software Download for interactive study and performance analysis.

STUDY UNIT SEVEN
PROPERTY, PLANT, AND EQUIPMENT

Definition and Initial Measurement

Property, plant, and equipment (PPE) are tangible, noncurrent assets held for use in ordinary operations. PPE include land, land improvements, buildings, machinery, equipment, furniture, fixtures, natural resources subject to depletion, leasehold improvements, leased assets held under capital leases, noncurrent assets under construction, and other depreciable assets. PPE normally are recorded at **historical cost minus depreciation or depletion** (amortized cost). Historical cost includes the purchase price plus other costs necessary to bring the asset to the location and condition necessary for its intended use. Thus, PPE are **not revalued upward** to reflect appraisal, market, current, or fair values above historical cost. Moreover, when two or more assets with varying estimated useful lives are acquired for a single price (a **basket purchase**), allocation of the cost is required. The basis of allocation is relative fair value. If an item of PPE is acquired in exchange for a **noncurrent note**, its cost is the present value of the consideration paid (the note). But the note's interest rate may be unstated or unreasonable, or the face amount may differ materially from the cash price of the PPE or the market value of the note. In these cases, the cost of the PPE should be the more clearly determinable of the cash price of the PPE or the market value of the note.

PPE may be donated to a business. In general, **contributions received** should be recognized as (1) revenues or gains in the period of receipt and (2) assets, decreases in liabilities, or expenses. They are measured at fair value. But this guidance does not apply to (1) contributions by governmental units to businesses or (2) tax exemptions, incentives, or abatements. Accordingly, a business may credit a contribution from a governmental unit to donated capital. However, treating contributions by governmental units as revenues or gains is not prohibited.

Capitalization of Interest

Capitalization of material interest costs is required for qualifying assets: (1) assets constructed for internal use, (2) assets constructed for sale or lease as discrete products, and (3) investments accounted for on the equity basis while the investee has activities in progress necessary to begin its planned principal operations. Capitalization of interest for a qualifying asset is required when (1) expenditures have been made, (2) activities are underway to prepare the asset for its intended use, and (3) interest cost is being incurred. The **amount capitalized** is intended to be the portion of interest costs incurred during a qualifying asset's acquisition period that theoretically could have been avoided if expenditures for the asset had not been made. The amount capitalized in an accounting period is determined by applying the capitalization rate to the **average amount of accumulated expenditures** for the asset during the period. The **capitalization** rate is based on rates applicable to borrowings outstanding during the period. The interest rate on construction loans specific to the qualifying asset is ordinarily used as the capitalization rate to the extent average accumulated expenditures for the period do not exceed the amount of the construction loan. A weighted-average rate on other borrowings outstanding during the period is used to the extent average accumulated expenditures for the period exceed the amount of the construction loan.

Costs Subsequent to Acquisition

Costs incurred **subsequent to acquisition** that significantly improve the future service potential of an asset by increasing the quality or quantity of its output or its estimated useful life are **capitalized** when incurred. But costs incurred to maintain an asset's operating condition (i.e., repairs and maintenance) are **expensed** when incurred.

A **replacement** substitutes a new component of an asset for a similar one, for example, a tile roof for a tile roof. But an **improvement** substitutes a better component, such as a more efficient heating system. Given accounting recognition of the old component, e.g., recording a central air conditioning system separately from the building, the procedure is to remove it from the ledger, along with accumulated depreciation, and to **substitute the cost of the new component**. A gain or loss may be recognized. The new component will be depreciated over the shorter of its useful life or that of the entire asset. **Rearranging** the configuration of plant assets, **reinstalling** such assets, or **relocating** operations also may require material outlays that are separable from recurring expenses and provide probable future benefits.

The following table summarizes the accounting for subsequent expenditures for PPE:

Action	Accounting Treatment	
Additions	Debit separate asset or debit old asset	
Replacements/Improvements – Carrying Amount Known	Substitution method	
Replacements/Improvements – Carrying Amount Not Known	Increase service potential only: debit asset	Extend useful life only: debit accum. depreciation
Rearrangements/Reinstallations	Cost known: substitution method	Otherwise, material costs debited to new asset
Repairs	Minor: expense	Major: treatment as addition, etc.

Impairment and Disposal

Long-lived assets that are to be held and used or disposed of may be included in a group with other assets and liabilities. The unit of accounting is the group. If a long-lived asset(s) is to be held and used, the **asset group** is the lowest level at which identifiable cash flows are largely independent of those of other groups. If a long-lived asset(s) is to be disposed of by sale or otherwise, the **disposal group** consists of assets to be disposed of together in one transaction and directly associated liabilities to be transferred in the same transaction. A long-lived asset (asset group) **to be held and used** is impaired when its carrying amount is greater than its **fair value**. However, an **impairment loss** equal to this excess is recognized only when the carrying amount is not **recoverable**. The carrying amount is not recoverable when it exceeds the sum of the undiscounted cash flows expected from the use and disposition of the asset (asset group). Recoverability is tested when events or changes in circumstances provide **indicators** that the carrying amount may not be recoverable.

Determination of an Impairment Loss
1. Events or changes in circumstances indicate a possible loss
2. Carrying amount > sum of undiscounted cash flows
3. Loss = carrying amount – fair value

A recognized impairment loss on a long-lived asset to be held and used is not reversible. Moreover, it decreases only the carrying amounts of the long-lived assets in the group on a pro rata basis according to their relative carrying amounts. However, the carrying amount of a given long-lived asset (its new **cost basis**) is not reduced below its fair value (if determinable without undue cost and effort). The new cost basis is depreciated over the remaining useful life of the asset (if the asset is depreciable). An entity **reports** an impairment loss in income from continuing operations before income taxes.

Long-lived assets may be **disposed of other than by sale**, for example, by abandonment, exchange (see next section), contribution, or a distribution to owners in a spinoff. They are classified as held and used and continue to be depreciated until disposal. An asset to be **abandoned** is disposed of when it is no longer used. If the asset is still in use, it is normally not immediately written down to zero. Continued use indicates that the asset has service potential. However, depreciation estimates should be revised to account for the reduced service period. A noncurrent asset that is temporarily idled is not treated as abandoned. **Contributions** made do not involve an exchange. They are recorded at fair value, and an expense and gain or loss are recognized. A **nonreciprocal transfer to owners** is accounted for based on the recorded amount (after recognition of impairment loss) in a distribution of nonmonetary assets to owners in a spinoff or other similar transaction.

An **involuntary conversion** of an item of PPE occurs when it is (1) lost through a casualty (flood, earthquake, fire, etc.), (2) expropriated (seized by a foreign government), or (3) condemned (through the governmental power of eminent domain). The accounting is the same as for other nonexchange dispositions. The **gain or loss** on an involuntary conversion is reported as an ordinary item unless the criteria for treatment as an extraordinary item are met. A nonmonetary asset may be involuntarily converted to monetary assets (e.g., insurance proceeds). Tax law may treat the gain as an adjustment of the basis of replacement property, not a currently taxable amount. Gain or loss recognition is required even though the entity reinvests or is required to reinvest the proceeds in replacement nonmonetary assets. Hence, the replacement property should be recorded at its **cost**. The involuntary conversion and replacement are not equivalent to a single exchange transaction between entities.

An asset (disposal group) is classified as **held for sale** when (1) management has committed to a plan to sell, (2) the asset is available for immediate sale in its current condition on usual and customary terms, (3) actions (such as actively seeking a buyer) have begun to complete the plan, (4) completion of sale within 1 year is probable (but this condition need not be met if certain events or circumstances occur that the entity cannot control), (5) the asset is actively marketed at a price reasonably related to current fair value, and (6) the likelihood is low of significant change in or withdrawal of the plan. Whenever these conditions are not met, the asset or disposal group must be **reclassified** as held and used. **Measurement** is at the **lower of carrying amount or fair value minus cost to sell**. An asset classified as held for sale is not depreciated, but expenses related to the liabilities of a disposal group are accrued. **Costs to sell** are the incremental direct costs. A **loss** is recognized for a write-down to fair value minus cost to sell. A **gain** is recognized for any subsequent increase, but only to the extent of previously recognized losses for write-downs. The loss or gain adjusts only the carrying amount of a long-lived asset even if it is included in a disposal group.

A **plan of sale may change** because of circumstances (previously unlikely) that result in a decision not to sell. The asset (disposal group) then must be **reclassified as held and used**. A reclassified long-lived asset is measured individually at the lower of (1) carrying amount before classification as held for sale, minus any depreciation (amortization) that would have been recognized if it had always been classified as held and used, or (2) fair value at the date of the decision not to sell.

A **reclassification adjustment** of the carrying amount is included in income from continuing operations in the period of the decision not to sell. If a **long-lived asset** is held for sale, it is **reported** separately in the balance sheet. If a **disposal group** is held for sale, its assets and liabilities are reported separately in the balance sheet and are not offset and presented as a single amount.

Exchanges of Nonmonetary Assets

Exchanges are classified as monetary or nonmonetary. **Monetary exchanges** involve assets fixed in terms of units of money. They are measured at the fair value of the assets involved, with gain or loss recognized in full immediately. The fair value of the assets given up generally is used unless the fair value of the assets received is more clearly evident. **Nonmonetary exchanges** also are measured at fair value. However, the accounting is based on the **carrying amount** of the assets given up when (1) neither the fair value of the assets given up nor the fair value of the assets received is reasonably determinable, (2) the exchange involves inventory sold in the same line of business that facilitates sales to customers not parties to the exchange, or (3) the exchange lacks commercial substance. An exchange **lacks commercial substance** when an entity's cash flows are not expected to change significantly.

In any exchange of nonmonetary assets that is not accounted for at fair value, partial monetary consideration **(boot)** may be paid by one party to the other. The recipient of boot must recognize a proportionate amount of any potential gain. But if a loss is indicated in an exchange (with or without boot) measured at the carrying amount of the assets given up, the **entire loss** is recognized. Any gain recognized by the recipient of boot equals the total potential gain (monetary consideration + fair value of assets received – carrying amount given up) times the ratio of

$$\frac{Boot}{Boot + Fair\ value\ of\ nonmonetary\ assets\ received}$$

The **entity paying boot** does not recognize gain. The new asset should be recorded at the carrying amount of the asset given plus boot paid. However, when this amount exceeds the fair value of the assets received, the assets received should be recorded at fair value, with the difference recognized as a loss.

If boot is **25% or more** of the total fair value of the exchange, both parties record a monetary exchange at fair value, with gains and losses recognized in full.

The following table summarizes gain or loss recognition in nonmonetary exchanges:

Measure of Exchange	Gain	Loss
Fair value	Full	Full
Carrying amount – no boot received	None	Full
Carrying amount – boot received	Partial	Full

Differences between GAAP and IFRS

Under IFRS:

- If the **fair value** of an item of PPE can be **reliably measured**, it may be accounted for in accordance with the revaluation model. It is carried at a **revalued** amount equal to **fair value at the revaluation date** (minus subsequent accumulated depreciation and impairment losses). Revaluation is needed whenever fair value and the asset's carrying amount differ materially. Some assets may be revalued as often as annually. Accumulated depreciation is restated proportionately or eliminated. If the revaluation model is the chosen accounting policy for an item of PPE, all items in its class (e.g., land and buildings) must be accounted for using the same model. If an item of PPE is revalued, all items in its class also must be revalued. A **revaluation increase** must be recognized in other comprehensive income and accumulated in equity as revaluation surplus. But the increase must be recognized in profit or loss to the extent it reverses a decrease of the same asset that was previously recognized in profit or loss. A **revaluation decrease** must be recognized in profit or loss. But the decrease must be recognized in other comprehensive income to the extent of any credit in revaluation surplus for the same asset. The **revaluation surplus** included in equity may be transferred directly to retained earnings (1) as the asset is used by the entity or (2) only when the asset is derecognized. However, no part of the revaluation surplus is required to be transferred to retained earnings.

- **Investment property** is land, a building, part of a building, or both held by the owner (or by the lessee under a finance lease) to earn rental income or for capital appreciation or both. Under **IAS 40**, *Investment Property*, such property must be accounted for according to the cost model or the fair value model. Under the **cost model**, all investment property must be carried at historical cost minus accumulated depreciation and impairment losses. Under the **fair value model**, all investment property must be measured at **fair value** at the end of the reporting period. A **gain or loss** from a change in the fair value of investment property must be recognized in profit or loss for the period in which it arises. Investment property that is accounted for according to the fair value model is not depreciated.

- **IAS 36**, *Impairment of Assets*, states that an asset is impaired when its **carrying amount exceeds its recoverable amount**. The entity assesses at each reporting date whether an indication of impairment exists. Given such an indication, the recoverable amount must be estimated. Moreover, **intangible assets** with indefinite useful lives or those not yet available for use and **goodwill** are tested for impairment at least annually. The **recoverable amount** of an asset is the greater of its fair value minus costs to sell or value in use. **Value in use** is the present value of the asset's expected cash flows. The recognized **impairment loss** is the excess of the asset's carrying amount over its recoverable amount. An impairment loss on an asset (except goodwill) may be reversed if a change in the estimates used to measure the recoverable amount has occurred.

QUESTIONS

7.1 Definition and Initial Measurement

1. Property, plant, and equipment are conventionally presented in the balance sheet at

A. Replacement cost minus accumulated depreciation.

B. Historical cost minus salvage value.

C. Original cost adjusted for general price-level changes.

D. Historical cost minus depreciated portion thereof.

Answer (D) is correct. *(CPA, adapted)*
REQUIRED: The conventional balance sheet presentation of property, plant, and equipment.
DISCUSSION: Property, plant, and equipment are recorded at their acquisition cost. They are then measured in accordance with SFAC 5 at their historical cost attribute. When property, plant, and equipment are used in normal operations, this historical cost must be allocated (depreciated) on a systematic and rational basis to the accounting periods in which they are used. Land is an exception because it is not depreciated.
Answer (A) is incorrect. Historical cost rather than replacement cost is the attribute at which property, plant, and equipment are measured. Answer (B) is incorrect. Assets appear in the balance sheet at historical cost with an offset for accumulated depreciation (not salvage value). Answer (C) is incorrect. The basic financial statements are not adjusted for price-level changes.

2. A contributed plant asset for which the fair value has been determined, and for which incidental costs were incurred in acceptance of the asset, should be recorded at an amount equal to its

A. Incidental costs incurred.

B. Fair value and incidental costs incurred.

C. Carrying amount on books of donor and incidental costs incurred.

D. Carrying amount on books of donor.

Answer (B) is correct. *(CPA, adapted)*
REQUIRED: The amount at which a contributed plant asset should be recorded.
DISCUSSION: A contributed plant asset should be debited at its fair value plus any incidental costs necessary to make the asset ready for its intended use. Contributions received ordinarily should be credited as revenues or gains in the periods they are received.
Answer (A) is incorrect. Any plant asset, including a contributed plant asset, should be recorded at fair value in addition to any incidental costs incurred. Answer (C) is incorrect. Any plant asset, including a contributed plant asset, should be debited at fair value plus costs necessary to render the asset operational. Answer (D) is incorrect. The carrying amount on the books of the donor has no impact on the recorded value of the asset.

3. When fixed assets are self-constructed, which costs should be expensed in the period of construction?

A. Excess of construction costs over third-party selling price.

B. Fixed and variable overhead costs.

C. Fees paid to outside consultants.

D. Cost of safety devices required by government agencies.

Answer (A) is correct. *(Publisher, adapted)*
REQUIRED: The costs of self-constructed fixed assets that should be expensed in the period of construction.
DISCUSSION: An asset should not be recorded in excess of its fair value. Thus, a self-constructed fixed asset should not be capitalized at an amount greater than that at which the asset could be purchased from a third party. Any excess cost is a loss that should not be deferred to future periods and should be expensed.
Answer (B) is incorrect. Some fixed costs may be expensed rather than capitalized when the construction reduces normal production. Answer (C) is incorrect. Fees paid to outside consultants are directly related to the construction of fixed assets and should be capitalized. Answer (D) is incorrect. The cost of safety devices required by government agencies are directly related to the construction of fixed assets and should be capitalized.

4. On December 1 of the current year, Horton Co. purchased a tract of land as a factory site for $300,000. The old building on the property was razed, and salvaged materials resulting from demolition were sold. Additional costs incurred and salvage proceeds realized during December were as follows:

Cost to raze old building	$25,000
Legal fees for purchase contract and to record ownership	5,000
Title guarantee insurance	6,000
Proceeds from sale of salvaged materials	4,000

In Horton's current-year balance sheet dated December 31, what amount should be reported as land?

A. $311,000

B. $321,000

C. $332,000

D. $336,000

Answer (C) is correct. *(CPA, adapted)*
REQUIRED: The amount to be reported as the cost of land.
DISCUSSION: When land is acquired as a factory site, the cost of the land should include the purchase price of the land and such additional expenses as legal fees, title insurance, recording fees, subsequent assumption of encumbrances on the property, and the costs incurred in preparing the property for its intended use. Because the land was purchased as a factory site, the cost of razing the old building, minus any proceeds received from the sale of salvaged materials, should be capitalized as part of the land account. Thus, the amount to be reported as land is $332,000 ($300,000 + $5,000 + $6,000 + $25,000 – $4,000).
Answer (A) is incorrect. The amount of $311,000 excludes the net cost of razing the old building. Answer (B) is incorrect. The amount of $321,000 excludes the legal fees and title insurance. Answer (D) is incorrect. The amount of $336,000 excludes the proceeds of razing the old building.

5. Meriadoc Co. purchased a machine costing $125,000 for its manufacturing operations and paid shipping costs of $20,000. It spent an additional $10,000 testing and preparing the machine for use. What amount should Meriadoc record as the cost of the machine?

A. $155,000

B. $145,000

C. $135,000

D. $125,000

Answer (A) is correct. *(CPA, adapted)*
REQUIRED: The amount to be recorded as the acquisition cost of the machine.
DISCUSSION: The amount to be recorded as the acquisition cost of a machine includes all costs necessary to prepare it for its intended use. Thus, the cost of a machine used in the manufacturing operations of a company includes the cost of testing and preparing the machine for use and the shipping costs. The acquisition cost is $155,000 ($125,000 + $20,000 + $10,000).
Answer (B) is incorrect. The amount of $145,000 does not include the $10,000 cost of testing and preparation. Answer (C) is incorrect. The amount of $135,000 does not include the shipping costs. Answer (D) is incorrect. The amount of $125,000 does not include the shipping, testing, and preparation costs.

6. Land was purchased to be used as the site for the construction of a plant. A building on the property was sold and removed by the buyer so that construction on the plant could begin. The proceeds from the sale of the building should be

A. Classified as other income.

B. Deducted from the cost of the land.

C. Netted against the costs to clear the land and expensed as incurred.

D. Netted against the costs to clear the land and amortized over the life of the plant.

Answer (B) is correct. *(CPA, adapted)*
REQUIRED: The treatment of proceeds from the sale of a building removed to prepare for construction.
DISCUSSION: Land obtained as a plant site should be recorded at its acquisition cost. This cost includes the purchase price of the land and any additional expenses such as legal fees, title insurance, recording fees, assumption of encumbrances on the property, and any other costs incurred in preparing the property for its intended use. Because the intended use of the land was as a site for the construction of a plant, the proceeds from the sale of the building removed to prepare the land for construction should be deducted from the cost of the land.
Answer (A) is incorrect. Proceeds from the sale of a building that is removed from a piece of land are not income. Answer (C) is incorrect. Proceeds from the sale of a building that is removed from a piece of land are not a cost. They are treated as a reduction in the cost of the land. Answer (D) is incorrect. Proceeds from the sale of a building that is removed from a piece of land are treated as a reduction in the cost of the land.

7. During the current year, Hamilton Co. had the following transactions pertaining to its new office building:

Purchase price of land	$120,000
Legal fees for contracts to purchase land	4,000
Architects' fees	16,000
Demolition of the old building on site	10,000
Sale of scrap from old building	6,000
Construction cost of new building (fully completed)	700,000

In Hamilton's current year balance sheet dated December 31, what amounts should be reported as the cost of land and cost of building?

	Land	Building
A.	$120,000	$720,000
B.	$124,000	$720,000
C.	$128,000	$716,000
D.	$130,000	$724,000

Answer (C) is correct. *(CPA, adapted)*
REQUIRED: The amounts reported as the cost of land and cost of building.
DISCUSSION: The cost of the land should include the purchase price of the land and additional expenses such as legal fees, title insurance, recording fees, subsequent assumption of encumbrances on the property, and the costs incurred in preparing the property for its intended use. Because the land was purchased as the site of an office building, the cost of razing the old building, minus any proceeds received from the sale of salvaged materials, should be capitalized as part of the land account. Thus, land should be reported as $128,000 ($120,000 + $4,000 + $10,000 – $6,000). The architects' fees are included in the cost of the building, which should be reported as $716,000 ($700,000 + $16,000).
Answer (A) is incorrect. A $120,000 land cost omits the legal fees and the net demolition cost, and a $720,000 building cost improperly includes the legal fees. Answer (B) is incorrect. A $124,000 land cost omits the legal fees or the net demolition cost, and a $720,000 building cost improperly includes the legal fees. Answer (D) is incorrect. A $130,000 land cost includes the gross demolition cost but not the legal fees. A $724,000 building cost includes the legal fees and the net demolition cost.

8. On July 1 of the current year, Degas Co. purchased a tract of land for $1,200,000. Degas incurred additional costs of $300,000 during the remainder of the year in preparing the land for sale. The tract was subdivided into residential lots as follows:

Lot Class	Number of Lots	Sales Price per Lot
A	100	$24,000
B	100	16,000
C	200	10,000

Using the relative sales value method, what amount of costs should be allocated to the Class A lots?

A. $300,000

B. $375,000

C. $600,000

D. $720,000

Answer (C) is correct. *(CPA, adapted)*
REQUIRED: The amount of costs allocated using the relative sales value method.
DISCUSSION: The relative sales value method allocates cost based on the relative value of assets in a group. The total sales value of the lots is $6,000,000 [(100 × $24,000) + (100 × $16,000) + (200 × $10,000)]. Class A represents 40% of the total value ($2,400,000 ÷ $6,000,000). Total costs equal $1,500,000 ($1,200,000 + $300,000). Thus, the amount of costs allocated to Class A is $600,000 ($1,500,000 × .40).
Answer (A) is incorrect. The additional costs incurred equal $300,000. Answer (B) is incorrect. The amount of $375,000 equals 25% of the total cost. Class A represents 25% of the lots but 40% of the total value. Answer (D) is incorrect. The amount of $720,000 equals 48% of the total cost. Class A's sales price per lot is 48% of the sum of the unit sales prices of Classes A, B, and C.

9. A company purchased a building for $45,000 cash and recorded its cost on the books at that amount. However, the fair value of the building was $46,500 on the date of purchase. How should the company account for this $1,500 difference?

A. Amortize it over the useful life of the building.

B. Capitalize it as goodwill.

C. Debit it to the building account.

D. Do not record the amount.

Answer (D) is correct. *(CIA, adapted)*
REQUIRED: The accounting treatment for an unrealized gain on a building.
DISCUSSION: Property, plant, and equipment should not be written up by an entity to reflect the appraisal, market, or current values that are above cost to the entity. The company should not recognize the unrealized gain of $1,500.
Answer (A) is incorrect. The unrealized gain should not be amortized. Answer (B) is incorrect. The unrealized gain is not goodwill. Answer (C) is incorrect. The recorded amount of the building should not exceed is acquisition cost.

10. Ismail Co. acquired two machines for $70,000. An appraisal costing $600 showed that the machines had fair values of $32,000 and $48,000, respectively. The carrying amounts for the machines were $20,000 and $40,000, respectively. The two assets should be individually recorded at costs of

- A. $20,000 and $40,000.
- B. $28,000 and $42,000.
- C. $28,240 and $42,360.
- D. $32,240 and $48,360.

Answer (C) is correct. *(Publisher, adapted)*
REQUIRED: The amount at which the two machines should be recorded.
DISCUSSION: The total acquisition cost for the two machines is $70,600 ($70,000 acquisition cost + $600 appraisal cost). When two or more assets with varying estimated useful lives are acquired for a single price (a basket purchase), allocation of the cost is required. The basis of allocation is relative fair value in accordance with current market prices, insurance appraisals, tax assessments, or other reasonable estimates. Thus, the allocation of the costs is as follows:

$$\frac{\$32,000}{\$32,000 + \$48,000} \times \$70,600 = \$28,240$$

$$\frac{\$48,000}{\$32,000 + \$48,000} \times \$70,600 = \$42,360$$

Answer (A) is incorrect. The total acquisition cost must be allocated to each machine based on fair value. Answer (B) is incorrect. The appraisal fees are a part of the acquisition cost of the machines. Answer (D) is incorrect. The machines should not be recorded at an amount above the cost to Ismail Co.

11. On July 1, Year 1, Colman Company sold land with a carrying amount of $75,000 to Monte Company in exchange for $50,000 in cash and a note calling for five annual $10,000 payments beginning on June 30, Year 2, and ending on June 30, Year 6. The fair value of the land is uncertain, and Monte can borrow long-term funds at 11%. What should be the amount capitalized as acquisition cost of the land by Monte Company? (The present value of $1 for five periods at 11% is 0.59345, and the present value of an ordinary annuity of $1 for five periods at 11% is 3.6959.)

- A. $55,935
- B. $75,000
- C. $86,959
- D. $100,000

Answer (C) is correct. *(S. Schultz)*
REQUIRED: The cost at which an asset should be capitalized when acquired under a financing agreement.
DISCUSSION: If an item of PPE is acquired in exchange for a noncurrent note, its cost is the present value of the consideration paid (the note). But the note's interest rate may be unstated or unreasonable, or the face amount may differ materially from the cash price of the PPE or the market value of the note. In these cases, the cost of the PPE should be the more clearly determinable of the cash price of the PPE or the market value of the note. The assets transferred included $50,000 in cash and a note with no stated interest rate. Given that Monte can borrow long-term funds at 11%, the market value of the note can be approximated by imputing an 11% rate and using it to calculate the present value of the five equal annual payments. The present value of this ordinary annuity is $36,959 ($10,000 payment × 3.6959), and the land should be recorded at $86,959 ($50,000 + $36,959).
Answer (A) is incorrect. The amount of $55,935 is the $50,000 in cash plus the present value of $10,000 to be received in 5 years. Answer (B) is incorrect. Colman Company's carrying amount of the land is $75,000. Answer (D) is incorrect. The amount of $100,000 is the $50,000 in cash plus $50,000 of payments that should have been calculated at present value.

12. Tioga City owned a vacant plot of land zoned for industrial use. Tioga gave this land to Haile Corp. solely as an incentive for Haile to build a factory on the site. The land had a fair value of $300,000 at the date of the gift. This nonmonetary transaction is most likely to be reported by Haile as

- A. An extraordinary gain.
- B. Donated capital.
- C. A credit to retained earnings.
- D. A memorandum entry.

Answer (B) is correct. *(CPA, adapted)*
REQUIRED: The accounting for a contributed asset.
DISCUSSION: Contributions received ordinarily should be accounted for as revenues and gains at fair value, but this guidance does not apply to a contribution from a government to a business. Nevertheless, it does not preclude accounting for the contribution as a revenue or gain. Such treatment is consistent with the accounting for most contributions. However, contributions have often been accounted for by crediting donated capital, an additional paid-in capital account. This approach is not currently prohibited by GAAP.
Answer (A) is incorrect. A contribution most likely does not meet the criteria of an extraordinary item. It is not unusual. Answer (C) is incorrect. A contribution from a government is not recorded directly in retained earnings. It should be reported in the income statement or as contributed capital. Answer (D) is incorrect. A contribution should be recognized in the accounts.

7.2 Capitalization of Interest

13. Interest should be capitalized for assets that are

A. In use or ready for their intended use in the earning activities of the entity.

B. Being constructed or otherwise being produced as discrete projects for an entity's own use.

C. Not being used in the earning activities of the entity and not undergoing the activities necessary to get them ready for use.

D. Routinely produced.

Answer (B) is correct. *(CMA, adapted)*
REQUIRED: The types of assets for which interest should be capitalized.
DISCUSSION: GAAP require capitalization of material interest costs for assets constructed for internal use and those constructed for sale or lease as discrete projects. It does not apply to products routinely produced for inventory, assets in use or ready for use, assets not being used or being prepared for use, and idle land.
Answer (A) is incorrect. Interest is not capitalized for assets in use or ready for use. Answer (C) is incorrect. Assets not being used and being prepared for use are not subject to interest capitalization rules. Answer (D) is incorrect. Capitalized interest should not be added to routinely produced inventory.

14. During the current year, Elbridge Co. constructed machinery for its own use and for sale to customers. Bank loans financed these assets both during construction and after construction was complete. How much of the interest incurred should be reported as interest expense in the current year income statement?

	Interest Incurred for Machinery for Elbridge's Own Use	Interest Incurred for Machinery Held for Sale
A.	All interest incurred	All interest incurred
B.	All interest incurred	Interest incurred after completion
C.	Interest incurred after completion	Interest incurred after completion
D.	Interest incurred after completion	All interest incurred

Answer (D) is correct. *(CPA, adapted)*
REQUIRED: The interest incurred reported as interest expense.
DISCUSSION: Interest should be capitalized for two types of assets: those constructed or otherwise produced for an entity's own use, including those constructed or produced by others, and those intended for sale or lease that are constructed or produced as discrete products (e.g., ships). Furthermore, equity-based investments also may be qualifying assets. Machinery constructed for an entity's own use qualifies for capitalization of interest if relevant expenditures have been made, activities necessary to prepare the asset for its intended use are in progress, and interest is being incurred. Machinery routinely constructed for sale to others does not qualify. Thus, interest incurred for machinery held for sale and interest incurred after an asset has been completed should be expensed.
Answer (A) is incorrect. Only interest incurred for machinery for Elbridge's own use after completion should be expensed. Answer (B) is incorrect. All interest incurred for machinery held for sale and interest incurred for machinery for Elbridge's own use after completion should be expensed. Answer (C) is incorrect. All interest incurred for machinery held for sale should be expensed.

15. During a calendar-year company's second quarter, the following expenditures were made relative to a qualifying asset on which interest is to be capitalized: $80,000 on April 1, $90,000 on May 1, and $100,000 incurred uniformly during the period. What was the average amount of accumulated expenditures for this quarterly accounting period?

A. $180,000

B. $190,000

C. $240,000

D. $270,000

Answer (B) is correct. *(Publisher, adapted)*
REQUIRED: The average accumulated expenditures.
DISCUSSION: To determine the average accumulated expenditures on which interest is to be capitalized, the expenditures must be weighted by the portion of the accounting period for which they were incurred. The $80,000 expended on April 1 was incurred during the entire period. The $90,000 expended on May 1 was incurred for two-thirds of the period. The $100,000 incurred uniformly throughout is equivalent to an expenditure of $50,000 for the whole period. The average amount of accumulated expenditures is equal to $190,000 [($80,000 × 1) + ($90,000 × 2/3) + ($100,000 × 1/2)].
Answer (A) is incorrect. The amount of $180,000 assumes the whole $100,000 is included and none of the $90,000. Answer (C) is incorrect. The amount of $240,000 assumes that the whole $100,000 is included. Answer (D) is incorrect. The amount of $270,000 is not the average amount of accumulated expenditures. It is the sum of the expenditures for a qualifying asset.

16. Which one of the following ways of determining an interest rate should be used when the average accumulated expenditures for the constructed asset exceed the amounts of specific new borrowings associated with the asset?

    A. Average rate of return on equity for the last 5 years.

    B. Cost of capital rate for the entity.

    C. Prime interest rate.

    D. Weighted average of the interest rates applicable to the other borrowings of the entity.

Answer (D) is correct. *(CMA, adapted)*
    REQUIRED: The method of determining the interest rate.
    DISCUSSION: The actual interest rate on specific new borrowings is used to capitalize construction expenditures to the extent of the new borrowings. If average accumulated construction expenditures for the period exceed the specific new borrowings related to the construction, interest on other borrowings must be capitalized. A weighted-average interest rate must be used to capitalize interest costs on accumulated construction expenditures in excess of the specific new borrowings associated with the asset.

17. Which of the following is not an accurate statement of a criterion that must be met before interest is required to be capitalized?

    A. Expenditures relative to a qualifying asset have been made.

    B. Activities necessary to prepare the asset for its intended use are in progress.

    C. Interest cost is incurred on borrowings.

    D. Debt is incurred for the project.

Answer (D) is correct. *(Publisher, adapted)*
    REQUIRED: The item not a criterion for capitalization of interest.
    DISCUSSION: Capitalization of interest for a qualifying asset is required when expenditures have been made, activities are in progress to ready the asset for its intended use, and interest cost is being incurred. The mere incurrence of debt is not sufficient. Capitalized interest is limited to interest on borrowings. Accordingly, the incurrence of debt, such as trade payables, upon which no interest cost is being incurred, is not sufficient to meet the required criteria, even if qualifying expenditures have been made and the appropriate activities are in progress.
    Answer (A) is incorrect. Having actually made expenditures is one of the qualifying criteria for capitalization of interest. Answer (B) is incorrect. Activities being underway to prepare the asset for its intended use is one of the qualifying criteria for interest capitalization. Answer (C) is incorrect. Incurring debt for the project is one of the qualifying criteria for interest capitalization.

18. Harbor Co. began constructing a building for its own use in January of the current year. During the current year, Harbor incurred interest of $100,000 on specific construction debt and $40,000 on other borrowings. Interest computed on the weighted-average amount of accumulated expenditures for the building during the current year was $80,000. What amount of interest cost should Harbor capitalize?

    A. $40,000

    B. $80,000

    C. $100,000

    D. $140,000

Answer (B) is correct. *(CPA, adapted)*
    REQUIRED: The amount of interest capitalized.
    DISCUSSION: Material interest costs incurred for the construction of certain assets for internal use are capitalized. The interest to be capitalized is determined by applying an interest rate (the capitalization rate) to the average qualifying expenditures accumulated during a given period. Thus, $80,000 of the interest incurred on the construction is capitalized.
    Answer (A) is incorrect. Interest on other borrowings equals $40,000. Answer (C) is incorrect. The total interest on specific construction debt equals $100,000. Answer (D) is incorrect. The sum of interest on other borrowings and the total interest on specific construction debt equals $140,000.

19. Sun Co. was constructing fixed assets that qualified for interest capitalization. Sun had the following outstanding debt issuances during the entire year of construction:

- $6,000,000 face value, 8% interest
- $8,000,000 face value, 9% interest

None of the borrowings were specified for the construction of the qualified fixed asset. Average expenditures for the year were $1,000,000. What interest rate should Sun use to calculate capitalized interest on the construction?

    A. 8.00%

    B. 8.50%

    C. 8.57%

    D. 9.00%

Answer (C) is correct. *(CPA, adapted)*
    REQUIRED: The interest rate used to calculate capitalized interest.
    DISCUSSION: The costs necessary to bring an asset to the condition and location of its intended use are part of the historical cost. Interest incurred during construction is such a cost and must be debited to the internally constructed asset. No new borrowings were outstanding during the period that can be identified with the ICA. Thus, the interest rate used is the weighted-average rate on other borrowings outstanding during the period. It is calculated as follows:

$$[\$6,000,000 \div (\$6,000,000 + \$8,000,000)] \times 8\% = \underline{3.43\%}$$
$$[\$8,000,000 \div (\$6,000,000 + \$8,000,000)] \times 9\% = \underline{5.14\%}$$
$$8.57\%$$

    Answer (A) is incorrect. This interest rate (8.00%) is for the $6,000,000 face amount debt issuance. Answer (B) is incorrect. This interest rate (8.50%) is the average of the two rates. The weighted-average rate on other borrowings is used to calculate the amount of interest that must be capitalized when no specific borrowing can be identified with the asset. Answer (D) is incorrect. This interest rate (9.00%) is for the $8,000,000 face amount debt issuance.

20. Which of the following items should not have been capitalized?

    A. The cost of reinstalling or rearranging equipment to facilitate more efficient future production.

    B. The cost of removing an old building from land that was purchased with the intent of constructing a new office building on the site.

    C. The estimated cost of equity capital during the construction period of a new office building.

    D. The cost of a new hospital wing.

Answer (C) is correct. *(CIA, adapted)*
    REQUIRED: The item that should not have been capitalized.
    DISCUSSION: GAAP require the capitalization of interest on debt incurred as a cost of acquiring an asset during the period in which an asset is being constructed for the company's own use. Imputed interest on equity capital is not capitalized. The view of the FASB is that recognizing the cost of equity capital would not conform to the current accounting framework.
    Answer (A) is incorrect. Such a cost will benefit future periods and thus should be capitalized. Answer (B) is incorrect. The removal cost is associated with preparing land for its intended use and therefore should be capitalized. Answer (D) is incorrect. A new hospital wing is an addition and should be capitalized.

7.3 Costs Subsequent to Acquisition

21. Charging the cost of ordinary repairs to the machinery and equipment asset account during the current year

    A. Understates net income for the current year.

    B. Understates equity at the end of the current year.

    C. Does not affect the total assets at the end of the current year.

    D. Does not affect the total liabilities at the end of the current year.

Answer (D) is correct. *(CMA, adapted)*
    REQUIRED: The effect of charging the cost of ordinary repairs to the machinery and equipment asset account.
    DISCUSSION: When an asset is acquired, the expenses of maintaining the asset are expenses of the period in which the ordinary repairs are rendered. Charging such ordinary repairs to the machinery and equipment asset account overstates total assets, the current year's net income, and equity. Liabilities are not affected.
    Answer (A) is incorrect. Net income is overstated (not understated). Answer (B) is incorrect. Equity is overstated (not understated). Answer (C) is incorrect. Assets are overstated.

22. On January 2, Novation Corp. replaced its boiler with a more efficient one. The following information was available on that date:

Purchase price of new boiler	$120,000
Carrying amount of old boiler	10,000
Fair value of old boiler	4,000
Installation cost of new boiler	16,000

The old boiler was sold for $4,000. What amount should Novation capitalize as the cost of the new boiler?

A. $136,000

B. $132,000

C. $126,000

D. $120,000

Answer (A) is correct. *(CPA, adapted)*
REQUIRED: The amount to be capitalized as the cost of the replacement asset.
DISCUSSION: When a fixed asset is replaced, the new asset should be recorded at its purchase price plus any incidental costs necessary to make the asset ready for its intended use. Consequently, the replacement boiler should be recorded at $136,000 ($120,000 purchase price + $16,000 installation cost). In addition, the $10,000 carrying amount of the old boiler should be removed from the accounts, and a loss of $6,000 ($4,000 proceeds – $10,000 carrying amount) should be recognized.
Answer (B) is incorrect. The amount of $132,000 improperly deducts the fair value of the old boiler. Answer (C) is incorrect. This figure results from deducting the carrying amount of the old boiler. Answer (D) is incorrect. The amount of $120,000 does not consider the installation costs.

23. A machine with an original estimated useful life of 10 years is moved to another location in the factory after it has been in service for 3 years. The efficiency of the machine is increased for its remaining useful life. The reinstallation costs should be capitalized if the remaining useful life of the machine is

	5 Years	10 Years
A.	No	No
B.	No	Yes
C.	Yes	No
D.	Yes	Yes

Answer (D) is correct. *(CPA, adapted)*
REQUIRED: The proper treatment of reinstallation costs that increase a machine's efficiency.
DISCUSSION: Costs that significantly improve the future service potential of an asset by increasing the quality or quantity of its output should be capitalized even though the machine's useful life is not extended. The reinstallation cost should be capitalized whether the remaining useful life is 5 or 10 years.
Answer (A) is incorrect. The reinstallation costs also should be capitalized when the remaining useful life is 5 or 10 years. Answer (B) is incorrect. The reinstallation costs should also be capitalized when the remaining useful life is 5 years. Answer (C) is incorrect. The reinstallation costs should also be capitalized if the remaining useful life is 10 years.

24. Chapeau Co. incurred costs to modify its building and to rearrange its production line. As a result, an overall reduction in production costs is expected. However, the modifications did not increase the building's market value, and the rearrangement did not extend the production line's life. Should the building modification costs and the production line rearrangement costs be capitalized?

	Building Modification Costs	Production Line Rearrangement Costs
A.	Yes	No
B.	Yes	Yes
C.	No	No
D.	No	Yes

Answer (B) is correct. *(CPA, adapted)*
REQUIRED: The accounting for building modification costs and production line rearrangement costs.
DISCUSSION: A rearrangement is the movement of existing assets to provide greater efficiency or to reduce production costs. If the rearrangement expenditure benefits future periods, it should be capitalized. If the building modification costs likewise improve future service potential, they too should be capitalized.
Answer (A) is incorrect. The production line rearrangement costs should be capitalized. Answer (C) is incorrect. The building modification costs and production line rearrangement costs should be capitalized. Answer (D) is incorrect. The building modification costs should be capitalized.

25. A building suffered uninsured fire damage. The damaged portion of the building was refurbished with higher quality materials. The cost and related accumulated depreciation of the damaged portion are identifiable. To account for these events, the owner should

A. Reduce accumulated depreciation equal to the cost of refurbishing.

B. Record a loss in the current period equal to the sum of the cost of refurbishing and the carrying amount of the damaged portion of the building.

C. Capitalize the cost of refurbishing and record a loss in the current period equal to the carrying amount of the damaged portion of the building.

D. Capitalize the cost of refurbishing by adding the cost to the carrying amount of the building.

Answer (C) is correct. *(CPA, adapted)*
REQUIRED: The proper accounting for a substitution.
DISCUSSION: When a substantial portion of a productive asset is replaced and the cost and related accumulated depreciation associated with the old component are identifiable, the substitution method of accounting is used. Under this approach, the asset account and accumulated depreciation should be reduced by the appropriate amounts and a gain or loss recognized. In this instance, the damages were uninsured, and a loss equal to the carrying amount of the damaged portion of the building should be recognized. In addition, the cost of refurbishing should be capitalized in the asset account.
Answer (A) is incorrect. Accumulated depreciation is not adjusted for the cost of refurbishing. Answer (B) is incorrect. The cost of refurbishing should be capitalized, and a loss equal to the carrying amount of the damaged portion of the building should be recognized. Answer (D) is incorrect. A loss equal to the carrying amount of the damaged portion of the building also should be recognized.

26. An expenditure subsequent to acquisition of assembly-line manufacturing equipment benefits future periods. The expenditure should be capitalized if it is a

	Betterment	Rearrangement
A.	No	No
B.	No	Yes
C.	Yes	No
D.	Yes	Yes

Answer (D) is correct. *(CPA, adapted)*
REQUIRED: The type(s) of expenditure that should be capitalized.
DISCUSSION: A betterment occurs when a replacement asset is substituted for an existing asset, and the result is increased productivity, capacity, or expected useful life. A rearrangement is the movement of existing assets to provide greater efficiency or to reduce production costs. If the betterment or rearrangement expenditure benefits future periods, it should be capitalized.
Answer (A) is incorrect. Betterments and rearrangements that benefit future periods should be capitalized. Answer (B) is incorrect. Betterments that benefit future periods also should be capitalized. Answer (C) is incorrect. Rearrangements that benefit future periods also should be capitalized.

27. During the current year, Murdock Company made the following expenditures relating to plant machinery and equipment:

● Renovation of a group of machines at a cost of $100,000 to secure greater efficiency in production over their remaining 5-year useful lives. The project was completed on December 31.

● Continuing, frequent, and low-cost repairs at a cost of $70,000.

● Replacement of a broken gear on a machine at a cost of $10,000.

What total amount should be charged to repairs and maintenance for the current year?

A. $70,000

B. $80,000

C. $170,000

D. $180,000

Answer (B) is correct. *(CPA, adapted)*
REQUIRED: The amount to be charged to repair and maintenance expense.
DISCUSSION: Repair and maintenance costs are incurred to maintain plant assets in operating condition. The continuing, frequent, and low-cost repairs and the replacement of a broken gear meet the definition of repairs and maintenance expense. Accordingly, the amount that should be charged to repairs and maintenance is $80,000 ($70,000 + $10,000). The renovation cost increased the quality of production during the expected useful life of the group of machines. Hence, this $100,000 cost should be capitalized.
Answer (A) is incorrect. The cost of a broken gear should also be charged to repairs and maintenance. Answer (C) is incorrect. The renovation of machines should not be charged to repairs and maintenance; it should be capitalized. The broken gear should be included in repairs and maintenance. Answer (D) is incorrect. The renovation of machines should be capitalized, not charged to repairs and maintenance.

28. On November 2, Corley Co. incurred the following costs for one of its printing presses:

Purchase of collating and stapling attachment	$168,000
Installation of attachment	72,000
Replacement parts for overhaul of press	52,000
Labor and overhead in connection with overhaul	28,000

The overhaul resulted in a significant increase in production. Neither the attachment nor the overhaul increased the estimated useful life of the press. What amount of the above costs should be capitalized?

A. $0

B. $168,000

C. $240,000

D. $320,000

Answer (D) is correct. *(CPA, adapted)*
REQUIRED: The amount of costs to be capitalized.
DISCUSSION: Expenditures that increase the quality or quantity of a machine's output should be capitalized whether or not its useful life is extended. Thus, the amount of the cost to be capitalized equals $320,000 ($168,000 + $72,000 + $52,000 + $28,000).
Answer (A) is incorrect. Costs in the amount of $320,000 should be capitalized. Answer (B) is incorrect. All of the costs associated with the purchase of the parts and the overhaul should be capitalized. Answer (C) is incorrect. The cost of replacement parts and labor and overhead should also be capitalized.

29. During Year 1, Kapital Company spent $2,700,000 to rearrange and $1,200,000 to reinstall the assembly line at one of its plants in order to convert the plant over to the manufacture of a new company product beginning in Year 2. The $1,200,000 in reinstallation costs were charged to the related machinery and equipment, which has an average remaining useful life of 15 years. The new product has an expected life of 9 years. The $2,700,000 in rearrangement costs should be charged in Year 1 to

A. A deferred expense account and expensed at a rate of $300,000 per year beginning in Year 2.

B. A deferred expense account that is never amortized.

C. An expense account.

D. Factory machinery and equipment and depreciated over 15 years.

Answer (A) is correct. *(CIA, adapted)*
REQUIRED: The proper accounting for rearrangement costs.
DISCUSSION: Costs that significantly improve the future service potential of an asset by increasing the quality or quantity of its output should be capitalized. Because the rearrangement and reinstallation costs were incurred to increase the productivity of the assembly line, both costs should be capitalized as part of the related machinery and equipment. These capitalized costs should then be amortized over the expected 9-year life of the new product. Thus, the $2,700,000 in rearrangement costs should be debited to either the asset account or a deferred expense account and then expensed over the 9 years at a rate of $300,000 per year.
Answer (B) is incorrect. The rearrangement costs should be capitalized and amortized over 9 years. Answer (C) is incorrect. The rearrangement costs increase the quality or quantity of output so the costs should not be treated as an expense. Answer (D) is incorrect. The rearrangement costs benefit the new product, which has an expected life of 9 years; therefore, the cost should not be amortized over 15 years (the life of the old equipment).

7.4 Impairment and Disposal

30. When should a long-lived asset be tested for recoverability?

A. When external financial statements are being prepared.

B. When events or changes in circumstances indicate that its carrying amount may not be recoverable.

C. When the asset's carrying amount is less than its fair value.

D. When the asset's fair value has decreased, and the decrease is judged to be permanent.

Answer (B) is correct. *(CPA, adapted)*
REQUIRED: The time when a long-lived asset should be tested for recoverability.
DISCUSSION: A long-lived asset is impaired when its carrying amount is greater than its fair value. However, a loss equal to this excess is recognized for the impairment only when the carrying amount is not recoverable. The carrying amount is not recoverable when it exceeds the sum of the undiscounted cash flows expected from the use and disposition of the asset. Testing should occur when events or changes in circumstances indicate that the carrying amount may not be recoverable.
Answer (A) is incorrect. Under U.S. GAAP, preparation of the external financial statements is not a reason to test for recoverability. Examples of events or changes in circumstances indicating nonrecoverability are a significant decrease in market price or a significant adverse change in use or condition of the asset. Answer (C) is incorrect. When the asset's carrying amount is less than its fair value, the asset is not impaired. Thus, the excess of the fair value over the carrying amount cannot be an indicator of impairment. Answer (D) is incorrect. Even though the asset's fair value has decreased permanently, the fair value may still exceed the carrying amount.

31. Tera Corporation owns a plant that produces baubles for a specialized market niche. This plant is part of an asset group that is the lowest level at which identifiable cash flows are largely independent of those of Tera's other holdings. The asset group includes long-lived assets X, Y, and Z, which are to be held and used. It also includes current assets and liabilities that are not subject to the guidance on accounting for the impairment or disposal of long-lived assets. The sum of the undiscounted cash flows expected to result from the use and eventual disposition of the asset group is $3,200,000, and its fair value is $2,900,000. The following are the carrying amounts ($000 omitted) of the assets and liabilities included in the asset group:

Current assets	$ 600
Liabilities	(200)
Long-lived asset X	1,500
Y	900
Z	600

If the fair value of X is determinable as $1,400,000 without undue cost and effort, what should be the carrying amount of Z?

A. $440,000

B. $500,000

C. $600,000

D. $660,000

Answer (A) is correct. *(Publisher, adapted)*
REQUIRED: The carrying amount of Z.
DISCUSSION: An impairment loss decreases only the carrying amounts of the long-lived assets in the group on a pro rata basis according to their relative carrying amounts. However, the carrying amount of a given long-lived asset is not reduced below its fair value if that fair value is determinable without undue cost and effort. Because the total carrying amount of the asset group of $3.4 million ($600 – $200 + $1,500 + $900 + $600) exceeds the $3.2 million sum of the undiscounted cash flows expected to result from the use and eventual disposition of the asset group, the carrying amount is not recoverable. Hence, an impairment loss equal to the excess of the total carrying amount of the group over its fair value ($3.4 million – $2.9 million = $500,000) must be recognized and allocated pro rata to the long-lived assets. The amounts allocated to X, Y, and Z are $250,000 [($1,500 ÷ $3,000) × $500], $150,000 [($900 ÷ $3,000) × $500], and $100,000 [($600 ÷ $3,000) × $500], respectively. The preliminary adjusted carrying amounts of X, Y, and Z are therefore $1,250,000 ($1,500 – $250), $750,000 ($900 – $150), and $500,000 ($600 – $100), respectively. However, the fair value of X determined without undue cost and effort is $1,400,000. Accordingly, $150,000 ($1,400 fair value of X – $1,250 preliminary adjusted carrying amount of X) must be reallocated to Y and Z. The amounts reallocated to Y and Z are $90,000 [($750 ÷ $1,250) × $150] and $60,000 [($500 ÷ $1,250) × $150], respectively. Thus, the carrying amount of Z should be $440,000 ($600 – $100 – $60).
Answer (B) is incorrect. The preliminary adjusted carrying amount of Z is $500,000. Answer (C) is incorrect. The carrying amount of Z before reduction for a proportionate share of the impairment loss is $600,000. Answer (D) is incorrect. The carrying amount of Z before reduction for a proportionate share of the impairment loss plus (rather than minus) Z's share of the reallocated amount is $660,000.

32. On January 2, Year 1, Clarinette Co. purchased assets for $400,000 that were to be depreciated over 5 years using the straight-line method with no salvage value. Taken together, these assets have identifiable cash flows that are largely independent of the cash flows of other asset groups. At the end of Year 2, Clarinette, as the result of certain changes in circumstances indicating that the carrying amount of these assets may not be recoverable, tested them for impairment. It estimated that it will receive net future cash inflows (undiscounted) of $100,000 as a result of continuing to hold and use these assets, which had a fair value of $80,000 at the end of Year 2. Thus, the impairment loss to be reported at December 31, Year 2, is

A. $0

B. $140,000

C. $160,000

D. $400,000

Answer (C) is correct. *(Publisher, adapted)*
REQUIRED: The carrying amount given estimated future net cash inflows and the fair value.
DISCUSSION: The carrying amount at December 31, Year 2, is $240,000 {$400,000 cost – [($400,000 ÷ 5 years) × 2 years]}, but the recoverable amount is only $100,000. Hence, the test for recognition of an impairment loss has been met. This loss is measured by the excess of the carrying amount over the fair value. Clarinette should therefore recognize a loss of $160,000 ($240,000 – $80,000 fair value).
Answer (A) is incorrect. The test for recognition of impairment has been met. Answer (B) is incorrect. The excess of the carrying amount over the undiscounted future net cash inflows is $140,000. Answer (D) is incorrect. The purchase price of the assets is $400,000.

33. An impairment loss on a long-lived asset (asset group) to be held and used is reported by a business enterprise in

    A. Discontinued operations.

    B. Extraordinary items.

    C. Other comprehensive income.

    D. Income from continuing operations.

Answer (D) is correct. *(Publisher, adapted)*
    REQUIRED: The reporting of an impairment loss on a long-lived asset (asset group) to be held and used.
    DISCUSSION: An impairment loss is included in income from continuing operations before income taxes by a business (income from continuing operations in the statement of activities by a not-for-profit entity). When a subtotal for "income from operations" is reported, the impairment loss is included.
    Answer (A) is incorrect. A long-lived asset (asset group) to be held and used is not a discontinued operation. Answer (B) is incorrect. An impairment loss does not meet the criteria for an extraordinary item (unusual in nature and infrequent in the environment in which the entity operates). Answer (C) is incorrect. An impairment loss is reported in the income statement. Items reported in OCI have bypassed the income statement.

34. According to U.S. GAAP, restorations of carrying value for long-lived assets are permitted if an asset's fair value increases subsequent to recording an impairment loss for which of the following?

	Held for use	Held for disposal
A.	Yes	Yes
B.	Yes	No
C.	No	Yes
D.	No	No

Answer (C) is correct. *(CPA, adapted)*
    REQUIRED: The long-lived assets for which restorations of carrying amounts are permitted.
    DISCUSSION: Under U.S. GAAP, a previously recognized impairment loss on a long-lived asset to be held and used must not be reversed. The carrying amount of the long-lived asset adjusted for an impairment loss is its new cost basis. However, if the long-lived asset is held for sale, a gain is recognized for a subsequent increase in fair value minus cost to sell. But the gain is limited to the extent of prior write-downs. Furthermore, if the long-lived asset is held to be disposed of other than by sale, it is classified as held and used until disposal.
    Answer (A) is incorrect. Under U.S. GAAP, a previously recognized impairment loss on a long-lived asset to be held and used must not be reversed. Answer (B) is incorrect. Under U.S. GAAP, a previously recognized impairment loss on a long-lived asset to be held and used must not be reversed. However, if the long-lived asset is held for sale, a gain is recognized for a subsequent increase in fair value minus cost to sell. But the gain is limited to the extent of prior write-downs. Answer (D) is incorrect. Under U.S. GAAP, if the long-lived asset is held for sale, a gain is recognized for a subsequent increase in fair value minus cost to sell. But the gain is limited to the extent of prior write-downs.

35. Four years ago on January 2, Randall Co. purchased a long-lived asset. The purchase price of the asset was $250,000, with no salvage value. The estimated useful life of the asset was 10 years. Randall used the straight-line method to calculate depreciation expense. An impairment loss on the asset of $30,000 was recognized on December 31 of the current year. The estimated useful life of the asset at December 31 of the current year did not change. What amount should Randall report as depreciation expense in its income statement for the next year?

    A. $20,000

    B. $22,000

    C. $25,000

    D. $30,000

Answer (A) is correct. *(CPA, adapted)*
    REQUIRED: The depreciation expense after recognition of an impairment loss.
    DISCUSSION: The depreciation expense reported in the year following the recognition of an impairment loss on the long-lived asset is $20,000. This amount is calculated as follows:

Initial depreciable amount ($250,000 – $0 residual value)	$250,000
Accumulated depreciation after 4 years [($250,000 ÷ 10 years) × 4 years]	(100,000)
	$150,000
Impairment loss	(30,000)
	$120,000
Remaining useful years of life	÷ 6
Revised annual depreciation expense	$ 20,000

    Answer (B) is incorrect. The amount of $22,000 is based on the assumption that the impairment loss was $18,000. Answer (C) is incorrect. The amount of $25,000 is the annual depreciation expense reported prior to recognition of the impairment loss. Answer (D) is incorrect. The amount of $30,000 equals $180,000 recognized over a remaining useful life of 6 years. This calculation is based on the assumption that a $30,000 revaluation increase was recognized. A revaluation increase is permitted under IFRS, not U.S. GAAP.

36. The guidance for the recognition and measurement of impairment losses on long-lived assets to be held and used applies to

A. Goodwill.

B. An asset group.

C. A financial instrument.

D. Any intangible asset not being amortized.

Answer (B) is correct. *(Publisher, adapted)*
REQUIRED: The item to which the guidance for the recognition and measurement of impairment losses on long-lived assets to be held and used applies.
DISCUSSION: Such guidance applies to the long-lived assets of an entity that are to be held and used or disposed of, including those that are part of a group with other assets and liabilities not subject to such guidance. The unit of accounting for such a long-lived asset is the asset group. If a long-lived asset(s) is to be held and used, the asset group is the lowest level at which identifiable cash flows are largely independent of those of other groups. If the carrying amount of a long-lived asset (asset group) is not recoverable, a loss equal to the excess of that carrying amount over the fair value is recognized.
Answer (A) is incorrect. The guidance does not apply to goodwill, which is tested for impairment at the reporting unit level. Answer (C) is incorrect. The guidance does not apply to financial instruments, servicing assets, deferred tax assets, and certain long-lived assets subject to Codification sections applicable to specialized industries (such as marketed software or oil and gas). Answer (D) is incorrect. The guidance does not apply to an intangible asset not being amortized that is to be held and used.

37. A long-lived asset (disposal group) classified as held for sale should be accounted for by

A. Subtracting expected future operating losses from its fair value.

B. Recognizing a write-down to fair value minus cost to sell as a credit to other comprehensive income.

C. Recognizing a gain for any increase in fair value minus cost to sale.

D. Adjusting only a long-lived asset for write-downs to fair value minus cost to sell or the reversal of such an adjustment.

Answer (D) is correct. *(Publisher, adapted)*
REQUIRED: The accounting for a long-lived asset classified as held for sale.
DISCUSSION: A loss is recognized for a write-down to fair value minus cost to sell. A gain is recognized for any subsequent increase but only to the extent of previously recognized losses for write-downs. The loss or gain adjusts only the carrying amount of a long-lived asset even if it is included in a disposal group.
Answer (A) is incorrect. A long-lived asset (disposal group) is measured at fair value minus cost to sell. Answer (B) is incorrect. A write-down to fair value minus cost to sell is recognized as a loss (a debit) in the income statement. Answer (C) is incorrect. The gain is limited to the cumulative loss previously recognized for write-downs.

38. If a long-lived asset satisfies the criteria for classification as held for sale,

A. Its carrying amount is the cost at the acquisition date if the asset is newly acquired.

B. It is not depreciated.

C. Interest attributable to liabilities of a disposal group to which the asset belongs is not accrued.

D. It is classified as held for sale even if the criteria are not met until after the balance sheet date but before issuance of the financial statements.

Answer (B) is correct. *(Publisher, adapted)*
REQUIRED: The treatment of a long-lived asset that meets the criteria for classification as held for sale.
DISCUSSION: A long-lived asset is not depreciated (amortized) while it is classified as held for sale and measured at the lower of carrying amount or fair value minus cost to sell. The reason is that depreciation (amortization) would reduce the carrying amount below fair value minus cost to sell. Furthermore, fair value minus cost to sell must be evaluated each period, so any future decline will be recognized in the period of decline.
Answer (A) is incorrect. The carrying amount of a newly acquired long-lived asset classified as held for sale is its fair value minus cost to sell at the acquisition date. Answer (C) is incorrect. Interest and other expenses attributable to liabilities of a disposal group to which the asset belongs are accrued. Answer (D) is incorrect. If the criteria are not met until after the balance sheet date but before issuance of the financial statements, the long-lived asset continues to be classified as held and used in those statements.

39. A long-lived asset is measured at the lower of carrying amount or fair value minus cost to sell if it is to be

I.   Held for sale
II. Abandoned
III. Exchanged for a similar productive asset
IV. Distributed to owners in a spinoff

    A. I only.

    B. I and III only.

    C. II, III, and IV only.

    D. I, II, III, and IV.

Answer (A) is correct. *(Publisher, adapted)*
    REQUIRED: The circumstances in which a long-lived asset is measured at the lower of carrying amount or fair value minus cost to sell.
    DISCUSSION: Disposal of a long-lived asset may be other than by sale, e.g., by abandonment, exchange, or distribution to owners in a spinoff. When disposal is to be other than by sale, the asset continues to be classified as held and used until disposal. A long-lived asset to be held and used is measured at the lower of its carrying amount or fair value if the carrying amount is not recoverable. An asset that meets the criteria for classification as held for sale is measured at the lower of its carrying amount or fair value minus cost to sell.
    Answer (B) is incorrect. A long-lived asset that is distributed to owners in a spinoff is not measured at the lower of carrying amount or fair value. Answer (C) is incorrect. A long-lived asset to be disposed of other than by sale is classified as held and used and is measured at the lower of carrying amount or fair value. Answer (D) is incorrect. Long-lived assets that are abandoned, exchanged for a similar productive asset, or distributed to owners in a spinoff are not measured at the lower of carrying amount or fair value.

40. An entity may decide not to sell a long-lived asset (disposal group) classified as held for sale. It should therefore reclassify the long-lived asset (disposal group) as held and used. As a result of reclassification,

    A. The disposal group will be measured at the lower of carrying amount or fair value at the date of the decision not to sell.

    B. The results of operations of a reclassified component of an entity will be reported prospectively in continuing operations.

    C. Depreciation on individual reclassified long-lived assets is reflected in their measurement.

    D. Any assets removed from a disposal group that are to be sold must continue to be measured as a group.

Answer (C) is correct. *(Publisher, adapted)*
    REQUIRED: The result of reclassifying a long-lived asset (disposal group) after a decision not to sell.
    DISCUSSION: Changes to a plan of sale may occur because of circumstances previously regarded as unlikely that result in a decision not to sell. In these circumstances, the asset (disposal group) is reclassified as held and used. A reclassified long-lived asset is measured individually at the lower of its (1) carrying amount before the asset (disposal group) was classified as held for sale, minus any depreciation (amortization) that would have been recognized if it had always been classified as held and used, or (2) fair value at the date of the decision not to sell.
    Answer (A) is incorrect. Individual long-lived assets are measured at the lower of carrying amount before classification as held for sale, adjusted for depreciation (amortization) that would otherwise have been recognized, or fair value at the date of the decision not to sell. Answer (B) is incorrect. When a component of an entity is reclassified as held and used, its results of operations previously reported in discontinued operations are reclassified and included in income from continuing operations for all periods presented. Answer (D) is incorrect. If the assets removed from a disposal group that are to be sold do not meet the criteria for classification as held for sale as a group, they are measured individually at the lower of their carrying amounts or fair values minus cost to sell at the date of removal.

41. How should a long-lived asset or disposal group classified as held for sale be reported?

    A. The major classes of assets and liabilities must be separately disclosed on the face of the balance sheet.

    B. Assets and liabilities of a disposal group may not be presented as one amount.

    C. A long-lived asset may be aggregated with similar items on the balance sheet if separate disclosure is made in the notes.

    D. The income statement must separately present a loss for a write-down to fair value minus cost to sell.

Answer (B) is correct. *(Publisher, adapted)*
    REQUIRED: The reporting of a long-lived asset or disposal group classified as held for sale.
    DISCUSSION: If a disposal group is held for sale, its assets and liabilities are reported separately in the balance sheet and are not offset and presented as a single amount.
    Answer (A) is incorrect. The major classes of assets and liabilities held for sale are separately disclosed on the face of the balance sheet or in the notes. Answer (C) is incorrect. If a long-lived asset is held for sale, it is reported separately in the balance sheet. Answer (D) is incorrect. The entity must disclose in the notes a loss recognized for a write-down to fair value minus cost to sell, and, if not separately presented on the income statement, the caption that includes the loss.

42. An entity disposes of a nonmonetary asset in a nonreciprocal transfer. A gain or loss should be recognized on the disposition of the asset when the fair value of the asset transferred is determinable and the nonreciprocal transfer is to

	Another Entity	A Shareholder of the Entity
A.	No	Yes
B.	No	No
C.	Yes	No
D.	Yes	Yes

Answer (D) is correct. *(CPA, adapted)*
REQUIRED: The circumstances under which gain or loss should be recorded in a nonreciprocal transfer.
DISCUSSION: A nonreciprocal transfer is a transfer of assets or services in one direction. A nonreciprocal transfer of a nonmonetary asset to a shareholder or to another entity should be recorded at the fair value of the asset transferred. A gain or loss should be recognized on the transfer. However, an exception to this general rule is provided for distributions of nonmonetary assets to owners in (1) a spin-off or other form of reorganization or liquidation or (2) a plan that is in substance the rescission of a prior business combination. In such cases, the transaction should be measured at the recorded amount (after any reduction for an impairment) of the nonmonetary assets distributed.

43. A state government condemned Epirus Co.'s parcel of real estate. Epirus will receive $1,500,000 for this property, which has a carrying amount of $1,150,000. Epirus incurred the following costs as a result of the condemnation:

Appraisal fees to support a $1,500,000 value	$5,000
Attorney fees for the closing with the state	7,000
Attorney fees to review contract to acquire replacement property	6,000
Title insurance on replacement property	8,000

What amount of cost should Epirus use to determine the gain on the condemnation?

A. $1,162,000

B. $1,164,000

C. $1,168,000

D. $1,176,000

Answer (A) is correct. *(CPA, adapted)*
REQUIRED: The amount of cost used to determine the gain on the condemnation.
DISCUSSION: Gain or loss must be recognized even though an enterprise reinvests or is obligated to reinvest the monetary assets in replacement nonmonetary assets. The determination of the gain is based on the carrying amount ($1,150,000) and the costs incurred as a direct result of the condemnation ($5,000 appraisal fees and $7,000 attorney fees), a total of $1,162,000. Because the recipient is not obligated to reinvest the condemnation proceeds in other nonmonetary assets, the costs associated with the acquisition of the replacement property (attorney fees and title insurance) should be treated as part of the consideration paid for that property.
Answer (B) is incorrect. The amount of $1,164,000 includes the costs associated with the replacement property but not the costs incurred as a direct result of the condemnation.
Answer (C) is incorrect. The amount of $1,168,000 includes the attorney fees associated with the replacement property.
Answer (D) is incorrect. The amount of $1,176,000 includes the costs associated with the replacement property.

44. On July 1 of the current year, one of Damon Co.'s delivery vans was destroyed in an accident. On that date, the van's carrying amount was $2,500. On July 15 of the current year, Damon received and recorded a $700 invoice for a new engine installed in the van in May, and another $500 invoice for various repairs. In August, Damon received $3,500 under its insurance policy on the van, which it plans to use to replace the van. What amount should Damon report as gain (loss) on disposal of the van in its current-year income statement?

A. $1,000

B. $300

C. $0

D. $(200)

Answer (B) is correct. *(CPA, adapted)*
REQUIRED: The gain (loss) on disposal of the van.
DISCUSSION: Gain (loss) is recognized on an involuntary conversion equal to the difference between the proceeds and the carrying amount. The carrying amount includes the carrying amount at July 1 ($2,500) plus the capitalizable cost ($700) of the engine installed in May. This cost increased the carrying amount because it improved the future service potential of the asset. Ordinary repairs, however, are expensed. Consequently, the gain is $300 [$3,500 – ($2,500 + $700)].
Answer (A) is incorrect. The amount of $1,000 results from expensing the cost of the engine. Answer (C) is incorrect. Gain (loss) is recognized on an involuntary conversion. Answer (D) is incorrect. The figure of $(200) assumes the cost of repairs increased the carrying amount.

45. Ocean Corp.'s comprehensive insurance policy allows its assets to be replaced at current value. The policy has a $50,000 deductible clause. One of Ocean's waterfront warehouses was destroyed in a winter storm. Such storms occur approximately every 4 years. Ocean incurred $20,000 of costs in dismantling the warehouse and plans to replace it. The following data relate to the warehouse:

Current carrying amount	$ 300,000
Replacement cost	1,100,000

The gain Ocean should report as a separate component of income before extraordinary items is

A. $1,030,000

B. $780,000

C. $730,000

D. $0

Answer (C) is correct. *(CPA, adapted)*
REQUIRED: The gain reported as a separate component of income before extraordinary items.
DISCUSSION: The gain or loss on an involuntary conversion is reported as an ordinary item unless the criteria for treatment as an extraordinary item are met. To be classified as an extraordinary item, a transaction must be both unusual in nature and infrequent in occurrence within the environment in which the business operates. If an item meets one but not both of these criteria, it should be presented separately as a component of income from continuing operations. The gain is presumably infrequent but is not unusual in the entity's operating environment. The gain does not possess a high degree of abnormality and is not clearly unrelated to, or only incidentally related to, the entity's ordinary and typical activities. Hence, Ocean should separately recognize a gain from continuing operations equal to $730,000 ($1,100,000 current value – $50,000 deductible – $300,000 carrying amount – $20,000 costs of dismantling).
Answer (A) is incorrect. The amount of $1,030,000 disregards the $300,000 carrying amount. Answer (B) is incorrect. The amount of $780,000 omits the deductible. Answer (D) is incorrect. A gain (loss) should be recognized for an involuntary conversion.

7.5 Exchanges of Nonmonetary Assets

46. Which of the following statements correctly describes the proper accounting for nonmonetary exchanges that are deemed to have commercial substance?

A. It defers any gains and losses.

B. It defers losses to the extent of any gains.

C. It recognizes gains and losses immediately.

D. It defers gains and recognizes losses immediately.

Answer (C) is correct. *(CPA, adapted)*
REQUIRED: The true statement about accounting for nonmonetary exchanges with commercial substance.
DISCUSSION: When the fair value of both assets in a nonmonetary exchange is determinable, the transaction is treated as a monetary exchange. Thus, it is measured at the fair value of the assets given up, and any gain or loss is recognized immediately. When certain exceptions apply, the accounting for a nonmonetary exchange is based on the carrying amount of the assets given up. Unless boot is received, no gain is recognized. The following are the exceptions: (1) neither the fair value of the assets given up nor the fair value of the assets received is reasonably determinable; (2) the exchange involves inventory sold in the same line of business that facilitates sales to customers, not parties to the exchange, or the exchange lacks commercial substance; that is, an entity's cash flows are not expected to change significantly.
Answer (A) is incorrect. Unless an exception applies, gains are recognized in full immediately. Losses always are recognized in full immediately. Answer (B) is incorrect. The full amount of a loss on a nonmonetary exchange always is recognized in full. Answer (D) is incorrect. All or part of a gain (but not a loss) is deferred if the transaction is measured at the carrying amount of the assets given up.

47. Campbell Corp. exchanged delivery trucks with Highway, Inc. Campbell's truck originally cost $23,000, its accumulated depreciation was $20,000, and its fair value was $5,000. Highway's truck originally cost $23,500, its accumulated depreciation was $19,900, and its fair value was $5,700. Campbell also paid Highway $700 in cash as part of the transaction. The transaction lacks commercial substance. What amount is the new book value for the truck Campbell received?

A. $5,700

B. $5,000

C. $3,700

D. $3,000

Answer (C) is correct. *(CPA, adapted)*
REQUIRED: The new carrying amount recognized by the payor of boot after a nonmonetary exchange.
DISCUSSION: If a nonmonetary exchange lacks commercial substance, it is measured at the carrying amount of the assets given up. Accordingly, unless boot is received, no gain is recognized. Campbell gave boot of $700 and a truck with a carrying amount of $3,000 ($23,000 cost – $20,000 accumulated depreciation). The carrying amount of the new truck is therefore $3,700.
Answer (A) is incorrect. The amount of $5,700 is the fair value of the truck received. Answer (B) is incorrect. The amount of $5,000 is the fair value of the truck given. Answer (D) is incorrect. The amount of $3,000 is the carrying amount of the truck given up.

48. Iona Co. and Siena Co. exchanged goods, held for resale, with equal fair values. Each will use the other's goods to promote its own products. The retail price of the wicket that Iona gave up is less than the retail price of the womble received. What gain should Iona recognize on the nonmonetary exchange?

A. A gain is not recognized.

B. A gain equal to the difference between the retail prices of the womble received and the wicket.

C. A gain equal to the difference between the retail price and the cost of the wicket.

D. A gain equal to the difference between the fair value and the cost of the wicket.

Answer (D) is correct. *(CPA, adapted)*
REQUIRED: The gain to be recognized on a nonmonetary exchange of inventory.
DISCUSSION: Accounting for both monetary and nonmonetary transactions generally should be based on fair value of the assets involved, with gain or loss recognized immediately. In certain circumstances, however, the accounting for a nonmonetary transaction should be based on the carrying amount of the asset relinquished. These circumstances include an exchange of a product or property held for sale in the ordinary course of business for a product to be sold in the same line of business. The exchange also must be designed to facilitate sales to customers other than the parties to the exchange. Because Iona will use the womble received to promote its own product, the requirement that the product be used to facilitate sales to customers other than Iona or Siena is not met. Facilitation entails, for example, meeting immediate inventory needs or reducing transportation costs. Hence, Iona should record a gain equal to the difference between the fair value (the same for both assets) and the cost (carrying amount) of the asset surrendered.
Answer (A) is incorrect. A gain should be recognized. Answer (B) is incorrect. Fair value, not retail prices, reduced by the cost of the wicket is the appropriate basis at which the asset received should be recognized. Answer (C) is incorrect. Fair value, not retail prices, is the appropriate basis at which the asset received should be recognized.

49. Jaffa Co. and Istria Co. exchanged similar trucks with fair values in excess of carrying amounts. In addition, Jaffa paid Istria to compensate for the difference in truck values. The amount paid was 20% of the fair value of the exchange. The exchange did not have commercial substance. As a consequence, Istria recognized

A. A gain equal to the difference between the fair value and carrying amount of the truck given up.

B. A gain determined by the proportion of the cash received to the total consideration.

C. A loss determined by the proportion of cash received to the total consideration.

D. Neither a gain nor a loss.

Answer (B) is correct. *(CPA, adapted)*
REQUIRED: The gain or loss, if any, to be recognized on a nonmonetary exchange of similar trucks involving boot if the transaction lacked commercial substance.
DISCUSSION: Accounting for both monetary and nonmonetary transactions generally should be based on fair value of the assets involved, with gain or loss recognized immediately. In certain circumstances, however, the accounting for a nonmonetary transaction should be based on the carrying amount of the asset relinquished. These circumstances include an exchange that lacks commercial substance. In addition, when the transaction includes a cash component (termed boot), if the boot is less than 25% of the fair value of the exchange, the recipient of the boot should adjust the carryover basis for the portion of the gain equal to the total gain times the ratio of the boot to the sum of the boot and the fair value of the asset received. However, the full amount of a loss is recognized as an adjustment of the carryover basis.
Answer (A) is incorrect. The proportion of the gain recognized is equal to the ratio of the boot to the sum of the boot and the fair value of the asset received. Answer (C) is incorrect. A gain should be recognized. Answer (D) is incorrect. Only a gain and no loss should be recognized.

50. Horn Co. and Book Co. exchanged nonmonetary assets in a transaction that did not have commercial substance for either party. Horn paid cash to Book that was equal to 15% of the fair value of the exchange. To the extent that the amount of cash exceeds a proportionate share of the carrying amount of the asset surrendered, a realized gain on the exchange should be recognized by

	Horn	Book
A.	Yes	Yes
B.	Yes	No
C.	No	Yes
D.	No	No

Answer (C) is correct. *(CPA, adapted)*
REQUIRED: The party(ies), if any, that should recognize a realized gain on a nonmonetary transaction involving boot that lacked commercial substance.
DISCUSSION: The accounting for a nonmonetary transaction should be based on the carrying amount of the asset(s) relinquished when the exchange lacks commercial substance. In addition, when the transaction includes a cash component (termed boot), if the boot is less than 25% of the fair value of the exchange, the recipient of the boot should adjust the carryover basis for the portion of the gain equal to the total gain times the ratio of the boot to the sum of the boot and the fair value of the asset received. However, the full amount of a loss is recognized as an adjustment of the carryover basis. In contrast, the payor of boot should measure the asset received at an amount equal to the carrying amount of the asset relinquished plus the amount of boot.
Answer (A) is incorrect. Horn does not recognize a proportionate gain. Answer (B) is incorrect. Book recognizes a proportionate gain, but Horn does not. Answer (D) is incorrect. The recipient of boot should recognize a gain.

51. Hagen Co. exchanged a truck with a carrying amount of $12,000 and a fair value of $20,000 for a truck and $5,000 cash. The fair value of the truck received was $15,000. The exchange was not considered to have commercial substance. At what amount should Hagen record the truck received in the exchange?

A. $7,000

B. $9,000

C. $12,000

D. $15,000

Answer (D) is correct. *(CPA, adapted)*
REQUIRED: The amount at which a nonmonetary asset should be recorded in a transaction involving boot that lacked commercial substance.
DISCUSSION: A transaction involving nonmonetary assets and boot is classified as monetary if the boot equals or exceeds 25% of the fair value of the exchange. In this exchange, the $5,000 of boot equals 25% of the $20,000 ($5,000 + $15,000) fair value of the exchange. Thus, the exchange is classified as monetary. Accounting for monetary transactions should be based on the fair value of the assets involved, with gain or loss recognized immediately. Hagen should record the truck received at its $15,000 fair value. Hagen also should record an $8,000 gain equal to the difference between the $20,000 fair value received and the $12,000 carrying amount of the truck relinquished.
Answer (A) is incorrect. This figure is equal to the $12,000 carrying amount of the asset relinquished minus the $5,000 boot received. Answer (B) is incorrect. This figure is equal to the $12,000 carrying amount of the truck relinquished, minus the $5,000 boot received, plus the $2,000 ($8,000 × 25%) proportionate gain that would have been recognized had the transaction been classified as nonmonetary. Answer (C) is incorrect. The carrying amount of the truck relinquished equals $12,000.

52. In an exchange of assets, Junger Co. received equipment with a fair value equal to the carrying amount of the equipment given up. Junger also contributed cash equal to 10% of the fair value of the exchange. If the exchange is not considered to have commercial substance, Junger should recognize

A. A loss equal to the cash (boot) given up.

B. A loss determined by the proportion of cash paid to the total transaction value.

C. A gain determined by the proportion of cash paid to the total transaction value.

D. Neither gain nor loss.

Answer (A) is correct. *(CPA, adapted)*
REQUIRED: The gain or loss to be recognized in a nonmonetary transaction involving boot that lacked commercial substance.
DISCUSSION: The accounting for a nonmonetary transaction should be based on the carrying amount of the asset(s) relinquished when the exchange lacks commercial substance. In addition, when the transaction includes cash consideration (boot), if the boot is less than 25% of the fair value of the exchange, the recipient (but not the payer) of the boot should adjust the carryover basis by a portion of the gain. This amount equals total gain times the ratio of the boot to the sum of the boot and the fair value of the asset received. However, the full amount of any loss is recognized as an adjustment of the carryover basis. In this situation, a loss should be recognized because the carrying amount of the asset relinquished plus the boot paid is greater than the fair value of the asset received. An asset should not be recognized at an amount higher than its fair value.
Answer (B) is incorrect. When a loss is indicated, the entire loss should be recognized. Answer (C) is incorrect. A gain equal to the amount of cash given up should not be recognized. Answer (D) is incorrect. A loss equal to the amount of cash given up should be recognized.

53. Bell and Mayo are independent companies. Each owns a tract of land being held for development. However, each would prefer to build on the other's land. Accordingly, the companies agreed to exchange their land. From an independent appraisal report and the companies' records, the following information was obtained:

	Bell's Land	Mayo's Land
Cost and carrying amount	$ 80,000	$50,000
Fair value based on appraisal	100,000	85,000

Based on the difference in appraisal values, Mayo paid $15,000 to Bell. If Mayo did not consider the exchange to have commercial substance, at what amount should Mayo record the receipt of the land from Bell?

A. $100,000

B. $85,000

C. $65,000

D. $50,000

Answer (C) is correct. *(W. Higley)*
REQUIRED: The amount at which the asset received should be recorded by the payer of boot in a nonmonetary exchange lacking commercial substance.
DISCUSSION: Accounting for a nonmonetary transaction should be based on the carrying amount of the asset(s) relinquished when the exchange lacks commercial substance. In addition, when the transaction includes cash consideration (boot), if the boot is less than 25% of the fair value of the exchange, the recipient (but not the payer) of the boot should adjust the carryover basis by a portion of the gain. This amount equals the total gain times the ratio of the boot to the sum of the boot plus the fair value of the asset received. The payer of boot should record the asset received at an amount equal to the carryover basis of the nonmonetary asset relinquished plus the boot paid. In this situation, because the boot equals 15% ($15,000 ÷ $100,000) of the fair value of the exchange, Mayo should record the land received from Bell at $65,000 ($50,000 carrying amount + $15,000 boot).
Answer (A) is incorrect. The fair value of the land received by Mayo is $100,000, the amount at which the land would be recorded if the exchange had commercial substance. Answer (B) is incorrect. The fair value of the land Mayo exchanged is $85,000. Answer (D) is incorrect. The carrying amount of the land Mayo exchanged is $50,000.

54. Minor Baseball Company had a player contract with Doe that was recorded in its accounting records at $145,000. Better Baseball Company had a player contract with Smith that was recorded in its accounting records at $140,000. Minor traded Doe to Better for Smith by exchanging player contracts. The fair value of each contract was $150,000. Evidence suggested that the contract exchange lacked commercial substance. At what amount should the contracts be valued in accordance with generally accepted accounting principles at the time of the exchange of the player contracts?

	Minor	Better
A.	$140,000	$140,000
B.	$140,000	$145,000
C.	$145,000	$140,000
D.	$150,000	$150,000

55. Essen Co. and Potsdam Co. are fuel oil distributors. To facilitate delivery of oil to their customers, Essen and Potsdam exchanged ownership of 1,200 barrels of oil without physically moving the oil. Essen paid Potsdam $30,000 to compensate for a difference in the grade of oil. On the date of the exchange, costs and fair values of the oil were as follows:

	Essen Co.	Potsdam Co.
Cost	$100,000	$126,000
Fair values	120,000	150,000

What amount of gain from the transaction should Potsdam report in its income statement?

A. $0

B. $4,800

C. $24,000

D. $30,000

Answer (C) is correct. *(CPA, adapted)*
REQUIRED: The amount at which to record an asset received in a nonmonetary exchange transaction that lacked commercial substance.
DISCUSSION: The accounting for a nonmonetary transaction should be based on the carrying amount of the asset(s) relinquished when the exchange lacks commercial substance. An exchange lacks commercial substance when an entity's cash flows are not expected to change significantly. Cash flows do not change significantly when (1) the configuration (risk, timing, and amount) of the entity's future cash flows is not expected to change significantly as a result of the exchange or (2) the entity-specific values of the assets involved do not differ significantly. Thus, Minor should record its contract with Smith at $145,000, and Better should record its contract with Doe at $140,000.
Answer (A) is incorrect. Minor should record its contract with Smith at $145,000, its previously recorded (carryover) amount for its contract with Doe. Answer (B) is incorrect. Minor should record its contract with Smith at $145,000, and Better should record its contract with Doe at $140,000. Answer (D) is incorrect. The fair value of each contract, $150,000, should be recorded if the exchange has commercial substance.

Answer (B) is correct. *(CPA, adapted)*
REQUIRED: The gain to be recognized in a nonmonetary exchange involving boot that facilitated sales to customers.
DISCUSSION: Accounting for an exchange of nonmonetary assets should be based on the carrying amount of the asset relinquished when the exchange involves inventory exchanged to facilitate sales to customers other than the parties to the exchange. In addition, when the transaction includes a cash component (termed boot), if the boot is less than 25% of the fair value of the exchange, the recipient of the boot should adjust its carryover basis for the portion of the gain equal to the total gain times the ratio of the boot to the sum of the boot and the fair value of the asset received. The boot in this exchange is equal to 20% [$30,000 ÷ ($30,000 + $120,000)]. Thus, Potsdam should record a $4,800 proportionate gain equal to 20% of the $24,000 ($150,000 – $126,000) difference between the fair value of the exchange and the cost of the inventory relinquished. Moreover, it should debit inventory for $100,800 ($126,000 carrying amount – $30,000 cash received + $4,800 gain recognized). The journal entry is

Inventory	$100,800	
Cash	30,000	
Inventory		$126,000
Gain		4,800

Answer (A) is incorrect. A proportionate gain should be recognized. Answer (C) is incorrect. The total potential gain is $24,000. Answer (D) is incorrect. The amount of boot is $30,000.

56. On July 1 of the current year, Trey Co. exchanged a truck for 25 shares of Deuce Corp.'s common stock. The fair value of this stock is not readily determinable. On that date, the truck's carrying amount was $2,500, and its fair value was $3,000. Also, the carrying amount of Deuce's stock was $50 per share. Trey cannot exercise significant influence over Deuce. What amount should Trey report in its December 31 current-year balance sheet as investment in Deuce?

- A. $3,000
- B. $2,500
- C. $1,250
- D. $1,750

Answer (A) is correct. *(CPA, adapted)*
REQUIRED: The amount reported for stock received in exchange for a nonmonetary asset.
DISCUSSION: Accounting for nonmonetary transactions usually should be based on the fair values of the assets or services involved. The exceptions arise when (1) the fair value of neither the asset(s) received nor the asset(s) relinquished is determinable within reasonable limits, (2) the exchange facilitates sales of inventory to customers, or (3) the exchange lacks commercial substance. No exception applies because the fair value of the asset relinquished is known, inventory is not involved, and no facts indicate that the exchange lacks commercial substance. Accordingly, the exchange is measured on July 1 at the $3,000 fair value of the asset relinquished. Moreover, this investment in equity securities is subsequently reported at cost (the fair value of the truck on July 1) because (1) their fair value is not readily determinable, and (2) the equity method does not apply because Trey cannot exercise significant influence over Deuce.
Answer (B) is incorrect. The truck's carrying amount, not its fair value, is $2,500. Answer (C) is incorrect. The carrying amount of 25 shares of Deuce's stock on July 1 on Deuce's books was $1,250. Answer (D) is incorrect. The fair value of the truck minus the carrying amount of 25 shares of Deuce's stock on July 1 is $1,750.

7.6 IFRS

57. Upon first-time adoption of IFRS, an entity may elect to use fair value as deemed cost for

- A. Biological assets related to agricultural activity for which there is no active market.
- B. Intangible assets for which there is no active market.
- C. Any individual item of property, plant, and equipment.
- D. Financial liabilities that are not held for trading.

Answer (C) is correct. *(CPA, adapted)*
REQUIRED: The assets or liabilities that may be measured at fair value as deemed cost upon first-time adoption of IFRS.
DISCUSSION: Under IFRS 1, *First-time Adoption of International Financial Reporting Standards*, a first-time adopter may elect to measure an item of PPE at (1) its fair value as deemed cost at the transition date or (2) a previous revaluation as deemed cost at the revaluation date.
Answer (A) is incorrect. The election of fair value or revaluation as deemed cost is available only for (1) PPE, (2) investment property accounted for at cost subsequent to recognition, and (3) intangible assets meeting the recognition and revaluation criteria. Answer (B) is incorrect. An active market for intangible assets is a requirement for the election. Answer (D) is incorrect. The election is not available for financial liabilities.

58. Under IFRS, when an entity chooses the revaluation model as its accounting policy for measuring property, plant, and equipment, which of the following statements is correct?

- A. When an asset is revalued, the entire class of property, plant, and equipment to which that asset belongs must be revalued.
- B. When an asset is revalued, individual assets within a class of property, plant, and equipment to which that asset belongs can be revalued.
- C. Revaluations of property, plant, and equipment must be made at least every 3 years.
- D. Increases in an asset's carrying amount as a result of the first revaluation must be recognized as a component of profit or loss.

Answer (A) is correct. *(CPA, adapted)*
REQUIRED: The true statement about revaluation of PPE.
DISCUSSION: Under IFRS, measurement of PPE subsequent to initial recognition may be at fair value at the revaluation date (minus subsequent depreciation and impairment losses). The assumption is that the PPE can be reliably measured. If an item of PPE is revalued, every item in its class also should be revalued.
Answer (B) is incorrect. If an item of PPE is revalued, every item in its class also should be revalued. Answer (C) is incorrect. Revaluation is needed whenever an asset's fair value and carrying amount differ materially. Answer (D) is incorrect. A revaluation increase (surplus) is credited directly to equity.

59. An entity bought a building for administrative purposes on January 1, Year 1, for $260,000. Its useful life is 20 years, with no residual value. The entity depreciates its items of PPE according to the straight-line (S-L) depreciation method, and its accounting policy for the building is the revaluation model with annual revaluations. The entity transfers the revaluation surplus directly to retained earnings as the asset is used by the entity. The fair values of the building on December 31, Year 1, and December 31, Year 2, are $285,000 and $261,000, respectively. On December 31, Year 1, the revaluation surplus is <List A> and the building's carrying amount is <List B>.

	List A	List B
A.	$13,000	$247,000
B.	$38,000	$285,000
C.	$25,000	$285,000
D.	$13,000	$261,000

Answer (B) is correct. *(Publisher, adapted)*
REQUIRED: The revaluation surplus and carrying amount at the end of the first year of the building's useful life.
DISCUSSION: The carrying amount of the building on December 31, Year 1, is $285,000 because it is the fair value on the revaluation date. The depreciation for Year 1 is $13,000 [($260,000 – $0 residual value) ÷ 20 years]. Thus, the carrying amount just prior to the revaluation is $247,000 ($260,000 – $13,000), and the revaluation surplus is $38,000 ($285,000 – $247,000).
Answer (A) is incorrect. The depreciation for Year 1 is $13,000. The carrying amount of the building is $247,000 ($260,000 – $13,000) on December 31, Year 1, before the revaluation. Answer (C) is incorrect. The difference between the fair value of the building on December 31, Year 1 ($285,000), and its cost ($260,000) is $25,000. Answer (D) is incorrect. The depreciation for Year 1 is $13,000, and the fair value at December 31, Year 2, is $261,000.

60. On December 31, Year 1, a company determined the following information for a long-lived asset:

Carrying amount	$80,000
Fair value	78,000
Costs to sell	3,000
Value in use	74,000
Undiscounted expected future cash flows	77,000

According to IFRS, what amount of impairment loss should the company recognize in the year-end financial statements?

A. $0

B. $6,000

C. $2,000

D. $5,000

Answer (D) is correct. *(Publisher, adapted)*
REQUIRED: The impairment loss.
DISCUSSION: Under IFRS, an impairment loss equals the excess of the carrying amount of the asset ($80,000) over its recoverable amount. The recoverable amount of the asset is the greater of its fair value minus costs to sell ($78,000 – $3,000 = $75,000) or its value in use ($74,000). Thus, the recoverable amount of the asset is $75,000, and the impairment loss is $5,000 ($80,000 – $75,000).
Answer (A) is incorrect. The carrying amount of the asset is higher than its recoverable amount. Thus, an impairment loss must be recognized. Answer (B) is incorrect. The recoverable amount of an asset is the greater, not the lower, of its fair value minus costs to sell or value in use. Answer (C) is incorrect. Under IFRS, an impairment loss of an asset is not the excess of the carrying amount and the fair value.

61. According to IFRS, which accounting policy may an entity apply to measure investment property in periods subsequent to initial recognition?

A. Cost model or revaluation model.

B. Cost model or fair value model.

C. Fair value model only.

D. Fair value model or revaluation model.

Answer (B) is correct. *(Publisher, adapted)*
REQUIRED: The accounting policy(ies) applicable to investment property.
DISCUSSION: An entity may choose either the cost model or the fair value model as its accounting policy. But it must apply that policy to all of its investment property. Under the cost model, investment property is carried at its cost minus any accumulated depreciation and impairment losses. Under the fair value model, investment property is measured at fair value, and gain or loss from a change in its fair value is recognized immediately in profit or loss.
Answer (A) is incorrect. Owner-occupied (not investment) property that is accounted for in accordance with IAS 16, *Property, Plant, and Equipment*, is measured in periods subsequent to initial recognition using the cost model or the revaluation model. Answer (C) is incorrect. An entity has a choose of models to use as its accounting policy for measuring investment property. Answer (D) is incorrect. The revaluation model may be applied to measure owner-occupied (not investment) property that is accounted for in accordance with IAS 16, *Property, Plant, and Equipment*.

62. Under IFRS, according to the revaluation model, an item of property, plant, and equipment must be carried at

A. Cost minus any accumulated depreciation.

B. Cost minus residual value.

C. Fair value minus any subsequent accumulated depreciation and impairment losses.

D. The lower of cost or net realizable value.

Answer (C) is correct. *(Publisher, adapted)*
REQUIRED: The measure of PPE according to the revaluation model.
DISCUSSION: Under the revaluation model, if the fair value of an item of property, plant, and equipment can be reliably measured, it must be carried subsequent to initial recognition at a revalued amount. This amount is fair value at the date of the revaluation minus any subsequent accumulated depreciation and impairment losses. The revaluation model is permitted by IFRS, not U.S. GAAP.
Answer (A) is incorrect. According to the cost model, an item of property, plant, and equipment must be carried at its cost minus any accumulated depreciation and impairment losses. Answer (B) is incorrect. Cost minus residual value is the depreciable amount of an item of property, plant, and equipment. Answer (D) is incorrect. Under IFRS, inventory must be measured at the lower of cost and net realizable value.

63. Under IFRS, an increase in the carrying amount of an item of property, plant, and equipment as a result of a first revaluation must be <List A> under the heading of <List B>.

	List A	List B
A.	Recognized in profit or loss	Gain on disposal
B.	Accumulated in equity	Revaluation surplus
C.	Accumulated in equity	Retained earnings
D.	Accumulated in current liabilities	Revaluation surplus

Answer (B) is correct. *(Publisher, adapted)*
REQUIRED: The accounting for an increase in the carrying amount after a first revaluation.
DISCUSSION: The net carrying amount of an item of property, plant, and equipment may increase as a result of a revaluation (fair value at the revaluation date – net carrying amount before revaluation). Given no prior revaluation, the increase must be credited directly to revaluation surplus in the equity section of the statement of financial position.
Answer (A) is incorrect. A revaluation decrease is recognized in profit or loss. A gain on disposal is recognized in profit or loss when the entity derecognizes the asset if the net proceeds are greater than the carrying amount of the asset. Answer (C) is incorrect. The increase in an asset's carrying amount as a result of revaluation may be transferred directly to retained earnings from revaluation surplus as the asset is used by the entity. But this transfer is not at the moment of revaluation. Answer (D) is incorrect. Revaluation surplus is an equity item, not a current liability.

64. Which of the following statements is false about an item of property, plant, and equipment (PPE)?

A. Under U.S. GAAP, such an item may be carried at an amount above its historical cost.

B. Under IFRS, such an item may be carried at an amount above its historical cost.

C. Under IFRS, such an item may be carried at its fair value.

D. Under U.S. GAAP, such an item may be carried at its historical cost.

Answer (A) is correct. *(Publisher, adapted)*
REQUIRED: The false statement about PPE.
DISCUSSION: Under U.S. GAAP, items of PPE cannot be carried above their historical cost. They are carried at historical cost minus accumulated depreciation and impairment losses.
Answer (B) is incorrect. Under IFRS, according to the revaluation model, an item of PPE is carried at its revalued amount, which can be greater than the historical cost. Answer (C) is incorrect. Under IFRS, according to the revaluation model, an item of PPE is measured at fair value on the revaluation date. Answer (D) is incorrect. If an item of PPE is acquired on the financial reporting date, it is carried at its historical cost because depreciation of the item has not yet begun.

65. Under IFRS, the recoverable amount of an asset is

   A. The higher of an asset's value in use or its fair value minus costs to sell.

   B. The estimated selling price in the ordinary course of business minus the estimated costs of completion and the estimated costs necessary to make the sale.

   C. The present value of the future cash flows expected to be derived from an asset.

   D. The amount obtainable from the sale of an asset in an arm's length transaction between knowledgeable, willing parties, minus the costs of disposal.

Answer (A) is correct. *(Publisher, adapted)*
   REQUIRED: The recoverable amount of an asset.
   DISCUSSION: Any indication that an asset may be impaired requires the entity to estimate its recoverable amount. The recoverable amount is the higher of an asset's fair value minus costs to sell and its value in use. Value in use is the present value of estimated future cash flows expected from (1) continuing use of an asset and (2) its disposal at the end of its useful life. Fair value minus costs to sell is the amount obtainable from the sale of an asset in an arm's length transaction between knowledgeable, willing parties, minus costs of disposal.
   Answer (B) is incorrect. The estimated selling price in the ordinary course of business minus the estimated costs of completion and the estimated costs necessary to make the sale is the net realizable value. Answer (C) is incorrect. The present value of the future cash flows expected to be derived from an asset is the value in use. Answer (D) is incorrect. Under IFRS, the amount obtainable from the sale of an asset in an arm's length transaction between knowledgeable, willing parties, minus the costs of disposal, is the fair value minus costs to sell, not the recoverable amount.

66. On January 1, Year 1, a company purchased a building for the purpose of earning rental income. The price paid was $100,000. The company classified the building as investment property and accounts for it using the fair value model. The fair values of the property on December 31, Year 1, and December 31, Year 2, are $80,000 and $110,000, respectively. Under IFRS, what effect does this property have on the company's Year 2 profit or loss?

   A. No effect on profit or loss.

   B. Appreciation gain of $10,000.

   C. Appreciation gain of $20,000.

   D. Appreciation gain of $30,000.

Answer (D) is correct. *(Publisher, adapted)*
   REQUIRED: The effect on profit or loss of property purchased to earn rental income.
   DISCUSSION: The changes in the fair value of investment property that is accounted for according to the fair value model are recognized as gain or loss in profit or loss for the period in which they occur. An appreciation gain of $30,000 ($110,000 – $80,000) is recognized for the Year 2 increase in the fair value of the investment property.
   Answer (A) is incorrect. The fair value of the property on December 31, Year 2, differs from the fair value on December 31, Year 1. Thus, the property affects profit or loss. Answer (B) is incorrect. Over the 2-year period, the total effect on the company's profit or loss is an appreciation gain of $10,000 ($110,000 – $100,000). Answer (C) is incorrect. The impairment loss recognized in Year 1 is $20,000. Under the fair value model, changes in the fair value of investment property are recognized in profit or loss. The gain recognized is not limited to impairment loss previously recognized.

67. On December 31, Year 1, indications are that an entity's asset may be impaired. The recoverable amount of that asset is $50,000. The entity applies the revaluation model for its assets and depreciates them using the straight-line method. The carrying amount of the asset on December 31, Year 1, before the test for impairment is $80,000 ($100,000 cost – $20,000 accumulated depreciation). The entity also has recognized a revaluation surplus from previous revaluations of the asset equal to $25,000. What impairment loss, if any, must be recognized in the entity's profit or loss on December 31, Year 1?

   A. No impairment loss.

   B. Impairment loss of $30,000.

   C. Impairment loss of $10,000.

   D. Impairment loss of $5,000.

Answer (D) is correct. *(Publisher, adapted)*
   REQUIRED: The impairment loss on a depreciable asset accounted for using the revaluation model.
   DISCUSSION: The reduction of the carrying amount of the asset to its recoverable amount results in an impairment loss of $30,000 ($80,000 carrying amount before impairment – $50,000 recoverable amount). An impairment loss on a revalued asset is recognized as a decrease in the credit balance of the revaluation surplus related to that asset. Any remainder after elimination of the revaluation surplus is recognized as a loss in profit or loss of $5,000 ($30,000 impairment of the asset – $25,000 revaluation surplus).
   Answer (A) is incorrect. The decrease in the carrying amount of the asset as a result of impairment is greater than the carrying amount of the revaluation surplus for the same asset. Thus, an impairment loss must be recognized in profit or loss. Answer (B) is incorrect. The difference between the recoverable amount and the carrying amount of the asset is $30,000. But an impairment loss on a revalued asset is first recognized as a decrease in the credit balance of any revaluation surplus related to the asset. Answer (C) is incorrect. The loss recognized in profit or loss for a revalued asset is the decrease in the carrying amount as a result of an impairment minus the credit balance of the revaluation surplus related to the asset. The amount of $10,000 is the difference between the $30,000 decrease in the carrying amount of the asset as a result of impairment and the $20,000 of accumulated depreciation.

68. An impairment loss on a <List A> must be recognized immediately in <List B>.

	List A	List B
A.	Revalued asset	Profit or loss
B.	Nonrevalued asset	Profit or loss
C.	Nonrevalued asset	Equity section
D.	Noncurrent asset held for sale	Equity section

Answer (B) is correct.   *(Publisher, adapted)*
   REQUIRED: The accounting for an impairment loss.
   DISCUSSION: An impairment loss on a nonrevalued asset must be recognized immediately in profit or loss. The entry is

| Impairment loss | XXX | |
| Provision for impairment | | XXX |

   Answer (A) is incorrect. An impairment loss on a revalued asset is recognized as a decrease in the credit balance of the revaluation surplus related to that asset. Any remainder after elimination of the revaluation surplus is recognized in profit or loss. Answer (C) is incorrect. An impairment loss on a nonrevalued asset must be recognized immediately in profit or loss. Answer (D) is incorrect. A noncurrent asset held for sale is outside of the impairment requirements of IAS 36. A noncurrent asset held for sale is measured at the end of the reporting period at the lower of its carrying amount immediately before the initial classification as held for sale and fair value minus costs to sell.

Use Gleim **EQE Test Prep** Software Download for interactive study and performance analysis.

STUDY UNIT EIGHT
DEPRECIATION AND DEPLETION

Depreciation Concepts

Depreciation is a noncash expense reflecting the consumption of the economic benefits represented by an assest's recorded amount. It results from the systematic and rational allocation of the **historical cost** of a long-lived, tangible, productive asset to the service (useful) life of the asset. The **depreciable base** of such an asset normally equals its original cost minus any estimated salvage value and recognized impairment losses. The **service life** of an asset may be time-based or activity-based. The service life is **time-based** when accounting periods define the expected useful life of the asset. It is **activity-based** when units of product or the output of service units (machine hours, miles driven, etc.) define the expected useful life.

Depreciation Calculations

During each accounting period, some portion of a depreciable asset's cost is debited to depreciation expense and credited to accumulated depreciation, a contra-asset. The net of historical cost and accumulated depreciation is the carrying amount. Four principal methods of depreciation are recognized under GAAP. The simplest is the **straight-line method**. It determines a constant periodic depreciation expense as follows:

$$\frac{Depreciable\ base}{Estimated\ useful\ life}$$

The **units-of-production (activity) method** matches depreciation expense with actual usage.

$$\frac{Depreciable\ base}{Estimated\ total\ lifetime\ units\ of\ output}$$

Annual depreciation expense equals this per-unit cost times the actual outputs for the year. An alternative is to use the estimated output of the service units (e.g., total machine hours) as the denominator.

Accelerated methods are used on tax returns as well as financial statements. But the same method need not be used on both. Accelerated methods are time-based. They result in decreasing depreciation charges over the life of the asset. The two major time-based methods are declining balance and sum-of-the-years' digits. **Declining balance (DB)** determines depreciation expense by multiplying the carrying amount (not a depreciable base equal to cost – salvage value) at the beginning of each period by some percentage (e.g., 200% or 150%) of the straight-line rate of depreciation. The carrying amount decreases by the depreciation recognized. The result is the use of a constant rate against a declining balance. Salvage value is ignored in determining the carrying amount, but the asset is not depreciated below salvage value.

The following schedule assumes a 5-year useful life, a $1,000,000 cost, a $100,000 salvage value, and 200% DB:

Year	Beginning Carrying Amount	DDB Rate	Depreciation	Accumulated Depreciation	Ending Carrying Amount
1	$1,000,000	40%	$400,000	$400,000	$600,000
2	600,000	40%	240,000	640,000	360,000
3	360,000	40%	144,000	784,000	216,000
4	216,000	40%	86,400	870,400	129,600
5	129,600	40%	29,600	900,000	100,000

Sum-of-the-years' digits (SYD) multiplies not the carrying amount but a constant depreciable base (cost – salvage value) by a declining fraction. It is a declining-rate, declining-charge method. The SYD fraction's **numerator** is the number of years of the useful life (n) minus the prior years elapsed. The formula for the **denominator** is

$$\frac{n\ (n\ +\ 1)}{2}$$

Thus, the denominator of the SYD fraction, given the facts for the DB schedule, is 15 {[5 × (5 + 1)] ÷ 2}, and the depreciation base is $900,000 ($1,000,000 – $100,000). The following is the depreciation schedule using the SYD method:

Year	Numerator	Base × Fraction	Expense	Accumulated Depreciation	Ending Carrying Amount
1	5	$900,000 × (5 ÷ 15)	$300,000	$300,000	$700,000
2	4	$900,000 × (4 ÷ 15)	240,000	540,000	460,000
3	3	$900,000 × (3 ÷ 15)	180,000	720,000	280,000
4	2	$900,000 × (2 ÷ 15)	120,000	840,000	160,000
5	1	$900,000 × (1 ÷ 15)	60,000	900,000	100,000

An entity must **disclose** (1) depreciation expense for the period, (2) balances of major classes of depreciable assets (by nature or function), (3) accumulated depreciation (either by major classes of depreciable assets or in total), and (4) descriptions of depreciation methods (for each major class of assets). Depreciation expense and accumulated depreciation should be the amounts at the balance sheet date.

Group and Composite Depreciation Methods

These methods apply straight-line accounting to a collection of assets depreciated as if they were a single asset. The **group method** applies to similar assets, and the **composite method** to dissimilar assets. They are efficient ways to account for large numbers of depreciable assets. They also result in offsetting of under- and overstated depreciation estimates. Each method calculates (1) the total depreciable cost (total acquisition cost – salvage value) for all the assets debited to a control account, (2) the weighted-average estimated useful life (total depreciable cost ÷ total annual straight-line depreciation), and (3) the weighted-average depreciation rate based on cost (total annual straight-line depreciation ÷ total acquisition cost). One accumulated depreciation account also is maintained. **Early and late retirements** are expected to offset each other. Thus, gains and losses on retirements of single assets are not recognized but are treated as adjustments of accumulated depreciation. The entry is

Cash (proceeds)	$XXX	
Asset (cost)		$XXX
Accumulated depreciation (dr or cr)		XXX

Periodic depreciation equals the weighted-average rate times the beginning balance of the asset for the period. Thus, depreciation is calculated based on the cost of assets in use during the period. Prior-period retirements are reflected in this balance.

Depletion

Depletion is similar to the units-of-production method of depreciation. It is the systematic allocation of the depletion base of a natural resource (a wasting asset such as oil, timber, and iron ore) to the estimated units of the resource expected to be produced. The **depletion base** is the sum of (1) the acquisition cost of land (but not the cost of extractive machinery), (2) development cost to prepare the site for extraction, and (3) restoration cost required by law to return the land to its original condition, minus the residual value of the property. Annual depletion expense per unit of output equals

$$\frac{\text{Historical cost + Reclamation costs - Salvage value}}{\text{Estimated total lifetime units of output}}$$

Differences between GAAP and IFRS

Under IFRS:

- Each part of an item with a cost significant to the total cost must be depreciated separately. But an entity may separately depreciate parts that are not significant.

QUESTIONS

8.1 Depreciation Concepts

1. A depreciable asset has an estimated 15% salvage value. At the end of its estimated useful life, the accumulated depreciation will equal the original cost of the asset under which of the following depreciation methods?

	Straight-Line	Activity
A.	Yes	No
B.	Yes	Yes
C.	No	Yes
D.	No	No

Answer (D) is correct. *(CPA, adapted)*
REQUIRED: The method(s), if any, under which accumulated depreciation will equal cost at the end of a salvageable asset's useful life.
DISCUSSION: The straight-line and activity depreciation methods subtract estimated salvage value from the original cost to determine the depreciable base. At the end of the asset's estimated useful life, the accumulated depreciation will equal the cost minus the salvage value under each of these methods. The net carrying amount (cost – accumulated depreciation) will equal the salvage value.
Answer (A) is incorrect. The straight-line method does not depreciate an asset beyond its salvage value. Answer (B) is incorrect. Neither the straight-line nor the activity method depreciates an asset beyond its salvage value. Answer (C) is incorrect. The activity method does not depreciate an asset beyond its salvage value.

2. Depreciation of a plant asset is the process of

A. Asset valuation for statement of financial position purposes.

B. Allocation of the asset's cost to the periods of use.

C. Fund accumulation for the replacement of the asset.

D. Asset valuation based on current replacement cost data.

Answer (B) is correct. *(CMA, adapted)*
REQUIRED: The purpose of depreciation of fixed assets.
DISCUSSION: In accounting, depreciation is the systematic and rational allocation of the cost of the productive capacity of a fixed asset to the accounting periods the asset benefits. The asset's historical cost minus expected salvage value is the basis for the allocation.
Answer (A) is incorrect. Depreciation is the allocation of a cost, not a process of valuation. Answer (C) is incorrect. Depreciation allocates cost. It does not provide for replacement. Answer (D) is incorrect. Plant assets are reported at historical cost rather than current replacement costs.

3. Net income is understated if, in the first year, estimated salvage value is excluded from the depreciation computation when using the

	Straight-Line Method	Activity
A.	Yes	No
B.	Yes	Yes
C.	No	No
D.	No	Yes

Answer (B) is correct. *(CPA, adapted)*
REQUIRED: The depreciation method(s) that understate(s) net income if estimated salvage value is excluded from the computation.
DISCUSSION: Under the straight-line method, the depreciable base of an asset is allocated uniformly over the time periods of the estimated use of the asset. Under the activity method, the depreciable base is allocated as a constant per-unit amount as goods are produced. For both methods, the depreciable base is equal to the original cost minus the salvage value. Thus, if the estimated salvage value is excluded from the depreciable base calculated using either method, the amount of depreciation is overstated. The result is an understatement of net income.
Answer (A) is incorrect. Under the activity depreciation method, excluding the salvage value from the depreciable base overstates depreciation expense and understates net income. Answer (C) is incorrect. Under both the straight-line and activity depreciation methods, excluding the salvage value from the depreciable base overstates depreciation expense and understates net income. Answer (D) is incorrect. Under the straight-line method, excluding the salvage value from the depreciable base overstates depreciation expense and understates net income.

4. Depreciation is computed on the original cost minus estimated salvage value under which of the following depreciation methods?

	Double-Declining Balance	Activity
A.	No	No
B.	No	Yes
C.	Yes	Yes
D.	Yes	No

Answer (B) is correct. *(CPA, adapted)*
REQUIRED: The method(s) under which depreciation is computed on original cost minus estimated salvage value.
DISCUSSION: Under the activity method, depreciation is determined by allocating the original cost minus the estimated salvage value to the projected units of output during the expected life of the asset. Under the double-declining-balance method, depreciation is determined by multiplying the carrying amount at the beginning of each period by a constant rate that is equal to twice the straight-line rate of depreciation. Each year, the carrying amount of the asset decreases by the depreciation expense recognized. The double-declining-balance calculation does not include salvage value in calculating depreciation. However, the asset may not be depreciated below the amount of the estimated salvage value.
Answer (A) is incorrect. The activity method does use a depreciable base equal to original cost minus salvage value. Answer (C) is incorrect. The DDB method excludes the salvage value from the depreciable base. Answer (D) is incorrect. The activity method uses a depreciable base equal to original cost minus salvage value, but the DDB method excludes the salvage value from the depreciable base.

5. Which of the following statements is the assumption on which straight-line depreciation is based?

A. The operating efficiency of the asset decreases in later years.

B. Service value declines as a function of time rather than use.

C. Service value declines as a function of obsolescence rather than time.

D. Physical wear and tear are more important than economic obsolescence.

Answer (B) is correct. *(CPA, adapted)*
REQUIRED: The assumption on which straight-line depreciation is based.
DISCUSSION: Under the straight-line method, depreciation expense is a constant amount for each period of the estimated useful life of the asset. The straight-line method ignores fluctuations in the use of an asset and in maintenance and service charges. The carrying amount is dependent upon the length of time the asset has been held rather than the amount of use.
Answer (A) is incorrect. If operating efficiency declines over time, an accelerated depreciation method may be appropriate. Answer (C) is incorrect. If obsolescence determines service value, a write-down method based on market values may be appropriate. Answer (D) is incorrect. Physical wear and tear is a justification for an activity method of depreciation, e.g., depreciation based on hours of machine use.

6. In which of the following situations is the activity method of depreciation most appropriate?

A. An asset's service potential declines with use.

B. An asset's service potential declines with the passage of time.

C. An asset is subject to rapid obsolescence.

D. An asset incurs increasing repairs and maintenance with use.

Answer (A) is correct. *(CPA, adapted)*
REQUIRED: The situation in which the units-of-production method of depreciation is most appropriate.
DISCUSSION: The activity depreciation method allocates asset cost based on the level of production. As production varies, so will the credit to accumulated depreciation. Consequently, when an asset's service potential declines with use, the activity method is the most appropriate method.
Answer (B) is incorrect. The straight-line method is appropriate when an asset's service potential declines with the passage of time. Answer (C) is incorrect. An accelerated method is best when an asset is subject to rapid obsolescence. Answer (D) is incorrect. The activity method does not allow for increasing repairs and maintenance.

7. Under which of the following depreciation methods is it possible for depreciation expense to be higher in the later years of an asset's useful life?

A. Straight-line.

B. Activity method based on units of production.

C. Sum-of-the-years'-digits.

D. Declining-balance.

Answer (B) is correct. *(CIA, adapted)*
REQUIRED: The depreciation method under which higher depreciation is possible later in an asset's useful life.
DISCUSSION: Under the activity method, depreciation is a function of use, not the passage of time. If the estimated activity level (stated, for example, in units of production) is higher in the later years of the asset's useful life, depreciation expense will be higher.
Answer (A) is incorrect. The straight-line method results in a constant depreciation expense. Answer (C) is incorrect. Depreciation expense diminishes over time when an accelerated method, such as SYD, is used. Answer (D) is incorrect. Depreciation expense diminishes over time when an accelerated method, such as declining-balance method, is used.

8. Which of the following reasons provides the best theoretical support for accelerated depreciation?

    A. Assets are more efficient in early years and initially generate more revenue.

    B. Expenses should be allocated in a manner that "smooths" earnings.

    C. Repairs and maintenance costs will probably increase in later periods, so depreciation should decline.

    D. Accelerated depreciation provides easier replacement because of the time value of money.

Answer (A) is correct. *(CPA, adapted)*
    REQUIRED: The best theoretical basis for accelerated depreciation.
    DISCUSSION: Accelerated depreciation methods result in decreasing depreciation charges over the life of the asset. Depreciation charges are greatest in the early years when the asset is presumably more efficient and generates more revenue. The effect of accelerated depreciation under this assumption is to match expenses and revenues more realistically.
    Answer (B) is incorrect. The smoothing of earnings is not a proper justification for making a choice among generally accepted accounting principles. Accounting theory requires that the results of operations be presented fairly, even though such presentation might produce considerable fluctuations in earnings. Answer (C) is incorrect. Although an anticipated increase in maintenance costs is a practical justification for accelerated depreciation, it is not the best theoretical support. Answer (D) is incorrect. Depreciation for financial reporting purposes has no effect on cash flow.

9. Quito Co. acquired a fixed asset with an estimated useful life of 5 years and no salvage value for $15,000 at the beginning of Year 1. For financial statement purposes, how would the depreciation expense calculated using the double-declining-balance (DDB) method compare with that calculated using the sum-of-the-years'-digits (SYD) method in Year 1 and Year 2, respectively?

	Year 1	Year 2
A.	Lower	Lower
B.	Lower	Higher
C.	Higher	Lower
D.	Higher	Higher

Answer (C) is correct. *(CIA, adapted)*
    REQUIRED: The comparison for 2 years of DDB and SYD depreciation expense.
    DISCUSSION: DDB is an accelerated depreciation method that determines periodic depreciation expense by multiplying the carrying amount at the beginning of each period by a constant rate that is equal to twice the straight-line rate of depreciation. Each year the carrying amount of the asset decreases by the depreciation expense recognized. Salvage value is ignored in determining the carrying amount except as a floor beneath which the asset may not be depreciated. SYD depreciation multiplies a constant depreciable base (cost – salvage value) by the SYD fraction. The SYD fraction's numerator is the number of years of the useful life (n) minus the prior years elapsed. The formula to compute the denominator in the SYD method is

$$n\left[\frac{(n+1)}{2}\right]$$

For a 5-year estimated useful life, the denominator of the fraction is 15 {5 × [(5 + 1) ÷ 2]}.

    DDB: Year 1 = $15,000(.4) = $6,000
             Year 2 = $9,000(.4)   = $3,600

    SYD: Year 1 = $15,000(5 ÷ 15) = $5,000
             Year 2 = $15,000(4 ÷ 15) = $4,000

    Answer (A) is incorrect. DDB depreciation is higher in Year 1. Answer (B) is incorrect. DDB depreciation is higher in Year 1 and lower in Year 2. Answer (D) is incorrect. DDB depreciation is lower in Year 2.

10. Ottawa Corp. uses the sum-of-the-years'-digits method of depreciation. In the third year of use of an asset with a 4-year estimated useful life, the portion of the depreciation cost for the asset that the entity will expense is

    A. 10%

    B. 20%

    C. 30%

    D. 33.33%

Answer (B) is correct. *(CIA, adapted)*
    REQUIRED: The SYD depreciation in the third year.
    DISCUSSION: The SYD fraction (remaining years of the useful life at the beginning of the year ÷ the sum of the years of the useful life) is applied to the constant depreciable base (cost – salvage). For the third year of use of an asset with a 4-year life, the percentage of the depreciable base to be recognized is 20% [2 years ÷ (1 + 2 + 3 + 4)].
    Answer (A) is incorrect. This percentage results from calculating the portion of depreciable cost to expense in any given year using the end of the current year in the numerator. Answer (C) is incorrect. This percentage uses the digit of the current year in the numerator. Answer (D) is incorrect. This percentage calculates the denominator as the sum of the years up to the end of the current year and uses the digit of the current year in the numerator.

11. A machine with a 5-year estimated useful life and an estimated 10% salvage value was acquired on January 1, Year 1. On December 31, Year 4, accumulated depreciation using the sum-of-the-years'-digits method is

A. (Original cost – salvage value) × (1 ÷ 15).

B. (Original cost – salvage value) × (14 ÷ 15).

C. Original cost × (14 ÷ 15).

D. Original cost × (1 ÷ 15).

Answer (B) is correct. *(CPA, adapted)*
REQUIRED: The accumulated depreciation at the end of 4 years under the SYD method.
DISCUSSION: SYD depreciation is calculated on a constant depreciable base equal to the original cost minus the salvage value, multiplied by the SYD fraction. The SYD fraction's numerator is the number of years of the useful life of the asset minus the prior years elapsed. The denominator is the sum of the digits of the total years of the expected useful life. In this case, the denominator is 15 (1 + 2 + 3 + 4 + 5). Thus, the accumulated depreciation at the end of the fourth year is (14 ÷ 15) of the depreciable base (original cost – salvage value), that is, the sum of the depreciation amounts calculated for each of the 4 years, or [(5 ÷ 15) + (4 ÷ 15) + (3 ÷ 15) + (2 ÷ 15)] times the depreciable base.
Answer (A) is incorrect. (Original cost – salvage value) × (1 ÷ 15) is the depreciation for Year 5. Answer (C) is incorrect. Original cost × (14 ÷ 15) is the accumulated depreciation on December 31, Year 4, assuming no salvage value. Answer (D) is incorrect. Original cost × (1 ÷ 15) is the depreciation for Year 5 assuming no salvage value.

12. Tunis Company purchased a van for $45,000. The estimated useful life of the van is 5 years or 80,000 miles, and the salvage value is $5,000. Actual mileage driven in the first year was 20,000 miles. Which of the following methods will result in the highest depreciation for the first year?

A. Straight-line.

B. Activity.

C. Sum-of-the-years'-digits.

D. Double-declining-balance.

Answer (D) is correct. *(J. Emig)*
REQUIRED: The method that will result in the highest depreciation for the first year.
DISCUSSION: Under the straight-line, activity, and SYD methods, the depreciable base is $40,000 ($45,000 original cost – $5,000 estimated salvage value). Under the straight-line method, this base is allocated equally to the 5 years, resulting in a depreciation expense of $8,000. Under the units-of-output method, the $40,000 is allocated evenly across the estimated mileage to produce a depreciation charge of $.50 per mile. Thus, first-year depreciation expense is $10,000 (20,000 miles × $.50). Under SYD, the depreciable base is multiplied by the SYD factor (years remaining at the beginning of the year ÷ the sum of the digits). SYD depreciation expense in the first year is therefore $13,333 [$40,000 × (5 ÷ 15)]. Under the DDB method, the $45,000 original cost is multiplied by a rate that is equal to twice the straight-line rate (2 × 20% = 40%). The result is a depreciation expense of $18,000 ($45,000 × 40%) in the first year.
Answer (A) is incorrect. Straight-line depreciation is $8,000. Answer (B) is incorrect. Activity method depreciation is $10,000. Answer (C) is incorrect. SYD depreciation is $13,333.

13. On January 1, Year 1, Nairobi, Inc., purchased equipment having an estimated salvage value equal to 20% of its original cost at the end of a 10-year life. The equipment was sold December 31, Year 5, for 50% of its original cost. If the equipment's disposition resulted in a reported loss, which of the following depreciation methods did Nairobi use?

A. Double-declining-balance.

B. Sum-of-the-years'-digits.

C. Straight-line.

D. Composite.

Answer (C) is correct. *(CPA, adapted)*
REQUIRED: The method that results in a reported loss upon disposition.
DISCUSSION: The straight-line method of depreciation yields the lowest amount of depreciation for the early part of the depreciable life of the asset. Because only 50% of the original cost was received and straight-line accumulated depreciation equaled 40% of cost {[(100% – 20%) ÷ 10 years] × 5 years} at the time of sale, a 10% loss [50% – (100% – 40%)] results.
Answer (A) is incorrect. The DDB method results in 5-year accumulated depreciation that is greater than 50% of cost. Answer (B) is incorrect. The SYD method results in 5-year accumulated depreciation that is greater than 50% of cost. Answer (D) is incorrect. The composite method of depreciation applies to the weighted average of multiple useful lives of assets, whereas only one asset is mentioned in this question. Moreover, it recognizes no gain or loss on disposition.

8.2 Depreciation Calculations

14. Pretoria Company acquired a new machine at a cost of $400,000 and incurred costs of $4,000 to have the machine shipped to its factory. Pretoria also paid $9,000 to construct and prepare a site for the new machine and $7,000 to install the necessary electrical connections. Pretoria estimates that the useful life of this new machine will be 5 years and that it will have a salvage value of $30,000 at the end of that period. Assuming that Pretoria acquired the machine on January 1 and will take a full year's depreciation, the proper amount of depreciation expense to be recorded by Pretoria if it uses the double-declining-balance method is

A. $148,000

B. $168,000

C. $160,000

D. $161,600

Answer (B) is correct. *(CMA, adapted)*
REQUIRED: The proper amount of depreciation under the double-declining-balance (DDB) method.
DISCUSSION: The acquisition cost of the machine includes all costs necessary to prepare it for its intended use. Hence, the depreciable cost is $420,000 ($400,000 invoice price + $4,000 delivery expense + $9,000 site preparation + $7,000 electrical work). Under the DDB method, salvage value is ignored at the beginning. Thus, the full $420,000 is subject to depreciation. Given a 5-year life, the annual straight-line rate is 20%, and the DDB rate is 40%. Depreciation for the first year is therefore $168,000 ($420,000 × 40%).
Answer (A) is incorrect. The amount of $148,000 assumes that the depreciable cost is the invoice price minus salvage value. Answer (C) is incorrect. The depreciable cost of the machine was $420,000, not the $400,000 invoice price. Answer (D) is incorrect. The amount of $161,600 assumes a depreciable cost of $404,000, which does not include the site preparation and electrical costs.

15. Sydney Co. purchased a machine that was installed and placed in service on January 1, Year 1, at a cost of $480,000. Salvage value was estimated at $80,000. The machine is being depreciated over 10 years by the double-declining-balance method. For the year ended December 31, Year 2, what amount should Sydney report as depreciation expense?

A. $96,000

B. $76,800

C. $64,000

D. $61,440

Answer (B) is correct. *(CPA, adapted)*
REQUIRED: The DDB depreciation expense reported in the second year.
DISCUSSION: DDB is an accelerated depreciation method that determines periodic depreciation expense by multiplying the carrying amount at the beginning of each period by a constant rate that is equal to twice the straight-line rate of depreciation. Given that this machine has a 10-year useful life, the DDB rate is 20%. Each year the carrying amount of the asset decreases by the depreciation expense recognized. Salvage value is ignored in determining the carrying amount except as a minimum below which the asset may not be depreciated. The carrying amount at the end of the first year was $384,000 [$480,000 cost × (100% – 20%)]. Thus, second-year depreciation is $76,800 ($384,000 × 20%).
Answer (A) is incorrect. The first-year depreciation was $96,000. Answer (C) is incorrect. The amount of $64,000 assumes that salvage value is included in the calculation. Answer (D) is incorrect. The third-year depreciation will be $61,440.

16. Khartoum Co. purchased equipment on January 2, Year 1, for $50,000. The equipment had an estimated 5-year service life. Khartoum's policy for 5-year assets is to use the 200%-double-declining-balance depreciation method for the first 2 years of the asset's life and then switch to the straight-line depreciation method. (Under GAAP, this practice consistently applied does not constitute a change in accounting principle.) In its December 31, Year 3, balance sheet, what amount should Khartoum report as accumulated depreciation for equipment?

A. $30,000

B. $38,000

C. $39,200

D. $42,000

Answer (B) is correct. *(CPA, adapted)*
REQUIRED: The amount of accumulated depreciation to be reported in the balance sheet.
DISCUSSION: Under the DDB method, the assets are depreciated at a constant rate of 40% (200% × 20% straight-line rate). This rate is applied in each of the first 2 years. For Year 3, straight-line is used based on the remaining carrying amount. The calculation is as follows:

Year 1:	$50,000 × 40%	$20,000
Year 2:	($50,000 – $20,000) × 40%	12,000
Year 3:	($50,000 – $20,000 – $12,000) ÷ 3	6,000
		$38,000

Answer (A) is incorrect. The accumulated straight-line depreciation for 3 years equals $30,000. Answer (C) is incorrect. DDB depreciation for 3 years equals $39,200. Answer (D) is incorrect. The amount of $42,000 includes third-year straight-line depreciation calculated without regard to DDB depreciation previously taken.

Questions 17 and 18 are based on the following information.

Since Year 1, Canberra Company has replaced all of its major manufacturing equipment and now has the following equipment recorded in the appropriate accounts. Canberra uses a calendar year as its fiscal year.

- A forge purchased January 1, Year 1, for $100,000. Installation costs were $20,000, and the forge has an estimated 5-year life with a salvage value of $10,000.
- A grinding machine costing $45,000 purchased January 1, Year 2. The machine has an estimated 5-year life with a salvage value of $5,000.
- A lathe purchased January 1, Year 4, for $60,000. The lathe has an estimated 5-year life with a salvage value of $7,000.

---

17. Using the straight-line depreciation method, Canberra's Year 4 depreciation expense is

A. $45,000

B. $40,334

C. $40,600

D. $40,848

Answer (C) is correct. *(CMA, adapted)*

REQUIRED: The Year 4 depreciation expense using the straight-line method.

DISCUSSION: The straight-line method allocates the depreciation evenly over the estimated useful life of an asset. The depreciable cost equals cost minus salvage value for each asset, and dividing that amount by the life of the asset gives the periodic depreciation as follows:

Asset	Cost	Salvage	C – S	Life	Expense
Forge	$120,000	$10,000	$110,000	5	$22,000
Grind	45,000	5,000	40,000	5	8,000
Lathe	60,000	7,000	53,000	5	10,600
Total					$40,600

Answer (A) is incorrect. The amount of $45,000 does not take into account the deduction for salvage value. Answer (B) is incorrect. The amount of $40,334 is based on the sum-of-the-years'-digits method. Answer (D) is incorrect. The amount of $40,848 is based on the double-declining-balance method.

---

18. Using the double-declining-balance method, Canberra's Year 4 depreciation expense is

A. $36,464

B. $40,334

C. $40,600

D. $40,848

Answer (D) is correct. *(CMA, adapted)*

REQUIRED: The Year 4 depreciation expense using the double-declining-balance method.

DISCUSSION: The DDB method allocates a series of decreasing depreciation charges over an asset's life. A percentage that is double the straight-line rate is multiplied each year by an asset's remaining carrying amount at the beginning of the year. Given that each asset has a 5-year life, the straight-line rate is 20%. The DDB rate is therefore 40%. The forge was purchased in Year 1 at a total cost of $120,000. The depreciation for each year is calculated as follows:

Year	Carrying Amount	%	Expense
Year 1	$120,000	40%	$48,000
Year 2	72,000	40%	28,800
Year 3	43,200	40%	17,280
Year 4	25,920	40%	10,368

For the grinding machine, the calculations are

Year	Carrying Amount	%	Expense
Year 2	$45,000	40%	$18,000
Year 3	27,000	40%	10,800
Year 4	16,200	40%	6,480

The Year 4 calculation for the new lathe requires multiplying the $60,000 cost by 40% to yield a $24,000 expense. Adding the Year 4 expense for each of the three machines ($10,368 + $6,480 + $24,000) produces total depreciation of $40,848.

Answer (A) is incorrect. The amount of $36,464 is based on the double-declining-balance method, but with salvage value deducted from the initial depreciable base. Answer (B) is incorrect. The amount of $40,334 is based on the sum-of-the-years'-digits method. Answer (C) is incorrect. The amount of $40,600 is based on the straight-line method.

Questions 19 through 21 are based on the following information.

Samoa Corporation's schedule of depreciable assets at December 31, Year 3, is shown in the next column. Samoa takes a full year's depreciation expense in the year of an asset's acquisition and no depreciation expense in the year of an asset's disposition. The estimated useful life of each depreciable asset is 5 years.

Asset	Cost	Accumulated Depreciation	Acquisition Date	Salvage Value
A	$100,000	$ 64,000	Year 2	$20,000
B	55,000	36,000	Year 1	10,000
C	70,000	33,600	Year 1	14,000
	$225,000	$133,600		$44,000

19. Samoa depreciates asset A on the double-declining-balance method. How much depreciation expense should Samoa record in Year 4 for asset A?

A. $32,000

B. $24,000

C. $14,400

D. $1,600

Answer (C) is correct. *(CPA, adapted)*
REQUIRED: The current depreciation expense.
DISCUSSION: DDB depreciation equals carrying amount at the beginning of the year times twice the straight-line rate. Salvage value is considered only as a minimum below which the carrying amount may not be reduced. Asset A has a useful life of 5 years, so the straight-line rate is 20%. The DDB rate is 40% (2 × 20%). The carrying amount is $36,000 ($100,000 cost – $64,000 accumulated depreciation). Annual depreciation expense for its third year is thus $14,400 ($36,000 × 40%).
Answer (A) is incorrect. First-year depreciation after subtracting salvage value from the depreciable base is $32,000. Answer (B) is incorrect. The Year 2 depreciation was $24,000. Answer (D) is incorrect. The difference between 12/31/Year 4 carrying amount and the salvage value that will be the Year 5 depreciation will be $1,600.

20. Using the same depreciation method as used in Year 1, Year 2, and Year 3, how much depreciation expense should Samoa record in Year 4 for asset B?

A. $6,000

B. $9,000

C. $12,000

D. $15,000

Answer (A) is correct. *(CPA, adapted)*
REQUIRED: The current depreciation expense.
DISCUSSION: The cost of asset B was $55,000, and the depreciation accumulated after 3 years of its 5-year life is $36,000. Under the straight-line method, depreciation would have totaled $27,000 [($55,000 – $10,000 salvage value) × 3 × 20%]. DDB depreciation would have been $43,120 (40% of a declining carrying amount each year). The SYD method multiplies a fraction (the years remaining ÷ the SYD) by a constant depreciable base (cost – salvage). The SYD is 15 [n(n + 1) ÷ 2 = 5(5 + 1) ÷ 2]. Total SYD depreciation after 3 years is $36,000. Thus, SYD should be used and Year 4 depreciation is $6,000 [$45,000 × (2 ÷ 15)].

Year 1:	[(5 ÷ 15) × ($55,000 – $10,000)]	=	$15,000
Year 2:	[(4 ÷ 15) × ($55,000 – $10,000)]	=	12,000
Year 3:	[(3 ÷ 15) × ($55,000 – $10,000)]	=	9,000
			$36,000

Answer (B) is incorrect. The third-year SYD depreciation was $9,000. Answer (C) is incorrect. The second-year depreciation was $12,000. Answer (D) is incorrect. The first-year depreciation was $15,000.

21. Samoa depreciates asset C by the straight-line method. On June 30, Year 4, Samoa sold asset C for $28,000 cash. How much gain or (loss) should Samoa record in Year 4 on the disposal of asset C?

A. $2,800

B. $(2,800)

C. $(5,600)

D. $(8,400)

Answer (D) is correct. *(CPA, adapted)*
REQUIRED: The gain (loss) on disposal of asset C.
DISCUSSION: Asset C had a carrying amount at the time of its disposition of $36,400 ($70,000 cost – $33,600 accumulated depreciation), given that no depreciation was recognized in the year of sale. The loss on the transaction was $8,400 ($36,400 carrying amount – $28,000 cash received).
Answer (A) is incorrect. The amount of $2,800 assumes that a year's depreciation was taken in Year 4. Answer (B) is incorrect. The amount of $(2,800) assumes depreciation was taken for the first half of the year. Answer (C) is incorrect. The amount of $(5,600) equals the accumulated depreciation balance minus the cash received.

Questions 22 and 23 are based on the following information. Roswell Company has the following information on one of its vehicles purchased on January 1, Year 1:

Vehicle cost	$50,000
Useful life, years, estimated	5
Useful life, miles, estimated	100,000
Salvage value, estimated	$10,000
Actual miles driven: Year 1	30,000
Year 2	20,000
Year 3	15,000
Year 4	25,000
Year 5	12,000

No estimates were changed during the life of the asset.

22. The Year 3 depreciation expense for Roswell's vehicle using the sum-of-the-years'-digits (SYD) method was

A. $6,000

B. $8,000

C. $10,000

D. $16,000

Answer (B) is correct. *(CMA, adapted)*
REQUIRED: The Year 3 depreciation expense under the SYD method.
DISCUSSION: Under the SYD method, the amount to be depreciated is $40,000 ($50,000 original cost – $10,000 salvage). The portion expensed each year is based on a fraction, the denominator of which is the summation of the years of life of the asset being depreciated. For an asset with a 5-year life, the denominator is 15 (5 + 4 + 3 + 2 + 1). The numerator equals the years remaining at the beginning of the year. For Year 3, the fraction is 3 ÷ 15, and depreciation expense is $8,000 [$40,000 × (3 ÷ 15)].
Answer (A) is incorrect. The amount of $6,000 is based on the units-of-production method. Answer (C) is incorrect. The amount of $10,000 omits the vehicle's salvage value from the calculation. Answer (D) is incorrect. The amount of $16,000 is the double-declining-balance method depreciation for Year 1 if the salvage value is subtracted from the cost.

23. Using the activity method, what was Roswell's Year 5 depreciation expense?

A. $4,000

B. $4,800

C. $5,000

D. $6,000

Answer (A) is correct. *(CMA, adapted)*
REQUIRED: The depreciation expense for Year 5 under the units-of-production method.
DISCUSSION: Under the activity method, periodic depreciation is based on the proportion of expected total production that occurred. For Years 1 through 4, the total depreciation was $36,000 {($50,000 – $10,000) × [(30,000 + 20,000 + 15,000 + 25,000) ÷ 100,000]}. Hence, the remaining depreciable base was $4,000 ($50,000 cost – $10,000 salvage – $36,000). Given that the 12,000 miles driven in Year 5 exceeded the remaining estimated production of 10,000 miles (100,000 – 30,000 – 20,000 – 15,000 – 25,000), only the $4,000 of the remaining depreciable base should be recognized in Year 5.
Answer (B) is incorrect. The amount of $4,800 is based on a Year 5 rate of 12% (12,000 miles ÷ 100,000 miles of estimated usage). It ignores the effects of depreciation expense deducted in prior years. Answer (C) is incorrect. The amount of $5,000 assumes that depreciation is based on original cost without regard to salvage value. Answer (D) is incorrect. The amount of $6,000 is based on a 12% rate and ignores salvage value.

24. On July 1, Year 1, Tungushka Corporation purchased factory equipment for $100,000. Salvage value was estimated at $4,000. The equipment will be depreciated over 10 years using the double-declining-balance method. Counting the year of acquisition as one-half year, Tungushka should record Year 2 depreciation expense of

A. $17,280

B. $18,000

C. $16,000

D. $20,000

Answer (B) is correct. *(CPA, adapted)*
REQUIRED: The DDB depreciation expense for an asset acquired in mid-year.
DISCUSSION: Using DDB when an asset is acquired in mid-year requires that each year's DDB depreciation be allocated to the accounting period in which it falls. Accordingly, the first year's depreciation must be prorated between the last half of Year 1 and the first half of Year 2. The second year's must be prorated between the second half of Year 2 and the first half of Year 3, etc. The Year 2 depreciation expense is the sum of half of the first year's and half of the second year's depreciation. The DDB depreciation for Years 1 and 2 computed below is based on the asset cost of $100,000 and a 10-year life (resulting in a DDB rate of 20%).

Year 1: $100,000 × 20% = $20,000
Year 2: ($100,000 − $20,000) × 20% = $16,000

$20,000 × 50%	=	$10,000
$16,000 × 50%	=	8,000
		$18,000

Answer (A) is incorrect. The amount of $17,280 is calculated by using a depreciable base of $100,000 reduced by the salvage value of $4,000. Answer (C) is incorrect. The total depreciation for the second year of the asset's life without proration is $16,000. Answer (D) is incorrect. The total depreciation for the first year of the asset's life without proration is $20,000.

25. Melbourne Co. uses straight-line depreciation for its property, plant, and equipment, which, stated at cost, consisted of the following:

	12/31/Year 2	12/31/Year 1
Land	$ 25,000	$ 25,000
Buildings	195,000	195,000
Machinery and equipment	695,000	650,000
	$915,000	$870,000
Minus accumulated depreciation	400,000	370,000
	$515,000	$500,000

Melbourne's depreciation expense for Year 2 and Year 1 was $55,000 and $50,000, respectively. What amount was debited to accumulated depreciation during Year 2 because of property, plant, and equipment retirements?

A. $40,000

B. $25,000

C. $20,000

D. $10,000

Answer (B) is correct. *(CPA, adapted)*
REQUIRED: The amount that was debited to accumulated depreciation because of retirements.
DISCUSSION: When an asset is depreciated, a debit is made to depreciation expense and a credit to accumulated depreciation. An equipment retirement results in a debit to accumulated depreciation. During Year 2, accumulated depreciation increased by $30,000 despite recognition of a $55,000 expense (a credit). Consequently, a $25,000 ($55,000 − $30,000) debit must have been made to the accumulated depreciation account.
Answer (A) is incorrect. The amount of $40,000 is equal to $55,000 minus the $15,000 increase in net property, plant, and equipment. Answer (C) is incorrect. The difference between Year 1 depreciation ($50,000) and the $30,000 increase in accumulated depreciation is $20,000. Answer (D) is incorrect. The amount of $10,000 is equal to $55,000 minus the $45,000 increase in the gross property, plant, and equipment.

26. Spiro Corp. uses the sum-of-the-years'-digits method to depreciate equipment purchased in January Year 1 for $20,000. The estimated salvage value of the equipment is $2,000, and the estimated useful life is 4 years. What should Spiro report as the asset's carrying amount as of December 31, Year 3?

    A. $1,800

    B. $2,000

    C. $3,800

    D. $4,500

Answer (C) is correct. *(CPA, adapted)*
    REQUIRED: The asset's carrying amount as of December 31, Year 3.
    DISCUSSION: The sum-of-the-years' digits (SYD) method multiplies a constant depreciable base (cost – salvage) by a declining fraction. It is a declining-rate, declining-charge method. The SYD fraction's numerator is the number of years of the useful life (n) minus the prior years elapsed. The formula to compute the (sum of the years' digits) denominator is

$$n\left[\frac{(n\ +\ 1)}{2}\right]$$

Consequently, the depreciable base is $18,000 ($20,000 – $2,000), the numerator is 1 year (4 – 3), and the denominator is 10 {[4 × (4 + 1)] ÷ 2}. The depreciation for the last year is $1,800 [$18,000 × (1 ÷ 10)], so the declining balance after 3 years of the 4-year period (Year 1-Year 3) is $3,800 ($1,800 remaining depreciable base + $2,000 salvage value).
    Answer (A) is incorrect. The final-year SYD depreciation is $1,800. Answer (B) is incorrect. The salvage value is $2,000. Answer (D) is incorrect. The annual straight-line depreciation is $4,500.

27. On January 2, Year 1, Osaka Co. purchased a machine for $800,000 and established an annual depreciation charge of $100,000 over an 8-year life. At the beginning of Year 4, after issuing its Year 3 financial statements, Osaka concluded that $250,000 was a reasonable estimate of the sum of the undiscounted net cash inflows expected to be recovered through use of the machine for the period January 1, Year 4 through December 31, Year 8. The machine's fair value was $200,000 at the beginning of Year 4. In Osaka's December 31, Year 4, balance sheet, the machine should be reported at a carrying amount of

    A. $0

    B. $100,000

    C. $160,000

    D. $400,000

Answer (C) is correct. *(CPA, adapted)*
    REQUIRED: The carrying amount of an asset.
    DISCUSSION: The asset should be written down to fair value if the carrying amount is not recoverable. Because the carrying amount ($800,000 cost – $300,000 accumulated depreciation = $500,000) exceeded the recoverable amount ($250,000) at the beginning of Year 4, Osaka should have recognized an impairment loss of $300,000 ($500,000 carrying amount – $200,000 fair value at the beginning of Year 4). Accordingly, the new carrying amount was $200,000, and the new annual depreciation expense for the remaining 5-year useful life (Year 4 - Year 8) was $40,000 ($200,000 ÷ 5 years). The machine should be reported at a carrying amount of $160,000 ($200,000 – $40,000 depreciation) on December 31, Year 4.
    Answer (A) is incorrect. The machine still has a carrying amount. Answer (B) is incorrect. This figure results from subtracting the originally computed annual depreciation from the new carrying amount. Answer (D) is incorrect. The amount of $400,000 assumes no impairment.

28. Auckland Co. determined that, because of obsolescence, equipment with an original cost of $1,800,000 and accumulated depreciation on the first day of the current fiscal year of $840,000 had suffered impairment and, as a result, should have a carrying amount of only $600,000 (the fair value) as of the beginning of the year. In addition, the remaining useful life of the equipment was reduced from 8 years to 3. In its year-end balance sheet, what amount should Auckland report as accumulated depreciation?

    A. $200,000

    B. $1,040,000

    C. $1,200,000

    D. $1,400,000

Answer (D) is correct. *(CPA, adapted)*
    REQUIRED: The accumulated depreciation given on impairment loss and a change in estimate.
    DISCUSSION: The carrying amount of the equipment before the impairment was $960,000 ($1,800,000 – $840,000). After the impairment, the carrying amount should be $600,000; therefore, $360,000 ($960,000 – $600,000) of additional accumulated depreciation should be recorded to reflect the impairment loss (assuming the entry is to debit the loss and credit accumulated depreciation). In addition, the depreciation for the year should be $200,000 ($600,000 ÷ 3). Hence, the accumulated depreciation in the year-end balance sheet is $1,400,000 ($840,000 + $360,000 impairment loss + $200,000 depreciation for the year).
    Answer (A) is incorrect. The depreciation for the year is $200,000. Answer (B) is incorrect. The sum of the accumulated depreciation at the beginning of the year and the revised annual depreciation is $1,040,000. Answer (C) is incorrect. The accumulated depreciation before adjusting the useful life and claiming current-year depreciation is $1,200,000.

29. On January 2, Rio Corp. bought machinery under a contract that required a down payment of $10,000, plus 24 monthly payments of $5,000 each, for total cash payments of $130,000. The cash equivalent price of the machinery was $110,000. The machinery has an estimated useful life of 10 years and estimated salvage value of $5,000. Rio uses straight-line depreciation. In its income statement for the year ended December 31, what amount should Rio report as depreciation for this machinery?

A. $10,500

B. $11,000

C. $12,500

D. $13,000

Answer (A) is correct. *(CPA, adapted)*
   REQUIRED: The depreciation on the machinery.
   DISCUSSION: The cash equivalent price of the machinery (present value), reduced by the salvage value, equals the depreciable base. The excess of the total cash to be paid over the cash equivalent price of the machinery will be recognized as interest expense, not depreciation. Accordingly, straight-line depreciation is $10,500 [($110,000 cash equivalent price – $5,000 salvage value) ÷ 10 years].
   Answer (B) is incorrect. The amount of $11,000 does not allow for the salvage value. Answer (C) is incorrect. The amount of $12,500 is based on the total cash payments minus salvage value. Answer (D) is incorrect. The amount of $13,000 is based on the total cash payments with no allowance for salvage value.

30. Caracas Corp. purchased a computer on January 1 for $108,000. It was estimated to have a 4-year useful life and a salvage value of $18,000. The double-declining-balance (DDB) method is to be used. The amount of depreciation to be reported at the end of the first year is

A. ($108,000 – $18,000) × (25% × 2)

B. ($108,000 – $18,000) × (25% × 1/2)

C. ($108,000) × (25% × 2)

D. ($108,000) × (25% × 1/2)

Answer (C) is correct. *(CIA, adapted)*
   REQUIRED: The computation to calculate the amount of depreciation under the double-declining-balance method.
   DISCUSSION: When using a declining-balance method, a constant rate is applied to the changing carrying amount of the asset. The carrying amount for the first period's calculation is the acquisition cost ($108,000). The constant rate for the DDB method is twice the straight-line rate [(100% ÷ 4 years) × 2].
   Answer (A) is incorrect. The salvage value is ignored in computing depreciation by use of a declining-balance method until the later years of the life. The asset should not be depreciated below its salvage value. Answer (B) is incorrect. The salvage value is ignored. Furthermore, the rate used should be twice the straight-line rate. Answer (D) is incorrect. The rate used should be twice the straight-line rate.

31. On the first day of its current fiscal year, Santiago Corporation purchased equipment costing $400,000 with a salvage value of $80,000. Depreciation expense for the year was $160,000. If Santiago uses the double-declining-balance (DDB) method of depreciation, what is the estimated useful life of the asset?

A. 5

B. 4

C. 2.5

D. 2

Answer (A) is correct. *(J. Hora)*
   REQUIRED: The estimated useful life of an asset being depreciated using the DDB method.
   DISCUSSION: DDB uses a depreciation rate that is twice the straight-line rate. In the first year of this equipment's life, the DDB depreciation rate is 40% ($160,000 ÷ $400,000). The straight-line rate is therefore 20% (40% ÷ 2). Accordingly, the expected useful life of the asset is 5 years.
   Answer (B) is incorrect. Four years assumes salvage value is subtracted from the cost to determine the depreciable base used to calculate DDB depreciation. Answer (C) is incorrect. A straight-line rate of 40% and a DDB rate of 80% is equivalent to 2.5 years. Hence, DDB depreciation would be $320,000 ($400,000 × 80%). Answer (D) is incorrect. If the useful life were 2 years, the depreciation expense would be $320,000 [($400,000 cost × 100%) – $80,000 salvage].

32. Lima Company is depreciating an asset with a 5-year useful life. It cost $100,000 and has no salvage value. If the <List A> method is used, depreciation expense in the second year will be <List B>.

	List A	List B
A.	Sum-of-years'-digits	$20,000
B.	Sum-of-years'-digits	$40,000
C.	Double-declining-balance	$16,000
D.	Double-declining-balance	$24,000

Answer (D) is correct. *(CIA, adapted)*
   REQUIRED: The proper match of depreciation method and expense amount.
   DISCUSSION: The DDB method uses twice the straight-line rate. In the first year of the asset's life, depreciation expense was $40,000 ($100,000 × 20% × 2 years). In the second year, the depreciation base is reduced by the amount of depreciation expense already taken in the first year, so depreciation expense in the second year is $24,000 [($100,000 – $40,000) × 20% × 2 years].
   Answer (A) is incorrect. Depreciation in the second year will be $20,000 under the straight-line method of depreciation. Under the SYD method, it is $26,667 [$100,000 × (4 ÷ 15)]. Answer (B) is incorrect. SYD depreciation in the second year is $26,667. Answer (C) is incorrect. The amount of $16,000 assumes the declining-balance method is used with the straight-line rate.

8.3 Group and Composite Depreciation Methods

Questions 33 through 35 are based on the following information.			
For its first year of operations, Falkland Co. decided to use the composite method of depreciation and prepared the schedule of machinery owned presented in the opposite column.	**Total Cost**	**Estimated Salvage Value**	**Estimated Life in Years**
Machine X	$550,000	$50,000	20
Machine Y	200,000	20,000	15
Machine Z	40,000	--	5

33. Falkland computes depreciation on the straight-line method. Based upon the information presented, the composite life of these assets (in years) should be

A. 13.3

B. 16.0

C. 17.6

D. 20.0

Answer (B) is correct. *(CPA, adapted)*
REQUIRED: The composite life of the assets in years.
DISCUSSION: The composite or average useful life of the assets is essentially a weighted average. As illustrated below, the annual straight-line depreciation for each asset should be calculated. The total cost, estimated salvage value, and depreciable base of the assets should then be computed. Dividing the composite depreciable base ($720) by the total annual straight-line depreciation ($45) gives the composite life (16 years) of these assets.

	Total Cost	Salvage Value	Dep. Base	Est. Life	Annual S-L Dep.
X	$550	$50	$500	20	$25
Y	200	20	180	15	12
Z	40	0	40	5	8
	$790	$70	$720		$45

Answer (A) is incorrect. The average useful life of the three assets is 13.3. Answer (C) is incorrect. The amount of 17.6 ignores salvage value in the calculation of total depreciable cost. Answer (D) is incorrect. The estimated life of asset X is 20.

34. At the start of the fifth year of operations, Falkland sold machine Z for $10,000. Assume that this change is not material. What are the depreciation expense and the ending balance in the accumulated depreciation account recorded for Year 5?

A. $45,000 and $225,000.

B. $45,000 and $195,000.

C. $42,750 and $222,750.

D. $42,750 and $192,750.

Answer (D) is correct. *(Publisher, adapted)*
REQUIRED: The depreciation expense and accumulated depreciation under the composite method when an asset is sold.
DISCUSSION: The straight-line depreciation rate is 5.70% ($45,000 annual depreciation ÷ $790,000 total cost). When an asset included in a composite group is sold, the original cost of that asset minus the amount received for it is debited to the accumulated depreciation account. No gain or loss is recorded. The depreciation rate is multiplied by the total cost of the remaining assets to determine the depreciation expense. Given that the asset disposal was not material to the total depreciable cost and the useful life composition of the group, the original depreciation rate continues to be used.
Thus, the depreciation expense for the fifth year is equal to $42,750 [($790,000 – $40,000) × 5.70%]. The accumulated depreciation at the start of Year 5 ($180,000) is increased by a credit for $42,750 of depreciation expense and decreased by a debit of $30,000 ($40,000 original cost – $10,000 cash received), leaving a year-end balance of $192,750.
Answer (A) is incorrect. The annual depreciation before the disposal is $45,000, and $225,000 is the ending accumulated depreciation for Year 5, assuming no disposal. Answer (B) is incorrect. The original annual depreciation is $45,000, and $195,000 equals the accumulated depreciation after 4 years, plus the original annual depreciation, minus $30,000 ($40,000 cost of Z – $10,000 sale price). Answer (C) is incorrect. The amount of $222,750 results from not adjusting accumulated depreciation for the difference between the cost and selling price of machine Z.

35. Refer to the information on the preceding page(s). Assume that, in addition to the sale of machine Z for $10,000 at the start of Year 5, Falkland purchased machine W for $60,000 to replace the machine that was sold. Machine W is expected to last 5 years with an expected salvage value of $10,000. If machine W is included in the composite asset group, the depreciation expense for the fifth year should be equal to which of the following amounts?

A. $42,750

B. $45,000

C. $45,600

D. $46,170

Answer (D) is correct. *(Publisher, adapted)*
REQUIRED: The depreciation expense under the composite method when a new asset is added.
DISCUSSION: When machine Z was sold, the total cost of the composite group was decreased from $790,000 to $750,000. The purchase of machine W adds $60,000 to the total cost. The new total cost ($810,000) is multiplied by the straight-line depreciation rate (5.70%), resulting in Year 5 depreciation of $46,170. Once a composite rate has been set, it continues to be used unless significant changes occur in the estimated lives or the composition of the assets through additions and retirements.
Answer (A) is incorrect. The depreciation expense excluding the new asset is $42,750. Answer (B) is incorrect. The amount of $45,000 fails to consider the effects of both the sale of Z and the purchase of W. Answer (C) is incorrect. The amount of $45,600 results from subtracting the salvage value of the new asset from the new total cost.

36. Asuncion Company, which uses the composite depreciation method for its fleet of trucks, cars, and campers, retired one of its trucks and received cash from a salvage company. The net carrying amount of these composite asset accounts was decreased by the

A. Cash proceeds received and original cost of the truck.

B. Cash proceeds received.

C. Original cost of the truck minus the cash proceeds.

D. Original cost of the truck.

Answer (B) is correct. *(CPA, adapted)*
REQUIRED: The effect of a retirement on the net carrying amount of a composite asset account.
DISCUSSION: Because both composite and group methods use weighted averages of useful lives and depreciation rates, early and late retirements are expected to offset each other. Consequently, gains and losses on retirements of single assets are treated as adjustments of accumulated depreciation. The entry is to credit the asset at cost, debit cash for any proceeds received, and debit accumulated depreciation for the difference. (A credit is unlikely. Proceeds of a retirement rarely exceed original cost.) Thus, the net carrying amount of the composite asset accounts is decreased by the amount of cash received. The net carrying amount of total assets is unchanged.
Answer (A) is incorrect. The net carrying amount of the composite asset accounts is decreased only by the cash proceeds received. Answer (C) is incorrect. Decreasing the net carrying amount by such an amount would reduce the asset account below the carrying value calculated using the weighted average of useful lives of all the composite assets. Answer (D) is incorrect. The original cost of the truck is used only to set up the net carrying amount and does not affect the value of composite assets upon retirement.

37. Which of the following uses the straight-line depreciation method?

	Group Depreciation	Composite Depreciation
A.	No	No
B.	Yes	No
C.	Yes	Yes
D.	No	Yes

Answer (C) is correct. *(CPA, adapted)*
REQUIRED: The method(s) using straight-line depreciation.
DISCUSSION: Both composite and group depreciation use the straight-line method. Both methods aggregate groups of assets. The composite method is used for a collection of dissimilar assets with varying useful lives, and the group method applies to similar assets. Each method involves the calculation of a total depreciable cost for all the assets included in one account and of a weighted-average estimated useful life.
Answer (A) is incorrect. Both methods use the straight-line method of depreciation. Answer (B) is incorrect. The composite method also uses straight-line depreciation. Answer (D) is incorrect. Group depreciations also uses the straight-line method of depreciation.

8.4 Depletion

38. Budapest Co., a calendar-year entity, purchased the rights to a copper mine on July 1. Of the total purchase price, $2.8 million was appropriately allocable to the copper. Estimated reserves were 800,000 tons of copper. Budapest expects to extract and sell 10,000 tons of copper per month. Production began immediately. The selling price is $25 per ton. Budapest uses percentage depletion (15%) for tax purposes. To aid production, Budapest also purchased some new equipment on July 1. The equipment cost $76,000 and had an estimated useful life of 8 years. After all the copper is removed from this mine, however, the equipment will be of no use to Budapest and will be sold for an estimated $4,000. If sales and production conform to expectations, what is Budapest's depletion expense on this mine for financial accounting purposes for the calendar year?

A. $105,000

B. $210,000

C. $215,400

D. $420,000

Answer (B) is correct. *(CPA, adapted)*
REQUIRED: The annual depletion expense for financial accounting purposes assuming accurate estimates of sales and production.
DISCUSSION: Depletion expense is based on the activity method. Assuming total reserves of 800,000 tons at a price of $2.8 million, the depletion charge per ton is $3.50. If 10,000 tons are extracted in each of the last 6 months of the year (60,000 tons), the depletion charge should be $210,000. The equipment cost is not included in the depletion base and is depreciated separately.
Answer (A) is incorrect. The depletion expense for 3 months is $105,000. Answer (C) is incorrect. The amount of $215,400 includes depreciation of the equipment based on the activity method. Answer (D) is incorrect. The 15% tax depletion is $420,000.

39. In January, Manila Co., a calendar-year entity, purchased a mineral mine for $2,640,000 with removable ore estimated at 1.2 million tons. After it has extracted all the ore, Manila will be required by law to restore the land to its original condition at an estimated cost of $180,000. Manila believes it will be able to sell the property afterwards for $300,000. During the year, Manila incurred $360,000 of development costs preparing the mine for production and removed and sold 60,000 tons of ore. In its annual income statement, what amount should Manila report as depletion?

A. $135,000

B. $144,000

C. $150,000

D. $159,000

Answer (B) is correct. *(CPA, adapted)*
REQUIRED: The amount of depletion to be reported.
DISCUSSION: The depletion base is the purchase price of the land ($2,640,000), minus the value of the land after restoration ($300,000 – $180,000 = $120,000), plus any costs necessary to prepare the property for the extraction of ore ($360,000). This depletion base must be allocated over the 1.2 million tons of ore that the land is estimated to yield. Accordingly, Manila's depletion charge per ton is $2.40 [($2,640,000 – $120,000 + $360,000) ÷ 1,200,000]. Manila should report $144,000 (60,000 tons removed × $2.40) as depletion in its annual income statement.
Answer (A) is incorrect. The amount of $135,000 does not include the $180,000 restoration costs. Answer (C) is incorrect. The amount of $150,000 does not consider the restoration costs and the residual value of the land. Answer (D) is incorrect. The amount of $159,000 adds the $180,000 restoration cost instead of deducting the $120,000 net residual value of the land.

8.5 IFRS

40. On January 1, Year 1, an entity acquires for $100,000 a new piece of machinery with an estimated useful life of 10 years. The machine has a drum that must be replaced every 5 years and costs $20,000 to replace. Continued operations of the machine requires an inspection every 4 years after purchase; the inspection cost is $8,000. The company uses the straight-line method of depreciation. Under IFRS, what is the depreciation expense for Year 1?

A. $10,000

B. $10,800

C. $12,000

D. $13,200

Answer (D) is correct. *(CPA, adapted)*
REQUIRED: The depreciation expense.
DISCUSSION: Under IFRS, each significant part of the item must be depreciated. For the machinery, the significant parts are (1) the inspection cost presumed to be included in the initial cost ($8,000 with a 4-year life), (2) the drum ($20,000 with a 5-year life), and (3) the machine parts excluding the drum ($100,000 – $8,000 – $20,000 = $72,000 with a 10-year life). Thus, first-year straight-line depreciation expense is $13,200 [($72,000 ÷ 10 years) + ($20,000 ÷ 5 years) + ($8,000 ÷ 4 years)].
Answer (A) is incorrect. The amount of $10,000 results from not separately depreciating the costs of the drum and the inspection. Answer (B) is incorrect. The amount of $10,800 equals $108,000 divided by 10 years. Answer (C) is incorrect. The amount of $12,000 equals $120,000 divided by 10 years.

Use Gleim **EQE Test Prep** Software Download for interactive study and performance analysis.

STUDY UNIT NINE
INTANGIBLE ASSETS AND
RESEARCH AND DEVELOPMENT COSTS

Accounting for Intangible Assets

An **intangible asset** is a nonfinancial asset without physical substance. If an intangible asset is acquired individually or with other assets but not in a business combination, it is initially recognized and measured at fair value. The costs of **internally developed intangible assets** and goodwill are expensed when incurred if they are not specifically identifiable, have indeterminate lives, or are inherent in a continuing business and related to the entity as a whole.

The **useful life** of an asset is the period during which it is expected to contribute either directly or indirectly to the future cash flows of the reporting entity. An intangible asset with a **finite useful life** to the reporting entity is amortized over that useful life. If the useful life is finite but not precisely known, the best estimate is the amortization period. The **pattern of consumption of economic benefits**, if it can be reliably ascertained, is reflected in the method of amortization. Otherwise, the **straight-line method** is required. The **amortizable amount** equals the amount initially assigned minus the residual value, which is the estimated fair value to the entity at the end of the asset's useful life, minus disposal costs. The **residual value** is zero unless a third party has committed to purchase the asset or it can be ascertained from an exchange transaction in an existing market for the asset that is expected to exist at the end of the useful life. The useful life should be reevaluated each reporting period.

An amortized intangible asset is reviewed for **impairment** when events or changes in circumstances indicate that its carrying amount may not be recoverable. An impairment loss is recognized only if the carrying amount is **not recoverable** and is greater than the asset's fair value. Thus, the test for recognition is met if the sum of the undiscounted expected future cash flows from the asset is less than the carrying amount. The measure of any loss recognized is the excess of that carrying amount over the fair value. This loss is irreversible.

Determination of an Impairment Loss
1. Events or changes in circumstances indicate a possible loss
2. Carrying amount > sum of undiscounted cash flows
3. Loss = carrying amount – fair value

An intangible asset with an **indefinite useful life** is not amortized. A nonamortized intangible asset is tested for impairment at least annually. It is tested more often if events or changes in circumstances suggest that the asset may be impaired. However, the impairment test differs from that for amortized intangible assets. If the carrying amount exceeds the fair value of the asset, that excess is the recognized loss. This loss is irreversible.

Determination of an Impairment Loss
1.   Review for impairment
2.   Loss = carrying amount − fair value

Subsequent Accounting for Goodwill

Goodwill is recognized only in a business combination. It is "an asset representing the future economic benefits arising from other assets acquired in a business combination that are not individually identified and separately recognized." Study Unit 24 covers the accounting for the initial recognition of goodwill.

Goodwill is not amortized. However, goodwill of a reporting unit is tested for impairment each year at the same time. A reporting unit is an operating segment or one of its components. A component is a reporting unit if (1) it is a business for which discrete financial information is available and (2) segment management regularly reviews its operating results. As part of testing goodwill for impairment, consolidated assets and liabilities must be assigned to reporting units. The assignment is made to the reporting unit if the assets and liabilities relate to its operations and are included in its fair value, and if the unit will benefit from the business combination. The assignment, in principle, should be done in the same manner as the determination of goodwill in a business combination. Thus, the **fair value of the acquired business** included in the reporting unit must be determined. An **excess** of this amount over the fair value of the net assets assigned to the reporting unit is the goodwill initially assigned. If no acquired assets or assumed liabilities are assigned to a reporting unit, the goodwill to be assigned equals the increase in the fair value of the reporting unit from the combination.

Goodwill Assigned to a Reporting Unit
FV of reporting unit − FV of net assets assigned

Potential impairment of goodwill exists only if the carrying amount (including goodwill) of a reporting unit is greater than its fair value. The goodwill impairment test includes an optional qualitative test and a two-step quantitative test. Prior to performing the quantitative goodwill impairment test, the entity may elect to make a **qualitative assessment**. Thus, the entity may choose to assess whether qualitative factors indicate that it is more likely than not (probability > 50%) that the fair value of the reporting unit is less than its carrying amount. The qualitative assessment considers relevant events and circumstances. Among many others, they may include (1) macroeconomic, industry, and market conditions; (2) cost increases; (3) overall financial performance; (4) other entity-specific events; and (5) events affecting the reporting unit. The quantitative test need not be performed if the qualitative assessment does not indicate impairment. If a potential impairment is found, the following two-step **quantitative test** is performed to determine any goodwill impairment.

- The fair value of the reporting unit is calculated and compared with its carrying amount (including goodwill). If the fair value exceeds the carrying amount, no impairment loss is recognized.
- If the fair value is less than the carrying amount, the **implied fair value** of reporting-unit goodwill is estimated by assigning the fair value of the reporting unit to its assets and liabilities. The excess of reporting-unit fair value over the sum of the amounts assigned equals the implied fair value. If the carrying amount of reporting-unit goodwill exceeds its implied fair value, an impairment loss is recognized. It equals any excess of that carrying amount over the implied fair value. This loss is **nonreversible**.

Determination of Impairment Loss
1. Carrying amount of reporting unit > its fair value
2. Carrying amount of reporting-unit goodwill > its implied fair value
3. Loss = excess in 2

EXAMPLE: On January 1, Year 1, Par Co. purchased Sub Co. for $200,000,000 and recognized $20,000,000 of goodwill. Sub is a reporting unit. On December 31, Year 2, the following information is available about Sub:

Carrying amount of net assets (including goodwill)	$190,000,000
Fair value	150,000,000
Fair value of net assets (excluding goodwill)	135,000,000

Par elected not to make a preliminary qualitative assessment of goodwill impairment. Instead, it performed the quantitative test. The carrying amount ($190,000,000) exceeds the fair value ($150,000,000). Thus, goodwill may be impaired.

The implied fair value of goodwill is $15,000,000 ($150,000,000 – $135,000,000). The impairment loss is $5,000,000 ($20,000,000 carrying amount of goodwill – $15,000,000 implied fair value).

Patents and Other Intangible Assets

An intangible asset distinct from goodwill is recognized if it arises from contractual or other legal rights even if it is not separable. If this criterion is not met, an intangible asset distinct from goodwill may still be recognized if it is separable. Examples of intangible assets meeting the **contractual-legal criterion** include (1) trade names and trademarks, (2) Internet domain names, (3) noncompetition agreements, (4) order or production backlogs, (5) artistic works, (6) licensing agreements, (7) service or supply contracts, (8) leases, (9) broadcast rights, (10) franchises, (11) patents, (12) computer software, and (13) trade secrets. The **separability criterion** may be met even if the intangible asset is not individually separable if it can be sold, transferred, licensed, rented, or exchanged along with a related item. Examples of intangible assets meeting the separability criterion include (1) customer lists, (2) noncontractual customer relationships, (3) unpatented technology, and (4) databases. An assembled workforce is an example of an item not recognizable as an intangible asset distinct from goodwill.

A **patent** is a right conferred upon application to and approval by the federal government (U.S. Patent and Trademark Office) for the exclusive use of an invention. An invention must (1) be for a patentable subject, (2) have utility, and (3) be novel and not obvious to a knowledgeable person. The right is given for a nonrenewable period, but an effective extension sometimes can be provided by obtaining a new patent that involves slight modifications of the old. **Utility patents** (the most common category) have a legal life ending 20 years after the application was filed. A design patent (as opposed to an invention) has a duration of 14 years. The **fair value** of a patent derives from the monopoly of a product or process. The initial capitalized cost of a **purchased patent** is normally the fair value of the consideration given, that is, its purchase price plus incidental costs, such as registration and attorneys' fees. **Internally developed patents** are less likely to be capitalized because related R&D costs must be expensed when incurred. Thus, only relatively minor costs can be capitalized, for example, patent registration fees and legal fees. Subsequent to the grant of a patent, its owner may need to bring or defend a **suit for patent infringement**. The net costs of successful litigation are capitalized because they will benefit future periods. The costs of unsuccessful litigation (damages, attorneys' fees) are expensed.

The **Copyright Act** provides broad rights to intellectual property consisting of "original works of authorship in any tangible medium of expression, now known or later developed." An **author's copyright** is for life plus 70 years. A **publisher's copyright** is for the earlier to expire of 95 years from publication or 120 years from creation. Among the works protected are literary, musical, and dramatic works; sound recordings; motion pictures and other audiovisual works; and computer software. The copyright holder has **exclusive rights** to reproduce, distribute, perform, display, and prepare derivative works from copyrighted material. **Limited exceptions** are allowed for library or archive reproduction and fair use for purposes of comment, criticism, news coverage, teaching, scholarship, or research. A **trademark** or other mark (e.g., a service mark or certification mark) is a distinctive design, word, symbol, mark, picture, etc. It is affixed to a product or placed on a tag, label, container, or associated display and adopted by the seller or manufacturer to identify it. A **trade name** is usually regarded as referring to a business and the goodwill it has generated, for example, Intel. Trademarks (but not trade names unless they also are trademarks or service marks) can be registered with the U.S. Patent and Trademark Office for **renewable periods of 10 years**. Registration requires that the trademark be in use or that the registrant intend to put it in use within 6 months. Trademarks and related property are safeguarded as long as they are used continuously.

Franchises

Franchise fees may be capitalized or expensed, depending upon the nature of the fees. The initial franchise fee includes the cost of establishing the franchise relationship and providing some initial services. The franchisee capitalizes this fee and amortizes the cost over the estimated useful life if it is finite. The continuing franchise fee includes the consideration paid for the continuing rights granted by the franchise arrangement and for general or specific services during its life. The franchisee expenses this fee as incurred. The franchisor recognizes franchise fee revenue at the earliest time that the franchisor has substantially performed or satisfied all material services or conditions relating to the franchise arrangement. The earliest time ordinarily is the beginning of operations by the franchisee, unless the franchisor can demonstrate that substantial performance of all obligations occurred previously.

R&D

Research is planned search or critical investigation aimed at discovery of new knowledge with the hope that such knowledge will aid in the development of a new product or service (product), or a new process or technique (process), or in the significant improvement of an existing product or process. **Development** is the translation of research findings or other knowledge into a plan or design for a new product or process or for the significant improvement of an existing product or process, whether for sale or use.

R&D costs are charged to expense when incurred. (However, this rule does not apply to R&D **conducted for others**. It also does not apply to assets acquired in a **business combination** that are used in R&D. These assets are initially recognized and measured at fair value even if they have no alternative use.) Disclosure of total R&D costs charged to expense is required for each period for which an income statement is presented. R&D costs include (1) materials, equipment, and facilities; (2) salaries, wages, and other related personnel costs; (3) costs of externally acquired intangible assets; (4) contract services; and (5) a reasonable allocation of indirect costs. The costs of materials, equipment, facilities, and intangible assets purchased from others that have alternative future uses (including other R&D projects) are capitalized when acquired or produced. These costs are expensed as R&D when consumed or depreciated as part of R&D activities. The costs of assets that are acquired or produced for a specific R&D project and that have no alternative future uses are expensed.

Activities typically classified as R&D (unless conducted for others under a contractual arrangement) include (1) laboratory research aimed at discovery of new knowledge; (2) searching for applications of new research findings or other knowledge; (3) conceptual formulation and design of possible product or process alternatives; (4) testing in search for or evaluation of product or process alternatives; (5) modification of the formulation or design of a product or process; (6) design, construction, and testing of preproduction prototypes and models; (7) design of tools, jigs, molds, and dies involving new technology; (8) design, construction, and operation of a pilot plant that is not of a scale economically feasible to the entity for commercial production; and (9) engineering activity required to advance the design of a product until it meets specific functional and economic requirements and is ready for manufacture.

Activities typically not classified as R&D include (1) engineering follow-through in an early phase of commercial production; (2) quality control during commercial production, including routine testing of products; (3) troubleshooting in connection with breakdowns during commercial production; (4) routine, ongoing efforts to refine, enrich, or otherwise improve upon the qualities of an existing product; (5) adaptation of an existing capability to a particular requirement or customer's need as part of a continuing commercial activity; (6) seasonal or other periodic design changes to existing products; (7) routine design of tools, jigs, molds and dies; (8) activity, including design and construction engineering, related to the construction, relocation, rearrangement, or start-up of facilities or equipment other than pilot plants and facilities or equipment whose sole use is for a particular R&D project; and (9) legal work in connection with patent applications or litigation, and the sale or licensing of patents.

Computer Software and Other Costs

The guidance addressing the accounting for the costs of computer software to be sold, leased, or otherwise marketed applies to software developed internally or purchased. All costs are expensed as R&D until technological feasibility has been established for the product. Costs incurred after technological feasibility is established are capitalized and amortized. Annual amortization is the greater of (1) total capitalized cost times the revenue ratio (annual gross software revenue ÷ total projected gross revenue) or (2) straight-line amortization over the estimated economic life of the software. Subsequent reporting is at the lower of unamortized cost or net realizable value. Capitalization ends when the product is available for general release. Costs incurred to produce the product for sale (e.g., duplication of software, training materials, and packaging) are capitalized as inventory. The guidance for the costs of computer software developed or obtained for internal use requires that software costs be expensed as incurred during the preliminary project stage. During the application development stage, internal and external costs are capitalized. During the post-implementation/operation stage, internal and external training and maintenance costs are expensed as incurred.

Organization costs are those incurred in the formation of a business entity. They include payments to promoters, legal and accounting fees, and costs of registering with the state of incorporation. **Start-up costs** are incurred to (1) investigate the creation or acquisition of an active trade or business, (2) create an active trade or business, or (3) engage in activities for profit prior to when they are expected to become an active trade or business. For financial accounting purposes, nongovernmental entities must expense such costs as incurred.

Advertising costs must be expensed, either as incurred or when advertising first occurs. The primary costs are production and communication. However, certain **direct response advertising** costs should be capitalized (deferred) if the primary purpose is to generate sales from customers who respond specifically to the advertising, and probable future economic benefits result.

Differences between GAAP and IFRS

Under IFRS:

- An intangible asset must be recognized only if (1) it is **probable** that the entity will receive the asset's expected economic benefits, and (2) the **cost** is reliably measurable.
- For the purpose of impairment testing, **goodwill** is allocated to the entity's **cash-generating units (CGUs)** that will benefit from the business combination. A CGU is the lowest level at which goodwill is monitored and must not be larger than an operating segment. The test for impairment of a CGU to which goodwill has been allocated is whether the carrying amount of the CGU (including allocated goodwill) exceeds its **recoverable amount** (greater of fair value minus costs to sell or value in use). Thus, the test has one step. An impairment loss for a CGU is allocated first to reduce allocated goodwill to zero and then pro rata to other assets of the CGU.
- An impairment loss for an asset (except goodwill) may be reversed if a change in the estimates used to measure the recoverable amount has occurred.
- The test for impairment of assets other than goodwill also has one step: whether an asset's carrying amount is greater than its recoverable amount.
- The **revaluation model** may be used for intangible assets if they are traded in active markets. (See Study Unit 7.)
- Development results in **recognition of an intangible asset** if the entity can demonstrate the (1) technical feasibility of completion of the asset, (2) intent to complete, (3) ability to use or sell the asset, (4) way in which it will generate probable future economic benefits, (5) availability of resources to complete and use or sell the asset, and (6) ability to measure reliably expenditures attributable to the asset.
- **Advertising costs** generally are expensed as incurred.

QUESTIONS

9.1 Accounting for Intangible Assets

1. Amortization of intangible assets, such as copyrights or patents, is the accounting process of

    A. Determining the cash flow from operations for the current period.

    B. Systematically allocating the cost of the intangible asset to the periods of use.

    C. Accumulating a fund for the replacement of the asset at the end of its useful life.

    D. Systematically reflecting the change in general price levels over the current period.

Answer (B) is correct. *(CMA, adapted)*
    REQUIRED: The meaning of amortization.
    DISCUSSION: Amortization is a means of allocating an initial cost to the periods that benefit from that cost. It is similar to depreciation, a term associated with long-lived tangible assets, and depletion, which is associated with natural resources.
    Answer (A) is incorrect. Amortization is an allocation process that is not cash-based. Answer (C) is incorrect. No funding is associated with amortization. Answer (D) is incorrect. Amortization has nothing to do with changes in price levels.

2. A recognized intangible asset is amortized over its useful life

    A. Unless the pattern of consumption of the economic benefits of the asset is not reliably determinable.

    B. If that life is determined to be finite.

    C. Unless the precise length of that life is not known.

    D. If that life is indefinite but not infinite.

Answer (B) is correct. *(Publisher, adapted)*
    REQUIRED: The circumstances in which a recognized intangible asset is amortized.
    DISCUSSION: A recognized intangible asset is amortized over its useful life if that useful life is finite, that is, unless the useful life is determined to be indefinite. The useful life of an intangible asset is indefinite if no foreseeable limit exists on the period over which it will contribute, directly or indirectly, to the reporting entity's cash flows.
    Answer (A) is incorrect. An intangible asset is amortizable if its useful life is finite. If the pattern of consumption of the economic benefits of such an intangible asset is not reliably determinable, the straight-line amortization method is applied. Answer (C) is incorrect. If the precise length of the useful life is not known, an intangible asset with a finite useful life is amortized over the best estimate of its useful life. Answer (D) is incorrect. A recognized intangible asset is not amortized if its useful life is indefinite.

3. Which of the following assets, if any, acquired this year in an exchange transaction is (are) potentially amortizable?

	Goodwill	Trademarks
A.	No	No
B.	No	Yes
C.	Yes	Yes
D.	Yes	No

Answer (B) is correct. *(CPA, adapted)*
    REQUIRED: The currently acquired assets that are potentially amortizable.
    DISCUSSION: Goodwill is tested for impairment at least annually but is never amortized. Trademarks, however, may be amortized, but only if they have finite useful lives.
    Answer (A) is incorrect. Trademarks are amortizable. Answer (C) is incorrect. Only trademarks with finite useful lives are amortizable. Answer (D) is incorrect. Goodwill is not amortizable, but trademarks may be amortized.

4. In accordance with generally accepted accounting principles, which of the following methods of amortization is required for amortizable intangible assets if the pattern of consumption of economic benefits is not reliably determinable?

    A. Sum-of-the-years'-digits.

    B. Straight-line.

    C. Units-of-production.

    D. Double-declining-balance.

Answer (B) is correct. *(CPA, adapted)*
    REQUIRED: The method of amortization of intangible assets if the pattern of consumption of economic benefits is not reliably determinable.
    DISCUSSION: The default method of amortization of intangible assets is the straight-line method.
    Answer (A) is incorrect. Sum-of-the-years'-digits may be used only if it is reliably determined to reflect the pattern of consumption of the economic benefits of the intangible asset. Answer (C) is incorrect. Units-of-production may be used only if it is reliably determined to reflect the pattern of consumption of the economic benefits of the intangible asset. Answer (D) is incorrect. Double-declining-balance may be used only if it is reliably determined to reflect the pattern of consumption of the economic benefits of the intangible asset.

5. Intangible assets acquired singly from other enterprises or individuals should be recorded at their cost at the date of acquisition. Cost may not be measured by which of the following?

A. Net carrying amount of the previous owner.

B. Amount of cash paid.

C. Present value of amounts to be paid for liabilities incurred.

D. Fair value of other assets distributed.

Answer (A) is correct. *(Publisher, adapted)*
REQUIRED: The method not allowed to measure the cost of intangible assets.
DISCUSSION: If cash is the consideration given in an exchange transaction, the cash paid is the measure of the transaction. If noncash consideration (noncash assets, liabilities incurred, or equity interests issued) is given, the measurement is based on the more reliably measurable of the fair value of the consideration given or the fair value of the asset or net assets acquired. Furthermore, the only objective of present value used in initial recognition and fresh-start measurements is to estimate fair value in the absence of a market price. Consequently, only the carrying amount of the previous owner is not a proper measurement of cost.
Answer (B) is incorrect. Amount of cash paid is an allowable measurement of fair value depending on the consideration given. Answer (C) is incorrect. Present value of amounts to be paid for liabilities incurred is an allowable measurement of fair value depending on the consideration given. Answer (D) is incorrect. Fair value of other assets distributed is an allowable measurement of fair value depending on the consideration given.

6. Which of the following is not a consideration in determining the useful life of an intangible asset?

A. Legal, regulatory, or contractual provisions.

B. Provisions for renewal or extension.

C. Expected actions of competitors.

D. Initial cost.

Answer (D) is correct. *(CPA, adapted)*
REQUIRED: The item not a consideration in determining the useful life of an intangible asset.
DISCUSSION: Initial cost is not a factor relevant to estimating the useful life of an intangible asset because it has no causal connection with the asset's contribution to the future cash flows of the reporting entity. The relevant factors for determining the useful life of an intangible asset include the expected use of the asset; the useful life of a related asset or assets; legal, regulatory, or contractual provisions that may limit the useful life or that may permit renewal or extension without substantial cost; economic factors (e.g., obsolescence, competition, or demand); and expenditures for maintenance.
Answer (A) is incorrect. The relevant factors for determining the useful life of an intangible asset include legal, regulatory, or contractual provisions that may limit the useful life or that may permit renewal or extension without substantial cost. Answer (B) is incorrect. The relevant factors for determining the useful life of an intangible asset include provisions that may limit the useful life or that may permit renewal or extension without substantial cost. Answer (C) is incorrect. The relevant factors for determining the useful life of an intangible asset include economic factors (e.g., obsolescence, competition, or demand).

7. When should leaseholds and leasehold improvements be amortized over different periods?

A. When the useful life of the leasehold improvement is less than the term of the leasehold.

B. When the term of the leasehold exceeds 40 years.

C. When the term of the leasehold is less than the useful life of the leasehold improvement.

D. If the company is in the development stage.

Answer (A) is correct. *(Publisher, adapted)*
REQUIRED: The reason the amortization periods of leaseholds and leasehold improvements may differ.
DISCUSSION: A leasehold is the property under lease. Leasehold improvements should be amortized over their useful life if it is less than the term of the lease. But if the useful life is greater than the term of the lease, the improvement should be amortized over the life of the lease because the property will revert to the lessor at the end of the lease. If an option exists for renewal of the lease and the lessee intends to renew, the leasehold improvements should be amortized over the option period as well, but not to exceed their useful life.
Answer (B) is incorrect. A leasehold should be amortized in the same way as other similar property. There is no minimum or maximum period. Answer (C) is incorrect. When the term of the lease is less than the improvement's useful life, amortization should occur over the shorter period. Answer (D) is incorrect. Development stage companies and established operating companies apply the same GAAP.

9.2 Subsequent Accounting for Goodwill

8. On January 1, Year 1, Chertco acquired an intangible asset for $500,000 and properly began amortizing it using the straight-line method over its estimated useful life of 10 years. The asset has no residual value. At December 31, Year 4, a significant change in the business climate caused Chertco to assess the recoverability of the carrying amount of the intangible asset. Chertco estimated that the undiscounted future net cash inflows from the intangible asset would be $325,000 and that its fair value was $275,000. Chertco must apply the principles of accounting for the impairment of long-lived assets. Accordingly, for the year ended December 31, Year 4, Chertco should recognize an impairment loss of

A. $225,000

B. $50,000

C. $25,000

D. $0

Answer (D) is correct. *(Publisher, adapted)*
REQUIRED: The impairment loss.
DISCUSSION: Events or changes in circumstances may indicate that the entity should assess the recoverability of the carrying amount of a recognized intangible asset subject to the principles of accounting for the impairment of long-lived assets. In that case, the entity should estimate the undiscounted future net cash inflows to be generated by the asset. If these cash flows are less than the carrying amount, an impairment loss, measured by the excess of the carrying amount over the fair value, is recognized. However, Chertco should recognize no impairment loss because the estimated undiscounted future net cash inflows ($325,000) exceed the carrying amount {$500,000 – [($500,000 ÷ 10 years) × 4 years] = $300,000}.
Answer (A) is incorrect. The amount of $225,000 is based on the assumption that the asset is not amortizable. Answer (B) is incorrect. The amount of $50,000 is the excess of the estimated undiscounted future net cash inflows over the fair value. Answer (C) is incorrect. The amount of $25,000 (carrying amount – fair value) would be the impairment loss if the carrying amount were not fully recoverable.

9. Which of the following costs of goodwill should be capitalized and amortized?

	Maintaining Goodwill	Developing Goodwill
A.	Yes	No
B.	No	No
C.	Yes	Yes
D.	No	Yes

Answer (B) is correct. *(CPA, adapted)*
REQUIRED: The costs of goodwill that should be capitalized and amortized.
DISCUSSION: Goodwill is not amortized. Moreover, the cost of internally developing, maintaining, or restoring intangible assets (including goodwill) that (1) are not specifically identifiable, (2) have indeterminate useful lives, or (3) are inherent in a continuing business and related to an entity as a whole should be expensed as incurred.
Answer (A) is incorrect. Costs of maintaining goodwill should not be capitalized. Answer (C) is incorrect. Costs of maintaining and developing goodwill should not be capitalized. Answer (D) is incorrect. Costs of developing goodwill should not be capitalized.

10. Dire Co. acquired Wall Co. in a transaction that resulted in recognition of goodwill having an expected 10-year benefit period. However, Dire plans to make additional expenditures to maintain goodwill for a total of 40 years. What amounts should be capitalized and over how many years should they be amortized?

	Amounts Capitalized	Amortization Period
A.	Recognized goodwill only	0 years
B.	Recognized goodwill only	40 years
C.	Recognized goodwill and maintenance costs	10 years
D.	Recognized goodwill and maintenance costs	40 years

Answer (A) is correct. *(CPA, adapted)*
REQUIRED: The costs to be capitalized and the amortization period.
DISCUSSION: Goodwill from a business combination must be capitalized. Subsequent to initial recognition, goodwill is tested for impairment but not amortized. But the cost of developing, maintaining, or restoring intangible assets (including goodwill) that (1) are not specifically identifiable, (2) have indeterminate lives, or (3) are inherent in a continuing business and related to an entity as a whole should be expensed as incurred.
Answer (B) is incorrect. The goodwill acquired externally is not amortized. Answer (C) is incorrect. The goodwill acquired externally is not amortized, and the costs of maintaining goodwill should be expensed as incurred. Answer (D) is incorrect. The goodwill acquired externally is not amortized, and the costs of maintaining goodwill should be expensed as incurred, no matter the length of the period.

11. A company reported $6 million of goodwill in last year's statement of financial position. How should the company account for the reported goodwill in the current year?

A. Determine the current year's amortizable amount and report the current year's amortization expense.

B. Determine whether the fair value of the reporting unit is greater than the carrying amount and report a gain on goodwill in the income statement.

C. Determine whether the fair value of the reporting unit is less than the carrying amount and report an impairment loss on goodwill in the income statement.

D. Determine whether the fair value of the reporting unit is greater than the carrying amount and report the recovery of any previous impairment in the income statement.

Answer (C) is correct. *(CPA, adapted)*
REQUIRED: The current accounting for goodwill reported in the prior year.
DISCUSSION: The goodwill impairment test includes an optional qualitative test and a two-step quantitative test. Potential impairment of goodwill exists only if the carrying amount of a reporting unit is greater than its fair value. The entity then calculates the implied fair value of reporting-unit goodwill. If the carrying amount of reporting-unit goodwill exceeds its implied fair value, an impairment loss is recognized.
Answer (A) is incorrect. Goodwill is not amortized. Answer (B) is incorrect. Goodwill is recognized only after applying the acquisition method to account for a business combination. Thus, recognition of impairment but not appreciation is allowed. Answer (D) is incorrect. An impairment of goodwill is not reversible.

12. On January 2, Year 1, Paye Co. acquired Shef Co. in a business combination that resulted in recognition of goodwill of $200,000 having an expected benefit period of 10 years. Shef is treated as a reporting unit, and the entire amount of the recognized goodwill is assigned to it. During the first quarter of Year 1, Shef spent an additional $80,000 on expenditures designed to maintain goodwill. Due to these expenditures, at December 31, Year 1, Shef estimated that the benefit period of goodwill was 40 years. In its consolidated December 31, Year 1, balance sheet, what amount should Paye report as goodwill?

A. $180,000

B. $200,000

C. $252,000

D. $280,000

Answer (B) is correct. *(CPA, adapted)*
REQUIRED: The amount of goodwill in the balance sheet.
DISCUSSION: Goodwill is not recorded except when an acquirer obtains control of a business. Thus, only the $200,000 recognized at the acquisition date should be recorded as goodwill. It should not be amortized but should be tested for impairment at the reporting-unit level. The facts given suggest that the fair value of the reporting unit (Shef) is not less than its carrying amount. Hence, no impairment of goodwill has occurred, and goodwill is unchanged at $200,000. Moreover, the cost of internally developing, maintaining, or restoring intangible assets (including goodwill) that are not specifically identifiable, have indeterminate useful lives, or are inherent in a continuing business and related to an entity as a whole should be expensed as incurred.
Answer (A) is incorrect. The amount of $180,000 results when goodwill is amortized on the straight-line basis over 10 years. Answer (C) is incorrect. The amount of $252,000 results from amortizing an additional $80,000 of expenditures to maintain goodwill over 10 years. Answer (D) is incorrect. The amount of $280,000 results from adding $80,000 of expenditures for the maintenance of goodwill.

13. What is the proper treatment of the recorded goodwill when an entity disposes of a portion of a reporting unit that constitutes a stand-alone acquired business?

A. All of the carrying amount of the goodwill of the reporting unit should be considered part of the cost of the assets sold.

B. The total carrying amount of the goodwill acquired with the business should be considered part of the cost of the assets sold.

C. Goodwill cannot be considered sold; it should be written off as a loss.

D. Goodwill cannot be sold; it should be amortized over its original useful life.

Answer (B) is correct. *(Publisher, adapted)*
REQUIRED: The true statement about goodwill when a portion of a reporting unit is sold.
DISCUSSION: If part of a reporting unit is to be disposed of and that part constitutes a business, goodwill related to the business is included in the carrying amount to be disposed of. The goodwill of the business and the goodwill retained by the reporting unit are determined based on relative fair values. However, when the business was not integrated with the other activities of the reporting unit, for example, because it is operated as a stand-alone entity, no allocation of the goodwill acquired with the business is made, and its carrying amount should be included in the carrying amount of the business to be disposed of.
Answer (A) is incorrect. The carrying amount of the goodwill acquired with the business should be considered sold. Answer (C) is incorrect. Goodwill can be considered sold as part of the business. Answer (D) is incorrect. Goodwill can be sold and cannot ever be amortized.

14. An entire acquired entity is sold. The goodwill remaining from the acquisition should be

    A. Included in the carrying amount of the net assets sold.

    B. Charged to retained earnings of the current period.

    C. Expensed in the period sold.

    D. Charged to retained earnings of prior periods.

Answer (A) is correct. *(Publisher, adapted)*
    REQUIRED: The accounting for goodwill when an acquired entity is sold.
    DISCUSSION: When a reporting unit is disposed of in its entirety, goodwill of that reporting unit (to the extent an impairment loss has not been recognized) is included in the carrying amount of the reporting unit to determine the gain or loss on disposal. Consequently, the unimpaired goodwill of each reporting unit of the acquired entity is included in the total carrying amount of that entity.
    Answer (B) is incorrect. Unimpaired goodwill of a reporting unit disposed of in its entirety is included in its carrying amount. Answer (C) is incorrect. Unimpaired goodwill is treated as an asset in accounting for the disposition. Answer (D) is incorrect. A prior-period adjustment is made only to correct an error.

9.3 Patents and Other Intangible Assets

15. A purchased utility patent has a remaining legal life of 15 years. It should be

    A. Expensed in the year of acquisition.

    B. Amortized over 15 years regardless of its useful life.

    C. Amortized over its useful life if less than 15 years.

    D. Amortized over 40 years.

Answer (C) is correct. *(CPA, adapted)*
    REQUIRED: The period over which a patent should be amortized.
    DISCUSSION: An intangible asset should be amortized over its useful life if that life is finite. A utility patent (the most common category) issued by the federal government after June 1995 is valid and legally enforceable for 20 years from the date of application. Thus, the useful life is limited by legal provisions, and the patent (an intangible asset) is therefore amortizable because its useful life is finite.
    Answer (A) is incorrect. An intangible asset acquired from another should be recorded as an asset. Answer (B) is incorrect. The amortization period is not to exceed the useful life. Answer (D) is incorrect. The remaining legal life of the patent is only 15 years.

16. Grayson Co. incurred significant costs in defending its patent rights. Which of the following is the appropriate treatment of the related litigation costs?

    A. Litigation costs would be capitalized regardless of the outcome of the litigation.

    B. Litigation costs would be expensed regardless of the outcome of the litigation.

    C. Litigation costs would be capitalized if the patent right is successfully defended.

    D. Litigation costs would be capitalized only if the patent was purchased rather than internally developed.

Answer (C) is correct. *(CPA, adapted)*
    REQUIRED: The accounting for litigation costs related to defending patent rights.
    DISCUSSION: Subsequent to the grant of a patent, its owner may need to bring or defend a suit for patent infringement. The unrecovered costs of successful litigation are capitalized because they will benefit future periods. They are amortized over the shorter of the remaining legal life or the estimated useful life of the patent. The costs of unsuccessful litigation (damages, attorneys' fees) are expensed. An unsuccessful suit also indicates that the unamortized cost of the patent has no value and should be recognized as a loss.
    Answer (A) is incorrect. The costs of unsuccessful litigation are expensed. Answer (B) is incorrect. The costs of successful litigation are capitalized. Answer (D) is incorrect. Whether the costs of litigation are capitalized does not depend on whether the patent was purchased or developed internally. This distinction is significant only for measurement at initial recognition. The costs of purchase but not internal development are capitalized under U.S. GAAP.

17. Espion Corp. bought Patent X for $80,000 and Patent Z for $120,000. Espion also paid acquisition costs of $10,000 for Patent X and $14,000 for Patent Z. Both patents were challenged in legal actions. Espion paid $40,000 in legal fees for a successful defense of Patent X and $60,000 in legal fees for an unsuccessful defense of Patent Z. What amounts should Espion capitalize for patents?

A. $324,000

B. $224,000

C. $130,000

D. $90,000

Answer (C) is correct. *(CPA, adapted)*
REQUIRED: The amount capitalized for patents.
DISCUSSION: When an intangible asset is acquired externally, it should be recorded at its cost at the date of acquisition. Cost is measured by the more reliably determinable of the fair value of the consideration given or the fair value of the net assets acquired. Moreover, an exchange transaction for which the consideration is cash is measured by the amount paid. Legal fees incurred in the successful defense of a patent should be capitalized as part of the cost of the patent and then amortized over its remaining useful life. Amortization is appropriate for a patent because its useful life is finite. Legal fees incurred in an unsuccessful defense should be expensed as the costs are incurred. Hence, the cost of Patent X ($80,000 + $10,000) and the legal fees for its successful defense ($40,000) should be capitalized in the amount of $130,000. The costs associated with Patent Z should be written off immediately. The unsuccessful defense suggests that no asset exists.
Answer (A) is incorrect. The amount of $324,000 includes all costs associated with Patent Z. Answer (B) is incorrect. The amount of $224,000 equals the total acquisition costs for Patents X and Z but excludes legal fees. Answer (D) is incorrect. The amount of $90,000 excludes the legal fees for a successful defense of Patent X.

18. On January 2, Year 1, Valhalla Corp. purchased a utility patent for a new consumer product for $180,000. At the time of purchase, the patent was valid for 15 years. However, the patent's useful life was estimated to be only 10 years due to the competitive nature of the product, with no residual value. On December 31, Year 4, the product was permanently withdrawn from sale under governmental order because of a potential health hazard in the product. Thus, no future positive cash flows will result from use of the patent, and its fair value is zero. What amount should Valhalla charge against income during Year 4, assuming straight-line amortization is appropriately recorded at the end of each year?

A. $18,000

B. $108,000

C. $126,000

D. $144,000

Answer (C) is correct. *(CPA, adapted)*
REQUIRED: The amount charged against income when a product is permanently withdrawn from sale.
DISCUSSION: A patent is an amortizable intangible asset because its useful life is finite. The straight-line method of amortization is used if the pattern of consumption of the economic benefits cannot be reliably determined. Because the patent was written off at the end of Year 4, the amount charged against income is equal to amortization expense plus the carrying amount of the asset at the time of the write-off. Amortization expense is $18,000 ($180,000 cost ÷ 10 years useful life). The remaining carrying amount of the asset is $108,000 ($180,000 cost – 4 years of amortization expense). This amount reflects an impairment loss ($108,000 carrying amount – $0 fair value). It is calculated in accordance with the principles of accounting for the impairment of long-lived assets when (1) the carrying amount is not recoverable and (2) the fair value of the asset is zero. Thus, the amount charged against income is $126,000 ($18,000 + $108,000).
Answer (A) is incorrect. The amount of $18,000 includes only amortization expense. Answer (B) is incorrect. It includes only the carrying amount of the asset before recognition of the impairment loss. Answer (D) is incorrect. The amount of $144,000 is based on a 15-year useful life.

19. Freya Co. has two patents that have allegedly been infringed by competitors. After investigation, legal counsel informed Freya that it had a weak case for Patent P and a strong case for Patent Q. Freya incurred additional legal fees to stop infringement on Patent Q. Both patents have a remaining legal life of 8 years. How should Freya account for these legal costs incurred relating to the two patents?

A. Expense costs for Patent P and capitalize costs for Patent Q.

B. Expense costs for both Patent P and Patent Q.

C. Capitalize costs for both Patent P and Patent Q.

D. Capitalize costs for Patent P and expense costs for Patent Q.

Answer (A) is correct. *(CPA, adapted)*
REQUIRED: The accounting for legal costs incurred.
DISCUSSION: Legal fees incurred in a successful defense of a patent should be capitalized and amortized. Legal fees incurred in an unsuccessful defense should be expensed as incurred. Hence, Freya should expense costs for Patent P and capitalize costs for Patent Q.
Answer (B) is incorrect. Freya should capitalize costs for Patent Q. Answer (C) is incorrect. Freya should expense costs for Patent P. Answer (D) is incorrect. Freya should expense costs for Patent P and capitalize costs for Patent Q.

20. A company recently acquired a copyright that now has a remaining legal life of 30 years. The copyright initially had a 38-year useful life assigned to it. An analysis of market trends and consumer habits indicated that the copyrighted material will generate positive cash flows for approximately 25 years. What is the remaining useful life, if any, over which the company can amortize the copyright for accounting purposes?

  A. 0 years.

  B. 25 years.

  C. 30 years.

  D. 38 years.

Answer (B) is correct. *(CPA, adapted)*
  REQUIRED: The remaining useful life over which a copyright can be amortized for accounting purposes.
  DISCUSSION: The useful life of an asset is the period during which it is expected to contribute either directly or indirectly to the future cash flows of the reporting entity. An intangible asset with a finite useful life to the reporting entity is amortized over that useful life. Because the entity expects the copyrighted material to generate positive cash flows for approximately 25 years, the copyright is amortized over 25 years.
  Answer (A) is incorrect. An intangible asset is not amortized if it has an indefinite useful life. The copyright does not have an indefinite useful life. Answer (C) is incorrect. The remaining legal life is not the useful life of the copyright. Answer (D) is incorrect. The useful life should be reevaluated each reporting period. Thus, the initial useful life is subject to revision.

21. Northstar Co. acquired a registered trademark for $600,000. The trademark has a remaining legal life of 5 years but can be renewed every 10 years for a nominal fee. Northstar expects to renew the trademark indefinitely. What amount of amortization expense should Northstar record for the trademark in the current year?

  A. $0

  B. $15,000

  C. $40,000

  D. $120,000

Answer (A) is correct. *(CPA, adapted)*
  REQUIRED: The amortization expense for a trademark.
  DISCUSSION: A trademark or other mark (e.g., a service mark or certification mark) is a distinctive design, word, symbol, mark, picture, etc. It is affixed to a product or placed on a tag, label, container, or associated display and adopted by the seller or manufacturer to identify it. The trademark is expected to be renewed indefinitely. Thus, it has an indefinite useful life and is not amortized. Amortization is recorded only for an intangible asset with a finite useful life.
  Answer (B) is incorrect. The amount of $15,000 equals annual amortization over 40 years. Answer (C) is incorrect. The amount of $40,000 is the annual amortization over a 15-year useful life (5-year remaining legal life + the first 10-year renewal). Answer (D) is incorrect. The amount of $120,000 equals annual amortization over the 5-year remaining legal life.

9.4 Franchises

22. On January 2, Year 1, Fafnir Co. purchased a franchise with a finite useful life of 10 years for $50,000. An additional franchise fee of 3% of franchise operation revenues must be paid each year to the franchisor. Revenues from franchise operations amounted to $400,000 during Year 1. The pattern of consumption of benefits of the franchise is not reliably determinable, and the residual value is zero. In its December 31, Year 1, balance sheet, what amount should Fafnir report as an intangible asset-franchise?

  A. $33,000

  B. $43,800

  C. $45,000

  D. $50,000

Answer (C) is correct. *(CPA, adapted)*
  REQUIRED: The amount of the intangible asset that is recorded for a franchise.
  DISCUSSION: Intangible assets acquired other than in a business combination are initially recognized and measured based on their fair value. This amortizable cost should be based on the more reliably measurable of the fair value of the consideration given or the fair value of the assets acquired. Franchise fees are capitalized and amortized over the finite useful life. Absent information about the fair value of the assets acquired, the capitalizable amount equals the consideration given, that is, the initial fee and other expenditures necessary to acquire the franchise. Future franchise fees are expensed as incurred. Because the pattern of consumption of benefits of the franchise is not reliably determinable, the straight-line method of amortization should be used. Thus, given no residual value, the amount that should be reported as an intangible asset is $45,000 [$50,000 – ($50,000 ÷10)].
  Answer (A) is incorrect. The amount of $33,000 results from subtracting the additional franchise fee. Answer (B) is incorrect. The amount of $43,800 includes amortization of the additional franchise fee. Answer (D) is incorrect. The amount of $50,000 is the unamortized initial fee.

23. Helsing Co. bought a franchise from Anya Co. on January 1, Year 1, for $204,000. An independent consultant retained by Helsing estimated that the remaining useful life of the franchise was a finite period of 50 years and that the pattern of consumption of benefits of the franchise is not reliably determinable. Its unamortized cost on Anya's books on January 1, Year 1, was $68,000. What amount should be amortized for the year ended December 31, Year 1, assuming no residual value?

A. $5,100

B. $4,080

C. $3,400

D. $1,700

Answer (B) is correct. *(CPA, adapted)*

REQUIRED: The first-year amortization expense of the cost of a franchise.

DISCUSSION: A franchise is an intangible asset. The initial measurement of an intangible asset is at fair value. Thus, the amortizable cost should be based on the more reliably measurable of the fair value of the consideration given or the fair value of the assets acquired. If the useful life is finite, the intangible asset is amortized over that period. Moreover, if the consumption pattern of benefits of the intangible asset is not reliably determinable, the straight-line method of amortization is used. Accordingly, given no residual value, the amortization expense is $4,080 ($204,000 consideration given ÷ 50-year finite useful life).

Answer (A) is incorrect. The amount of $5,100 is based on a 40-year period. Answer (C) is incorrect. The amount of $3,400 is the difference between the $204,000 franchise price and Anya's $68,000 unamortized cost, divided by 40 years. Answer (D) is incorrect. The amount of $1,700 equals the unamortized cost on Anya's books amortized over 40 years.

24. On December 31, Year 1, Sigrid Corp. authorized Vortigern to operate as a franchisee for an initial franchise fee of $300,000. Of this amount, $120,000 was received upon signing the agreement, and the balance, represented by a note, is due in three annual payments of $60,000 each, beginning December 31, Year 2. The present value on December 31, Year 1, of the three annual payments appropriately discounted is $144,000. According to the agreement, the nonrefundable down payment represents a fair measure of the services already performed by Sigrid; however, substantial future services are required of Sigrid. Collectibility of the note is reasonably certain. In Sigrid's December 31, Year 1, balance sheet, unearned franchise fees from Vortigern's franchise should be reported as

A. $300,000

B. $264,000

C. $180,000

D. $144,000

Answer (D) is correct. *(CPA, adapted)*

REQUIRED: The amount at which the franchisor should report unearned franchise fees.

DISCUSSION: Franchise fee revenue ordinarily should be recognized at the earliest time when the franchisor has substantially performed or satisfied all material services or conditions relating to the franchise sale. The earliest time usually is the beginning of operations by the franchisee unless it can be demonstrated that substantial performance of all obligations occurred previously. Hence, Sigrid should recognize $120,000 of revenue. The note is a long-term receivable that should be reported at its present value. However, this amount ($144,000) should be recorded as unearned revenue because the franchisor has not substantially performed (completed the earning process).

Answer (A) is incorrect. The amount of $300,000 is the total undiscounted initial fee. Answer (B) is incorrect. The amount of $264,000 includes $120,000 for services already performed. Answer (C) is incorrect. The amount of $180,000 is the undiscounted total of the annual payments.

25. Each of Thaumatic Co.'s 42 new franchisees contracted to pay an initial franchise fee of $60,000. By December 31, Year 1, each franchisee had paid a nonrefundable $20,000 fee and signed a note to pay $20,000 principal plus the market rate of interest on December 31, Year 2, and December 31, Year 3. Experience indicates that two franchisees will default on the additional payments. Services for the initial fee will be performed in Year 2. What amount of net unearned franchise fees would Thaumatic report at December 31, Year 1?

A. $1,600,000

B. $2,420,000

C. $2,440,000

D. $2,520,000

Answer (C) is correct. *(CPA, adapted)*

REQUIRED: The net unearned franchise fees reported at year end by the franchisor.

DISCUSSION: Franchise fee revenue ordinarily should be recognized at the earliest time when the franchisor has substantially performed or satisfied all material services or conditions relating to the franchise sale. Thaumatic should not recognize revenue from initial franchise fees because the related services will not be performed until Year 2, and the earning process is therefore not complete. The franchisor should recognize the cash received (42 × $20,000 = $840,000), a net receivable for the principal amounts estimated to be collected (40 × $40,000 = $1,600,000), and unearned franchise fees ($840,000 + $1,600,000 = $2,440,000).

Answer (A) is incorrect. The principal amount that the franchisor estimates will be collected is $1,600,000. Answer (B) is incorrect. The amount of $2,420,000 omits the nonrefundable fee paid by one franchisee. Answer (D) is incorrect. The amount of $2,520,000 is based on the assumption that all franchisees will pay in full.

26. Which of the following should be expensed as incurred by the franchisee for a franchise with an estimated useful life of 10 years?

    A. Amount paid to the franchisor for the franchise.

    B. Periodic payments to a company, other than the franchisor, for that company's franchise.

    C. Legal fees paid to the franchisee's lawyers to obtain the franchise.

    D. Periodic payments to the franchisor based on the franchisee's revenues.

Answer (D) is correct. *(CPA, adapted)*
    REQUIRED: The payment that should be expensed as incurred by the franchisee.
    DISCUSSION: Payments under a franchise agreement made to a franchisor based on the franchisee's revenues do not create benefits in future periods and should not be treated as an asset. These payments should be treated as operating expenses in the period in which incurred.
    Answer (A) is incorrect. The amount paid as an initial franchise fee benefits future periods and should therefore be capitalized and amortized over the useful life of the franchise. Answer (B) is incorrect. Periodic payments to another franchise holder benefit future periods and should therefore be capitalized and amortized over the useful life of the franchise. Answer (C) is incorrect. Legal fees constitute a cost of acquiring the franchise. This cost benefits future periods and should therefore be capitalized and amortized over the useful life of the franchise.

9.5 R&D

27. Which one of the following is not considered a research and development activity?

    A. Laboratory research intended for the discovery of a new product.

    B. Testing in search of product processing alternatives.

    C. Modification of the design of a process.

    D. Periodic design changes to existing products.

Answer (D) is correct. *(CMA, adapted)*
    REQUIRED: The item not considered an R&D activity.
    DISCUSSION: R&D costs must be expensed as incurred. Research is planned search or critical investigation aimed at discovery of new knowledge with the hope that such knowledge will be useful in developing a new product or service or a new process or technique or in bringing about a significant improvement in an existing product or process. Development is the translation of research findings or other knowledge into a plan or design for a new product or process or for a significant improvement in an existing product or process whether intended for sale or use. Seasonal or other periodic design changes in existing products do not meet either of these definitions.
    Answer (A) is incorrect. Laboratory research aimed at discovery of a new product is an R&D activity. Answer (B) is incorrect. Testing in search of product or process alternatives is an R&D activity. Answer (C) is incorrect. Modification of the formulation or design of a product or process is an R&D activity.

28. Le Sud Co. made the following expenditures relating to product THX-1138:

- Legal costs to file a patent on the product – $10,000. Production of the finished product would not have been undertaken without the patent.
- Special equipment to be used solely for development of the product – $60,000. The equipment has no other use and has an estimated useful life of 4 years.
- Labor and material costs incurred in producing a prototype model – $200,000.
- Cost of testing the prototype – $80,000.

What is the total amount of costs that will be expensed when incurred?

    A. $280,000

    B. $295,000

    C. $340,000

    D. $350,000

Answer (C) is correct. *(CPA, adapted)*
    REQUIRED: The total amount of costs that will be expensed when incurred.
    DISCUSSION: R&D costs are expensed as incurred. R&D costs do not include legal work in connection with patent applications or litigation and the sale or licensing of patents from the definition of R&D. Thus, the legal costs of filing a patent should be capitalized. The company's R&D costs include the cost of equipment used solely for a specific project and those incurred for the design, construction, and testing of preproduction prototypes. Thus, the total amount of costs that will be expensed when incurred is $340,000 ($60,000 + $200,000 + $80,000).
    Answer (A) is incorrect. The amount of $280,000 omits the cost of the special equipment. Answer (B) is incorrect. The amount of $295,000 includes 1 year's straight-line depreciation on the special equipment instead of the full cost. Answer (D) is incorrect. The amount of $350,000 includes the legal costs of filing a patent.

29. During the current year, Beta Motor Co. incurred the following costs related to a new solar-powered car:

Salaries of laboratory employees researching how to build the new car	$250,000
Legal fees for the patent application for the new car	20,000
Engineering follow-up during the early stages of commercial production (the follow-up occurred during the current year)	50,000
Marketing research to promote the new car	30,000
Design, testing, and construction of a prototype	400,000

What amount should Beta Motor report as research and development expense in its income statement for the current year?

A. $250,000

B. $650,000

C. $720,000

D. $750,000

Answer (B) is correct. *(CPA, adapted)*
REQUIRED: The research and development (R&D) expense.
DISCUSSION: Salaries, wages, and other related costs of personnel engaged in R&D and the design, construction, and testing of preproduction prototypes and models are activities typically included in R&D. These costs are expensed when incurred. Thus, R&D expense for the current year is $650,000 ($250,000 + $400,000).
Answer (A) is incorrect. Costs for design, testing, and construction of a prototype are included in R&D costs and expensed when incurred. Answer (C) is incorrect. Legal work in connection with patent applications and engineering follow-through in an early phase of commercial production are not R&D activities. Answer (D) is incorrect. Legal work in connection with patent applications, engineering follow-through in an early phase of commercial production, and marketing research are not R&D activities.

30. During the current year, Narn Co. incurred the following costs:

Research and development services performed by Molari Corp. for Narn	$150,000
Design, construction, and testing of preproduction prototypes and models	200,000
Testing in search for new products of process alternatives	175,000

In its current-year income statement, what should Narn report as research and development expense?

A. $150,000

B. $200,000

C. $350,000

D. $525,000

Answer (D) is correct. *(CPA, adapted)*
REQUIRED: The R&D expense.
DISCUSSION: Research is planned search or critical investigation aimed at discovery of new knowledge useful in developing a new product, service, process, or technique, or in bringing about a significant improvement to an existing product, etc. Development is translation of research findings or other knowledge into a plan or design for a new or improved product or process. R&D expenses include R&D performed under contract by others; design, construction, and testing of prototypes; and testing in search for new products. Thus, R&D expense of $525,000 ($150,000 + $200,000 + $175,000) should be recognized.
Answer (A) is incorrect. The amount of $150,000 does not include design, construction, and testing of preproduction prototypes or testing in search of new products. Answer (B) is incorrect. The amount of $200,000 does not include R&D performed under contract by others or testing in search for new products. Answer (C) is incorrect. The amount of $350,000 does not include testing in search for new products.

31. Jakar Co. made the following expenditures during the current year:

Costs to develop computer software for internal use in Jakar's general management information system	$200,000
Costs of market research activities	150,000

What amount of these expenditures should Jakar report in its current-year income statement as research and development expenses?

A. $350,000

B. $200,000

C. $150,000

D. $0

Answer (D) is correct. *(CPA, adapted)*
REQUIRED: The amount of research and development expenses.
DISCUSSION: Under GAAP, the costs of market research are not R&D costs. Costs to develop software for the entity's own general management information system are also not R&D costs.
Answer (A) is incorrect. R&D expenses do not include costs to develop software for internal use in a general management information system or the costs of market research. Answer (B) is incorrect. R&D costs do not include costs to develop software for internal use in a general management information system. Answer (C) is incorrect. R&D costs do not include market research costs.

32. In the current year, Devlin Research Station incurred the following costs:

Direct costs of doing contract research
and development work for the
government to be reimbursed by
governmental unit $400,000

Research and development costs not included above were

Depreciation	$300,000
Salaries	700,000
Indirect costs appropriately allocated	200,000
Materials	180,000

What was Devlin's total research and development expense in the current year?

   A. $1,080,000

   B. $1,380,000

   C. $1,580,000

   D. $1,780,000

Answer (B) is correct. *(CPA, adapted)*
   REQUIRED: The total research and development expense.
   DISCUSSION: Materials used in R&D, compensation costs of personnel, and indirect costs appropriately allocated are R&D costs that should be expensed immediately. The costs of equipment and facilities that are used for R&D activities and have alternative future uses, whether for other R&D projects or otherwise, are to be capitalized as tangible assets when acquired or constructed. Depreciation on this equipment is to be expensed as R&D expense. However, R&D expense does not include the reimbursable costs of R&D activities conducted for others. The total R&D expense is therefore $1,380,000 ($300,000 + $700,000 + $200,000 + $180,000).
   Answer (A) is incorrect. The amount of $1,080,000 omits the depreciation. Answer (C) is incorrect. The amount of $1,580,000 includes the reimbursable costs of R&D conducted for others but omits the indirect costs. Answer (D) is incorrect. The amount of $1,780,000 includes the reimbursable costs of R&D conducted for others.

33. During Year 1, Scios Co. incurred $204,000 of research and development costs in its laboratory to develop a patent that was granted on July 1, Year 1. Legal fees and other costs associated with registration of the patent totaled $41,000. The estimated economic life of the patent is 10 years. What amount should Scios capitalize for the patent on July 1, Year 1?

   A. $0

   B. $41,000

   C. $204,000

   D. $245,000

Answer (B) is correct. *(CPA, adapted)*
   REQUIRED: The amount to be capitalized for an internally developed patent.
   DISCUSSION: R&D costs must be expensed as they are incurred. Legal fees and registration fees are excluded from the definition of R&D. Thus, the $41,000 in legal fees and other costs associated with the registration of the patent should be capitalized. The $204,000 in R&D costs should be expensed.
   Answer (A) is incorrect. Legal fees and other costs associated with the registration of the patent should be capitalized. Answer (C) is incorrect. Legal fees and other costs associated with the registration of the patent should be capitalized, whereas R&D costs must be expensed as incurred. Answer (D) is incorrect. R&D costs must be expensed as incurred.

34. If a company constructs a laboratory building to be used as a research and development facility, the cost of the laboratory building is matched against earnings as

   A. Research and development expense in the period(s) of construction.

   B. Depreciation deducted as part of research and development costs.

   C. Depreciation or immediate write-off depending on company policy.

   D. An expense at such time as productive research and development has been obtained from the facility.

Answer (B) is correct. *(CPA, adapted)*
   REQUIRED: The proper treatment of the cost of a laboratory building used as an R&D facility.
   DISCUSSION: The costs of equipment and facilities that are used for R&D activities and have alternative future uses, whether for other R&D projects or otherwise, are to be capitalized as tangible assets when acquired or constructed. The depreciation of a facility such as a laboratory building used for R&D is an R&D expense.
   Answer (A) is incorrect. The cost should be matched against earnings in the period of construction only if the building is usable for a particular research project and has no alternative use. Answer (C) is incorrect. A company has no discretion regarding R&D costs. Answer (D) is incorrect. The cost should be capitalized.

Questions 35 and 36 are based on the following information. Partnership A advances $1 million to Corporation B to perform research and development. The terms of the agreement specify that B must repay the funds upon successful completion of the project.

35. Corporation B accounts for the $1 million as

A. A liability.

B. Income from operations.

C. Deferred contract revenue.

D. Shareholders' equity.

Answer (C) is correct. *(E. Spede/J. Sperry)*
REQUIRED: The classification of an R&D advance in the accounts of the recipient.
DISCUSSION: If the entity is obligated to repay any of the funds provided by the other party, regardless of the outcome of the project, it recognizes a liability. If repayment depends solely on the results of the R&D having future economic benefit, the entity accounts for its obligation as a contract to perform R&D for others. Given that B must repay only on successful completion of the project, the advance should be recorded as deferred contract revenue.
Answer (A) is incorrect. The entity is not obligated to repay if the R&D has no future economic benefit. Answer (B) is incorrect. No services have yet been performed. Answer (D) is incorrect. The transaction is a contract to perform services, not an investment by Partnership A.

36. Partnership A accounts for the $1 million as

A. Accounts receivable.

B. Research and development expense.

C. Deferred research and development costs.

D. Advances on contract.

Answer (B) is correct. *(E. Spede/J. Sperry)*
REQUIRED: The classification of the advance in the accounts of the lender.
DISCUSSION: If repayment to the entity of any advance to other parties depends solely on the results of the R&D having future economic benefits, the advance is accounted for as a cost incurred. Furthermore, the costs are charged to R&D expense. B's repayment depends solely on the successful completion of the R&D, and Partnership A should treat the advance as R&D expense.
Answer (A) is incorrect. Corporation B does not have an unconditional obligation to repay the advance. Answer (C) is incorrect. The $1 million must be expensed. Answer (D) is incorrect. When repayment depends solely on the results of the R&D having future economic benefits, the advance must be expensed.

37. On January 1, Year 1, Cybience purchased equipment for use in developing a new product. Cybience uses the straight-line depreciation method. The equipment could provide benefits over a 10-year period. However, the new product development is expected to take 5 years, and the equipment can be used only for this project. Cybience's Year 1 expense equals

A. The total cost of the equipment.

B. One-fifth of the cost of the equipment.

C. One-tenth of the cost of the equipment.

D. Zero.

Answer (A) is correct. *(CPA, adapted)*
REQUIRED: The expense for equipment usable only for developing a new product.
DISCUSSION: The costs of materials, equipment, or facilities that are acquired or constructed for a particular R&D project and that have no alternative future uses and therefore no separate economic values are R&D costs when incurred. R&D costs are expensed in full when incurred.
Answer (B) is incorrect. None of the cost can be capitalized. Answer (C) is incorrect. The total cost of the equipment should be expensed in Year 1. Answer (D) is incorrect. There is no alternative future use for the equipment, so it may not be capitalized.

9.6 Computer Software and Other Costs

38. On December 31, Year 1, Byte Co. had capitalized software costs of $600,000 with an economic life of 4 years. Sales for Year 2 were 10% of expected total sales of the software. At December 31, Year 2, the software had a net realizable value of $480,000. In its December 31, Year 2, balance sheet, what amount should Byte report as net capitalized cost of computer software?

A. $432,000

B. $450,000

C. $480,000

D. $540,000

Answer (B) is correct. *(CPA, adapted)*
REQUIRED: The net capitalized cost of computer software.
DISCUSSION: The annual amortization is the greater of (1) the amount determined using the ratio of current gross revenues to the sum of current gross revenues and anticipated future gross revenues or (2) the straight-line amount. At year end, the unamortized cost must be compared with the net realizable value (NRV). Any excess of unamortized cost over NRV must be written off. The straight-line amortization is greater than the amount determined using the 10% ratio of current sales to expected total sales. Thus, the unamortized cost of software is $450,000 [$600,000 capitalized cost − ($600,000 ÷ 4)] at December 31, Year 2. This amount is less than the $480,000 NRV, so $450,000 is the amount reported in the year-end balance sheet.
Answer (A) is incorrect. The amount of $432,000 equals the NRV at December 31, Year 2, minus amortization calculated as 10% of NRV. Answer (C) is incorrect. The amount of $480,000 is the NRV at December 31, Year 2. Answer (D) is incorrect. The amount of $540,000 assumes amortization at 10% with no adjustment for NRV.

39. Miller Co. incurred the following computer software costs for the development and sale of software programs during the current year:

Planning costs	$ 50,000
Design of the software	150,000
Substantial testing of the project's initial stages	75,000
Production and packaging costs for the first month's sales	500,000
Costs of producing product masters after technological feasibility was established	200,000

The project was not under any contractual arrangement when these expenditures were incurred. What amount should Miller report as research and development expense for the current year?

A. $200,000

B. $275,000

C. $500,000

D. $975,000

Answer (B) is correct. *(CPA, adapted)*
REQUIRED: The R&D expense.
DISCUSSION: R&D costs of software are all costs incurred to establish technological feasibility. Technological feasibility is established when the enterprise has completed all planning, designing, coding, and testing necessary to establish that the product can be produced to meet its design specifications, including functions, features, and technical performance requirements. Consequently, Miller's R&D cost is $275,000 ($50,000 planning + $150,000 design + $75,000 initial testing).
Answer (A) is incorrect. The amount of $200,000 does not include the cost for substantial testing of the project's initial stages. Answer (C) is incorrect. Production and packaging costs for the first month's sales are capitalized as inventory. Answer (D) is incorrect. The amount of $975,000 includes production and packaging costs for the first month's sales that should be inventoried. Costs of producing product masters after technological feasibility was established should be capitalized as software costs.

40. Certain costs of internal-use software not qualifying as R&D costs should be capitalized in which stage(s), if any, of software development?

	Preliminary Project Stage	Application Development Stage	Post-Implementation Operation Stage
A.	Yes	Yes	Yes
B.	Yes	Yes	No
C.	No	Yes	No
D.	No	No	No

Answer (C) is correct. *(Publisher, adapted)*
REQUIRED: The stage(s), if any, of development of internal-use software in which costs are capitalized.
DISCUSSION: Certain internal and external development costs of internal-use software not qualifying as R&D costs should be expensed during the preliminary project and post-implementation/operation stages. However, they should be capitalized during the application development stage. Costs capitalizable include external direct costs of materials and services consumed, payroll and payroll-related costs for employees to the extent they spend time directly on the project, and interest costs. Furthermore, costs to develop or obtain software allowing for access or conversion of old data by a new system are also capitalized.
Answer (A) is incorrect. Only certain costs are capitalized during the application development stage. Answer (B) is incorrect. Costs are expensed during the preliminary project stage. Certain costs are capitalized during the application development stage. Answer (D) is incorrect. Certain costs are capitalized during the application development stage.

Questions 41 and 42 are based on the following information. During Year 1, Microcomp Corp. incurred costs to develop and produce a routine, low-risk computer software product, as described below.

Completion of detail program design	$13,000
Costs incurred for coding and testing to establish technological feasibility	10,000
Other coding costs after establishment of technological feasibility	24,000
Other testing costs after establishment of technological feasibility	20,000
Costs of producing product masters for training materials	15,000
Duplication of computer software and training materials from product masters (1,000 units)	25,000
Packaging product (500 units)	9,000

41. In Microcomp's December 31, Year 1, balance sheet, what amount should be reported in inventory?

A. $25,000

B. $34,000

C. $40,000

D. $49,000

Answer (B) is correct. *(CPA, adapted)*
REQUIRED: The amount reported in inventory.
DISCUSSION: Costs incurred internally in creating a computer software product must be charged to expense when incurred as R&D until technological feasibility has been established. Thereafter, all software production costs incurred until the product is available for general release to customers must be capitalized and amortized. The costs of duplicating the software, documentation, and training materials from the product masters and of physically packaging the product for distribution are capitalized as inventory. Hence, inventory should be reported at $34,000 ($25,000 duplication costs + $9,000 packaging costs).
Answer (A) is incorrect. The amount of $25,000 excludes packaging costs. Answer (C) is incorrect. The amount of $40,000 excludes packaging costs but includes costs of producing product masters. Answer (D) is incorrect. The amount of $49,000 includes costs of producing product masters.

42. In Microcomp's December 31, Year 1, balance sheet, what amount should be capitalized as software cost subject to amortization?

A. $54,000

B. $57,000

C. $59,000

D. $69,000

Answer (C) is correct. *(CPA, adapted)*
REQUIRED: The amount capitalized as software cost subject to amortization.
DISCUSSION: Costs incurred internally in creating a computer software product shall be charged to expense when incurred as research and development until technological feasibility has been established for the product. Thereafter, all software production costs incurred until the product is available for general release to customers shall be capitalized and subsequently reported at the lower of unamortized cost or net realizable value. Hence, the costs of completing the detail program design and establishing technological feasibility are expensed, the costs of duplicating software and training materials and packaging the product are inventoried, and the costs of coding and other testing after establishing technological feasibility and the costs of producing product masters are capitalized and amortized. The amount capitalized as software cost subject to amortization is therefore $59,000 ($24,000 + $20,000 + $15,000).
Answer (A) is incorrect. The amount of $54,000 equals inventoriable costs plus the other testing costs. Answer (B) is incorrect. The amount of $57,000 is the sum of the costs expensed and the costs inventoried. Answer (D) is incorrect. The amount of $69,000 assumes the costs of coding and testing to establish feasibility are capitalized and amortized.

43. Direct response advertising costs are capitalized (deferred) to provide an appropriate expense in each period for

	Interim Financial Reporting	Year-End Financial Reporting
A.	Yes	No
B.	Yes	Yes
C.	No	No
D.	No	Yes

Answer (B) is correct. *(CPA, adapted)*
REQUIRED: The type(s) of reporting in which direct response advertising costs may be accrued or deferred.
DISCUSSION: Direct response advertising costs are capitalized (deferred) if the primary purpose is to make sales to customers who respond specifically to the advertising, and probable future economic benefits result. An entity that capitalizes these costs must document that customers have specifically responded to the advertising. It also must document the benefits from prior direct response advertising. The deferral of advertising costs is appropriate for both interim and year-end financial reporting if their benefits clearly apply to more than one period. Moreover, if a cost that would be fully expensed in an annual report benefits more than one interim period, it may be allocated to those interim periods.

44. Wind Co. incurred organization costs of $6,000 at the beginning of its first year of operations. How should Wind treat the organization costs in its financial statements in accordance with GAAP?

A. Never amortized.

B. Amortized over 180 months.

C. Amortized over 40 years.

D. Expensed immediately.

Answer (D) is correct. *(CPA, adapted)*
REQUIRED: The accounting for organization costs.
DISCUSSION: Organization costs are those incurred in the formation of a business entity. For financial statement purposes, nongovernmental entities must expense all start-up costs and organization costs as incurred.
Answer (A) is incorrect. Organization costs are never capitalized. Answer (B) is incorrect. Organization costs are amortized over a minimum of 15 years (180 months) for federal income tax purposes. Answer (C) is incorrect. Organization costs are expensed as incurred under GAAP.

45. Neue Co., a developmental stage enterprise, incurred the following costs during its first year of operations:

Legal fees for incorporation and other
 related matters $55,000
Underwriters' fees for initial stock offering 40,000
Exploration costs and purchases of
 mineral rights 60,000

Neue had no revenue during its first year of operation. What amount must Neue expense as organization costs?

A. $155,000

B. $100,000

C. $95,000

D. $55,000

Answer (D) is correct. *(CPA, adapted)*
REQUIRED: The organization costs to be expensed.
DISCUSSION: Organization costs are those incurred in the formation of a business entity. For financial accounting purposes, nongovernmental entities must expense all start-up and organization costs as incurred. Thus, the legal fees ($55,000) should be expensed because they are organization costs. Fees for an initial stock offering are customarily treated as a reduction in the proceeds rather than as organization costs, and exploration costs and purchases of mineral rights are capitalizable items that are not organization costs.
Answer (A) is incorrect. Fees for an initial stock offering are customarily treated as a reduction of the proceeds, and exploration costs and purchases of mineral rights are capitalizable items. Answer (B) is incorrect. The legal fees for incorporation and other related matters are the only organization costs. Answer (C) is incorrect. The underwriters' fees for initial stock offering are not organization costs.

9.7 IFRS

46. Under IFRS, an entity that acquires an intangible asset may use the revaluation model for subsequent measurement only if

A. The useful life of the intangible asset can be reliably determined.

B. An active market exists for the intangible asset.

C. The cost of the intangible asset can be measured reliably.

D. The intangible asset is a monetary asset.

Answer (B) is correct. *(CPA, adapted)*
REQUIRED: The condition for use of the revaluation model for subsequent measurement of an intangible asset.
DISCUSSION: An intangible asset is carried at cost minus any accumulated amortization and impairment losses, or at a revalued amount. The revaluation model is similar to that for items of PPE (initial recognition of an asset at cost). However, fair value must be determined based on an active market.
Answer (A) is incorrect. An intangible asset may have an indefinite life. Answer (C) is incorrect. Initial recognition of an intangible asset is at cost. Recognition is permitted only when it is probable that the entity will receive the expected economic benefits, and the cost is reliably measurable. The revaluation model applies only to subsequent measurement. Answer (D) is incorrect. An intangible asset is nonmonetary.

47. Under IFRS, which of the following is a criterion that must be met in order for an item to be recognized as an intangible asset other than goodwill?

A. The item's fair value can be measured reliably.

B. The item is part of the entity's activities aimed at gaining new scientific or technical knowledge.

C. The item is expected to be used in the production or supply of goods or services.

D. The item is identifiable and lacks physical substance.

Answer (D) is correct. *(CPA, adapted)*
REQUIRED: The criterion for recognizing an intangible asset other than goodwill.
DISCUSSION: IAS 38, *Intangible Assets*, defines an intangible asset as an identifiable nonmonetary asset without physical substance.
Answer (A) is incorrect. Initial recognition of an intangible asset is at cost. Recognition is permitted only when it is probable that the entity will receive the expected economic benefits, and the cost is reliably measurable. Answer (B) is incorrect. Research is undertaken to gain new scientific or technical knowledge and understanding. Expenditures for research are expensed as incurred. Answer (C) is incorrect. Property, plant, and equipment are expected to be used in the production or supply of goods or services.

48. An entity purchases a trademark and incurs the following costs in connection with the trademark:

One-time trademark purchase price	$100,000
Nonrefundable VAT taxes	5,000
Training sales personnel on the use of the new trademark	7,000
Research expenditures associated with the purchase of the new trademark	24,000
Legal costs incurred to register the trademark	10,500
Salaries of the administrative personnel	12,000

Applying IFRS and assuming that the trademark meets all of the applicable initial asset recognition criteria, the entity should recognize an asset in the amount of

A. $100,000

B. $115,500

C. $146,500

D. $158,500

Answer (B) is correct. *(CPA, adapted)*
REQUIRED: The initial amount recognized for an intangible asset.
DISCUSSION: Cost includes the purchase price (including purchase taxes and import duties) and any directly attributable costs to prepare the asset for its intended use, such as legal fees. Thus, the intangible asset is initially recognized at $115,500 ($100,000 price + $5,000 value-added taxes + $10,500 of legal costs).
Answer (A) is incorrect. Purchase taxes and legal fees for registration also are capitalized. Answer (C) is incorrect. Training and research costs are expensed as incurred. Answer (D) is incorrect. Training and research costs and administrative salaries and other overhead costs are not directly attributable costs.

Use Gleim **EQE Test Prep** Software Download for interactive study and performance analysis.

STUDY UNIT TEN
INVESTMENTS

Held-to-Maturity, Trading, and Available-for-Sale Securities

The guidance addressing the accounting for most investments in debt and equity securities that are not derivatives applies to equity securities with readily determinable fair values (quoted market prices) and to all debt securities. An **equity security** represents an ownership interest in an entity or a right to acquire or dispose of such an interest. Convertible debt and preferred stock that must be redeemed by the issuer or is redeemable at the investor's option are not considered equity securities. A **debt security** represents a creditor relationship with the security's issuer. This definition excludes (1) trade receivables and loans, (2) leases, (3) options, (4) financial futures contracts, and (5) forward contracts.

The guidance referred to above does not apply to investments in **subsidiaries** or interests in **variable interest entities (VIEs)** (see Study Unit 24) that the entity must consolidate. It also does not apply to (1) entities with specialized accounting practices that include accounting for all investments at fair or market value, (2) not-for-profit entities, (3) most derivatives, and (4) equity-method investments. The securities to which the guidance applies are classified at acquisition in one of three categories. The classification is reassessed at each reporting date. Held-to-maturity securities are debt securities that the reporting entity has the positive intent and ability to hold to maturity. Trading securities are primarily intended to be sold in the near term. Available-for-sale securities are those that are not classified as held-to-maturity or trading.

Held-to-maturity securities. If the investing entity intends to hold a **debt security** for an indefinite period, or the possibility exists that it may need to be sold before maturity (to supply needed cash, avoid interest rate risk, etc.), the security cannot be classified as held-to-maturity. If circumstances change, for example, because of the election of the fair value option (see page 252), an entity can change its intent with respect to a given debt security "without calling into question the intent to hold other debt securities to maturity in the future." If a sale is before maturity, the security still can be classified as held-to-maturity if (1) sale is near enough to the maturity (e.g., within 3 months) so that interest rate risk (change in the market rate) does not have a significant effect on fair value, or (2) sale is after collection of 85% or more of the principal. Held-to-maturity securities are normally reported at amortized cost.

Presentation: Held-to-Maturity Securities

Balance sheet. Held-to-maturity securities are presented net of any unamortized premium or discount. No valuation account is used. Amortization of any discount (premium) is reported by a debit (credit) to held-to-maturity securities and a credit (debit) to interest income. Individual securities are presented as current or noncurrent.

Income statement. Realized gains and losses and interest income (including amortization of premium or discount) are included in earnings.

Cash flow statement. Cash flows are from investing activities.

Trading securities. Trading securities are purchased and sold frequently. Each trading security is initially recorded at **cost** (including brokerage commissions and taxes). At each balance sheet date, trading securities are **remeasured at fair value**. Quoted market prices are easy to obtain and are the most reliable and verifiable measure of fair value. An **unrealized holding gain or loss** is recognized in earnings. It is the net change in fair value during the period, not including recognized dividends or interest not received. A valuation account may be used to adjust the carrying amount to reflect the net change.

Presentation: Trading Securities

Balance sheet. The balances of the securities and valuation allowances are netted. One amount is displayed for fair value. Assets similar to those classified as trading that are not measured subsequently at fair value are reported separately. Individual securities are presented as current or noncurrent.

Income statement. Unrealized and realized holding gains and losses, dividends, and interest income (including premium or discount amortization) are included in earnings.

Cash flow statement. Classification of cash flows depends on the nature of the securities and the purpose of their acquisition. They are typically considered to be from operating activities.

Available-for-sale securities. Available-for-sale securities are not classified as held-to-maturity or trading. The accounting is similar to that for trading securities. The initial acquisition is recorded at **cost** by a debit to available-for-sale securities and a credit to cash. Amortization of any discount (premium) is reported as an increase (decrease) in available-for-sale securities by a credit (debit) to interest income. Receipt of cash dividends is recorded by a debit to cash and a credit to dividend income. The major difference is that **unrealized holding gains and losses** are reported in **other comprehensive income (OCI)**, not earnings. Tax effects are debited or credited directly to OCI. However, all or part of unrealized gains and losses for an available-for-sale security that is the hedged item in a fair value hedge are recognized in earnings (see page 254).

Presentation: Available-for-Sale Securities

Balance sheet. The balances of the securities and valuation allowances are netted. One amount is displayed for fair value. Assets similar to those classified as available-for-sale that are not measured subsequently at fair value are reported separately. Individual securities are presented as current or noncurrent. In the equity section, unrealized holding gains and losses are reported in accumulated OCI (the real account to which OCI is closed).

Income statement. Realized gains and losses, dividends, and interest income (including premium or discount amortization) are included in earnings.

Cash flow statement. Cash flows are from investing activities.

Statement of other comprehensive income. Unrealized holding gains and losses are included in OCI. Reclassification adjustments also must be made for each component of OCI. Their purpose is to avoid double counting when an item included in net income also was included in OCI for the same or a prior period. For example, if a gain on available-for-sale securities is realized in the current period, the prior-period recognition of an unrealized holding gain must be eliminated by debiting OCI and crediting a gain.

The following table summarizes the guidance in this study unit when the fair value option has not been elected:

Category	Held-to-maturity		Trading		Available-for-sale	
Definition	Debt securities that the entity has the positive intent and ability to hold to maturity		Bought and held for near-term sale and frequently traded		All securities not in the other categories	
Type of security	**Debt**	**Equity**	**Debt**	**Equity**	**Debt**	**Equity**
Recognize holding G/L?	No	--	Yes	Yes	Yes	Yes
Recognize unrealized holding G/L in	--	--	Earnings	Earnings	OCI	OCI
Measured at	Amortized cost	--	Fair value	Fair value	Fair value	Fair value

Transfers between categories. Transfers are recorded at fair value. Unrealized holding gains and losses on securities transferred from the trading category will have already been recognized and are not reversed. The portion of unrealized holding gains and losses on securities transferred to the trading category not previously recognized in earnings is recognized in earnings immediately. The unrealized holding gain or loss on held-to-maturity debt securities transferred to the available-for-sale category is recognized in OCI. The unrealized holding gain or loss on the date of transfer for available-for-sale securities transferred to the held-to-maturity category continues to be reported in OCI. However, it is amortized in the same manner as the amortization of any discount or premium. This amortization at least partly offsets the amortization of the premium or discount. Fair value accounting may result in a premium or discount when a debt security is transferred to the held-to-maturity category. Transfers from the held-to-maturity category or into or from the trading category should be rare.

From	To	Earnings Recognition
Trading	Any category	Already recognized, not reversed
Any category	Trading	If not already recognized
Held-to-maturity	Available-for-sale	Unrealized gain (loss) recognized in OCI
Available-for-sale	Held-to-maturity	Amounts in OCI not reversed but are amortized in same way as premium (discount)

The **amortized cost basis** is used to calculate any **impairment**. The amortized cost basis differs from fair value, which equals the cost basis plus or minus the net unrealized holding gain or loss. If a decline in fair value of an individual held-to-maturity or available-for-sale security below its amortized cost basis is other than temporary, the amortized cost basis is written down to fair value as a new cost basis. However, if a security has been the hedged item in a fair value hedge, its amortized cost basis will reflect adjustments in its carrying amount for changes in fair value attributable to the hedged risk. The impairment is a realized loss and is included in earnings. The new cost basis is not affected by subsequent recoveries in fair value. Subsequent changes in fair value of available-for-sale securities are included in OCI, except for other-than-temporary declines.

Fair Value Option (FVO)

Election of the FVO allows entities to measure most **financial assets and liabilities** at **fair value** and report unrealized gains and losses in earnings. The FVO **may not be elected** for (1) an investment in a subsidiary or an interest in a variable interest entity that must be consolidated (i.e., the FVO is not an alternative to consolidation), (2) obligations or assets for funding of postretirement employee benefits and other deferred compensation, (3) most financial assets and liabilities under leases, (4) demand deposit liabilities, and (5) financial instruments at least partly classified in equity. The decision whether to elect the FVO is made irrevocably at an election date (unless a new election date occurs). The decision is ordinarily made instrument by instrument and only for an entire instrument. However, the FVO generally need not be applied to all instruments in a single transaction. **Election dates** include the dates of (1) initial recognition of an eligible item, (2) entry into an eligible firm commitment involving only financial instruments, (3) a change in accounting for an investment because it becomes subject to the equity method, (4) deconsolidation of a subsidiary or a variable interest entity (with retention of an interest), and (5) an event requiring fair value measurement when it occurs but not subsequently (excluding recognition of nontemporary impairment, e.g., of inventory or long-lived assets). Examples of events requiring either remeasurement at fair value or initial recognition (or both) of eligible items and that result in an election date are (1) a business combination, (2) a consolidation or deconsolidation, or (3) a significant modification of debt.

In the **balance sheet**, assets and liabilities measured using the FVO are reported in a way that separates their fair values from the carrying amounts of similar items measured using another attribute. In the **income statement**, unrealized gains and losses on items measured using the FVO are recognized at subsequent reporting dates. Upfront costs and fees related to those items are recognized as incurred. In the **statement of cash flows**, cash flows related to items measured at fair value are classified according to their nature and purpose.

Equity Method

The accounting method used by the investor depends on the influence presumed to be exercised based on its voting interest. The following depicts the possibilities:

Percentage Voting Interest	Presumed Influence	Accounting Method
100%		
	Control	Consolidation
50%		
	Significant	Equity Method or FVO
20%		
	Little or none	Fair Value
0%		

The fair value method is used when the investor does not have significant influence. It was addressed in the preceding sections. The equity method is used when the investor has significant influence. It is discussed further on the following page. Consolidation is ordinarily required when the investor owns more than 50% of the outstanding voting interests. It is covered in Study Unit 24. However, consolidation is not required if the majority owner does not have control.

Under the **equity method**, the investor's share of the investee's earnings and losses is adjusted to eliminate interentity profits and losses not realized in third-party transactions. It is also reduced by any dividends on cumulative preferred stock, whether or not declared. The adjusted share of the investee's earnings is a debit (losses and dividends are credits) to the carrying amount of the investment. The receipt of a cash dividend from the investee is treated as a return of an investment. Thus, it is credited to the investment account but does not affect equity-based earnings.

When an investor obtains **significant influence** over an investee, it must elect either the equity method or the FVO. A **20% or greater** voting interest is presumed to permit such influence. An investor that elects the equity method must retroactively adjust (1) the carrying amount of the investment, (2) results of operations for current and prior periods presented, and (3) retained earnings. The adjustment is made as if the equity method had been in effect during all of the previous periods in which any percentage was held. An investor may account for an investment by the equity method and then sell shares such that significant influence can no longer be presumed to be exerted. This change from the equity method is not a basis for an FVO election. It is accounted for on a prospective basis. The shares retained normally will be accounted for using the fair value method as available for sale or trading securities.

If the equity method is not appropriate (or not elected), equity securities are accounted for based on fair values. However, if such equity securities do **not have readily determinable fair values**, they are accounted for after acquisition using the **cost method**. Under the cost method, an investment in stock is initially recorded at cost, but subsequent unrealized changes in fair value are not recognized unless they represent nontemporary declines. Moreover, dividends from an investee are accounted for by the investor as dividend income under both the cost and fair-value methods unless a liquidating dividend is received. A **liquidating dividend** occurs when the total accumulated dividends received since the date of acquisition exceed the investor's proportionate share of the investee's net accumulated earnings during that time. A liquidating dividend is a return of, not a return on, the investment. It reduces the carrying amount of the investment.

Investments in Bonds

Assuming no FVO election, noncurrent debt securities (e.g., bonds) theoretically should be recorded at the present value of the future cash flows discounted at the market rate. In practice (again assuming no FVO election), they are recorded at their **historical cost** (including brokerage fees but excluding accrued interest at purchase). Any **discount or premium** (difference between the purchase price and maturity amount) is amortized over the remaining life of the debt. If the reporting entity has the positive intent and ability to hold bonds to maturity, they are classified as held-to-maturity. A separate premium or discount account is seldom used. The carrying amount equals the face amount plus any unamortized premium or minus any unamortized discount. The **effective interest method** of amortization must be used unless the straight-line method gives results that do not differ materially. This method multiplies the security's carrying amount by the effective interest rate at the time of purchase to determine the interest revenue for the period. The difference between interest revenue and the actual cash received is the amount of amortization of discount or premium. If the security was purchased at a premium (discount), interest will be less (greater) than the amount of cash debited. The effective interest rate is the rate the instrument was purchased to yield. If it is greater than the stated rate, the security was purchased at a discount. If the effective rate is lower than the stated rate, the security was purchased at a premium. Cash paid to the seller includes interest accrued since the last payment date. Interest accrued at the date of purchase is debited to interest receivable.

When debt securities with **detachable stock warrants** are purchased, the price should be allocated between the warrants and the securities based upon their **relative fair values** at issuance. The amount debited to investment in stock warrants relative to the total amount paid increases the discount or decreases the premium on the investment. A contract with the bondholders (bond indenture) may require a sinking fund (a long-term investment). The objective of making payments into the fund is to accumulate sufficient assets to pay bond interest and principal. The amounts transferred plus the revenue earned on the investments provide the necessary funds.

Cash Surrender Value

The cash surrender value of **life insurance** policies on key executives is a **noncurrent asset**. The policy typically contains a schedule specifying the cash surrender value and loan value for each year. The annual premium for life insurance is allocated between expense and the cash surrender value. The **expense** recognized equals the difference between the premiums paid (cash) and the cash surrender value. Thus, an increase in the policy's cash surrender value decreases insurance expense. If the entity is the beneficiary, the premiums are not deductible on the tax return, and the proceeds of the policy are not taxable. When proceeds from the policy are received, cash is debited, and cash surrender value and insurance income are credited.

Derivatives and Hedges

Entities must recognize all derivatives as either **assets or liabilities** and measure them at **fair value**. A **derivative** is a financial instrument or other contract that (1) has (a) one or more underlyings or (b) one or more notional amounts or payment provisions, or both; (2) requires either no initial net investment or an immaterial net investment; and (3) requires or permits net settlement. An underlying may be a(n) (1) specified interest rate, (2) security price, (3) commodity price, (4) foreign exchange rate, (5) index of prices or rates, or (6) other variable. A notional amount is a number of currency units, shares, bushels, pounds, or other units specified. Settlement of a derivative is based on the interaction of the notional amount and the underlying.

Certain derivatives may be **designated as hedges** of (1) the exposure to changes in the fair value of a recognized asset or liability or an unrecognized firm commitment; (2) the exposure to the variability of the cash flows of a recognized asset or liability or a forecasted transaction; or (3) the foreign currency exposure of (a) a net investment in a foreign operation, (b) an unrecognized firm commitment, (c) a recognized asset or liability, or (d) a forecasted transaction. An entity electing to designate a derivative as a hedge must establish at that time the method for assessing the effectiveness of the hedge and the measurement approach for determining any ineffective aspect of the hedge. Gains and losses from changes in fair value of a derivative not designated as a hedge are included in earnings in the period of change.

A **fair value hedge** includes a hedge of an exposure to changes in the fair value of (1) a recognized asset or liability or (2) an unrecognized firm commitment with fixed cash flows. A foreign currency fair value hedge includes a hedge of a foreign currency exposure of either (1) an unrecognized firm commitment or (2) a recognized asset or liability (including an available-for-sale security). Gains and losses arising from changes in fair value of a derivative classified as either a fair value or a foreign currency fair value hedge are included in the determination of **earnings** in the period of change. They are offset by losses or gains on the hedged item attributable to the risk being hedged. Thus, earnings of the period of change are affected only by the net gain or loss attributable to the ineffective aspect of the hedge.

A **cash flow hedge** is a hedge of an exposure to variability in the cash flows of (1) a recognized asset or liability or (2) a forecasted transaction with variable cash flows. A foreign currency cash flow hedge is a hedge of the foreign currency exposure to variability in the functional-currency equivalent cash flows associated with (1) a forecasted transaction, (2) a recognized asset or liability, (3) an unrecognized firm commitment, or (4) a forecasted interentity transaction (e.g., a forecasted sale to a foreign subsidiary). The accounting treatment of gains and losses arising from changes in fair value of a derivative designated as either a cash flow or a foreign currency cash flow hedge varies for the effective and ineffective portions. The effective portion initially is reported in **other comprehensive income**. It is reclassified into earnings when the hedged transaction affects earnings. The ineffective portion is immediately included in earnings.

Ordinarily, nonderivatives may not be designated as hedging instruments. The exceptions are for (1) nonderivative financial instruments that hedge the foreign currency exposure of an unrecognized firm commitment (a fair value hedge) and (2) a net investment in a foreign operation. In the second case, the gain or loss on a hedging derivative (or the foreign currency transaction gain or loss on a nonderivative hedging instrument) is reported as a component of the **cumulative translation adjustment** in other comprehensive income.

Embedded derivatives must be accounted for separately from the related **host contract** if three conditions are met: (1) The economic characteristics and risks of the embedded derivative are not clearly and closely related to the economic characteristics of the host; (2) the hybrid instrument is not remeasured at fair value under otherwise applicable GAAP, with changes in fair value reported in earnings as they occur; and (3) a freestanding instrument with the same terms as the embedded derivative would be subject to the requirements of GAAP for derivatives. If an embedded derivative is accounted for separately, the host contract is accounted for based on the accounting standards that are applicable to instruments of its type. The **separated derivative** should be accounted for under GAAP for derivatives. If separating the two instruments is impossible, the **entire contract** must be measured **at fair value**, with gains and losses recognized **in earnings**. It may not be designated as a hedging instrument because nonderivatives usually do not qualify as hedging instruments.

Hedging Summary

	What is it?	Requirements	Hedged Asset, Liability, Forecasted Transaction, or Firm Commitment	Hedging Instrument
			Initial Recognition	
1. Cash flow hedge	The hedging instrument must offset the variability of the cash flows of a recognized asset or liability or a forecasted transaction. In a foreign currency cash flow hedge, the hedged item also may be an unrecognized firm commitment.	The hedging instrument must be designated as part of a hedge and meet the criteria for a cash flow hedge.	Recognize receivable or payable.	No journal entry is made. The contract has no initial fair value because it is unperformed at its inception.
Journal entry			A/R $XXX Sales $XXX	
2. Fair value hedge	A fair value hedge must offset the changes in fair value of a recognized asset or liability or an unrecognized firm commitment.	The hedging instrument must be designated as part of a hedge and meet the criteria for a fair value hedge.	Recognize receivable or payable.	No journal entry is made. The contract has no initial fair value because it is unperformed at its inception.
Journal entry			A/R $XXX Sales $XXX	

Balance Sheet Date

	Hedged Asset, Liability, Forecasted Transaction, or Firm Commitment	Hedging Instrument		Amortization of Discount/Premium
1. Cash flow hedge	Adjusted to fair value. Recognized in earnings.	Adjusted to fair value. An asset/liability is recognized on balance sheet. Offsetting entry is an adjustment to other comprehensive income (OCI).		The discount/premium (forward contract) or the time value (option) must be amortized over the life of the derivative. This amount is recognized in earnings and offset by an entry to OCI.

Journal entry	A/R \$XXX
	     Gain \$XXX
		OCI \$XXX
		     Derivative \$XXX
				Discount amortization \$XXX
				     OCI \$XXX

2. Fair value hedge	Adjusted to fair value. Change is recognized in earnings.	Adjusted to fair value. An asset/liability is recognized on balance sheet. Offsetting entry is gain/loss and is recognized in earnings.		

Journal entry	A/R \$XXX
	     Gain \$XXX
		Loss on derivative \$XXX
		     Derivative \$XXX		

Expiration Date

	Hedged Asset, Liability, Forecasted Transaction, or Firm Commitment	Hedging Instrument	OCI Entry	Amortization of Discount/Premium
1. Cash flow hedge	Adjusted to fair value. Recognized in earnings.	Adjusted to fair value. The offsetting entry is to OCI.	The adjustment of OCI is transferred to earnings. This allows the gain/loss on the hedged item to be offset by the change in fair value of the derivative.	The discount/premium (forward contract) or the time value (option) must be amortized over the life of the derivative. This amount is recognized in earnings and offset by an entry to OCI.

Journal entry	Loss \$XXX
	     A/R \$XXX
		Derivative \$XXX
		     OCI \$XXX
			OCI \$XXX
			     Gain on derivative \$XXX
				Discount amortization \$XXX
				     OCI \$XXX

2. Fair value hedge	Adjusted to fair value. Offsetting entry is to gain/loss recognized in earnings.	Adjusted to fair value. Offsetting entry is to gain/loss recognized in earnings.	N/A	N/A

Journal entry	Loss \$XXX
	     A/R \$XXX
		Derivative \$XXX
		     Gain on derivative \$XXX		

Financial Instrument Disclosures

A financial instrument is cash, evidence of an ownership interest in an entity, or a contract that both (1) imposes on one entity a **contractual obligation** to (a) deliver cash or another financial instrument to a second entity or (b) exchange other financial instruments on potentially unfavorable terms with the second entity, **and** (2) conveys to that second entity a **contractual right** to (a) receive cash or another financial instrument from the first entity or (b) exchange other financial instruments on potentially favorable terms with the first entity. Certain entities must disclose the **fair value** of financial instruments. This rule applies whether or not they are recognized if (1) it is feasible to estimate such fair values and (2) the total fair value is material. If estimating fair value is not feasible, disclosures include information pertinent to estimating fair value, such as the carrying amount, effective interest rate, and maturity. The reasons that estimating the fair value is not feasible also should be disclosed. See Study Unit 1 for the framework for determining fair values, including approaches to measurement and a hierarchy of inputs to those approaches. Ordinarily, disclosures should not net the fair values of instruments even if they are of the same class or are related, e.g., by a risk management strategy.

Differences between GAAP and IFRS

Under IFRS:

- When the investor has significant influence, the equity method must be applied unless (1) the investment is classified as held for sale, or (2) conditions exist similar to those that would exempt a parent from preparing consolidated statements.

  - The investor applies the equity method prospectively from the moment that significant influence is achieved.
  - In assessing the investor's influence, the entity also considers potential voting rights (share call options, share warrants, or other instruments convertible into ordinary shares). These must be currently exercisable or convertible and must be considered even if held by other entities.
  - When significant influence is lost, any retained investment is measured at fair value.
  - Under the equity method, the investor's statements must use uniform accounting policies. Thus, adjustments must be made to conform the investee's policies to the investor's.

- A financial asset not at fair value through profit or loss is **measured initially** at fair value plus transaction costs. Other financial assets are measured at fair value.

- Unless the fair value option has been elected, financial assets are classified as subsequently measured at either (1) amortized cost or (2) fair value. This determination is made on the basis of the business model test and the contractual cash flow test.

- A financial asset is **measured subsequently** at amortized cost if it meets the business model test (objective: collect the contractual cash flows) and the cash flow test (contract provides for specific dates for cash flows that are principal and interest payments only).

- Equity investments are measured at fair value through profit or loss unless the entity has elected at initial recognition to recognize holding gains or losses in other comprehensive income. This irrevocable election may be made for an equity investment not held for trading. But dividend income is still recognized in profit or loss.

- Financial assets are **reclassified** only if the entity changes its business model for managing them.

QUESTIONS

10.1 Held-to-Maturity, Trading, and Available-for-Sale Securities

1. Investments in equity securities that have readily determinable fair values may be classified as

I.   Available-for-sale securities
II. Held-to-maturity securities
III. Trading securities

   A. I only.

   B. I and II only.

   C. I and III only.

   D. I, II, and III.

Answer (C) is correct. *(Publisher, adapted)*
REQUIRED: The possible classification(s) of equity securities.
DISCUSSION: Equity securities with readily determinable fair values that are held principally for sale in the near term are classified as trading securities. Equity securities not classified as trading securities are classified as available-for-sale securities. Held-to-maturity securities are debt securities only.
Answer (A) is incorrect. Equity securities also may be classified as trading. Answer (B) is incorrect. Only debt securities may be classified as held-to-maturity. Answer (D) is incorrect. Equity securities are classified as trading or available-for-sale, but only debt securities may be classified as held-to-maturity.

2. At year end, Slim Co. held several investments with the intent of selling them in the near term. The investments consisted of $100,000, 8%, 5-year bonds, purchased for $92,000, and equity securities purchased for $35,000. At year end, the bonds were selling on the open market for $105,000, and the equity securities had a market value of $50,000. The fair value option was not elected. What amount should Slim report as trading securities in its year-end balance sheet?

   A. $50,000

   B. $127,000

   C. $142,000

   D. $155,000

Answer (D) is correct. *(CPA, adapted)*
REQUIRED: The amount of trading securities at year end.
DISCUSSION: Trading securities are debt securities not classified as held-to-maturity and equity securities with readily determinable fair values that are bought and held primarily for sale in the near term. Hence, the bonds and the equity securities are trading securities. They are initially recorded at cost but are subsequently measured at fair value at each balance sheet date. Quoted market prices in active markets are the best evidence of fair value. Based on market quotes at year end, the bonds had a fair value of $105,000, and the equity securities had a fair value of $50,000. The total is $155,000.
Answer (A) is incorrect. The fair value of the bonds is also included. Answer (B) is incorrect. Trading securities are reported at their fair value, not historical cost. Answer (C) is incorrect. The bonds should be measured at fair value, not historical cost.

3. A company should report the marketable equity securities that it has classified as trading at

   A. Lower of cost or market, with holding gains and losses included in earnings.

   B. Lower of cost or market, with holding gains included in earnings only to the extent of previously recognized holding losses.

   C. Fair value, with holding gains included in earnings only to the extent of previously recognized holding losses.

   D. Fair value, with holding gains and losses included in earnings.

Answer (D) is correct. *(CPA, adapted)*
REQUIRED: The correct reporting method for marketable equity securities classified as trading.
DISCUSSION: Trading securities are those held principally for sale in the near term. They are classified as current and consist of debt securities and equity securities with readily determinable fair values. Unrealized holding gains and losses on trading securities are reported in earnings. On a statement of financial position, these securities are reported at fair value.
Answer (A) is incorrect. Trading securities are recorded at fair value. Answer (B) is incorrect. Trading securities are recorded at fair value, with unrealized gains/losses recognized in earnings. Answer (C) is incorrect. Unrealized gains/losses on trading securities are recognized in earnings.

4. Investments classified as held-to-maturity securities should be measured at

   A. Acquisition cost.

   B. Amortized cost.

   C. Lower of cost or market.

   D. Fair value.

Answer (B) is correct. *(Publisher, adapted)*
REQUIRED: The attribute for measuring held-to-maturity securities.
DISCUSSION: Debt securities classified as held-to-maturity are measured at amortized cost if the reporting entity has the positive intent and ability to hold them to maturity.
Answer (A) is incorrect. The acquisition cost of held-to-maturity securities is adjusted for amortization. Answer (C) is incorrect. Held-to-maturity securities are written down below amortized cost only when a decline in fair value below amortized cost is other than temporary. Answer (D) is incorrect. Debt securities classified as held-to-maturity are reported at amortized cost.

5. On July 2, Year 4, Wynn, Inc., purchased as a short-term investment a $1 million face amount Kean Co. 8% bond for $910,000 plus accrued interest to yield 10%. The bonds mature on January 1, Year 11, and pay interest annually on January 1. On December 31, Year 4, the bonds had a fair value of $945,000. On February 13, Year 5, Wynn sold the bonds for $920,000. In its December 31, Year 4, balance sheet, what amount should Wynn report for the bond if it is classified as an available-for-sale security?

A. $910,000

B. $920,000

C. $945,000

D. $950,000

Answer (C) is correct. *(CPA, adapted)*
REQUIRED: The amount to be reported for a bond classified as an available-for-sale security.
DISCUSSION: Available-for-sale securities should be measured at fair value in the balance sheet. Hence, the bond should be reported at its fair value of $945,000 to reflect the unrealized holding gain (change in fair value).
Answer (A) is incorrect. The cost is $910,000 (accrued interest is not recorded as part of the cost but as an adjustment of interest income). Answer (B) is incorrect. The sale price is $920,000. Answer (D) is incorrect. This amount equals the cost plus accrued interest (the total price paid) on 7/2/Year 4.

6. When the fair value of an investment in debt securities exceeds its amortized cost, how should each of the following debt securities be reported at the end of the year?

	Debt Securities Classified As	
	Held-to-Maturity	Available-for-Sale
A.	Amortized cost	Amortized cost
B.	Amortized cost	Fair value
C.	Fair value	Fair value
D.	Fair value	Amortized cost

Answer (B) is correct. *(CPA, adapted)*
REQUIRED: The reporting of debt securities classified as held-to-maturity and available-for-sale.
DISCUSSION: Investments in debt securities are classified as held-to-maturity and measured at amortized cost in the balance sheet if the reporting entity has the positive intent and ability to hold them to maturity. Marketable equity securities can be classified as either trading or available-for-sale. Equity securities that are not expected to be sold in the near term should be classified as available-for-sale (unless the FVO election has been made). These securities should be reported at fair value, with unrealized holding gains and losses (except those on securities designated as being hedged in a fair value hedge) excluded from earnings and reported in OCI.
Answer (A) is incorrect. Available-for-sale securities are recorded at fair value. Answer (C) is incorrect. Held-to-maturity securities are recorded at amortized cost. Answer (D) is incorrect. Available-for-sale securities are recorded at fair value, and held-to-maturity securities are recorded at amortized cost.

7. A decline in the fair value of an available-for-sale security below its amortized cost basis that is deemed to be other than temporary should

A. Be accumulated in a valuation allowance.

B. Be treated as a realized loss and included in the determination of net income for the period.

C. Not be realized until the security is sold.

D. Be treated as an unrealized loss and included in the equity section of the balance sheet as a separate item.

Answer (B) is correct. *(CMA, adapted)*
REQUIRED: The accounting for a nontemporary impairment of an available-for-sale security.
DISCUSSION: Any other-than-temporary decline in the fair value of an available-for-sale security below its amortized cost basis should be considered a realized loss. The amortized cost basis should be written down to fair value and is not adjusted for subsequent recoveries in fair value. Realized gains and losses should be included in income in the period in which they occur. However, if a security has been the hedged item in a fair value hedge, its amortized cost basis will reflect adjustments in its carrying amount for changes in fair value attributable to the hedged risk. The amortized cost basis should be distinguished from the fair value, which equals the cost basis plus or minus the net unrealized holding gain or loss. The cost basis, not the fair value, is used to determine the amount of any other-than-temporary decline in fair value that will be treated as a realized loss.
Answer (A) is incorrect. A valuation allowance is used to record changes in fair value regarded as temporary. Answer (C) is incorrect. A permanent decline in fair value is treated as a realized loss. Answer (D) is incorrect. A temporary decline in fair value is debited to other comprehensive income (OCI). Accumulated OCI is a component of equity on the balance sheet.

8. The following information pertains to Lark Corp.'s available-for-sale securities:

	December 31	
	Year 2	Year 3
Cost	$100,000	$100,000
Fair value	90,000	120,000

Differences between cost and fair values are considered to be temporary. The decline in fair value was properly accounted for at December 31, Year 2. Ignoring tax effects, by what amount should other comprehensive income (OCI) be credited at December 31, Year 3?

A. $0

B. $10,000

C. $20,000

D. $30,000

Answer (D) is correct. *(CPA, adapted)*
REQUIRED: The credit to OCI if fair value exceeds cost.
DISCUSSION: Unrealized holding gains and losses on available-for-sale securities, including those classified as current assets, are not included in earnings but ordinarily are reported in OCI, net of tax effects (ignored in this question). At 12/31/Year 2, (assuming the securities are not designated as being hedged in a fair value hedge), OCI should have been debited for $10,000 for the excess of cost over fair value to reflect an unrealized holding loss. At 12/31/Year 3, OCI should be credited to reflect a $30,000 unrealized holding gain ($120,000 fair value at 12/31/Year 3 – $90,000 fair value at 12/31/Year 2).
Answer (A) is incorrect. Unrealized holding gains on available-for-sale securities are recognized. Answer (B) is incorrect. The amount of $10,000 is merely the recovery of the previously recognized unrealized holding loss. The recognition of gain is not limited to that amount. Answer (C) is incorrect. The amount of $20,000 is merely the excess of fair value over cost.

9. For available-for-sale securities included in noncurrent assets, which of the following amounts should be included in the period's net income?

I. Unrealized holding losses during the period
II. Realized gains during the period
III. Changes in fair value during the period

A. III only.

B. II only.

C. I and II.

D. I, II, and III.

Answer (B) is correct. *(CPA, adapted)*
REQUIRED: The amounts included in the period's net income for available-for-sale securities included in noncurrent assets.
DISCUSSION: The temporary decline below cost of the fair value of available-for-sale securities is recorded in OCI, assuming they are not designated as being hedged in a fair value hedge. Thus, temporary changes in the measurement of these securities do not flow through net income. A realized gain occurs when securities are sold at an amount greater than their cost basis. Realized gains are included in net income regardless of the classification of the securities.
Answer (A) is incorrect. Changes in fair value during the period that are unrealized gains or temporary losses are included in OCI. Answer (C) is incorrect. Unrealized holding losses during the period that are temporary are included in OCI, assuming they are not designated as being hedged in a fair value hedge. Answer (D) is incorrect. Most unrealized holding losses during the period and changes in fair value during the period are included in OCI.

10. On December 31, Year 1, Ott Co. had investments in trading securities as follows:

	Cost	Fair Value
Man Co.	$10,000	$ 8,000
Kemo, Inc.	9,000	11,000
Fenn Corp.	11,000	9,000
	$30,000	$28,000

Ott's December 31, Year 1, balance sheet should report the trading securities as

A. $26,000

B. $28,000

C. $29,000

D. $30,000

Answer (B) is correct. *(CPA, adapted)*
REQUIRED: The amount at which the trading securities should be reported.
DISCUSSION: Trading securities are reported at fair value, and unrealized holding gains and losses are included in earnings. Consequently, the securities should be reported as $28,000.
Answer (A) is incorrect. The amount of $26,000 is the lower of cost or fair value determined on an individual security basis. Answer (C) is incorrect. The amount of $29,000 is the average of the aggregate cost and aggregate fair value. Answer (D) is incorrect. The amount of $30,000 is the aggregate cost.

11. Zinc Co.'s adjusted trial balance at December 31, Year 1, includes the following account balances:

Common stock, $3 par	$600,000
Additional paid-in capital	800,000
Treasury stock, at cost	50,000
Accumulated other comprehensive income: net unrealized loss on available-for-sale equity securities	20,000
Retained earnings: appropriated for uninsured earthquake losses	150,000
Retained earnings: unappropriated	200,000

What amount should Zinc report as total equity in its December 31, Year 1, balance sheet?

- A. $1,680,000
- B. $1,720,000
- C. $1,780,000
- D. $1,820,000

Answer (A) is correct. *(CPA, adapted)*
REQUIRED: The total equity.
DISCUSSION: Total credits to equity equal $1,750,000 ($600,000 common stock at par + $800,000 additional paid-in capital + $350,000 retained earnings). Total debits equal $70,000 ($50,000 cost of treasury stock + $20,000 unrealized loss on available-for-sale securities). Thus, total equity equals $1,680,000.
Answer (B) is incorrect. The amount of $1,720,000 treats the unrealized loss as a credit. Answer (C) is incorrect. The amount of $1,780,000 treats the treasury stock as a credit. Answer (D) is incorrect. The amount of $1,820,000 treats the treasury stock and the unrealized loss as credits.

12. On January 2, Year 1, Adam Co. purchased as a long-term investment 10,000 shares of Mill Corp.'s common stock for $40 a share. These securities were properly classified as available for sale. On December 31, Year 1, the market price of Mill's stock was $35 a share, reflecting a temporary decline in market price. On January 28, Year 2, Adam sold 8,000 shares of Mill stock for $30 a share. For the year ended December 31, Year 2, Adam should report a realized loss on disposal of a long-term investment of

- A. $100,000
- B. $80,000
- C. $60,000
- D. $40,000

Answer (B) is correct. *(CPA, adapted)*
REQUIRED: The loss on disposal of a noncurrent investment.
DISCUSSION: A realized loss or gain is recognized when an individual security is sold or otherwise disposed of. The investment was acquired for $40 per share. Because the shares were purchased as a noncurrent investment, they should be classified as available-for-sale securities. Thus, the temporary decline in fair value at 12/31/Year 1 was debited to other comprehensive income and was not included in earnings. Accordingly, the realized loss included in earnings at 12/31/Year 2 was $80,000 [8,000 shares × ($40 – $30)].
Answer (A) is incorrect. The amount of $100,000 assumes disposal of 10,000 shares. Answer (C) is incorrect. The amount of $60,000 is the fair value of the remaining shares. Answer (D) is incorrect. The amount of $40,000 was the temporary decline in value of 8,000 shares at 12/31/Year 1.

13. In Year 1, a company reported in other comprehensive income an unrealized holding loss on an investment in available-for-sale securities. During Year 2, these securities were sold at a loss equal to the unrealized loss previously recognized. The reclassification adjustment should include which of the following?

- A. The unrealized loss should be credited to the investment account.
- B. The unrealized loss should be credited to the other comprehensive income account.
- C. The unrealized loss should be debited to the other comprehensive income account.
- D. The unrealized loss should be credited to beginning retained earnings.

Answer (B) is correct. *(CPA, adapted)*
REQUIRED: The reclassification adjustment for a sale of available-for-sale securities at a loss.
DISCUSSION: Available-for-sale securities are measured at fair value, with unrealized holding gains and losses recognized in OCI. The Year 1 entry to recognize the loss was a debit to OCI for a loss and a credit to the allowance for securities fair value adjustments (or directly to available-for-sale securities). The Year 2 sale of the securities was at a loss equal to the recognized unrealized loss. Accordingly, the sale was at their carrying amount. Assuming the securities had a cost of $100 and the unrealized loss was $10, the Year 2 entry was

Cash	$90	
Allowance	10	
Loss	10	
Securities		$100
OCI		10

This entry reclassifies the loss from OCI to earnings.
Answer (A) is incorrect. The investment is credited for the initial cost, assuming an allowance account is used. Answer (C) is incorrect. The now-realized loss must be reclassified by crediting OCI to remove the effect of the previously recognized unrealized loss. Answer (D) is incorrect. Retained earnings is not directly affected by the loss.

14. The following information was extracted from Gil Co.'s December 31, Year 1, financial statements:

Noncurrent assets:
Long-term investments in available-for-
sale equity securities (at fair value) $96,450
Accumulated other comprehensive income:
Net unrealized loss on long-term
investments in available-for-sale
equity securities   (19,800)

Historical cost of the long-term investments in available-for-sale equity securities was

A. $63,595

B. $76,650

C. $96,450

D. $116,250

Answer (D) is correct. *(CPA, adapted)*
REQUIRED: The historical cost of the available-for-sale securities.
DISCUSSION: The existence of a debit balance for a classification of a separate component of equity (accumulated other comprehensive income) signifies that the available-for-sale securities are reported at fair value that is less than historical cost. The difference is the net unrealized loss balance. Hence, historical cost must have been $116,250 ($96,450 available-for-sale securities at fair value + $19,800 net unrealized loss).
Answer (A) is incorrect. The amount of $63,595 is a nonsense figure. Answer (B) is incorrect. The amount of $76,650 results from subtracting the unrealized loss instead of adding. Answer (C) is incorrect. The amount of $96,450 ignores the unrealized loss balance.

15. Jay Company acquired a wholly owned foreign subsidiary on January 1. The equity section of the December 31 consolidated balance sheet follows:

Common stock	$ 500,000
Additional paid-in capital	200,000
Retained earnings	900,000
	$1,600,000
Minus: Contra accounts	600,000
Total equity	$1,000,000

The contra account balance appropriately represents adjustments in translating the foreign subsidiary's financial statements into U.S. dollars.

The consolidated income statement included the excess of cost of investments in certain debt and equity securities over their fair values, which is considered temporary, as follows:

Available-for-sale securities	$200,000
Trading securities	100,000

The amounts for retained earnings and the contra accounts in the consolidated statement of equity for the year ended December 31 are

	Retained Earnings	Contra Accounts
A.	$900,000	$600,000
B.	$1,000,000	$700,000
C.	$1,100,000	$800,000
D.	$1,200,000	$900,000

Answer (C) is correct. *(CPA, adapted)*
REQUIRED: The amounts of retained earnings and the contra accounts in the consolidated statement of equity.
DISCUSSION: The unrealized holding loss on available-for-sale securities does not flow through net income (unless the securities are designated as being hedged in a fair value hedge). Instead, it is charged to OCI. This amount is closed to accumulated OCI, a contra account reported in the equity section. Accordingly, retained earnings and the contra accounts were understated by $200,000. Their amounts should be $1,100,000 and $800,000, respectively.
Answer (A) is incorrect. The amounts of $900,000 and $600,000 are unadjusted retained earnings and the contra accounts, respectively. Answer (B) is incorrect. The amount of $1,000,000 equals total equity. Moreover, $700,000 assumes that the unrealized holding loss on the trading securities, not the available-for-sale securities, is charged to an equity account. Answer (D) is incorrect. The amount of $1,200,000 assumes that the unrealized holding losses on both classes of securities are charged to an equity account. A contra accounts balance of $900,000 reflects the same assumption.

16. Data regarding Ball Corp.'s available-for-sale securities follow:

	Cost	Fair Value
December 31, Year 1	$150,000	$130,000
December 31, Year 2	150,000	160,000

Differences between cost and fair values are considered temporary. The decline in fair value was properly accounted for at December 31, Year 1. Ball's Year 2 statement of changes in equity would report an increase of

A. $30,000

B. $20,000

C. $10,000

D. $0

Answer (A) is correct. *(CPA, adapted)*
REQUIRED: The increase reported in the statement of changes in equity because of a change in the fair value of available-for-sale securities.
DISCUSSION: Unrealized holding gains and losses on available-for-sale securities classified as temporary are excluded from earnings, assuming these securities are not being hedged in a fair-value hedge. They are reported in other comprehensive income. At 12/31/Year 2, the fair value was greater than the cost. Consequently, the net amount reported (an unrealized net holding gain) is a credit of $10,000 ($160,000 fair value – $150,000 cost). At 12/31/Year 1, the balance would have been a debit of $20,000 ($150,000 cost – $130,000 fair value). Thus, the change from a debit of $20,000 to a credit of $10,000 increases accumulated other comprehensive income and therefore total equity by $30,000.
Answer (B) is incorrect. The amount of $20,000 is the excess of cost over fair value on 12/31/Year 1. Answer (C) is incorrect. The amount of $10,000 is the excess of fair value over cost on 12/31/Year 2. Answer (D) is incorrect. Equity increases when other comprehensive income is credited.

17. On December 1, Year 1, Wall Company purchased equity securities and properly classified them as trading securities. Pertinent data are as follows:

Security	Cost	Fair Value at 12/31/Year 1
A	$39,000	$36,000
B	50,000	55,000
C	96,000	85,000

On December 31, Year 1, Wall reclassified its investment in security C from trading to available-for-sale because Wall intends to retain security C. What net loss on its securities should be included in Wall's income statement for the year ended December 31, Year 1?

A. $0

B. $9,000

C. $11,000

D. $14,000

Answer (B) is correct. *(CPA, adapted)*
REQUIRED: The net loss to be included in net income when a trading security is reclassified.
DISCUSSION: Unrealized holding gains and losses on trading securities are included in earnings, and reclassification is at fair value. Furthermore, for a security transferred from the trading category, the unrealized holding gain or loss at the date of transfer will have already been recognized in earnings and is not reversed. Thus, the net unrealized holding loss at 12/31/Year 1 recognized in income is $9,000 ($3,000 loss on A – $5,000 gain on B + $11,000 loss on C).
Answer (A) is incorrect. The amount of $0 ignores the unrealized losses. Answer (C) is incorrect. The amount of $11,000 ignores the loss on A and the gain on B. Answer (D) is incorrect. The amount of $14,000 ignores the gain on B.

18. A reclassification of available-for-sale securities to the held-to-maturity category will result in

A. The amortization of an unrealized gain or loss in the same way as premium (discount).

B. The recognition in earnings on the transfer date of an unrealized gain or loss.

C. The reversal of any unrealized gain or loss previously recognized in earnings.

D. The reversal of any unrealized gain or loss previously recognized in other comprehensive income.

Answer (A) is correct. *(Publisher, adapted)*
REQUIRED: The true statement about a reclassification of available-for-sale securities to the held-to-maturity category.
DISCUSSION: The unrealized holding gain or loss on the date of transfer for available-for-sale securities transferred to the held-to-maturity category continues to be reported in OCI, assuming these securities were not designated as being hedged in a fair value hedge. In that case, the unrealized holding gain or loss would have previously been recognized in earnings. However, it is amortized in the same manner as the amortization of any discount or premium. This amortization at least partly offsets the effect on interest income of the amortization of the premium or discount.
Answer (B) is incorrect. Only transfers to the trading securities category result in immediate recognition in earnings of an unrealized gain or loss. Answer (C) is incorrect. No reversals are required by reclassification. Answer (D) is incorrect. The reclassification does not require reversal of any previously recognized amounts.

10.2 The Fair Value Option

19. Election of the fair value option (FVO)

- A. Permits only for-profit entities to measure eligible items at fair value.
- B. Results in recognition of unrealized gains and losses in earnings of a business entity.
- C. Requires deferral of related upfront costs.
- D. Results in recognition of unrealized gains and losses in other comprehensive income of a business entity.

Answer (B) is correct. *(Publisher, adapted)*
REQUIRED: The accounting for the FVO.
DISCUSSION: A business measures at fair value the eligible items for which the FVO election was made at a specified election date. The unrealized gains and losses on those items are reported in earnings at each subsequent reporting date.
Answer (A) is incorrect. The FVO may be elected by all entities. Answer (C) is incorrect. Upfront costs and fees are recognized in earnings of a business as they are incurred if they relate to eligible items for which the FVO election was made. Answer (D) is incorrect. The unrealized gains and losses are recognized in earnings, not OCI.

20. The decision whether to elect the fair value option (FVO)

- A. Is irrevocable until the next election date, if any.
- B. May be applied to a portion of a financial instrument.
- C. Must be applied only to classes of financial instruments.
- D. Must be applied to all instruments issued in a single transaction.

Answer (A) is correct. *(Publisher, adapted)*
REQUIRED: The scope of the decision to elect the FVO.
DISCUSSION: The decision whether to elect the FVO is final and cannot be revoked unless a new election date occurs. For example, an election date occurs when an entity recognizes an investment in equity securities with readily determinable fair values issued by another entity. A second election date occurs when the accounting changes because the investment later becomes subject to equity-method accounting. An original decision to classify the equity securities as available-for-sale may then be revoked at the second election date by choosing the FVO instead of the equity method.
Answer (B) is incorrect. The decision whether to elect the FVO applies only to an entire instrument and not to only specified risks, specific cash flows, or portions of it. Answer (C) is incorrect. The decision whether to elect the FVO may be applied to individual eligible items. Thus, identical items may be treated differently. However, certain exceptions apply. For example, the FVO may be applied to an investment to which the equity method would otherwise apply. This election must be applied to all financial interests held by the investor in the investee that are eligible items. Answer (D) is incorrect. With certain exceptions (e.g., multiple advances to one debtor under a single construction loan that merge into a larger balance), the FVO need not be applied to all eligible items acquired or issued in the same transaction. For example, an acquirer of registered bonds may apply the FVO to only some of the bonds.

21. Which of the following is an election date for the purpose of determining whether to elect the fair value option (FVO)?

- A. The accounting treatment of an equity investment changes because the entity no longer has significant influence.
- B. The entity enters into a firm commitment to purchase soybeans in 3 months.
- C. The accounting for an equity investment changes because the entity no longer consolidates a subsidiary.
- D. The accounting treatment of an equity investment changes because the entity must consolidate the investee.

Answer (C) is correct. *(Publisher, adapted)*
REQUIRED: The election date.
DISCUSSION: An entity may choose the FVO only on an election date. For example, an election date occurs when the accounting for an equity investment in another entity changes because the investor retains an interest but no longer consolidates a subsidiary or a variable interest entity.
Answer (A) is incorrect. An election date occurs when the accounting changes because the investment becomes subject to equity-method accounting. Loss of significant influence does not result in an election date. Answer (B) is incorrect. A firm commitment is not an eligible item unless it involves financial instruments only. Answer (D) is incorrect. The FVO is not an alternative to consolidation.

10.3 Equity Method

22. If the reporting entity has not elected the fair value option, the equity method of accounting for investments in common stock

    A. Should be used in accounting for investments in common stock of corporate joint ventures.

    B. Should be used only for investments in common stock of unconsolidated domestic subsidiaries reported in consolidated financial statements.

    C. Is a valid substitute for consolidation.

    D. May not be used when accounting for an investment of less than 25% of the voting stock of an investee.

Answer (A) is correct. *(Publisher, adapted)*
REQUIRED: The true statement about the equity method.
DISCUSSION: Investors should account for investments in common stock of corporate joint ventures by the equity method because it best enables them to reflect the underlying nature of their investments. Usually, the investors have the ability to exert significant influence on the operation of the joint venture.
Answer (B) is incorrect. Investments in which the investor has significant influence must be accounted for by the equity method whether the unconsolidated subsidiaries are domestic or foreign. Answer (C) is incorrect. Application of the equity method is not a valid substitute for consolidation. Answer (D) is incorrect. The equity method would most likely be used if ownership were 20% or greater.

23. X Company owns 15% of the voting stock of Y Co. and 25% of the voting stock of Z Co. X has not elected the fair value option. Under what circumstances should X account for each investment using the equity method?

	Investment in Y	Investment in Z
A.	In all cases	In all cases
B.	Never	In all cases
C.	Never	Only if X has the ability to exercise significant influence over Z
D.	Only if X has the ability to exercise significant influence over Y	Only if X has the ability to exercise significant influence over Z

Answer (D) is correct. *(S. Rubin)*
REQUIRED: The circumstances in which the equity method of accounting for a stock investment should be used.
DISCUSSION: The equity method is used when an investee has the ability to exercise significant influence. An investment of 20% or more of the voting stock of an investee leads to a presumption that an investor has the ability to exercise significant influence. An investment of less than 20% leads to a presumption that an investor does not have such ability. However, those presumptions can be overcome by predominant evidence to the contrary. See the guidance on the criteria for applying the equity method.
Answer (A) is incorrect. The equity method should be used only if X has the ability to exercise significant influence over Y or Z. Answer (B) is incorrect. The equity method should be used if X has the ability to exercise significant influence over Y even though its holding is below the 20% threshold. The equity method should not be used if X cannot exercise significant influence over Y even though its holding exceeds the 20% threshold. Answer (C) is incorrect. The equity method should be used if X has the ability to exercise significant influence over Y even though its holding is below the 20% threshold.

24. When an investor uses the equity method to account for investments in common stock, the investment account will be increased when the investor recognizes

    A. A proportionate interest in the net income of the investee.

    B. A cash dividend received from the investee.

    C. Periodic amortization of the goodwill related to the purchase.

    D. Depreciation related to the excess of fair value over the carrying amount of the investee's depreciable assets at the date of purchase by the investor.

Answer (A) is correct. *(CPA, adapted)*
REQUIRED: The basis for increasing the investment account when the investor uses the equity method.
DISCUSSION: Under the equity method, the investor's share of the investee's net income is accounted for as an addition to the carrying amount of the investment on the investor's books. Losses and dividends are reflected as reductions of the carrying amount.
Answer (B) is incorrect. Recognition of a cash dividend received from the investee reduces the carrying amount. Answer (C) is incorrect. Goodwill is not amortized. Moreover, equity method goodwill is not separately reviewed for impairment because it is not separate from the investment. Answer (D) is incorrect. Recognition of depreciation related to the excess of fair value over the carrying amount of the investee's depreciable assets at the date of purchase by the investor reduces the carrying amount.

25. When the equity method is used to account for investments in common stock, which of the following affects the investor's reported investment income?

	Goodwill Amortization Related to the Purchase	Cash Dividends from Investee
A.	Yes	Yes
B.	No	Yes
C.	No	No
D.	Yes	No

Answer (C) is correct.   *(CPA, adapted)*
REQUIRED: The transaction(s) affecting the investor's reported investment income when the equity method is used.
DISCUSSION: The difference between the cost of an investment and the investee's underlying equity should be accounted for as if the investee were a consolidated subsidiary. Thus, the difference is assigned first to any undervalued or overvalued assets, with the remainder allocated to goodwill. Amortization of goodwill is prohibited and therefore does not reduce investment income. Moreover, equity method goodwill is not separately reviewed for impairment because it is not separate from the investment. The receipt of a cash dividend from the investee also does not affect equity-based earnings. The entry is to debit cash and credit the investment.
Answer (A) is incorrect. Goodwill related to the purchase is not amortized, and cash dividends do not affect investment income. Answer (B) is incorrect. Cash dividends do not affect investment income. Answer (D) is incorrect. Goodwill is not amortized.

26. In its financial statements, Pulham Corp. uses the equity method of accounting for its 30% ownership of Angles Corp. At December 31, Year 1, Pulham has a receivable from Angles. How should the receivable be reported in Pulham's Year 1 financial statements?

A. None of the receivable should be reported, but the entire receivable should be offset against Angles' payment to Pulham.

B. 70% of the receivable should be separately reported, with the balance offset against 30% of Angles' payment to Pulham.

C. The total receivable should be disclosed separately.

D. The total receivable should be included as part of the investment in Angles, without separate disclosure.

Answer (C) is correct.   *(CPA, adapted)*
REQUIRED: The method of reporting a receivable from a 30%-owned company.
DISCUSSION: Related parties include an entity and its equity-based investees. A receivable from a related party should be separately disclosed in full.
Answer (A) is incorrect. Elimination of intercompany transactions is inappropriate except in the case of combined or consolidated statements. Answer (B) is incorrect. A general principle of accounting is that assets and liabilities should not be offset in the balance sheet unless a right of offset exists. Answer (D) is incorrect. The investment balance equals cost plus the investor's share of earnings and losses, minus any return of the investment. Also, separate disclosure is required.

27. The criterion for determining whether an entity may apply the equity method is the ability to exercise significant influence over the investee. An investor who owns 30% of the voting common stock of the investee is most likely to exercise significant influence when

A. The investor and investee sign an agreement under which the investor surrenders significant rights.

B. The investor tries and fails to obtain representation on the investee's board of directors.

C. Opposition by the investee, such as litigation, challenges the investor's exercise of significant influence.

D. The majority ownership of the investee is spread among a large group of shareholders who have objectives with respect to the investee that differ from those of the investor.

Answer (D) is correct.   *(Publisher, adapted)*
REQUIRED: The situation that indicates ability to exercise significant influence.
DISCUSSION: If the investor owns 20% to 50% of an investee and the remainder of the ownership is spread among a large group of shareholders, the investee will be able to exert significant influence even though most of the other owners have objectives contrary to those of the investor. The presumption of significant influence can be overcome by evidence that majority ownership is held by a small number of shareholders who operate the investee without regard to the investor's views.
Answer (A) is incorrect. When the investor and investee sign an agreement under which the investor surrenders significant rights, the investor cannot exercise significant influence. Answer (B) is incorrect. When the investor tries and fails to obtain representation on the investee's board of directors, the investor cannot exercise significant influence. Answer (C) is incorrect. When opposition by the investee, such as litigation or complaints to governmental regulatory authorities, challenges the investor's exercise of significant influence, the investor cannot exercise significant influence.

28. On January 2, Year 1, Well Co. purchased 10% of Rea, Inc.'s outstanding common shares for $400,000. Well is the largest single shareholder in Rea, and Well's officers are a majority on Rea's board of directors. Rea reported net income of $500,000 for Year 1 and paid dividends of $150,000. In its December 31, Year 1, balance sheet, what amount should Well report as investment in Rea if it has not elected the fair value option?

A. $450,000

B. $435,000

C. $400,000

D. $385,000

Answer (B) is correct. *(CPA, adapted)*
REQUIRED: The amount reported in the investment account.
DISCUSSION: The equity method should be used because Well Co. exercises significant influence over Rea. The investment in Rea equals $435,000 [$400,000 investment + ($500,000 net income × 10%) – ($150,000 of dividends × 10%)].
Answer (A) is incorrect. The amount of $450,000 does not deduct Well's dividends. Answer (C) is incorrect. The amount of $400,000 does not include Well's share of net income or deduct Well's dividends. Answer (D) is incorrect. The amount of $385,000 does not include Well's share of net income.

29. Which procedure mentioned below is a requirement in the application of the equity method of accounting for investments?

A. The investor's share of extraordinary items should be classified in a similar manner, if material, in the income statement of the investor.

B. The difference between the cost of an investment and the amount of the underlying equity in net assets of the investee should be permanently capitalized in the balance sheet of the investor.

C. Even if the percentage ownership of the investee's common stock held by the investor falls below the level needed to exercise significant influence, the equity method should still be employed.

D. The investor should continue using the equity method even when the investee's losses are large enough to cause the investment account to be reduced below a zero balance.

Answer (A) is correct. *(Publisher, adapted)*
REQUIRED: The proper procedure in applying the equity method.
DISCUSSION: The income statement of an investor reflects investment income resulting from the investor's share of the earnings of the investee company. The investor's share of the investee's extraordinary items must be reported as extraordinary items in the investor's income statement.
Answer (B) is incorrect. The difference between the cost of an investment and the investee's underlying equity should be assigned first to any undervalued or overvalued assets, with the remainder allocated to goodwill, which is nonamortizable. Moreover, equity method goodwill is not separately reviewed for impairment. Answer (C) is incorrect. If an investment falls below the level needed to exert significant influence, the investor should discontinue use of the equity method and change to the fair-value method (assuming the stock has a readily determinable fair value). Answer (D) is incorrect. When the investment is reduced to zero by the losses of the investee, the investor should discontinue using the equity method.

30. An investor uses the equity method to account for an investment in common stock. After the date of acquisition, the investment account of the investor is

A. Not affected by its share of the earnings or losses of the investee.

B. Not affected by its share of the earnings of the investee but is decreased by its share of the losses of the investee.

C. Increased by its share of the earnings of the investee but is not affected by its share of the losses of the investee.

D. Increased by its share of the earnings of the investee and is decreased by its share of the losses of the investee.

Answer (D) is correct. *(CPA, adapted)*
REQUIRED: The effect(s) on an equity-based investment in common stock of investee earnings and losses.
DISCUSSION: After the date of acquisition, an equity-based investment-in-common-stock account of an investor is increased by its share of the earnings of the investee, decreased by its share of the losses of the investee, and decreased by its share of cash dividends received from the investee.
Answer (A) is incorrect. The investment is increased by the investor's share of earnings and decreased by its share of losses. Answer (B) is incorrect. The investment is increased by the investor's share of investee earnings. Answer (C) is incorrect. The investment is decreased by the investor's share of investee losses.

31. The investor's accounting procedure under the equity method is to debit the investment account to record its share of investee income and to credit the investment account to record its share of investee dividends. In substance, the net effect is to

A. Recognize only distributed income of the investee.

B. Not consider distributed income of the investee as income.

C. Increase the investment account for investee distributed income.

D. Recognize both distributed and undistributed income of the investee.

Answer (D) is correct. *(Publisher, adapted)*
REQUIRED: The substance of the entries to record investee income and dividends under the equity method.
DISCUSSION: The traditional journal entries for the equity method are

Investment in investee	$XXX	
Investment income		$XXX
Cash	$XXX	
Investment in investee		$XXX

If they are combined in a single entry, the net effect is to debit the investment account for undistributed income, to debit cash for distributed income, and to credit investment income for total income.
Answer (A) is incorrect. The cost method and the fair value method recognize only distributed income of the investee. Answer (B) is incorrect. Both distributed and undistributed income are recognized by the investor. Answer (C) is incorrect. The investment account is increased only by the investor's share of the investee's undistributed income.

32. Company A holds an investment in another entity but does not elect the fair value option. Which of the following is false?

A. Company A owns 19% of Company B's voting common stock and acquires 1% more. Company A's investment, results of operations (current and prior periods presented), and retained earnings should be adjusted retroactively.

B. Depending on the circumstances, an investor may be required to account for an investment in voting common stock under the fair-value method even though the investor owns more than 20% of the voting common stock.

C. Company A owns 20% of Company B's voting common stock and sells 1%. Company A's investment, results of operations (current and prior periods presented), and retained earnings should be adjusted retroactively.

D. One of the disclosures necessary under the equity method of accounting for investments is the difference, if any, between the amount at which an investment is carried and the amount of underlying equity in net assets and the accounting treatment of the difference.

Answer (C) is correct. *(Publisher, adapted)*
REQUIRED: The false statement regarding the equity method of accounting.
DISCUSSION: Unless an investor entity has elected the fair value option, it must apply the equity method if it can exercise significant influence over the investee (presumed at a level of 20% ownership or greater). If the investor subsequently sells shares so that significant influence is no longer presumed, the investment is accounted for using the fair-value method if the shares retained have a readily determinable fair value. The change is accounted for on a prospective basis. The carrying amount of the investment subsequently will be changed by transactions in the stock and by changes in its fair value. The investment will be classified as available-for-sale or trading securities, but the fair value option cannot be elected when the investment ceases to be subject to equity-method accounting.
Answer (A) is incorrect. Achieving significant influence subsequent to the initial purchase of an investment requires retroactive application of the equity method. Answer (B) is incorrect. When significant influence cannot be exerted over the investee despite 20% or greater ownership, the fair-value method should be used if the stock has a readily determinable fair value. Answer (D) is incorrect. GAAP require disclosure of (1) the difference, if any, between the amount of the investment and the underlying equity in the net assets of the investee and (2) the accounting treatment of the difference.

33. Peel Co. received a cash dividend from a common stock investment with a readily determinable fair value. Should Peel report an increase in the investment account if it accounts for the security as available-for-sale or uses the equity method of accounting?

	Available- for-Sale	Equity
A.	No	No
B.	Yes	Yes
C.	Yes	No
D.	No	Yes

Answer (A) is correct. *(CPA, adapted)*
REQUIRED: The effect of a cash dividend on the investment account.
DISCUSSION: If a stock investment is classified as available-for-sale, it is accounted for using the fair-value method. Hence, dividends from an investee should be accounted for by the investor as dividend income unless a liquidating dividend is received. Thus, assuming that the dividend is not liquidating, it has no effect on the investment. Under the equity method, cash dividends decrease the investment because the dividend is considered to be a return of investment.
Answer (B) is incorrect. A cash dividend does not increase the investment under either the fair-value method or the equity method. Answer (C) is incorrect. A cash dividend does not increase the investment under the fair-value method. Answer (D) is incorrect. A cash dividend does not increase the investment account under the equity method.

34. On January 1, Year 1, Point, Inc., purchased 10% of Iona Co.'s common stock. Point purchased additional shares, bringing its ownership up to 40% of Iona's common stock outstanding on August 1, Year 1. Point did not elect the fair value option. During October Year 1, Iona declared and paid a cash dividend on all of its outstanding common stock. How much income from the Iona investment should Point's Year 1 income statement report?

A. 10% of Iona's income for January 1 to July 31, Year 1, plus 40% of Iona's income for August 1 to December 31, Year 1.

B. 40% of Iona's income for August 1 to December 31, Year 1, only.

C. 40% of Iona's Year 1 income.

D. Amount equal to dividends received from Iona.

35. A corporation that uses the equity method of accounting for its investment in a 40%-owned investee that earned $20,000 and paid $5,000 in dividends made the following entries:

Investment in subsidiary $8,000
     Equity in earnings of subsidiary $8,000

Cash $2,000
     Dividend revenue $2,000

What effect will these entries have on the parent's statement of financial position?

A. Investment understated, retained earnings understated.

B. Investment overstated, retained earnings overstated.

C. Investment overstated, retained earnings understated.

D. Financial position will be fairly stated.

36. Park Co. uses the equity method to account for its January 1, Year 1, purchase of Tun, Inc.'s common stock. On January 1, Year 1, the fair values of Tun's FIFO inventory and land exceeded their carrying amounts. How do these excesses of fair values over carrying amounts affect Park's reported equity in Tun's Year 1 earnings?

	Inventory Excess	Land Excess
A.	Decrease	Decrease
B.	Decrease	No effect
C.	Increase	Increase
D.	Increase	No effect

Answer (A) is correct. *(CPA, adapted)*
REQUIRED: The income from an investment that has increased from less than 20% to more than 20% during the period.
DISCUSSION: Once the ownership percentage increased from 10% to 40%, Point was presumed to exercise significant influence over Iona. Because the fair value option was not elected, the investment should be accounted for retroactively under the equity method. Given that Point held 10% of Iona's common stock for the first 7 months of the year, it should recognize in earnings 10% of Iona's income for that period. It should recognize 40% of Iona's income for the balance of the year. Point's share of the dividend is credited to the investment account and is not included in earnings.
Answer (B) is incorrect. Adoption of the equity method is retroactive to the acquisition of the first shares of stock of the investee. Answer (C) is incorrect. Point held only 10% of Iona's stock for the January-July period. Answer (D) is incorrect. Iona's dividends do not affect Point's net income.

Answer (B) is correct. *(CPA, adapted)*
REQUIRED: The effect of an error in recording investment income or dividends received.
DISCUSSION: In the case of 40% ownership, the equity method of accounting for the investment in the investor's books should be applied. The 40% share of the investee's $20,000 net income ($8,000) is correctly recorded.
Dividends received from an investee must be recorded in the books of the investor as a decrease in the carrying amount of the investment and an increase in assets (cash). Hence, dividend revenue was incorrectly credited with the $2,000 dividend resulting in an overstatement of retained earnings. The investment should have been credited for $2,000. Thus, the effect on the investment is also an overstatement.
Answer (A) is incorrect. The $2,000 of dividend revenue should have been credited to the investment in subsidiary. Thus, both the investment and retained earnings are overstated. Answer (C) is incorrect. The entries overstated retained earnings. Answer (D) is incorrect. Financial position is misstated. The investment (an asset) and retained earnings (an equity account) are overstated.

Answer (B) is correct. *(CPA, adapted)*
REQUIRED: The effect on equity in investee earnings of the excess of the fair values of the investee's FIFO inventory and land over their carrying amounts.
DISCUSSION: The equity method of accounting requires the investor's proportionate share of the investee's reported net income to be adjusted for certain acquisition differentials. Thus, the difference at the date of acquisition of the investee's stock between the fair value and carrying amount of inventory is such an adjustment when the inventory is sold. A similar adjustment for land is required when the land is sold. Assuming that the FIFO inventory was sold in Year 1 and the land was not, Park's proportionate share of Tun's reported net income is decreased by the inventory differential allocated at the date of acquisition.
Answer (A) is incorrect. The land excess has no effect. Answer (C) is incorrect. The inventory excess decreases equity in the investee's earnings, but the land excess has no effect. Answer (D) is incorrect. The inventory excess decreases equity in the investee's earnings.

37. On January 2, Year 1, Kean Co. purchased a 30% interest in Pod Co. for $250,000. On this date, Pod's equity was $500,000. The carrying amounts of Pod's net assets approximated their fair values except for land, for which fair value exceeded its carrying amount by $200,000. Pod reported net income of $100,000 for Year 1 and paid no dividends. Kean accounts for this investment using the equity method. In its December 31, Year 1, balance sheet, what amount should Kean report as an equity method investment?

A. $210,000

B. $220,000

C. $276,000

D. $280,000

Answer (D) is correct. *(CPA, adapted)*
REQUIRED: The amount reported as investment in subsidiary under the equity method.
DISCUSSION: The purchase price is allocated to the fair value of the net assets acquired, with the remainder allocated to goodwill. The fair value of Kean's 30% interest in Pod's net assets is $210,000 [($500,000 + $200,000) × 30%]. Goodwill is $40,000 ($250,000 – $210,000). The equity method requires the investor's share of subsequent net income reported by the investee to be adjusted for the difference at acquisition between the fair value and the carrying amount of the investee's net assets when the net assets are sold or consumed in operations. The land is assumed not to be sold, and the equity method goodwill is not amortized or separately reviewed for impairment. Thus, Kean's share of Pod's net income is $30,000 ($100,000 declared income × 30%), and the investment account at year end is $280,000 ($250,000 acquisition balance + $30,000 investment income).
Answer (A) is incorrect. The amount of $210,000 equals the fair value of the identifiable net assets acquired. Answer (B) is incorrect. The amount of $220,000 equals the price minus Kean's equity in Pod's net income. Answer (C) is incorrect. The amount of $276,000 assumes amortization of goodwill over 10 years.

38. Green Corp. owns 30% of the outstanding common stock and 100% of the outstanding noncumulative nonvoting preferred stock of Axel Corp. In Year 1, Axel declared dividends of $100,000 on its common stock and $60,000 on its preferred stock. Green exercises significant influence over Axel's operations and uses the equity method to account for the investment in the common stock. What amount of dividend revenue should Green report in its income statement for the year ended December 31, Year 1?

A. $0

B. $30,000

C. $60,000

D. $90,000

Answer (C) is correct. *(CPA, adapted)*
REQUIRED: The dividend revenue reported given declaration of common and preferred dividends by an investee.
DISCUSSION: Under the equity method, the receipt of a cash dividend from the investee should be credited to the investment account. It is a return of, not a return on, the investment. However, the equity method is not applicable to preferred stock. Thus, Green should report $60,000 of revenue when the preferred dividends are declared.
Answer (A) is incorrect. The preferred, not the common, dividends should be credited to revenue. Answer (B) is incorrect. The amount of $30,000 is Green's share of the common dividends. The cash dividends on common stock should be credited to the investment account. Answer (D) is incorrect. The amount of $90,000 is the sum of the preferred dividends ($60,000) and 30% of the common dividends ($100,000 × 30%).

39. Sage, Inc., bought 40% of Adams Corp.'s outstanding common stock on January 2, Year 1, for $400,000. The carrying amount of the net assets at the purchase date totaled $900,000. Fair values and carrying amounts were the same for all items except for plant and inventory, for which fair values exceeded their carrying amounts by $90,000 and $10,000, respectively. The plant has an 18-year life. All inventory was sold during Year 1. During Year 1, Adams reported net income of $120,000 and paid a $20,000 cash dividend. What amount should Sage report in its income statement from its investment in Adams for the year ended December 31, Year 1, if it did not elect the fair value option?

A. $48,000

B. $42,000

C. $36,000

D. $32,000

Answer (B) is correct. *(CPA, adapted)*
REQUIRED: The amount reported as investment income.
DISCUSSION: Sage holds 40% of the investee's stock and is assumed to exercise significant influence. Given that it did not elect the fair value method, Sage must account for the investment on the equity basis by recognizing its proportionate share of the investee's net income. To determine the amount of investment income the investor should report, the investee's net income of $120,000 should be adjusted for the $10,000 excess of fair value over the carrying amount of the inventory acquired because this inventory was sold. The investee's reported net income also should be adjusted for the share of the difference between the fair value and carrying amount of the plant that has been consumed (depreciated), or $5,000 ($90,000 difference ÷ 18 years). No goodwill is recognized because the $400,000 purchase price equals a proportionate share of the fair value of the net assets {[($900,000 + $90,000 + $10,000) × 40%] = $400,000}. Thus, Sage should report investment income of $42,000 [($120,000 – $10,000 – $5,000) × 40%].
Answer (A) is incorrect. The amount of $48,000 equals the proportionate share of the investee's reported net income. Answer (C) is incorrect. The amount of $36,000 adjusts the reported net income for the dividend disclosed and does not adjust for the plant depreciation. Answer (D) is incorrect. The amount of $32,000 assumes the plant's useful life is 3 years.

40. Pare, Inc., purchased 10% of Tot Co.'s 100,000 outstanding shares of common stock on January 2, Year 1, for $50,000. On December 31, Year 1, Pare purchased an additional 20,000 shares of Tot for $150,000. There was no goodwill as a result of either acquisition, and Tot had not issued any additional stock during Year 1. Tot reported earnings of $300,000 for Year 1. What amount should Pare report in its December 31, Year 1, balance sheet as investment in Tot if it did not elect the fair value option?

    A. $170,000

    B. $200,000

    C. $230,000

    D. $290,000

Answer (C) is correct. *(CPA, adapted)*
REQUIRED: The amount reported in the investment account.
DISCUSSION: Given that Pare owned 30% of Tot at year end, Pare presumably can exercise significant influence. Given also that it did not elect the fair value option, the equity method should be used. Although Pare held 20% or greater ownership only on the last day of Year 1, the adoption of the equity method must be retroactive. However, the retroactive effect is based on the percentage of ownership held prior to the adoption of the equity method. Consequently, Pare should recognize its equity in the earnings of Tot as if the equity method had been in effect since 1/2/Year 1. Accordingly, its share of Tot's Year 1 earnings will be $30,000 ($300,000 × 10%), and the investment account balance at year end will be $230,000 ($150,000 + $50,000 + $30,000).
Answer (A) is incorrect. The amount of $170,000 results from subtracting the equity in Tot's earnings. Answer (B) is incorrect. The amount of $200,000 ignores the equity in Tot's earnings. Answer (D) is incorrect. The amount of $290,000 assumes Pare held a 30% interest throughout the year.

41. On January 1, Year 1, Mega Corp. acquired 10% of the outstanding voting stock of Penny, Inc. On January 2, Year 2, Mega gained the ability to exercise significant influence over financial and operating control of Penny by acquiring an additional 20% of Penny's outstanding stock. Mega did not elect the fair value option. The two purchases were made at prices proportionate to the value assigned to Penny's net assets, which equaled their carrying amounts. For the years ended December 31, Year 1 and Year 2, Penny reported the following:

	Year 1	Year 2
Dividends paid	$200,000	$300,000
Net income	600,000	650,000

In Year 2, what amounts should Mega report as current-year investment income and as an adjustment, before income taxes, to Year 1 investment income?

	Year 2 Investment Income	Adjustment to Year 1 Investment Income
A.	$195,000	$160,000
B.	$195,000	$120,000
C.	$195,000	$40,000
D.	$105,000	$40,000

Answer (C) is correct. *(CPA, adapted)*
REQUIRED: The amounts reported as current-year investment income and as an adjustment, before income taxes, to the previous year's investment income.
DISCUSSION: When ownership of an investee reaches the level of significant influence, the investor must adopt the equity method if it did not elect the fair value option. The investor must also retroactively adjust the carrying amount of the investment, results of operations, and retained earnings as if the equity method had been in effect during all of the previous periods in which any percentage was held. Consequently, Mega should report Year 2 investment income before taxes equal to $195,000 ($650,000 net income reported by Penny for Year 2 × 30%). Ignoring taxes, it should retroactively adjust Year 1 investment income by $40,000 [($600,000 investee net income in Year 1 × 10% interest held in Year 1) – ($200,000 dividends paid by investee in Year 1 × 10%)].
Answer (A) is incorrect. The amount of $160,000 equals 30% of Penny's Year 1 net income minus 10% of Penny's Year 1 dividends. Answer (B) is incorrect. The amount of $120,000 equals 30% of Penny's Year 1 net income minus 30% of Penny's Year 1 dividends. Answer (D) is incorrect. The amount of $105,000 equals Mega's share of Year 2 net income minus its share of dividends.

42. On July 1, Year 1, Denver Corp. purchased 3,000 shares of Eagle Co.'s 10,000 outstanding shares of common stock for $20 per share but did not elect the fair value option. On December 15, Year 1, Eagle paid $40,000 in dividends to its common shareholders. Eagle's net income for the year ended December 31, Year 1, was $120,000, earned evenly throughout the year. In its Year 1 income statement, what amount of income from this investment should Denver report?

    A. $36,000

    B. $18,000

    C. $12,000

    D. $6,000

Answer (B) is correct. *(CPA, adapted)*
REQUIRED: The income reported from an investment in common stock.
DISCUSSION: Denver Corp.'s purchase of 30% of Eagle presumably allows it to exercise significant influence. Hence, it should apply the equity method. The investor's share of the investee's income is a function of the percentage of ownership and the length of time the investment was held. The income from this investment was therefore $18,000 [$120,000 × 30% × (6 months ÷ 12 months)].
Answer (A) is incorrect. The amount of $36,000 assumes Denver owned the stock for the full year. Answer (C) is incorrect. The amount of $12,000 equals 30% of the dividend. Dividends do not affect income under the equity method. Answer (D) is incorrect. The amount of $6,000 equals 50% of 30% of the dividends.

43. Pear Co.'s income statement for the year ended December 31, Year 1, as prepared by Pear's controller, reported income before taxes of $125,000. The auditor questioned the following amounts that had been included in income before taxes:

Equity in earnings of Cinn Co.	$40,000
Dividends received from Cinn	8,000
Adjustments to profits of prior years for arithmetical errors in depreciation	(35,000)

Pear owns 40% of Cinn's common stock but did not elect the fair value option. Pear's December 31, Year 1, income statement should report income before taxes of

A. $85,000

B. $117,000

C. $120,000

D. $152,000

Answer (D) is correct. *(CPA, adapted)*
REQUIRED: The amount reported as income before taxes on the income statement.
DISCUSSION: Under the equity method, the investor's share of the investee's net income is accounted for as an addition to the carrying amount of the investment, and losses and dividends are reflected as reductions. Consequently, the equity in earnings of Cinn Co. was correctly included in income, but the dividends received should have been excluded. In addition, error corrections related to earlier periods are treated as prior-period adjustments and are not included in net income. Thus, income before taxes should have been $152,000 ($125,000 – $8,000 dividends + $35,000 depreciation error).
Answer (A) is incorrect. The amount of $85,000 subtracts the equity in earnings of Cinn Co. and includes the dividends and the effects of the prior-period adjustment. Answer (B) is incorrect. The amount of $117,000 includes the prior-period adjustment. Answer (C) is incorrect. The amount of $120,000 equals the computed income, minus the equity in the earnings of Cinn, plus the depreciation error.

44. Band Co. uses the equity method to account for its investment in Guard, Inc., common stock. How should Band record a 2% stock dividend received from Guard?

A. As dividend revenue at Guard's carrying amount of the stock.

B. As dividend revenue at the fair value of the stock.

C. As a reduction in the total cost of Guard stock owned.

D. As a memorandum entry reducing the unit cost of all Guard stock owned.

Answer (D) is correct. *(CPA, adapted)*
REQUIRED: The entry to record a stock dividend received from an equity investee.
DISCUSSION: No entries are made to record the receipt of stock dividends. However, a memorandum entry should be made in the investment account to record additional shares owned. This treatment applies whether the investment is accounted for by the fair-value method or the equity method.
Answer (A) is incorrect. The receipt of a stock dividend is not a revenue. The shareholder has the same proportionate interest in the investee. Answer (B) is incorrect. The stock dividend received from Guard is not recorded in the accounts. Answer (C) is incorrect. The cost per share, not the total cost, is reduced.

10.4 Investments in Bonds

45. When bond interest payments are sent to the owner of the bonds by the debtor, the bonds are called

A. Participating bonds.

B. Coupon bonds.

C. Registered bonds.

D. Debenture bonds.

Answer (C) is correct. *(Publisher, adapted)*
REQUIRED: The bonds on which interest payments are sent to the owner by the debtor.
DISCUSSION: Registered bonds are issued in the name of the owner. Thus, interest payments are sent directly to the owner. When the owner sells registered bonds, the bond certificates must be surrendered and new certificates issued. They differ from coupon (bearer) bonds, which can be freely transferred and have a detachable coupon for each interest payment.
Answer (A) is incorrect. Participating bonds participate in excess earnings of the debtor as defined in the contractual agreement. Answer (B) is incorrect. The debtor does not keep records of the owners of coupon (bearer) bonds. Answer (D) is incorrect. Debenture bonds are unsecured bonds.

46. Bonds that investors may present for payment prior to maturity are

A. Callable bonds.

B. Redeemable bonds.

C. Convertible bonds.

D. Income bonds.

Answer (B) is correct. *(Publisher, adapted)*
REQUIRED: The type of bond that may be presented for payment prior to maturity.
DISCUSSION: Redeemable bonds may be presented for payment by the creditor prior to the maturity date. The bonds usually are redeemable only after a specified period of time.
Answer (A) is incorrect. Callable bonds may be redeemed by the debtor. Answer (C) is incorrect. Convertible bonds may be exchanged, usually at the option of the creditor, for common stock or other equity securities. Answer (D) is incorrect. The distinctive feature of income bonds is that interest is paid only if income is earned by the debtor.

47. On January 1, Welling Company purchased 100 of the $1,000 face amount, 8%, 10-year bonds of Mann, Inc. The bonds mature on January 1 in 10 years, and pay interest annually on January 1. Welling purchased the bonds to yield 10% interest.

Present value of $1 at 8% for 10 periods	0.4632
Present value of $1 at 10% for 10 periods	0.3855
Present value of an annuity of $1 at 8% for 10 periods	6.7101
Present value of an annuity of $1 at 10% for 10 periods	6.1446

How much did Welling pay for the bonds?

- A. $87,707
- B. $92,230
- C. $95,477
- D. $100,000

Answer (A) is correct. *(CPA, adapted)*
REQUIRED: The present value to the investor (price paid) of an investment in long-term bonds.
DISCUSSION: An investment in a bond should be recorded at its fair value, i.e., the present value of its cash flows discounted at the market (yield) rate of interest. The present value of the investment has two components: the value of the periodic cash interest payments and the value of the bond proceeds at maturity. The interest payment at 8% on each bond will be $80 per year for 10 years. Applying a present value factor of 6.1446 (annuity, 10 periods, 10%) gives a present value of the periodic interest payments of $491.57. The proceeds of each bond at maturity of $1,000 are multiplied by a factor of .3855 (10%, 10 periods) for a present value of $385.50. The resulting total price per bond of $877.07 ($491.57 + $385.50) multiplied by 100 bonds gives a total payment of $87,707.
Answer (B) is incorrect. The amount of $92,230 is based on a present value of an annuity factor of 6.7101. Answer (C) is incorrect. The amount of $95,477 results from using a present value factor of .4632. Answer (D) is incorrect. This figure is the face amount of the bonds, which were purchased at a discount.

48. Loan origination fees are charged to the borrower in connection with originating, refinancing, or restructuring a loan (e.g., points, lending fees, etc.). Loan origination fees should be

- A. Recognized in income when collected.
- B. Recognized in income on a straight-line basis during the life of the loan but over no more than 5 years.
- C. Deferred and recognized in income over the life of the loan using the straight-line method.
- D. Deferred and recognized in income over the life of the loan by the interest method.

Answer (D) is correct. *(Publisher, adapted)*
REQUIRED: The lender accounting procedure for loan origination fees.
DISCUSSION: Loan origination fees must be recognized in income over the life of the loan using the interest method. The objective is to achieve a constant effective yield over the life of the loan.
Answer (A) is incorrect. The fees are deferred, not recognized immediately. Answer (B) is incorrect. The effective interest method is used and no 5-year maximum is prescribed. Answer (C) is incorrect. The effective interest method is used, not straight-line amortization.

49. An investor purchased a bond classified as a long-term investment between interest dates at a discount. At the purchase date, the carrying amount of the bond is more than the

	Cash Paid to Seller	Face Amount of Bond
A.	No	Yes
B.	No	No
C.	Yes	No
D.	Yes	Yes

Answer (B) is correct. *(CPA, adapted)*
REQUIRED: The carrying amount of a bond purchased at a discount between interest dates.
DISCUSSION: At the date of purchase, the carrying amount of the bond equals its face amount minus the discount. The cash paid equals the initial carrying amount plus accrued interest. Hence, the initial carrying amount is less than the cash paid by the amount of the accrued interest and less than the face amount by the amount of the discount.
Answer (A) is incorrect. The carrying amount is less than the face amount. Answer (C) is incorrect. The carrying amount is less than the cash paid. Answer (D) is incorrect. The carrying amount is less than either the face amount or the cash paid.

50. On September 1, the Consul Company acquired $10,000 face amount, 8% bonds of Envoy Corporation at 104. The bonds were dated May 1 and mature in 5 years on April 30, with interest payable each October 31 and April 30. What entry should Consul make to record the purchase of the bonds?

A. Investment in bonds $10,400
    Interest receivable   266
      Cash $10,666

B. Investment in bonds $10,666
     Cash $10,666

C. Investment in bonds $10,666
    Accrued interest receivable $ 266
      Cash   10,400

D. Investment in bonds $10,000
    Premium on bonds   666
      Cash $10,666

Answer (A) is correct. *(CPA, adapted)*
REQUIRED: The entry to record a bond purchased at a premium with accrued interest.
DISCUSSION: At 104, the price paid for the bonds is $10,400 in the absence of any accrued interest. Because the bonds were purchased between interest dates, cash interest accrued for the 4 months from May 1 to September 1 (date of purchase) must be computed and included in the purchase price. The interest for 4 months at 8% is $266.67 [$10,000 × 8% × (4 months ÷ 12 months)], which is recorded as interest receivable and added to the $10,400 purchase price, for a total amount paid of $10,666. When interest is received on October 31, the $266 in interest receivable will be credited.
Answer (B) is incorrect. Interest receivable should be recognized in the amount of $266. The purchase was between interest dates. Answer (C) is incorrect. Interest receivable should be debited. Answer (D) is incorrect. The premium paid was $400. The interest receivable of $266 should be recorded separately from bond premium.

51. Cap Corp. reported accrued investment interest receivable of $38,000 and $46,500 at January 1 and December 31, Year 1, respectively. During Year 1, cash collections from the investments included the following:

Capital gains distributions $145,000
Interest   152,000

What amount should Cap report as interest revenue from investments for Year 1?

A. $160,500
B. $153,500
C. $152,000
D. $143,500

Answer (A) is correct. *(CPA, adapted)*
REQUIRED: The interest revenue from debt investments.
DISCUSSION: When a receivable increases, revenue exceeds collections. Given that the accrued interest receivable balance increased by $8,500 ($46,500 – $38,000), and interest collected equaled $152,000, interest revenue equals $160,500 ($152,000 + $8,500). Capital gains distributions do not affect interest.
Answer (B) is incorrect. The amount of $153,500 equals capital gains plus the increase in accrued interest receivable. Answer (C) is incorrect. The amount of $152,000 equals collections. Answer (D) is incorrect. The amount of $143,500 equals collections of interest minus the increase in accrued interest receivable.

52. On July 1, Year 1, York Co. purchased as a long-term investment $1 million of Park, Inc.'s 8% bonds for $946,000, including accrued interest of $40,000. The bonds were purchased to yield 10% interest and were properly classified as held-to-maturity securities. The bonds mature on January 1, Year 8, and pay interest annually on January 1. York uses the effective interest method of amortization. In its December 31, Year 1, balance sheet, what amount should York report as investment in bonds?

A. $911,300
B. $916,600
C. $953,300
D. $960,600

Answer (A) is correct. *(CPA, adapted)*
REQUIRED: The amount reported as bond investment at year end.
DISCUSSION: The bond investment's original balance was $906,000 ($946,000 price – $40,000 accrued interest) because the carrying amount does not include accrued interest. Under the effective interest method, interest income equals the yield or effective interest rate times the carrying amount of the bonds at the beginning of the interest period. The amortization of premium or discount is the difference between this interest income and the periodic cash payments. For the period 7/1 to 12/31/Year 1, interest income is $45,300 [$906,000 × 10% × (6 months ÷ 12 months)], and the actual interest is $40,000 [$1,000,000 × 8% × (6 months ÷ 12 months)]. Hence, the carrying amount at year end is $911,300 [$906,000 + ($45,300 – $40,000)].
Answer (B) is incorrect. The amount of $916,600 amortizes the discount for 12 months. Answer (C) is incorrect. The amount of $953,300 includes the accrued interest. Answer (D) is incorrect. The amount of $960,600 includes the accrued interest and amortizes the discount for 12 months.

53. On July 1, Year 1, Cody Co. paid $1,198,000 for 10%, 20-year bonds with a face amount of $1 million. Interest is paid on December 31 and June 30. The bonds were purchased to yield 8%. Cody uses the effective interest rate method to recognize interest income from this investment. The bonds are properly classified as held-to-maturity. What should be reported as the carrying amount of the bonds in Cody's December 31, Year 1, balance sheet?

 A. $1,207,900

 B. $1,198,000

 C. $1,195,920

 D. $1,193,050

Answer (C) is correct. *(CPA, adapted)*
 REQUIRED: The amount reported as bond investment at year end.
 DISCUSSION: Under the effective interest method, interest income equals the yield or effective interest rate times the carrying amount of the bonds at the beginning of the interest period. The amortization of premium or discount is the difference between this interest income and the periodic cash payments. For Year 1, interest income is $47,920 [$1,198,000 × 8% × (6 months ÷ 12 months)], and interest received is $50,000 [$1,000,000 × 10% × (6 months ÷ 12 months)]. Hence, the carrying amount at year end is 1,195,920 [$1,198,000 – ($50,000 – $47,920)].
 Answer (A) is incorrect. The amount of $1,207,900 equals the investment if interest income is determined using a 10% rate, and the difference between actual interest and interest income is added to the carrying amount. Answer (B) is incorrect. This figure is the carrying amount before adjustment for the premium amortization. Answer (D) is incorrect. The amount of $1,193,050 assumes that interest income is based on a 10% rate and that the bonds have been outstanding for 3 months.

54. On July 1, Year 1, Pell Co. purchased Green Corp. 10-year, 8% bonds with a face amount of $500,000 for $420,000. The bonds mature on June 30, Year 9, and pay interest semiannually on June 30 and December 31. Using the interest method, Pell recorded bond discount amortization of $1,800 for the 6 months ended December 31, Year 1. From this held-to-maturity investment, Pell should report Year 1 revenue of

 A. $16,800

 B. $18,200

 C. $20,000

 D. $21,800

Answer (D) is correct. *(CPA, adapted)*
 REQUIRED: The interest revenue when amortization of bond discount is known.
 DISCUSSION: Interest income for a bond issued at a discount is equal to the sum of the periodic cash flows and the amount of bond discount amortized during the interest period. The periodic cash flows are equal to $20,000 ($500,000 face amount × 8% coupon rate × .5 year). The discount amortization is given as $1,800. Thus, revenue for the 6-month period from 7/1 to 12/31/Year 1 is $21,800 ($20,000 + $1,800).
 Answer (A) is incorrect. The amount of $16,800 is 50% of 8% of $420,000. Answer (B) is incorrect. The amount of $18,200 equals the cash flow minus discount amortization. Answer (C) is incorrect. The amount of $20,000 equals the cash flow.

55. In Year 1, Lee Co. acquired, at a premium, Enfield, Inc., 10-year bonds as a long-term investment. At December 31, Year 1, Enfield's bonds were quoted at a small discount. Which of the following situations is the most likely cause of the decline in the bonds' fair value?

 A. Enfield issued a stock dividend.

 B. Enfield is expected to call the bonds at a premium, which is less than Lee's carrying amount.

 C. Interest rates have declined since Lee purchased the bonds.

 D. Interest rates have increased since Lee purchased the bonds.

Answer (D) is correct. *(CPA, adapted)*
 REQUIRED: The most likely cause of a decline in a bond's fair value.
 DISCUSSION: Bonds selling at a premium have a nominal rate in excess of the market rate. Bonds selling at a discount have a nominal rate less than the market rate. Thus, interest rates in the market must have increased in order for a bond originally acquired at a premium to be currently quoted at a discount.
 Answer (A) is incorrect. A stock dividend has no effect on quoted fair values of bonds. Answer (B) is incorrect. Bonds expected to be called at a premium would not be quoted at a discount. Answer (C) is incorrect. If interest rates decline below the stated rate, the bonds will be quoted at a higher premium.

56. When bonds with detachable stock warrants are purchased, the amount debited to investment in stock warrants relative to the total amount paid

A. Increases the premium on the investment in bonds.

B. Increases the discount on investment in bonds.

C. Increases any premium or decreases any discount on the bonds.

D. Has no effect on the investment of bond premium or discount because the warrants are purchased separately.

Answer (B) is correct. *(Publisher, adapted)*
REQUIRED: The effect on the carrying amount of bonds of debiting investment in stock warrants.
DISCUSSION: The portion of the price allocated to the detachable stock warrants decreases the allocation to investment in bonds. Thus, amounts debited to investment in stock warrants increase the discount or decrease the premium recorded for the investment in bonds.
Answer (A) is incorrect. The allocation to detachable stock warrants decreases the premium. Answer (C) is incorrect. The allocation to detachable stock warrants decreases the premium or increases any discount. Answer (D) is incorrect. The price should be allocated between the warrants and the bonds based upon their relative market values at issuance. The allocation to detachable stock warrants decreases the premium or increases any discount.

10.5 Cash Surrender Value

57. On January 2, Year 1, Beal, Inc., acquired a $70,000 whole-life insurance policy on its president. The annual premium is $2,000. The company is the owner and beneficiary. Beal charged officer's life insurance expense as follows:

Year	Life Insurance Expense
1	$2,000
2	1,800
3	1,500
4	1,100
Total	$6,400

In Beal's December 31, Year 4, balance sheet, the investment in cash surrender value should be

A. $0

B. $1,600

C. $6,400

D. $8,000

Answer (B) is correct. *(CPA, adapted)*
REQUIRED: The investment in cash surrender value.
DISCUSSION: Cash surrender value is the loan value or surrender value of a whole-life insurance policy. It is equal to the difference between the premiums paid and the life insurance expense recognized. Because the total of premiums paid is $8,000 ($2,000 × 4 years) and the total life insurance expense is $6,400, the investment in cash surrender value is $1,600. This amount is classified as a noncurrent asset on a classified balance sheet because management purchases life insurance policies for the life insurance aspect rather than as a short-term investment.
Answer (A) is incorrect. The excess of the premiums over the expenses is the cash surrender value. Answer (C) is incorrect. The amount of $6,400 is the total insurance expense for 4 years. Answer (D) is incorrect. The amount of $8,000 is the sum of the premiums for 4 years.

58. An increase in the cash surrender value of a life insurance policy owned by a company is recorded by

A. Decreasing annual insurance expense.

B. Increasing investment income.

C. Recording a memorandum entry only.

D. Decreasing a deferred charge.

Answer (A) is correct. *(CPA, adapted)*
REQUIRED: The proper recording of an increase.
DISCUSSION: The cash surrender value of the policy is an asset of the company. Thus, part of the premium paid is not expense. As the cash surrender value increases, the annual insurance expense decreases, assuming a constant premium.
Answer (B) is incorrect. Investment income is not affected by life insurance. Answer (C) is incorrect. As the cash surrender value increases, the annual insurance expense decreases. Answer (D) is incorrect. Cash surrender value should be classified as an asset, not a deferred charge. The deferred charge category should be avoided.

59. In Year 1, Chain, Inc., purchased a $1 million life insurance policy on its president, of which Chain is the beneficiary. Information regarding the policy for the year ended December 31, Year 6, follows:

Cash surrender value, 1/1/Year 6	$ 87,000
Cash surrender value, 12/31/Year 6	108,000
Annual advance premium paid 1/1/Year 6	40,000

During Year 6, dividends of $6,000 were applied to increase the cash surrender value of the policy. What amount should Chain report as life insurance expense for Year 6?

- A. $40,000
- B. $21,000
- C. $19,000
- D. $13,000

Answer (C) is correct. *(CPA, adapted)*
REQUIRED: The life insurance expense to be reported.
DISCUSSION: Life insurance expense is equal to the excess of the premiums paid over the increase in cash surrender value and dividends received. Because the dividends were applied to increase the cash surrender value, they were therefore not received. Hence, Chain's life insurance expense is $19,000.

Premium	$40,000
Less:	
Increase in cash surrender value	
($108,000 – $87,000)	(21,000)
Life insurance expense	$19,000

Answer (A) is incorrect. The amount of $40,000 is the premium paid. Answer (B) is incorrect. The amount of $21,000 is the change in the cash surrender value. Answer (D) is incorrect. The amount of $13,000 results from subtracting the dividends applied.

60. In Year 1, Gar Corp. collected $300,000 as beneficiary of a key person life insurance policy carried on the life of Gar's controller, who had died in Year 1. The life insurance proceeds are not subject to income tax. At the date of the controller's death, the policy's cash surrender value was $90,000. What amount should Gar report as revenue in its Year 1 income statement?

- A. $0
- B. $90,000
- C. $210,000
- D. $300,000

Answer (C) is correct. *(CPA, adapted)*
REQUIRED: The revenue reported from collection of life insurance.
DISCUSSION: Upon receipt of life insurance proceeds, cash is debited for the amount received. Cash surrender value is credited for the amount of the asset on the books, and the balancing credit is to insurance income (a revenue account). Hence, revenue equals $210,000 ($300,000 cash – $90,000 cash surrender value).
Answer (A) is incorrect. Cash collected exceeded the asset. Answer (B) is incorrect. The amount of $90,000 is the cash surrender value. Answer (D) is incorrect. The amount of $300,000 equals the cash collected.

10.6 Derivatives and Hedges

61. A derivative financial instrument is best described as

- A. Evidence of an ownership interest in an entity such as shares of common stock.
- B. A contract that has its settlement value tied to an underlying notional amount.
- C. A contract that conveys to a second entity a right to receive cash from a first entity.
- D. A contract that conveys to a second entity a right to future collections on accounts receivable from a first entity.

Answer (B) is correct. *(CPA, adapted)*
REQUIRED: The best description of a derivative.
DISCUSSION: A derivative is a bet on whether the value of something (underlying notional amount) will go up or down. A derivative has at least one underlying (interest rate, currency exchange rate, price of a specific financial instrument, etc.) and at least one notional amount (number of units specified in the contract) or payment provision, or both. No initial net investment, or one smaller than that necessary for contracts with similar responses to the market, is required. Furthermore, a derivative's terms require or permit net settlement or provide for the equivalent. Net settlement means that the derivative can be readily settled with only a net delivery of assets. Thus, neither party must deliver (1) an asset associated with its underlying or (2) an asset that has a principal, stated amount, etc., equal to the notional amount.
Answer (A) is incorrect. Financial instruments include cash, evidence of an ownership interest in an entity, and certain contracts. A derivative is a contract. Answer (C) is incorrect. Any financial instrument (not just a derivative) that is a contract conveys to a second entity a right to receive cash or another financial instrument from a first entity or to exchange other financial instruments on potentially favorable terms with the first entity. Answer (D) is incorrect. A contract that conveys to a second entity a right to future collections on accounts receivable from a first entity is not, by itself, a derivative. It is not a bet on whether the price of something will go up or down. Instead, it may be a factoring arrangement.

62. Garcia Corporation has entered into a binding agreement with Hernandez Company to purchase 400,000 pounds of Colombian coffee at $2.53 per pound for delivery in 90 days. This contract is accounted for as a

A. Financial instrument.

B. Firm commitment.

C. Forecasted transaction.

D. Fair value hedge

Answer (B) is correct. *(Publisher, adapted)*
REQUIRED: The type of transaction defined.
DISCUSSION: A firm commitment is an agreement with an unrelated party, binding on both parties and usually legally enforceable, that specifies all significant terms and includes a disincentive for nonperformance.
Answer (A) is incorrect. A financial instrument does not involve the delivery of a product. Answer (C) is incorrect. A forecasted transaction is a transaction that is expected to occur for which no firm commitment exists. Answer (D) is incorrect. The transaction does not hedge an exposure to risk.

63. Neron Co. has two derivatives related to two different financial instruments, instrument A and instrument B, both of which are debt instruments. The derivative related to instrument A is a fair value hedge, and the derivative related to instrument B is a cash flow hedge. Neron experienced gains in the value of instruments A and B due to a change in interest rates. Which of the gains should be reported by Neron in its income statement?

	Gain in Value of Debt Instrument A	Gain in Value of Debt Instrument B
A.	Yes	Yes
B.	Yes	No
C.	No	Yes
D.	No	No

Answer (B) is correct. *(CPA, adapted)*
REQUIRED: The gain(s), if any, reported in the income statement.
DISCUSSION: In a fair value hedge, the change in fair value of the hedged item (instrument A) is an adjustment of the carrying amount that is recognized currently in earnings. The same treatment applies to the change in fair value of the hedging instrument. The earnings effect of (gain on) the hedged item (instrument B) in this cash flow hedge occurs in a future reporting period.
Answer (A) is incorrect. The earnings effect of (gain on) the hedged item (instrument B) in this cash flow hedge occurs in a future reporting period. Answer (C) is incorrect. The gain in fair value of instrument B is recognized in a future period. The gain in fair value of instrument A is recognized currently in earnings. Answer (D) is incorrect. The gain in fair value of instrument A is recognized currently in earnings.

64. To the extent the hedge is effective, a loss arising from the decrease in fair value of a derivative is included in current earnings if the derivative qualifies and is designated as a

	Fair-Value Hedge	Cash-Flow Hedge
A.	Yes	No
B.	No	Yes
C.	Yes	Yes
D.	No	No

Answer (A) is correct. *(Publisher, adapted)*
REQUIRED: The treatment of a loss arising from a decrease in fair value of a derivative qualified and designated as either a fair-value or a cash-flow hedge.
DISCUSSION: A fair-value hedge includes a hedge of an exposure to changes in the fair value of a recognized asset or liability or of an unrecognized firm commitment. Changes in both (1) the fair value of a derivative that qualifies and is designated as a fair-value hedge and (2) the fair value of the hedged item attributable to the hedged risk are included in earnings in the period of change. Thus, the net effect on earnings is limited to the ineffective portion, i.e., the difference between the changes in fair value. A cash-flow hedge includes a hedge of an exposure to variability in the cash flows of a recognized asset or liability or a forecasted transaction. Changes in the fair value of a derivative that qualifies and is designated as a cash-flow hedge are recognized in OCI to the extent the hedge is effective. The ineffective portion of the hedge is recognized in current earnings. The amounts accumulated in OCI are reclassified to earnings in the period(s) the hedged transaction affects earnings. For example, accumulated amounts related to a forecasted purchase of equipment are reclassified as the equipment is depreciated.
Answer (B) is incorrect. To the extent the hedge is effective, the changes in fair value of a hedge qualified and designated as a fair-value hedge are included in earnings in the periods the changes take place. The changes in the fair value of a derivative that qualifies and is designated as a cash-flow hedge are recognized as in OCI to the extent the hedge is effective. Answer (C) is incorrect. Changes in the fair value of a derivative that qualifies and is designated as a cash-flow hedge are recognized to the extent the hedge is effective. Answer (D) is incorrect. The changes in fair value of a hedge qualified, designated, and effective as a fair-value hedge are included in earnings in the periods when they occur.

65. On October 1, Year 1, Bordeaux, Inc., a calendar year-end firm, invested in a derivative designed to hedge the risk of changes in fair value of certain assets, currently estimated at $1.5 million. The derivative is structured to result in an effective hedge. However, some ineffectiveness may result. On December 31, Year 1, the fair value of the hedged assets has decreased by $350,000. The fair value of the derivative has increased by $325,000. Bordeaux should recognize a net effect on Year 1 earnings of

A. $0

B. $25,000

C. $325,000

D. $350,000

Answer (B) is correct. *(Publisher, adapted)*
REQUIRED: The net effect on earnings of a partially effective hedge of changes in fair value of a recognized asset.
DISCUSSION: A hedge of an exposure to changes in the fair value of a recognized asset or liability is classified as a fair value hedge. Gains and losses arising from changes in fair value of a derivative classified as a fair value hedge are included in the determination of earnings in the period of change. They are offset by losses or gains on the hedged item attributable to the risk being hedged. Thus, earnings of the period of change are affected only by the net gain or loss attributable to the ineffective aspect of the hedge. The ineffective portion is equal to $25,000 ($350,000 – $325,000).
Answer (A) is incorrect. The net effect is equal to the ineffective portion of the hedge. Answer (C) is incorrect. The amount of $325,000 is the increase in the derivative's fair value. Answer (D) is incorrect. The amount of $350,000 is the decrease in the hedged assets' fair value.

10.7 Financial Instrument Disclosures

66. Which of the following is a financial instrument?

A. Merchandise inventory.

B. Deferred subscription revenue.

C. A note payable in U.S. Treasury bonds.

D. A warranty payable.

Answer (C) is correct. *(Publisher, adapted)*
REQUIRED: The item meeting the definition of a financial instrument.
DISCUSSION: A financial instrument is cash, evidence of an ownership interest in an entity, or a contract that both (1) imposes on one entity a contractual obligation (a) to deliver cash or another financial instrument to a second entity or (b) to exchange financial instruments on potentially unfavorable terms with the second entity, and (2) conveys to that second entity a contractual right (a) to receive cash or another financial instrument from the first entity or (b) to exchange other financial instruments on potentially favorable terms with the first entity. A note payable in U.S. Treasury bonds gives the holder the contractual right to receive and imposes on the issuer the contractual obligation to deliver bonds that are themselves financial instruments. Thus, given that one entity has a contractual obligation to deliver another financial instrument and the second entity has a contractual right to receive another financial instrument, the note payable in U.S. Treasury bonds meets the definition of a financial instrument.
Answer (A) is incorrect. Although the sale of inventory could result in the receipt of cash, the holder of the inventory has no current contractual right to receive cash. Answer (B) is incorrect. Deferred subscription revenue will result in the delivery of goods or services. Answer (D) is incorrect. A warranty payable will result in the delivery of goods or services.

67. Whether recognized or unrecognized in an entity's financial statements, disclosure of the fair values of the entity's financial instruments is required when

A. It is practicable to estimate those values.

B. The entity maintains accurate cost records.

C. Aggregated fair values are material to the entity.

D. Individual fair values are material to the entity.

Answer (A) is correct. *(CPA, adapted)*
REQUIRED: The circumstances in which disclosure of the fair values of the entity's financial instruments is required.
DISCUSSION: Certain entities must disclose the fair value of financial instruments, whether or not they are recognized in the balance sheet, if it is practicable to estimate such fair values. If estimating fair value is not practicable, disclosures include information pertinent to estimating the fair value of the financial instrument or class of financial instruments, such as the carrying amount, effective interest rate, and maturity. The reasons that estimating the fair value is not practicable also should be disclosed.
Answer (B) is incorrect. The disclosure requirement is based on a practicability standard, not whether the entity maintains accurate cost records. Answer (C) is incorrect. Disclosure is based on practicability, not whether aggregated fair values are material to the entity. Answer (D) is incorrect. Disclosure is based on practicability, not whether individual fair values are material to the entity.

68. Disclosure of information about significant concentrations of credit risk is required for

A. Most financial instruments.

B. Financial instruments with off-balance-sheet credit risk only.

C. Financial instruments with off-balance-sheet market risk only.

D. Financial instruments with off-balance-sheet risk of accounting loss only.

Answer (A) is correct. *(CPA, adapted)*
REQUIRED: The financial instruments for which disclosure of significant concentrations of credit risk is required.
DISCUSSION: GAAP require the disclosure of information about the fair value of financial instruments, whether recognized or not (certain nonpublic entities and certain instruments, such as leases and insurance contracts, are exempt from the disclosure requirements). Furthermore, GAAP require disclosure of all significant concentrations of credit risk for most financial instruments (except for obligations for deferred compensation, certain instruments of a pension plan, insurance contracts, warranty obligations and rights, and unconditional purchase obligations).
Answer (B) is incorrect. Disclosure of significant concentrations of credit risk is required for most financial instruments. Answer (C) is incorrect. Disclosure about market risk is encouraged, not required. Answer (D) is incorrect. Disclosure is not limited to unrecognized risks of accounting loss.

10.8 IFRS

69. Under IFRS, an entity may elect the fair value option

A. For any financial asset or liability.

B. To reduce an accounting mismatch.

C. Whenever an embedded derivative cannot feasibly be separated from the host.

D. As an alternative to consolidation.

Answer (B) is correct. *(Publisher, adapted)*
REQUIRED: The circumstance in which an entity may elect the FVO.
DISCUSSION: The fair value option is available if it significantly reduces an accounting mismatch, that is, a measurement or recognition inconsistency. A mismatch results from measuring assets or liabilities (not just those that are financial) or recognizing gain or loss on them using different methods.
Answer (A) is incorrect. IFRS permit the FVO in limited circumstances. GAAP permit the FVO for most but not all financial assets or liabilities. Answer (C) is incorrect. The FVO is not available if the host contract of the embedded derivative is not an asset and (1) the embedded derivative does not significantly affect the related cash flows or (2) separation of the embedded derivative from the host contract is clearly inappropriate. Answer (D) is incorrect. Neither GAAP nor IFRS treat the FVO as an alternative to consolidation.

Use Gleim **EQE Test Prep** Software Download for interactive study and performance analysis.

STUDY UNIT ELEVEN
CURRENT LIABILITIES, COMPENSATED ABSENCES, AND CONTINGENCIES

Current Liabilities

Current liabilities include obligations that are expected to be paid using current assets or by creating other current liabilities within 1 year from the balance sheet date (or **operating cycle**, if longer). Thus, current liabilities include (1) obligations to pay for items to be used in producing goods or providing services (e.g., accounts payable), (2) obligations to pay for operations directly related to the operating cycle (e.g., wages or taxes payable), (3) collections in advance of delivering goods or providing services (e.g., deferred rent revenue), and (4) other obligations expected to be paid within 1 year (or operating cycle, if longer) from the balance sheet date. Examples of other obligations are (1) current debt, (2) the current portion of noncurrent debt, (3) payments required under sinking-fund requirements, and (4) agency obligations incurred by the collection of assets for third parties.

Current liabilities also include obligations that, by their terms, are **due on demand** within 1 year (or the operating cycle, if longer). Liquidation need not be expected. Noncurrent obligations that are **callable** at the balance sheet date because the debtor has violated the debt agreement are reclassified as current if the violation is not remedied within any specified period. However, such obligations are not classified as current if either (1) the creditor has waived or subsequently lost the right to demand repayment for more than 1 year (or operating cycle, if longer), or (2) it is probable that the violation will be remedied during a grace period. Furthermore, current liabilities do not include (1) obligations that are expected to be satisfied using **noncurrent assets** or (2) current obligations that an entity intends, and has demonstrated the ability, to **refinance on a long-term basis**.

Measurement of current liabilities is customarily at the undiscounted face amount (e.g., accounts payable) or net settlement value (warranties). However, GAAP allow an entity to measure most recognized financial liabilities at fair value.

Certain Taxes Payable

Federal unemployment tax and the employer's share of **FICA taxes** are expenses incurred as employees earn wages. But they are paid only on a periodic basis to the federal government. Accordingly, liabilities should be accrued for both expenses, as well as for wages earned but not paid. Income taxes withheld and the employees' share of FICA taxes are accrued as withholding taxes (payroll deductions), not as employer payroll taxes. Most states impose **sales taxes**. Ordinarily, the tax is paid by the buyer but is collected and remitted by the seller. Most states require quarterly or monthly filing of sales tax returns and remittance of taxes collected. **Property taxes** are usually expensed by monthly accrual over the fiscal period of the taxing authority.

Refinancing of Current Debt

If an entity intends to refinance current debt on a **noncurrent basis** and demonstrates the ability to do so, the obligation should be reclassified as **noncurrent**. The ability to refinance may be demonstrated by issuing noncurrent obligations or equity securities after the end of the reporting period but before issuance of the balance sheet. The ability to refinance also may be shown by entering into a financing agreement that meets the following criteria: (1) The agreement does not expire within the longer of 1 year or the operating cycle, (2) it is noncancelable by the lender, (3) no violation of the agreement exists at the end of the reporting period, and (4) the lender is financially capable of honoring the agreement.

Compensated Absences and Postemployment Benefits

Compensated absences are absences from work (e.g., illness, vacations, holidays) for which employees will be paid. Accrual of a liability for compensated absences is required when (1) the compensation relates to services already provided, (2) payment is probable, (3) the amount can be reasonably estimated, and (4) the benefits either vest or accumulate. However, accrual of compensated absences for **sick pay benefits** are required only if the benefits vest.

The accounting for postemployment benefits by employers applies to all benefits provided after employment but before retirement to former or inactive employees, their beneficiaries, and their covered dependents. **Postemployment benefits** include (1) salary continuation, (2) supplemental unemployment benefits, (3) severance benefits, (4) disability-related benefits, (5) job training and counseling, and (6) the continuation of healthcare benefits and insurance coverage. Postemployment benefits may be paid as a result of a disability, layoff, death, or other event. They are accrued if (1) the employer's obligation is attributable to employees' services already rendered, (2) the obligation relates to rights that **vest or accumulate**, (3) payment of the compensation is probable, and (4) the amount is reasonably estimable. If these conditions are not met, postemployment benefits must be accrued if it is probable that a liability has been incurred and the amount is reasonably estimable.

Contingencies

A contingency involves uncertainty as to possible loss (a loss contingency) or gain (a gain contingency). It ultimately will be resolved when one or more future events occur or fail to occur. A loss (gain) contingency involves either a potentially overstated (understated) asset or a potentially understated (overstated) liability.

Accrual of a **contingent loss** is required if information available prior to the issuance of financial statements indicates that it is **probable** that an asset is overstated or a liability is understated and the amount of the loss can be **reasonably estimated**. If the estimate of the loss is stated within a given range and an amount within that range is considered to be a better estimate than any other, that amount must be accrued. If no amount within the range is considered to be a better estimate than any other, the minimum of the range must be accrued. Disclosure of the nature of the loss also is required, and disclosure of the amount accrued is required if nondisclosure might make the financial statements misleading.

If the existence of a contingent loss is **reasonably possible**, disclosure of the nature of the contingency and an estimate of the potential loss or range of loss, if available, are required. If an estimate cannot be made, the disclosure must include a statement to that effect.

Disclosure ordinarily is not required if the possibility of a loss is **remote**. However, disclosure of the nature and amount of remote contingencies involving **guarantees** is required, for example, for (1) direct or indirect guarantees of the indebtedness of others or (2) guarantees to repurchase receivables that have been sold or otherwise assigned. A guarantee is a noncontingent obligation to be ready to perform after a triggering event or condition. It is combined with a contingent obligation to make payments if the event or condition occurs. Thus, recognition of a liability at the effective date of a guarantee is required even when it is not probable that payments will be made. The initial measurement ordinarily is at **fair value**. If a contingent loss and liability also are required to be recognized under GAAP, the liability recognized by the guarantor is the greater of the fair value or the contingent liability amount. Examples are (1) a stand-alone guarantee given for a premium (debit cash or a receivable), (2) a stand-alone guarantee to an unrelated party without consideration (debit expense), or (3) an operating (not a capital) lessee's guarantee of residual value (debit prepaid rent). However, the requirement for recognition of a noncontingent obligation does not apply to certain guarantees, e.g., product warranties, derivatives, or obligations payable in the guarantor's equity shares. Many **disclosures** are required, such as the terms of the guarantee, how it arose, the triggering events, and maximum payments.

When a loss contingency involves an unasserted claim or assessment, neither accrual nor disclosure is required unless it is probable that a claim or assessment will be asserted. Also, **general or unspecified business risks** are not considered loss contingencies. Thus, no accrual or disclosure is required.

Contingent gains are not recognized until they are realized, but the existence of contingent gains must be disclosed. However, misleading implications as to the likelihood of realization should be avoided.

Warranties

A **warranty** is a written guarantee of the integrity of a product or service. The seller agrees to repair or replace a product, refund all or part of the price, or provide additional service. It is customarily offered for a limited time, such as 90 days. A warranty may or may not be separable from the product or service. When the warranty **is not separable**, the liability is treated as a **loss contingency**. Hence, the criteria for accrual of a loss contingency apply. If incurrence of warranty expense is probable, the amount can be reasonably estimated, and the amount is material, accrual accounting methods should be used. Otherwise, warranty expense should be recorded as incurred, that is, on the cash basis. The accounting for **separately extended** warranty and product maintenance contracts applies when the contract is separately priced. Revenue on the warranty is deferred and is ordinarily recognized on the straight-line basis over the term of the contract. Costs are not deferred and amortized unless directly related. The main example is the cost of commissions. Furthermore, if service costs are not incurred on a straight-line basis, revenue recognition over the contract's term should be proportionate to the estimated service costs. Moreover, under GAAP applying to guarantees, a product warrantor (a guarantor) must **disclose** (1) its accounting policy, (2) its method of calculating the liability, and (3) a reconciliation of the changes in the total for the period. Also, other required disclosures for guarantees must be made except for the maximum potential amount of future payments.

Coupons and Premiums

The liability for coupons is treated as a loss contingency. Many sellers include stamps, coupons, special labels, etc., with merchandise that can be redeemed for premiums (cash or goods). The purpose is to increase sales. In accordance with the **matching principle**, the expense associated with premium offers is recognized in the same period as the related revenue. Moreover, (1) the premiums must be purchased and recorded as inventory, (2) the expense of redemptions must be debited, and (3) a liability for estimated redemptions must be credited at the end of the accounting period.

Differences between GAAP and IFRS

Under IFRS:

- **Current liabilities** are (1) expected to be settled in the normal course of the operating cycle, (2) due to be settled within 12 months after the reporting period, (3) held primarily to be traded, or (4) obligations for which the entity does not have an unconditional right to defer payment for 12 months after the reporting period.

- Financial liabilities due to be settled within 12 months should continue to be classified as current. This treatment applies even if (1) the original term exceeded 12 months and (2) an agreement to refinance, or reschedule payments, on a noncurrent basis is completed after the reporting period and before the financial statements are authorized for issue. An entity that expects and has discretion to refinance or roll over the liability under an **existing** loan agreement classifies it as noncurrent.

- For **short-term compensated absences**, the timing of recognition depends on whether the benefits **accumulate**. If they do not accumulate, recognition of the expected cost is when the absences occur. If they accumulate, recognition is when services are rendered that increase the employees' entitlement to future compensated absences. The accumulating obligation is recognized whether it is vesting (the employee is entitled to a cash payment for an unused entitlement upon leaving the entity) or not vesting, and the amount should not be discounted. It equals the additional amount expected to be paid as a result of the unused accumulated entitlement at the balance sheet date.

- **Provisions** are liabilities of uncertain timing or amount except (1) those resulting from executory (unperformed) contracts (unless their unavoidable costs exceed their expected benefits) or (2) those covered by other IFRS. Examples are liabilities for violations of environmental law, nuclear plant decommissioning costs, warranties, and restructurings.

  1) Provisions differ from trade payables and accruals because of their greater uncertainty. They differ from contingent liabilities because they are present obligations that meet the recognition criteria.

  2) **Recognition** of provisions is appropriate when (a) the entity has a legal or constructive present obligation resulting from a past event (called an obligating event), (b) it is probable that an outflow of economic benefits will be necessary to settle the obligation, and (c) its amount can be reliably estimated.

  3) If the estimate of a provision is stated within a continuous range of possible outcomes, and each point in the range is as likely as any other, the midpoint is used.

  4) Provisions must be discounted if the effect of the time value of money is material. The amount of a provision must be the present value of the expenditures expected to be required to settle the obligation.

- A **contingent liability** is a possible obligation arising from past events. Its existence will be confirmed only by uncertain future events not wholly within the entity's control. A liability also is contingent if it is a present obligation arising from past events but does not meet the recognition criteria. For example, if the entity and other parties are jointly and severally liable on an obligation, the amount expected to be paid by the other parties is a contingent liability. A **contingent liability must not be recognized**. However, it is disclosed unless the possibility of resource outflows is **remote**.

- A **contingent asset** is a possible asset arising from past events, the existence of which will be confirmed only by uncertain future events not wholly within the entity's control. An example is a potential recovery on a legal claim with an uncertain outcome. A **contingent asset must not be recognized**, but it is disclosed if an inflow of economic benefits is **probable**.

QUESTIONS

11.1 Current Liabilities

1. Acme Co.'s accounts payable balance at December 31 was $850,000 before necessary year-end adjustments, if any, related to the following information:

- At December 31, Acme has a $50,000 debit balance in its accounts payable resulting from a payment to a supplier for goods to be manufactured to Acme's specifications.
- Goods shipped FOB destination on December 20 were received and recorded by Acme on January 2. The invoice cost was $45,000.

In its December 31 balance sheet, what amount should Acme report as accounts payable?

A. $850,000

B. $895,000

C. $900,000

D. $945,000

Answer (C) is correct. *(CPA, adapted)*
REQUIRED: The amount of accounts payable after year-end adjustments.
DISCUSSION: The payment to a supplier for goods to be manufactured to specifications should have been recorded by a debit to a prepaid asset, not accounts payable. Accordingly, accounts payable should be $900,000 ($850,000 + $50,000 error correction). The goods shipped FOB destination were not received until January 2, so they were appropriately excluded from accounts payable at year end. When the shipping term is FOB destination, the buyer records inventory and a payable when the goods are tendered at the destination (when title and risk of loss pass).
Answer (A) is incorrect. The amount of $850,000 does not reflect the necessary year-end adjustment to remove the erroneous charge for the prepayment. Answer (B) is incorrect. The amount of $895,000 includes $45,000 for the goods shipped FOB destination and received after the cutoff date. It does not include the adjustment for the erroneous charge to accounts payable for the prepayment. Answer (D) is incorrect. The amount of $945,000 includes $45,000 for the goods shipped FOB destination and received after the cutoff date.

2. Seoul Corp. had the following liabilities at December 31, Year 1:

Accounts payable	$ 110,000
Unsecured notes, 8%, due 7/1/Year 2	800,000
Accrued expenses	70,000
Contingent liability	900,000
Deferred income tax liability	50,000
Senior bonds, 7%, due 3/31/Year 2	2,000,000

The contingent liability is an accrual for possible losses on a $2 million lawsuit filed against Seoul. Seoul's legal counsel expects the suit to be settled in Year 3 and has estimated that Seoul will be liable for damages in the range of $900,000 to $1,500,000. The deferred income tax liability is not related to an asset for financial reporting and is expected to reverse in Year 3. What amount should Seoul report in its December 31, Year 1, balance sheet for current liabilities?

A. $1,030,000

B. $1,880,000

C. $2,980,000

D. $3,030,000

Answer (C) is correct. *(CPA, adapted)*
REQUIRED: The amount reported for current liabilities.
DISCUSSION: A current liability is an obligation that will be either liquidated using a current asset or replaced by another current liability. The following are current liabilities: (1) obligations that, by their terms, are due on demand within 1 year (or the operating cycle if longer) and (2) obligations that are callable by the creditor within 1 year because of a violation of a debt covenant. Thus, the current liabilities are calculated as

Accounts payable	$ 110,000
Unsecured notes, 8%, due 7/1/Year 2	800,000
Accrued expenses	70,000
Senior bonds, 7%, due 3/31/Year 2	2,000,000
	$2,980,000

Answer (A) is incorrect. The amount of $1,030,000 excludes the senior bonds due within 1 year and includes the deferred income tax liability that will not reverse within 1 year. Whether a deferred tax asset or liability is current depends on the classification of the related asset or liability. If it is not related to an asset or liability, the expected reversal date of the temporary difference determines the classification. Answer (B) is incorrect. The amount of $1,880,000 includes the contingent liability not expected to be settled until Year 3 and excludes the senior bonds. Answer (D) is incorrect. The amount of $3,030,000 includes the deferred income tax liability not expected to reverse until Year 3.

3. On September 30, World Co. borrowed $1,000,000 on a 9% note payable. World paid the first of four quarterly payments of $264,200 when due on December 30. In its December 31 balance sheet, what amount should World report as note payable?

   A. $735,800

   B. $750,000

   C. $758,300

   D. $825,800

Answer (C) is correct. *(CPA, adapted)*
   REQUIRED: The amount of a note payable.
   DISCUSSION: This interest-bearing 1-year note with four quarterly payments is a current liability because it is expected to be liquidated using current assets. Each payment of $264,200 consists of interest and principal. Only the principal component reduces the liability. The interest component equals $22,500 [$1,000,000 face amount × 9% × (1 ÷ 4 quarters)]. Thus, the principal is reduced by $241,700 ($264,200 payment – $22,500 interest). The note payable is reported as $758,300 ($1,000,000 carrying amount – $241,700 principal reduction) at year end.
   Answer (A) is incorrect. The amount of $735,800 results from treating the entire payment as principal. Answer (B) is incorrect. The amount of $750,000 is simply 75% of the face amount of the note. Answer (D) is incorrect. The amount of $825,800 is based on the assumption that the annual interest of $90,000 is included in the first payment.

4. Wilk Co. reported the following liabilities at December 31, Year 1:

Accounts payable-trade	$ 750,000
Short-term borrowings	400,000
Bank loan, current portion $100,000	3,500,000
Other bank loan, matures June 30, Year 2	1,000,000

The bank loan of $3,500,000 was in violation of the loan agreement. The creditor had not waived the rights under the loan. What amount should Wilk report as current liabilities at December 31, Year 1?

   A. $1,250,000

   B. $2,150,000

   C. $2,250,000

   D. $5,650,000

Answer (D) is correct. *(CPA, adapted)*
   REQUIRED: The current liabilities to be reported at year end.
   DISCUSSION: Obligations are liabilities when they are callable by the creditor within 1 year because of a violation of a debt covenant. Noncurrent debt need not be classified as current if it is probable that a violation existing at the balance sheet date will be remedied within a specified period. Absent a probable remedy of Wilk's violation of the loan agreement, current liabilities to be reported at year end are $5,650,000 ($750,000 trade payables + $400,000 current borrowings + $3,500,000 bank loan + $1,000,000 other bank loan due within 1 year).
   Answer (A) is incorrect. Both the entire $3,500,000 bank loan and the other bank loan must be included as current liabilities. Answer (B) is incorrect. The $3,500,000 bank loan must be included as a current liability. Answer (C) is incorrect. The entire $3,500,000 bank loan must be recorded as a current liability.

5. On March 31, Year 1, Koala Co. received an advance payment of 60% of the sales price for special order goods to be manufactured and delivered within 5 months. At the same time, Koala subcontracted for production of the special-order goods at a price equal to 40% of the main contract price. What liabilities should be reported in Koala's March 31, Year 1, balance sheet?

	Payables to Deferred Revenues	Subcontractor
A.	None	None
B.	60% of main contract price	40% of main contract price
C.	60% of main contract price	None
D.	None	40% of main contract price

Answer (C) is correct. *(CPA, adapted)*
   REQUIRED: The liabilities to be reported in the balance sheet.
   DISCUSSION: The 60% advance payment is a deferred revenue (liability) because it has been realized but not earned. The entity has not substantially accomplished what it must do to be entitled to the benefits represented by the prepayment. The agreement with the subcontractor does not create a liability because the entity has no current obligation to transfer assets or provide services. That obligation will not arise until the subcontractor has performed.
   Answer (A) is incorrect. The 60% prepayment should be credited to deferred revenue. Answer (B) is incorrect. Koala has no liability to the subcontractor. Answer (D) is incorrect. The 60% prepayment should be credited to deferred revenue, and Koala has no liability to the subcontractor.

6. Nepal Co. requires advance payments with special orders for machinery constructed to customer specifications. These advances are nonrefundable. Information for Year 2 is as follows:

Customer advances--balance 12/31/Year 1	$236,000
Advances received with orders in Year 2	368,000
Advances applied to orders shipped in Year 2	328,000
Advances applicable to orders canceled in Year 2	100,000

In Nepal's December 31, Year 2, balance sheet, what amount should be reported as a current liability for advances from customers?

A. $0

B. $176,000

C. $276,000

D. $296,000

Answer (B) is correct. *(CPA, adapted)*
REQUIRED: The current liability for advances.
DISCUSSION: The amount of $176,000 ($236,000 beginning balance + $368,000 advances received – $328,000 advances credited to revenue after shipment of orders – $100,000 for canceled orders) should be reported as a current liability for customer advances. Deposits or other advance payments are liabilities because they involve a probable future sacrifice of economic benefits arising from a current obligation. The advances applicable to canceled orders are not refundable. Thus, no future sacrifice of economic benefits is necessary.
Answer (A) is incorrect. Deposits or other advance payments should be recognized as liabilities. Answer (C) is incorrect. The amount of $276,000 includes $100,000 applicable to orders canceled. Answer (D) is incorrect. The amount of $296,000 results from subtracting advances received and adding advances applied to shipments and advances for canceled orders.

7. Harare Company maintains escrow accounts and pays real estate taxes for its mortgage customers. Escrow funds are kept in interest-bearing accounts. Interest, minus a 10% service fee, is credited to the customer's account and used to reduce future escrow payments. Additional information follows:

Escrow accounts liability, 1/1/Year 1	$ 700,000
Escrow payments received during Year 1	1,580,000
Real estate taxes paid during Year 1	1,720,000
Interest on escrow funds during Year 1	50,000

What amount should Harare report as escrow accounts liability in its December 31, Year 1, balance sheet?

A. $510,000

B. $515,000

C. $605,000

D. $610,000

Answer (C) is correct. *(CPA, adapted)*
REQUIRED: The amount of escrow accounts liability.
DISCUSSION: The liability at the beginning of the year was $700,000. Escrow payments of $1,580,000 were credited and taxes paid of $1,720,000 were debited to the account during the year. Furthermore, interest of $45,000 [$50,000 – ($50,000 × 10%) service fee] was credited. Thus, the year-end balance was $605,000 ($700,000 + $1,580,000 – $1,720,000 + $45,000).
Answer (A) is incorrect. The amount of $510,000 results from debiting $50,000 rather than crediting $45,000. Answer (B) is incorrect. The amount of $515,000 results from debiting $45,000 rather than crediting $45,000. Answer (D) is incorrect. The amount of $610,000 omits the adjustment for the service fee.

8. Sudan Co. sells major household appliance service contracts for cash. The service contracts are for a 1-year, 2-year, or 3-year period. Cash receipts from contracts are credited to unearned service contract revenues. This account had a balance of $1,440,000 at December 31, Year 1, before year end adjustment. Service contract costs are charged as incurred to the service contract expense account, which had a balance of $360,000 at December 31, Year 1. Outstanding service contracts at December 31, Year 1, expire as follows:

During Year 2	$300,000
During Year 3	450,000
During Year 4	200,000

What amount should be reported as unearned service contract revenues in Sudan's December 31, Year 1, balance sheet?

A. $1,080,000

B. $950,000

C. $590,000

D. $490,000

Answer (B) is correct. *(CPA, adapted)*
REQUIRED: The amount to be reported as unearned service contract revenues at year end.
DISCUSSION: Unearned service contract revenues relate to outstanding contracts for which the agreed service has not yet been provided. Thus, the amount to be reported as unearned service contract revenues is the $950,000 ($300,000 + $450,000 + $200,000) of service contracts outstanding at 12/31/Year 1.
Answer (A) is incorrect. The amount of $1,080,000 is the difference between the unearned service contract revenue before adjustment and the balance in the service contract expense account. Answer (C) is incorrect. The amount of $590,000 is the difference between the $360,000 balance in service contract expense and the $950,000 of unearned service contract revenue reported in the 12/31/Year 1 balance sheet. Answer (D) is incorrect. The amount of $490,000 is the change in the unearned service contract revenue account ($1,440,000 – $950,000).

9. Noncurrent obligations that are or will become callable by the creditor because of the debtor's violation of a provision of the debt agreement at the balance sheet date should be classified as

A. Noncurrent liabilities.

B. Current liabilities unless the creditor has waived the right to demand repayment for more than 1 year from the balance sheet date.

C. Contingent liabilities until the violation is corrected.

D. Current liabilities unless it is reasonably possible that the violation will be corrected within the grace period.

Answer (B) is correct.   *(CMA, adapted)*
REQUIRED: The proper classification of noncurrent debt callable by the creditor because of a violation of an agreement.
DISCUSSION: A current liability is an obligation that will be either liquidated using a current asset or replaced by another current liability. Current liabilities include (1) obligations that by their terms are due on demand within 1 year (or the operating cycle, if longer) and (2) obligations that are callable by the creditor within 1 year because of a violation of a debt agreement. An exception exists, however, if the creditor has waived or subsequently lost the right to demand repayment for more than 1 year (or the operating cycle, if longer) from the balance sheet date.
Answer (A) is incorrect. This kind of obligation should be classified as a current liability. Answer (C) is incorrect. The liability is not contingent. Answer (D) is incorrect. The obligation may be classified as noncurrent if it is probable that the violation will be corrected within the specified period.

10. On January 3, Year 1, North Company issued noncurrent bonds due January 3, Year 6. The bond agreement includes a call provision that is effective if the firm's current ratio falls below 2:1. On June 30, Year 1, the fiscal year end for the company, its current ratio was 1.5:1. The bonds should be reported on the financial statements as a

A. Noncurrent liability because their maturity date is January 3, Year 6.

B. Noncurrent liability if it is reasonably possible that North can remedy the violation of the agreement before the end of any allowed grace period.

C. Current liability if the violation of the agreement is not remedied.

D. Current liability, regardless of any action by the bondholder, because the company was in violation of the agreement on the balance sheet date.

Answer (C) is correct.   *(R.B. Posey)*
REQUIRED: The proper classification of callable obligations.
DISCUSSION: Noncurrent liabilities that are callable by the creditor because of the debtor's violation of the debt agreement at the balance sheet date must be classified as current.
Answer (A) is incorrect. The violation of the debt agreement allows the creditor to accelerate the maturity date. Answer (B) is incorrect. The debt should be classified as current unless it is probable that the violation will be remedied within any specified period. Answer (D) is incorrect. A creditor's waiver of the right to demand repayment of the debt allows North to classify the bonds as noncurrent.

11.2 Certain Taxes Payable

11. Florence Co.'s payroll for the month ended January 31 is summarized as follows:

Total wages	$10,000
Federal income tax withheld	1,200

All wages paid were subject to FICA taxes. Assume FICA tax rates were 7% each for employee and employer. Florence remits payroll taxes on the 15th of the following month. In its financial statements for the month ended January 31, what amounts should Florence report as total payroll tax liability and as payroll tax expense?

	Liability	Expense
A.	$1,200	$1,400
B.	$1,900	$1,400
C.	$1,900	$700
D.	$2,600	$700

Answer (D) is correct.   *(CPA, adapted)*
REQUIRED: The amounts reported as total payroll tax liability and as payroll tax expense.
DISCUSSION: The payroll liability is $2,600 ($1,200 federal income tax withheld + $700 employer's FICA + $700 employees' FICA). The payroll tax expense consists of the employer's share of FICA. The employees' share is considered a withholding, not an expense.
Answer (A) is incorrect. The amount of $1,200 does not include employer and employee shares of current FICA taxes, and $1,400 includes the employees' share of FICA taxes. Answer (B) is incorrect. The amount of $1,900 does not include $700 of FICA taxes, and $1,400 includes the employees' share of FICA taxes. Answer (C) is incorrect. The amount of $1,900 does not include $700 of FICA taxes.

12. Hudson Hotel collects 15% in city sales taxes on room rentals, in addition to a $2 per room, per night, occupancy tax. Sales taxes for each month are due at the end of the following month, and occupancy taxes are due 15 days after the end of each calendar quarter. On January 3, Year 2, Hudson paid its November Year 1 sales taxes and its fourth quarter Year 1 occupancy taxes. Additional information pertaining to Hudson's operations is

Year 1	Room Rentals	Room Nights
October	$100,000	1,100
November	110,000	1,200
December	150,000	1,800

What amounts should Hudson report as sales taxes payable and occupancy taxes payable in its December 31, Year 1, balance sheet?

	Sales Taxes	Occupancy Taxes
A.	$39,000	$6,000
B.	$39,000	$8,200
C.	$54,000	$6,000
D.	$54,000	$8,200

Answer (B) is correct. *(CPA, adapted)*
REQUIRED: The sales taxes payable and occupancy taxes payable.
DISCUSSION: Hudson presumably paid its October sales taxes during Year 1, but it did not pay sales taxes for November and December and occupancy taxes for October, November, and December until Year 2. Consequently, it should accrue a liability for sales taxes in the amount of $39,000 [($110,000 November rentals + $150,000 December rentals) × 15%] and a liability for occupancy taxes in the amount of $8,200 [(1,100 + 1,200 + 1,800) room nights × $2].
Answer (A) is incorrect. The amount of $6,000 excludes October room nights. Answer (C) is incorrect. The amount of $54,000 includes October room rentals, and $6,000 excludes October room nights. Answer (D) is incorrect. The amount of $54,000 includes October room rentals.

13. On July 1, Year 1, Wessex County issued real estate tax assessments for its fiscal year ended June 30, Year 2. On September 1, Year 1, Milan Co. purchased a warehouse in Wessex County. The purchase price was reduced by a credit for accrued realty taxes. Milan did not record the entire year's real estate tax obligation but instead records tax expenses at the end of each month by adjusting prepaid real estate taxes or real estate taxes payable, as appropriate. On November 1, Year 1, Milan paid the first of two equal installments of $24,000 for real estate taxes. What amount of this payment should Milan record as a debit to real estate taxes payable?

A. $8,000
B. $16,000
C. $20,000
D. $24,000

Answer (B) is correct. *(CPA, adapted)*
REQUIRED: The amount to be debited to real estate taxes payable.
DISCUSSION: The credit balance in real estate taxes payable at 11/1/Year 1 is $16,000. This amount reflects accrued real estate taxes of $4,000 a month [(2 × $24,000) ÷ 12 months] for 4 months (July through October). This payable should be debited for $16,000 when the real estate taxes are paid.
Answer (A) is incorrect. The amount of $8,000 includes real estate taxes for September and October only. Answer (C) is incorrect. The amount of $20,000 includes real estate taxes for November. Answer (D) is incorrect. The amount of $24,000 equals 6 months of real estate taxes.

11.3 Refinancing of Current Debt

14. At December 31, Year 1, Telemark Co. owed notes payable of $1,750,000, due on May 15, Year 2. Telemark expects to retire this debt with proceeds from the sale of 100,000 shares of its common stock. The stock was sold for $15 per share on March 10, Year 2, prior to the issuance of the year-end financial statements. In Telemark's December 31, Year 1, balance sheet, what amount of the notes payable should be excluded from current liabilities?

A. $0
B. $250,000
C. $1,500,000
D. $1,750,000

Answer (C) is correct. *(CPA, adapted)*
REQUIRED: The amount of notes payable that should be excluded from current liabilities.
DISCUSSION: If an entity intends to refinance current obligations on a noncurrent basis and demonstrates an ability to do so, the obligation should be excluded from current liabilities and reclassified as noncurrent. The ability to refinance may be demonstrated by issuing noncurrent obligations or equity securities after the end of the reporting period but before issuance of the balance sheet. Thus, $1,500,000 (100,000 shares × $15) of the notes payable should be excluded from current liabilities and reclassified as noncurrent.
Answer (A) is incorrect. The amount of $1,500,000 should be excluded from current liabilities. Answer (B) is incorrect. The amount that should be classified as a current liability is $250,000. Answer (D) is incorrect. The full amount of notes payable, which should be allocated between current and noncurrent liabilities, is $1,750,000.

15. On December 31, Year 1, Lapp Co. had a $750,000 note payable outstanding, due July 31, Year 2. Lapp borrowed the money to finance construction of a new plant. Lapp planned to refinance the note by issuing noncurrent bonds. Because Lapp temporarily had excess cash, it prepaid $250,000 of the note on January 12, Year 2. In February Year 2, Lapp completed a $1.5 million bond offering. Lapp will use the bond offering proceeds to repay the note payable at its maturity and to pay construction costs during Year 2. On March 3, Year 2, Lapp issued its Year 1 financial statements. What amount of the note payable should Lapp include in the current liabilities section of its December 31, Year 1, balance sheet?

   A. $750,000

   B. $500,000

   C. $250,000

   D. $0

Answer (C) is correct. *(CPA, adapted)*
REQUIRED: The amount that should be classified as current obligations.
DISCUSSION: The portion of debt scheduled to mature in the following fiscal year ordinarily should be classified as a current liability. However, if an entity intends to refinance current obligations on a noncurrent basis and demonstrates an ability to do so, the obligation should be excluded from current liabilities and reclassified as noncurrent. One method of demonstrating the ability to refinance is to issue noncurrent obligations or equity securities after the end of the reporting period but before issuance of the balance sheet. Lapp intended, and demonstrated an ability, to refinance $500,000 of the note payable. Thus, the portion prepaid ($250,000) is a current liability because the assets used for the prepayment were current. The remaining $500,000 should be classified as noncurrent.
Answer (A) is incorrect. The amount of $750,000 includes the $500,000 that was refinanced. Answer (B) is incorrect. The amount that should be reclassified as noncurrent is $500,000. Answer (D) is incorrect. The amount of $250,000 should be classified as a current liability.

16. Scotia, Inc., has $1 million of notes payable due June 15, Year 2. At the financial statement date of December 31, Year 1, Scotia signed an agreement to borrow up to $1 million to refinance the notes payable on a noncurrent basis. The financing agreement called for borrowings not to exceed 80% of the value of the collateral Scotia was providing. At the date of issue of the December 31, Year 1, financial statements, the value of the collateral was $1.2 million and was not expected to fall below this amount during Year 2. In its December 31, Year 1, balance sheet, Scotia should classify the notes payable as

	Current Obligations	Noncurrent Obligations
A.	$0	$1,000,000
B.	$40,000	$960,000
C.	$200,000	$800,000
D.	$1,000,000	$0

Answer (B) is correct. *(CPA, adapted)*
REQUIRED: The proper classification of notes payable subject to a refinancing agreement.
DISCUSSION: The portion of debt scheduled to mature in the following fiscal year ordinarily should be classified as a current liability. However, if an entity intends to refinance current obligations on a noncurrent basis and demonstrates an ability to do so, the obligation should be excluded from current liabilities and classified as noncurrent. Scotia has signed an agreement to borrow up to $1 million to refinance the notes payable on a noncurrent basis, but the borrowings may not exceed 80% of the value of the collateral. Consequently, Scotia has demonstrated an ability to refinance $960,000 ($1,200,000 collateral × 80% ceiling) of the notes payable. This amount should be classified as a noncurrent obligation. The remaining $40,000 ($1,000,000 − $960,000) should be reported as a current obligation.
Answer (A) is incorrect. Scotia has not demonstrated an ability to refinance $40,000 of the notes payable. This amount should thus be classified as current obligations and the remainder ($960,000) as noncurrent obligations. Answer (C) is incorrect. Scotia has demonstrated an ability to refinance $960,000 of the notes payable. This amount should thus be classified as noncurrent obligations and the remainder ($40,000) as current obligations. Answer (D) is incorrect. Of the notes payable, $960,000 should be classified as noncurrent obligations. Scotia has demonstrated an ability to refinance this amount. The remainder ($40,000) should be classified as current obligations.

17. Included in Sapporo Corp.'s liability account balances at December 31, Year 3, were the following:

14% note payable issued October 1, Year 3,
maturing September 30, Year 4 $125,000

16% note payable issued April 1, Year 1,
payable in six equal annual installments
of $50,000 beginning April 1, Year 2   200,000

Sapporo's December 31, Year 3, financial statements were issued on March 31, Year 4. On January 15, Year 4, the entire $200,000 balance of the 16% note was refinanced by issuance of a noncurrent obligation payable in a lump sum. In addition, on March 10, Year 4, Sapporo consummated a noncancelable agreement with the lender to refinance the 14%, $125,000 note on a noncurrent basis, on readily determinable terms that have not yet been implemented. Both parties are financially capable of honoring the agreement, and there have been no violations of the agreement's provisions. On the December 31, Year 3, balance sheet, the amount of the notes payable that Sapporo should classify as current obligations is

- A. $175,000
- B. $125,000
- C. $50,000
- D. $0

Answer (D) is correct. *(CPA, adapted)*
REQUIRED: The amount that should be classified as current obligations.
DISCUSSION: If an entity intends to refinance current obligations on a noncurrent basis and demonstrates an ability to do so, the obligation should be excluded from current liabilities and reclassified as noncurrent. The ability to refinance may be demonstrated by issuance of noncurrent obligations or equity securities after the end of the reporting period but before issuance of the balance sheet. Thus, the 16% note payable should be classified as noncurrent. The ability to refinance also may be shown by entering into a financing agreement that meets the following criteria: (1) The agreement does not expire within the longer of 1 year or the operating cycle, (2) it is noncancelable by the lender, (3) no violation of the agreement exists at the balance sheet date, and (4) the lender is financially capable of honoring the agreement. For this reason, the 14% note payable also is excluded from current obligations. The amount of the notes payable classified as current is therefore $0.
Answer (A) is incorrect. The amount of $175,000 is the sum of the installment payment of $50,000 due 4/1/Year 3 and the $125,000 of the 14% note. Answer (B) is incorrect. The amount of the 14% note is $125,000. Answer (C) is incorrect. The amount of $50,000 is the installment payment on the 16% note due 4/1/Year 3.

11.4 Compensated Absences and Postemployment Benefits

18. If the payment of employees' compensation for future absences is probable, the amount can be reasonably estimated, and the obligation relates to rights that vest, the compensation should be

- A. Recognized when paid.
- B. Accrued if attributable to employees' services whether or not already rendered.
- C. Accrued if attributable to employees' services already rendered.
- D. Accrued if attributable to employees' services not already rendered.

Answer (C) is correct. *(CPA, adapted)*
REQUIRED: The additional criterion to be met to accrue an expense for compensated absences.
DISCUSSION: An accrual is required when four criteria are met: (1) The payment of compensation is probable, (2) the amount can be reasonably estimated, (3) the benefits either vest or accumulate, and (4) the compensation relates to employees' services that have already been rendered.
Answer (A) is incorrect. The cash basis is not appropriate for recognizing expenses related to compensated absences. Answer (B) is incorrect. The services must be rendered before the compensation is accrued. Answer (D) is incorrect. The services must have been previously rendered.

19. At December 31, Year 1, Murmansk Co. estimates that its employees have earned vacation pay of $100,000. Employees will receive their vacation pay in Year 2. Should Murmansk accrue a liability at December 31, Year 1, if the rights to this compensation accumulated over time or if the rights are vested?

	Accumulated	Vested
A.	Yes	No
B.	No	No
C.	Yes	Yes
D.	No	Yes

Answer (C) is correct. *(CPA, adapted)*
REQUIRED: The effect of accumulation and vesting on accrual of a liability for vacation pay.
DISCUSSION: An accrual for compensated services is required when the compensation relates to services previously provided, the benefits either vest or accumulate, and payment is both probable and reasonably estimable. The single exception is for sick pay benefits, which must be accrued only if the rights vest.
Answer (A) is incorrect. Vesting meets one of the criteria for accrual of a liability. Answer (B) is incorrect. Either vesting or accumulation meets one of the criteria for accrual of a liability. Answer (D) is incorrect. Accumulation meets one of the criteria for accrual of a liability.

20. Employers must accrue a liability for employees' compensation for future absences. The item that requires accrual is

    A. Stock compensation.

    B. Termination benefits.

    C. Postretirement benefits.

    D. Vacation pay based on past service.

Answer (D) is correct. *(CMA, adapted)*
    REQUIRED: The item that requires accrual.
    DISCUSSION: The accounting for compensated absences applies to such items as sick pay benefits, holidays, and vacations. The criteria for accrual are that the obligation arose from past services, the employees' rights vest or accumulate, payment is probable, and an amount can be reasonably estimated.
    Answer (A) is incorrect. The GAAP for compensated absences does not apply to stock compensation plans, which are addressed by GAAP for share-based payment. Answer (B) is incorrect. The GAAP for compensated absences does not apply to special or contractual termination benefits. Answer (C) is incorrect. The GAAP for compensated absences does not apply to pension and other postretirement benefits.

21. On January 1, Year 1, Toledo Co. decided to grant its employees 10 vacation days and 5 sick days each year. Vacation days, but not sick days, may be carried over to the next year. However, sick pay benefits are vested. Each employee received payment for an average of 3 sick days in Year 1. During Year 1, each of Toledo's six employees earned $100 per day and earned 10 vacation days. These vacation days were taken during Year 2. What amount should Toledo report for accrued compensated absence expense for the year ended December 31, Year 1?

    A. $0

    B. $6,000

    C. $7,200

    D. $9,000

Answer (C) is correct. *(CPA, adapted)*
    REQUIRED: The accrued compensated absence expense.
    DISCUSSION: An accrual is required for compensated services when the compensation relates to services previously provided, the benefits either vest or accumulate, and payment is both probable and reasonably estimable. The single exception is for sick pay benefits, which must be accrued only if the rights vest. Accordingly, Toledo should report accrued compensated absence expense of $7,200 [(6 employees × $100 × 10 days) vacation pay + (6 employees × $100 × 2 days) sick pay].
    Answer (A) is incorrect. Toledo must accrue accumulated vacation pay and vested sick pay benefits. Answer (B) is incorrect. The amount of $6,000 omits sick pay. Answer (D) is incorrect. The amount of $9,000 includes 5 days of sick pay per employee.

22. Berne Co. has an employee benefit plan for compensated absences that gives employees 10 paid vacation days and 10 paid sick days. Both vacation and sick days can be carried over indefinitely. Employees can elect to receive payment in lieu of vacation days; however, no payment is given for sick days not taken. At December 31 of the current year, Berne's unadjusted balance of liability for compensated absences was $21,000. Berne estimated that there were 150 vacation days and 75 sick days available at December 31. Berne's employees earn an average of $100 per day. In its December 31 balance sheet, what amount of liability for compensated absences is Berne required to report?

    A. $36,000

    B. $22,500

    C. $21,000

    D. $15,000

Answer (D) is correct. *(CPA, adapted)*
    REQUIRED: The amount of liability for compensated absences.
    DISCUSSION: Vacation benefits earned but not yet taken must be accrued. However, a liability is not accrued for future sick pay unless the rights are vested. Thus, the estimated vacation days available at December 31 require a liability of $15,000 ($100 × 150 days).
    Answer (A) is incorrect. The amount of $36,000 is the sum of the $15,000 liability for compensated absences and the unadjusted balance of liability for compensated absences. Answer (B) is incorrect. The sick days are not required to be included in the liability for compensated absences. Answer (C) is incorrect. The amount of $21,000 is the unadjusted balance of liability for compensated absences.

23. Employers' accounting for postemployment benefits applies to

A. Pension benefits provided to spouses of retired employees.

B. Salary continuation benefits provided to employees on disability leave.

C. Counseling benefits provided to employees nearing retirement age.

D. Healthcare benefits provided to dependents of retired employees.

Answer (B) is correct. *(Publisher, adapted)*
REQUIRED: The type of benefits to which employers' accounting applies.
DISCUSSION: Benefits to former or inactive employees, their beneficiaries, and their covered dependents after employment but before retirement include, but are not limited to, (1) salary continuation, (2) supplemental unemployment benefits, (3) severance benefits, (4) disability-related benefits (including workers' compensation), (5) job training and counseling, and (6) continuation of benefits, such as healthcare and life insurance coverage.
Answer (A) is incorrect. The former employees have retired and thus are not covered. Answer (C) is incorrect. The employees are still employed. Answer (D) is incorrect. Healthcare benefits provided to dependents of retired employees are not covered.

24. Sanders Co. has determined that its payment of postemployment benefits is probable, the amount can be reasonably estimated, and the obligation relates to rights that vest or accumulate. The company's obligation for postemployment benefits should

A. Be recognized when the benefits are paid.

B. Be accrued at the date of the event giving rise to the payment of benefits.

C. Be accrued if attributable to employees' services already rendered.

D. Not be recognized.

Answer (C) is correct. *(Publisher, adapted)*
REQUIRED: The treatment of postemployment benefits by the employer.
DISCUSSION: Employers must recognize the obligation to provide postemployment benefits if (1) the obligation is attributable to employees' services already rendered, (2) employees' rights accumulate or vest, (3) payment is probable, and (4) the amount of the benefits can be reasonably estimated.
Answer (A) is incorrect. If the services have been performed, a liability must be recognized. Answer (B) is incorrect. If the definition of a liability is met, an obligation is accrued even if an event triggering payment (e.g., severance) has not occurred. Answer (D) is incorrect. The obligation should be accrued.

25. At December 31 of this year, Medina Corporation reasonably estimates that its obligations for postemployment benefits include

Severance pay	$120,000
Job training benefits	90,000

These benefits relate to employees' services already rendered, and payment is probable. The severance pay benefits vest; the job training benefits accumulate. In its December 31 balance sheet, Medina should report a liability for postemployment benefits of

A. $0

B. $90,000

C. $120,000

D. $210,000

Answer (D) is correct. *(Publisher, adapted)*
REQUIRED: The amount of liability that should be recorded for postemployment benefits.
DISCUSSION: If postemployment benefits are attributable to employees' services already rendered, employees' rights accumulate or vest, payment is probable, and the amount of the benefits can be reasonably estimated, the employer should recognize a liability for the obligation. Thus, the full amount of the severance pay and job training benefits of $210,000 ($120,000 + $90,000) should be reported as a liability.
Answer (A) is incorrect. The full amount of both benefits should be included in the liability. Answer (B) is incorrect. The amount of $90,000 excludes the severance pay. Answer (C) is incorrect. The amount of $120,000 excludes the training benefits.

11.5 Contingencies

26. A loss contingency should be accrued on an entity's records only if it is

A. Reasonably possible that a liability has been incurred and the amount of the loss is known.

B. Probable that a liability has been incurred and the amount of the loss is unknown.

C. Probable that a liability has been incurred and the amount of the loss can be reasonably estimated.

D. Remotely probable that a liability has been incurred but the amount of the loss can be reasonably estimated.

Answer (C) is correct. *(CMA, adapted)*
REQUIRED: The circumstance under which a loss contingency should be accrued.
DISCUSSION: Loss contingencies should be accrued when information available prior to issuance of financial statements indicates that it is probable that an asset has been impaired or a liability has been incurred, and the amount of loss can be reasonably estimated. Probable is defined as a condition in which future events are likely to occur.
Answer (A) is incorrect. An event is reasonably possible if the chance of occurrence is more than remote but less than probable. Accrual requires that the event be probable. Answer (B) is incorrect. The amount of the loss must be capable of reasonable estimation. Answer (D) is incorrect. An event is remote if the chance of occurrence is slight.

27. Conlon Co. is the plaintiff in a patent-infringement case. Conlon has a high probability of a favorable outcome and can reasonably estimate the amount of the settlement. What is the proper accounting treatment of the patent-infringement case?

A. A gain contingency for the minimum estimated amount of the settlement.

B. A gain contingency for the estimated probable settlement.

C. Disclosure in the notes only.

D. No reporting is required at this time.

Answer (C) is correct. *(CPA, adapted)*
REQUIRED: The plaintiff's accounting for a patent-infringement suit if a favorable outcome is probable and the amount can be reasonably estimated.
DISCUSSION: Under the conservatism restraint, when alternative accounting methods are appropriate, the one having the less favorable effect on net income and total assets is preferable. Thus, a loss, not a gain, contingency may be recorded in the financial statements. If the probability of realization of a gain is high, the contingency is disclosed in the notes.
Answer (A) is incorrect. A gain contingency is never recognized. Answer (B) is incorrect. A gain contingency is never recognized. Answer (D) is incorrect. Although contingencies that might result in gains are not accrued, some minimum disclosure is required.

28. Management can estimate the amount of loss that will occur if a foreign government expropriates some company assets. If expropriation is reasonably possible, a loss contingency should be

A. Disclosed but not accrued as a liability.

B. Disclosed and accrued as a liability.

C. Accrued as a liability but not disclosed.

D. Neither accrued as a liability nor disclosed.

Answer (A) is correct. *(CPA, adapted)*
REQUIRED: The reporting of a loss contingency that is reasonably possible.
DISCUSSION: A contingent loss that is reasonably possible but not probable is disclosed but not accrued. The disclosure should describe the nature of the contingency and provide an estimate of the loss or range of loss or state that an estimate cannot be made.
Answer (B) is incorrect. A contingent loss is accrued only if it is probable and reasonably estimable. Answer (C) is incorrect. If a loss is reasonably possible, it is disclosed but not accrued. Answer (D) is incorrect. If a loss is reasonably possible, it is disclosed.

29. A manufacturer of household appliances may incur a loss due to the discovery of a defect in one of its products. The occurrence of the loss is reasonably possible, and the resulting costs can be reasonably estimated. This possible loss should be

	Accrued	Disclosed in Notes
A.	Yes	No
B.	Yes	Yes
C.	No	Yes
D.	No	No

Answer (C) is correct. *(CPA, adapted)*
REQUIRED: The accounting for a contingent loss that is reasonably possible and reasonably estimable.
DISCUSSION: A contingent loss must be accrued when two conditions are met: (1) It is probable that, at a balance sheet date, an asset is overstated or a liability has been incurred, and (2) the amount of the loss can be reasonably estimated. If one or both conditions are not met, but the probability of the loss is at least reasonably possible, the amount of the loss must be disclosed. This loss is reasonably possible and reasonably estimable, and it therefore should be disclosed but not accrued as a liability. The financial statements should disclose the nature of the loss contingency and the amount or range of the possible loss. If an estimate cannot be made, the note should so state.
Answer (A) is incorrect. The contingent loss should be disclosed but not accrued. Answer (B) is incorrect. The contingent loss should not be accrued. Answer (D) is incorrect. The contingent loss should be disclosed.

30. When reporting contingencies,

A. A guarantee of another's indebtedness is accrued as a loss contingency only if the loss is considered imminent.

B. Disclosure of a loss contingency is to be made if there is a remote possibility that the loss has been incurred.

C. Disclosure of a loss contingency must include a dollar estimate of the loss.

D. A loss that is probable but not estimable must be disclosed with a notation that the amount of the loss cannot be estimated.

Answer (D) is correct. *(CMA, adapted)*
REQUIRED: The true statement about reporting contingencies.
DISCUSSION: Contingencies are probable (likely to occur), reasonably possible, or remote. When contingent losses are probable and the amount can be reasonably estimated, the amount of the loss should be recognized. If the amount cannot be reasonably estimated but the loss is at least reasonably possible, full disclosure should be made, including a statement that an estimate cannot be made.
Answer (A) is incorrect. A loss contingency is accrued when (1) it is probable (not necessarily imminent) that an asset has been impaired or a liability incurred and (2) the loss is reasonably estimable. Moreover, a guarantee of another's indebtedness must be disclosed even if the possibility of loss is remote. Answer (B) is incorrect. Remote contingencies ordinarily need not be disclosed. Answer (C) is incorrect. Disclosure need not include an amount when that amount cannot be reasonably estimated.

31. On December 20, an uninsured property damage loss was caused by a company car's being driven on company business by a company sales agent. The company did not become aware of the loss until January 25, but the amount of the loss was reasonably estimable before the financial statements were issued. The company's December 31 financial statements should report an estimated loss as

A. A disclosure but not an accrual.

B. An accrual.

C. Neither an accrual nor a disclosure.

D. An appropriation of retained earnings.

Answer (B) is correct. *(CPA, adapted)*
REQUIRED: The manner of disclosure of a loss contingency.
DISCUSSION: A loss contingency involves uncertainty as to the impairment of an asset or the incurrence of a liability at the balance sheet date. Resolution of the uncertainty depends on the occurrence or nonoccurrence of one or more future events. A loss should be debited and either an asset valuation allowance or a liability credited when the loss contingency is both probable and reasonably estimable. The loss should be accrued even though the company was not aware of the contingency at the balance sheet date.
Answer (A) is incorrect. Disclosure alone would suffice only if the loss had occurred after December 31. Answer (C) is incorrect. A loss that is both probable and reasonably estimable must always be disclosed. Accrual depends on the timing of the loss. Answer (D) is incorrect. The loss must be charged to income.

32. Ace Co. settled litigation on February 1, Year 2, for an event that occurred during Year 1. An estimated liability was determined as of December 31, Year 1. This estimate was significantly less than the final settlement. The transaction is considered to be material. The year-end financial statements for Year 1 have not been issued. How should the settlement be reported in Ace's Year 1 financial statements?

A. Disclosure only of the settlement.

B. Only an accrual of the settlement.

C. Neither a disclosure nor an accrual.

D. Both a disclosure and an accrual.

Answer (D) is correct. *(CPA, adapted)*
REQUIRED: The treatment of a loss contingency.
DISCUSSION: A contingent loss must be accrued when, based on information available prior to the issuance of the financial statements, two conditions are met: (1) It is probable that an asset has been impaired or a liability has been incurred at a balance sheet date, and (2) the amount of the loss can be reasonably estimated. Because the liability was settled before the financial statements were issued, it was certain that a liability had been incurred, and the amount could be specifically determined. Thus, the contingent loss must be accrued. Disclosure of the amount of the accrual is necessary to keep the financial statements from being misleading, given that the settlement was significantly greater than expected.
Answer (A) is incorrect. The settlement amount must also be accrued. Answer (B) is incorrect. The settlement must also be disclosed. Answer (C) is incorrect. The settlement must be disclosed and accrued.

33. During Year 1, Strasbourg Corp. guaranteed a supplier's $500,000 loan from a bank. At the time of the guarantee, the likelihood of default was not probable. On October 1, Year 2, Strasbourg was notified that the supplier had defaulted on the loan and filed for bankruptcy protection. Counsel believes Strasbourg will probably have to pay between $250,000 and $450,000 under its guarantee. As a result of the supplier's bankruptcy, Strasbourg entered into a contract in December Year 2 to retool its machines so that it could accept parts from other suppliers. Retooling costs are estimated to be $300,000. What amount should Strasbourg report as a contingent liability in its December 31, Year 2, balance sheet?

    A. $250,000

    B. $450,000

    C. $550,000

    D. $750,000

Answer (A) is correct. *(CPA, adapted)*
    REQUIRED: The amount reported as a contingent liability.
    DISCUSSION: A contingent loss must be accrued when two conditions are met: It is probable that at a balance sheet date an asset is overstated or a liability has been incurred, and the amount of the loss can be reasonably estimated. If the estimate is stated within a given range, and no amount within that range appears to be a better estimate than any other, the minimum of the range should be accrued. Hence, the minimum amount ($250,000) of the probable payment under the guarantee should be accrued as a liability. The retooling costs will be charged to the equipment account when incurred because they significantly improve the future service of the machines. The guarantor would have recorded the fair value of a noncontingent liability in Year 1 for the guarantee. If a contingent liability and loss also have to be recognized, the liability is measured at the greater of the fair value or the contingent liability at the inception of the guarantee.
    Answer (B) is incorrect. The amount of $450,000 is the maximum estimated range of loss. Answer (C) is incorrect. The amount of $550,000 includes the retooling costs. Answer (D) is incorrect. The amount of $750,000 equals the retooling costs plus the maximum estimated range of loss.

34. In January Year 2, an explosion occurred at Zurich Co.'s plant, causing damage to area properties. By March 10, Year 2, no claims had yet been asserted against Zurich. However, Zurich's management and legal counsel concluded that it was reasonably possible that Zurich would be held responsible for negligence and that $3 million would be a reasonable estimate of the damages. Zurich's $5 million comprehensive public liability policy contains a $300,000 deductible clause. In Zurich's December 31, Year 1, financial statements, for which the auditor's field work was completed in April Year 2, how should this casualty be reported?

    A. As a note disclosing a possible liability of $3 million.

    B. As an accrued liability of $300,000.

    C. As a note disclosing a possible liability of $300,000.

    D. No note disclosure or accrual is required for Year 1 because the event occurred in Year 2.

Answer (C) is correct. *(CPA, adapted)*
    REQUIRED: The proper accounting for a reasonably possible contingent loss covered under a liability policy.
    DISCUSSION: A loss contingency involving an unasserted claim should be disclosed if it is considered probable that the claim will be asserted and at least reasonably possible that an unfavorable outcome will result. The amount of the loss to be disclosed equals the amount of the company's potential liability. The comprehensive public liability policy has a $300,000 deductible clause, and the policy is sufficient to cover the reasonable estimate of the liability. The company should therefore disclose in a note the possible loss of $300,000.
    Answer (A) is incorrect. The possible loss to the company is limited to the $300,000 deductible. Answer (B) is incorrect. A reasonably possible loss should not be accrued. Answer (D) is incorrect. Note disclosure is required to prevent the financial statements from being misleading even though no asset was impaired and no liability was incurred at the balance sheet date.

35. On February 5, Year 2, an employee filed a $2 million lawsuit against Vienna Co. for damages suffered when one of Vienna's plants exploded on December 29, Year 1. Vienna's legal counsel expects the company will lose the lawsuit and estimates the loss to be between $500,000 and $1 million. The employee has offered to settle the lawsuit out of court for $900,000, but Vienna will not agree to the settlement. In its December 31, Year 1, balance sheet, what amount should Vienna report as liability from lawsuit?

    A. $2,000,000

    B. $1,000,000

    C. $900,000

    D. $500,000

Answer (D) is correct. *(CPA, adapted)*
    REQUIRED: The contingent loss that should be accrued when a range of estimates is provided.
    DISCUSSION: Because the loss is probable and can be reasonably estimated, it should be accrued if the amount is material. If the estimate is stated within a given range, and no amount within that range appears to be a better estimate than any other, the minimum of the range should be accrued. Thus, Vienna should report a $500,000 contingent liability.
    Answer (A) is incorrect. The amount of $2,000,000 is above the maximum range, and only the minimum of the range should be accrued. Answer (B) is incorrect. The minimum of the range should be accrued. Answer (C) is incorrect. The proposed settlement amount is $900,000.

36. On November 10, Year 1, a Warsaw Corp. truck was in an accident with an auto driven by Krzyzewski. On January 10, Year 2, Warsaw received notice of a lawsuit seeking $800,000 in damages for personal injuries suffered by Krzyzewski. Warsaw Corp.'s counsel believes it is reasonably possible that Krzyzewski will be awarded an estimated amount in the range between $250,000 and $500,000 and that $400,000 is a better estimate of potential liability than any other amount. Warsaw's accounting year ends on December 31, and the Year 1 financial statements were issued on March 6, Year 2. What amount of loss should Warsaw accrue at December 31, Year 1?

A. $0

B. $250,000

C. $400,000

D. $500,000

Answer (A) is correct. *(CPA, adapted)*
REQUIRED: The proper accounting for a contingent loss that is reasonably possible and can be estimated within a range.
DISCUSSION: A contingent loss must be accrued when it is probable that, at a balance sheet date, an asset is overstated or a liability has been incurred and the amount of the loss can be reasonably estimated. If both conditions are not met but the probability of the loss is at least reasonably possible, the amount of the loss must be disclosed. This loss is reasonably possible and reasonably estimable. Hence, it should be disclosed but not accrued.
Answer (B) is incorrect. The amount of $250,000 would be disclosed in a note if a better estimate did not exist. Answer (C) is incorrect. The amount of $400,000 should be disclosed. It is the best estimate. It is not accrued. Answer (D) is incorrect. The amount of $500,000 is the maximum loss in the range. It is not the amount used in a note disclosure.

37. Tyrol, Inc., has a self-insurance plan. Each year, retained earnings is appropriated for contingencies in an amount equal to insurance premiums saved minus recognized losses from lawsuits and other claims. As a result of a current-year accident, Tyrol is a defendant in a lawsuit in which it will probably have to pay damages of $190,000. What are the effects of this lawsuit's probable outcome on Tyrol's current-year financial statements?

A. An increase in expenses and no effect on liabilities.

B. An increase in both expenses and liabilities.

C. No effect on expenses and an increase in liabilities.

D. No effect on either expenses or liabilities.

Answer (B) is correct. *(CPA, adapted)*
REQUIRED: The effect on the financial statements of litigation with a probable unfavorable outcome.
DISCUSSION: A loss contingency involves uncertainty as to the impairment of an asset or the incurrence of a liability at the balance sheet date. Resolution of the uncertainty depends on the occurrence or nonoccurrence of one or more future events. A loss should be debited and either an asset valuation allowance or a liability credited when the loss contingency is both probable and reasonably estimable. Thus, the company should accrue a loss and a liability. Appropriations of retained earnings have no effect on these accounting treatments.
Answer (A) is incorrect. The company should accrue a liability. Answer (C) is incorrect. The company should accrue a loss. Answer (D) is incorrect. The company should accrue a loss and a liability.

38. Seller-Guarantor sold an asset with a carrying amount at the time of sale of $500,000 to Buyer for $650,000 in cash. Seller also provided a guarantee to Guarantee Bank of the $600,000 loan that Guarantee made to Buyer to finance the sale. The probability that Seller will become liable under the guarantee is remote. In a stand-alone arm's-length transaction with an unrelated party, the premium required by Seller to provide the same guarantee would have been $40,000. The entry made by Seller at the time of the sale should include a

A. Gain of $150,000.

B. Noncontingent liability of $40,000.

C. Contingent liability of $600,000.

D. Loss of $450,000.

Answer (B) is correct. *(Publisher, adapted)*
REQUIRED: The entry made to reflect sale of an asset and the seller's guarantee of the buyer's debt.
DISCUSSION: No contingent liability results because the likelihood of payment by the guarantor is remote. However, a noncontingent liability is recognized at the effective date of the seller's guarantee. This liability is initially measured at fair value. In a multiple-element transaction with an unrelated party, the fair value is estimated, for example, as the premium required by the guarantor to provide the same guarantee in a stand-alone arm's-length transaction with an unrelated party. The amount of that premium is given as $40,000. Hence, Seller debits cash for the total received ($650,000), credits the asset sold for its carrying amount ($500,000), credits the noncontingent liability for its estimated fair value ($40,000), and credits a gain for $110,000 ($650,000 – $500,000 – $40,000).
Answer (A) is incorrect. A gain of $150,000 assumes neither a noncontingent nor a contingent liability is recognized. Answer (C) is incorrect. No contingent liability is recognized. The likelihood of payment is remote, not probable. Answer (D) is incorrect. A loss of $450,000 assumes recognition of a contingent liability of $600,000.

39. In Year 1, a contract dispute between Loch Co. and Lomond Co. was submitted to binding arbitration. In Year 1, each party's attorney indicated privately that the probable award in Loch's favor could be reasonably estimated. In Year 2, the arbitrator decided in favor of Loch. When should Loch and Lomond recognize their respective gain and loss?

	Loch's Gain	Lomond's Loss
A.	Year 1	Year 1
B.	Year 1	Year 2
C.	Year 2	Year 1
D.	Year 2	Year 2

Answer (C) is correct. *(CPA, adapted)*
REQUIRED: The accounting for a contingent gain or loss that is probable and capable of reasonable estimation.
DISCUSSION: A contingent loss must be accrued when two conditions are met: It is probable that, at a balance sheet date, an asset is overstated or a liability has been incurred, and the amount of the loss can be reasonably estimated. But gain contingencies should not be recognized until they are realized. A gain contingency should be disclosed, but misleading implications as to the likelihood of realization should be avoided. Because the award in favor of Loch is probable and can be reasonably estimated, a loss should be recognized in Year 1 by Lomond. However, Loch should not recognize the gain until Year 2.
Answer (A) is incorrect. Loch should recognize a gain in Year 2. Answer (B) is incorrect. Loch should recognize a gain in Year 2, and Lomond should recognize a loss in Year 1. Answer (D) is incorrect. Lomond should recognize a loss in Year 1.

40. During January of the current year, Kiev Corp. won a litigation award for $15,000 that was tripled to $45,000 to include punitive damages. The defendant, who is financially stable, has appealed only the $30,000 of punitive damages. Kiev was awarded $50,000 in an unrelated suit it filed, which is being appealed by the defendant. Counsel is unable to estimate the outcome of these appeals. In its current-year financial statements, Kiev should report what amount of pretax gain?

A. $15,000

B. $45,000

C. $50,000

D. $95,000

Answer (A) is correct. *(CPA, adapted)*
REQUIRED: The amount of pretax gain from litigation.
DISCUSSION: Gain contingencies must not be recognized until they are realized. A gain contingency should be disclosed, but care should be taken to avoid misleading implications as to the likelihood of realization. Consequently, the only litigation award to be recognized in income in the current year is the $15,000 amount that has not been appealed. The other awards have not been realized because they have been appealed.
Answer (B) is incorrect. The amount of $45,000 includes the punitive damages that have been appealed. Answer (C) is incorrect. The amount of $50,000 is the award in the unrelated suit that has been appealed. Answer (D) is incorrect. The amount of $95,000 includes the punitive damages and the award in the unrelated suit. Both have been appealed.

41. In May of Year 1, Caso Co. filed suit against Wayne, Inc., seeking $1.9 million damages for patent infringement. A court verdict in November Year 4 awarded Caso $1.5 million in damages, but Wayne's appeal is not expected to be decided before Year 6. Caso's counsel believes it is probable that Caso will be successful against Wayne for an estimated amount in the range between $800,000 and $1.1 million, with $1 million considered the most likely amount. What amount should Caso record as income from the lawsuit in the year ended December 31, Year 4?

A. $0

B. $800,000

C. $1,000,000

D. $1,500,000

Answer (A) is correct. *(CPA, adapted)*
REQUIRED: The amount of income recorded from the lawsuit.
DISCUSSION: Gain contingencies must not be recognized until they are realized. Because the appeal is not expected to be decided before Year 6, Caso should not record any revenue from the lawsuit in the Year 4 income statement. This gain contingency should be disclosed. However, misleading implications as to the likelihood of realization should be avoided.
Answer (B) is incorrect. Gains should not be recognized until they are realized. Answer (C) is incorrect. The gain is not realized and therefore cannot be recognized. Answer (D) is incorrect. Realization before recognition is required.

11.6 Warranties

42. Kamchatka sells a durable good on January 1, Year 1, and the customer is automatically given a 1-year warranty. The customer also buys an extended warranty package, extending the coverage for an additional 2 years to the end of Year 3. At the time of the original sale, the company expects warranty costs to be incurred evenly over the life of the warranty contracts. The customer has only one warranty claim during the 3-year period, and the claim occurs during Year 2. The company will recognize revenue from the sale of the extended warranty

    A. On January 1, Year 1.

    B. In Years 2 and 3.

    C. At the time of the claim in Year 2.

    D. December 31, Year 3, when the warranty expires.

Answer (B) is correct. *(CIA, adapted)*
REQUIRED: The recognition of revenue from the sale of an extended warranty.
DISCUSSION: Because warranty costs are expected to be incurred evenly over the life of the warranty contracts, the revenue should be recognized on the straight-line basis over the life of the extended warranty contract.
Answer (A) is incorrect. The recognition of revenue from the sale of the extended warranty is deferred until the extended warranty period begins. Answer (C) is incorrect. The revenue should be recognized evenly over the life of the contract. It is not related to the timing of the claims. Answer (D) is incorrect. Revenue is recognized over the life of the warranty, not at expiration.

43. San Marino Co. sells appliances that include a 3-year warranty. Service calls under the warranty are performed by an independent mechanic under a contract with San Marino. Based on experience, warranty costs are estimated at $30 for each machine sold. When should San Marino recognize these warranty costs?

    A. Evenly over the life of the warranty.

    B. When the service calls are performed.

    C. When payments are made to the mechanic.

    D. When the machines are sold.

Answer (D) is correct. *(CPA, adapted)*
REQUIRED: The proper recording of warranty costs.
DISCUSSION: Under the accrual method, a provision for warranty costs is made when the related revenue is recognized. Revenue is recognized when the machines are sold, so warranty costs also should be recognized.
Answer (A) is incorrect. The accrual method matches the costs and the related revenues. Answer (B) is incorrect. When the warranty costs can be reasonably estimated, the accrual method should be used. Recognizing the costs when the service calls are performed is the cash basis. Answer (C) is incorrect. Recognizing costs when paid is the cash basis.

44. Salvador Co. sold 800,000 electronic can openers in Year 1. Based on past experience, the company estimated that 10,000 of the 800,000 would prove to be defective and that 60% of these would be returned for replacement under the company's warranty. The cost to replace an electronic can opener is $6.00.

On January 1, Year 1, the balance in the company's estimated liability for warranties account was $3,000. During Year 1, 5,000 electronic can openers were replaced under the warranty. The estimated liability for warranties reported on December 31, Year 1, should be

    A. $6,000

    B. $9,000

    C. $36,000

    D. $39,000

Answer (B) is correct. *(O. Broome, Jr.)*
REQUIRED: The year-end estimated liability for warranties.
DISCUSSION: At the time of the sale of each electronic can opener, it is probable that a warranty liability has been incurred and its amount can be reasonably estimated. Consequently, a warranty expense should be recognized with a corresponding credit to an estimated liability for warranties account. As indicated below, the 1/1/Year 1 balance in this account is $3,000. It was increased during Year 1 by $36,000 (10,000 estimated defective can openers × $6 replacement fee × 60% estimated replacement rate). The account should be decreased by $30,000 (5,000 openers replaced × $6). Thus, the ending balance is $9,000.

Estimated Liability for Warranties		
	$ 3,000	1/1/Year 1
Replacements $30,000	36,000	Warranty expense
	$ 9,000	12/31/Year 1

Answer (A) is incorrect. The amount of $6,000 is the balance if you ignore the $3,000 balance already in the account. Answer (C) is incorrect. The amount of $36,000 is the estimated liability recorded when the can openers are sold. Answer (D) is incorrect. The amount of $39,000 is the balance in the estimated liability for warranties account before it is adjusted for the actual replacement costs incurred.

45. During Year 1, Brunei Co. introduced a new product carrying a 2-year warranty against defects. The estimated warranty costs related to dollar sales are 2% within 12 months following the sale and 4% in the second 12 months following the sale. Sales and actual warranty expenditures for the years ended December 31, Year 1 and Year 2, are as follows:

	Sales	Actual Warranty Expenditures
Year 1	$150,000	$2,250
Year 2	250,000	7,500
	$400,000	$9,750

What amount should Brunei report as estimated warranty liability in its December 31, Year 2, balance sheet?

A. $2,500

B. $3,250

C. $11,250

D. $14,250

Answer (D) is correct. *(CPA, adapted)*
REQUIRED: The estimated warranty liability at the end of the second year.
DISCUSSION: Because this product is new, the beginning balance in the estimated warranty liability account at the beginning of Year 1 is $0. For Year 1, the estimated warranty costs related to dollar sales are 6% (2% + 4%) of sales, or $9,000 ($150,000 × 6%). For Year 2, the estimated warranty costs are $15,000 ($250,000 × 6%). These amounts are charged to warranty expense and credited to the estimated warranty liability account. This liability account is debited for expenditures of $2,250 and $7,500 in Year 1 and Year 2, respectively. Hence, the estimated warranty liability at 12/31/Year 2 is $14,250.

Estimated Liability for Warranties			
		$ 0	1/1/Year 2
Year 1 expenditures	$2,250	9,000	Year 1 expense
Year 2 expenditures	$7,500	15,000	Year 2 expense
		$14,250	12/31/Year 2

Answer (A) is incorrect. The amount of $2,500 is equal to 10% of Year 2 sales. Answer (B) is incorrect. The amount of $3,250 is equal to 2% of Year 1 sales, plus 4% of Year 2 sales, minus the $9,750 in actual expenses incurred. Answer (C) is incorrect. The amount of $11,250 is the sum of Year 1's actual expenditures of $2,250 and the Year 1 warranty expense of $9,000.

46. The selling price of a new company's units is $20,000 each. The buyers are provided with a 2-year warranty that is expected to cost the company $500 per unit in the year of the sale and $1,500 per unit in the year following the sale. The company sold 160 units in the first year of operation and 200 units in the second year. Actual payments for warranty claims were $40,000 and $260,000 in Years 1 and 2, respectively. The amount charged to warranty expense during the second year of operation is

A. $100,000

B. $260,000

C. $340,000

D. $400,000

Answer (D) is correct. *(CIA, adapted)*
REQUIRED: The amount charged to warranty expense during the second year of operation.
DISCUSSION: Under the accrual method, the total estimated warranty costs are charged to operating expense in the year of sale. The total estimated warranty cost per unit is $2,000 ($500 + $1,500). In Year 2, 200 units were sold, so the warranty expense recognized is $400,000.

Answer (A) is incorrect. The expected amount of warranty claims for the first year of the warranty from second-year sales is $100,000. Answer (B) is incorrect. The actual amount of claims in the second year is $260,000. Answer (C) is incorrect. The expected amount of warranty claims in the second year is $340,000.

11.7 Coupons and Premiums

47. A department store sells gift cards that may be redeemed for merchandise. Each card expires 3 years after issuance. The revenue from the gift cards should be recognized

A. Evenly over 3 years from the date of issuance.

B. In the period the cards are sold.

C. In the period the cards expire.

D. In the period the cards are redeemed or in the period they expire if they are allowed to lapse.

Answer (D) is correct. *(CIA, adapted)*
REQUIRED: The timing of revenue recognition for gift cards.
DISCUSSION: SFAC 5, *Recognition and Measurement in Financial Statements of Business Enterprises*, states that revenue should be recognized when realized or realizable and earned. Revenue from gift cards is realized when the cash is received. It is earned when the cards are redeemed or allowed to lapse. Thus, the criteria of being both realized and earned are satisfied when the cards are redeemed or allowed to lapse.

Answer (A) is incorrect. The revenue from the cards is not earned evenly over 3 years. Answer (B) is incorrect. The revenue from the cards is not earned when the cards are sold. Answer (C) is incorrect. The revenue is also recognized in the period the cards are redeemed.

48. Conch Shell Company sells gift cards, redeemable for merchandise, that expire 1 year after their issuance. Conch Shell has the following information pertaining to its gift cards sales and redemptions:

Unredeemed at 12/31/Year 1	$150,000
Year 2 sales	500,000
Year 2 redemptions of prior-year sales	50,000
Year 2 redemptions of current-year sales	350,000

Conch Shell's experience indicates that 10% of gift certificates sold will not be redeemed. In its December 31, Year 2, balance sheet, what amount should Conch Shell report as unearned revenue?

A. $250,000

B. $200,000

C. $150,000

D. $100,000

Answer (D) is correct. *(CPA, adapted)*
REQUIRED: The amount reported as unearned revenue at year end.
DISCUSSION: Because the cards expire after 1 year, all revenue from sales prior to Year 2 has been earned. Hence, the unearned revenue balance for gift card sales at the end of Year 2 relates solely to Year 2 sales. Given Year 2 sales of $500,000 and redemptions of $350,000, $150,000 of cards are unredeemed at year end. However, 10% of total cards sold in Year 2 ($500,000 × 10% = $50,000) are not expected to be redeemed. Accordingly, unearned revenue is $100,000 ($150,000 – $50,000).
Answer (A) is incorrect. The amount of $250,000 is the sum of the beginning and ending balances. Answer (B) is incorrect. The amount of $200,000 assumes that none of the cards reflected in the beginning balance have lapsed but that 10% of the cards sold in Year 2 are expected to lapse. Answer (C) is incorrect. The amount of $150,000 does not consider the 10% of cards sold in Year 2 that are estimated not to be redeemed.

49. Amman Company records stamp service revenue and provides for the cost of redemptions in the year stamps are sold to licensees. Amman's past experience indicates that only 80% of the stamps sold to licensees will be redeemed. Amman's liability for stamp redemptions was $6 million at December 31, Year 1. Additional information for Year 2 is as follows:

Stamp service revenue from stamps sold to licensees	$4,000,000
Cost of redemptions (stamps sold prior to 1/1/Year 2)	2,750,000

If all the stamps sold in Year 2 were presented for redemption in Year 3, the redemption cost would be $2,250,000. What amount should Amman report as a liability for stamp redemptions at December 31, Year 2?

A. $7,800,000

B. $5,500,000

C. $5,050,000

D. $3,250,000

Answer (C) is correct. *(CPA, adapted)*
REQUIRED: The reported liability for stamp redemptions at year end.
DISCUSSION: The liability for stamp redemptions at the beginning of Year 2 is given as $6 million. This liability would be increased in Year 2 by $2.25 million if all stamps sold in Year 2 were presented for redemption. However, because only 80% are expected to be redeemed, the liability should be increased by $1,800,000 ($2,250,000 × 80%). The liability was decreased by the $2,750,000 attributable to the costs of redemptions. Thus, the liability for stamp redemptions at 12/31/Year 2 is $5,050,000 ($6,000,000 + $1,800,000 – $2,750,000).
Answer (A) is incorrect. The amount of $7,800,000 omits the Year 2 redemptions from the calculation. Answer (B) is incorrect. The amount of $5,500,000 assumes a 100% redemption rate. Answer (D) is incorrect. The amount of $3,250,000 omits the expected Year 3 redemptions from the calculation.

50. In June Year 1, Haifa Retailers sold refundable merchandise coupons. Haifa received $10 for each coupon redeemable from July 1 to December 31, Year 1, for merchandise with a retail price of $11. At June 30, Year 1, how should Haifa report these coupon transactions?

A. Unearned revenues at the merchandise's retail price.

B. Unearned revenues at the cash received amount.

C. Revenues at the merchandise's retail price.

D. Revenues at the cash received amount.

Answer (B) is correct. *(CPA, adapted)*
REQUIRED: The reporting of refundable merchandise coupons.
DISCUSSION: Revenue should not be recognized until it is realized or realizable and earned. Because the earning process is not complete until the coupons lapse or are redeemed, an unearned revenue (liability) account should be credited at the time of sale for the amount received.
Answer (A) is incorrect. The transaction is measured at the amount received, not the nominal retail price. Answer (C) is incorrect. Revenue is not realized or realizable and earned at June 30, Year 1, so it cannot be recognized. Answer (D) is incorrect. Revenue should not be recognized until it is realized or realizable and earned.

51. Negev Co. frequently distributes coupons to promote a new product. On October 1, Year 1, Negev mailed 1 million coupons for $.90 off each box of the product purchased. Negev expects 240,000 of these coupons to be redeemed before the December 31, Year 1, expiration date. It takes 30 days from the redemption date for Negev to receive the coupons from the retailers. Negev reimburses the retailers an additional $.10 for each coupon redeemed. As of December 31, Year 1, Negev had paid retailers $100,000 related to these coupons and had 100,000 coupons on hand that had not been processed for payment. What amount should Negev report as a liability for coupons in its December 31, Year 1, balance sheet?

A. $140,000

B. $116,000

C. $100,000

D. $90,000

Answer (A) is correct. *(CPA, adapted)*
REQUIRED: The liability for coupons at year end.
DISCUSSION: The company pays $1.00 ($.90 + $.10) for the redemption of a coupon, and it expects 240,000 to be redeemed at a total cost of $240,000 (240,000 × $1.00). Given that payments of $100,000 have been made, the liability at year end must be $140,000 ($240,000 – $100,000). The cost associated with the unprocessed coupons on hand does not reduce the liability because payment for these coupons has not yet been made.
Answer (B) is incorrect. The amount of $116,000 ignores the additional $.10 per coupon paid to retailers. Answer (C) is incorrect. The amount of $100,000 is the cost of the coupons on hand that have not yet been processed for payment. Negev expects to receive additional redeemed coupons for 30 days after the balance sheet date. Answer (D) is incorrect. The amount of $90,000 equals $.90 times 100,000 coupons.

52. In packages of its products, the Kirghiz Company includes coupons that may be presented to grocers for discounts of certain products on or before a stated expiration date. The grocers are reimbursed when they send the coupons to Kirghiz. In the company's experience, 40% of such coupons are redeemed, and 1 month usually elapses between the date a grocer receives a coupon from a consumer and the date Kirghiz receives it. During Year 1, Kirghiz issued two series of coupons as follows:

Issued on	Total Face Amount	Consumer Expiration Date	Amount Disbursed as of 12/31/Year 1
1/1/Year 1	$100,000	6/30/Year 1	$34,000
7/1/Year 1	120,000	12/31/Year 1	40,000

The company's December 31, Year 1, balance sheet should include a liability for unredeemed coupons of

A. $0

B. $8,000

C. $14,000

D. $48,000

Answer (B) is correct. *(CPA, adapted)*
REQUIRED: The year-end liability for unredeemed coupons.
DISCUSSION: No liability should be reported for unredeemed coupons at December 31 with regard to the coupons issued on 1/1/Year 1 because more than 1 month has elapsed since their expiration date. The total estimated liability for the coupons issued on 7/1/Year 1 is equal to $48,000 ($120,000 total face amount of coupons issued × 40%) minus the $40,000 disbursed as of 12/31/Year 1. Consequently, the liability is $8,000 ($48,000 – $40,000).
Answer (A) is incorrect. The amount disbursed was less than the total estimated liability. Answer (C) is incorrect. The amount of $14,000 assumes that less than 1 month has elapsed since the expiration date of the coupons issued on 1/1/Year 1. Answer (D) is incorrect. The amount of $48,000 is the total estimated liability for the coupons issued on 7/1/Year 1.

11.8 IFRS

53. Because of a defect discovered in its seat belts in December Year 1, an automobile manufacturer believes it is probable that it will be required to recall its products. The final decision on the recall is expected to be made in March Year 2. The cost of the recall is reliably estimated to be $2.5 million. How should this information be reported in the December 31, Year 1, financial statements?

A. As a loss of $2.5 million and a provision of $2.5 million.

B. As an adjustment of the opening balance of retained earnings equal to $2.5 million.

C. As an appropriation of retained earnings of $2.5 million.

D. It should not be disclosed because it has not yet happened.

Answer (A) is correct. *(CIA, adapted)*
REQUIRED: The reporting of a probable loss from a product recall.
DISCUSSION: A provision is a liability of uncertain timing or amount. Recognition of provisions is appropriate when (1) the entity has a legal or constructive present obligation resulting from a past event (called an obligating event), (2) it is probable that an outflow of economic benefits will be necessary to settle the obligation, and (3) its amount can be reliably estimated. Consequently, the entity must recognize a loss and a liability for $2.5 million.
Answer (B) is incorrect. An adjustment of beginning retained earnings is not appropriate. A loss should be recognized because it is probable and can be reliably estimated. Answer (C) is incorrect. An appropriation of retained earnings is permissible although not required, but the entity must still recognize a loss and a provision. Moreover, no part of the appropriation may be transferred to income, and no loss may be charged to an appropriation of retained earnings. Answer (D) is incorrect. If the loss is probable and can be reliably estimated, it should be recognized by a charge to income.

54. An entity has been sued for $100 million for producing and selling an unsafe product. Attorneys for the entity cannot reliably predict the outcome of the litigation. In its financial statements, the entity should

A. Make the following journal entry, and disclose the existence of the lawsuit in a note.

| Estimated loss from litigation | $100,000,000 | |
| Estimated provision for litigation loss | | $100,000,000 |

B. Disclose the existence of the lawsuit in a note without making a journal entry.

C. Neither make a journal entry nor disclose the lawsuits in a note because bad publicity will hurt the entity.

D. Make the following journal entry, and disclose the existence of the lawsuit in a note.

| Cost of goods sold | $100,000,000 | |
| Estimated provision for litigation loss | | $100,000,000 |

Answer (B) is correct. *(CIA, adapted)*
REQUIRED: The financial statement treatment of a loss from pending litigation.
DISCUSSION: In the very rare case in which a reliable estimate of an obligation that otherwise qualifies for treatment as a provision cannot be determined, no liability is recognized. Instead, the existing liability is disclosed as a contingent liability (unless the possibility of any outflow in settlement is remote).
Answer (A) is incorrect. A journal entry is made when the outflow in settlement is probable and can be reliably estimated. Answer (C) is incorrect. A disclosure must be made of a contingent liability. Answer (D) is incorrect. A journal entry is made when the outflow in settlement is probable and can be reliably estimated.

55. An entity is currently being sued by a customer. A reliable estimate can be made of the costs that would result from a ruling unfavorable to the entity, and the amount involved is material. The entity's managers, lawyers, and auditors agree that the likelihood of an unfavorable ruling is remote. This contingent liability

A. Should be disclosed in a note.

B. Should be disclosed as a parenthetical comment in the balance sheet.

C. Need not be disclosed.

D. Should be disclosed by an appropriation of retained earnings.

Answer (C) is correct. *(Publisher, adapted)*
REQUIRED: The treatment of a contingent liability that is reliably estimable but remote in probability.
DISCUSSION: A contingent liability includes a present obligation for which an outflow of resources embodying economic benefits is not probable. A contingent liability is not recognized but is disclosed unless the possibility of the outflow is remote.

56. A company had $100,000 in current liabilities at the end of the current year. The company refinanced this liability on a noncurrent basis subsequent to the end of the year but before the financial statements were issued. How should this liability be presented, according to IFRS and U.S. GAAP, in the company's year-end financial statements?

A. In current liabilities under IFRS and in noncurrent liabilities under U.S. GAAP.

B. In current liabilities under both IFRS and U.S. GAAP.

C. In noncurrent liabilities under both IFRS and U.S. GAAP.

D. In noncurrent liabilities under IFRS and in current liabilities under U.S. GAAP.

Answer (A) is correct. *(Publisher, adapted)*
REQUIRED: The presentation of a current liability that was refinanced after the end of the reporting but before the issuance of the statements.
DISCUSSION: Under U.S. GAAP, if an entity (1) intends to refinance current debt on a noncurrent basis and (2) demonstrates an ability to do so, the obligation must be reclassified as noncurrent. The ability to refinance may be demonstrated by entering into an agreement to refinance or reschedule payments on a noncurrent basis even if such an agreement is completed after the reporting date but before the financial statements are issued or available to be issued. Under IFRS, a current liability may be reclassified as noncurrent only if the agreement to refinance or reschedule payments on a noncurrent basis is completed before the end of the reporting period.
Answer (B) is incorrect. Under U.S. GAAP, the liability must be reported as noncurrent because the refinancing agreement was completed before the financial statements were issued or available to be issued. Answer (C) is incorrect. Under IFRS, the liability must continue to be presented in current liabilities because the refinancing agreement was completed after the end of the reporting period. Answer (D) is incorrect. Because the refinancing agreement was completed after the end of the reporting period, this liability must continue to be reported as current under IFRS. Under U.S. GAAP, it is reported in noncurrent liabilities because the liability was refinanced before the financial statements were issued.

Use Gleim **EQE Test Prep** Software Download for interactive study and performance analysis.

STUDY UNIT TWELVE
NONCURRENT LIABILITIES

Traditional noncurrent liabilities (bonds and notes) are recognized and measured in accordance with the guidance applicable to interest on receivables and payables unless the **fair value option** has been elected (see Study Unit 10).

Bonds

A bond is a formal contract to pay an amount of money (face amount) at the maturity date plus interest at the stated rate at specific intervals. All of the terms are stated in an agreement (an indenture) with the bondholders. The proceeds received from the sale of a bond equal the sum of the present values of the face amount and the interest payments (if the bond is interest-bearing). When the proceeds differ from the face amount, the difference is a discount or premium. Bonds are sold at a **premium** when the contract (stated) rate exceeds the market (effective) rate. Cash is debited, and bonds payable and premium on bonds payable are credited. Bonds are sold at a **discount** when the contract (stated) rate is less than the market (effective) rate. Cash and discount on bonds payable are debited, and bonds payable is credited.

Bond discount or premium must be amortized using the **effective interest method**. Under the interest method, interest expense changes every period, but the interest rate is constant. When bonds are issued between interest payment dates, the buyer includes accrued interest in the purchase price. **Interest expense** for a period is equal to the carrying amount of the bonds at the beginning of the period (face amount – unamortized discount or + unamortized premium) times the yield (market) interest rate. The **cash paid** for periodic interest is equal to the face amount of the bonds times the stated rate. It remains constant over the life of the bonds.

The difference between interest expense and cash interest paid is the discount or premium amortization. When the entity amortizes a **discount**, discount amortized, total interest expense, and the carrying amount of the bonds **increase** each period. Interest expense is debited and cash and discount are credited. When the entity amortizes a **premium**, premium amortized, total interest expense, and the carrying amount of the bonds **decrease** each period. Interest expense and premium are debited and cash is credited. At the maturity date, the discount or premium will be fully amortized to zero, and the net carrying amount of the bonds will equal the face amount. Bond discount or premium appears as a direct subtraction from, or addition to, the face amount of the bonds payable in the balance sheet.

Debt issue costs are incurred to bring a bond to market. They include (1) printing and engraving costs, (2) legal fees, (3) accountants' fees, (4) underwriters' commissions, (5) registration fees, and (6) promotion costs. Issue costs should be reported in the balance sheet as **deferred charges** and amortized over the life of the bonds, not combined with bond premium or discount. Although the interest method is theoretically preferable, issue costs may be amortized on a straight-line basis if the results are not materially different.

Convertible Debt

When convertible bonds are issued, the entire proceeds are reported as a noncurrent liability until the bonds are converted or redeemed. When bonds are converted under the **book value method** (the generally accepted approach), the stock issued is recorded at the carrying amount of the bonds with no recognition of gain or loss. When bonds are converted under the **market value method**, the stock issued is recorded at fair value with recognition of gain or loss equal to the difference between fair value and the carrying amount of the bonds. A debtor issuing additional securities or paying other consideration to **induce conversion** recognizes the fair value of the inducements (sweeteners) as an expense.

Debt that must be surrendered to exercise **attached warrants** is accounted for as **convertible**. Thus, the entire proceeds are reported as a noncurrent liability until the debt is surrendered or redeemed. However, when debt is issued with **detachable warrants**, the proceeds are allocated between the debt and the warrants based on their relative fair values at the time of issuance. The portion allocated to the warrants is accounted for as additional paid-in capital – warrants.

Extinguishment of Debt

All **debt extinguishments** are fundamentally alike. The difference between the reacquisition price and the net carrying amount should be recognized in income for the period of extinguishment. A liability is derecognized only if it has been extinguished. Extinguishment occurs when either (1) the debtor pays the creditor and is relieved of its obligation for the liability, or (2) the debtor is legally released from being the primary obligor under the liability, either judicially or by the creditor. Thus, GAAP prohibit the recognition of a gain or loss from an **in-substance defeasance**. In-substance defeasance occurs when the debtor irrevocably sets aside assets to be used for satisfying the debt.

Noncurrent Notes Payable

Noncurrent notes payable are essentially the same as bonds. However, a note is payable to a single creditor, and bonds are payable to many creditors. In practice, notes are usually of shorter duration than bonds. Noncurrent notes, such as **mortgage notes**, that are payable in installments are classified as current to the extent of any payments due in the coming year. Payments not due in the current year are classified as noncurrent. For a full summary, see Study Unit 5.

Troubled Debt Restructuring

A troubled debt restructuring (TDR) occurs when the creditor for economic or legal reasons related to the debtor's financial difficulties grants a concession to the debtor that it would not otherwise consider. A TDR can consist of either a **settlement of the debt in full** or a continuation of the debt with a **modification of terms**. TDRs almost always involve a loss to the creditor and a gain to the debtor.

Given a settlement in full with a **transfer of assets**, the **creditor** recognizes a **loss** equal to the difference between the fair value of the assets received and the carrying amount of the receivable. If the allowance method is used for recording bad debts, the loss is debited to the allowance account to the extent of its credit balance. If the creditor receives long-lived assets to be sold in full satisfaction, the assets are recorded at fair value minus cost to sell. The **debtor** recognizes a **gain** when the carrying amount of the debt (adjusted face amount) exceeds the fair value of the asset(s) given. The debtor also recognizes a **gain (loss)** equal to the difference between the fair value of the assets given and their carrying amount.

Given a settlement in full with a **transfer of an equity interest**, the **creditor** again recognizes a **loss** equal to the difference between the assets received and the carrying amount of the receivable. The **debtor** recognizes a **gain** only on the restructuring. The creditor's loss equals the debtor's gain.

Given a **modification of terms**, three changes in the terms of the loan are common: (1) a reduction in the principal, (2) an extension of the maturity date, and (3) a lowering of the interest rate. The **debtor** recognizes **no gain** when the **undiscounted total future cash flows (UCF)** that the debtor has committed to pay exceed the carrying amount of the debt. A **creditor** must recognize the impairment of a loan when it is probable that the creditor will not be able to collect all amounts due in accordance with the original terms of the loan. The **loss** is the difference between the **discounted total future cash flows (DCF)** and the carrying amount of the receivable. The discount rate is the original contract rate. The creditor treats the loss as an ordinary debit to bad debt expense. Because the creditor uses the time value of money in this calculation, its loss does not equal the debtor's gain (the debtor may have no gain). A creditor measures **impairment** based on the present value of expected future cash flows discounted at the loan's effective rate. An alternative is to use the loan's observable market price or the fair value of the collateral, if the loan is collateral dependent. If foreclosure is probable, impairment is based on the fair value of the collateral.

When a TDR involves a modification of terms and the UCF are **less than** the carrying amount of the debt, the **debtor** recognizes a **gain**. As stated above, the **creditor's loss** is the difference between the DCF and the carrying amount of the receivable. Again, the creditor treats the loss as an ordinary debit to bad debt expense. Moreover, the creditor's loss does not equal the debtor's gain (if any).

Debt restructuring expenses are expensed as incurred, except by debtors issuing equity securities (restructuring expenses reduce paid-in capital from these securities).

Asset Retirement Obligations (AROs)

GAAP for AROs apply to (1) obligations associated with the retirement of tangible noncurrent assets and (2) the related asset retirement cost. The fair value of a **legal obligation** for an ARO is recognized as a liability when incurred if fair value can be reasonably estimated. An expected present value technique ordinarily should be used to estimate the fair value of an ARO. The liability is subsequently increased (credited) periodically for the passage of time. The offsetting debit for this adjustment is to **accretion expense** (an operating item). The related **asset retirement cost (ARC)** is recorded as an increase in the carrying amount of the long-lived asset by an amount equal to the ARO. Thus, when the ARO is initially recognized, the entry is to debit a long-lived asset (ARC) and credit the ARO. The ARC is systematically and rationally allocated over its useful life. The periodic change in the ARO due to the passage of time (accretion expense) is included in the carrying amount of the liability. The entity then revises the ARO and the ARC for changes in the estimated undiscounted cash flows. The legal obligation to be ready to perform the obligation is **unconditional**, even though the timing or method of settlement is conditional. Hence, a liability is recognized for a conditional asset retirement obligation if its fair value can be reasonably estimated.

Differences between GAAP and IFRS

Under IFRS:

- For a discussion of provisions (liabilities of uncertain timing or amount), see the differences between GAAP and IFRS in Study Unit 11.

- A compound financial instrument (e.g., bonds convertible into stock) has liability and equity components. The issuer allocates to the liability component its fair value. The equity component is allocated the residual amount of the initial carrying amount of the instrument.

- **Derecognition of a financial liability** (or a part) occurs only by **extinguishment**. This condition is satisfied only when the debtor pays the creditor or is legally released from primary responsibility either by the creditor or through the legal process. An extinguishment of the old debt and recognition of new debt occurs when the borrower and lender exchange debt instruments with **substantially different terms**. A **substantial modification of terms** of an existing financial liability or a part of it must be accounted for as an extinguishment of the original financial liability and a recognition of a new one. The difference between the carrying amount of a liability (or a part) that has been extinguished or transferred and the amount paid is included in profit or loss.

QUESTIONS

12.1 Bonds

1. When purchasing a bond, the present value of the bond's expected net future cash inflows discounted at the market rate of interest provides what information about the bond?

- A. Price.
- B. Par.
- C. Yield.
- D. Interest.

Answer (A) is correct. *(CPA, adapted)*
REQUIRED: The information about a bond provided by the present value of the bond's expected net future cash inflows discounted at the market rate of interest.
DISCUSSION: The issue price of a bond is based on the market interest rate and reflects its fair value. The proceeds received from the sale of a bond equal the sum of the present values of the face amount and the interest payment (if the bond is interest-bearing). When bonds are issued between interest payment dates, the buyer includes accrued interest in the purchase price.
Answer (B) is incorrect. Par is the maturity amount.
Answer (C) is incorrect. Yield is the effective interest rate.
Answer (D) is incorrect. Interest is the amount of cash paid as interest.

2. When the effective interest method of amortization is used for bonds issued at a premium, the amount of interest payable for an interest period is calculated by multiplying the

- A. Face value of the bonds at the beginning of the period by the contractual interest rate.
- B. Face value of the bonds at the beginning of the period by the effective interest rates.
- C. Carrying value of the bonds at the beginning of the period by the contractual interest rate.
- D. Carrying value of the bonds at the beginning of the period by the effective interest rates.

Answer (A) is correct. *(CPA, adapted)*
REQUIRED: The calculation of the amount of interest payable for an interest period.
DISCUSSION: Interest payable does not vary with the issue price of bonds. It equals their face amount times the stated (contractual) rate at the beginning of the period.
Answer (B) is incorrect. The contractual rate and the face amount determine the amount payable. The effective rate and the carrying amount determine the amount of interest expense. Answer (C) is incorrect. The contractual rate and nominal (face) amount determine the amount of bonds payable. The carrying amount and the effective rate determine the amount of interest expense. Answer (D) is incorrect. The carrying amount and the effective rate determine the amount of interest expense.

Stated ↗

market ↗

3. Perk, Inc., issued $500,000, 10% bonds to yield 8%. Bond issuance costs were $10,000. How should Perk calculate the net proceeds to be received from the issuance?

A. Discount the bonds at the stated rate of interest.

B. Discount the bonds at the market rate of interest.

C. Discount the bonds at the stated rate of interest and deduct bond issuance costs.

D. Discount the bonds at the market rate of interest and deduct bond issuance costs.

Answer (D) is correct. *(CPA, adapted)*
REQUIRED: The net proceeds to be received from the issuance.
DISCUSSION: Bonds are sold at the sum of the present values of the maturity amount and the interest payments (if interest-bearing). The difference between the face amount and the selling price of bonds is either a discount or a premium. Bonds are sold at a discount when they sell for less than face amount, that is, when the contract (stated) interest rate is less than the market (effective) interest rate. Bonds are sold at a premium (in excess of face amount) when the stated rate exceeds the effective rate. To determine the present value of the bonds' future cash flows, the market rate of interest is used as the discount rate. The result is the market price of the bonds at the issue date. The net proceeds equal the price of the bonds minus the issue costs. Issue costs are incurred to bring a bond to market and include printing and engraving costs, legal fees, accountants' fees, underwriters' commissions, registration fees, and promotion costs.
Answer (A) is incorrect. The bonds should be discounted at the market rate, and the net proceeds equal the price (cash flows discounted at the market rate) minus the issue costs. Answer (B) is incorrect. The net proceeds equal the price (cash flows discounted at the market rate) minus the issue costs. Answer (C) is incorrect. The bonds should be discounted at the market rate.

4. York Corp.'s December 31, Year 3, balance sheet contained the following items in the noncurrent liabilities section:

9 3/4% registered debentures, callable in Year 14, due in Year 19	$1,400,000
9 1/2% collateral trust bonds, convertible into common stock beginning in Year 12, due in Year 22	1,200,000
10% subordinated debentures ($60,000 maturing annually beginning in Year 9)	600,000

What is the total amount of York's term bonds?

A. $1,200,000

B. $1,400,000

C. $2,000,000

D. $2,600,000

Answer (D) is correct. *(CPA, adapted)*
REQUIRED: The total amount of term bonds.
DISCUSSION: Term bonds mature on a single date. Hence, the registered bonds and the collateral trust bonds are term bonds, a total of $2,600,000 ($1,400,000 + $1,200,000).
Answer (A) is incorrect. The registered bonds are also term bonds. Answer (B) is incorrect. The collateral trust bonds are also term bonds. Answer (C) is incorrect. The collateral trust bonds, not the subordinated debentures, are term bonds.

5. A bond issued on June 1, Year 1, has interest payment dates of April 1 and October 1. Bond interest expense for the year ended December 31, Year 1, is for a period of

A. 7 months.

B. 6 months.

C. 4 months.

D. 3 months.

Answer (A) is correct. *(CPA, adapted)*
REQUIRED: The period for which interest is paid when a bond is issued between payment dates.
DISCUSSION: Interest expense should be recorded on a systematic and rational basis. The basis used is the passage of time. Because the period from June 1 to December 31 includes 7 months, 7 months of interest expense should be recorded for the year of issuance. The determination of interest expense is not dependent on the interest payment dates. The length of time outstanding determines the interest expense.
Answer (B) is incorrect. Six months assumes a July 1 issuance. Answer (C) is incorrect. Four months is the time to the next payment date. Answer (D) is incorrect. The length of time outstanding determines the interest expense.

6. Cornwall Co.'s December 31, Year 3, balance sheet contained the following items in the noncurrent liabilities section:

Unsecured

9.375% registered bonds ($50,000 maturing annually beginning in Year 7)	$550,000
11.5% convertible bonds, callable beginning in Year 12, due Year 23	250,000

Secured

9.875% guaranty security bonds, due Year 23	$500,000
10.0% commodity-backed bonds ($100,000 maturing annually beginning in Year 8)	400,000

What are the total amounts of serial bonds and debenture bonds?

	Serial Bonds	Debenture Bonds
A.	$950,000	$800,000
B.	$950,000	$250,000
C.	$900,000	$800,000
D.	$400,000	$1,300,000

Answer (A) is correct. *(CPA, adapted)*
REQUIRED: The total amounts of serial bonds and debenture bonds.
DISCUSSION: Serial bonds mature in installments at various dates. Debentures are unsecured bonds. The commodity-backed bonds and the registered bonds are serial bonds. They total $950,000 ($550,000 + $400,000). The registered bonds and the convertible bonds are debentures. They total $800,000 ($550,000 + $250,000).
Answer (B) is incorrect. The registered bonds also are debentures. Answer (C) is incorrect. The registered bonds, not the guaranty security bonds, are serial bonds. Answer (D) is incorrect. The registered bonds are serial bonds, and the guaranty security bonds are not debentures.

7. Unamortized bond discount should be reported on the balance sheet of the issuer as a

A. Direct deduction from the face amount of the debt.

B. Direct deduction from the present value of the debt.

C. Deferred charge.

D. Part of the issue costs.

Answer (A) is correct. *(CPA, adapted)*
REQUIRED: The issuer's balance sheet presentation of unamortized discount.
DISCUSSION: Bond discount must appear as a direct deduction from the face amount of the bond payable to report the effective liability for the bonds. Hence, the bond liability is shown net of unamortized discount.
Answer (B) is incorrect. The face amount minus the unamortized discount is equal to the present value (carrying amount) of the bond. Answer (C) is incorrect. Bond issue costs, not unamortized discount, appear as a deferred charge in the balance sheet. Answer (D) is incorrect. Unamortized discount is segregated from issue costs.

8. The following information pertains to Wales Corp.'s issuance of bonds on July 1, Year 1:

Face amount	$800,000
Term	10 years
Stated interest rate	6%
Interest payment dates	Annually on July 1
Yield	9%

	At 6%	At 9%
Present value of 1 for 10 periods	0.558	0.422
Future value of 1 for 10 periods	1.791	2.367
Present value of ordinary annuity of 1 for 10 periods	7.360	6.418

What should be the issue price for each $1,000 bond?

A. $1,000

B. $943

C. $864

D. $807

Answer (D) is correct. *(CPA, adapted)*
REQUIRED: The issue price for each bond.
DISCUSSION: The issue price for each bond reflects the fair value. It equals the sum of the present values of the future cash flows (principal + interest). This amount is $807 {($1,000 face amount × .422 PV of 1 for 10 periods at 9%) + [($1,000 × 6% interest) × 6.418 PV of an ordinary annuity for 10 periods at 9%]}.
Answer (A) is incorrect. The face amount is $1,000. Answer (B) is incorrect. The amount of $943 is the result of discounting the interest payments at 9% and the face amount at 6%. Answer (C) is incorrect. The amount of $864 is the result of discounting the interest payments at 6% and the face amount at 9%.

9. On January 2, Year 1, Tintagel Co. issued 8% bonds with a face amount of $1 million that mature on January 2, Year 6. The bonds were issued to yield 12%, resulting in a discount of $150,000. Tintagel incorrectly used the straight-line method instead of the effective-interest method to amortize the discount. How is the carrying amount of the bonds affected by the error?

	At December 31, Year 1	At January 2, Year 6
A.	Overstated	Understated
B.	Overstated	No effect
C.	Understated	Overstated
D.	Understated	No effect

Answer (B) is correct. *(CPA, adapted)*
REQUIRED: The effect of amortizing bond discount using the straight-line method.
DISCUSSION: The carrying amount of a bond issued at a discount equals its maturity amount minus the unamortized discount. Under the effective-interest method, periodic interest expense equals the carrying amount times the effective (yield) rate. Discount amortization is the excess of interest expense over actual interest paid. When bonds are issued at a discount, the carrying amount increases over time as the discount is amortized, thereby increasing interest expense and the amount of amortization. Discount amortization under the straight-line method is a constant periodic amount. Thus, in the first year, straight-line amortization of the discount exceeds the amount determined under the interest method. The effect of the error is to overstate the carrying amount by this excess. At the due date of the bonds, however, the discount is fully amortized, and the carrying amount is the same under both methods.
Answer (A) is incorrect. The error has no effect at 1/2/Year 6. Answer (C) is incorrect. The error overstates the carrying amount at 12/31/Year 1 but has no effect at 1/2/Year 6. Answer (D) is incorrect. The error overstates the carrying amount at 12/31/Year 1.

10. Kent Co. issued 6,000 of its 9%, $1,000 face amount bonds at 101 1/2. In connection with the sale of these bonds, Kent paid the following expenses:

Promotion costs	$ 40,000
Engraving and printing	50,000
Underwriters' commissions	400,000

What amount should Kent record as bond issue costs to be amortized over the term of the bonds?

A. $0

B. $440,000

C. $450,000

D. $490,000

Answer (D) is correct. *(CPA, adapted)*
REQUIRED: The amount to be recorded as bond issue costs.
DISCUSSION: Bond issue costs include printing costs, underwriters' commissions, attorney's fees, and promotion costs (including preparation of a prospectus). The issue costs to be amortized equal $490,000 ($40,000 promotion costs + $50,000 printing costs + $400,000 underwriters' commissions).
Answer (A) is incorrect. The amount of $490,000 of bond issue costs should be amortized. Answer (B) is incorrect. The $50,000 printing cost should be amortized. Answer (C) is incorrect. The $40,000 promotion costs should be amortized.

11. On May 1, Year 1, a company issued, at 103 plus accrued interest, 500 of its 12%, $1,000 bonds. The bonds are dated January 1, Year 1, and mature on January 1, Year 5. Interest is payable semiannually on January 1 and July 1. The journal entry to record the issuance of the bonds and the receipt of the cash proceeds is

A. Cash	$515,000	
Interest payable	20,000	
Bonds payable		$500,000
Premium on bonds payable		35,000

B. Cash	$525,000	
Bonds payable		$500,000
Premium on bonds payable		15,000
Interest payable		10,000

C. Cash	$535,000	
Bonds payable		$500,000
Premium on bonds payable		15,000
Interest payable		20,000

D. Cash	$535,000	
Bonds payable		$500,000
Premium on bonds payable		35,000

Answer (C) is correct. *(CIA, adapted)*
REQUIRED: The journal entry to record the issuance of a bond at a premium plus accrued interest.
DISCUSSION: The face amount of the 500 bonds is equal to $500,000 (500 × $1,000). The cash proceeds excluding interest from the issuance of the bonds are $515,000 ($500,000 × 103%). The $15,000 premium is the difference between the cash issuance proceeds and the face amount of the bonds. Because the bonds were issued between interest payment dates, the issuer is also entitled to receive cash for the accrued interest for the 4 months between the prior interest date and the issuance date. The accrued interest is $20,000 [500 bonds × $1,000 face amount × 12% stated rate × (4 months ÷ 12 months)]. The issuing company will therefore receive $535,000 in cash ($515,000 + $20,000). The resulting journal entry includes a $535,000 debit to cash, a $500,000 credit to bonds payable, a $15,000 credit to premium, and a $20,000 credit to either interest payable or interest expense.
Answer (A) is incorrect. The bond premium is $15,000 ($500,000 × 3%), and interest payable should be credited. Answer (B) is incorrect. Interest payable should be $20,000 [$500,000 × 12% × (4 months ÷ 12 months)]. Answer (D) is incorrect. The premium on bonds payable should not include interest payable.

12. If the market rate of interest is <List A> the coupon rate when bonds are issued, then the bonds will sell in the market at a price <List B> the face amount, and the issuing firm will record a <List C> on bonds payable.

	List A	List B	List C
A.	Equal to	Equal to	Premium
B.	Greater than	Greater than	Premium
C.	Greater than	Less than	Discount
D.	Less than	Greater than	Discount

Answer (C) is correct. *(CIA, adapted)*
REQUIRED: The relationship of the market rate, the coupon rate, and the recording of a discount or premium.
DISCUSSION: If the market rate exceeds the coupon rate, the price of the bonds must decline to a level that equates the yield on the bonds with the market rate of interest. Accordingly, the bonds will be recorded by a debit to cash for the proceeds, a debit to discount on bonds payable, and a credit to bonds payable at face amount.
Answer (A) is incorrect. If the market rate equals the coupon rate, the bonds will not sell at a premium or discount. Answer (B) is incorrect. If the market rate exceeds the coupon rate, the bond issue will sell at a discount. Answer (D) is incorrect. If the market rate is less than the coupon rate, the bonds will sell at a premium.

13. How is the carrying amount of a bond payable affected by amortization of the following?

	Discount	Premium
A.	Increase	Increase
B.	Decrease	Decrease
C.	Increase	Decrease
D.	Decrease	Increase

Answer (C) is correct. *(CPA, adapted)*
REQUIRED: The effect of discount and premium amortization on the carrying amount of a bond payable.
DISCUSSION: The carrying amount of a bond payable is equal to its maturity (face) amount plus any unamortized premium or minus any unamortized discount. Amortization results in a reduction of the discount or premium. Consequently, the carrying amount of a bond is increased when discount is amortized and decreased when premium is amortized.
Answer (A) is incorrect. The carrying amount of a bond payable is decreased by the amortization of a premium. Answer (B) is incorrect. The carrying amount of a bond payable is increased by the amortization of a discount. Answer (D) is incorrect. The carrying amount of a bond payable is increased by the amortization of a discount and decreased by the amortization of a premium.

14. Midland, Inc., had the following amounts of noncurrent debt outstanding at December 31, Year 1:

14 1/2% term note, due Year 2	$ 6,000
11 1/8% term note, due Year 4	214,000
8% note, due in 11 equal annual principal payments, plus interest beginning December 31, Year 2	220,000
7% guaranteed debentures, due Year 5	200,000
Total	$640,000

Midland's annual sinking-fund requirement on the guaranteed debentures is $8,000 per year. What amount should Midland report as current maturities of noncurrent debt in its December 31, Year 1, balance sheet?

A. $8,000

B. $14,000

C. $20,000

D. $26,000

Answer (D) is correct. *(CPA, adapted)*
REQUIRED: The amount to be reported as current maturities of noncurrent debt in the balance sheet.
DISCUSSION: A noncurrent liability that will become due within 1 year or the firm's operating cycle, whichever is longer, should be reclassified as a current liability, except when (1) the portion currently due will be refinanced on a noncurrent basis, (2) the assets that will be used to retire the currently due portion are classified as noncurrent assets, or (3) capital stock will be issued to retire the portion currently due. In this case, the obligations that should be reclassified as current are the $6,000 balance of the 14 1/2% term note due in Year 2 and $20,000 of the 8% note (the payment is made to reduce principal in 11 equal payments), a total of $26,000. No exception applies.
Answer (A) is incorrect. The amount of $8,000 is Midland's annual sinking-fund requirement on the guaranteed debentures. Answer (B) is incorrect. The amount of $14,000 is the difference between the $20,000 due in Year 2 on the 8% note and the $6,000 due in Year 2 on the 14 1/2% note. Answer (C) is incorrect. The 14 1/2% note should be reclassified as a current liability.

15. On July 1, Dover Co. received $206,576 for $200,000 face amount, 12% bonds, a price that yields 10%. Interest expense for the 6 months ended December 31 should be

A. $12,394

B. $12,000

C. $10,328

D. $10,000

Answer (C) is correct. *(CPA, adapted)*
REQUIRED: The amount of interest expense.
DISCUSSION: Under the interest method, interest expense for the 6 months since the bond was issued is equal to the carrying amount of the bond multiplied by the effective interest rate for half a year. Thus, interest expense is $10,328 [$206,576 × 10% × (6 months ÷ 12 months)].
Answer (A) is incorrect. The carrying amount multiplied by the coupon rate is $12,394. Answer (B) is incorrect. The face amount multiplied by the coupon rate is $12,000. Answer (D) is incorrect. The face amount multiplied by the yield rate is $10,000.

16. On January 2, Year 1, Kerry Co. issued $4 million of 10-year, 8% bonds at par. The bonds, dated January 1, Year 1, pay interest semiannually on January 1 and July 1. Bond issue costs were $500,000. In accordance with current practice, what amount of bond issue costs is unamortized at June 30, Year 2?

A. $475,000

B. $450,000

C. $441,600

D. $425,000

Answer (D) is correct. *(CPA, adapted)*
REQUIRED: The amount to be recorded as unamortized bond issue costs.
DISCUSSION: Bond issue costs are customarily amortized using the straight-line method for the term of the bond, although the interest method is theoretically superior. The rationale for the current practice is that the results do not differ materially from the interest method. Thus, the amortization is $50,000 per year ($500,000 ÷ 10 years). Because the bond has been held for 18 months, $75,000 ($50,000 + $25,000) of issue costs has been amortized by 6/30/Year 2. The unamortized issue costs are $425,000 ($500,000 – $75,000).
Answer (A) is incorrect. An additional full year of amortization should have been claimed. Answer (B) is incorrect. Six more months of issue costs should have been amortized for the time between 1/1/Year 2 through 6/30/Year 2. Answer (C) is incorrect. The amount of $441,600 results from amortization using the interest method.

17. On January 1, Year 1, Cork Corporation issued 1,000 of its 9%, $1,000 callable bonds for $1,030,000. The bonds are dated January 1, Year 1, and mature on December 31, Year 15. Interest is payable semiannually on January 1 and July 1. The bonds can be called by the issuer at 102 on any interest payment date after December 31, Year 5. The unamortized bond premium was $14,000 at December 31, Year 8, and the market price of the bonds was 99 on this date. In its December 31, Year 8, balance sheet, at what amount should Cork report the carrying amount of the bonds?

A. $1,020,000

B. $1,016,000

C. $1,014,000

D. $990,000

Answer (C) is correct. *(CPA, adapted)*
REQUIRED: The carrying amount of bonds issued at a premium.
DISCUSSION: The face amount of the bonds is $1,000,000 (1,000 × $1,000), and the unamortized premium is $14,000 (given). The carrying amount is thus $1,014,000. The other data are irrelevant.
Answer (A) is incorrect. The amount of $1,020,000 is to be paid if the bonds are called. Answer (B) is incorrect. The amount of $1,016,000 is the issue price minus the unamortized premium ($1,030,000 – $14,000). Answer (D) is incorrect. The amount of $990,000 is the market price.

18. A company issues 10-year bonds with a face amount of $1 million, dated January 1, Year 1, and bearing interest at an annual rate of 12% payable semiannually on January 1 and July 1. The full interest amount will be paid each due date. The market rate of interest on bonds of similar risk and maturity, with the same schedule of interest payments, is also 12%. If the bonds are issued on February 1, Year 1, the amount the issuing company receives from the buyers of the bonds on that date is

A. $990,000

B. $1,000,000

C. $1,010,000

D. $1,020,000

Answer (C) is correct. *(CIA, adapted)*
REQUIRED: The amount received when bonds are issued subsequent to the date printed on the face of the bonds.
DISCUSSION: The market rate of interest is equal to the stated interest rate. Thus, the amount the issuing company receives on 2/1/Year 1 is the face amount of the issue plus 1 month of accrued interest, or $1,010,000 {$1,000,000 + [($1,000,000 × 12%) ÷ 12]}.
Answer (A) is incorrect. The amount of $990,000 is the result if 1 month of accrued interest is deducted from, rather than added to, the face amount. Answer (B) is incorrect. The purchasers must pay for the accrued interest from the last interest date to the issue date. They will receive 6 months' interest on July 1 despite holding the bonds for 5 months. Answer (D) is incorrect. The amount of $1,020,000 results from adding 2 months of accrued interest to the face amount.

19. Derry Corp.'s liability account balances at June 30, Year 2, included a 10% note payable in the amount of $3.6 million. The note is dated October 1, Year 1, and is payable in three equal annual payments of $1.2 million plus interest. The first interest and principal payment was made on October 1, Year 2. In Derry's June 30, Year 3, balance sheet, what amount should be reported as accrued interest payable for this note?

A. $270,000

B. $180,000

C. $90,000

D. $60,000

Answer (B) is correct. *(CPA, adapted)*
REQUIRED: The amount that should be reported as accrued interest payable.
DISCUSSION: Accrued interest on the note payable at the balance sheet date is the carrying amount of the note multiplied by the interest rate on the note. Because the first payment was made 10/1/Year 2, the carrying amount of the note is $2,400,000 ($3,600,000 – $1,200,000). Also, interest has accrued for only 9 months since the first payment. As a result, accrued interest payable is $180,000 [$2,400,000 × 10% × (9 months ÷ 12 months)].
Answer (A) is incorrect. The figure of $270,000 assumes that the carrying amount of the note was not reduced by the payment of $1,200,000 made on 10/1/Year 2. Answer (C) is incorrect. The figure of $90,000 assumes that the carrying amount of the note was not reduced by the first payment of $1,200,000 and that interest was accrued for 9 months instead of 3. Answer (D) is incorrect. Interest should be accrued for 9 months instead of 3.

20. On December 31, Year 1, Ulster Co. issued $200,000 of 8% serial bonds, to be repaid in the amount of $40,000 each year. Interest is payable annually on December 31. The bonds were issued to yield 10% a year. The bond proceeds were $190,280 based on the present values at December 31, Year 1, of the five annual payments:

Due Date	Principal	Interest	Present Value at 12/31/Year 1
		Amounts Due	
12/31/Year 2	$40,000	$16,000	$ 50,900
12/31/Year 3	40,000	12,800	43,610
12/31/Year 4	40,000	9,600	37,250
12/31/Year 5	40,000	6,400	31,690
12/31/Year 6	40,000	3,200	26,830
			$190,280

Ulster amortizes the bond discount by the interest method. In its December 31, Year 2, balance sheet, at what amount should Ulster report the carrying amount of the bonds?

A. $139,380

B. $149,100

C. $150,280

D. $153,308

Answer (D) is correct. *(CPA, adapted)*
REQUIRED: The carrying amount after Year 1 of bonds issued at a discount.
DISCUSSION: The carrying amount of the bonds for Year 1 equals the proceeds of $190,280. Interest expense at the 10% effective rate is $19,028. Actual interest paid is $16,000, and discount amortization is $3,028 ($19,028 – $16,000). Thus, the discount remaining at year end is $6,692 [($200,000 face amount – $190,280 issue proceeds) – $3,028 discount amortization]. Given that $40,000 in principal is paid at year end, the carrying amount is $153,308 ($160,000 face amount – $6,692 unamortized discount).
Answer (A) is incorrect. The carrying amount of the bonds at 12/31/Year 1 minus the present value of the bonds due 12/31/Year 2 is $139,380. Answer (B) is incorrect. The difference between the face amount of the bonds and the present value of the bonds due 12/31/Year 2 is $149,100. Answer (C) is incorrect. Reducing the carrying amount at 12/31/Year 1 by the payment due 12/31/Year 2 results in $150,280.

21. On July 1, Year 3, Calais Company issued 500 of its 8%, $1,000 bonds for $438,000. The bonds were issued to yield 10%. The bonds are dated July 1, Year 3, and mature on July 1, Year 13. Interest is payable semiannually on January 1 and July 1. Using the interest method, how much of the bond discount should be amortized for the 6 months ended December 31, Year 3?

A. $3,800

B. $3,100

C. $2,480

D. $1,900

Answer (D) is correct. *(CPA, adapted)*
REQUIRED: The amount of bond discount to be amortized using the interest method.
DISCUSSION: Under the interest method, interest expense is equal to the carrying amount of the bonds at the beginning of the interest period times the yield rate. Because interest is paid semiannually, the semiannual interest rate is equal to one-half of the annual rate. Interest expense is therefore $21,900 [$438,000 × 10% × (6 months ÷ 12 months)]. The periodic cash payment is $20,000 [$500,000 face amount × 8% stated rate × (6 months ÷ 12 months)]. The $1,900 ($21,900 – $20,000) difference is the amount of discount to be amortized during this 6-month interest period.
Answer (A) is incorrect. The amount of $3,800 is the discount amortized for a full year. Answer (B) is incorrect. The amount of $3,100 is the difference between interest expense calculated at 10% and interest payable calculated at 10% for half a year. Answer (C) is incorrect. The amount of $2,480 is equal to the difference between interest expense calculated at 8% and interest payable calculated at 8% for half a year.

Questions 22 and 23 are based on the following information. Clare Co. issued $6 million of 12% bonds on December 1, Year 1, due on December 1, Year 6, with interest payable each December 1 and June 1. The bonds were sold for $5,194,770 to yield 16%.

22. If the discount were amortized by the straight-line method, Clare's interest expense for the fiscal year ended November 30, Year 2, related to its $6 million bond issue would be

A. $558,954

B. $623,372

C. $720,000

D. $881,046

Answer (D) is correct. *(CMA, adapted)*
REQUIRED: The interest expense under the straight-line amortization method.
DISCUSSION: Under the straight-line method, interest expense is the sum of the periodic cash flows plus the discount amortization. The periodic cash flows are equal to $720,000 ($6,000,000 face amount × 12% coupon rate). The discount at the time of issuance was $805,230 ($6,000,000 face amount – $5,194,770 issuance price). Because the term of the bonds is 5 years, amortization by the straight-line method each year will be $161,046 ($805,230 discount ÷ 5 years). Thus, interest expense is $881,046 ($720,000 + $161,046) for the fiscal year ended 11/30/Year 2. Under the straight-line method, interest expense will be the same for each year in which the bonds are outstanding. However, the straight-line method is allowable only when it does not differ materially from the interest method.
Answer (A) is incorrect. The amount of $558,954 results from subtracting the amortization of the discount. Answer (B) is incorrect. The carrying amount of the bonds multiplied by the coupon rate is $623,372. Answer (C) is incorrect. The amount of $720,000 is interest payable.

23. If the discount were amortized by the effective-interest method, Clare's interest expense for the fiscal year ended November 30, Year 2, related to its $6 million bond issue would be

A. $623,372

B. $720,000

C. $831,163

D. $835,610

Answer (D) is correct. *(CMA, adapted)*
REQUIRED: The interest expense for the first year under the effective-interest method.
DISCUSSION: Under the interest method, interest expense is equal to the carrying amount of the bonds at the beginning of the interest period times the effective interest rate. The carrying amount of the bonds at December 1, Year 1 (the issuance date), was $5,194,770. The annual yield rate was 16%. Interest expense is therefore equal to $415,582 [$5,194,770 × 16% × (6 months ÷ 12 months)] for the first 6 months of the year. For the same period, interest paid was $360,000 [$6,000,000 × 12% × (6 months ÷ 12 months)]. Hence, the semiannual discount amortization was $55,582 ($415,582 interest expense – $360,000 interest paid), and the carrying amount of the bonds for the second 6-month period was $5,250,352 ($5,194,770 + $55,582). For this period, the semiannual interest expense was $420,028 [$5,250,352 × 16% × (6 months ÷ 12 months)]. Total interest expense for the year is equal to $835,610 ($415,582 + $420,028).
Answer (A) is incorrect. The carrying amount of the bond multiplied by the coupon rate is $623,372. Answer (B) is incorrect. The amount of $720,000 is interest payable. Answer (C) is incorrect. The amount of $831,163 results from calculating interest expense as if interest is payable annually.

24. On January 1, Year 4, Dundee Corp. issued 9% bonds in the face amount of $1 million, which mature on January 1, Year 14. The bonds were issued for $939,000 to yield 10%, resulting in a bond discount of $61,000. Dundee uses the interest method of amortizing bond discount. Interest is payable annually on December 31. At December 31, Year 4, Dundee's unamortized bond discount should be

A. $51,000

B. $51,610

C. $52,000

D. $57,100

Answer (D) is correct. *(CPA, adapted)*
REQUIRED: The amount of unamortized bond discount at the end of the first year.
DISCUSSION: Under the interest method, interest expense is equal to the carrying amount of the bonds at the beginning of the period times the market (yield) rate of interest. For the first year, interest expense is $93,900 ($939,000 carrying amount × 10% yield rate). The periodic interest payment is $90,000 ($1,000,000 face amount × 9% coupon rate). The $3,900 ($93,900 – $90,000) difference is the amount of bond discount to be amortized. Thus, the $61,000 unamortized bond discount at the beginning of the year should be reduced by $3,900 to a year-end balance of $57,100.
Answer (A) is incorrect. This figure results from reducing the discount by the face amount times the market (yield) rate, minus the interest payment. Answer (B) is incorrect. This figure results from reducing the discount by the carrying amount times the yield, minus the carrying amount times the coupon rate. Answer (C) is incorrect. The bond discount is reduced by the interest payment.

25. Karrie Co. has outstanding a 7%, 10-year bond with a $100,000 face amount. The bond was originally sold to yield 6% annual interest. Karrie uses the effective-interest method to amortize bond premium. On June 30, Year 1, the carrying amount of the outstanding bond was $105,000. What amount of unamortized premium on the bond should Karrie report in its June 30, Year 2, balance sheet?

A. $1,050

B. $3,950

C. $4,300

D. $4,500

Answer (C) is correct. *(CPA, adapted)*
REQUIRED: The amount of unamortized premium.
DISCUSSION: Under the interest method, interest expense is equal to the carrying amount of the bonds at the beginning of the interest period times the market (yield) rate of interest. Interest expense for the year ended 6/30/Year 2 is $6,300 ($105,000 carrying amount × 6%), and the periodic interest payment is $7,000 ($100,000 × 7%). The difference ($7,000 – $6,300 = $700) is the amount of premium amortized. The unamortized premium is therefore $4,300 ($5,000 – $700).
Answer (A) is incorrect. This amount is the carrying amount of the bond times the stated interest rate, minus the carrying amount times the market rate. Answer (B) is incorrect. The amount of $3,950 equals the premium minus the carrying amount of the bond times the stated interest rate, minus the carrying amount times the market rate. Answer (D) is incorrect. The amount of $4,500 assumes straight-line amortization and a 6/30/Year 1 issue date.

26. On January 2, Year 5, Ost Co. issued 9% bonds in the amount of $500,000, which mature on January 2, Year 15. The bonds were issued for $469,500 to yield 10%. Interest is payable annually on December 31. Ost uses the interest method of amortizing bond discount. In its June 30, Year 5, balance sheet, what amount should Ost report as bonds payable?

A. $469,500

B. $470,475

C. $471,450

D. $500,000

Answer (B) is correct. *(CPA, adapted)*
REQUIRED: The amount to be reported as bonds payable at an interim date.
DISCUSSION: Accrued interest expense is $23,475 [$469,500 × 10% × (6 months ÷ 12 months)]. Accrued interest payable is $22,500 [$500,000 × 9% × (6 months ÷ 12 months)]. The difference of $975 is the amount of discount amortization for the period. Bonds payable equal $470,475 ($469,500 + $975).
Answer (A) is incorrect. The amount of $469,500 is the issue price unadjusted for discount amortization. Answer (C) is incorrect. The amount of $471,450 reflects a full year's discount amortization. Answer (D) is incorrect. The face amount of the bonds is $500,000.

12.2 Convertible Debt

Questions 27 and 28 are based on the following information. On January 2, Year 1, Kiril Co. issued 10-year convertible bonds at 105. During Year 4, these bonds were converted into common stock having an aggregate par value equal to the total face amount of the bonds. At conversion, the market price of Kiril's common stock was 50% above its par value.

27. On January 2, Year 1, cash proceeds from the issuance of the convertible bonds should be reported as

A. Contributed capital for the entire proceeds.

B. Contributed capital for the portion of the proceeds attributable to the conversion feature and as a liability for the balance.

C. A liability for the face amount of the bonds and contributed capital for the premium.

D. A liability for the entire proceeds.

Answer (D) is correct. *(CPA, adapted)*
REQUIRED: The proper accounting for cash proceeds received from the issuance of convertible bonds.
DISCUSSION: The entire proceeds from the issuance of convertible bonds must be reported as a liability until such time as the bonds are converted into stock.
Answer (A) is incorrect. The cash proceeds from the issuance of the convertible bonds must be treated as a liability for the entire amount. Answer (B) is incorrect. Allocation of the proceeds between equity and debt is not permitted. Answer (C) is incorrect. The premium also is treated as debt.

28. Depending on whether the book-value method or the market-value method was used, Kiril should recognize gains or losses on conversion when using the

	Book-Value Method	Market-Value Method
A.	Either gain or loss	Gain
B.	Either gain or loss	Loss
C.	Neither gain nor loss	Loss
D.	Neither gain nor loss	Gain

Answer (C) is correct. *(CPA, adapted)*
REQUIRED: The accounting method(s) that recognizes gains or losses on the conversion of the convertible bonds.
DISCUSSION: Under the book-value method for recognizing the conversion of outstanding bonds payable to common stock, the stock issued is recorded at the carrying amount of the bonds with no recognition of gain or loss. Under the market-value method, the stock is recorded at the market value of the stock (or of the bonds). A gain or loss is recognized equal to the difference between the market value recorded and the carrying amount of the bonds payable. At the time of the conversion, Kiril's common stock had an aggregate par value equal to the total face amount of the bonds, and the market price of the stock was 50% above its par value. Thus, a loss should have been recognized upon conversion in accordance with the market-value method. The total of the credits to equity accounts exceeds the total of the debits to bonds payable and unamortized premium. The difference is the amount of the loss.
Answer (A) is incorrect. Under the book-value method, no gain or loss is recognized at conversion. Under the market-value method, a loss would result. Answer (B) is incorrect. Under the book-value method, no gain or loss is recognized at conversion. Answer (D) is incorrect. Under the market-value method, a loss would result.

29. An issuer of a convertible security may attempt to induce prompt conversion of its convertible debt to equity securities by offering additional securities or other consideration as a sweetener. The additional consideration used to induce conversion should be reported as a(n)

A. Reduction of the paid-in capital recognized for the new equity securities.

B. Reduction of retained earnings.

C. Extraordinary item in the current income statement.

D. Expense of the current period, but not an extraordinary item.

Answer (D) is correct. *(CMA, adapted)*
REQUIRED: The proper treatment of a convertible debt sweetener.
DISCUSSION: A debtor may induce conversion of convertible debt by offering additional securities or other consideration to the holders of convertible debt. This convertible debt sweetener must be recognized as an ordinary expense. It is equal to the fair value of the securities or other consideration transferred in excess of the fair value of the securities that would have been issued under the original conversion privilege.
Answer (A) is incorrect. The additional consideration is expensed. Answer (B) is incorrect. The excess of the transferred consideration over the fair value of the securities issuable under the original terms is an expense. Answer (C) is incorrect. The sweetener must be recognized as an ordinary item.

30. What is the preferred method of accounting for unamortized discount, unamortized issue costs, and the costs of implementing a conversion of debt into common stock?

A. Expense them in the period bonds are converted.

B. Amortize them over the remaining life of the issue retired.

C. Amortize them over a period not to exceed 40 years.

D. Charge them to paid-in capital in excess of the par value of the stock issued.

31. On July 1, after recording interest and amortization, Lancaster Co. converted $2 million of its 12% convertible bonds into 100,000 shares of $1 par value common stock. On the conversion date, the carrying amount of the bonds was $2.6 million, the market value of the bonds was $2.8 million, and Lancaster's common stock was publicly trading at $30 per share. Using the book-value method, what amount of additional paid-in capital should Lancaster record as a result of the conversion?

A. $1,900,000

B. $2,500,000

C. $2,700,000

D. $3,000,000

32. Any gains or losses from the early extinguishment of convertible debt should be

A. Recognized in current income of the period of extinguishment.

B. Treated as an increase or decrease in paid-in capital.

C. Classified as extraordinary.

D. Amortized over the remaining original life of the extinguished convertible debt.

Answer (D) is correct. *(Publisher, adapted)*
REQUIRED: The preferred method of accounting for unamortized discount, unamortized issue costs, and the costs of converting debt into common stock.
DISCUSSION: The conversion of debt into common stock is ordinarily based upon the carrying amount of the debt at the time of issuance. Because the carrying amount is based on all related accounts, the debit balances of unamortized bond discount, unamortized issue costs, and conversion costs should be considered reductions in the net carrying amount at the time of conversion. Consequently, these items should be reflected as reductions in the additional paid-in capital account.
Answer (A) is incorrect. Unamortized discount, issue costs, and conversion costs are not expensed. In effect, each reduces the amount at which the stock is issued. Answer (B) is incorrect. Unamortized discount, issue costs, and conversion costs are credited and additional paid-in capital is debited. Answer (C) is incorrect. No pronouncement requires amortization over 40 years.

Answer (B) is correct. *(CPA, adapted)*
REQUIRED: The amount of additional paid-in capital reported on the conversion of bonds when the book-value method is used.
DISCUSSION: Under the book-value method for recognizing the conversion of outstanding bonds payable to common stock, the stock issued is recorded at the carrying amount of the bonds with no recognition of a gain or loss. Accordingly, the conversion should be recorded at $2.6 million. However, this amount must be allocated between common stock and additional paid-in capital. The common stock account is always measured at par value. Thus, $100,000 (100,000 shares × $1) will be credited to common stock and $2,500,000 to additional paid-in capital.
Answer (A) is incorrect. The face amount of the bonds minus the par value of the stock is $1,900,000. Answer (C) is incorrect. The amount of $2,700,000 is the market value of the bonds minus the par value of the stock. Answer (D) is incorrect. The amount of $3,000,000 is the market value of the stock.

Answer (A) is correct. *(Publisher, adapted)*
REQUIRED: The treatment of gains or losses from early extinguishment of convertible debt.
DISCUSSION: The accounting for the extinguishment of convertible debt and for ordinary debt is the same. A difference between the cash reacquisition price of the debt and its net carrying amount should be recognized in current income of the period of extinguishment.
Answer (B) is incorrect. The debt and equity features are treated as inseparable. The convertible debt should be accounted for as if it were ordinary debt. Answer (C) is incorrect. Gains and losses from debt extinguishment are not automatically classified as extraordinary. Answer (D) is incorrect. Amortization was rejected by the accounting standard setter in favor of current recognition in income of the full gain or loss.

12.3 Bonds and Warrants

33. How should warrants attached to a debt security be accounted for?

A. No amount assigned.

B. A separate portion of paid-in capital.

C. An appropriation of retained earnings.

D. As a separate liability.

Answer (A) is correct. *(CPA, adapted)*
REQUIRED: The accounting for the value of warrants attached to a debt security.
DISCUSSION: Assuming the warrants are not detachable and the debt security must be surrendered to exercise the warrants, the securities are substantially equivalent to convertible debt. No portion of the proceeds from the issuance should be accounted for as attributable to the conversion feature or the warrants.
Answer (B) is incorrect. The portion of the proceeds allocable to the warrants should be accounted for as paid-in capital only if the warrants are detachable. Answer (C) is incorrect. Nondetachable warrants are not separately recognized, but detachable warrants are recognized as paid-in capital. Answer (D) is incorrect. The attached equity instruments are not separately recognized.

34. When bonds are issued with stock purchase warrants, a portion of the proceeds should be allocated to paid-in capital for bonds issued with

	Detachable Stock Purchase Warrants	Nondetachable Stock Purchase Warrants
A.	No	Yes
B.	No	No
C.	Yes	No
D.	Yes	Yes

Answer (C) is correct. *(CPA, adapted)*
REQUIRED: The circumstances in which proceeds from the issuance of a bond should be allocated between the bond and stock warrants.
DISCUSSION: The proceeds from debt securities issued with detachable warrants must be allocated between the debt securities and the warrants based on their relative fair values at the time of issuance. The portion allocated to the warrants should be accounted for as paid-in capital. However, when debt securities are issued with nondetachable warrants, no part of the proceeds should be allocated to the warrants.
Answer (A) is incorrect. A portion of the proceeds should be allocated to paid-in capital for bonds with detachable stock purchase warrants, and no part of the proceeds should be allocated if the warrants are nondetachable. Answer (B) is incorrect. A portion of the proceeds should be allocated to paid-in capital for bonds with detachable stock purchase warrants. Answer (D) is incorrect. No part of the proceeds should be allocated if the warrants are nondetachable.

35. Bonds with detachable stock warrants were issued by Flack Co. Immediately after issue, the aggregate fair value of the bonds and the warrants exceeds the proceeds. Is the portion of the proceeds allocated to the warrants less than their fair value, and is that amount recorded as contributed capital?

	Less than Warrants' Fair Value	Contributed Capital
A.	No	Yes
B.	Yes	No
C.	Yes	Yes
D.	No	No

Answer (C) is correct. *(CPA, adapted)*
REQUIRED: The allocation of proceeds to detachable warrants and the recording of the allocation.
DISCUSSION: The proceeds from debt securities issued with detachable warrants must be allocated between the debt securities and the warrants based on their relative fair values at the time of issuance. The portion allocated to the warrants should be accounted for as paid-in (contributed) capital. Assuming that the fair values of both the bonds and the warrants are known and the proceeds are less than their sum, the allocation process must result in crediting paid-in (contributed) capital from stock warrants (stock warrants outstanding) for less than their fair value. If the fair value of the bonds is not known, the warrants will be credited at their value.
Answer (A) is incorrect. The warrants will be credited at less than fair value. Answer (B) is incorrect. The amount allocated to the warrants is credited to paid-in (contributed) capital. Answer (D) is incorrect. The warrants will be credited at less than fair value, and the amount allocated to the warrants is credited to paid-in (contributed) capital.

36. On December 30, Worcester, Inc., issued 1,000 of its 8%, 10-year, $1,000 face amount bonds with detachable stock warrants at par. Each bond carried a detachable warrant for one share of Worcester's common stock at a specified option price of $25 per share. Immediately after issuance, the market value of the bonds without the warrants was $1,080,000, and the market value of the warrants was $120,000. In its December 31 balance sheet, what amount should Worcester report as bonds payable?

   A. $1,000,000

   B. $975,000

   C. $900,000

   D. $880,000

Answer (C) is correct. *(CPA, adapted)*
   REQUIRED: The amount reported for bonds payable with detachable stock warrants.
   DISCUSSION: The issue price of the bonds is allocated between the bonds and the detachable stock warrants based on their relative fair values. The market price of bonds without the warrants is $1,080,000, which is 90% [$1,080,000 ÷ ($1,080,000 + $120,000)] of the total fair value of the bonds without warrants plus the value of the warrants. Consequently, 90% of the issue price should be allocated to the bonds, and they should be reported at $900,000 ($1,000,000 × 90%) in the balance sheet.
   Answer (A) is incorrect. The amount of $1,000,000 equals the total proceeds. Answer (B) is incorrect. The amount of $975,000 is the result of deducting the option price of the stock from the total proceeds. Answer (D) is incorrect. The amount of $880,000 is the result of deducting the fair value of the warrants from the total proceeds.

37. Armagh Corp. issued bonds with a face amount of $200,000. Each $1,000 bond contained detachable stock warrants for 100 shares of Armagh's common stock. Total proceeds from the issue amounted to $240,000. The fair value of each warrant was $2, and the fair value of the bonds without the warrants was $196,000. The bonds were issued at a discount of

   A. $0

   B. $678

   C. $4,000

   D. $40,678

Answer (B) is correct. *(CPA, adapted)*
   REQUIRED: The amount of the bond discount.
   DISCUSSION: The proceeds of bonds issued with detachable stock warrants must be allocated based on their relative fair values at the time of issuance. The fair values are $196,000 for the bonds and $40,000 for the warrants (200 bonds × 100 shares × 1 warrant per share × $2). Of the total proceeds of $240,000, $199,322 should be allocated to the bonds. Hence, bond discount is $678 ($200,000 face amount – $199,322 allocated proceeds).

$$\frac{\$196,000}{\$196,000 + \$40,000} \times \$240,000 = \$199,322$$

   Answer (A) is incorrect. The allocation to the bonds was less than their face amount. Answer (C) is incorrect. The difference between the face amount and the fair value of the bonds is $4,000. Answer (D) is incorrect. The amount allocated to the warrants is $40,678.

38. On March 1, Year 2, Quebec Corp. issued $1 million of 10%, nonconvertible bonds at 103. They were due on February 28, Year 12. Each $1,000 bond was issued with 30 detachable stock warrants, each of which entitled the holder to purchase, for $50, one share of Quebec common stock, par value $25. On March 1, Year 2, the quoted market value of Quebec's common stock was $20 per share, and the value of each warrant was $4. What amount of the bond issue proceeds should Quebec record as an increase in equity?

   A. $120,000

   B. $90,000

   C. $30,000

   D. $0

Answer (A) is correct. *(CPA, adapted)*
   REQUIRED: The proceeds from bonds issued with detachable stock warrants to be recorded as equity.
   DISCUSSION: When bonds are issued with detachable stock warrants, the proceeds must be allocated between the warrants and the bonds on the basis of their relative fair values. When the fair value of the warrants but not the bonds is known, paid-in capital from stock warrants should be credited (increased) for the fair value of the warrants, with the remainder credited to the bonds. Quebec issued 1,000 bonds ($1,000,000 ÷ 1,000); therefore, 30,000 warrants (1,000 bonds × 30 warrants) must also have been issued. Their fair value was $120,000 (30,000 warrants × $4), which is the amount of the credit to paid-in capital from stock warrants. The remainder of the proceeds [($1,000,000 × 103%) – $120,000 = $910,000] is allocated to bonds payable.
   Answer (B) is incorrect. The amount of $90,000 equals the discount on the bonds. Answer (C) is incorrect. The amount of $30,000 is the difference between the fair value of the warrants and the discount on the bonds. Answer (D) is incorrect. Stock warrants outstanding (paid-in capital from stock warrants) is an equity account.

39. Winnipeg Company issued bonds with detachable stock warrants. Each warrant granted an option to buy one share of $40 par value common stock for $75 per share. Five hundred warrants were originally issued, and $4,000 was appropriately credited to warrants. If 90% of these warrants are exercised when the market price of the common stock is $85 per share, how much should be credited to capital in excess of par on this transaction?

- A. $19,350
- B. $19,750
- C. $23,850
- D. $24,250

Answer (A) is correct. *(CPA, adapted)*
REQUIRED: The credit to capital in excess of par upon exercise of 90% of the warrants.
DISCUSSION: If 90% of the warrants are exercised, 450 shares must be issued at $75 per share. The total debit to cash is $33,750. The debit to stock warrants outstanding reflects the exercise of 90% of $4,000 of warrants, or $3,600. The par value of the common stock issued is credited for $18,000 (450 shares × $40 par). The balance of $19,350 ($33,750 + $3,600 – $18,000) is credited to capital in excess of par. The transaction is based on the exercise price, not the fair value of the stock or warrants at the time of issuance.

Cash	$33,750
Warrants	3,600
Common stock at par	$18,000
Capital in excess of par	19,350

Answer (B) is incorrect. The amount of $19,750 results from assuming all of the warrants were exercised with the same amount of stock being issued. Answer (C) is incorrect. The amount of $23,850 results from issuing the stock for $85 per share instead of $75. Answer (D) is incorrect. The amount of $24,250 results from issuing the stock for $85 per share, instead of $75, and assuming all of the warrants were exercised with the same amount of stock being issued.

12.4 Extinguishment of Debt

40. PPF partnership purchased land for $1,000,000 on May 1, Year 1, paying $200,000 cash and giving an $800,000 note payable to Lender Bank. PPF made three annual payments on the note totaling $358,000, which included interest of $178,000. PPF then defaulted on the note. Title to the land was transferred by PPF to Lender, which canceled the note, releasing the partnership from further liability. At the time of the default, the fair value of the land approximated the note balance. In PPF's Year 4 income statement, the amount of the loss should be

- A. $558,000
- B. $442,000
- C. $380,000
- D. $200,000

Answer (C) is correct. *(CPA, adapted)*
REQUIRED: The amount of the loss after default on a note and repossession of the land.
DISCUSSION: The principal of the note had been reduced to $620,000 [$800,000 – ($358,000 total payments – $178,000 interest)] at the time of default. The resultant $380,000 loss is equal to the difference between the $1,000,000 carrying amount (cost) of the land and the $620,000 carrying amount of the note.
Answer (A) is incorrect. This amount results from subtracting the total payments ($358,000) in determining the remaining principal. Answer (B) is incorrect. The amount of $442,000 is the note payable balance after subtracting the $178,000 of interest. Answer (D) is incorrect. The amount of $200,000 is the initial payment.

41. Paris Co. issued a 10-year, $100,000, 9% note on January 1, Year 1. The note was issued to yield 10% for proceeds of $93,770. Interest is payable semiannually. The note is callable after 2 years at a price of $96,000. Due to a decline in the market rate to 8%, Paris retired the note on December 31, Year 3. On that date, the carrying amount of the note was $94,582, and the discounted amount of its cash flows based on the market rate was $105,280. What amount should Paris report as gain (loss) from extinguishment of the note for the year ended December 31, Year 3?

- A. $9,280
- B. $4,000
- C. $(2,230)
- D. $(1,418)

Answer (D) is correct. *(CPA, adapted)*
REQUIRED: The amount of gain (loss) from the extinguishment of a note.
DISCUSSION: The amount of gain or loss resulting from the extinguishment of debt is the difference between the amount paid and the carrying amount of the note. Thus, a loss of $1,418 ($94,582 carrying amount – $96,000 amount paid) results from the extinguishment.
Answer (A) is incorrect. The difference between the discounted amount based on the market rate and the call price is $9,280. Answer (B) is incorrect. The difference between the face amount of the note and the call price is $4,000. Answer (C) is incorrect. The difference between the original amount received and the call price is $(2,230).

42. An entity should not derecognize an existing liability under which of the following circumstances?

A. The entity exchanges convertible preferred stock for its outstanding debt securities. The debt securities are not canceled but are held as treasury bonds.

B. Because of financial difficulties being experienced by the entity, a creditor accepts a parcel of land as full satisfaction of an overdue loan. The value of the land is less than 50% of the loan balance.

C. The entity irrevocably places cash into a trust that will be used solely to satisfy scheduled principal and interest payments of a specific bond obligation. Because the trust investments will generate a higher return, the amount of cash is less than the carrying amount of the debt.

D. As part of the agreement to purchase a shopping center from the entity, the buyer assumes without recourse the mortgage for which the center serves as collateral.

Answer (C) is correct. *(Publisher, adapted)*
REQUIRED: The circumstances under which an existing liability should not be derecognized.
DISCUSSION: A liability is derecognized only if it has been extinguished. Extinguishment occurs when either (1) the debtor pays the creditor and is relieved of its obligation for the liability, or (2) the debtor is legally released from being the primary obligor under the liability, either judicially or by the creditor. Thus, the recognition of a gain or loss from an in-substance defeasance (e.g., placing cash in an irrevocable trust) is prohibited.
Answer (A) is incorrect. The debt is extinguished when the entity exchanges convertible preferred stock for its outstanding debt securities. This exchange is at fair value. Debt-equity swaps are rare because they are not tax-exempt. Answer (B) is incorrect. The debt is extinguished when a creditor accepts a parcel of land as full satisfaction of an overdue loan. Answer (D) is incorrect. The debt is extinguished when a buyer assumes without recourse the mortgage for which the property sold is collateral.

43. On June 2, Year 1, Danube Co. issued $500,000 of 10%, 15-year bonds at par. Interest is payable semiannually on June 1 and December 1. Bond issue costs were $6,000. On June 2, Year 6, Danube retired half of the bonds at 98. What is the net amount that Danube should use in computing the gain or loss on extinguishment of debt?

A. $250,000

B. $248,000

C. $247,000

D. $246,000

Answer (B) is correct. *(CPA, adapted)*
REQUIRED: The net amount used in computing the gain or loss on the extinguishment of debt.
DISCUSSION: The gain or loss on the extinguishment of debt is equal to the difference between the proceeds paid and the carrying amount of the debt. The carrying amount of the debt is equal to the face amount plus any unamortized premium or minus any unamortized discount. In addition, any unamortized issue costs are considered in effect a reduction of the carrying amount even though they are accounted for separately from the bond discount or premium. The amortization of the issue costs is $400 per year ($6,000 ÷ 15). Because accumulated amortization is $2,000 ($400 × 5 years), the unamortized issue costs are $4,000 ($6,000 – $2,000), of which 50%, or $2,000, should be subtracted in determining the carrying amount of the bonds retired. Consequently, the net carrying amount that should be used in computing the gain or loss on this early extinguishment of debt is $248,000 ($250,000 face amount – $2,000 unamortized deferred bond issue costs).
Answer (A) is incorrect. The amount of $250,000 is half of the par value. Answer (C) is incorrect. The amount of $247,000 is half of the par value minus half of the issue costs. Answer (D) is incorrect. The amount of $246,000 results from subtracting 100% of the unamortized issue costs.

44. On July 31, Year 3, Nile Co. issued $1 million of 10%, 15-year bonds at par and used a portion of the proceeds to call its 600 outstanding 11%, $1,000 face amount bonds, due on July 31, Year 13, at 102. On that date, unamortized bond premium relating to the 11% bonds was $65,000. In its Year 3 income statement, what amount should Nile report as gain or loss, before income taxes, from extinguishment of bonds?

A. $53,000 gain.

B. $0

C. $(65,000) loss.

D. $(77,000) loss.

Answer (A) is correct. *(CPA, adapted)*
REQUIRED: The amount to be reported for the extinguishment of bonds.
DISCUSSION: The excess of the net carrying amount of the bonds over the reacquisition price is a gain from extinguishment. The carrying amount of the bonds equals $665,000 ($600,000 face amount + $65,000 unamortized premium). The reacquisition price is $612,000 (600 bonds × $1,000 × 102%). Thus, the gain from extinguishment is $53,000 ($665,000 – $612,000).
Answer (B) is incorrect. The excess of the carrying amount over the reacquisition cost is a gain. Answer (C) is incorrect. The amount of $65,000 is the unamortized premium. Answer (D) is incorrect. The amount of $77,000 equals the reacquisition price of $612,000, minus the face amount of $600,000, plus $65,000 unamortized premium.

45. On June 30, Year 7, Rhine Co. had outstanding 9%, $5,000,000 face amount bonds maturing on June 30, Year 9. Interest was payable semiannually every June 30 and December 31. On June 30, Year 7, after amortization was recorded for the period, the unamortized bond premium and bond issue costs were $30,000 and $50,000, respectively. On that date, Rhine acquired all its outstanding bonds on the open market at 98 and retired them. At June 30, Year 7, what amount should Rhine recognize as gain before income taxes on redemption of bonds?

A. $20,000

B. $80,000

C. $120,000

D. $180,000

Answer (B) is correct. *(CPA, adapted)*
REQUIRED: The amount of gain from the redemption of bonds.
DISCUSSION: The amount of gain or loss on the redemption of bonds is equal to the difference between the proceeds paid and the carrying amount of the debt. The carrying amount of the bonds is equal to the face amount, plus unamortized bond premium, minus unamortized bond issue costs. Thus, the carrying amount of the bonds is $4,980,000 ($5,000,000 + $30,000 – $50,000). The $80,000 gain is the difference between the carrying amount ($4,980,000) and the amount paid $4,900,000 ($5,000,000 × 98%).
Answer (A) is incorrect. The amount of $20,000 results from subtracting the unamortized bond premium and bond issue costs from the face amount of the bond. Answer (C) is incorrect. The amount of $120,000 results from adding the unamortized bond issue costs and subtracting the unamortized bond premium to find the carrying amount. Answer (D) is incorrect. The amount of $180,000 results from adding the unamortized bond issue costs and bond premium to find the carrying amount of the bond.

46. On January 2, Year 9, Seine Corporation entered into an in-substance debt defeasance transaction by placing cash of $875,000 into an irrevocable trust. The trust assets are to be used solely for satisfying the interest and principal payments on Seine's 6%, $1.1 million, 30-year bond payable. Seine has not been legally released under the bond agreement, but the probability is remote that Seine will be required to place additional cash in the trust. On December 31, Year 8, the bond's carrying amount was $1,050,000; its fair value was $800,000. Disregarding income taxes, what amount of gain (loss) should Seine report in its Year 9 income statement?

A. $(75,000)

B. $0

C. $175,000

D. $225,000

Answer (B) is correct. *(Publisher, adapted)*
REQUIRED: The amount of gain (loss) to be recognized on an in-substance defeasance.
DISCUSSION: A debtor derecognizes a liability only if it has been extinguished. Extinguishment results only if (1) the debtor pays the creditor and is relieved of its obligation with respect to the liability, or (2) the debtor is legally released from being the primary obligor, either judicially or by the creditor.
Answer (A) is incorrect. The amount of $(75,000) is the excess of cash paid over the fair value of the bond, but no loss is recognized. Seine has not been legally released under the bond agreement. Answer (C) is incorrect. An in-substance defeasance does not result in the derecognition of a liability. Answer (D) is incorrect. No gain is recognized. However, if a gain or loss were recognized, it would equal the difference between the carrying amount and the amount paid ($1,050,000 – $875,000 = $175,000).

47. A debtor should derecognize a liability in which circumstances?

I. The debtor pays the creditor and is relieved of its obligation with respect to the liability.

II. The debtor is legally released from being the primary obligor.

III. The debtor irrevocably places cash or other assets in a trust to be used solely for satisfying scheduled payments of interest and principal of a specific obligation.

A. I only.

B. I and II only.

C. II and III only.

D. I, II, and III.

Answer (B) is correct. *(Publisher, adapted)*
REQUIRED: The circumstances in which a debtor should derecognize a liability.
DISCUSSION: A debtor derecognizes a liability only if it has been extinguished. Extinguishment results only if (1) the debtor pays the creditor and is relieved of its obligation with respect to the liability, or (2) the debtor is legally released from being the primary obligor, either judicially or by the creditor.
Answer (A) is incorrect. A legal release also permits derecognition. Answer (C) is incorrect. Paying the creditor and being relieved of the obligation also permits derecognition. Moreover, an in-substance defeasance (III) is not an extinguishment. Answer (D) is incorrect. An in-substance defeasance (III) is not an extinguishment.

48. Columbia Corporation extinguished an issue of bonds before its maturity date through a direct exchange of securities. The new issue of debt is best measured by the

A. Maturity amount of the new issue.

B. Net carrying amount of the old issue.

C. Fair value of the new issue.

D. Maturity amount of the old issue.

Answer (C) is correct. *(CPA, adapted)*
REQUIRED: The best measure of a new issue of debt used to extinguish an issue of bonds.
DISCUSSION: All extinguishments are fundamentally alike. Thus, the accounting should be the same however the extinguishment is accomplished. Any difference between the reacquisition price (e.g., the new issue of debt) and the carrying amount of the debt extinguished is recognized in current income as a loss or gain. A debtor that transfers its assets in full settlement recognizes a gain measured by the excess of the carrying amount of the payable settled over the fair value of the assets transferred. The customary estimate of the fair value of debt is present value. According to SFAC 7, *Using Cash Flow Information and Present Value in Accounting Measurements,* "The only objective of present value, when used in accounting measurements at initial recognition [e.g., for a new issue of debt] and fresh start measurements, is to estimate fair value."
Answer (A) is incorrect. The present value of the new issue must be used. Answer (B) is incorrect. The net carrying amount of the old issue is eliminated when the extinguishment is recognized. It is not carried over. Answer (D) is incorrect. The net carrying amount of the old issue, not the maturity amount of the old issue, is relevant to accounting for the extinguishment, but it is not the measure of the new issue.

49. A 15-year bond was issued in Year 1 at a discount. During Year 11, a 10-year bond was issued at face amount with the proceeds used to retire the 15-year bond at its face amount. The net effect of the Year 11 bond transactions was to increase noncurrent liabilities by the excess of the 10-year bond's face amount over the 15-year bond's

A. Face amount.

B. Carrying amount.

C. Face amount minus the deferred loss on bond retirement.

D. Carrying amount minus the deferred loss on bond retirement.

Answer (B) is correct. *(CPA, adapted)*
REQUIRED: The net effect of the bond transactions.
DISCUSSION: The 10-year bond was issued at its face amount, that is, at neither a premium nor a discount. Its face amount therefore equaled its proceeds, which were used to retire the 15-year bond at its face amount. The 15-year bond was carried at a discount (face amount – unamortized discount). Consequently, net noncurrent liabilities must have increased by the amount of the unamortized discount on the 15-year bond, which is the excess of the 10-year bond's face amount over the carrying amount of the 15-year bond.
Answer (A) is incorrect. The face amount of the 10-year bond equaled the face amount of the 15-year bond. Answer (C) is incorrect. The 15-year bond was carried not at its face amount but net of the unamortized discount. The loss equals the unamortized discount. Answer (D) is incorrect. The loss on early extinguishment is not deferred.

12.5 Noncurrent Notes Payable

50. A company issued a noninterest-bearing note payable due in 1 year in exchange for land. Which of the following statements is true concerning the accounting for the transaction?

A. The land should be recorded at the future value of the note, and interest should be imputed at the prevailing rate on similar notes.

B. No interest should be recognized on the note, and the land should be recorded at the present value of the note.

C. Interest on the note should be imputed at the prime rate, and the land should be recorded at the discounted value of the note.

D. Interest on the note should be imputed at the prevailing rate for similar notes, and the land should be recorded at the present value of the note.

Answer (D) is correct. *(CIA, adapted)*
REQUIRED: The proper accounting for a noninterest-bearing note.
DISCUSSION: If interest on a note is not stated, it is imputed by recording the note at the fair value of the property, goods, or services exchanged, or at the fair value of the note itself. If these values are not determinable, an interest rate must be imputed. GAAP include certain guidelines for imputing an interest rate. The rate should be at least equal to that at which the debtor could obtain financing of a similar nature from other sources. Other considerations are the market rate for an exchange of the note, the prime or higher rate for notes discounted with banks in light of the credit standing of the maker, and the current rates for debt instruments with substantially identical terms and risks that are traded in open markets. Accordingly, if the fair value of the note or the land is not determinable, the transaction will be recorded at the present value of the note based on an imputed rate.
Answer (A) is incorrect. The land is recorded at present value. Answer (B) is incorrect. Interest should be recognized on the note. Answer (C) is incorrect. The proper discount rate is the prevailing rate for similar notes, not the prime rate.

51. When it is necessary to impute interest on a note payable, the imputed rate should be

   A. Influenced by the prevailing market rate for debt instruments with substantially identical terms and risks.

   B. Two-thirds of the prime rate effective at the time the note is received.

   C. Equal to the rate obtainable on government securities with comparable due dates.

   D. The minimum rate allowed by the Internal Revenue Code.

Answer (A) is correct. *(Publisher, adapted)*
   REQUIRED: The true statement about imputation of an interest rate in connection with a note payable.
   DISCUSSION: GAAP include certain guidelines for selecting an interest rate. The rate should be at least equal to that at which the debtor could obtain financing of a similar nature from other sources. Other considerations are the market rate for an exchange of the note, the prime or higher rate for notes discounted with banks in light of the credit standing of the maker, and the current rates for debt instruments with substantially identical terms and risks that are traded in open markets.
   Answer (B) is incorrect. GAAP do not specify any particular interest rate. Answer (C) is incorrect. The prime rate is given to the most credit-worthy borrowers. Answer (D) is incorrect. The IRC does not specify interest rates.

52. When a note payable has properly been recorded at its present value, any resulting discount should be disclosed in the financial statements

   A. As a separate asset or liability.

   B. As a deferred charge or credit.

   C. In a summary caption along with any related issue costs.

   D. As a direct reduction of the face amount of the note.

Answer (D) is correct. *(Publisher, adapted)*
   REQUIRED: The proper financial statement disclosure of a discount related to a note payable.
   DISCUSSION: Discount or premium is not an asset or liability separable from the related note. A discount should therefore be reported in the balance sheet as a direct reduction of the face amount of the note.
   Answer (A) is incorrect. The discount is disclosed as a direct adjustment to the face amount of the note. Answer (B) is incorrect. GAAP also explicitly prohibit treating a discount or premium as a deferred charge or a deferred credit. Answer (C) is incorrect. A discount and issue costs are separately reported. Debt issue costs are reported as deferred charges.

53. Which of the following is reported as interest expense?

   A. Pension cost interest.

   B. Postretirement healthcare benefits interest.

   C. Imputed interest on a noninterest-bearing note.

   D. Interest incurred to finance construction of machinery for an entity's own use.

Answer (C) is correct. *(CPA, adapted)*
   REQUIRED: The item reported as interest expense.
   DISCUSSION: When a noninterest-bearing note is exchanged for property, and neither the note nor the property has a clearly determinable exchange price, the present value of the note should be determined by discounting all future payments using an appropriately imputed interest rate. Periodic interest expense must be calculated and recognized in accordance with the effective-interest method.
   Answer (A) is incorrect. Interest cost for a defined benefit pension plan is reported as a component of the net periodic pension cost. Answer (B) is incorrect. Interest cost for a defined benefit postretirement plan is reported as a component of the net postretirement benefit cost. Answer (D) is incorrect. Interest incurred to finance construction of machinery for an entity's own use is capitalized.

54. On September 1, Year 1, Brok Co. issued a note payable to Federal Bank in the amount of $900,000, bearing interest at 12%, and payable in three equal annual principal payments of $300,000. On this date, the bank's prime rate was 11%. The first interest and principal payment was made on September 1, Year 2. At December 31, Year 2, Brok should record accrued interest payable of

   A. $36,000

   B. $33,000

   C. $24,000

   D. $22,000

Answer (C) is correct. *(CPA, adapted)*
   REQUIRED: The amount to be recorded as accrued interest payable.
   DISCUSSION: Under the interest method, accrued interest payable is equal to the face amount of the note at the beginning of the interest period, times the stated interest rate, times the portion of the interest period that is included within the accounting period. At 9/1/Year 1, the face amount of the note was $900,000. After the first $300,000 principal payment at 9/1/Year 2, the face amount of the note was $600,000 ($900,000 – $300,000). Accrued interest payable for the period 9/1/Year 2 to 12/31/Year 2 was thus $24,000 [$600,000 face amount × 12% stated interest rate × (4 months ÷ 12 months)]. The prime rate is irrelevant to the calculation of accrued interest payable.
   Answer (A) is incorrect. The amount of $36,000 was the accrued interest payable at 12/31/Year 1. Answer (B) is incorrect. The amount of $33,000 would have been the accrued interest payable at 12/31/Year 1 if the interest rate had been 11%. Answer (D) is incorrect. The amount of $22,000 would have been the accrued interest payable at 12/31/Year 2 if the interest rate had been 11%.

Questions 55 and 56 are based on the following information. House Publishers offered a contest in which the winner would receive $1 million, payable over 20 years. On December 31, Year 4, House announced the winner of the contest and signed a note payable to the winner for $1 million, payable in $50,000 installments every January 2. Also on December 31, Year 4, House purchased an annuity for $418,250 to provide the $950,000 prize monies remaining after the first $50,000 installment, which was paid on January 2, Year 5.

55. In its December 31, Year 4, balance sheet, what amount should House report as note payable-contest winner, net of current portion?

  A. $368,250

  B. $418,250

  C. $900,000

  D. $950,000

Answer (B) is correct. *(CPA, adapted)*
REQUIRED: The amount of the note payable.
DISCUSSION: Noninterest-bearing notes payable should be measured at their present value rather than their face amount. Thus, House should report the note payable at $418,250 (the present value of the remaining payments).
  Answer (A) is incorrect. The amount of $368,250 includes a reduction of $50,000 for the first installment. Answer (C) is incorrect. The amount of $900,000 equals the face amount of the note payable minus two installments. Answer (D) is incorrect. The amount of $950,000 equals the face amount of the note payable minus the first installment.

56. In its Year 4 income statement, what should House report as contest prize expense?

  A. $0

  B. $418,250

  C. $468,250

  D. $1,000,000

Answer (C) is correct. *(CPA, adapted)*
REQUIRED: The contest prize expense.
DISCUSSION: The contest prize expense equals $468,250 ($418,250 cost of the annuity + $50,000 first installment).
  Answer (A) is incorrect. The amount of $0 does not include the purchase of the annuity or the first installment as an expense in Year 4. Answer (B) is incorrect. The amount of $418,250 does not include the $50,000 installment due in Year 5. Answer (D) is incorrect. The face amount of the note is $1,000,000.

57. On January 1 of the current year, Parke Company borrowed $360,000 from a major customer evidenced by a noninterest-bearing note due in 3 years. Parke agreed to supply the customer's inventory needs for the loan period at less than the market price. At the 12% imputed interest rate for this type of loan, the present value of the note is $255,000 at January 1 of the current year. What amount of interest expense should be included in Parke's current-year income statement?

  A. $43,200

  B. $35,000

  C. $30,600

  D. $0

Answer (C) is correct. *(CPA, adapted)*
REQUIRED: The amount of interest expense recognized by the maker of a noninterest-bearing note.
DISCUSSION: A note issued solely for cash equal to its face amount is presumed to earn the stated rate of interest, even if that rate is zero. If, however, the parties have also exchanged stated or unstated rights or privileges, these must be recognized by determining the fair value (present value) of the note based on an appropriate interest rate. Interest income or expense should be calculated and the discount amortized using the effective interest rate. Parke agreed to supply the customer's inventory needs for the loan period at less than the market price. Hence, the initial carrying amount of the note is $255,000, with the $105,000 ($360,000 – $255,000) discount recognized as the measure of the price concession. The entry is to debit cash and credit notes payable for $360,000 and to debit discount and credit unearned revenue for $105,000. The unearned revenue is recognized as sales revenue in proportion to periodic sales to the creditor-buyer. The discount is amortized as interest expense using the effective interest method. Interest expense is equal to the carrying amount of the note at the beginning of the interest period times the 12% imputed interest rate. The interest expense for the year should therefore be $30,600 ($255,000 carrying amount × 12% imputed interest rate).
  Answer (A) is incorrect. This figure results from applying the imputed interest rate to the face amount of the note instead of to the carrying amount. Answer (B) is incorrect. The amount of $35,000 results from recognizing interest expense using the straight-line method. Answer (D) is incorrect. Interest expense must be imputed on a noninterest-bearing note.

58. On January 31, Year 3, Beau Corp. issued $300,000 maturity amount, 12% bonds for $300,000 cash. The bonds are dated December 31, Year 2, and mature on December 31, Year 12. Interest will be paid semiannually on June 30 and December 31. What amount of accrued interest payable should Beau report in its September 30, Year 3, balance sheet?

A. $27,000

B. $24,000

C. $18,000

D. $9,000

Answer (D) is correct. *(CPA, adapted)*
REQUIRED: The amount of accrued interest payable that should be reported in the balance sheet.
DISCUSSION: Given that interest is paid semiannually on June 30 and December 31, the amount of each payment is $18,000 [($300,000 × 12%) ÷ 2]. On June 30, $18,000 was paid. From 7/1/Year 3 to 9/30/Year 3 (3 months), interest accrued. Thus, $9,000 [$18,000 × (3 months ÷ 6 months)] of accrued interest payable should be reported.
Answer (A) is incorrect. The amount of $27,000 includes the $18,000 already paid on June 30. Answer (B) is incorrect. The amount of $24,000 includes the $18,000 already paid on June 30 and erroneously records $6,000, which is the accrued interest for 2 months. Answer (C) is incorrect. The amount of $18,000 is the semiannual interest payable.

12.6 Troubled Debt Restructurings

59. A troubled debt restructuring (TDR) is one in which the

A. Fair value of cash, other assets, or an equity interest accepted by a creditor from a debtor in full satisfaction of its receivable at least equals the creditor's recorded investment in the receivable.

B. Creditor reduces the effective interest rate on the debt primarily to reflect a decrease in market interest rates in general.

C. Debtor issues, in exchange for its existing debt, new marketable debt having an effective interest rate that is at or near the current market interest rates for debt with similar maturity dates and stated interest rates issued by nontroubled debtors.

D. Creditor, for economic or legal reasons related to the debtor's financial difficulties, grants a concession to the debtor that it would not otherwise consider.

Answer (D) is correct. *(CMA, adapted)*
REQUIRED: The definition of a troubled debt restructuring.
DISCUSSION: A TDR occurs when the creditor, for economic or legal reasons related to the debtor's financial difficulties, grants a concession to the debtor that it would not otherwise consider. TDRs usually involve a continuation of debt with modified terms, a settlement at an amount less than the amount of the debt owed, or a combination. The concession involved may be imposed by law or a court, or it may arise from an agreement between the creditor and the debtor. The creditor's purpose is to reduce the loss it would otherwise incur if it did not grant the concession.
Answer (A) is incorrect. A TDR does not arise when the fair value of cash, other assets, or an equity interest accepted by a creditor from a debtor in full satisfaction of its receivable at least equals the creditor's recorded investment in the receivable. Answer (B) is incorrect. A TDR does not arise when the creditor reduces the effective interest rate on the debt primarily to reflect a decrease in market interest rates in general. Answer (C) is incorrect. Refunding does not constitute a TDR when the new effective rate is at or near current market rates.

60. Which of the following situations that arise because of a debtor's financial difficulties and would not otherwise be acceptable to the creditor must be accounted for as a troubled debt restructuring (TDR)?

A. Because of a court order, a creditor accepts as full satisfaction of its receivable a building the fair value of which equals the creditor's recorded investment in the receivable.

B. As part of a negotiated settlement, a creditor accepts as full satisfaction of its receivable a building the fair value of which equals the debtor's carrying amount of the payable.

C. Because of a court order, a creditor reduces the stated interest rate for the remaining original life of the debt.

D. As part of a negotiated settlement designed to maintain a relationship with a debtor, a creditor reduces the effective interest rate on debt outstanding to reflect the lower market interest rate currently applicable to debt of that risk class.

Answer (C) is correct. *(Publisher, adapted)*
REQUIRED: The situation that must be accounted for as a troubled debt restructuring.
DISCUSSION: A TDR occurs when the creditor, for economic or legal reasons related to the debtor's financial difficulties, grants a concession to the debtor that it would not otherwise consider. TDRs usually involve a continuation of debt with modified terms, a settlement at an amount less than the amount of the debt owed, or a combination. A court order reducing a creditor's interest rate creates a TDR (assuming the reduction would not be otherwise acceptable to the creditor).
Answer (A) is incorrect. No TDR exists if, because of a court order, a creditor accepts as full satisfaction of its receivable a building the fair value of which equals the creditor's recorded investment in the receivable. Answer (B) is incorrect. No TDR exists if the creditor receives full payment. Answer (D) is incorrect. If the debtor could refund the debt at the lower market rate, the creditor is not making a substantive concession.

61. All of the following disclosures are required by debtors involved in a troubled debt restructuring except disclosure of

- A. A description of the major changes in terms, major features of settlement, or both.

- B. The aggregate gain on restructuring and the related tax effect.

- C. The aggregate net gain or loss on transfer of assets.

- D. The gross interest revenue that would have been recorded in the period.

Answer (D) is correct. *(CMA, adapted)*
REQUIRED: The disclosure that is not required of debtors following a troubled debt restructuring.
DISCUSSION: Debtors must, in subsequent periods, disclose the extent to which contingent amounts are included in the carrying amount of restructured payables. The gross interest revenue that would have been recorded in the period is not a required disclosure for debtors because interest revenue is applicable to receivables, not payables.
Answer (A) is incorrect. A description of the major changes in terms or major features of settlement must be disclosed. Answer (B) is incorrect. The aggregate gain on restructuring and the related tax effect must be disclosed. Answer (C) is incorrect. The gain or loss on transfer of assets must be disclosed.

62. In Year 18, May Corp. acquired land by paying $75,000 down and signing a note with a maturity amount of $1 million. On the note's due date, December 31, Year 23, May owed $40,000 of accrued interest and $1 million principal on the note. May was in financial difficulty and was unable to make any payments. May and the bank agreed to amend the note as follows:

- The $40,000 of interest due on December 31, Year 23, was forgiven.

- The principal of the note was reduced from $1 million to $950,000 and the maturity date extended 1 year to December 31, Year 24.

- May would be required to make one interest payment totaling $30,000 on December 31, Year 24.

As a result of the troubled debt restructuring (TDR), May should report a gain, before taxes, in its Year 23 income statement of

- A. $40,000

- B. $50,000

- C. $60,000

- D. $90,000

Answer (C) is correct. *(CPA, adapted)*
REQUIRED: The amount of gain to be recognized from a troubled debt restructuring.
DISCUSSION: When a TDR is structured as a modification of terms that results in future undiscounted cash flows less than the carrying amount of the debt, a debtor should recognize a gain equal to the difference if it is material. Accordingly, May should report a gain of $60,000 ($1,000,000 principal + $40,000 accrued interest – $950,000 new principal – $30,000 interest payment). In addition, the future payments of $980,000 ($950,000 + $30,000) should be recorded as further reductions of the debt.
Answer (A) is incorrect. The amount of $40,000 is the interest forgiven. Answer (B) is incorrect. The amount of $50,000 is the reduction of the principal forgiven. Answer (D) is incorrect. The amount of $90,000 does not include the required interest payment of $30,000 in the calculation of the gain.

63. On May 30 of the current year, Nathan Corp. paid $400,000 cash and issued 80,000 shares of its $1 par value common stock to its unsecured creditors on a pro rata basis pursuant to a reorganization plan under Chapter 11 of the bankruptcy statutes. Nathan owed these unsecured creditors a total of $1,200,000. Nathan's common stock was trading at $1.25 per share on May 30 of the current year. As a result of this transaction, Nathan's total equity had a net increase of

- A. $1,200,000

- B. $800,000

- C. $100,000

- D. $80,000

Answer (B) is correct. *(CPA, adapted)*
REQUIRED: The net increase in equity immediately after the Chapter 11 reorganization.
DISCUSSION: A debtor that grants an equity interest in settlement of a payable should account for the equity interest at fair value. The result is an increase in equity of $100,000 (80,000 shares × $1.25). Because $400,000 in cash and a $100,000 equity interest are accepted as settlement of a $1,200,000 debt, a $700,000 ($1,200,000 – $400,000 – $100,000) gain will also be recognized and result in an increase in equity (retained earnings). Accordingly, the net increase in total equity is $800,000 ($100,000 + $700,000).
Answer (A) is incorrect. The amount of $1,200,000 is the debt. Answer (C) is incorrect. The amount of $100,000 is the increase in contributed capital. Answer (D) is incorrect. The amount of $80,000 is the increase in common stock.

64. Smokey Joe Corp., a debtor-in-possession under Chapter 11 of the Federal Bankruptcy Code, granted an equity interest to a creditor in full settlement of a $56,000 debt owed to the creditor. At the date of this transaction, the equity interest had a fair value of $50,000. What amount should Smokey Joe recognize as a gain on restructuring of debt?

A. $0

B. $6,000

C. $50,000

D. $56,000

Answer (B) is correct. *(CPA, adapted)*
REQUIRED: The amount recognized as a gain on restructuring of debt by a debtor that has granted an equity interest.
DISCUSSION: A debtor that grants an equity interest in full settlement of a payable should account for the equity interest at fair value. The difference between the fair value of the equity interest and the carrying amount of the payable is a gain. Consequently, Smokey Joe will recognize a gain of $6,000 ($56,000 debt – $50,000 fair value of the equity interest).
Answer (A) is incorrect. A gain should be recognized. Answer (C) is incorrect. The amount of $50,000 is the fair value of the equity interest. Answer (D) is incorrect. The carrying amount of the debt is $56,000.

65. Franco Corporation owes Chester National Bank (CNB) on a 10-year, 15% note in the amount of $100,000, plus $30,000 accrued interest. Because of financial difficulty, Franco has been unable to make annual interest payments for the past 2 years, and the note is due today. Accordingly, CNB restructured Franco Corporation's debt as follows:

● The $30,000 of accrued interest was forgiven.

● Franco was given 3 more years to pay off the debt at 8% interest. Payments are to be made annually at year end.

Franco would properly record the restructuring and the payment for the first year as

A. An increase in interest expense of $8,000 and a gain of $2,000.

B. A decrease in accrued interest of $8,000.

C. A decrease in accrued interest of $8,000 and a gain of $2,000.

D. A decrease in accrued interest of $30,000 and a gain of $6,000.

Answer (D) is correct. *(CMA, adapted)*
REQUIRED: The entry for the restructuring of a debt if accrued interest is forgiven, the interest rate is lowered, and the payment period is extended.
DISCUSSION: When modified terms of a restructured troubled debt provide for future undiscounted cash payments that are less than the carrying amount of the debt, the debtor should record the difference as a gain if it is material. Franco's future cash payments will total $124,000 after the restructuring ($100,000 of principal + 3 years of interest at $8,000 per year). Given a $130,000 carrying amount ($100,000 principal + $30,000 interest), the result is a gain of $6,000 ($130,000 – $124,000). Following a restructuring of this type, all future payments on the debt (principal and interest) are treated as reductions of the carrying amount. Consequently, no interest expense is recorded in the years following this restructuring. The entry to recognize the restructuring and the gain is

Note payable	$100,000	
Accrued interest	30,000	
Restructured note payable		$124,000
Gain		6,000

The entry to record the first payment is to debit restructured note payable for $8,000 and credit cash for $8,000.
Answer (A) is incorrect. No interest expense is recognized on a restructuring, and the gain is $6,000. Answer (B) is incorrect. Accrued interest is reduced by $30,000 (the amount forgiven). Answer (C) is incorrect. Accrued interest is reduced by $30,000, and the gain is $6,000.

66. An entity incurs legal fees amounting to $2,000 in granting an equity interest to a creditor in a troubled debt restructuring. In its financial statements, the entity should

A. Capitalize the $2,000 and amortize it over a period not to exceed 40 years.

B. Treat the $2,000 as an expense of the period.

C. Subtract the $2,000 from the $8,000 gain resulting from the restructuring of payables.

D. Reduce by $2,000 the amount that would otherwise be recorded for the equity interest.

Answer (D) is correct. *(Publisher, adapted)*
REQUIRED: The debtor's accounting for legal fees incurred in granting an equity interest to a creditor in a troubled debt restructuring.
DISCUSSION: Legal fees and other direct costs that a debtor incurs in granting an equity interest to a creditor in a troubled debt restructuring reduce the amount otherwise recorded for the interest. Other direct costs a debtor incurs to effect a troubled debt restructuring are deducted in measuring the gain on the restructuring of the payables. If no such gain is recognized, these costs are expensed as they are incurred.
Answer (A) is incorrect. The legal fees should be applied to reduce the amount of the equity interest. Answer (B) is incorrect. Treating the $2,000 as an expense of the period is the proper accounting for direct debt restructuring costs incurred other than in granting an equity interest. Answer (C) is incorrect. Deducting the $2,000 from the $8,000 gain resulting from the restructuring of payables is the proper accounting for direct debt restructuring costs incurred other than in granting an equity interest.

67. On December 31 of the current year, X Corp. was indebted to Zyland Company on a $100,000, 10% note. Only interest had been paid to date, and the remaining life of the note was 2 years. Because X Corp. was in financial difficulties, the parties agreed that X Corp. would settle the debt on the following terms:

1. Settle one-half of the note by transferring land with a recorded amount of $40,000 and a fair value of $45,000

2. Settle one-fourth of the note by transferring 1,000 shares of $1 par common stock with a fair value of $15 per share

3. Modify the terms of the remaining one-fourth of the note by reducing the interest rate to 5% for the remaining 2 years and reducing the principal to $15,000

What total gain should X Corp. record in the current year from this troubled debt restructuring?

    A. $10,000

    B. $13,500

    C. $23,500

    D. $28,500

Answer (D) is correct. *(T. Miller)*
    REQUIRED: The total gains recorded from a troubled debt restructuring.
    DISCUSSION: A debtor must recognize a gain upon restructuring a troubled debt. X Corp. should recognize a gain of $5,000 ($45,000 fair value – $40,000 cost) when recording the land at its fair value and a gain of $5,000 when exchanging the land for a portion of the note worth $50,000 ($100,000 face amount × 50%). A gain of $10,000 should be recognized on the exchange of stock with a fair value of $15,000 (1,000 shares × $15) for the portion of the note worth $25,000 ($100,000 face amount × 25%). Accordingly, the carrying amount of the balance of the note before the modification of its terms equals the remaining $25,000 principal of the original note. Because total cash payments after the restructuring will include principal of $15,000 and 2 years of interest equal to $1,500 ($15,000 × 5% × 2 years), the difference between the $25,000 carrying amount and the total cash payments of $16,500 is a gain of $8,500. The total gain is therefore $28,500 ($5,000 + $5,000 + $10,000 + $8,500).
    Answer (A) is incorrect. The amount of $10,000 is the gain on the exchange of stock. Answer (B) is incorrect. The amount of $13,500 equals 50% of the gain that should be recognized on the transfer of land and the gain from reducing the rate on 25% of the note. Answer (C) is incorrect. The amount of $23,500 includes only 50% of the gain that should be recognized on the transfer of the land.

68. Casey Corp. entered into a troubled debt restructuring agreement with First State Bank. First State agreed to accept land with a carrying amount of $85,000 and a fair value of $120,000 in exchange for a note with a carrying amount of $185,000. Disregarding income taxes, what amount should Casey report as an extraordinary gain in its income statement?

    A. $0

    B. $35,000

    C. $65,000

    D. $100,000

Answer (A) is correct. *(CPA, adapted)*
    REQUIRED: The extraordinary gain reported by a debtor after a troubled debt restructuring.
    DISCUSSION: The debtor must recognize a gain as a result of the extinguishment of debt because the creditor settled the debt by accepting assets with a fair value less than the carrying amount of the debt. However, no extraordinary gain is recognized. An event or transaction is presumed to be ordinary and usual absent clear evidence to the contrary. Accordingly, Casey should recognize an ordinary gain of $100,000 attributable to the $35,000 appreciation of the land ($120,000 fair value – $85,000 carrying amount) and the $65,000 excess of the carrying amount of the debt over the fair value of the land ($185,000 – $120,000).
    Answer (B) is incorrect. The amount of $35,000 is the part of the ordinary gain attributable to appreciation of the land. Answer (C) is incorrect. The amount of $65,000 is the part of the ordinary gain attributable to the excess of the debt's carrying amount over the fair value of the land. Answer (D) is incorrect. The amount of $100,000 is the total ordinary gain recognized.

12.7 Asset Retirement Obligations (AROs)

69. GAAP for asset retirement obligations apply to obligations related to the retirement of long-lived tangible assets. A liability for an asset retirement obligation (ARO) within the scope of this guidance may arise solely from

    A. A plan to sell a long-lived asset.

    B. The improper operation of a long-lived asset.

    C. The temporary idling of a long-lived asset.

    D. The acquisition, construction, development, or normal operation of a long-lived asset.

Answer (D) is correct. *(Publisher, adapted)*
    REQUIRED: The source of a liability for an ARO.
    DISCUSSION: An ARO is recognized for a legal obligation relating to the retirement of a tangible long-lived asset. This obligation results from the acquisition, construction, development, or normal operation of such an asset.
    Answer (A) is incorrect. The scope of GAAP for AROs does not extend to obligations arising solely from a plan to sell or otherwise dispose of a long-lived asset. Answer (B) is incorrect. The scope of GAAP for AROs does not extend to obligations arising from the improper operation of an asset. Answer (C) is incorrect. Retirement is the nontemporary removal of the asset from service, for example, by sale, abandonment, or recycling.

70. An entity is most likely to account for an asset retirement obligation (ARO) by

A. Recognizing the fair value of the liability using an expected present value technique.

B. Recognizing a liability equal to the sum of the net undiscounted future cash flows associated with the ARO.

C. Decreasing the carrying amount of the related long-lived asset.

D. Decreasing the liability for the ARO to reflect the accretion expense.

Answer (A) is correct. *(Publisher, adapted)*
REQUIRED: The proper accounting for an ARO.
DISCUSSION: The fair value of the ARO liability is recognized when incurred. If a reasonable estimate of the fair value cannot be made at that time, the ARO will be recognized when such an estimate can be made. An expected present value technique ordinarily should be used to estimate the fair value. A credit-adjusted risk-free rate is the appropriate discount rate.
Answer (B) is incorrect. A present value method may be used to estimate the fair value. Probability-weighted present values, not undiscounted amounts, are ordinarily used to measure the ARO. Answer (C) is incorrect. The associated asset retirement cost (ARC) is added (debited) to the carrying amount of the tangible long-lived asset when the ARO is recognized (credited). Answer (D) is incorrect. Accretion expense is debited when the ARO is credited to reflect its increase due to passage of time.

71. A business acquired a tangible long-lived asset with an asset retirement obligation (ARO) and included asset retirement cost (ARC) in the asset's carrying amount. The entity also recorded a liability for the ARO on the acquisition date. Subsequently, the entity should

A. Test the ARC for impairment but not amortize it.

B. Test the tangible long-lived asset for impairment and exclude ARC from the carrying amount for this purpose.

C. Recognize accretion expense before the periodic change in the ARO due to revised estimates of cash flows.

D. Discount upward revisions of the undiscounted estimated cash flows relating to the ARO by using the original credit-adjusted risk-free rate.

Answer (C) is correct. *(Publisher, adapted)*
REQUIRED: The subsequent accounting for a tangible long-lived asset with an ARO.
DISCUSSION: A change from one period to the next in the ARO due to passage of time is added to the liability. It is measured by applying an interest method of allocation to the ARO's beginning balance for the period. The rate is the credit-adjusted risk-free (CARF) rate used at the ARO's initial measurement. The offsetting debit is to accretion expense, which is classified as an operating item. After the periodic change resulting from the passage of time has been recognized, the periodic change in the ARO due to revised estimates of the timing or amount of the undiscounted cash flows is accounted for as an adjustment of the capitalized ARC and the carrying amount of the ARO. Increases in those estimated undiscounted cash flows are discounted using the current CARF rate, and decreases are discounted using the original CARF rate.
Answer (A) is incorrect. The ARC is expensed over its useful life using a systematic and rational method, but the entity is permitted to expense the amount that is capitalized in the same period. Answer (B) is incorrect. The carrying amount of the tangible long-lived asset includes ARC for the purpose of impairment testing. Answer (D) is incorrect. The original CARF rate is used to discount downward revisions of the undiscounted estimated cash flows relating to an ARO.

72. A business acquired a long-lived tangible asset on January 1, Year 3. On that date, it recorded a liability for an asset retirement obligation (ARO) and capitalized asset retirement cost (ARC). The estimated useful life of the long-lived tangible asset is 5 years, the credit-adjusted risk-free (CARF) rate used for initial measurement of the ARO is 10%, the initial fair value of the ARO liability based on an expected present value calculation is $250,000, and no changes occur in the undiscounted estimated cash flows used to calculate that fair value. If the entity settles the ARO on December 31, Year 7, for $420,000, what is the settlement gain or loss (rounded)?

A. $(17,372)

B. $25,000

C. $(152,628)

D. $(170,000)

Answer (A) is correct. *(Publisher, adapted)*
REQUIRED: The gain (loss) on settlement of an ARO.
DISCUSSION: Given no changes in the undiscounted estimated cash flows used to calculate the fair value of the ARO on 1/1/Year 3, the only adjustment to the ARO during its useful life is for the passage of time (debit accretion expense, credit ARO). This adjustment is recognized each period in an amount equal to the beginning ARO balance times the initial CARF rate. Consequently, the ARO at 12/31/Year 7 is

	Beginning Balance	Accretion Adjustment	Ending Balance
Year 3	$250,000	$25,000	$275,000
Year 4	275,000	27,500	302,500
Year 5	302,500	30,250	332,750
Year 6	332,750	33,275	366,025
Year 7	366,025	36,602.5	402,627.5

The settlement loss is $17,372 ($420,000 – $402,628 ARO balance at 12/31/Year 7).
Answer (B) is incorrect. The amount of $25,000 is the accretion expense for Year 3. Answer (C) is incorrect. The amount of $(152,628) is the difference between the ARO balance at 1/1/Year 3 and the ARO balance at 12/31/Year 7. Answer (D) is incorrect. The amount of $(170,000) equals the difference between the settlement and the initial balance.

73. Finch Co. reported a total asset retirement obligation of $257,000 in last year's financial statements. This year, Finch acquired assets subject to unconditional retirement obligations measured at undiscounted cash flow estimates of $110,000 and discounted cash flow estimates of $68,000. Finch paid $87,000 toward the settlement of previously recorded asset retirement obligations and recorded an accretion expense of $26,000. What amount should Finch report for the asset retirement obligation in this year's balance sheet?

- A. $238,000
- B. $264,000
- C. $280,000
- D. $306,000

Answer (B) is correct. *(CPA, adapted)*
REQUIRED: The ARO given acquisition of a new ARO, a partial settlement, and accretion expense.
DISCUSSION: An asset retirement obligation (ARO) reflects a legal obligation arising from the acquisition, construction, development, or normal operation of an asset. The ARO is recorded initially as a liability at fair value when incurred, and the liability is adjusted periodically. The liability decreases when the entity settles part of the ARO. It increases because of incurrence of a new ARO and the passage of time (accretion expense). The ARO and the asset retirement cost (the increase in the related long-lived tangible asset equal to the initial ARO) also are adjusted for changes in estimates. An expected present value technique ordinarily is used to estimate the fair value of the ARO. In this question, the fair value of the acquired ARO is meant to be approximated by the discounted cash flow estimate ($68,000). Thus, the ARO at year end is $264,000.

Beginning balance	$257,000
New ARO (FV)	68,000
Partial settlement	(87,000)
Accretion expense	26,000
Ending balance	$264,000

Answer (A) is incorrect. The amount of $238,000 does not include the accretion expense. Answer (C) is incorrect. The amount of $280,000 includes the undiscounted cash flow estimate of $110,000 instead of the discounted cash flow and does not reflect the accretion expense. Answer (D) is incorrect. The amount of $306,000 includes the undiscounted cash flow estimate instead of the discounted estimate.

12.8 IFRS

74. An entity most likely may derecognize a financial liability if it

- A. Transfers amounts to a trust to be used to repay the obligation.
- B. Exchanges debt instruments with the lender with substantially similar terms.
- C. Exchanges debt instruments with the lender with substantially different terms.
- D. Transfers amounts in a transaction that meets the requirements of an in-substance defeasance.

Answer (C) is correct. *(Publisher, adapted)*
REQUIRED: The circumstances in which an entity may derecognize a financial liability.
DISCUSSION: Derecognition of a financial liability (or a part) occurs only by means of extinguishment. This condition is satisfied only when the debtor pays the creditor or is legally released from primary responsibility either by the creditor or through the legal process. An extinguishment and derecognition of the old debt and recognition of new debt occurs when the borrower and lender exchange debt instruments with substantially different terms, that is, when the respective discounted cash flows differ by at least 10%.
Answer (A) is incorrect. Payment to a third party, such as a trust (also known as an in-substance defeasance), does not by itself extinguish the obligation absent a legal release. Answer (B) is incorrect. The terms should be substantially different. Answer (D) is incorrect. Payment to a third party, such as a trust (also known as an in-substance defeasance), does not by itself extinguish the obligation absent a legal release.

75. Debtor owes Bank on a 10-year, 15% note in the amount of $100,000, plus $30,000 accrued interest. Because of financial difficulty, Debtor has been unable to make annual interest payments for the past 2 years, and the note is due today. Accordingly, Bank legally agreed to restructure Debtor's debt as follows:

- The $30,000 of accrued interest was forgiven.

- Debtor was given 3 more years to pay off the debt at 8% interest. Payments are to be made annually at year end. The present value of the payments using the prevailing rate for similar instruments of an issuer with a similar credit rating is $84,018.

At the date of the restructuring, Debtor properly records

    A. A loss of $30,000.

    B. A gain of $30,000.

    C. A gain of $45,982.

    D. No gain or loss because no extinguishment occurred.

Answer (C) is correct. *(Publisher, adapted)*
    REQUIRED: The entry for the restructuring of a debt if accrued interest is forgiven, the interest rate is lowered, and the payment period is extended.
    DISCUSSION: Derecognition of a financial liability (or a part) occurs only by means of extinguishment. This condition is satisfied only when the debtor pays the creditor or is legally released from primary responsibility either by the creditor or through the legal process. An extinguishment and derecognition of the old debt and recognition of new debt occurs when the borrower and lender exchange debt instruments with substantially different terms, that is, when the respective discounted cash flows differ by at least 10%. A substantial modification of terms is also accounted for as an extinguishment. The difference between the carrying amount (including unamortized costs) of a liability (or part) that has been extinguished or transferred and the amount paid is included in profit or loss. This transaction qualifies as an extinguishment based on a substantial modification of terms because the discounted cash flow from the old debt ($130,000 due immediately) and the new debt (given as $84,018) differ by at least 10%. Hence, the amount included by Debtor in profit or loss at the date of the restructuring is a $45,982 gain ($130,000 – $84,018), that is, the difference between the carrying amount extinguished and the amount paid (the present value of the new debt instrument determined by discounting the cash outflows at the prevailing rate for similar instruments of an issuer with a similar credit rating). The entry is to debit the extinguished liability for accrued interest and principal ($130,000), debit discount on note payable ($15,982), credit note payable ($100,000), and credit gain ($45,982).
    Answer (A) is incorrect. The amount of $30,000 is the difference between the sum of the existing liabilities and the face amount of the note with modified terms. Moreover, a gain should be recognized. Answer (B) is incorrect. The amount of $30,000 is the difference between the sum of the existing liabilities and the face amount of the note with modified terms. Moreover, a gain should be recognized. Answer (D) is incorrect. The terms were substantially different. Thus, an extinguishment occurred.

76. Cuddy Corp. issued bonds with a face amount of $200,000. Each $1,000 bond contained detachable share purchase warrants for 100 shares. Total proceeds from the issue amounted to $240,000. The fair value of each warrant was $2, and the fair value of the bonds without the warrants was $196,000. Under IFRS, the bonds were issued at a discount of

    A. $0

    B. $678

    C. $4,000

    D. $40,678

Answer (C) is correct. *(Publisher, adapted)*
    REQUIRED: The amount of the bond discount.
    DISCUSSION: Under IFRS, the proceeds of bonds issued with detachable share purchase warrants must be assigned based on the residual allocation method. The liability component is measured at its fair value ($196,000), and the equity component is measured at the residual amount ($240,000 proceeds – $196,000 assigned to the liability component = $44,000). Accordingly, the bonds were issued at a discount of $4,000 ($200,000 face amount – $196,000). The entry is

Cash	$240,000	
Discount on bonds payable	4,000	
Bonds payable		$200,000
Share premium – warrants		44,000

    Answer (A) is incorrect. The allocation to the bonds was less than their face amount. Answer (B) is incorrect. The discount given an allocation based on relative fair values is $678. Answer (D) is incorrect. The amount allocated to the warrants based on relative fair values is $40,678.

Use Gleim **EQE Test Prep** Software Download for interactive study and performance analysis.

STUDY UNIT THIRTEEN
PENSIONS AND OTHER POSTRETIREMENT BENEFITS

Postretirement benefit plans are **deferred compensation** arrangements by which an employer promises to provide future benefits in exchange for current services of its employees. The primary objective of accounting for these benefits is to recognize the compensation cost over the employees' approximate service periods. The two major types of postretirement benefit arrangements are pension plans and other postretirement employee benefit (OPEB) plans.

Pensions

The two most common types of pension plans are defined contribution plans and defined benefit plans. Under a **defined contribution plan**, the employer deposits an amount into the employee pension trust each period. Pension expense for the period is the amount of the contribution determined by the plan's formula. Under a **defined benefit plan**, the employer guarantees each eligible employee a certain payment throughout retirement. Benefits are based on a complex formula involving years of service rendered, employee life expectancy, and levels of compensation. Because total benefits cannot be precisely determined in advance, the amount must be estimated. Each year, entities with defined benefit plans must recognize pension expense, the funding provided, and any unfunded liability.

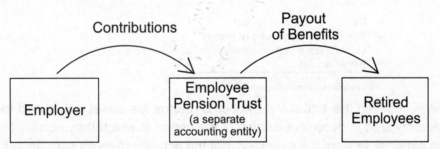

The principal measure of the defined benefit pension liability is the **projected benefit obligation (PBO)**. The PBO at a certain date is the actuarial present value of all benefits attributed by the pension benefit formula to employee services rendered prior to that date. The measurement date for benefit obligations and plan assets is generally the balance sheet date. The PBO is measured using assumptions about future as well as past and current compensation. Moreover, assumptions about discount (interest) rates must be made to calculate the PBO. The PBO at the end of a period equals the following:

```
+ Beginning PBO
+ Service cost
+ Interest cost
+ Prior service cost
– Prior service credit
– Benefits paid
± Changes in the PBO resulting from (a) experience different from that assumed or
    (b) changes in assumptions
Ending PBO
```

The **minimum** annual pension expense that must be recognized has five elements:

```
+   Service cost
+   Interest cost
−   Expected return on plan assets
−/+ Amortization of net gain or loss
−/+ Amortization of prior service cost or credit
    Pension expense
```

Service cost is the present value of the benefits earned during the current period by employees. It is calculated by the plan's actuary using the plan's benefit formula.

Interest cost is the increase in the PBO resulting from the passage of time. It equals the PBO at the beginning of the year multiplied by the current discount rate. The PBO and the discount rate are provided by the plan's actuary.

The **expected return on plan assets** is the market-related value of plan assets (MRV) at the beginning of the period multiplied by the expected long-term rate of return. The expected return (if positive) decreases pension expense. The MRV may be either fair value or a calculated value that recognizes changes in fair value systematically and rationally. (In this text, the MRV is assumed to be fair value.)

Amortization of net gain or loss. Changes in the PBO or plan assets result from (1) changes in actuarial assumptions (what actuaries call liability gains and losses and (2) experience different from that expected (asset gains and losses). The **actual return on plan assets** is based on the **fair value** of the plan assets at the beginning and end of the accounting period, adjusted for contributions and payments.

```
+   Fair value − end of period
−   Fair value − beginning of period
−   Contributions to plan assets
+   Benefits paid
    Actual return on plan assets
```

The differences between the actual and expected returns are **asset gains and losses**. They are not required to be amortized in pension expense of the period in which they occur. Thus, the required minimum pension expense reflects the expected, not the actual, return on plan assets. Gains and losses not recognized in pension expense must be recognized in **other comprehensive income (OCI)**, net of tax, when they occur. OCI is a nominal account that is closed to accumulated OCI, a real account, at the end of the period. The entry for a loss not recognized in pension expense (excluding the deferred tax effect) is

OCI	$XXX	
Pension liability		XXX

A **corridor approach** may be used to reduce the volatility of the pension expense caused by gains and losses. The net of the liability and asset gains and losses included in accumulated OCI is subject to required amortization in pension expense. However, only the amount that exceeds (at the beginning of the year) 10% of the greater of the PBO or the MRV must be amortized.

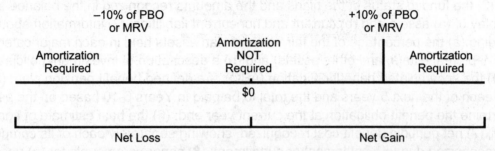

The minimum required amortization equals the excess described above divided by the **average remaining service period** of active employees expected to receive benefits. Amortization of a net gain (loss) decreases (increases) pension expense. OCI is debited (credited), net of tax, each period for required amortization of net gain (loss) arising in prior periods. The entry for amortization of a net loss from a prior period is

Pension expense	$XXX	
OCI		XXX

This entry reclassifies the amortized amount from OCI to net income.

Amortization of prior service cost. Prior service cost is recognized if a plan has been amended to increase benefits for past service. This cost is allocated to the future periods of service of employees active at the date of the amendment who are expected to receive benefits. The total cost is debited to OCI, net of tax, at the amendment date. The entry at the amendment date is

OCI	$XXX	
Pension liability		XXX

Required amortization of prior service cost assigns an equal amount to each future period of service of each qualifying employee. But any alternative that more rapidly amortizes the cost is allowed if applied consistently. The entry is

Pension expense	$XXX	
OCI		XXX

Amortization of prior service credit. A plan amendment that retroactively decreases benefits reduces the PBO. This decrease (a prior service credit) is **credited to OCI**, net of tax. First, it is used to reduce any prior service cost in accumulated OCI. Second, any remaining prior service credit is amortized as part of pension expense on the same basis as prior service cost. Amortization of prior service cost (credit) increases (decreases) pension expense.

Employers must recognize the **over- or underfunded status** of a defined benefit pension plan. It is the difference between the fair value of the plan assets and the PBO. If the plan is overfunded (fair value of plan assets > PBO), the excess is reported in the balance sheet as a pension asset. If the plan is underfunded (fair value of plan assets < PBO), the deficit must be reported in the balance sheet as a pension liability. The fair value of the plan assets at the end of a period equals the following:

　　　　+　Fair value – beginning of period
　　　　+　Contributions
　　　　–　Benefits paid
　　+/–　Actual return on plan assets
　　　　　Fair value – end of period

Many **employer disclosures** about postretirement benefits [pension and other post-retirement employee benefit plans (OPEB)] must be included in the notes. (However, required disclosures for nonpublic entities are less extensive than for public entities.) Examples of disclosures for public entities are (1) reconciliations of beginning and ending balances of the benefit obligation and the fair value of plan assets; (2) the funded status of the plans and the amounts recognized in the balance sheet, with separate display of (a) assets and (b) current and noncurrent liabilities; (3) information about plan assets, including (a) the percentage of the fair value of plan assets held in each major category (e.g., equity, debt, real estate, and other assets) and (b) a description of investment policies and strategies; (4) the accumulated benefit obligation (ABO) of a defined benefit pension plan; (5) benefits to be paid in each of the next 5 years and the total to be paid in Years 6-10 based on the assumptions used to determine the benefit obligation at the current year end; (6) the best estimate of contributions in the next year; (7) net periodic benefit cost recognized, showing separately each of its components and gain or loss recognized due to a settlement or curtailment; (8) separate amounts for (a) net gain (loss) and prior service cost (credit) recognized in OCI for the period, (b) reclassification adjustments of OCI recognized in net periodic benefit cost for the period, and (c) items still in accumulated OCI; and (9) information about rates used in the benefit formula, such as the discount rate, expected long-term rate of return, and healthcare cost trend rates.

The diagram on page 340 summarizes the accounting for defined benefit pension plans.

Postretirement Benefits Other Than Pensions

Examples of other postretirement employee benefit plans (OPEBs) are healthcare and life insurance.

Basic elements of OPEB accounting are the **expected postretirement benefit obligation (EPBO)** and the **accumulated postretirement benefit obligation (APBO)**. The EPBO and the APBO are the same after the full eligibility date. The EPBO, APBO, and service cost include consideration of future salary progression. The EPBO and APBO are illustrated in the following diagram:

Postretirement benefit expense is similar to pension expense. It also is the **minimum** amount that must be recognized and consists of the same five basic components: (1) service cost (the part of the EPBO attributed to employee service during the period); (2) interest cost (the change in the APBO resulting from the passage of time); (3) expected return on plan assets; (4) amortization of prior service cost or credit included in accumulated OCI; and (5) the gain or loss component, which equals any gain or loss immediately recognized in postretirement benefit cost or the amortization of the net gain or loss included in accumulated OCI. The most significant difference between pension accounting and OPEB accounting is that an OPEB plan's funding status is measured based on the APBO. If the plan is **overfunded** (fair value of plan assets > APBO), the excess is reported in the balance sheet as a **postretirement asset**. If the plan is **underfunded** (fair value of plan assets < APBO), the deficit must be reported in the balance sheet as a **postretirement liability**. The **EPBO is not reported** in the financial statements or disclosed in the notes.

A **settlement** of a postretirement plan is a transaction that is irrevocable, relieves the employer of the primary responsibility for its benefit obligation, and eliminates significant risks related to the obligation and the assets used to make the settlement. A **curtailment** is an event that (1) significantly reduces the expected years of future service of active plan participants or (2) eliminates the accrual of defined benefits for some or all of the future services of a significant number of active plan participants. **Special termination benefits** are benefits offered only for a short period of time in connection with a termination of employment.

Guidance for accounting and reporting by defined benefit pension plans applies to plans that issue financial statements except for those of state and local governments, which are covered by GASB pronouncements. The objective of these statements is to provide information useful in assessing the plan's ability to pay benefits.

Differences between GAAP and IFRS

Under IFRS:

- On June 16, 2011, the IASB issued a revision of IAS 19, *Employee Benefits*. The new standard is effective for annual periods beginning on or after January 1, 2013. Earlier application is permitted. Thus, it is testable on the CPA examination in 2012.

- Interest income on plan assets for the period is a component of the return on plan assets. It is recognized in profit or loss. It equals the fair value of the plan assets at the beginning of the year (adjusted for contributions and benefits paid during the year) times the same rate used to discount the defined benefit obligation. Under U.S. GAAP, different interest rates may be used to calculate interest cost and the expected return on plan assets.

- The following is an example of the calculation of the remeasurement of plan assets:

Fair value of plan assets end of the year	$ 1,200
Fair value of plan assets beginning of the year	(1,000)
Interest income (included in profit or loss)	(100)
Contributions	(200)
Benefit payments	150
Remeasurement of plan assets	$ 50

- Remeasurements of the net defined benefit liability (asset) are recognized in OCI. They are never reclassified to profit or loss in subsequent periods. Remeasurements include actuarial gains and losses. These are changes in the benefit obligation from (1) adjustments for the differences between assumptions and actual results and (2) changes in assumptions. Remeasurements also include the remeasurement of plan assets. Accordingly, the corridor approach is not used.

- Past service cost is recognized as an expense at the earlier of (1) when the plan amendment or curtailment occurs and (2) an entity recognizes related restructuring costs or termination benefits. Thus, past service cost is never included in OCI and never reclassified to profit or loss as it is amortized.

Pension Accounting

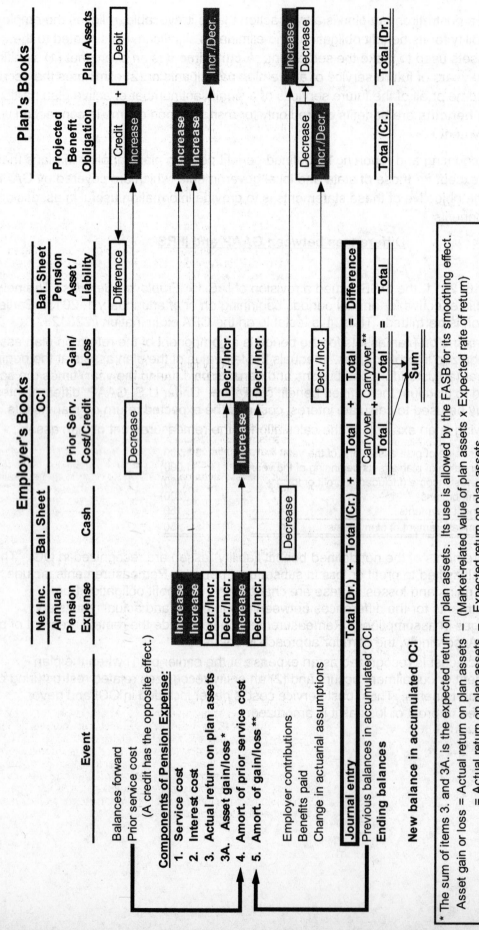

QUESTIONS
13.1 Pensions

1. An employer's accounting for a single-employer defined benefit pension plan is based on the fundamental assumption that such a plan is part of an employee's compensation incurred when the

    A. Defined pension benefit becomes vested.

    B. Defined pension benefit is paid.

    C. Defined pension benefit becomes a legal obligation.

    D. Employee's services are rendered.

Answer (D) is correct. *(Publisher, adapted)*
    REQUIRED: The basic assumption underlying pension accounting.
    DISCUSSION: The fundamental assumption an employer's accounting for a single-employer defined benefit pension plan is that the plan is part of an employee's compensation incurred when the services provided to the employer by the employee are rendered. The defined pension benefit is provided in the form of a deferred payment. It is not precisely determinable. It can only be estimated based on the plan benefit formula and relevant future events, such as (1) future compensation levels, (2) mortality rates, (3) ages at retirement, and (4) vesting schedules.
    Answer (A) is incorrect. A defined benefit pension plan is part of an employee's compensation received when the services provided to the employer by the employee are rendered. Answer (B) is incorrect. Net periodic pension cost may be accrued. Answer (C) is incorrect. Recognition of a liability requires a "present obligation" but not a legal obligation (SFAC 6, *Elements of Financial Statements*).

2. Certain accounting treatments not ordinarily allowed under GAAP are allowed in an employer's accounting for pensions. Which of the following accounting treatments is generally allowed in accounting for defined benefit pension plans?

    A. The tax basis of accounting.

    B. The cash or modified cash basis of accounting.

    C. The offsetting of assets and liabilities.

    D. The immediate recognition of all costs.

Answer (C) is correct. *(Publisher, adapted)*
    REQUIRED: The accounting treatment ordinarily allowed under GAAP only for pension accounting.
    DISCUSSION: GAAP for accounting for defined benefit pension plans permit (1) the delayed recognition of certain events, (2) the reporting of a net cost, and (3) the offsetting of assets and liabilities. "Delayed recognition" means that certain changes in the pension obligation and in the value of the plan assets are not recognized as they occur. They are recognized on a systematic and gradual basis over subsequent accounting periods. "Net costs" means that various pension costs (service cost, interest, actuarial gains and losses, etc.) reflected in the income statement are reported as one expense. The "offsetting feature" means that the recognized values of the plan assets contributed to the plan are offset in the statement of financial position against the recognized liabilities.
    Answer (A) is incorrect. The tax basis of accounting is not appropriate under GAAP. Answer (B) is incorrect. The accrual basis of accounting is required. Answer (D) is incorrect. Delayed, rather than immediate, recognition is allowed for certain events.

3. GAAP relevant to employers' accounting for pensions apply primarily to defined benefit pension plans. It defines the projected benefit obligation as the

    A. Present value of benefits accrued to date based on future compensation levels.

    B. Present value of benefits accrued to date based on current compensation levels.

    C. Increase in retroactive benefits at the date of the amendment of the plan.

    D. Amount of the adjustment necessary to reflect the difference between actual and estimated actuarial returns.

Answer (A) is correct. *(CMA, adapted)*
    REQUIRED: The definition of the projected benefit obligation.
    DISCUSSION: The projected benefit obligation (PBO) as of a date is equal to the actuarial present value of all benefits attributed by the pension benefit formula to employee service rendered prior to that date. The PBO is measured using assumptions about future compensation levels.
    Answer (B) is incorrect. The accumulated benefit obligation (ABO) is the present value of benefits accrued to date based on current compensation levels. Answer (C) is incorrect. Prior service cost is the increase in retroactive benefits at the date of the amendment of the plan. Answer (D) is incorrect. The gain or loss component of net periodic pension cost is the amount of the adjustment necessary to reflect the difference between actual and estimated actuarial returns.

4. Timor Co. sponsors a defined benefit pension plan. The accumulated benefit obligation (ABO) arising under the plan includes benefit obligations to <List A> employees at <List B> salary levels.

	List A	List B
A.	Vested but not nonvested	Current
B.	Vested but not nonvested	Future
C.	Vested and nonvested	Current
D.	Vested and nonvested	Future

Answer (C) is correct. *(CIA, adapted)*
REQUIRED: The nature of the ABO.
DISCUSSION: The ABO is the present value of benefits accrued to date based on past and current compensation levels. Whether benefits are vested is irrelevant to the computation. Thus, the ABO includes both vested and nonvested benefits and is calculated at current, not future, salary levels.
Answer (A) is incorrect. Vested and nonvested benefits are included in the ABO. Answer (B) is incorrect. Vested and nonvested benefits are included in the ABO at current salary levels. Answer (D) is incorrect. The PBO is measured using assumptions about future salary levels.

5. An employee's right to obtain pension benefits regardless of whether (s)he remains employed is the

A. Prior service cost.

B. Defined benefit.

C. Vested interest.

D. Minimum liability.

Answer (C) is correct. *(CIA, adapted)*
REQUIRED: The term defined as the right to obtain pension benefits regardless of future employment.
DISCUSSION: Vested benefits (vested interest) are those earned pension benefits owed to an employee regardless of the employee's continued service. The employer's vested benefit obligation (VBO) is the actuarial present value of these vested benefits.
Answer (A) is incorrect. Prior service cost relates to benefits for employee service provided prior to the adoption or amendment of a defined benefit pension plan. Answer (B) is incorrect. A defined benefit pension plan provides a defined pension benefit based on one or more factors, such as level of compensation, years of service, or age. Answer (D) is incorrect. Recognition of a minimum liability equal to the unfunded ABO was replaced by full recognition of funded status. An employer now must recognize an asset (liability) for the overfunded (underfunded) PBO.

6. Which of the following defined benefit pension plan disclosures should be made in a public company's financial statements?

I. A reconciliation of the beginning and ending balances of the benefit obligation

II. A general description of the employer's funding policy

III. A reconciliation of the beginning and ending balances of the fair value of plan assets

A. I and II.

B. I and III.

C. II and III.

D. I only.

Answer (B) is correct. *(CPA, adapted)*
REQUIRED: The disclosure(s) about a defined benefit pension plan made in a public company's statements.
DISCUSSION: Among other things, a public entity must disclose (1) reconciliations of beginning and ending balances of the benefit obligation and the fair value of plan assets; (2) the funded status of the plans and amounts recognized in the balance sheet, with separate display of (a) assets and (b) current and noncurrent liabilities; (3) information about plan assets, including (a) the percentage of the fair value of plan assets held in each major category (e.g., equity, debt, real estate, and other assets) and (b) a description of investment policies and strategies; (4) the ABO of a defined benefit pension plan; (5) benefits to be paid in each of the next 5 years and the total to be paid in Years 6-10 based on the assumptions used to determine the benefit obligation at the current year end; (6) the best estimate of contributions in the next year; (7) net periodic benefit cost recognized, showing separately each of its components and gain or loss recognized due to a settlement or curtailment; (8) separate amounts for (a) net gain (loss) and prior service cost (credit) recognized in OCI for the period, (b) reclassification adjustments of OCI recognized in net periodic benefit cost for the period, and (c) items still in accumulated OCI; and (9) information about rates used in the benefit formula, such as the discount rate, expected long-term rate of return, and healthcare cost trend rates.
Answer (A) is incorrect. A reconciliation of the beginning and ending balances of the fair value of plan assets must be disclosed. However, general descriptive information about the employer's benefit plans need not be disclosed. Answer (C) is incorrect. A reconciliation of the beginning and ending balances of the benefit obligation must be disclosed. General descriptive information about the employer's benefit plans need not be disclosed. Answer (D) is incorrect. A reconciliation of the beginning and ending balances of the fair value of plan assets must be disclosed.

7. Which of the following is a true statement about the employer's reporting of the assets of a defined benefit pension plan?

A. Market-related value should be used for all purposes except determining asset gains and losses.

B. All assets should be measured at cost.

C. Plan assets that constitute plan investments should be measured at fair value for disclosure purposes.

D. Plan assets used in plan operations should be measured at market value.

Answer (C) is correct. *(Publisher, adapted)*
REQUIRED: The true statement about the measurement of plan assets.
DISCUSSION: For disclosure purposes and for determination of the plan's funded status, plan investments are measured at their fair values. For calculating the expected return on plan assets and thus for determining asset gains and losses, the market-related value is used. Market-related value may be either fair value or a calculated value that recognizes changes in fair value systematically and rationally over not more than 5 years, e.g., a 5-year moving average.
Answer (A) is incorrect. Market-related value (fair value or a calculated value) is used for calculating the expected return on plan assets and asset gains and losses (actual return – expected return). Answer (B) is incorrect. An employer discloses plan assets at fair value. Furthermore, the employer may use market-related value for certain purposes. Answer (D) is incorrect. Plan assets used in operations, e.g., an administration building, should be reported at cost minus accumulated depreciation by the plan, not the employer-sponsor.

8. Entities that sponsor defined benefit pension plans must recognize the actuarial present value of the increase in pension benefits payable to employees because of their services rendered during the current period. This element of pension expense is the

A. Amortization of prior service credit.

B. Service cost.

C. Accumulated benefit obligation (ABO).

D. Projected benefit obligation (PBO).

Answer (B) is correct. *(CMA, adapted)*
REQUIRED: The term for the actuarial present value of the pension benefits attributable to employee services during the current period.
DISCUSSION: Service cost is the present value of the future benefits earned in the current period (as calculated according to the plan's benefit formula). This amount is usually calculated by the plan's actuary. Service cost is a component of net periodic pension cost. It is also a portion of the PBO.
Answer (A) is incorrect. A plan amendment that retroactively reduces benefits results in a prior service credit. It decreases the PBO. This decrease is credited to OCI, net of tax. Any credit remaining after reducing prior service cost in accumulated OCI is amortized as part of pension expense. Answer (C) is incorrect. The ABO is the same as the PBO except that it is limited to past and current compensation levels. Answer (D) is incorrect. The PBO is the actuarial present value of all future benefits attributed to past employee service at a moment in time. It is based on assumptions as to future compensation if the plan formula is based on future compensation.

9. Janney Co. sponsors a defined benefit pension plan. The discount rate used by Janney to calculate the projected benefit obligation is determined by the

	Expected Return on Plan Assets	Actual Return on Plan Assets
A.	Yes	Yes
B.	No	No
C.	Yes	No
D.	No	Yes

Answer (B) is correct. *(CPA, adapted)*
REQUIRED: The basis for determining the discount rate used to calculate the projected benefit obligation.
DISCUSSION: Assumed discount rates are used to measure the PBO. They reflect the rates at which benefit obligations can be settled. In estimating these rates, it is appropriate to consider current prices of annuity contracts that could be used to settle pension obligations as well as the rates on high-quality fixed investments. Neither the expected nor the actual return on plan assets determines the rate used to calculate the PBO.
Answer (A) is incorrect. The expected return on plan assets equals the expected long-term rate of return times the market-related value of plan assets. The actual return on plan assets is based on their fair values at the beginning and end of the period. Neither determines the discount rates used to calculate the PBO. Answer (C) is incorrect. The rates used to calculate the PBO reflect the rates at which benefit obligations can be settled, not the rate used to calculate the expected return on plan assets. Answer (D) is incorrect. The actual return on plan assets is based on their fair values at the beginning and end of the period. However, the rate implicit in the actual return is unrelated to the rates at which the PBO could be settled.

10. Interest cost included in the pension expense recognized by an employer sponsoring a defined benefit pension plan is the

A. Difference between the expected and actual return on plan assets.

B. Increase in the projected benefit obligation resulting from the passage of time.

C. Increase in the fair value of plan assets resulting from the passage of time.

D. Amortization of the discount on unrecognized prior service costs.

Answer (B) is correct. *(CPA, adapted)*
REQUIRED: The definition of interest cost.
DISCUSSION: The interest cost component of net periodic pension cost is defined as the increase in the PBO resulting from the passage of time. The PBO is a discounted amount of benefits to be paid. As the time to payment is reduced, the present value increases. Interest cost is calculated by applying an appropriate discount rate to the beginning balance of the PBO for the period.
Answer (A) is incorrect. The difference between the expected and actual return on plan assets is an asset gain or loss. Answer (C) is incorrect. The increase in the fair value of plan assets resulting from the passage of time is not an element of pension expense. An element of the required minimum pension expense related to plan assets is the expected return on plan assets. This amount equals the market-related value of plan assets at the beginning of the period times the expected long-term rate of return. Answer (D) is incorrect. Interest cost is unrelated to prior service cost. Furthermore, it is the prior service cost recognized in accumulated OCI that is amortized as part of pension expense, not a pension expense "discount."

11. Amortization of the cumulative net gain or loss is a possible component of the pension expense recognized by an employer sponsoring a defined benefit pension plan. Which of the following amortization policies is required?

A. If amortization is required, it will be over the average life expectancy of the plan's employee-participants.

B. Any systematic amortization method may be used, provided the amortized amount does not exceed the prescribed minimum.

C. Amortization of a net unrecognized loss results in an increase in pension expense.

D. No amortization is required if the net gain or loss falls within a certain range.

Answer (D) is correct. *(G. Westmoreland)*
REQUIRED: The required amortization of unrecognized net gain or loss.
DISCUSSION: A corridor approach is followed to reduce the volatility of the pension expense. The cumulative net gain or loss included in accumulated OCI at the beginning of the period (excluding asset gains and losses not reflected in the market-related value of plan assets) is subject to required amortization in pension expense only to the extent it exceeds 10% of the greater of the PBO or the market-related value of plan assets.
Answer (A) is incorrect. Unless almost all participants are inactive, the amortization period is the average remaining service period of active employees expected to receive benefits under the plan. Answer (B) is incorrect. The amortized amount may be greater but not less than the minimum prescribed. Answer (C) is incorrect. All gains and losses are recognized in other comprehensive income.

12. On January 1, Whitford Co. amended its single-employer defined benefit pension plan by granting increased benefits for services provided prior to the current year. This prior service cost will be reflected in the financial statements for

A. Years before the current year only.

B. The current year only.

C. The current year and years before and following the current year.

D. The current year and following years only.

Answer (D) is correct. *(CPA, adapted)*
REQUIRED: The year(s) in which prior service cost will be reflected in the financial statement(s).
DISCUSSION: The amortization of prior service cost should be recognized as a component of pension expense during the future service periods of those employees active at the date of the plan amendment who are expected to receive benefits under the plan. The cost of retroactive benefits is the increase in the PBO at the date of the amendment (debit OCI, net of tax, and credit pension asset or liability). It should be amortized by assigning an equal amount to each future period of service of each employee active at the date of the amendment who is expected to receive benefits under the plan. However, to reduce the burden of these allocation computations, any alternative amortization approach (e.g., averaging) that more rapidly reduces the unrecognized prior service cost is acceptable provided it is applied consistently.
Answer (A) is incorrect. Prior service cost is not recognized as a prior-period adjustment. Answer (B) is incorrect. Prior service cost is allocated to future service periods on a systematic and rational basis. Answer (C) is incorrect. Prior service cost will be amortized in pension expense beginning in the current year.

13. Sheen Company maintains a defined benefit pension plan for its employees. For the fiscal year ended December 31 of the current year, it reported a pension liability. This liability is the amount by which the

A. Projected benefit obligation exceeds the fair value of plan assets.

B. Projected benefit obligation exceeds the vested benefit obligation.

C. Vested benefit obligation exceeds the fair value of plan assets.

D. Accumulated benefit obligation exceeds contributions to the plan.

Answer (A) is correct. *(CPA, adapted)*
REQUIRED: The amount that the unfunded accrued pension cost represents in a defined benefit pension plan.
DISCUSSION: If the PBO is overfunded (fair value of plan assets > PBO), the excess is recognized in the balance sheet as an asset. If the PBO is underfunded (fair value of plan assets < PBO), the excess is recognized in the balance sheet as a liability.
Answer (B) is incorrect. The VBO is not used to determine the funded status of the plan. Answer (C) is incorrect. The liability is the excess of the PBO over the fair value of plan assets. Answer (D) is incorrect. The factors used in measuring the funded status of the plan are the PBO and the fair value of plan assets.

14. Which of the following describes a fundamental aspect of accounting for defined benefit pension plans by employers?

A. Changes in pension assets and obligations are recognized immediately.

B. The amount of pension benefits is not precisely determinable.

C. Net periodic pension cost (pension expense) may be reported within maximum and minimum limits.

D. An employer that funds multiple pension plans may calculate its funded status based on accumulated benefit obligation if some of the plans are overfunded and others are underfunded.

Answer (B) is correct. *(Publisher, adapted)*
REQUIRED: The statement of a fundamental aspect of pension accounting.
DISCUSSION: The total pension benefit to be provided in the form of deferred payments is not precisely determinable and can only be estimated based on the plan's benefit formula and relevant future events, many of which are not controllable by the employer. Such events include how long the employee and survivors live, years of service rendered, and levels of compensation.
Answer (A) is incorrect. Certain changes in the pension obligation and in the value of the assets set aside to meet those obligations are not recognized as they occur. They are recognized on a systematic and gradual basis over subsequent accounting periods. All changes ultimately will be recognized except to the extent they may be offset by subsequent changes. Answer (C) is incorrect. A standard method (not a range) is prescribed for measuring pension expense. Answer (D) is incorrect. A defined-benefit pension plan's funded status must be measured using the projected, not accumulated, benefit obligation.

15. Spencer Company sponsors a defined benefit pension plan for its employees. What pension-related information must it disclose?

	Amount of Prior Service Cost in Accumulated Other Comprehensive Income	Reclassification Adjustments of Other Comprehensive Income
A.	Yes	Yes
B.	Yes	No
C.	No	No
D.	No	Yes

Answer (A) is correct. *(CPA, adapted)*
REQUIRED: The disclosure(s), if any, required of an employer sponsoring a defined benefit pension plan.
DISCUSSION: A public or nonpublic entity that sponsors a defined benefit pension plan must disclose, among other things, separate amounts for (1) net gain (loss) and prior service cost (credit) recognized in OCI for the period, (2) reclassification adjustments of OCI recognized in net periodic benefit cost for the period, and (3) items still in accumulated OCI (showing separately net gain or loss, net prior service cost or credit, and net transition asset or obligation).
Answer (B) is incorrect. Reclassification adjustments of OCI recognized in pension expense (for example, debit pension expense and credit OCI, net of tax for amortization of prior service cost recorded in a prior period) must be disclosed. Answer (C) is incorrect. Prior service cost in accumulated OCI and reclassification adjustments of OCI must be disclosed. Answer (D) is incorrect. Prior service cost in accumulated OCI must be disclosed.

16. In a business combination, Ryan Co. acquired Pichardo Co., which sponsors a single-employer defined benefit pension plan. Ryan should

    A. Recognize any previously existing net gain or loss.

    B. Assign part of the purchase price to the prior service cost as an intangible asset.

    C. Assign part of the purchase price to the excess of plan assets over the projected benefit obligation.

    D. Recognize a previously existing transition net asset or obligation of the plan.

Answer (C) is correct. *(Publisher, adapted)*
    REQUIRED: The acquiring company's accounting when the acquired company sponsors a pension plan.
    DISCUSSION: In a business combination, the acquiring entity should recognize a pension liability if the PBO of the acquired entity is in excess of its plan assets. Likewise, a pension asset should be recognized if plan assets exceed the PBO.
    Answer (A) is incorrect. In a business combination, previously existing net gains and losses recognized in accumulated OCI are eliminated by the assignment of part of the purchase price to a liability (excess of PBO over plan assets) or an asset (excess of plan assets over the PBO). Answer (B) is incorrect. In a business combination, previously existing prior service costs recognized in accumulated OCI are eliminated by the assignment of part of the purchase price to a liability (excess of PBO over plan assets) or an asset (excess of plan assets over the PBO). Answer (D) is incorrect. In a business combination, a previously existing transition net asset or obligation of the acquired company's defined benefit plan recognized in accumulated OCI is eliminated by the assignment of part of the purchase price to a liability (excess of PBO over plan assets) or an asset (excess of plan assets over the PBO).

17. Dawson Co. sponsors an arrangement that provides pension benefits in return for services rendered, provides an individual account for each participant, and specifies how contributions to the individual accounts are to be determined. This arrangement is a

    A. Defined benefit pension plan.

    B. Defined contribution plan.

    C. Multiemployer plan.

    D. Multiple-employer plan.

Answer (B) is correct. *(Publisher, adapted)*
    REQUIRED: The type of plan defined.
    DISCUSSION: A defined contribution plan specifies how contributions to an individual's account are to be determined. The benefits a participant will receive depend solely on the amount contributed, the returns earned on investments of those contributions, and forfeitures of other participants' benefits that may be allocated to his/her account. The pension expense is the contribution called for in the particular accounting period.
    Answer (A) is incorrect. A defined benefit pension plan is a plan that provides a defined pension benefit based on one or more factors. Answer (C) is incorrect. A multiemployer plan is a plan to which two or more unrelated employers contribute, usually pursuant to one or more collective bargaining agreements. Assets are not segregated and may be used to provide benefits to employees of any of the participating employers. Answer (D) is incorrect. A multiple-employer plan is a pension plan to which two or more unrelated employers contribute, usually to allow pooling of assets for investment purposes and to reduce administrative costs. Assets are segregated, and contributions may be based on benefit formulas that differ.

18. The following information pertains to McNeil Co.'s defined benefit pension plan:

Actuarial estimate of projected benefit obligation at January 1	$144,000
Assumed discount rate	10%
Service cost for the year	36,000
Pension benefits paid during the year	30,000

If no change in actuarial estimates occurred during the year, McNeil's PBO at December 31 was

    A. $128,400

    B. $150,000

    C. $158,400

    D. $164,400

Answer (D) is correct. *(CPA, adapted)*
    REQUIRED: The projected benefit obligation at the end of the year.
    DISCUSSION: The ending balance of the PBO is the beginning balance plus the service cost and interest cost components, minus the benefits paid. The interest cost component is equal to the PBO's beginning balance times the discount rate.

Beginning PBO balance	$144,000
Service cost	36,000
Interest cost ($144,000 × 10%)	14,400
Benefits paid	(30,000)
Ending PBO balance	$164,400

    Answer (A) is incorrect. The amount of $128,400 excludes the current year's service cost component. Answer (B) is incorrect. The amount of $150,000 excludes the interest cost component. Answer (C) is incorrect. The amount of $158,400 excludes both the service cost component and the benefits paid.

19. The following information pertains to Beltran Co.'s defined benefit pension plan for the current year:

Fair value of plan assets, beginning of year	$ 700,000
Fair value of plan assets, end of year	1,050,000
Employer contributions	220,000
Benefits paid	170,000

In computing pension expense, what amount should Beltran use as actual return on plan assets?

A. $130,000

B. $300,000

C. $350,000

D. $520,000

Answer (B) is correct. *(CPA, adapted)*
REQUIRED: The actual return on plan assets.
DISCUSSION: The actual return on plan assets is based on the fair value of plan assets at the beginning and end of the accounting period adjusted for contributions and payments during the period. The actual return is $300,000 ($1,050,000 – $700,000 – $220,000 + $170,000).
Answer (A) is incorrect. The amount of $130,000 results when benefits paid to employees are not included. Answer (C) is incorrect. The amount of $350,000 is the change in the fair value of plan assets without adjustment for contributions or benefits paid. Answer (D) is incorrect. The amount of $520,000 does not deduct employer contributions.

20. At the beginning of the current year, the market-related value of the plan assets of Janeway Company's defined benefit pension plan was $1,000,000. Janeway uses a 5-year weighted-average method to determine market-related values. The company, however, had not previously experienced any asset gains or losses. The expected long-term rate of return on plan assets is 10%. The actual return during the year was $50,000. Contributions and benefits paid were $150,000 and $200,000, respectively. At year end, the market-related value (MRV) of Janeway's plan assets is

A. $1,140,000

B. $1,040,000

C. $1,000,000

D. $950,000

Answer (B) is correct. *(Publisher, adapted)*
REQUIRED: The market-related value of plan assets at year end.
DISCUSSION: If market-related value is defined as fair value, the ending market-related value of the plan assets is the beginning amount, plus the actual returns, plus the contributions, minus the benefits paid. However, in this case, the company uses an alternative method to determine market-related value. This alternative includes 20% of the sum of the differences between the actual and the expected returns (asset gains and losses) over the last 5 years. The year-end market-related value is the beginning amount, plus the expected return, plus the contributions, minus the benefits paid, minus 20% of the difference between the actual return ($50,000) and the expected return ($1,000,000 × 10% = $100,000) for the current year only.

Beginning market-related value	$1,000,000
Expected return ($1,000,000 × 10%)	100,000
Contributions	150,000
Benefits paid	(200,000)
20% of $50,000 loss	(10,000)
Year-end market-related value	$1,040,000

Answer (A) is incorrect. The amount of $1,140,000 excludes the expected returns and benefits paid. Answer (C) is incorrect. The amount of $1,000,000 is the fair value and not the MRV of plan assets at year end. Answer (D) is incorrect. The amount of $950,000 excludes the expected return and 20% of the loss.

21. The following information relates to the current-year activity of the defined benefit pension plan of Kim Company, whose stock is publicly traded:

Service cost	$240,000
Expected return on plan assets	60,000
Interest cost on pension benefit obligation	80,000
Amortization of actuarial loss	20,000
Amortization of prior service cost	10,000

Kim's pension cost for the current year is

A. $240,000

B. $260,000

C. $270,000

D. $290,000

Answer (D) is correct. *(A. Oddo)*
REQUIRED: The pension expense for the year.
DISCUSSION: Components of pension expense are service cost, interest cost, the expected return on plan assets, and amortization of any (1) prior service cost or credit or (2) net gain (loss). Service cost, interest cost, and the amortization of actuarial loss and prior service cost increase the pension expense. The expected return on plan assets decreases pension expense. As indicated below, pension expense is $290,000.

Service cost	$240,000
Expected return on plan assets	(60,000)
Interest cost	80,000
Amortization of actuarial loss	20,000
Amortization of prior service cost	10,000
Pension expense	$290,000

Answer (A) is incorrect. The amount of $240,000 includes only the service cost component. Answer (B) is incorrect. The amount of $260,000 excludes the amortization of prior service cost and the actuarial loss. Answer (C) is incorrect. The amount of $270,000 excludes the amortization of the actuarial loss.

22. Schiff Co. sponsors a defined benefit pension plan. For the current year, the expected return on plan assets was $100,000. The actual return was $150,000. The company's actuary estimates an increase of $600,000 in the projected benefit obligation. The amount of the projected benefit obligation determined at year end reflected an increase of only $400,000. If no net gain (loss) was carried in accumulated OCI at the beginning of the year, the amount of net gain (loss) subject to required amortization for the current year is

A. $0

B. $400,000

C. $50,000

D. $250,000

Answer (A) is correct. *(Publisher, adapted)*
REQUIRED: The amount of net gain (loss) subject to required amortization for the current year.
DISCUSSION: Gains and losses need not be recognized in pension expense of the period in which they arise. The $50,000 asset gain ($150,000 actual return – $100,000 expected return) and the liability gain (the PBO at year end was $200,000 less than estimated) are therefore not required to be included in pension expense of the current year. Given that no net gain (loss) was carried in accumulated OCI at the beginning of the year, the required amortization for the current year is $0.
Answer (B) is incorrect. The amount of $400,000 is the year-end estimate of the PBO increase. This amount is not subject to required amortization when it occurs. Answer (C) is incorrect. The amount of $50,000 is the asset gain. No amortization is currently required. Answer (D) is incorrect. The amount of $250,000 is the sum of the asset gain and the liability gain. No amortization is currently required.

23. The following is the only information pertaining to Kane Co.'s defined benefit pension plan:

Pension asset, January 1, Year 1	$ 2,000
Service cost	19,000
Interest cost	38,000
Actual and expected return on plan assets	22,000
Amortization of prior service cost arising in a prior period	52,000
Employer contributions	40,000

In its December 31, Year 1, balance sheet, what amount should Kane report as the underfunded or overfunded projected benefit obligation (PBO)?

A. $7,000 overfunded.

B. $15,000 underfunded.

C. $45,000 underfunded.

D. $52,000 underfunded.

Answer (A) is correct. *(CPA, adapted)*
REQUIRED: The underfunded or overfunded PBO.
DISCUSSION: The employer must recognize the funded status of the plan as the difference between the fair value of plan assets and the PBO. That amount is an asset or a liability. Current service cost and interest cost increase the PBO. The actual return on plan assets and contributions increase plan assets. Amortization of prior service cost arising in a prior period and recognized in accumulated OCI has no additional effect on the PBO or plan assets. However, it is a component of pension expense. The PBO was overfunded by $2,000 on January 1. It increased during the year by $57,000 ($19,000 + $38,000). Plan assets increased by $62,000 ($22,000 + $40,000). Accordingly, the plan is overfunded by $7,000 [$2,000 + ($62,000 – $57,000)] at year end. Kane should recognize a pension asset of $7,000 at year end.
Answer (B) is incorrect. The return on plan assets should be added to plan assets. Answer (C) is incorrect. The amount of $45,000 underfunded includes prior service cost amortization. Prior service cost that arose in a prior period was reflected in the asset or liability recognized for the funded status of the plan at the beginning of the year. When prior service cost arises, the entry is to debit OCI, net of tax, and credit pension liability. Answer (D) is incorrect. The amount of $52,000 is the prior service cost amortization.

24. An entity sponsors a defined benefit pension plan that is underfunded by $800,000. A $500,000 increase in the fair value of plan assets would have which of the following effects on the financial statements of the entity?

A. An increase in the assets of the entity.

B. An increase in accumulated other comprehensive income of the entity for the full amount of the increase in the value of the assets.

C. A decrease in accumulated other comprehensive income of the entity for the full amount of the increase in the value of the assets.

D. A decrease in the liabilities of the entity.

Answer (D) is correct. *(CPA, adapted)*
REQUIRED: The effect of an increase in the fair value of plan assets on the financial statements of an entity with an underfunded defined benefit pension plan.
DISCUSSION: If a pension benefit obligation (PBO) exceeds the fair value of plan assets, the amount of the underfunding must be recognized as a liability. If the pension plan is underfunded by $800,000, an increase in the fair value of plan assets of $500,000 reduces the underfunding by $500,000. Thus, the increase in the fair value of plan assets decreases but does not eliminate the pension liability.
Answer (A) is incorrect. Given that the PBO is underfunded by $800,000, the fair value of plan assets would have to increase by more than $800,000 to increase the assets of the entity. For example, if the fair value of the plan assets, which are not assets of the sponsor, had increased by $900,000, the entity would recognize an asset of $100,000 for the overfunding. Answer (B) is incorrect. The full over- or underfunded status of the plan is reported as an asset or liability, respectively. Unamortized gains or losses, prior service cost, and prior service credit are reported in OCI. The total OCI for the period is transferred to accumulated OCI (a component of equity in the statement of financial position). Thus, the funded status of the plan does not affect accumulated OCI. Answer (C) is incorrect. The funded status of the plan does not affect accumulated OCI.

25. A company has a defined benefit pension plan for its employees. On December 31, Year 1, the accumulated benefit obligation (ABO) is $45,900, the projected benefit obligation (PBO) is $68,100, and the fair value of the plan assets is $62,000. What amount, if any, related to the defined benefit plan should be recognized in the balance sheet at December 31, Year 1?

A. An asset of $16,100.

B. A liability of $6,100.

C. Nothing, as the fair value of the plan assets exceeds the accumulated benefit obligation.

D. An unrealized loss of $6,100.

Answer (B) is correct. *(CPA, adapted)*
REQUIRED: The amount related to a defined benefit pension plan given the ABO, PBO, and the fair value of plan assets.
DISCUSSION: The balance sheet must report the full overfunded or underfunded status of the defined benefit pension plan as an asset or a liability. Other comprehensive income (OCI) (presented in equity) must report unamortized gains or losses, prior service cost, and prior service credit. The funded status of a pension plan is the difference between the fair value of plan assets and the projected benefit obligation. Accordingly, the balance sheet must report a liability of $6,100 ($68,100 PBO – $62,000 FV of plan assets) for the amount by which the defined benefit pension plan is underfunded.
Answer (A) is incorrect. The fair value of plan assets exceeds the accumulated benefit obligation by $16,100. But the PBO, not the ABO, is used to measure the funded status of the defined benefit pension plan. Answer (C) is incorrect. The ABO was used to measure the additional minimum liability required to be recognized under prior U.S. GAAP. However, current U.S. GAAP require recognition of the full funded status of the defined benefit pension plan. Answer (D) is incorrect. The funded status of the plan is recognized as an asset or liability, and an unamortized gain or loss is recognized in OCI. Pension accounting does not use the term "unrealized loss." Amortized liability gains and losses (from changes in actuarial assumptions) and amortized asset gains and losses (from experience different from that expected) are recognized in pension expense.

26. On January 1 of the current year, Kohl Corp. adopted a defined benefit pension plan. The plan's service cost of $75,000 was fully funded at the end of the current year. Prior service cost was fully funded by a contribution of $30,000 in the current year. Amortization of prior service cost was $12,000 for the current year. Pension expense has no other components. What is the amount of Kohl's pension asset at December 31 of the current year?

A. $0

B. $18,000

C. $42,000

D. $105,000

Answer (A) is correct. *(CPA, adapted)*
REQUIRED: The pension asset at year end.
DISCUSSION: The projected benefit obligation is increased by the recognition of $30,000 of prior service cost and $75,000 of service cost, leaving a PBO of $105,000. The plan assets were increased by the full funding of both components of pension expense ($30,000 + $75,000 = $105,000). Thus, the PBO is equal to the plan assets at year end, and no pension asset or liability is reported.
Answer (B) is incorrect. The amount of $18,000 is the excess of the prior service cost over the amortization of prior service cost ($30,000 – $12,000). Answer (C) is incorrect. The amount of $42,000 is the sum of the prior service cost and the amortization of prior service cost ($30,000 + $12,000). Answer (D) is incorrect. The amount of $105,000 equals the PBO or the plan assets at year end ($30,000 + $75,000).

27. Jan Corp. amended its defined benefit pension plan, granting a total credit of $100,000 to four employees for services rendered prior to the plan's adoption. The employees, A, B, C, and D, are expected to retire from the company as follows:

A will retire after 3 years.
B and C will retire after 5 years.
D will retire after 7 years.

What is the amount of prior service cost amortization in the first year?

A. $0

B. $5,000

C. $20,000

D. $25,000

Answer (C) is correct. *(CPA, adapted)*
REQUIRED: The amount of prior service cost amortization in the first year after amendment of a defined benefit pension plan.
DISCUSSION: The cost of retroactive benefits is the increase in the PBO at the date of the amendment (debit OCI, net of tax, and credit pension liability or asset). It should be amortized by assigning an equal amount to each future period of service of each employee active at the date of the amendment who is expected to receive benefits under the plan. However, to reduce the burden of these allocation computations, any alternative amortization approach (e.g., averaging) that more rapidly reduces the unrecognized prior service cost is acceptable, provided that it is applied consistently. The total service years to be rendered by the employees equals 20 (3 + 5 + 5 + 7). Hence, the amortization percentage for the first year is 20% (4 ÷ 20), and the minimum amortization is $20,000 ($100,000 × 20%).
Answer (A) is incorrect. Amortization of prior service cost is a component of pension expense. Answer (B) is incorrect. The amount of $5,000 is assigned to each period of service by each employee. Answer (D) is incorrect. The figure of $25,000 results from assigning an equal amount to each employee.

28. On January 2 of the current year, Walesa Co. established a noncontributory defined benefit plan covering all employees and contributed $1,000,000 to the plan. At December 31 of the current year, Walesa determined that the current year service and interest costs for the plan were $620,000. The expected and the actual rate of return on plan assets for the current year was 10%. There are no other components of pension expense. What amount should Walesa report in its balance sheet for the current year as a pension asset?

A. $280,000

B. $380,000

C. $480,000

D. $620,000

Answer (C) is correct. *(CPA, adapted)*
REQUIRED: The pension asset.
DISCUSSION: A pension asset is recognized when the fair value of the plan assets exceeds the projected benefit obligation. Two of the components of pension expense ($620,000 service and interest costs) increase the projected benefit obligation. The third component, the actual and expected return on plan assets, increases the plan assets by $100,000 ($1,000,000 beginning balance × 10% expected rate of return). Thus, at December 31, the fair value of the plan assets exceeds the projected benefit obligation by $480,000 ($1,100,000 – $620,000). This amount is reported as a pension asset.
Answer (A) is incorrect. The amount of $280,000 is the difference between the contributed amount and the service and interest costs, with 10% of $1,000,000 subtracted from the difference. Answer (B) is incorrect. The amount of $380,000 is the difference between the contributed amount and the sum of the service and interest costs. Answer (D) is incorrect. The amount of $620,000 is the sum of the service and interest costs.

29. At end of the year, Nickel Company's projected benefit obligation (PBO) was determined to be $1,500,000, which was $200,000 higher than had been expected. The market-related value of the defined benefit plan's assets was equal to its fair value of $1,250,000. No other gains and losses have occurred. If the average remaining service life is 20 years, the minimum required amortization of the net gain (loss) in the next year will be

A. $20,000

B. $3,750

C. $2,500

D. $0

Answer (C) is correct. *(Publisher, adapted)*
REQUIRED: The minimum required amortization of net gain (loss) next year.
DISCUSSION: At a minimum, amortization of net gain or loss included in accumulated OCI at the beginning of the year (excluding asset gains and losses not yet reflected in market-related value) must be included as a component of pension expense for a year if, as of the beginning of the year, that gain or loss exceeds 10% of the greater of the PBO or the market-related value (MRV) of plan assets. At year end, Nickel's PBO was $200,000 greater than estimated (a $200,000 liability loss). Given that no other gain or loss has occurred, the net loss to be amortized beginning next year is $200,000. The corridor amount is $150,000 (10% of the greater of $1,500,000 PBO or $1,250,000 MRV of plan assets). The amount outside the corridor is $50,000 ($200,000 – $150,000), and the amount to be amortized is thus $2,500 ($50,000 ÷ 20 years of average remaining service life).
Answer (A) is incorrect. The amount of $20,000 is the result of using the full $200,000 liability loss without regard to the corridor amount. It also assumes an amortization period of 10 years instead of 20. Answer (B) is incorrect. The amount of $3,750 is the result of using $125,000 ($1,250,000 plan assets × 10%) as the corridor amount instead of $150,000. Answer (D) is incorrect. The amount of $50,000 of the liability loss must be amortized over the average remaining service life beginning the year following the loss.

30. On June 1, Year 1, Cleaver Corp. established a defined benefit pension plan for its employees. The following information was available at May 31, Year 3:

Projected benefit obligation	$29,000,000
Accumulated benefit obligation	24,000,000
Plan assets at fair value	14,000,000
Accumulated OCI – prior service cost	3,100,000

To report the proper pension liability in Cleaver's May 31, Year 3, balance sheet, what is the amount of the adjustment required?

A. $3.1 million.

B. $11.9 million.

C. $15.0 million.

D. $17.1 million.

Answer (B) is correct. *(CPA, adapted)*
REQUIRED: The amount of the adjustment required to reflect pension liability properly on the balance sheet.
DISCUSSION: A pension liability must be recognized in the amount of the underfunded PBO (PBO – fair value of plan assets). The PBO is underfunded by $15 million ($29 million PBO – $14 million FV of plan assets). However, the recording of OCI – prior service cost (a component of the PBO) required a credit to pension liability (net of tax) of $3.1 million. Accordingly, the adjustment is a credit of $11.9 million ($29 million PBO – $14 million plan assets at fair value – $3.1 million pension liability related to prior service cost).
Answer (A) is incorrect. The amount of $3.1 million equals accumulated OCI – prior service cost. Answer (C) is incorrect. The amount of $15.0 million is the total pension liability. Answer (D) is incorrect. The amount of $17.1 million is the sum of the fair value of plan assets and the accumulated OCI – prior service cost.

31. Worldwide Co. implemented a defined benefit pension plan for its employees on January 1, Year 4. During Year 4 and Year 5, Worldwide's contributions fully funded the plan. The following data are provided for Year 6:

	Year 6 Actual
Projected benefit obligation, December 31	$700,000
Accumulated benefit obligation, December 31	500,000
Plan assets at fair value, December 31	600,000
Projected benefit obligation in excess of plan assets	100,000

During Year 7, Worldwide recognized service cost of $120,000 and interest cost of $100,000. Its actual return on plan assets was $130,000. Worldwide had no recognized asset gain or loss and did not need to amortize prior service cost (credit), gain (loss), or a transition amount. To report a pension liability of $75,000 at December 31, Year 7, Worldwide must contribute what amount to the plan?

A. $75,000

B. $115,000

C. $165,000

D. $265,000

Answer (B) is correct. *(CPA, adapted)*
REQUIRED: The amount contributed to report a given pension liability.
DISCUSSION: The pension liability on January 1, Year 7, was $100,000. It increased during the year by $220,000 ($120,000 service cost + $100,000 interest cost) and decreased during the year by the actual return on plan assets of $130,000. The actual return on plan assets equaled the expected return because Worldwide had no asset gain or loss. Thus, the amount of pension liability before the adjustment for contributions is $190,000 ($100,000 + $220,000 – $130,000). To report a pension liability of $75,000, the contribution during Year 7 must be $115,000 ($190,000 – $75,000).
Answer (A) is incorrect. A contribution of $75,000 results in a pension liability of $115,000. Answer (C) is incorrect. A contribution of $165,000 results in a pension liability of $25,000. Answer (D) is incorrect. A contribution of $265,000 results in a pension asset of $75,000.

32. On September 1, Year 1, Howe Corp. offered special termination benefits to employees who had reached the early retirement age specified in the company's pension plan. The termination benefits consisted of lump-sum and periodic future payments. Additionally, the employees accepting the company offer receive the usual early retirement pension benefits. The offer expired on November 30, Year 1. Actual or reasonably estimated amounts at December 31, Year 1, relating to the employees accepting the offer are as follows:

- Lump-sum payments totaling $475,000 were made on January 1, Year 2.
- Periodic payments of $60,000 annually for 3 years will begin January 1, Year 3. The present value at December 31, Year 1, of these payments was $155,000.
- Reduction of accrued pension costs at December 31, Year 1, for the terminating employees was $45,000.

At December 31, Year 1, Howe should report a total liability for special termination benefits of

A. $475,000

B. $585,000

C. $630,000

D. $655,000

Answer (C) is correct. *(CPA, adapted)*
REQUIRED: The total liability for special termination benefits.
DISCUSSION: The liability and expense arising from special termination benefits should be recognized by an employer when the employees accept the offer and the amount can be reasonably estimated. The amount should include the lump-sum payments and the present value of any future payments. Thus, Howe should report a total liability for special termination benefits of $630,000 ($475,000 lump-sum payments + $155,000 present value of future payments) in its 12/31/Year 1 balance sheet. The reduction of accrued pension costs is recognized by a debit for $45,000. After crediting the liability for $630,000, the debit to a loss account will be $585,000.
Answer (A) is incorrect. The amount of $475,000 omits the present value of the future benefits. Answer (B) is incorrect. The amount of $585,000 is the loss, not the liability. Answer (D) is incorrect. The figure of $655,000 is the undiscounted amount of the payments for termination benefits.

33. Which of the following components must be included in the calculation of pension expense recognized for a period by an employer sponsoring a defined benefit pension plan?

	Interest Cost	Actual Return on Plan Assets
A.	Yes	No
B.	Yes	Yes
C.	No	Yes
D.	No	No

Answer (B) is correct. *(CPA, adapted)*
REQUIRED: The component(s), if any, to be included in pension expense.
DISCUSSION: The interest cost component of pension expense is the addition to the beginning balance of the PBO as a result of the passage of time. According to GAAP, (1) the actual return on plan assets is included in pension expense, (2) the difference between the actual and expected returns is included in the gain or loss component of pension expense, and (3) gains and losses (e.g., the difference between the actual and expected returns) are not required to be recognized in pension expense of the period in which they occur. Thus, the net effect on the required minimum pension expense is to decrease it by the amount of the expected, not the actual, return on plan assets. The current asset gain or loss, that is, the difference between the actual and expected returns, is deferred for the purpose of calculating the required minimum pension expense. For example, if the actual return exceeds the expected return, the gain is debited to the liability for pension benefits (or to an asset if the plan is overfunded). The credit is to OCI, net of tax.
Answer (A) is incorrect. The actual return is included. Answer (C) is incorrect. Interest cost is included. Answer (D) is incorrect. The actual return and interest cost are included.

34. The following information pertains to Lee Corp.'s defined benefit pension plan for Year 1:

Service cost	$160,000
Actual and expected gain on plan assets	35,000
Unexpected loss on plan assets related to a Year 1 disposal of a subsidiary	40,000
Amortization of prior service cost	5,000
Annual interest on pension obligation	50,000

What amount must Lee report as pension expense in its Year 1 income statement?

A. $250,000
B. $220,000
C. $210,000
D. $180,000

Answer (D) is correct. *(CPA, adapted)*
REQUIRED: The pension expense for the year.
DISCUSSION: The components of the required minimum pension expense are (1) service cost, (2) interest cost, (3) return on plan assets, (4) amortization of the net gain or loss recognized in accumulated OCI, and (5) amortization of any prior service cost or credit. Accordingly, the service cost, actual and expected gain on plan assets, interest cost, and amortization of prior service cost are included in the computation. Gains and losses arising from changes in the PBO or plan assets resulting from experience different from that assumed and from changes in assumptions about discount rates, life expectancies, etc., are not required to be included in the calculation of the required minimum pension expense when they occur. Accordingly, the unexpected Year 1 loss on plan assets is included in the gain or loss recognized in OCI (debit OCI, net of tax, and credit pension liability or asset). It must be amortized beginning in Year 2. Pension expense is therefore $180,000 ($160,000 service cost – $35,000 actual and expected return on plan assets + $5,000 prior service cost amortization + $50,000 interest cost).
Answer (A) is incorrect. The amount of $250,000 results from adding, not subtracting, the expected gain on plan assets. Answer (B) is incorrect. The amount of $220,000 includes the unexpected loss. Answer (C) is incorrect. The amount of $210,000 includes the unexpected loss and subtracts instead of adding the amortization of prior service cost.

35. How should plan investments be reported in a defined benefit plan's financial statements?

A. At actuarial present value.
B. At cost.
C. At net realizable value.
D. At fair value.

Answer (D) is correct. *(CPA, adapted)*
REQUIRED: The accounting for plan investments by a defined benefit plan.
DISCUSSION: The annual financial statements of a defined benefit plan must include information about the net assets available for benefits at the end of the plan year. Plan investments, whether equity or debt securities, real estate, or other (excluding insurance contracts) must be presented at their fair value at the reporting date.
Answer (A) is incorrect. Accumulated plan benefits are measured at actuarial present value at the benefit information date. Answer (B) is incorrect. Plan operating assets must be presented at cost minus accumulated depreciation or amortization. Answer (C) is incorrect. The plan does not measure assets or benefits at net realizable value.

36. On January 2, Loch Co. established a noncontributory defined-benefit pension plan covering all employees and contributed $400,000 to the plan. At December 31, Loch determined that the annual service and interest costs of the plan were $720,000. The expected and the actual rate of return on plan assets for the year was 10%. Loch's pension expense has no other components. What amount should Loch report in its December 31, balance sheet as liability for pension benefits?

- A. $280,000
- B. $320,000
- C. $360,000
- D. $720,000

Answer (A) is correct. *(CPA, adapted)*
REQUIRED: The pension liability.
DISCUSSION: Service and interest costs and the return on plan assets are the entity's only components of pension expense in the plan's first year. The return on plan assets is $40,000 ($400,000 contributed to the plan × 10%). The pension expense is therefore $680,000 ($720,000 service and interest costs – $40,000 actual and expected return on plan assets). Because the actual and expected returns were the same, no gain or loss occurred. The funded status of the plan is the difference between plan assets at fair value ($400,000 + $40,000 = $440,000 at year end) and the projected benefit obligation ($720,000 service and interest costs, given no prior service cost or credit). Consequently, the liability recognized to record the unfunded status of the plan at year end is $280,000 ($720,000 – $440,000).
Answer (B) is incorrect. The amount of $320,000 is the result if the return on plan assets is not added to plan assets at year end. Answer (C) is incorrect. The amount of $360,000 results when the return on plan assets is subtracted from plan assets at year end. Answer (D) is incorrect. The amount of $720,000 is the sum of service and interest costs.

37. A curtailment of a defined benefit pension plan is an event that significantly reduces the expected years of future service of current employees or eliminates for a significant number of employees the accrual of defined benefits for some or all of their future service. Which statement is descriptive of a curtailment?

- A. It occurs only when a plan is terminated.
- B. If the amount of net curtailment loss is less than or equal to the sum of the interest cost and service cost components of net periodic pension cost, recognition is not mandatory.
- C. A curtailment gain resulting from a decrease in the projected benefit obligation is offset by any transition obligation remaining in accumulated OCI.
- D. It involves recognition of unamortized prior service cost.

Answer (D) is correct. *(Publisher, adapted)*
REQUIRED: The statement descriptive of a curtailment.
DISCUSSION: A curtailment net gain or loss equals the sum of (1) the prior service cost remaining in accumulated OCI associated with years of service no longer expected to be rendered and (2) the change in the PBO that does not represent a reversal of net gains or losses remaining in accumulated OCI. Any transition asset remaining in accumulated OCI is treated as a net gain. For this purpose, prior service cost includes any transition obligation remaining in accumulated OCI.
Answer (A) is incorrect. Termination of a plan is not required for a curtailment. Answer (B) is incorrect. Recognition is not mandatory for a settlement (not a curtailment) gain or loss. However, recognition of a settlement gain or loss is required if the cost of all settlements in a year exceeds the sum of the interest cost and the service cost components. Answer (C) is incorrect. A curtailment gain resulting from a decrease in the PBO is offset only by any net loss remaining in accumulated OCI.

38. Termination benefits are provided to employees in connection with their termination of employment. Termination benefits may be classified as either special termination benefits offered only for a short period or contractual termination benefits required by the terms of a pension plan only if a specified event occurs. The liability and loss arising from termination benefits should be recognized by an employer when the employees accept the offer and the amount can be reasonably estimated for

	Special Benefits	Contractual Benefits
A.	No	No
B.	No	Yes
C.	Yes	No
D.	Yes	Yes

Answer (C) is correct. *(Publisher, adapted)*
REQUIRED: The termination benefits that should be recognized by the employer when the employees accept the offer and the amount is reasonably estimable.
DISCUSSION: The liability and loss arising from special termination benefits should be recognized by an employer when the employees accept the offer and the amount can be reasonably estimated. The liability and loss arising from contractual termination benefits should be recognized when it is probable that employees will be entitled to benefits and the amount can be reasonably estimated.
Answer (A) is incorrect. The liability and loss arising from special termination benefits should be recognized by an employer when the employees can accept the offer and the amount can be reasonably estimated. Answer (B) is incorrect. The recognition criteria for special benefits, not contractual benefits, are offer acceptance and reasonable estimation. Answer (D) is incorrect. The liability and loss arising from contractual termination benefits should be recognized when it is probable that employees will be entitled to benefits and the amount can be reasonably estimated.

39. The following information pertains to Gali Co.'s defined benefit pension plan for Year 1:

Fair value of plan assets, beginning of year	$350,000
Fair value of plan assets, end of year	525,000
Employer contributions	110,000
Benefits paid	85,000

In computing pension expense, what amount should Gali use as actual return on plan assets?

- A. $65,000
- B. $150,000
- C. $175,000
- D. $260,000

Answer (B) is correct. *(CPA, adapted)*
REQUIRED: The actual return on plan assets.
DISCUSSION: The actual return on plan assets is based on the fair value of plan assets at the beginning and end of the accounting period adjusted for contributions and payments during the period. The actual return for Gali is $150,000 ($525,000 – $350,000 – $110,000 + $85,000).
Answer (A) is incorrect. The amount of $65,000 results when benefits paid to employees are not included. Answer (C) is incorrect. The amount of $175,000 is the change in the fair value of plan assets without adjustment for contributions or benefits paid. Answer (D) is incorrect. The amount of $260,000 does not deduct employer contributions.

13.2 Postretirement Benefits Other Than Pensions

40. The guidance applying to employers' accounting for postretirement benefits other than pensions emphasizes an employer's accounting for a single-employer plan that defines other postretirement employee benefits (OPEB). The basic elements of accounting for OPEB include

- A. The expected postretirement benefit obligation (EPBO), which equals the accumulated postretirement benefit obligation (APBO) after the full eligibility date.
- B. The APBO, which is the actuarial present value at a given date of the benefits projected to be earned after the full eligibility date.
- C. Required recognition of a minimum liability for any excess of the EPBO over the APBO.
- D. The projected benefit obligation (PBO) and the vested benefit obligation (VBO).

Answer (A) is correct. *(Publisher, adapted)*
REQUIRED: The true statement about the elements of accounting for OPEB.
DISCUSSION: The EPBO for an employee is the actuarial present value at a given date of the OPEB expected to be paid. Its measurement depends on the anticipated amounts and timing of future benefits, the costs to be incurred to provide those benefits, and the extent the costs are shared by the employee and others (such as governmental programs). The APBO for an employee is the actuarial present value at a given date of future benefits attributable to the employee's service as of that date. The determination of the APBO (as well as of the EPBO and service cost) implicitly includes the consideration of future salary progression to the extent the benefit formula defines benefits as a function of future compensation levels. The full eligibility date is reached when the employee has rendered all the services necessary to earn all of the benefits expected to be received by that employee. After the full eligibility date, the EPBO and APBO are equal. Prior to that date, the EPBO exceeds the APBO.
Answer (B) is incorrect. The full eligibility date is the date when an employee has earned all the benefits expected to be received. Answer (C) is incorrect. The full funded status of the plan must be recognized. Answer (D) is incorrect. The PBO and the VBO relate to pension accounting only.

41. Ethelred Co. is an employer sponsoring a defined benefit postretirement healthcare plan. Which of the following components might be included in its postretirement benefit expense?

	Amortization of Prior Service Credit Remaining in Accumulated OCI	Interest Cost
A.	No	No
B.	Yes	No
C.	No	Yes
D.	Yes	Yes

Answer (D) is correct. *(Publisher, adapted)*
REQUIRED: The true statement about the elements of postretirement benefit expense.
DISCUSSION: The six possible components of the required minimum postretirement benefit expense are (1) service cost, (2) interest on the APBO, (3) expected return on plan assets, (4) amortization of prior service cost or credit remaining in accumulated OCI, (5) amortization of the transition obligation or asset remaining in accumulated OCI, and (6) the gain or loss component. The postretirement benefit expense is very similar to pension expense.
Answer (A) is incorrect. Amortization of prior service credit remaining in accumulated OCI and interest cost should be included in the net periodic postretirement benefit cost of an employer sponsoring a defined benefit healthcare plan.
Answer (B) is incorrect. Interest cost should be included in the postretirement benefit expense. Answer (C) is incorrect. Amortization of prior service credit remaining in accumulated OCI should be included in the postretirement benefit expense.

42. Li Co. is a publicly traded entity that sponsors both a pension plan and a postretirement plan providing other, nonpension benefits. The following information relates to the current year's activity of Li's defined benefit postretirement plan:

Service cost	$240,000
Return on plan assets	60,000
Interest cost on accumulated benefit obligation	80,000
Amortization of actuarial loss	20,000
Amortization of prior service cost	10,000

Li's nonpension postretirement benefit cost is

A. $240,000

B. $280,000

C. $350,000

D. $290,000

Answer (D) is correct. *(A. Oddo)*
REQUIRED: The postretirement benefit cost for the year.
DISCUSSION: The components of the postretirement benefit cost are service cost, interest cost, the expected return on plan assets, and amortization of (1) any prior service cost remaining in accumulated OCI, and (2) any net gain (loss) from prior periods remaining in accumulated OCI. Service cost, interest cost, and the amortization of actuarial loss and prior service cost increase the postretirement benefit cost. The expected return on plan assets decreases the postretirement benefit cost. As indicated below, the amount for the year is $290,000.

Service cost	$240,000
Return on plan assets	(60,000)
Interest cost	80,000
Amortization of actuarial loss	20,000
Amortization of prior service cost	10,000
Postretirement benefit cost	$290,000

Answer (A) is incorrect. The amount of $240,000 includes only the service cost component. Answer (B) is incorrect. The amount of $280,000 excludes the amortization of the prior service cost. Answer (C) is incorrect. The amount of $350,000 excludes the return on plan assets from the calculation of the postretirement benefit cost.

43. Gallaher Co. sponsors a single-employer defined benefit postretirement plan that provides nonpension benefits. The service cost component of its postretirement benefit expense is

A. Included in the APBO but not in the EPBO.

B. The portion of the EPBO attributed to employee service for a period.

C. Included in the EPBO but not the APBO.

D. Measured using implicit and explicit actuarial assumptions and present value techniques.

Answer (B) is correct. *(Publisher, adapted)*
REQUIRED: The definition of the service cost component of the NPPBC.
DISCUSSION: Service cost is the actuarial present value of benefits attributed to services rendered by employees during the period. It is the portion of the EPBO attributed to service in the period and is not affected by the level of funding.
Answer (A) is incorrect. The service cost for the most recently completed period is included in the EPBO. Answer (C) is incorrect. The service cost for the most recently completed period is included in the APBO. Answer (D) is incorrect. The use of explicit assumptions, each of which is the best estimate of a particular event, is required.

44. Hubbard Co. sponsors a single-employer defined benefit postretirement plan that provides nonpension benefits. Its prior service cost is the cost of benefit improvements attributable to plan participants' prior service pursuant to a plan amendment or a plan initiation that provides benefits in exchange for plan participants' prior service. Hubbard ordinarily should recognize prior service cost in postretirement benefit expense

A. By assigning an equal amount to each remaining year of service to the full eligibility date of each participant active at the amendment date who was not yet fully eligible for benefits.

B. In full in the accounting period in which the plan is amended.

C. By amortizing it over the remaining life expectancy of the participants.

D. In accordance with straight-line amortization over the average remaining years to full eligibility of the active participants.

Answer (A) is correct. *(Publisher, adapted)*
REQUIRED: The general rule for recognition of prior service cost.
DISCUSSION: The effect of a plan amendment on a participant's EPBO should be attributed to each year of service in that individual's attribution period (ordinarily from the date of hire or a later date specified by the benefit formula to the full eligibility date). This period may include years of service already rendered. The cost of benefit improvements for years of service already rendered is the increase in the APBO as a result of an amendment and measured at the date of the amendment. The general rule is that equal amounts of this cost should be assigned to each remaining year of service to the full eligibility date for each active plan participant at the date of the amendment who was not yet fully eligible.
Answer (B) is incorrect. Prior service cost is deemed to provide economic benefits to the employer in future periods. Thus, recognition in full in the year of the amendment is prohibited. Answer (C) is incorrect. Amortization over the remaining life expectancy of the participants is appropriate only if all or almost all of the participants are fully eligible. Answer (D) is incorrect. Recognizing prior service cost in accordance with straight-line amortization over the average remaining years to full eligibility of the active participants is a pragmatic exception to the general rule. An alternative, consistently applied amortization method that more rapidly reduces prior service cost remaining in accumulated OCI is permitted to reduce complexity and detail.

45. Campbell Co. sponsors a single-employer defined benefit postretirement plan that provides nonpension benefits. The interest cost component of its postretirement benefit expense is the

A. Increase in the EPBO because of the passage of time.

B. Increase in the APBO because of the passage of time.

C. Product of the market-related value of plan assets and the expected long-term rate of return on plan assets.

D. Change in the APBO during the period.

Answer (B) is correct. *(Publisher, adapted)*
REQUIRED: The definition of the interest cost component of the postretirement benefit expense.
DISCUSSION: Interest cost reflects the change in the APBO during the period resulting solely from the passage of time. It equals the APBO at the beginning of the period times the assumed discount rate used in determining the present value of future cash outflows currently expected to be required to satisfy the obligation.
Answer (A) is incorrect. Interest cost is a function of the APBO. Answer (C) is incorrect. The expected return on plan assets is the product of the market-related value of plan assets and the expected long-term rate of return on plan assets. Answer (D) is incorrect. The change in the obligation reflects many factors, of which interest cost is one.

46. Which of the following items of information should be disclosed by Purpura Company, which provides healthcare benefits to its retirees under a single-employer defined benefit plan?

I. The assumed healthcare cost trend rate used to measure the expected cost of benefits covered by the plan

II. The assumptions about the discount rate, rate of compensation increase, and expected long-term rate of return on plan assets

A. I and II.

B. I only.

C. II only.

D. Neither I nor II.

Answer (A) is correct. *(CPA, adapted)*
REQUIRED: The information that should be disclosed by an entity providing healthcare benefits to its retirees.
DISCUSSION: The disclosure requirements for pensions and other postretirement employee benefits include

● "The assumed healthcare cost trend rate(s) for the next year used to measure the expected cost of benefits covered by the plan (gross eligible charges), and a general description of the direction and pattern of change in the assumed trend rates thereafter, together with the ultimate trend rate(s) and when that rate is expected to be achieved."

● "On a weighted-average basis, the following assumptions used in accounting for a plan: assumed discount rates, rates of compensation increase (for pay-related plans), and expected long-term rates of return on plan assets specifying, in a tabular format, the assumptions used to determine the benefit obligation and the assumptions used to determine net benefit cost."

Disclosures about assumed healthcare cost trend rates and certain other assumptions used in accounting for a plan must be made by public and nonpublic entities.
Answer (B) is incorrect. The assumptions about the discount rate, rate of compensation increase, and expected long-term rate of return on plan assets also must be disclosed. Answer (C) is incorrect. The assumed healthcare cost trend rate used to measure the expected cost of benefits covered by the plan also must be disclosed. Answer (D) is incorrect. The assumed healthcare cost trend rate used to measure the expected cost of benefits covered by the plan and the assumptions about the discount rate, rate of compensation increase, and expected long-term rate of return on plan assets also must be disclosed.

47. Griffin Co. provides postretirement healthcare benefits to employees under a single-employer defined benefit plan. To be eligible, employees must have completed at least 10 years service and be aged 55 years or older when retiring. Employees retiring from Griffin have a median age of 62, and no one has worked beyond age 65. Hera Hurlbert was hired when she was 48 years old. The attribution period for accruing Griffin's expected postretirement healthcare benefit obligation to Hurlbert is during the period when Hurlbert is aged

A. 48 to 65.

B. 48 to 58.

C. 55 to 65.

D. 55 to 62.

Answer (B) is correct. *(CPA, adapted)*
REQUIRED: The attribution period for accruing the expected postretirement healthcare benefit obligation to an employee.
DISCUSSION: The attribution period begins on the date of hire unless the plan's benefit formula grants credit for service only from a later date. The end of the period is the full eligibility date. If the exception does not apply, Hurlbert's attribution is from age 48, the date of hire, to age 58, the date of full eligibility.
Answer (A) is incorrect. The attribution period is 10 years. Furthermore, it ends on the date of full eligibility. Answer (C) is incorrect. The attribution period is from the date of hire to the date of full eligibility. Answer (D) is incorrect. The attribution period is 10 years.

48. Which of the following costs is unique to postretirement healthcare benefits?

- A. Per capita claims.
- B. Service.
- C. Prior service.
- D. Interest.

Answer (A) is correct. *(CPA, adapted)*
REQUIRED: The cost unique to postretirement healthcare benefits.
DISCUSSION: A per capita claim (capitation fee) is a fixed amount per individual paid periodically to a healthcare provider as payment for services for the period (ordinarily monthly).
Answer (B) is incorrect. Service cost is an element of pension expense and postretirement benefit expense.
Answer (C) is incorrect. Amortization of prior service cost is an element of pension expense and postretirement benefit expense. Answer (D) is incorrect. Interest cost is an element of pension expense and postretirement benefit expense.

Use Gleim **EQE Test Prep** Software Download for interactive study and performance analysis.

STUDY UNIT FOURTEEN
LEASES

A lease is a **contract**. It transfers from the **lessor** (owner) to the **lessee** the right to use specific property for a stated period in exchange for a stated payment. The basic issue is whether the lease is a long-term rental contract or a purchase-and-financing agreement. Lessees prefer to treat leases as rental contracts to avoid reporting debt on the balance sheet.

Capital Leases – Lessee Accounting

A lessee classifies a lease as an operating lease or a capital lease. In an **operating lease**, the lessor retains substantially all of the benefits and risks of ownership. Such a lease is a rental agreement. The lessee records the periodic payments (debit rental expense, credit cash) and recognizes no noncurrent liability. In a **capital lease**, the lessor transfers substantially all of the benefits and risks of ownership to the lessee. Such a lease is a purchase-and-financing agreement. A lessee classifies a lease as a capital lease if **one of the following criteria** indicates that substantially all of the benefits and risks of ownership have been transferred:

1. The lease provides for the transfer of ownership of the leased property.
2. The lease contains a bargain purchase option (BPO).
3. The lease term is 75% or more of the estimated economic life of the leased property.
4. The present value of the minimum lease payments (excluding executory costs) is at least 90% of the fair value of the leased property to the lessor at the inception of the lease.

The last two criteria do not apply if the beginning of the lease term is within the last 25% of the property's total estimated economic life. If a lease covers **only land** and contains either a transfer of ownership at the end of its term or a BPO, the lessee capitalizes the lease. Otherwise, it is accounted for as an operating lease.

The lessee must record a capital lease as an asset (e.g., debit lease equipment) and an obligation (e.g., credit lease obligation) at an amount equal to the **present value of the minimum lease payments**. The discount rate used in calculating this amount is the lower of (1) the lessor's implicit rate if it is known to the lessee and (2) the lessee's incremental borrowing rate. The lessor's implicit rate is the rate at which the sum of the present values of (1) the minimum lease payments and (2) the unguaranteed residual value at the beginning of the lease equals the fair value of the leased property. The higher the rate, the lower the present value of the minimum lease payments and the less likely that the lease will be capitalized. Thus, if the lessee and lessor use different rates, one might recognize an operating lease and the other a capital lease. The present value of the minimum lease payments cannot exceed the fair value of the leased property at the beginning of the lease.

The **lessee's minimum lease payments** include (1) minimum rental payments, (2) a BPO, (3) any guaranteed residual value, and (4) a nonrenewal penalty. The minimum rental payments are the periodic amounts owed by the lessee, minus any executory costs (such as insurance, maintenance, taxes, etc.) that will be paid by the lessor. A BPO gives the lessee the right to purchase the leased property. The price must be sufficiently lower than its expected fair value at the exercise date that exercise is reasonably assured. Any guaranteed residual value is generally the estimated fair value of the leased property at the end of the lease that the lessee must pay. A guarantee of residual value may be obtained by the lessee from an unrelated third party for the benefit of the lessor. This third-party guarantee is specifically excluded from the minimum lease payments if the lessor releases the lessee from liability. Furthermore, amounts paid for this third-party guarantee also are excluded. A nonrenewal penalty is any payment that the lessee must make if it does not renew or extend the lease.

Given a BPO, the present value of the minimum lease payments equals the sum of the present values of (1) the minimum rental payments (excluding executory costs) and (2) the BPO. If no BPO exists, this amount equals the sum of the present values of (1) the minimum rental payments, (2) the amount of residual value guaranteed by the lessee, and (3) any nonrenewal penalty.

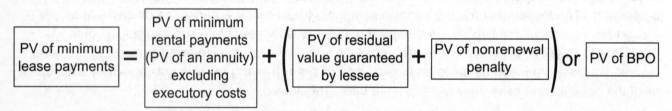

Each periodic **lease payment** has two components: interest and the reduction of the lease liability. The **effective-interest method** is required. Interest expense equals the appropriate interest rate times the carrying amount of the lease liability at the beginning of each period. The effect is a constant periodic rate of interest on the remaining balance. The portion of the minimum lease payment in excess of interest expense reduces the balance sheet liability. In a classified balance sheet, the lease liability must be allocated between current and noncurrent portions. The current portion at a balance sheet date is the reduction of the lease liability in the next year.

The **term of a lease** may not extend beyond the date a BPO becomes exercisable. Absent a BPO, the term of the lease includes the fixed noncancelable lease term. It also may include any periods covered by (1) bargain renewal options and (2) ordinary renewal options. Furthermore, the lease may include a nonrenewal penalty so large that renewal appears to be reasonably assured. Finally, the lease term may include periods for renewals or extensions of the lease at the lessor's option.

If a **lease of land and a building** transfers ownership or contains a BPO, the lessee should (1) separately capitalize the land and building, (2) allocate the present value of the minimum lease payments based on fair values, and (3) amortize the building.

An asset recorded under a capital lease by the lessee should be **depreciated** in a manner consistent with the lessee's **normal policy**. Thus, the lease liability is accounted for under lease accounting, but the depreciation is the same as that of an entity-owned asset. If the lease is capitalized because the lease either transfers ownership or contains a BPO, the depreciation of the asset is over its estimated economic life. If the lease is capitalized because another criterion is met, the asset is depreciated over the lease term to its expected value to the lessee at the end of that term. A lessee does not recognize depreciation for an operating lease. If the lease provisions are changed and the result is a new agreement classified as an operating lease, the sale and leaseback rules are applied.

Future minimum lease payments as of the latest balance sheet presented must be **disclosed** in the aggregate and for each of the 5 succeeding fiscal years. This disclosure is required whether the lease is a capital or an operating lease.

Capital Leases – Lessor Accounting

A lessor capitalizes a lease only if (1) it meets one of the four capitalization criteria, and (2)(a) **collectibility** of the remaining payments is reasonably predictable, and (b) no material **uncertainties** exist regarding the lessor's unreimbursable costs.

A lessor must further classify a capital lease as either a direct financing lease or a sales-type lease. If the asset's fair value at the beginning of the lease equals its carrying amount, the lease is a direct financing lease. If the asset's fair value at the beginning of the lease is not equal to its carrying amount, the lease is a sales-type lease. In a **direct financing lease**, the lessor does not recognize a manufacturer's or dealer's profit (loss). The lessor's economic interest is financing the purchase. The lessor debits a lease receivable and credits the asset leased. The difference between the **gross investment** (minimum lease payments + unguaranteed residual value) and the cost or carrying amount is credited to **unearned income**. The unearned income and the initial direct costs of a direct financing lease are amortized to income over the lease term using the interest method. The result is a constant rate of return on the net investment. This equals the gross investment, plus unamortized initial direct costs, minus unearned income. **Initial direct costs** include the lessor's costs to originate a lease in essential dealings with independent third parties that directly result from the acquisition of the lease. They also include certain costs directly related to specified activities performed for that lease, e.g., evaluating lessee financial condition and security arrangements, negotiating terms, preparing documents, and closing.

EXAMPLE: On January 2, Year 1, Lessee leased a machine for 3 years from Lessor. Lessee must pay $100,000 at the end of each year. The machine has zero residual value after 3 years, no initial direct costs are recorded, and the rate implicit in the lease is 10%. The present value of the minimum lease payments is $248,690.

Lessor's journal entry on January 2, Year 1:

Lease payments receivable*	$300,000	
Asset		$248,690
Unearned interest income		51,310

*This entry reflects the gross method. It records the gross receivable (gross investment). An alternative is the direct method. It debits the receivable for an amount net of unearned interest (net investment).

Lessor's journal entry on December 31, Year 1:

Cash	$100,000	
Lease payments receivable		$100,000
Unearned interest income	$24,869	
Interest income		$24,869

Date	Net Investment	Times: Effective Rate	Equals: Interest Income	Cash Receipt	Difference: Reduction of Net Investment Receivable	Net Investment
1/2/Year 1						$248,690
12/31/Year 1	$248,690	10%	$24,869	$100,000	$(75,131)	173,559
12/31/Year 2	173,559	10%	17,356	100,000	(82,644)	90,915
12/31/Year 3	90,915	10%	9,091	100,000	(90,915)	0

In a **sales-type lease**, the lessor recognizes a **manufacturer's or dealer's profit (loss)**. The fair value of the leased property at the beginning of the lease differs from its cost or carrying amount. The following summarizes the initial entry for a sales-type lease:

Debit	Credit	Amount
Cost of goods sold		Cost or carrying amount + initial direct costs – PV of unguaranteed residual value
Lease payments receivable		Gross or net investment depending on whether unearned income recognized
	Asset	Cost or carrying amount
	Sales revenue	PV of minimum lease payments
	Unearned income	If gross method is used, difference between lease payments receivable (gross investment) and sum of PVs of its components.

Assuming no initial direct costs, the **gross profit** on the sale equals sales revenue minus cost of goods sold. Profit is not affected if **residual value is unguaranteed**. In that case, the present value of the residual value is not included in the present value of the minimum lease payments. Thus, cost of goods sold and sales revenue are lower. Minimum lease payments include any residual value guaranteed by the lessee. Unearned income is amortized to income over the lease term using the **interest method**. The result is a constant rate of return on the net investment. The estimate of residual value is reviewed at least annually. A nontemporary decrease results in revision of the accounting for the transaction and recognition of a nonreversible loss because of the reduction in the net investment. The **lessor's minimum lease payments** are the same as those for the lessee except that they include any residual value or rental payments beyond the lease term guaranteed by a financially capable third party unrelated to the lessor or the lessee.

$$
\begin{array}{ccccc}
\textit{Lessor's PV of} & & \textit{Lessee's PV of} & & \textit{Amounts Guaranteed} \\
\textit{Minimum Lease} & = & \textit{Minimum Lease} & + & \textit{by Independent} \\
\textit{Payments} & & \textit{Payments} & & \textit{Third Party}
\end{array}
$$

The effect of this difference may be that the fourth capitalization criterion is met by the lessor but not the lessee.

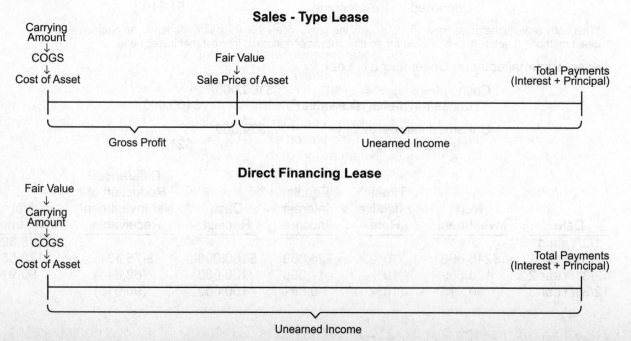

Operating Leases

Operating leases do not meet the criteria for capitalization. They are transactions in which lessees rent the right to use lessor assets without acquiring a substantial portion of the benefits and risks of ownership of those assets. Thus, the lessor does not record a sale or financing. **Rent** is reported as income by the lessor in accordance with the lease agreement. If rental payments vary, for example, if the first month is free, the **straight-line basis** should be used unless another systematic and rational basis is more representative of the time pattern in which the use benefit from the property is reduced. The lessor should report the leased property near property, plant, and equipment in the balance sheet and should depreciate the property according to its **normal depreciation policy** for owned assets. **Initial direct costs**, such as realtor fees, should be deferred and amortized by the lessor over the lease term in proportion to the recognition of rental income.

Sale-Leaseback Transactions

A sale-leaseback involves the sale of property by the owner and a lease of the property back to the seller. If the lease qualifies as a **capital lease**, the gain or loss on the sale is normally deferred and amortized by the seller-lessee in proportion to the depreciation of the leased asset. The **gain deferred** may be reported as an asset valuation allowance (a contra asset with a credit balance). A **loss** occurs when the carrying amount is greater than the fair value, and is recognized in full immediately. However, if the carrying amount is greater than the sale price, but the fair value exceeds the carrying amount, the loss is deferred and amortized as prepaid rent. If the carrying amount is greater, the full loss is recognized immediately. If the lease qualifies as an **operating lease**, a gain or loss on the sale normally should be deferred and amortized in proportion to the gross rental payments expensed over the lease term.

When the seller-lessee classifies the lease as an operating lease, no asset is reported on the balance sheet. Thus, the deferral cannot be presented as a contra asset. Accordingly, the usual practice is to report the gain (loss) as a deferred credit (debit). The **purchaser-lessor** accounts for a sale-leaseback transaction as a purchase and a direct financing lease if the capitalization criteria are satisfied. If these criteria are not met, the lessor records a purchase and an operating lease.

Differences between GAAP and IFRS

Under IFRS:

- A lease is classified as a finance lease if it transfers substantially all the risks and rewards of ownership to the lessee. Whether the lease is a finance lease (a capital lease under U.S. GAAP) or an operating lease depends on the substance of the transaction. IFRS provide examples and indicators of situations that individually or together can result in classification as a finance lease. Thus, a lease is classified at its inception as a finance lease if, for example, (1) it provides for the transfer of ownership of the leased asset by the end of the lease term, (2) it contains a bargain purchase option, (3) the lease term is for the major part of the economic life of the leased asset, (4) the present value of the minimum lease payments is at least substantially all of the fair value of the leased asset at the inception of the lease, and (5) the leased asset is such that it can be used only by the lessee without major modification. Other factors also may indicate classification as a finance lease: (1) lessor losses from cancelation of the lease are borne by the lessee, (2) the lessee bears the risk of fluctuations in the fair value of the residual value, and (3) the lessee may renew the lease at a rent substantially below the market rent.
- If a sale and leaseback transaction results in an operating lease, and the transaction is at fair value, any profit or loss must be recognized immediately.

QUESTIONS

14.1 Capital Leases -- Lessee Accounting

1. Leases should be classified by the lessee as either operating leases or capital leases. Which of the following statements best characterizes operating leases?

- A. The benefits and risks of ownership are transferred from the lessor to the lessee.

- B. The lessee records an asset and a liability for the present value of the lease payments.

- C. Operating leases transfer ownership to the lessee, contain a bargain purchase option, are for more than 75% of the leased property's useful life, or have lease payments with a present value in excess of 90% of the value of the leased property.

- D. The lessor records lease revenue, asset depreciation, maintenance, etc., and the lessee records lease payments as rental expense.

Answer (D) is correct. *(Publisher, adapted)*
REQUIRED: The true statement about operating leases.
DISCUSSION: Operating leases are transactions in which lessees rent the right to use lessor assets without acquiring a substantial portion of the benefits and risks of ownership of those assets.
Answer (A) is incorrect. When the benefits and risks of ownership are transferred from the lessor to the lessee, the transaction is a capital lease. Answer (B) is incorrect. The lessee records an asset and a liability for the present value of the lease payments if the transaction is accounted for as a capital lease. However, this amount may not exceed the fair value of the leased property. Answer (C) is incorrect. Satisfaction of any one of four criteria requires the lease to be treated as a capital lease.

2. The present value of minimum lease payments should be used by the lessee in determining the amount of a lease liability under a lease classified by the lessee as a(n)

	Capital Lease	Operating Lease
A.	Yes	Yes
B.	Yes	No
C.	No	No
D.	No	Yes

Answer (B) is correct. *(CPA, adapted)*
REQUIRED: The lease for which the lessee's liability is based on the present value of the minimum lease payments.
DISCUSSION: The lessee must record a capital lease as an asset and a liability at an amount equal to the present value of the minimum lease payments. However, this amount may not exceed the fair value of the leased property. Under an operating lease, the lessee records no liability except for rental expense accrued at the end of an accounting period. Such accrual would be at settlement value rather than present value.
Answer (A) is incorrect. An operating lease does not result in a lease liability for the lessee. Answer (C) is incorrect. The lease liability under a capital lease is the present value of minimum lease payments. Answer (D) is incorrect. The lease liability under a capital lease is the present value of minimum lease payments. Also, an operating lease does not result in a lease liability.

3. On January 1, Year 1, Cutlip Co. signed a 7-year lease for equipment having a 10-year economic life. The present value of the monthly lease payments equals 80% of the equipment's fair value. The lease agreement provides for neither a transfer of title to Cutlip nor a bargain purchase option. In its Year 1 income statement, Cutlip should report

- A. Rent expense equal to the Year 1 lease payments.

- B. Rent expense equal to the Year 1 lease payments minus interest.

- C. Lease amortization equal to one-tenth of the equipment's fair value.

- D. Lease amortization equal to one-seventh of 80% of the equipment's fair value.

Answer (A) is correct. *(CPA, adapted)*
REQUIRED: The income statement effect of the lease.
DISCUSSION: A lease is either a capital lease or an operating lease. A lease must be classified as a capital lease by a lessee if, at its beginning, any one of four criteria is satisfied. Each of these criteria indicates that a substantial transfer of the benefits and risks of ownership has occurred. The following are the four criteria: (1) The lease provides for the transfer of ownership of the leased property, (2) the lease contains a bargain purchase option, (3) the lease term is 75% or more of the estimated economic life of the leased property, or (4) the present value of the minimum lease payments (excluding executory costs) is at least 90% of the fair value of the leased property to the lessor at the inception of the lease minus any related investment tax credit. (The last two criteria do not apply if the lease term begins within the last 25% of the total estimated economic life.) Because none of these criteria is satisfied, the lease must be treated as an operating lease. Under an operating lease, the lessee recognizes periodic rental expense but records neither an asset nor a liability (except for accrued rental expense at the end of a period).
Answer (B) is incorrect. Cutlip should not recognize interest on an operating lease. Answer (C) is incorrect. The lease is an operating lease. Moreover, operating leases do not require amortization using the interest method. Answer (D) is incorrect. Operating leases do not require amortization.

4. GAAP require that certain lease agreements be accounted for as purchases. The theoretical basis for this treatment is that a lease of this type

    A. Conveys substantially all of the benefits and risks incident to the ownership of property.

    B. Is an example of form over substance.

    C. Provides the use of the leased asset to the lessee for a limited period of time.

    D. Must be recorded in accordance with the concept of cause and effect.

Answer (A) is correct. *(CPA, adapted)*
    REQUIRED: The theoretical justification for capitalization of certain leases.
    DISCUSSION: A lease transferring substantially all of the benefits and risks of the ownership of property should be accounted for as the acquisition of an asset and the incurrence of a liability by the lessee. The lessor should account for the transaction as a sale or financing.
    Answer (B) is incorrect. A lease is not a purchase in form, although transfer of substantially all of the benefits and risks of ownership make it similar to a purchase in substance. Answer (C) is incorrect. Although a lease is a contract covering the use of property for a specified time period, other aspects of the lease justify the capitalization treatment. Answer (D) is incorrect. The concept of cause and effect is not relevant to accounting for leases.

5. Guilford Co. has leased property and accounted for the transaction as a capital lease. The amount recorded initially by Guilford as a liability should normally

    A. Exceed the total of the minimum lease payments.

    B. Exceed the present value of the minimum lease payments at the beginning of the lease.

    C. Equal the total of the minimum lease payments.

    D. Equal the present value of the minimum lease payments at the beginning of the lease.

Answer (D) is correct. *(CPA, adapted)*
    REQUIRED: The amount recorded initially by the lessee as a liability.
    DISCUSSION: The lessee must record a capital lease as an asset and a liability at the present value of the minimum lease payments during the lease term. The discount rate is the lower of the lessor's implicit interest rate (if known) or the lessee's incremental borrowing rate of interest. The present value cannot exceed the fair value of the leased property at the inception of the lease.
    Answer (A) is incorrect. Minimum lease payments are undiscounted amounts. Answer (B) is incorrect. The amount recorded initially should equal the present value of the minimum lease payments. Answer (C) is incorrect. The amount recorded initially should be a present value. Hence, it will be less than the total of the minimum lease payments.

6. A 12-year capital lease expiring on December 31 specifies equal minimum annual lease payments. Part of this payment represents interest and part represents a reduction in the net lease liability. The portion of the minimum lease payment in Year 10 applicable to the reduction of the net lease liability should be

    A. Less than in Year 8.

    B. More than in Year 8.

    C. The same as in Year 12.

    D. More than in Year 12.

Answer (B) is correct. *(CPA, adapted)*
    REQUIRED: The trend of the change, if any, in the periodic reduction of the net lease liability.
    DISCUSSION: A lease payment has two components: interest and the portion applied to the reduction of the lease obligation. The effective interest method requires that the carrying amount of the liability at the beginning of each interest period be multiplied by the appropriate interest rate to determine the interest. The difference between the minimum lease payment and the interest is the reduction in the carrying amount of the lease obligation. Because the carrying amount declines with each payment, interest in future years also declines, resulting in an increase in the amount applied to reduce the lease obligation. The Year 10 minimum lease payment therefore will result in a greater reduction in the liability than the Year 8 payment.
    Answer (A) is incorrect. More of the lease payment in Year 10 is applied to the lease liability than in Year 8. Answer (C) is incorrect. More of the lease payment in Year 12 is applied to the lease liability than in Year 10. Answer (D) is incorrect. The carrying amount of the lease liability declines with each payment, which reduces interest in future periods. As a result, more of the lease payment is applied to the lease liability in future years.

7. Quick Company's lease payments are made at the end of each period. Quick's liability for a capital lease will be reduced periodically by the

A. Minimum lease payment minus the portion of the minimum lease payment allocable to interest.

B. Minimum lease payment plus the amortization of the related asset.

C. Minimum lease payment minus the amortization of the related asset.

D. Minimum lease payment.

Answer (A) is correct. *(CPA, adapted)*
REQUIRED: The reduction of the liability for a capital lease after payments at the end of each period.
DISCUSSION: The lease liability consists of the present value of the minimum lease payments. The lease liability is reduced by the portion of the lease payment attributable to the lease liability. This amount is the lease payment minus the interest component of the payment. Thus, the liability is decreased by the minimum lease payment each period minus the portion of the payment allocable to interest.
Answer (B) is incorrect. The lease liability cannot be reduced by an amount greater than the minimum lease payment. Answer (C) is incorrect. The amortization of the related asset is based on the entity's depreciation policy. Answer (D) is incorrect. The portion of the minimum lease payment allocated to interest does not reduce the liability.

8. Cott, Inc., prepared an interest amortization table for a 5-year lease payable with a bargain purchase option of $2,000, exercisable at the end of the lease. At the end of the 5 years, the balance in the leases payable column of the spreadsheet was zero. Cott has asked Grant, CPA, to review the spreadsheet to determine the error. Only one error was made on the spreadsheet. Which of the following statements represents the best explanation for this error?

A. The beginning present value of the lease did not include the present value of the payment called for by the bargain purchase option.

B. Cott subtracted the annual interest amount from the lease payable balance instead of adding it.

C. The present value of the payment called for by the bargain purchase option was subtracted from the present value of the annual payments.

D. Cott discounted the annual payments as an ordinary annuity, when the payments actually occurred at the beginning of each period.

Answer (A) is correct. *(CPA, adapted)*
REQUIRED: The best explanation for an error in an interest amortization table for a lease payable with a bargain purchase option.
DISCUSSION: This lessee must record a capital lease as an asset and a liability at an amount equal to the present value of the minimum lease payments (minimum rental payments, excluding executory costs, and the payment called for by the bargain purchase option). The effect of including the present value of the payment called for by the bargain purchase option is that, at the end of the 5-year amortization period, the lease obligation should equal that payment.
Answer (B) is incorrect. The amount of the minimum lease payment that is greater than the periodic interest is subtracted from the lease payable balance. Answer (C) is incorrect. If the present value of the payment called for by the bargain purchase option were subtracted from the present value of the annual payments, the lease payable balance would be reduced to zero in fewer than 5 years, assuming the correct amounts were amortized each period, that is, amounts based on the correct (higher) balance of the lease obligation. At the lease's inception, the present value of the payment called for by the bargain purchase option should be added to the present value of the minimum payments. Answer (D) is incorrect. Treating the lease payments as an ordinary annuity instead of an annuity due would result in an amount different from zero at the end of 5 years.

9. On July 1, Year 1, Maryann Company leased equipment under a 5-year, noncancelable, nonrenewable agreement. The company paid a consultant a commission of $3,000 for arranging the lease. The lessee incurred $900 in installation and $600 in pre-operational testing costs. The equipment has an expected life of 7 years and a total expected life of 10 years. The lease does not contain a bargain purchase option, and, at the expiration of the lease, the equipment reverts to the lessor. The fair value of the equipment is $300,000, and the present value of the future minimum lease payments is $280,000. At the inception of the lease, the company should classify this lease as a(n)

A. Leveraged lease.

B. Operating lease.

C. Sale and leaseback.

D. Capital lease.

Answer (D) is correct. *(P. McBrayer)*
REQUIRED: The proper classification of a lease at its inception.
DISCUSSION: A lease must be classified as a capital lease by a lessee if, at its beginning, any one of four criteria is satisfied. Each of these criteria indicates that a substantial transfer of the benefits and risks of ownership has occurred. The following are the four criteria: (1) The lease provides for the transfer of ownership of the leased property, (2) the lease contains a bargain purchase option, (3) the lease term is 75% or more of the estimated economic life of the leased property, or (4) the present value of the minimum lease payments (excluding executory costs) is at least 90% of the excess of the fair value of the leased property to the lessor at the beginning of the lease over any related investment tax credit. (The last two criteria do not apply if the lease term begins within the last 25% of the total estimated economic life.) The first three criteria are not satisfied. The fourth criterion is satisfied, however, because the $280,000 present value of the future minimum lease payments is greater than 90% of the $300,000 fair value of the equipment. Hence, this lease should be classified as a capital lease.
Answer (A) is incorrect. A leveraged lease involves financing the transaction with substantial leverage (i.e., nonrecourse debt). Answer (B) is incorrect. The lease qualifies as a capital lease. Answer (C) is incorrect. No sale occurred.

10. Scott Co. entered into a 5-year capital lease requiring it to make equal annual payments. The reduction of the lease liability in Year 2 should equal

    A. The current liability shown for the lease at the end of Year 1.

    B. The current liability shown for the lease at the end of Year 2.

    C. The reduction of the lease obligation in Year 1.

    D. One-tenth of the original lease liability.

Answer (A) is correct. *(CPA, adapted)*
    REQUIRED: The reduction of a capital lease liability in the second year.
    DISCUSSION: At the beginning of a capital lease, a lessee should record a fixed asset and a lease liability equal to the present value of the minimum lease payments. However, this amount may not exceed the fair value of the leased property. In a classified balance sheet, the lease liability must be allocated between the current and noncurrent portions. The current portion at a balance sheet date is the reduction of the lease liability in the forthcoming year.
    Answer (B) is incorrect. The current liability at the end of Year 2 is equal to the reduction that will be recorded in Year 3. Answer (C) is incorrect. The reduction of the lease liability will increase in each subsequent year. Answer (D) is incorrect. The interest method is used to determine the reduction in the lease liability.

11. The terms of a 6-year, noncancelable lease include a guarantee by Lessee of Lessor's 7-year bank loan obtained to finance construction of the leased equipment, a termination penalty assuring that the lease will be renewed for 3 years following the expiration of the initial lease, and an option that allows Lessor to extend the lease for 3 years following the last renewal option exercised by Lessee. The lease term as defined by current authoritative literature is

    A. 6 years.

    B. 7 years.

    C. 9 years.

    D. 12 years.

Answer (D) is correct. *(Publisher, adapted)*
    REQUIRED: The number of years in the lease term.
    DISCUSSION: The term of a lease includes not only the fixed noncancelable lease term but also any periods (1) covered by bargain renewal options, (2) covered by ordinary renewal options preceding the date at which a bargain purchase option is exercisable, (3) covered by ordinary renewal options during which a guarantee by the lessee of the lessor's debt or a loan from the lessee to the lessor related to the leased property is expected to be in effect, (4) for which failure to renew the lease imposes a penalty on the lessee in an amount such that renewal appears to be reasonably assured, and (5) representing renewals or extensions of the lease at the lessor's option. In no case can the lease term extend beyond the date a bargain purchase option becomes exercisable.
    The termination penalty covers the 3 years immediately following the initial 6-year lease term. The renewal option by Lessor at the end of the first 9 years covers an additional 3 years, resulting in a lease term of 12 years. The 7-year period of the bank loan is included in the 6-year term and the first 3-year renewal period.
    Answer (A) is incorrect. Six years includes only the fixed term. Answer (B) is incorrect. Seven years is the debt term. Answer (C) is incorrect. The lease term includes both the period that would result in a penalty to the lessee and the period that is at the option of the lessor.

12. At its beginning, the lease term of Lease G is 65% of the estimated remaining economic life of the leased property. This lease contains a bargain purchase option. The lessee should record Lease G as

    A. Neither an asset nor a liability.

    B. An asset but not a liability.

    C. An asset and a liability.

    D. An expense.

Answer (C) is correct. *(CPA, adapted)*
    REQUIRED: The proper accounting for a lease containing a bargain purchase option.
    DISCUSSION: A lease must be classified as a capital lease by a lessee if, at its beginning, any one of four criteria is satisfied. Each of these criteria indicates that a substantial transfer of the benefits and risks of ownership has occurred. One test is whether the lease contains a bargain purchase option, which is a provision that permits the lessee to purchase the leased property at a price significantly lower than the expected fair value of the property at the date the option becomes exercisable. A capital lease must be recorded by the lessee as both an asset and a liability at an amount equal to the present value of the minimum lease payments, but this amount should not exceed the fair value at the beginning of the lease.
    Answer (A) is incorrect. The lease qualifies as a capital lease due to the bargain purchase option. A capital lease should be recorded as both an asset and a liability at the present value of minimum lease payments, but this amount should not exceed the fair value at the beginning of the lease. Answer (B) is incorrect. The lease must be recorded as an asset and a liability. Answer (D) is incorrect. If the lease were an operating lease, rent expense would be recorded periodically but not at the lease's beginning.

13. Zubenko Co. has leased equipment from Lessor Co. under two leases. Lease A does not contain a bargain purchase option, but the lease term is equal to 90% of the total estimated economic life of the leased property. Lease B does not transfer ownership of the property to the lessee by the end of the lease term, but the lease term is equal to 75% of the total estimated economic life of the leased property. How should Zubenko classify these leases?

	Lease A	Lease B
A.	Operating lease	Capital lease
B.	Operating lease	Operating lease
C.	Capital lease	Capital lease
D.	Capital lease	Operating lease

Answer (C) is correct. *(CPA, adapted)*
REQUIRED: The proper classification of leases.
DISCUSSION: For a lease to be classified as a capital lease by the lessee, any one of four criteria must be met. One of these criteria is that the lease term equal 75% or more of the estimated remaining economic life of the leased property, but this criterion does not apply if the lease term begins in the final 25% of the total estimated economic life. Both leases meet the 75% criterion and should be properly classified as capital leases.
Answer (A) is incorrect. Lease A's term is 90% of the estimated economic life. Answer (B) is incorrect. Both leases meet the 75% criterion for capitalization. Answer (D) is incorrect. Lease B's term is 75% of the estimated economic life.

14. On January 1, Year 1, Fitzpatrick Co. signed a contract to lease equipment to Hom Co. for 8 years. The leased equipment has an estimated remaining economic life of 10 years. Collectibility of the remaining payments is reasonably predictable, and no material uncertainties exist regarding unreimbursable costs to be incurred by the lessor. The present value of the 16 equal semiannual payments in advance equaled 85% of the equipment's fair value. The contract had no provision for the lessor to transfer legal ownership of the equipment. Should Fitzpatrick recognize rent or interest revenue in Year 3, and should the revenue recognized in Year 3 be the same or less than the revenue recognized in Year 2?

	Year 3 Revenues Recognized	Year 3 Amount Recognized Compared with Year 2
A.	Rent	The same
B.	Rent	Less
C.	Interest	The same
D.	Interest	Less

Answer (D) is correct. *(CPA, adapted)*
REQUIRED: The type of revenue recognized and the amount compared with the previous year.
DISCUSSION: A lease must be classified as a capital lease by a lessor if, at its beginning, any one of the four capitalization criteria is satisfied and if, in addition, collectibility of the remaining payments is reasonably predictable, and no material uncertainties exist regarding unreimbursable costs to be incurred by the lessor. One of the capitalization criteria is that the lease term be 75% or more of the estimated economic life of the leased property, but this criterion does not apply if the lease term begins in the final 25% of the total estimated economic life. Because the lease term is 80% (8 years ÷ 10 years) of the total estimated life of the equipment, the lease is a capital lease. Whether the lessor treats the capital lease as a direct-financing or sales-type lease, it will recognize interest revenue. The amount declines over the lease term because the effective-interest method is used. As the carrying amount decreases, the interest component (applicable interest rate × carrying amount) of the periodic lease payment also decreases.
Answer (A) is incorrect. The lessor should recognize interest revenue, which will decline over the lease term. Answer (B) is incorrect. The interest revenue should be recognized, not rent. Answer (C) is incorrect. The interest revenue will decrease as the liability decreases.

15. Wilson leased a new machine having a total and remaining expected useful life of 30 years from Tehi. Terms of the noncancelable, 25-year lease were that Wilson would gain title to the property upon payment of a sum equal to the fair value of the machine at the termination of the lease. Wilson accounted for the lease as a capital lease and recorded an asset and a liability in the financial records. The asset recorded under this lease should properly be amortized over

A. 5 years.

B. 22.5 years.

C. 25 years.

D. 30 years.

Answer (C) is correct. *(Publisher, adapted)*
REQUIRED: The proper amortization period for a lease with a purchase option.
DISCUSSION: When a lease transfers ownership of the property to the lessee at the end of the lease or contains a bargain purchase option, the lessee will own the asset at the end of the lease. Hence, such a lease is capitalized and amortized over the expected useful life of the leased property. Because the purchase price is not lower than the expected fair value of the machine at the termination of the lease, no bargain purchase option exists. If the lease meets either the 75% lease term test or the 90% fair value test, it will be accounted for as a capital lease and will be amortized over the lease term, assuming the lease term does not begin in the final 25% of the total estimated economic life. Because the lease term is more than 75% of the total expected useful life of the leased property, the lease should be amortized over the lease term (25 years).
Answer (A) is incorrect. Five years is the period of ownership after expiration of the lease. Answer (B) is incorrect. Twenty-two and a half years is 75% of the asset's useful life. However, the lessee's amortization period covers the entire period of the lease. Answer (D) is incorrect. Thirty years is the total asset life. A lease is amortized over the expected useful life of the leased property only when a bargain purchase option exists or ownership is transferred at the end of the lease.

16. Douglas Co. leased machinery with an economic useful life of 6 years. For tax purposes, the depreciable life is 7 years. The lease is for 5 years, and Douglas can purchase the machinery at fair market value at the end of the lease. What is the depreciable life of the leased machinery for financial reporting purposes?

A. 0 years.

B. 5 years.

C. 6 years.

D. 7 years.

Answer (B) is correct. *(CPA, adapted)*
REQUIRED: The depreciable life of the leased machinery for financial reporting purposes.
DISCUSSION: If a lessee capitalizes a lease because the lease term is at least 75% of the expected remaining life, or the present value of the minimum lease payments is at least 90% of the fair value at the inception of the lease, the asset should be amortized over the lease term. These capitalization criteria do not apply when the beginning of the lease term is within the last 25% of the total estimated economic life. Douglas Co.'s lease is for a period that exceeds 75% of the expected remaining life (5 years ÷ 6 years = 83 1/3%). Thus, the depreciable life is the lease term of 5 years.
Answer (A) is incorrect. Leased equipment is amortized over its depreciable life. Answer (C) is incorrect. Six years would be the depreciable life only if the lease contained a bargain purchase option. Answer (D) is incorrect. Seven years is the depreciable life for tax purposes, not financial reporting purposes.

17. On January 1, Year 1, Hall Co. entered into a 10-year lease for a manufacturing plant. The annual minimum lease payments are $100,000. In the notes to the December 31, Year 2, financial statements, what amounts of subsequent years' lease payments should be disclosed?

	Total of Annual Disclosed Amounts for Required Period	Aggregate Amount for the Period Thereafter
A.	$100,000	$0
B.	$300,000	$500,000
C.	$500,000	$300,000
D.	$500,000	$0

Answer (C) is correct. *(CPA, adapted)*
REQUIRED: The amounts of subsequent years' lease payments to be disclosed.
DISCUSSION: The future minimum lease payments as of the date of the latest balance sheet presented must be disclosed in total and for each of the 5 succeeding fiscal years. This disclosure is required whether the lease is classified as a capital lease or as an operating lease. Hence, the total liability is $800,000 ($100,000 × 8 years remaining), consisting of the future payments for the next 5 years in the amount of $500,000 ($100,000 × 5 years), and for the period thereafter in the amount of $300,000.
Answer (A) is incorrect. The total of the annual disclosures for the next 5 years is $500,000, and the remaining amount is $300,000. Answer (B) is incorrect. The required period for annual disclosure is 5 years. Answer (D) is incorrect. The remaining $300,000 for the lease's last 3 years must be disclosed as part of the aggregate amount.

18. On January 1, Year 1, Rice Co. acquired a land lease for a 21-year period with no option to renew. The lease required Rice to construct a building in lieu of rent. The building, completed on January 1, Year 2, at a cost of $840,000, will be depreciated using the straight-line method. At the end of the lease, the building's estimated fair value will be $420,000. What is the building's carrying amount in Rice's December 31, Year 2, balance sheet?

A. $798,000

B. $800,000

C. $819,000

D. $820,000

Answer (A) is correct. *(CPA, adapted)*
REQUIRED: The building's carrying amount after 2 years.
DISCUSSION: The lease is an operating lease because it involves land only and does not transfer ownership or contain a bargain purchase option. Moreover, the general improvements to the leased property should be capitalized as leasehold improvements and amortized in accordance with the straight-line method over the shorter of their expected useful life or the lease term. Given no renewal option, the amortization period is 20 years, the shorter of the expected useful life or the remaining lease term at the date of completion. The amortizable base is $840,000 even though the building will have a fair value of $420,000 at the end of the lease. The latter amount is not a salvage value because the building will become the lessor's property when the lease expires. Consequently, Year 2 straight-line amortization is $42,000 ($840,000 ÷ 20 years), and the year-end carrying amount is $798,000 ($840,000 – $42,000).
Answer (B) is incorrect. The amount of $800,000 assumes a 21-year remaining lease term at 1/1/Year 2. Answer (C) is incorrect. The amount of $819,000 assumes no amortization of an amount equal to the fair value at the end of the lease term. Answer (D) is incorrect. The amount of $820,000 assumes a 21-year remaining lease term at 1/1/Year 2 and no amortization of an amount equal to the fair value at the end of the lease term.

19. Terry Co. leases a building for its product showroom. The 10-year nonrenewable lease will expire on December 31, Year 10. In January Year 5, Terry redecorated its showroom and made leasehold improvements of $48,000. The estimated useful life of the improvements is 8 years. Terry uses the straight-line method of amortization. What amount of leasehold improvements, net of amortization, should Terry report in its June 30, Year 5, balance sheet?

- A. $45,600
- B. $45,000
- C. $44,000
- D. $43,200

Answer (C) is correct. *(CPA, adapted)*
REQUIRED: The net amount of leasehold improvements reported in the balance sheet.
DISCUSSION: General improvements to leased property should be capitalized as leasehold improvements and amortized in accordance with the straight-line method over the shorter of their expected useful life or the lease term. Because the remaining lease term is less than the estimated life of the improvements, the cost should be amortized equally over 6 years. On June 30, Year 5, $44,000 {$48,000 − [($48,000 ÷ 6 years) × .5 year]} should be reported for net leasehold improvements.
Answer (A) is incorrect. The amount of $45,600 assumes the amortization period is 10 years. Answer (B) is incorrect. The amount of $45,000 assumes the amortization period is 8 years. Answer (D) is incorrect. The amount of $43,200 assumes that 1 year's amortization has been recorded and that the amortization period is 10 years.

20. Schwass Corporation has leased manufacturing equipment from Riley Corporation in a transaction that is to be accounted for as a capital lease. Schwass has guaranteed Riley a residual value for the equipment. How should this guarantee be reflected in the financial statements of Schwass?

- A. The full amount of the residual guarantee should be capitalized as part of the cost of the equipment.
- B. The present value of the residual guarantee should be capitalized as part of the cost of the equipment.
- C. The guarantee will not be reflected in the body of the financial statements but should be disclosed in the notes.
- D. The guarantee should not be reflected in the financial statements.

Answer (B) is correct. *(CIA, adapted)*
REQUIRED: The effect of a guaranteed residual value on lessee accounting for a capital lease.
DISCUSSION: For lessee accounting, a guaranteed residual value is defined as the portion of the expected salvage value that is guaranteed by the lessee. This portion of the expected salvage value is included with the periodic rental payments in the definition of minimum lease payments. Because the lessee should record an asset and an obligation in an amount equal to the lower of the fair value of the leased property or the present value of the minimum lease payments, the guaranteed residual value is included in the capitalized cost of the equipment at an amount equal to its present value if that amount does not exceed fair value.
Answer (A) is incorrect. The present value should be capitalized as part of the cost of the equipment. Answer (C) is incorrect. The residual guarantee should be reflected in the body of the financial statements. Answer (D) is incorrect. The residual guarantee is included with the periodic rental payments in the definition of minimum lease payments.

21. On April 1, the first day of its fiscal year, Jaymarr Co. signed a 5-year lease for a major piece of equipment. Terms of the lease require a fixed annual payment of $12,000 plus $100 for each 1% of a specific bank's prime interest rate. If the prime interest rate is 14% on April 1, is expected to rise to 16% by July 1, and is expected to average 10% for the life of the lease, the total minimum lease payments for the life of the lease should be

- A. $60,000
- B. $65,000
- C. $67,000
- D. $68,000

Answer (C) is correct. *(Publisher, adapted)*
REQUIRED: The total minimum lease payments over the life of the lease.
DISCUSSION: Contingent rentals are excluded from minimum lease payments. Contingent rentals are the changes in lease payments resulting from changes occurring subsequent to the inception of the lease. But lease payments that are based on a factor that exists and is measurable at the inception of the lease are not contingent rentals. Thus, total minimum lease payments for this piece of equipment should include the five annual payments of $12,000 per year ($60,000) plus $7,000, which is the sum of the five annual $1,400 payments. This amount is based on the prime interest rate (14%) existing at the inception of the lease ($100 × 14% = $1,400). As the prime rate changes during the lease term, the corresponding increase or decrease of $100 for each 1% of the prime rate should be charged or credited to income as appropriate. Minimum lease payments, however, should not be adjusted.
Answer (A) is incorrect. The amount of $60,000 excludes the $7,000 ($100 × 14% × 5 years) measurable at the inception of the lease. Answer (B) is incorrect. The amount of $65,000 is based on the average expected prime rate of 10%. Answer (D) is incorrect. The amount of $68,000 is based on the 16% prime rate in July.

22. Which one of the following items is not part of the minimum lease payments recorded by the lessee?

A. The minimum rental payments called for by the lease.

B. A guarantee by the lessee of the lessor's debt.

C. The specified maximum amount of any deficiency in the lessor's realization of the residual value that the lessee is required to make up.

D. Any payment the lessee must make at the end of the lease term either to purchase the leased property or to satisfy a penalty for failure to renew the lease.

Answer (B) is correct. *(CMA, adapted)*
REQUIRED: The item that is not a component of minimum lease payments.
DISCUSSION: The lease term includes not only the fixed, noncancelable term of the lease but also those years for which there is reasonable assurance that the lease will remain in effect. A guarantee by the lessee of the lessor's debt related to the leased property provides such assurance and thus may affect the term over which the minimum lease payments are calculated. Otherwise, such a guarantee does not affect the computation of minimum lease payments.
Answer (A) is incorrect. The minimum rental payments are included by the lessee in the computation of the minimum lease payments for a capital lease. Answer (C) is incorrect. Any guaranteed residual value is included by the lessee in the computation of the minimum lease payments for a capital lease. Answer (D) is incorrect. A bargain purchase option or nonrenewal penalty is included by the lessee in the computation of the minimum lease payments for a capital lease.

23. On October 1, the first day of its fiscal year, Heather Co., a retail outlet, entered into a lease of a building. Terms of the 5-year, noncancelable lease require monthly payments of $600 plus 1% of sales. Sales have been averaging $15,000 per month and are expected to remain constant or increase. What monthly amount(s) should be included in minimum lease payments?

A. Only the $150 payment based on expected sales.

B. Only the $600 monthly payment.

C. Both the $150 and $600 payments.

D. Neither the $150 nor $600 payments.

Answer (B) is correct. *(Publisher, adapted)*
REQUIRED: The amount(s) to be included in minimum lease payments on a lease containing a contingent payment term.
DISCUSSION: Contingent rentals are lease payments based on a factor that does not exist or is not measurable at the inception of the lease. Future sales do not exist at the inception of the lease and meet the definition of a contingent rental. Contingent rentals are excluded from minimum lease payments. Because the $150 based on expected future sales is a contingent rental, only the $600 periodic payment is included in minimum lease payments.
Answer (A) is incorrect. The minimum lease payment includes only those payments that are measurable at the inception of the lease. Answer (C) is incorrect. The $150 payment is not measurable at the inception of the lease. Answer (D) is incorrect. The $600 payment is included in minimum lease payments because it is measurable.

24. Jennifer Co. intends to lease a machine from Jan Corp. Jennifer's incremental borrowing rate is 14%. The prime rate of interest is 8%. Jan's implicit rate in the lease is 10%, which is known to Jennifer. Jennifer computes the present value of the minimum lease payments using which rate?

A. 8%

B. 10%

C. 12%

D. 14%

Answer (B) is correct. *(CPA, adapted)*
REQUIRED: The discount rate used by the lessee in determining the present value of minimum lease payments.
DISCUSSION: A lessee should compute the present value of the minimum lease payments using its incremental borrowing rate unless the lessee knows the lessor's implicit rate, and the implicit rate is less than the lessee's incremental borrowing rate. Because both conditions are met, Jennifer must use the 10% implicit rate. The effect of using the lower rate is to increase the probability that the lessee will capitalize the lease.
Answer (A) is incorrect. Eight percent is the prime rate. Answer (C) is incorrect. Twelve percent is the average of the implicit and incremental rates. Answer (D) is incorrect. Fourteen percent is the incremental rate, which is higher.

25. On January 1, Year 1, Hombob Co. as lessee signed a 5-year noncancelable equipment lease with annual payments of $100,000 beginning December 31, Year 1. Hombob treated this transaction as a capital lease. The five lease payments have a present value of $379,000 at January 1, Year 1, based on interest of 10%. What amount should Hombob report as interest for the year ended December 31, Year 1?

A. $37,900

B. $27,900

C. $24,200

D. $0

Answer (A) is correct. *(CPA, adapted)*
REQUIRED: The interest to be recognized in the first year of a capital lease.
DISCUSSION: The lease liability at the beginning of the lease is $379,000. Under the effective-interest method, the lease liability balance (the carrying amount) at the beginning of each year should be multiplied by the appropriate interest rate to determine the interest for that year. Accordingly, the interest for the first year is $37,900 ($379,000 × 10%).
Answer (B) is incorrect. The amount of $27,900 assumes the initial payment was made immediately. Answer (C) is incorrect. The amount of $24,200 is one-fifth of the total interest ($500,000 – $379,000). Answer (D) is incorrect. Interest must be accrued.

26. On December 29, Year 1, Strickland Corp. signed a 7-year capital lease for an airplane to transport its professional volleyball team around the country. The airplane's fair value was $841,500. Strickland made the first annual lease payment of $153,000 on December 31, Year 1. Strickland's incremental borrowing rate was 12%, and the interest rate implicit in the lease, which was known by Strickland, was 9%. The following are the rounded present value factors for an annuity due:

9% for 7 years	5.5
12% for 7 years	5.1

What amount should Strickland report as capital lease liability in its December 31, Year 1, balance sheet?

- A. $841,500
- B. $780,300
- C. $688,500
- D. $627,300

Answer (C) is correct. *(CPA, adapted)*
REQUIRED: The amount that should be reported as a capital lease liability in the balance sheet.
DISCUSSION: The capital lease liability is recorded at the present value of the minimum lease payments. The lease payments due should be discounted at the lesser of the borrower's incremental borrowing rate or the rate implicit in the lease, if known by the borrower. In this situation, the lease should be recorded at the present value of minimum lease payments discounted at the implicit rate of 9% because this rate is known by the lessee and is lower than the incremental rate. The amount is $841,500 ($153,000 × 5.5), which must then be reduced by the payment made at the inception of the lease of $153,000. The capital lease liability thus should be $688,500 ($841,500 – $153,000) in the December 31, Year 1, balance sheet.
Answer (A) is incorrect. The liability must be reduced by the payment made at the inception of the lease. Answer (B) is incorrect. The present value of minimum lease payments should be discounted at 9% instead of 12%. Also, the liability should be reduced by the payment made at the beginning of the lease. Answer (D) is incorrect. The lease liability should be recorded at 9% instead of 12%.

27. On January 1, Jessie Co. (lessee) entered into a 5-year lease for equipment. Jessie accounted for the acquisition as a capital lease for $120,000, which includes a $5,000 bargain purchase option. At the end of the lease, Jessie expects to exercise the bargain purchase option. Jessie estimates that the equipment's fair value will be $10,000 at the end of its 8-year life. Jessie regularly uses straight-line depreciation on similar equipment. For the year ended December 31, what amount should Jessie recognize as amortization of the asset recorded under the capital lease?

- A. $13,750
- B. $15,000
- C. $23,000
- D. $24,000

Answer (A) is correct. *(CPA, adapted)*
REQUIRED: The amortization of the asset recorded under a lease.
DISCUSSION: When a lease is capitalized because title passes to the lessee at the end of the lease term or because the lease contains a bargain purchase option, the amortization period is the estimated economic life of the underlying property. The asset recorded under the capital lease should be amortized in accordance with the lessee's normal depreciation policy for owned assets. Jessie regularly uses the straight-line method. Hence, amortization is $13,750 [($120,000 asset recorded under the lease – $10,000 salvage value) ÷ 8-year economic life].
Answer (B) is incorrect. The amount of $15,000 does not consider salvage value. Answer (C) is incorrect. The amount of $23,000 subtracts the bargain purchase option from the present value of the minimum lease payments, uses a 5-year life, and does not consider salvage value. Answer (D) is incorrect. The amount of $24,000 uses a 5-year life and does not consider salvage value.

28. Law Co. leased a machine from Order Co. The lease qualifies as a capital lease and requires 10 annual payments of $10,000 beginning immediately. The lease specifies an interest rate of 12% and a purchase option of $10,000 at the end of the 10th year, even though the machine's estimated value on that date is $20,000. Law's incremental borrowing rate is 14%.

The present value of an annuity due of 1 at:
        12% for 10 years is 6.328
        14% for 10 years is 5.946

The present value of 1 at:
        12% for 10 years is .322
        14% for 10 years is .270

What amount should Law record as lease liability at the beginning of the lease term?

- A. $62,160
- B. $64,860
- C. $66,500
- D. $69,720

Answer (C) is correct. *(CPA, adapted)*
REQUIRED: The amount that should be reported as a capital lease liability.
DISCUSSION: The capital lease liability should be recorded at the present value of the minimum lease payments. The lease liability should be calculated using the lesser of the implicit interest rate, if known to the lessee, or the incremental borrowing rate of the lessee. The minimum lease payments should include the present value of the payment required by the bargain purchase option of $10,000 at 12% and the present value of an annuity due of $10,000 at 12% for 10 years. Thus, the lease liability is equal to $66,500 [($10,000 × 6.328) + ($10,000 × .322)].
Answer (A) is incorrect. The present value of the payment required by the bargain purchase option and the annual lease payments should be discounted at 12% instead of 14%. Answer (B) is incorrect. The amount of the bargain purchase option is $10,000, not the estimated value at that date. Also, the discount rate for both the option amount and the annual payments should be 12% instead of 14%. Answer (D) is incorrect. The payment required by the bargain purchase option should be included in the present value of minimum lease payments, not the estimated value of the asset at the end of the lease.

29. Collis Corporation leased equipment under a 4-year, noncancelable lease properly classified as a capital lease. The lease does not transfer ownership or contain a bargain purchase option. The equipment had an estimated economic life of 5 years and an estimated salvage value of $20,000. Terms of the lease included a guaranteed residual value of $50,000. If Collis initially recorded an asset under the lease of $240,000, the amount of amortization that should be charged each year under the lessee's usual depreciation method (straight-line) is

   A. $55,000

   B. $47,500

   C. $44,000

   D. $38,000

Answer (B) is correct. *(H.F. Bush)*
   REQUIRED: The amount of amortization to be recorded on a capital lease.
   DISCUSSION: The lease does not transfer ownership or contain a bargain purchase option. Accordingly, the period of amortization should be the lease term. Given that the lessee's normal depreciation policy is to apply the straight-line method, the amortization base for the asset recorded under this capital lease is equal to the $240,000 initially recorded value, minus the $50,000 guaranteed residual value, allocated equally over the 4-year lease term. Consequently, annual amortization is $47,500 [($240,000 – $50,000) ÷ 4 years].
   Answer (A) is incorrect. The guaranteed residual value, not the estimated salvage value, must be subtracted from the initially recorded value. Answer (C) is incorrect. The guaranteed residual value, not the estimated salvage value, must be subtracted from the initially recorded value, and the term of the lease, not the estimated economic life, is used as the denominator in the calculation. Answer (D) is incorrect. The amount of $38,000 results from using the estimated economic life as the denominator in the calculation.

30. Allen Co. leased equipment for its entire 9-year useful life, agreeing to pay $50,000 at the start of the lease term on December 31, Year 1, and $50,000 annually on each December 31 for the next 8 years. The present value on December 31, Year 1, of the nine lease payments over the lease term, using the rate implicit in the lease was $316,500. Allen knows that this rate is 10%. The December 31, Year 1, present value of the lease payments using Allen's incremental borrowing rate of 12% was $298,500. Allen made a timely second lease payment. What amount should Allen report as capital lease liability in its December 31, Year 2, balance sheet?

   A. $350,000

   B. $243,150

   C. $228,320

   D. $0

Answer (B) is correct. *(CPA, adapted)*
   REQUIRED: The amount to be reported as a capital lease liability.
   DISCUSSION: The lease is a capital lease because the lease term is at least 75% of the estimated economic life of the property, and the beginning of the lease term does not fall within the last 25% of the total estimated economic life. The lessee must use the lower of the lessor's implicit interest rate (if known) or the lessee's incremental borrowing rate of interest. Allen knows the implicit rate; therefore, the present value of the minimum lease payments of this capital lease is $316,500, the amount based on the lessor's implicit rate. After the initial payment of $50,000, which contains no interest component, is deducted, the carrying amount during Year 2 is $266,500. Accordingly, the interest component of the next payment is $26,650 ($266,500 × 10% implicit rate), and the capital lease liability on December 31, Year 2, is $243,150 [$266,500 – ($50,000 – $26,650)].
   Answer (A) is incorrect. The amount of $350,000 is the sum of the seven lease payments. Answer (C) is incorrect. The amount of $228,320 is based on a 12% rate. Answer (D) is incorrect. The amount of $0 is based on the assumption that the lease is an operating lease.

31. On December 30, Year 1, Riley Corp. leased equipment under a capital lease. Annual lease payments of $20,000 are due December 31 for 10 years. The equipment's useful life is 10 years, and the interest rate implicit in the lease is 10%. The capital lease obligation was recorded on December 30, Year 1, at $135,000, and the first lease payment was made on that date. What amount should Riley include in current liabilities for this capital lease in its December 31, Year 1, balance sheet?

   A. $6,500

   B. $8,500

   C. $11,500

   D. $20,000

Answer (B) is correct. *(CPA, adapted)*
   REQUIRED: The current liability for the capital lease.
   DISCUSSION: At the beginning of a capital lease, a lessee should record a fixed asset and a lease obligation equal to the present value of the minimum lease payments. In a classified balance sheet, the lease liability must be allocated between the current and noncurrent portions. The current portion at a balance sheet date is the reduction of the lease liability in the forthcoming year. A periodic lease payment has two components: interest and the reduction of the lease obligation. Under the effective interest method, the appropriate interest rate is applied to the carrying amount of the lease obligation at the beginning of the interest period to calculate interest. The portion of the minimum lease payment greater than the amount of interest is the reduction of the liability in the forthcoming year. At the beginning of Year 2, the lease obligation is $115,000 ($135,000 – $20,000 initial payment). Thus, Year 1 interest will be $11,500 ($115,000 × 10%), and the reduction of the liability when the next payment is made will be $8,500 ($20,000 – $11,500 interest).
   Answer (A) is incorrect. The amount of $6,500 results from assuming that the carrying amount of the lease in Year 1 will be $135,000. Answer (C) is incorrect. The amount of $11,500 is the interest. Answer (D) is incorrect. The amount of $20,000 is the full payment due.

32. Bodhran Corp. entered into a 9-year capital lease on a warehouse on December 31, Year 1. The land and building are capitalized as a single unit. Lease payments of $52,000, which include real estate taxes of $2,000, are due annually, beginning on December 31, Year 2, and every December 31 thereafter. Bodhran does not know the interest rate implicit in the lease; Bodhran's incremental borrowing rate is 9%. The rounded present value of an ordinary annuity for 9 years at 9% is 5.6. What amount should Bodhran report as capitalized lease liability at December 31, Year 1?

A. $280,000

B. $291,200

C. $450,000

D. $468,000

Answer (A) is correct. *(CPA, adapted)*
REQUIRED: The amount reported as capitalized lease liability.
DISCUSSION: For a capital lease, the present value of the minimum lease payments should be recorded at the beginning date. The minimum lease payments exclude executory costs, such as insurance, maintenance, and taxes. The capitalized lease liability is therefore $280,000 [($52,000 – $2,000) × 5.6].
Answer (B) is incorrect. The amount of $291,200 is based on a $52,000 annual payment. Answer (C) is incorrect. This figure is the total undiscounted amount of the minimum lease payments. Answer (D) is incorrect. This figure is the total undiscounted amount of the minimum lease payments plus real estate taxes.

14.2 Capital Leases -- Lessor Accounting

33. In a lease that is recorded as a sales-type lease by the lessor, interest income

A. Should be recognized in full as income at the lease's inception.

B. Should be recognized over the period of the lease using the straight-line method.

C. Should be recognized over the period of the lease using the effective-interest method.

D. Does not arise.

Answer (C) is correct. *(CPA, adapted)*
REQUIRED: The proper accounting for interest income in a sales-type lease.
DISCUSSION: The difference between the gross investment in the lease and the sum of the present values of the components of the gross investment must be recorded as unearned income. This unearned income is amortized to income over the lease term using the effective-interest method, which produces a constant periodic rate of return on the net investment.
Answer (A) is incorrect. The interest income should be recognized over the period of the lease using the effective-interest method. Answer (B) is incorrect. The straight-line method is appropriate only if its results are not materially different from those of the effective-interest method. Answer (D) is incorrect. The difference between the gross investment in the lease and the sum of the present values of the components of the gross investment is recognized over the lease term as interest income.

34. What is the difference between a direct financing lease and a sales-type lease?

A. Lessees usually amortize direct financing leases over the term of the lease and sales-type leases over the useful life of the leased asset.

B. The difference between the gross investment and the cost of the leased property to the lessor is unearned income for direct financing leases, and is part unearned income and part profit or loss for sales-type leases.

C. The lease payments receivable on the books of a lessor are recorded at their present value for sales-type leases and at their gross value for direct financing leases.

D. The lessor records the present value of the residual value of the leased property for direct financing leases, but records the undiscounted (gross) residual value for sales-type leases.

Answer (B) is correct. *(Publisher, adapted)*
REQUIRED: The difference between direct financing leases and sales-type leases.
DISCUSSION: Both direct financing and sales-type leases are accounted for by the lessee as capital leases. The difference between the two arises only for lessor accounting. In a direct financing lease, the difference between the gross investment (minimum lease payments + unguaranteed residual value) and its cost or carrying amount is recorded as unearned income. No manufacturer's or dealer's profit or loss is recognized. In a sales-type lease, the lessor records manufacturer's or dealer's profit or loss, and unearned income equals the gross investment minus the sum of the present values of its components. The cost or carrying amount, plus initial direct costs, minus the present value of the unguaranteed residual value, is debited to income when the sales price (present value of the minimum lease payments) is recognized. The difference between a direct financing and a sales-type lease is that the cost used in accounting for a direct-financing lease is ordinarily the fair value. But the cost for a sales-type lease differs from the fair value.
Answer (A) is incorrect. Lessees use the same amortization methods for both kinds of leases. Answer (C) is incorrect. The receivable for the lease payments is recorded at gross on the books of the lessor for both the sales-type and direct financing leases. Answer (D) is incorrect. The undiscounted (gross) residual value is recorded by the lessor for both direct financing and sales-type leases. It is included as part of the gross investment, i.e., in lease payments receivable.

35. What are the components of the lease receivable for a lessor involved in a direct-financing lease?

- A. The minimum lease payments plus any executory costs.
- B. The minimum lease payments plus residual value.
- C. The minimum lease payments less residual value.
- D. The minimum lease payments less initial direct costs.

Answer (B) is correct. *(CPA, adapted)*
REQUIRED: The components of the lease receivable for a lessor involved in a direct-financing lease.
DISCUSSION: The lessor may use the net method or the gross method of accounting for a direct-financing lease. If the lessor elects the net method, it debits the receivable at the beginning of the lease for the sum of the present values of (1) the minimum lease payments (including any guaranteed residual value) and (2) any unguaranteed residual value. The credit is to the leased asset. No sales revenue is recognized because the lease is a direct-financing, not a sales-type, lease. If the lessor elects the gross method, the lease receivable equals the sum of the undiscounted lease payments, and an additional credit is made to unearned income.
Answer (A) is incorrect. If the lessor is responsible for executory costs of the lease (e.g., taxes, maintenance, and insurance), they are excluded from the minimum lease payments. They are not payments on the obligation. Answer (C) is incorrect. The minimum lease payments include any guaranteed residual value, and any unguaranteed residual value is added to the minimum lease payments. Answer (D) is incorrect. Initial direct costs are certain lessor's costs to originate a lease. They are amortized over the lease term using the interest method to produce a constant rate of return on the net investment [gross investment (minimum lease payments – unguaranteed residual value) + unamortized direct costs – unearned income].

36. Able Co. leased equipment to Baker under a noncancelable lease with a transfer of title. Will Able record depreciation expense on the leased asset and interest revenue related to the lease?

	Depreciation expense	Interest revenue
A.	Yes	Yes
B.	Yes	No
C.	No	No
D.	No	Yes

Answer (D) is correct. *(CPA, adapted)*
REQUIRED: The accounting by a lessor under a noncancelable lease with a transfer of title.
DISCUSSION: The lease provides for the transfer of ownership. Accordingly, the lease is recognized as a capital lease by the lessor and lessee. For capital leases, depreciation is recorded by the lessee, not the lessor, because substantially all of the benefits and risks of ownership have been transferred. Furthermore, the lessor records interest revenue (income) under a capital lease whether it is a sales-type lease or a direct-financing lease.
Answer (A) is incorrect. The lessor does not recognize depreciation expense. Answer (B) is incorrect. The lessor does not recognize depreciation expense but does recognize interest revenue. Answer (C) is incorrect. The lessor recognizes interest revenue.

37. Initial direct costs incurred by the lessor under a sales-type lease should be

- A. Deferred and allocated over the economic life of the leased property.
- B. Expensed in the period incurred.
- C. Deferred and allocated over the term of the lease in proportion to the recognition of rental income.
- D. Added to the gross investment in the lease and amortized over the term of the lease as a yield adjustment.

Answer (B) is correct. *(CMA, adapted)*
REQUIRED: The accounting for initial direct costs in a sales-type lease.
DISCUSSION: Initial direct costs have two components: (1) the lessor's external costs to originate a lease incurred in dealings with independent third parties and (2) the internal costs directly related to specified activities performed by the lessor for that lease. In a sales-type lease, the cost, or carrying amount if different, plus any initial direct costs, minus the present value of any unguaranteed residual value, is charged against income in the same period that the sales price (present value of the minimum lease payments) is credited to income. The result is the recognition of a net profit or loss on the sales-type lease.
Answer (A) is incorrect. Initial direct costs are considered an expense in the period of sale. Answer (C) is incorrect. The initial direct costs of an operating lease are deferred and allocated over the term of the lease in proportion to the recognition of rental income. Answer (D) is incorrect. The initial direct costs of a direct financing lease are added to the gross investment in the lease and amortized over the term of the lease as a yield adjustment.

38. For a direct financing lease, the gross investment (lease payments receivable) recorded by the lessor is equal to the

A. Present value of the minimum lease payments minus the unguaranteed residual value accruing to the lessor at the end of the lease term.

B. Lower of 90% of the present value of the minimum lease payments or the fair value of the leased property.

C. Difference between the fair value of the leased property and the unearned interest income.

D. Minimum lease payments plus the unguaranteed residual value accruing to the lessor at the end of the lease term.

Answer (D) is correct. *(CMA, adapted)*
REQUIRED: The amount to be recorded as the gross investment in a direct financing lease.
DISCUSSION: The lessor should record as the gross investment in a direct financing lease the amount of the minimum lease payments plus any unguaranteed residual value. For a lessee, minimum lease payments include the minimum rental payments (excluding executory costs such as insurance, maintenance, and taxes) required during the lease term and the payment called for by a bargain purchase option. If no such option exists, the lessee's minimum lease payments equal the sum of the minimum rental payments, the amount of residual value guaranteed by the lessee, and any nonrenewal penalty imposed. The minimum lease payments calculated by the lessor are the same as those for the lessee except that they include any residual value or rental payments beyond the lease term guaranteed by a financially capable third party unrelated to the lessor or the lessee. The net investment in the lease is equal to the gross investment, plus any unamortized initial direct costs, minus the unearned income.
Answer (A) is incorrect. The unguaranteed residual value should be added, and the minimum lease payments should not be discounted. Answer (B) is incorrect. One of the capitalization criteria, not the gross investment, includes the following elements: (1) the present value of the minimum lease payments and (2) 90% of the fair value of the leased property. Answer (C) is incorrect. The gross investment in a direct financing lease equals the minimum lease payments plus any unguaranteed residual value.

39. Fraser Co. has agreed to lease equipment under a direct financing lease. As lessor, Fraser has incurred a material amount of initial direct costs. What is the proper accounting for these initial direct costs by Fraser?

A. Initial direct costs must be offset against unearned income so as to produce a constant periodic rate of return on the lease.

B. Initial direct costs must be capitalized as part of the net investment in the lease.

C. Initial direct costs must be capitalized as a deferred charge and written off at the end of the lease term.

D. Initial direct costs must be written off immediately.

Answer (B) is correct. *(T.J. Phillips, Jr.)*
REQUIRED: The proper accounting for initial direct costs in a direct financing lease.
DISCUSSION: The initial direct costs of a direct financing lease must be amortized to income over the lease term so as to produce a constant periodic rate of return on the net investment in the lease. The net investment is the gross investment (minimum lease payments + any unguaranteed residual value), plus any unamortized initial direct costs, minus the unearned income. The unearned income equals the gross investment minus the cost or carrying amount, if different, of the leased property.
Answer (A) is incorrect. Offsetting initial direct costs against unearned income is not permitted. Answer (C) is incorrect. The initial direct costs should be capitalized as part of the net investment in the lease. Answer (D) is incorrect. The initial direct costs should be amortized to income over the lease term.

40. Mark Co. leases computer equipment to customers under direct financing leases. The equipment has no residual value at the end of the lease, and the leases do not contain bargain purchase options. Mark wishes to earn 8% interest on a 5-year lease of equipment with a fair value of $323,400. The present value of an annuity due of $1 at 8% for 5 years is 4.312. What is the total amount of interest income that Mark will earn over the life of the lease?

A. $51,600

B. $75,000

C. $129,360

D. $164,825

Answer (A) is correct. *(CPA, adapted)*
REQUIRED: The interest income earned over the life of a lease.
DISCUSSION: To earn 8% interest over the lease term, the annual payment must be $75,000 ($323,400 fair value at the inception of the lease ÷ 4.312 annuity factor). Given no residual value and no bargain purchase option, total lease payments will be $375,000 ($75,000 payment × 5 years). Because no profit is recognized on a direct financing lease, the fair value is presumably the carrying amount. The difference between the gross lease payments to be received and their present value is the total interest of $51,600 ($375,000 − $323,400).
Answer (B) is incorrect. The amount of $75,000 is the annual lease payment. Answer (C) is incorrect. Interest revenue equals the total lease payments of $375,000 minus the fair value of $323,400. Answer (D) is incorrect. The amount of $164,825 results from using an interest factor of 3.312.

Questions 41 and 42 are based on the following information. Odom Company leased a machine to Rapp Company on January 1. The lease was for a 10-year period, which approximated the useful life of the machine. Odom purchased the machine for $80,000 and expects to earn a 10% return on its investment, based upon an annual rental of $11,836 payable in advance each January 1. The lease was a direct financing lease.

41. What should be the interest entry in Odom's books on December 31 of the first year of the lease?

| A. Cash | $3,836 | |
| Interest income | | $3,836 |

| B. Unearned income | $6,816 | |
| Income | | $6,816 |

| C. Cash | $8,000 | |
| Interest income | | $8,000 |

D. Cash	$11,836	
Interest income		$8,000
Equipment		3,836

Answer (B) is correct. *(CPA, adapted)*
REQUIRED: The interest income from a direct financing lease during the first year of the lease.
DISCUSSION: The annual $11,836 lease payment to Odom is payable at the beginning of each period. The first payment received from Rapp reduces Odom's lease investment by the full amount of the payment, leaving a carrying amount of $68,164 ($80,000 – $11,836) at the beginning of the first year. Because the appropriate rate of return to Odom on this lease investment is 10%, interest earned in the first year is $6,816 ($68,164 × 10%). The difference between the gross investment and the lessor's cost or carrying amount, if different, of the leased property is reflected in the lessor's books as unearned income. Hence, the journal entry debit recognizing first-year income is to unearned income.
Answer (A) is incorrect. The amount of $3,836 is equal to the $11,836 rental payment minus $8,000 ($80,000 cost × 10%) and cash is received January 1. Answer (C) is incorrect. The amount of $8,000 is equal to the $80,000 cost unadjusted by the $11,836 initial payment times 10%. Moreover, the annual rental payment (cash) is received on January 1. Answer (D) is incorrect. Equipment is not affected by the rental payment.

42. What is the initial journal entry by Odom Company to record the lease on January 1?

A. Leased property	$ 80,000	
Lease payment		
obligation		$68,164
Cash		11,836

B. Lease payments		
receivable	$ 80,000	
Leased property		$80,000

C. Lease payments		
receivable	$ 68,164	
Cash	11,836	
Leased property		$80,000

D. Cash	$ 11,836	
Lease payments		
receivable	106,524	
Leased property		$80,000
Unearned income		38,360

Answer (D) is correct. *(Publisher, adapted)*
REQUIRED: The lessor's journal entry to record a direct financing lease.
DISCUSSION: For a direct financing lease, the lessor should record the total amount of the minimum lease payments, net of executory costs (10 × $11,836 = $118,360), plus any unguaranteed residual value ($0) as the gross investment in the lease (lease payments receivable). In this case, cash also must be debited and lease payments receivable credited for the first payment ($11,836) because the payments are made at the beginning of each year. The leased property should be credited at its cost ($80,000), with the difference between the initial gross investment and cost ($118,360 – $80,000 = $38,360) recorded as unearned income.
Answer (A) is incorrect. The lessee records a capital lease as an asset and an obligation. Answer (B) is incorrect. The lease payments receivable are recorded at their gross amount rather than at their present value. Furthermore, the initial payment and unearned income must be recognized. Answer (C) is incorrect. The lease receivable should equal the gross amount of 9 more payments, and unearned income must be recognized.

43. The excess of the fair value of leased property at the inception of the lease over its cost or carrying amount should be classified by the lessor as

A. Unearned income from a sales-type lease.

B. Unearned income from a direct financing lease.

C. Manufacturer's or dealer's profit from a sales-type lease.

D. Manufacturer's or dealer's profit from a direct financing lease.

Answer (C) is correct. *(CPA, adapted)*
   REQUIRED: The classification by the lessor of the excess of the fair value of leased property over its cost or carrying amount.
   DISCUSSION: In a sales-type lease, the cost, or carrying amount if different, plus any initial direct costs, minus the present value of any unguaranteed residual value, is charged against income in the same period that the sales price (present value of the minimum lease payments) is recognized. The result is the recognition of a net profit or loss on the sales-type lease. Thus, by definition, a sales-type lease is one that gives rise to a manufacturer's or dealer's profit (or loss) because the fair value of the leased property at the inception of the lease (the present value of the minimum lease payments) differs from its cost or carrying amount.
   Answer (A) is incorrect. Unearned income from a sales-type lease is equal to the difference between the gross investment and the present value of its components (minimum lease payments, which include any guaranteed residual value and are netted against executory costs, and the unguaranteed residual value). The net investment for a sales-type lease equals gross investment minus unearned income. Answer (B) is incorrect. Unearned income in a direct financing lease equals the difference between the gross investment (minimum lease payments + unguaranteed residual value) and the cost or carrying amount. Answer (D) is incorrect. No manufacturer's or dealer's profit arises in a direct financing lease.

44. Skor Co. leased equipment to Douglas Corp. on January 2, Year 1, for an 8-year period expiring December 31, Year 8. Equal payments under the lease are $600,000 and are due on January 2 of each year. The first payment was made on January 2, Year 1. The list selling price of the equipment is $3,520,000, and its carrying cost on Skor's books is $2,800,000. The lease is appropriately accounted for as a sales-type lease. The present value of the lease payments at an imputed interest rate of 12% (Skor's incremental borrowing rate) is $3,300,000. What amount of profit on the sale should Skor report for the year ended December 31, Year 1?

A. $720,000

B. $500,000

C. $90,000

D. $0

Answer (B) is correct. *(CPA, adapted)*
   REQUIRED: The amount of profit on a sales-type lease.
   DISCUSSION: Skor Co., the lessor, should report a profit from a sales-type lease. The gross profit equals the difference between the sales price (present value of the minimum lease payments) and the cost. Consequently, the profit on the sale equals $500,000 ($3,300,000 – $2,800,000).
   Answer (A) is incorrect. The amount of $720,000 is the result of using the list selling price instead of the present value of the lease payments. Answer (C) is incorrect. The amount of $90,000 is one-eighth of the difference between the list price and the cost. Answer (D) is incorrect. A profit of $500,000 should be reported.

45. On January 1 of the current year, Clouser Co. leased a machine to Cohen Co. for 10 years, with $10,000 payments due at the beginning of each year effective at the inception of the lease. The machine cost Clouser $55,000. The lease is appropriately accounted for as a sales-type lease by Clouser. The present value of the 10 rent payments over the lease term discounted appropriately at 10% was $67,600. The estimated salvage value of the machine at the end of 10 years is equal to the disposal costs. How much interest income should Clouser record from the lease for the current year ended December 31?

A. $5,500

B. $5,760

C. $6,760

D. $7,020

Answer (B) is correct. *(CPA, adapted)*
   REQUIRED: The interest income recognized by the lessor in the first year of a sales-type lease.
   DISCUSSION: In accordance with the effective-interest method, the interest income is equal to the carrying amount of the net investment in the lease at the beginning of the interest period multiplied by the interest rate used to calculate the present value of the lease payments. The present value of $67,600 is reduced by the $10,000 payment made at the inception of the lease, leaving a carrying amount of $57,600. This balance multiplied by 10% yields $5,760 to be reflected as interest income for the first year of the lease.
   Answer (A) is incorrect. Interest income is calculated using the present value of the lease payments. The machine cost is irrelevant for this calculation. Answer (C) is incorrect. The carrying amount of the lease must first be reduced by the $10,000 payment at the inception of the lease. Answer (D) is incorrect. Interest income is based on the carrying amount of the lease multiplied by the discount rate. Therefore, the amount of interest income is $5,760 [($67,600 – $10,000) × 10%].

46. Fletcher Company leased a machine to Leavergood Company on January 1. The lease meets the criteria for a sales-type lease. Title to the asset will automatically pass to the lessee at the end of the lease term. Other details are as follows:

Lease term	10 years
Useful life of the asset	10 years
Cost of the leased property to the lessor	$55,000
Annual payment payable at the beginning of each year, beginning January 1	$10,000
Implicit interest rate	10%
Present value of an annuity due of $1 discounted for 10 years at 10%	$6.7590
Present value of $1 due in 10 years discounted at 10%	$.3855

The journal entry to record the inception of this lease on the lessor's books at January 1 is

A. Leased machine $67,590
　　Lease obligation　　　　　　$57,590
　　Cash　　　　　　　　　　　　10,000

B. Lease payments receivable $90,000
　　Cash　　　　　　　　　　　10,000
　　Cost of sales　　　　　　　55,000
　　　Inventory　　　　　　　　　　$55,000
　　　Unearned income -- leases　　45,000
　　　Sales　　　　　　　　　　　　55,000

C. Lease payments receivable $90,000
　　Cash　　　　　　　　　　　10,000
　　　Interest income　　　　　　　$32,410
　　Gross profit on sales -- type lease　　　　　　　　　　　　12,590
　　　Inventory　　　　　　　　　　55,000

D. Lease payments receivable $90,000
　　Cash　　　　　　　　　　　10,000
　　Cost of sales　　　　　　　55,000
　　　Sales　　　　　　　　　　　　$67,590
　　　Inventory　　　　　　　　　　55,000
　　　Unearned income -- leases　　32,410

Answer (D) is correct. *(CIA, adapted)*
REQUIRED: The lessor's journal entry at the inception of a sales-type lease.
DISCUSSION: For a sales-type lease, the lessor should record

1. As gross investment, the minimum lease payments plus any unguaranteed residual value (the latter element is $0 in this case)

2. As unearned income, the difference between the gross investment in the lease and the present value of its components

3. As the sales price, the present value of the minimum lease payments computed at the interest rate implicit in the lease

4. As a charge to income, the cost of the leased property, plus any initial direct costs ($0 in this case), minus the present value of the unguaranteed residual value ($0 in this case)

Because the first payment is made at the inception of the lease, the payment structure is that of an annuity due. Sales revenue is therefore equal to the $10,000 periodic payment times the present value of an annuity due of $1 discounted for 10 years at 10% ($10,000 × 6.7590 = $67,590). Given that cash is paid at the beginning of the year, the initial $10,000 cash debit immediately decreases the gross investment in the lease (lease payments receivable) from $100,000 to $90,000. The cost of the leased property ($55,000) must also be charged to cost of sales and credited to inventory. Finally, at the inception of the lease, unearned income equals the difference between the gross investment and the present value of its components ($100,000 – $67,590 = $32,410).
Answer (A) is incorrect. The lessee's journal entry is to debit an asset and credit a liability. Answer (B) is incorrect. The sale should be recorded at the present value of the minimum lease payments, and the unearned income should be recorded as the difference between the gross lease payments receivable and the present value of this gross investment. Answer (C) is incorrect. The lease should reflect both cost of goods sold and sales, not the netted gross profit on the sales-type lease.

47. Avizinis Co. manufactures equipment that is sold or leased. On December 31, Year 1, Avizinis leased equipment to Anderson for a 5-year period ending December 31, Year 6, at which date ownership of the leased asset will be transferred to Anderson. Equal periodic payments under the lease are $22,000 (including $2,000 of executory costs) and are due on December 31 of each year. The first payment was made on December 31, Year 1. Collectibility of the remaining lease payments is reasonably assured, and Avizinis has no material cost uncertainties. The normal sales price of the equipment is $77,000, and cost is $60,000. For the year ended December 31, Year 1, what amount of income should Avizinis realize from the lease transaction?

A. $17,000

B. $20,000

C. $22,000

D. $33,000

Answer (A) is correct. *(CPA, adapted)*
REQUIRED: The income to be recognized.
DISCUSSION: For a lessor to treat a lease as a capital lease, it must first meet one of four criteria. That ownership of the leased equipment transfers to the lessee at the end of the lease term is one of the four criteria. In addition, the lessor cannot treat the lease as a capital lease unless collectibility of the remaining lease payments is reasonably assured and there are no material cost uncertainties. These conditions also are met. Because the $77,000 fair value is greater than the $60,000 recorded cost of the equipment on the lessor's books, the lease should be accounted for as a sales-type lease. In a sales-type lease, two components of income may be recognized. These are the profit on the sale and interest income. The profit on the sale recorded at the inception of the lease is $17,000 ($77,000 normal sales price – $60,000 cost). At the inception of the lease, no interest income should be recorded. Thus, Avizinis should realize $17,000 of income from this lease transaction in Year 1.
Answer (B) is incorrect. The amount of $20,000 is the annual payment minus executory costs. Answer (C) is incorrect. The amount of $22,000 is the annual payment. Answer (D) is incorrect. The amount of $33,000 is the difference between the sales price ($77,000) and the sum of the rental payments ($22,000 × 5 = $110,000).

48. On August 1, Mansfield Corporation leased property to Park Company for a 5-year period. The annual $20,000 lease payment is payable at the end of each year. The expected residual value at the end of the lease term is $10,000. Mansfield Company's implicit interest rate is 12%. The cost of the property to Mansfield was $50,000, which is the fair value at the lease date. The present value of an ordinary annuity of 1 for five periods is 3.605. The present value of 1 at the end of five periods is .567. At the beginning of the lease, the recorded gross investment is

A. $110,000

B. $100,000

C. $72,100

D. $90,000

Answer (A) is correct. *(J.O. Hall)*
REQUIRED: The amount to be recorded as gross investment at the beginning of the lease.
DISCUSSION: For a direct financing or a sales-type lease, the lessor should record the gross investment in the lease at the undiscounted sum of the minimum lease payments and any unguaranteed residual value. For a lessee, minimum lease payments include the minimum rental payments (excluding executory costs such as insurance, maintenance, and taxes) required during the lease term and the payment called for by a bargain purchase option. If no such option exists, the lessee's minimum lease payments equal the sum of the minimum rental payments, the amount of residual value guaranteed by the lessee, and any nonrenewal penalty imposed. The minimum lease payments calculated by the lessor are the same as those for the lessee except that they include any residual value or rental payments beyond the lease term guaranteed by a financially capable third party unrelated to the lessor or the lessee. Accordingly, the gross investment is the same regardless of whether any residual value is guaranteed. The five periodic payments of $20,000 equal $100,000. The expected residual value, including both guaranteed and unguaranteed portions, equals $10,000. Thus, the gross investment in this lease should be $110,000 ($100,000 + $10,000).
Answer (B) is incorrect. The amount of $100,000 fails to include the residual value in the gross investment. Answer (C) is incorrect. The annual lease payments should be recorded at their undiscounted amount. Answer (D) is incorrect. The residual value is added to, not subtracted from, the undiscounted lease payments.

49. Bailey Company leased equipment to Greco, Inc., on January 1, Year 2. The lease is for an 8-year period expiring December 31, Year 9. The first of eight equal annual payments of $600,000 was made on January 1, Year 2. Bailey had purchased the equipment on December 29, Year 1, for $3,200,000. The lease is appropriately accounted for as a sales-type lease by Bailey. Assume that the present value at January 1, Year 2, of all rent payments over the lease term discounted at a 10% interest rate was $3,520,000. What amount of interest income should Bailey record in Year 3 (the second year of the lease period) as a result of the lease?

A. $261,200

B. $292,000

C. $320,000

D. $327,200

Answer (A) is correct. *(CPA, adapted)*
REQUIRED: The interest income during the second year of a sales-type lease.
DISCUSSION: The net investment to be recorded by the lessor at 1/1/Year 2 is given as $3,520,000, the present value of the minimum lease payments discounted at 10%. The net investment is immediately reduced by the $600,000 lease payment on 1/1/Year 2, resulting in a carrying amount for Year 2 of $2,920,000. Interest earned for the Year 2 at a rate of 10% ($2,920,000 × 10%) is $292,000. Thus, the $600,000 1/1/Year 3 lease payment consists of the $292,000 interest component and a $308,000 reduction of the net investment. Because the Year 3 net investment balance is $2,612,000 ($2,920,000 – $308,000), interest income for Year 3 is $261,200 ($2,612,000 × 10%).
Answer (B) is incorrect. The amount of $292,000 is the interest income in Year 2. Answer (C) is incorrect. The amount of $320,000 is based on original cost of the leased property. Answer (D) is incorrect. Interest income is calculated as the carrying amount of the lease multiplied by the discount rate. Thus, the amount of interest income is $261,200 [($2,920,000 – $308,000) × 10%].

50. On the first day of its fiscal year, Miller Co. leased certain property at an annual rental of $100,000 receivable at the beginning of each year for 10 years. The first payment was received immediately. The leased property is new, had cost $650,000, and has an estimated useful life of 13 years with no salvage value. Miller's borrowing rate is 8%. The present value of an annuity of $1 payable at the beginning of the period at 8% for 10 years is 7.247. Miller had no other costs associated with this lease. Miller should have accounted for this lease as a sale but mistakenly treated the lease as an operating lease. Thus, Miller recognized depreciation using the straight-line method, its normal policy for owned assets. What was the effect on net earnings during the first year of treating this lease as an operating lease rather than as a sale?

A. No effect.

B. Understated.

C. Overstated.

D. The effect depends on the method selected for income tax purposes.

Answer (B) is correct. *(CPA, adapted)*
REQUIRED: The effect of accounting for a lease as an operating rather than as a sales-type lease.
DISCUSSION: Accounting for the lease as an operating lease during the first year generated $50,000 of income, the $100,000 lease payment minus $50,000 of depreciation ($650,000 ÷ 13). In a sales-type lease, the lessor recognizes two income components: profit on the sale and interest income. Total income from accounting for the lease as a sale would have been $124,676 ($74,700 + $49,976). The effect of the error on net earnings was therefore an understatement.

Net investment			Net investment		
($100,000 × 7.247)	$724,700		($100,000 × 7.247)	$724,700	
Carrying amount	(650,000)		First lease payment	(100,000)	
Profit on sale	$ 74,700		Lease balance	$624,700	
			Interest rate	×	.08
			Interest income	$ 49,976	

Answer (A) is incorrect. The effect of the accounting error will be an understatement of net earnings before taxes and after taxes. Answer (C) is incorrect. Net earnings is understated, not overstated. Answer (D) is incorrect. The effect of the accounting error will be an understatement of net earnings before taxes and after taxes.

14.3 Operating Leases

51. During January of the current year, Pauzouskie Co. made long-term improvements to a recently leased building. The lease agreement provides for neither a transfer of title to Pauzouskie nor a bargain purchase option. Moreover, the fair value of the land is less than 25% of the value of the leased property at the inception of the lease. The present value of the minimum lease payments equals 85% of the fair value of the leased property, and the lease term equals 70% of the building's economic life. Should assets be recognized for the lease and the leasehold improvements?

	Lease	Leasehold Improvements
A.	Yes	Yes
B.	No	Yes
C.	Yes	No
D.	No	No

Answer (B) is correct. *(CPA, adapted)*
REQUIRED: The item(s) for which an asset should be recognized.
DISCUSSION: A lease must be classified as a capital lease by a lessee if, at its inception, (1) the lease provides for the transfer of ownership of the leased property, (2) the lease contains a bargain purchase option, (3) the lease term is 75% or more of the estimated economic life of the leased property, or (4) the present value of the minimum lease payments (excluding executory costs) is at least 90% of the excess of the fair value of the leased property to the lessor at the inception of the lease over any related investment tax credit. (The last two criteria do not apply if the lease term begins within the last 25% of the total estimated economic life.) If a lease involves land and a building, and the fair value of the land is less than 25% of the fair value of the leased property at the inception of the lease, the land and building are deemed to be a single unit for purposes of applying criteria (3) and (4). Thus, none of the criteria is satisfied, and the lessee should not recognize an asset and an obligation for the lease. However, general improvements to leased property should be capitalized as leasehold improvements and amortized in accordance with the straight-line method over the shorter of their expected useful life or the lease term.
Answer (A) is incorrect. An asset is not recognized for an operating lease. Answer (C) is incorrect. An asset is not recognized for the improvements, not the lease. Answer (D) is incorrect. An asset is recognized for the improvement, even though the lease is an operating lease.

52. On July 1, Year 1, Rebstock Co. entered into a 10-year operating lease for a warehouse facility. The annual minimum lease payments are $100,000. In addition to the base rent, Rebstock pays a monthly allocation of the building's operating expenses, which amounted to $20,000 for the year ended June 30, Year 2. In the notes to Rebstock's June 30, Year 2, financial statements, what amounts of subsequent years' lease payments should be disclosed?

A. $100,000 per annum for each of the next 5 years and $500,000 in the aggregate.

B. $120,000 per annum for each of the next 5 years and $600,000 in the aggregate.

C. $100,000 per annum for each of the next 5 years and $900,000 in the aggregate.

D. $120,000 per annum for each of the next 5 years and $1,080,000 in the aggregate.

Answer (C) is correct. *(CPA, adapted)*
REQUIRED: The amounts of subsequent years' lease payments to be disclosed.
DISCUSSION: The future minimum lease payments as of the date of the latest balance sheet presented must be disclosed in the aggregate and for each of the 5 succeeding fiscal years. This disclosure is required whether the lease is classified as a capital lease or as an operating lease. Thus, Rebstock should disclose that annual minimum lease payments are $100,000 for each of the next 5 years and that the aggregate is $900,000. The operating expenses are executory costs that are not included in the minimum lease payments.
Answer (A) is incorrect. The aggregate is $900,000. Answer (B) is incorrect. The operating expenses should not be included and the aggregate amount is $900,000. Answer (D) is incorrect. The operating expenses should not be included.

53. On June 1, Rogers Co. entered into a 5-year nonrenewable lease for office space, commencing on that date, and made the following payments to Rose Properties:

Bonus to obtain lease	$30,000
First month's rent	10,000
Last month's rent	10,000

In its income statement for the year ended June 30, what amount should Rogers report as rent expense?

A. $10,000

B. $10,500

C. $40,000

D. $50,000

Answer (B) is correct. *(CPA, adapted)*
REQUIRED: The amount to be reported as rent expense for an operating lease.
DISCUSSION: Rent expense is recognized as services are used. Payments that benefit the entire lease term should be amortized over the lease period. Accordingly, the rent expense will include the rent payment for June and the amount of the bonus amortized for that period. Rent expense for June is thus $10,500 {$10,000 for the month's rent + [($30,000 ÷ 5) ÷ 12 amortization of the bonus]}.
Answer (A) is incorrect. The expense should include amortization of the bonus. Answer (C) is incorrect. The bonus should be amortized over the lease term benefited. Answer (D) is incorrect. The last month's rent payment should be deferred and expensed in the period it benefits. Also, the bonus should be amortized over the lease term.

54. Sunhachawi Apparel, Inc., leases and operates a retail store. The following information relates to the lease for the year ended December 31:

- The store lease, an operating lease, calls for a base monthly rent of $1,500 due the first day of each month.
- Additional rent is computed at 6% of net sales over $300,000 up to $600,000 and 5% of net sales over $600,000, per calendar year.
- Net sales for Year 1 were $900,000.
- Sunhachawi paid executory costs to the lessor for property taxes of $12,000 and insurance of $5,000.

For the year, Sunhachawi's expenses relating to the store lease are

A. $71,000

B. $68,000

C. $54,000

D. $35,000

Answer (B) is correct. *(CPA, adapted)*
REQUIRED: The lessee's expenses relating to a store lease.
DISCUSSION: This lease is properly classified as an operating lease. The expenses relating to this lease should include the fixed monthly rental payment, the contingent rental payments, and the executory costs. The expenses, as indicated below, amount to $68,000.

Monthly rent	$18,000	($1,500 × 12 months)
Additional rent	18,000	($600,000 – $300,000) × 6%
	15,000	($900,000 – $600,000) × 5%
Executory costs	12,000	(property taxes)
	5,000	(insurance)
Total expenses	$68,000	

Answer (A) is incorrect. The amount of $71,000 includes the contingent rent at 6%. Answer (C) is incorrect. The amount of $54,000 includes the contingent rent at 6% and excludes the executory costs. Answer (D) is incorrect. The amount of $35,000 excludes the contingent rent.

55. On January 1, Year 1, Masingil Co. leased a building to Leavengood Corp. for a 10-year term at an annual rental of $50,000. At the inception of the lease, Masingil received $200,000 covering the first 2 years' rent and a security deposit of $100,000. This deposit will not be returned to Leavengood upon expiration of the lease but will be applied to payment of rent for the last 2 years of the lease. What portions of the $200,000 should be shown as a current and a noncurrent liability, respectively, in Masingil's December 31, Year 1, balance sheet?

	Current Liability	Noncurrent Liability
A.	$0	$200,000
B.	$50,000	$100,000
C.	$100,000	$100,000
D.	$100,000	$50,000

Answer (B) is correct. *(CPA, adapted)*
REQUIRED: The allocation of an advance payment between current and noncurrent.
DISCUSSION: Of the $200,000 received at the beginning of the lease, $50,000 should be recognized as rental income for the year ended 12/31/Year 1. At 12/31/Year 1, the $50,000 attributable to rent for Year 2 should be classified as a current liability, and the $100,000 applicable to the last 2 years of the lease should be classified as a noncurrent liability.
Answer (A) is incorrect. A current liability should be recognized at 12/31/Year 1 for the amount prepaid for Year 2. Moreover, $200,000 is the incorrect amount of the noncurrent liability. Answer (C) is incorrect. The amount of $50,000 should be classified as current. Answer (D) is incorrect. The amount of $50,000 should be classified as current and $100,000 as noncurrent.

56. On January 1 of the current year, Sharp Company leased a building to Schlachtman under an operating lease for 10 years at $50,000 per year, payable the first day of each lease year. Sharp paid $15,000 to a real estate broker as a finder's fee. The annual depreciation on the building is $12,000. Sharp incurred insurance and property tax expenses totaling $9,000 during the current year. Sharp's net rental income for the year should be

A. $27,500
B. $29,000
C. $35,000
D. $36,500

Answer (A) is correct. *(CPA, adapted)*
REQUIRED: The net rental income that should be recorded for the first year.
DISCUSSION: Net rental income is equal to the $50,000 annual payment minus any expenses incurred during the year. These expenses include $12,000 of depreciation, $9,000 for insurance and property taxes, and $1,500 ($15,000 ÷ 10 years) amortization of the finder's fee. In an operating lease, a finder's fee is an initial direct cost that should be deferred and allocated over the lease term in proportion to the recognition of rental income. Accordingly, the net rental income for the year is $27,500.

Rental income	$50,000
Depreciation	(12,000)
Insurance and property tax expenses	(9,000)
Amortization	(1,500)
Net rental income	$27,500

Answer (B) is incorrect. The amount of $29,000 excludes amortization of the finder's fee. Answer (C) is incorrect. The amount of $35,000 includes the entire finder's fee and excludes depreciation and the insurance and property tax expenses. Answer (D) is incorrect. The amount of $36,500 excludes the insurance and property tax expenses.

57. On December 1, King Co. leased office space for 5 years at a monthly rental of $60,000. On the same date, King paid the lessor the following amounts:

First month's rent	$ 60,000
Last month's rent	60,000
Security deposit (refundable at lease expiration)	80,000
Installation of new walls and offices	360,000

King's expense relating to use of the office space for the year should be

A. $140,000
B. $120,000
C. $66,000
D. $60,000

Answer (C) is correct. *(CPA, adapted)*
REQUIRED: The amount to be included as rent expense in relation to the lease.
DISCUSSION: Rent expense should be recognized as the services are used. Payments that benefit future periods should be deferred and recognized when incurred. Leasehold improvements (i.e., installation of new walls and offices) should be capitalized and amortized over the term of the lease. Thus, the expense should include $60,000 rent for the first month of the lease and amortization of the leasehold improvement of $6,000 [($360,000 ÷ 5 years) ÷ 12 months]. Total expense recognized should be $66,000 ($60,000 + $6,000).
Answer (A) is incorrect. The amount of $140,000 includes the security deposit and excludes amortization of the leasehold improvements. Answer (B) is incorrect. The amount of $120,000 includes the last month's rent and excludes amortization of the leasehold improvements. Answer (D) is incorrect. The amount of $60,000 excludes amortization of the leasehold improvements.

58. Greco Co. leased office premises to Houghton, Inc., for a 5-year term beginning January 2, Year 1. Under the terms of the operating lease, rent for the first year is $8,000 and rent for Years 2 through 5 is $12,500 per annum. However, as an inducement to enter the lease, Greco granted Houghton the first 6 months of the lease rent-free. In its December 31, Year 1, income statement, what amount should Greco report as rental income?

A. $12,000

B. $11,600

C. $10,800

D. $8,000

Answer (C) is correct. *(CPA, adapted)*
REQUIRED: The rental revenue reported for the first year of an operating lease given a varying annual rental.
DISCUSSION: For an operating lease, rent is reported as income in accordance with the lease agreement. However, if rentals vary from a straight-line basis, the straight-line basis should be used unless another systematic and rational basis is more representative of the time pattern in which the use benefit from the property is reduced. No basis other than straight-line is more representative of the reduction in the use benefit of office space. Because rent for the first year is $4,000 [$8,000 × (6 ÷ 12)], Greco should report rental revenue of $10,800 {[$4,000 + (4 × $12,500)] ÷ 5 years}.
Answer (A) is incorrect. The amount of $12,000 equals the first year's rent payment plus 6 months of free rent. Answer (B) is incorrect. The amount of $11,600 does not adjust for the 6 months of free rent. Answer (D) is incorrect. The amount of $8,000 is equal to the first year's unadjusted rental payment.

59. On July 1, Year 1, Danner, Inc., leased a delivery truck from Cerrato Corp. under a 3-year operating lease. Total rent for the term of the lease will be $36,000, payable as follows:

$ 500 × 12 months = $ 6,000
$ 750 × 12 months =   9,000
$1,750 × 12 months =   21,000

All payments were made when due. In Cerrato's June 30, Year 3, balance sheet, the accrued rent receivable should be reported as

A. $0

B. $9,000

C. $12,000

D. $21,000

Answer (B) is correct. *(CPA, adapted)*
REQUIRED: The amount to be included as rent receivable in the balance sheet.
DISCUSSION: For an operating lease, rent revenue is recognized in accordance with the straight-line method unless another systematic and rational basis is more representative of the benefits realized. Thus, monthly rent revenue of $1,000 [($6,000 + $9,000 + $21,000) ÷ 36 months] should be recognized. At 6/30/Year 3, cumulative revenue recognized is $24,000 ($1,000 × 24 months). Because cumulative cash received is $15,000 ($6,000 + $9,000), an accrued receivable for the $9,000 ($24,000 – $15,000) difference should be recognized.
Answer (A) is incorrect. The amount of $9,000 is equal to rent received during the year ended 6/30/Year 3. Answer (C) is incorrect. The amount of $12,000 is rent revenue recognized each year. Answer (D) is incorrect. The amount of $21,000 is equal to the rent payments to be received in the following fiscal year.

60. On April 1, Year 1, Hall Fitness Center leased its gym to Dunn Fitness Center under a 4-year operating lease. Hall normally charges $6,000 per month to lease its gym, but as an incentive, Hall gave Dunn half off the first year's rent and one quarter off the second year's rent. Dunn's rental payments were as follows:

Year 1: 12 × $3,000 = $36,000

Year 2: 12 × $4,500 = $54,000

Year 3: 12 × $6,000 = $72,000

Year 4: 12 × $6,000 = $72,000

Dunn's rent payments were due on the first day of the month, beginning on April 1, Year 1. What amount should Dunn report as rent expense in its monthly income statement for April, Year 3?

A. $3,000

B. $4,500

C. $4,875

D. $6,000

Answer (C) is correct. *(CPA, adapted)*
REQUIRED: The rent expense reported by a lessee under an operating lease.
DISCUSSION: Under an operating lease, rent is reported as an expense by the lessee in accordance with the lease agreement. If rental payments vary from a straight-line basis, rent expense must be recognized over the full lease term on the straight-line basis. However, another systematic and rational basis may be used if it is more representative of the time pattern in which the benefit of the property is reduced. The annual rent before incentives is $72,000 (12 months × $6,000), but the first year's rent is $36,000 ($72,000 × 50%), and the second year's rent is $54,000 ($72,000 × 75%). Consequently, the straight-line monthly rent expense over the 4-year term of the operating lease is $4,875 [($36,000 + $54,000 + $72,000 + $72,000) ÷ (12 months per year × 4 years)].
Answer (A) is incorrect. The amount of $3,000 is the monthly rent to be paid in the first year of the lease. Answer (B) is incorrect. The amount of $4,500 is the monthly rent to be paid in the second year of the lease. Answer (D) is incorrect. The amount of $6,000 is the monthly rent to be paid in the third and fourth years of the lease.

61. A company enters into a 3-year operating lease agreement effective January 1, Year 1. The amounts due on the first day of each year are $25,000 in Year 1, $30,000 in Year 2, and $35,000 in Year 3. What amount, if any, is the related liability on the first day of Year 2?

A. $0

B. $5,000

C. $60,000

D. $65,000

Answer (B) is correct. *(CPA, adapted)*
REQUIRED: The lessee's liability under an operating lease at the beginning of the second year.
DISCUSSION: An operating lease is a simple rental agreement, and no asset is recognized by the lessee. Rent is reported as an expense by the lessee in accordance with the lease agreement. If rental payments vary from a straight-line basis, rent expense must be recognized over the full lease term on the straight-line basis. However, another systematic and rational basis may be used if it is more representative of the time pattern in which the benefit of the property is reduced. The total rent due is $90,000 ($25,000 + $30,000 + $35,000), and the annual straight-line expense is $30,000 ($90,000 ÷ 3 years). In Year 1, the entity recognized rent expense of $30,000, a cash payment of $25,000, and a liability of $5,000.
Answer (A) is incorrect. The amount of $0 does not reflect use of the straight-line method. Answer (C) is incorrect. The amount of $60,000 is the total rent expense for 2 years. Answer (D) is incorrect. The amount of $65,000 is the total to be paid in Years 2 and 3.

62. Clark Corp. owns an office building and normally charges tenants $30 per square foot per year for office space. Because the occupancy rate is low, Clark agreed to lease 10,000 square feet to Fletcher Co. at $12 per square foot for the first year of a 3-year operating lease. Rent for remaining years will be at the $30 rate. Fletcher moved into the building on January 1, Year 1, and paid the first year's rent in advance. What amount of rental revenue should Clark report from Fletcher in its income statement for the year ended September 30, Year 1?

A. $90,000

B. $120,000

C. $180,000

D. $240,000

Answer (C) is correct. *(CPA, adapted)*
REQUIRED: The amount of rent revenue to be included in the income statement.
DISCUSSION: In an operating lease, when payments differ from year to year, revenue is recognized by allocating the total amount of revenue to be received evenly over the lease term. At 9/30/Year 1, the amount of revenue to be recognized is for 9 months. Thus, rent revenue is $180,000 {[$10,000 square feet × ($12 + $30 + $30)] × (9 ÷ 36)}.
Answer (A) is incorrect. The amount of $90,000 recognizes rent equal to the rental payments. Answer (B) is incorrect. The amount of $120,000 recognizes rent equal to rent payments for 12 months. Answer (D) is incorrect. The amount of $240,000 recognizes rent for 12 months.

14.4 Sale-Leaseback Transactions

63. In a sale-leaseback transaction, the seller-lessee has retained the property. The gain on the sale should be recognized at the time of the sale-leaseback when the lease is classified as a(n)

	Capital Lease	Operating Lease
A.	Yes	Yes
B.	No	No
C.	No	Yes
D.	Yes	No

Answer (B) is correct. *(CPA, adapted)*
REQUIRED: The lease for which a gain on a sale-leaseback should be recognized at the time of the transaction.
DISCUSSION: A gain on the sale in a sale-leaseback transaction normally should be deferred and amortized in proportion to the amortization of the leased asset if the leaseback is classified as a capital lease. The amortization is in proportion to the gross rental payments expensed over the lease term if the leaseback is classified as an operating lease. The gain on the sale is normally not recognized at the time of the sale-leaseback.
Answer (A) is incorrect. The gain is normally deferred and amortized over the lease term regardless of the classification of the leaseback. Answer (C) is incorrect. If the leaseback is an operating lease, the gain is normally deferred and amortized over the lease term in proportion to the gross rental payments expensed. Answer (D) is incorrect. If the leaseback is a capital lease, the gain is normally deferred and amortized over the lease term in proportion to the amortization of the leased asset.

64. On December 31, Dirk Corp. sold Smith Co. two airplanes and simultaneously leased them back. Additional information pertaining to the sale-leasebacks follows:

	Plane #1	Plane #2
Sales price	$600,000	$1,000,000
Carrying amount, 12/31	$100,000	$550,000
Remaining useful life, 12/31	10 years	35 years
Lease term	8 years	3 years
Annual lease payments	$100,000	$200,000

In its December 31 balance sheet, what amount should Dirk report as deferred gain on these transactions?

A. $950,000

B. $500,000

C. $450,000

D. $0

Answer (A) is correct. *(CPA, adapted)*
REQUIRED: The amount to be recorded as deferred gain in a sale and leaseback.
DISCUSSION: The lease of Plane #1 is a capital lease. Its 8-year term exceeds 75% of the 10-year estimated remaining useful life of the plane. In a sale and leaseback, any gain or loss on the sale ordinarily is deferred and amortized in proportion to the amortization of the leased asset if the lease is a capital lease. If a leaseback of the entire property sold (e.g., Plane #1) qualifies as a capital lease, the seller-lessee is presumed to retain substantially all of the remaining use of the property. Thus, no exception to deferral of gain or loss applies. At the inception of this lease, the $500,000 gain ($600,000 sales price – $100,000 carrying amount) should be deferred. The lease of Plane #2 is an operating lease that may be subject to an exception. The seller-lessee has agreed to make $600,000 ($200,000 × 3 years) of undiscounted lease payments. Thus, no capital lease criterion is met. No bargain purchase option or transfer of ownership is stated, the lease term is less than 75% of the useful life, and the present value of the lease payments is less than 90% of the fair value of the property (presumably $1,000,000). When the seller-lessee retains less than substantially all of the remaining use of the property sold (the present value of the lease payments is less than 90% of the fair value) but more than a minor portion (the present value of the lease payments is more than 10% of the fair value), the seller-lessee should recognize any excess gain (for an operating lease, in excess of the present value of the minimum lease payments). The present value of the $600,000 of payments under the leaseback of Plane #2 is clearly less than 90% of the $1,000,000 fair value of the leased property and clearly more than 10% ($1,000,000 × 10% = $100,000) of that fair value. However, the present value of the lease payments will exceed the gain ($1,000,000 – $550,000 = $450,000) unless the discount rate is very high (about 16%). Accordingly, the gain on the sale of Plane #2 also is deferred (assuming the applicable interest rate is less than 16%). The total deferred gain is therefore $950,000 ($500,000 + $450,000). The gain on Plane #2 also is recognized.
Answer (B) is incorrect. The gain on Plane #2 also is recognized. Answer (C) is incorrect. The gain on Plane #1 also is recognized. Answer (D) is incorrect. The gain on both planes is recognized.

65. McKenzie Co. sold its factory at a gain and simultaneously leased it back for 10 years. The factory's remaining economic life is 20 years. The lease was reported as an operating lease. At the time of sale, McKenzie should report the gain as

A. An extraordinary item, net of income tax.

B. An asset valuation allowance.

C. A separate component of shareholders' equity.

D. A deferred credit.

Answer (D) is correct. *(CPA, adapted)*
REQUIRED: The proper treatment of a gain on a sale-leaseback.
DISCUSSION: A gain on the sale in a sale-leaseback normally should be deferred and amortized. When the seller-lessee classifies the lease arising from the sale-leaseback as an operating lease, no asset is shown on the balance sheet, and the deferral cannot be presented as a contra asset. Accordingly, the usual practice is to report the gain as a deferred credit.
Answer (A) is incorrect. The gain is ordinarily deferred. Answer (B) is incorrect. An asset valuation allowance would be reported if the lease qualified as a capital lease. Answer (C) is incorrect. The gain is usually reported as a deferred credit.

66. On December 31, Joseenrique Corp. sold equipment to Dorr and simultaneously leased it back for 3 years. The following data pertain to the transaction at this date:

Sales price	$220,000
Carrying amount	150,000
Present value of lease rentals	
($2,000 for 36 months at 12%)	60,800
Estimated remaining useful life	10 years

At December 31 what amount should Joseenrique report as deferred revenue from the sale of the equipment?

A. $0

B. $9,200

C. $60,800

D. $70,000

Answer (C) is correct. *(CPA, adapted)*

REQUIRED: The amount to be reported as deferred revenue in a sale-leaseback.

DISCUSSION: In an ordinary sale and leaseback, any profit or loss on the sale is amortized over the life of the lease. But exceptions exist. One exception applies when a seller-lessee retains more than a minor part but less than substantially all of the use of the property through the leaseback. If the seller-lessee in this situation realizes a profit on the sale in excess of either (1) the present value of the minimum lease payments over the lease term if the leaseback is an operating lease or (2) the recorded amount of the leased asset if the leaseback is classified as a capital lease, the "excess" profit on the sale is recognized at the date of the sale. "Substantially all" has essentially the same meaning as the "90% test" used in determining whether a lease is a capital or operating lease (the present value of the lease payments is 90% or more of the fair value of the leased property). "Minor" refers to a transfer of 10% or less of the use of the property in the lease.

For Joseenrique Corp., the $60,800 present value of the lease rentals is greater than 10% and less than 90% of the fair value of the leased property as measured by the sales price. Thus, $9,200 in excess profit should be recognized.

Sales price	$220,000
Carrying amount	(150,000)
Profit	$ 70,000
Minus: PV of lease payments	(60,800)
Profit recognized	$ 9,200

The $60,800 remaining gain on the sale-leaseback should be amortized in proportion to the gross rentals expensed over the lease term because the leaseback is classified as an operating lease (none of the criteria for a capital lease is met). At 12/31, the date of the inception of the lease, the entire $60,800 should be reported in the balance sheet as deferred revenue from the sale of the equipment.

Answer (A) is incorrect. More than a minor part but less than substantially all of the use of the property has been retained. Accordingly, only the excess profit is recognized immediately, and the remaining portion is deferred. Answer (B) is incorrect. The amount of $9,200 is the profit that is recognized immediately. Answer (D) is incorrect. The amount of $70,000 is the total profit.

67. The following information pertains to a sale and leaseback of equipment by Joshua Co. on December 31:

Sales price	$400,000
Carrying amount	300,000
Monthly lease payment	3,250
Present value of lease payments	36,900
Estimated remaining life	25 years
Lease term	1 year
Implicit rate	12%

What amount of deferred gain on the sale should Joshua report at December 31?

A. $0

B. $36,900

C. $63,100

D. $100,000

Answer (A) is correct. *(CPA, adapted)*

REQUIRED: The amount of gain to defer resulting from a sale-leaseback transaction.

DISCUSSION: In a sale-leaseback transaction, a seller will defer all gains and losses, recognize all gains and losses, or recognize only excess gains. The rules for these recognition principles are based on the rights the seller retains in the property. If the seller-lessee retains substantially all rights in the property (present value of the minimum lease payments is 90% or more of the fair value of the leased asset), all gains and losses are deferred. If minor rights are retained (present value of the minimum lease payments is 10% or less of the fair value of the leased asset), all gains and losses are recognized. If the rights retained are between these two thresholds, only excess gains are recognized. In this situation, minor rights are retained, so the entire gain of $100,000 ($400,000 sales price – $300,000 carrying amount) is recognized, and none is deferred.

Answer (B) is incorrect. The amount of $36,900 is the present value of the lease payments. Answer (C) is incorrect. The amount of $63,100 is the difference between the $100,000 gain and the present value of the minimum lease payments. Answer (D) is incorrect. The amount of $100,000 is the gain recognized immediately.

68. On June 30, Travis Co. sold equipment with an estimated useful life of 11 years and immediately leased it back for 10 years. The equipment's carrying amount was $450,000; the sales price was $430,000; and the present value of the lease payments, which is equal to the fair value of the equipment, was $465,000. In its June 30 balance sheet, what amount should Travis report as deferred loss?

A. $35,000

B. $20,000

C. $15,000

D. $0

Answer (B) is correct. *(CPA, adapted)*
REQUIRED: The amount of deferred loss.
DISCUSSION: Any profit or loss on the sale in a sale-leaseback transaction is ordinarily deferred and amortized. Immediate recognition of the loss is permitted, however, when the fair value at the time of the transaction is less than the undepreciated cost. Given a fair value of $465,000 and a carrying amount of $450,000, that exception does not apply. Consequently, the $20,000 ($450,000 − $430,000) excess of the carrying amount over the sales price should be deferred.
Answer (A) is incorrect. The amount of $35,000 is the excess of the fair value over the sales price. Answer (C) is incorrect. The amount of $15,000 is the excess of the fair value over the carrying amount. Answer (D) is incorrect. Full recognition of the loss is not appropriate when the fair value is greater than the carrying amount.

Use Gleim **EQE Test Prep** Software Download for interactive study and performance analysis.

STUDY UNIT FIFTEEN
CORPORATE EQUITY

General

The equity accounts of a corporation include contributed capital, treasury stock, retained earnings, and items included in accumulated other comprehensive income (see Study Unit 3). **Contributed capital** is primarily the result of transactions by an enterprise in its own stock. The principal classes of stock are common and preferred. Preferred stock generally has a preference in liquidation and may be callable or redeemable. These amounts must be disclosed. Transactions in stock may include issuances, repurchases, and retirements. Gains and losses must not be recognized from (1) transactions by an enterprise in its own stock or (2) the reporting of its holdings of its own stock (treasury stock) as an asset.

The issuance of **par-value or stated-value stock** is recorded as an increase in (credit to) capital stock equal to the number of shares issued times the par or stated value. The excess of the issuance price over the par or stated value is recorded by a credit to **additional paid-in capital**. The issuance of no-par-value stock is recorded by a credit to capital stock. The issuance price ordinarily is determined by the transaction giving rise to the issuance. For example, stock issued in exchange for cash or property is recorded at the fair value of the proceeds received, stock issued in a lump-sum transaction is recorded at the allocated amount of the lump-sum proceeds, and common stock issued upon conversion of convertible debt or preferred stock is recorded at the carrying amount or the fair value of the security converted.

Cash and Property Dividends

Cash and property (in-kind) dividends are nonreciprocal transfers from an enterprise to its shareholders. A property dividend is recorded at the fair value of the asset transferred, with a gain or loss recognized equal to the difference between its fair value and carrying amount. Cash and property dividends are recorded as liabilities on the date of declaration by the board of directors. These liabilities are satisfied on the date of payment. Dividends on preferred stock ordinarily must be paid before dividends on common stock. In addition, dividends on preferred stock usually are cumulative. **Cumulative** unpaid dividends from previous years (dividends in arrears) must be disclosed. They also must be paid before dividends for the current year. Moreover, dividends on preferred stock also may be, but usually are not, participating. **Participating** preferred shareholders fully or partially participate in additional dividends with common shareholders after the latter have received an initial dividend that proportionally equals the preferred shareholders' dividend for the current year.

Stock Dividends and Stock Splits

Stock dividends and stock splits do not increase net assets. They also do not change the proportionate interests of shareholders. The purpose of a **stock dividend** is to provide the shareholders with additional evidence of their interests in the retained earnings of the business without distribution of cash or other assets. The purpose of a **stock split** is to materially reduce the market price per share by increasing the number of shares outstanding, thereby obtaining wider distribution and improved marketability.

A stock dividend is recognized by capitalizing retained earnings in an amount equal to the **fair value** of the additional shares distributed. Capitalizing retained earnings results in a debit to retained earnings and credits to common stock and additional paid-in capital. A stock split is recognized by a decrease in the par or stated value of the common stock, resulting in a proportionate increase in the number of shares of stock outstanding. In some circumstances, legal requirements of the state in which an entity is incorporated may require the capitalization of retained earnings when a stock split occurs. Moreover, use of the term "dividend" may be required. Under these circumstances, the stock split preferably should be described as a **split-up effected in the form of a dividend**, and retained earnings should be capitalized in an amount equal to the legal requirement, usually the par or stated value of the additional shares distributed.

The entity's description of the intent of the distribution normally determines whether the distribution should be accounted for as a stock dividend or a stock split. However, an issuance of shares **less than 20% or 25%** of the previously outstanding shares usually should be recognized as a stock dividend. The SEC provides that an issuance of less than 25% should be treated as a stock dividend.

Treasury Stock Transactions

When an entity reacquires its previously issued and outstanding shares, these shares may be retired or held as **treasury stock**. However, the stock is not an asset of the corporation, and no dividends are paid on it. To record the **retirement** of shares, the common stock and additional paid-in capital accounts that were credited when the stock was originally issued are debited. An excess of the amounts debited over the purchase cost is credited to additional paid-in capital arising from treasury stock transactions. An excess of the purchase cost over the amounts debited is recorded first as a debit to any additional paid-in capital arising from previous treasury stock transactions, with any remainder recorded as a debit to retained earnings.

The most common method to record shares held as treasury stock is the **cost method**. The reacquired shares are recorded at their acquisition cost as an offset to the sum of capital stock, capital surplus (additional paid-in capital), and retained earnings. When the stock is subsequently reissued for an amount greater than its acquisition cost, the excess is credited to additional paid-in capital from treasury stock transactions. If stock is subsequently reissued for an amount less than its acquisition cost, the difference is recorded first as a debit to any additional paid-in capital arising from treasury stock transactions, with any remainder debited to retained earnings.

An alternative method of accounting for shares held as treasury stock is the **par-value method**. It accounts for a treasury stock transaction as a constructive retirement. In accordance with this method, the reacquired shares first are recorded at par value as an offset to the contributed capital account representing issued stock of the same type. The additional paid-in capital and retained earnings accounts are then treated as if the reacquired shares were retired. When the treasury shares are subsequently reissued, the treasury stock account is eliminated (credited), with any excess of the reissuance price over the par value recorded as a credit to additional paid-in capital in excess of par.

Adjustments or debits or credits resulting from transactions in the entity's own stock are excluded from the earnings or the results of operations. Thus, the receipt of a **contribution of an entity's own stock** is recorded at fair value as increases in both contributed capital and treasury stock. Because these accounts offset, the transaction has no net effect on equity.

Rights and Warrants

When a corporation issues **stock rights and warrants** for no consideration, it makes a memorandum entry. When consideration is received, the issuance is credited to additional paid-in capital – rights and warrants. When securities are issued with **detachable warrants**, the proceeds are allocated between the securities and warrants based on their relative fair values at issuance. When rights and warrants are exercised and stock is issued, capital stock and additional paid-in capital are credited for the proceeds and any amount previously credited to additional paid-in capital – rights and warrants.

QUESTIONS

15.1 General

1. Which of the following is the primary element that distinguishes accounting for corporations from accounting for other legal forms of business entity (such as partnerships)?

   A. The entity theory relates primarily to the other forms of business entity.

   B. The corporation draws a sharper distinction in accounting for sources of capital.

   C. In a corporation, retained earnings may be reduced only by the declaration of dividends.

   D. Generally accepted accounting principles apply to corporations but have relatively little applicability to other forms of business entity.

Answer (B) is correct. *(CPA, adapted)*
   REQUIRED: The primary distinguishing feature of accounting for corporations.
   DISCUSSION: The three primary forms of business entity are the corporation, the partnership, and the proprietorship. Of the three, only the corporation sharply differentiates between contributed equity and equity earned and retained in the business. Contributed capital is reflected in the various capital stock and additional paid-in capital (additional contributed capital) accounts. Earned capital is reflected in the retained earnings accounts.
   Answer (A) is incorrect. The entity theory relates primarily to the corporation. It achieves a greater degree of separation from its owners than any other form of business entity. Answer (C) is incorrect. Retained earnings may be reduced by numerous transactions, including a net operating loss. Answer (D) is incorrect. GAAP apply to all forms of business entity.

2. The issuance of shares of preferred stock to shareholders

   A. Increases preferred stock outstanding.

   B. Has no effect on preferred stock outstanding.

   C. Increases preferred stock authorized.

   D. Decreases preferred stock authorized.

Answer (A) is correct. *(CPA, adapted)*
   REQUIRED: The effect of the issuance of shares of preferred stock to shareholders.
   DISCUSSION: The charter (articles of incorporation) filed with the secretary of state of the state of incorporation indicates the classes of stock that may be issued and their authorized amounts in terms of shares and/or total dollar value. When authorized shares are issued, the effect is to increase the amount of that class of stock outstanding.
   Answer (B) is incorrect. The effect of the issuance of shares is to increase the stock outstanding. Answer (C) is incorrect. The issuance of shares has no effect on the preferred stock authorized. Answer (D) is incorrect. Preferred stock authorized is not affected by the issuance of shares.

3. Bier Corp. issued 400,000 shares of common stock when it began operations in Year 1 and issued an additional 200,000 shares in Year 2. Bier also issued preferred stock convertible to 200,000 shares of common stock. In Year 3, Bier purchased 150,000 shares of its common stock and held it in treasury. At the end of Year 3, how many shares of Bier's common stock were outstanding?

   A. 800,000

   B. 650,000

   C. 600,000

   D. 450,000

Answer (D) is correct. *(CPA, adapted)*
   REQUIRED: The number of shares of outstanding common stock.
   DISCUSSION: Bier issued 400,000 shares of common stock in Year 1 and 200,000 shares in Year 2. The purchase of 150,000 shares of treasury stock decreased the number of shares of common stock outstanding in Year 3 to 450,000 (400,000 + 200,000 – 150,000). The convertible preferred stock is not considered common stock.
   Answer (A) is incorrect. This amount includes the convertible preferred stock and the treasury stock. Answer (B) is incorrect. This amount includes the convertible preferred stock. Answer (C) is incorrect. This amount includes the treasury stock.

4. The preemptive right of shareholders is the right to

A. Share equally in dividend distributions.

B. Purchase shares of stock on a pro rata basis when new issues are offered for sale.

C. Share in the distribution of assets on liquidation of the corporation.

D. Participate in the management of the corporation.

Answer (B) is correct. *(Publisher, adapted)*
REQUIRED: The definition of the preemptive right of shareholders.
DISCUSSION: The preemptive right refers to each shareholder's right to maintain proportionate ownership in the corporation if additional shares are offered for sale.
Answer (A) is incorrect. Sharing equally in dividend distributions is a shareholder right distinct from the preemptive right. Answer (C) is incorrect. Sharing in the distribution of assets on liquidation of the corporation is a shareholder right distinct from the preemptive right. Answer (D) is incorrect. Participating in management is a shareholder right distinct from the preemptive right. Shareholders participate in management of the corporation by electing a board of directors and by voting on referendums presented by management and the directors.

5. On December 1, Circle Corp. received a contribution of 4,000 shares of its $10 par value common stock from a shareholder. On that date, the stock's market value was $70 per share. The stock was originally issued for $50 per share. By what amount does this contribution cause total equity to decrease?

A. $280,000

B. $200,000

C. $40,000

D. $0

Answer (D) is correct. *(CPA, adapted)*
REQUIRED: The decrease in equity from receipt of a contribution of the company's own stock.
DISCUSSION: Contributions received ordinarily are recorded as revenues or gains in the period received. However, adjustments or debits or credits resulting from transactions in the entity's own stock are excluded from earnings or the results of operations. Thus, the receipt of a contribution of a company's own stock is recorded at fair value as increases in both contributed capital and treasury stock. Because these accounts offset, the net effect on equity is $0.
Answer (A) is incorrect. The amount of $280,000 records an effect equal to the current market price. Answer (B) is incorrect. The amount of $200,000 records an effect equal to the original issuance price. Answer (C) is incorrect. The amount of $40,000 records an effect equal to the par value.

6. East Co. issued 2,000 shares of its $5 par common stock to Krannik as compensation for 1,000 hours of legal services performed. Krannik usually bills $200 per hour for legal services. On the date of issuance, the stock was trading on a public exchange at $160 per share. By what amount should the additional paid-in capital account increase?

A. $320,000

B. $310,000

C. $200,000

D. $190,000

Answer (B) is correct. *(CPA, adapted)*
REQUIRED: The increase in additional paid-in capital.
DISCUSSION: When stock is issued for property or services, the transaction is recorded at the fair value of the stock or of the property or services received. In this case, the value of the stock is used because it is more objective. The $320,000 (2,000 shares × $160 market price) should be allocated as follows: $10,000 (2,000 shares × $5 par) to common stock and $310,000 to additional paid-in capital.
Answer (A) is incorrect. An amount of $10,000 should be allocated to common stock. Answer (C) is incorrect. Additional paid-in capital should increase by $310,000. Answer (D) is incorrect. The value of the stock should be used to record the transaction.

7. Ricky Corp. had 700,000 shares of common stock authorized and 300,000 shares outstanding at December 31, Year 1. The following events occurred during Year 2:

January 31	Declared 10% stock dividend
June 30	Purchased 100,000 shares
August 1	Reissued 50,000 shares
November 30	Declared 2-for-1 stock split

At December 31, Year 2, how many shares of common stock did Ricky have outstanding?

A. 560,000

B. 600,000

C. 630,000

D. 660,000

Answer (A) is correct. *(CPA, adapted)*
REQUIRED: The number of outstanding shares of common stock.
DISCUSSION: Ricky had 300,000 shares outstanding at the beginning of the year. The 10% stock dividend (300,000 shares × 10% = 30,000) increased the shares outstanding to 330,000. The purchase reduced shares outstanding to 230,000. The reissuance increased these shares to 280,000. The 2-for-1 stock split increased shares outstanding to 560,000 (280,000 × 2).
Answer (B) is incorrect. The amount of 600,000 ignores all transactions except the stock split. Answer (C) is incorrect. The amount of 630,000 ignores the purchase and reissuance and assumes that the shares of the stock dividend were not split. Answer (D) is incorrect. The amount of 660,000 excludes the treasury stock purchase and the reissuance of 50,000 shares.

Questions 8 and 9 are based on the following information. Anand Co. reported the following in its statement of equity on January 1:

Common stock, $5 par value, authorized 200,000 shares, issued 100,000 shares	$ 500,000
Additional paid-in capital	1,500,000
Retained earnings	516,000
	$2,516,000
Minus treasury stock, at cost, 5,000 shares	40,000
Total equity	$2,476,000

The following events occurred during the year:

May 1	-- 1,000 shares of treasury stock were sold for $10,000. *$10/sh*
July 9	-- 10,000 shares of previously unissued common stock sold for $12 per share.
October 1	-- The distribution of a 2-for-1 stock split resulted in the common stock's per-share par value being halved.

Anand accounts for treasury stock under the cost method. Laws in the state of Anand's incorporation protect shares held in treasury from dilution when stock dividends or stock splits are declared.

8. In Anand's December 31 statement of equity, the par value of the issued common stock should be

A. $550,000

B. $530,000

C. $275,000

D. $265,000

Answer (A) is correct. *(CPA, adapted)*
REQUIRED: The par value of the issued common stock.
DISCUSSION: At the beginning of the year, 100,000 shares with a par value of $500,000 had been issued. These shares included the treasury stock (issued but not outstanding) accounted for at cost. Under the cost method, the par value recorded in the common stock account is unaffected by purchases and sales of treasury stock. On July 9, 10,000 shares of previously unissued common stock were sold. This transaction increased the aggregate par value to $550,000 (110,000 shares issued × $5). The 2-for-1 stock split reduced the par value per share by 50% but did not affect the aggregate par value of the issued stock. Thus, state law presumably did not require capitalization of retained earnings as a result of the stock split.
Answer (B) is incorrect. The par value of the issued and outstanding shares is $530,000. Answer (C) is incorrect. Half the par value of the issued stock is $275,000. Answer (D) is incorrect. Half the par value of the issued and outstanding stock is $265,000.

9. The number of outstanding common shares at December 31 should be

A. 222,000

B. 220,000

C. 212,000

D. 210,000

Answer (C) is correct. *(CPA, adapted)*
REQUIRED: The number of outstanding shares.
DISCUSSION: On January 1, 95,000 shares (100,000 issued – 5,000 treasury shares) were outstanding. The treasury stock sale and the issuance of previously unissued shares increased that amount to 106,000 shares (95,000 + 1,000 + 10,000). The stock split doubled the shares outstanding to 212,000 (106,000 × 2).
Answer (A) is incorrect. This amount assumes 100,000 shares were outstanding on January 1. Answer (B) is incorrect. This amount assumes 100,000 shares were outstanding on January 1 but omits the treasury stock sale. Answer (D) is incorrect. This amount omits the treasury stock sale.

10. The December 31, Year 7, condensed balance sheet of Moore and Daughter, a partnership, follows:

Current assets	$280,000
Equipment (net)	260,000
	$540,000
Liabilities	$140,000
Moore and Daughter, capital	400,000
	$540,000

Fair values at December 31, Year 7, are as follows:

Current assets	$320,000
Equipment	420,000
Liabilities	140,000

On January 2, Year 8, Moore and Daughter was incorporated, with 10,000 shares of $10 par value common stock issued. How much should be credited to additional contributed capital?

A. $640,000

B. $600,000

C. $500,000

D. $400,000

Answer (C) is correct. *(CPA, adapted)*
REQUIRED: The amount credited to additional contributed capital upon incorporation.
DISCUSSION: When assets of a partnership are contributed to a corporation in exchange for par value common stock, the contributed capital account should be credited for the fair value of the net assets. The fair value of the net assets equals $600,000 ($320,000 + $420,000 – $140,000). Of this amount, $100,000 (10,000 shares × $10 par value) should be credited to the capital stock account, with the remaining $500,000 credited to additional contributed capital.
Answer (A) is incorrect. This amount equals the total fair value of the assets minus the $100,000 allocated to capital stock. Answer (B) is incorrect. This amount is the fair value of the net assets. Answer (D) is incorrect. This amount is the partnership capital at its carrying amount.

11. On February 1, Lopez Corporation issued 1,000 shares of its $10 par common and 2,000 shares of its $10 par convertible preferred stock for a lump sum of $40,000. At this date, Lopez's common stock was selling for $18 per share and the convertible preferred stock for $13.50 per share. The amount of proceeds allocated to Lopez's preferred stock should be

A. $22,000

B. $24,000

C. $27,000

D. $30,000

Answer (B) is correct. *(CPA, adapted)*
REQUIRED: The proceeds to be allocated to preferred stock in a lump-sum issuance.
DISCUSSION: Given that the 1,000 shares of common stock and 2,000 shares of preferred stock were issued for a lump sum of $40,000, the proceeds should be allocated based on the relative fair values of the securities issued. The fair value of the common stock is $18,000 (1,000 shares × $18). The fair value of the preferred stock is $27,000 (2,000 shares × $13.50). Because 60% [$27,000 ÷ ($27,000 + $18,000)] of the total fair value is attributable to the preferred stock, $24,000 ($40,000 × 60%) of the proceeds should be allocated to this stock.
Answer (A) is incorrect. This amount equals the lump sum received minus the fair value of the common stock. Answer (C) is incorrect. The fair value of the preferred stock is $27,000. Answer (D) is incorrect. The sum of the par values of the stock issued is $30,000.

12. When collectibility is reasonably assured, the excess of the subscription price over the stated value of no-par common stock subscribed should be recorded as

A. No-par common stock.

B. Additional paid-in capital when the subscription is recorded.

C. Additional paid-in capital when the subscription is collected.

D. Additional paid-in capital when the common stock is issued.

Answer (B) is correct. *(CPA, adapted)*
REQUIRED: The recording of the excess of the subscription price over the stated value of no-par common stock subscribed.
DISCUSSION: The accounting for subscriptions of no-par stock with a stated value is the same as for par value stock. When stock is subscribed, the corporation recognizes an obligation to issue stock, and the subscriber undertakes the legal obligation to pay for the shares subscribed. If collectibility of the subscription price is reasonably assured on the date the subscription is received, the issuing corporation should recognize the cash collected and a subscription receivable for the remainder. In addition, the common stock subscribed account should be credited for the stated value of the shares subscribed, with the excess of the subscription price over the stated value recognized as additional paid-in capital.
Answer (A) is incorrect. A credit is recorded to additional paid-in capital. Answer (C) is incorrect. Additional paid-in capital is not credited when the subscription is collected. Answer (D) is incorrect. Additional paid-in capital is not credited when the common stock is issued.

13. On December 1, Year 3, shares of authorized common stock were issued on a subscription basis at a price in excess of par value. A total of 20% of the subscription price of each share was collected as a down payment on December 1, Year 3, with the remaining 80% of the subscription price of each share due in Year 4. Collectibility was reasonably assured. At December 31, Year 3, the equity section of the balance sheet should report additional paid-in capital for the excess of the subscription price over the par value of the shares of common stock subscribed and

A.   Common stock issued for 20% of the par value of the shares of common stock subscribed.

B.   Common stock issued for the par value of the shares of common stock subscribed.

C.   Common stock subscribed for 80% of the par value of the shares of common stock subscribed.

D.   Common stock subscribed for the par value of the shares of common stock subscribed.

14. Of the 125,000 shares of common stock issued by Maddux Corp., 25,000 shares were held as treasury stock at December 31, Year 4. During Year 5, transactions involving Maddux's common stock were as follows:

January 1 through October 31 -- 13,000 treasury shares were distributed to officers as part of a stock compensation plan.

November 1 -- A 3-for-1 stock split took effect.

December 1 -- Maddux purchased 5,000 of its own shares to discourage an unfriendly takeover. These shares were not retired.

At December 31, Year 5, how many of Maddux's common stock were issued and outstanding?

	Shares Issued	Outstanding
A.	375,000	334,000
B.	375,000	324,000
C.	334,000	334,000
D.	324,000	324,000

Answer (D) is correct. *(CPA, adapted)*
REQUIRED: The proper recording of subscribed stock in the equity section.
DISCUSSION: When stock is subscribed, the corporation recognizes an obligation to issue stock, and the subscriber undertakes the legal obligation to pay for the shares subscribed. If collectibility of the subscription price is reasonably assured on the date the subscription is received, the issuing corporation should recognize the cash collected and a subscription receivable for the remainder. In addition, the common stock subscribed account should be credited for the par value of the shares subscribed, with the excess of the subscription price over the par value recognized as additional paid-in capital.
Answer (A) is incorrect. The equity section of the balance sheet should report the common stock subscribed account for the par value of the shares subscribed and additional paid-in capital for the excess of the subscription price over the par value. Answer (B) is incorrect. The equity section of the balance sheet should report the common stock subscribed account for the par value of the shares subscribed and additional paid-in capital for the excess of the subscription price over the par value. Answer (C) is incorrect. The equity section of the balance sheet should report the common stock subscribed account for 100% of the par value of the shares subscribed.

Answer (A) is correct. *(CPA, adapted)*
REQUIRED: The number of shares issued and outstanding.
DISCUSSION: Given that 125,000 shares have been issued and that the stock has been split 3-for-1, the shares issued at year end equal 375,000 (125,000 × 3). At the beginning of the year, 100,000 shares were outstanding (125,000 issued – 25,000 treasury shares). After 13,000 treasury shares were distributed, 113,000 were outstanding, an amount that increased to 339,000 (113,000 × 3) after the stock split. The purchase on December 1 reduced the shares outstanding to 334,000 (339,000 – 5,000).
Answer (B) is incorrect. If the 5,000-share purchase had been made before the split, 324,000 shares would be outstanding. Answer (C) is incorrect. Shares issued exceed shares outstanding. Answer (D) is incorrect. Shares issued exceed shares outstanding.

15. Galarraga Co. completed a number of capital transactions during the fiscal year ended September 30 as follows:

- An issue of 8% debentures was converted into common stock.
- An issue of $2.50 preferred stock was called and retired.
- A 10% common stock dividend was distributed on November 30.
- Warrants for 200,000 shares of common stock were exercised on September 20.

For the year-end financial statements to be sufficiently informative, Galarraga's most satisfactory method of presenting the effects of these events is

A. A formal retained earnings statement and general description in the notes to the financial statements.

B. A formal statement of changes in equity that discloses changes in the various equity accounts.

C. A detailed inclusion of each event or transaction in the statement of cash flows.

D. Comparative statements of income, financial position, and retained earnings for this year and last year.

Answer (B) is correct. *(CMA, adapted)*
REQUIRED: The most satisfactory method of presenting the effects of the listed capital transactions.
DISCUSSION: When both financial position and results of operations are presented, the entity must disclose changes in (1) the accounts included in equity (in addition to retained earnings) and (2) the number of shares of equity securities during at least the most recent annual fiscal period and any subsequent interim periods presented. The required disclosure may be made in the basic financial statements, in the notes, or in a formal statement of changes in equity (which is preferable).
Answer (A) is incorrect. A general description is inadequate. Answer (C) is incorrect. Events or transactions not resulting in cash flows (e.g., conversion of debt to equity or a stock dividend) are not included in the statement of cash flows. Answer (D) is incorrect. Presenting disclosures about changes in equity in a separate statement gives them greater prominence than if they were contained in the basic statements.

16. At the end of the current year, Peek Corp., a newly formed company, had the following stock issued and outstanding:

- Common stock, no par, $1 stated value, 10,000 shares originally issued for $15 per share
- Preferred stock, $10 par value, 3,000 shares originally issued for $25 per share

Peek's statement of equity for the year should report

	Common Stock	Preferred Stock	Additional Paid-In Capital (APIC)
A.	$150,000	$30,000	$45,000
B.	$150,000	$75,000	$0
C.	$10,000	$75,000	$140,000
D.	$10,000	$30,000	$185,000

Answer (D) is correct. *(CPA, adapted)*
REQUIRED: The amounts of common stock, preferred stock, and APIC reported in the statement of equity.
DISCUSSION: The common stock was issued for a total of $150,000 (10,000 shares × $15). Of this amount, $10,000 (10,000 shares × $1 stated value) should be allocated to the common stock, with the remaining $140,000 ($150,000 – $10,000) credited to APIC. The preferred stock was issued for $75,000 (3,000 shares × $25), of which $30,000 (3,000 shares × $10 par value) should be allocated to the preferred stock and $45,000 ($75,000 – $30,000) to APIC. In the Year 1 statement of equity, Peek therefore should report $10,000 in the common stock account, $30,000 in the preferred stock account, and $185,000 ($140,000 + $45,000) as APIC.
Answer (A) is incorrect. The total received for the common stock is $150,000, and $45,000 omits the APIC for the common stock. Answer (B) is incorrect. The total received for the common stock is $150,000, $75,000 includes the APIC for the preferred stock, and $0 omits the APIC for the common and preferred stock. Answer (C) is incorrect. The amount of $75,000 includes the APIC for the preferred stock, and $140,000 omits the APIC for the preferred stock.

17. During Year 1, Andruw Co. issued 5,000 shares of $100 par convertible preferred stock for $110 per share. One share of preferred stock can be converted into three shares of Andruw's $25 par common stock at the option of the preferred shareholder. On December 31, Year 2, when the market value of the common stock was $40 per share, all of the preferred stock was converted. What amount should Andruw credit to common stock and to additional paid-in capital as a result of the conversion?

	Common Stock	Additional Paid-In Capital
A.	$375,000	$175,000
B.	$375,000	$225,000
C.	$500,000	$50,000
D.	$600,000	$0

Answer (A) is correct. *(CPA, adapted)*
　REQUIRED: The amounts credited to common stock and additional paid-in capital.
　DISCUSSION: Andruw received $550,000 (5,000 × $110) for the preferred stock converted to common stock. The par value of the 15,000 shares (5,000 × 3) of common stock is $375,000 (15,000 × $25). The remaining $175,000 ($550,000 – $375,000) is credited to additional paid-in capital.
　Answer (B) is incorrect. An amount of $175,000 is credited to additional paid-in capital ($550,000 – $375,000). Answer (C) is incorrect. The par value of the preferred stock, not the common stock, is $500,000. Answer (D) is incorrect. The fair value of the common stock at the date of conversion is $600,000.

18. Sanders Company effects self-insurance against loss from fire by appropriating an amount of retained earnings each year equal to the amount that would otherwise be paid out as fire insurance premiums. According to current accounting literature, the procedure used by Sanders is

A. Prohibited for external reporting purposes.

B. Acceptable provided that fire losses are not charged against the appropriation.

C. Acceptable provided that fire losses are charged against the appropriation.

D. Acceptable if the amount is shown outside the equity section of the balance sheet.

Answer (B) is correct. *(Publisher, adapted)*
　REQUIRED: The true statement about an appropriation of retained earnings to disclose self-insurance against fire loss.
　DISCUSSION: GAAP permit no accrual of an expense prior to the occurrence of the event for which an entity self-insures. The reason is that the value of the property diminishes only if the event actually occurs. But an appropriation of retained earnings is acceptable to disclose the self-insurance policy if, when a fire loss occurs, (1) the entry appropriating retained earnings is reversed, and (2) the loss is charged against income of the period of loss and not against retained earnings.
　Answer (A) is incorrect. An appropriation of retained earnings for self-insurance is permissible. Answer (C) is incorrect. Fire losses may never be charged against the appropriation of retained earnings. Answer (D) is incorrect. The procedure is acceptable only if the appropriation is shown within the equity section of the balance sheet.

19. In Year 1, Veras Corp. reported $3,500,000 of appropriated retained earnings for the construction of a new office building, which was completed in Year 2 at a total cost of $3,000,000. In Year 2, Veras appropriated $2,400,000 of retained earnings for the construction of a new plant. Also, $4,000,000 of cash was restricted for the retirement of bonds due in Year 3. In its Year 2 balance sheet, Veras should report what amount of appropriated retained earnings?

A. $2,400,000

B. $2,900,000

C. $5,900,000

D. $6,400,000

Answer (A) is correct. *(CPA, adapted)*
　REQUIRED: The amount of appropriated retained earnings reported.
　DISCUSSION: Appropriating retained earnings is a formal way of marking a portion of retained earnings for other uses. A journal entry is used to reclassify retained earnings to appropriated retained earnings. When the appropriation is no longer necessary, the entry is reversed. The original appropriation of $3,500,000 in Year 1 would have been reversed for that amount in Year 2. The cash restriction is not included in appropriated retained earnings. If the amount is material, the restriction will require separate reporting of the cash item in the balance sheet, footnote disclosure, and reclassification as noncurrent. Thus, appropriated retained earnings in Year 2 should be reported at $2,400,000.
　Answer (B) is incorrect. This amount includes the previous year's excess of appropriated retained earnings over the actual cost. Answer (C) is incorrect. This amount includes the cash restriction and subtracts the previous year's excess of appropriated retained earnings over the actual cost. Answer (D) is incorrect. This amount includes the $4,000,000 restriction on cash for bond retirement.

20. At December 31, Year 5, Chipper Corporation has the following account balances:

Common stock ($10 par, 50,000 shares issued)	$500,000
8% preferred stock ($50 par, 10,000 shares issued)	500,000
Paid-in capital in excess of par on common stock	640,000
Paid-in capital in excess of par on preferred stock	20,000
Retained earnings	600,000

The preferred stock is cumulative, nonparticipating, and has a call price of $55 per share. Chipper's journal entry to record the redemption of all preferred stock on January 2, Year 6, pursuant to the call provision is

A.
Preferred stock	$500,000	
Paid-in capital in excess of par: preferred	20,000	
Discount on preferred stock	30,000	
Cash		$550,000

B.
Preferred stock	$500,000	
Paid-in capital in excess of par: preferred	20,000	
Loss on redemption of preferred stock	30,000	
Cash		$550,000

C.
Preferred stock	$500,000	
Loss on redemption of preferred stock	50,000	
Retained earnings	300,000	
Cash		$550,000
Paid-in capital in excess of par: preferred		300,000

D.
Preferred stock	$500,000	
Paid-in capital in excess of par: preferred	20,000	
Retained earnings	30,000	
Cash		$550,000

Answer (D) is correct. *(CIA, adapted)*
REQUIRED: The journal entry to record the redemption of preferred stock pursuant to the call provision.
DISCUSSION: The exercise of the call provision resulted in the redemption of the 10,000 shares of preferred stock issued and outstanding at the call price of $550,000 (10,000 shares × $55 call price per share). To eliminate the carrying amount of the preferred stock and recognize the cash paid in this transaction, the required journal entry is to debit preferred stock for $500,000, debit paid-in capital in excess of par: preferred for $20,000, and credit cash for $550,000. The difference of $30,000 ($550,000 cash – $520,000 carrying amount of the preferred stock) is charged to retained earnings. No loss is reported because GAAP do not permit the recognition of a gain or loss on transactions involving a company's own stock.
Answer (A) is incorrect. The $30,000 excess of cash paid over the carrying amount of the redeemed stock should not be debited to a discount on preferred stock account. Answer (B) is incorrect. The $30,000 excess of cash paid over the carrying amount of the redeemed stock should be debited to retained earnings. Answer (C) is incorrect. The $30,000 excess of cash paid over the carrying amount of the redeemed stock should be debited to retained earnings. Also, paid-in capital in excess of par: preferred, should be debited for $20,000.

15.2 Cash and Property Dividends

21. On January 15, Rico Co. declared its annual cash dividend on common stock for the year ended January 31. The dividend was paid on February 9 to shareholders of record as of January 28. On what date should Rico decrease retained earnings by the amount of the dividend?

A. January 15.

B. January 31.

C. January 28.

D. February 9.

Answer (A) is correct. *(CPA, adapted)*
REQUIRED: The date to decrease retained earnings by the amount of the dividend.
DISCUSSION: Unlike stock dividends, cash dividends cannot be rescinded. A liability to the shareholders is created because the dividends must be paid once they are declared. At the declaration date, retained earnings must be debited, resulting in a decrease.

Retained earnings	$XXX	
Dividends payable		$XXX

The declaration date was January 15.
Answer (B) is incorrect. The entry should not be an adjusting entry. Answer (C) is incorrect. The liability and the reduction in retained earnings should be recognized on the declaration date. Answer (D) is incorrect. The liability was never recorded.

22. Glavine Corp., a company with a fiscal year end on October 31, had sufficient retained earnings as a basis for dividends but was temporarily short of cash. Glavine declared a dividend of $100,000 on February 1, Year 3, and issued promissory notes to its shareholders in lieu of cash. The notes, which were dated February 1, Year 3, had a maturity date of January 31, Year 4, and a 10% interest rate. How should Glavine account for the scrip dividend and related interest?

A. Debit retained earnings for $110,000 on February 1, Year 3.

B. Debit retained earnings for $110,000 on January 31, Year 4.

C. Debit retained earnings for $100,000 on February 1, Year 3, and debit interest expense for $10,000 on January 31, Year 4.

D. Debit retained earnings for $100,000 on February 1, Year 3, and debit interest expense for $7,500 on October 31, Year 3.

Answer (D) is correct. *(CPA, adapted)*
REQUIRED: The accounting for a scrip dividend and its related interest.
DISCUSSION: When a scrip dividend is declared, retained earnings should be debited and scrip dividends (or notes) payable should be credited for the amount of the dividend ($100,000) excluding interest. Interest accrued on the scrip dividend is recorded as a debit to interest expense up to the balance sheet date with a corresponding credit for interest payable. Thus, interest expense will be debited and interest payable credited for $7,500 [$100,000 × 10% × (9 months ÷ 12 months)] on 10/31/Year 3.
Answer (A) is incorrect. Interest expense is recognized on the balance sheet date and on the date of payment, not on the date of declaration. Answer (B) is incorrect. At year end, $7,500 of the $10,000 interest expense should be recognized, and retained earnings should be debited on the date of declaration. Answer (C) is incorrect. At year end, $7,500 of the $10,000 interest expense should be recognized.

23. Weiss Company declared a cash dividend on its common stock on December 15, Year 1, payable on January 12, Year 2. How would this dividend affect equity on the following dates?

	December 15, Year 1	December 31, Year 1	January 12, Year 2
A.	Decrease	No effect	Decrease
B.	Decrease	No effect	No effect
C.	No effect	Decrease	No effect
D.	No effect	No effect	Decrease

Answer (B) is correct. *(CPA, adapted)*
REQUIRED: The effect on retained earnings of a cash dividend.
DISCUSSION: When cash dividends are declared, a liability to the shareholders is created because the dividends must be paid once they are declared. At the declaration date, retained earnings must be debited, resulting in a decrease in retained earnings. The effect is to decrease total equity (assets – liabilities) because liabilities are increased with no corresponding increase in assets. At the balance sheet date, no entry is made and there is no effect on equity. When the cash dividends are subsequently paid, the dividends payable account is debited and a cash account credited. Thus, at the payment date, equity is also not affected.
Answer (A) is incorrect. Payment has no effect on equity. Answer (C) is incorrect. Declaration decreases equity, but at year end has no effect. Answer (D) is incorrect. Declaration decreases equity, but payment has no effect.

24. On June 1, Ligtenberg Company's board of directors declared a cash dividend of $1.00 per share on the 50,000 shares of common stock outstanding. The company also has 5,000 shares of treasury stock. Shareholders of record on June 15 are eligible for the dividend, which is to be paid on July 1. On June 1, the company should

A. Make no accounting entry.

B. Debit retained earnings for $50,000.

C. Debit retained earnings for $55,000.

D. Debit retained earnings for $50,000 and paid-in capital for $5,000.

Answer (B) is correct. *(CMA, adapted)*
REQUIRED: The proper journal entry on the declaration date of a dividend.
DISCUSSION: Dividends are recorded on their declaration date by a debit to retained earnings and a credit to dividends payable. The dividend is the amount payable to all shares outstanding. Treasury stock is not eligible for dividends because it is not outstanding. Thus, the June 1 entry is to debit retained earnings and credit dividends payable for $50,000 (50,000 × $1).
Answer (A) is incorrect. A liability should be recorded. Answer (C) is incorrect. The treasury stock is not eligible for a dividend. Answer (D) is incorrect. Paid-in capital is not affected by the dividend declaration.

25. Lunar Corp.'s outstanding capital stock at September 15 of the current year consisted of the following:

- 30,000 shares of 5% cumulative preferred stock, par value $10 per share, fully participating as to dividends. No dividends were in arrears.
- 200,000 shares of common stock, par value $1 per share.

On September 15 of the current year, Lunar declared dividends of $100,000. What was the amount of dividends payable to Lunar's common shareholders?

- A. $10,000
- B. $34,000
- C. $40,000
- D. $60,000

Answer (C) is correct. *(CPA, adapted)*
REQUIRED: The amount of dividends payable to common shareholders.
DISCUSSION: The stated rate of dividends must be paid to preferred shareholders before any amount is paid to common shareholders. Because no dividends are in arrears, this amount is $15,000 (30,000 shares × $10 par × 5%). The preferred stock is also fully participating. The preferred will participate equally in the cash dividend after a 5% return is paid on the common. The basic return to common shareholders is $10,000 (200,000 shares × $1 par × 5%). The total of the basic distributions to the shareholders is $25,000 ($15,000 + $10,000). The remaining $75,000 ($100,000 – $25,000) of the total cash dividend will be shared by all shareholders in proportion to the par values of the shares outstanding.
The aggregate par value of the preferred is $300,000 (30,000 shares × $10 par). The aggregate par value of the common is $200,000 (200,000 shares × $1 par). The distribution will therefore be in the ratio of 3:2, and $45,000 ($75,000 × 60%) is the participating share of the preferred shareholders. The balance of $30,000 ($75,000 – $45,000) will be paid to the common shareholders. The total amount of dividends payable on the common stock is $40,000 ($10,000 + $30,000).
Answer (A) is incorrect. The basic return to common shareholders is $10,000. Answer (B) is incorrect. The amount of $34,000 results from assuming that no basic return is paid to the common shareholders. Answer (D) is incorrect. The amount paid to the preferred shareholders is $60,000.

26. At December 31, Year 2 and Year 3, Perigel Co. had 3,000 shares of $100 par, 5% cumulative preferred stock outstanding. No dividends were in arrears as of December 31, Year 1. Perigel did not declare a dividend during Year 2. During Year 3, Perigel paid a cash dividend of $10,000 on its preferred stock. Perigel should report dividends in arrears in its Year 3 financial statements as a(n)

- A. Accrued liability of $15,000.
- B. Disclosure of $15,000.
- C. Accrued liability of $20,000.
- D. Disclosure of $20,000.

Answer (D) is correct. *(CPA, adapted)*
REQUIRED: The amount and means of reporting preferred dividends in arrears.
DISCUSSION: Dividends in arrears on preferred stock are not an obligation of the company and are not recognized in the financial statements. However, the aggregate and per-share amounts of arrearages in cumulative preferred dividends should be disclosed on the face of the balance sheet or in the notes. The aggregate amount in arrears is $20,000 [(3,000 shares × $100 par × 5% × 2 years) – $10,000 paid in Year 3].
Answer (A) is incorrect. Dividends in arrears do not meet recognition criteria for a liability. Answer (B) is incorrect. The amount of $15,000 is the arrearage for 1 year. Answer (C) is incorrect. Dividends in arrears do not meet recognition criteria for a liability.

27. Instead of the usual cash dividend, Smalty Corp. declared and distributed a property dividend from its overstocked merchandise. The excess of the merchandise's carrying amount over its fair value should be

- A. Ignored.
- B. Reported as a separately disclosed reduction of retained earnings.
- C. Reported as an extraordinary loss, net of income taxes.
- D. Reported as a reduction in income before extraordinary items.

Answer (D) is correct. *(CPA, adapted)*
REQUIRED: The method of accounting for the excess of the carrying amount of a property dividend over its fair value.
DISCUSSION: A nonreciprocal transfer of nonmonetary assets to owners ordinarily must be recorded at the fair value of the asset transferred on the declaration date. But the transfer is accounted for at the recorded amount of the assets given up if it is made in (1) a spinoff (or other form of reorganization or liquidation) or (2) a plan that effectively rescinds a business combination. This property dividend qualifies for fair value measurement. Thus, a loss should be recognized on the disposition of the asset. This loss on merchandise is an operating item, not an extraordinary loss.
Answer (A) is incorrect. This property dividend qualifies as a nonreciprocal transfer and should be accounted for as such. Answer (B) is incorrect. Accounting for the property dividend at fair value gives rise to a loss that should be reported in the income statement. Answer (C) is incorrect. The loss does not meet the criteria of an extraordinary item.

28. A property dividend should be recorded in retained earnings at the property's

    A. Fair value at date of declaration.

    B. Fair value at date of issuance (payment).

    C. Carrying amount at date of declaration.

    D. Carrying amount at date of issuance.

Answer (A) is correct. *(CPA, adapted)*
REQUIRED: The method of accounting for the value of property dividend.
DISCUSSION: When a property dividend is declared, the property to be distributed should be restated at fair value. Any gain or loss should be recognized. The declared dividend is then recorded as a debit to retained earnings and a credit to property dividends payable.
Answer (B) is incorrect. The fair value is determined as of the declaration date. Answer (C) is incorrect. Fair value at the date of declaration is used. Answer (D) is incorrect. Fair value at the date of declaration is the preferred alternative.

29. On June 27, Year 1, Marquis Co. distributed to its common shareholders 100,000 outstanding common shares of its investment in Chen Co., an unrelated party. The carrying amount on the books of Chen's $1 par common stock was $2 per share. Immediately after the distribution, the market price of Chen's stock was $2.50 per share. In its income statement for the year ended June 30, Year 1, what amount should Marquis report as gain before income taxes on disposal of the stock?

    A. $250,000

    B. $200,000

    C. $50,000

    D. $0

Answer (C) is correct. *(CPA, adapted)*
REQUIRED: The amount to be reported as gain before income taxes on disposal of stock.
DISCUSSION: When a property dividend is declared, the property to be distributed should be restated from carrying amount to fair value, with the resultant gain or loss recognized. Thus, Marquis should report a gain of $50,000 [100,000 shares × ($2.50 − $2.00)].
Answer (A) is incorrect. The fair value of the property dividend is $250,000. Answer (B) is incorrect. The book value of the property dividend is $200,000. Answer (D) is incorrect. A $50,000 gain should be recognized.

30. Orr Corporation owned 1,000 shares of Vee Corporation. These shares were purchased for $9,000. On September 15, Orr declared a property dividend of one share of Vee for every 10 shares of Orr held by a shareholder. On that date, when the market price of Vee was $14 per share, 9,000 shares of Orr were outstanding. This transaction did not constitute a spin-off or other form of reorganization or liquidation and was not part of a plan that was in substance a rescission of a prior business combination. What gain and net reduction in retained earnings would result from this property dividend?

	Gain	Net Reduction in Retained Earnings
A.	$0	$8,100
B.	$0	$12,600
C.	$4,500	$3,600
D.	$4,500	$8,100

Answer (D) is correct. *(CPA, adapted)*
REQUIRED: The gain and net reduction in retained earnings from a property dividend.
DISCUSSION: The Vee shares had a carrying amount of $9 per share ($9,000 ÷ 1,000 shares). Because 900 shares were distributed by Orr as a property dividend (9,000 shares ÷ 10), the shares used as a property dividend had a total carrying amount of $8,100. The fair value of the 900 shares on the date of declaration was $12,600 (900 shares × $14 per share). The transaction is not effectively a reorganization, liquidation, or rescission of a business combination. Thus, a nonreciprocal transfer of a nonmonetary asset to a shareholder must be recorded at the fair value of the asset transferred, and a gain or loss must be recognized on the disposition. The gain is $4,500 ($12,600 fair value − $8,100 carrying amount). The net reduction in retained earnings is $8,100 ($12,600 dividend − $4,500 gain). The journal entries are

Retained earnings	$12,600	
Property dividend payable		$12,600
Property dividend payable	$12,600	
Investment in Vee		$ 8,100
Gain on Vee disposition		4,500

Answer (A) is incorrect. A gain must be recognized when the fair value of a property dividend is higher than its carrying amount. Answer (B) is incorrect. A gain must be recognized. It affects part of the reduction of retained earnings. Answer (C) is incorrect. The gain is $3,600 if the full amount of the $9,000 of Vee Corporation stock is subtracted from the $12,600 dividend.

15.3 Stock Dividends and Stock Splits

31. The following data are extracted from the equity section of the balance sheet of Ebbs Corporation:

	12/31/Yr 6	12/31/Yr 7
Common stock ($2 par value)	$100,000	$102,000
Paid-in capital in excess of par	50,000	58,000
Retained earnings	100,000	104,600

During Year 7, the corporation declared and paid cash dividends of $15,000 and also declared and issued a stock dividend. There were no other changes in stock issued and outstanding during Year 7. Net income for Year 7 was

A. $4,600

B. $19,600

C. $21,600

D. $29,600

Answer (D) is correct. *(CIA, adapted)*
REQUIRED: The net income for Year 7 after payment of cash and stock dividends.
DISCUSSION: The cash dividends reduced retained earnings by $15,000. The stock dividend reduced retained earnings by $10,000, as determined from the changes in the contributed capital accounts [($102,000 + $58,000) – ($100,000 – $50,000)]. Hence, as shown below, net income was $29,600.

Retained earnings			
		$100,000	Beginning
Cash dividend	$15,000		
Stock dividend	10,000		
		29,600	Net income
		$104,600	Ending

Answer (A) is incorrect. The increase in retained earnings for the year is $4,600. Answer (B) is incorrect. The amount of $19,600 results from not reducing retained earnings by the stock dividend. Answer (C) is incorrect. The amount of $21,600 results from reducing retained earnings for a $2,000 stock dividend.

32. The following information was abstracted from the accounts of the Moore Corp. at year end:

Total income since incorporation	$840,000
Total cash dividends paid	260,000
Proceeds from sale of donated Travis Co. stock	90,000
Total value of stock dividends distributed	60,000
Excess of proceeds over cost of treasury stock sold	140,000

What should be the current balance of retained earnings?

A. $520,000

B. $580,000

C. $610,000

D. $670,000

Answer (A) is correct. *(CPA, adapted)*
REQUIRED: The current balance of retained earnings.
DISCUSSION: To compute the current balance, one must know which transactions affected retained earnings. Total income since incorporation ($840,000) increased retained earnings, whereas both the cash dividends and the stock dividends ($260,000 + $60,000) decreased it. Proceeds from the sale of the donated stock (given that it was not Moore Corp. stock) already would have been included in income to the extent of gain or loss. The excess of proceeds over the cost of treasury stock also does not affect retained earnings because the credit is to additional paid-in capital from treasury stock transactions. The current balance of retained earnings is therefore equal to $520,000 ($840,000 – $260,000 – $60,000).
Answer (B) is incorrect. This amount results from not reducing retained earnings by the value of stock dividends distributed. Answer (C) is incorrect. This amount results from adding the proceeds from the sale of donated stock. Answer (D) is incorrect. This amount results from including the proceeds from the sale of donated stock and not subtracting the total value of the stock dividends distributed.

33. Jordan Corp. declared a 5% stock dividend on its 10,000 issued and outstanding shares of $2 par value common stock, which had a fair value of $5 per share before the stock dividend was declared. This stock dividend was distributed 60 days after the declaration date. By what amount did Jordan's current liabilities increase as a result of the stock dividend declaration?

A. $0

B. $500

C. $1,000

D. $2,500

Answer (A) is correct. *(CPA, adapted)*
REQUIRED: The increase in current liabilities as a result of the stock dividend declaration.
DISCUSSION: Declaration of an issuance of fewer than 20% to 25% of the shares outstanding is a stock dividend. It is not accounted for as a liability but as a reclassification of equity. The entry is to debit retained earnings for the fair value of the stock (10,000 shares × $5 fair value × 5% = $2,500), credit stock dividend distributable at par (10,000 shares × $2 × 5% = $1,000), and credit additional paid-in capital for the excess of fair value over par value ($2,500 – $1,000 = $1,500).
Answer (B) is incorrect. There is no liability, only a reclassification of equity. Answer (C) is incorrect. Retained earnings should be debited and capital stock credited. Answer (D) is incorrect. No liability is recognized.

34. A corporation issuing stock should charge retained earnings for the market value of the shares issued in a

    A. Reverse stock split.

    B. 2-for-1 stock split accounted for as a stock dividend.

    C. 10% stock dividend.

    D. 2-for-1 stock split.

Answer (C) is correct. *(CPA, adapted)*
    REQUIRED: The basis for charging retained earnings when stock is issued.
    DISCUSSION: A stock dividend is a stock issuance of fewer than 20% to 25% of the shares outstanding. It generally should be accounted for by charging (debiting) retained earnings for the fair value of the stock and crediting a capital stock account for the par or stated value. A difference between the fair value and the par or stated value is credited to an additional paid-in capital account. Hence, retained earnings decreases, but total equity does not change.
    Answer (A) is incorrect. A reverse stock split has no effect on the capital accounts. Answer (B) is incorrect. When an issuance exceeds 20% to 25% of the shares outstanding and capitalization of retained earnings is required by law, the transaction should be accounted for as a stock split-up effected in the form of a dividend. Retained earnings should be charged for the amount required by state law, usually the par or stated value of the shares issued. Answer (D) is incorrect. A stock split has no effect on the capital accounts.

35. Unlike a stock split, a stock dividend requires a formal journal entry in the financial accounting records because stock

    A. Dividends increase the relative book value of an individual's stock holding.

    B. Splits increase the relative book value of an individual's stock holdings.

    C. Dividends are payable on the date they are declared.

    D. Dividends represent a transfer from retained earnings to capital stock.

Answer (D) is correct. *(CIA, adapted)*
    REQUIRED: The reason a stock dividend requires a formal journal entry and a stock split does not.
    DISCUSSION: The purpose of a stock dividend is to provide evidence to the shareholders of their interest in accumulated earnings without distribution of cash or other property.
    Answer (A) is incorrect. Stock dividends have no effect on total equity or on the book value of an individual shareholder's investment. Answer (B) is incorrect. Stock splits have no effect on total equity or on the book value of an individual shareholder's investment. Answer (C) is incorrect. Dividends, whether stock, cash, or property, are usually payable on a date different from the declaration date.

36. On December 31, Year 4, the equity section of Spitz Co. was as follows:

Common stock, par value $10; authorized 30,000 shares; issued and outstanding 9,000 shares	$ 90,000
Additional paid-in capital	116,000
Retained earnings	146,000
Total equity	$352,000

On March 31, Year 5, Spitz declared a 10% stock dividend. Accordingly, 900 shares were issued when the fair value was $16 per share. For the 3 months ended March 31, Year 5, Spitz sustained a net loss of $32,000. The balance of Spitz's retained earnings as of March 31, Year 5, should be

    A. $99,600

    B. $105,000

    C. $108,600

    D. $114,000

Answer (A) is correct. *(CPA, adapted)*
    REQUIRED: The retained earnings balance after a stock dividend and incurrence of a net loss.
    DISCUSSION: When the number of shares issued is fewer than 20% to 25% of the outstanding stock, the issuance generally is considered a stock dividend. Retained earnings should be debited for the fair value of the stock distributed as a stock dividend. Thus, $14,400 (900 Spitz shares × $16 fair value) should be debited to retained earnings. Retained earnings should also be decreased by the net loss of $32,000. Thus, the balance of Spitz's retained earnings as of March 31 is $99,600 ($146,000 beginning balance – $14,400 stock dividend – $32,000 net loss).
    Answer (B) is incorrect. The amount of $105,000 results from reducing retained earnings by the par value of the stock dividend. Answer (C) is incorrect. The amount of $108,600 results from reducing retained earnings by the difference between the fair value and the par value. Answer (D) is incorrect. The amount of $114,000 results from not reducing retained earnings for the stock dividend.

37. Effective April 27, the shareholders of Wuerffel Corp. approved a 2-for-1 split of the company's common stock and an increase in authorized common shares from 100,000 shares (par value $20 per share) to 200,000 shares (par value $10 per share). No state legal requirements apply to this stock split. Wuerffel's equity accounts immediately before issuance of the shares were as follows:

Common stock, par value $20;
  100,000 shares authorized;
  50,000 shares outstanding
	$1,000,000

Additional paid-in capital ($3 per share on issuance of common stock)	150,000
Retained earnings	1,350,000

The shares were issued on June 30. In Wuerffel's June 30 statement of equity, the balances of additional paid-in capital and retained earnings are

	Additional Paid-In Capital	Retained Earnings
A.	$0	$500,000
B.	$150,000	$350,000
C.	$150,000	$1,350,000
D.	$1,150,000	$350,000

Answer (C) is correct. *(CPA, adapted)*
REQUIRED: The effect of a stock split on additional paid-in capital and retained earnings.
DISCUSSION: A stock split is a nonreciprocal transfer of a company's own shares to its common shareholders in order to reduce the unit market price of the shares. The purpose is to increase the shares' marketability and broaden their distribution. Given this clear intent by Wuerffel, no transfer from retained earnings is necessary unless required by law. Hence, absent state legal requirements, the transaction described will increase the number of shares outstanding to 100,000 (50,000 shares × 2), the par value will be reduced to $10 ($20 ÷ 2), but the capital accounts will be unaffected. To effect this stock split, no formal entry is necessary because no capitalization of retained earnings occurs. Thus, additional paid-in capital ($150,000) and retained earnings ($1,350,000) will not change.
Answer (A) is incorrect. A stock split will affect only the number of shares outstanding and the par value. Answer (B) is incorrect. The capital accounts will remain unaffected in total. Answer (D) is incorrect. A stock split will affect only the number of shares outstanding and the par value. The capital accounts will remain unaffected in total.

15.4 Treasury Stock Transactions

38. An amount representing the difference between the carrying amount and the proceeds from the purchase and resale of treasury stock may be reflected only in

A. Paid-in capital accounts.

B. Income, paid-in capital, and retained earnings accounts.

C. Retained earnings and paid-in capital accounts.

D. Income and retained earnings accounts.

Answer (C) is correct. *(Publisher, adapted)*
REQUIRED: The accounts affected by treasury stock transactions.
DISCUSSION: Adjustments, debits, or credits resulting from transactions in the entity's own stock are always excluded from earnings or the results of operations. Hence, an excess of the proceeds over the carrying amount of treasury stock must be credited to additional paid-in capital. An excess of the carrying amount over the proceeds of treasury stock may be debited to either retained earnings or additional paid-in capital, depending on the circumstances.
Answer (A) is incorrect. Retained earnings may sometimes be charged as a result of treasury stock transactions. Answer (B) is incorrect. Transactions in treasury stock do not affect income. Answer (D) is incorrect. Transactions in treasury stock may only be reflected in paid-in capital and retained earnings.

39. The acquisition of treasury stock will cause the number of shares outstanding to decrease if the treasury stock is accounted for by the

	Cost Method	Par-Value Method
A.	Yes	No
B.	No	No
C.	Yes	Yes
D.	No	Yes

Answer (C) is correct. *(CPA, adapted)*
REQUIRED: The effect of the acquisition of treasury stock on the number of shares outstanding.
DISCUSSION: When treasury stock is acquired, the effect will be to decrease the number of shares of common stock outstanding whether the treasury stock is accounted for by the cost method or the par-value method.
Answer (A) is incorrect. When treasury stock is acquired, the number of shares outstanding will decrease under the par-value method. Answer (B) is incorrect. When treasury stock is acquired, the number of shares outstanding will decrease under both the cost method and the par-value method. Answer (D) is incorrect. When treasury stock is acquired, the number of shares outstanding will decrease under the cost method.

40. Treasury stock transactions may result in

A. Increases in the balance of retained earnings.

B. Increases or decreases in the amount of net income.

C. Decreases in the balance of retained earnings.

D. Increases or decreases in the amount of shares authorized to be issued.

Answer (C) is correct. *(J.N. McKenna)*
REQUIRED: The effect of treasury stock transactions.
DISCUSSION: Under the par-value method, when treasury shares are purchased for a price greater than the par value, retained earnings is debited for the excess of the purchase price over the par value if there is no existing paid-in capital from past treasury stock transactions or if the existing credit balance is insufficient to absorb the excess. Under the cost method, if the subsequent resale price of the treasury shares is less than the original acquisition price, it may be necessary to charge retained earnings for a portion or all of the excess of the original purchase price over the sales price.
Answer (A) is incorrect. Equity credits from treasury stock transactions would affect paid-in capital accounts, not retained earnings. Answer (B) is incorrect. Treasury stock transactions have no effect on net income. Answer (D) is incorrect. Treasury stock transactions affect only the number of outstanding shares, not the authorized number.

41. In Year 1, Phineas Co. issued $10 par value common stock for $25 per share. No other common stock transactions occurred until March 31, Year 3, when Phineas acquired some of the issued shares for $20 per share and retired them. Which of the following statements correctly states an effect of this acquisition and retirement?

A. Year 3 net income is decreased.

B. Year 3 net income is increased.

C. Additional paid-in capital is decreased.

D. Retained earnings is increased.

Answer (C) is correct. *(CPA, adapted)*
REQUIRED: The effect of the acquisition and retirement of a company's stock for less than the issue price.
DISCUSSION: When shares of common stock are reacquired and retired, contributed capital should be debited for the amount that was credited upon the issuance of the securities. In addition, because the acquisition of a company's own shares is an equity transaction, no gain or loss should be reflected in the determination of income. The entry is to debit common stock at par (number of shares × $10) and additional paid-in capital [number of shares × ($25 − $10)], and to credit additional paid-in capital from retirement of common stock [number of shares × ($25 − $20)] and cash (number of shares × $20). The effect is to decrease additional paid-in capital.
Answer (A) is incorrect. Contributed capital is the affected account. Answer (B) is incorrect. Net income is not affected. Answer (D) is incorrect. Retained earnings may not be increased because of treasury stock transactions.

42. Knight Corp. holds 20,000 shares of its $10 par value common stock as treasury stock reacquired in Year 1 for $240,000. On December 12, Year 3, Knight reissued all 20,000 shares for $380,000. Under the cost method of accounting for treasury stock, the reissuance resulted in a credit to

A. Common stock of $200,000.

B. Retained earnings of $140,000.

C. Gain on sale of investments of $140,000.

D. Additional paid-in capital of $140,000.

Answer (D) is correct. *(CPA, adapted)*
REQUIRED: The effect of the reissuance of treasury stock accounted for under the cost method.
DISCUSSION: When treasury stock accounted for under the cost method is acquired, the treasury stock account is debited for the amount of the purchase price. If it is subsequently reissued for a price greater than its carrying amount, the excess is credited to additional paid-in capital. For this transaction, the excess is $140,000 ($380,000 − $240,000).
Answer (A) is incorrect. The common stock account is unaffected by purchases and subsequent resales of treasury stock accounted for by the cost method. Answer (B) is incorrect. Gains on treasury stock transactions may not be credited to retained earnings. Answer (C) is incorrect. Gains on sale of investments may not be credited to income.

43. McGlinchy Company had 100,000 shares of $4 par value common stock outstanding on June 12 of the current year. On this date, McGlinchy acquired 1,000 of its own shares as treasury stock at a cost of $12 per share. The acquisition was accounted for by the cost method. As a result of this treasury stock purchase,

A. Total assets and total equity decreased.

B. Total assets and total equity were unaffected.

C. Total assets, retained earnings, and total equity decreased.

D. Total assets were unaffected, but retained earnings decreased.

Answer (A) is correct. *(CMA, adapted)*
REQUIRED: The effect on the balance sheet of an acquisition of treasury stock accounted for by the cost method.
DISCUSSION: Under the cost method, the acquisition of treasury stock is recorded as a debit to treasury stock and a credit to cash equal to the amount of the purchase price. This transaction results in a decrease in both total assets and total equity.
Answer (B) is incorrect. Both total assets and total equity decrease. Answer (C) is incorrect. Retained earnings are unaffected. Answer (D) is incorrect. Total assets decrease and retained earnings are unaffected.

44. Daniel Corp. had outstanding 2,000 shares of 11% preferred stock, $50 par. On September 17 of the current year, Daniel redeemed and retired 25% of these shares for $22,500. On that date, Daniel's additional paid-in capital from preferred stock totaled $30,000. To record this transaction, Daniel should debit (credit) its capital accounts as follows:

	Preferred Stock	Additional Paid-In Capital	Retained Earnings
A.	$25,000	$ 7,500	$(10,000)
B.	$25,000	--	$ (2,500)
C.	$25,000	$(2,500)	--
D.	$22,500	--	--

Answer (C) is correct. *(CPA, adapted)*
REQUIRED: The accounting for redemption and retirement of preferred stock.
DISCUSSION: Under the cost method, the entry to record a treasury stock purchase is to debit treasury stock at cost ($22,500) and credit cash. The entry to retire this stock is to debit preferred stock at par [(2,000 shares × 25%) × $50 = $25,000], credit treasury stock at cost ($22,500), and credit additional paid-in capital from preferred stock ($2,500). No entry to retained earnings is necessary.
Answer (A) is incorrect. The capital accounts are affected, but retained earnings is not. Answer (B) is incorrect. Retained earnings is not affected. Answer (D) is incorrect. Preferred stock is debited for the par value of the retired shares.

45. On December 31 of the current year, Remlinger Corp.'s board of directors canceled 50,000 shares of $2.50 par value common stock held in treasury at an average cost of $13 per share. Before recording the cancelation of the treasury stock, Remlinger had the following balances in its equity accounts:

Common stock	$540,000
Additional paid-in capital	750,000
Retained earnings	900,000
Treasury stock, at cost	650,000

In its balance sheet at December 31 of the current year, Remlinger should report common stock outstanding of

A. $0

B. $250,000

C. $415,000

D. $540,000

Answer (C) is correct. *(CPA, adapted)*
REQUIRED: The common stock outstanding after cancelation of the treasury stock.
DISCUSSION: The treasury shares had an aggregate par value of $125,000 (50,000 shares × $2.50). Consequently, the common stock outstanding after their retirement is $415,000 ($540,000 par value of issued common stock – $125,000).
Answer (A) is incorrect. There are 166,000 shares ($415,000 ÷ $2.50) of common stock outstanding. Answer (B) is incorrect. This amount is the difference between retained earnings and the cost of the treasury stock. Answer (D) is incorrect. This amount is the par value of the issued shares prior to cancelation of the treasury stock.

46. In Year 1, Rattana Corp. acquired 6,000 shares of its own $1 par value common stock at $18 per share. In Year 2, Rattana reissued 3,000 of these shares at $25 per share. Rattana uses the cost method to account for its treasury stock transactions. What accounts and amounts should Rattana credit in Year 2 to record the reissuance of the 3,000 shares?

	Treasury Stock	Additional Paid-In Capital	Retained Earnings	Common Stock
A.	$54,000	--	$21,000	--
B.	$54,000	$21,000	--	--
C.	--	$72,000	--	$3,000
D.	--	$51,000	$21,000	$3,000

Answer (B) is correct. *(CPA, adapted)*
REQUIRED: The accounts and amounts to be credited when treasury stock is reissued.
DISCUSSION: Under the cost method, the treasury stock account should be debited for the purchase price. When this stock is subsequently reissued for an amount greater than its acquisition cost, the excess should be credited to additional paid-in capital. The 3,000 shares were purchased as treasury stock for $54,000 (3,000 shares × $18 per share). They were reissued for $75,000 (3,000 shares × $25 per share). Under the cost method, the carrying amount of the 3,000 shares was $54,000. When these shares are reissued, the treasury stock account should be credited for $54,000, with the remaining $21,000 ($75,000 – $54,000) credited to additional paid-in capital.
Answer (A) is incorrect. Additional paid-in capital, not retained earnings, should be credited. Answer (C) is incorrect. Additional paid-in capital should be credited for $21,000 and treasury stock for $54,000. Common stock is unaffected. Answer (D) is incorrect. Additional paid in capital should be credited for $21,000, and retained earnings and common stock are unaffected.

47. Burkett, Inc., initially issued 100,000 shares of its $10 par common stock at $11 per share. During the current year, Burkett acquired 30,000 shares of its common stock at a price of $16 per share and accounted for them by the cost method. Subsequently, these shares were reissued at a price of $12 per share. Burkett had made no other issuances or acquisitions of its own common stock. What effect does the reissuance of the stock have on the following accounts?

	Additional Paid-In Capital	Retained Earnings
A.	Decrease	Decrease
B.	No effect	Decrease
C.	Decrease	No effect
D.	No effect	No effect

48. Lem Co., which accounts for treasury stock under the par-value method, acquired 100 shares of its $6 par value common stock for $10 per share. The shares had originally been issued by Lem for $7 per share. By what amount would Lem's additional paid-in capital from common stock decrease as a result of the acquisition?

A. $0

B. $100

C. $300

D. $400

49. Mulholland Corp. acquired treasury shares at an amount greater than their par value but less than their original issue price. Compared with the cost method of accounting for treasury stock, does the par value method report a greater amount for additional paid-in capital and a greater amount for retained earnings?

	Additional Paid-In Capital	Retained Earnings
A.	Yes	Yes
B.	Yes	No
C.	No	No
D.	No	Yes

Answer (B) is correct. *(CPA, adapted)*
REQUIRED: The effect of a reissuance of treasury stock on retained earnings and additional paid-in capital.
DISCUSSION: When shares are issued for an amount greater than their par value, the difference is credited to additional paid-in capital. Under the cost method, the treasury stock account should be debited for the price of reacquired shares. If the treasury stock is subsequently reissued for an amount less than its acquisition cost but greater than its original issuance price, the difference between the acquisition cost and the reissuance price should be recorded as a decrease in additional paid-in capital from treasury stock transactions. However, if this account has a $0 balance, retained earnings is decreased. Thus, Burkett must debit cash for $360,000 (30,000 shares × $12 reissuance price per share), debit (decrease) retained earnings for $120,000 [30,000 shares × ($16 cost per share – $12)], and credit treasury stock for $480,000 (30,000 shares × $16 cost per share). As long as the reissuance price is greater than the original issuance price, additional paid-in capital will not be affected.
Answer (A) is incorrect. Additional paid-in capital is not affected. Answer (C) is incorrect. Additional paid-in capital is not affected, but retained earnings is decreased. Answer (D) is incorrect. Retained earnings is decreased.

Answer (B) is correct. *(CPA, adapted)*
REQUIRED: The decrease in APIC after an acquisition of treasury stock accounted for under the par-value method.
DISCUSSION: The entry for issuance of the stock was

Cash	$700	
Common stock ($6 per share)		$600
Additional paid-in capital		$100

The par-value method treats a treasury stock purchase as a constructive retirement. Assuming no balance in paid-in capital from treasury stock transactions, the entry for the treasury stock purchase using the par-value method is

Treasury stock-common stock	$600	
Additional paid-in capital	100	
Retained earnings	300	
Cash		$1,000

Answer (A) is incorrect. Under the par-value method, the acquisition of treasury stock is accounted for by reducing additional paid-in capital by the amount recorded when the shares were originally issued. Answer (C) is incorrect. The amount of $300 is the debit to retained earnings. Answer (D) is incorrect. The amount of $400 is the sum of the debit to additional paid-in capital and the debit to retained earnings.

Answer (C) is correct. *(CPA, adapted)*
REQUIRED: The effect of the par value method on additional paid-in capital and retained earnings compared with that of the cost method.
DISCUSSION: Under the cost method, the purchase of treasury stock has no effect on additional paid-in capital and retained earnings. Under the par value method, given that the acquisition cost is greater than par but less than the original issue price, treasury stock is debited at par and cash is credited for the purchase price. Additional paid-in capital is debited and additional paid-in capital from treasury stock transactions is credited for the difference between par value and the purchase price. Hence, additional paid-in capital is lower under the par value method, and retained earnings are not affected under either method.
Answer (A) is incorrect. The par value method does not report a greater amount for additional paid-in capital or retained earnings. Answer (B) is incorrect. The par value method does not report a greater amount for additional paid-in capital. Answer (D) is incorrect. The par value method does not report a greater amount for retained earnings.

50. On incorporation, Genomenon, Inc., issued common stock at a price in excess of its par value. No other stock transactions occurred except that treasury stock was acquired for an amount exceeding this issue price. If Genomenon uses the par value method of accounting for treasury stock appropriate for retired stock, what is the effect of the acquisition on the following?

	Net Common Stock	Additional Paid-In Capital	Retained Earnings
A.	No effect	Decrease	No effect
B.	Decrease	Decrease	Decrease
C.	Decrease	No effect	Decrease
D.	No effect	Decrease	Decrease

Answer (B) is correct. *(CPA, adapted)*
REQUIRED: The effects of a purchase of treasury stock accounted for under the par value method.
DISCUSSION: Under the par value method, treasury stock is debited at par value, and the amount is reported as a reduction of common stock. The purchase also results in the removal of the additional paid-in capital associated with the original issue of the shares. Given that no other stock transactions occurred and that treasury stock was acquired for an amount exceeding the issue price, the balancing debit for the excess of the acquisition price over the issue price is to retained earnings. If additional paid-in capital from treasury stock transactions had been previously recorded, the balancing debit would be to that account but only to the extent of its credit balance. Thus, retained earnings is also decreased.
Answer (A) is incorrect. Net common stock and retained earnings are decreased. Answer (C) is incorrect. Additional paid-in capital is decreased. Answer (D) is incorrect. Net common stock is decreased.

51. Treasury stock was acquired for cash at a price in excess of its original issue price. The treasury stock was subsequently reissued for cash at a price in excess of its acquisition price. Assuming that the par value method of accounting for treasury stock transactions is used, what is the effect on total equity of each of the following events?

	Acquisition of Treasury Stock	Reissuance of Treasury Stock
A.	Decrease	No effect
B.	Decrease	Increase
C.	Increase	Decrease
D.	No effect	No effect

Answer (B) is correct. *(CPA, adapted)*
REQUIRED: The effect on total equity of treasury stock transactions accounted for under the par value method.
DISCUSSION: The par value method treats the acquisition of treasury stock as a constructive retirement and its resale as a new issuance of stock. Thus, the acquisition of treasury stock will be reflected as a decrease in total equity. The reissuance will be accounted for as an increase in total equity.
Answer (A) is incorrect. Under the par value method, the reissuance of treasury stock is treated as a resale and will increase total equity. Answer (C) is incorrect. Under the par value method, acquisition of treasury stock will reduce total equity, while the reissuance of treasury stock will increase total equity. Answer (D) is incorrect. Under the par value method, acquisition of treasury stock is treated as a constructive retirement which will reduce total equity. The reissuance of treasury stock is treated as a resale and will increase total equity.

15.5 Rights and Warrants

52. On December 1, Year 1, Lombard, Inc., issued warrants to its shareholders giving them the right to purchase additional $20 par value common shares at a price of $30. The shareholders exercised all warrants on April 1, Year 2. The shares had market prices of $33, $35, and $40 on December 1, Year 1; December 31, Year 1; and April 1, Year 2, respectively. What were the effects of the warrants on Lombard's additional paid-in capital and net income?

	Additional Paid-In Capital	Net Income
A.	Increased in Year 2	No effect
B.	Increased in Year 1	No effect
C.	Increased in Year 2	Decreased in Year 1 and Year 2
D.	Increased in Year 1	Decreased in Year 1 and Year 2

Answer (A) is correct. *(CPA, adapted)*
REQUIRED: The effects on additional paid-in capital and net income when warrants are issued and exercised.
DISCUSSION: When stock rights and warrants are issued for no consideration, only a memorandum entry is made. Consequently, common stock and additional paid-in capital are not affected. However, when warrants are exercised and stock is issued, the issuing company will reflect the proceeds as an increase in common stock and additional paid-in capital. Consequently, Lombard will increase additional paid-in capital in Year 2 when stock is issued, but net income will not be affected.
Answer (B) is incorrect. Only a memorandum entry is made in Year 1. Answer (C) is incorrect. Net income is not affected. Answer (D) is incorrect. Only a memorandum entry is made in Year 1, and net income is not affected.

53. Quilvio Co. issued rights to its existing shareholders without consideration. A shareholder received a right to buy one share for each 20 shares held. The exercise price was in excess of par value but less than the current market price. Retained earnings decreases when

	Rights Are Issued	Rights Are Exercised
A.	Yes	Yes
B.	Yes	No
C.	No	Yes
D.	No	No

54. Merrilea Goings, Inc., issued preferred stock with detachable common stock warrants. The issue price exceeded the sum of the warrants' fair value and the preferred stocks' par value. The preferred stocks' fair value was not determinable. What amount should be assigned to the warrants outstanding?

A. Total proceeds.

B. Excess of proceeds over the par value of the preferred stock.

C. The proportion of the proceeds that the warrants' fair value bears to the preferred stocks' par value.

D. The fair value of the warrants.

55. On September 1, Poilu Corp. issued rights to shareholders to subscribe to additional shares of its common stock. One right was issued for each share owned. A shareholder could purchase one additional share for 10 rights plus $15 cash. The rights expired on November 30. On September 1, the market price of a share with the right attached was $40, while the market price of one right alone was $2. Poilu's equity on August 31 included the following:

Common stock, $25 par value,
  4,000 shares issued and outstanding $100,000
Additional paid-in capital   60,000
Retained earnings   80,000

By what amount should Poilu's retained earnings decrease as a result of issuance of the stock rights on September 1?

A. $0

B. $5,000

C. $8,000

D. $10,000

Answer (D) is correct. *(CPA, adapted)*
REQUIRED: The effect on retained earnings when rights are issued and exercised.
DISCUSSION: When stock rights are issued for no consideration, only a memorandum entry is made. When stock rights are exercised and stock is issued, the issuing company will reflect the proceeds as an increase in common stock and additional paid-in capital. Thus, retained earnings will not be affected when rights are issued or exercised.
Answer (A) is incorrect. Retained earnings will not be affected when rights are issued or exercised. Answer (B) is incorrect. Retained earnings will not be affected when rights are issued. Answer (C) is incorrect. Retained earnings will not be affected when rights are exercised.

Answer (D) is correct. *(CPA, adapted)*
REQUIRED: The amount assigned to outstanding warrants when the preferred stocks' fair value is not determinable.
DISCUSSION: When securities are issued with detachable stock warrants, the proceeds should generally be allocated between the securities and the warrants based on their relative fair values at issuance. However, if the fair value of only the warrants is known, the warrants should be recorded at fair value, with the remainder allocated to the securities.
Answer (A) is incorrect. The total proceeds need to be allocated between the warrants and the preferred stock. Answer (B) is incorrect. Par value is not an appropriate basis for allocation. Answer (C) is incorrect. The fair value of the warrants is not related to the par value of the preferred stock.

Answer (A) is correct. *(CPA, adapted)*
REQUIRED: The effect on retained earnings when stock rights are issued.
DISCUSSION: When stock rights are issued for no consideration, only a memorandum entry is made. When stock rights are exercised and stock is issued, the issuing company will reflect the proceeds as an increase in common stock and additional paid-in capital. Thus, retained earnings will not be affected when rights are either issued or exercised.
Answer (B) is incorrect. Stock rights will have no effect on retained earnings. Answer (C) is incorrect. When stock rights are issued, only a memorandum entry is made, having no effect on retained earnings. Answer (D) is incorrect. When stock rights are issued, only a memorandum entry is made.

56. On June 4, Year 3, Bastet Co. purchased 1,000 shares of Angkor Co.'s common stock at $80 per share. On December 26, Year 3, Bastet received 1,000 stock rights to purchase an additional 1,000 shares at $90 per share. The stock rights had an expiration date of May 1, Year 4. On December 26, Year 3, Angkor's common stock had a market value, ex-rights, of $95 per share, and the stock rights had a market value of $5 each. What amount should Bastet record on December 26, Year 3, for the investment in stock rights?

A. $4,000

B. $5,000

C. $10,000

D. $15,000

Answer (A) is correct. *(CPA, adapted)*
REQUIRED: The amount to be recorded for the investment in stock rights on the balance sheet.
DISCUSSION: The $80 original cost of each share of stock should be allocated between the stock and the stock right based on their relative fair values.

Stock:	$80 cost × [$95 ÷ ($95 + $5)] = $76
Right:	$80 cost × [$ 5 ÷ ($95 + $5)] = $\underline{\quad 4}$
	$\underline{\underline{\$80}}$

Thus, the stock rights should be recorded at $4,000 (1,000 rights × $4) on the balance sheet.
Answer (B) is incorrect. The fair value of the rights is $5,000. Answer (C) is incorrect. This amount is the difference between the cost of the 1,000 shares of stock and the exercise price for an additional 1,000 shares. Answer (D) is incorrect. This amount is the difference between the cost of the 1,000 shares of stock and their fair value.

57. In September Year 5, Felinity Corp. made a dividend distribution of one right for each of its 240,000 shares of outstanding common stock. Each right was exercisable for the purchase of 1% of a share of Felinity's $50 variable rate preferred stock at an exercise price of $80 per share. On March 20, Year 10, none of the rights had been exercised, and Felinity redeemed them by paying each shareholder $0.10 per right. As a result of this redemption, Felinity's equity was reduced by

A. $240

B. $24,000

C. $48,000

D. $72,000

Answer (B) is correct. *(CPA, adapted)*
REQUIRED: The effect on equity of the redemption of stock rights.
DISCUSSION: When rights are issued for no consideration, only a memorandum entry is made. Consequently, neither common stock nor additional paid-in capital is affected by the issuance of rights in a nonreciprocal transfer. The redemption of the rights reduces equity by the amount of their cost (240,000 × $.10 = $24,000).
Answer (A) is incorrect. The amount of $240 equals $.10 times the number of shares (2,400) that could have been purchased. Answer (C) is incorrect. If the rights were initially credited to paid-in capital at $72,000, or $.30 each [($80 exercise price – $50 par value) ÷ 100], and paid-in capital was reduced by the redemption price of $.10 each (240,000 × $.10 = $24,000), the balance remaining would be $48,000. Answer (D) is incorrect. This amount assumes a price per right of $.30 [($80 exercise price – $50 par value) ÷ 100].

Use Gleim **EQE Test Prep** Software Download for interactive study and performance analysis.

STUDY UNIT SIXTEEN
EPS AND SHARE-BASED PAYMENT

Earnings per share (EPS) is the amount of earnings attributable to a share of common stock. Investors commonly use this ratio to measure the performance of an entity over an accounting period. The two forms of EPS are basic and diluted.

Basic Earnings per Share (BEPS)

BEPS measures earnings performance based on common stock outstanding during all or part of the reporting period.

$$BEPS = \frac{Income\ available\ to\ common\ shareholders}{Weighted\text{-}average\ common\ shares\ outstanding}$$

Income available to common shareholders is determined by subtracting current dividends accumulated on cumulative preferred stock (arrearages would have been subtracted in prior periods) and current dividends declared on noncumulative preferred stock from income from continuing operations, other income components, and net income. When either a loss from continuing operations or a net loss is reported, dividends on preferred stock (if applicable) increase the amount of the loss.

The **weighted-average number of shares of common stock outstanding** is equal to the shares of common stock outstanding during the entire period, plus the shares issued or minus those reacquired during the period. The latter shares are weighted according to the portion of the period they were outstanding.

Diluted Earnings per Share (DEPS)

BEPS is the only EPS measure reported by an entity with a **simple capital structure**, that is, one with only common stock outstanding. All other entities must report BEPS and DEPS. DEPS includes the effects of dilutive **potential common stock**, a security or other contract that may entitle the holder to obtain common stock. It includes (1) convertible securities (convertible preferred stock and convertible debt), (2) stock options and warrants, and (3) contingently issuable common stock. Potential common stock is **dilutive** if its inclusion in EPS decreases EPS or increases loss per share. In determining whether potential common stock is dilutive, each issue or series of issues must be considered separately and in sequence from the most dilutive to the least dilutive.

DEPS is computed by (1) increasing the BEPS denominator for the weighted-average number of additional shares of common stock that would have been outstanding if the dilutive potential common stock had been issued and (2) adding back to the BEPS numerator any dividends on convertible preferred stock and after-tax interest related to any convertible debt. The numerator also must be adjusted for other changes in income or loss, such as profit-sharing expenses, that would result from the assumed issuance of common stock. DEPS is based on the holder's most advantageous conversion rate or exercise price. Previously reported DEPS is not retroactively adjusted for subsequent conversions or changes in the market price of the common stock.

$$DEPS = \frac{BEPS\ numerator + Effect\ of\ dilutive\ PCS}{BEPS\ denominator + Effect\ of\ dilutive\ PCS}$$

The **if-converted** method is used to determine the dilutive effect of **convertible securities**. It assumes that the convertible security was converted at the beginning of the period or time of issuance, if later. Conversion is not assumed if the effect is antidilutive. As a result, to arrive at the DEPS denominator, the BEPS denominator is increased by the weighted-average number of shares of common stock assumed to be issued. To determine the DEPS numerator, the BEPS numerator is increased by the dividends on convertible preferred stock and by the after-tax amounts of interest (after amortization of discount or premium) related to convertible debt for which the denominator was increased. The numerator is also adjusted for other changes in income or loss, such as profit-sharing expenses, that would result from the assumed issuance of common shares.

The **treasury stock method** is used to determine the dilutive effect of outstanding **call options and warrants**. Dilution occurs if the average market price for the period exceeds the exercise price. The treasury stock method assumes that (1) the options and warrants were exercised at the beginning of the period or time of issuance, if later; (2) the proceeds (weighted-average number of shares issuable upon exercise × price) were used to purchase common stock at the **average market price** during the period; and (3) to arrive at the DEPS denominator, the BEPS denominator is increased by the excess, if any, of shares issued over the shares purchased.

If a potential common stock has a dilutive effect on DEPS for **income from continuing operations**, the number of shares used to adjust the denominator for that calculation is used to adjust the denominator for the calculation of DEPS for all other reported earnings amounts. If a loss from continuing operations or a loss from continuing operations available to common shareholders is reported, potential common stock is not included in the calculation of DEPS for any reported earnings amount because the effect would be antidilutive.

If the number of common shares outstanding changes because of a **stock dividend, a stock split, or a reverse stock split**, EPS amounts for all periods presented are adjusted retroactively to reflect the change in capital structure as if it had occurred at the beginning of the first period presented. These adjustments are made even if the change occurs after the close of the current period but before the issuance of the financial statements.

All entities must present EPS amounts for both income from continuing operations and net income on the face of the income statement. An entity with a **simple capital structure** (only common stock and nondilutive potential common stock outstanding) must report BEPS amounts. An entity with a **complex capital structure** (one with dilutive securities) must present BEPS and DEPS amounts with equal prominence. An entity that reports a discontinued operation or an extraordinary item must report the applicable EPS amount(s) on the face of the income statement or in the notes.

An entity must **disclose** (1) EPS data for all periods for which either an income statement or a summary of earnings is presented; (2) for all periods for which an income statement is presented, (a) a reconciliation by individual security of the numerators and denominators of the BEPS and DEPS computations for income from continuing operations (including income and share effects), (b) the effect of preferred dividends on the BEPS numerator, and (c) potential common shares not included in DEPS because their inclusion would have had an antidilutive effect in the periods reported; and (3) for the latest period for which an income statement is presented, any transaction occurring after the end of the most recent period but before the issuance of the financial statements that would have had a material effect on common shares or potential common shares outstanding had the transaction occurred prior to the balance sheet date. If DEPS data are reported for at least one period, they must be reported for all periods presented, even if they are equal to BEPS amounts.

Public and private entities must disclose the following **information about capital structure**: (1) rights and privileges of outstanding securities, (2) information about the number of shares issued, (3) information about liquidation preferences of preferred stock, and (4) redemption requirements for the next 5 years.

Share-Based Payment

The guidance for share-based payment applies to receipt by the entity of goods or services in return for (1) its **equity instruments**, e.g., shares or share options, or (2) incurrence of **liabilities** to suppliers that (a) are based on the **price** of the entity's equity instruments or (b) may require share settlement. Initial recognition of goods or services occurs when they are received. The credit is to equity or a liability depending on which classification criteria are met. Cost is recognized upon disposal or consumption of the goods or services. In a transaction with **nonemployees**, the more reliably measurable of the fair value of the equity instruments issued or the consideration received is used to measure the transaction. In a transaction with **employees**, the fair value of the equity instruments issued ordinarily is the basis for measurement. The fair value of the services they render ordinarily is not readily determinable.

Employee compensation cost for an award classified as **equity** is recognized over the **requisite service period (RSP)**. The credit is usually to paid-in capital. The following are typical entries:

Compensation expense	$XXX	
Paid-in capital – equity award		$XXX
(recognition of expense)		
Cash	$XXX	
Paid-in capital – equity award	XXX	
Common stock		$XXX
Paid-in capital in excess of par		XXX
(issuance of shares)		
Paid-in capital – equity award	$XXX	
Paid-in capital – forfeitures		$XXX
(forfeitures, expiration of options, etc.,		
result in **renaming of paid-in capital**)		

The RSP is the period during which employees must perform services. It is most often the **vesting period**. The beginning of the RSP is usually the grant date. The **grant date** is when (1) a mutual understanding of key terms of the award has been reached and (2) the employer is obligated if the employee renders the requisite service. Vesting conditions may be performance conditions or service conditions or both. **Performance conditions** relate to rendering services for a specified period and reaching objectives that relate solely to the employer's activities (e.g., achieving a stated rate of growth). **Service conditions** pertain solely to rendering services for the designated period. **Market conditions** (e.g., attaining a specified share price) do not affect vesting. Hence, an entity must not reverse previously recognized compensation cost solely because a market condition is unsatisfied.

Total compensation cost at the end of the RSP is based on the **number of equity instruments** for which the requisite service was completed. The entity must estimate this number when initial accruals are made. Changes in the estimate result in recognition of the cumulative effect on prior and current periods in the calculation of compensation cost for the period of change. The cost of employee services performed in exchange for awards of share-based compensation normally is measured at the **grant-date fair value** of the equity instruments issued or **fair value** of the liabilities incurred. Such liabilities are remeasured at each reporting date. The fair value of an equity share option (i.e., one with time value) is determined using an observable market price of an option with similar terms if available. In other cases, a valuation method, such as an option-pricing model (for example, the Black-Scholes-Merton model or a binomial model) may be used. **Nonpublic entities** may be unable to determine the expected volatility of their share prices. Such entities must substitute the historical volatility of their industry sector index. The resulting measure is **calculated value**. When an entity cannot reasonably estimate the fair value of equity instruments at the grant date, the accounting is based on **intrinsic value**.

Fair value of an underlying share – Exercise price of an option

Remeasurement is required at each reporting date and on final settlement. Periodic compensation cost is based on the change in intrinsic value. The final measure of compensation cost is the intrinsic value on the settlement date. An award may meet the criteria for classification as a **liability**. The measurement date for liabilities is the settlement date. Thus, after initial recognition, liabilities are remeasured at each reporting date. A public entity remeasures liabilities based on their fair values. Periodic compensation cost depends on the change (or part of the change, depending on the requisite service performed to date) in fair value. A **nonpublic entity** may elect to measure all such liabilities at **fair value** or **intrinsic value**. The percentage of fair value or intrinsic value accrued as compensation cost equals the percentage of required service rendered to date.

Share appreciation rights (SARs) allow employees to receive the increase in value of the shares directly from the employer rather than having to purchase the shares and sell them to receive the benefit. The covered employee receives the appreciation of the market price on the exercise date over the option price. The award may be distributed with cash or shares of the entity's stock. If the employer has the right to settle the award in shares, an **equity transaction** is reported. The fair value of the SARs is measured at the grant date in the same way as share options, and the compensation cost is recognized over the service period. If the employee has the right to choose to receive cash on the exercise date, the SARs are considered to be a **liability**. The liability is estimated at the grant date but continually adjusted to recognize the fair value of the liability at the balance sheet date. Compensation cost is recognized every year of the service period as a fraction of total compensation cost. The estimate of total compensation cost changes every year, so the accounting for a change in estimate must be applied.

QUESTIONS

16.1 Basic Earnings per Share (BEPS)

1. With respect to the computation of earnings per share, which of the following would be most indicative of a simple capital structure?

- A. Common stock, preferred stock, and convertible debt outstanding.
- B. Common stock, convertible preferred stock, and debt outstanding.
- C. Common stock, preferred stock, and debt outstanding.
- D. Common stock, preferred stock, and stock options outstanding.

Answer (C) is correct. *(CPA, adapted)*
REQUIRED: The situation most indicative of a simple capital structure.
DISCUSSION: A simple capital structure has only common stock outstanding. A complex capital structure contains potential common stock. Potential common stock includes options, warrants, convertible securities, contingent stock requirements, and any other security or contract that may entitle the holder to obtain common stock.
Answer (A) is incorrect. A simple capital structure does not include convertible debt outstanding. Answer (B) is incorrect. A simple capital structure does not include convertible preferred stock. Answer (D) is incorrect. A simple capital structure does not include stock options.

2. The disclosure requirements for earnings per share do not apply to

- A. Statements presented by corporations whose capital structures contain only common stock.
- B. Statements presented by wholly owned subsidiaries.
- C. Statements presented by corporations whose capital structures contain both common stock and potential common stock.
- D. Summaries of financial statements that purport to present the results of operations of publicly held corporations in conformity with generally accepted accounting principles.

Answer (B) is correct. *(Publisher, adapted)*
REQUIRED: The type of capital structure or financial statement presentation to which EPS disclosure requirements do not apply.
DISCUSSION: EPS disclosure requirements apply to companies whose securities trade in a public market. Specifically exempted are investment companies (such as mutual funds) and wholly owned subsidiaries from these disclosure requirements.
Answer (A) is incorrect. EPS disclosure requirements apply to companies whose capital structures only contain common stock. Answer (C) is incorrect. EPS disclosure requirements apply to companies whose capital structures contain both common stock and potential common stock. Answer (D) is incorrect. EPS data of companies subject to EPS disclosure requirements must be presented for all periods for which an income statement or a summary of earnings is presented.

3. Earnings-per-share data must be reported on the face of the income statement for

	Income from Continuing Operations	Cumulative Effect of a Change in Accounting Principle
A.	Yes	Yes
B.	Yes	No
C.	No	No
D.	No	Yes

Answer (B) is correct. *(CPA, adapted)*
REQUIRED: The EPS data that must be reported on the face of the income statement.
DISCUSSION: EPS data for income from continuing operations and net income must be reported on the face of the income statement. EPS data for a discontinued operation or an extraordinary item may be disclosed on the face of the income statement or in a note.
Answer (A) is incorrect. EPS data is not reported for the effect of an accounting change. Answer (C) is incorrect. EPS data must be reported on the face of the income statement for income from continuing operations and net income. Answer (D) is incorrect. EPS data must be reported on the face of the income statement for income from continuing operations and net income but not for the effect of an accounting change.

4. What is the required financial statement presentation of earnings per share?

- A. Restatement of EPS data of a prior period if the earnings of the prior period have been restated by a prior-period adjustment.
- B. Dual presentation of BEPS and DEPS for the current period only.
- C. The presentation of BEPS only for prior periods presented for comparative purposes.
- D. Disclosure of the effect of a restatement of prior-period earnings from a prior-period adjustment in the current period, but not in EPS form.

Answer (A) is correct. *(Publisher, adapted)*
REQUIRED: The financial statement presentation of EPS.
DISCUSSION: When the results of operations of a prior period are restated in the financial statements, the EPS data for those prior periods must also be restated.
Answer (B) is incorrect. Both BEPS and DEPS must be disclosed for all periods presented if a corporation has a complex capital structure. Answer (C) is incorrect. BEPS must be disclosed for all periods presented if a corporation has a complex capital structure. Answer (D) is incorrect. Presentation of the effect of a prior-period adjustment on EPS is required for all prior periods affected by such restatement.

5. With regard to stock dividends and stock splits, current authoritative literature contains what general guideline for the computation of EPS?

A. If changes in common stock resulting from stock dividends, stock splits, or reverse splits have been consummated after the close of the period but before completion of the financial report, the per-share computations should be based on the new number of shares.

B. It is not necessary to give recognition to the effect on prior periods' computations of EPS for stock dividends or stock splits consummated in the current period.

C. Computations of EPS for prior periods must give recognition to changes in common shares due to stock splits, but not stock dividends, because stock dividends have an immaterial effect on EPS.

D. Footnote disclosure is necessary for anticipated stock dividends and stock splits and their effect on BEPS and DEPS.

Answer (A) is correct. *(Publisher, adapted)*
   REQUIRED: The treatment of stock dividends and stock splits in the calculation of the weighted-average number of shares.
   DISCUSSION: When a stock dividend, stock split, or reverse split occurs at any time before issuance of the financial statements, restatement of EPS is required for all periods presented. The purpose is to promote comparability of EPS data among reporting periods.
   Answer (B) is incorrect. The effect of stock dividends and stock splits on prior-period earnings must be calculated, and EPS data should be restated for all periods presented in the financial statements. Answer (C) is incorrect. Stock dividends and stock splits are treated the same for EPS purposes regardless of their amounts. Answer (D) is incorrect. A stock dividend or stock split is not accounted for or disclosed until it occurs.

6. In computing the loss per share of common stock, cumulative preferred dividends not earned should be

A. Deducted from the loss for the year.

B. Added to the loss for the year.

C. Deducted from income in the year paid.

D. Added to income in the year paid.

Answer (B) is correct. *(CPA, adapted)*
   REQUIRED: The effect of unearned cumulative preferred dividends on the loss-per-share calculation.
   DISCUSSION: When preferred stock is cumulative, the dividend, whether earned or not, is deducted from income from continuing operations and net income, or added to any loss for the year, in computing earnings or loss, per share of common stock. When preferred stock is noncumulative, an adjustment is made for dividends declared. If the dividend is cumulative only if earned, no adjustment is necessary except to the extent of available income; that is, the preferred dividends accumulate only to the extent of net income.
   Answer (A) is incorrect. It has the effect of reducing loss per share. Answer (C) is incorrect. Cumulative preferred dividends are a necessary adjustment for the year in which they accumulate. Answer (D) is incorrect. Cumulative preferred dividends are a necessary adjustment for the year in which they accumulate, regardless of when paid.

7. Snell Co. had 300,000 shares of common stock issued and outstanding at December 31, Year 2. No common stock was issued during Year 3. On January 1, Year 3, Snell issued 200,000 shares of nonconvertible preferred stock. During Year 2, Snell declared and paid $75,000 of cash dividends on the common stock and $60,000 on the preferred stock. Net income for the year ended December 31, Year 3, was $330,000. What is Snell's Year 3 basic earnings per share?

A. $1.10

B. $0.90

C. $0.85

D. $0.65

Answer (B) is correct. *(CPA, adapted)*
   REQUIRED: The amount of BEPS.
   DISCUSSION: BEPS is equal to the amount of earnings available to the common shareholders divided by the weighted-average number of shares of common stock outstanding during the year. To calculate earnings available to holders of common stock, dividends on cumulative preferred stock must be subtracted from net income whether or not the dividends were declared. Earnings per common share for Year 3 thus amounted to $0.90.

$$\frac{\$330,000 - \$60,000}{300,000} = \$0.90$$

   Answer (A) is incorrect. This amount assumes no preferred dividends were declared. Answer (C) is incorrect. This amount assumes the common but not the preferred dividends were subtracted from the numerator. Answer (D) is incorrect. This amount assumes all dividends are subtracted from the numerator.

8. Chape Co. had the following information related to common and preferred shares during the year:

Common shares outstanding, 1/1	700,000
Common shares repurchased, 3/31	20,000
Conversion of preferred shares, 6/30	40,000
Common shares repurchased, 12/1	36,000

Chape reported net income of $2,000,000 at December 31. What amount of shares should Chape use as the denominator in the computation of basic earnings per share?

A. 684,000

B. 700,000

C. 702,000

D. 740,000

Answer (C) is correct. *(CPA, adapted)*
REQUIRED: The amount of shares used as the BEPS denominator.
DISCUSSION: Basic earnings per share (BEPS) equals income available to common shareholders divided by the weighted average of common shares outstanding. The BEPS denominator is weighted because some shares may have been issued or reacquired during the period. The weights are the fractions of the period that different amounts of shares are outstanding.

Dates Outstanding	Shares Outstanding	Fraction of Period	Weighted-Average Shares
1/1-3/31	700,000	(3 ÷ 12)	175,000
Repurchase 3/31	(20,000)		
4/1-6/30	680,000	(3 ÷ 12)	170,000
Conversion of preferred shares 6/30	40,000		
7/1-11/30	720,000	(5 ÷ 12)	300,000
Repurchase 12/1	(36,000)		
12/1-12/31	684,000	(1 ÷ 12)	57,000
			702,000

Answer (A) is incorrect. The amount of 684,000 shares is the number outstanding during December. Answer (B) is incorrect. The amount of 700,000 shares is the number outstanding on January 1. Answer (D) is incorrect. The amount of 740,000 shares is the number that would have been deemed to be outstanding on January 1 if the conversion of preferred shares had related back to that date.

9. The following information pertains to Tidwell Corp.'s outstanding stock for the year just ended:

Common stock, $5 par value:

Shares outstanding, 1/1	20,000
2-for-1 stock split, 4/1	20,000
Shares issued, 7/1	10,000

Preferred stock, $10 par value, 5% cumulative:

Shares outstanding, 1/1	4,000

How many shares should Tidwell use to calculate BEPS?

A. 40,000

B. 45,000

C. 50,000

D. 54,000

Answer (B) is correct. *(CPA, adapted)*
REQUIRED: The number of shares used to calculate BEPS.
DISCUSSION: BEPS is equal to the amount of earnings available to the common shareholders divided by the weighted-average number of shares of common stock outstanding during the year. When a stock dividend, a stock split, or a reverse split occurs other than at the beginning of a year, a retroactive adjustment for the change in capital structure should be made as of the beginning of the earliest accounting period presented. Shares outstanding during the year must then be weighted by the number of months for which they were outstanding in calculating the weighted-average number of shares to be used in determining BEPS. Hence, the new shares issued on 7/1 are included in year-end BEPS at their weighted average of 5,000 shares [10,000 shares × (6 months ÷ 12 months)]. Preferred stock is not included even if convertible because the BEPS calculation excludes the effects of potential common stock. Consequently, the total shares used to calculate BEPS equals 45,000 (20,000 shares outstanding at 1/1 + 20,000 stock-split shares + 5,000 shares issued 7/1).
Answer (A) is incorrect. The amount of 40,000 assumes that the stock split is not treated as though it occurred at the beginning of the period. Answer (C) is incorrect. The amount of 50,000 assumes that the shares issued on 7/1 were outstanding for 12 months. Answer (D) is incorrect. The amount of 54,000 includes the preferred stock and assumes that the shares issued on 7/1 were outstanding for 12 months.

Questions 10 through 13 are based on the following information.

Colon Co. uses a calendar year for financial reporting. The company is authorized to issue 5 million shares of $10 par common stock. At no time has Colon issued any potentially dilutive securities. A two-for-one stock split of Colon's common stock took place on March 31, Year 4. Additional information is in the next column.

Number of common shares issued and outstanding at 12/31/Year 1	1,000,000
Shares issued as a result of a 10% stock dividend on 9/30/Year 2	100,000
Shares issued for cash on 3/31/Year 3	1,000,000
Number of common shares issued and outstanding at 12/31/Year 3	2,100,000

10. The weighted-average number of common shares used in computing basic earnings per common share for Year 2 on the Year 3 comparative income statement was

A. 1,100,000

B. 1,050,000

C. 1,025,000

D. 1,000,000

Answer (A) is correct. *(CMA, adapted)*
REQUIRED: The weighted-average number of shares used in the BEPS computation for Year 2 on the Year 3 comparative income statement.
DISCUSSION: At the beginning of Year 2, 1 million shares were outstanding. Another 100,000 were issued as a result of a stock dividend on September 30. The stock dividend is assumed to have occurred at the beginning of the year. Accordingly, the number of shares outstanding throughout Year 2 would have been 1.1 million. No stock dividends or stock splits occurred in Year 3. Thus, the same 1.1 million shares used in the BEPS calculation on the Year 2 income statement would be used to determine the Year 2 BEPS in the Year 3 comparative statements.
Answer (B) is incorrect. This figure assumes the stock dividend affects shares outstanding for 6 months. Answer (C) is incorrect. This figure assumes the stock dividend affects shares outstanding for 3 months. Answer (D) is incorrect. This figure does not consider the stock dividend.

11. The weighted-average number of common shares used in computing BEPS for Year 3 on the Year 3 comparative income statement was

A. 1,600,000

B. 1,850,000

C. 2,100,000

D. 3,700,000

Answer (B) is correct. *(CMA, adapted)*
REQUIRED: The weighted-average number of shares used in computing BEPS for Year 3 on the Year 3 income statement.
DISCUSSION: At the beginning of Year 3, 1.1 million shares were outstanding. This figure remained unchanged for 3 months until March 31, when an additional 1 million shares were issued. Hence, for the last 9 months of the year, 2.1 million shares were outstanding. Weighting the shares outstanding by the amount of time they were outstanding results in a weighted average of 1,850,000 shares {[1,100,000 × (3 months ÷ 12 months)] + [2,100,000 × (9 months ÷ 12 months)]}.
Answer (A) is incorrect. The 1,000,000 shares issued on 3/31/Yr 3 are assumed to be outstanding for 6 months. Answer (C) is incorrect. The 1,000,000 shares issued on 3/31/Yr 3 are assumed to be outstanding for the entire year. Answer (D) is incorrect. This number of shares is used in computing BEPS for Year 3 on the Year 4 comparative income statement.

12. The weighted-average number of common shares to be used in computing BEPS for Year 4 on the Year 4 comparative income statement is

A. 2,100,000

B. 3,150,000

C. 3,675,000

D. 4,200,000

Answer (D) is correct. *(CMA, adapted)*
REQUIRED: The weighted-average number of shares used in computing BEPS for Year 4 on the Year 4 comparative income statement.
DISCUSSION: At the beginning of Year 4, 2.1 million shares were outstanding. Because of the March 31 two-for-one stock split, that number increased to 4.2 million. The stock split is assumed to have occurred on the first day of the year. Consequently, the number of shares outstanding throughout Year 4 was 4.2 million.
Answer (A) is incorrect. The amount of 2,100,000 ignores the 3/31/Yr 4 stock split. Answer (B) is incorrect. The amount of 3,150,000 assumes the stock split increases shares outstanding for 6 months. Answer (C) is incorrect. The amount of 3,675,000 assumes the stock split increases shares outstanding from the date the split occurred.

13. The weighted-average number of common shares to be used in computing BEPS for Year 3 on the Year 4 comparative income statement is

A. 1,850,000

B. 2,100,000

C. 3,700,000

D. 4,200,000

Answer (C) is correct. *(CMA, adapted)*
REQUIRED: The weighted-average number of shares used in computing BEPS for Year 3 on the Year 4 comparative income statement.
DISCUSSION: A stock dividend or split occurring at any time must be treated as though it occurred at the beginning of the earliest period presented for purposes of computing the weighted-average number of shares. Thus, prior-period BEPS figures presented for comparative purposes must be retroactively restated for the effects of a stock dividend or a stock split. The number of shares used in computing the Year 3 BEPS on the Year 3 income statement was 1,850,000 {[1,100,000 shares × (3 months ÷ 12 months)] + [2,100,000 × (9 months ÷ 12 months)]}. However, because of the stock split on March 31, Year 4, the number of shares doubled. Thus, the BEPS calculation for Year 3 on the Year 4 comparative income statement should be based on 3,700,000 shares (1,850,000 × 2).
Answer (A) is incorrect. The number of shares used in computing BEPS for Year 3 on the Year 3 income statement is 1,850,000. Answer (B) is incorrect. The amount of 2,100,000 is the number of shares in Year 4. It does not reflect the 3/31/Yr 4 stock split. Answer (D) is incorrect. The number of shares used in computing BEPS for Year 4 on the Year 4 comparative income statement is 4,200,000.

Question 14 is based on the following information. Smith Corporation had net income for the year of $101,504 and a simple capital structure consisting of the following common shares outstanding:

Months Outstanding	Number of Shares
January - February	24,000
March - June	29,400
July - November	36,000
December	35,040
Total	124,440

---

14. Smith Corporation's basic earnings per share (rounded to the nearest cent) were

A. $2.90

B. $3.20

C. $3.26

D. $3.45

Answer (B) is correct. *(CMA, adapted)*
REQUIRED: The BEPS for a company with a simple capital structure.
DISCUSSION: BEPS equals net income divided by the weighted-average number of shares outstanding. The latter is calculated as follows:

24,000 × (2 ÷ 12) =	4,000
29,400 × (4 ÷ 12) =	9,800
36,000 × (5 ÷ 12) =	15,000
35,040 × (1 ÷ 12) =	2,920
	31,720

Accordingly, BEPS is $3.20 ($101,504 NI ÷ 31,720 shares).
Answer (A) is incorrect. This amount is based on the shares outstanding at year end. Answer (C) is incorrect. This amount is based on an unweighted average of the four levels of shares outstanding during the year. Answer (D) is incorrect. This amount is based on the shares outstanding March through June.

15. In computing earnings-per-share data, which of the following is true regarding the weighted-average computation of shares outstanding?

    A. Reacquired shares should be excluded from the date of their acquisition.

    B. Reacquired shares should be excluded from the beginning of the period in which they were acquired.

    C. Stock dividends and stock splits consummated after the close of the period do not affect EPS computations, even though they may have been consummated before issuance of the financial statements.

    D. The shares issued during the period as a result of a stock dividend are weighted according to the portion of the period for which they were actually outstanding.

Answer (A) is correct. *(Publisher, adapted)*
    REQUIRED: The true statement concerning the computation of the weighted average of shares outstanding.
    DISCUSSION: Reacquired shares, or treasury shares, no longer represent outstanding stock to the company as of the date of their repurchase. Thus, they should be excluded from the calculation of the weighted-average number of shares as of their reacquisition date.
    Answer (B) is incorrect. Until the date of their repurchase, the shares represent outstanding ownership. Answer (C) is incorrect. Stock dividends and stock splits occurring anytime before the issuance of the statements require retroactive adjustment of EPS for all periods presented. Answer (D) is incorrect. Shares issued in a stock dividend are assumed to have been outstanding from the beginning of all periods presented.

16.2 Diluted Earnings per Share (DEPS)

16. In the computation of diluted earnings per share, convertible securities are

    A. Ignored.

    B. Recognized whether they are dilutive or antidilutive.

    C. Recognized only if they are antidilutive.

    D. Recognized only if they are dilutive.

Answer (D) is correct. *(CPA, adapted)*
    REQUIRED: The true statement about the treatment of convertible securities in computing DEPS.
    DISCUSSION: The objective of DEPS is to measure the performance of an entity during an accounting period while giving effect to all dilutive potential common shares that were outstanding during the period. Convertible securities are potential common stock.
    Answer (A) is incorrect. Convertible securities are included in the computation of diluted earnings per share if they are dilutive. Answer (B) is incorrect. Convertible securities are included in the computation of diluted earnings per share only when they are dilutive. Answer (C) is incorrect. Convertible securities are included in the computation of diluted earnings per share only when they are dilutive.

17. In calculating annual diluted earnings per share, which of the following should not be considered?

    A. The weighted-average number of common shares outstanding.

    B. The amount of dividends declared on nonconvertible cumulative preferred shares.

    C. The amount of cash dividends declared on common shares.

    D. The number of common shares resulting from the assumed conversion of debentures outstanding.

Answer (C) is correct. *(CIA, adapted)*
    REQUIRED: The information not included in the calculation of DEPS.
    DISCUSSION: The numerator of the DEPS calculation represents the residual income for the period available to holders of common stock and potential common stock. A cash dividend on common stock has no effect on earnings available to common shareholders. Thus, earnings are included whether they are distributed or undistributed.
    Answer (A) is incorrect. The weighted-average number of common shares outstanding is included in the denominator of DEPS. Answer (B) is incorrect. The dividend on nonconvertible cumulative preferred stock, whether declared or not, must be deducted from income from continuing operations and also from net income to arrive at earnings available to common shareholders. Answer (D) is incorrect. The assumed conversion of debentures requires adjusting both the numerator (for interest, net of tax effect) and the denominator (for the shares assumed issued) of DEPS.

18. In the computation of DEPS for a complex capital structure, which of the following is a potential common stock?

	Nonconvertible Preferred Stock	Stock Option
A.	Yes	No
B.	Yes	Yes
C.	No	Yes
D.	No	No

Answer (C) is correct. *(CPA, adapted)*
REQUIRED: The potential common stock.
DISCUSSION: Potential common stock is a security or other contract that may entitle its holder to obtain common stock during either the reporting period or some future accounting period. Potential common stocks include options, warrants, convertible preferred stock, convertible debt, and contingent stock agreements.
Answer (A) is incorrect. Unlike a stock option, nonconvertible preferred stock is never potential common stock. Moreover, potential common stock includes options. Answer (B) is incorrect. Unlike a stock option, nonconvertible preferred stock is never potential common stock. Answer (D) is incorrect. Potential common stock includes options.

19. In the calculation of diluted earnings per share, a convertible bond was found to be antidilutive in Year 2 and dilutive in Year 3. The convertible bond is included in the computation for

	Year 2	Year 3
A.	Yes	Yes
B.	No	Yes
C.	No	No
D.	Yes	No

Answer (B) is correct. *(CPA, adapted)*
REQUIRED: The circumstances under which potential common stock is included in the determination of DEPS.
DISCUSSION: DEPS is based on the number of common shares outstanding during the period plus the common shares that would have been outstanding if dilutive potential common shares had been issued. Thus, in a period in which the effect of potential common stock is antidilutive, it is not included in the determination of DEPS. It is included, however, in those periods in which its effect is dilutive.
Answer (A) is incorrect. The convertible bond is not included in the calculation of DEPS for Year 2. Answer (C) is incorrect. The convertible bond is included in the calculation of DEPS for Year 3. Answer (D) is incorrect. The convertible bond is included in the calculation of DEPS for Year 3.

20. The nature of the adjustment for stock options in the calculation of diluted earnings per share can be described as

A. Historical because earnings are historical.

B. Historical because it indicates the firm's valuation.

C. Pro forma because it indicates potential changes in the number of shares.

D. Pro forma because it indicates potential changes in earnings.

Answer (C) is correct. *(CPA, adapted)*
REQUIRED: The nature of the adjustment required for stock options in calculating DEPS.
DISCUSSION: The denominator in the DEPS calculation is adjusted for the assumed exercise of outstanding call options and warrants issued by the entity if the exercise would have a dilutive effect. The change in the number of shares has not occurred and is only assumed, so the calculation is essentially pro forma.
Answer (A) is incorrect. The conversion of stock options into common shares has not occurred, and the required adjustment is hypothetical. Answer (B) is incorrect. The conversion of stock options into common shares has not occurred, and the required adjustment is hypothetical. Answer (D) is incorrect. The assumed exercise of the options affects only the denominator of the DEPS ratio.

21. When a company reports amounts for basic and diluted earnings per share,

A. They should be presented with equal prominence on the face of the income statement.

B. They need not be shown on the face of the income statement but must be disclosed in the notes to the financial statements.

C. They need to be reported for net income only.

D. BEPS should be presented on the face of the income statement. DEPS may be disclosed either on the face of the income statement or in the notes.

Answer (A) is correct. *(CMA, adapted)*
REQUIRED: The true statement about the reporting of BEPS and DEPS.
DISCUSSION: An entity whose stock is publicly traded must report EPS information on the face of the income statement for both income from continuing operations and net income. In addition, EPS data for any discontinued operation or extraordinary item must be presented on the face of the income statement or in a note. When the entity does not have a simple capital structure, it must present BEPS and DEPS with equal prominence.
Answer (B) is incorrect. Certain EPS amounts must be presented on the face of the income statement. Answer (C) is incorrect. EPS must also be presented for income from continuing operations, discontinued operations, and extraordinary items. Answer (D) is incorrect. BEPS and DEPS are to be presented on the face of the income statement with equal prominence.

22. Under the treasury stock method, the DEPS calculation is based on the assumption that call options and warrants issued by the reporting entity and outstanding for the entire year were exercised at the

A. End of the period and that the funds obtained thereby were used to purchase common stock at the average market price during the period.

B. Beginning of the period and that the funds obtained thereby were used to purchase common stock at the average market price during the period.

C. End of the period and that the funds obtained thereby were used to purchase common stock at the current market price in effect at the end of the period.

D. Beginning of the period and that the funds obtained thereby were used to purchase common stock at the current market price in effect at the end of the period.

Answer (B) is correct. *(Publisher, adapted)*
REQUIRED: The proper application of the treasury stock method to the assumed exercise of options and warrants in the calculation of DEPS.
DISCUSSION: The treasury stock method of accounting for dilutive call options and warrants issued by the reporting entity assumes the exercise of outstanding options and warrants at the beginning of the period or at time of issuance, if later. The treasury stock method assumes that the proceeds from the exercise are used to purchase common stock at the average market price during the period. The incremental shares, that is, the excess of those assumed issued over those assumed purchased, are included in the DEPS denominator.
Answer (A) is incorrect. The options and warrants are assumed to have been exercised at the beginning of the period. Answer (C) is incorrect. The options and warrants are assumed to have been exercised at the beginning of the period, and the average market price during the period is used. Answer (D) is incorrect. The average market price during the period is used.

23. Deaton, Inc., had 300,000 shares of common stock issued and outstanding at January 1. On July 1, an additional 50,000 shares of common stock were issued for cash. Deaton also had issued unexercised stock options to purchase 40,000 shares of common stock at $15 per share outstanding at the beginning and end of the year. The average market price of Deaton's common stock was $20 during the year. What number of shares should be used in computing diluted earnings per share for the year ended December 31?

A. 325,000

B. 335,000

C. 360,000

D. 365,000

Answer (B) is correct. *(CPA, adapted)*
REQUIRED: The number of shares to be used in computing DEPS.
DISCUSSION: On July 1, 50,000 shares of common stock were issued. Hence, for the purpose of calculating Deaton's weighted-average number of shares, 300,000 shares should be considered outstanding for the first 6 months and 350,000 shares for the second 6 months, a weighted average of 325,000 shares.
Dilutive call options and warrants are included in DEPS. These options are assumed to be exercised at the beginning of the period using the treasury stock method. This method assumes the options are exercised and the $600,000 of proceeds (40,000 options × $15) is used to repurchase shares. In the DEPS computation, the assumed repurchase price is the average market price for the period ($20), so 30,000 shares are assumed to be repurchased ($600,000 ÷ $20). The difference between the shares assumed to be issued and those repurchased (40,000 − 30,000 = 10,000) is added to the weighted average of common shares outstanding to determine the DEPS denominator. Thus, 335,000 (325,000 + 10,000) shares should be used in computing DEPS for the year ending December 31.
Answer (A) is incorrect. The amount of 325,000 does not include the 10,000 shares includible due to the stock option. Answer (C) is incorrect. The amount of 360,000 includes the full 50,000 shares sold on July 1 instead of the weighted-average number of shares of 25,000. Answer (D) is incorrect. The amount of 365,000 includes the full 40,000 shares covered by the stock options instead of the amount computed under the treasury stock method.

24. How are partially paid stock subscriptions treated in the computation of EPS?

A. By use of the treasury stock method.

B. By not including them until issuance.

C. By disclosure only.

D. By use of the if-converted method.

Answer (A) is correct. *(Publisher, adapted)*
REQUIRED: The treatment of stock subscriptions in EPS computations.
DISCUSSION: Stock purchase contracts, partially paid stock subscriptions, and nonvested stock granted to employees are equivalent to stock options and warrants. Thus, the treasury stock method is used to account for partially paid stock subscriptions.
Answer (B) is incorrect. If the stock subscriptions are dilutive, they must be included in the calculation of EPS. Answer (C) is incorrect. If the stock subscriptions are dilutive, they must be included in the calculation of EPS. Answer (D) is incorrect. The if-converted method applies to convertible securities.

25. In a diluted earnings-per-share computation, the effect of outstanding call options and warrants issued by the reporting entity is reflected by applying the treasury stock method. If the exercise price of these options or warrants exceeds the average market price, the computation would

A. Fairly present diluted earnings per share on a prospective basis.

B. Fairly present the maximum potential dilution of diluted earnings per share on a prospective basis.

C. Reflect the excess of the number of shares assumed issued over the number of shares assumed reacquired as the potential dilution of earnings per share.

D. Be antidilutive.

Answer (D) is correct. *(CPA, adapted)*
REQUIRED: The effect on DEPS of an exercise price above the average market price for options and warrants.
DISCUSSION: Under the treasury stock method, call options and warrants issued by the reporting entity are assumed to be exercised at the beginning of the period or at time of issuance, if later. The proceeds are then assumed to be used to reacquire common shares outstanding at the average market price for the period. The effect on the denominator in the DEPS calculation is the difference between the shares assumed to be issued and the treasury shares assumed to be acquired. If the exercise price exceeds the average market price, more shares would be purchased than issued. Because these assumed transactions would increase DEPS by decreasing the denominator, their effect would be antidilutive.
Answer (A) is incorrect. When the exercise price exceeds the average market price, the result is antidilutive. Answer (B) is incorrect. When the exercise price exceeds the average market price, the result is antidilutive. Answer (C) is incorrect. The number of shares reacquired would exceed the number issued.

26. Troupe Company had 100,000 shares of common stock issued and outstanding at January 1. On July 1, Troupe issued a 10% stock dividend. Unexercised call options to purchase 20,000 shares of Troupe's common stock (adjusted for the stock dividend) at $20 per share were outstanding at the beginning and end of the year. The average market price of Troupe's common stock (which was not affected by the stock dividend) was $25 per share during the year. Net income for the year ended December 31 was $550,000. What should be Troupe's DEPS for the year?

A. $4.82

B. $5.00

C. $5.05

D. $5.24

Answer (A) is correct. *(CPA, adapted)*
REQUIRED: The DEPS for the year given a mid-year stock dividend and unexercised stock options.
DISCUSSION: A stock dividend occurring at any time before issuance of the financial statements must be reflected as a retroactive adjustment of the capital structure at the beginning of the first period presented. Hence, the 110,000 shares outstanding after the stock dividend are deemed to have been outstanding during the entire year.
The options are not antidilutive because the exercise price was less than the average market price. Accordingly, exercise of the options is assumed to have occurred at the beginning of the year at the exercise price of $20. Under the treasury stock method, the assumed proceeds of $400,000 (20,000 shares × $20) are used to repurchase 16,000 shares ($400,000 ÷ $25) at the average market price during the period. The difference between the 20,000 shares assumed to be issued and the 16,000 shares assumed to be repurchased increases the DEPS denominator from 110,000 shares to 114,000 shares. Thus, DEPS equals $4.82 ($550,000 income ÷ 114,000 shares).
Answer (B) is incorrect. Five dollars does not include the stock options in the calculation of shares outstanding for the year. Answer (C) is incorrect. The amount of $5.05 assumes the shares issued as a stock dividend were outstanding for 6 months. Answer (D) is incorrect. The amount of $5.24 assumes the shares issued as a stock dividend were outstanding for 6 months. This amount also excludes the stock options.

27. Starks Corporation has 300,000 shares of common stock outstanding. The only other securities outstanding are 10,000 shares of 9% cumulative preferred stock with detachable warrants (10 warrants per preferred share). Each warrant provides for the purchase of one share of common stock at $72. For the year, net income was $1.6 million. During the year, the average market price of common stock was $125. The price at December 31 was $120. What number of shares should be used to determine diluted earnings per share?

A. 340,000

B. 342,400

C. 357,600

D. 400,000

Answer (B) is correct. *(L. Krueger)*
REQUIRED: The number of shares to be used to determine DEPS.
DISCUSSION: The treasury stock method of accounting for the dilutive effect of call options and warrants issued by the reporting entity assumes they are exercised at the beginning of the period at the exercise price, with the proceeds being used to repurchase shares in the market. The assumed repurchase price is the average market price. Because the $7.2 million of hypothetical proceeds (10,000 shares of preferred × 10 warrants per share × $72 exercise price) can be used to purchase 57,600 shares ($7,200,000 ÷ 125), the DEPS denominator will be 342,400 shares (300,000 common shares outstanding + 100,000 assumed issued upon conversion – 57,600 assumed repurchased).
Answer (A) is incorrect. This figure is based on the 12/31 price of $120. Answer (C) is incorrect. This figure includes the 57,600 shares assumed to be repurchased. Answer (D) is incorrect. This figure does not adjust for treasury stock assumed to have been repurchased.

Questions 28 through 30 are based on the following information.

Collins Corp.'s capital structure was as follows:

	December 31	
	Year 4	Year 5
Outstanding shares of stock:		
Common	100,000	100,000
Convertible preferred	10,000	10,000
9% convertible bonds	$1,000,000	$1,000,000

During Year 5, Collins paid dividends of $3 per share on its preferred stock. The preferred shares are convertible into 20,000 shares of common stock, and the 9% bonds are convertible into 30,000 shares of common stock. Assume that the income tax rate is 30%.

28. If net income for Year 5 is $350,000, Collins should report DEPS as

A. $3.20

B. $2.95

C. $2.92

D. $2.75

Answer (D) is correct. *(CPA, adapted)*

REQUIRED: The DEPS given convertible preferred stock, convertible bonds, and net income of $350,000.

DISCUSSION: Potential common stock is included in the calculation of DEPS if it is dilutive. When two or more issues of potential common stock are outstanding, each issue is considered separately in sequence from the most to the least dilutive. This procedure is necessary because a convertible security may be dilutive on its own but antidilutive when included with other potential common shares in the calculation of DEPS. The incremental effect on EPS determines the degree of dilution. The lower the incremental effect, the more dilutive.

The incremental effect of the convertible preferred stock is $1.50 [($3 preferred dividend × 10,000) ÷ 20,000 potential common shares]. The incremental effect of the convertible debt is $2.10 {[$1,000,000 × 9% × (1.0 – .30)] ÷ 30,000 potential common shares}. Because the $1.50 incremental effect of the convertible preferred is lower, it is the more dilutive, and its incremental effect is compared with BEPS, which equals $3.20 [($350,000 – 30,000) ÷ 100,000]. Because $1.50 is lower than $3.20, the convertible preferred is dilutive and is included in a trial calculation of DEPS. The result is $2.92 [($350,000 – $30,000 + $30,000) ÷ (100,000 + 20,000)]. However, the $2.10 incremental effect of the convertible debt is lower than the $2.92 trial calculation, so the convertible debt is also dilutive and should be included in the calculation of DEPS. Thus, DEPS is $2.75 as indicated below.

$$\frac{\$350,000 - \$30,000 + \$30,000 + \$63,000}{100,000 + 20,000 + 30,000} = \$2.75$$

Answer (A) is incorrect. This amount equals BEPS. Answer (B) is incorrect. This amount excludes the convertible preferred stock. Answer (C) is incorrect. This amount excludes the convertible debt.

29. If net income for Year 5 is $245,000, Collins should report DEPS as

A. $2.15

B. $2.14

C. $2.05

D. $2.04

Answer (D) is correct. *(Publisher, adapted)*

REQUIRED: The DEPS given convertible preferred stock, convertible debt, and net income of $245,000.

DISCUSSION: The incremental effect of the convertible preferred is $1.50 and of the convertible debt is $2.10. Given net income of $245,000, BEPS equals $2.15 [($245,000 – $30,000) ÷ 100,000]. The $1.50 incremental effect of the convertible preferred stock is lower than BEPS, so it is dilutive and should be included in a trial calculation of DEPS. The result is $2.04 [($245,000 – $30,000 + $30,000) ÷ (100,000 + 20,000)]. Because the $2.10 incremental effect of the convertible debt is higher than $2.04, the convertible debt is antidilutive and should not be included in the DEPS calculation. Thus, DEPS should be reported as $2.04.

Answer (A) is incorrect. This amount equals BEPS. Answer (B) is incorrect. This amount excludes the convertible preferred stock. Answer (C) is incorrect. This amount includes the convertible debt.

30. If net income for Year 5 is $170,000, Collins should report DEPS as

A. $1.40

B. $1.42

C. $1.56

D. $1.70

Answer (A) is correct. *(Publisher, adapted)*
REQUIRED: The DEPS given convertible preferred stock, convertible debt, and net income of $170,000.
DISCUSSION: Given net income of $170,000, BEPS equals $1.40 [($170,000 – $30,000) ÷ 100,000]. This amount is lower than both the $2.10 incremental effect of the convertible debt and the $1.50 incremental effect of the convertible preferred. Thus, both convertible securities are antidilutive, and Collins should report that DEPS is equal to BEPS. This dual presentation may be displayed on one line of the income statement.
Answer (B) is incorrect. The amount of $1.42 includes the convertible preferred stock. Answer (C) is incorrect. The amount of $1.56 includes the convertible debt. Answer (D) is incorrect. The amount of $1.70 results from not adjusting the $170,000 of net income for the $30,000 of preferred dividends in determining income available to common shareholders.

31. A firm has basic earnings per share of $1.29. If the tax rate is 30%, which of the following securities would be dilutive?

A. Cumulative 8%, $50 par preferred stock.

B. Ten percent convertible bonds, issued at par, with each $1,000 bond convertible into 20 shares of common stock.

C. Seven percent convertible bonds, issued at par, with each $1,000 bond convertible into 40 shares of common stock.

D. Six percent, $100 par cumulative convertible preferred stock, issued at par, with each preferred share convertible into four shares of common stock.

Answer (C) is correct. *(CPA, adapted)*
REQUIRED: The dilutive securities.
DISCUSSION: The calculation of dilutive EPS (DEPS) gives effect to dilutive potential common shares (e.g., options and convertible securities). Dilution is a reduction in basic EPS (BEPS) resulting from the assumption that (1) convertible securities were converted, (2) options or warrants were exercised, or (3) contingently issuable shares were issued. The conversion of the bonds would eliminate after-tax interest expense per bond of $49 [($1,000 par × 7%) × (1.0 – 30% tax rate)]. (The bonds were issued at par, so amortization of premium or discount does not affect the calculation.) The per-share effect is $1.225 ($49 ÷ 40 shares per bond). Thus, the convertible debt is dilutive ($1.225 < $1.29 BEPS).
Answer (A) is incorrect. Unless the preferred stock is convertible, it is not dilutive. Nonconvertible preferred shares are not potential common stock and therefore are not considered in the calculation of DEPS. Answer (B) is incorrect. The conversion of the bonds would eliminate after-tax interest expense per bond of $70 [($1,000 par × 10%) × (1.0 – 30% tax rate)]. (The bonds were issued at par, so amortization of premium or discount does not affect the calculation.) The per-share effect is $3.50 ($70 ÷ 20 shares per bond). Thus, the convertible debt is antidilutive ($3.50 > $1.29 BEPS). Answer (D) is incorrect. If the preferred stock is converted, the EPS numerator increases by the dividend savings of $6 ($100 par × 6%) per share of preferred stock (the additional income available to common shareholders). The per-share effect is $1.50 ($6 ÷ 4 common shares per share of preferred stock). Thus, the preferred stock is antidilutive ($1.50 > $1.29 BEPS).

32. In determining earnings per share, interest expense, net of applicable income taxes, on dilutive convertible debt should be

A. Added back to net income for BEPS and ignored for DEPS.

B. Added back to net income for both BEPS and DEPS.

C. Deducted from net income for DEPS.

D. Added back to net income for DEPS.

Answer (D) is correct. *(CPA, adapted)*
REQUIRED: The correct treatment of after-tax interest on dilutive convertible debt.
DISCUSSION: In accordance with the if-converted method, the DEPS calculation assumes that dilutive convertible debt is converted into common stock at the beginning of the period or at the time of issuance, if later. Given the assumed conversion, no debt would exist upon which interest could have been paid. Interest is a deduction in arriving at net income. Accordingly, that interest savings, net of tax effect, should be added back to net income in the DEPS computation.
Answer (A) is incorrect. The interest, net of tax effect, should be added to the numerator for DEPS but not for BEPS.
Answer (B) is incorrect. The interest, net of tax effect, should be added to the numerator for DEPS. Answer (C) is incorrect. The interest, net of tax effect, should be added to the numerator for DEPS.

33. The Fleming Corporation had 200,000 shares of common stock and 10,000 shares of cumulative, 6%, $100 par preferred stock outstanding during the year just ended. The preferred stock is convertible at the rate of three shares of common per share of preferred. For the year, the company had a $30,000 net loss from continuing operations. Fleming should report loss per share for the year of

A. $(.13)

B. $(.15)

C. $(.39)

D. $(.45)

Answer (D) is correct.   *(Publisher, adapted)*
REQUIRED: The loss per share given convertible preferred stock outstanding.
DISCUSSION: Potential common stock always has an antidilutive effect if an entity has a loss from continuing operations or a loss from continuing operations available to common shareholders (after an adjustment for preferred dividends). Thus, the loss per share reported should be based on common shares outstanding. When preferred stock is cumulative, the dividend, whether earned or not, is deducted from income from continuing operations and net income or added to any loss for the year in computing earnings or loss, respectively, per share of common stock. When preferred stock is noncumulative, an adjustment is made for dividends declared. If the dividend is cumulative only if earned, no adjustment is necessary except to the extent of available income; that is, the preferred dividends accumulate only to the extent of net income. Accordingly, the loss per share is $(.45) {[[$30,000 + 10,000 preferred shares × ($100 × 6%)] ÷ 200,000 shares of common stock}.
Answer (A) is incorrect. This figure includes the convertible preferred stock. Answer (B) is incorrect. This figure does not include the cumulative preferred dividends in the computation. Answer (C) is incorrect. This figure includes 200,000 shares of common stock as preferred stock convertible 3-for-1 into common stock (200,000 ÷ 3 = 66,666) and the 10,000 shares of preferred stock as common stock.

34. A company's convertible debt securities are dilutive for EPS purposes. What is the effect of these securities on the calculation of BEPS and DEPS?

	BEPS	DEPS
A.	Decrease	Decrease
B.	Increase	No effect
C.	No effect	Decrease
D.	Decrease	Increase

Answer (C) is correct.   *(CPA, adapted)*
REQUIRED: The effect of dilutive convertible securities on the calculation of BEPS and DEPS.
DISCUSSION: Securities classified as potential common stock be included in the computation of the number of common shares outstanding for DEPS if the effect of the inclusion is dilutive. Dilutive potential common stock decreases DEPS. BEPS is not affected by potential common stock.
Answer (A) is incorrect. Dilutive potential common stock has no effect on BEPS. Answer (B) is incorrect. Dilutive potential common stock decreases DEPS and has no effect on BEPS. Answer (D) is incorrect. Dilutive potential common stock decreases DEPS and has no effect on BEPS.

35. In the computation of DEPS, the number of common shares into which convertible preferred stock is assumed to be converted is added as an adjustment to the denominator (number of shares outstanding). If the preferred stock is preferred as to dividends, which amount should be added as an adjustment to the numerator (earnings available to common shareholders)?

A. Annual preferred dividend.

B. Annual preferred dividend times (1 – the income tax rate).

C. Annual preferred dividend times the income tax rate.

D. Annual preferred dividend divided by the income tax rate.

Answer (A) is correct.   *(CPA, adapted)*
REQUIRED: The adjustment to the numerator for preferred dividends in the DEPS computation.
DISCUSSION: If a capital structure has convertible preferred stock with a dilutive effect on DEPS, the if-converted method is used. This method assumes the conversion of the preferred stock occurred at the beginning of the accounting period or at issuance, if later. The annual preferred dividend is accordingly added back to earnings available to common shareholders (the numerator of the DEPS ratio).
Answer (B) is incorrect. The annual preferred dividend is not multiplied by (1 – the income tax rate). The preferred dividend is paid with after-tax dollars; i.e., preferred dividends are not tax-deductible. Answer (C) is incorrect. The annual preferred dividend is not multiplied by the income tax rate. The preferred dividend is paid with after-tax dollars; i.e., preferred dividends are not tax-deductible. Answer (D) is incorrect. The annual preferred dividend is not divided by the income tax rate. The preferred dividend is paid with after-tax dollars; i.e., preferred dividends are not tax-deductible.

36. During the current year, Green Corp. had the following two classes of stock issued and outstanding for the entire year:

- 100,000 shares of common stock, $1 par.
- 1,000 shares of 4% preferred stock, $100 par, convertible share for share into common stock. This stock is cumulative, whether or not earned, and no preferred dividends are in arrears.

Green's current-year net income was $900,000, and its income tax rate for the year was 30%. Diluted earnings per share for the current year are

    A. $9.00

    B. $8.96

    C. $8.91

    D. $8.87

Answer (C) is correct. *(CPA, adapted)*
    REQUIRED: The DEPS given convertible preferred stock.
    DISCUSSION: DEPS is equal to the amount of earnings available to common shareholders and to holders of dilutive potential common stock, divided by the weighted-average number of shares of common stock and additional common shares that would have been outstanding if dilutive potential common shares had been issued. Dilution is tested by calculating EPS and the incremental effect of the potential common shares on EPS. BEPS equals income available to common shareholders (net income – cumulative preferred dividend) divided by the weighted average of common shares outstanding. Thus, BEPS is $8.96 {[$900,000 NI – (1,000 preferred shares × $100 par × 4%)] ÷ 100,000 common shares}. The incremental effect of the potential common shares equals the preferred dividends added back to the numerator if conversion is assumed divided by the potential common shares, or $4.00 ($4,000 ÷ 1,000). Because $4.00 is less than $8.96, the potential common shares are dilutive. Accordingly, the convertible preferred stock is assumed to be converted at the beginning of the year, and no dividends are deemed to have been paid. The DEPS calculation therefore adds the $4,000 preferred dividend to the BEPS numerator and the 1,000 common shares into which the preferred stock can be converted to the BEPS denominator. DEPS is $8.91 [($896,000 + $4,000) ÷ (100,000 + 1,000)].
    Answer (A) is incorrect. Nine dollars is equal to $900,000 net income divided by 100,000 common shares. Answer (B) is incorrect. The amount of $8.96 is equal to BEPS. Answer (D) is incorrect. The amount of $8.87 is equal to $900,000 net income minus the $4,000 preferred dividend, divided by 101,000 shares.

37. The if-converted method of computing DEPS amounts assumes conversion of convertible securities at the

    A. Beginning of the earliest period reported (or at time of issuance, if later).

    B. Beginning of the earliest period reported (regardless of time of issuance).

    C. Middle of the earliest period reported (regardless of time of issuance).

    D. End of the earliest period reported (regardless of time of issuance).

Answer (A) is correct. *(CPA, adapted)*
    REQUIRED: The conversion assumption underlying the if-converted method.
    DISCUSSION: The if-converted method of computing DEPS assumes that convertible securities are included in the determination of DEPS if dilutive. Conversion is assumed to have occurred at the beginning of the earliest period reported or, if the security was issued at a later time, at the date of issuance.
    Answer (B) is incorrect. Conversion is assumed at the beginning of the earliest period reported but not regardless of time of issuance. Answer (C) is incorrect. Conversion is assumed at the beginning of the earliest period reported (or at the time of issuance, if later). Answer (D) is incorrect. Conversion is assumed at the beginning of the earliest period reported (or at the time of issuance, if later).

38. During all of the year just ended, Berlin Co. had outstanding 100,000 shares of common stock and 5,000 shares of noncumulative, $7 preferred stock. Each share of the latter is convertible into three shares of common. For the year, Berlin had $230,000 income from continuing operations and $575,000 of extraordinary losses; no dividends were paid or declared. Berlin should report diluted earnings (loss) per share for income from continuing operations and for net income (loss), respectively, of

    A. $2.30 and $(3.45).

    B. $2.00 and $(3.00).

    C. $2.19 and $(3.29).

    D. $2.26 and $(3.39).

Answer (B) is correct. *(CPA, adapted)*
    REQUIRED: The diluted earnings (loss) per share from continuing operations and net income (loss).
    DISCUSSION: The noncumulative convertible preferred stock is dilutive because its assumed conversion will have no effect on the DEPS numerator and will increase the denominator by 15,000 (5,000 × 3) shares. DEPS for income from continuing operations is $2.00 ($230,000 ÷ 115,000 shares). Net loss equals the $230,000 income from continuing operations minus the $575,000 extraordinary loss, or $345,000. This amount divided by the 115,000 shares results in a diluted net loss per share of $3.00.
    The effect of including the convertible preferred in the calculation of the net loss per share is antidilutive. However, potential common stock that is dilutive for purposes of determining DEPS from continuing operations must be included in all calculations of diluted per-share amounts.
    Answer (A) is incorrect. The convertible preferred stock is excluded from the calculation of shares outstanding for the year. Answer (C) is incorrect. Each share of preferred stock is convertible into three shares of common stock. Answer (D) is incorrect. The number of shares outstanding is calculated as if three shares of preferred stock were convertible into one share of common stock.

Questions 39 through 45 are based on the following information.

Carolina Company is a calendar-year entity with a complex capital structure. Carolina reported no discontinued operations, but it had an extraordinary loss (net of tax) of $1,200,000 in the first quarter when its income before the extraordinary item was $1,000,000.

The average market price of Carolina's common stock for the first quarter was $25, the shares outstanding at the beginning of the period equaled 300,000, and 12,000 shares were issued on March 1.

At the beginning of the quarter, Carolina had outstanding $2,000,000 of 5% convertible bonds, with each $1,000 bond convertible into 10 shares of common stock. No bonds were converted.

At the beginning of the quarter, Carolina also had outstanding 120,000 shares of preferred stock paying a dividend of $.10 per share at the end of each quarter and convertible to common stock on a one-to-one basis. Holders of 60,000 shares of preferred stock exercised their conversion privilege on February 1.

Throughout the first quarter, warrants to buy 50,000 shares of Carolina's common stock for $28 per share were outstanding but unexercised. Carolina's tax rate was 30%.

39. The weighted-average number of shares used to calculate BEPS amounts for the first quarter is

A. 444,000

B. 372,000

C. 344,000

D. 300,000

Answer (C) is correct.   *(Publisher, adapted)*
REQUIRED: The weighted-average number of shares used to calculate BEPS amounts for the first quarter.
DISCUSSION: The number of shares outstanding at January 1 was 300,000, 12,000 shares were issued on March 1, and 60,000 shares of preferred stock were converted to 60,000 shares of common stock on February 1. Thus, the weighted-average number of shares used to calculate BEPS amounts for the first quarter is 344,000 {300,000 + [12,000 × (1 ÷ 3)] + [60,000 × (2 ÷ 3)]}.
Answer (A) is incorrect. The adjusted weighted-average number of shares used in the DEPS calculation is 444,000. Answer (B) is incorrect. The total outstanding at March 31 is 372,000. Answer (D) is incorrect. The shares outstanding at January 1 equals 300,000.

40. The control number for determining whether potential common shares are dilutive or antidilutive is

A. $1,000,000

B. $994,000

C. $(206,000)

D. $(1,200,000)

Answer (B) is correct.   *(Publisher, adapted)*
REQUIRED: The control number for determining whether potential common shares are dilutive or antidilutive.
DISCUSSION: GAAP requires that a company use income from continuing operations (in Carolina's case, income before extraordinary item), adjusted for preferred dividends, as the control number for determining whether potential common shares are dilutive or antidilutive. Hence, the number of potential common shares used in calculating DEPS for income from continuing operations is also used in calculating the other DEPS amounts even if the effect is antidilutive with respect to the corresponding BEPS amounts. However, if the entity has a loss from continuing operations available to common shareholders, no potential common shares are included in the calculation of any DEPS amount. The control number for Carolina is $994,000 {$1,000,000 income before extraordinary item – [(120,000 preferred shares – 60,000 preferred shares converted) × $.10 per share dividend]}.
Answer (A) is incorrect. The amount of $1,000,000 is unadjusted income from continuing operations. Answer (C) is incorrect. The amount of $(206,000) is the net loss available to common shareholders after subtracting the extraordinary loss. Answer (D) is incorrect. The amount of $(1,200,000) is the extraordinary loss.

41. BEPS for net income or loss is

A. $2.89

B. $(0.46)

C. $(0.60)

D. $(3.49)

Answer (C) is correct. *(Publisher, adapted)*

REQUIRED: The BEPS for net income or loss.

DISCUSSION: The weighted-average of shares used in the BEPS denominator is 344,000 {300,000 + [12,000 × (1 month ÷ 3 months)] + [60,000 × (2 months ÷ 3 months)]}. The numerator equals income before extraordinary item minus preferred dividends of $6,000 [(120,000 preferred shares – 60,000 preferred shares converted) × $.10] minus the extraordinary loss. Thus, the numerator equals $(206,000) [$1,000,000 – $6,000 – $1,200,000]. BEPS for net loss is $(0.60) [$(206,000) ÷ 344,000 shares].

Answer (A) is incorrect. BEPS for income before the extraordinary item is $2.89. Answer (B) is incorrect. This figure uses the denominator of the DEPS calculation. Answer (D) is incorrect. The BEPS amount for the extraordinary loss is $(3.49).

42. The weighted-average number of shares used to calculate DEPS amounts for the first quarter is

A. 444,000

B. 438,000

C. 372,000

D. 344,000

Answer (A) is correct. *(Publisher, adapted)*

REQUIRED: The weighted-average number of shares used to calculate DEPS amounts for the first quarter.

DISCUSSION: The denominator of DEPS equals the weighted-average number of shares used in the BEPS calculation (344,000) plus dilutive potential common shares (assuming the control number is not a loss). The incremental shares from assumed conversion of warrants is zero because they are antidilutive. The $25 market price is less than the $28 exercise price. The assumed conversion of all the preferred shares at the beginning of the quarter results in 80,000 incremental shares {[120,000 shares × (3 ÷ 3)] – [60,000 shares × (2 ÷ 3)]}. The assumed conversion of all the bonds at the beginning of the quarter results in 20,000 incremental shares [($2,000,000 ÷ $1,000 per bond) × 10 common shares per bond]. Consequently, the weighted-average number of shares used to calculate DEPS amounts for the first quarter is 444,000 (344,000 + 0 + 80,000 + 20,000).

Answer (B) is incorrect. This amount assumes the hypothetical exercise of all the warrants at the beginning of the period at a price of $28 and the repurchase of shares using the proceeds at a price of $25. Answer (C) is incorrect. The total outstanding at March 31 is 372,000. Answer (D) is incorrect. The denominator of the BEPS fraction is 344,000.

43. The difference between BEPS and DEPS for the extraordinary item is

A. $2.89

B. $2.10

C. $.79

D. $.60

Answer (C) is correct. *(Publisher, adapted)*

REQUIRED: The difference between BEPS and DEPS for the extraordinary item.

DISCUSSION: BEPS for the extraordinary loss is $(3.49) [$(1,200,000) ÷ 344,000], and DEPS is $(2.70) [$(1,200,000) ÷ 444,000 shares].

Answer (A) is incorrect. The BEPS for income before the extraordinary item is $2.89. Answer (B) is incorrect. The difference between DEPS for the extraordinary loss and the BEPS for the net loss available to common shareholders after the extraordinary loss is $2.10. Answer (D) is incorrect. The BEPS for the net loss available to common shareholders after the extraordinary loss is $.60.

44. DEPS for net income or loss is

A. $2.29

B. $(0.41)

C. $(0.53)

D. $(2.70)

Answer (B) is correct. *(Publisher, adapted)*

REQUIRED: The DEPS for net income or loss.

DISCUSSION: The numerator equals the income available to common shareholders, plus the effect of the assumed conversions, minus the extraordinary loss. The denominator equals the weighted-average of shares outstanding plus the dilutive potential common shares. Hence, DEPS for net loss is $(.41) [($994,000 + $23,500 – $1,200,000) ÷ 444,000].

Answer (A) is incorrect. DEPS for income before the extraordinary item is $2.29. Answer (C) is incorrect. This figure is based on the BEPS denominator. Answer (D) is incorrect. DEPS for the extraordinary item is $(2.70).

45. Refer to the information on the preceding page(s). The effect of assumed conversions on the numerator of the DEPS fraction is

    A. $31,000

    B. $25,000

    C. $23,500

    D. $17,500

Answer (C) is correct. *(Publisher, adapted)*
    REQUIRED: The effect of assumed conversions on the numerator of the DEPS fraction.
    DISCUSSION: If all of the convertible preferred shares are assumed to be converted on January 1, $6,000 of dividends [(120,000 – 60,000) preferred shares × $.10] will not be paid. Furthermore, if the bonds are assumed to be converted on January 1, interest of $17,500 {[($2,000,000 × 5% ÷ 4] × (1.0 – .30 tax rate)} will not be paid. Accordingly, the effect of assumed conversions on the numerator of the DEPS fraction is an addition of $23,500 ($6,000 + $17,500) to the income available to common shareholders.
    Answer (A) is incorrect. This amount disregards the tax shield provided by bond interest. Answer (B) is incorrect. This amount equals one quarter's bond interest payment. Answer (D) is incorrect. This amount is the effect of the assumed conversion of the bonds alone.

46. At the beginning of the fiscal year, June 1, Year 3, Piotrowski Corporation had 80,000 shares of common stock outstanding. Also outstanding was $200,000 of 8% convertible bonds that had been issued at $1,000 par. The bonds were convertible into 20,000 shares of common stock; however, no bonds were converted during the year. The company's tax rate is 34%. Piotrowski's net income for the year was $107,000. Diluted earnings per share of Piotrowski common stock for the fiscal year ended May 31, Year 4, was

    A. $1.07

    B. $1.18

    C. $1.23

    D. $1.34

Answer (B) is correct. *(CMA, adapted)*
    REQUIRED: The DEPS given convertible bonds outstanding.
    DISCUSSION: Potential common shares that have a dilutive effect are included in the determination of DEPS. The calculation of DEPS assumes the conversion of the bonds at the beginning of the year, so the assumption is that no interest would be paid. Because bond interest was subtracted in determining net income, the DEPS numerator should be increased by the interest paid (net of tax effect). This after-tax effect was a $10,560 reduction of net income [($200,000 × 8%) × (1.0 – .34 tax rate)]. The denominator of the DEPS calculation is 100,000 shares (80,000 common shares outstanding + 20,000 shares that would be issued if the bonds were converted as of the beginning of the year). Hence, DEPS is equal to $1.18 per share [($107,000 NI + $10,560) ÷ (80,000 + 20,000)]. The convertible bonds are dilutive because their incremental inclusion reduces the corresponding BEPS amount.
    Answer (A) is incorrect. The amount of $1.07 fails to adjust the numerator for the interest savings and extra taxes. Answer (C) is incorrect. The amount of $1.23 fails to consider the additional taxes that would have to be paid on the interest savings. Answer (D) is incorrect. The amount of $1.34 equals BEPS.

47. Bilco had 10,000 shares of common stock outstanding throughout Year 3. There was no potential dilution of earnings per share except that, in Year 2, Bilco agreed to issue 2,000 additional shares of its stock to the former shareholders of an acquired company if the acquired company's earnings for any of the 5 years, Year 3 through Year 8, exceed $5,000. Results of operations for Year 3 were

Net income of Bilco	$10,000
Net income of acquired company	4,000
Consolidated net income	$14,000

Diluted earnings per share for Year 3 on a consolidated basis is

    A. $14,000 ÷ 10,000 = $1.40

    B. $14,000 ÷ 12,000 = $1.17

    C. $15,000 ÷ 10,000 = $1.50

    D. $15,000 ÷ 12,000 = $1.25

Answer (A) is correct. *(CPA, adapted)*
    REQUIRED: The consolidated DEPS when contingent shares are outstanding.
    DISCUSSION: If all necessary conditions have not been met at the end of the reporting period, the number of contingently issuable shares included in the DEPS denominator equals the number issuable if the end of the reporting period were the end of the contingency period. Because the acquired company earned only $4,000 for Year 3, no contingent shares would be issued if the end of Year 3 were the end of the contingency period. Thus, the contingent shares are disregarded. DEPS equals BEPS of $1.40 ($14,000 consolidated net income ÷ 10,000 shares issued and outstanding).
    Answer (B) is incorrect. DEPS is calculated using 10,000 common shares outstanding. Answer (C) is incorrect. Consolidated net income of $14,000 is used to calculate DEPS. Answer (D) is incorrect. Consolidated net income of $14,000 is used to calculate DEPS.

48. On June 30, Year 2, Kight Co. issued 20 $10,000, 7% bonds at par. Each bond was convertible into 200 shares of common stock. On January 1, Year 3, 10,000 shares of common stock were outstanding. The bondholders converted all the bonds on July 1, Year 3. The following amounts were reported in Kight's income statement for the year ended December 31, Year 3:

Revenues	$977,000
Operating expenses	(920,000)
Interest on bonds	(7,000)
Income before income tax	50,000
Income tax at 30%	(15,000)
Net income	$ 35,000

What amount should Kight report as its Year 3 diluted earnings per share?

A. $2.50

B. $2.85

C. $3.00

D. $3.50

Answer (B) is correct. *(CPA, adapted)*
REQUIRED: The DEPS given convertible bonds.
DISCUSSION: DEPS should be calculated even though no potential common shares were outstanding at year end. The reason is that the purpose of DEPS is to measure the performance of the entity over the reporting period while giving effect to all potential common shares that were outstanding during the period. The bonds were converted into 4,000 (20 bonds × 200 shares) shares of common stock on July 1, Year 3. Thus, the weighted-average number of shares of common stock outstanding is 12,000 shares [(10,000 × 12 ÷ 12) + (4,000 × 6 ÷ 12)]. BEPS therefore equals $2.92 ($35,000 net income ÷ 12,000). To determine if the potential common shares are dilutive, their incremental effect on EPS is calculated. This effect is equal to the after-tax interest that would be added back to net income divided by the potential common shares that would be added to the denominator. After-tax interest equals $4,900 [$7,000 × (1.0 − .30 tax rate)], and the dilutive potential common shares equal 2,000 [20 bonds × 200 shares × (6 months ÷ 12 months)]. The latter computation is a weighted average because the convertible bonds were outstanding for only 6 months. The incremental effect on EPS of the assumed conversion at the beginning of the year is $2.45 ($4,900 ÷ 2,000 shares). This amount is less than BEPS, so the convertible bonds are dilutive. Thus, DEPS equals $2.85 [($35,000 + $4,900) ÷ (12,000 + 2,000)].
Answer (A) is incorrect. This amount is based on a numerator of $35,000. Answer (C) is incorrect. This amount is based on a numerator of $42,000 (not net of tax). Answer (D) is incorrect. This amount is based on net income of $35,000 and 10,000 shares.

49. The senior accountant for Carlton Co., a public company with a complex capital structure, has just finished preparing Carlton's income statement for the current fiscal year. While reviewing the income statement, Carlton's finance director noticed that the earnings-per-share data has been omitted. What changes will have to be made to Carlton's income statement as a result of the omission of the earnings-per-share data?

A. No changes will have to be made to Carlton's income statement. The income statement is complete without the earnings-per-share data.

B. Carlton's income statement will have to be revised to include the earnings-per-share data.

C. Carlton's income statement will only have to be revised to include the earnings-per-share data if Carlton's market capitalization is greater than $5,000,000.

D. Carlton's income statement will only have to be revised to include the earnings-per-share data if Carlton's net income for the past 2 years was greater than $5,000,000.

Answer (B) is correct. *(CPA, adapted)*
REQUIRED: The changes needed when a public company with a complex capital structure has omitted EPS data.
DISCUSSION: A public entity must report EPS data on the face of the income statement. A public entity with only common stock outstanding must report basic earnings per share (BEPS) but not diluted earnings per share (DEPS) for income from continuing operations and net income. All other public entities must present BEPS and DEPS for income from continuing operations and net income with equal prominence. A nonpublic entity must follow the guidance for calculation and presentation of EPS only if it elects to report EPS.
Answer (A) is incorrect. A public entity must report EPS data on the face of the income statement. Answer (C) is incorrect. Market capitalization does not affect whether EPS must be disclosed in the income statement. Answer (D) is incorrect. Net income does not affect whether EPS must be disclosed in the income statement.

16.3 Share-Based Payment

50. On which of the following dates is a public entity required to measure the cost of employee services in exchange for an award of equity interests, based on the fair market value of the award?

A. Date of grant.

B. Date of restriction lapse.

C. Date of vesting.

D. Date of exercise.

Answer (A) is correct. *(CPA, adapted)*
REQUIRED: The measurement date for the cost of employee services in exchange for an award of equity interests.
DISCUSSION: The cost of employee services performed in exchange for an award of equity interests (share-based compensation) is recognized over the requisite service period. The beginning of this period is usually at the grant date. For equity awards, the entity estimates the fair value at the grant date of the equity instruments it is obligated to issue when employees meet the necessary conditions. The grant date is when (1) a mutual understanding of key terms of the award has been reached, (2) the employer is obligated if the employee provides the requisite service, (3) any needed approvals are obtained, and (4) an employee begins to be affected by changes in the price of the shares. Under U.S. GAAP, this guidance applies to equity awards by public and nonpublic entities.
Answer (B) is incorrect. Sale of shares issued to employees may be restricted (prohibited) for a specified period. For example, the ability to sell vested shares or share options may be restricted. This restriction is a factor in the measurement of their fair value at the grant date. But a restriction on nonvested shares is not considered. The date of restriction lapse is not the measurement date. Answer (C) is incorrect. Measurement must precede the date of vesting. Answer (D) is incorrect. Measurement must precede the date of exercise.

51. In a share-based payment transaction (SBPT) involving the receipt of goods or services by the reporting entity,

A. Initial recognition of the goods or services occurs when the entity issues its equity instruments.

B. Equity or a liability may be credited in appropriate circumstances.

C. Measurement of the SBPT is normally at the fair value of the services provided by employees.

D. The cost of goods or services received is recognized when they are received.

Answer (B) is correct. *(Publisher, adapted)*
REQUIRED: The true statement about an SBPT involving the receipt of goods or services by the reporting entity.
DISCUSSION: The relevant guidance applies to all SBPTs involving receipt by the entity of goods or services in return for its equity instruments, e.g., most shares or share options. It also applies to incurrence of liabilities that (1) are based wholly or in part on the price of the entity's equity instruments or (2) may require share settlement. Initial recognition of goods or services occurs when they are received. The credit is to equity or a liability depending on which classification criteria are met. Cost is recognized upon disposal or consumption of the goods or services.
Answer (A) is incorrect. Initial recognition occurs when goods or services are received. Answer (C) is incorrect. In an SBPT with nonemployees, the more reliably measurable of the fair value of the equity instruments issued or the consideration received is used to measure the SBPT. In an SBPT with employees, the fair value of the equity instruments issued ordinarily is the basis for measurement. The fair value of the services they render ordinarily is not readily determinable. Answer (D) is incorrect. The cost of goods or services received is recognized when they are disposed of or consumed.

52. Entities ordinarily must account for share-based employee compensation awards classified as equity in accordance with which of the following methods?

	Fair-Value Method	Intrinsic-Value Method
A.	Yes	Yes
B.	Yes	No
C.	No	Yes
D.	No	No

Answer (B) is correct. *(Publisher, adapted)*
REQUIRED: The method(s) prescribed for accounting for share-based employee compensations awards.
DISCUSSION: Entities must account for share-based payments classified as equity in accordance with the fair-value method except in the rare cases in which a nonpublic entity cannot reasonably estimate the fair value of the equity instruments at the grant date. In these cases, entities must account for such payments in accordance with the intrinsic-value method.
Answer (A) is incorrect. Election of either method is no longer permitted. An award classified as equity now must be measured at fair value except in rare cases. Answer (C) is incorrect. Election of either method is no longer permitted. An award classified as equity now must be measured at fair value except in rare cases. Answer (D) is incorrect. The fair-value method is used except in rare cases.

53. A reporting entity classifies as equity an award of share-based employee compensation in the form of share options. To account for this award, the entity

A. Recognizes changes in estimated total cost by retrospective application to prior periods affected.

B. Recognizes no cost for an award with a performance condition until the condition is satisfied.

C. Credits other comprehensive income.

D. Recognizes total compensation cost based on the number of equity instruments for which the requisite service was performed.

Answer (D) is correct. *(Publisher, adapted)*
REQUIRED: The accounting for an equity award of share-based employee compensation in the form of share options.
DISCUSSION: Compensation cost for an award classified as equity is recognized over the requisite service period. The credit is usually to paid-in capital. This period is the period during which employees must perform services. It is most often the vesting period. The requisite service period begins at the service inception date. The service required is called the requisite service. Total compensation cost at the end of the requisite service period is determined by the number of equity instruments for which the requisite service was completed and their grant-date fair value. The entity must estimate this number when initial accruals are made.
Answer (A) is incorrect. Changes in the estimate result in recognition of the cumulative effect on prior and current periods in calculation of compensation cost of the period of change. Answer (B) is incorrect. An accrual for an award with a performance condition is made if it is probable that the condition will be satisfied. Answer (C) is incorrect. The credit is usually to paid-in capital.

54. A reporting entity has entered into a share-based payment transaction (SBPT) with employees. In exchange for services to be performed, the entity will issue instruments properly classified as liabilities. For this SBPT,

A. The measurement date is the settlement date.

B. The measurement date is the service inception date.

C. A public entity may elect to measure the liabilities at intrinsic value.

D. A nonpublic entity must measure the liabilities at intrinsic value.

Answer (A) is correct. *(Publisher, adapted)*
REQUIRED: The true statement regarding this SBPT.
DISCUSSION: The measurement date for liabilities is the settlement date. Thus, after initial recognition, liabilities are remeasured at each reporting date.
Answer (B) is incorrect. The measurement date for liabilities is the settlement date. Answer (C) is incorrect. A public entity remeasures liabilities based on their fair values. Periodic compensation cost depends on the change (or part of the change, depending on the requisite service performed to date) in fair value. Answer (D) is incorrect. A nonpublic entity may elect to measure all such liabilities at fair value or intrinsic value. Fair value is preferable for the purpose of justifying a change in accounting principle. The percentage of fair value or intrinsic value accrued as compensation cost equals the percentage of required service rendered to date.

55. The service inception date is the date at which the requisite service period begins for a share-based payment transaction. The service inception date generally

A. Precedes the grant date.

B. Is the same as the grant date.

C. Follows the grant date.

D. Differs from the grant date.

Answer (B) is correct. *(Publisher, adapted)*
REQUIRED: The relationship between the grant date and the service inception date.
DISCUSSION: For most share-based payments, the service inception date is the same as the grant date. However, the service inception date precedes the grant date if (1) an award is authorized; (2) service begins before the employer and employee reach a mutual understanding of the terms of the award; and (3) either (a) the terms of the award do not require substantive services to be rendered after the grant date, or (b) the terms include a market or performance condition that will result in forfeiture of the award if it is not satisfied during the service period preceding the grant date.
Answer (A) is incorrect. The service inception date usually is the grant date, but it will precede the grant date under certain conditions. Answer (C) is incorrect. The service inception date usually is the grant date, but it will precede the grant date under certain conditions. Answer (D) is incorrect. The service inception date usually is the grant date, but it will precede the grant date under certain conditions.

Questions 56 through 59 are based on the following information. On December 21, Year 1, the board of directors of Oak Corporation approved a plan to award 600,000 share options to 20 key employees as additional compensation. Effective January 1, Year 2, each employee was granted the right to purchase 30,000 shares of the company's $2 par value stock at an exercise price of $36 per share. The market price on that date was $32 per share. All share options vest at December 31, Year 4, the end of the 3-year requisite service period. They expire on December 31, Year 11. Based on an appropriate option-pricing formula, the fair value of the options on the grant date was estimated at $12 per option.

56. What amount of compensation expense should Oak Corporation recognize in its annual income statement for the year ended December 31, Year 2?

    A. $7,200,000

    B. $6,400,000

    C. $2,400,000

    D. $1,200,700

Answer (C) is correct. *(Publisher, adapted)*
REQUIRED: The compensation expense recognized in Year 2.
DISCUSSION: Total compensation cost recognized during the requisite service period should equal the grant-date fair value of all share options for which the requisite service is rendered. GAAP require an entity to (1) estimate the number of share options for which the requisite service is expected to be rendered, (2) measure the cost of employee services received in exchange for those options at their fair value on the grant date, and (3) allocate that cost to the requisite service period. Given that all options vest at the same time (known as cliff vesting), the $7,200,000 (600,000 shares × $12 estimated fair value) total compensation cost should be allocated proportionately to the 3-year requisite service period. Thus, $2,400,000 ($7,200,000 ÷ 3) should be expensed in the annual income statement for the year ended December 31, Year 2.
    Answer (A) is incorrect. The amount of $7,200,000 is the total estimated compensation cost for the entire requisite service period. Answer (B) is incorrect. The amount of $6,400,000 is total compensation expense based on the $32 market price. Answer (D) is incorrect. The amount of $1,200,000 is 600,000 shares times the $2 par value.

57. On January 1, Year 3, five key employees left Oak Corporation. What amount of compensation expense should Oak report in the income statement for the year ended December 31, Year 3?

    A. $5,400,000

    B. $3,600,000

    C. $2,400,000

    D. $1,200,000

Answer (D) is correct. *(Publisher, adapted)*
REQUIRED: The compensation expense recognized in Year 3 after a change in estimate.
DISCUSSION: Given that all options vest at the same time (known as cliff vesting), the $7,200,000 (600,000 shares × $12 estimated fair value) total compensation cost should be allocated proportionately to the 3-year requisite service period. Thus, $2,400,000 ($7,200,000 ÷ 3) should be expensed in the annual income statement for the year ended December 31, Year 2. However, only 15 key employees are covered in Year 3. The total compensation expense for these employees is $5,400,000 [(30,000 options × 15 employees) × $12 fair value]. The amount to be recognized each year of the requisite service period is $1,800,000 ($5,400 ÷ 3). The revised cumulative amount to be recognized at the end of Year 3 is therefore $3,600,000 ($1,800,000 × 2 years). Because $2,400,000 was expensed in Year 2, Year 3 expense is $1,200,000 ($3,600,000 revised cumulative expense – $2,400,000).
    Answer (A) is incorrect. The total compensation expense for the entire requisite service period is $5,400,000. Answer (B) is incorrect. The total compensation expense that should be recognized in Years 2 and 3 combined is $3,600,000. Answer (C) is incorrect. The amount of $2,400,000 is based on the assumption that all 20 key employees remain employed.

58. On January 1, Year 3, five key employees left Oak Corporation. During the period from January 1, Year 5, through December 31, Year 11, 400,000 of the share options that vested were exercised. At the end of this period, the cumulative amount that should have been credited to additional paid-in capital is

- A. $19,200,000
- B. $18,400,000
- C. $13,600,000
- D. $4,000,000

Answer (B) is correct. *(Publisher, adapted)*
REQUIRED: The credit to additional paid-in capital at the end of the period.
DISCUSSION: Additional paid-in capital–share options was credited for $5,400,000 (450,000 × $12) as compensation expense was recognized during the requisite service period. During the period from January 1, Year 5, through December 31, Year 11, 400,000 options were exercised. Hence, additional paid-in capital should be credited for $18,400,000 [400,000 shares × ($36 exercise price + $12 previously credited to additional paid-in capital–stock options – $2 par value allocated to common stock)].
Answer (A) is incorrect. The amount of $19,200,000 includes the $2 par value allocated to the common stock account. Answer (C) is incorrect. The amount of $13,600,000 does not include the $12 fair value of the options determined at the grant date. Answer (D) is incorrect. The amount of $4,000,000 does not include the $36 exercise price.

59. On January 1, Year 3, five key employees left Oak Corporation. During the period from January 1, Year 5, through December 31, Year 11, 400,000 of the share options that vested were exercised. The remaining options were not exercised. What amount of the previously recognized compensation expense should be adjusted upon expiration of the share options?

- A. $2,400,000
- B. $2,300,000
- C. $100,000
- D. $0

Answer (D) is correct. *(Publisher, adapted)*
REQUIRED: The adjustment to previously recognized compensation expense when share options are not exercised.
DISCUSSION: Total compensation expense for the requisite service period is not adjusted for expired options.
Answer (A) is incorrect. This amount is the annual compensation expense recognized during each of the years of the requisite service period assuming no forfeitures. Answer (B) is incorrect. This amount is the additional amount that would have been credited to additional paid-in capital if the 50,000 expired options had been exercised. Answer (C) is incorrect. This amount is the additional amount that would have been credited to common stock if the 50,000 expired options had been exercised.

60. On January 1, Year 1, the grant date, Public Entity entered into an equity-settled share-based payment transaction with its senior executives. This award of 1,000 share options has a 4-year vesting period. The market prices of the options and the related shares on the grant date are $20 and $80, respectively. The exercise price is $85. Assuming that the requisite service was not completed for 100 of the options because of unexpected events in Year 4, the entry to debit option expense at

- A. December 31, Year 4, is for $5,000.
- B. December 31, Year 3, is for $4,500.
- C. December 31, Year 2, is for $5,000.
- D. January 1, Year 1, is for $20,000.

Answer (C) is correct. *(Publisher, adapted)*
REQUIRED: The entry to debit option expense given that requisite service was not completed for some options.
DISCUSSION: The fair value of each share option is determined at the measurement date, which is usually the grant date for transactions with employees. Thus, the fair value of each share option was set at its market price of $20 on January 1, Year 1. The periodic expense varies only with the expected number of equity instruments for which the requisite service is expected to be completed. Because the events causing the requisite service not to be completed for 100 options occurred unexpectedly in Year 4, the entity presumably expected at each balance sheet date for the first 3 years of the requisite service period that all options would be expensed. Total expected expense was therefore $20,000, and the proportional expense recognized in each of the first 3 years was $5,000 [(1,000 options × $20) ÷ 4 years].
Answer (A) is incorrect. The Year 4 expense is $3,000 [$20,000 total expected – $15,000 recognized in the first 3 years – (100 × $20) not vested]. Answer (B) is incorrect. No retrospective adjustment is made. The Year 3 entry would have been $5,000 based on a then-expected total expense of $20,000. Answer (D) is incorrect. If the options had vested immediately, $20,000 would have been recognized at January 1, Year 1.

61. On January 2, Kine Co. granted Morgan, its president, fully vested share options to buy 1,000 shares of Kine's $10 par common stock. The options have an exercise price of $20 per share and are exercisable for 3 years following the grant date. Morgan exercised the options on December 31. The market price of the shares was $50 on January 2, and $70 on the following December 31. If the fair value of the options is not reasonably estimable at the grant date, by what net amount should equity increase as a result of the grant and exercise of the options?

A. $20,000

B. $30,000

C. $50,000

D. $70,000

Answer (A) is correct. *(CPA, adapted)*
    REQUIRED: The amount equity increases as a result of the grant and exercise of share options.
    DISCUSSION: In the rare case in which an entity cannot reasonably estimate the fair value of equity instruments at the grant date, the accounting is based on intrinsic value (fair value of the underlying shares – exercise price of an option). Remeasurement is required at each reporting date and on final settlement. The measurement date is January 2. At that date, the intrinsic value of the options is $30,000 [1,000 shares × ($50 market price – $20 option price)]. The entry is

Compensation expense	$30,000	
Additional paid-in		
capital (share options)		$30,000

When the options are exercised, compensation expense will be debited and additional paid-in capital (share options) will be credited for $20,000 [1,000 shares × ($70 –$50)] to reflect the final measure of intrinsic value.

Compensation expense	$20,000	
Additional paid-in		
capital (share options)		$20,000

The final entry records the receipt of payment and the issuance of shares.

Cash	$20,000	
Additional paid-in capital		
(share options)	50,000	
Common stock		
(1,000 shares × $10 par)		$10,000
Additional paid-in capital		60,000

The net effect on equity is an increase of $20,000 ($10,000 common stock + $60,000 additional paid-in capital – $50,000 compensation expense).
    Answer (B) is incorrect. The amount of $30,000 is the initial debit to compensation expense and credit to options outstanding. Answer (C) is incorrect. The final measure of intrinsic value is $50,000. Answer (D) is incorrect. The market price of the shares issued on the settlement date is $70,000.

Use Gleim **EQE Test Prep** Software Download for interactive study and performance analysis.

STUDY UNIT SEVENTEEN
ACCOUNTING FOR INCOME TAXES

Objectives and Principles

The objectives of accounting for income taxes are to recognize (1) the amount of taxes payable or refundable for the current year and (2) deferred tax liabilities and assets for the future tax consequences of events recognized in financial statements or tax returns. The **asset and liability method** is used in accounting for income taxes. The following are the basic principles: (1) a **current tax liability or asset** is recognized for the estimated taxes payable or refundable on tax returns for the current year, (2) a **deferred tax liability or asset** is recognized for the estimated future tax effects attributable to temporary differences and carryforwards, (3) measurement of tax liabilities and assets is based on enacted tax law without regard to future changes in that law, and (4) a deferred tax asset is reduced by a valuation allowance if it is more likely than not that some portion will not be realized. Accordingly, income tax expense or benefit has two components: (1) current tax expense or benefit and (2) deferred tax expense or benefit. Current tax expense or benefit is the tax paid or payable (or refundable) based on enacted tax laws. Deferred tax expense or benefit is the net change during the year in an entity's deferred tax amounts (deferred tax liabilities and assets). A deferred tax liability records the deferred tax consequences of taxable temporary differences. A deferred tax asset records the deferred tax consequences of deductible temporary differences and carryforwards.

Temporary and Permanent Differences

Income reported under **GAAP** (accrual basis) differs from income reported for **tax purposes** (modified cash basis) because some items are included in taxable income (loss) of an earlier or later year than the year they are recognized in earnings. Moreover, other tax consequences result from (1) other events that create differences between the tax bases of assets and liabilities and their financial statement amounts, and (2) operating loss or tax credit carrybacks for refunds of taxes paid in prior years and carryforwards to reduce taxes payable in future years. A **temporary difference (TD)** results when (1) the GAAP basis and the tax basis of an asset or liability differ, and (2) the effect is a taxable or deductible amount in future years when the asset is recovered or the liability is settled.

TDs result in deferred tax liabilities or deferred tax assets. **Deferred tax liabilities** arise when the recovery of an asset will result in **future taxable amounts**.

$$DTL = Future\ taxable\ amount \times Enacted\ tax\ rate$$

Taxable TDs are of two kinds: One includes items recognized when **revenues or gains** are included in taxable income **after** they are recognized under GAAP. An example is income recognized under the equity method for financial statement purposes and at the time of distribution in taxable income. Another example is sales revenue accrued in full for financial reporting and recognized on the installment basis for tax purposes. The second includes items recognized when **expenses or losses** are deductible for tax purposes **before** they are recognized under GAAP. An example is property depreciated more rapidly for tax purposes than for financial reporting.

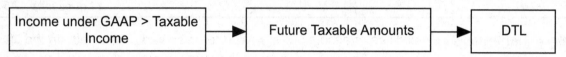

Deferred tax assets arise when TDs result in **future deductible amounts**.

$$DTA = Future\ deductible\ amount \times Enacted\ tax\ rate$$

Deductible TDs also are of two kinds. One includes items recognized when **revenues or gains** are included in taxable income **before** they are recognized under GAAP. An example is subscription revenue received in advance. The second includes items recognized when **expenses or losses** are deductible for tax purposes **after** they are recognized under GAAP. Examples include bad debt expense recognized under the allowance method and warranty costs.

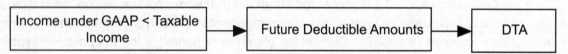

Some TDs result from assets or liabilities that are **recognized for tax purposes** but **not for financial reporting purposes**. One example of future deductible amounts that arise from such circumstances is organizational costs. They are deferred and amortized for tax purposes. But they must be expensed when incurred for financial reporting purposes. A second example is an operating loss carryforward. It is carried forward as deductions in future years for tax purposes but must be recognized immediately under GAAP. A deferred tax liability must be recognized for the taxable TD arising from tax deductions for **goodwill**, which is not amortizable for financial statement purposes. This treatment is required even though the deferred tax liability will not be settled until some indefinite future period when goodwill is impaired, sold, or otherwise disposed of. The same treatment applies to other intangible assets that are not amortizable because their useful lives are indefinite.

A **permanent difference** is an event that is recognized either in pretax financial income or in taxable income but never in both. One kind of permanent difference consists of items **included in income for financial reporting** purposes but not for tax purposes. Examples include state and municipal bond interest and proceeds from life insurance on key employees. Another kind consists of items **deducted from income for financial reporting purposes** but not for tax purposes. Examples include premiums paid for life insurance on key employees and fines resulting from violation of law. A third kind consists of items **deducted from income for tax purposes** but not for financial reporting purposes. Examples include percentage depletion of natural resources and the dividends received deduction.

Recognition and Measurement of Deferred Income Taxes

The computation of deferred tax amounts is based on the following procedures: (1) Identify the types and amounts of existing TDs; (2) identify the nature, amount, and remaining carryforward period of each type of operating loss and tax credit carryforward; (3) measure the total deferred tax liability for taxable TDs using the applicable tax rate; (4) measure the total deferred tax asset for deductible TDs and operating loss carryforwards using the applicable tax rate; (5) measure deferred tax assets for each type of tax credit carryforward; and (6) recognize a **valuation allowance** (if necessary).

The **applicable tax rate** is the **enacted tax rate** expected to apply to taxable income in the periods in which deferred tax liabilities or assets are expected to be settled or realized. In the U.S., the applicable tax rate is the regular rate. The tax rate used in the measurement of deferred tax amounts is, in essence, a flat rate if graduated rates are **not** significant to the entity. Otherwise, an average of the applicable graduated rates is used.

A valuation allowance reduces a **deferred tax asset**. It is recognized if, based on the weight of all available evidence, it is **more likely than not** (probability > 50%) that some portion of the asset will not be realized. The allowance should reduce the deferred tax asset to the amount that is more likely than not to be realized.

The basic entry to record taxes in accordance with the asset and liability method is

Income tax expense (or benefit)	debit (or credit)
Income tax payable (or refundable)	credit (or debit)
Deferred income tax liability (or asset)	credit (or debit)

Current tax expense or benefit is

Current tax expense (benefit) = Taxable income (or excess of deductions over revenue) × Enacted rate

Deferred tax expense or benefit is

Deferred tax expense (benefit) = Changes in DTL balances ± Changes in DTA balances

The following are entries reflecting changes in the deferred tax liability (DTL) or the deferred tax asset (DTA):

If the DTL balance increased during the year:			If the DTA balance increased during the year:		
Income tax expense	$xx,xxx		Income tax expense	$x,xxx	
Deferred tax liability		$x,xxx	Deferred tax asset	x,xxx	
Income tax payable		x,xxx	Income tax payable		$xx,xxx
If the DTL balance decreased during the year:			**If the DTA balance decreased during the year:**		
Income tax expense	$x,xxx		Income tax expense	$xx,xxx	
Deferred tax liability	x,xxx		Deferred tax asset		$x,xxx
Income tax payable		$xx,xxx	Income tax payable		x,xxx

Additional Income Tax Issues

Deferred tax liabilities and assets are classified as **current or noncurrent** based on the classification of the related asset or liability for financial reporting. Deferred tax amounts not related to an asset or liability for financial reporting, such as deferred tax assets related to carryforwards, are classified based on the expected reversal date. A valuation allowance for a specific tax jurisdiction is allocated pro rata between current and noncurrent deferred tax assets. Deferred tax amounts are **offset** and classified as net current and net noncurrent amounts for a given tax-paying entity within a specific tax jurisdiction.

A deferred tax amount is adjusted for the effect of an **enacted change in tax law or rates**. The effect is included in income from continuing operations for the period that includes the date of enactment.

Intraperiod tax allocation is required. Total income tax expense or benefit is allocated among (1) continuing operations, (2) discontinued operations, (3) extraordinary items, (4) other comprehensive income, and (5) items charged or credited directly to equity.

Required **disclosures** include (1) total deferred tax liabilities, (2) total deferred tax assets, (3) the total valuation allowance for deferred tax assets and the net annual change in it, and (4) the significant components of income tax expense related to continuing operations. Public entities also must disclose the tax effect of each TD or carryforward resulting in a significant deferred tax amount. However, a nonpublic entity must disclose only the types of significant TDs and carryforwards. No disclosures about permanent differences are required.

Differences between GAAP and IFRS

Under IFRS:

- Deferred tax amounts are measured based on the enacted tax rates or the substantively enacted tax rates at the end of the reporting period.
- With limited exceptions (e.g., initial recognition of goodwill), all deferred tax liabilities must be recognized.
- All deferred tax amounts are noncurrent.
- A deferred tax asset is recognized for most deductible temporary differences (TDs) and for the carryforward of unused tax losses and credits, but only to the extent it is probable that taxable profit will be available. Thus, no valuation allowance is recognized. Moreover, IFRS do not define probable.

QUESTIONS

17.1 Objectives and Principles

1. Under current generally accepted accounting principles, which approach is used to determine income tax expense?

A. Asset and liability approach.

B. "With and without" approach.

C. Net-of-tax approach.

D. Deferred approach.

Answer (A) is correct. *(CPA, adapted)*
REQUIRED: The current approach used to determine income tax expense.
DISCUSSION: The asset and liability approach accrues liabilities or assets (taxes payable or refundable) for the current year. It also recognizes deferred tax liabilities and assets for the future tax consequences of events that have been previously recognized in the financial statements or tax returns. These liabilities and assets recognize the effects of temporary differences measured using the tax rate(s) expected to apply when the liabilities and assets are expected to be settled or realized.
Answer (B) is incorrect. Superseded guidance stated that the tax effect of a timing difference should "be measured by the differential between income taxes computed with and without inclusion of the transaction creating the difference between taxable income and pretax accounting income." Answer (C) is incorrect. The net-of-tax approach accounts for the effects of taxability or deductibility on assets and liabilities as reductions in their reported amounts. Answer (D) is incorrect. The deferred method used in superseded guidance recognized deferred tax credits and charges. It attempted to match income tax expense with related revenues and expenses for the year when they were recognized in pretax financial income. Thus, no measurement was made of the cumulative taxes payable or refundable when temporary differences reverse in the future. Income tax expense was determined by multiplying pretax financial income by the current tax rate, with the difference between taxes payable (refundable) and income tax expense (benefit) being recorded as a deferred credit or charge.

17.2 Temporary and Permanent Differences

2. When accounting for income taxes, a temporary difference occurs in which of the following scenarios?

    A. An item is included in the calculation of net income but is neither taxable nor deductible.

    B. An item is included in the calculation of net income in one year and in taxable income in a different year.

    C. An item is **no** longer taxable due to a change in the tax law.

    D. The accrual method of accounting is used.

Answer (B) is correct. *(CPA, adapted)*
REQUIRED: The circumstances resulting in a temporary difference.
DISCUSSION: A temporary difference (TD) results when the GAAP basis and the tax basis of an asset or liability differ. The effect is that a taxable or deductible amount will occur in future years when the asset is recovered or the liability is settled. But some TDs are not related to an asset or liability for financial reporting. Thus, TDs occur when revenues or gains, or expenses or losses, are used to calculate net income under GAAP in a year before or after being used to calculate taxable income.
Answer (A) is incorrect. A permanent difference is an event that is recognized either in pretax financial income or in taxable income, but never in both. It does not result in a deferred tax amount. Answer (C) is incorrect. An item that is no longer taxable results in a permanent difference. Answer (D) is incorrect. The accrual method and the tax basis recognize many items in the same period.

3. In its income statement for the year just ended, Small Co. reported income before income taxes of $600,000. Small estimated that, because of permanent differences, taxable income for the year would be $560,000. During the year, Small made estimated tax payments of $100,000, which were debited to income tax expense. Small is subject to a 30% tax rate. What amount should Small report as income tax expense?

    A. $68,000

    B. $100,000

    C. $168,000

    D. $180,000

Answer (C) is correct. *(CPA, adapted)*
REQUIRED: The amount to be reported for income tax expense.
DISCUSSION: Income tax expense or benefit is the sum of current tax expense or benefit and deferred tax expense or benefit. A deferred tax expense or benefit is the change in an entity's deferred tax assets and liabilities. However, a permanent difference does not result in a change in a deferred tax asset or liability. Thus, income tax expense equals current income tax expense, which is the amount of taxes paid or payable for the year. Income taxes payable for the year equal $168,000 ($560,000 taxable income × 30%).
Answer (A) is incorrect. The amount of $68,000 equals the $168,000 of income taxes payable minus the $100,000 of income taxes paid. Answer (B) is incorrect. The amount of $100,000 equals income taxes paid, not the total current income tax expense. Answer (D) is incorrect. The amount of $180,000 is equal to the reported income of $600,000 times the tax rate.

4. Fern Co. has net income, before taxes, of $200,000, including $20,000 interest revenue from municipal bonds and $10,000 paid for officers' life insurance premiums where the company is the beneficiary. The tax rate for the current year is 30%. What is Fern's effective tax rate?

    A. 27.0%

    B. 28.5%

    C. 30.0%

    D. 31.5%

Answer (B) is correct. *(CPA, adapted)*
REQUIRED: The effective tax rate given pretax net income, interest from municipal bonds, officers' life insurance premiums, and the current tax rate.
DISCUSSION: The municipal bond revenue (nontaxable) and key-person life insurance premiums (an expense that is nondeductible) are permanent differences. Thus, pretax income is adjusted to eliminate both items.

Pretax income	$200,000
Municipal bond income	(20,000)
Life insurance premiums	10,000
Taxable income	$190,000

Assuming no temporary differences and deferred taxes, income tax is $57,000 ($190,000 × 30%). Accordingly, the effective tax rate is 28.5% ($57,000 income tax expense ÷ $200,000 pretax net income).
Answer (A) is incorrect. The amount of 27.0% [($180,000 × 30%) ÷ $200,000] results from treating the insurance premiums as deductible. Answer (C) is incorrect. The amount of 30.0% [($200,000 × 30%) ÷ $200,000] results from treating pretax net income as taxable income. Answer (D) is incorrect. The amount of 31.5% [($210,000 × 30%) ÷ $200,000] results from adding the insurance premiums to pretax income to determine taxable income.

5. In Year 2, Ajax, Inc., reported taxable income of $400,000 and pretax financial statement income of $300,000. The difference resulted from $60,000 of nondeductible premiums on Ajax's officers' life insurance and $40,000 of rental income received in advance. Rental income is taxable when received. Ajax's effective tax rate is 30%. In its Year 2 income statement, what amount should Ajax report as income tax expense--current portion?

A. $90,000

B. $102,000

C. $108,000

D. $120,000

Answer (D) is correct. *(CPA, adapted)*
   REQUIRED: The current income tax expense given taxable income, pretax net income, officers' life insurance premiums, and rent received in advance.
   DISCUSSION: Current income tax expense or benefit is the amount of taxes paid or payable (or refundable) for the year based on enacted tax law applied to taxable income (excess of deductions over revenues). Thus, current income tax expense is $120,000 ($400,000 taxable income × 30%).
   Answer (A) is incorrect. The amount of $90,000 equals the effective tax rate times pretax financial statement income. Answer (B) is incorrect. The amount of $102,000 equals the effective tax rate times the excess of reported taxable income over the nondeductible insurance premiums. Answer (C) is incorrect. The amount of $108,000 equals the effective tax rate times the excess of reported taxable income over rent received in advance.

6. Temporary differences arise when expenses are deductible for tax purposes

	After They Are Recognized in Financial Income	Before They Are Recognized in Financial Income
A.	No	No
B.	No	Yes
C.	Yes	Yes
D.	Yes	No

Answer (C) is correct. *(CPA, adapted)*
   REQUIRED: The situations in which temporary differences arise.
   DISCUSSION: A temporary difference exists when (1) the reported amount of an asset or liability in the financial statements differs from the tax basis of that asset or liability, and (2) the difference will result in taxable or deductible amounts in future years when the asset is recovered or the liability is settled at its reported amount. A temporary difference may also exist although it cannot be identified with a particular asset or liability recognized for financial reporting purposes. A temporary difference relates to an asset or liability if reduction of the asset or liability causes the temporary difference to reverse. An example of a temporary difference not related to an asset or liability because it is not reduced when the asset or liability is reduced is a long-term contract accounted for by the percentage-of-completion method for financial reporting and the completed-contract method for tax purposes. In this case, the temporary difference reverses only when the contract is completed, not from collection of receivables resulting from progress billings. Such a temporary difference must result from an event recognized in the financial statements and must also result in taxable or deductible amounts in future years based on the provisions of the tax laws. Temporary differences commonly arise when either expenses or revenues are recognized for tax purposes either earlier or later than in the determination of financial income.

7. Among the items reported on Perez Company's income statement for the year ended December 31 were the following:

Compensation expense for a stock option plan	$50,000
Insurance premium on the life of an officer (Perez is the owner and beneficiary.)	25,000

Neither is deductible for tax purposes. Temporary differences amount to

A. $0

B. $25,000

C. $50,000

D. $75,000

Answer (A) is correct. *(CPA, adapted)*
   REQUIRED: The amount of temporary differences.
   DISCUSSION: Temporary differences arise when (1) the reported amount of an asset or a liability in the financial statements differs from the tax basis of that asset or liability, and (2) the difference will result in taxable or deductible amounts in future years when the asset is recovered or the liability is settled at its reported amount. It is given that expenses for compensation expense for a stock option plan and payment of the premium for life insurance covering a key executive are recognized in the financial statements but are not deductible for tax purposes. Because neither will result in taxable or deductible amounts in future years, they are permanent, not temporary differences.
   Answer (B) is incorrect. The insurance premium on the life of an officer is not deductible for tax purposes. Hence, it results in a permanent difference. Answer (C) is incorrect. The compensation expense for a stock option plan is not deductible for tax purposes. Hence, it results in a permanent difference. Answer (D) is incorrect. Neither expense is deductible for tax purposes.

8. Which one of the following temporary differences will result in a deferred tax asset?

A. Use of the straight-line depreciation method for financial statement purposes and the Modified Accelerated Cost Recovery System (MACRS) for income tax purposes.

B. Installment sale profits accounted for on the accrual basis for financial statement purposes and on a cash basis for income tax purposes.

C. Advance rental receipts accounted for on the accrual basis for financial statement purposes and on a cash basis for tax purposes.

D. Prepaid expenses accounted for on the accrual basis for financial statement purposes and on a cash basis for income tax purposes.

Answer (C) is correct. *(CMA, adapted)*
REQUIRED: The temporary difference that will result in a deferred tax asset.
DISCUSSION: A deferred tax asset records the deferred tax consequences attributable to deductible temporary differences and carryforwards. Advance rental receipts accounted for on the accrual basis for financial statement purposes and on a cash basis for tax purposes result in a deferred tax asset. The financial statements report no income and no related tax expense because the rental payments apply to future periods. The tax return, however, reports the rent as income when the cash is received, and a tax is due in the year of receipt. Because the tax is paid prior to recording the income for financial statement purposes, it represents an asset that will be recognized as an expense when income is finally recorded.
Answer (A) is incorrect. Using accelerated depreciation on the tax return results in a deferred tax liability. Answer (B) is incorrect. Recognizing installment income on the financial statements but not the tax return results in a taxable temporary difference. Answer (D) is incorrect. Recognizing prepaid expenses earlier on the tax return than on the financial statements (a situation akin to the accelerated depreciation of fixed assets) gives rise to a deferred tax liability.

9. On December 31, Year 3, Thomas Company reported a $150,000 warranty expense in its income statement. The expense was based on actual warranty costs of $30,000 in Year 3 and expected warranty costs of $35,000 in Year 4, $40,000 in Year 5, and $45,000 in Year 6. At December 31, Year 3, deferred taxes should be based on a

A. $120,000 deductible temporary difference.

B. $150,000 deductible temporary difference.

C. $120,000 taxable temporary difference.

D. $150,000 taxable temporary difference.

Answer (A) is correct. *(Publisher, adapted)*
REQUIRED: The taxable (deductible) temporary difference resulting from a warranty expense.
DISCUSSION: At year-end Year 3, Thomas Company should report a $120,000 warranty liability in its balance sheet. The warranty liability is equal to the $150,000 warranty expense minus the $30,000 warranty cost actually incurred in Year 3. Because warranty costs are not deductible until actually incurred, the tax basis of the warranty liability is $0. The result is a $120,000 temporary difference ($120,000 carrying amount – $0 tax basis). When the liability is settled through the actual incurrence of warranty costs, the amounts will be deductible. Thus, the temporary difference should be classified as a deductible temporary difference.
Answer (B) is incorrect. The warranty expense, not the payable, equals $150,000. Answer (C) is incorrect. Warranty costs will result in a deductible amount. Answer (D) is incorrect. The warranty costs will result in a deductible amount, and the $30,000 actual warranty costs are currently deductible.

17.3 Recognition and Measurement of Deferred Income Taxes

10. Jackson Corp. leased a building and received the $36,000 annual rental payment on June 15. The beginning of the lease was July 1. Rental income is taxable when received. Jackson's tax rates are 30% for the current year and 40% thereafter. Jackson had no other permanent or temporary differences. Jackson determined that no valuation allowance was needed. What amount of deferred tax asset should Jackson report in its December 31 balance sheet?

A. $5,400

B. $7,200

C. $10,800

D. $14,400

Answer (B) is correct. *(CPA, adapted)*
REQUIRED: The amount of deferred tax asset reported at year end.
DISCUSSION: The $36,000 rental payment is taxable in full when received but only $18,000 [$36,000 × (6 ÷ 12)] should be recognized in financial accounting income for the year. The result is a deductible temporary difference arising from the difference between the tax basis ($0) of the liability for unearned rent and its reported amount in the year-end balance sheet ($36,000 – $18,000 = $18,000). A deductible temporary difference results in a deferred tax asset. The income tax payable for the current year based on the rental payment is $10,800 ($36,000 × 30% tax rate for the current year), the deferred tax asset is $7,200 ($18,000 future deductible amount × 40% enacted tax rate applicable after the current year when the asset will be realized), and the income tax expense is $3,600 ($10,800 current tax expense – $7,200 deferred tax benefit). The deferred tax benefit equals the net change during the year in the entity's deferred tax liabilities and assets ($7,200 deferred tax asset recognized in the current year – $0).
Answer (A) is incorrect. The amount of $5,400 is based on a 30% tax rate. Answer (C) is incorrect. Income tax payable is $10,800. Answer (D) is incorrect. The income tax payable would be $14,400 if the 40% tax rate applied in the current year.

11. Vickers, Inc., reported deferred tax assets and deferred tax liabilities at the end of both Year 4 and Year 5. For the year ended in Year 5, Vickers should report deferred income tax expense or benefit equal to the

A. Sum of the net changes in deferred tax assets and deferred tax liabilities.

B. Decrease in the deferred tax assets.

C. Increase in the deferred tax liabilities.

D. Current income tax liability plus the sum of the net changes in deferred tax assets and deferred tax liabilities.

Answer (A) is correct. *(CPA, adapted)*
REQUIRED: The method of determining deferred income tax expense or benefit.
DISCUSSION: The deferred tax expense or benefit recognized is the sum of the net changes in the deferred tax assets and deferred tax liabilities. The deferred income tax expense or benefit is aggregated with the income taxes currently payable or refundable to determine the amount of income tax expense or benefit for the year to be recorded in the income statement.
Answer (B) is incorrect. The deferred income tax expense or benefit equals the sum of the net changes in the deferred tax assets and deferred tax liabilities. Answer (C) is incorrect. The calculation also includes any decrease in deferred tax liabilities and changes in deferred tax assets. Answer (D) is incorrect. The current income tax liability plus the sum of the net changes in deferred tax assets and deferred tax liabilities is the income tax expense or benefit for the year.

12. A deferred tax asset must be reduced by a valuation allowance if it is

A. Probable that some portion will not be realized.

B. Reasonably possible that some portion will not be realized.

C. More likely than not that some portion will not be realized.

D. Likely that some portion will not be realized.

Answer (C) is correct. *(Publisher, adapted)*
REQUIRED: The standard for recognizing a valuation allowance for a deferred tax asset.
DISCUSSION: A deferred tax asset is reduced by a valuation allowance if the weight of the available evidence, both positive and negative, indicates that it is more likely than not (that is, the probability is greater than 50%) that some portion will not be realized. The allowance should suffice to reduce the deferred tax asset to the amount that is more likely than not to be realized.
Answer (A) is incorrect. The FASB specifically rejected the term "probable" (likely) as used in the guidance applying to accounting for contingencies. Answer (B) is incorrect. The FASB believes that the appropriate criterion is the one that produces results that are closest to the expected outcome. A reasonable possibility does not meet that standard. Answer (D) is incorrect. It must be "more likely than not" that some portion of the deferred tax asset will not be realized.

13. Deferred tax assets must be reduced by a valuation allowance if, based on the weight of the evidence, it is more likely than not that some portion or all of the deferred tax assets will not be realized. Which of the following kinds of evidence is considered in making this determination?

	Positive Evidence	Negative Evidence
A.	Yes	No
B.	Yes	Yes
C.	No	Yes
D.	No	No

Answer (B) is correct. *(Publisher, adapted)*
REQUIRED: The evidence to be considered in determining whether a valuation allowance should be recognized.
DISCUSSION: In determining whether a valuation allowance is required to reduce deferred tax assets to the amount that is more likely than not to be realized, all available evidence should be considered. Available evidence includes both positive and negative evidence. In considering the relative impact of positive and negative evidence, the weight given to the potential effect of the evidence should be commensurate with the extent to which the evidence can be objectively verified. However, the more negative evidence in existence, the more positive evidence is necessary and the more difficult it is to support a conclusion that a valuation allowance is not necessary.
Answer (A) is incorrect. Negative evidence also should be considered. Answer (C) is incorrect. Positive evidence also should be considered. Answer (D) is incorrect. All available evidence should be considered in determining whether a valuation allowance is required, including both positive and negative evidence.

14. Ray Co. began operations in the current year and reported $225,000 in income before income taxes for the year. Ray's current-year tax depreciation exceeded its book depreciation by $25,000. Ray also had nondeductible book expenses of $10,000 related to permanent differences. Ray's tax rate for the current year was 40%, and 35% for the following years. In its current-year balance sheet, what amount of deferred income tax liability should Ray report?

   A. $8,750

   B. $10,000

   C. $12,250

   D. $14,000

Answer (A) is correct. *(CPA, adapted)*
   REQUIRED: The deferred income tax liability reported on the balance sheet.
   DISCUSSION: In measuring a deferred tax liability or asset, the objective is to use the enacted tax rate(s) expected to apply to taxable income in the periods in which the deferred tax liability or asset is expected to be settled or realized. At the end of the current year, the only temporary difference is the $25,000 excess of tax depreciation over the book depreciation. This temporary difference will give rise to a $25,000 taxable amount in the years following the current year. Given the enacted tax rate of 35% applicable after the current year, the total tax consequence attributable to the taxable temporary difference (the deferred tax liability) is $8,750 ($25,000 × 35%).
   Answer (B) is incorrect. The 35% tax rate applicable when the deferred tax liability is expected to be settled should be used. Answer (C) is incorrect. Permanent differences do not create deferred tax liabilities. Answer (D) is incorrect. Permanent differences do not create deferred tax liabilities, and the 35% tax rate applicable when the deferred tax liability is expected to be settled should be used.

15. Based on its current operating levels, Ellis Corporation estimates that its annual level of taxable income (including reversing temporary differences) in the foreseeable future will be $200,000 annually. Enacted tax rates for the tax jurisdiction in which Ellis operates are 15% for the first $50,000 of taxable income, 25% for the next $50,000 of taxable income, and 35% for taxable income in excess of $100,000. Which tax rate should Ellis use to measure a deferred tax liability or asset?

   A. 15%

   B. 25%

   C. 27.5%

   D. 35%

Answer (C) is correct. *(Publisher, adapted)*
   REQUIRED: The tax rate applicable to the measurement of a deferred tax liability or asset.
   DISCUSSION: In measuring a deferred tax liability or asset, the objective is to use the enacted tax rate(s) expected to apply to taxable income in the periods in which the deferred tax liability or asset is expected to be settled or realized. If graduated tax rates are a significant factor for an entity, the applicable tax rate is the average graduated tax rate applicable to the amount of estimated future annual taxable income. As indicated, the applicable tax rate is 27.5%.

Taxable Income			Tax Rate		
$ 50,000	×	15%	=	$ 7,500
50,000	×	25%	=	12,500
100,000	×	35%	=	35,000
$200,000				$55,000

$55,000 ÷ $200,000 = 27.5%

   Answer (A) is incorrect. Fifteen percent is the tax rate for the first $50,000 of income. Answer (B) is incorrect. Twenty-five percent is the tax rate for income over $50,000 but less than $100,000. Answer (D) is incorrect. Thirty-five percent is the tax rate for income over $100,000.

16. In its Year 3 income statement, Orr Corp. reported depreciation of $400,000. Orr reported depreciation of $550,000 on its Year 3 income tax return. The difference in depreciation is the only temporary difference, and it will reverse equally over the next 3 years. Assume that the enacted income tax rates are 35% for Year 3, 30% for Year 4, and 25% for Year 5 and Year 6. What amount should be included in the deferred income tax liability in Orr's December 31, Year 3, balance sheet?

   A. $37,500

   B. $40,000

   C. $45,000

   D. $52,500

Answer (B) is correct. *(CPA, adapted)*
   REQUIRED: The amount to be included in the deferred income tax liability at year end.
   DISCUSSION: At 12/31/Year 3, the only temporary difference is the $150,000 ($550,000 – $400,000) excess of the tax depreciation over the book depreciation. This temporary difference will give rise to a $50,000 taxable amount in each of the years Year 4 through Year 6. Given the enacted tax rates of 30% in Year 4 and 25% in Year 5 and Year 6, the total tax consequences are $40,000, which is the balance that should be reported in the deferred income tax liability at year end.

Year	Taxable Amount	Enacted Tax Rates	Tax Consequences
4	$50,000	30%	$15,000
5	50,000	25%	12,500
6	50,000	25%	12,500
			$40,000

   Answer (A) is incorrect. The amount of $37,500 is based on a 25% tax rate. Answer (C) is incorrect. The amount of $45,000 is based on a 30% tax rate. Answer (D) is incorrect. The amount of $52,500 is based on a 35% tax rate.

17. Tharris Corp. uses the equity method to account for its 25% investment in Bailey, Inc. During the current year, Tharris received dividends of $30,000 from Bailey and recorded $180,000 as its equity in the earnings of Bailey. Additional information follows:

● All the undistributed earnings of Bailey will be distributed as dividends in future periods.

● The dividends received from Bailey are eligible for the 80% dividends received deduction.

● There are no other temporary differences.

● Enacted income tax rates are 30% for the current year and thereafter.

In its current-year balance sheet, what amount should Tharris report for deferred income tax liability?

A. $9,000

B. $10,800

C. $45,000

D. $54,000

Answer (A) is correct. *(CPA, adapted)*
REQUIRED: The deferred income tax liability reported on the balance sheet.
DISCUSSION: The deferred tax liability constitutes the deferred tax consequences attributable to taxable temporary differences. A deferred tax liability is measured using the applicable enacted tax rate and the enacted tax law. The recognition of $180,000 of equity-based earnings creates a temporary difference that will result in taxable amounts in future periods when dividends are distributed. The deferred tax liability arising from this temporary difference is measured using the 30% enacted tax rate and the dividends received deduction. Accordingly, given that all the undistributed earnings will be distributed, a deferred tax liability of $9,000 [($180,000 equity – $30,000 dividends received) × 20% not deductible × 30% tax rate applicable after the current year] should be reported.
Answer (B) is incorrect. The amount of $10,800 equals 30% of 20% of the equity in the earnings of Bailey. Answer (C) is incorrect. The amount of $45,000 is the net increase in the investment in Bailey account under the equity method multiplied by the 30% tax rate. Answer (D) is incorrect. The amount of $54,000 equals 30% of $180,000.

18. Ratliff Co., organized on January 2, Year 3, had pretax accounting income of $500,000 and taxable income of $800,000 for the year ended December 31, Year 3. Ratliff expected to maintain this level of taxable income in future years. The only temporary difference is for accrued product warranty costs expected to be paid as follows:

Year 4	$100,000
Year 5	50,000
Year 6	50,000
Year 7	100,000

The applicable enacted income tax rate is 30%. In Ratliff's December 31, Year 3, balance sheet, the deferred income tax asset and related valuation allowance should be

	Deferred Tax Asset	Valuation Allowance
A.	$0	$0
B.	$90,000	$90,000
C.	$90,000	$0
D.	$0	$90,000

Answer (C) is correct. *(CPA, adapted)*
REQUIRED: The deferred tax asset and valuation allowance to be recognized at 12/31/Year 3.
DISCUSSION: At 12/31/Year 3, Ratliff should report an accrued product warranty liability of $300,000. The result is a deductible temporary difference of $300,000 because the liability will be settled and related amounts will be tax deductible when the warranty costs are incurred. A deferred tax asset should be measured for deductible temporary differences using the applicable tax rate. Hence, Ratliff should record a $90,000 ($300,000 × 30%) deferred tax asset. A valuation allowance should be used to reduce a deferred tax asset if, based on the weight of the available evidence, it is more likely than not that some portion will not be realized. In this case, however, Ratliff had taxable income of $800,000 for Year 3 and expects to maintain that level of taxable income in future years. The positive evidence therefore indicates that sufficient taxable income will be available for the future realization of the tax benefit of the existing deductible temporary differences. Given no negative evidence, a valuation allowance is not necessary.
Answer (A) is incorrect. A deferred tax asset should be recognized. Answer (B) is incorrect. A valuation allowance should not be recognized. Answer (D) is incorrect. A deferred tax asset but not a valuation allowance should be recognized.

19. Which of the following items should affect current income tax expense for Year 3?

A. Interest on a Year 1 tax deficiency paid in Year 3.

B. Penalty on a Year 1 tax deficiency paid in Year 3.

C. Change in income tax rate for Year 3.

D. Change in income tax rate for Year 4.

Answer (C) is correct. *(CPA, adapted)*
REQUIRED: The item that affects current income tax expense for Year 3.
DISCUSSION: Current tax expense is the amount of income taxes paid or payable for a year as determined by applying the provisions of the enacted tax law to the taxable income for that year.
Answer (A) is incorrect. Interest on a prior-year tax deficiency does not affect current income tax expense. Answer (B) is incorrect. Penalties on a prior-year tax deficiency do not affect current income tax expense. Answer (D) is incorrect. A change in income tax rate for Year 4 would affect the deferred tax expense or benefit for Year 3, assuming scheduled effects of a temporary difference will occur in Year 4.

20. In preparing its current year-end financial statements, Guss Corp. must determine the proper accounting treatment of a $180,000 loss carryforward available to offset future taxable income. There are no temporary differences. The applicable current and future income tax rate is 30%. Available evidence is not conclusive as to the future existence of sufficient taxable income to provide for the future realization of the tax benefit of the $180,000 loss carryforward. However, based on the available evidence, Guss believes that it is more likely than not that future taxable income will be available to provide for the future realization of $100,000 of this loss carryforward. In its current-year statement of financial condition, Guss should recognize what amounts?

	Deferred Tax Asset	Valuation Allowance
A.	$0	$0
B.	$30,000	$0
C.	$54,000	$24,000
D.	$54,000	$30,000

Answer (C) is correct. *(Publisher, adapted)*
REQUIRED: The amounts to be recognized as a deferred tax asset and related valuation allowance.
DISCUSSION: The applicable tax rate should be used to measure a deferred tax asset for an operating loss carryforward that is available to offset future taxable income. Guss should therefore recognize a $54,000 ($180,000 × 30%) deferred tax asset. A valuation allowance should be recognized to reduce the deferred tax asset if, based on the weight of the available evidence, it is more likely than not (the likelihood is more than 50%) that some portion or all of a deferred tax asset will not be realized. The valuation allowance should be equal to an amount necessary to reduce the deferred tax asset to the amount that is more likely than not to be realized. Based on the available evidence, Guss believes that it is more likely than not that the tax benefit of $100,000 of the operating loss will be realized. Thus, the company should recognize a $24,000 valuation allowance to reduce the $54,000 deferred tax asset to $30,000 ($100,000 × 30%), the amount of the deferred tax asset that is more likely than not to be realized.
Answer (A) is incorrect. A deferred tax asset equal to $54,000 should be recognized, and a valuation allowance should be recognized equal to $24,000 to reduce the deferred tax asset to $30,000. Answer (B) is incorrect. A deferred tax asset of $30,000 results from netting the valuation allowance against the deferred tax asset. Answer (D) is incorrect. The amount of $30,000 is the deferred tax asset, not the valuation allowance, after the two are netted.

21. Carter Corp.'s pretax income in the current year was $100,000. The temporary differences between amounts reported in the financial statements and the tax return are as follows:

- Depreciation in the financial statements was $8,000 more than tax depreciation.
- The equity method of accounting resulted in financial statement income of $35,000. A $25,000 dividend was received during the year, which is eligible for the 80% dividends-received deduction (DRD).

Carter's effective income tax rate was 30% in the current year. In its current-year income statement, Carter should report a current provision for income taxes of

A. $26,400

B. $23,400

C. $21,900

D. $18,600

Answer (B) is correct. *(CPA, adapted)*
REQUIRED: The current provision for income taxes.
DISCUSSION: Current tax expense is the amount of income taxes paid or payable for a year as determined by applying the provisions of the enacted tax law to the taxable income for that year. Pretax accounting income is given as $100,000. Financial statement depreciation exceeds tax depreciation by $8,000. Accounting income includes $35,000 of income determined in accordance with the equity method, but taxable income includes only $5,000 of this amount [$25,000 dividend received – ($25,000 × 80%) dividends-received deduction]. The reconciliation of pretax accounting income to taxable income is as follows:

Pretax accounting income	$100,000
Financial statement – tax depreciation	8,000
Equity-based income – taxable dividends	(30,000)
Taxable income	$ 78,000

Accordingly, the current provision for income taxes is $23,400 ($78,000 × 30% applicable tax rate).
Answer (A) is incorrect. The amount of $26,400 is based on the assumption that taxable income includes equity-based income minus the 80% DRD. Answer (C) is incorrect. The amount of $21,900 assumes a 100% DRD. Answer (D) is incorrect. The amount of $18,600 results from subtracting, not adding, the excess financial statement depreciation.

Questions 22 and 23 are based on the following information. Zeff Co. prepared the following reconciliation of its pretax financial statement income to taxable income for the current year, its first year of operations:

Pretax financial income	$160,000
Nontaxable interest received on municipal securities	(5,000)
Long-term loss accrual in excess of deductible amount	10,000
Depreciation in excess of financial statement amount	(25,000)
Taxable income	$140,000

Zeff's tax rate is 40%.

22. In its current-year income statement, what amount should Zeff report as income tax expense – current portion?

A. $52,000

B. $56,000

C. $62,000

D. $64,000

Answer (B) is correct. *(CPA, adapted)*
REQUIRED: The current portion of income tax expense.
DISCUSSION: Pretax financial income is adjusted for permanent and temporary differences to arrive at the current taxable income. The current portion of income tax expense equals income taxes paid or payable as determined by applying enacted tax law. Thus, the current portion of income tax expense equals $56,000 ($140,000 × 40% tax rate).
Answer (A) is incorrect. The amount of $52,000 results from using taxable income of $130,000. Answer (C) is incorrect. The amount of $62,000 excludes the temporary differences from consideration. Answer (D) is incorrect. The amount of $64,000 is based on pretax financial income.

23. In its current-year balance sheet, what should Zeff report as deferred income tax liability?

A. $2,000

B. $4,000

C. $6,000

D. $8,000

Answer (C) is correct. *(CPA, adapted)*
REQUIRED: The amount of deferred income tax liability.
DISCUSSION: A deferred income tax liability arises from a taxable temporary difference. The $10,000 long-term loss accrual (a deductible temporary difference) results in a deferred tax asset. The $25,000 excess depreciation (a taxable temporary difference) is also a noncurrent item. It results in a deferred tax liability. These items should be netted because all noncurrent deferred tax assets and liabilities should be offset and presented as a single amount. Accordingly, the net deferred tax liability is $6,000 [($25,000 – $10,000) × 40%].
Answer (A) is incorrect. The amount of $2,000 is 40% times the $5,000 permanent difference. Answer (B) is incorrect. The amount of $4,000 equals 40% of the deductible temporary difference. Answer (D) is incorrect. The amount of $8,000 results from combining the temporary differences and the permanent difference (municipal bond interest).

17.4 Additional Income Tax Issues

24. When a change in the tax law or rates occurs, the effect of the change on a deferred tax liability or asset is

A. Not recognized.

B. Recognized as an adjustment as of the effective date of the change.

C. Recognized as an adjustment as of the enactment date of the change.

D. Recognized as a prior-period adjustment.

Answer (C) is correct. *(Publisher, adapted)*
REQUIRED: The effect on a deferred tax liability or asset of a change in the tax law or rates.
DISCUSSION: When a change in the tax law or rates occurs, the effect of the change on a deferred tax liability or asset is recognized as an adjustment in the period that includes the enactment date of the change. The adjustment is allocated to income from continuing operations. It is not treated as an extraordinary item.
Answer (A) is incorrect. The change is recognized currently and prospectively. Answer (B) is incorrect. The change is recognized in the period that includes the enactment date. Answer (D) is incorrect. A prior-period adjustment is recognized only as an error correction.

25. Because Pittman Co. uses different methods to depreciate equipment for financial statement and income tax purposes, Pittman has temporary differences that will reverse during the next year and add to taxable income. Deferred income taxes that are based on these temporary differences should be classified in Pittman's balance sheet as a

    A. Contra account to current assets.

    B. Contra account to noncurrent assets.

    C. Current liability.

    D. Noncurrent liability.

Answer (D) is correct. *(CPA, adapted)*
    REQUIRED: The classification of deferred income taxes based on temporary differences.
    DISCUSSION: These temporary differences arise from use of an accelerated depreciation method for tax purposes. Future taxable amounts reflecting the difference between the tax basis and the reported amount of the asset will result when the reported amount is recovered. Accordingly, Pittman must recognize a deferred tax liability to record the tax consequences of these temporary differences. This liability is noncurrent because the related asset (equipment) is noncurrent.
    Answer (A) is incorrect. A deferred tax liability is not a valuation account. Furthermore, the liability is noncurrent. Answer (B) is incorrect. A liability is not reported as an offset to assets. However, for a given taxpayer and a specific jurisdiction, current (noncurrent) deferred tax amounts are netted. Answer (C) is incorrect. The classification of the deferred tax liability is determined by the classification of the asset to which it relates. Thus, it is noncurrent.

26. At the end of the current year, the tax effects of Scottco's temporary differences were as follows:

	Deferred Tax Assets (Liabilities)	Related Asset Classification
Accelerated tax depreciation	($150,000)	Noncurrent asset
Additional costs in inventory for tax purposes	50,000	Current asset
	($100,000)	

A valuation allowance was not considered necessary. Scottco anticipates that $20,000 of the deferred tax liability will reverse next year. In Scottco's current-year balance sheet, what amount should Scottco report as noncurrent deferred tax liability?

    A. $80,000

    B. $100,000

    C. $130,000

    D. $150,000

Answer (D) is correct. *(CPA, adapted)*
    REQUIRED: The amount of noncurrent deferred tax liability.
    DISCUSSION: In a classified balance sheet, deferred tax assets and liabilities are separated into current and noncurrent amounts. Classification as current or noncurrent is based on the classification of the related asset or liability. Because the $150,000 deferred tax liability is related to a noncurrent asset, it should be classified as noncurrent.
    Answer (A) is incorrect. The amount of $80,000 equals the $100,000 net deferred tax liability minus the $20,000 expected to reverse next year. Answer (B) is incorrect. The net deferred tax liability equals $100,000. Answer (C) is incorrect. The amount of $130,000 equals the $150,000 noncurrent deferred tax liability minus the $20,000 expected to reverse next year.

27. On June 15, Year 2, the county in which Mills Company operates enacted changes in the county's tax law. These changes are to become effective on January 1, Year 3. They will have a material effect on the deferred tax accounts that Mills reported. In which of the following interim and annual financial statements issued by Mills should the effect of the changes in tax law initially be reported?

    A. The interim financial statements for the 3-month period ending June 30, Year 2.

    B. The annual financial statements for the year ending December 31, Year 2.

    C. The interim financial statements for the 3-month period ending September 30, Year 2.

    D. The annual financial statements for the year ending December 31, Year 3.

Answer (A) is correct. *(Publisher, adapted)*
    REQUIRED: The financial statements in which the effects of a change in tax law should initially be reported.
    DISCUSSION: The effects of a change in tax law or rates initially should be included in income from continuing operations in the first financial statements issued for the period that includes the enactment date.
    Answer (B) is incorrect. The effect should initially be reported in the first statements issued for the period that includes the enactment date. If the entity issues interim statements for that period, they must report the effect of the change. Answer (C) is incorrect. The interim financial statements for the 3-month period ending September 30, Year 2, are not for the period that includes the enactment date. Answer (D) is incorrect. The effect of the change will be reported in the second quarter interim statements.

28. Which one of the following is true regarding disclosure of income taxes, including deferred taxes?

A. The manner of reporting the tax benefit of an operating loss carryforward or carryback is determined by the source of the income or loss in the current year.

B. The manner of reporting the tax benefit of an operating loss carryforward or carryback is determined by the source of expected future income that will result in realization of a deferred tax asset for an operating loss carryforward from the current year.

C. The tax benefit of an operating loss carryforward or carryback is disclosed only in a note to the financial statements.

D. The tax benefit of an operating loss carryforward or carryback is a component of net tax expense and is not separately disclosed.

Answer (A) is correct. *(CMA, adapted)*
REQUIRED: The true statement about disclosures relating to income taxes.
DISCUSSION: With certain exceptions, the tax benefit of an operating loss carryforward is reported in the same manner as the source of the income offset by the carryforward in the current year. Similarly, the tax benefit of an operating loss carryback is reported in the same manner as the source of the current-year loss.
Answer (B) is incorrect. The manner of reporting is controlled by the source of the income or loss in the current year. Answer (C) is incorrect. The tax benefit is recorded. Answer (D) is incorrect. Operating loss carryforwards and carrybacks should be separately disclosed.

29. Which of the following should be disclosed in a company's financial statements related to deferred taxes?

I. The types and amounts of existing temporary differences.

II. The types and amounts of existing permanent differences.

III. The nature and amount of each type of operating loss and tax credit carryforward.

A. I and II only.

B. I and III only.

C. II and III only.

D. I, II, and III.

Answer (B) is correct. *(CPA, adapted)*
REQUIRED: The necessary disclosures about deferred taxes.
DISCUSSION: A public entity discloses the tax effects of each type of temporary difference and carryforward resulting in a significant deferred tax amount. A nonpublic entity discloses the types of significant temporary differences and carryforwards but may omit the tax effects. Other required disclosures include the amounts and expiration dates of operating loss and tax credit carryforwards for tax purposes. No disclosure is required about the types and amounts of existing permanent differences.
Answer (A) is incorrect. Disclosures about permanent differences are not required, but an entity must disclose the amounts and expiration dates of operating loss and tax credit carryforwards for tax purposes. Answer (C) is incorrect. Disclosures about significant temporary differences also are required. Answer (D) is incorrect. Disclosures about permanent differences are not required.

30. Intraperiod income tax allocation arises because

A. Items included in the determination of taxable income may be presented in different sections of the financial statements.

B. Income taxes must be allocated between current and future periods.

C. Certain revenues and expenses appear in the financial statements either before or after they are included in taxable income.

D. Certain revenues and expenses appear in the financial statements but are excluded from taxable income.

Answer (A) is correct. *(CPA, adapted)*
REQUIRED: The accounting reason for intraperiod allocation of income taxes.
DISCUSSION: To provide a fair presentation of the various components of the results of operations, income tax expense for the period must be allocated among (1) income from continuing operations, (2) discontinued operations, (3) extraordinary items, (4) other comprehensive income, and (5) items charged or credited directly to equity.
Answer (B) is incorrect. Interperiod tax allocation allocates income taxes between current and future periods. Answer (C) is incorrect. Differences in the timing of revenues and expenses for financial statement and tax return purposes create the need for interperiod income tax allocation. Interperiod tax allocation affects two or more periods. Intraperiod tax allocation affects only one period. Answer (D) is incorrect. Revenues and expenses included in the financial statements but never in taxable income cause permanent differences between the financial statements and tax returns. They do not create a need for tax allocation.

31. Last year, before providing for taxes, Dixon Company had income from continuing operations of $930,000 and an extraordinary gain of $104,000. The current effective tax rate on continuing operations income was 40% and the total tax liability was $398,000 ignoring any temporary differences. The amount of the extraordinary gain net of tax effect was

A. $41,600

B. $62,400

C. $78,000

D. $104,000

Answer (C) is correct. *(Publisher, adapted)*
REQUIRED: The amount of extraordinary gain net of the tax effect.
DISCUSSION: Given that the effective tax rate for continuing operations was 40%, the related tax expense was $372,000 ($930,000 × 40%). Because the total tax liability was $398,000, $26,000 ($398,000 – $372,000) was applicable to the extraordinary item. Accordingly, the extraordinary gain net of tax effect was $78,000 ($104,000 – $26,000).
Answer (A) is incorrect. The amount of $41,600 results from multiplying the extraordinary gain times the effective tax rate. Answer (B) is incorrect. The amount of $62,400 results from subtracting the extraordinary gain times the effective tax rate from the extraordinary gain. Answer (D) is incorrect. The amount of $104,000 results from not accounting for the tax effect.

17.5 IFRS

32. Under IFRS, a deferred tax asset is

A. Required to be reduced by a valuation allowance if it is more likely than not that some portion will not be realized.

B. Measured by applying the tax rates effective when the asset is realized.

C. Recognized to the extent that realization is probable.

D. Recognized to reflect the deferred tax consequences of a taxable temporary difference.

Answer (C) is correct. *(Publisher, adapted)*
REQUIRED: The amount recorded for a deferred tax asset.
DISCUSSION: Under IFRS, a deferred tax asset is recognized for most deductible TDs and for the carryforward of unused tax losses and credits, but only to the extent it is probable that taxable profit will be available to permit the use of those amounts. Probable means more likely than not. Thus, no valuation allowance is separately recognized under IFRS.
Answer (A) is incorrect. Under U.S. GAAP, a deferred tax asset is reduced by a credit to a separate valuation allowance. This credit equals the amount needed to reduce the asset to the amount more likely than not (the probability exceeds 50%) to be realized. Under IFRS, the presentation of a separate allowance is not necessary. Instead, the deferred tax asset is recognized to the extent it is probable that taxable profit will be available against which tax deductions may be taken. Answer (B) is incorrect. According to IAS 12, deferred tax assets and liabilities ordinarily are measured using the tax rates that (1) have been enacted or substantively enacted as of the end of the reporting period and (2) apply when the asset is realized or the liability is settled. Thus, a tax rate effective when the asset is realized may not have been enacted or substantively enacted as of the end of the reporting period. Answer (D) is incorrect. A deferred tax liability is recognized to reflect the deferred tax consequences of a taxable temporary difference.

Use Gleim **EQE Test Prep** Software Download for interactive study and performance analysis.

STUDY UNIT EIGHTEEN
ACCOUNTING CHANGES AND ERROR CORRECTIONS

GAAP for accounting changes and error corrections apply to businesses and not-for-profit entities. An **accounting change** is a change in (1) an accounting principle, (2) an accounting estimate, or (3) the reporting entity. An accounting change does not include a correction of an accounting error in previously issued financial statements.

Changes in Accounting Principle or the Reporting Entity

A **change in accounting principle** occurs when an entity (1) adopts a generally accepted accounting principle different from the one previously used, (2) changes the method of applying a generally accepted principle, or (3) changes to a generally accepted principle when the principle previously used is no longer generally accepted. A change in principle does not include the initial adoption of a principle because of an event or transaction (1) occurring for the first time or (2) that previously had an immaterial effect. It also does not include adoption of a principle to account for an event or transaction that clearly differs in substance from the one previously occurring.

The general presumption is that a principle once adopted must be **applied consistently**. However, a change in principle is appropriate if (1) the change is required by a newly issued official pronouncement or (2) the entity is able to justify it as **preferable**.

Retrospective application is required for all **direct effects** and the related income tax effects of a change in principle unless it is impracticable to determine (1) the cumulative effect or (2) the period-specific effects of the change. But retrospective application must not include **indirect effects**. These effects are changes in current or future cash flows resulting from retrospective application. An example is a required profit-sharing payment based on a reported amount (e.g., revenue). Thus, only current and future expenses are affected by this retrospective change in the measurement of revenue. Recognized indirect effects are reported in the period of change.

The carrying amounts of assets, liabilities, and retained earnings (or other components of equity or net assets) at the beginning of the first period reported must be adjusted for the **cumulative effect (CE)** of the new principle on all periods not reported. Moreover, all periods reported must be individually adjusted for the **period-specific effects (PSE)** of the new principle.

It may be **impracticable** to determine the **cumulative effect** of a new principle on any prior period (for example, when the change is from FIFO to LIFO). In that case, the new principle must be applied as if the change had been made prospectively at the **earliest date practicable**. It may be practicable to determine the cumulative effect on all prior periods but not the **period-specific effects** on all prior periods presented. Cumulative-effect adjustments then must be made to the beginning balances for the first period to which the new principle can be applied.

IMPRACTICABILITY EXCEPTIONS

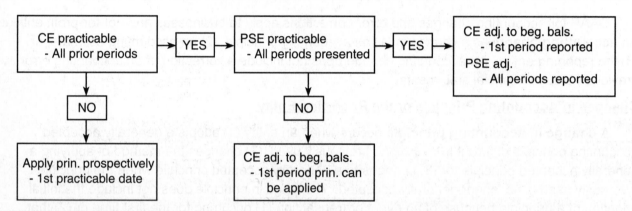

A **change in reporting entity** results in statements that effectively are those of a different entity. Most such changes occur when (1) consolidated or combined statements replace those of individual entities, (2) consolidated statements include different subsidiaries, or (3) combined statements include different entities. A change in reporting entity does not result from a business combination or consolidation of a variable interest entity. This change is retrospectively applied to interim and annual statements.

Changes in Accounting Estimates

A change in accounting estimate results from new information. It is a reassessment of the status and future benefits and obligations of assets and liabilities. Its effects must be accounted for only in the period of change and any future periods affected **prospectively**. A **change in estimate inseparable from (effected by) a change in principle** must be accounted for as a change in estimate. An example is a change in a method of depreciation, amortization, or depletion of long-lived, nonfinancial assets.

Corrections of Errors in Prior Statements

An error in prior statements results from (1) a mathematical mistake, (2) a mistake in the application of GAAP, or (3) an oversight or misuse of facts existing when the statements were prepared. A change to an accounting principle that is generally accepted from one that is not is the correction of an error. An error related to a prior period discovered after the statements are (or available to) be issued must be reported as an error correction by restating the prior-period statements. **Restatement** requires the same adjustments as retrospective application of a new principle. But corrections of prior-period errors must not be included in current net income. Error corrections must be reported in single-period statements as adjustments of the opening balance of retained earnings. If comparative statements are presented, corresponding adjustments must be made to net income (and its components) and retained earnings (and other affected balances) for all periods reported. In this context, the term **period** includes annual and interim periods.

Error Analysis. A correcting journal entry combines the reversal of the error with the correct entry. Thus, it requires a determination of the (1) journal entry originally recorded, (2) event or transaction that occurred, and (3) correct journal entry.

EXAMPLE: If the purchase of a fixed asset on account had been debited to purchases:

Incorrect Entry	Correct Entry	Correcting Entry
Purchases	Fixed asset	Fixed asset
Payables	Payables	Purchases

If cash had been incorrectly credited:

Incorrect Entry	Correct Entry	Correcting Entry
Purchases	Fixed asset	Fixed Asset
Cash	Payables	Cash
		Purchases
		Payables

Error analysis addresses (1) whether an error affects prior-period statements, (2) the timing of error detection, (3) whether comparative statements are presented, and (4) whether the error is counterbalancing. An error affecting **prior-period statements** may or may not affect prior-period net income. For example, misclassifying an item as a gain rather than a revenue does not affect income and is readily correctable. No prior-period adjustment to retained earnings is required. An error that affects prior-period net income is **counterbalancing** if it self-corrects over two periods. See Study Unit 6 for an illustration of the effects of an overstatement of ending inventory on the financial statements of the period of the error and the next period. An example of a **noncounterbalancing** error is a misstatement of depreciation. Such an error does not self-correct over two periods. Thus, a prior-period adjustment will be necessary.

Differences between GAAP and IFRS

Under IFRS:

- A prior period error must be corrected by restatement unless it is impracticable to do so.
- A change in accounting policy must be made only if it (1) is required by a new standard or interpretation or (2) results in reliable and more relevant information about transactions, financial condition, financial performance, and cash flows.
- The indirect effects of a change in accounting policy are not addressed.

QUESTIONS

18.1 Changes in Accounting Principle or the Reporting Entity

1. Which of the following transactions should be classified as an accounting change?

I. Change from a previously generally accepted accounting principle to a new accounting principle.

II. Change from an accounting principle not generally accepted to a generally accepted accounting principle.

III. Change in the percentage used to determine an allowance for uncollectible accounts.

    A. I, II, and III.

    B. I and II only.

    C. I and III only.

    D. II and III only.

Answer (C) is correct. *(Publisher, adapted)*
    REQUIRED: The transactions properly classified as accounting changes.
    DISCUSSION: An accounting change is a change in an accounting principle, an accounting estimate, or the reporting entity. A correction of an error in previously issued financial statements is not an accounting change. A transition to newly prescribed guidance is a change in accounting principle. A change from an accounting principle not generally accepted to one that is generally accepted is a correction of an accounting error. A change in the percentage used to determine an allowance for uncollectible accounts is a change in estimate.
    Answer (A) is incorrect. A correction of an error is not an accounting change. Answer (B) is incorrect. A change in the percentage used to determine an allowance for uncollectible accounts is a change in accounting estimate. Furthermore, the change from an accounting principle not generally accepted to a generally accepted accounting principle is a correction of an error. Answer (D) is incorrect. A change from a previously generally accepted accounting principle to a new accounting principle is a change in accounting principle. Furthermore, the change from an accounting principle not generally accepted to a generally accepted accounting principle is a correction of an error.

2. For which of the following justified changes should previously issued financial statements be adjusted to report the effects of a newly adopted accounting principle as if the new principle had always been used?

    A. A change from an accelerated method of depreciation of productive assets to the straight-line method.

    B. A change from the weighted-average method of inventory measurement to the FIFO method.

    C. A change in the percentages used to determine warranty expense.

    D. Adoption of an accounting principle to account for a transaction clearly different in substance from previously occurring transactions.

Answer (B) is correct. *(Publisher, adapted)*
    REQUIRED: The change that results in a retrospective adjustment.
    DISCUSSION: Retrospective application changes previously issued financial statements to report the effects of a newly adopted accounting principle as if the new principle had always been used. It is required for all direct effects and the related income tax effects of a change in accounting principle, such as a change in inventory measurement methods, unless it is impracticable to determine either the cumulative effect or the period-specific effects of the change. An accounting principle is changed (1) to account for transition to a newly issued official pronouncement (unless the pronouncement prescribes a different method) or (2) when the entity justifies the change on the basis that it is preferable.
    Answer (A) is incorrect. A change from an accelerated method of depreciation of productive assets to the straight-line method is a change in accounting estimate effected by a change in accounting principle. Answer (C) is incorrect. A change in the percentages used to determine warranty expense is a change in accounting estimate. Answer (D) is incorrect. The adoption of an accounting principle to account for a transaction clearly different in substance from previously occurring transactions is not considered a change in accounting principle.

3. When reporting a change in accounting principle, the usual approach is to report the change

    A. Prospectively, in the period of change and future periods affected by the change.

    B. As a cumulative effect included in net income of the period of change.

    C. By retrospective application to previously issued financial statements to report the effects of the new principle.

    D. As a cumulative effect included in net income of the period of change and prospective application in future periods.

Answer (C) is correct. *(CMA, adapted)*
    REQUIRED: The accounting for a change in accounting principle.
    DISCUSSION: A change in accounting principle is applied retrospectively to previously issued financial statements unless it is impracticable to determine either the cumulative effect or the period-specific effects of the change. However, a newly issued official pronouncement may prescribe a different transition method.
    Answer (A) is incorrect. Application is prospective for changes in estimate, not changes in principle. Answer (B) is incorrect. Including the cumulative effect of a change in accounting principle in net income in the period of the change is not the generally accepted method of accounting for a change in principle. Answer (D) is incorrect. Retrospective application is required.

4. The general presumption in preparing financial statements in accordance with generally accepted accounting principles is that

    A. A change in accounting principle is permissible if the entity is able to justify the new principle as preferable to the existing principle.

    B. A change in accounting principle is permissible only to correct the effect of an error in previously issued financial statements.

    C. A change in previously issued financial statements is never permissible.

    D. A change in accounting principle is permissible only when a newly issued official pronouncement requires a change in accounting principle.

Answer (A) is correct. *(Publisher, adapted)*
    REQUIRED: The general presumption regarding when changes to previously issued financial statements are permitted.
    DISCUSSION: The general presumption in preparing financial statements in accordance with GAAP is that an accounting principle once adopted must be applied on a consistent basis. However, a change in principle is appropriate if the change is required by a newly issued official pronouncement, or the entity is able to justify the new principle as preferable to the existing principle. In addition, when an error is discovered, the error must be corrected by a restatement of all periods presented.
    Answer (B) is incorrect. Correction of an error is not a change in accounting principle. Answer (C) is incorrect. A change in accounting principle may be justified, and a correction of an error is required. Answer (D) is incorrect. An accounting principle also may be changed if it can be justified as preferable.

5. J. Will Company has justifiably changed its method of accounting for inventory. Retrospective application of the change is practicable. The cumulative effect on all prior periods of changing to the new accounting principle is included in the first period reported as an adjustment of

    A. Retained earnings at the end of the year.

    B. Retained earnings at the beginning of the year.

    C. Net income.

    D. Comprehensive income.

Answer (B) is correct. *(Publisher, adapted)*
    REQUIRED: The proper accounting for the cumulative effect of a change in accounting principle.
    DISCUSSION: A change in accounting principle is accounted for by retrospective application unless it is impracticable to determine either the cumulative effect or the period-specific effects of the change. Furthermore, a newly issued official pronouncement may prescribe a different transition method. Retrospective application changes previously issued financial statements to report the effects of the newly adopted principle as if it had always been used. Retrospective application requires that the carrying amounts of assets, liabilities, and retained earnings at the beginning of the first period reported be adjusted for the cumulative effect of the new principle on periods prior to the first period reported. Moreover, all periods reported must be individually adjusted for the period-specific effects of applying the new principle.
    Answer (A) is incorrect. Retained earnings at the beginning of the first period reported is adjusted. Answer (C) is incorrect. Net income is adjusted for the period-specific effects. Answer (D) is incorrect. Comprehensive income is adjusted for the period-specific effects.

6. Retrospective application of a change in accounting principle is impracticable when

I.   The costs of applying the new accounting principle to prior period financial statements are material.

II.   Retrospective application requires that management's intent in a prior period be assumed without independent substantiation.

    A. I only.

    B. II only.

    C. Both I and II.

    D. Neither I nor II.

Answer (B) is correct. *(Publisher, adapted)*
    REQUIRED: The condition(s) indicating that retrospective application is impracticable.
    DISCUSSION: Retrospective application of a change in an accounting principle is deemed to be impracticable when (1) the entity cannot apply the new principle after making every reasonable effort; (2) assumptions about management's intent in a prior period are required that cannot be independently substantiated; or (3) significant estimates are required, and it is not possible to obtain objective evidence (a) about circumstances existing when amounts would have been recognized, measured, or disclosed, and (b) that would have been available when the prior statements were issued.
    Answer (A) is incorrect. Retrospective application requires that management's intent in a prior period be assumed without and independent substantiation. But whether the costs of applying the new accounting principle to prior period financial statements are material is not considered in determining impracticability. Answer (C) is incorrect. Cost is not a condition of impracticability. Answer (D) is incorrect. Retrospective application is deemed to be impracticable when management's intent in a prior period must be assumed without independent substantiation.

Questions 7 through 9 are based on the following information. Loire Co., a calendar year-end firm, has used the FIFO method of inventory measurement since it began operations in Year 3. Loire changed to the weighted-average method for determining inventory costs at the beginning of Year 6. Justification for this change was that it better reflected inventory flow. The following schedule shows year-end inventory balances under the FIFO and weighted-average methods:

Year	FIFO	Weighted-Average
Year 3	$ 90,000	$108,000
Year 4	156,000	142,000
Year 5	166,000	150,000

In its Year 6 financial statements, Loire included comparative statements for both Year 5 and Year 4.

7. What adjustment, before taxes, should Loire make retrospectively to the balance reported for retained earnings at the beginning of Year 4?

A. $18,000 increase.

B. $18,000 decrease.

C. $4,000 increase.

D. $0.

Answer (A) is correct. *(CPA, adapted)*
REQUIRED: The pretax retrospective adjustment to retained earnings as of the beginning of the first period reported.
DISCUSSION: Retrospective application requires that the carrying amounts of assets, liabilities, and retained earnings as of the beginning of the first period reported be adjusted for the cumulative effect of the new accounting principle on periods prior to the first period reported. Moreover, all periods reported must be individually adjusted for the period-specific effects of applying the new principle. The pretax cumulative-effect adjustment to retained earnings reported at the beginning of Year 4 is equal to the $18,000 increase ($108,000 – $90,000) in inventory. If the weighted-average method had been applied in the first year of operations (Year 3), cost of goods sold would have been $18,000 lower. Pretax net income and ending retained earnings for Year 3 and beginning retained earnings for Year 4 would have been $18,000 greater.
Answer (B) is incorrect. Beginning retained earnings as of the beginning of the first period reported (Year 4) is increased. Ending inventory would have been higher and cost of goods sold lower for Year 3. Answer (C) is incorrect. The amount of $4,000 is equal to the difference between FIFO and weighted-average inventory amounts at December 31, Year 3, minus the difference at December 31, Year 4. Answer (D) is incorrect. A cumulative-effect adjustment should be recorded.

8. What amount should Loire report as inventory in its financial statements for the year ended December 31, Year 4, presented for comparative purposes?

A. $90,000

B. $108,000

C. $142,000

D. $156,000

Answer (C) is correct. *(Publisher, adapted)*
REQUIRED: The amount to be reported as inventory at December 31, Year 4.
DISCUSSION: Retrospective application results in changing previously issued financial statements to reflect the direct effects of the newly adopted accounting principle as if it had always been used. Retrospective application requires that the carrying amounts of assets, liabilities, and retained earnings as of the beginning of the first period reported be adjusted for the cumulative effect of the new principle on periods prior to the first period reported. Moreover, all periods reported must be individually adjusted for the period-specific effects of applying the new principle. Thus, the December 31, Year 4, inventory following the retrospective adjustment should be reported as the weighted-average amount of $142,000.
Answer (A) is incorrect. The FIFO amount at December 31, Year 3, is $90,000. Answer (B) is incorrect. The weighted-average amount at December 31, Year 3, is $108,000. Answer (D) is incorrect. The FIFO amount at December 31, Year 4, is 156,000.

9. By what amount should cost of sales be retrospectively adjusted for the year ended December 31, Year 5?

A. $0.

B. $2,000 increase.

C. $14,000 increase.

D. $16,000 increase.

Answer (B) is correct. *(Publisher, adapted)*
REQUIRED: The retrospective adjustment to cost of sales for the year ended December 31, Year 5.
DISCUSSION: Retrospective application changes previously issued financial statements to reflect the direct effects of the newly adopted principle as if it had always been used. Retrospective application requires that all periods reported be individually adjusted for the period-specific effects of applying the new principle. Cost of sales equals beginning inventory, plus purchases, minus ending inventory. Purchases are the same under FIFO and weighted average. Thus, the retrospective adjustment to cost of sales is equal to the change in beginning inventory resulting from the change from FIFO to weighted average minus the change in ending inventory. This adjustment equals an increase in cost of sales of $2,000 [($156,000 – $142,000) – ($166,000 – $150,000)].
Answer (A) is incorrect. Period-specific adjustments are required. Answer (C) is incorrect. The difference between FIFO and weighted-average inventory amounts at December 31, Year 4, is $14,000. Answer (D) is incorrect. The difference between FIFO and weighted-average inventory amounts at December 31, Year 5, is $16,000.

10. P. Werner and Co. has made a justifiable change in an accounting principle. The cumulative effect of applying the change to all prior periods is determinable. However, it is not practicable to determine the period-specific effects on all prior periods presented. Consequently, the reported carrying amounts of the assets and liabilities must be adjusted for the cumulative effect of applying the new principle at the

A. Beginning of the earliest accounting period presented to which the new principle can be applied.

B. End of the latest accounting period presented for which retrospective application is impracticable.

C. Beginning of the current accounting period.

D. Beginning of the earliest accounting period presented.

Answer (A) is correct. *(Publisher, adapted)*
REQUIRED: The accounting when period-specific effects are not determinable.
DISCUSSION: When it is impracticable to determine the cumulative effect of applying a change in principle to any prior period, it must be applied prospectively at the earliest date practicable. However, it may be practicable to determine the cumulative effect but impracticable to determine the period-specific effects on all prior periods presented. In this case, cumulative effect adjustments must be made to the reported carrying amounts of assets and liabilities at the beginning of the earliest period to which the new principle can be applied. An offsetting adjustment also may need to be made to beginning retained earnings.
Answer (B) is incorrect. Cumulative-effect adjustments must be made at the beginning of the earliest accounting period presented to which the new principle can be applied. Answer (C) is incorrect. The adjustments must be made at the beginning of the current accounting period, not for any prior period applied, but only if it is the earliest period to which the new principle can be applied. Answer (D) is incorrect. The adjustments must be made at the beginning of the earliest accounting period presented when it is practicable to determine the cumulative effect on all prior periods and the period-specific effects on all prior periods presented.

11. JKC Corporation, a calendar year-end firm, changed its method for measuring inventory from FIFO to LIFO, effective January 1, Year 6. Records of inventory purchases and sales were not available for certain earlier years of its existence. Accordingly, it was impracticable for JKC to determine the cumulative effect of applying the change in accounting principle retrospectively. If records of inventory purchases and sales are available for recent years, JKC must apply LIFO at the

A. End of the latest accounting period presented for which retrospective application is impracticable.

B. Beginning of the earliest accounting period presented for which full retrospective application is practicable.

C. Beginning of the current accounting period.

D. Earliest date practicable.

Answer (D) is correct. *(CPA, adapted)*
REQUIRED: The accounting for a change in accounting principle.
DISCUSSION: When it is impracticable to determine the cumulative effect of applying a new accounting principle to any prior period, it must be applied as if the change had been made prospectively at the earliest date practicable. For example, if JKC has all the required information for applying LIFO beginning on January 1, Year 4, it will carry forward the Year 3 FIFO ending inventory balance. It will then begin using LIFO on January 1, Year 4.
Answer (A) is incorrect. When it is impracticable to determine the cumulative effect of a change in accounting principle on any prior period, the new principle must be applied as if the change had been made prospectively at the earliest date practicable. Answer (B) is incorrect. The new principle must be applied in the earliest period for which prospective application is practicable. Answer (C) is incorrect. The new principle must be applied at the beginning of the current accounting period, not to any prior period, but only if it is the earliest date practicable. An earlier date is practicable because JKC has inventory information for recent years.

12. When the Kenya Leopard Corporation began business in Year 1, its accountants decided to include such indirect costs of manufacturing as factory janitorial expenses, depreciation of machinery, and insurance on the factory as elements of inventory costs. At the beginning of Year 14, the company began expensing all insurance costs in the period in which they are incurred. To comply with current standards, the company must justify and disclose the reason for the change. The reason that is most appropriate is that the new principle

A. Is preferable to the alternative.

B. Has been and continues to be the treatment used for tax purposes.

C. Is easier to apply because no assumptions about allocation must be made.

D. Is one used by the company for insurance costs other than those on factory-related activities.

Answer (A) is correct. *(Publisher, adapted)*
REQUIRED: The most appropriate reason for making a change in accounting principle.
DISCUSSION: The presumption is that, once adopted, an accounting principle must not be changed in accounting for events and transactions of a similar type. This presumption in favor of consistency may be overcome if the entity justifies the use of another principle. The new principle must be preferable. Sufficient support for a change in principle is the issuance of an Accounting Standards Update that (1) requires use of a new principle, (2) expresses a preference for a principle not being used, (3) interprets an existing principle, or (4) rejects a specific principle.
Answer (B) is incorrect. Use for tax purposes does not constitute sufficient justification. Answer (C) is incorrect. Ease of application does not constitute sufficient justification. Answer (D) is incorrect. Use for other insurance costs does not constitute sufficient justification.

13. Volga Co. included a foreign subsidiary in its Year 6 consolidated financial statements. The subsidiary was acquired in Year 4 and was excluded from previous consolidations. The change was caused by the elimination of foreign currency controls. Including the subsidiary in the Year 6 consolidated financial statements results in an accounting change that should be reported

A. By note disclosure only.

B. Currently and prospectively.

C. Currently with note disclosure of pro forma effects of retrospective application.

D. By retrospective application to the financial statements of all prior periods presented.

Answer (D) is correct. *(CPA, adapted)*
REQUIRED: The reporting of the change in the subsidiaries included in consolidated financial statements.
DISCUSSION: A change in the reporting entity requires retrospective application to all prior periods presented to report information for the new entity. The following are changes in the reporting entity: (1) presenting consolidated or combined statements in place of statements of individual entities, (2) changing the specific subsidiaries included in the group for which consolidated statements are presented, and (3) changing the entities included in combined statements.
Answer (A) is incorrect. The change requires recognition in the financial statements. Answer (B) is incorrect. A change in reporting entity requires retrospective application. Answer (C) is incorrect. The change must apply to the financial statements for all periods presented.

18.2 Changes in Accounting Estimates

14. How should the effect of a change in accounting estimate be accounted for?

A. By retrospectively applying the change to amounts reported in financial statements of prior periods.

B. By reporting pro forma amounts for prior periods.

C. As a prior-period adjustment to beginning retained earnings.

D. By prospectively applying the change to current and future periods.

Answer (D) is correct. *(CPA, adapted)*
REQUIRED: The accounting for the effect of a change in accounting estimate.
DISCUSSION: The effect of a change in accounting estimate is accounted for in the period of change, if the change affects that period only, or in the period of change and future periods, if the change affects both. For a change in accounting estimate, the entity may not (1) restate or retrospectively adjust prior-period statements or (2) report pro forma amounts for prior periods.
Answer (A) is incorrect. A change in an accounting principle or the reporting entity is applied retrospectively. Answer (B) is incorrect. Disclosure of pro forma amounts for prior periods is not required. Answer (C) is incorrect. A prior-period adjustment is appropriate for an error correction.

15. For Year 2, Suwanee Co. estimated its 2-year equipment warranty costs based on $100 per unit sold in Year 2. Experience during Year 3 indicated that the estimate should have been based on $110 per unit. The effect of this $10 difference from the estimate is reported

A. In Year 3 income from continuing operations.

B. As an accounting change, net of tax, below Year 3 income from continuing operations.

C. As an accounting change requiring Year 2 financial statements to be retrospectively adjusted.

D. As a correction of an error requiring Year 2 financial statements to be restated.

Answer (A) is correct.   *(CPA, adapted)*
REQUIRED: The accounting for a change in estimate.
DISCUSSION: The effect of a change in accounting estimate is accounted for in the period of change, if the change affects that period only, or in the period of change and future periods, if the change affects both. For a change in accounting estimate, the entity may not (1) restate or retrospectively adjust prior-period statements or (2) report pro forma amounts for prior periods. A change in warranty costs is a change in estimate because it results from an assessment of the current status and expected future benefits and obligations associated with assets and liabilities. Thus, it affects income from continuing operations.

Answer (B) is incorrect. The effect of a change in accounting estimate for a period is included in the determination of income from continuing operations for that period. No cumulative effect is reported. Answer (C) is incorrect. A change in estimate is not reported retrospectively. Answer (D) is incorrect. A change in estimate is not a correction of an error.

16. On July 1, Year 1, Allegheny Corp. purchased computer equipment at a cost of $360,000. This equipment was estimated to have a 6-year life with no residual value and was depreciated by the straight-line method. On January 3, Year 4, Allegheny determined that this equipment could no longer process data efficiently, its value had been permanently impaired, and $70,000 could be recovered over the remaining useful life of the equipment. What carrying amount should Allegheny report on its December 31, Year 4, balance sheet for this equipment?

A. $0

B. $50,000

C. $70,000

D. $150,000

Answer (B) is correct.   *(CPA, adapted)*
REQUIRED: The carrying amount following a change in estimate.
DISCUSSION: At 1/3/Year 4, the carrying amount of the computer equipment should be written down to $70,000. This $70,000 is expected to be recovered over the 3.5-year remaining useful life of the equipment. Under the straight-line method, the depreciation expense for the year ending 12/31/Year 4 is $20,000 [($70,000 ÷ 42 months) × 12 months]. Thus, the carrying amount in the year-end balance sheet should be $50,000 ($70,000 – $20,000).

Answer (A) is incorrect. The computer should have a carrying amount of $50,000. Answer (C) is incorrect. For Year 4, $20,000 of depreciation must be taken on the asset. Answer (D) is incorrect. The amount of $150,000 reflects continued depreciation based on the original assumptions.

17. Missouri Company bought a machine on January 1, Year 1, for $24,000, at which time it had an estimated useful life of 8 years, with no residual value. Straight-line depreciation is used for all of Missouri's depreciable assets. On January 1, Year 3, the machine's estimated useful life was determined to be only 6 years from the acquisition date. Accordingly, the appropriate accounting change was made in Year 3. The direct effects of this change were limited to the effect on depreciation and the related provision for income tax. Missouri's income tax rate was 40% in all the affected years. In Missouri's Year 3 financial statements, how much should be reported as the cumulative effect on prior years because of the change in the estimated useful life of the machine?

A. $0

B. $1,200

C. $2,000

D. $2,700

Answer (A) is correct.   *(CPA, adapted)*
REQUIRED: The accounting for a change in estimate.
DISCUSSION: An adjustment arising from a revision in an asset's estimated useful life is a change in accounting estimate that must be accounted for on a prospective basis. The remaining depreciable base must be allocated over the revised remaining life with no adjustment to the depreciation accumulated at the time of the change. Because no retrospective adjustment is made, the cumulative effect on prior years is $0. The remaining depreciable base of $18,000 ($24,000 cost – $6,000 accumulated depreciation based on a 6-year life) is allocated over the remaining expected life at $4,500 per year ($18,000 ÷ 4).

Answer (B) is incorrect. The total depreciation expense for Years 1 and 2, net of tax, for a 6-year useful life minus the amount for an 8-year life is $1,200. Answer (C) is incorrect. The total pretax depreciation for Years 1 and 2 for a 6-year useful life minus the amount for an 8-year life is $2,000. Answer (D) is incorrect. The depreciation expense, net of tax, for the current year is $2,700.

18. Tone Company is the defendant in a lawsuit filed by Witt in Year 2, disputing the validity of a copyright held by Tone. At December 31, Year 2, Tone determined that Witt would probably be successful against Tone for an estimated amount of $400,000. Appropriately, a $400,000 loss was accrued by a charge to income for the year ended December 31, Year 2. On December 15, Year 3, Tone and Witt agreed to a settlement providing for a cash payment of $250,000 by Tone to Witt and the transfer of Tone's copyright to Witt. The carrying amount of the copyright on Tone's accounting records was $60,000 at December 15, Year 3. The settlement's effect on Tone's income before income tax in Year 3 is

A. No effect.

B. $60,000 decrease.

C. $90,000 increase.

D. $150,000 increase.

Answer (C) is correct. *(CPA, adapted)*
REQUIRED: The accounting for the effect of a settlement at an amount different from that previously accrued.
DISCUSSION: In Year 2, a $400,000 contingent loss and an accrued liability in the amount of $400,000 were properly recognized. In Year 3, the actual loss of $310,000 ($250,000 cash + $60,000 carrying amount of the copyright) was $90,000 less than the previously estimated amount. This new information must be treated as a change in estimate and accounted for in the period of change. Consequently, the $90,000 difference will be credited to Year 3 income as a recovery of a previously recognized loss.
Answer (A) is incorrect. Tone's income before income tax will increase by $90,000. Answer (B) is incorrect. The carrying amount of the copyright is $60,000. Answer (D) is incorrect. A $150,000 increase does not include the carrying amount of the copyright.

19. The effect of a change in accounting principle that is inseparable from the effect of a change in accounting estimate should be reported

A. By restating the financial statements of all prior periods presented.

B. As a correction of an error.

C. In the period of change and future periods if the change affects both.

D. As a separate disclosure after income from continuing operations, in the period of change and future periods if the change affects both.

Answer (C) is correct. *(CPA, adapted)*
REQUIRED: The reporting of the effect of a change in principle inseparable from a change in estimate.
DISCUSSION: When the effect of a change in principle is inseparable from the effect of a change in estimate, it must be accounted for in the same manner as a change in estimate only. An example of such a change is a change in the method of depreciation. Because the new method is adopted to recognize (1) a change in estimated future benefits, (2) their pattern of consumption, or (3) the information available to the entity about them, the effect of the change in principle is inseparable from the change in estimate. The effect of a change in estimate is accounted for in the period of change if the change affects that period only, or in the period of change and in future periods, if the change affects both.
Answer (A) is incorrect. Prospective treatment is accorded to a change in principle inseparable from a change in estimate. Answer (B) is incorrect. A correction of an error is accounted for as a prior-period adjustment. Answer (D) is incorrect. The effect of the change in estimate is included in the determination of income from continuing operations. Moreover, disclosures about a change in estimate are made in the notes.

20. On January 1, Year 4, Vicar Company purchased a machine for $240,000 with a useful life of 10 years and no salvage value. The machine was depreciated using the double-declining-balance (DDB) method, and the carrying amount of the machine was $153,600 on December 31, Year 5. Vicar changed to the straight-line method on January 1, Year 6. Vicar can justify the change. What should be the depreciation expense on this machine for the year ended December 31, Year 6?

A. $15,360

B. $19,200

C. $24,000

D. $30,720

Answer (B) is correct. *(CPA, adapted)*
REQUIRED: The depreciation expense in the year in which a change in depreciation method is made.
DISCUSSION: A change in accounting estimate inseparable from (effected by) a change in accounting principle includes a change in depreciation, amortization, or depletion method. When a change in estimate and a change in principle are inseparable, the change must be accounted for as a change in estimate. The effects of a change in estimate must be accounted for prospectively. Thus, the effects should be recognized in the period of change and any future periods affected by the change. The effects should not be recognized in prior periods. Consequently, depreciation expense for the year ended December 31, Year 6, should be $19,200 ($153,600 carrying amount at December 31, Year 5 ÷ 8-year remaining useful life).
Answer (A) is incorrect. The figure of $15,360 is equal to the carrying amount at December 31, Year 5, allocated using the straight-line method and assuming a 10-year remaining useful life. Answer (C) is incorrect. The amount of $24,000 is equal to the cost of the machine allocated using the straight-line method and assuming a 10-year remaining useful life. Answer (D) is incorrect. The amount of $30,720 is the result of continuing to depreciate the machine under the DDB method.

21. On January 2, Year 7, Monongahela Co. purchased a machine for $264,000 and depreciated it by the straight-line method using an estimated useful life of 8 years with no salvage value. On January 2, Year 10, the company determined that the machine had a useful life of 6 years from the date of acquisition and will have a salvage value of $24,000. An accounting change was made in Year 10 to reflect the additional data. The accumulated depreciation for this machine should have a balance at December 31, Year 10, of

    A. $179,000

    B. $160,000

    C. $154,000

    D. $146,000

Answer (D) is correct. *(CPA, adapted)*
    REQUIRED: The accumulated depreciation for a machine given changes in estimates.
    DISCUSSION: A change in estimated life is accounted for on a prospective basis. The new estimate affects the year of the change and subsequent years. For Year 7 through Year 9, the amount of depreciation was $33,000 per year ($264,000 ÷ 8). In Year 10, the new estimates change annual depreciation to $47,000 [($264,000 – $99,000 accumulated depreciation – $24,000 expected salvage) ÷ 3 years remaining]. Thus, accumulated depreciation for Year 10 is $146,000 ($99,000 + $47,000).
    Answer (A) is incorrect. The amount of $179,000 does not include accumulated depreciation in calculating depreciation for Year 10. Answer (B) is incorrect. The amount of $160,000 would be the accumulated depreciation if the revised estimates had been used from the date of acquisition. Answer (C) is incorrect. The amount of $154,000 does not include salvage value in calculating depreciation for Year 10.

22. On January 1, Year 4, Dickey Co. purchased a machine for $450,000 with an estimated life of 5 years with no salvage value. Dickey depreciated this machine under the sum-of-the-years'-digits method (SYD) for 2 years. At January 1, Year 6, when the carrying amount of the machine was $180,000 ($450,000 – $150,000 depreciation for Year 4 – $120,000 depreciation for Year 5), Dickey changed to the straight-line method. Dickey can justify the change. Dickey also determined that the remaining useful life of the machine had increased from 3 to 4 years. What is the amount of depreciation that Dickey should record in its income statement for the year ending December 31, Year 6?

    A. $90,000

    B. $75,000

    C. $60,000

    D. $45,000

Answer (D) is correct. *(CPA, adapted)*
    REQUIRED: The depreciation expense in the year in which a change in depreciation method is made.
    DISCUSSION: A change in accounting estimate inseparable from (effected by) a change in accounting principle includes a change in depreciation, amortization, or depletion method. When a change in estimate and a change in principle are inseparable, the change must be accounted for as a change in estimate. The effects of a change in estimate must be accounted for prospectively. Thus, the effects must be recognized in the period of change and any future periods affected by the change. The effects must not be recognized in prior periods. Consequently, depreciation expense for the year ended December 31, Year 6, should be $45,000 ($180,000 carrying amount at December 31, Year 5 ÷ 4-year remaining useful life).
    Answer (A) is incorrect. The amount of $90,000 is based on the $450,000 original cost allocated to the 5-year useful life under the straight-line method. Answer (B) is incorrect. The amount of $75,000 is equal to the original cost of the machine allocated under the straight-line method over its revised 6-year useful life. Answer (C) is incorrect. The figure of $60,000 is equal to the December 31, Year 5, carrying amount allocated under the straight-line method over 3 years.

23. In early January Year 6, Off-Line Co. changed its method of accounting for demo costs from writing off the costs over 2 years to expensing the costs immediately. Off-Line made the change in recognition that an increasing number of demos placed with potential customers did not result in sales. Off-Line had deferred demo costs of $500,000 at December 31, Year 5, of which $300,000 were to be written off in Year 6 and the remainder in Year 7. Off-Line's income tax rate is 30%. In its Year 6 statement of retained earnings, what amount should Off-Line report as a retrospective adjustment of its January 1, Year 6, retained earnings?

    A. $0

    B. $210,000

    C. $300,000

    D. $500,000

Answer (A) is correct. *(CPA, adapted)*
    REQUIRED: The retrospective adjustment of retained earnings at the beginning of the year in which an entity changed from capitalizing a cost to expensing it as incurred.
    DISCUSSION: In general, the retrospective application method is used to account for a change in accounting principle. However, a change in accounting estimate inseparable from (effected by) a change in accounting principle must be accounted for as a change in accounting estimate. A change in estimate results from new information, such as the decreasing sales resulting from the demo placements. The effects of a change in estimate must be accounted for prospectively. Thus, the effects should be recognized in the period of change and any future periods affected by the change. Accordingly, the write-off of the $500,000 in deferred demo costs should be reported in the Year 6 income statement. Retained earnings at the beginning of the year must not be retrospectively adjusted.
    Answer (B) is incorrect. The after-tax effect of expensing $300,000 of the deferred costs in Year 6 is $210,000. Answer (C) is incorrect. The amount that had been scheduled to be expensed in Year 6 is $300,000. Answer (D) is incorrect. The pretax write-off to be recorded in the Year 6 income statement is $500,000.

24. In January, based on evidence that justified the change, Urban Corporation changed its method of depreciation of its productive assets from an accelerated method to the straight-line method. Urban must account for this accounting change as a

A. Change in accounting estimate.

B. Correction of an error.

C. Change in accounting principle.

D. Change in the reporting entity.

Answer (A) is correct. *(Publisher, adapted)*
REQUIRED: The accounting for a change in depreciation method.
DISCUSSION: A change in a depreciation, amortization, or depletion method reflects recognition of a change in the estimated future benefits of an asset, the pattern of consumption of those benefits, or the information available about those benefits. Thus, the effect of the change in accounting principle is considered to be inseparable from the effect of the change in accounting estimate. When a change in estimate is inseparable from (effected by) a change in principle, the change must be accounted for as a change in estimate. The effects of a change in estimate must be accounted for prospectively, that is, by recognition in the period of change and any future periods affected by the change. The effects should not be recognized in prior periods.
Answer (B) is incorrect. The correction of an error is not an accounting change. Answer (C) is incorrect. A change in a depreciation, amortization, or depletion method must be accounted for as a change in accounting estimate, not a change in accounting principle. Answer (D) is incorrect. A change in reporting entity results from (1) presenting consolidated or combined statements in place of statements of individual entities, (2) changing the specific subsidiaries included in the group for which consolidated statements are presented, and (3) changing the entities included in combined statements.

25. On January 1, Year 4, Colorado Corp. purchased a machine having an estimated useful life of 8 years and no salvage value. The machine was depreciated by the double-declining-balance (DDB) method for both financial statement and income tax reporting. On January 1, Year 6, Colorado changed with justification to the straight-line method for both financial statement and income tax reporting. Accumulated depreciation at December 31, Year 5, was $525,000. If the straight-line method had been used, the accumulated depreciation at December 31, Year 5, would have been $300,000. The amount to be reported as a retroactive adjustment to the accumulated depreciation account as of January 1, Year 6, as a result of the change in depreciation method is

A. $0

B. $225,000

C. $300,000

D. $525,000

Answer (A) is correct. *(CPA, adapted)*
REQUIRED: The retroactive adjustment to accumulated depreciation at the beginning of the year in which a change in depreciation method was made.
DISCUSSION: A change in accounting estimate inseparable from (effected by) a change in accounting principle includes a change in depreciation, amortization, or depletion method. When a change in accounting estimate and a change in accounting principle are inseparable, the transaction must be accounted for as a change in accounting estimate. The effects of a change in accounting estimate must be accounted for prospectively. Thus, the effects must be recognized in the period of change and any future periods affected by the change. The effects must not be recognized in prior periods. Consequently, the accumulated depreciation at January 1, Year 6, should carry forth the $525,000 balance determined in accordance with the DDB method as of December 31, Year 5.
Answer (B) is incorrect. The difference between the DDB and straight-line methods is equal to $225,000. Answer (C) is incorrect. The balance determined under the straight-line method is $300,000. Answer (D) is incorrect. The balance under the DDB method is $525,000.

18.3 Corrections of Errors in Prior Statements

26. The correction of an error in the financial statements of a prior period should be reported, net of applicable income taxes, in the current

A. Retained earnings statement after net income but before dividends.

B. Retained earnings statement as an adjustment of the opening balance.

C. Income statement after income from continuing operations and before extraordinary items.

D. Income statement after income from continuing operations and after extraordinary items.

Answer (B) is correct. *(CPA, adapted)*
REQUIRED: The proper recording of a correction of a prior-period error.
DISCUSSION: Error corrections must be reported in single period statements net of applicable income taxes as changes in the opening balance in the statement of retained earnings of the current period. In comparative financial statements, all prior periods affected by the error correction must be restated to reflect the adjustment.
Answer (A) is incorrect. The correction of the error must be reported as an adjustment of beginning retained earnings. Answer (C) is incorrect. Discontinued operations is reported in the income statement after income from continuing operations and before extraordinary items. Answer (D) is incorrect. An error correction is not included in current net income. It is reported in the current retained earnings statement.

27. Which of the following errors results in an overstatement of both current assets and equity?

- A. Accrued sales expenses are understated.
- B. Noncurrent note receivable principal is misclassified as a current asset.
- C. Annual depreciation on manufacturing machinery is understated.
- D. Holiday pay expense for administrative employees is misclassified as manufacturing overhead.

Answer (D) is correct. *(CIA, adapted)*
    REQUIRED: The error that results in an overstatement of both current assets and equity.
    DISCUSSION: The classification of holiday pay expense as manufacturing overhead overstates both current assets and equity. Holiday pay expense for administrative employees should be expensed as incurred. By classifying the expense as manufacturing overhead, inventory (a current asset) is overstated. If this inventory is not sold in the period, ending inventory will be overstated and expenses for the period will be understated. The effect is to overstate current assets, net income, retained earnings, and equity.
    Answer (A) is incorrect. An understatement of accrued sales overstates equity but affects current liabilities, not current assets. Answer (B) is incorrect. A misclassification of a noncurrent note receivable as a current asset does not affect equity. Answer (C) is incorrect. An understatement of depreciation on equipment does not affect current assets.

28. The Year 1 financial statements of Essen Company reported net income for the year ended December 31, Year 1, of $2 million. On July 1, Year 2, subsequent to the issuance of the Year 1 financial statements, Essen changed from an accounting principle that is not generally accepted to one that is generally accepted. If the generally accepted accounting principle had been used in Year 1, net income for the year ended December 31, Year 1, would have been decreased by $1 million. On August 1, Year 2, Essen discovered a mathematical error relating to its Year 1 financial statements. If this error had been discovered in Year 1, net income for the year ended December 31, Year 1, would have been increased by $500,000. What amount, if any, should be included in net income for the year ended December 31, Year 2, because of the items noted above?

- A. $0
- B. $500,000 decrease.
- C. $500,000 increase.
- D. $1,000,000 decrease.

Answer (A) is correct. *(CPA, adapted)*
    REQUIRED: The amount that should be included in net income because of an accounting change and a prior-period error.
    DISCUSSION: A change from an accounting principle that is not generally accepted to one that is generally accepted must be accounted for as the correction of an error. Corrections of errors in financial statements of prior periods must be accounted for by restatement and thus excluded from the determination of net income for the current period. Accordingly, the mathematical error and the change in accounting method have no effect on Year 2 net income.
    Answer (B) is incorrect. The $500,000 decrease is the net amount by which Year 1 income should be restated. Answer (C) is incorrect. A mathematical error caused a $500,000 increase in Year 1 net income. Answer (D) is incorrect. A $1,000,000 decrease in Year 1 income was the result of using an incorrect accounting principle.

29. At the end of Year 2, Dnieper Co. failed to accrue sales commissions earned during Year 2 but paid in Year 3. The error was not repeated in Year 3. What was the effect of this error on Year 2 ending working capital and on the Year 3 ending retained earnings balance?

	Year 2 Ending Working Capital	Year 3 Ending Retained Earnings
A.	Overstated	Overstated
B.	No effect	Overstated
C.	No effect	No effect
D.	Overstated	No effect

Answer (D) is correct. *(CPA, adapted)*
    REQUIRED: The effect of failure to accrue sales commissions.
    DISCUSSION: The Year 2 ending working capital (current assets – current liabilities) is overstated because the error understates current liabilities. The Year 3 ending retained earnings balance is unaffected because it is a cumulative amount. Whether the sales commission expense is recognized in Year 2 when it should have been accrued or in Year 3 when it was paid affects the net income amounts for Year 2 and Year 3 but not Year 3 ending retained earnings.
    Answer (A) is incorrect. Year 3 ending retained earnings is unaffected. Answer (B) is incorrect. Year 2 ending working capital is overstated, and Year 3 ending retained earnings is unaffected. Answer (C) is incorrect. Year 2 ending working capital is overstated.

30. Eiger Co. reported a retained earnings balance of $400,000 at December 31, Year 2. In August Year 3, Eiger determined that insurance premiums of $60,000 for the 3-year period beginning January 1, Year 2, had been paid and fully expensed in Year 2. Eiger has a 30% income tax rate. What amount should Eiger report as adjusted beginning retained earnings in its Year 3 statement of retained earnings?

A. $420,000

B. $428,000

C. $440,000

D. $442,000

Answer (B) is correct. *(CPA, adapted)*
REQUIRED: The beginning retained earnings after correction of an error.
DISCUSSION: Correction of prior-period errors must be reflected net of applicable income taxes as changes in the opening balance in the statement of retained earnings. The $60,000 insurance prepayment in Year 2 should have been expensed ratably over the 3-year period. Consequently, Year 2 net income was understated by $40,000, before tax effect, and $40,000 [$60,000 – ($60,000 ÷ 3)] should have been reported as a prepaid expense (an asset) at the beginning of Year 3. The error correction to the beginning balance of retained earnings is therefore a credit of $28,000 [$40,000 × (1.0 – 0.3 tax rate)]. The adjusted balance is $428,000 ($400,000 + $28,000).
Answer (A) is incorrect. The sum of the beginning balance of retained earnings and the expense that should have been recognized in Year 2 is $420,000. Answer (C) is incorrect. The amount of $440,000 does not consider the tax effect. Answer (D) is incorrect. The amount of $442,000 assumes that no insurance expense should have been recognized in Year 2.

31. On January 1, Year 1, Newport Corp. purchased a machine for $100,000. The machine was depreciated using the straight-line method over a 10-year period with no residual value. Because of a bookkeeping error, no depreciation was recognized in Newport's Year 1 financial statements, resulting in a $10,000 overstatement of the book value of the machine on December 31, Year 1. The oversight was discovered during the preparation of Newport's Year 2 financial statements. What amount should Newport report for depreciation expense on the machine in the Year 2 financial statements?

A. $9,000

B. $10,000

C. $11,000

D. $20,000

Answer (B) is correct. *(CPA, adapted)*
REQUIRED: The reported depreciation expense in the Year 2 financial statements.
DISCUSSION: Error corrections related to prior periods are not included in net income. They are reported in single-period statements as adjustments of the opening balance of retained earnings. If comparative statements are presented, corresponding adjustments should be made to net income (and its components) and retained earnings (and other affected balances) for all periods reported. Accordingly, the error in Year 1 does not affect depreciation expense in Year 2 regardless of whether single-year or comparative statements are presented. It equals $10,000 [($100,000 – $0 residual value) ÷ 10 years].
Answer (A) is incorrect. The amount of $9,000 equals the appropriate carrying amount at the beginning of Year 2 ($90,000) divided by 10 years. Answer (C) is incorrect. The amount of $11,000 equals initial carrying amount ($100,000 divided by 9 years and rounded to the nearest thousand). Answer (D) is incorrect. The amount of $20,000 is the total depreciation expense for Years 1 and 2. However, no catch-up adjustment for the omission in Year 1 is recognized in income for Year 2.

32. An audit of Fundy Co. for its first year of operations detected the following errors made at December 31:

- Failed to accrue $50,000 interest expense
- Failed to record depreciation expense on office equipment of $80,000
- Failed to amortize prepaid rent expense of $100,000
- Failed to delay recognition of prepaid insurance expense of $60,000

The net effect of these errors was to overstate net income for the year by

A. $130,000

B. $170,000

C. $230,000

D. $290,000

Answer (B) is correct. *(CIA, adapted)*
REQUIRED: The effect of certain errors on net income.
DISCUSSION: The failure to accrue interest expense, record depreciation expense on office equipment, and amortize prepaid rent expense overstates net income. Expensing the full amount of prepaid insurance instead of deferring recognition understates net income. Thus, net income is overstated by $170,000 ($50,000 + $80,000 + $100,000 – $60,000).
Answer (A) is incorrect. The amount of $130,000 includes only the interest expense and depreciation expense. Answer (C) is incorrect. The amount of $230,000 results from not subtracting the prepaid insurance expense. Answer (D) is incorrect. The amount of $290,000 results from adding prepaid insurance expense.

33. Eure's Year 3 cost of goods sold for the holiday merchandise was

A. Overstated by the difference between the note's face amount and the note's October 1, Year 3, present value.

B. Overstated by the difference between the note's face amount and the note's October 1, Year 3, present value plus 11% interest for 2 months.

C. Understated by the difference between the note's face amount and the note's October 1, Year 3, present value.

D. Understated by the difference between the note's face amount and the note's October 1, Year 3, present value plus 16% interest for 2 months.

Answer (C) is correct. *(CPA, adapted)*
REQUIRED: The cost of goods sold.
DISCUSSION: The general presumption when a note is exchanged for property, goods, or services in an arm's-length transaction is that the rate of interest is fair and adequate. If the rate is not stated or the stated rate is unreasonable, the note and the property, goods, or services should be recorded at the fair value of the property, goods, or services or the market value of the note, whichever is more clearly determinable. In the absence of these values, the present value of the note should be used as the basis for recording both the note and the property, goods, or services. This present value is obtained by discounting all future payments on the note using the market rate of interest. Because the imputed rate (11%) is less than the nominal rate (16%), the note (and the purchase) should be recorded at a premium. The face amount is the present value at the nominal rate. The face amount plus a premium is the present value at the (lower) market rate. Thus, recording the note and purchase at the face amount of the note understates the cost of the inventory sold.
Answer (A) is incorrect. The cost of goods sold was understated by the amount of the premium that should have been recognized. Answer (B) is incorrect. The cost of goods sold was understated. Answer (D) is incorrect. The understatement was equal to the note's present value at 11% on the date of purchase minus the face amount (present value at the 16% nominal rate).

34. As a result of Eure's accounting treatment of the note, interest, and merchandise, which of the following item(s) was (were) reported correctly?

	12/31/Year 3 Retained Earnings	12/31/Year 3 Interest Payable
A.	Yes	Yes
B.	No	No
C.	Yes	No
D.	No	Yes

Answer (D) is correct. *(CPA, adapted)*
REQUIRED: The item correctly reported as a result of incorrectly recording a note payable.
DISCUSSION: If the note's rate is not stated, or the stated rate is unreasonable, the note and any related property, goods, or services should be recorded at the fair value of the property, goods, services, or the market value of the note, whichever is more clearly determinable. Because the note was recorded at its face amount, cost of goods sold was understated by the difference between the note's face amount and its present value. Interest expense should be calculated based on the present value of the note at the market rate of interest. Interest payable is the stated rate times the face amount, and amortization of premium or discount is the difference between the payable and interest expense. In this situation, interest expense and interest payable are both recorded at the stated rate multiplied by the face amount. Thus, retained earnings is misstated as a result of the error in calculating cost of goods sold and interest expense. Interest payable is correctly reported.
Answer (A) is incorrect. Retained earnings is misstated. Answer (B) is incorrect. Interest payable is correctly stated. Answer (C) is incorrect. Retained earnings is misstated, and interest payable is correctly stated.

Questions 35 and 36 are based on the following information. An audit of Brasilia Company has revealed the following four errors that have occurred but have not been corrected:

1. Inventory at December 31, Year 2 -- $40,000, Understated

2. Inventory at December 31, Year 3 -- $15,000, Overstated

3. Depreciation for Year 2 -- $7,000, Understated

4. Accrued expenses at December 31, Year 3 -- $10,000, Understated

35. The errors cause the reported net income for the year ending December 31, Year 3, to be

    A. Overstated by $72,000.

    B. Overstated by $65,000.

    C. Understated by $28,000.

    D. Understated by $45,000.

Answer (B) is correct. *(CIA, adapted)*
REQUIRED: The effect of certain errors on net income.
DISCUSSION: Both the understatement of beginning inventory and the overstatement of ending inventory will understate cost of goods sold. The result understates cost of goods sold and overstates net income by $55,000 ($40,000 + $15,000). The understatement of Year 2's depreciation has no effect on Year 3's net income, but results in an overstatement of Year 2 and Year 3 retained earnings of $7,000. The understatement of accrued expenses overstates net income by $10,000. Thus, net income is overstated by $65,000 ($40,000 + $15,000 + $10,000).
Answer (A) is incorrect. The amount of $72,000 results from including the $7,000 depreciation. Answer (C) is incorrect. A $28,000 understatement results from taking the difference between inventory errors ($40,000 – $15,000) and adding accrued expenses and subtracting depreciation expense. Answer (D) is incorrect. A $45,000 understatement results from adding beginning inventory and ending inventory and subtracting accrued expenses.

36. The errors cause the reported retained earnings at December 31, Year 3, to be

    A. Overstated by $65,000.

    B. Overstated by $32,000.

    C. Overstated by $25,000.

    D. Understated by $18,000.

Answer (B) is correct. *(CIA, adapted)*
REQUIRED: The effect of errors on retained earnings.
DISCUSSION: The error in 12/31/Year 2, inventory understates income in Year 2 (cost of goods sold is overstated by $40,000) and overstates income in Year 3 (cost of goods sold is understated by $40,000). The error in 12/31/Year 3, inventory understates cost of goods sold, which overstates net income in Year 3 by $15,000. The understatement of depreciation of $7,000 overstates Year 2 net income. The understatement of accrued expenses overstates income in Year 3 by $10,000. The effect of these errors on net income is reflected in retained earnings at 12/31/Year 3. The result is an overstatement of retained earnings by $32,000 ($40,000 + $15,000 + $7,000 + $10,000 – $40,000).
Answer (A) is incorrect. An overstatement of $65,000 is the effect of the errors on Year 3 net income. Answer (C) is incorrect. An overstatement of $25,000 results from taking into account only the ending inventory in Year 3 and the accrued expenses. Answer (D) is incorrect. The amount of $18,000 results from subtracting, not adding, the effect of depreciation expense.

37. For the past 3 years, Gainesville Co. has failed to accrue unpaid wages earned by workers during the last week of the year. The amounts omitted, which are considered material, were as follows:

December 31, Year 1	$56,000
December 31, Year 2	51,000
December 31, Year 3	64,000

The entry on December 31, Year 3, to correct for these omissions would include a

A. Credit to wage expense for $64,000.

B. Debit to wage expense for $51,000.

C. Debit to wage expense for $13,000.

D. Credit to retained earnings for $64,000.

38. While preparing its Year 3 financial statements, Fulda Corp. discovered computational errors in its Year 2 and Year 1 depreciation expense. These errors resulted in overstatement of each year's income by $25,000, net of income taxes. The following amounts were reported in the previously issued financial statements:

	Year 2	Year 1
Retained earnings, 1/1	$700,000	$500,000
Net income	150,000	200,000
Retained earnings, 12/31	$850,000	$700,000

Fulda's Year 3 net income is correctly reported at $180,000. Which of the following amounts should be reported as prior-period adjustments and net income in Fulda's Year 3 and Year 2 comparative financial statements?

	Year	Prior-Period Adjustment	Net Income
A.	Year 2	--	$150,000
	Year 3	$(50,000)	180,000
B.	Year 2	$(50,000)	$150,000
	Year 3	--	180,000
C.	Year 2	$(25,000)	$125,000
	Year 3	--	180,000
D.	Year 2	--	$125,000
	Year 3	--	180,000

Answer (C) is correct. *(CMA, adapted)*
REQUIRED: The entry to correct for failure to accrue wages.
DISCUSSION: Failing to record accrued wages is a self-correcting error. Expenses are understated in one year and overstated in the next. The Year 1 error overstated Year 1 earnings and understated Year 2 earnings by $56,000. The Year 2 error overstated Year 2 earnings and understated Year 3 earnings by $51,000. The Year 3 error overstated Year 3 earnings by $64,000. Thus, the net effect in Year 3 of the Year 2 and Year 3 errors is a $13,000 ($64,000 – $51,000) overstatement. The correcting entry is to debit expense for $13,000, debit retained earnings for $51,000, and credit wages payable for $64,000.
Answer (A) is incorrect. The accrued wages payable, not the amount of the adjustment, is $64,000. Answer (B) is incorrect. The correct wage accrual for Year 2 is $51,000. Answer (D) is incorrect. Retained earnings should be debited.

Answer (C) is correct. *(CPA, adapted)*
REQUIRED: The amounts that should be reported as prior-period adjustments and net income in comparative financial statements.
DISCUSSION: In the comparative financial statements presented for Year 2 and Year 3, the Year 2 statements must be restated to reflect the adjustment. The beginning balance of retained earnings for Year 2 must be adjusted to correct the $25,000 overstatement of after-tax income for Year 1, a year for which financial statements are not presented. The statements for Year 2 must be restated to reflect the correction of the error in Year 2 net income. This amount will be correctly reported in the Year 3 and Year 2 financial statements as $125,000 ($150,000 in the previously issued Year 2 statements – $25,000 overstatement). No corrections of the Year 3 financial statements are necessary.
Answer (A) is incorrect. Restated Year 2 net income is $125,000, and the beginning balance of retained earnings for Year 2 is restated. Answer (B) is incorrect. Restated Year 2 net income is $125,000, and the correction of Year 2 retained earnings is for $25,000 (the overstatement of Year 1 net income). Answer (D) is incorrect. A $25,000 error correction must be made in the Year 2 statements.

18.4 IFRS

39. Under IAS 8, *Accounting Policies, Changes in Accounting Estimates and Errors*, an impracticability exception applies to which of the following?

I.   Retrospective application of a new accounting policy

II. Retrospective application of a change in estimate

III. Retrospective restatement of a prior period error

   A. I and II only.

   B. I and III only.

   C. II and III only.

   D. I only.

Answer (B) is correct. *(Publisher, adapted)*
REQUIRED: The item(s) to which an impracticability exception applies.
DISCUSSION: Retrospective application of a new accounting policy is not done if it is impracticable to determine period-specific effects or the cumulative effect. Impracticable means that the entity cannot apply a requirement after making every reasonable effort. Accordingly, retrospective application to a prior period is impracticable unless the cumulative effects on the opening and closing statements of financial position for the period are practically determinable. The impracticability exception also applies to retrospective restatement of a prior period error. However, a change in estimate is applied prospectively in profit or loss.
Answer (A) is incorrect. A change in estimate is applied prospectively, and retrospective restatement of a prior period error is subject to an impracticability exception. Answer (C) is incorrect. Retrospective application of a new accounting policy is subject to an impracticability exception, and a change in estimate is applied prospectively. Answer (D) is incorrect. Retrospective restatement of a prior period error is subject to an impracticability exception.

40. Under IFRS, changes in accounting policies are

   A. Permitted if the change will result in a more reliable and more relevant presentation of the financial statements.

   B. Permitted if the entity encounters new transactions, events, or conditions that are substantively different from existing or previous transactions.

   C. Required on material transactions if the entity had previously accounted for similar, though immaterial, transactions under an unacceptable accounting method.

   D. Required if an alternate accounting policy gives rise to a material change in assets, liabilities, or the current-year net income.

Answer (A) is correct. *(CPA, adapted)*
REQUIRED: The true statement about changes in accounting policies.
DISCUSSION: A change in policy must be made only if it (1) is required by a new standard or interpretation or (2) results in reliable and more relevant information about transactions, financial condition, financial performance, and cash flows.
Answer (B) is incorrect. Applying a new policy to new transactions, events, or conditions that are substantively different from existing or previous transactions is not a change in policy. Answer (C) is incorrect. A change in policy does not occur when a new policy is applied to transactions that were immaterial. Answer (D) is incorrect. A change is made only if required by a pronouncement or the result is reliable and more relevant information.

Use Gleim **EQE Test Prep** Software Download for interactive study and performance analysis.

STUDY UNIT NINETEEN
STATEMENT OF CASH FLOWS

Statement of Cash Flows -- General

The reporting standards for the statement of cash flows apply to businesses and not-for-profit entities (NFPs). This reporting for NFPs is covered in Study Unit 28. The **primary purpose** of the statement of cash flows is to provide relevant information about the cash receipts and cash payments of an entity during an accounting period. An entity that issues financial statements that report both financial position and results of operations must present a statement of cash flows for each accounting period for which results of operations are presented. The presentation must **reconcile beginning and ending cash and cash equivalents**. Cash equivalents are readily convertible to known amounts of cash and so near their maturity that they present insignificant risk of changes in value because of changes in interest rates. Moreover, cash equivalents ordinarily include only investments with original maturities to the holder of 3 months or less. The totals are the same amounts as similarly titled line items or subtotals presented in the beginning and ending statements of financial position. But the entity must not report cash flows per share.

Classification of Cash Flows

Cash flows are classified as operating, investing, and financing. They are normally reported at **gross amounts**.

Operating activities are all transactions and other events that are not classified as either financing or investing activities. In general, operating activities involve producing and delivering goods and providing services. Thus, their effects normally are reported in earnings or an NFP's change in net assets. Moreover, certain items related to investing and financing also are classified as operating. The reason is that they are reported in GAAP-based net income or the change in net assets. Examples of cash flows from such items are (1) interest received on debt investments, (2) dividends received on equity investments, and (3) interest paid on debt obligations. However, cash flows from purchases, sales, and maturities of **trading securities** are classified based on the nature and purpose for which the securities were acquired.

Cash flows from **investing activities** include those from (1) purchases and sales of property, plant, and equipment; (2) purchases, sales, and maturities of available-for-sale and held-to-maturity securities; and (3) loans to other entities and collections of the principal (collections and payments of interest are cash flows from operating activities).

Cash flows from investing activities:	
Purchase of land	$(XX,XXX)
Purchase of building	(XX,XXX)
Sale of equipment	XX,XXX
Purchase of available-for-sale securities	(XX,XXX)
Sale of held-to-maturity securities	XX,XXX
Net cash used in investing activities	**$ (X,XXX)**

Cash flows from **financing activities** include (1) proceeds from borrowing money and repayments of amounts borrowed, (2) proceeds from issuing stock and payments to reacquire it, and (3) payments of dividends on stock (the receipt of cash dividends is an operating activity).

Cash flows from financing activities:	
Issuance of equity securities	$X,XXX,XXX
Retirement of bonds payable	(XXX,XXX)
Payment of dividends	(XX,XXX)
Net cash provided by financing activities	**$XXX,XXX**

Significant **noncash financing and investing activities** that affect recognized assets or liabilities must be disclosed. Given only a few transactions, disclosure may be on the same page as the statement of cash flows. Otherwise, they may be reported elsewhere in the statements with a clear reference to the statement of cash flows. The presentation must clearly relate the cash and noncash aspects of transactions involving similar items. Examples of noncash financing and investing activities include (1) converting debt to equity; (2) acquiring assets through the assumption of related liabilities, such as purchasing a building by incurring a mortgage to the seller; (3) exchanging noncash assets or liabilities for other noncash assets or liabilities; (4) recognizing a capital lease of an asset; and (5) obtaining a building or investment asset by gift.

Operating Activities -- Indirect Presentation

The FASB prescribes two approaches to presenting cash flows from operating activities: the direct method and the indirect method. The **direct method** reports the major classes of gross cash receipts and payments and reports net cash flow as the difference between them. At a minimum, the following must be reported: (1) cash collected from customers, (2) interest and dividends received (unless donor-restricted for long-term purposes), (3) other operating cash receipts, (4) cash paid to employers and other suppliers of goods or services, (5) interest paid, (6) income taxes paid, and (7) other operating cash payments. The **indirect method** (also called the reconciliation method) begins with GAAP-based net income or the change in net assets and removes items that did not affect operating cash flow. The two methods always produce the same net amount.

DIRECT METHOD				INDIRECT METHOD		
Cash flows from operating activities:				**Cash flows from operating activities:**		
Cash receipts from:				**Accrual-basis net income**		$XX,XXX
Customers	$XX,XXX			**Additions:**		
Sale of trading securities	XX,XXX			Decrease in receivables	$X,XXX	
Interest on loans to other entities	XX,XXX			Decrease in inventories	X,XXX	
Dividends on equity investments	XX,XXX			Increase in payables	X,XXX	
Other operating cash receipts	XX,XXX			Depreciation expense	X,XXX	
Net cash inflows		$XXX,XXX		Amortization of bond discount	X,XXX	
Cash payments for:				Loss on sale of plant assets	X,XXX	
Inventory	$XX,XXX			Loss on investment in equity-		
Purchase of trading securities	XX,XXX			method investees	X,XXX	
Salaries and wages	XX,XXX			**Net additions**		XX,XXX
Interest	XX,XXX			**Subtractions:**		
Taxes	XX,XXX			Increase in receivables	$X,XXX	
Other operating cash payments	XX,XXX			Increase in inventories	X,XXX	
Net cash outflows		(XXX,XXX)		Decrease in payables	X,XXX	
Net cash provided by operating activities		$ X,XXX		Amortization of bond premium	X,XXX	
				Gain on sale of plant assets	X,XXX	
				Income from investment in equity-		
				method investees	X,XXX	
				Net subtractions		(XX,XXX)
				Net cash provided by operating activities		$ X,XXX

Operating Activities -- Direct Presentation

The FASB prefers the **direct method**. However, if the direct method is used, a **separate reconciliation** based on the indirect method must be provided in a separate schedule. For this reason, most entities use the indirect method on the face of the statement.

Differences between GAAP and IFRS

Under IFRS:

- Cash flows from **interest and dividends** should be separately disclosed and consistently classified. Total interest paid is disclosed whether it was expensed or capitalized. A **financial institution** customarily classifies interest paid or received and dividends received as operating items. For **entities other than financial institutions**, the following are the appropriate classifications:

	Operating	Financing	Investing
Interest paid	Yes	Yes	No
Interest received	Yes	No	Yes
Dividends paid	Yes	Yes	No
Dividends received	Yes	No	Yes

- Reporting cash flow per share is not prohibited.
- An entity must disclose in the notes or the statements the operating, investing, and financing cash flows of a discontinued operation.
- Noncash investing and financing transactions must be excluded from the statement of cash flows and disclosed elsewhere in the statements.
- If bank overdrafts that are repayable on demand are part of an entity's cash management program, they are included in cash and cash equivalents, not in cash flows from financing activities.

QUESTIONS

19.1 Statement of Cash Flows -- General

1. A statement of cash flows is to be presented in general-purpose external financial statements by which of the following?

A. Publicly held business enterprises only.

B. Privately held business enterprises only.

C. All businesses.

D. All businesses and not-for-profit entities.

Answer (D) is correct. *(Publisher, adapted)*
REQUIRED: The entities required to present a statement of cash flows.
DISCUSSION: A statement of cash flows is required as part of a full set of financial statements of all businesses (both publicly held and privately held) and not-for-profit entities. Defined benefit pension plans, certain other employee benefit plans, and certain highly liquid investment companies are exempt from this requirement.
Answer (A) is incorrect. All businesses are required to present a statement of cash flows. Answer (B) is incorrect. Publicly held businesses also must present a statement of cash flows. Answer (C) is incorrect. Not-for-profit entities also must present a statement of cash flows.

2. The primary purpose of a statement of cash flows of a business is to provide relevant information about

A. Differences between net income and associated cash receipts and disbursements.

B. An entity's ability to generate future positive net cash flows.

C. The cash receipts and cash disbursements of an enterprise during a period.

D. An enterprise's ability to meet cash operating needs.

Answer (C) is correct. *(CPA, adapted)*
REQUIRED: The purpose of a statement of cash flows.
DISCUSSION: The primary purpose is to provide information about the cash receipts and cash payments during a period. This information helps investors, creditors, and other users to assess the ability of the business to (1) generate net cash inflows, (2) meet its obligations, (3) pay dividends, and (4) obtain external financing. It also helps assess the reasons for the differences between net income and net cash flow and the effects of cash and noncash financing and investing activities.
Answer (A) is incorrect. Reconciling net income with cash flows is a secondary purpose. Answer (B) is incorrect. Assessing the ability to generate cash flows is a secondary purpose. Answer (D) is incorrect. Assessing the ability to meet cash needs is a secondary purpose.

3. A corporation issues a balance sheet and income statement for the current year. It also issues comparative income statements for each of the 2 previous years and a comparative balance sheet for 1 previous year. A statement of cash flows

    A. Must be issued for the current year only.

    B. Must be issued for the current and the previous year only.

    C. Must be issued for all 3 years.

    D. May be issued at the company's option for any or all of the 3 years.

Answer (C) is correct. *(Publisher, adapted)*
    REQUIRED: The circumstances in which a statement of cash flows must be issued.
    DISCUSSION: When a business provides a set of financial statements that reports both financial position and results of operations, it also must present a statement of cash flows for each period for which the results of operations are provided.
    Answer (A) is incorrect. A statement of cash flows must be provided for all 3 years. Answer (B) is incorrect. An income statement was issued for the 2 previous years. Answer (D) is incorrect. The statement of cash flows is mandatory when an income statement is issued.

4. Which of the following should be reported in a statement of cash flows issued by Grady Company?

    A. Basic cash flows per share only.

    B. Diluted cash flows per share only.

    C. Both basic and diluted cash flows per share.

    D. Cash flows per share should not be reported.

Answer (D) is correct. *(CPA, adapted)*
    REQUIRED: The cash flows per share reported in a statement of cash flows.
    DISCUSSION: Reporting cash flow per share is prohibited. Reporting a per-share amount might improperly imply that cash flow is an alternative to net income as a performance measure.
    Answer (A) is incorrect. Basic cash flow per share must not be reported. However, an entity with a simple capital structure must report basic EPS. Answer (B) is incorrect. Cash flow per share must not be reported. However, an entity with a complex capital structure reports basic and diluted EPS. Answer (C) is incorrect. Basic and diluted cash flow per share must not be reported.

5. Ghent Co. purchased a 3-month U.S. Treasury bill. In preparing Ghent's statement of cash flows, this purchase would

    A. Have no effect.

    B. Be treated as an outflow from financing activities.

    C. Be treated as an outflow from investing activities.

    D. Be treated as an outflow from lending activities.

Answer (A) is correct. *(CPA, adapted)*
    REQUIRED: The effect of purchasing a 3-month T-bill.
    DISCUSSION: Cash equivalents are readily convertible to known amounts of cash and so near their maturity that they present insignificant risk of changes in value because of changes in interest rates. Moreover, cash equivalents ordinarily include only investments with original maturities to the holder of 3 months or less. The T-bill is therefore a cash equivalent and has no effect on the statement of cash flows.
    Answer (B) is incorrect. A purchase of a security ordinarily is an investing activity. However, no outflow occurred because the 3-month T-bill is a cash equivalent. Answer (C) is incorrect. Cash was paid for a cash equivalent. Answer (D) is incorrect. Cash flows are classified as operating, financing, and investing.

19.2 Classification of Cash Flows

6. Which of the following would be reported as an investing activity in a company's statement of cash flows?

    A. Collection of proceeds from a note payable.

    B. Collection of a note receivable from a related party.

    C. Collection of an overdue account receivable from a customer.

    D. Collection of a tax refund from the government.

Answer (B) is correct. *(CPA, adapted)*
    REQUIRED: The collection reported as an investing activity.
    DISCUSSION: Investing activities include making and collecting loans. Whether the debtor is a related party affects disclosure requirements, not the classification of the cash inflow.
    Answer (A) is incorrect. A note payable is a liability of an entity. Collection of proceeds from the borrowing is a cash inflow from a financing activity. Answer (C) is incorrect. Collection of an overdue account receivable from a customer is not related to the financing or investing activities of the business. Thus, it is reported in the operating activities section. Answer (D) is incorrect. Collection of a tax refund from the government is not related to the financing or investing activities of the business. Thus, it is reported in the operating activities.

7. Which of the following transactions should be classified as an investing activity on an entity's statement of cash flows?

A. Increase in accounts receivable.

B. Sale of property, plant, and equipment.

C. Payment of cash dividend to the shareholders.

D. Issuance of common stock to the shareholders.

Answer (B) is correct. *(CPA, adapted)*
REQUIRED: The transaction classified as an investing activity.
DISCUSSION: Investing activities include (1) making and collecting loans; (2) acquiring and disposing of debt or equity instruments; and (3) acquiring and disposing of property, plant, and equipment and other productive assets (but not materials in inventory) held for or used in the production of goods and services.
Answer (A) is incorrect. An increase in accounts receivable affects cash flows from operating activities. Answer (C) is incorrect. Payment of dividends is a financing activity. Answer (D) is incorrect. Issuance of stock is a financing activity.

8. Gascony Co. had the following activities during the current year:

- Acquired 2,000 shares of the common stock of Garmisch, Inc. (classified as available-for-sale), for $26,000.
- Sold common stock of Gastineau Motors (classified as available-for-sale) for $35,000 when the carrying amount was $33,000.
- Acquired a $50,000, 4-year certificate of deposit from a bank. (During the year, interest of $3,750 was paid to Gascony.)
- Collected dividends of $1,200 on stock investments.

In Gascony's current-year statement of cash flows, net cash outflow for investing activities should be

A. $37,250

B. $38,050

C. $39,800

D. $41,000

Answer (D) is correct. *(CPA, adapted)*
REQUIRED: The net cash outflow for investing activities.
DISCUSSION: Investing activities include (1) making and collecting loans; (2) acquiring and disposing of debt and equity instruments; and (3) acquiring and disposing of property, plant, equipment, and other productive assets held for, or used in, the production of goods or services (excluding inventory). However, transactions in cash equivalents and certain loans or other instruments acquired specifically for resale are operating, not investing, activities. Cash flows from purchases, sales, and maturities of available-for-sale and held-to-maturity securities are cash flows from investing activities and are reported gross for each classification of security in the cash flows statement. Thus, the purchase of available-for-sale securities, the sale of available-for-sale securities, and the acquisition of a long-term certificate of deposit (not a cash equivalent) are investing activities. The receipts of interest and dividends are cash flows from operating activities. The net cash used in investing activities therefore equals $41,000 ($26,000 – $35,000 + $50,000).
Answer (A) is incorrect. The amount of $37,250 treats interest received as an investing cash inflow. Answer (B) is incorrect. The amount of $38,050 treats interest and dividends received as investing cash inflows and uses the carrying amount of the investment sold. Answer (C) is incorrect. The amount of $39,800 treats dividends received as an investing cash inflow.

9. On September 1, Year 1, Gardd Co. signed a 20-year building lease that it reported as a capital lease. Gardd paid the monthly lease payments when due. How should Gardd report the effect of the lease payments in the financing activities section of its Year 1 statement of cash flows?

A. An inflow equal to the present value of future lease payments at September 1, Year 1, minus Year 1 principal and interest payments.

B. An outflow equal to the Year 1 principal and interest payments on the lease.

C. An outflow equal to the Year 1 principal payments only.

D. The lease payments should not be reported in the financing activities section.

Answer (C) is correct. *(CPA, adapted)*
REQUIRED: The effect of lease payments on the financing activities section in the statement of cash flows.
DISCUSSION: Financing activities include the repayment or settlement of debt obligations. Financing activities do not include the payment of interest. Thus, the payment of principal is an outflow from financing activities. The payments for interest are operating cash flows.
Answer (A) is incorrect. The payments made in Year 1 are cash outflows, but the present value of future payments is not a cash item. Answer (B) is incorrect. The interest payments should not be included as cash flows from a financing activity. Answer (D) is incorrect. Lease payments are considered cash outflows from financing activities.

10. Abbott Co. is preparing its statement of cash flows for the year. Abbott's cash disbursements during the year included the following:

Payment of interest on bonds payable	$500,000
Payment of dividends to stockholders	300,000
Payment to acquire 1,000 shares of Marks Co. common stock	100,000

What should Abbott report as total cash outflows for financing activities in its statement of cash flows under U.S. GAAP?

A. $0

B. $300,000

C. $800,000

D. $900,000

Answer (B) is correct. *(CPA, adapted)*
REQUIRED: The total cash outflows from financing activities.
DISCUSSION: The $300,000 dividend should be classified as a financing cash outflow. Other financing activities include (1) the issuance of stock, (2) treasury stock transactions, (3) incurrence of debt, (4) settlement of debt, and (5) exercise of share options resulting in excess tax benefits. The payment of interest is an operating cash outflow under U.S. GAAP, and the payment to acquire the common stock of Marks is an investing cash outflow. Under IFRS, payment of dividends may be classified as an operating or a financing activity.
Answer (A) is incorrect. The $300,000 dividend is a financing cash outflow. Answer (C) is incorrect. The $500,000 payment of interest, although related to a financing activity, is reported under U.S. GAAP as an operating cash outflow. Answer (D) is incorrect. The $100,000 payment to acquire another entity's common stock is an investing activity, and the $500,000 payment of interest, although related to a financing activity, is reported under U.S. GAAP as an operating cash outflow.

11. The following information was taken from the accounting records of Gorky Corporation for the year ended December 31, Year 1:

Proceeds from issuance of preferred stock	$8,000,000
Dividends paid on preferred stock	800,000
Bonds payable converted to common stock	4,000,000
Payment for purchase of machinery	1,000,000
Proceeds from sale of plant building	2,400,000
2% stock dividend on common stock	600,000
Gain on sale of plant building	400,000

The net cash flows from investing and financing activities that should be presented on Gorky's statement of cash flows for the year ended December 31, Year 1, are respectively

A. $1,400,000 and $7,200,000.

B. $1,400,000 and $7,800,000.

C. $1,800,000 and $7,800,000.

D. $1,800,000 and $7,200,000.

Answer (A) is correct. *(CMA, adapted)*
REQUIRED: The respective net cash flows from investing and financing activities.
DISCUSSION: Investing activities include (1) making and collecting loans; (2) acquiring and disposing of debt and equity instruments; and (3) acquiring and disposing of property, plant, equipment, and other productive assets held for, or used in, the production of goods or services (excluding inventory). However, transactions in cash equivalents and certain loans or other instruments acquired specifically for resale are operating, not investing, activities. Financing activities include the issuance of stock, the payment of dividends, treasury stock transactions, the issuance of debt, the receipt of donor-restricted resources to be used for long-term purposes, and the repayment or other settlement of debt obligations. Investing activities include the purchase of machinery and the sale of a building. The net inflow from these activities is $1,400,000 ($2,400,000 – $1,000,000). Financing activities include the issuance of preferred stock and the payment of dividends. The net inflow is $7,200,000 ($8,000,000 – $800,000). The conversion of bonds into common stock and the stock dividend do not affect cash.
Answer (B) is incorrect. The stock dividend has no effect on cash flows from financing activities. Answer (C) is incorrect. The gain on the sale of the building is double counted in determining the net cash flow from investing activities, and the stock dividend has no effect on cash flows from financing activities. Answer (D) is incorrect. The gain on the sale of the building is double counted in determining the net cash flow from investing activities.

12. In a statement of cash flows, which of the following items is reported as a cash outflow from financing activities?

I.   Payments to retire mortgage notes
II. Interest payments on mortgage notes
III. Dividend payments

A. I, II, and III.

B. II and III only.

C. I only.

D. I and III only.

Answer (D) is correct. *(CPA, adapted)*
REQUIRED: The cash outflows from financing activities.
DISCUSSION: Financing activities include issuance of stock, payment of dividends and other distributions to owners, treasury stock transactions, issuance of debt, receipt of donor-restricted resources to be used for long-term purposes, and repayment or other settlement of debt obligations. Thus, payment of the principal of a note and payment of dividends are outflows from financing activities.
Answer (A) is incorrect. Interest payments are outflows from operating activities. Answer (B) is incorrect. Payments to retire mortgage notes are outflows from financing activities, and interest payments are outflows from operating activities. Answer (C) is incorrect. Dividend payments are outflows from financing activities.

13. In preparing its statement of cash flows, if Harlingen Co. omits the payment of cash dividends, the net cash provided by <List A> activities will be <List B>.

	List A	List B
A.	Operating	Understated
B.	Investing	Understated
C.	Investing	Overstated
D.	Financing	Overstated

Answer (D) is correct. *(CIA, adapted)*
REQUIRED: The effect of omitting payment of cash dividends.
DISCUSSION: Cash flows from financing activities include (1) obtaining resources from owners and providing them with a return on their investment, (2) borrowing from and repaying creditors, and (3) receiving restricted resources that by donor stipulation must be used for long-term purposes. This category of cash flows will be overstated if the use of cash to pay dividends to equity holders is omitted from the statement of cash flows.
Answer (A) is incorrect. Cash flows from operating activities ordinarily arise from transactions that enter into the determination of net income. Cash dividends paid do not affect the cash flows from operating activities. Answer (B) is incorrect. Cash flows from investing activities arise from making and collecting loans and acquiring and disposing of investments (both debt and equity) and property, plant, and equipment. Cash dividends do not affect the cash flows from investing activities. Answer (C) is incorrect. Cash dividends do not affect the cash flows from investing activities and therefore do not misstate the net cash provided by investing activities.

14. Hanford Co. reported bonds payable of $47,000 on December 31, Year 1, and $50,000 on December 31, Year 2. During Year 2, Hanford issued $20,000 of bonds payable in exchange for equipment. There was no amortization of bond premium or discount during the year. What amount should Hanford report in its Year 2 statement of cash flows for redemption of bonds payable?

A. $3,000

B. $17,000

C. $20,000

D. $23,000

Answer (B) is correct. *(CPA, adapted)*
REQUIRED: The amount reported in the statement of cash flows for redemption of bonds payable.
DISCUSSION: Assuming no amortization of premium or discount, the net amount of bonds payable reported was affected solely by the issuance of bonds for equipment and the redemption of bonds. Given that $20,000 of bonds were issued and that the amount reported increased by only $3,000, $17,000 of bonds must have been redeemed. This amount should be reported in the statement of cash flows as a cash outflow from a financing activity.
Answer (A) is incorrect. The amount of $3,000 equals the increase in bonds payable. Answer (C) is incorrect. The amount of bonds issued is $20,000. Answer (D) is incorrect. The amount of $23,000 is the sum of the bonds issued and the increase in bonds payable.

15. A company calculated the following data for the period:

Cash received from customers	$25,000
Cash received from sale of equipment	1,000
Interest paid to bank on note	3,000
Cash paid to employees	8,000

What amount should the company report as net cash provided by operating activities in its statement of cash flows?

A. $14,000

B. $15,000

C. $18,000

D. $26,000

Answer (A) is correct. *(CPA, adapted)*
REQUIRED: The net cash provided by operating activities.
DISCUSSION: Operating activities are all transactions and other events that are not financing or investing activities. In general, operating activities involve producing and delivering goods and providing services. Their effects normally are reported in earnings. Cash inflows from operating activities include receipts from collection or sale of accounts and notes resulting from sales to customers ($25,000). Cash outflows from operating activities include cash payments to employees for services ($8,000) and creditors for interest ($3,000). Thus, the net cash provided by operating activities is $14,000. The cash received from sale of equipment is an investing cash inflow.

Cash from customers	$25,000
Cash paid to employees	(8,000)
Interest paid	(3,000)
	$14,000

Answer (B) is incorrect. The amount of $15,000 includes cash received from sale of equipment, an investing cash inflow. Answer (C) is incorrect. The amount of $18,000 excludes interest paid but includes cash from the equipment sale. Answer (D) is incorrect. The amount of $26,000 equals cash from customers plus cash from sale of equipment.

19.3 Operating Activities -- Indirect Presentation

16. Helicon Co. accrued a gain from the sale of used equipment for cash. The gain should be reported in a statement of cash flows using the indirect method in

A. Investment activities as a reduction of the cash inflow from the sale.

B. Investment activities as a cash outflow.

C. Operating activities as a deduction from income.

D. Operating activities as an addition to income.

Answer (C) is correct. *(CPA, adapted)*
REQUIRED: The presentation of a gain on the sale of used equipment in a statement of cash flows (indirect method).
DISCUSSION: Cash received from the sale of equipment is ordinarily classified in a statement of cash flows as a cash inflow from an investing activity. The cash inflow is equal to the carrying amount of the equipment plus any gain or minus any loss realized. Because the gain will be included in the determination of net income, it must be subtracted from the net income amount presented in the statement of cash flows (indirect method) in the reconciliation of net income to net cash flow from operating activities. The purpose of the adjustment is to remove the effect of the gain from both net income and the cash inflows from operating activities. In the cash flows from investing activities section, the amount reported is the sum of the gain and the carrying amount of the equipment.
Answer (A) is incorrect. The gain should be reported in the statement of cash flows as a cash flow from investing activities. Answer (B) is incorrect. The gain is a cash inflow. Answer (D) is incorrect. The gain is a cash inflow from an investing activity. Thus, it is subtracted from income.

17. If the indirect method is used to present the statement of cash flows of a business, depreciation expense is

A. Presented as an addition to net income in the operating section of the statement.

B. Presented as a deduction from net income in the operating section of the statement.

C. Reported as a cash outflow in the investing section of the statement.

D. Not disclosed on the statement.

Answer (A) is correct. *(R. Derstine)*
REQUIRED: The presentation of depreciation when the indirect method is used.
DISCUSSION: In an indirect presentation of net cash flows from operating activities by a business, the statement of cash flows should begin with net income adjusted for certain items, including those recognized in the determination of net income that did not affect cash during the period. The recognition of depreciation expense reduces net income without directly affecting cash. Thus, depreciation must be added back to net income in the determination of cash flows from operating activities.
Answer (B) is incorrect. Depreciation is an addition to net income. Answer (C) is incorrect. Depreciation is not a cash flow. Answer (D) is incorrect. Depreciation is disclosed as an adjustment to net income.

18. Hellespont Company uses the indirect method to prepare its statement of cash flows. It should present the recognition of a loss from the impairment of goodwill as a(n)

A. Cash flow from investing activities.

B. Cash flow from financing activities.

C. Deduction from net income.

D. Addition to net income.

Answer (D) is correct. *(CMA, adapted)*
REQUIRED: The treatment of goodwill impairment in a statement of cash flows based on the indirect method.
DISCUSSION: The statement of cash flows may report operating activities in the form of either an indirect or a direct presentation. An indirect presentation by a business removes from net income the effects of all non-cash items, all deferrals of past operating cash flows, all accruals of expected future operating cash flows, and all items whose cash effects are financing or investing cash flows. The result is net operating cash flow. Goodwill impairment is a noncash loss and should be added to net income.
Answer (A) is incorrect. Goodwill impairment is not a cash flow. Answer (B) is incorrect. Goodwill impairment is not a cash flow. Answer (C) is incorrect. Goodwill impairment is added to net income.

19. In a statement of cash flows (indirect method) of a business, an increase in inventories should be presented as a(n)

A. Outflow of cash.

B. Inflow and outflow of cash.

C. Addition to income from continuing operations.

D. Deduction from income from continuing operations.

Answer (D) is correct. *(CPA, adapted)*

REQUIRED: The presentation of an increase in inventories in a statement of cash flows (indirect method).

DISCUSSION: Under the indirect method, net operating cash flow is determined by adjusting net income. Cost of goods sold is included in net income. Cash paid to suppliers, however, is the amount included in net operating cash flows. The difference between cost of goods sold and cash paid to suppliers requires a two-step adjustment. The first step is to adjust net income for the change in inventory. This step adjusts for the difference between cost of goods sold and purchases. The second step is to adjust for the change in accounts payable. This step adjusts for the difference between purchases and the amounts paid to suppliers. An increase in inventories indicates that purchases were greater than cost of goods sold. Thus, as part of the first step, an increase in inventories must be subtracted from net income.

Answer (A) is incorrect. An increase in inventory must be subtracted from income from continuing operations under the indirect method. Answer (B) is incorrect. An increase in inventory implies that cost of goods sold is less than purchases. Answer (C) is incorrect. An addition to income from continuing operations results from a decrease in inventory.

20. The net income for Hudson Co. was $3 million for the year ended December 31, Year 1. Additional information is as follows:

Depreciation on fixed assets	$1,500,000
Gain from cash sale of land	200,000
Increase in accounts payable	300,000
Dividends paid on preferred stock	400,000

The net cash provided by operating activities in the statement of cash flows for the year ended December 31, Year 1, should be

A. $4,200,000

B. $4,500,000

C. $4,600,000

D. $4,800,000

Answer (C) is correct. *(CMA, adapted)*

REQUIRED: The net cash provided by operations.

DISCUSSION: The statement of cash flows may be in the form of an indirect or a direct presentation. The indirect presentation by a business removes from net income the effects of all non-cash items, all deferrals of past operating cash flows, all accruals of expected future operating cash flows, and all items whose cash effects are financing or investing cash flows. The result is net operating cash flow. Depreciation is an expense not directly affecting cash flows that should be added back to net income. The increase in accounts payable is added to net income because it indicates that an expense has been recorded but not paid. The gain on the sale of land is an inflow from an investing, not an operating, activity and should be subtracted from net income. The dividends paid on preferred stock do not affect net income or net cash flow from operating activities and do not require an adjustment. Thus, net cash flow from operations is $4,600,000 ($3,000,000 + $1,500,000 – $200,000 + $300,000).

Answer (A) is incorrect. Net income plus depreciation, minus the increase in accounts payable, equals $4,200,000. Answer (B) is incorrect. Net income plus depreciation equals $4,500,000. Answer (D) is incorrect. Net income, plus depreciation, plus the increase in accounts payable, equals $4,800,000.

21. Ionia Company reports operating activities in its statement of cash flows using the indirect method. Which of the following items, if any, should Ionia add back to net income to arrive at net operating cash flow?

	Excess of Treasury Stock Acquisition Cost over Sales Proceeds (Cost Method)	Bond Discount Amortization
A.	Yes	Yes
B.	No	No
C.	No	Yes
D.	Yes	No

Answer (C) is correct. *(CPA, adapted)*

REQUIRED: The item(s), if any, added back to net income when a business reports net operating cash flow by the indirect method.

DISCUSSION: Bond discount amortization is a noncash component of interest expense. Because the amortization decreases net income, it is added back in the reconciliation of net income to net operating cash flow. Treasury stock transactions involve cash flows that do not affect net income. They are also classified as financing activities, not operating activities.

Answer (A) is incorrect. Cash flows from treasury stock transactions do not affect net income. Answer (B) is incorrect. The bond discount amortization should be added to net income. Answer (D) is incorrect. The bond discount amortization should be added to net income, and cash flows from treasury stock transactions do not affect net income.

22. Honshu Co. has provided the following current account balances for the preparation of the annual statement of cash flows:

	January 1	December 31
Accounts receivable	$11,500	$14,500
Allowance for uncollectible accounts	400	500
Prepaid rent expense	6,200	4,100
Accounts payable	9,700	11,200

Honshu's current-year net income is $75,000. Net cash provided by operating activities in the statement of cash flows should be

A. $72,700

B. $74,300

C. $75,500

D. $75,700

Answer (D) is correct. *(CPA, adapted)*
REQUIRED: The net cash provided by operating activities.
DISCUSSION: The net income of a business should be adjusted for the effects of items properly included in the determination of net income but having either a different effect or no effect on net operating cash flow. The increase in gross accounts receivable should be subtracted from net income. The increase indicates that sales exceeded cash received. The increase in the allowance for uncollectible accounts should be added to net income. This amount reflects a noncash expense. The decrease in prepaid rent expense should be added to net income. The cash was disbursed in a prior period, but the expense was recognized currently as a noncash item. The increase in accounts payable indicates that liabilities and related expenses were recognized without cash outlays. Thus, the change in this account should be added to net income. The net cash provided by operating activities is $75,700 ($75,000 NI – $3,000 change in A/R + $100 change in allowance + $2,100 decrease in prepaid rent + $1,500 increase in A/P).
Answer (A) is incorrect. The amount of $72,700 results from subtracting the increase in accounts payable. Answer (B) is incorrect. The amount of $74,300 results from adding the change in accounts receivable and subtracting the changes in the other balances. Answer (C) is incorrect. The amount of $75,500 results from subtracting the change in the allowance.

Questions 23 and 24 are based on the following information. Ithaca Co. reported net income of $300,000 for the current year. Changes occurred in several balance sheet accounts as follows:

Equipment	$25,000 increase
Accumulated depreciation	40,000 increase
Note payable	30,000 increase

Additional Information:

• During the current year, Ithaca sold equipment costing $25,000, with accumulated depreciation of $12,000, for a gain of $5,000.

• In December of the current year, Ithaca purchased equipment costing $50,000 with $20,000 cash and a 12% note payable of $30,000.

• Depreciation expense for the year was $52,000.

23. In Ithaca's current-year statement of cash flows, net cash provided by operating activities should be

A. $340,000

B. $347,000

C. $352,000

D. $357,000

Answer (B) is correct. *(CPA, adapted)*
REQUIRED: The net cash provided by operating activities in the statement of cash flows.
DISCUSSION: A business should adjust net income for the effects of items included in the determination of net income that have no effect on net cash provided by operating activities. Depreciation is included in the determination of net income but has no cash effect. Thus, depreciation should be added to net income. The sale of equipment resulted in a gain included in the determination of net income, but the cash effect is classified as an inflow from an investing activity. Thus, the gain should be subtracted from net income. The cash outflow for the purchase of equipment is from an investing activity and has no effect on net income. Hence, it requires no adjustment. Thus, the net cash provided by operating activities is $347,000 ($300,000 NI + $52,000 depreciation – $5,000 gain).
Answer (A) is incorrect. The amount of $340,000 reflects addition of the accumulated depreciation. Answer (C) is incorrect. The amount of $352,000 results from not deducting the gain. Answer (D) is incorrect. The amount of $357,000 results from adding the gain.

24. In Ithaca's current-year statement of cash flows, net cash used in investing activities should be

A. $2,000

B. $12,000

C. $18,000

D. $20,000

Answer (A) is correct. *(CPA, adapted)*
REQUIRED: The net cash used in investing activities.
DISCUSSION: Cash flows from investing activities include the cash inflow from the sale of equipment and the cash outflow from the purchase of equipment. The issuance of a note payable as part of the acquisition price of equipment is classified as a noncash financing and investing activity. The cash inflow from the sale of equipment (carrying amount + gain) is $18,000 [($25,000 – $12,000) + $5,000]. The cash outflow from the purchase of equipment is $20,000. Thus, net cash used is $2,000 ($20,000 – $18,000).
Answer (B) is incorrect. The amount of $12,000 assumes a $30,000 cash payment for the equipment. Answer (C) is incorrect. The amount of $18,000 is the cash inflow from the sale of equipment. Answer (D) is incorrect. The cash outflow from the purchase of equipment is $20,000.

25. Jungfrau Company had net income of $150,000 for the year ended December 31, Year 2, and paid $125,000 of dividends during Year 2. The following is its comparative balance sheet:

	12/31/Year 2	12/31/Year 1
Cash	$150,000	$180,000
Accounts receivable	200,000	220,000
Total assets	$350,000	$400,000
Payables	$ 80,000	$160,000
Capital stock	130,000	125,000
Retained earnings	140,000	115,000
Total	$350,000	$400,000

The amount of net cash provided by operating activities during Year 2 was

A. $70,000

B. $90,000

C. $150,000

D. $210,000

Answer (B) is correct. *(CIA, adapted)*
REQUIRED: The amount of net cash provided by operating activities during Year 2.
DISCUSSION: A business adjusts net income to determine the net cash provided by operations. The payment of cash dividends is a cash flow from a financing activity. Hence, it is not a reconciling item. However, the decrease in accounts receivable ($220,000 – $200,000 = $20,000) during the period represents a cash inflow (collections of pre-Year 1 receivables) not reflected in Year 1 net income. Moreover, the decrease in payables ($160,000 – $80,000 = $80,000) indicates a cash outflow (payment of pre-Year 1 liabilities) that also is not reflected in Year 1 net income. Accordingly, net cash provided by operations was $90,000 ($150,000 + $20,000 – $80,000).
Answer (A) is incorrect. The amount of $70,000 fails to add to net income the reduction in accounts receivable. Answer (C) is incorrect. Net income is $150,000. Answer (D) is incorrect. The amount of $210,000 subtracts the reduction in receivables and adds the reduction in payables.

26. In its statement of cash flows issued for the year ending September 30, Berne Company reported a net cash inflow from operating activities of $123,000. The following adjustments were included in the supplementary schedule reconciling cash flow from operating activities with net income:

Depreciation	$38,000
Increase in net accounts receivable	31,000
Decrease in inventory	27,000
Increase in accounts payable	48,000
Increase in interest payable	12,000

Net income is

A. $29,000

B. $41,000

C. $79,000

D. $217,000

Answer (A) is correct. *(Publisher, adapted)*
REQUIRED: The net income given cash flow from operating activities and reconciling adjustments.
DISCUSSION: For a business to derive net income from net cash inflow from operating activities, various adjustments are necessary. The depreciation of $38,000 should be subtracted because it is a noncash item included in the determination of net income. The increase in net accounts receivable of $31,000 should be added because it signifies that sales revenue was greater than the cash collections from customers. The increase in accounts payable should be subtracted because it indicates that purchases were $48,000 greater than cash disbursements to suppliers. The second step of the transformation from cash paid to suppliers to cost of goods sold is to subtract the decrease in inventory. This change means that cost of goods sold was $27,000 greater than purchases. The $12,000 increase in interest payable should also be subtracted because it indicates that interest expense was greater than the cash paid to the lenders. Thus, the net adjustment to net cash inflow from operating activities is –$94,000 (–$38,000 + $31,000 – $27,000 – $48,000 – $12,000). Net income is $29,000 ($123,000 net cash inflow – $94,000 net adjustment).
Answer (B) is incorrect. The increase in interest payable is not subtracted. Answer (C) is incorrect. Depreciation and the increase in interest payable are not subtracted. Answer (D) is incorrect. Depreciation, the increase in accounts payable, the decrease in inventory, and the increase in interest payable should be subtracted. The increase in net accounts receivable should be added.

27. In the indirect presentation of cash flows from operating activities, net income of a business is adjusted for noncash revenues, gains, expenses, and losses to determine the cash flows from operating activities. A reconciliation of net cash flows from operating activities to net income

A. Must be reported in the statement of cash flows.

B. Must be presented separately in a related disclosure.

C. May be either reported in the statement of cash flows or presented separately in a related disclosure.

D. Need not be presented.

Answer (C) is correct. *(Publisher, adapted)*
REQUIRED: The reporting of a reconciliation of net cash flows from operating activities to net income.
DISCUSSION: When an indirect presentation of net cash flows from operating activities is made by a business, a reconciliation with net income must be provided for all noncash revenues, gains, expenses, and losses. This reconciliation may be either (1) reported in the statement of cash flows or (2) provided separately in related disclosures, with the statement of cash flows presenting only the net cash flows from operating activities.
Answer (A) is incorrect. A reconciliation may be presented in a related disclosure. Answer (B) is incorrect. A reconciliation may be reported in the statement of cash flows. Answer (D) is incorrect. A reconciliation must be reported in an indirect presentation of the statement of cash flows.

19.4 Operating Activities -- Direct Presentation

28. In a statement of cash flows of a business enterprise, which of the following will increase reported cash flows from operating activities using the direct method? (Ignore income tax considerations.)

A. Dividends received from investments.

B. Gain on sale of equipment.

C. Gain on early retirement of bonds.

D. Change from straight-line to accelerated depreciation.

Answer (A) is correct. *(CPA, adapted)*
REQUIRED: The item that will increase reported cash flows from operating activities using the direct method.
DISCUSSION: Operating activities are transactions and other events not classified as investing and financing activities. In general, the cash effects of operating activities (other than gains and losses) enter into the determination of the net income of a business enterprise or the change in net assets of a not-for-profit entity. Thus, cash receipts from dividends are cash flows from an operating activity.
Answer (B) is incorrect. The sale of equipment is an investing activity. Answer (C) is incorrect. An early retirement of bonds is a financing activity. Answer (D) is incorrect. A change in accounting principle is a noncash event.

29. Manitoba Company acquired copyrights from authors, in some cases paying advance royalties and in others paying royalties within 30 days of year end. Manitoba reported royalty expense of $375,000 for the year ended December 31, Year 2. The following data are included in Manitoba's balance sheet:

	Year 1	Year 2
Prepaid royalties	$60,000	$50,000
Royalties payable	75,000	90,000

In its Year 2 statement of cash flows, Manitoba should report cash disbursements for royalty payments of

A. $350,000

B. $370,000

C. $380,000

D. $400,000

Answer (A) is correct. *(CPA, adapted)*
REQUIRED: The cash payments for royalty payments.
DISCUSSION: A decrease in a prepaid royalties asset account implies that royalty expense was greater than the related cash disbursements. Similarly, an increase in a royalties payable liability account indicates that royalties expense exceeded cash disbursements. Royalty expense therefore exceeds the amount of cash payments for royalty payments by the amount of the decrease in the prepaid royalties account plus the increase in the royalties payable account. Thus, Manitoba's Year 2 cash payments for royalty payments total $350,000 ($375,000 royalty expense – $10,000 decrease in prepaid royalties – $15,000 increase in royalties payable).
Answer (B) is incorrect. The $10,000 decrease in prepaid royalties should be subtracted, not added. Answer (C) is incorrect. The $15,000 increase in royalties payable should be subtracted from royalty expense, not added. Answer (D) is incorrect. The decrease in prepaid royalties and the increase in royalties payable should be subtracted, not added.

30. Mukden Co. reported cost of goods sold of $270,000 for the year just ended. Additional information is as follows:

	December 31	January 1
Inventory	$60,000	$45,000
Accounts payable	26,000	39,000

If Mukden uses the direct method, what amount should Mukden report as cash paid to suppliers in its statement of cash flows for the year?

A. $242,000

B. $268,000

C. $272,000

D. $298,000

Answer (D) is correct. *(CPA, adapted)*
REQUIRED: The amount reported as cash paid to suppliers in the statement of cash flows.
DISCUSSION: To reconcile cost of goods sold to cash paid to suppliers, a two-step adjustment is needed. First, determine purchases by adding the increase in inventory to cost of goods. Second, determine cash paid for goods sold by adding the decrease in accounts payable to purchases. Thus, cash paid for goods sold equals $298,000 [$270,000 + ($60,000 – $45,000) + ($39,000 – $26,000)].
Answer (A) is incorrect. The amount of $242,000 results from subtracting the changes in inventory and accounts payable. Answer (B) is incorrect. The amount of $268,000 results from subtracting the change in inventory. Answer (C) is incorrect. The amount of $272,000 results from subtracting the change in accounts payable.

31. The Marburg Corporation owns extensive rental property. For some of this property, rent is paid in advance. For other property, rent is paid following the end of the year. In the income statement for the year ended December 31, Year 2, Marburg reported $140,000 in rental income. The following data are included in Marburg's December 31 balance sheets:

	Year 2	Year 1
Rent receivable	$95,000	$120,000
Deferred rent income	40,000	50,000

In its statement of cash flows for the year ended December 31, Year 2, Marburg should report cash receipts from rental properties totaling

A. $105,000

B. $125,000

C. $155,000

D. $175,000

Answer (C) is correct. *(K.M. Boze)*
REQUIRED: The amount of total rental cash receipts.
DISCUSSION: No write-offs of rent receivables are mentioned. Consequently, a decrease in the rent receivable asset account implies that Marburg collected more in cash receipts from rental customers than it recognized as rental income in Year 2. In contrast, a decrease in the deferred rent income liability account signifies that Marburg recognized more rental income than it received in cash payments. To determine cash receipts from rental properties, the rental income of $140,000 should be increased by the $25,000 change in the rent receivable account and decreased by the $10,000 reduction in the deferred rent income account. Cash receipts from rental properties were therefore $155,000.
Answer (A) is incorrect. The $25,000 decrease in rent receivable should be added to rental income, not subtracted. Answer (B) is incorrect. The $25,000 decrease in rent receivable should be added to rental income, not subtracted, and the $10,000 decrease in deferred rental income should be subtracted, not added. Answer (D) is incorrect. The $10,000 decrease in deferred rental income should be subtracted from rental income, not added.

32. Cash flows from operating activities may be presented in either a direct or an indirect (reconciliation) format. In which of these formats is cash collected from customers presented as a gross amount?

	Direct	Indirect
A.	No	No
B.	No	Yes
C.	Yes	Yes
D.	Yes	No

Answer (D) is correct. *(R. O'Keefe)*
REQUIRED: The format in which cash collected from customers is presented as a gross amount.
DISCUSSION: The statement of cash flows may report cash flows from operating activities in either an indirect (reconciliation) or a direct format. The direct format reports the major classes of operating cash receipts and cash payments as gross amounts. The indirect presentation reconciles net income (or the change in net assets of a not-for-profit entity) to the same amount of net cash flow from operations that would be determined in accordance with the direct method. To arrive at net operating cash flow, the indirect method adjusts net income by removing the effects of (1) all deferrals of past operating cash receipts and payments, (2) all accruals of expected future operating cash receipts and payments, and (3) all items whose cash effects are financing and investing cash flows.
Answer (A) is incorrect. The direct-method format for the statement of cash flows presents cash collected from customers as a gross amount. Answer (B) is incorrect. The direct-method format presents cash collected from customers as a gross amount, but the indirect method format arrives at net operating cash flow by adjusting net income (or the change in net assets of an NFP). Answer (C) is incorrect. The indirect-method format is based on a reconciliation.

Questions 33 through 36 are based on the following information.

Pimlico Corp. uses the direct method to prepare its statement of cash flows. Pimlico's trial balances at December 31, Year 2 and Year 1, are as follows:

	December 31	
	Year 2	Year 1
Debits		
Cash	$ 35,000	$ 32,000
Accounts receivable	33,000	30,000
Inventory	31,000	47,000
Property, plant, & equipment	100,000	95,000
Unamortized bond discount	4,500	5,000
Cost of goods sold	250,000	380,000
Selling expenses	141,500	172,000
General and administrative expenses	137,000	151,300
Interest expense	4,300	2,600
Income tax expense	20,400	61,200
	$756,700	$976,100

Credits		
Allowance for uncollectible accounts	$ 1,300	$ 1,100
Accumulated depreciation	16,500	15,000
Trade accounts payable	25,000	17,500
Income taxes payable	21,000	27,100
Deferred income taxes	5,300	4,600
8% callable bonds payable	45,000	20,000
Common stock	50,000	40,000
Additional paid-in capital	9,100	7,500
Retained earnings	44,700	64,600
Sales	538,800	778,700
	$756,700	$976,100

- Pimlico purchased $5,000 in equipment during Year 2.
- Pimlico allocated one-third of its depreciation expense to selling expenses and the remainder to general and administrative expenses.

33. What amounts should Pimlico report in its statement of cash flows for the year ended December 31, Year 2, for cash collected from customers?

A. $541,800

B. $541,600

C. $536,000

D. $535,800

Answer (D) is correct. *(CPA, adapted)*
REQUIRED: The cash collected from customers.
DISCUSSION: Collections from customers equal sales minus the increase in gross accounts receivable, or $535,800 ($538,800 – $33,000 + $30,000).
Answer (A) is incorrect. This amount results from adding the increase in receivables. Answer (B) is incorrect. This amount results from adding the increase in receivables and subtracting the increase in the allowance for uncollectible accounts, that is, from adding net accounts receivable. Answer (C) is incorrect. This amount results from subtracting net accounts receivable.

34. What amounts should Pimlico report in its statement of cash flows for the year ended December 31, Year 2, for cash paid for interest?

A. $4,800

B. $4,300

C. $3,800

D. $1,700

Answer (C) is correct. *(CPA, adapted)*
REQUIRED: The cash paid for interest.
DISCUSSION: Interest expense is $4,300. This amount includes $500 of discount amortization, a noncash item. Hence, the cash paid for interest was $3,800 ($4,300 – $500).
Answer (A) is incorrect. This figure results from adding the amortized discount. Answer (B) is incorrect. This figure is the total interest expense. Answer (D) is incorrect. This figure is the increase in interest expense.

35. What amounts should Pimlico report in its statement of cash flows for the year ended December 31, Year 2, for cash paid for income taxes?

A. $25,800

B. $20,400

C. $19,700

D. $15,000

Answer (A) is correct. *(CPA, adapted)*
REQUIRED: The cash paid for income taxes.
DISCUSSION: To reconcile income tax expense to cash paid for income taxes, a two-step adjustment is needed. The first step is to add the decrease in income taxes payable. The second step is to subtract the increase in deferred income taxes. Hence, cash paid for income taxes equals $25,800 [$20,400 + ($27,100 – $21,000) – ($5,300 – $4,600)].
Answer (B) is incorrect. This amount is income tax expense. Answer (C) is incorrect. This amount equals income tax expense minus the increase in deferred income taxes. Answer (D) is incorrect. This amount results from subtracting the decrease in income taxes payable and adding the increase in deferred taxes payable.

36. What amounts should Pimlico report in its statement of cash flows for the year ended December 31, Year 2, for cash paid for selling expenses?

A. $142,000

B. $141,500

C. $141,000

D. $140,000

Answer (C) is correct. *(CPA, adapted)*
REQUIRED: The cash paid for selling expenses.
DISCUSSION: Cash paid for selling expenses equals selling expenses minus the depreciation allocated to selling expenses. Total depreciation expense equals the $1,500 ($16,500 – $15,000) change in accumulated depreciation. Thus, cash paid for selling expenses equals $141,000 ($141,500 expense for Year 2 – $1,500 depreciation for Year 2 × 33 1/3% allocated to selling).
Answer (A) is incorrect. The amount of $142,000 results from adding the depreciation allocated to selling expenses. Answer (B) is incorrect. The amount of $141,500 equals the selling expenses for Year 2. Answer (D) is incorrect. The amount of $140,000 results from subtracting 100% of depreciation expense from selling expenses.

37. The following information was taken from the financial statements of Hofburg Corp. for the year just ended:

Accounts receivable, January 1	$ 21,600
Accounts receivable, December 31	30,400
Sales on account and cash sales	438,000
Uncollectible accounts	1,000

No accounts receivable were written off or recovered during the year. If the direct method is used in its statement of cash flows, Hofburg should report cash collected from customers as

A. $447,800

B. $446,800

C. $429,200

D. $428,200

Answer (C) is correct. *(CPA, adapted)*
REQUIRED: The cash collected from customers.
DISCUSSION: Collections from customers equal sales revenue adjusted for the change in gross accounts receivable and write-offs and recoveries. Because no accounts receivable were written off or recovered during the year, no adjustment for these transactions is needed. Accounts receivable increased by $8,800 ($30,400 – $21,600), which represents an excess of revenue recognized over cash received. Hofburg thus should report cash collected from customers of $429,200 ($438,000 – $8,800).
Answer (A) is incorrect. This figure results from adding the increase in accounts receivable and the uncollectible accounts balance. Answer (B) is incorrect. This figure results from adding the increase in accounts receivable. Answer (D) is incorrect. This figure results from subtracting the uncollectible accounts balance.

38. The following balances were reported by Oland Co. at December 31, Year 2 and Year 1:

	12/31/Year 2	12/31/Year 1
Inventory	$260,000	$290,000
Accounts payable	75,000	50,000

Oland paid suppliers $490,000 during the year ended December 31, Year 2. What amount should Oland report for cost of goods sold in Year 2?

A. $545,000

B. $495,000

C. $485,000

D. $435,000

Answer (A) is correct. *(CPA, adapted)*
REQUIRED: The cost of goods sold.
DISCUSSION: If trade accounts increased by $25,000, purchases must have been $25,000 higher than the disbursements for purchases. Purchases thus are $515,000 ($490,000 + $25,000). The decrease in merchandise inventory indicates that cost of goods sold must have been $30,000 higher than purchases. Hence, COGS equals $545,000 ($515,000 + $30,000).
Answer (B) is incorrect. The amount of $495,000 results from subtracting the increase in accounts payable. Answer (C) is incorrect. The amount of $485,000 results from subtracting the decrease in inventory. Answer (D) is incorrect. The amount of $435,000 results from subtracting the decrease in inventory and the increase in accounts payable.

19.5 IFRS

39. Which combination below explains the effect of credit card interest incurred and paid during the period on (1) equity on the statement of financial position and (2) the statement of cash flows?

	(1) Effect on Equity on Statement of Financial Position	(2) Reflected on Statement of Cash Flows as a(n)
A.	Decrease	Investing outflow
B.	Decrease	Operating or financing outflow
C.	No effect	Financing or investing outflow
D.	No effect	Operating outflow

Answer (B) is correct. *(CIA, adapted)*
REQUIRED: The effect of interest paid on the statement of financial position and cash flow statement.
DISCUSSION: Interest incurred is classified as interest expense on the income statement, which in turn reduces equity on the statement of financial position by reducing retained earnings. According to IAS 7, cash payments for interest made by an entity that is not a financial institution may be classified on the statement of cash flows as an outflow of cash from operating or financing activities.
Answer (A) is incorrect. Interest payments are classified as an operating or financing outflow on the statement of cash flows. Answer (C) is incorrect. Credit card interest charges reduce equity. Answer (D) is incorrect. Credit card interest charges reduce equity.

40. In the statement of cash flows, the payment of cash dividends appears in the <List A> activities section as a <List B> of cash.

	List A	List B
A.	Operating or investing	Source
B.	Operating or financing	Use
C.	Investing or financing	Use
D.	Investing	Source

Answer (B) is correct. *(CIA, adapted)*
REQUIRED: The treatment of cash dividends in a statement of cash flows.
DISCUSSION: According to IAS 7, dividends paid may be treated as a cash outflow from financing activities because they are a cost of obtaining resources from owners. However, they also may be treated as operating items to help determine the entity's ability to pay dividends from operating cash flows.

41. The comparative statement of financial position for an entity that had profit of $150,000 for the year ended December 31, Year 2, and paid $125,000 of dividends during Year 2 is as follows:

	12/31/Yr 2	12/31/Yr 1
Cash	$150,000	$180,000
Accounts receivable	200,000	220,000
Total assets	$350,000	$400,000
Payables	$ 80,000	$160,000
Share capital	130,000	125,000
Retained earnings	140,000	115,000
Total	$350,000	$400,000

If dividends paid are treated as an operating item, the amount of net cash from operating activities during Year 2 was

A. –$35,000

B. $90,000

C. $150,000

D. $210,000

Answer (A) is correct. *(CIA, adapted)*
REQUIRED: The amount of net cash from operating activities during Year 2.
DISCUSSION: Profit is adjusted to determine the net cash from operations. The payment of cash dividends is regarded as a cash flow from an operating activity. Hence, it is a reconciling item requiring a $35,000 reduction of profit. However, the decrease in accounts receivable ($220,000 – $200,000 = $20,000) during the period represents a cash inflow (collections of pre-Year 2 receivables) not reflected in Year 2 profit. Moreover, the decrease in payables ($160,000 – $80,000 = $80,000) indicates a cash outflow (payment of pre-Year 2 liabilities) that also is not reflected in Year 2 profit. Accordingly, net cash from operations was –$35,000 ($150,000 – $125,000 + $20,000 – $80,000).
Answer (B) is incorrect. The amount of $90,000 assumes that dividends paid were a financing item. Answer (C) is incorrect. The amount of $150,000 is profit. Answer (D) is incorrect. The amount of $210,000 subtracts the reduction in receivables and adds the reduction in payables.

STUDY UNIT TWENTY
FINANCIAL STATEMENT DISCLOSURES

Disclosure of Accounting Policies

Entities must disclose significant accounting policies involving (1) a selection from existing acceptable policies, (2) those unique to the industry in which the entity operates, and (3) any unusual or innovative applications. The summary of accounting policies preferably is included as a separate section preceding the notes or as the first note.

Development Stage Entities

An entity must disclose whether it is in the development stage. An entity is in this stage if (1) planned principal operations have not begun or (2) these operations have not yet generated significant revenue. The financial statements are presented in conformity with GAAP. However, while in the development stage, an entity also must disclose (1) the nature of its development stage activities and (2) certain additional information accumulated since its inception. This information includes (1) cumulative net losses, (2) cumulative revenue and expense, (3) cumulative cash flows, and (4) information about stock issuances.

Related Party Disclosures

Material related party transactions other than compensation arrangements, expense allowances, and similar items occurring in the ordinary course of business must be disclosed. Required disclosures include (1) the nature of the relationship involved, (2) information about each transaction for each period an income statement is presented, (3) the dollar amount of each transaction for each period an income statement is presented, (4) related party receivables and payables at the date of each balance sheet, and (5) certain tax information.

Segment Information

A public entity must disclose information about its different types of business activities and the different economic environments in which it operates. The disclosures must be made in annual and interim financial statements issued to shareholders. These disclosures include certain information about operating segments and related information about (1) products and services, (2) countries in which the entity earns revenues and holds assets, and (3) major customers. This information should reflect management's approach to organizing segments for making operating decisions and assessing performance. Consistent with the **management approach**, the segment information disclosed ordinarily must be on the same basis as that used internally by the chief operating decision maker. **Operating segments** are components of a public entity (1) that earn revenues and incur expenses by engaging in business activities (including intersegment activities) and (2) for which separate financial information is available that is evaluated regularly by the chief operating decision maker (CODM). This person (or function) decides how to allocate resources and assesses performance.

An entity must report information separately for each operating segment for which a **materiality threshold** is reached: (1) Reported **revenue**, including both sales to external customers and intersegment sales or transfers, is at least 10% of the combined revenue, external and internal, of all operating segments; (2) **assets** are at least 10% of the combined assets of all operating segments; or (3) the absolute amount of reported **profit or loss** is at least 10% of the greater, in absolute terms, of (a) the combined reported profit of all operating segments that did not report a loss or (b) the combined reported loss of all operating segments that reported a loss. How segment profit (loss) is calculated is not specified. This amount depends upon the measure reviewed by the CODM. However, the following is the general approach:

Sales
(Traceable costs)
(Allocated costs)
Profit (loss)

Test Amount	% of Relevant Amount
Revenue	≥ 10% of all operating segments
Assets	≥ 10% of all operating segments
Absolute Profit or Loss	≥ 10% of greater of absolute sum of (1) all profitable OSs or (2) all loss-reporting OSs

However, an operating segment not meeting one of these criteria may be treated as reportable, and may be separately disclosed, if management believes that information about that segment would be useful. Moreover, nonqualifying operating segments may be combined if they share a majority of certain criteria. If the **total external revenue** of the entity's operating segments is **less than 75%** of total consolidated revenue, additional operating segments must be treated as reportable even if they do not meet the specified criteria. The entity must report combined information for nonreportable operating segments and other business activities in an all other category as a reconciling item.

Reportable Segments

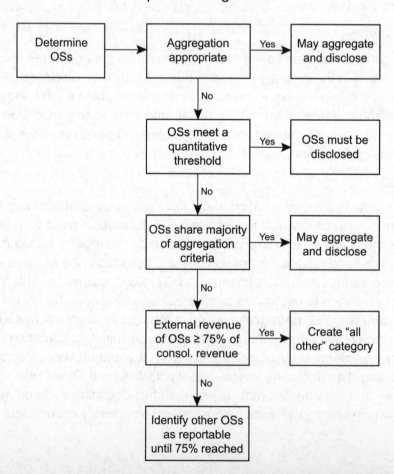

An entity also must disclose for **each period for which an income statement is presented** (1) the factors it used to identify its reportable segments; (2) the types of products and services from which each reportable segment derives its revenues; (3) information about each segment's operating profit or loss, total assets, and the basis of measurement of these amounts; and (4) reconciliations of the totals of segment revenues, reported profit or loss, assets, and other significant items to corresponding amounts in the entity's general-purpose financial statements. However, **reconciliations** of balance sheet items are required only for years in which a balance sheet is presented. Moreover, an entity is not required to disclose information that is not prepared for internal use if reporting it would be impracticable.

Risks and Uncertainties

Disclosure of certain risks and uncertainties is required if they could significantly affect reported amounts in the near term. One set of nonquantified disclosures relates to the **nature of operations**: (1) major products or services, (2) principal markets, (3) industries in which the entity operates and the relative importance of each, and (4) the basis for determining the relative importance. A second type of disclosure addresses the **use of estimates** in the preparation of financial statements. Conformity with GAAP requires management to use numerous estimates. A third category concerns certain **significant estimates**. Disclosure of an estimate used to measure assets, liabilities, or contingencies is required when the estimate is subject to a **reasonable possibility** of change in the near term and the effect of the change will be material. If an estimate is of a **loss contingency**, the disclosure should include the estimated range of loss or a statement that an estimate cannot be made. A fourth set of disclosures consists of information about current vulnerability due to **concentrations**, for example, when entities fail to diversify. Disclosure is necessary if (1) management knows prior to issuance of the statements that the concentration exists at the balance sheet date, (2) it makes the entity vulnerable to a near-term severe impact, and (3) such impact is at least reasonably possible in the near term. Disclosable concentrations include (1) volume of business with a given customer, supplier, lender, grantor, or contributor; (2) revenue from given products, services, or fund-raising events; (3) the available suppliers of materials, labor, services, or rights (e.g., licenses) used in operations; and (4) the market or geographic area where the entity operates.

Unconditional Purchase Obligations

Disclosure of commitments under unconditional purchase obligations associated with suppliers is required. Such obligations are commitments to transfer funds in the future for fixed or minimum amounts of goods or services at fixed or minimum prices. An unconditional purchase obligation has the following characteristics: it (1) was negotiated as part of the financing arrangement for facilities that will provide contracted goods or services, (2) has a remaining term of more than 1 year, and (3) is either noncancelable or cancelable only under terms that make continuation or replacement (but not cancelation) of the agreement reasonably assured. A purchase obligation cancelable upon the payment of a nominal penalty is not unconditional. If an unconditional purchase obligation is **recognized**, the total payments for unconditional purchase obligations must be disclosed for each of the 5 years following the date of the latest balance sheet. If an unconditional purchase obligation is **not recognized**, the disclosures required are (1) the nature and term of the obligation; (2) its variable components; (3) the amounts purchased under the obligation for each period; and (4) the amount of the fixed and determinable portion of the obligation at the latest balance sheet date and, if determinable, for each of the 5 succeeding fiscal years.

Subsequent Events

The guidance in this summary applies to accounting and disclosure issues for subsequent events not covered by other GAAP (e.g., the principles related to contingencies). Subsequent events are events or transactions that occur **after the balance sheet date** and **prior to the issuance or availability for issuance of the financial statements**. An **SEC filer** evaluates subsequent events through the date the statements are issued (become widely available for general use). **Other entities** evaluate subsequent events through the date statements are available for issuance (are complete in accordance with GAAP and approved). The entity must disclose the **date** through which subsequent events have been evaluated. One type of subsequent event provides additional evidence about **conditions at the date of the balance sheet**, including the estimates inherent in statement preparation. This type of event must be recognized in the financial statements. Subsequent events affecting the realization of assets (such as receivables and inventories) or the settlement of estimated liabilities ordinarily require recognition. They usually reflect the resolution of conditions that existed over a relatively long period. Examples are (1) the settlement of a lawsuit for an amount differing from the liability recorded in the statements and (2) a loss on a receivable resulting from a customer's bankruptcy. The second type of subsequent event provides evidence about **conditions that did not exist at the date of the balance sheet**. Some of these events require disclosure but not recognition. Examples of nonrecognized subsequent events requiring disclosure only include (1) sale of a bond or capital stock issue, (2) a business combination, (3) settlement of a lawsuit when the event resulting in the claim occurred after the balance sheet date, (4) loss of plant or inventories as a result of a fire or natural disaster, and (5) losses on receivables resulting from conditions (e.g., a customer's major casualty) occurring after the balance sheet date. Some events of the second type may be so significant that the most appropriate disclosure is to supplement the historical statements with **pro forma financial data**.

Difference between GAAP and IFRS

Under IFRS:

- The entity must disclose the compensation of key management personnel in total and by components.

QUESTIONS

20.1 Disclosure of Accounting Policies

1. The specific accounting policies and methods considered to be appropriate by management and used for reporting purposes

A. Should be disclosed parenthetically in the tabular portion of the financial statements.

B. Should be disclosed in a separate summary of significant accounting policies preceding the notes to the financial statements or in the initial note to the financial statements.

C. Should be disclosed in management's discussion of operations.

D. Need not be disclosed unless they are at variance with generally accepted accounting principles.

Answer (B) is correct. *(CMA, adapted)*
REQUIRED: The most appropriate statement concerning disclosure of accounting policies.
DISCUSSION: All significant accounting policies of a reporting entity must be disclosed as an integral part of its financial statements. The preferred presentation is inclusion of a summary of accounting policies in a separate section preceding the notes or in the initial note. Disclosure should encompass those principles and methods that involve a selection from existing acceptable alternatives, those methods peculiar to the industry in which the entity operates, and any unusual or innovative applications of GAAP.
Answer (A) is incorrect. Specific accounting policies and methods should not be disclosed parenthetically in the tabular portion of the financial statements. Answer (C) is incorrect. Specific accounting policies and methods should not be disclosed in management's discussion of operations. Answer (D) is incorrect. Accounting policies and methods must be disclosed.

2. Which of the following facts concerning fixed assets should be included in the summary of significant accounting policies?

	Depreciation Method	Composition
A.	No	Yes
B.	Yes	Yes
C.	Yes	No
D.	No	No

Answer (C) is correct. *(CPA, adapted)*
REQUIRED: The fact(s) concerning fixed assets disclosed in the summary of significant accounting policies.
DISCUSSION: Disclosure of significant accounting policies is required when (1) a selection has been made from existing acceptable alternatives; (2) a policy is unique to the industry in which the entity operates, even if the policy is predominantly followed in that industry; and (3) GAAP have been applied in an unusual or innovative way. A depreciation method is a selection from existing acceptable alternatives and should be included in the summary of significant accounting policies. Financial statement disclosure of accounting policies should not duplicate details presented elsewhere in the financial statements, such as composition of plant assets.

3. Disclosure of accounting policies is not necessary when

A. Selection of an accounting principle or method has been made from existing acceptable alternatives.

B. The accounting principles and methods used by an entity are peculiar to the entity's industry, provided that such principles and methods are predominantly followed in that industry.

C. Unaudited financial statements are issued as of a date between annual reporting dates and the reporting entity has not changed its accounting policies since the end of its preceding fiscal year.

D. An entity makes unusual or innovative applications of GAAP.

Answer (C) is correct. *(Publisher, adapted)*
REQUIRED: The situation in which disclosure of accounting policies is not necessary.
DISCUSSION: Disclosure of accounting policies is not required in unaudited interim financial statements when the reporting entity has not changed its policies since the end of the preceding fiscal year. Users of such interim statements will presumably consult the disclosure concerning significant accounting policies in the statements issued at the close of the preceding fiscal year.
Answer (A) is incorrect. Disclosure is required when an accounting principle or method has been selected from existing acceptable alternatives. Answer (B) is incorrect. Disclosure is required when the accounting principles and methods used are peculiar to the entity's industry. Answer (D) is incorrect. Disclosure is required when an entity makes unusual or innovative applications of GAAP.

4. Which of the following information should be disclosed in the summary of significant accounting policies?

A. Refinancing of debt subsequent to the balance sheet date.

B. Guarantees of indebtedness of others.

C. Criteria for determining which investments are treated as cash equivalents.

D. Adequacy of pension plan assets relative to vested benefits.

Answer (C) is correct. *(CPA, adapted)*
REQUIRED: The disclosure of the summary of significant accounting policies.
DISCUSSION: All significant accounting policies must be disclosed as an integral part of the financial statements. Also required is disclosure of the policy for determining which investments are treated as cash equivalents.
Answer (A) is incorrect. The refinancing of debt subsequent to the balance sheet date is not an accounting policy but is an item disclosed in the notes. Answer (B) is incorrect. Guarantees of the indebtedness of others is not an accounting policy but is an item disclosed in the notes. Answer (D) is incorrect. The adequacy of pension plan benefits is not an accounting policy but is an item disclosed in the notes.

5. Which of the following information should be included in Mariah Company's current-year summary of significant accounting policies?

A. Property, plant, and equipment is recorded at cost with depreciation computed principally by the straight-line method.

B. During the current year, the consulting services operating segment was sold.

C. Operating segment current-year sales are $2 million for the software segment, $4 million for the book production segment, and $6 million for the technical services segment.

D. Future common share dividends are expected to approximate 60% of earnings.

Answer (A) is correct. *(CPA, adapted)*
REQUIRED: The item properly disclosed in the summary of significant accounting policies.
DISCUSSION: The commonly required disclosures in a summary of significant accounting policies include (1) the basis of consolidation, (2) depreciation methods, (3) amortization of intangible assets, (4) inventory pricing, (5) recognition of profit on long-term construction-type contracts, (6) recognition of revenue from franchising and leasing operations, and (7) the policy for defining cash equivalents. Hence, the summary of significant accounting policies should include information about property, plant, and equipment depreciated by the straight-line method.
Answer (B) is incorrect. The sale of an operating segment is a transaction, not an accounting principle. It is reflected in the discontinued operations section of the income statement. Answer (C) is incorrect. Specific operating segment information does not constitute an accounting policy. An accounting policy is a specific principle or a method of applying it. Answer (D) is incorrect. Future dividend policy is not an accounting policy.

6. Which of the following should be disclosed in the summary of significant accounting policies?

	Composition of Inventories	Maturity Dates of Noncurrent Debt
A.	Yes	Yes
B.	Yes	No
C.	No	No
D.	No	Yes

Answer (C) is correct.   *(CPA, adapted)*
REQUIRED: The item(s) properly disclosed in the summary of significant accounting policies.
DISCUSSION: Certain limits are commonly required disclosures in a summary of significant accounting policies. These include (1) the basis of consolidation, (2) depreciation methods, (3) amortization of intangible assets, (4) inventory pricing, (5) recognition of profit on long-term construction-type contracts, (6) recognition of revenue from franchising and leasing operations, and (7) the policy for defining cash equivalents. However, financial statement disclosure of accounting policies should not duplicate details presented elsewhere in the financial statements. Details about the composition of inventories and the maturity dates of noncurrent debts are disclosed elsewhere in the financial statements. Hence, the summary of significant accounting policies should refer to these details but need not duplicate them.
Answer (A) is incorrect. Neither the composition of inventories nor the maturity dates of noncurrent debt should be disclosed in the summary of significant accounting policies. Answer (B) is incorrect. The composition of inventories should not be disclosed in the summary of significant accounting policies. Answer (D) is incorrect. The maturity dates of noncurrent debt should not be disclosed in the summary of significant accounting policies.

7. When financial statements are issued, a statement identifying the accounting policies adopted by the reporting entity preferably should be presented as part of the financial statements. All of the following are required to be disclosed with respect to accounting policies except the

A. Depreciation methods used for plant assets.

B. Accounting for long-term construction contracts.

C. Estimated lives of depreciable assets.

D. Principles of consolidation.

Answer (C) is correct.   *(CMA, adapted)*
REQUIRED: The item not a required disclosure.
DISCUSSION: Disclosure of accounting policies is required to be made in a separate summary of significant accounting policies or in the initial note to the financial statements. The disclosures should identify the principles followed and the methods of applying them that materially affect the statements. Moreover, the disclosures should encompass (1) principles and methods involving a selection from acceptable alternatives, (2) accounting principles unique to a particular industry, and (3) innovative or unusual applications of GAAP. However, the disclosures should not repeat details presented elsewhere, e.g., the estimated lives of depreciable assets.
Answer (A) is incorrect. Examples of required disclosures include depreciation and amortization methods. Answer (B) is incorrect. Examples of required disclosures include means of accounting for long-term construction contracts. Answer (D) is incorrect. Examples of required disclosures include basis of consolidation.

8. The summary of significant accounting policies should disclose the

A. Prior-period information retrospectively adjusted because of a change in accounting principle.

B. Basis of profit recognition on long-term construction contracts.

C. Adequacy of pension plan assets in relation to vested benefits.

D. Future minimum lease payments in the aggregate and for each of the 5 succeeding fiscal years.

Answer (B) is correct.   *(CPA, adapted)*
REQUIRED: The item disclosed in the summary of significant accounting policies.
DISCUSSION: Certain items are commonly required disclosures in a summary of significant accounting policies. These items include (1) the basis of consolidation, (2) depreciation methods, (3) amortization of intangible assets, (4) inventory pricing, (5) recognition of profit on long-term construction-type contracts, (6) recognition of revenue from franchising and leasing operations, and (7) the policy for defining cash equivalents.
Answer (A) is incorrect. Prior-period information retrospectively adjusted because of a change in accounting principle must be disclosed. However, the disclosure is in the notes, not in the summary of significant accounting policies. Answer (C) is incorrect. The adequacy of pension plan assets in relation to vested benefits is not a required disclosure. Answer (D) is incorrect. The future minimum lease payments in the aggregate and for each of the 5 succeeding fiscal years should be disclosed in the notes, but not in the summary of significant accounting policies.

20.2 Development Stage Entities

9. A statement of cash flows for a development stage entity

A. Is the same as that of an established operating entity and, in addition, reports cumulative amounts from the entity's inception.

B. Reports only cumulative amounts from the entity's inception.

C. Is the same as that of an established operating entity, but does not show cumulative amounts from the entity's inception.

D. Is not presented.

Answer (A) is correct. *(CPA, adapted)*
REQUIRED: The true statement about a statement of cash flows for a development stage entity.
DISCUSSION: A development stage entity must present financial statements in conformity with GAAP together with certain additional information accumulated since the entity's inception. The additional disclosures include (1) cumulative net losses in the equity section of the balance sheet, (2) cumulative amounts of revenue and expense in the income statement, (3) cumulative amounts of cash inflows and outflows in the statement of cash flows, and (4) information about each issuance of stock in the statement of equity.
Answer (B) is incorrect. The statement of cash flows also must conform with GAAP applicable to established entities. Answer (C) is incorrect. The statement of cash flows also must report cumulative amounts from the entity's inception. Answer (D) is incorrect. A statement of cash flows is required as part of a full set of financial statements.

10. An entity is considered to be in the development stage if

A. 12 months of operations have not been completed.

B. Planned principal operations have commenced but have not yet begun to produce significant revenue.

C. The entity has not previously shown a profit from operations.

D. The entity has not obtained 50% of the initial planned activity level.

Answer (B) is correct. *(Publisher, adapted)*
REQUIRED: The statement that describes the development stage of an entity.
DISCUSSION: An entity is considered to be in the development stage if planned principal operations have not yet commenced or if they have not yet begun to generate significant revenue.
Answer (A) is incorrect. The development stage has no time limit. Answer (C) is incorrect. Amounts of profit or loss do not define the development stage. Answer (D) is incorrect. The development stage is not defined by a level of planned activity.

11. Juris Corp. was a development stage entity from October 10, Year 1, (inception) through December 31, Year 2. The year ended December 31, Year 3, was the first year in which Juris qualified as an established operating entity. The following are among the costs incurred by Juris:

	For the Period 10/10/Yr 1 through 12/31/Yr 2	For the Year Ended 12/31/Yr 3
Leasehold improvements, equipment, and furniture	$1,000,000	$ 300,000
Security deposits	60,000	30,000
Research and development	750,000	900,000
Laboratory operations	175,000	550,000
General and administrative	225,000	685,000
Depreciation	25,000	115,000
	$2,235,000	$2,580,000

From its inception through the period ended December 31, Year 3, what is the total amount of costs incurred by Juris that should be charged to operations?

A. $3,425,000

B. $2,250,000

C. $1,775,000

D. $1,350,000

Answer (A) is correct. *(CPA, adapted)*
REQUIRED: The total amount of costs that a development stage entity should charge to operations.
DISCUSSION: A development stage entity must use the same GAAP as an established operating entity. An established operating entity would have capitalized the entire $1,300,000 of leasehold improvements, equipment, and furniture, as well as the $90,000 of security deposits. Consequently, Juris Corp., a development stage entity, should also capitalize these costs. An established operating entity would have expensed the $1,650,000 of research and development costs, the $725,000 of laboratory operations costs, the $910,000 of general and administrative costs, and the $140,000 of depreciation. Juris Corp. should also expense these costs. The total to be expensed by Juris therefore equals $3,425,000 ($1,650,000 + $725,000 + $910,000 + $140,000).
Answer (B) is incorrect. The amount of $2,250,000 equals costs incurred in Year 3 minus security deposits and leasehold improvements, equipment, and furniture. Answer (C) is incorrect. The amount of $1,775,000 excludes R&D costs. Answer (D) is incorrect. The amount of $1,350,000 equals costs incurred during the development stage, minus leasehold improvements, equipment, and furniture, plus Year 3 depreciation.

12. Financial reporting by a development stage entity differs from financial reporting for an established operating entity in regard to note disclosures

    A. Only.

    B. And expense recognition principles only.

    C. And revenue recognition principles only.

    D. And revenue and expense recognition principles.

Answer (A) is correct. *(CPA, adapted)*
    REQUIRED: The way in which financial reporting by a development stage entity differs from financial reporting for an established operating entity.
    DISCUSSION: A development stage entity must present financial statements in conformity with GAAP together with certain additional information accumulated since the entity's inception. The additional disclosures include (1) cumulative net losses in the equity section of the balance sheet, (2) cumulative amounts of revenue and expense in the income statement, (3) cumulative amounts of cash inflows and outflows in the statement of cash flows, and (4) information about each issuance of stock in the statement of equity.

20.3 Related Party Disclosures

13. Dex Co. has entered into a joint venture with an affiliate to secure access to additional inventory. Under the joint venture agreement, Dex will purchase the output of the venture at prices negotiated on an arm's-length basis. Which of the following is(are) required to be disclosed about the related party transaction?

    I. The amount due to the affiliate at the balance sheet date.

    II. The dollar amount of the purchases during the year.

    A. I only.

    B. II only.

    C. Both I and II.

    D. Neither I nor II.

Answer (C) is correct. *(CPA, adapted)*
    REQUIRED: The disclosures for a related party transaction.
    DISCUSSION: Required disclosures include (1) the nature of the relationship involved; (2) a description of the transactions for each period an income statement is presented and such other information as is deemed necessary to an understanding of the effects of the transactions; (3) the dollar amounts of transactions for each period an income statement is presented and the effects of any change in the method of establishing their terms; (4) amounts due from or to related parties as of the date of each balance sheet, including the terms of settlement; and (5) certain tax information if the entity is part of a group that files a consolidated tax return.
    Answer (A) is incorrect. The dollar amount of the purchases during the year must be disclosed. Answer (B) is incorrect. The amount due to the affiliate at the balance sheet date must be disclosed. Answer (D) is incorrect. The amount due to the affiliate at the balance sheet date and the dollar amount of the purchases during the year must be disclosed.

14. Related party transactions include transactions between the entity and

    A. The principal owners, management, and any of their relatives.

    B. Affiliates.

    C. Trusts for the benefit of employees whether or not the trustee is independent of management.

    D. Beneficial owners of at least 5% of the voting interests of the entity.

Answer (B) is correct. *(Publisher, adapted)*
    REQUIRED: The parties to related party transactions.
    DISCUSSION: Related party transactions include transactions between

1. A parent and its subsidiaries
2. Subsidiaries of a common parent
3. An entity and employee trusts managed by or under the trusteeship of the entity's management
4. An entity and its principal owners, management, or members of their immediate families
5. Affiliates
6. An entity and (a) its equity-based investees or (b) investees that would be accounted for using the equity method if not for the election of the fair value option
7. An entity and any other entity if one party can significantly influence the other to the extent that one party may be prevented from fully pursuing its own interests
8. Parties all of which can be significantly influenced by another party

    Answer (A) is incorrect. Only immediate family members of the principal owners and management are considered related parties. Answer (C) is incorrect. Employee benefit trusts that are not managed by the entity are not related parties. Answer (D) is incorrect. Only those owners of record or known beneficial owners of more than 10% of the voting interests of the entity are related parties.

15. For purposes of related party disclosures, principal owners are

A. Parties that, directly or indirectly, through one or more intermediaries, control, are controlled by, or are under common control with an entity.

B. Owners of record or known beneficial owners of more than 10% of the voting interests of that entity.

C. Owners of record or known beneficial owners of more than 30% of the voting interests of that entity.

D. Persons who are responsible for achieving the objectives of the entity and who have the authority to establish policies and make decisions by which those objectives are pursued.

Answer (B) is correct. *(Publisher, adapted)*
REQUIRED: The definition of a principal owner for the purpose of disclosing related party transactions.
DISCUSSION: Principal owners are owners of record or known beneficial owners of more than 10% of the voting interests of the entity.
Answer (A) is incorrect. Affiliates are parties that, directly or indirectly, through one or more intermediaries, control, are controlled by, or are under common control with an entity. Answer (C) is incorrect. The threshold percentage of ownership is 10%, not 30%. Answer (D) is incorrect. Management consists of persons who are responsible for achieving the objectives of the entity and who have the authority to establish policies and make decisions by which those objectives are pursued.

16. The disclosure of certain related party transactions is required. Which of the following is not a related party transaction?

A. The Eli Company borrowed money from the Peyton Company at the prevailing market rate of interest. Both companies are subsidiaries of the Arch Corporation.

B. The Kerwin Corporation established a profit-sharing trust fund administered by an independently owned bank located in the same community. The trustees invested part of the trust fund in Kerwin Corporation's outstanding bonds.

C. The Perry Company provided management services to its subsidiary without charge.

D. The Peace Company lent $25,000 to the son of the company's president at the prevailing market rate of interest.

Answer (B) is correct. *(Publisher, adapted)*
REQUIRED: The transaction not between related parties.
DISCUSSION: Related parties include

1. A parent and its subsidiaries
2. Subsidiaries of a common parent
3. An entity and employee trusts managed by or under the trusteeship of the entity's management
4. An entity and its principal owners, management, or members of their immediate families
5. Affiliates
6. An entity and (a) its equity-based investees or (b) investees that would be accounted for using the equity method if not for the election of the fair value option
7. An entity and any other entity if one party can significantly influence the other to the extent that one party may be prevented from fully pursuing its own interests
8. Parties all of which can be significantly influenced by another party

If a trust fund established to benefit employees is administered by an independent party (the bank), the investment of trust assets in the bonds of the reporting entity is not a transaction between related parties.
Answer (A) is incorrect. Subsidiaries of a common parent are related parties even if they do business at arm's length and at prevailing market interest rates. Answer (C) is incorrect. Transactions between a parent and subsidiary are considered related party transactions even if they are not recorded when they occur. Answer (D) is incorrect. A reporting entity and a member of the immediate family of one of its policy makers are related parties.

17. The material transaction between related parties that must be disclosed in financial statements is the

A. Compensation arrangement between a company and its president.

B. Loan made by a parent to its consolidated subsidiary.

C. Loan between a parent entity and its unconsolidated equity-based investee.

D. Expense allowance provided by a company to its chief executive officer.

Answer (C) is correct. *(Publisher, adapted)*
REQUIRED: The transaction between related parties that must be disclosed.
DISCUSSION: The disclosure of material related party transactions is required. Exceptions are compensation arrangements, expense allowances, and other similar items in the ordinary course of business. Related party transactions that are eliminated in the preparation of consolidated or combined financial statements also are not required to be disclosed in those financial statements. A loan made by a parent to an unconsolidated equity-based investee (or vice versa) is not eliminated, so the transaction must be disclosed.
Answer (A) is incorrect. A compensation agreement in the ordinary course of business need not be disclosed. Answer (B) is incorrect. Transactions that will be eliminated in the preparation of consolidated statements need not be disclosed. Answer (D) is incorrect. Expense allowances in the ordinary course of business need not be disclosed.

18. The disclosure of certain related party transactions is considered useful to financial statement users in formulating their investment and credit decisions. Which of the following statements about related party transactions is true?

A. A reporting entity need only disclose that it is the subsidiary of another company when transactions have taken place between it and its parent.

B. Representations about transactions between related parties may not indicate that they were equivalent to arm's-length transactions.

C. Transactions between related parties are not considered to be related party transactions unless they are given accounting recognition.

D. Transactions between related parties cannot ordinarily be presumed to be carried out on an arm's-length basis.

Answer (D) is correct. *(Publisher, adapted)*
REQUIRED: The true statement about related party transactions.
DISCUSSION: Transactions reflected in financial statements are usually presumed to have been consummated between independent parties on an arm's-length basis. When transactions occur between related parties, the required conditions of competitive, free-market dealings may not be present, and this general presumption is not applicable.
Answer (A) is incorrect. Even if there were no transactions between the entities, disclosure of the control relationship is required when common ownership or management control could result in financial position or operating results of a reporting entity materially different from those obtainable if the entities were independent. Answer (B) is incorrect. Representations about transactions between related parties may be made if they can be substantiated. Answer (C) is incorrect. Accounting recognition is not a requirement of a related party transaction.

19. Julia Co. acquired 100% of Amsterdam Corp. prior to the current year. During the current year, the individual companies included in their financial statements the following:

	Julia	Amsterdam
Officers' salaries	$150,000	$100,000
Officers' expenses	40,000	20,000
Loans to officers	250,000	100,000
Intercompany sales	300,000	--

What amount should be reported as related party disclosures in the notes to Julia's current year consolidated financial statements?

A. $300,000

B. $310,000

C. $350,000

D. $660,000

Answer (C) is correct. *(CPA, adapted)*
REQUIRED: The amount to be reported as related party disclosures.
DISCUSSION: The disclosure of material related party transactions is required. Exceptions are compensation arrangements, expense allowances, and other similar items in the ordinary course of business. Related party transactions that are eliminated in the preparation of consolidated or combined financial statements also are not required to be disclosed in those financial statements. Accordingly, the compensation arrangements (officers' salaries and expenses) and the intercompany sales, which will be eliminated in the consolidated financial statements, need not be disclosed. However, other transactions between an entity and its management, such as borrowings and lendings, must be disclosed. Julia should therefore report as related party disclosures the $350,000 ($250,000 + $100,000) of loans to officers.
Answer (A) is incorrect. The intercompany sales equals $300,000. Answer (B) is incorrect. The officers' salaries and officers' expenses equal $310,000. Answer (D) is incorrect. The officers' salaries and officers' expenses plus the loans to officers equal $660,000.

20. Lemu Co. and Young Co. are under the common management of Ego Co. Ego can significantly influence the operating results of both Lemu and Young. While Lemu had no transactions with Ego during the year, Young sold merchandise to Ego under the same terms given to unrelated parties. In the notes to their respective financial statements, should Lemu and Young disclose their relationship with Ego?

	Lemu	Young
A.	Yes	Yes
B.	Yes	No
C.	No	Yes
D.	No	No

Answer (A) is correct. *(CPA, adapted)*
REQUIRED: The disclosure(s), if any, by entities under common management regarding an entity that can significantly influence them.
DISCUSSION: Financial statements should disclose material related party transactions. A related party is essentially any party that controls or can significantly influence the management or operating policies of the reporting entity. Moreover, two or more entities may be under common ownership or management control such that the results of the reporting entity might vary significantly from those obtained if the entities were autonomous. In these circumstances, the relationship should be disclosed even though no transactions occurred between the parties.

20.4 Segment Information

21. GAAP require the disclosure of information about operating segments in financial statements of

A. Public business entities.

B. Public and nonpublic business entities.

C. Public business entities, nonpublic business entities, and not-for-profit entities.

D. Public business entities and not-for-profit entities.

Answer (A) is correct. *(Publisher, adapted)*
REQUIRED: The entities for which operating segment disclosures are required in annual financial statements.
DISCUSSION: GAAP require public business entities to disclose information about operating segments in their financial statements.
Answer (B) is incorrect. Required disclosure of segment information is not applicable to nonpublic business entities. Answer (C) is incorrect. Required disclosure of segment information is not applicable to nonpublic business entities or not-for-profit entities. Answer (D) is incorrect. Required disclosure of segment information is not applicable to not-for-profit entities.

22. The disclosure of information about major customers is required when the amount of sales to a single customer is 10% or more of the revenue of an entity. Which of the following must be disclosed?

A. The identity of the major customer.

B. The amount of revenues that each segment reports from that customer.

C. The operating segment or segments making the sale.

D. The geographic area or areas from which the sales were made.

Answer (C) is correct. *(Publisher, adapted)*
REQUIRED: The required disclosure for sales to major customers.
DISCUSSION: If 10% or more of the revenue of an entity is derived from sales to any single customer, that fact and the amount of revenue from each such customer (without disclosing the identity of the customer) must be disclosed. The identity of the operating segment or segments making the sales must also be disclosed.
Answer (A) is incorrect. The identity of a major customer is not a required disclosure. Answer (B) is incorrect. The amount of revenues that each segment reports from that customer is not a required disclosure. Answer (D) is incorrect. The geographic area from which a major sale is made is not a required disclosure.

23. In determining the segment profit or loss to be included in the annual performance review of reportable operating segments, a public company's chief operating decision maker receives information about both unusual items and extraordinary items. Which of these items, if any, must be disclosed?

	Unusual Items	Extraordinary Items
A.	Yes	No
B.	No	Yes
C.	Yes	Yes
D.	No	No

Answer (C) is correct. *(Publisher, adapted)*
REQUIRED: The item(s), if any, required to be disclosed about reportable operating segments.
DISCUSSION: Required disclosures include the measure of operating profit or loss and the total assets evaluated by the chief operating decision maker in deciding resource allocations and performance evaluations. Further disclosures of certain items are required if they are included in the measure of operating segment profit or loss. These items include (1) revenues from unaffiliated customers; (2) revenues from affiliated customers; (3) interest revenue; (4) interest expense; (5) depreciation, depletion, amortization, and other significant noncash items; (6) unusual items; (7) income from equity-basis investees; (8) income tax provisions; and (9) extraordinary items.
Answer (A) is incorrect. Disclosure of extraordinary items is required. Answer (B) is incorrect. Disclosure of unusual items is required. Answer (D) is incorrect. Disclosure of unusual items and extraordinary items is required.

24. Which of the following is not one of the three criteria used to define an operating segment?

    A. Discrete financial information about the segment is available.

    B. The segment's operating results are regularly reviewed by the chief operating decision maker (CODM).

    C. The segment is involved with business activities from which it may earn revenues and incur expenses.

    D. The segment is primarily involved in business activities with unaffiliated entities.

Answer (D) is correct. *(Publisher, adapted)*
    REQUIRED: The criterion not included in the definition of an operating segment.
    DISCUSSION: An operating segment is a component of an entity (1) engaged in business activities from which it may earn revenues and incur expenses, (2) whose operating results regularly are reviewed by the chief operating officer as a basis for allocating resources and assessing performance, and (3) for which discrete information is available. The segment's business activities may involve affiliated components as well as unaffiliated entities.
    Answer (A) is incorrect. Availability of discrete financial information about a segment is one of the three definitional criteria of an operating segment. Answer (B) is incorrect. The CODM's regular review of operating results is one of the three definitional criteria of an operating segment. Answer (C) is incorrect. Involvement in revenue-generating and expense-incurring activities is one of the three definitional criteria of an operating segment.

25. Arktos Co. is a multidivisional corporation that makes both intersegment sales and sales to unaffiliated customers. Arktos should report operating segment financial information for each segment meeting which one of the following criteria?

    A. Segment operating profit or loss is 10% or more of consolidated profit or loss.

    B. Segment operating profit or loss is 10% or more of combined operating profit or loss of all entity segments.

    C. Segment revenue is 10% or more of combined revenue of all operating segments.

    D. Segment revenue is 10% or more of consolidated revenue.

Answer (C) is correct. *(CPA, adapted)*
    REQUIRED: The criterion used to identify operating segments as reportable segments.
    DISCUSSION: An operating segment is classified as a reportable when it is significant to the entity. An operating segment is considered significant if it satisfies one or more of three tests: (1) Its revenue (including sales to both affiliated and unaffiliated customers) is at least 10% of the combined revenue (including sales to both affiliated and unaffiliated customers) of all the entity's operating segments; (2) its assets are at least 10% of the combined assets of all its operating segments; or (3) the absolute amount of its operating profit or operating loss is at least 10% of the greater, in absolute amount, of the combined operating profit of all operating segments that did not incur an operating loss or the combined loss of all operating segments that did incur an operating loss.
    Answer (A) is incorrect. Operating segment financial information is not required when segment operating profit or loss is 10% or more of consolidated profit or loss. Answer (B) is incorrect. Operating segment financial information is not required when segment operating profit or loss is 10% or more of combined operating profit or loss of all entity segments. Answer (D) is incorrect. Operating segment financial information is not required when segment revenue is 10% or more of consolidated revenue.

26. The following information pertains to revenue earned by Meadows Co.'s operating segments for the year ended December 31:

Segment	Sales to Unaffiliated Customers	Intersegment Sales	Total Revenue
Alpha	$ 5,000	$ 3,000	$ 8,000
Beta	8,000	4,000	12,000
Delta	4,000	--	4,000
Gamma	43,000	16,000	59,000
Combined	60,000	$23,000	83,000
Elimination	--	(23,000)	(23,000)
Consolidated	$60,000	--	$60,000

In conformity with the revenue test, the entity's reportable segments were

    A. Only Gamma.

    B. Only Beta and Gamma.

    C. Only Alpha, Beta, and Gamma.

    D. Alpha, Beta, Delta, and Gamma.

Answer (B) is correct. *(CPA, adapted)*
    REQUIRED: The reportable segments in conformity with the revenue test.
    DISCUSSION: For the purpose of identifying reportable operating segments, revenue includes sales to unaffiliated customers and intersegment sales. In accordance with the revenue test, a reportable operating segment has revenue equal to 10% or more of the total combined revenue of all of the entity's operating segments. Given combined revenue of $83,000, only Beta ($12,000) and Gamma ($59,000) qualify because their revenues are at least $8,300 ($83,000 × 10%). Moreover, their total external revenue of $51,000 ($8,000 + $43,000) is not less than 75% of total consolidated revenue of $45,000 ($60,000 × 75%).
    Answer (A) is incorrect. Beta also qualifies. Answer (C) is incorrect. Alpha does not qualify. Answer (D) is incorrect. Alpha and Delta do not qualify.

27. An enterprise must separately report information about an operating segment when the segment's revenue meets what minimum percentage of the combined revenue of all operating segments?

A. 5%

B. 10%

C. 20%

D. 50%

Answer (B) is correct. *(CPA, adapted)*
REQUIRED: The percentage of the combined revenue of all operating segments that requires separate reporting of an operating segment.
DISCUSSION: Reportable segments are operating segments that must be separately disclosed if (1) reported revenue is at least 10% of the combined revenue of all operating segments, (2) assets are at least 10% of the combined assets of all operating segments, and (3) the absolute amount of reported profit or loss is at least 10% of the greater (in absolute amount) of either (a) the combined profit of all profitable operating segments or (b) the combined loss of all operating segments that reported a loss.

28. Greque Co. operates in four industries. Which of the following operating segments should be identified as a reportable segment under the operating profit or loss test?

Segment	Operating Profit (Loss)
Rho	$ 90,000
Sigma	(100,000)
Tau	910,000
Upsilon	(420,000)

A. Segment Tau only.

B. Segments Tau and Upsilon.

C. Segments Sigma, Tau, and Upsilon.

D. Segments Rho, Sigma, Tau, and Upsilon.

Answer (C) is correct. *(Publisher, adapted)*
REQUIRED: The reportable segments under the operating profit or loss test.
DISCUSSION: An operating segment is identified as a reportable segment if it meets the profit or loss test (among others). The segment is reportable if the absolute amount of the operating profit or loss equals at least 10% of the greater, in absolute amount, of (1) the combined operating profit of all operating segments not reporting an operating loss or (2) the combined operating loss of all operating segments reporting an operating loss.
Segments Sigma, Tau, and Upsilon are reportable operating segments. As shown below, the sum of the operating profits of Rho and Tau ($1,000,000) is greater than the sum of the operating losses of Sigma and Upsilon ($520,000). Consequently, the test criterion is $100,000 ($1,000,000 × 10%).

Segment	Operating Profit	Operating Loss
Rho	$ 90,000	$ 0
Sigma	0	100,000
Tau	910,000	0
Upsilon	0	420,000
	$1,000,000	$520,000

Answer (A) is incorrect. Segments Sigma and Upsilon also meet the operating profit or loss test. Answer (B) is incorrect. Segment Sigma also meets the operating profit or loss test. Answer (D) is incorrect. Segment Rho does not meet the operating profit or loss test.

29. Salaam Co.'s four operating segments have revenues and identifiable assets expressed as percentages of Salaam's total revenues and total assets as follows:

	Revenues	Assets
Un	64%	66%
Deux	14%	18%
Trois	14%	4%
Quatre	8%	12%
	100%	100%

Which of these operating segments are deemed to be reportable segments?

A. Un only.

B. Un and Deux only.

C. Un, Deux, and Trois only.

D. Un, Deux, Trois, and Quatre.

Answer (D) is correct. *(CPA, adapted)*
REQUIRED: The operating segment(s) deemed to be reportable.
DISCUSSION: An operating segment is a reportable segment if it satisfies one or more of three criteria. One test is whether its revenue is 10% or more of the combined revenue of all the entity's operating segments. According to the identifiable assets test, an operating segment with identifiable assets equal to 10% or more of the combined identifiable assets of all operating segments is a reportable segment. Un, Deux, and Trois meet the revenue test, and Un, Deux, and Quatre meet the identifiable assets test.
Answer (A) is incorrect. Deux, Trois, and Quatre also meet at least one of the criteria. Answer (B) is incorrect. Trois and Quatre also meet at least one of the criteria. Answer (C) is incorrect. Quatre also meets at least one of the criteria.

30. Dillon Corp. and its divisions are engaged solely in manufacturing operations. The following data (consistent with prior years' data) pertain to the operating segments for the year ended December 31:

Industry	Total Revenue	Operating Profit	Identifiable Assets at 12/31
A	$10,000,000	$1,750,000	$20,000,000
B	8,000,000	1,400,000	17,500,000
C	6,000,000	1,200,000	12,500,000
D	3,000,000	550,000	7,500,000
E	4,250,000	675,000	7,000,000
F	1,500,000	225,000	3,000,000
	$32,750,000	$5,800,000	$67,500,000

In its operating segment information for the year, how many reportable operating segments does Dillon have?

    A. Three.

    B. Four.

    C. Five.

    D. Six.

Answer (C) is correct. *(CPA, adapted)*
    REQUIRED: The number of reportable operating segments.
    DISCUSSION: Four operating segments (A, B, C, and E) have segment revenue equal to or greater than 10% of the $32,750,000 total revenue of all operating segments. These four operating segments also have segment operating profit equal to or greater than 10% of the $5,800,000 total operating profit of all operating segments. Five operating segments (A, B, C, D, and E) have identifiable assets greater than 10% of the $67,500,000 total identifiable assets of all operating segments. Because an operating segment is reportable if it meets one or more of three tests, Dillon Corp. has five reportable segments for the year.
    Answer (A) is incorrect. An operating segment must meet one of three tests to be considered a reportable segment. Dillon has more than three reportable segments. Answer (B) is incorrect. An operating segment must meet one of three tests to be considered a reportable segment. Dillon has more than four reportable segments. Answer (D) is incorrect. An operating segment must meet one of three tests to be considered a reportable segment. Dillon has fewer than six reportable segments.

31. Which of the following materiality tests is required to determine whether the operating segments of an entity that have been identified as reportable operating segments represent a substantial portion of the total operations of the entity?

    A. The combined revenue of all reportable segments equals or exceeds 75% of the combined revenue of all operating segments.

    B. The combined revenue from sales to unaffiliated customers by all reportable segments equals or exceeds 75% of the combined revenue of all operating segments.

    C. The combined revenue from sales to unaffiliated customers by all reportable segments equals or exceeds 75% of total consolidated revenue.

    D. The combined revenue of all reportable segments equals or exceeds 75% of the combined revenue from sales to unaffiliated customers by all operating segments.

Answer (C) is correct. *(Publisher, adapted)*
    REQUIRED: The test for determining whether the reportable segments represent a substantial portion of the entity's total operations.
    DISCUSSION: The reportable segments must represent a substantial portion of the entity's total operations. To determine materiality, the combined revenue from sales to unaffiliated customers by all reportable segments must equal or exceed 75% of total consolidated revenue. The test should be applied separately for each fiscal year for which financial statements are presented. When the test criterion is not met, additional segments must be identified as reportable until the criterion is met.

32. Zan Corp., a publicly owned corporation, is subject to the requirements for segment reporting. In its income statement for the current year end, Zan reported revenues of $100,000,000, operating expenses of $94,000,000, and net income of $6,000,000. Operating expenses include payroll costs of $30,000,000. Zan's combined identifiable assets of all operating segments in the current year were $80,000,000. In its current-year financial statements, Zan should disclose major customer data if sales to any single customer amount to at least

    A. $600,000

    B. $3,000,000

    C. $8,000,000

    D. $10,000,000

Answer (D) is correct. *(CPA, adapted)*
    REQUIRED: The sales level requiring disclosure of major customer data.
    DISCUSSION: If 10% or more of the revenue of an entity is derived from sales to any single customer, that fact and the amount of revenue from each such customer (without disclosing the identity of the customer) must be disclosed. The identity of the operating segment or segments making the sales also must be disclosed. Hence, Zan's sales to a single customer of $10,000,000 ($100,000,000 total revenue × 10%) will necessitate disclosure of major customer data.
    Answer (A) is incorrect. The amount of $600,000 is 10% of net income. Answer (B) is incorrect. The amount of $3,000,000 is 10% of payroll costs. Answer (C) is incorrect. The amount of $8,000,000 is 10% of combined identifiable assets of all industry segments.

33. Listed below are the most recent year's sales to the three largest customers of the Oxford Company, a publicly held firm.

Federal government	$5,000,000
State of Florina	4,000,000
State of Carolida	3,000,000

If Oxford's total revenue amounts to $44,000,000, Oxford should disclose the total amount of sales to major customers as which of the following amounts?

- A. $0
- B. $5,000,000
- C. $9,000,000
- D. $12,000,000

Answer (B) is correct. *(Publisher, adapted)*
REQUIRED: The total amount of sales to major customers required to be separately reported.
DISCUSSION: An entity should disclose information about the extent of its reliance on its major customers. If 10% or more of the revenue of an entity is derived from sales to any single customer, that fact, the identity of the operating segment or segments making the sale, and the amount of revenue from such customer must be disclosed. A single customer includes a group of entities under common control, the federal government, a state government, a local government, or a foreign government. Total revenue for Oxford is $44,000,000. Thus, Oxford should disclose the amount of sales to any major customer from whom sales revenue totals $4,400,000 ($44,000,000 × 10%). Because the year's sales to the federal government totaled $5,000,000, such disclosure must be made (but not necessarily identifying the customer).
Answer (A) is incorrect. Sales to the federal government of $5,000,000 meet or exceed the 10% of total revenues test. Answer (C) is incorrect. Sales to the state of Florina do not meet or exceed the 10% of total revenues test. Answer (D) is incorrect. Sales to the states of Florina and Carolida do not meet or exceed the 10% of total revenues test.

20.5 Risks and Uncertainties

34. Neely Co. disclosed in the notes to its financial statements that a significant number of its unsecured trade account receivables are with companies that operate in the same industry. This disclosure is required to inform financial statement users of the existence of

- A. Concentration of credit risk.
- B. Concentration of market risk.
- C. Risk of measurement uncertainty.
- D. Off-balance-sheet risk of accounting loss.

Answer (A) is correct. *(CPA, adapted)*
REQUIRED: The purpose of disclosing that a significant number of unsecured accounts are with entities in the same industry.
DISCUSSION: Credit risk is the risk of accounting loss from a financial instrument because of the possible failure of another party to perform. An entity must disclose most significant concentrations of credit risk arising from instruments. Group concentrations arise when multiple counterparties have similar characteristics that cause their ability to meet obligations to be similarly affected by changes in conditions. An example of such a group is an industry.
Answer (B) is incorrect. Market risk is the risk of loss from the change in market value of assets or liabilities. Answer (C) is incorrect. That a significant number of unsecured trade accounts receivable are with companies that operate in the same industry has no bearing on the risk of measurement uncertainty. Answer (D) is incorrect. The entity's trade accounts receivable are on the balance sheet. Moreover, the risk of accounting loss is reflected in the recognition of an allowance for bad debts.

20.6 Unconditional Purchase Obligations

35. Denmark Corp. has unconditional purchase obligations associated with product financing arrangements. These obligations are reported as liabilities on Denmark's balance sheet, with the related assets also recognized. In the notes to Denmark's financial statements, the aggregate amount of payments for these obligations should be disclosed for each of how many years following the date of the balance sheet?

- A. 0
- B. 1
- C. 5
- D. 10

Answer (C) is correct. *(CPA, adapted)*
REQUIRED: The disclosure about reported unconditional purchase obligations.
DISCUSSION: The following disclosures must be made for recorded unconditional purchase obligations for each of the 5 years after the date of the latest balance sheet: (1) the aggregate amount of the payments for the recognized obligations and (2) the combined amount of maturities and sinking fund requirements for all noncurrent borrowing.
Answer (A) is incorrect. Disclosures are required for 5 years. Answer (B) is incorrect. Disclosures are required for 5 years, not 1 year. Answer (D) is incorrect. Disclosures are required for 5 years, not 10 years.

36. Witt Corp. has outstanding at December 31, Year 3, two long-term borrowings with annual sinking-fund requirements and maturities as follows:

	Sinking-Fund Requirements	Maturities
Year 4	$1,000,000	$ --
Year 5	1,500,000	2,000,000
Year 6	1,500,000	2,000,000
Year 7	2,000,000	2,500,000
Year 8	2,000,000	3,000,000
	$8,000,000	$9,500,000

In the notes to its December 31, Year 3, balance sheet, how should Witt report the above data?

A.   No disclosure is required.

B.   Only sinking-fund payments totaling $8,000,000 for the next 5 years detailed by year need be disclosed.

C.   Only maturities totaling $9,500,000 for the next 5 years detailed by year need be disclosed.

D.   The combined aggregate of $17,500,000 of maturities and sinking-fund requirements detailed by year should be disclosed.

Answer (D) is correct. *(CPA, adapted)*
REQUIRED: The required note disclosure of sinking fund payments and maturities for long-term borrowings.
DISCUSSION: The following information for recorded obligations for each of the 5 years following the date of the latest balance sheet presented must be disclosed: (1) the aggregate amount of payments for unconditional purchase obligations and (2) the aggregate amount of maturities and sinking-fund requirements for all long-term borrowings. Thus, Witt Corp. should disclose in the notes to the December 31, Year 3, balance sheet the combined aggregate of $17,500,000 ($8,000,000 + $9,500,000) of maturities and sinking-fund requirements detailed by year.
Answer (A) is incorrect. The combined aggregate amount of maturities and sinking-fund payments for all borrowings must be disclosed. Answer (B) is incorrect. The amount of maturities also must be disclosed. Answer (C) is incorrect. The sinking-fund payments also must be disclosed.

37. A purchase obligation is not unconditional if it is cancelable under which of the following conditions?

A.   Upon the occurrence of a remote contingency.

B.   With the permission of the other party.

C.   If a replacement agreement is signed between the same parties.

D.   Upon payment of a nominal penalty.

Answer (D) is correct. *(Publisher, adapted)*
REQUIRED: The condition preventing a purchase obligation from being unconditional.
DISCUSSION: An unconditional purchase obligation

1.   Was negotiated as part of the financing arrangement for (a) facilities that will provide contracted goods or services or (b) costs related to those goods or services,

2.   Has a remaining term of more than 1 year, and

3.   Is either noncancelable or cancelable only under specific terms that make continuation or replacement of the agreement reasonably assured.

A purchase obligation cancelable upon the payment of a nominal penalty is not unconditional.
Answer (A) is incorrect. Cancelability only upon the occurrence of a remote contingency is a condition indicating that the obligation is noncancelable in substance. Answer (B) is incorrect. Cancelability only with the permission of the other party is a condition indicating that the obligation is noncancelable in substance. Answer (C) is incorrect. Cancelability only if a replacement agreement is signed between the same parties is a condition indicating that the obligation is noncancelable in substance.

38. An entity discloses the imputed interest rate necessary to reduce an unconditional purchase obligation, not recorded in the balance sheet, to its present value. The interest rate disclosed should be

A.   If known by the purchaser, the effective initial rate of the debt that financed the facilities providing the contracted goods or services.

B.   The purchaser's incremental borrowing rate.

C.   The prime rate.

D.   The current Aa bond interest rate.

Answer (A) is correct. *(Publisher, adapted)*
REQUIRED: The interest rate to be used in determining the present value of an unconditional purchase obligation.
DISCUSSION: GAAP encourage, but do not require, disclosure of the imputed interest rate. If known by the purchaser, the rate disclosed should be the initial effective rate of the debt that financed the facilities providing the contracted goods or services. If that rate cannot be determined by the purchaser, the purchaser's incremental borrowing rate should be used.
Answer (B) is incorrect. The purchaser's incremental borrowing rate is used only if the purchaser does not know the initial rate on the debt that financed the facilities providing the contracted goods or services. Answer (C) is incorrect. The prime rate is not relevant. Answer (D) is incorrect. The current Aa bond interest rate is not relevant.

20.7 Subsequent Events

39. Zero Corp. suffered a loss that would have a material effect on its financial statements on an uncollectible trade account receivable due to a customer's bankruptcy. This occurred suddenly due to a natural disaster 10 days after Zero's balance sheet date but 1 month before the issuance of the financial statements. Under these circumstances,

	The Loss Must be Recognized in the Financial Statements	The Event Requires Financial Statement Disclosure Only
A.	Yes	Yes
B.	Yes	No
C.	No	No
D.	No	Yes

Answer (D) is correct. *(CPA, adapted)*
REQUIRED: The effect on the financial statements of a customer's bankruptcy after the balance sheet date but before the issuance of the statements.
DISCUSSION: Certain subsequent events may provide additional evidence about conditions at the date of the balance sheet, including estimates inherent in the preparation of statements. These events require recognition in the statements at year end. Other subsequent events provide evidence about conditions not existing at the date of the balance sheet but arising (1) subsequent to that date and (2) before the issuance of the statements or their availability for issuance (date of issuance for an SEC filer). These events may require disclosure but not recognition in the statements. Thus, the loss must not be recognized in Zero's statements, but disclosure must be made.

40. On January 15, Year 7, before the Mapleview Co. released its financial statements for the year ended December 31, Year 6, it settled a long-standing lawsuit. A material loss resulted, and no prior liability had been recorded. How should this loss be disclosed or recognized?

A. The loss should be disclosed in notes to the financial statements, but the financial statements themselves need not be adjusted.

B. The loss should be recognized in the financial statements for Year 7.

C. No disclosure or recognition is required.

D. The financial statements should be adjusted to recognize the loss.

Answer (D) is correct. *(Publisher, adapted)*
REQUIRED: The proper disclosure of a material loss on an existing lawsuit after year end.
DISCUSSION: Subsequent events that provide additional evidence with the respect to conditions that existed at the balance sheet date and that affect the estimates inherent in the process of preparing the financial statements should be reflected in the current financial statements. Settlement of a lawsuit is indicative of conditions existing at year end and calls for adjustment of the statements.
Answer (A) is incorrect. The financial statements should be adjusted to reflect the loss. Answer (B) is incorrect. The settlement of the lawsuit was a subsequent event. Thus, recognition in the financial statements for Year 6 is required. Occurrence of an event after the issuance of the statements may require reissuance of the statements to disclose the event and avoid misleading users. But recognition in reissued statements is not permitted unless required by GAAP or a regulation. Answer (C) is incorrect. Failure to adjust the statements for a material loss on an asset that existed at year end would be misleading.

Use Gleim **EQE Test Prep** Software Download for interactive study and performance analysis.

STUDY UNIT TWENTY-ONE
LONG-TERM CONSTRUCTION-TYPE
CONTRACTS, INSTALLMENT SALES,
AND CONSIGNMENTS

Long-Term Construction-Type Contracts

The **percentage-of-completion method** is preferred. It records all contract costs in the inventory account **construction-in-progress**. It also recognizes periodic gross profit.

Construction in progress	$XXX	
Cash or accounts payable		$XXX
Construction in progress	XXX	
Construction gross profit		XXX

The following are the entries to record progress billings made and payments received during a period:

Accounts receivable	$XXX	
Progress billings		$XXX
Cash	XXX	
Accounts receivable		XXX

If progress billings exceed (are less than) construction in progress, the entity recognizes a liability (an asset). Progress billings (a debit) and construction in progress (a credit) are closed at the end of the project.

A variation on the entries above is to credit periodic gross revenue instead of gross profit. This practice requires a debit to a cost of revenue earned account similar to cost of goods sold. The debit equals the costs incurred in the current period.

Construction in progress (gross profit)	$XXX	
Construction expenses (a nominal account)	XXX	
Gross revenue		$XXX

The percentage-of-completion method recognizes revenue and gross profit (total revenue – total costs) on long-term contracts when the (1) extent of progress toward completion, contract revenue, and contract costs are reasonably estimable; (2) enforceable rights under the contract are clearly specified; and (3) obligations of the buyer and the contractor are expected to be fulfilled. **Revenue or gross profit** is measured based upon the (1) estimated total revenue or gross profit, (2) percentage completed based on the **progress toward completion** (the relationship of costs incurred to estimated total costs is the recommended basis for determining progress), and (3) revenue or gross profit recognized to date. The **estimated total gross profit** equals the contract price minus total estimated costs. The percentage completed times the total expected revenue or gross profit equals the total revenue or gross profit to be recognized to date. The total recognized in prior periods is then subtracted from the total to date to determine the amount to be recognized in the current period.

The **completed-contract method** is used when the percentage-of-completion method is inappropriate. It recognizes revenue and gross profit when the contract is complete or substantially complete.

Under both methods, the **full estimated loss** on any project is recognized as soon as it becomes apparent. When estimated revenue and costs are revised, a **change in accounting estimate** is recognized. Recognition of the change is prospective.

Installment Sales

An **installment sale** occurs when the receivable associated with the sale will be collected over an extended period of time. Revenue from an installment sale is recognized when realized and earned, usually at the point of sale. Under unusual circumstances, when no reasonable basis exists for estimating the degree of collectibility of the receivable, recognition of the gross profit may be deferred until cash is collected. Either the installment method or the cost-recovery method may be appropriate in these circumstances. Under the **installment-sales method**, a proportional amount of installment gross profit is realized as each installment is collected. This amount is equal to the gross profit rate associated with the receivable multiplied by the amount of the receivable collected. Under the **cost-recovery method**, gross profit is not realized until the full cost of the item sold is recovered. Subsequent amounts collected are recognized as realized gross profit.

Consignments

In a consignment, the consignor ships goods to the consignee, who acts as agent for the consignor in selling the goods. The goods are held by the consignee but remain the property of the consignor and are **included in the consignor's inventory** at cost. Costs incurred by a consignor on the transfer of goods to a consignee are costs necessary to their sale. Thus, the costs are inventoriable. Because consigned goods remain in the consignor's inventory, shipping costs, in-transit insurance premiums, etc., must be debited to **consignment-out** (inventory on consignment). When goods are shipped on consignment, consignment-out is debited and inventory is credited. Sales revenue and the related cost of goods sold from consigned goods are recognized by the consignor only when notification is received that the consignee has sold the goods. The basic account used in consignee accounting is **consignment-in**, a receivable/payable. Its balance is the amount payable to the consignor (a credit) or the amount receivable from the consignor (a debit). Before consigned goods are sold, expenses chargeable to the consignor are recorded in consignment-in as a receivable. After the consigned goods are sold, the balance is the consignee's net liability to the consignor.

Differences between GAAP and IFRS

Under IFRS:

- The completed-contract method is not used. When the outcome of a long-term construction contract cannot be estimated reliably, revenue recognized is limited to recoverable costs incurred. Contract costs must be recognized as an expense in the period in which they are incurred.
- See the revenue recognition criteria described in Study Unit 1.
- The term **installment sale** applies not to the use of the installment method but to a sale in which the consideration is receivable in installments. The sale price is the present value of the consideration and is recognized as revenue at the time of sale. Interest is recognized as earned under the effective interest method.

QUESTIONS

21.1 Long-Term Construction-Type Contracts

1. A building contractor has a contract to construct a large building. It is estimated that the building will take 2 years to complete. Progress billings will be sent to the customer at quarterly intervals. Which of the following describes the preferable point for revenue and gross profit recognition for this contract?

A. After the contract is signed.

B. As progress is made toward completion of the contract.

C. As cash is received.

D. When the contract is completed.

Answer (B) is correct. *(CIA, adapted)*
REQUIRED: The timing of recognition of revenue and gross profit.
DISCUSSION: Two methods are used for revenue and gross profit recognition for long-term construction-type contracts: the percentage-of-completion method and the completed-contract method. Under the percentage-of-completion method, revenue and gross profit are recognized each period based upon the progress of the construction. The presumption is that the percentage-of-completion approach is the better method and that the completed-contract method should be used only when the percentage-of-completion method is inappropriate.
Answer (A) is incorrect. Revenue and gross profit are not earned until progress has been made toward completion. Answer (C) is incorrect. An accrual method, such as the percentage-of-completion method, should be used. Answer (D) is incorrect. The completed-contract method should be used only if conditions for using the percentage-of-completion method cannot be met.

2. Saskia Company's construction projects extend over several years, and collection of receivables is reasonably certain. Each project has a firm contract price, reliable estimates of the extent of progress and cost to finish, and a contract that is specific as to the rights and obligations of all parties. The contractor and the buyer are expected to fulfill their contractual obligations on each project. The method that the company should use to account for construction revenue and gross profit is

A. Installment sales.

B. Percentage-of-completion.

C. Completed-contract.

D. Point-of-sale.

Answer (B) is correct. *(CIA, adapted)*
REQUIRED: The method appropriate to account for construction revenue.
DISCUSSION: Revenue should be recognized when it is both realized or realizable and earned. If a project is contracted for before production and is long in relation to reporting periods, revenue and gross profit may be recognized by a percentage-of-completion method as they are earned (as production occurs), provided reasonable estimates of results at completion and reliable measures of progress are available. This information is more relevant and representationally faithful than information based on waiting for delivery, completion of the project, or payment.
Answer (A) is incorrect. The installment method is appropriate if collectibility is doubtful. Answer (C) is incorrect. The completed-contract method is appropriate if reasonable estimates of results at completion and reliable measures of progress are not available. Answer (D) is incorrect. The point-of-sale method is appropriate when the product or merchandise is delivered or services are rendered directly to customers.

3. The calculation of the gross profit recognized in the third year of a 5-year construction contract accounted for using the percentage-of-completion method includes the ratio of

A. Total costs incurred to date to total estimated costs.

B. Total costs incurred to date to total billings to date.

C. Costs incurred in Year 3 to total estimated costs.

D. Costs incurred in Year 3 to total billings to date.

Answer (A) is correct. *(CPA, adapted)*
REQUIRED: The ratio used in the calculation of gross profit recognized for a construction contract using the percentage-of-completion method.
DISCUSSION: The percentage-of-completion method provides for the recognition of gross profit based on the relationship between costs incurred to date and estimated total costs for completion of the contract. (But other measures of progress are permitted.) The amount recognized in the third year of a 5-year contract is calculated as follows: The total anticipated gross profit (based on the latest available estimated costs) is multiplied by the ratio of costs incurred to date to the latest available total estimated costs, and the product is reduced by previously recognized gross profit.
Answer (B) is incorrect. The ratio of total costs incurred to date to total billings to date is not relevant. Answer (C) is incorrect. Total costs incurred must be used. Answer (D) is incorrect. Neither the issuance nor the collection of billings results in income recognition.

4. How should the balances of progress billings and construction in progress be shown at reporting dates prior to the completion of a long-term contract?

A. Progress billings as deferred income, construction in progress as a deferred expense.

B. Progress billings as income, construction in progress as inventory.

C. Net, as a current asset if debit balance and current liability if credit balance.

D. Net, as gross profit from construction if credit balance, and loss from construction if debit balance.

Answer (C) is correct. *(CPA, adapted)*
REQUIRED: The proper balance sheet presentation of progress billings and construction in progress.
DISCUSSION: The difference between construction in progress (costs and recognized gross profit) and progress billings to date must be reported as a current asset if construction in progress exceeds total billings, and as a current liability if billings exceed construction in progress. Separate recognition is required for each project.
Answer (A) is incorrect. Progress billings and construction in progress should be netted for balance sheet presentation as a current asset or liability. Answer (B) is incorrect. Progress billings are not yet income, and construction in progress is not inventory; it uses inventory. Answer (D) is incorrect. Neither gross profit nor loss results from progress billings.

5. A company used the percentage-of-completion method of accounting for a 4-year construction contract. Which of the following items should be used to calculate the gross profit recognized in the second year?

	Gross Profit Previously Recognized	Progress Billings to Date
A.	Yes	Yes
B.	No	Yes
C.	Yes	No
D.	No	No

Answer (C) is correct. *(CPA, adapted)*
REQUIRED: The item(s) used in computing gross profit in the second year.
DISCUSSION: The percentage-of-completion method provides for the recognition of gross profit based on the relationship between the costs incurred to date and estimated total costs for the completion of the contract. The amount of gross profit (based on the latest available estimated costs) recognized in the second year of a 4-year contract is calculated as follows: The total anticipated gross profit is multiplied by the ratio of the costs incurred to date to the total estimated costs, and the product is reduced by previously recognized gross profit. Gross profit previously recognized is therefore used to calculate gross profit to be recognized in the second year. However, progress billings to date have no effect on the amount of gross profit to be recognized in the second year.
Answer (A) is incorrect. Progress billings to date are not used to calculate the amount recognized. Answer (B) is incorrect. Gross profit previously recognized is used to calculate the amount recognized, but progress billings are not. Answer (D) is incorrect. The gross profit previously recognized must be included in the calculation of current period gross profit.

6. Felis Corp. began construction work under a 3-year contract this year. The contract price is $800,000. Felis uses the percentage-of-completion method for financial accounting purposes. The gross profit to be recognized each year is based on the proportion of costs incurred to total estimated costs for completing the contract. The following financial statement presentations relate to this contract at December 31 of the first year:

Accounts receivable-- construction contract billings		$30,000
Construction in progress	$100,000	
Minus contract billings	(94,000)	
Costs of uncompleted contract in excess of billings		6,000
Gross profit (before tax) on the contract recognized in Year 1		$20,000

How much cash was collected in the first year on this contract?

A. $30,000

B. $64,000

C. $70,000

D. $94,000

Answer (B) is correct. *(CPA, adapted)*
REQUIRED: The cash collections in the first year on a contract accounted for under the percentage-of-completion method.
DISCUSSION: Billings on a construction contract are debited to a receivable and credited to a cumulative contract billings account (progress billings). Collections are debited to cash and credited to the receivable. The billings account, however, will not be reduced until it is closed at the end of the contract. Consequently, the difference between the billings and receivable accounts is the amount collected. For Felis Corp., collections equal $64,000 ($94,000 contract billings – $30,000 accounts receivable).
Answer (A) is incorrect. The accounts receivable balance for the contract billings is $30,000. Answer (C) is incorrect. The difference between construction in progress and the accounts receivable balance is $70,000. Answer (D) is incorrect. The amount of contract billings is $94,000.

7. During Year 1, Lynx Co. began construction on a project scheduled for completion in Year 3. At December 31, Year 1, an overall loss was anticipated at contract completion. What would be the effect of the project on Year 1 operating income under the percentage-of-completion method and the completed-contract method?

	Percentage-of-Completion	Completed-Contract
A.	No effect	No effect
B.	No effect	Decrease
C.	Decrease	No effect
D.	Decrease	Decrease

Answer (D) is correct. *(CPA, adapted)*
REQUIRED: The effect of the project on Year 1 operating income under the percentage-of-completion method and the completed-contract method.
DISCUSSION: When the current estimate of total contract costs indicates a loss, an immediate provision for the entire loss should be made regardless of method. Thus, under either method, Year 1 operating income is decreased by the projected loss.
Answer (A) is incorrect. Under either method, Year 1 operating income is decreased by the projected loss. Answer (B) is incorrect. Under the percentage-of-completion method, Year 1 operating income is decreased by the projected loss. Answer (C) is incorrect. Under the completed-contract method, Year 1 operating income is decreased by the projected loss.

8. Cinnabar Construction Company has consistently used the percentage-of-completion method of recognizing gross profit. During Year 1, Cinnabar entered into a fixed-price contract to construct an office building for $10 million. Information relating to the contract is as follows:

	December 31	
	Year 1	Year 2
Percentage of completion	20%	60%
Estimated total costs at completion	$7,500,000	$8,000,000
Gross profit recognized (cumulative)	500,000	1,200,000

Contract costs incurred during Year 2 were

A. $3,200,000
B. $3,300,000
C. $3,500,000
D. $4,800,000

Answer (B) is correct. *(CPA, adapted)*
REQUIRED: The contract cost incurred during the second year of a long-term contract.
DISCUSSION: If the percentage of completion is based on the relationship of the cumulative costs incurred to date to estimated total costs at completion, the cumulative amount incurred at 12/31/Year 1 was $1,500,000 ($7,500,000 × 20%). At 12/31/Year 2, the cumulative amount incurred was $4,800,000 ($8,000,000 × 60%). The difference of $3,300,000 ($4,800,000 – $1,500,000) equals contract costs incurred during Year 2.
Answer (A) is incorrect. The amount of $3,200,000 equals the $8,000,000 estimated total costs multiplied by the 40% (60% – 20%) change in the percentages of completion. Answer (C) is incorrect. The amount of $3,500,000 equals the $10,000,000 contract price multiplied by the 40% change in the percentage of completion minus the $500,000 gross profit recognized in Year 1. Answer (D) is incorrect. The amount of $4,800,000 equals the $8,000,000 estimated total costs multiplied by the 60% percentage of completion.

9. Kechara Corp. started a long-term construction project in Year 1. The following data relate to this project:

Contract price	$4,200,000
Costs incurred in Year 1	1,750,000
Estimated costs to complete	1,750,000
Progress billings	900,000
Collections on progress billings	800,000

The project is accounted for by the percentage-of-completion method of accounting. In Kechara's Year 1 income statement, what amount of gross profit should be reported for this project?

A. $350,000
B. $700,000
C. $900,000
D. $100,000

Answer (A) is correct. *(CPA, adapted)*
REQUIRED: The gross profit for the first year of a long-term construction contract.
DISCUSSION: In Year 1, one-half of the estimated costs of this construction project were incurred [$1,750,000 ÷ ($1,750,000 + $1,750,000)]. The company should therefore recognize one-half of the estimated gross profit in Year 1. At year end, the estimated gross profit is $700,000, equal to the contract price minus total estimated costs [$4,200,000 – ($1,750,000 + $1,750,000)]. In Year 1, $350,000 should be recognized as gross profit ($700,000 × 50%).
Answer (B) is incorrect. The estimated gross profit at year end is $700,000. Answer (C) is incorrect. Progress billings equal $900,000. They are not used in the calculation of gross profit under any method. Answer (D) is incorrect. Uncollected billings of $100,000 have no effect on the gross profit.

10. Ashke Co. recognizes construction revenue and gross profit using the percentage-of-completion method. During Year 1, a single long-term project was begun, which continued through Year 2. Information on the project follows:

	Year 1	Year 2
Accounts receivable from construction contract	$100,000	$300,000
Construction costs	105,000	192,000
Construction in progress	122,000	364,000
Partial billings on contract	100,000	420,000

Gross profit recognized on the long-term construction contract in Year 2 should be

A. $50,000

B. $108,000

C. $120,000

D. $228,000

Answer (A) is correct. *(CPA, adapted)*
REQUIRED: The gross profit recognized on the long-term construction contract.
DISCUSSION: Construction in progress includes gross profit recognized and costs incurred. Costs incurred through Year 2 equal $297,000 ($105,000 + $192,000). Hence, gross profit recognized in Year 1 and Year 2 is $67,000 ($364,000 construction in progress – $297,000 cumulative costs). Because gross profit of $17,000 was recognized in Year 1 ($122,000 construction in progress – $105,000 of costs), $50,000 ($67,000 – $17,000) should be recognized in Year 2.
Answer (B) is incorrect. The Year 2 accounts receivable minus Year 2 costs equals $108,000. Answer (C) is incorrect. Year 2 billings minus Year 2 accounts receivable equals $120,000. Answer (D) is incorrect. Year 2 billings minus Year 2 costs equals $228,000.

11. Ailouros Construction, Inc., has consistently used the percentage-of-completion method of recognizing gross profit. During Year 1, Ailouros started work on a $6 million fixed-price construction contract. The accounting records disclosed the following data for the year ended December 31, Year 1:

Costs incurred	$1,860,000
Estimated costs to complete	4,340,000
Progress billings	2,200,000
Collections	1,400,000

How much loss should Ailouros have recognized in Year 1?

A. $460,000

B. $200,000

C. $60,000

D. $0

Answer (B) is correct. *(CPA, adapted)*
REQUIRED: The loss to be recorded in the first year of a long-term construction contract.
DISCUSSION: The total of the costs incurred in Year 1 plus estimated costs to complete is $6,200,000 ($1,860,000 + $4,340,000). Because this sum exceeds the $6 million fixed-price construction contract amount, a $200,000 loss should be recognized.
Answer (A) is incorrect. The difference between the costs incurred and the collections ($1,860,000 – $1,400,000) is $460,000. Answer (C) is incorrect. The amount of $60,000 results from multiplying the loss that should be recognized by the ratio of estimated costs incurred to total costs [$1,860,000 ÷ ($1,860,000 + $4,340,000) × $200,000 = $60,000]. Answer (D) is incorrect. A loss is recognized in the period in which it occurs.

12. A company uses the completed-contract method to account for a long-term construction contract. Revenue and gross profit are recognized when recorded progress billings

	Are Collected	Exceed Recorded Costs
A.	Yes	Yes
B.	No	No
C.	Yes	No
D.	No	Yes

Answer (B) is correct. *(CPA, adapted)*
REQUIRED: The effect of the completed-contract method on revenue recognition.
DISCUSSION: Under the completed-contract method of accounting for long-term construction contracts, recorded progress billings have no effect on the recognition of revenue and gross profit.
Answer (A) is incorrect. Progress billings are accrued until the end of the project. Answer (C) is incorrect. Collection of progress billings have no effect on the completed contract's revenue recognition. Answer (D) is incorrect. The excess of billings over costs will be closed out at the completion of the contract.

13. A company uses the percentage-of-completion method to account for a 4-year construction contract. Which of the following should be used in the calculation of the gross profit recognized in the first year?

	Progress Billings	Collections on Progress Billings
A.	Yes	Yes
B.	Yes	No
C.	No	No
D.	No	Yes

Answer (C) is correct. *(CPA, adapted)*
REQUIRED: The effect that progress billings and collections have on the determination of gross profit.
DISCUSSION: Under GAAP, revenue should be recognized when it is realized or realizable and earned. For long-term construction contracts, these criteria are met in accordance with either the percentage-of-completion or the completed-contract method. Neither the issuance of a progress billing (debit accounts receivable, credit progress billings) nor the collection of cash (debit cash, credit accounts receivable) results in recognition of gross profit.
Answer (A) is incorrect. Neither progress billings nor collections on progress billings are a part of the two allowable methods: percentage-of-completion or completed-contract. Answer (B) is incorrect. Progress billings should not be used to calculate gross profit. Answer (D) is incorrect. Collections on progress billings should not be used to calculate gross profit.

14. Frame construction company's contract requires the construction of a bridge in 3 years. The expected total cost of the bridge is $2,000,000, and Frame will receive $2,500,000 for the project. The actual costs incurred to complete the project were $500,000, $900,000, and $600,000, respectively, during each of the 3 years. Progress payments received by Frame were $600,000, $1,200,000, and $700,000, respectively. Assuming that the percentage-of-completion method is used, what amount of gross profit would Frame report during the last year of the project?

A. $120,000

B. $125,000

C. $140,000

D. $150,000

Answer (D) is correct. *(CPA, adapted)*
REQUIRED: The recognized gross profit during the last year of the project.
DISCUSSION: The expected gross profit is $500,000 ($2,500,000 price – $2,000,000 expected cost). Recognized gross profit in Year 1 is $125,000 [$500,000 × ($500,000 ÷ $2,000,000)]. Cumulative recognized gross profit in Year 2 is $350,000 {$500,000 × [($500,000 + $900,000) ÷ $2,000,000]}. Recognized gross profit in Year 3 is $150,000 [($2,500,000 price – $500,000 – $900,000 – $600,000) actual gross profit – $350,000 previously recognized].
Answer (A) is incorrect. The amount of $120,000 is the recognized gross profit in the first year based on the percentage of the price paid ($600,000 ÷ $2,500,000). Answer (B) is incorrect. The amount of $125,000 is the amount recognized in the first year. Answer (C) is incorrect. The amount of $140,000 is the recognized gross profit in the third year based on the percentage of the price paid ($700,000 ÷ $2,500,000).

15. Haft Construction Co. has consistently used the percentage-of-completion method. On January 10, Year 1, Haft began work on a $3 million construction contract. At the inception date, the estimated cost of construction was $2,250,000. The following data relate to the progress of the contract:

Gross profit recognized at 12/31/Year 1	$ 300,000
Costs incurred 1/10/Year 1 through 12/31/Year 2	1,800,000
Estimated cost to complete at 12/31/Year 2	600,000

In its income statement for the year ended December 31, Year 2, what amount of gross profit should Haft report?

A. $450,000

B. $300,000

C. $262,500

D. $150,000

Answer (D) is correct. *(CPA, adapted)*
REQUIRED: The amount of gross profit reported using the percentage-of-completion method.
DISCUSSION: The percentage-of-completion method normally provides for the recognition of gross profit based on the relationship between the costs incurred to date and estimated total costs for the completion of the contract. The total anticipated gross profit is multiplied by the ratio of the costs incurred to date to the total estimated costs, and the product is reduced by previously recognized gross profit. The percentage-of-completion at 12/31/Year 2 is 75% [$1,800,000 ÷ ($1,800,000 + $600,000)]. The total anticipated gross profit is $600,000 ($3,000,000 contract price – $2,400,000 expected total costs). Consequently, a gross profit of $150,000 [($600,000 total gross profit × 75%) – $300,000 previously recognized gross profit] is recognized for Year 2.
Answer (A) is incorrect. The Year 2 gross profit equals the cumulative gross profit minus the previously recognized gross profit. Answer (B) is incorrect. The previously recognized gross profit is $300,000. Answer (C) is incorrect. The amount of $262,500 assumes the total estimated gross profit is $750,000 ($3,000,000 price – $2,250,000 originally estimated total cost).

Questions 16 and 17 are based on the following information. Data pertaining to Catus Co.'s construction jobs, which commenced during Year 1, are as follows:

	Project 1	Project 2
Contract price	$420,000	$300,000
Costs incurred during Year 1	240,000	280,000
Estimated costs to complete	120,000	40,000
Billed to customers during Year 1	150,000	270,000
Received from customers during Year 1	90,000	250,000

16. If Catus uses the completed-contract method, what amount of gross profit (loss) should Catus report in its Year 1 income statement?

A. $(20,000)

B. $0

C. $40,000

D. $420,000

Answer (A) is correct. *(CPA, adapted)*
REQUIRED: The amount of gross profit (loss) reported in the income statement under the completed-contract method.
DISCUSSION: Under the completed-contract method, gross profit is recognized when the contract is completed. Neither project will be completed by the end of Year 1. Hence, no gross profit is recognized for Project 1 even though estimated data predict a gross profit of $60,000 ($420,000 contract price – $240,000 costs incurred – $120,000 additional estimated costs). However, when the current estimate of total contract costs indicates a loss, an immediate provision for the entire loss should be made regardless of the method of accounting used. Thus, a $20,000 loss ($300,000 contract price – $280,000 costs incurred – $40,000 additional estimated costs) will be reported for Project 2.
Answer (B) is incorrect. Estimated losses must be recognized. Answer (C) is incorrect. This amount is the estimated gross profit, not what is recognized. Answer (D) is incorrect. Gross profit is not recognized until the contract is completed.

17. If Catus uses the percentage-of-completion method, what amount of gross profit (loss) should Catus report in its Year 1 income statement?

A. $(20,000)

B. $20,000

C. $22,500

D. $40,000

Answer (B) is correct. *(CPA, adapted)*
REQUIRED: The amount of gross profit (loss) reported in the income statement using the percentage-of-completion method.
DISCUSSION: Percentages of completion are normally based on the ratio of cumulative costs incurred to date to the total estimated costs. At the end of Year 1, Project 1 is 66 2/3% complete [$240,000 ÷ ($240,000 + $120,000)] and Project 2 is 87 1/2% complete [$280,000 ÷ ($280,000 + $40,000)]. Each project's percentage of completion is multiplied by its expected total gross profit. Accordingly, Catus recognizes $40,000 [($420,000 contract price – $240,000 costs incurred – $120,000 additional estimated costs) × 66 2/3%] of gross profit for Project 1. However, Project 2 estimates indicate a loss of $20,000 ($300,000 – $280,000 – $40,000). Because the full amount of a loss is reported immediately irrespective of the accounting method used, a gross profit of $20,000 [$40,000 Project 1 + $(20,000) Project 2] is recognized.
Answer (A) is incorrect. The amount of $(20,000) does not include the gross profit from Project 1. Answer (C) is incorrect. The entire loss projected for Project 2 is reported. Answer (D) is incorrect. The amount of $40,000 excludes the loss on Project 2.

18. Felidae Company uses the completed-contract method to account for a 4-year construction contract that is currently in its third year. Progress billings were recorded and collected in the third year. Based on events occurring in the third year, a loss is now anticipated on the contract. When will the effect of each of the following be reported in the company's income statement?

	Third-Year Progress Billings	Anticipated Loss
A.	Not third year	Third year
B.	Not third year	Fourth year
C.	Third year	Third year
D.	Third year	Fourth year

Answer (A) is correct. *(CPA, adapted)*
REQUIRED: The effect of progress billings and an anticipated loss on the company's income statement.
DISCUSSION: Under the completed-contract method, the gross profit on the contract should be recognized upon the completion of the contract. If a loss is anticipated, however, the loss should be recognized immediately. Under GAAP, the entries to record progress billings and their collection do not affect the recognition of gross profit or loss. Thus, the third-year progress billings have no effect on the income statement, but the loss anticipated in the third year should be recognized in full in that year.
Answer (B) is incorrect. Under the completed-contract method, an anticipated loss should be recognized in the year it occurs. Answer (C) is incorrect. Under the completed-contract method, progress billings have no effect on the recognition of gross profit. Answer (D) is incorrect. An anticipated loss is recognized immediately under the percentage-of-completion or completed-contract method.

19. Falton Co. had the following first-year amounts related to its $9,000,000 construction contract:

Actual costs incurred and paid	$2,000,000
Estimated costs to complete	6,000,000
Progress billings	1,800,000
Cash collected	1,500,000

What amount should Falton recognize as a current liability at year end, using the percentage-of-completion method?

A. $0

B. $200,000

C. $250,000

D. $300,000

Answer (A) is correct. *(CPA, adapted)*
REQUIRED: The current liability at year end, using the percentage-of-completion method.
DISCUSSION: Accumulated costs and recognized gross profit are debited to construction in progress. If the balance in this inventory account exceeds progress billings, a current asset is recorded. A liability is recorded when progress billings exceed the balance in construction in progress. Total estimated gross profit is $1,000,000 ($9,000,000 price – $2,000,000 costs – $6,000,000 estimated costs). Gross profit for the first year is $250,000 {$1,000,000 total GP × [$2,000,000 first-year costs ÷ ($2,000,000 + $6,000,000 costs to complete)]}. Thus, the balance in construction in progress ($2,000,000 + $250,000 = $2,250,000) exceeds progress billings ($1,800,000). No current liability is recognized.
Answer (B) is incorrect. The amount of $200,000 is the excess of actual paid costs over progress billings. Answer (C) is incorrect. The amount of $250,000 is the first-year gross profit recorded under the percentage-of-completion method. Answer (D) is incorrect. The amount of $300,000 is the excess of the amount billed over the amount collected.

21.2 Installment Sales

20. Cash collection is a critical event for income recognition in the

	Cost-Recovery Method	Installment Method
A.	No	No
B.	Yes	Yes
C.	No	Yes
D.	Yes	No

Answer (B) is correct. *(CPA, adapted)*
REQUIRED: The method(s), if any, under which cash collection is important for recognizing income.
DISCUSSION: When receivables are collected over an extended period and no reasonable basis exists for estimating the degree of collectibility, the installment method or the cost-recovery method of accounting may be used. Under the installment method, gross profit recognized during each period of the term of an installment receivable is equal to the gross profit ratio on the installment sales for the period in which the receivable is recognized multiplied by the amount of cash collected on that receivable during the period. The cost-recovery method recognizes gross profit only after collections exceed the cost of the item sold, that is, when the full cost has been recovered. Subsequent amounts collected are treated entirely as realized gross profit.
Answer (A) is incorrect. Cash collections are critical to the cost-recovery and installment methods. Answer (C) is incorrect. Cash collections must exceed the cost of the item sold to recognize income under the cost-recovery method. Answer (D) is incorrect. The installment method recognizes income equal to the product of cash collected and the gross profit ratio.

21. On January 2, Year 1, Ishmael Co. sold a plant to Merchant Co. for $1.5 million. On that date, the plant's carrying cost was $1 million. Merchant gave Ishmael $300,000 cash and a $1.2 million note, payable in four annual installments of $300,000 plus 12% interest. Merchant made the first principal and interest payment of $444,000 on December 31, Year 1. Ishmael uses the installment method of revenue recognition. In its Year 1 income statement, what amount of realized gross profit should Ishmael report?

A. $344,000

B. $200,000

C. $148,000

D. $100,000

Answer (B) is correct. *(CPA, adapted)*
REQUIRED: The amount of realized gross profit under the installment method of revenue recognition.
DISCUSSION: The installment method recognizes gross profit on a sale as the related receivable is collected. The amount recognized each period is the gross profit ratio (gross profit ÷ selling price) multiplied by the cash collected. In addition, interest income must be accounted for separately from the gross profit on the sale. The cash collected is the $300,000 paid to Ishmael on 1/2/Year 1, plus the $300,000 principal paid on 12/31/Year 1. The gross profit is $500,000 ($1,500,000 – $1,000,000), and the gross profit ratio is 33 1/3% ($500,000 ÷ $1,500,000). Thus, the amount of realized profit is $200,000 ($600,000 × 33 1/3%).
Answer (A) is incorrect. The amount of $344,000 includes the interest income of $144,000 ($1,200,000 × 12%). Answer (C) is incorrect. The amount of $148,000 equals the gross profit ratio applied to the total payment of interest and principal ($444,000 × 33 1/3%). Answer (D) is incorrect. The amount of $100,000 is equal to the gross profit ratio applied to $300,000.

22. Leopard Co. uses the installment sales method to recognize revenue. Customers pay the installment notes in 24 equal monthly amounts, which include 12% interest. What is the balance of an installment note receivable 6 months after the sale?

A. 75% of the original sales price.

B. Less than 75% of the original sales price.

C. The present value of the remaining monthly payments discounted at 12%.

D. Less than the present value of the remaining monthly payments discounted at 12%.

Answer (C) is correct. *(CPA, adapted)*
REQUIRED: The balance of an installment note 6 months after sale.
DISCUSSION: The balance of an installment note receivable equals the unpaid principal. The difference between the gross receivable and the unpaid principal equals interest. Thus, the balance of the note is equal to the present value of the remaining payments discounted at the contract interest rate.
Answer (A) is incorrect. The balance will be greater than 75% of the price. Because early payments contain a greater interest component than later payments, the sum of the principal components of the first six payments will be less than 25% of the price. Answer (B) is incorrect. In the early months of the note's term, the interest component of a payment is relatively high. Thus, the reduction in the principal will be lower (not greater) than the proportion of time expired. Answer (D) is incorrect. The principal balance equals the present value of the remaining payments.

23. Decorum Co., which began operations on January 1, Year 1, appropriately uses the installment method of accounting to record revenues. The following information is available for the years ended December 31, Year 1 and Year 2:

	Year 1	Year 2
Sales	$1,000,000	$2,000,000
Gross profit realized on sales made in:		
Year 1	150,000	90,000
Year 2	--	200,000
Gross profit percentages	30%	40%

What amount of installment accounts receivable should Decorum report in its December 31, Year 2, balance sheet?

A. $1,100,000

B. $1,300,000

C. $1,700,000

D. $1,900,000

Answer (C) is correct. *(CPA, adapted)*
REQUIRED: The amount of installment accounts receivable.
DISCUSSION: Gross profit realized equals the gross profit percentage times cash collected. Cash collected may be calculated by dividing gross profit realized by the gross profit percentage. Hence, cash collected on Year 1 sales was $800,000 [($150,000 + $90,000) ÷ 30%], and cash collected on Year 2 sales was $500,000 ($200,000 ÷ 40%). Because installment accounts receivable equals sales minus collections, the remaining balance of installment receivables is $1,700,000 ($1,000,000 + $2,000,000 – $800,000 – $500,000).
Answer (A) is incorrect. The amount of $1,100,000 equals total gross profit (both realized and unrealized) for Year 1 and Year 2. Answer (B) is incorrect. Total cash collected is $1,300,000. Answer (D) is incorrect. The amount of $1,900,000 equals total sales minus total gross profit for Year 1 and Year 2.

24. Curling Co., which began operations on January 2, Year 1, appropriately uses the installment sales method of accounting. The following information is available for Year 1:

Installment accounts receivable, December 31, Year 1	$800,000
Deferred gross profit, December 31, Year 1 (before recognition of realized gross profit for Year 1)	$560,000
Gross profit on sales	40%

For the year ended December 31, Year 1, cash collections and realized gross profit on sales should be

	Cash Collections	Realized Gross Profit
A.	$480,000	$320,000
B.	$480,000	$240,000
C.	$600,000	$320,000
D.	$600,000	$240,000

Answer (D) is correct. *(CPA, adapted)*

REQUIRED: The amount of cash collections and realized gross profit under the installment sales method.

DISCUSSION: Under the installment method, the periodic recognition of gross profit over the term of the installment receivable is equal to the gross profit margin on the sale multiplied by the amount of cash collected. Given that Year 1 was the first year of operations for Curling, the $560,000 of total deferred gross profit before recognition of realized gross profit represents 40% of all sales. Hence, sales during Year 1 were $1,400,000 ($560,000 ÷ 40%). The $800,000 in accounts receivable at year end is the difference between total sales and cash collections; therefore, cash collections must have been $600,000 ($1,400,000 – $800,000). Because gross profit is recognized in proportion to cash collections, the realized gross profit for Year 1 is equal to $240,000 ($600,000 cash collections × 40% gross margin).

Answer (A) is incorrect. The amount of $320,000 is the deferred gross profit after recognition of the realized gross profit, and $480,000 equals year-end installment receivables minus the deferred gross profit. Answer (B) is incorrect. The amount of $480,000 equals year-end installment receivables minus the deferred gross profit. Answer (C) is incorrect. The amount of $320,000 is the deferred gross profit after recognition of the realized gross profit.

25. On January 1, Year 1, Seven Co. sold a used machine to Union, Inc., for $525,000. On this date, the machine had a depreciated cost of $367,500. Union paid $75,000 cash on January 1, Year 1, and signed a $450,000 note bearing interest at 10%. The note was payable in three annual installments of $150,000 beginning January 1, Year 2. Seven appropriately accounted for the sale under the installment method. Union made a timely payment of the first installment on January 1, Year 2, of $195,000, which included interest of $45,000 to date of payment. At December 31, Year 2, Seven has deferred gross profit of

A. $105,000

B. $99,000

C. $90,000

D. $76,500

Answer (C) is correct. *(CPA, adapted)*

REQUIRED: The deferred gross profit.

DISCUSSION: The deferred gross profit balance at the end of Year 2 is equal to the amount of installment sales for which cash has not been collected times the gross profit margin. The uncollected amount of installment sales is $300,000 ($525,000 price – $75,000 down payment – $150,000 installment payment). The gross profit margin is 30% [($525,000 price – $367,500 carrying amount) ÷ $525,000]. Hence, the deferred gross profit is $90,000 ($300,000 × 30%).

Answer (A) is incorrect. The amount of $105,000 is equal to the $150,000 first installment payment minus the $45,000 interest. Answer (B) is incorrect. The amount of $99,000 includes 30% of the interest that will be due on January 1, Year 3. Answer (D) is incorrect. The amount of $76,500 results from deducting the interest paid as part of the first installment from the balance of the installment receivable.

26. Several of Pitt, Inc.'s customers are having cash flow problems. Information pertaining to these customers for the years ended March 31, Year 1 and Year 2, follows:

	3/31/Year 1	3/31/Year 2
Sales	$10,000	$15,000
Cost of sales	8,000	9,000
Cash collections		
on Year 1 sales	7,000	3,000
on Year 2 sales	--	12,000

If the cost-recovery method is used, what amount should Pitt report as gross profit from sales to these customers for the year ended March 31, Year 2?

A. $2,000

B. $3,000

C. $5,000

D. $15,000

Answer (C) is correct. *(CPA, adapted)*

REQUIRED: The gross profit from sales if the cost-recovery method is used.

DISCUSSION: The cost-recovery method recognizes profit only after collections exceed the cost of the item sold, that is, when the full cost has been recovered. Subsequent amounts collected are treated entirely as realized gross profit. The sum of collections in excess of costs to be recognized as gross profit is $5,000 [($3,000 of Year 2 collections on Year 1 sales + $7,000 of Year 1 collections on Year 1 sales – $8,000 cost) + ($12,000 of collections on Year 2 sales – $9,000 cost)].

Answer (A) is incorrect. The amount of $2,000 excludes the profit on Year 2 sales. Answer (B) is incorrect. The amount of $3,000 excludes the gross profit on Year 1 sales. Answer (D) is incorrect. Year 2 sales equal $15,000.

27. Feld Co., which began operations on January 1, Year 1, appropriately uses the installment method of accounting. The following information pertains to its operations for the Year 1:

Installment sales	$1,000,000
Regular sales	600,000
Cost of installment sales	500,000
Cost of regular sales	300,000
General and administrative expenses	100,000
Collections on installment sales	200,000

The balance in the deferred gross profit account in Feld's December 31, Year 1, balance sheet should be

A. $200,000

B. $320,000

C. $400,000

D. $500,000

Answer (C) is correct. *(CPA, adapted)*
REQUIRED: The deferred gross profit at the end of the first year of operations.
DISCUSSION: The installment method recognizes gross profit as collections on installment sales are made. Gross profit recognized equals the cash collected multiplied by the gross profit margin on the installment sale that gave rise to the receivable. The ending balance in the deferred gross profit account equals the year-end balance of installment accounts receivable times the gross profit margin on the installment sales. The installment accounts receivable have a year-end balance of $800,000 ($1,000,000 installment sales – $200,000 collections on installment sales). The gross profit margin is equal to the installment sales minus their cost, divided by the installment sales. As indicated below, the gross profit margin on Year 1 installment sales is 50%. At 12/31/Year 1, Feld should record a deferred gross profit of $400,000 ($800,000 × 50%).

$$\frac{\$1,000,000 - \$500,000}{\$1,000,000} = 50\% \text{ gross profit margin}$$

Answer (A) is incorrect. Collections on installment sales equal $200,000. Answer (B) is incorrect. The amount of $320,000 results from including the general and administrative expenses in the cost of installment sales. Answer (D) is incorrect. The total of deferred and recognized gross profit is $500,000.

28. Christopher Co. sells equipment on installment contracts. Which of the following statements best justifies Christopher's use of the cost-recovery method of revenue recognition to account for these installment sales?

A. The sales contract provides that title to the equipment passes to the purchaser only when all payments have been made.

B. No cash payments are due until 1 year from the date of sale.

C. Sales are subject to a high rate of return.

D. There is no reasonable basis for estimating collectibility.

Answer (D) is correct. *(CPA, adapted)*
REQUIRED: The best justification for the cost-recovery method.
DISCUSSION: Revenues ordinarily should be accounted for when a transaction is completed, with appropriate provision for uncollectible accounts. However, when no reasonable basis exists for estimating the degree of collectibility, either the installment method or the cost-recovery method may be used. The cost-recovery method recognizes gross profit only after collections exceed the cost of the item sold.
Answer (A) is incorrect. Passage of title is not a recognition criterion. Answer (B) is incorrect. A delayed due date does not necessarily indicate that collectibility cannot be reasonably estimated. Answer (C) is incorrect. A high rate of return does not necessarily indicate that collectibility cannot be reasonably estimated.

29. The following information pertains to a sale of real estate by South Co. to Nordstrom Co. on December 31, Year 1:

Carrying amount		$4,000,000
Sales price:		
Cash	$ 600,000	
Purchase money mortgage	5,400,000	6,000,000

The mortgage is payable in nine annual installments of $600,000 beginning December 31, Year 2, plus interest of 10%. The December 31, Year 2, installment was paid as scheduled, together with interest of $540,000. South uses the cost-recovery method to account for the sale. What amount of gross profit should South recognize in Year 2 from the real estate sale and its financing?

A. $1,200,000

B. $2,800,000

C. $4,800,000

D. $0

Answer (D) is correct. *(CPA, adapted)*
REQUIRED: The gross profit recognized under the cost-recovery method.
DISCUSSION: Under the cost-recovery method, gross profit is not recognized until collections exceed the cost of the item sold, that is, when the full cost has been recovered. As of 12/31/Year 2, only $1,200,000 ($600,000 + $600,000) of the $4,000,000 cost has been recovered. Consequently, no gross profit should be recognized. The $540,000 of interest received is recognized as interest income, not gross profit (price – carrying amount).
Answer (A) is incorrect. The cost recovered equals $1,200,000. Answer (B) is incorrect. The cost yet to be recovered is $2,800,000. Answer (C) is incorrect. The amount of $4,800,000 equals the price minus principal payments to date.

21.3 Consignments

30. What is the appropriate treatment for goods held on consignment?

- A. The goods should be included in ending inventory of the consignor.
- B. The goods should be included in ending inventory of the consignee.
- C. The goods should be included in cost of goods sold of the consignee only when sold.
- D. The goods should be included in cost of goods sold of the consignor when transferred to the consignee.

Answer (A) is correct. *(CPA, adapted)*
REQUIRED: The appropriate treatment of goods held on consignment.
DISCUSSION: A consignment sale is an arrangement between the owner of goods and a sales agent. Consigned goods are not sold but rather transferred to the agent (consignee) for possible sale. The consignor records sales only when the goods are sold to third parties by the consignee. Thus, unsold consigned goods are included in inventory at cost.
Answer (B) is incorrect. The consignee never records the consigned goods as an asset, but it does record an asset for the amount receivable from the consignor. Answer (C) is incorrect. The goods are not an asset of the consignee, so it cannot recognize cost of goods sold. Answer (D) is incorrect. The transfer to the consignee is not a sale. Hence, the goods are included in the cost of goods sold of the consignor only when sold to a third party.

31. Consignor Co. paid the in-transit insurance premium for consignment goods shipped to Consignee Co. In addition, Consignor advanced part of the commissions that will be due when Consignee sells the goods. Should Consignor include the in-transit insurance premium and the advanced commissions in inventory costs?

	Insurance Premiums	Advanced Commissions
A.	Yes	Yes
B.	No	No
C.	Yes	No
D.	No	Yes

Answer (C) is correct. *(CPA, adapted)*
REQUIRED: The item(s) included in a consignor's inventory costs.
DISCUSSION: Inventoriable costs include all costs of making the inventory ready for sale. Costs incurred by a consignor on the transfer of goods to a consignee are costs necessary to prepare the inventory for sale. Consequently, these costs are inventoriable, and therefore the in-transit insurance premium is inventoried. The advanced commissions constitute a receivable or prepaid expense, not an element of inventory cost.
Answer (A) is incorrect. The advanced commissions are not an element of inventory cost. Answer (B) is incorrect. The in-transit insurance premium is inventoried. Answer (D) is incorrect. The in-transit insurance premium is inventoried, but the advanced commissions are not an element of inventory cost.

32. In accounting for sales on consignment, sales revenue and the related cost of goods sold should be recognized by the

- A. Consignor when the goods are shipped to the consignee.
- B. Consignee when the goods are shipped to the third party.
- C. Consignor when notification is received that the consignee has sold the goods.
- D. Consignee when cash is received from the customer.

Answer (C) is correct. *(CIA, adapted)*
REQUIRED: The basis for recognition of sales revenue and related cost of goods sold for goods on consignment.
DISCUSSION: Under a consignment sales arrangement, the consignor ships merchandise to the consignee, who acts as agent for the consignor in selling the goods. The goods are in the physical possession of the consignee but remain the property of the consignor and are included in the consignor's inventory count. Sales revenue and the related cost of goods sold from these consigned goods should be recognized by the consignor only when the merchandise is sold and delivered to the ultimate customer. Accordingly, recognition occurs when notification is received that the consignee has sold the goods.
Answer (A) is incorrect. At the date of shipment to the consignee, the goods are still the property of the consignor. Answer (B) is incorrect. The consignee does not recognize sales revenue or cost of goods sold for these goods. The consignee recognizes commission revenue only. Answer (D) is incorrect. The consignee does not recognize sales revenue or cost of goods sold for these goods. The consignee recognizes commission revenue only when the goods are sold and delivered to the third party.

Questions 33 and 34 are based on the following information. Glazier Co. sells all of its glassware on a consignment basis. The consignees receive reimbursement of expenses plus a sales commission of 10% of retail value. During the current year, Glazier shipped 11,800 units with a cost of $24 per unit and a retail value of $44 per unit to the Glass Retailers. Freight paid by Glazier on these shipments totaled $26,600. Glass reported that it sold 9,500 units and incurred expenses relating to the sold units, exclusive of commissions, in the amount of $19,200. Glass remitted cash for the units sold minus commissions and expenses.

33. The cash collected during the year by Glazier from Glass is

  A. $208,800

  B. $357,000

  C. $186,000

  D. $398,800

Answer (B) is correct. *(CMA, adapted)*
  REQUIRED: The cash collected by the consignor.
  DISCUSSION: The consignor will receive cash equal to the sales price of the units sold, minus expenses of $19,200, minus a 10% sales commission. The units sold for $418,000 (9,500 units × $44). Cash collected equaled $357,000 [$418,000 – ($418,000 × 10%) – $19,200].
  Answer (A) is incorrect. The amount of $208,800 is based on the cost of $24 per unit, not the retail selling price, and ignores the sales commissions. Answer (C) is incorrect. The amount of $186,000 is based on the cost of $24 per unit, not the retail selling price of $44. Answer (D) is incorrect. The amount of $398,800 omits the 10% sales commission.

34. Glazier's profit before taxes from consignment sales made by Glass for the current year is

  A. $129,000

  B. $138,280

  C. $102,400

  D. $107,585

Answer (D) is correct. *(CMA, adapted)*
  REQUIRED: The consignor's profit before taxes.
  DISCUSSION: The consignor will receive cash equal to the sales price of the units sold, minus expenses of $19,200, minus a 10% sales commission. The units sold for $418,000 (9,500 units × $44). Cash collected equaled $357,000 [$418,000 – ($418,000 × 10%) – $19,200]. Freight costs attributable to the units sold were $21,415 [(9,500 units sold ÷ 11,800 units consigned) × $26,600]. Thus, pretax profit is $107,585 [$357,000 – $21,415 freight costs – (9,500 units × $24 unit cost)].
  Answer (A) is incorrect. The amount of $129,000 ignores the freight costs of $26,600. Answer (B) is incorrect. The amount of $138,280 assumes 11,800 units were sold. Answer (C) is incorrect. The amount of $102,400 expenses all of the freight costs (inventoriable costs).

35. Jel Co., a consignee, paid the freight costs for goods shipped from Dale Co., a consignor. These freight costs are to be deducted from Jel's payment to Dale when the consignment goods are sold. Until Jel sells the goods, the freight costs should be included in Jel's

  A. Cost of goods sold.

  B. Freight-out costs.

  C. Selling expenses.

  D. Accounts receivable.

Answer (D) is correct. *(CPA, adapted)*
  REQUIRED: The consignee's classification of freight costs paid by the consignee on behalf of the consignor.
  DISCUSSION: The consignee should debit consignment-in for the freight costs. Consignment-in is a receivable/payable account used by consignees. It represents the amount payable to the consignor if it has a credit balance. If it has a debit balance, it reflects the amount receivable from the consignor. Before consigned goods are sold, expenditures chargeable to the consignor are recorded in the consignment-in account as a receivable. After the consigned goods are sold, the consignee's net liability to the consignor is reflected in the account.
  Answer (A) is incorrect. A consignee does not recognize cost of goods sold. Answer (B) is incorrect. A consignee recognizes freight-in by a debit to consignment-in. Answer (C) is incorrect. The freight costs are inventoriable costs of the consignor and a receivable of the consignee.

36. On October 1, the Ajax Company consigned 100 television sets to M & R Retailers, Inc. Each television set had a cost of $150. Freight on the shipment was paid by Ajax in the amount of $200. On December 1, M & R submitted an "account sales" stating that it had sold 60 sets, and it remitted the $12,840 balance due. The remittance was net of the following deductions from the sales price of the televisions sold:

Commission	20% of sales price
Advertising	$500
Delivery and installation charges	$100

What was the total sales price of the television sets sold by M & R?

A. $13,440

B. $15,000

C. $16,800

D. $17,000

Answer (C) is correct. *(CPA, adapted)*

REQUIRED: The total sales price of the consigned goods sold during the period.

DISCUSSION: Because the television sets are on consignment from Ajax, M & R should make no accounting entry to record the receipt of the sets. The inventory should remain on the books of Ajax. A consignment-in account is used by M & R to record reimbursable expenses in connection with the consignment and sales of the consigned goods. Assuming the advertising and delivery and installation charges are expenses of Ajax, they are debits to consignment-in (reimbursable cash outlays). Moreover, the commission of 20% of the sales price due M & R should be debited to the account. The calculation of sales price is given below:

Consignment-In			
Adv.	$ 500	X	Sales
Del. & inst.	100		
Commission	.2X		
Remit to Ajax	$12,840		

$$\$500 + \$100 + .2X + \$12,840 = X$$
$$\$13,440 = X - .2X$$
$$\$13,440 = .8X$$
$$\$16,800 = X$$

Answer (A) is incorrect. The total sales price if the amount of commission is excluded is $13,440. Answer (B) is incorrect. The amount of consigned television sets multiplied by the cost per set (100 × $150) is $15,000. Answer (D) is incorrect. The total sales price plus the freight costs paid by Ajax ($16,800 + $200) is $17,000.

37. The following information was derived from the current-year accounting records of Niche Co.:

	Niche's Central Warehouse	Niche's Goods Held by Consignees
Beginning inventory	$110,000	$12,000
Purchases	480,000	60,000
Freight-in	10,000	
Transportation to consignees		5,000
Freight-out	30,000	8,000
Ending inventory	145,000	20,000

Niche's cost of sales for the current year is

A. $455,000

B. $485,000

C. $507,000

D. $512,000

Answer (D) is correct. *(CPA, adapted)*

REQUIRED: The total cost of sales for goods sold from a central warehouse and by consignees.

DISCUSSION: Cost of sales is equal to the cost of goods available for sale minus the ending inventory. Cost of goods available for sale is equal to beginning inventory, plus purchases, plus additional costs (such as freight-in and transportation to consignees) that are necessary to prepare the inventory for sale. As indicated below, the cost of sales for the inventory items held in the central warehouse is $455,000. The cost of sales for the inventory held by consignees is $57,000. Hence, total cost of sales equals $512,000 ($455,000 + $57,000). Freight-out is a selling cost and therefore not included in the determination of cost of sales.

Central Warehouse Inventory			
1/1	$110,000	$455,000	Cost of sales
Purchases	480,000		
Freight-in	10,000		
12/31	$145,000		

Consigned Inventory			
1/1	$12,000	$57,000	Cost of sales
Purchases	60,000		
Transportation	5,000		
12/31	$20,000		

Answer (A) is incorrect. The cost of sales for the central warehouse inventory is $455,000. Answer (B) is incorrect. The amount of $485,000 is the cost of sales for the central warehouse inventory assuming freight-out is included as a cost of sales. Answer (C) is incorrect. The amount of $507,000 is the cost of sales minus the cost of transportation to consignees ($512,000 – $5,000).

38. On December 1, New Co. received 505 sweaters on consignment from Olden. Olden's cost for the sweaters was $80 each, and they were priced to sell at $100. New's commission on consigned goods is 10%. At December 31, five sweaters remained. In its December 31 balance sheet, what amount should New report as payable for consigned goods?

A. $49,000

B. $45,400

C. $45,000

D. $40,400

Answer (C) is correct.   *(CPA, adapted)*
REQUIRED: The payable reported by the consignee for consigned goods.
DISCUSSION: Consignment-in is a receivable/payable account used by consignees. It is the amount payable to the consignor if it has a credit balance. The amount of the payable equals total sales minus 10% commission on the goods sold, or $45,000 {(500 × $100) sales – [(500 × $100) × 10%] commission}.
Answer (A) is incorrect. The amount of $49,000 equals sales minus 10% of the gross margin on sales. Answer (B) is incorrect. The amount of $45,400 equals the cost of 505 sweaters, plus the commissions on the 500 sweaters sold. Answer (D) is incorrect. The cost of 505 sweaters is $40,400.

39. Mora Co.'s December 31 balance sheet reported the following current assets:

Cash	$ 70,000
Accounts receivable	120,000
Inventories	60,000
Total	$250,000

An analysis of the accounts disclosed that accounts receivable consisted of the following:

Trade accounts	$ 96,000
Allowance for uncollectible accounts	(2,000)
Selling price of Mora's unsold goods out on consignment, at 130% of cost, not included in Mora's ending inventory	26,000
Total	$120,000

At December 31, the total of Mora's current assets is

A. $224,000

B. $230,000

C. $244,000

D. $270,000

Answer (C) is correct.   *(CPA, adapted)*
REQUIRED: The amount of total current assets to be reported at year end.
DISCUSSION: Under a consignment sales agreement, the goods are in the physical possession of the consignee but remain the property of the consignor and are included in the consignor's inventory. Thus, unsold consigned goods should be included in inventory at cost ($26,000 ÷ 130% = $20,000), not in receivables at their sale price. Current assets should therefore be $244,000 ($70,000 cash + $94,000 net receivables + $80,000 inventory).
Answer (A) is incorrect. The amount of $224,000 does not include the cost of the consigned goods in inventory. Answer (B) is incorrect. The amount of $230,000 results from subtracting the cost of the consigned goods from the total reported current assets. Answer (D) is incorrect. The amount of $270,000 results from adding the cost of the consigned goods to the total reported current assets.

40. Petra Co. had the following consignment transactions during December:

Inventory shipped on consignment to Rock Co.	$18,000
Freight paid by Petra	900
Inventory received on consignment from Jeter Co.	12,000
Freight paid by Jeter	500

No sales of consigned goods were made through December 31. Petra's December 31 balance sheet should include consigned inventory at

A. $12,000

B. $12,500

C. $18,000

D. $18,900

Answer (D) is correct.   *(CPA, adapted)*
REQUIRED: The recognition of inventory for consignment sales.
DISCUSSION: In a consignment, the consignor ships merchandise to the consignee, who acts as agent for the consignor in selling the goods. The goods are in the physical possession of the consignee but remain the physical property of the consignor and are included in the consignor's inventory. Costs incurred by a consignor on the transfer of goods to a consignee are inventoriable. Thus, Petra's inventory account should include $18,900 equal to the $18,000 inventory shipped to Rock on consignment and the $900 associated freight charges.
Answer (A) is incorrect. The amount of $12,000 is the inventory received from Jeter, which is not the property of Petra. Answer (B) is incorrect. The amount of $12,500 is the inventory received from Jeter and the associated freight charges. Answer (C) is incorrect. The amount of $18,000 does not include the $900 freight cost.

21.4 IFRS

41. A building contractor has a fixed-price contract to construct a large building. It is estimated that the building will take 2 years to complete. Progress billings will be sent to the customer at quarterly intervals. Which of the following describes the preferable point for revenue recognition for this contract if the outcome of the contract can be estimated reliably?

    A. After the contract is signed.

    B. As progress is made toward completion of the contract.

    C. As cash is received.

    D. When the contract is completed.

Answer (B) is correct. *(CIA, adapted)*
REQUIRED: The moment when revenue should be recognized.
DISCUSSION: Under the percentage-of-completion method, revenues and expenses are recognized based on the stage of completion at the balance sheet date if the outcome of the contract can be estimated reliably. For a fixed-price contract, the outcome can be estimated reliably if (1) total revenue can be measured reliably, (2) it is probable that the economic benefits of the contract will flow to the enterprise, (3) contract costs to complete and stage of completion can be measured reliably, and (4) contract costs can be clearly identified and measured reliably so that actual and estimated costs can be compared.
Answer (A) is incorrect. Revenue is not recognized until progress has been made toward completion. Answer (C) is incorrect. The cash basis is inappropriate. An accrual method, that is, the percentage-of-completion method, should be used. Answer (D) is incorrect. The completed-contract method is not a permissible method.

Use Gleim **EQE Test Prep** Software Download for interactive study and performance analysis.

STUDY UNIT TWENTY-TWO
FINANCIAL STATEMENT ANALYSIS

Converting the information contained in financial statements to percentage relationships often enhances financial statement analysis. Common-size analysis and ratio analysis are the primary methods based on percentage relationships.

Common-Size Analysis

Common-size financial statements are expressed in percentages. **Horizontal common-size analysis** focuses on changes in operating results and financial position during two or more accounting periods. The changes are expressed in terms of percentages of corresponding amounts in a base period.

Vertical common-size analysis concerns the relationships among financial statement items of a single accounting period expressed in terms of a percentage relationship to a base item. For example, income statement items may be expressed as percentages of sales or cost of goods sold, and balance sheet items may be expressed as a percentage of total assets.

Ratio Analysis

Ratio analysis focuses on the relationship of two or more related financial statement items. Ratios commonly measure financial attributes, such as liquidity, activity, profitability, and stability. They are used for internal comparisons of an enterprise's operations over a number of accounting periods; they also are used for external comparisons of an enterprise's performance with that of other enterprises.

Liquidity (solvency) ratios, e.g., current ratio and quick (acid-test) ratio, analyze short-term viability, that is, the ability of the entity to satisfy its short-term obligations. **Activity ratios**, e.g., receivables turnover ratio and inventory turnover ratio, analyze the enterprise's ability to generate revenue and operating income. **Profitability ratios**, e.g., earnings per share, rate of return, and price-earnings ratio, analyze the firm's effectiveness in meeting its return objectives. **Leverage ratios**, e.g., debt ratio and times-interest-earned ratio, analyze the entity's long-term solvency.

Free cash flow is an analytical measure of financial flexibility. It is the cash from operations remaining after subtracting amounts that must be paid to sustain the current level of productive capacity. The elements subtracted, however, vary in practice. Most models subtract all **capital expenditures** to arrive at free cash flow. But some authorities treat capital expenditures to increase capacity as discretionary items and do not subtract them. Some models also subtract **interest, dividends, and taxes** to arrive at free cash flow because these amounts may be viewed as nondiscretionary.

Although ratio analysis provides useful information about the efficiency of operations and the stability of financial condition, it has many **limitations**. For example, comparing ratios with **industry averages** is more useful for entities that operate within a particular industry than for conglomerates (entities that operate in a variety of industries). The effects of **inflation** on fixed assets and depreciation, inventory costs, noncurrent debt, and profitability cause misstatement of the balance sheet and income statement. Thus, fixed assets and depreciation will be understated, and inventory also will be understated if LIFO is used. Moreover, the **interest-rate** increases that accompany inflation will decrease the fair value of outstanding noncurrent debt. Many assets are recorded at historical cost, so their true fair value may not be reflected on the balance sheet. Ratio analysis may be affected by **seasonal factors**. For example, inventory and receivables may vary widely, and year-end balances may not reflect the averages for the period. Still another limitation is that **geographical locations** may affect comparability because of differences in labor markets, price levels, governmental regulation, taxation, and other factors. **Size differentials** among entities affect comparability because of differences in access to and cost of capital, economies of scale, and width of markets. Management also has an incentive to improve financial results. For example, if the current ratio is greater than 1.0, paying liabilities on the last day of the year will increase it. **Comparability** of financial statement amounts and the ratios derived from them is impaired if different entities choose different **accounting policies**. Also, changes in accounting policies may create some distortion in the comparison of the results over a period of years. In addition, ratios are based on **accounting data**, much of which is subject to **estimation**, and current performance and trends may be misinterpreted if **sufficient years** of historical analysis are not considered. Also, some data may be presented either **before or after taxes** or entities may have different **fiscal years**. Furthermore, whether a certain level of a ratio is favorable depends on the **underlying circumstances**. For example, a high quick ratio indicates high liquidity, but it may also imply that excessive cash is being held. Different ratios may yield opposite conclusions about financial health. Accordingly, the **net effects** of a set of ratios should be analyzed.

QUESTIONS

22.1 General

1. A useful tool in financial statement analysis is the common-size financial statement. What does this tool enable the financial analyst to do?

A. Evaluate financial statements of companies within a given industry of approximately the same value.

B. Determine which companies in the same industry are at approximately the same stage of development.

C. Compare the mix of assets, liabilities, capital, revenue, and expenses within a company over time or between companies within a given industry without respect to relative size.

D. Ascertain the relative potential of companies of similar size in different industries.

Answer (C) is correct. *(CPA, adapted)*
REQUIRED: The purposes of a common-size financial statement.
DISCUSSION: A common-size financial statement presents the items in a financial statement as percentages of a common base amount. In vertical common-size analysis, the items in a balance sheet are usually stated in percentages of total assets, and the items in the income statement are usually expressed as a percentage of sales. Thus, comparisons among firms in the same industry are made possible despite differences in size. Comparison of firms in different industries has drawbacks because the optimum mix of assets, liabilities, etc., will vary from industry to industry. Horizontal common-size analysis focuses on changes in operating results and financial position during two or more accounting periods. The changes are expressed in terms of percentages of corresponding amounts in a base period.
Answer (A) is incorrect. Common-size statements are designed to permit comparison of different-sized companies. Answer (B) is incorrect. Common-size statements do not reveal the stage of development of a company. Answer (D) is incorrect. Common-size statements are more useful for comparing companies in the same industries than in different ones.

2. In financial statement analysis, the expression of all financial statement figures as a percentage of base-year figures is

A. Horizontal common-size analysis.

B. Vertical common-size analysis.

C. Cross-sectional analysis.

D. Ratio analysis.

Answer (A) is correct. *(CMA, adapted)*
REQUIRED: The financial statement analysis based on the expression of financial statement figures as a percentage of base-year figures.
DISCUSSION: Horizontal common-size analysis is a percentage analysis technique in which financial data from two or more accounting periods are expressed in terms of a single designated base. Percentage analysis is a technique used to highlight trends in individual line items or accounts of financial statements.
Answer (B) is incorrect. In vertical analysis, all of the line items or accounts in a particular financial statement are presented as a percentage of a single designated line item or account in that financial statement. Answer (C) is incorrect. Cross-sectional analysis is a technique that is not time related. Answer (D) is incorrect. Ratio analysis is an analysis technique that concerns the relationship between two or more line items or accounts in the financial statements.

3. The relationship of the total debt to the total equity of a corporation is a measure of

A. Liquidity.

B. Profitability.

C. Creditor risk.

D. Solvency.

Answer (C) is correct. *(CMA, adapted)*
REQUIRED: The information provided by the debt-to-equity ratio.
DISCUSSION: The ratio of total debt to total equity is a measure of risk to creditors. It helps in the evaluation of a company's relative reliance on debt and equity financing (leverage).
Answer (A) is incorrect. Liquidity measures describe the ability of a company to meet its short-term obligations. Answer (B) is incorrect. Profitability ratios measure the relative success of a firm in earning a return on its assets, sales, equity, etc. Answer (D) is incorrect. Solvency measures describe the ability of a company to meet its short-term obligations.

4. What type of ratio is earnings per share?

A. Profitability ratio.

B. Activity ratio.

C. Liquidity ratio.

D. Leverage ratio.

Answer (A) is correct. *(Publisher, adapted)*
REQUIRED: The proper classification of the earnings-per-share ratio.
DISCUSSION: Earnings per share is a profitability ratio. It measures the level of profitability of the entity on a per-share basis.
Answer (B) is incorrect. Activity ratios measure management's efficiency in using specific resources. Answer (C) is incorrect. Liquidity ratios indicate the ability of an entity to meet short-term obligations. Answer (D) is incorrect. Leverage ratios concern the relationship of debt to equity and measure the impact of the debt on profitability and risk.

5. Are the following ratios useful in assessing the liquidity position of a company?

	Defensive-Interval Ratio	Return on Equity
A.	Yes	Yes
B.	Yes	No
C.	No	Yes
D.	No	No

Answer (B) is correct. *(CPA, adapted)*
REQUIRED: The ratio(s) useful in assessing the liquidity position of a company.
DISCUSSION: The defensive-interval ratio is equal to defensive assets divided by average daily expenditures for operations. Defensive assets include cash, short-term marketable securities, and net short-term receivables. This ratio provides information about a company's ability to survive in the absence of external cash flows. It is therefore useful in assessing liquidity (the ability to meet obligations as they mature). In contrast, return on equity is equal to net income minus preferred dividends, divided by average common equity. Return on equity provides information about the profitability of the firm. It does not provide information that is useful in assessing liquidity.
Answer (A) is incorrect. Return on equity is useful in measuring the profitability, not the liquidity, of a company. Answer (C) is incorrect. Return on equity is not useful in assessing the liquidity position. Answer (D) is incorrect. The defensive-interval ratio is useful in assessing the liquidity position.

22.2 Quick (Acid-Test) Ratio

6. Which of the following ratios is(are) useful in assessing a company's ability to meet currently maturing or short-term obligations?

	Acid-Test Ratio	Debt-to-Equity Ratio
A.	No	No
B.	No	Yes
C.	Yes	Yes
D.	Yes	No

Answer (D) is correct. *(CPA, adapted)*
REQUIRED: The ratio(s) useful in assessing a company's ability to meet currently maturing obligations.
DISCUSSION: Liquidity ratios measure the ability of a company to meet its short-term obligations. A commonly used liquidity ratio is the acid-test or quick ratio, which equals quick assets (net accounts receivable, current marketable securities, and cash) divided by current liabilities. The debt-to-equity ratio is a leverage ratio. Leverage ratios measure the impact of debt on profitability and risk.
Answer (A) is incorrect. The acid-test ratio is useful in assessing a company's ability to meet currently maturing or short-term obligations. Answer (B) is incorrect. The acid-test ratio is useful in assessing a company's ability to meet currently maturing or short-term obligations, but the debt-to-equity ratio does not exclude long-term obligations. Answer (C) is incorrect. The debt-to-equity ratio includes long-term obligations.

7. How is the average inventory used in the calculation of each of the following?

	Acid-Test (Quick) Ratio	Inventory Turnover Ratio
A.	Numerator	Numerator
B.	Numerator	Denominator
C.	Not used	Denominator
D.	Not used	Numerator

Answer (C) is correct. *(CPA, adapted)*
REQUIRED: The use of average inventories in the acid-test (quick) ratio and the inventory turnover ratio.
DISCUSSION: Assets included in the numerator of the acid-test (quick) ratio include cash, current marketable securities, and net accounts receivable. The inventory turnover ratio is equal to cost of goods sold divided by average inventory. Thus, average inventory is included in the denominator of the inventory turnover ratio but is not used in the acid-test ratio.
Answer (A) is incorrect. Average inventory is the denominator of the inventory turnover ratio. Answer (B) is incorrect. Average inventory is not used to calculate the acid-test ratio. Answer (D) is incorrect. Average inventory is not liquid enough to calculate the acid-test ratio.

8. Selected financial data from Barrymore Co. are

	As of December 31
Cash	$ 75,000
Accounts receivable (net)	225,000
Merchandise inventory	270,000
Trading securities (current)	40,000
Land and building (net)	500,000
Mortgage payable-current portion	30,000
Accounts payable and accrued liabilities	120,000
Short-term notes payable	50,000

	Year Ended December 31
Sales	$1,500,000
Cost of goods sold	900,000

Barrymore's quick (acid-test) ratio as of December 31 is

A. 3.6 to 1.

B. 3.1 to 1.

C. 2.0 to 1.

D. 1.7 to 1.

Answer (D) is correct. *(CPA, adapted)*
REQUIRED: The company's quick (acid-test) ratio.
DISCUSSION: The quick or acid-test ratio is a measure of the firm's ability to pay its maturing liabilities in the short run. It is defined as quick assets divided by current liabilities. Quick assets are current monetary assets, such as cash, current marketable securities, and net accounts receivable. The company's quick assets equal $340,000 ($75,000 + $225,000 + $40,000). The current liabilities equal $200,000 ($30,000 + $120,000 + $50,000). Dividing the $340,000 of quick assets by the $200,000 of current liabilities results in a quick (acid-test) ratio of 1.7 to 1.
Answer (A) is incorrect. The ratio of 3.6 to 1 includes inventory in the quick assets and does not include the current portion of the mortgage payable in the current liabilities. Answer (B) is incorrect. The ratio of 3.1 to 1 includes inventory in the current monetary assets. Answer (C) is incorrect. The ratio of 2.0 to 1 does not include the current portion of the mortgage payable in the current liabilities.

9. North Bank is analyzing Belle Corp.'s financial statements for a possible extension of credit. Belle's quick ratio is significantly better than the industry average. Which of the following factors should North consider as a possible limitation of using this ratio when evaluating Belle's creditworthiness?

A. Fluctuating market prices of short-term investments may adversely affect the ratio.

B. Increasing market prices for Belle's inventory may adversely affect the ratio.

C. Belle may need to sell its available-for-sale investments to meet its current obligations.

D. Belle may need to liquidate its inventory to meet its long-term obligations.

Answer (A) is correct. *(CPA, adapted)*
REQUIRED: The possible limitation of using the quick ratio to evaluate creditworthiness.
DISCUSSION: The quick ratio equals current assets minus inventory, divided by current liabilities. Because short-term marketable securities are included in the numerator, fluctuating market prices of short-term investments may adversely affect the ratio if Belle holds a substantial amount of such current assets.
Answer (B) is incorrect. Inventory is excluded from the calculation of the quick ratio. Answer (C) is incorrect. If the available-for-sale securities are not current, they are not included in the calculation of the ratio. If they are classified as current, their sale to meet current obligations is consistent with normal current assets management practices. Answer (D) is incorrect. Inventory is not liquid enough to include in the calculation of the quick ratio.

10. Given an acid-test ratio of 2.0, current assets of $5,000, and inventory of $2,000, and assuming no prepaid expenses, the value of current liabilities is

A. $1,500

B. $2,500

C. $3,500

D. $6,000

Answer (A) is correct. *(CIA, adapted)*
REQUIRED: The value of current liabilities given the acid-test ratio, current assets, and inventory.
DISCUSSION: The acid-test or quick ratio equals the ratio of the quick assets divided by current liabilities. Current assets equal the quick assets plus inventory and prepaid expenses. This question assumes that the entity has no prepaid expenses. Given current assets of $5,000, inventory of $2,000, and no prepaid expenses, the quick assets must be $3,000. Because the acid-test ratio is 2.0, the quick assets are double the current liabilities. Current liabilities therefore are equal to $1,500 ($3,000 quick assets ÷ 2.0).
Answer (B) is incorrect. The amount of $2,500 results from dividing the current assets by 2.0. Current assets include inventory, which should not be included in the calculation of the acid-test ratio. Answer (C) is incorrect. The amount of $3,500 results from adding inventory to current assets rather than subtracting it. Answer (D) is incorrect. The amount of $6,000 results from multiplying the quick assets by 2 instead of dividing by 2.

22.3 Current Ratio and Net Working Capital

11. Badoglio Co.'s current ratio is 3:1. Which of the following transactions would normally increase its current ratio?

A. Purchasing inventory on account.

B. Selling inventory on account for profit.

C. Collecting an account receivable.

D. Purchasing machinery for cash.

Answer (B) is correct. *(CPA, adapted)*
REQUIRED: The transaction that would increase a current ratio.
DISCUSSION: The current ratio is equal to current assets divided by current liabilities. Given that the company has a current ratio of 3:1, an increase in current assets or decrease in current liabilities would cause this ratio to increase. If the company sold merchandise on open account that earned a normal gross margin, receivables would be increased at the time of recording the sales revenue in an amount greater than the decrease in inventory from recording the cost of goods sold. The effect would be an increase in the current assets and no change in the current liabilities. Thus, the current ratio would be increased.
Answer (A) is incorrect. The purchase of inventory on open account increases current assets and current liabilities by the same amount. Equal increases in the numerator and denominator of a fraction that exceeds one decrease the fraction. Answer (C) is incorrect. Collecting an account receivable decreases one current asset and increases another by the same amount. Answer (D) is incorrect. Purchasing machinery for cash decreases a current asset and increases a noncurrent asset, thereby decreasing the ratio.

12. Information from Dominic Company's year-end financial statements is as follows:

	Year 1	Year 2
Current assets	$ 4,000,000	$ 4,200,000
Current liabilities	2,000,000	1,800,000
Equity	5,000,000	5,400,000
Net sales	16,600,000	17,600,000
Cost of goods sold	12,400,000	12,800,000
Operating income	1,000,000	1,100,000

What is the current ratio at December 31, Year 2?

A. 1.38 to 1.

B. 2.94 to 1.

C. 2.33 to 1.

D. 3.00 to 1.

Answer (C) is correct. *(CPA, adapted)*
REQUIRED: The current ratio at the end of the second year.
DISCUSSION: The current ratio equals current assets divided by current liabilities. For Year 2, the current ratio equals $4,200,000 divided by $1,800,000, or 2.33. The other information is irrelevant.
Answer (A) is incorrect. The current ratio is not net sales divided by cost of goods sold. Answer (B) is incorrect. The current ratio does not include income. Answer (D) is incorrect. The current ratio does not include equity.

13. At December 30, Agnon Co. had cash of $200,000, a current ratio of 1.5:1, and a quick ratio of .5:1. On December 31, all cash was used to reduce accounts payable. How did these cash payments affect the ratios?

	Current Ratio	Quick Ratio
A.	Increased	Decreased
B.	Increased	No effect
C.	Decreased	Increased
D.	Decreased	No effect

Answer (A) is correct. *(CPA, adapted)*
REQUIRED: The effect of the cash payments on the current and quick ratios.
DISCUSSION: The current ratio (1.5) equals current assets (cash, net accounts receivable, current marketable securities, certain available-for-sale and held-to-maturity securities, inventory, prepaid expenses) divided by current liabilities (accounts payable, etc.). If a ratio is greater than 1.0, equal decreases in the numerator and denominator (debit accounts payable and credit cash for $200,000) increase the ratio. The quick ratio (.5) equals quick assets divided by current liabilities. If a ratio is less than 1.0, equal decreases in the numerator and denominator (debit accounts payable and credit cash for $200,000) decrease the ratio.
Answer (B) is incorrect. The quick ratio decreased. Answer (C) is incorrect. Cash paid out for accounts payable has exactly the opposite effect. Answer (D) is incorrect. The current ratio increased.

14. In comparing the current ratios of two companies, why is it invalid to assume that the company with the higher current ratio is the better company?

A. The current ratio includes assets other than cash.

B. A high current ratio may indicate inadequate inventory on hand.

C. A high current ratio may indicate inefficient use of various assets and liabilities.

D. The two companies may define working capital in different terms.

Answer (C) is correct. *(CPA, adapted)*
REQUIRED: The reason comparison of firms' current ratios does not indicate the better company.
DISCUSSION: The current ratio measures only the ratio of current assets to current liabilities. It does not measure the efficiency of handling the individual current asset accounts. A high ratio may indicate, for example, holding of excess inventory, or retention of more cash than needed for the cash flow requirements of the firm. The weaker and less efficient company may have the higher current ratio.
Answer (A) is incorrect. The composition of the assets in the current ratio does not, by itself, indicate whether a higher or lower ratio is preferable. Answer (B) is incorrect. A high ratio more likely indicates excess inventory on hand. Answer (D) is incorrect. Working capital is always defined as the excess of current assets over current liabilities.

15. Mogul Co. wrote off obsolete inventory during the current year. What was the effect of this write-off on Mogul's ratio analysis?

A. Decrease in current ratio but not in quick ratio.

B. Decrease in quick ratio but not in current ratio.

C. Increase in current ratio but not in quick ratio.

D. Increase in quick ratio but not in current ratio.

Answer (A) is correct. *(CPA, adapted)*
REQUIRED: The effect of writing off obsolete inventory.
DISCUSSION: The entry is to debit a loss and credit inventory, an asset that is included in the numerator of the current ratio, but not the quick ratio. Hence, the write-off decreases the current ratio, but not the quick ratio.
Answer (B) is incorrect. The write-off does not affect the quick ratio. Answer (C) is incorrect. The write-off decreases the current ratio. Answer (D) is incorrect. Inventory does not affect the quick ratio.

16. Galad Corp. has current assets of $180,000 and current liabilities of $360,000. Which of the following transactions would improve Galad's current ratio?

A. Refinancing a $60,000 long-term mortgage with a short-term note.

B. Purchasing $100,000 of merchandise inventory with a short-term account payable.

C. Paying $40,000 of short-term accounts payable.

D. Collecting $20,000 of short-term accounts receivable.

Answer (B) is correct. *(CPA, adapted)*
REQUIRED: The transaction that improves the current ratio.
DISCUSSION: If a current ratio is less than 1.0, a transaction that results in equal increases in the numerator and denominator will improve the ratio. The current ratio is .5 ($180,000 ÷ $360,000). Debiting inventory and crediting accounts payable increases the ratio to .61 ($280,000 ÷ $460,000).
Answer (A) is incorrect. Refinancing a $60,000 long-term mortgage with a short-term note results in an increase in the denominator and no change in the numerator. Answer (C) is incorrect. Decreasing the denominator and the numerator by the same amount decreases a current ratio that is lower than 1.0. Answer (D) is incorrect. Collecting $20,000 of short-term accounts receivable has no effect on the amount of the numerator or denominator.

17. A company has a current ratio of 1.5. This ratio will decrease if the company

A. Receives a 10% stock dividend on one of its marketable securities.

B. Pays a large account payable that had been a current liability.

C. Borrows cash on a 9-month note.

D. Sells merchandise for more than cost and records the sale using the perpetual inventory method.

Answer (C) is correct. *(CPA, adapted)*
REQUIRED: The transaction reducing a positive current ratio.
DISCUSSION: If a current ratio is greater than 1.0, an equal increase in current assets and current liabilities, like borrowing cash on a short-term basis, decreases the ratio.
Answer (A) is incorrect. Stock dividends do not affect the carrying value of the securities. Answer (B) is incorrect. Paying a current liability decreases current assets and liabilities equally, thereby increasing the ratio. Answer (D) is incorrect. It increases the numerator with no effect on the denominator, which causes the ratio to increase.

18. Austen, Inc., uses the allowance method to account for uncollectible accounts. An account receivable that was previously determined to be uncollectible and written off was collected during September. The effect of the collection on Austen's current ratio and total working capital is

	Current Ratio	Working Capital
A.	None	None
B.	Increase	Increase
C.	Decrease	Decrease
D.	None	Increase

Answer (A) is correct. *(CMA, adapted)*
REQUIRED: The effect of the collection of a previously written off account receivable on the current ratio and total working capital.
DISCUSSION: The current ratio is the ratio of current assets to current liabilities. Working capital is equal to the difference between current assets and current liabilities. When an account receivable is written off, the allowance for uncollectible accounts and the gross receivables are decreased by the same amount. Thus, there is no effect on net accounts receivable. When an account receivable that was previously determined to be uncollectible and written off is collected, the amounts previously written off must be reestablished (debit accounts receivable, credit the allowance). This entry also has no net effect on net accounts receivable. The collection is then recorded as an equal increase in cash and a decrease in accounts receivable. The changes in these accounts are equal, so net current assets is unchanged. Because the net amount of current assets remains the same, neither the current ratio nor working capital is affected.
Answer (B) is incorrect. There is no increase in either of these accounts. Answer (C) is incorrect. There is no decrease in either of these accounts. Answer (D) is incorrect. The net amount of current assets remains the same, so neither the current ratio nor the working capital is affected.

19. If a company converts a short-term note payable into a long-term note payable, this transaction will

A. Decrease working capital only.

B. Decrease both working capital and the current ratio.

C. Increase working capital only.

D. Increase both working capital and the current ratio.

Answer (D) is correct. *(CPA, adapted)*
REQUIRED: The effect of converting a short-term note to a long-term note.
DISCUSSION: Converting a short-term note to a long-term note reduces current liabilities but not current assets. Thus, the transaction increases both working capital and the current ratio.
Answer (A) is incorrect. A reduction in current liabilities increases working capital. Answer (B) is incorrect. A reduction in current liabilities with no change in current assets increases both working capital and the current ratio. Answer (C) is incorrect. A decrease in current liabilities increases the current ratio as well as working capital.

Questions 20 and 21 are based on the following information. Calculation of ratios and the determination of other factors are considered important in analysis of financial statements. Prior to the independent events described below, the corporation concerned had current and quick ratios in excess of one to one and reported a net income (as opposed to a loss) for the period just ended. Income tax effects are to be ignored. The corporation had only one class of shares outstanding.

20. The effect of recording a 2-for-1 stock split is to

A. Decrease the current ratio, decrease working capital, and decrease book value per share.

B. Leave inventory turnover unaffected, decrease working capital, and decrease book value per share.

C. Leave working capital unaffected, decrease earnings per share, and decrease book value per share.

D. Leave working capital unaffected, decrease earnings per share, and decrease the debt-to-equity ratio.

Answer (C) is correct. *(CPA, adapted)*
REQUIRED: The effect of recording a 2-for-1 stock split.
DISCUSSION: A 2-for-1 stock split involves an increase in shares outstanding with no increase in the capital stock account. Thus, the par or stated value of the shares is adjusted so that the total is unchanged. It has no effect on assets, liabilities, working capital, or total equity. Thus, the current ratio, the working capital, and the debt-to-equity ratio are unaffected. EPS and book value per share decline because more shares are outstanding.
Answer (A) is incorrect. The current ratio, the working capital, and the debt-to-equity ratio are unaffected. Answer (B) is incorrect. None of these accounts change. Answer (D) is incorrect. The debt-to-equity ratio is unaffected.

21. Recording the payment (as distinguished from the declaration) of a cash dividend, the declaration of which was already recorded, will

A. Increase the current ratio but have no effect on working capital.

B. Decrease both the current ratio and working capital.

C. Increase both the current ratio and working capital.

D. Have no effect on the current ratio or earnings per share.

Answer (A) is correct. *(CPA, adapted)*
REQUIRED: The effect of the payment of a cash dividend.
DISCUSSION: The payment of a previously declared cash dividend reduces current assets and current liabilities equally. An equal reduction in current assets and current liabilities causes an increase in a positive (greater than 1.0) current ratio.
Answer (B) is incorrect. Working capital is not affected by the dividend payment. Answer (C) is incorrect. Paying a dividend does not increase working capital. Answer (D) is incorrect. The current ratio is increased.

22.4 Receivable and Inventory Ratios

22. The following information is available from Alden Corp.'s financial records for the current year:

Sales:

Net credit sales	$500,000
Net cash sales	250,000
	$750,000

Accounts Receivable:

Balance, January 1	$ 75,000
Balance, December 31	50,000

How many times did Alden's accounts receivable turn over in the current year?

A. 15

B. 12

C. 10

D. 8

Answer (D) is correct. *(CPA, adapted)*
REQUIRED: The accounts receivable turnover.
DISCUSSION: The accounts receivable turnover is equal to net credit sales divided by the average accounts receivable. Net credit sales is $500,000. The average accounts receivable is $62,500 [($75,000 + $50,000) ÷ 2]. Accounts receivable turnover is 8 ($500,000 ÷ $62,500).
Answer (A) is incorrect. Fifteen results from dividing total sales by ending accounts receivable. Answer (B) is incorrect. Twelve results from dividing total sales by average accounts receivable. Answer (C) is incorrect. Ten results from dividing net credit sales by ending accounts receivable.

23. Kline Co. had the following sales and accounts receivable balances at the end of the current year:

Cash sales	$1,000,000
Net credit sales	3,000,000
Net accounts receivable, 1/1	100,000
Net accounts receivable, 12/31	400,000

Assuming a 360-day year, what is Kline's average collection period for its accounts receivable?

A. 48.0 days.

B. 30.0 days.

C. 22.5 days.

D. 12.0 days.

Answer (B) is correct. *(CPA, adapted)*
REQUIRED: The average collection period for accounts receivable.
DISCUSSION: The average collection period for accounts receivable is calculated by dividing 360 days by the accounts receivable turnover. Accounts receivable turnover is equal to net credit sales divided by average accounts receivable. Average accounts receivable equals $250,000 [($100,000 beginning balance + $400,000 ending balance) ÷ 2]. Accounts receivable turnover is 12 times ($3,000,000 ÷ $250,000). Thus, the average collection period for accounts receivable is 30 days (360 days ÷ 12).
Answer (A) is incorrect. The figure of 48 days is based on a turnover rate calculated using ending accounts receivable instead of average accounts receivable. Answer (C) is incorrect. Cash sales should not be included when calculating the turnover ratio. Answer (D) is incorrect. The receivables turnover ratio is 12.

24. During the current year, Rand Co. purchased $960,000 of inventory. The cost of goods sold for the year was $900,000, and the ending inventory at December 31 was $180,000. What was the inventory turnover for the year?

A. 6.4

B. 6.0

C. 7.2

D. 5.0

Answer (B) is correct. *(CPA, adapted)*
REQUIRED: The inventory turnover.
DISCUSSION: Inventory turnover is equal to cost of goods sold divided by the average inventory. Average inventory is equal to the average of beginning inventory and ending inventory [(BI + EI) ÷ 2]. As calculated below, beginning inventory is equal to $120,000. Average inventory is therefore equal to $150,000 [($120,000 + $180,000) ÷ 2]. Inventory turnover is 6.0 ($900,000 cost of goods sold ÷ $150,000 average inventory).

Cost of goods sold	$ 900,000
Ending inventory	180,000
Goods available	$1,080,000
Purchases	(960,000)
Beginning inventory	$ 120,000

Answer (A) is incorrect. Purchases divided by average inventory equals 6.4. Answer (C) is incorrect. This figure results from dividing goods available for sale by average inventory. Answer (D) is incorrect. This figure results from dividing cost of goods sold by ending inventory.

25. On July 14, Avila Co. collected a receivable due from a major customer. Which of the following ratios is increased by this transaction?

A. Inventory turnover ratio.

B. Receivable turnover ratio.

C. Current ratio.

D. Quick ratio.

Answer (B) is correct. *(CPA, adapted)*
REQUIRED: The ratio increased by collection of a receivable.
DISCUSSION: The accounts receivable turnover is equal to net credit sales divided by the average accounts receivable. Collection of a receivable decreases the denominator and increases the ratio.
Answer (A) is incorrect. The inventory turnover ratio equals the cost of goods sold divided by the average inventory. Collection of a receivable does not affect it. Answer (C) is incorrect. A decrease in a receivable and an equal increase in cash have no effect on the current ratio. Answer (D) is incorrect. A decrease in a receivable and an equal increase in cash have no effect on the quick ratio.

26. Selected data from Baez Corporation's year-end financial statements are presented below. The difference between average and ending inventory is immaterial.

Current ratio	3.0
Quick ratio	2.0
Current liabilities	$120,000
Inventory turnover (based on cost of goods sold)	6 times
Gross profit margin	50%

Net sales for the year were

- A. $1,440,000
- B. $720,000
- C. $1,800,000
- D. $360,000

Answer (A) is correct. *(CMA, adapted)*
REQUIRED: The net sales for the year.
DISCUSSION: Net sales may be calculated indirectly from the inventory turnover ratio and the other ratios given. If the current ratio is 3.0 and current liabilities are $120,000, current assets must be $360,000 (3.0 × $120,000). Similarly, if the quick ratio is 2.0, the total quick assets must be $240,000 (2.0 × $120,000). The major difference between quick assets and current assets is that inventory is not included in the definition of quick assets. Consequently, ending inventory must be $120,000 ($360,000 – $240,000). The inventory turnover ratio (COGS ÷ average inventory) is 6. Thus, cost of goods sold must be 6 times average inventory, or $720,000, given no material difference between average and ending inventory. If the gross profit margin is 50%, the cost of goods sold percentage is 50%, cost of goods sold equals 50% of sales, and sales must be $1,440,000 ($720,000 ÷ 50%).
Answer (B) is incorrect. Cost of goods sold is $720,000. Answer (C) is incorrect. The amount of $1,800,000 is based on a 60% gross profit margin. Answer (D) is incorrect. Current assets equals $360,000.

27. Which one of the following inventory cost flow assumptions will result in a higher inventory turnover ratio in an inflationary economy?

- A. FIFO.
- B. LIFO.
- C. Weighted average.
- D. Specific identification.

Answer (B) is correct. *(CMA, adapted)*
REQUIRED: The cost flow assumption that will result in a higher inventory turnover ratio in an inflationary economy.
DISCUSSION: The inventory turnover ratio equals the cost of goods sold divided by the average inventory. LIFO assumes that the last goods purchased are the first goods sold and that the oldest goods purchased remain in inventory. The result is a higher cost of goods sold and a lower average inventory than under other inventory cost flow assumptions if prices are rising. Because cost of goods sold (the numerator) will be higher and average inventory (the denominator) will be lower than under other inventory cost flow assumptions, LIFO produces the highest inventory turnover ratio.
Answer (A) is incorrect. When prices are rising, FIFO results in a lower cost of goods sold and a higher average inventory than LIFO. Answer (C) is incorrect. When prices are rising, weighting the average dilutes the cost effect on total inventory. Answer (D) is incorrect. When prices are rising, LIFO results in a higher cost of goods sold and a lower average inventory than under other inventory cost flow assumptions.

28. Selected information from the accounting records of Bolingbroke Company follows:

Net sales	$1,800,000
Cost of goods sold	1,200,000
Inventories at January 1	336,000
Inventories at December 31	288,000

Assuming there are 300 working days per year, what is the number of days' sales in average inventories for the year?

- A. 78
- B. 72
- C. 52
- D. 48

Answer (A) is correct. *(CPA, adapted)*
REQUIRED: The number of days' sales in average inventories.
DISCUSSION: The number of days' sales in average inventories (average number of days to sell inventories) equals the number of working days in the year (300) divided by the inventory turnover ratio (COGS ÷ average inventory). COGS is given as $1,200,000, and average inventory is $312,000 [($336,000 + $288,000) ÷ 2]. The number of days' sales in average inventories is therefore 78 [300 ÷ ($1,200,000 ÷ $312,000)].
Answer (B) is incorrect. This figure results from using ending inventory rather than average inventory in the inventory turnover ratio. Answer (C) is incorrect. This figure results from using net sales rather than cost of goods sold in the inventory turnover ratio. Answer (D) is incorrect. This figure results from using net sales and ending inventory rather than cost of goods sold and average inventory in the inventory turnover ratio.

29. Which of the following ratios should be used in evaluating the effectiveness with which the company uses its assets?

	Receivables Turnover	Dividend Payout Ratio
A.	Yes	Yes
B.	No	No
C.	Yes	No
D.	No	Yes

Answer (C) is correct. *(CPA, adapted)*
REQUIRED: The ratios that should be used in evaluating the effectiveness with which assets are used by a company.
DISCUSSION: The receivables turnover is equal to net credit sales divided by average accounts receivable, which is an estimate of the number of times a year that receivables are collected. It may indicate the quality of receivables and the success of collection efforts. Accordingly, this ratio is a measure of the effectiveness with which a company uses its assets. In contrast, the dividend payout ratio is equal to the declared cash dividends divided by income available to common shareholders (net income – preferred dividends). It measures the extent to which a company distributes its assets and may be useful to investors desiring regular income from equity securities. However, the payout ratio does not reflect the efficiency and effectiveness of management.
Answer (A) is incorrect. The dividend payout ratio is not useful in evaluating the effectiveness with which the company uses its assets. Answer (B) is incorrect. The receivables turnover is useful in evaluating the effectiveness with which the company uses its assets. Answer (D) is incorrect. The receivables turnover is useful in evaluating the effectiveness with which the company uses its assets, but the dividend payout ratio is not.

30. Selected information from the accounting records of the Blackwood Company is as follows:

Net A/R at December 31, Year 7	$900,000
Net A/R at December 31, Year 8	$1,000,000
Accounts receivable turnover	5 to 1
Inventories at December 31, Year 7	$1,100,000
Inventories at December 31, Year 8	$1,200,000
Inventory turnover	4 to 1

All of the company's sales are on credit. What was the gross margin for Year 8?

A. $150,000

B. $200,000

C. $300,000

D. $400,000

Answer (A) is correct. *(CPA, adapted)*
REQUIRED: The gross margin given inventory, receivables, and the related turnover ratios.
DISCUSSION: Gross margin is net sales minus cost of goods sold. Net sales are equal to sales on credit and may be calculated from the accounts receivable turnover ratio, which is net sales divided by average receivables. The average accounts receivable is $950,000 [($900,000 + $1,000,000) ÷ 2]. Sales equal average receivables multiplied by the related turnover ratio, or $4,750,000 (5 × $950,000).
Cost of goods sold may be calculated from the inventory turnover ratio, which is cost of goods sold divided by average inventory. Average inventory is $1,150,000 [($1,100,000 + $1,200,000) ÷ 2]. Cost of goods sold equals average inventory multiplied by the inventory turnover ratio, or $4,600,000 (4 × $1,150,000). Thus, the gross margin is $150,000 ($4,750,000 net sales – $4,600,000 cost of goods sold).
Answer (B) is incorrect. The amount of $200,000 results from subtracting the ending inventory times the inventory turnover from the ending accounts receivable times the accounts receivable turnover. Answer (C) is incorrect. The amount of $300,000 results from subtracting the sum of the beginning and ending inventories times the inventory turnover from the sum of the beginning and ending accounts receivable times the accounts receivable turnover. Answer (D) is incorrect. The amount of $400,000 results from subtracting the sum of the beginning and ending accounts receivable from the sum of the beginning and ending inventories.

31. In a comparison of Year 2 with Year 1, Baliol Co.'s inventory turnover ratio increased substantially although sales and inventory amounts were essentially unchanged. Which of the following statements explains the increased inventory turnover ratio?

A. Cost of goods sold decreased.

B. Accounts receivable turnover increased.

C. Total asset turnover increased.

D. Gross profit percentage decreased.

Answer (D) is correct. *(CPA, adapted)*
REQUIRED: The statement that explains the increased inventory turnover ratio.
DISCUSSION: The inventory turnover ratio is equal to cost of goods sold divided by average inventory. If inventory is unchanged, an increase in cost of goods sold increases the inventory turnover ratio. A decrease in the gross profit percentage [(sales – cost of goods sold) ÷ sales] signifies an increase in cost of goods sold given that the amount of sales is constant.
Answer (A) is incorrect. A decrease in cost of goods sold results in a decrease in the inventory turnover ratio. Answer (B) is incorrect. The accounts receivable turnover does not affect the inventory turnover ratio. Answer (C) is incorrect. Total asset turnover does not affect the inventory turnover ratio.

32. Blasso Company's net accounts receivable were $500,000 at December 31, Year 3, and $600,000 at December 31, Year 4. Net cash sales for Year 4 were $200,000. The accounts receivable turnover for Year 4 was 5.0. What were Blasso's total net sales for Year 4?

A. $2,950,000

B. $3,000,000

C. $3,200,000

D. $5,500,000

Answer (A) is correct. *(CPA, adapted)*
REQUIRED: The net sales given accounts receivable, net cash sales, and the accounts receivable turnover.
DISCUSSION: Total sales equal cash sales plus credit sales. Blasso's cash sales were $200,000. Credit sales may be determined from the accounts receivable turnover formula, which equals net credit sales divided by average accounts receivable. Net credit sales are equal to 5.0 times average receivables [($500,000 + $600,000) ÷ 2], or $2,750,000. Total sales were equal to $2,950,000 ($2,750,000 + $200,000).
Answer (B) is incorrect. Ending accounts receivable multiplied by the accounts receivable turnover ratio equals $3,000,000. Answer (C) is incorrect. Cash sales plus the product of ending accounts receivable and the accounts receivable turnover ratio equals $3,200,000. Answer (D) is incorrect. Beginning accounts receivable plus ending accounts receivable multiplied by the accounts receivable turnover ratio equals $5,500,000.

33. If a company changes from the first-in, first-out (FIFO) inventory method to the last-in, first-out (LIFO) method during a period of rising prices, its

A. Current ratio will be reduced.

B. Inventory turnover ratio will be reduced.

C. Cash flow will be decreased.

D. Debt-to-equity ratio will be decreased.

Answer (A) is correct. *(CMA, adapted)*
REQUIRED: The effect of changing from FIFO to LIFO during a period of rising prices.
DISCUSSION: Changing from FIFO to LIFO during a period of rising prices will result in a lower inventory valuation and a higher cost of goods sold. Thus, the current ratio will be reduced because current assets are lower under LIFO.
Answer (B) is incorrect. Inventory turnover will increase. Cost of goods sold (the numerator) will increase, and the average inventory (the denominator) will decline. Answer (C) is incorrect. Cash flow will be unchanged except for the tax savings from switching to LIFO. The tax savings will result in increased cash flow. Answer (D) is incorrect. The debt-to-equity ratio will increase. Assets and equity will be lower, but debt will be unchanged.

34. Based on the data presented below, what is the cost of sales for the Canfield Corporation for Year 5?

Current ratio	3.5
Acid-test ratio	3.0
Current liabilities 12/31/Year 5	$600,000
Inventory 12/31/Year 4	$500,000
Inventory turnover	8.0

A. $1,600,000

B. $2,400,000

C. $3,200,000

D. $6,400,000

Answer (C) is correct. *(CMA, adapted)*
REQUIRED: The cost of sales given various ratios, ending liabilities, and beginning inventory.
DISCUSSION: Inventory turnover equals cost of sales divided by average inventory. The turnover ratio and the beginning inventory are known. If ending inventory can be determined, average inventory and cost of sales can also be calculated. The relationship among the current ratio, acid-test ratio, and current liabilities facilitates this calculation. The current ratio is the ratio of current assets to current liabilities. Thus, current assets are 3.5 times current liabilities. Given that current liabilities at year end are $600,000, current assets at year end must be $2,100,000 (3.5 × $600,000). The acid-test ratio is equal to the ratio of the sum of cash, net accounts receivable, and short-term marketable securities to current liabilities. Accordingly, quick assets are 3.0 times current liabilities. If current liabilities at year end are $600,000, the quick assets are $1,800,000 (3.0 × $600,000). The difference between current assets and quick assets is equal to inventory (assuming no prepaid expenses are included in current assets). Because current assets at year end are $2,100,000 and quick assets are $1,800,000, ending inventory must be $300,000. Average inventory is equal to $400,000 [($500,000 beginning inventory + $300,000 ending inventory) ÷ 2]. An inventory turnover (cost of sales ÷ average inventory) of 8.0 indicates that cost of sales is 8.0 times average inventory. Cost of sales is therefore equal to $3,200,000 (8.0 × $400,000).
Answer (A) is incorrect. The amount of $1,600,000 incorrectly uses half of average inventory in the denominator. Answer (B) is incorrect. The amount of $2,400,000 incorrectly uses ending, not average, inventory in the denominator. Answer (D) is incorrect. The amount of $6,400,000 incorrectly uses the sum, rather than the average, of beginning and ending inventory.

35. The following computations were made from Bruckner Co.'s current-year books:

| Number of days' sales in inventory | 55 |
| Number of days' sales in trade accounts receivable | 26 |

What was the number of days in Bruckner's current-year operating cycle?

A. 26

B. 40.5

C. 55

D. 81

Answer (D) is correct. *(CPA, adapted)*
REQUIRED: The number of days in the operating cycle.
DISCUSSION: The operating cycle is the time needed to turn cash into inventory, inventory into receivables, and receivables back into cash. It is equal to the sum of the number of days' sales in inventory (average number of days to sell inventory) and the number of days' sales in receivables (the average collection period). The number of days' sales in inventory is given as 55 days. The number of days' sales in receivables is given as 26 days. Hence, the number of days in the operating cycle is 81 (55 + 26).
Answer (A) is incorrect. The number of days' sales in receivables is 26. Answer (B) is incorrect. The figure of 40.5 equals the sum of the number of days' sales in inventory and the number of days' sales in receivables, divided by 2. Answer (C) is incorrect. The number of days' sales in inventory is 55.

22.5 Leverage and Profitability Ratios

36. Calderone Corp.'s equity balances, which include no accumulated other comprehensive income, were as follows at December 31:

6% noncumulative preferred stock, $100 par (liquidation value $105 per share)	$100,000
Common stock, $10 par	300,000
Retained earnings	95,000

At December 31, book value per common share was

A. $13.17

B. $13.00

C. $12.97

D. $12.80

Answer (B) is correct. *(CPA, adapted)*
REQUIRED: The book value per share of common stock at year end.
DISCUSSION: The preferred stock is noncumulative, so the equity of the preferred shareholders equals the liquidation value. The liquidation value is $105,000 (1,000 shares × $105 per share). Given total equity of $495,000 ($100,000 + $300,000 + $95,000), common equity is $390,000 ($495,000 – $105,000). Therefore, book value per share of common stock equals $13.00 ($390,000 ÷ 30,000 shares).
Answer (A) is incorrect. The sum of common stock and retained earnings divided by the shares outstanding of common stock equals $13.17. Answer (C) is incorrect. The sum of common stock and retained earnings, minus the preferred stock dividend, divided by the number of common stock shares outstanding equals $12.97. Answer (D) is incorrect. The amount of $12.80 results from deducting the preferred stock dividend from common equity and dividing by the number of common shares outstanding.

37. The ratio of earnings before interest and taxes to total interest expense is a measure of

A. Liquidity.

B. Solvency.

C. Activity.

D. Profitability.

Answer (B) is correct. *(CPA, adapted)*
REQUIRED: The function of the times-interest-earned ratio.
DISCUSSION: The ratio of earnings before interest and taxes to total interest expense is the times-interest-earned ratio. This ratio assists a creditor in estimating risk by measuring a firm's ability to pay interest expense.
Answer (A) is incorrect. The current (liquidity) ratio measures the ability to pay short-term liabilities out of current assets. Answer (C) is incorrect. Turnover ratios measure a firm's activity. Answer (D) is incorrect. EPS measures return to owners.

38. The following data pertain to Canova, Inc., for the year ended December 31:

Net sales	$ 600,000
Net income	150,000
Total assets, January 1	2,000,000
Total assets, December 31	3,000,000

What was Canova's rate of return on assets for the year?

A. 5%

B. 6%

C. 20%

D. 24%

Answer (B) is correct. *(CPA, adapted)*
REQUIRED: The rate of return on assets.
DISCUSSION: Return on assets equals net income divided by average total assets, or 6% ($150,000 ÷ $2,500,000).
Answer (A) is incorrect. Five percent results from using ending total assets instead of the average total assets. Answer (C) is incorrect. Twenty percent results from dividing net sales by ending total assets. Answer (D) is incorrect. Twenty-four percent results from dividing net sales by average total assets.

39. Cloisters Corp.'s current balance sheet reports the following equity:

5% cumulative preferred stock, par value $100 per share; 2,500 shares issued and outstanding	$250,000
Common stock, par value $3.50 per share; 100,000 shares issued and outstanding	350,000
Additional paid-in capital in excess of par value of common stock	125,000
Retained earnings	300,000
Accumulated other comprehensive income	100,000

Dividends in arrears on the preferred stock amount to $25,000. If Cloisters were to be liquidated, the preferred shareholders would receive par value plus a premium of $50,000. The book value per share of common stock is

A. $8.75

B. $8.50

C. $8.25

D. $8.00

Answer (D) is correct. *(CPA, adapted)*
REQUIRED: The book value per share of common stock upon liquidation.
DISCUSSION: Given that the preferred stock is cumulative, the liquidation value of the preferred stock equals the par value, plus the premium, plus the dividends in arrears. Liquidation value equals $325,000 ($250,000 + $50,000 + $25,000). Given total equity of $1,125,000 ($250,000 + $350,000 + $125,000 + $300,000 + $100,000), common equity is $800,000 ($1,125,000 − $325,000). Thus, book value per share of common stock equals $8.00 ($800,000 ÷ 100,000 shares outstanding).
Answer (A) is incorrect. The amount of $8.75 does not include the dividends in arrears or the premium. Answer (B) is incorrect. The amount of $8.50 does not include the premium. Answer (C) is incorrect. The amount of $8.25 does not include the dividends in arrears.

40. If Day Company has a higher rate of return on assets than Night Company, the reason may be that Day has a <List A> profit margin on sales, or a <List B> asset turnover ratio, or both.

	List A	List B
A.	Higher	Higher
B.	Higher	Lower
C.	Lower	Higher
D.	Lower	Lower

Answer (A) is correct. *(CIA, adapted)*
REQUIRED: The reason for a higher rate of return on assets.
DISCUSSION: The return on assets equals the product of the profit margin and the asset turnover.

$$Return\ on\ assets\ =\ Profit\ margin\ \times\ Asset\ turnover$$

$$\frac{Net\ income}{Assets} = \frac{Net\ income}{Sales} \times \frac{Sales}{Assets}$$

If one company has a higher return on assets than another, it may have a higher profit margin, a higher asset turnover, or both.
Answer (B) is incorrect. The asset turnover ratio does not explain a higher return on assets. Answer (C) is incorrect. A lower profit margin on sales does not explain a higher return on assets. Answer (D) is incorrect. A higher profit margin on sales or a higher asset turnover ratio may explain a higher return on assets.

41. Selected information for Dayan Company is as follows:

	December 31, Year 5	Year 6
Preferred stock, 8%, par $100, nonconvertible, noncumulative	$125,000	$125,000
Common stock	300,000	400,000
Retained earnings	75,000	185,000
Accumulated other comprehensive income	0	40,000
Dividends paid on preferred stock for year ended	10,000	10,000
Net income for year ended	60,000	120,000

Dayan's return on common equity, rounded to the nearest percentage point, for Year 6 is

A. 16%

B. 17.6%

C. 22%

D. 24%

Answer (C) is correct. *(CPA, adapted)*
REQUIRED: The return on common equity for the year.
DISCUSSION: Return on common equity is equal to the earnings available to common shareholders divided by average common equity. The numerator is therefore net income ($120,000) minus preferred dividends ($125,000 × 8% = $10,000), that is, $110,000. Average common equity is equal to the average of beginning and ending common equity, or $500,000 [($375,000 + $625,000) ÷ 2]. Thus, return on common equity equals 22% ($110,000 ÷ $500,000).
Answer (A) is incorrect. Sixteen percent results from dividing net income for Year 6 by total equity. Answer (B) is incorrect. This percentage results from dividing earnings available to common shareholders by ending common equity. Answer (D) is incorrect. This percentage results from dividing net income for Year 6 by average common equity without subtracting the preferred dividends from net income.

42. Sharif Co. has total debt of $420,000 and equity of $700,000. Sharif is seeking capital to fund an expansion. Sharif is planning to issue common stock for an additional $300,000 and is negotiating with a bank to borrow additional funds. The bank requires a debt-to-equity ratio of .75. What is the maximum additional amount Sharif will be able to borrow?

A. $225,000

B. $330,000

C. $525,000

D. $750,000

Answer (B) is correct. *(CPA, adapted)*
REQUIRED: The maximum additional borrowing allowed to satisfy a specific debt-to-equity ratio.
DISCUSSION: Sharif will have $1 million ($700,000 + $300,000) in total equity. The debt-to-equity restriction allows up to $750,000 ($1,000,000 × .75) in debt. Sharif already has $420,000 in debt, so the additional borrowing cannot exceed $330,000 ($750,000 – $420,000).
Answer (A) is incorrect. The amount of $225,000 results from multiplying the $300,000 of additional common stock by the debt-to-equity ratio. Answer (C) is incorrect. The $700,000 of equity times the debt-to-equity ratio equals $525,000. Answer (D) is incorrect. The total debt allowed is $750,000.

43. A company has 100,000 outstanding common shares with a market value of $20 per share. Dividends of $2 per share were paid in the current year, and the company has a dividend-payout ratio of 40%. The price-earnings (P-E) ratio of the company is

A. 2.5

B. 4

C. 10

D. 50

Answer (B) is correct. *(CIA, adapted)*
REQUIRED: The P-E ratio.
DISCUSSION: The P-E ratio equals the share price divided by EPS. If the dividends per share equaled $2 and the dividend-payout ratio was 40%, EPS must have been $5 ($2 ÷ .4). Accordingly, the P-E ratio is 4 ($20 share price ÷ $5 EPS).
Answer (A) is incorrect. This ratio equals EPS divided by dividends per share. Answer (C) is incorrect. Share price divided by dividends per share equals 10. Answer (D) is incorrect. Price per share divided by the dividend-payout percentage equals 50.

44. How are the following used in the calculation of the dividend-payout ratio for a company with only common stock outstanding?

	Dividends per Share	Earnings per Share	Book Value per Share
A.	Denominator	Numerator	Not used
B.	Denominator	Not used	Numerator
C.	Numerator	Denominator	Not used
D.	Numerator	Not used	Denominator

Answer (C) is correct. *(CPA, adapted)*
REQUIRED: The components of the dividend-payout ratio.
DISCUSSION: In the absence of preferred stock, the dividend-payout ratio may be stated as the dividends per share (numerator) divided by the earnings per share (denominator).
Answer (A) is incorrect. Dividends per share is the numerator and earnings per share is the denominator in the dividend-payout ratio. Answer (B) is incorrect. Dividends per share is the numerator, earnings per share is the denominator, and book value per share is not used in the dividend-payout ratio. Answer (D) is incorrect. Earnings per share is the denominator and book value per share is not used in the dividend-payout ratio.

45. Ehrenburg Company had net income of $5.3 million and earnings per share on common stock of $2.50. Included in the net income was $500,000 of bond interest expense related to its long-term debt. The income tax rate was 50%. Dividends on preferred stock were $300,000. The dividend-payout ratio on common stock was 40%. What were the dividends on common stock?

A. $1,000,000

B. $1,900,000

C. $2,000,000

D. $2,120,000

Answer (C) is correct. *(CPA, adapted)*
REQUIRED: The dividends on common stock given the dividend-payout ratio.
DISCUSSION: The dividend-payout ratio is equal to the dividends on common stock divided by the earnings available to common. If earnings available to common were $5,000,000 ($5,300,000 net income – $300,000 preferred dividends) and the payout ratio was 40%, the dividends on common stock were $2,000,000.
Answer (A) is incorrect. Taxes should not be included in this calculation. Answer (B) is incorrect. The dividends on common stock are determined by multiplying the earnings available to common shareholders by the dividend-payout ratio. Answer (D) is incorrect. The preferred dividends must be subtracted out.

46. Information concerning Rashad Company's common stock is presented below for the fiscal year ended May 31, Year 9.

Common shares outstanding	750,000
Stated value per share	$15.00
Market price per share	45.00
Year 8 dividends paid per share	4.50
Year 9 dividends paid per share	7.50
Basic earnings per share	11.25
Diluted earnings per share	9.00

The price-earnings ratio for Rashad's common stock is

A. 3.0 times.

B. 4.0 times.

C. 5.0 times.

D. 6.0 times.

Answer (C) is correct. *(CMA, adapted)*
REQUIRED: The price-earnings ratio for the common stock.
DISCUSSION: The price-earnings ratio is calculated by dividing the current market price of the stock by the earnings per share. Diluted earnings per share is used if disclosed. Thus, Rashad's price-earnings ratio is 5.0 ($45 market price ÷ $9 DEPS).
Answer (A) is incorrect. The 3.0 figure is based on the stated value per share in the denominator. Answer (B) is incorrect. The ratio of 4.0 is based on the basic earnings per share in the denominator. Answer (D) is incorrect. The ratio of 6.0 is derived by using Year 9 dividends per share in the denominator.

47. Selected financial data of Draco Corporation for the year ended December 31 are as follows. Common stock dividends were $120,000.

Operating income	$900,000
Interest expense	(100,000)
Income before income tax	$800,000
Income tax expense	(320,000)
Net income	$480,000
Preferred stock dividends	(200,000)
Net income available to common shareholders	$280,000

The times-interest-earned ratio is

A. 2.8 to 1.

B. 4.8 to 1.

C. 8.0 to 1.

D. 9.0 to 1.

Answer (D) is correct. *(CPA, adapted)*
REQUIRED: The times-interest-earned ratio.
DISCUSSION: The times-interest-earned ratio is a measure of the firm's ability to pay interest on debt. It equals earnings before interest and taxes divided by the amount of interest.

$$\frac{\$900,000}{\$100,000} = 9.0$$

Answer (A) is incorrect. The ratio of 2.8 to 1 results from dividing net income available to common shareholders by interest expense. Answer (B) is incorrect. The ratio of 4.8 to 1 results from dividing net income by interest expense. Answer (C) is incorrect. The ratio of 8.0 to 1 results from dividing income before income tax by interest expense.

22.6 Questions on More than One Ratio

Questions 48 and 49 are based on the following information. Selected data pertaining to Castile Co. for the current calendar year is as follows:

Net cash sales	$ 3,000
Cost of goods sold	18,000
Inventory at beginning of year	6,000
Purchases	24,000
Accounts receivable at beginning of year	20,000
Accounts receivable at end of year	22,000

48. The accounts receivable turnover for the current year was 5.0 times. What were Castile's current-year net credit sales?

A. $105,000

B. $107,000

C. $110,000

D. $210,000

Answer (A) is correct. *(CPA, adapted)*
REQUIRED: The net credit sales.
DISCUSSION: Credit sales may be determined from the accounts receivable turnover formula (credit sales ÷ average accounts receivable). Credit sales are equal to 5.0 times average receivables [($20,000 + $22,000) ÷ 2], or $105,000.
Answer (B) is incorrect. Ending accounts receivable multiplied by the accounts receivable turnover ratio, minus cash sales equals $107,000. Answer (C) is incorrect. Ending accounts receivable multiplied by the accounts receivable turnover ratio equals $110,000. Answer (D) is incorrect. Beginning accounts receivable plus ending accounts receivable, multiplied by the accounts receivable turnover ratio equals $210,000.

49. What was the inventory turnover for the current year?

A. 1.2 times.

B. 1.5 times.

C. 2.0 times.

D. 3.0 times.

Answer (C) is correct. *(CPA, adapted)*
REQUIRED: The inventory turnover ratio.
DISCUSSION: Inventory turnover is equal to cost of goods sold divided by average inventory. Ending inventory equals beginning inventory, plus purchases, minus cost of goods sold, or $12,000 ($6,000 + $24,000 – $18,000). Average inventory is $9,000 [($6,000 + $12,000) ÷ 2]. Inventory turnover is 2.0 times ($18,000 cost of goods sold ÷ $9,000 average inventory).
Answer (A) is incorrect. This figure uses the average of beginning inventory and purchases. Answer (B) is incorrect. This figure uses ending inventory instead of average inventory. Answer (D) is incorrect. This figure uses beginning inventory instead of average inventory.

Questions 50 through 52 are based on the following information. The following inventory and sales data are available for the current year for Dylan Company, which uses a 365-day year when computing ratios.

	November 30, Year 2	November 30, Year 1
Net credit sales	$6,205,000	
Gross receivables	350,000	$320,000
Inventory	960,000	780,000
Cost of goods sold	4,380,000	

50. Dylan Company's average number of days to collect accounts receivable for the current year is

A. 18.82 days.

B. 19.43 days.

C. 19.71 days.

D. 20.59 days.

Answer (C) is correct. *(CMA, adapted)*
REQUIRED: The average collection period.
DISCUSSION: The average collection period (the number of days' sales in receivables) equals 365 days divided by the receivables turnover (net credit sales ÷ average accounts receivable). Turnover is 18.52 times {$6,205,000 sales ÷ [($350,000 + $320,000) ÷ 2]}. Hence, the average collection period is 19.71 days (365 ÷ 18.52).
Answer (A) is incorrect. The number of 18.82 days is based on receivables of $320,000. Answer (B) is incorrect. The number of 19.43 days is based on a 360-day year. Answer (D) is incorrect. The number of 20.59 days is based on receivables of $350,000.

51. Dylan Company's average number of days to sell inventory for the current year is

A. 51.18 days.

B. 65.00 days.

C. 71.51 days.

D. 72.50 days.

Answer (D) is correct. *(CMA, adapted)*
REQUIRED: The average days to sell inventory.
DISCUSSION: The average number of days to sell inventory (the number of days' sales in inventory) equals 365 days divided by the inventory turnover (cost of goods sold ÷ average inventory). Thus, turnover is 5.0345 times {$4,380,000 COGS ÷ [($960,000 + $780,000) ÷ 2]}. The average number of days to sell inventory is 72.5 days (365 ÷ 5.0345).
Answer (A) is incorrect. The number of 51.18 days is based on sales, not cost of sales. Sales are recorded at retail prices. Answer (B) is incorrect. The number of 65.00 days is based on the beginning inventory. Answer (C) is incorrect. The number of 71.51 days is based on a 360-day year, not a 365-day year.

52. Dylan Company's operating cycle for the current year is

A. 70.61 days.

B. 93.09 days.

C. 92.21 days.

D. 99.71 days.

Answer (C) is correct. *(CMA, adapted)*
REQUIRED: The length of the firm's operating cycle.
DISCUSSION: The operating cycle is the length of time required to complete normal operating activities. Thus, the operating cycle is a cash-to-cash cycle equivalent to the average time that inventory is held plus the average time that receivables are held. Dylan holds its inventory 72.50 days [365 days ÷ ($4,380,000 COGS ÷ $870,000 average inventory)] and its receivables 19.71 days [365 days ÷ ($6,205,000 sales ÷ $335,000 average receivables)]. Its operating cycle is 92.21 days (72.50 + 19.71).
Answer (A) is incorrect. The inventory alone is held for 72.50 days. Answer (B) is incorrect. The number of 93.09 days is based on the ending receivables balance. Answer (D) is incorrect. The number of 99.71 days is based on the ending inventory.

Questions 53 through 55 are based on the following information. The selected data below pertain to Patel Company at December 31:

Quick assets	$208,000
Acid-test ratio	2.6 to 1
Current ratio	3.5 to 1
Net sales for the year	$1,800,000
Cost of sales for the year	$990,000
Average total assets for the year	$1,200,000

---

53. Patel's current liabilities at December 31 amount to

A. $59,429

B. $80,000

C. $311,538

D. $231,429

Answer (B) is correct. *(CIA, adapted)*
REQUIRED: Current liabilities at year end.
DISCUSSION: The acid-test ratio is equal to quick assets divided by current liabilities. Thus, current liabilities equal the $208,000 of quick assets divided by the 2.6 acid-test ratio. Hence, current liabilities equal $80,000.
Answer (A) is incorrect. The amount of $59,429 improperly divides the $208,000 of quick assets by the current ratio instead of by the acid-test ratio. Answer (C) is incorrect. The current liabilities at year end are not determined using the gross margin. Answer (D) is incorrect. The current liabilities at year end are not determined using the gross margin or the current ratio.

54. Patel's asset turnover for the year is

A. .667

B. 1.82

C. 0.825

D. 1.50

Answer (D) is correct. *(CIA, adapted)*
REQUIRED: The asset turnover for the year.
DISCUSSION: Asset turnover equals $1,800,000 of net sales divided by $1,200,000 of average total assets. The asset turnover for the year is therefore equal to 1.5.
Answer (A) is incorrect. Asset turnover does not equal average total assets divided by net sales. Answer (B) is incorrect. Asset turnover does not equal net sales divided by cost of sales. Answer (C) is incorrect. Asset turnover does not equal cost of sales divided by average total assets.

55. Patel's inventory balance at December 31 is

A. $72,000

B. $282,857

C. $280,000

D. $342,857

Answer (A) is correct. *(CIA, adapted)*
REQUIRED: The inventory balance at year end.
DISCUSSION: Inventory is equal to the difference between current assets and quick assets (assuming no prepaid expenses are included in current assets). The current ratio is equal to current assets divided by current liabilities. Accordingly, multiplying the current liabilities of $80,000 (determined by dividing the quick assets by the acid-test ratio) by the current ratio of 3.5 gives current assets of $280,000. Subtracting the $208,000 of quick assets from the $280,000 of current assets results in an inventory balance of $72,000.
Answer (B) is incorrect. Inventory does not equal cost of sales divided by current ratio. Answer (C) is incorrect. Inventory equals the difference between current assets and quick assets (assuming no prepaid expenses). Multiplying the current liabilities by the current ratio gives the current assets. Answer (D) is incorrect. Inventory does not equal the average assets divided by the current ratio.

Questions 56 and 57 are based on the following information. Eisenstein Co. had the following account information:

Accounts receivable	$200,000
Accounts payable	80,000
Bonds payable, due in 10 years	300,000
Cash	100,000
Interest payable, due in 3 months	10,000
Inventory	400,000
Land	250,000
Notes payable, due in 6 months	50,000
Prepaid expenses	40,000

The company has an operating cycle of 5 months.

56. The current ratio for Eisenstein is

    A. 1.68

    B. 2.14

    C. 5.00

    D. 5.29

Answer (D) is correct. *(CMA, adapted)*
    REQUIRED: The current ratio.
    DISCUSSION: The current ratio equals current assets divided by current liabilities. This company's current assets consist of accounts receivable, cash, inventory, and prepaid expenses, which total $740,000 ($200,000 + $100,000 + $400,000 + $40,000). The current liabilities consist of accounts payable, interest payable, and notes payable, which total $140,000 ($80,000 + $10,000 + $50,000). Thus, the current ratio is 5.29 ($740,000 ÷ $140,000).
    Answer (A) is incorrect. The ratio of 1.68 treats bonds payable as a current liability. Answer (B) is incorrect. The quick ratio is 2.14. Answer (C) is incorrect. This ratio excludes prepaid expenses from current assets.

57. What is the company's acid-test (quick) ratio?

    A. 0.68

    B. 1.68

    C. 2.14

    D. 2.31

Answer (C) is correct. *(CMA, adapted)*
    REQUIRED: The acid-test (quick) ratio.
    DISCUSSION: The acid-test, or quick, ratio equals quick assets divided by current liabilities. Quick assets consist of cash ($100,000) and accounts receivable ($200,000), for a total of $300,000. The current liabilities consist of accounts payable, interest payable, and notes payable, for a total of $140,000 ($80,000 + $10,000 + $50,000). Hence, the quick ratio is 2.14 ($300,000 ÷ $140,000).
    Answer (A) is incorrect. This ratio equals the quick assets divided by the sum of the current liabilities and the bonds payable. Answer (B) is incorrect. This ratio equals current assets divided by the sum of current liabilities and the bonds payable. Answer (D) is incorrect. This ratio omits interest payable from the current liabilities.

58. Obsolete inventory of $125,000 was written off during the year. This transaction

    A. Decreased the quick ratio.

    B. Increased the quick ratio.

    C. Increased net working capital.

    D. Decreased the current ratio.

Answer (D) is correct. *(CMA, adapted)*
    REQUIRED: The effect of writing off obsolete inventory.
    DISCUSSION: Writing off obsolete inventory reduced current assets but not quick assets (cash, receivables, and marketable securities). Thus, the current ratio was reduced, and the quick ratio was unaffected.
    Answer (A) is incorrect. Inventory is not included in the quick ratio calculation. Answer (B) is incorrect. The quick ratio was not affected. Answer (C) is incorrect. Working capital was decreased.

Questions 59 through 61 are based on the following information. Hopper Company is a manufacturer of industrial products and employs a calendar year for financial reporting purposes. These questions present several of Hopper's transactions during the year. Assume that total quick assets exceeded total current liabilities both before and after each transaction described. Further assume that Hopper has positive profits during the year and a credit balance throughout the year in its retained earnings account.

59. Hopper's payment of a trade account payable of $64,500 will

A. Increase the current ratio, but the quick ratio would not be affected.

B. Increase the quick ratio, but the current ratio would not be affected.

C. Increase both the current and quick ratios.

D. Decrease both the current and quick ratios.

Answer (C) is correct. *(CMA, adapted)*
REQUIRED: The effect of paying a trade account payable on the current and quick ratios.
DISCUSSION: Given that the quick assets exceed current liabilities, both the current and quick ratios exceed one because the numerator of the current ratio includes other current assets in addition to the quick assets of cash, net accounts receivable, and short-term marketable securities. An equal reduction in the numerator and the denominator, such as a payment of a trade payable, will cause each ratio to increase.
Answer (A) is incorrect. The quick ratio also would increase. Answer (B) is incorrect. The current ratio also would increase. Answer (D) is incorrect. Both the current ratio and the quick ratio would increase.

60. Hopper's purchase of raw materials for $85,000 on open account will

A. Increase the current ratio.

B. Decrease the current ratio.

C. Increase net working capital.

D. Decrease net working capital.

Answer (B) is correct. *(CMA, adapted)*
REQUIRED: The effect of a credit purchase of raw materials on the current ratio and working capital.
DISCUSSION: The purchase increases both the numerator and denominator of the current ratio by adding inventory to the numerator and payables to the denominator. Because the ratio before the purchase was greater than one, the ratio is decreased.
Answer (A) is incorrect. The current ratio is decreased. Answer (C) is incorrect. The purchase of raw materials on account has no effect on working capital. Answer (D) is incorrect. Current assets and current liabilities change by the same amount.

61. Hopper's collection of a current accounts receivable of $29,000 will

A. Increase the current ratio.

B. Decrease the current ratio and the quick ratio.

C. Increase the quick ratio.

D. Not affect the current or quick ratios.

Answer (D) is correct. *(CMA, adapted)*
REQUIRED: The effect of collection of a current account receivable on the current and quick ratios.
DISCUSSION: Collecting current accounts receivable has no effect on either the current ratio or the quick ratio because current assets, quick assets, and current liabilities are unchanged by the collection.
Answer (A) is incorrect. Collecting current accounts receivable does not change the current ratio. Answer (B) is incorrect. Collecting current accounts receivable does not change current assets, quick assets, or current liabilities, which means the current and quick ratios are not changed. Answer (C) is incorrect. Collecting current accounts receivable does not change quick assets or current liabilities, so the quick ratio is not changed.

Questions 62 through 64 are based on the following information. Ellington Company reports the following account balances at year end:

Account	Balance
Long-term debt	$200,000
Cash	50,000
Net sales	600,000
Fixed assets (net)	370,000
Tax expense	67,500
Inventory	25,000
Common stock	100,000
Interest expense	20,000
Administrative expense	35,000
Retained earnings	150,000
Accumulated other comprehensive income	50,000
Accounts payable	65,000
Accounts receivable	120,000
Cost of goods sold	400,000
Depreciation expense	10,000

Additional Information:

- The opening balance of common stock was $100,000.
- The opening balance of retained earnings was $82,500.
- The opening balance of accumulated other comprehensive income was $17,500.
- The company had 10,000 common shares outstanding all year.
- No dividends were paid during the year.

62. For the year just ended, Ellington has times-interest-earned of

A. 3.375 times.

B. 6.75 times.

C. 7.75 times.

D. 9.5 times.

Answer (C) is correct. *(CIA, adapted)*
REQUIRED: The times-interest-earned ratio (TIE).
DISCUSSION: The TIE ratio is a leverage ratio. It indicates the company's ability to pay interest expense. The ratio equals income before interest and taxes divided by interest.

$$= \frac{(\text{Sales} - \text{COGS} - \text{Administrative expense} - \text{Depreciation})}{(\text{Interest expense})}$$

$$= \frac{\$600,000 - \$400,000 - \$35,000 - \$10,000}{\$20,000}$$

$$= 7.75 \text{ times}$$

Answer (A) is incorrect. This number results from including deductions for taxes and interest in the numerator. Answer (B) is incorrect. This number results from including a deduction for interest in the numerator. Answer (D) is incorrect. This number results from failing to deduct the administrative expenses from the numerator.

63. At year end, Ellington has a book value per share of

A. $15

B. $20

C. $25

D. $30

Answer (D) is correct. *(CIA, adapted)*
REQUIRED: The book value per share at year end.
DISCUSSION: Book value per share, based on balance sheet amounts, measures the per-share amount that would be received if the company were liquidated. The ratio is calculated as common equity divided by the number of outstanding shares.

$$= \frac{\text{Common stock} + \text{Retained earnings} + \text{AOCI}}{\text{Outstanding shares}}$$

$$= \frac{\$100,000 + \$150,000 + \$50,000}{10,000 \text{ shares}}$$

$$= \underline{\$30}$$

Answer (A) is incorrect. The amount of $15 excludes retained earnings from the numerator. Answer (B) is incorrect. The amount of $20 excludes common stock from the numerator. Answer (C) is incorrect. The amount of $25 is based on average equity.

64. For the year just ended, Ellington had a rate of return on common equity, rounded to two decimals, of

   A. 27.00%

   B. 45.00%

   C. 50.47%

   D. 62.00%

Answer (A) is correct. *(CIA, adapted)*
   REQUIRED: The rate of return on common equity for the year just ended.
   DISCUSSION: Rate of return on common equity, a profitability ratio, measures the rate of return on investment. The ratio equals net income divided by average equity.

$$= \frac{(\text{Sales} - \text{COGS} - \text{Adm. expense} - \text{Deprec.} - \text{Interest} - \text{Tax})}{(\text{Beginning equity} + \text{Ending equity}) \div 2}$$

$$= \frac{\$600,000 - \$400,000 - \$35,000 - \$10,000 - \$20,000 - \$67,500}{(\$200,000 + 300,000) \div 2}$$

$$= \frac{\$67,500}{250,000}$$

$$= 27.00\%$$

   Answer (B) is incorrect. Forty-five percent excludes common stock from the denominator. Answer (C) is incorrect. This percentage excludes retained earnings from the denominator. Answer (D) is incorrect. Sixty-two percent excludes interest expense and tax expense from the numerator.

65. The issuance of new shares in a five-for-one split of common stock

   A. Decreases the book value per share of common stock.

   B. Increases the book value per share of common stock.

   C. Increases total equity.

   D. Decreases total equity.

Answer (A) is correct. *(CMA, adapted)*
   REQUIRED: The effect of a five-for-one split of common stock.
   DISCUSSION: Given that five times as many shares of stock are outstanding after the split, the book value per share of common stock is one-fifth of the former value.
   Answer (B) is incorrect. The book value per share is decreased. Answer (C) is incorrect. The stock split does not change the amount of equity. Answer (D) is incorrect. The stock split has no effect on the amount of equity it represents.

66. The issuance of serial bonds in exchange for an office building, with the first installment of the bonds due late this year,

   A. Decreases net working capital.

   B. Decreases the current ratio.

   C. Decreases the quick ratio.

   D. Affects all of the above as indicated.

Answer (D) is correct. *(CMA, adapted)*
   REQUIRED: The effect of issuing serial bonds with the first installment due late this year.
   DISCUSSION: The first installment is a current liability; thus, the amount of current liabilities increases with no corresponding increase in current assets. The effect is to decrease working capital, the current ratio, and the quick ratio.
   Answer (A) is incorrect. The bond issuance also decreases the current ratio and the quick ratio. Answer (B) is incorrect. The bond issuance also decreases the quick ratio and net working capital. Answer (C) is incorrect. The bond issuance also decreases the current ratio and net working capital.

67. The early liquidation of a noncurrent note with cash affects the

   A. Current ratio to a greater degree than the quick ratio.

   B. Quick ratio to a greater degree than the current ratio.

   C. Current and quick ratio to the same degree.

   D. Current ratio but not the quick ratio.

Answer (B) is correct. *(CMA, adapted)*
   REQUIRED: The effect of an early liquidation of a noncurrent note with cash.
   DISCUSSION: The numerators of the quick and current ratios are decreased when cash is expended. Early payment of a noncurrent liability has no effect on the denominator (current liabilities). Because the numerator of the quick ratio, which includes cash, net receivables, and marketable securities, is less than the numerator of the current ratio, which includes all current assets, the quick ratio is affected to a greater degree.
   Answer (A) is incorrect. This is the opposite of what happens. Answer (C) is incorrect. The quick ratio is affected to a greater degree than the current ratio. Answer (D) is incorrect. The quick ratio is affected.

STUDY UNIT TWENTY-THREE
GAAP ACCOUNTING FOR PARTNERSHIPS

Partnership law in the U.S. is based on the Uniform Partnership Act (UPA). However, a later version of this act, the **Revised Uniform Partnership Act (RUPA)**, has been widely adopted. Accordingly, this summary is based on the RUPA to the extent it is relevant. A **partnership**, as defined by the RUPA, is "the association of two or more persons to carry on as co-owners a business for profit." GAAP ordinarily is the same for partnerships as for corporations and proprietorships. But GAAP accounting for partners' interests is different. These differences involve the use of individual capital and drawing accounts for each partner. **Capital accounts** record the partners' initial contributions, additional investments, shares of profits and losses, withdrawals, and adjustments for ownership changes. They facilitate the accounting for partnership interests when partners elect to share differently in profits or losses. Partners' withdrawals are recorded in **drawing accounts**. Drawing accounts are nominal accounts that are closed to partnership capital at the end of each period.

Partnership Formation

Partners **contribute** cash and other property as the basis of their equity in a partnership. Cash is recorded at its nominal amount and property at its **fair value**. The equity section of the partnership balance sheet includes only the partners' capital accounts. The partners may decide that a partner's contribution exceeds the fair value of cash and tangible property contributed, e.g., because of a special talent or an established customer list. Two accounting treatments are available. Under the **bonus method**, only the fair values of cash and tangible property contributed are recorded on the partnership's books. The partners then apportion the capital accounts to reflect a partner's special contribution. Under the **goodwill method**, the partners record an asset for the perceived fair value of the intangible benefit contributed by a given partner. In practice, no objective basis is needed for this measure of the goodwill. Existing partners may make additional contributions to the partnership. The appropriate asset is debited for the nominal amount of cash or fair value of property, and that partner's capital account is credited. No reallocation of equity among the partners is made.

Distribution of Income

Distributions of profits or losses ordinarily are determined in accordance with a **profit-and-loss ratio**. Different shares also may include adjustments for salaries, bonuses, and returns on capital balances in addition to a residual profit-and-loss ratio. Returns on capital are provided to reward levels of capital investment, and provisions for salaries and bonuses usually are included to reward partners for their involvement in partnership activities. Still another possibility employed by many international accounting firms is to allocate profits and losses exclusively on the basis of capital balances, with partners required to maintain minimum balances related to levels of responsibility. However, unless the partnership agreement states otherwise, the RUPA requires partners to share profits equally and to share losses in proportion to their shares of the profits.

Admission of New Partners

New partners may contribute cash, property, or services. A partner's tangible and intangible contributions may be recognized using one of four accounting methods. (1) A **bonus** may be credited to the original partners. If the fair value of the new partner's contribution exceeds the amount credited to his/her capital account, the excess is a bonus to the existing partners. (2) **Goodwill** may be credited to the original partners. If the original partners wish to recognize an increase in total partnership capital in excess of the new partner's contribution, the excess is debited to goodwill. (3) The existing partners may **revalue** the partnership assets and recognize any increase as a **bonus** in their respective capital accounts. (4) A **bonus or goodwill** may be credited to the new partner. The existing partners acknowledge an intangible benefit brought to the partnership in addition to cash or property.

Withdrawal of Partners

When a partner withdraws, the transaction is in essence a buy-out by the remaining partners. An appraisal determines the fair values of the partnership assets, and the withdrawing partner receives cash or other property equal to his/her capital balance after the appraisal. One of three accounting methods may be used. (1) The **bonus method** does not formally recognize the results of the appraisal. The allocation of the withdrawing partner's share of the revaluation and recognition of any new goodwill is an adjustment of the remaining partners' capital based on the relative profit-and-loss percentages. (2) The **goodwill method** formally recognizes a revaluation of tangible assets, and any goodwill is recognized. (3) The **hybrid method** formally recognizes a revaluation of tangible assets, but goodwill is not recognized. When an existing partner sells his/her interest in a partnership to an outside party, the new partner is entitled to share in the partnership's profits and losses. However, (s)he is not allowed to participate in management decisions until the remaining partners agree to admit the new partner to the partnership.

Liquidation of Partnerships

When the partnership ends, the process of liquidating noncash assets and settling liabilities begins. The liquidation process has four steps. (1) **First**, any gain or loss realized from the actual sale of assets is allocated to the partners' capital accounts in accordance with the profit-and-loss ratio. (2) **Second**, remaining noncash assets are assumed to have a fair value of $0, which results in an **assumed loss** equal to their carrying amounts. This amount is allocated to the partners' accounts in accordance with the profit-and-loss ratio. (3) **Third**, if at least one of the partners' capital accounts has a deficit balance, the deficit is allocated to the remaining partners' accounts. (4) **Fourth**, the final balances in the partnership accounts equal the amounts of cash, if any, that may be distributed to the partners. **Creditors**, including partners, are paid in full before any distributions to partners. However, in practice, because partners are liable for all partnership debts, partnership creditors are paid first. After payment of creditors, any **surplus** is paid in cash to the partners. To settle partnership accounts with **credit balances**, each partner receives a distribution equal to the excess of credits over debits to his/her account. Thus, no distinction is made between distributions of capital and of profits. **Profits and losses** from liquidation of assets are credits and debits, respectively. **Prior credits** to an account include contributions made and the share of profits. **Prior debits** include distributions received and the share of losses. If a partnership account has a **debit balance**, the partner is liable to **contribute** the amount of the balance. If a partner does not make a required contribution, the other partners must pay the difference in the same proportion in which they share losses. However, a partner making an **excess contribution** may recover the excess from the other partners.

A **cash predistribution plan** (a schedule of possible losses) is prepared at the beginning of the liquidation process to avoid preparing new schedules after each transaction during the liquidation period. The plan consists of a series of maximum incremental losses potentially to be incurred during liquidation. Thus, it indicates the amount of loss that would eliminate each partner's capital balance in sequence. The purpose of the plan is to determine the amount of **cash that can safely be distributed** to the partners.

EXAMPLE: William Rosecrans, Braxton Bragg, and George Thomas decide to dissolve their partnership.

	Assets		Liabilities and Equity
Cash	$ 20,000	Accounts payable	$ 10,000
Inventory	4,000	Loan from Rosecrans	40,000
Equipment	6,000	Bragg, capital	20,000
Building	110,000	Rosecrans, capital	60,000
		Thomas, capital	10,000
Total	$140,000	Total	$140,000

The maximum loss that would eliminate each partner's capital balance is calculated.

	Beginning of Liquidation	Profit/Loss Allocation	Maximum Loss
Bragg, capital	$20,000	25%	$ 80,000
Rosecrans, capital	60,000	50%	120,000
Thomas, capital	10,000	25%	40,000

George Thomas is the most vulnerable. A loss of $40,000 eliminates his interest in the partnership.

	Bragg, Capital	Rosecrans, Capital	Thomas, Capital
Beginning balances	$20,000	$60,000	$10,000
Assumed $40,000 loss	(10,000)	(20,000)	(10,000)
Balances after Step 1	$10,000	$40,000	$ 0

The next maximum loss is calculated. Bragg's share is 33% (25% ÷ 75%). Rosecrans' is 67% (50% ÷ 75%).

	Beginning of Step 2	Loss Allocation	Maximum Loss
Bragg, capital	$10,000	33%	$30,303
Rosecrans, capital	40,000	67%	59,701

Bragg is the next most vulnerable. A further loss of $30,303 eliminates his interest.

	Bragg, Capital	Rosecrans, Capital
Beginning balances	$10,000	$40,000
Assumed $30,303 loss	(10,000)	(20,303)
Balances after Step 2	$ 0	$19,697

Given three partners, only three incremental losses will eliminate the partnership's capital.

	Bragg, Capital	Rosecrans, Capital	Thomas, Capital
Beginning balances	$20,000	$60,000	$10,000
Assumed $40,000 loss	(10,000)	(20,000)	(10,000)
Balances after Step 1	$10,000	$40,000	$ 0
Assumed $30,303 loss	(10,000)	(20,303)	
Balances after Step 2	$ 0	$19,697	
Assumed $19,697 loss		(19,697)	
Final balance		$ 0	

If each successive loss in reverse does not occur, that amount of cash may safely be distributed to the partners. As cash becomes available after the partnership's liabilities are settled, it is safe to distribute the first $19,697 to Rosecrans. If a further $30,303 becomes available, it can be distributed $20,303 to Rosecrans and $10,000 to Bragg. Any additional cash may be distributed to all three partners.

QUESTIONS

23.1 Partnership Formation

1. The Revised Uniform Partnership Act defines a partnership as

A. Any association of two or more persons or entities.

B. An association of two or more persons to carry on as co-owners a business for profit.

C. A separate legal entity for most legal purposes.

D. An entity created by following statutory requirements.

Answer (B) is correct. *(Publisher, adapted)*
REQUIRED: The definition of a partnership.
DISCUSSION: A partnership, as defined by the Revised Uniform Partnership Act, is "the association of two or more persons to carry on as co-owners a business for profit."
Answer (A) is incorrect. A partnership must be a profit-oriented business arrangement among co-owners. Answer (C) is incorrect. A partnership is viewed for most legal purposes as a group of individuals rather than a separate entity. Answer (D) is incorrect. No statutory requirements need be met to create a general partnership. A partnership may arise regardless of the intent of the parties when an arrangement satisfies the definition. However, specific statutory requirements must be followed to create a limited partnership.

2. Pilates and Wesson drafted a partnership agreement that lists the following assets contributed at the partnership's formation:

	Contributed by	
	Pilates	Wesson
Cash	$40,000	$60,000
Inventory	--	30,000
Building	--	80,000
Furniture and equipment	30,000	--

The building is subject to a mortgage of $20,000, which the partnership has assumed. The partnership agreement also specifies that profits and losses are to be distributed evenly. What amounts should be recorded as capital for Pilates and Wesson at the formation of the partnership?

	Pilates	Wesson
A.	$70,000	$170,000
B.	$70,000	$150,000
C.	$110,000	$110,000
D.	$120,000	$120,000

Answer (B) is correct. *(CPA, adapted)*
REQUIRED: The capital balances of partners at the formation of the partnership.
DISCUSSION: The balances should reflect the fair values of the assets contributed. The building should be valued net of the mortgage. Hence, the capital balances for Pilates and Wesson are $70,000 ($40,000 + $30,000) and $150,000 ($60,000 + $30,000 + $80,000 – $20,000), respectively.
Answer (A) is incorrect. The building should be included net of the mortgage. Answer (C) is incorrect. The partners did not agree to divide capital equally. Answer (D) is incorrect. The partners did not agree to divide capital equally, and the building should be included net of the mortgage.

3. The Gray-Redd Partnership was formed on January 2 of the current year. Under the partnership agreement, each partner has an equal initial capital balance accounted for under the goodwill method. Partnership net income or loss is allocated 60% to Gray and 40% to Redd. To form the partnership, Gray originally contributed assets costing $30,000 with a fair value of $60,000 on January 2 of the current year, and Redd contributed $20,000 in cash. Drawings by the partners during the current year totaled $3,000 by Gray and $9,000 by Redd. The partnership's current-year net income was $25,000. Redd's initial capital balance in the partnership is

A. $20,000

B. $25,000

C. $40,000

D. $60,000

Answer (D) is correct. *(CPA, adapted)*
REQUIRED: The initial capital balance credited to Redd based on the goodwill method.
DISCUSSION: If $60,000 (the fair value of Gray's original contribution) is 50% of the partnership capital, the total initial capital is $120,000, and goodwill of $40,000 should be recognized ($120,000 – $60,000 – $20,000 cash contributed by Redd). Thus, Redd's initial capital is $60,000.
Answer (A) is incorrect. Redd's initial cash contribution is $20,000. Answer (B) is incorrect. The amount of $25,000 equals 50% of the cost of assets contributed by Gray plus the cash contributed by Redd. Answer (C) is incorrect. The goodwill recorded is $40,000.

4. Byrd and Katt formed a partnership and agreed to divide initial capital equally, even though Byrd contributed $200,000 and Katt contributed $168,000 in identifiable assets. Under the bonus approach to adjust the capital accounts, Katt's unidentifiable asset should be debited for

- A. $92,000
- B. $32,000
- C. $16,000
- D. $0

Answer (D) is correct. *(CPA, adapted)*
REQUIRED: The unidentifiable asset debited under the bonus approach.
DISCUSSION: The goodwill and the bonus methods are two means of adjusting for differences between the carrying amount and the fair value of partnership net assets. Under the goodwill method, assets are revalued. Under the bonus method, assets are not revalued. Instead, adjustments are made to partnership capital accounts. Consequently, total partnership capital differs between the two methods, and an unidentifiable asset may be debited under the goodwill but not the bonus method.
Answer (A) is incorrect. The amount of $92,000 is 50% of the balance in each partner's capital account under the bonus method. Answer (B) is incorrect. The unidentifiable asset recognized under the goodwill method is $32,000. Answer (C) is incorrect. The amount transferred from Byrd's capital account to Katt's capital account under the bonus method is $16,000.

5. When property other than cash is invested in a partnership, at what amount should the noncash property be credited to the contributing partner's capital account?

- A. Fair value at the date of contribution.
- B. Contributing partner's original cost.
- C. Assessed valuation for property tax purposes.
- D. Contributing partner's tax basis.

Answer (A) is correct. *(CPA, adapted)*
REQUIRED: The credit to the contributing partner's capital account when noncash assets are invested.
DISCUSSION: The capital account should be credited for the current fair value of the assets at the date of the contribution.
Answer (B) is incorrect. Cost does not reflect depreciation or appreciation of the property. Answer (C) is incorrect. Fair value best reflects the economic substance of the transaction. Answer (D) is incorrect. Tax basis is determined differently than the true economic value of the property.

6. Partnership capital and drawing accounts are similar to the corporate

- A. Paid-in capital, retained earnings, and dividends accounts.
- B. Retained earnings account.
- C. Paid-in capital and retained earnings accounts.
- D. Preferred and common stock accounts.

Answer (A) is correct. *(Publisher, adapted)*
REQUIRED: The corporate accounts similar to partnership capital and drawing accounts.
DISCUSSION: Partnership capital accounts are similar to corporate paid-in capital and retained earnings accounts. Partnership drawing accounts are similar to corporate dividends accounts. They are nominal accounts that are closed to partnership capital and corporate retained earnings, respectively, at the end of each period.

23.2 Distribution of Income

7. The partnership agreement of Moe, Berg & Tyrus provides for the year-end allocation of net income in the following order:

- First, Moe is to receive 10% of net income up to $100,000 and 20% over $100,000.
- Second, Berg and Tyrus are each to receive 5% of the remaining income over $150,000.
- The balance of income is to be allocated equally among the three partners.

The partnership's net income was $250,000 before any allocations to partners. What amount should be allocated to Moe?

- A. $101,000
- B. $106,667
- C. $108,000
- D. $110,000

Answer (C) is correct. *(CPA, adapted)*
REQUIRED: The amount of partnership net income allocated to Moe.
DISCUSSION: Partners may elect to allocate income on any basis that is legal. Common elements of an income distribution are salary, bonus, return on capital, and a residual ratio. This agreement includes bonus and residual ratio provisions. Moe initially receives $40,000 {($100,000 × 10%) + [($250,000 – $100,000) × 20%]}. The remaining income is $210,000 ($250,000 – $40,000). Of this amount, Berg and Tyrus each receive $3,000 [($210,000 – $150,000) × 5%], a total of $6,000. The balance is allocated equally [($250,000 – $40,000 – $6,000) ÷ 3 = $68,000]. Thus, Moe receives a total of $108,000 ($40,000 + $68,000).
Answer (A) is incorrect. The amount of $101,000 omits the 10% of net income up to $100,000 paid to Moe. Answer (B) is incorrect. The amount of $106,667 assumes, in the calculation of amounts paid to Berg and Tyrus, that the remaining income over $150,000 is $100,000. Answer (D) is incorrect. The amount of $110,000 omits the 5% of remaining income over $150,000 paid to both Berg and Tyrus.

8. If the partnership agreement does not specify how income is to be allocated, profits should be allocated

    A. Equally.

    B. In proportion to the weighted average of capital invested during the period.

    C. Equitably so that partners are compensated for the time and effort expended on behalf of the partnership.

    D. In accordance with an established ratio.

Answer (A) is correct. *(Publisher, adapted)*
    REQUIRED: The profit and loss allocation among partners absent a provision in the partnership agreement.
    DISCUSSION: Under the RUPA, profits are to be distributed equally among partners, and losses are to be distributed in the same manner as profits unless the partnership agreement provides otherwise. This equal distribution should be based on the number of partners rather than in proportion to the partners' capital balances.
    Answer (B) is incorrect. The RUPA assumes that the partners intended an equal distribution if their agreement is silent on the issue. Answer (C) is incorrect. An equitable distribution depends on the circumstances of the individual partnership. Thus, a distribution on all equitable basis must be defined in the partnership agreement. Answer (D) is incorrect. Whenever a partnership agreement is silent on the matter, profits and losses are distributed equally.

9. Moore, the active partner in Moore & Besser, receives an annual bonus of 25% of partnership net income after deducting the bonus. For the current year ended December 31, partnership net income before the bonus amounted to $300,000. Moore's current-year bonus should be

    A. $56,250

    B. $60,000

    C. $75,000

    D. $100,000

Answer (B) is correct. *(CPA, adapted)*
    REQUIRED: The amount of a bonus defined as a percentage of income after deduction of the bonus.
    DISCUSSION: Calculating the bonus requires formulating an equation with one unknown. The bonus is formulated by subtracting the bonus variable B from net income and multiplying the result by 25%.

$$
\begin{aligned}
B &= .25(NI - B) \\
B &= .25(\$300,000 - B) \\
B &= \$75,000 - .25B \\
1.25B &= \$75,000 \\
B &= \$60,000
\end{aligned}
$$

    Answer (A) is incorrect. The amount of $56,250 is the result of taking 25% of $300,000, subtracting that amount from $300,000, and then multiplying the remainder by 25%. Answer (C) is incorrect. The amount of $75,000 is 25% of the net income before the bonus. Answer (D) is incorrect. The amount of $100,000 is 25% of the sum of net income plus the bonus.

10. Kaspar and Karp formed a partnership on January 2 and agreed to share profits 90% and 10%, respectively. Kaspar contributed capital of $25,000. Karp contributed no capital but has a specialized expertise and manages the firm full-time. There were no withdrawals during the year. The partnership agreement provides that capital accounts are to be credited annually with interest at 5% of beginning capital; Karp is to be paid a salary of $1,000 a month; Karp is to receive a bonus of 20% of income calculated before deducting her salary, the bonus, and interest on both capital accounts; and bonus, interest, and Karp's salary are to be considered partnership expenses. The partnership annual income statement follows:

Revenues	$96,450
Expenses (including salary, interest, and bonus)	(49,700)
Net income	$46,750

What is Karp's bonus?

    A. $11,688

    B. $12,000

    C. $14,687

    D. $15,000

Answer (D) is correct. *(CPA, adapted)*
    REQUIRED: The amount of a bonus calculated as a percentage of income before salary and interest.
    DISCUSSION: The bonus payable to Karp is equal to 20% of the income before deduction of her salary and interest on both capital accounts. Net income after deduction of salary, interest, and the bonus is $46,750. The solution requires adding back salary ($1,000 × 12 months), interest ($25,000 × 5%), and the bonus (B) to the net income. The bonus (B) equals 20% of the sum of these items.

$$
\begin{aligned}
B &= .2(\$46,750 + \$12,000 + \$1,250 + B) \\
B &= .2(\$60,000 + B) \\
B &= \$12,000 + .2B \\
.8B &= \$12,000 \\
B &= \$15,000
\end{aligned}
$$

    Answer (A) is incorrect. The amount of $11,688 results from omitting salary and interest from the bonus computation. Answer (B) is incorrect. The salary is $12,000. Answer (C) is incorrect. The amount of $14,687 results from omitting interest from the bonus computation.

11. The Oxide and Ferris partnership agreement provides for Oxide to receive a 20% bonus on profits before the bonus. Remaining profits and losses are divided between Oxide and Ferris in the ratio of 2 to 3, respectively. Which partner has a greater advantage when the partnership has a profit and when it has a loss?

	Profit	Loss
A.	Oxide	Ferris
B.	Oxide	Oxide
C.	Ferris	Oxide
D.	Ferris	Ferris

Answer (B) is correct. *(CPA, adapted)*
REQUIRED: The partner with a greater advantage when the partnership has a profit and when it has a loss.
DISCUSSION: When the partnership has a loss, Ferris is allocated 60% and Oxide 40%. Hence, Oxide has the advantage when the partnership has a loss. When the partnership has a profit, Oxide receives 20% plus 40% of the remaining 80%, a total of 52% [20% + (40% × 80%)]. Thus, Oxide also has the advantage in this situation.
Answer (A) is incorrect. Oxide has the advantage in the case of a loss. Answer (C) is incorrect. Oxide has the advantage in the case of a profit. Answer (D) is incorrect. Oxide has the advantage in the case of either a profit or a loss. Oxide's bonus is computed before any distribution of profit or loss.

12. The partnership agreement of Orion and Hunt provides that interest at 10% per year is to be credited to each partner on the basis of weighted-average capital balances. A summary of Hunt's capital account for the current year ended December 31 is as follows:

Balance, January 1	$280,000
Additional investment, July 1	80,000
Withdrawal, August 1	(30,000)
Balance, December 31	330,000

What amount of interest should be credited to Hunt's capital account for the current year?

A. $28,000

B. $30,750

C. $33,000

D. $36,000

Answer (B) is correct. *(CPA, adapted)*
REQUIRED: The amount of interest credited to Hunt's capital account.
DISCUSSION: Hunt's balance was $280,000 for 6 months, $360,000 for 1 month, and $330,000 for 5 months. Consequently, the weighted-average balance was $307,500, as shown below, and interest was $30,750 ($307,500 × 10%).

$$\$280,000 \times (6 \div 12) = \$140,000$$
$$\$360,000 \times (1 \div 12) = 30,000$$
$$\$330,000 \times (5 \div 12) = \underline{137,500}$$
$$\underline{\$307,500}$$

Answer (A) is incorrect. The amount of $28,000 is based on the beginning balance. Answer (C) is incorrect. The amount of $33,000 is based on the year-end balance. Answer (D) is incorrect. The amount of $36,000 is based on the July 1 balance.

13. Porter and Saint-Lucie are partners who share profits and losses in the ratio of 6:4, respectively. Porter's salary is $20,000 and Saint-Lucie's is $10,000. The partners also are paid interest on their average capital balances. In the year just ended, Porter received $10,000 of interest and Saint-Lucie $4,000. The profit and loss allocation is determined after deductions for the salary and interest payments. If Saint-Lucie's share of partnership income was $40,000 for the year, what was the total partnership income?

A. $65,000

B. $95,000

C. $100,000

D. $109,000

Answer (D) is correct. *(P. Lockett)*
REQUIRED: The partnership income given the distribution of income to one partner.
DISCUSSION: Given that Saint-Lucie's share of partnership income was $40,000, her share of residual income must have been $26,000 ($40,000 – $10,000 salary – $4,000 interest on his average capital balance). This amount represents 40% of the residual income, so total residual income was $65,000 ($26,000 ÷ 40%). Consequently, Porter's share of residual income was $39,000 ($65,000 × 60%). Moreover, Porter's share of partnership income was equal to $69,000 ($10,000 interest + $20,000 salary + $39,000 residual income). Total partnership income was therefore $109,000 ($69,000 + $40,000).
Answer (A) is incorrect. The residual income was $65,000. Answer (B) is incorrect. The sum of residual income and salaries was $95,000. Answer (C) is incorrect. Assuming Saint-Lucie's share of residual income was $40,000, the residual income was $100,000.

14. During the current year, Jung and Freud maintained average capital balances in their partnership of $160,000 and $100,000, respectively. The partners receive 10% interest on average capital balances, and residual profit or loss is divided equally. Partnership profit before interest was $4,000. By what amount should Freud's capital account change for the year?

A. $1,000 decrease.

B. $2,000 increase.

C. $11,000 decrease.

D. $12,000 increase.

Answer (A) is correct. *(CPA, adapted)*
REQUIRED: The change in a partner's capital account.
DISCUSSION: The partners are to receive 10% interest and then split the residual profit or loss. Because interest exceeds partnership profit before interest, the residual loss is $22,000 {[($160,000 + $100,000) × 10%] – $4,000}. Freud's account is increased by $10,000 ($100,000 × 10%) and decreased by $11,000 ($22,000 loss × 50%), a net decrease of $1,000.
Answer (B) is incorrect. The amount of $2,000 is 50% of the partnership profit before interest. Answer (C) is incorrect. An $11,000 decrease does not include the $10,000 of interest owed to Freud. Answer (D) is incorrect. A $12,000 increase equals 10% of capital plus 50% of the partnership profit before interest.

23.3 Admission of New Partners

15. The goodwill and bonus methods are two means of adjusting for differences between the net book value and the fair value of partnerships when new partners are admitted. Which of the following statements about these methods is true?

A. The bonus method does not revalue assets to market values.

B. The bonus method revalues assets to market values.

C. Both methods result in the same balances in partner capital accounts.

D. Both methods result in the same total value of partner capital accounts, but the individual capital accounts vary.

Answer (A) is correct. *(Publisher, adapted)*
REQUIRED: The true statement about the bonus and goodwill methods.
DISCUSSION: The goodwill method revalues assets to adjust the total value of partnership capital. The bonus method simply readjusts capital accounts and makes no changes in existing asset accounts.
Answer (B) is incorrect. The bonus method does not revalue assets. Answer (C) is incorrect. The goodwill method revalues assets and the bonus method adjusts capital accounts. Answer (D) is incorrect. The goodwill method revalues assets where bonus method adjusts capital accounts. Consequently, total partnership capital differs between the two methods.

16. Presented below is the condensed balance sheet of the partnership of Charles, Foster, and Welles, who share profits and losses in the ratio of 6:3:1, respectively:

Cash	$ 85,000
Other assets	415,000
	$500,000
Liabilities	$ 80,000
Charles, capital	252,000
Foster, capital	126,000
Welles, capital	42,000
	$500,000

Assume that the partners agree to sell to Orson 20% of their respective capital and profit and loss interests for a total payment of $90,000. The payment by Orson is to be made directly to the individual partners. The partners agree that implied goodwill is to be recorded prior to the acquisition by Orson. What are the capital balances of Charles, Foster, and Welles, respectively, after the acquisition by Orson?

A. $198,000; $99,000; $33,000

B. $201,600; $100,800; $33,600

C. $216,000; $108,000; $36,000

D. $270,000; $135,000; $45,000

Answer (C) is correct. *(CPA, adapted)*
REQUIRED: The capital balances of the original partners after recording goodwill and selling an interest to a new partner.
DISCUSSION: If Orson is to purchase a 20% interest in the partnership for $90,000, the partnership is estimated to be worth $450,000 ($90,000 ÷ 20%). But the sum of the original capital balances is only $420,000. Because goodwill is to be recognized prior to the purchase, $30,000 must be allocated to the capital accounts of the original partners. This amount will be shared in the profit and loss ratio of 6:3:1. The final step is to debit the capital accounts of the original partners for 20% of their respective interests and to credit the new partner's account for $90,000.

	Charles	Foster	Welles	Orson
Beginning capital	$252	$126	$42	
Goodwill	18	9	3	
	$270	$135	$45	
Minus 20% sold	(54)	(27)	(9)	$90
Ending capital	$216	$108	$36	$90

Answer (A) is incorrect. The amounts of $198,000, $99,000, and $33,000 equal the balances of Charles, Foster, and Welles, respectively, if $90,000 is allocated according to the profit-and-loss ratio from the partners' original balances to Orson's account. Answer (B) is incorrect. The amounts of $201,600, $100,800, and $33,600 are the original partners' balances if no goodwill is recognized and if 20% of the original balances ($420,000 × 20% = $84,000) is deemed to have been sold. Answer (D) is incorrect. The amounts of $270,000, $135,000, and $45,000 are the original partners' balances after allocation of goodwill but before deduction of the interest sold.

17. Tinker and Evers are partners with capital balances of $60,000 and $20,000, respectively. Profits and losses are divided in the ratio of 60:40. Tinker and Evers decided to admit Chance as a new partner. Chance invested land valued at $15,000 for a 20% capital interest in the new partnership. The cost of the land was $12,000. The partnership elected to use the bonus method to record the admission of Chance into the partnership. Chance's capital account should be credited for

A. $12,000

B. $15,000

C. $16,000

D. $19,000

Answer (D) is correct. *(CPA, adapted)*
REQUIRED: The amount to be credited to a new partner's capital account.
DISCUSSION: This transaction is to be accounted for under the bonus method. The incoming partner invests $15,000 fair value of land for a 20% interest in the capital of the new partnership. Hence, the incoming partner's capital account should be credited for 20% of the total capital following the investment. The total capital following the investment by the new partner equals $95,000 ($60,000 + $20,000 + $15,000). Because 20% of this amount is $19,000, Chance's capital account should be credited for $19,000.
Answer (A) is incorrect. The cost of the land is $12,000. Answer (B) is incorrect. The fair value of the land is $15,000. Answer (C) is incorrect. The amount of $16,000 equals 20% of the capital of the original partners.

18. Redd and White are partners with capital account balances of $60,000 and $90,000, respectively. They agree to admit Blue as a partner with a one-third interest in capital and profits, for an investment of $100,000, after revaluing the assets of Redd and White. Goodwill to the original partners should be

A. $0

B. $33,333

C. $50,000

D. $66,667

Answer (C) is correct. *(CPA, adapted)*
REQUIRED: The goodwill to the original partners.
DISCUSSION: If a one-third interest is worth an investment of $100,000, the value of the partnership must be $300,000 ($100,000 ÷ 33 1/3%). The total of the existing capital balances and Blue's investment is $250,000 ($60,000 + $90,000 + $100,000). Thus, goodwill is $50,000 ($300,000 – $250,000). The entry will be to debit cash (or property at fair value) for $100,000 and goodwill for $50,000, and to credit Blue's capital balance for $100,000 and the capital balances of Redd and White for a total of $50,000.
Answer (A) is incorrect. Goodwill should be recognized and credited to the capital balances of Redd and White. Answer (B) is incorrect. The amount of $33,333 is one-third of the new partner's investment. Answer (D) is incorrect. The amount of $66,667 is two-thirds of the new partner's investment.

19. Presented below is the condensed balance sheet for the partnership of Lever, Polen, and Quint, who share profits and losses in the ratio of 4:3:3, respectively.

Cash	$ 90,000
Other assets	830,000
Lever, loan	20,000
	$940,000
Accounts payable	$210,000
Quint, loan	30,000
Lever, capital	310,000
Polen, capital	200,000
Quint, capital	190,000
	$940,000

Assume that the assets and liabilities are fairly valued on the balance sheet and that the partnership decides to admit Fahn as a new partner with a 20% interest. No goodwill or bonus is to be recorded. How much should Fahn contribute in cash or other assets?

A. $140,000

B. $142,000

C. $175,000

D. $177,500

Answer (C) is correct. *(CPA, adapted)*
REQUIRED: The amount to be contributed by a new partner when neither goodwill nor bonus is to be recorded.
DISCUSSION: The carrying amount of the partnership is the sum of the capital accounts of Lever, Polen, and Quint, i.e., $700,000. If Fahn is to have a 20% interest without recording goodwill or bonus, the current sum of the capital accounts will be equal to 80% of the carrying amount after the admission of Fahn. Dividing the original carrying amount of $700,000 by 80% yields the new carrying amount after Fahn's admission ($875,000). The difference between the respective carrying amounts is the amount the new partner must contribute.

New partnership ($700,000 ÷ 80%)	$875,000
Old partnership	(700,000)
Fahn's contribution	$175,000

Answer (A) is incorrect. The amount of $140,000 equals 20% of the $700,000 carrying amount. Answer (B) is incorrect. The amount of $142,000 equals 20% of the $700,000 carrying amount plus the $10,000 excess of the Quint payable over the Lever receivable. Answer (D) is incorrect. The amount of $177,500 assumes that the $10,000 excess of the Quint payable over the Lever receivable is added to the sum of the existing capital accounts before being divided by 80%.

20. Gordon and Rogers are partners who share profits and losses in the ratio of 6:4, respectively. On May 1 of the current year, their respective capital accounts were as follows:

Gordon	$60,000
Rogers	50,000

On that date, Corbett was admitted as a partner with a one-third interest in capital and profits for an investment of $40,000. The new partnership began with total capital of $150,000. Immediately after Corbett's admission, Gordon's capital should be

A. $50,000

B. $54,000

C. $56,667

D. $60,000

Answer (B) is correct. *(CPA, adapted)*
REQUIRED: The capital balance of an existing partner following the admission of a new partner.
DISCUSSION: Following the entrance of Corbett, the partnership began with total capital of $150,000. Corbett received a one-third interest; therefore, the new partner's capital balance must be credited for $50,000 ($150,000 ÷ 3). But Corbett contributed only $40,000, so the $10,000 difference ($50,000 – $40,000) must be allocated to the existing partners in the ratio of 6:4. The result will be debits to the capital accounts of Gordon and Rogers of $6,000 ($10,000 × 60%) and $4,000 ($10,000 × 40%), respectively. Consequently, immediately after Corbett's admission, Gordon's capital is $54,000 ($60,000 – $6,000).
Answer (A) is incorrect. Corbett's capital balance is $50,000. Answer (C) is incorrect. The amount of $56,667 assumes Gordon's balance was reduced by one-third of the difference between Corbett's balance and his contribution. Answer (D) is incorrect. Gordon's original capital balance was $60,000.

21. Orange and Blue have a partnership with capital balances of $50,000 and $70,000, respectively. They wish to admit Jeri White into the partnership partly because of the prestige that she will bring to the partnership. If White purchases a one-fourth interest in capital and future profit and loss for $25,000, her capital account should reflect assigned goodwill in what amount?

A. $10,000

B. $11,250

C. $15,000

D. $25,000

Answer (C) is correct. *(Publisher, adapted)*
REQUIRED: The goodwill assigned to a new partner.
DISCUSSION: The partnership capital is $120,000 prior to the admission of White, and she is to receive 25% of the capital for her contribution of cash and goodwill. Thus, $120,000 equals 75% of the new capital after her admission. The total capital will therefore be $160,000 ($120,000 ÷ 75%), and White's capital account will be credited for $40,000. Because she contributed only $25,000 in cash, a debit to goodwill of $15,000 also is required.
Answer (A) is incorrect. The amount of $10,000 is the difference between the cash contribution and the goodwill assigned. Answer (B) is incorrect. The amount of $11,250 equals 25% of the capital excluding goodwill, minus the cash contribution. Answer (D) is incorrect. The cash contribution equals $25,000.

22. In the Alex and Amy partnership, Alex and Amy had a capital ratio of 3:1 and a profit and loss ratio of 2:1, respectively. The bonus method was used to record Mark's admittance as a new partner. What ratio would be used to allocate to Alex and Amy the excess of Mark's contribution over the amount credited to Mark's capital account?

A. Alex and Amy's new relative capital ratio.

B. Alex and Amy's new relative profit and loss ratio.

C. Alex and Amy's old capital ratio.

D. Alex and Amy's old profit and loss ratio.

Answer (D) is correct. *(CPA, adapted)*
REQUIRED: The ratio used to allocate to the original partners the excess of the new partner's contribution over the amount credited to his/her capital account.
DISCUSSION: The bonus method makes no changes in existing asset accounts. Capital accounts of existing partners are adjusted in accordance with the old profit and loss ratio to reflect the bonus. The entry will be to debit cash (or the fair value of the property) contributed and to credit Mark's capital account for a lesser amount. The excess will be credited in the ratio of 2:1 to the original partners' capital balances.
Answer (A) is incorrect. The bonus to the original partners should not be allocated based on the new capital ratio. Answer (B) is incorrect. The bonus to the original partners should be allocated based on the old profit and loss ratio. Answer (C) is incorrect. The bonus to the original partners should be allocated based on the old profit and loss ratio, not the old capital ratio.

23.4 Withdrawal of Partners

23. Hi Shade, a partner in an accounting firm, decided to withdraw from the partnership. Shade's share of the partnership profits and losses was 20%. Upon withdrawing from the partnership, he was paid $74,000 in final settlement of his interest. The total of the partners' capital accounts before recognition of partnership goodwill prior to Shade's withdrawal was $210,000. After his withdrawal, the remaining partners' capital accounts, excluding their share of goodwill, totaled $160,000. The total agreed upon goodwill of the firm was

A. $120,000

B. $160,000

C. $210,000

D. $250,000

Answer (A) is correct. *(CPA, adapted)*
REQUIRED: The amount of goodwill agreed upon prior to Shade's withdrawal.
DISCUSSION: The balance in Shade's account prior to recognition of goodwill was $50,000 ($210,000 – $160,000). Given that he was paid $74,000 upon withdrawing, Shade's account must have been credited with $24,000 in goodwill. If his share of partnership profits and losses was 20%, the total agreed upon goodwill equals $120,000 ($24,000 ÷ 20%).
Answer (B) is incorrect. The amount of $160,000 was the sum of the remaining partners' capital balances exclusive of goodwill. Answer (C) is incorrect. The amount of $210,000 was the sum of the partners' capital balances prior to Shade's withdrawal. Answer (D) is incorrect. The amount of $250,000 assumes that Shade was assigned $50,000 of goodwill.

24. On June 30, the condensed balance sheet for the partnership of Anna Lowe, Ben High, and Cam Meany, together with their respective profit-and-loss sharing percentages, was as follows:

Assets, net of liabilities	$320,000
Lowe, capital (50%)	$160,000
High, capital (30%)	96,000
Meany, capital (20%)	64,000
	$320,000

Lowe decided to retire from the partnership and by mutual agreement is to be paid $180,000 out of partnership funds for her interest. Total goodwill implicit in the agreement is to be recorded. After Lowe's retirement, what are the capital balances of the other partners?

	High	Meany
A.	$84,000	$56,000
B.	$102,000	$68,000
C.	$108,000	$72,000
D.	$120,000	$80,000

Answer (C) is correct. *(CPA, adapted)*
REQUIRED: The capital balances of the remaining partners following the retirement of a partner.
DISCUSSION: The $180,000 paid to Lowe represents Lowe's 50% interest in the partnership. The total value of the partnership is therefore $360,000 ($180,000 ÷ 50%), and the goodwill implicit in the retirement agreement is $40,000 ($360,000 total value – $320,000 net assets prior to the recording of goodwill). This $40,000 should be allocated 50% ($20,000) to Lowe, 30% ($12,000) to High, and 20% ($8,000) to Meany. High's capital balance following the recording of goodwill is $108,000 ($96,000 + $12,000), and Meany's is $72,000 ($64,000 + $8,000).
Answer (A) is incorrect. It assumes no goodwill is recognized, and the additional $20,000 paid to Lowe is deducted from the balances of High and Meany in the ratio of 3:2. Answer (B) is incorrect. The amount of $20,000, not $10,000, of goodwill should be allocated to High and Meany. Answer (D) is incorrect. The entire amount of goodwill should not be allocated to High and Meany.

25. When Brown retired from the partnership of Brown, Dart, and Prince, the final settlement of Brown's interest exceeded Brown's capital balance. Under the bonus method, the excess

A. Was recorded as goodwill.

B. Was recorded as an expense.

C. Reduced the capital balances of Dart and Prince.

D. Had no effect on the capital balances of Dart and Prince.

Answer (C) is correct. *(CPA, adapted)*
REQUIRED: The treatment of the excess of the settlement of a partner's interest over the capital balance.
DISCUSSION: The bonus method reduces the capital accounts of the other partners because the bonus, that is, the excess of settlement value over the retiring partner's capital balance, is deemed to be paid to the withdrawing partner by the remaining partners.
Answer (A) is incorrect. Goodwill is not recorded under the bonus method. Answer (B) is incorrect. The excess is not an expense. Answer (D) is incorrect. The excess reduces the capital accounts.

26. On June 30, the balance sheet for the partnership of Ace, Deuce, and Trey, including their respective profit-and-loss ratios, was as follows:

Assets, at cost	$300,000
Ace, loan	$ 15,000
Ace, capital (20%)	70,000
Deuce, capital (20%)	65,000
Trey, capital (60%)	150,000
Total	$300,000

Ace has decided to retire from the partnership and by mutual agreement the assets are to be adjusted to their fair value of $360,000 at June 30. It was agreed that the partnership would pay Ace $102,000 cash for Ace's partnership interest exclusive of the amount due on the loan, which is to be repaid in full. No goodwill is to be recorded in this transaction. After Ace's retirement, what are the capital account balances of Deuce and Trey, respectively?

A. $65,000 and $150,000.

B. $72,000 and $171,000.

C. $73,000 and $174,000.

D. $77,000 and $186,000.

Answer (B) is correct. *(CPA, adapted)*
REQUIRED: The capital account balances of the remaining partners after a partner's retirement.
DISCUSSION: The first step is to record $60,000 to reflect the appreciation of the assets. This amount should be allocated according to the profit-and-loss ratio of 2:2:6. Writeup of specific assets has nothing to do with the recording of goodwill.
After the distribution, Ace has an account balance of $82,000. If Ace is to be paid $102,000, exclusive of the repayment of the loan and without recording goodwill, a $20,000 bonus must be deducted from the capital accounts of Deuce and Trey. Because they share profits and losses in the ratio of 2:6, their accounts will be reduced by $5,000 and $15,000, respectively.

	Ace	Deuce	Trey
Beginning capital	$ 70	$65	$150
Appreciation	12	12	36
	$ 82	$77	$186
Bonus	20	(5)	(15)
Ending capital	$102	$72	$171

Answer (A) is incorrect. The accounts must be adjusted for appreciation and bonus. Answer (C) is incorrect. The accounts must be increased for appreciation in the ratio of 2:2:6 and decreased in Deuce's and Trey's accounts for the bonus in the ratio of 2:6. Answer (D) is incorrect. The accounts must be reduced by the amount of the bonus.

23.5 Liquidation of Partnerships

27. On January 1, the partners of Hornsby, Wagner, and Waner, who share profits and losses in the ratio of 5:3:2, respectively, decided to liquidate their partnership. On this date, the partnership condensed balance sheet was as follows:

Assets

Cash	$ 50,000
Other assets	250,000
	$300,000

Liabilities and Capital

Liabilities	$ 60,000
Hornsby, capital	80,000
Wagner, capital	90,000
Waner, capital	70,000
	$300,000

On January 15, the first cash sale of other assets with a carrying amount of $150,000 realized $120,000. Safe installment payments to the partners were made the same date. How much cash should be distributed to each partner?

	Hornsby	Wagner	Waner
A.	$15,000	$51,000	$44,000
B.	$40,000	$45,000	$35,000
C.	$55,000	$33,000	$22,000
D.	$60,000	$36,000	$24,000

Answer (A) is correct. *(CPA, adapted)*
REQUIRED: The safe installment payments to partners after the initial sale of assets.
DISCUSSION: When the liquidation of a partnership proceeds over time, a conservative approach must be taken to the distribution of assets (cash) to partners. This conservative approach incorporates three steps. In the first step, a gain or loss realized from the actual sale of assets ($120,000 – $150,000 = $30,000 loss) is allocated to the partners' capital accounts in accordance with the profit-and-loss ratio. In the second step, remaining assets are assumed to have a fair value of $0, which results in an assumed loss equal to their carrying amount. For this partnership, an assumed loss of $100,000 ($250,000 of other assets – $150,000 of other assets sold) results. This assumed loss is also allocated to the partners' accounts in accordance with the profit-and-loss ratio. The third step is taken only if at least one of the partners' capital accounts has a deficit balance. If a deficit results, the conservative approach requires allocation of the deficit to the remaining partners' accounts. This step is not necessary in this example. The final balances in the partnership accounts equal the amounts of cash that may be distributed in a safe installment payment schedule.

	Hornsby	Wagner	Waner
Beginning capital	$80,000	$90,000	$70,000
Realized loss ($30,000)	(15,000)	(9,000)	(6,000)
Assumed loss ($100,000)	(50,000)	(30,000)	(20,000)
Resulting capital	$15,000	$51,000	$44,000

Answer (B) is incorrect. A maximum of $110,000 in cash can be distributed given available cash of $170,000 and liabilities of $60,000. Answer (C) is incorrect. The amounts of $55,000, $33,000, and $22,000 are equal to 50%, 30%, and 20%, respectively, of the excess of the total cash available over the liabilities. Answer (D) is incorrect. The amounts of $60,000, $36,000, and $24,000 are equal to 50%, 30%, and 20%, respectively, of the $120,000 of cash realized from the sale of other assets.

28. The following condensed balance sheet is presented for the Iota and Theta partnership, who share profits and losses in the ratio of 60:40, respectively:

Other assets	$450,000
Iota, loan	20,000
	$470,000

Accounts payable	$120,000
Iota, capital	195,000
Theta, capital	155,000
	$470,000

The partners have decided to liquidate. If the other assets are sold for $385,000, what amount of the available cash should be distributed to Iota?

- A. $136,000
- B. $156,000
- C. $159,000
- D. $195,000

Answer (A) is correct. *(CPA, adapted)*
REQUIRED: The amount of cash to be distributed to a partner.
DISCUSSION: When the partnership sells the other assets, it must recognize a loss of $65,000 ($450,000 – $385,000). This loss must be allocated to the partners based on their loss ratio of 60:40. Thus, Iota's capital account is reduced to $156,000 [$195,000 – ($65,000 × 60%)] and Theta's to $129,000 [$155,000 – ($65,000 × 40%)]. The accounts payable are then paid, leaving assets of $265,000. Finally, the balance of the loan is subtracted from Iota's capital account balance, and each partner receives the balance in his/her capital account. Thus, Iota should receive $136,000 in cash ($156,000 – $20,000).
Answer (B) is incorrect. The amount of $156,000 results from not subtracting the loan from Iota's capital account.
Answer (C) is incorrect. The amount of $159,000 equals 60% of the assets remaining after the liabilities have been settled.
Answer (D) is incorrect. Iota's unadjusted capital balance equals $195,000.

29. The following condensed balance sheet is presented for the partnership of Axel, Barr, and Cain, who share profits and losses in the ratio of 4:3:3, respectively:

Cash	$100,000
Other assets	300,000
	$400,000

Liabilities	$150,000
Axel, capital	40,000
Barr, capital	180,000
Cain, capital	30,000
	$400,000

The partners agreed to wind up the partnership after selling the other assets for $200,000. Upon winding up, Axel should have received

- A. $0
- B. $40,000
- C. $60,000
- D. $70,000

Answer (A) is correct. *(CPA, adapted)*
REQUIRED: The amount Axel should receive upon liquidation.
DISCUSSION: When the other assets with a carrying value of $300,000 were sold for $200,000, a loss of $100,000 resulted. When this loss is distributed in the ratio of 4:3:3 to the capital balances, Axel's and Cain's capital balances are eliminated. Thus, upon winding up of the partnership, neither Axel nor Cain will receive any cash. Of the $300,000 available ($100,000 cash on hand + $200,000 proceeds from the sale of other assets), $150,000 will be distributed to creditors (liabilities) and $150,000 to Barr.

	Axel	Barr	Cain
Beginning capital	$40,000	$180,000	$30,000
Loss on sale	(40,000)	(30,000)	(30,000)
Distribution of cash	$ 0	$150,000	$ 0

Answer (B) is incorrect. The beginning balance in Axel's capital account is $40,000. Answer (C) is incorrect. The amount of $60,000 assumes that Axel is due 40% of the $150,000 available to distribute to partners. Answer (D) is incorrect. The sum of the capital balances of Axel and Cain is $70,000.

Questions 30 and 31 are based on the following information.

December 31 balance sheet accounts of the Dan, Jim, and Mary Partnership follow:

Cash	$ 20,000
Inventory	120,000
Plant assets – net	300,000
Accounts payable	170,000
Dan, capital	100,000
Jim, capital	90,000
Mary, capital	80,000

The partners' profit and loss percentages are Dan, 50%; Jim, 30%; and Mary, 20%.

On January 1 of the next year, the partners decide to liquidate the partnership. They agree that all cash should be distributed as soon as it becomes available during the liquidation process. They also agree that a cash predistribution plan is necessary to facilitate the distribution of cash.

30. If cash of $220,000, including the $20,000 cash on hand, becomes available, it should be distributed in accordance with the cash predistribution plan. How much should be distributed to the creditors and partners respectively?

	Creditors	Dan	Jim	Mary
A.	$170,000	$25,000	$15,000	$10,000
B.	$170,000	$0	$26,000	$24,000
C.	$170,000	$10,000	$32,000	$8,000
D.	$170,000	$0	$18,000	$32,000

Answer (D) is correct. *(Publisher, adapted)*
REQUIRED: The distribution of cash to partners and creditors using a cash predistribution plan.
DISCUSSION: To prepare a cash predistribution plan, the smallest projected loss that will eliminate the partner most vulnerable to losses is allocated in the profit-loss ratio. Then, based on the newly calculated capital balances, the projected loss that will eliminate the next most vulnerable partner is allocated. The projected loss and its allocation are based on a profit-and-loss ratio adjusted for the previous elimination of more vulnerable partners. Once projected losses to eliminate all partners are calculated, the plan sets forth a distribution of cash that prevents an overpayment to an insolvent partner. Liabilities to outside creditors must be satisfied before cash is distributed to the partners. After satisfying the accounts payable of $170,000, $50,000 remains to be distributed to partners. The first $20,000 is to be distributed to Mary. Of the remaining $30,000, 60% ($18,000) will be distributed to Jim and 40% ($12,000) to Mary. The $50,000 should therefore be distributed $0 to Dan, $18,000 to Jim, and $32,000 to Mary.

Cash Predistribution Plan

Projected Loss	Dan-50%	Jim-30%	Mary-20%
	$100,000	$90,000	$80,000
$200,000	(100,000)	(60,000)	(40,000)
	$ --	$30,000	$40,000
$ 50,000		(30,000)	(20,000)
		$ --	$20,000
$ 20,000			(20,000)
			$ --

Cash Distribution	Creditors	Dan	Jim	Mary
First $170,000	100%			
Next 20,000				100%
Next 50,000			60%	40%
Then		50%	30%	20%

Answer (A) is incorrect. A 5:3:2 distribution is appropriate only for amounts in excess of $240,000. Answer (B) is incorrect. The first $170,000 must go to creditors, the next $20,000 must go to Mary, and the remaining $30,000 should be distributed to Jim and Mary in the ratio of 3:2. Answer (C) is incorrect. Mary did not receive the $20,000 distribution, Dan does not receive a distribution until Jim and Mary receive theirs, and Jim and Mary have not fulfilled a 3:2 distribution of $50,000.

31. The predistribution plan should be based on relative vulnerability to losses. For the Dan, Jim, and Mary Partnership, the relative vulnerability should show that

    A. Dan is the most vulnerable.

    B. Dan is the least vulnerable.

    C. Jim is the most vulnerable.

    D. Jim is the least vulnerable.

Answer (A) is correct. *(Publisher, adapted)*

    REQUIRED: The true statement about relative vulnerability.

    DISCUSSION: A cash predistribution plan is based on the partners' relative vulnerability to losses under the assumption that a partner would not repay a deficit capital balance. This vulnerability is determined by projecting the loss that, in accordance with the profit-and-loss ratio, would eliminate each partner's account. Because Dan would be allocated 50% of each loss, a projected loss of $200,000 ($100,000 capital balance ÷ 50%) would eliminate his account. Projected losses of $300,000 ($90,000 ÷ 30%) and $400,000 ($80,000 ÷ 20%) would eliminate Jim's and Mary's balances, respectively. Accordingly, Dan is the most vulnerable because his capital balance would be eliminated by the smallest projected loss.

32. Prior to partnership liquidation, a schedule of possible losses is frequently prepared to determine the amount of cash that may be safely distributed to the partners. The schedule of possible losses

    A. Consists of each partner's capital account plus loan balance, divided by that partner's profit-and-loss sharing ratio.

    B. Shows the successive losses necessary to eliminate the capital accounts of partners (assuming no contribution of personal assets by the partners).

    C. Indicates the distribution of successive amounts of available cash to each partner.

    D. Assumes contribution of personal assets by partners unless there is a substantial presumption of personal insolvency by the partners.

Answer (B) is correct. *(Publisher, adapted)*

    REQUIRED: The true statement about a schedule of possible losses.

    DISCUSSION: A schedule of possible losses presents a series of incremental losses to indicate the amount of loss in a liquidation that will eliminate each partner's capital account. The presumption is that losses or partners' capital deficits will not be repaid by individual partners. The schedule is used to determine the amount of cash that may be safely distributed to the individual partners without potential impairment of the rights of any party.

    Answer (A) is incorrect. It describes the computation that determines the order in which partners' capital accounts will be eliminated by losses, not the amounts thereof. Answer (C) is incorrect. It describes a cash distribution schedule. Answer (D) is incorrect. The presumption (for the schedule) is that losses or deficits will not be repaid by individual partners.

Use Gleim **EQE Test Prep** Software Download for interactive study and performance analysis.

STUDY UNIT TWENTY-FOUR
BUSINESS COMBINATIONS AND CONSOLIDATED FINANCIAL REPORTING

Nature of a Business Combination

A business combination is "a transaction or other event in which an acquirer obtains control of one or more businesses" (FASB Codification). An **acquirer** gains control of the **acquiree** in a combination.

Control is a **controlling financial interest**. This usually means one entity's direct or indirect ownership of more than 50% of the outstanding voting shares of another entity.

A **business** consists of integrated activities and assets that can be conducted to provide a return in the form of dividends, lower costs, or other economic benefits directly to investors or others. Thus, the essential elements of a business are inputs and processes. Processes are applied to inputs to generate outputs. **Outputs** are direct returns to investors and others, but a business need **not** have outputs as long as it is capable of being managed to provide them. Moreover, a set of assets and activities that includes **goodwill** is assumed to be a business, but a business need not have goodwill. When the assets acquired and liabilities assumed do **not** constitute a business, an **asset acquisition**, not a business combination, occurs.

BUSINESS

INPUTS	→	PROCESSES	→	POTENTIAL outputs

A combination may be **structured** in many ways. For example, a business(es) may be **legally merged** with the acquirer or become its **subsidiary** (an entity controlled by the parent-acquirer). In a **merger**, the assets and liabilities of one combining entity are transferred to the books of the surviving entity. The first entity ceases to have a separate legal existence. A merger may result from (1) a direct acquisition of the net assets of the acquiree or (2) an acquisition of all of the acquiree's shares followed by transfer of the net assets. Another possibility is **consolidation**. In this arrangement, the combining entities are dissolved, and a new legal entity is created with their assets and liabilities. A combination effected as a consolidation should not be confused with the **accounting process** to prepare statements for entities that are legally separate. The acquirer (parent) and the acquiree (subsidiary) may remain **legally separate**, although the parent has control.

Combination	Surviving Entity(ies)
Merger	Acquirer
Consolidation	New entity
Voting interest > 50%	Acquirer and acquiree

Acquisition Method

A combination involves (1) determining the acquirer and the acquisition date and (2) recognizing and measuring (a) identifiable assets acquired, (b) liabilities assumed, (c) any noncontrolling interest, and (d) goodwill or a gain from a bargain purchase.

One of the combining entities must be identified as the **acquirer**. When the combination is accomplished primarily by the transfer of assets or incurrence of liabilities, the entity that does so ordinarily is the acquirer.

The **acquisition date** is the date the acquirer obtains control of the acquiree. Control is usually obtained on the closing date.

As of the acquisition date, the acquirer **recognizes** (1) identifiable assets acquired (separately from goodwill), (2) liabilities assumed, and (3) any **noncontrolling interest** in the acquiree. Their measurement is customarily at acquisition-date fair values. A **noncontrolling interest (NCI)** is the part of a subsidiary's equity not directly or indirectly attributable to the parent.

Assets and liabilities must meet the definitions of **elements of financial statements** (see Study Unit 1). For example, restructuring costs the acquirer expects but is not required to pay are not covered by the definition of a liability. They are not "present obligations" and are **not** accounted for as part of the combination. The assets and liabilities **recognized** also must be **part of the exchange** for the acquiree, not a distinct transaction. Thus, the acquirer must recognize **only** the consideration transferred for the acquiree. A precombination transaction that primarily benefits the acquirer, not the acquiree, is most likely to be accounted for separately from the exchange. An example is an agreement by the acquiree to make severance payments to its executives when an expected combination occurs. If the main purpose is to benefit the acquirer, the payments are not part of the exchange.

The acquirer may recognize some **assets and liabilities not recognized by the acquiree**. Examples are certain operating leases and intangible assets. Ordinarily, no asset (liability) is recognized if the acquiree is a lessee. However, an acquiree (as lessor or lessee) may have a favorable or unfavorable **operating lease**. The acquirer recognizes an intangible asset or liability to the extent that the lease is favorable or unfavorable, respectively. The acquirer also separately recognizes identifiable **intangible assets**. An intangible asset is identifiable if it meets either (1) the contractual-legal criterion or (2) the separability criterion. (See Study Unit 9.)

Specific rules apply to **measuring specific assets**. For example, **no valuation allowance** is recognized because assets measured at acquisition-date fair value reflect the uncertainty of cash flows. Thus, no allowance for uncollectible receivables is recognized. Also, the acquisition-date fair value of an asset is not affected by whether it is **subject to an operating lease** under which the acquiree is the **lessor**.

If the acquisition-date fair value of an asset or liability arising from a **contingency** can be determined, it must be recognized. If it cannot, it still must be recognized if (1) the amount can be reasonably estimated, and (2) it is probable that an asset existed or a liability had been incurred at the acquisition date. If this criterion is **not** met, no asset or liability is recorded at the acquisition date. Other GAAP (see Study Unit 14) are then applied.

The seller in a combination may contractually undertake to pay the acquirer for the result of a **contingency or uncertainty** related to an asset (liability). An example is a guarantee that the acquirer's assumed liability will not be greater than an agreed amount. The **indemnification asset** and the indemnified item generally are recognized at the same time.

When **consideration** is transferred by the acquirer, the amount is the sum of the acquisition-date **fair values** of the acquirer's (1) assets transferred, (2) liabilities incurred to former owners of the acquiree, (3) equity interests issued, and (4) any asset or liability resulting from a contingent consideration arrangement.

The **carrying amounts** of consideration transferred often differ from their acquisition-date fair values. Thus, they are remeasured, and the **gains or losses** are included in earnings. However, the acquirer retains **control** of transferred items that are **within the combined entity**, such as those transferred to the acquiree rather than to its former owners. Accordingly, these items are measured at their carrying amounts just before the acquisition date, and **no gain or loss** is recognized.

Contingent consideration given in exchange for the acquiree usually creates an obligation to transfer additional assets or equity interests to the former owners if certain requirements are met. But an acquirer also may have a right to the return of previously transferred consideration in certain circumstances. Thus, an **asset** is recognized for a contingent right of return of transferred consideration.

Goodwill and Bargain Purchases

Goodwill is an asset. It reflects the future economic benefits arising from other assets acquired in a business combination that are not individually identified and separately recognized. Goodwill is the **excess** of (1) over (2):

(1) The sum of (a) the consideration transferred (normally at acquisition-date fair value), (b) the fair value of a noncontrolling interest (NCI), and (c) the acquisition-date fair value of a previously held equity interest in the acquiree over

(2) The **net** of acquisition-date fair values of identifiable assets acquired and liabilities assumed.

$$Goodwill = (Consid. + NCI + prev. eq. int.) > Net\ ident.\ assets$$

In an acquisition **achieved in stages** (a step acquisition), the acquirer has an equity interest in the acquiree just before obtaining control. This interest must be remeasured at acquisition-date fair value. The gain or loss is included in **earnings**. If changes in fair value have been recognized in **other comprehensive income**, they are reclassified and included in gain or loss at the acquisition date.

If a combination involves an exchange only of equity interests, and the fair value of the **acquiree's equity interests** is more reliably measurable than the acquirer's, it is used to determine goodwill.

A **bargain purchase** results when (2) exceeds (1) above. The excess is **recognized in earnings as a gain**. Prior to gain recognition, the acquirer must reevaluate whether all assets and liabilities have been identified. It also must review the procedures for measuring (1) the consideration transferred, (2) assets acquired, (3) liabilities, (4) the NCIs, and (5) a previously held equity interest in the acquiree.

Acquisition-Related Costs

Acquisition-related costs, such as finder's fees, professional and consulting fees, and general administrative costs (e.g., for an acquisitions department), are **expensed as incurred**. However, **issuance costs** for securities are accounted for under other GAAP. Direct issuance costs of **equity** (underwriting, legal accounting, tax, registration, etc.) are debited to additional paid-in capital. Indirect costs of issuance, records maintenance, and ownership transfers (e.g., a stock transfer agent's fees) are expenses. Issuance costs of **debt** are reported in the balance sheet as deferred charges and amortized over the life of the debt using the interest method. They are not combined with premium or discount.

Consolidated Reporting

Subsidiaries must be consolidated. The assumption is that consolidated statements are needed for fair presentation if one entity in a group (the parent) controls the others (subsidiaries). However, a majority-owned subsidiary must not be consolidated if the majority owner does not have control. For example, control is lacking when the subsidiary is (1) in bankruptcy, (2) in legal reorganization, or (3) under severe governmentally imposed uncertainties.

Consolidation is an **accounting process** to prepare statements for a business combination when the combined entities remain legally separate. Consolidated statements primarily benefit the owners and creditors of the parent. They report the results of operations, financial position, and cash flows of a consolidated entity (a parent and its subsidiaries) as if it were one **economic entity**. The basic consolidation procedure begins by **eliminating** intraentity balances and transactions (those within the economic entity). Examples of eliminations are (1) reciprocal payables and receivables, (2) the parent's investment in the subsidiary, (3) sales and purchases, (4) intraentity gross profit or loss on assets remaining in the consolidated entity, (5) interest and dividends, and (6) investments in and issuances of securities. The basic consolidation procedure also excludes the subsidiary's equity balances (including retained earnings) and recognizes any noncontrolling interest (NCI) in consolidated equity. When a subsidiary is **initially consolidated** during the year, its revenues, expenses, gains, and losses are included in the consolidated statements only from the consolidation date.

Intraentity balances and transactions are **eliminated in full** even if an NCI exists. Elimination means debits are credited and credits are debited.

Gross profit or loss (sales – cost of goods sold) is the usual basis for an elimination entry. However, if **income taxes** have been paid on intraentity gain related to assets still held by the consolidated group, the taxes must be deferred, or the profits to be eliminated must be reduced.

An NCI must be separately reported and clearly identified in the equity section of the consolidated balance sheet, e.g., as **NCI in subsidiaries**. Thus, the equity section of the consolidated balance sheet at the acquisition date is not the same as the equity section of the parent's separate balance sheet. Consolidated equity includes any NCI in the fair value of the acquiree's identifiable net assets presented separately from the parent's equity.

The initial amount of the NCI equals its **acquisition date fair value**. Subsequently, it is adjusted for its share of the subsidiary's net income included in consolidated net income, comprehensive income, and dividends. On consolidating worksheets, an adjustment to the NCI also is needed for unrealized gains and losses on (1) upstream (subsidiary to parent) sales of inventory and fixed assets and (2) purchases of combining entity debt.

In the **consolidated income statement**, the NCI's share of a subsidiary's net income that is included in consolidated net income is subtracted from consolidated net income to determine the **net income attributable to the parent**. A similar presentation is required for **comprehensive income**. Thus, (1) revenue and expenses, (2) gains and losses, (3) net income or loss, and (4) other comprehensive income (OCI) or loss are reported at consolidated amounts.

A business combination is an acquisition of net assets. Thus, only the fair value of the net assets of a subsidiary is included in a consolidated balance sheet prepared using the acquisition method. Its equity, including retained earnings, is excluded. In the absence of a bargain purchase, total equity of the consolidated entity immediately after acquisition is the same as the parent's total equity, which includes any NCI.

A **parent's ownership interest may change** without loss of its controlling financial interest. For example, the parent or subsidiary may buy or sell the subsidiary's ownership interests. These changes are **equity transactions**. No gain or loss is recognized in the consolidated statements, and the carrying amount of the noncontrolling interest (NCI) is adjusted. The difference between the consideration given or received and the adjustment is recognized in equity attributable to the parent. If the subsidiary has accumulated other comprehensive income (AOCI), its carrying amount is adjusted by a debit or credit to equity attributable to the parent.

A parent **deconsolidates a subsidiary** when it no longer has a controlling financial interest. The parent records the deconsolidation by recognizing a **gain or loss**. The gain or loss equals the difference between (1) the sum of (a) the fair value of consideration received, (b) the fair value of any retained investment, and (c) the carrying amount of any NCI (including AOCI attributable to it), **and** (2) the carrying amount of the former subsidiary's assets and liabilities.

A parent may deconsolidate a subsidiary during the year while retaining **significant influence**. If the fair value option is not elected, the **equity method** should be applied to account for such a retained interest but only from the date of the deconsolidation.

A **variable interest entity (VIE)** is an off-balance-sheet arrangement that may take any legal form (e.g., corporation, partnership, not-for-profit entity, limited liability company, or trust). Moreover, the equity investors (1) have insufficient equity at risk (the entity is undercapitalized) or (2) lack one of the following characteristics: (a) the power through voting (or similar) rights to direct the most significant economic activities (voting rights), (b) an obligation to absorb expected losses (risk of loss), or (c) the right to receive expected residual returns (rewards of ownership).

Variable interests are ownership, contractual, or monetary interests that vary with changes in the fair value of the VIE's net assets (excluding variable interests). Examples are (1) common stock in a VIE formed as a corporation, (2) subordinated debt issued by the VIE, and (3) guarantees of the VIE's assets or liabilities.

An **entity must be consolidated as a VIE** if, by design, the equity investors meet one of the conditions above. Equity investors as a group also lack the voting rights characteristic and consolidation is required if (1) voting rights of some investors are disproportionate to their risk of loss or their rights to expected returns and (2) substantially all of the VIE's activities involve or are performed for an investor with disproportionately few voting rights.

An entity consolidates a VIE when its variable interest(s) provides a **controlling financial interest**. This entity is the **primary beneficiary** of the VIE. It must have (1) the power to direct the activities of the VIE that most significantly affect its economic performance and (2) risk of loss or the right to benefits with potential significance to the VIE.

Combined Financial Statements

Consolidated statements must be prepared only when the controlling financial interest is held by one of the consolidated entities. When consolidated statements are not prepared, combined statements may be more meaningful than the separate statements of commonly controlled entities. For example, combined statements are useful when one individual owns a controlling financial interest in several entities with related operations. They also may be used to present the statements of entities under common management. Combined statements are prepared in the same way as consolidated statements. When they are prepared for related entities, e.g., commonly controlled entities, intraentity transactions and gains or losses are eliminated. Moreover, consolidation procedures are applied to such matters as (1) noncontrolling interests, (2) foreign operations, (3) different fiscal periods, and (4) income taxes.

Differences between GAAP and IFRS

Under IFRS:

- A noncontrolling interest (NCI) may be measured at (1) fair value or (2) a proportionate share of the fair value of the acquiree's identifiable net assets.

- Control is defined as "the power to govern the financial and operating policies of an entity so as to obtain benefits from its activities." Potential voting rights that are currently exercisable must be considered when assessing control.

- Consolidated financial statements must be prepared using uniform accounting policies. If a member of the consolidated group uses different policies, adjustments must be made to its statements when preparing the consolidated statements.

- An acquirer must recognize a contingent liability at the acquisition date if (1) it is a present obligation arising from past events and (2) its fair value can be measured reliably. Recognition occurs even if it is not probable that an outflow of economic benefits will be needed to settle the obligation. In circumstances other than a business combination, a liability (called a provision) is recognized only if (1) the outflow of benefits is probable and (2) the other criteria are met.

QUESTIONS

24.1 Nature of a Business Combination

1. Primor, a manufacturer, owns 75% of the voting interests of Sublette, an investment firm. Sublette owns 60% of the voting interests of Minos, an insurer. In Primor's consolidated financial statements, should consolidation accounting or equity method accounting be used for Sublette and Minos?

A. Consolidation used for Sublette and equity method used for Minos.

B. Consolidation used for both Sublette and Minos.

C. Equity method used for Sublette and consolidation used for Minos.

D. Equity method used for both Sublette and Minos.

Answer (B) is correct. *(CPA, adapted)*
REQUIRED: The method of accounting used by an entity that has a direct controlling interest in one entity and an indirect interest in another.
DISCUSSION: All entities in which a parent has a controlling financial interest through direct or indirect ownership of a majority voting interest ordinarily must be consolidated. However, a subsidiary is not consolidated when control does not rest with the majority owner. Primor has direct control of Sublette and indirect control of Minos and should consolidate both.
Answer (A) is incorrect. Primor has a controlling interest in Minos as well. Answer (C) is incorrect. Primor has a controlling interest in Sublette as well. Answer (D) is incorrect. Primor should consolidate both Sublette and Minos.

2. A parent-subsidiary relationship most likely arises from a

A. Tax-free reorganization.

B. Vertical business combination.

C. Horizontal business combination.

D. Greater than 50% ownership of the voting interests of another entity.

Answer (D) is correct. *(Publisher, adapted)*
REQUIRED: The situation creating a parent-subsidiary relationship.
DISCUSSION: A parent-subsidiary relationship usually arises from an effective ownership of more than 50% of the voting interests of another entity. The financial statements for the two entities must be presented on a consolidated basis unless control does not rest with the majority owner. To the extent the acquiree is not wholly owned, a noncontrolling interest is presented.
Answer (A) is incorrect. A tax-free reorganization may or may not be a combination, and it may or may not result in a parent-subsidiary relationship. Answer (B) is incorrect. Vertical combinations also may be accomplished by a merger or a consolidation, in which case the combining entities become one. A vertical combination combines a supplier and customer. Answer (C) is incorrect. Horizontal combinations also may be accomplished by a merger or a consolidation, in which case the combining entities become one. A horizontal combination combines competitors.

3. According to the guidance applicable to accounting and reporting for business combinations, a business must

    A. Have goodwill.

    B. Generate a return.

    C. Be capable of being managed to provide economic benefits.

    D. Have inputs, outputs, and processes.

Answer (C) is correct. *(CPA, adapted)*
    REQUIRED: The element of a business.
    DISCUSSION: The activities and assets of a business are capable of being managed to provide economic benefits (returns such as dividends, lower costs, and other economic benefits). Processes are applied to inputs to generate outputs. Outputs are direct returns to investors and other participants.
    Answer (A) is incorrect. A set of activities and assets that includes goodwill is presumed to be a business. However, a business need not have goodwill. Answer (B) is incorrect. A business must be capable of being managed to provide economic benefits (a return). It need not have outputs or returns. Answer (D) is incorrect. A business need not have outputs if it is capable of being managed to provide them.

4. A business combination in which the surviving entity is not one of the two combining entities is a(n)

    A. Investment in stock.

    B. Consolidation.

    C. Merger.

    D. Acquisition.

Answer (B) is correct. *(Publisher, adapted)*
    REQUIRED: The combination in which the survivor is not a combining entity.
    DISCUSSION: In a consolidation, the combining entities are dissolved, and the assets and liabilities of the combining entities are used to create a new legal entity.
    Answer (A) is incorrect. An investment in stock is not always associated with a business combination. Answer (C) is incorrect. In a merger, one of the combining entities survives. Answer (D) is incorrect. In an acquisition, one entity typically exchanges cash, equity securities, debt securities, or other considerations for the majority of the outstanding voting interests of another entity, and both continue to operate separately.

5. Which of the following describes a business combination that is structured as a merger?

    A. The surviving entity is one of the two combining entities.

    B. The surviving entity is neither of the two combining entities.

    C. An investor-investee relationship is established.

    D. A parent-subsidiary relationship is established.

Answer (A) is correct. *(Publisher, adapted)*
    REQUIRED: The business combination that is structured as a merger.
    DISCUSSION: In a business combination structured as a merger, the assets and liabilities of one of the combining entities are transferred to the other combining entity (the surviving entity). The surviving entity continues to exist as a separate legal entity. The nonsurviving entity generally ceases to exist as a separate entity, and its books are closed.
    Answer (B) is incorrect. In a consolidation, a new entity is formed to account for the assets and liabilities of the combining entities. This term should not be confused with the consolidation of the financial statements of legally separate entities. Answer (C) is incorrect. An investor-investee relationship is established in an investment. Answer (D) is incorrect. A parent-subsidiary relationship exists when one entity (the parent) holds a controlling financial interest in the other (the subsidiary). This usually means that the parent has direct or indirect ownership of more than 50% of the outstanding voting interests of the subsidiary.

24.2 Acquisition Method

6. Parent Co. acquires a controlling financial interest in Sub Co., a business entity. However, part of the equity in Sub is not attributable, directly or indirectly, to Parent. The NCI must be

    A. Measured at its acquisition-date fair value.

    B. Greater if goodwill is recognized.

    C. Lower if the acquirer previously held an equity interest in the acquiree.

    D. Excluded from the measurement of goodwill.

Answer (A) is correct. *(Publisher, adapted)*
    REQUIRED: The accounting for an NCI.
    DISCUSSION: A business combination has occurred because the acquirer has obtained control of a business. The acquirer measures the identifiable assets acquired, liabilities assumed, and any NCI in the acquiree at their acquisition-date fair values.
    Answer (B) is incorrect. NCI is measured at its fair value on the acquisition date regardless of whether goodwill is recognized. Answer (C) is incorrect. The amount of the NCI initially recognized bears no necessary relationship to the acquirer's equity interest held prior to the combination. Answer (D) is incorrect. The acquisition-date fair value of the NCI is an element of the calculation of goodwill.

7. Rolan Corporation issued 10,000 shares of common stock in exchange for all of Sandin Corporation's outstanding stock on September 1. Rolan's common stock had a market price of $60 per share on September 1. The market price of Sandin's stock was not readily ascertainable. Condensed balance sheets of Rolan and Sandin immediately prior to the combination are indicated below.

	Rolan	Sandin
Total assets	$1,000,000	$500,000
Liabilities	$ 300,000	$150,000
Common stock ($10 par)	200,000	100,000
Retained earnings	500,000	250,000
Total liabilities and shareholder's equity	$1,000,000	$500,000

Rolan's investment in Sandin's stock will be stated in Rolan's parent-only balance sheet immediately after the combination in the amount of

A. $100,000

B. $350,000

C. $500,000

D. $600,000

Answer (D) is correct. *(CPA, adapted)*
REQUIRED: The recorded amount of the acquired entity.
DISCUSSION: A business combination is accounted for as an acquisition because the essence of the acquisition method of accounting is the measurement principle. The acquirer measures the identifiable assets acquired, the liabilities assumed, and any noncontrolling interest at acquisition-date fair value. Goodwill or a gain also will be recognized based on fair-value measurements. However, in a parent-only balance sheet, the acquirer recognizes only an investment and the issuance of equity. Thus, given that the fair value of Rolan's shares is known but Sandin's is not, the fair value of the consideration transferred (10,000 shares × $60 = $600,000) is the measure of the investment. In a consolidated balance sheet, no investment in the subsidiary would be recognized.
Answer (A) is incorrect. The par value of the stock issued equals $100,000. Answer (B) is incorrect. The carrying amount of Sandin's net assets equals $350,000. Answer (C) is incorrect. The fair value of the stock issued minus its par value equals $500,000.

8. For the past several years, Mozza Company has invested in the common stock of Chedd Company, a wholesaler of imported cheeses. As of July 1, Mozza owned approximately 13% of the total of Chedd's outstanding voting common stock. Recently, managements of the two companies have discussed a possible combination of the two entities. However, no public announcement has been made, and no notice to owners has been given. The business combination that may result must be accounted for using the

A. Pooling-of-interests method.

B. Acquisition method.

C. Part pooling, part acquisition method.

D. Joint venture method.

Answer (B) is correct. *(Publisher, adapted)*
REQUIRED: The accounting for a business combination.
DISCUSSION: A business combination is "a transaction or other event in which an acquirer obtains control of one or more businesses" (FASB Codification). An entity must account for a combination using the following steps of the acquisition method: (1) identify the acquirer; (2) determine the acquisition date; (3) recognize and measure the identifiable assets acquired, liabilities assumed, and any noncontrolling interest; and (4) recognize and measure goodwill or a gain from a bargain purchase.
Answer (A) is incorrect. The pooling-of-interests method may no longer be used to account for a business combination. Answer (C) is incorrect. Accounting for a business combination as part pooling and part acquisition is not allowed. Answer (D) is incorrect. A joint venture does not meet the definition of a business combination.

9. Acquirer and Acquiree are the combining entities in a business combination. As part of the bargain, Acquirer assumed a contingent liability based on a suit brought against Acquiree because of a defect in one of its products. However, the former owner of Acquiree has agreed to pay the amount of any damages in excess of $5,000,000. In the consolidated balance sheet issued on the acquisition date, the contingent liability is reported at acquisition-date fair value. Accordingly,

A. An indemnification asset is recognized at acquisition-date fair value.

B. A valuation allowance is reported for the indemnification asset.

C. An exception to the customary accounting for a business combination applies.

D. No indemnification asset is recognized until the contingency is resolved.

Answer (A) is correct. *(CPA, adapted)*
REQUIRED: The effect of the acquiree's promise to pay excess damages under a contingent liability assumed by the acquirer.
DISCUSSION: If the acquisition-date fair value of an asset or liability arising from a contingency can be determined, it must be recognized. If it cannot, it still must be recognized if (1) the amount can be reasonably estimated and (2) it is probable that an asset existed or a liability had been incurred at the acquisition date. Moreover, the indemnification asset and the indemnified item are recognized at the same time and on the same basis. Thus, the indemnification asset also is recognized at acquisition-date fair value.
Answer (B) is incorrect. No valuation allowance is necessary when an item is recognized at acquisition-date fair value. The effects of uncertainty are reflected in the fair value measurement. Answer (C) is incorrect. The asset is recognized at acquisition-date fair value. The exception for items measured using U.S. GAAP for contingencies does not apply. Answer (D) is incorrect. The indemnification asset and the indemnified item are recognized at the same time.

10. Acquirer Co. and Acquiree Co. are in negotiations for a business combination. Acquirer suggested to Acquiree that it reach agreements with certain key executives to make payments with a total amount of $5,000,000 if negotiations succeed. Acquiree already had a contract with its chief executive to make a $10,000,000 payment if the company was acquired. This contract was agreed to several years before any acquisition was contemplated. What amount, if any, of these payments most likely is part of the exchange for the acquiree?

A. $15,000,000

B. $10,000,000

C. $5,000,000

D. 0

Answer (B) is correct. *(CPA, adapted)*
REQUIRED: The payment, if any, part of the exchange for the acquiree.
DISCUSSION: Under the acquisition method, one recognition condition is that assets and liabilities be part of the exchange (part of the consideration transferred for the acquiree). The assumption of the $10,000,000 liability to the chief executive of Acquiree is not part of a separate arrangement with Acquirer reached before or during the negotiations for the combination. Moreover, the purpose was apparently to obtain (or retain) the services of the chief executive, a benefit to Acquiree. However, the agreement with other key executives was made by Acquiree at the suggestion of Acquirer to provide termination payments, a likely benefit to Acquirer. Accordingly, the acquisition-date fair value of the $10,000,000 liability is included in the accounting for the combination. The $5,000,000 of other termination payments will be accounted for separately.
Answer (A) is incorrect. The $5,000,000 in payments apparently is for the benefit of Acquirer. Answer (C) is incorrect. The assumption of the $10,000,000 liability to the chief executive is part of the consideration transferred for the acquiree. The assumption of the $5,000,000 liability is postcombination compensation for the departures of certain key executives. Answer (D) is incorrect. The assumption of the $10,000,000 liability to the chief executive is part of the consideration transferred for the acquiree.

11. Damon Co. purchased 100% of the outstanding common stock of Smith Co. in an acquisition by issuing 20,000 shares of its $1 par common stock that had a fair value of $10 per share and providing contingent consideration that had a fair value of $10,000 on the acquisition date. Damon also incurred $15,000 in direct acquisition costs. On the acquisition date, Smith had assets with a book value of $200,000, a fair value of $350,000, and related liabilities with a book and fair value of $70,000. What amount of gain should Damon report related to this transaction?

A. $55,000

B. $70,000

C. $80,000

D. $250,000

Answer (B) is correct. *(CPA, adapted)*
REQUIRED: The gain on a bargain purchase arising from a business combination.
DISCUSSION: The gain on a bargain purchase arising from a business combination equals the excess of 1) over 2):

1) The net of the acquisition-date fair value of

- The identifiable assets acquired and
- Liabilities assumed

2) The sum of the acquisition-date fair value of

- The consideration transferred
- Any noncontrolling interest
- Any previously held equity interest in the acquiree

The net of the acquisition-date fair value of the identifiable assets acquired and the liabilities assumed was $280,000 ($350,000 FV of assets – $70,000 FV of liabilities). The acquisition-date fair value of the consideration transferred was $210,000 [(20,000 shares × $10 FV per share) + $10,000 FV of contingent consideration]. Contingent consideration given in exchange for the acquiree is usually an obligation to transfer something to the former owners if a specified condition is met. But the acquirer also may have a right to the return of the consideration if a specified condition is met. The fair value of contingent consideration reflects the probability that it will be paid (or returned). Because the acquirer received 100% of the voting interests of the acquiree, no noncontrolling interest or previously held equity interest in the acquiree existed. Consequently, the acquiree recognizes an ordinary gain in earnings of $70,000 ($280,000 FV net identifiable assets – $210,000 FV consideration transferred).
Answer (A) is incorrect. The amount of $55,000 includes $15,000 of direct acquisition costs, an expense not included in the calculation of the gain on a bargain purchase. Answer (C) is incorrect. The amount of $80,000 omits the fair value of the contingent consideration. Answer (D) is incorrect. The amount of $250,000 equals the $280,000 fair value of the net identifiable assets acquired, minus the $20,000 par value of the common stock issued, minus the $10,000 fair value of the contingent consideration.

24.3 Goodwill and Bargain Purchases

12. On November 30, Pindar Co. purchased for cash at $30 per share all 250,000 shares of the outstanding common stock of Shimoda Co., a business entity. Shimoda reported net assets on that date with a carrying amount of $6 million. This amount reflected acquisition-date fair value except for property, plant, and equipment, which had a fair value that exceeded its carrying amount by $800,000. In its November 30 consolidated balance sheet, what amount should Pindar report as goodwill?

A. $1,500,000

B. $800,000

C. $700,000

D. $0

Answer (C) is correct. *(CPA, adapted)*
   REQUIRED: The amount Pindar should report as goodwill.
   DISCUSSION: A business combination is accounted for as an acquisition. Goodwill is the excess of (1) the sum of the acquisition-date fair values (with some exceptions) of (a) the consideration transferred, (b) any noncontrolling interest in the acquiree, and (c) the acquirer's previously held equity interest in the acquiree over (2) the net of the acquisition-date fair values (with some exceptions) of the identifiable assets acquired and liabilities assumed. Given no noncontrolling interest or previously held equity interest, goodwill is $700,000.

Consideration transferred (250,000 shares × $30 market price)	$7,500,000
Acquisition-date fair value of the net assets acquired:	
Carrying amount	(6,000,000)
Undervaluation of PP&E	(800,000)
Goodwill	$ 700,000

   Answer (A) is incorrect. The excess of the consideration transferred over the carrying amount equals $1,500,000. Answer (B) is incorrect. The fair value in excess of the carrying amount of the acquired net assets is $800,000. Answer (D) is incorrect. Goodwill must be recognized. The consideration transferred exceeds the fair value of the net assets acquired.

13. Pellew Corp. paid $600,000 for all of the outstanding common stock of Samos Co. in a business combination initiated and completed in December. At that time, Samos had the following condensed balance sheet:

	Carrying Amounts
Current assets	$ 80,000
Plant and equipment, net	760,000
Liabilities	400,000
Equity	440,000

The acquisition-date fair value of the plant and equipment was $120,000 more than its carrying amount. The acquisition-date fair values and carrying amounts were equal for all other assets and liabilities. What amount of goodwill, related to Samos's acquisition, must Pellew report in its December 31 consolidated balance sheet?

A. $40,000

B. $80,000

C. $120,000

D. $160,000

Answer (A) is correct. *(CPA, adapted)*
   REQUIRED: The amount of goodwill reported in the consolidated balance sheet.
   DISCUSSION: A business combination is accounted for as an acquisition. Goodwill is the excess of (1) the sum of the acquisition-date fair values (with some exceptions) of (a) the consideration transferred, (b) any noncontrolling interest in the acquiree, and (c) the acquirer's previously held equity interest in the acquiree over (2) the net of the acquisition-date fair values (with some exceptions) of the identifiable assets acquired and liabilities assumed. After adjusting the net plant and equipment, goodwill is $40,000.

Consideration transferred	$600,000
Acquisition-date fair value of the net assets acquired	
Current assets	(80,000)
Plant and equipment, carrying amount	(760,000)
Plant and equipment, undervaluation	(120,000)
Liabilities	400,000
Goodwill	$ 40,000

   Answer (B) is incorrect. The amount of current assets is $80,000. Answer (C) is incorrect. The amount of plant and equipment is undervalued is $120,000. Answer (D) is incorrect. The difference between the $600,000 cost and the $440,000 carrying amount of the net assets is $160,000.

14. MAJ Corporation acquired 90% of the common stock of Min Co. for $420,000. MAJ previously held no equity interest in Min. On the date of acquisition, the carrying amount of Min's identifiable net assets equaled $300,000. The acquisition-date fair values of Min's inventory and equipment exceeded their carrying amounts by $60,000 and $40,000, respectively. The carrying amounts of the other assets and liabilities were equal to their acquisition-date fair values, and the fair value of the noncontrolling interest was $45,000. What amount should MAJ recognize as goodwill immediately after the acquisition?

A. $150,000

B. $90,000

C. $65,000

D. $114,000

Answer (C) is correct. *(Publisher, adapted)*
REQUIRED: The goodwill recognized given an NCI.
DISCUSSION: Goodwill is the excess of (1) the sum of the acquisition-date fair values (with some exceptions) of (a) the consideration transferred, (b) any NCI in the acquiree, and (c) the acquirer's previously held equity interest in the acquiree over (2) the net of the acquisition-date fair values (with some exceptions) of the identifiable assets acquired and liabilities assumed. Goodwill is therefore $66,667.

Consideration transferred	$ 420,000
Fair value of NCI	45,000
Carrying amount of net assets	(300,000)
Understatement of inventory	(60,000)
Understatement of equipment	(40,000)
Goodwill	$ 65,000

Answer (A) is incorrect. The difference between consideration transferred and 90% of the carrying amount of Min's identifiable net assets is $150,000. Answer (B) is incorrect. The excess of the consideration transferred over the carrying amount of 90% of the net assets acquired minus the amount allocated to inventory is $90,000. Answer (D) is incorrect. The excess of the consideration transferred over 90% of the carrying amount of Min's identifiable net assets, minus 90% of the excess fair value of the equipment is $114,000.

15. Psyops Corporation acquired for cash at $10 per share all 100,000 shares of the outstanding common stock of Spondee Company. The total fair value of the identifiable assets acquired minus liabilities assumed of Spondee was $1.4 million on the acquisition date, including the fair value of its property, plant, and equipment (its only noncurrent asset) of $250,000. The consolidated financial statements of Psyops Corporation and its wholly owned subsidiary must reflect

A. A deferred credit of $150,000.

B. Goodwill of $150,000.

C. A gain of $150,000.

D. A gain of $400,000.

Answer (D) is correct. *(CPA, adapted)*
REQUIRED: The accounting for a bargain purchase.
DISCUSSION: In a bargain purchase, the gain is recognized in earnings. The gain equals the excess of (1) the net of the acquisition-date fair values (with some exceptions) of the identifiable assets acquired and liabilities assumed over (2) the sum of the acquisition-date fair values (with some exceptions) of (a) the consideration transferred, (b) any noncontrolling interest in the acquiree, and (c) the acquirer's previously held equity interest in the acquiree. Consequently, the gain is $400,000 ($1.4 million – (100,000 shares × $10)].

Acquisition-date fair value of net assets acquired	$1,400,000
Consideration transferred (100,000 × $10)	(1,000,000)
Gain from bargain purchase	$ 400,000

Answer (A) is incorrect. A deferred credit is never recognized for a bargain purchase. Answer (B) is incorrect. Goodwill is the excess of (1) the sum of the acquisition-date fair values (with some exceptions) of (a) the consideration transferred, (b) any noncontrolling interest in the acquiree, and (c) the acquirer's previously held equity interest in the acquiree over (2) the net of the acquisition-date fair values (with some exceptions) of the identifiable assets acquired and liabilities assumed. Answer (C) is incorrect. A gain of $150,000 results from assuming that the fair value of the property, plant, and equipment was reduced to zero.

16. If a business combination results in a bargain purchase, the acquirer

A. Recognizes a deferred credit.

B. Reduces the amounts assigned to current assets and recognizes a deferred credit for any unallocated portion.

C. Recognizes a gain after reassessment of the identification of assets and liabilities and the procedures for measurement.

D. Records a pro rata reduction of the amounts assigned to all acquired assets and an extraordinary gain for any unallocated portion.

Answer (C) is correct. *(CPA, adapted)*
REQUIRED: The accounting for the excess of the fair value of acquired net assets over cost.
DISCUSSION: In a bargain purchase, the gain is recognized in earnings. Prior to gain recognition, the acquirer must re-evaluate whether all assets and liabilities have been identified. It also must review the procedures for measuring (1) the consideration transferred, (2) assets acquired, (3) liabilities, (4) the noncontrolling interests, and (5) a previously held equity interest in the acquiree.
Answer (A) is incorrect. A deferred credit is never recognized in a bargain purchase. Answer (B) is incorrect. Identifiable assets acquired and liabilities assumed are (with certain exceptions) measured at acquisition-date fair value. Moreover, a deferred credit is never recognized in a bargain purchase. Answer (D) is incorrect. The amounts assigned to acquired assets are not reduced, and the gain is ordinary.

17. Plume Co. acquired all of the outstanding voting stock of Sumir Co. for $6 million. The identifiable net assets of Sumir were appropriately measured at an acquisition-date fair value of $7.5 million. Moreover, the business combination was completed in the period in which it was initiated, and no contingent consideration or preacquisition contingency existed. Below are Sumir's only assets. They are measured at acquisition-date fair values.

Financial assets (not accounted for by the equity method)	$3 million
Deferred tax assets	.5 million
Assets to be disposed of by sale	3 million
Other current assets	2 million
Property, plant, and equipment	1 million

The consolidated income statement for the period in which the combination was completed must reflect

A. An extraordinary gain of $500,000.

B. An ordinary gain of $1.5 million.

C. Goodwill of $150,000.

D. No gain or goodwill.

Answer (B) is correct. *(Publisher, adapted)*
REQUIRED: The accounting for a business combination.
DISCUSSION: In a bargain purchase, the gain is recognized in earnings. The gain equals the excess of (1) the net of the acquisition-date fair values (with some exceptions) of the identifiable assets acquired and liabilities assumed over (2) the sum of the acquisition-date fair values (with some exceptions) of (a) the consideration transferred, (b) any NCI in the acquiree, and (c) the acquirer's previously held equity interest in the acquiree. Consequently, the gain was $1.5 million ($7.5 million – $6 million).

Answer (A) is incorrect. The gain is not allocated to reduce specified assets and is not extraordinary. Answer (C) is incorrect. Goodwill is the excess of (1) the sum of the acquisition-date fair values (with some exceptions) of (a) the consideration transferred, (b) any NCI in the acquiree, and (c) the acquirer's previously held equity interest in the acquiree over (2) the net of the acquisition-date fair values (with some exceptions) of the identifiable assets acquired and liabilities assumed. Answer (D) is incorrect. A gain is recognized.

18. Practicum Co. paid $1.2 million for an 80% interest in the common stock of Sarong Co. Practicum had no previous equity interest in Sarong. On the acquisition date, Sarong's identifiable net assets had a $1.3 million carrying amount, and their fair value equaled $1.4 million. The fair value of the noncontrolling interest (NCI) equals 20% of the implied fair value of the acquiree. Practicum should record goodwill of

A. $(200,000)

B. $(100,000)

C. $100,000

D. $160,000

Answer (C) is correct. *(Publisher, adapted)*
REQUIRED: The calculation of goodwill recorded using the acquisition method.
DISCUSSION: In a business combination, goodwill is the excess of (1) the sum of the acquisition-date fair values (with some exceptions) of (a) the consideration transferred, (b) any NCI in the acquiree, and (c) the acquirer's previously held equity interest in the acquiree over (2) the net of the acquisition-date fair values (with some exceptions) of the identifiable assets acquired and liabilities assumed. Goodwill is therefore $100,000.

Consideration transferred	$1,200,000
NCI [($1,200,000 ÷ 80%) × 20%]	300,000
Previously held equity interest	0
Fair value of identifiable net assets acquired	(1,400,000)
Goodwill	$ 100,000

Answer (A) is incorrect. The amount of $(200,000) is the difference between the fair value of Sarong's identifiable net assets and the consideration transferred. Answer (B) is incorrect. The amount of $(100,000) is the difference between the carrying amount of Sarong's identifiable net assets and their fair value. Answer (D) is incorrect. The amount of $160,000 is the difference between the consideration transferred and 80% of the carrying amount of the identifiable net assets.

19. On the last day of its fiscal year, Packwood Co. gave cash and other property for all of the common stock of Silvertown Co. The fair value of Silvertown's identifiable net assets exceeded the fair value of the consideration transferred. After reassessing the identification of assets and liabilities and the procedures for their measurement, Packwood concluded that the initial accounting for this business combination was correct. Accordingly, the difference should be

A. Recognized as an ordinary gain.

B. Treated as goodwill to be amortized over the period benefited.

C. Allocated on a pro rata basis to all of the assets of the acquired entity.

D. Applied pro rata to reduce, but not below zero, the amounts initially assigned to certain acquired assets.

Answer (A) is correct. *(CMA, adapted)*
REQUIRED: The accounting for a business combination.
DISCUSSION: If the net of the acquisition-date fair values of the identifiable assets acquired and liabilities assumed exceeds the fair value of the sum of the consideration transferred, any previously held equity interest, and any NCI, Packwood should recognize an ordinary gain for the difference.
Answer (B) is incorrect. Goodwill results when the fair value of the consideration transferred (assuming no NCI or previously held equity interest in the acquiree) exceeds the fair value of the identifiable net assets acquired and it is not amortized. Answer (C) is incorrect. The difference is recognized as an ordinary gain. Answer (D) is incorrect. Allocation to certain acquired assets is an accounting treatment that is not permitted.

24.4 Acquisition-Related Costs

20. On August 31, Planar Corp. exchanged 100,000 shares of its $40 par value common stock for all of the net assets of Sistrock Co. The fair value of Planar's common stock on August 31 was $72 per share. Planar paid a fee of $320,000 to the consultant who arranged this acquisition. Direct costs of registering and issuing the equity securities amounted to $160,000. No goodwill or bargain purchase was involved in the acquisition. At what amount should Planar record the acquisition of Sistrock's net assets?

A. $7,200,000

B. $7,360,000

C. $7,520,000

D. $7,680,000

Answer (A) is correct. *(CPA, adapted)*
REQUIRED: The fair value of the net assets acquired.
DISCUSSION: Acquisition-related costs, such as the $320,000 consultant's fee, are, with one exception, expensed as incurred. Issuance costs for debt or equity securities are accounted for under other GAAP. Thus, the direct issuance costs of equity ($160,000) are debited to additional paid-in capital. The consideration transferred in a business combination is measured at acquisition-date fair value. It may consist of assets, liabilities incurred, or equity interests (including preferred stock) issued. Thus, the consideration transferred is measured at its fair value of $7,200,000 (100,000 shares of common stock issued × $72). Furthermore, given that no goodwill or bargain purchase was involved, neither goodwill nor a gain is recognized. Consequently, because the identifiable assets acquired and liabilities assumed must be measured at fair value, the debit recording their net amount is $7,200,000, the fair value of the consideration transferred. The compound entry is

Net of assets acquired and liabilities assumed	$7,200,000	
Expense for consulting fee	320,000	
Additional paid-in capital (direct registration and issue costs)	160,000	
Common stock ($40 par)		$4,000,000
Additional paid-in capital ($72 – $40)		3,200,000
Cash		480,000

Answer (B) is incorrect. The fair value of the net assets acquired plus the registration and issuance costs equals $7,360,000. Answer (C) is incorrect. The fair value of the net assets acquired plus the consultant's fee equals $7,520,000. Answer (D) is incorrect. The fair value of the net assets acquired plus the registration and issuance costs and the consultant's fee equals $7,680,000.

21. Pendragon Co. issues 200,000 shares of $5 par value common stock to acquire Squire Co. in a business combination. The market value of Pendragon's common stock is $12. Legal and consulting fees incurred in relationship to the combination are $110,000. Direct registration and issuance costs for the common stock are $35,000. What should be recorded in Pendragon's additional paid-in capital (APIC) for this business combination?

A. $1,545,000

B. $1,400,000

C. $1,365,000

D. $1,255,000

Answer (C) is correct. *(CPA, adapted)*
REQUIRED: The effect of the business combination on APIC.
DISCUSSION: Acquisition-related costs, such as finder's fees, professional (e.g., legal) and consulting fees, and general administrative costs (e.g., for an acquisitions department), are expensed as incurred. The one exception is for the issuance costs of debt or equity securities. These are accounted for under other GAAP. Thus, direct issuance costs of equity (underwriting, legal, accounting, tax, registration, etc.) are debited to additional paid-in capital. Accordingly, the amount recorded in APIC for the combination should be $1,365,000 {[200,000 shares × ($12 market value – $5 par value)] – $35,000 direct issuance costs}.
Answer (A) is incorrect. The amount of $1,545,000 equals $1,400,000 [200,000 × ($12 – $5)] plus legal and consulting fees ($110,000) and direct issuance costs ($35,000). Answer (B) is incorrect. APIC without an adjustment for direct issuance costs equals $1,400,000. Answer (D) is incorrect. The amount of $1,255,000 equals $1,400,000 [200,000 × ($12 – $5)], minus legal and consulting fees ($110,000), minus direct issuance costs ($35,000).

22. Costs incurred in completing a business combination are listed below.

General administrative costs	$240,000
Consulting fees	120,000
Direct cost to register and issue equity securities	80,000

The amount charged to the expenses of the business combination is

A. $80,000

B. $120,000

C. $240,000

D. $360,000

Answer (D) is correct. *(CMA, adapted)*
REQUIRED: The expenses of a business combination.
DISCUSSION: Acquisition-related costs, such as finder's fees, professional and consulting fees, and general administrative costs (e.g., for an acquisitions department) are expensed as incurred. The one exception is for issuance costs of debt or equity securities. These are accounted for under other GAAP. Direct issuance costs of equity (underwriting, legal, accounting, tax, registration, etc.) are debited to additional paid-in capital. Indirect costs of issuance, records maintenance, and ownership transfers (e.g., a stock transfer agent's fees) are expensed. Accordingly, the amount expensed is $360,000 ($240,000 + $120,000).
Answer (A) is incorrect. The direct cost to register and issue equity securities equals $80,000. This cost is a reduction of additional paid-in capital, not an expense. Answer (B) is incorrect. The amount of $120,000 does not include the general and administrative costs. Costs of registering and issuing equity securities should be treated as a reduction of their otherwise determinable fair value. Thus, only the $120,000 in indirect acquisition expenses should be charged to the expenses of the business combination. Answer (C) is incorrect. The amount of $240,000 does not include the consulting fees.

23. In a business combination, Major Corporation issued nonvoting, nonconvertible preferred stock with a fair value of $8 million in exchange for all of the outstanding common stock of Minor Corporation. On the acquisition date, Minor had identifiable net assets with a carrying amount of $4 million and a fair value of $5 million. In addition, Major issued preferred stock with a fair value of $800,000 to an individual as a finder's fee in arranging the transaction. As a result of this transaction, Major should record an increase in net assets of

A. $4,000,000

B. $5,000,000

C. $8,000,000

D. $8,800,000

Answer (C) is correct. *(CPA, adapted)*
REQUIRED: The initial amount recorded for net assets acquired in a business combination.
DISCUSSION: Goodwill is the excess of (1) the sum of the acquisition-date fair values (with some exceptions) of (a) the consideration transferred, (b) any noncontrolling interest in the acquiree, and (c) the acquirer's previously held equity interest in the acquiree over (2) the net of the acquisition-date fair values (with some exceptions) of the identifiable assets acquired and liabilities assumed. In the absence of a noncontrolling interest and a previously held equity interest, goodwill is therefore the excess of the fair value of the consideration transferred ($8 million) over the fair value of the net assets acquired ($5 million), or $3 million. Thus, the increase in net assets is $8 million. The acquisition-related cost (the finder's fee) is expensed.
Answer (A) is incorrect. The carrying amount of Minor's identifiable net assets is $4,000,000. Answer (B) is incorrect. The fair value of Minor's identifiable net assets is $5,000,000. Answer (D) is incorrect. The amount of $8,800,000 results from treating the finder's fee as part of the consideration transferred.

24. The following costs were incurred by the acquirer in business combinations:

Legal fees	$3,000,000
Cost of an internal acquisitions department	10,000,000
Issuance cost of debt securities	180,000

Which costs related to effecting business combinations are expensed in full by the controlled group for the period in which they are incurred?

A. $180,000

B. $3,180,000

C. $13,000,000

D. $13,180,000

Answer (C) is correct. *(Publisher, adapted)*
REQUIRED: The amount of costs related to business combinations that are fully expensed.
DISCUSSION: Acquisition-related costs, such as finder's fees, professional and consulting fees, and general administrative costs (e.g., for an acquisitions department), are expensed as incurred. The one exception is for issuance costs of debt or equity securities. These are accounted for under other GAAP. Issue costs of debt should be reported in the balance sheet as deferred charges and amortized over the life of the debt using the interest method. They are not commingled with premium or discount. Thus, the amount expensed as incurred is $13,000,000 ($3,000,000 + $10,000,000).
Answer (A) is incorrect. Costs to register and issue debt securities are reported as a deferred charge and amortized over the life of the debt using the interest method. Answer (B) is incorrect. The amount of $3,180,000 results from failing to include the cost of the acquisitions department and from improperly including the cost of the debt securities. Answer (D) is incorrect. The amount of $13,180,000 results from improperly including the cost of issuing the debt securities.

24.5 Consolidated Reporting

25. When a parent-subsidiary relationship exists, consolidated financial statements are prepared in recognition of the accounting concept of

A. Reliability.

B. Materiality.

C. Legal entity.

D. Economic entity.

Answer (D) is correct. *(CPA, adapted)*
REQUIRED: The accounting concept reflected in preparation of consolidated statements.
DISCUSSION: Consolidated statements primarily benefit the owners and creditors of the parent. They report the results of operations, financial position, and cash flows of a consolidated entity (a parent and its subsidiaries) as if it were one economic entity. The presumption is that consolidated statements are needed for fair presentation when one of the entities in the consolidated group directly or indirectly has a controlling financial interest in the other combined entities.
Answer (A) is incorrect. Reliability reflects the quality of information assuring that it is reasonably free from error and bias and faithfully represents what it purports to represent. Answer (B) is incorrect. Materiality requires reporting of information that has a value significant enough to affect decisions of those using the financial statements. Answer (C) is incorrect. The boundaries of the legal entity are disregarded in the preparation of consolidated financial statements.

26. A parent need not consolidate a subsidiary for financial reporting purposes if

A. The subsidiary's operations differ greatly from those of the parent.

B. The subsidiary operates in a country different from that of the parent.

C. A noncontrolling interest holds 45% of the subsidiary's outstanding common stock.

D. It is in legal reorganization.

Answer (D) is correct. *(N. Powell)*
REQUIRED: The exception to mandatory consolidation.
DISCUSSION: A parent is defined as an entity that holds a controlling financial interest in a subsidiary. The usual condition for a controlling financial interest is a majority voting interest. Thus, consolidation of all majority-owned subsidiaries ordinarily is required unless control does not rest with the majority owner. Circumstances in which control does not rest with the majority owner include when the subsidiary is (1) in bankruptcy, (2) in legal reorganization, or (3) subject to severe government-imposed uncertainties.
Answer (A) is incorrect. Whether the subsidiary's operations differ greatly from those of the parent does not affect the consolidation requirements. Answer (B) is incorrect. Whether the subsidiary operates in a country different from that of the parent does not affect the consolidation requirements. Answer (C) is incorrect. A noncontrolling interest does not prevent the need for consolidation.

27. Which subsidiary is most likely to meet the criteria for mandatory consolidation?

A. A 55%-owned subsidiary in bankruptcy.

B. A 49%-owned domestic subsidiary.

C. A 51%-owned foreign subsidiary.

D. A 90%-owned subsidiary subject to severe governmentally imposed uncertainties.

Answer (C) is correct. *(Publisher, adapted)*
REQUIRED: The subsidiary most likely to be consolidated.
DISCUSSION: All entities in which a parent has a controlling financial interest through direct or indirect ownership of a majority voting interest ordinarily must be consolidated. However, a subsidiary is not consolidated when control does not rest with the majority owner. Circumstances in which control does not rest with the majority owners include when the subsidiary is (1) in bankruptcy, (2) in legal reorganization, or (3) subject to foreign exchange restrictions or other government imposed restrictions that preclude exercise of control.
Answer (A) is incorrect. The majority-owned subsidiary is in bankruptcy. Answer (B) is incorrect. Over 50% of the outstanding voting interests are not owned by this investor. Answer (D) is incorrect. The government-imposed restrictions preclude exercise of control.

28. Consolidated financial statements are typically prepared when one entity has a majority voting interest in another unless

A. The subsidiary is a finance entity.

B. The fiscal year ends of the two entities are more than 3 months apart.

C. Control does not rest with the majority owner(s).

D. The two entities are in unrelated industries, such as manufacturing and real estate.

Answer (C) is correct. *(CPA, adapted)*
REQUIRED: The circumstance in which a majority-owned entity is not consolidated.
DISCUSSION: Consolidated financial reporting is required when one entity owns, directly or indirectly, more than 50% of the outstanding voting interests of another entity. However, a majority-owned subsidiary is not consolidated if control does not rest with the majority owner.
Answer (A) is incorrect. The nature of the subsidiary's business is irrelevant. Answer (B) is incorrect. A difference in fiscal periods is irrelevant. Answer (D) is incorrect. Whether the parent and subsidiary are in related industries is irrelevant.

29. According to GAAP relative to consolidation of variable interest entities,

A. A not-for-profit organization may not be treated as a variable interest entity.

B. A variable interest entity has an equity investment of more than 10% of its total assets.

C. A variable interest entity is consolidated by its primary beneficiary when the beneficiary becomes involved with the entity.

D. Corporations may not be organized as variable interest entities.

Answer (C) is correct. *(Publisher, adapted)*
REQUIRED: The true statement about VIEs.
DISCUSSION: In essence, a variable interest entity (VIE) is any legal structure (including, but not limited to, those previously described as special-purpose entities) with insufficient equity investment or whose equity investors lack one of the essential characteristics of financial control. When an entity becomes involved with a VIE, it must determine whether it is the primary beneficiary and therefore must consolidate the VIE. A primary beneficiary holds a variable interest(s) that will absorb a majority of the VIE's expected losses or receive a majority of its expected residual returns (or both).
Answer (A) is incorrect. The guidance for VIEs applies to NFPs if they are used to avoid the requirements of GAAP. Answer (B) is incorrect. An entity qualifies as a VIE if the equity at risk does not suffice to finance entity activities without additional subordinated financial support. An equity investment of less than 10% of total assets is usually considered to be insufficient. But a greater investment also may not suffice if, for example, assets or entity activities are high risk. Answer (D) is incorrect. A VIE may take any form.

24.6 Consolidated Reporting -- Balance Sheet

30. Pent Corp. acquired 100% of Subtle Corp.'s outstanding capital stock for $890,000 cash. Immediately before the acquisition, the balance sheets of both corporations reported the following:

	Pent	Subtle
Assets	$4,000,000	$1,500,000
Liabilities	$1,400,000	$ 720,000
Common stock	2,000,000	620,000
Retained earnings	500,000	80,000
Accumulated other comprehensive income	100,000	80,000
Liabilities and equity	$4,000,000	$1,500,000

At the date of purchase, the fair value of Subtle's assets was $100,000 more than the aggregate carrying amounts. In the consolidated balance sheet prepared immediately after the purchase, the consolidated equity should equal

- A. $3,490,000
- B. $3,480,000
- C. $3,380,000
- D. $2,600,000

Answer (D) is correct. *(CPA, adapted)*
REQUIRED: The consolidated equity after the acquisition.
DISCUSSION: A business combination is an acquisition of net assets. Thus, only the fair value of the net assets of a subsidiary is included in a consolidated balance sheet prepared using the acquisition method. Its equity, including retained earnings, is excluded. Accordingly, in the absence of a bargain purchase, total equity of the consolidated entity attributable to the owners immediately after acquisition is the same as the parent's total equity. Consequently, equity is $2,600,000 ($2,000,000 common stock + $500,000 retained earnings + $100,000 accumulated OCI).
Answer (A) is incorrect. The sum of the equity of Pent plus the cash price is $3,490,000. Answer (B) is incorrect. The sum of the equity of Pent and Subtle plus the excess fair value of Subtle's assets is $3,480,000. Answer (C) is incorrect. The sum of the equity of Pent and Subtle is $3,380,000.

31. On December 31, Poe Corporation exchanged 200,000 shares of its $10 par common stock, with a market price of $18 per share, for all of Saxe Corporation's common stock. The equity section of each entity's balance sheet immediately before the combination is presented below:

	Poe	Saxe
Common stock	$3,000,000	$1,500,000
Additional paid-in capital	1,300,000	150,000
Retained earnings	2,500,000	850,000
Totals	$6,800,000	$2,500,000

In the December 31 consolidated balance sheet, additional paid-in capital should be reported at

- A. $3,600,000
- B. $1,300,000
- C. $1,450,000
- D. $2,900,000

Answer (D) is correct. *(CPA, adapted)*
REQUIRED: The additional paid-in capital to be reported in the consolidated balance sheet.
DISCUSSION: To effect the acquisition, Poe records the following journal entry in its separate books:

Investment in Saxe Corp.		
(200,000 shares × $18 market price)	$3,600,000	
Common stock (200,000 shares × $10 par value)		$2,000,000
Additional paid-in capital (difference)		1,600,000

The additional paid-in capital carried on Poe's (the parent's) books is therefore $2,900,000 ($1,300,000 + $1,600,000). This balance also is reported on the consolidated balance sheet.
Answer (A) is incorrect. The consideration transferred for all of Saxe's common stock is $3,600,000. Answer (B) is incorrect. The amount reported by Poe immediately before the combination is $1,300,000. Answer (C) is incorrect. The sum of the amounts reported by Poe and Saxe immediately before the combination is $1,450,000.

Questions 32 through 36 are based on the following information. On January 2, Parma borrowed $60,000 and used the proceeds to purchase 90% of the outstanding common shares of Seville. Parma had no prior equity interest in Seville. Ten equal principal and interest payments begin December 30. The excess of the implied fair value of Seville over the carrying amount of its identifiable net assets should be assigned 60% to inventory and 40% to goodwill. Moreover, the fair value of the noncontrolling interest (NCI) is 10% of the implied fair value of the acquiree.

The following are the balance sheets of Parma and Seville on January 1:

	Parma	Seville
Current assets	$ 70,000	$20,000
Noncurrent assets	90,000	40,000
Total assets	$160,000	$60,000
Current liabilities	$ 30,000	$10,000
Noncurrent liabilities	50,000	--
Equity	80,000	50,000
Total liabilities and equity	$160,000	$60,000

---

32. On Parma's January 2 consolidated balance sheet, current assets equal

A. $100,000

B. $96,000

C. $90,000

D. $80,000

Answer (A) is correct. *(CPA, adapted)*
   REQUIRED: The consolidated current assets.
   DISCUSSION: The implied fair value of the subsidiary is $66,667 ($60,000 cash paid by the parent ÷ 90%). The excess of this amount over the carrying amount of the subsidiary's identifiable net assets is $16,667 ($66,667 – $50,000). This amount is allocated $10,000 to inventory ($16,667 × 60%) and $6,667 to goodwill ($16,667 × 40%). Thus, the reported amount of the current assets is $100,000.

Current assets of Parma	$ 70,000
Current assets of Seville	20,000
Understatement of inventory	10,000
Consolidated current assets	$100,000

   Answer (B) is incorrect. The amount of $96,000 assumes an assignment of $6,000 to inventory. Answer (C) is incorrect. The amount of $90,000 ignores the $10,000 excess of the fair value of inventory over its carrying amount. Answer (D) is incorrect. The amount of $80,000 results from subtracting the excess of the fair value of inventory over its carrying amount.

---

33. On Parma's January 2 consolidated balance sheet, noncurrent assets equal

A. $130,000

B. $134,000

C. $136,667

D. $140,000

Answer (C) is correct. *(CPA, adapted)*
   REQUIRED: The consolidated noncurrent assets.
   DISCUSSION: The implied fair value of the subsidiary is $66,667 ($60,000 cash paid by the parent ÷ 90%). The excess of this amount over the carrying amount of the subsidiary's identifiable net assets is $16,667 ($66,667 – $50,000). This amount is allocated $10,000 to inventory ($16,667 × 60%) and $6,667 to goodwill ($16,667 × 40%). Thus, reported noncurrent assets equal $136,667.

Noncurrent assets of Parma	$ 90,000
Noncurrent assets of Seville	40,000
Goodwill	6,667
Consolidated noncurrent assets	$136,667

   Answer (A) is incorrect. The amount of $130,000 ignores goodwill. Answer (B) is incorrect. The amount of $134,000 assumes that a 100% interest was acquired and that goodwill was therefore $4,000 [($60,000 – $50,000) × 40%]. Answer (D) is incorrect. The amount of $140,000 assumes that a 100% interest was acquired and that goodwill was $10,000.

34. On Parma's January 2 consolidated balance sheet, current liabilities equal

A. $50,000

B. $46,000

C. $40,000

D. $30,000

Answer (B) is correct. *(CPA, adapted)*

REQUIRED: The consolidated current liabilities.

DISCUSSION: Consolidated current liabilities contain the current portion of the debt issued by Parma to finance the acquisition ($60,000 ÷ 10 equal principal payments = $6,000). Reported current liabilities equal $46,000.

Current liabilities of Parma	$30,000
Current liabilities of Seville	10,000
Current component of new debt	6,000
Consolidated current liabilities	$46,000

Answer (A) is incorrect. The pre-existing noncurrent debt is $50,000. Answer (C) is incorrect. The amount of $40,000 ignores the new borrowing. Answer (D) is incorrect. The amount of Parma's pre-existing current liabilities is $30,000.

35. On Parma's January 2 consolidated balance sheet, the sum of the noncurrent liabilities and the NCI equal

A. $116,667

B. $110,667

C. $104,000

D. $50,000

Answer (B) is correct. *(CPA, adapted)*

REQUIRED: The sum of the noncurrent liabilities and the NCI.

DISCUSSION: Consolidated noncurrent liabilities include the noncurrent portion of the debt issued by Parma to finance the acquisition ($60,000 – $6,000 = $54,000). Thus, reported noncurrent liabilities equal $104,000.

Noncurrent liabilities of Parma	$ 50,000
Noncurrent component of new debt	54,000
Consolidated noncurrent liabilities	$104,000

The implied fair value of the subsidiary is $66,667 ($60,000 cash paid by the parent ÷ 90%), and the NCI is $6,667 ($66,667 × 10%). The sum of the noncurrent liabilities and the NCI is therefore $110,667 ($104,000 + $6,667).

Answer (A) is incorrect. The amount of $116,667 is the sum of noncurrent liabilities (excluding the new borrowing) and the implied fair value of the subsidiary. Answer (C) is incorrect. The amount of $104,000 omits the NCI. Answer (D) is incorrect. The amount of $50,000 ignores the new borrowing and the NCI.

36. On Parma's January 2 consolidated balance sheet, Parma's equity should be

A. $80,000

B. $86,667

C. $90,000

D. $130,000

Answer (A) is correct. *(CPA, adapted)*

REQUIRED: The equity in the consolidated balance sheet.

DISCUSSION: An NCI is the equity of a subsidiary not directly or indirectly attributable to the parent. Accordingly, the equity section of the consolidated balance sheet at the acquisition date is not the same as the equity section of the parent's separate balance sheet. Consolidated equity includes any NCI in the fair value of the acquiree's identifiable net assets presented separately from the parent's equity. Thus, Parma's equity on the consolidated balance sheet is calculated as follows:

Consolidated current assets	$ 100,000
Consolidated noncurrent assets	136,667
Consolidated current liabilities	(46,000)
Consolidated noncurrent liabilities	(104,000)
NCI	(6,667)
Parma's equity	$ 80,000

Answer (B) is incorrect. Parma's equity at 1/1 plus the fair value of the NCI equals $86,667. Answer (C) is incorrect. The total liabilities of the two entities at 1/1 equal $90,000. Answer (D) is incorrect. The sum of the equity amounts for Parma and Seville at 1/1 is $130,000.

Questions 37 through 39 are based on the following information. The separate condensed balance sheets and income statements of Pater Corp. and its wholly owned subsidiary, Subito Corp., are as follows:

BALANCE SHEETS
As of December 31

Assets	Pater	Subito
Current assets		
Cash	$ 80,000	$ 60,000
Accounts receivable (net)	140,000	25,000
Inventories	90,000	50,000
Total current assets	$ 310,000	$135,000
Property, plant, and		
equipment (net)	515,000	280,000
Intangible assets	100,000	--
Investment in Subito		
(equity method)	400,000	--
Total assets	$1,325,000	$415,000

Liabilities and Equity	Pater	Subito
Current liabilities		
Accounts payable	$ 160,000	$ 95,000
Accrued liabilities	110,000	30,000
Total current liabilities	$ 270,000	$125,000
Equity		
Common stock ($10 par)	$ 300,000	$ 50,000
Additional paid-in capital		10,000
Retained earnings	755,000	230,000
Total equity	$1,055,000	$290,000
Total liabilities and equity	$1,325,000	$415,000

INCOME STATEMENTS
For the Year Ended December 31

	Pater	Subito
Sales	$2,000,000	$750,000
Cost of goods sold	1,540,000	500,000
Gross margin	$ 460,000	$250,000
Operating expenses	260,000	150,000
Operating income	$ 200,000	$100,000
Equity in earnings of Subito	70,000	--
Income before income taxes	$ 270,000	$100,000
Provision for income taxes	70,000	30,000
Net income	$ 200,000	$ 70,000

Additional Information:

- On January 1, Pater purchased for $360,000 all of Subito's $10 par, voting common stock. On January 1, the fair value of Subito's assets and liabilities equaled their carrying amounts of $410,000 and $160,000, respectively, except that the fair values of certain items in Subito's inventory were $10,000 more than their carrying amounts. These items were still on hand on December 31. Pater amortizes intangible assets over a 10-year period.

- During the year, Pater and Subito paid cash dividends of $100,000 and $30,000, respectively. For tax purposes, Pater receives the 100% exclusion for dividends received from Subito.

- There were no intraentity transactions, except for Pater's receipt of dividends from Subito and Pater's recording of its share of Subito's earnings.

- No transactions affected other comprehensive income.

- Both Pater and Subito paid income taxes at the rate of 30%.

- Pater treats Subito as a reporting unit, and all goodwill acquired in the business combination is assigned to Subito for the purpose of testing impairment. However, goodwill was not impaired on December 31.

- Assume that the consolidation did not affect the net incomes of Pater and Subito.

37. In the December 31 consolidated financial statements of Pater and its subsidiary, total current assets should be

A. $455,000

B. $445,000

C. $310,000

D. $135,000

Answer (A) is correct. *(CPA, adapted)*
REQUIRED: The total current assets.
DISCUSSION: Consolidated current assets are calculated as follows:

Current assets of Pater	$310,000
Current assets of Subito	135,000
Undervalued inventory	10,000
Consolidated current assets	$455,000

Answer (B) is incorrect. The amount of $445,000 does not reflect the fair value of the inventory. Answer (C) is incorrect. The parent's current assets equal $310,000. Answer (D) is incorrect. The unadjusted current assets of the subsidiary equal $135,000.

38. In the December 31 consolidated financial statements of Pater and its subsidiary, total assets should be

   A. $1,740,000

   B. $1,450,000

   C. $1,350,000

   D. $1,325,000

Answer (B) is correct. *(CPA, adapted)*
   REQUIRED: The total assets.
   DISCUSSION: Goodwill is the excess of (1) the sum of the acquisition-date fair values (with some exceptions) of (a) the consideration transferred, (b) any NCI in the acquiree, and (c) the acquirer's previously held equity interest in the acquiree over (2) the net of the acquisition-date fair values (with some exceptions) of the identifiable assets acquired and liabilities assumed. Goodwill is therefore $100,000.

Consideration transferred	$360,000
Carrying amount of net assets acquired	(250,000)
Undervaluation of inventory	(10,000)
Goodwill	$100,000

December 31 consolidated total assets are calculated as follows:

Assets of Pater	$1,325,000
Assets of Subito	415,000
Investment in Subito	(400,000)
Undervalued inventory	10,000
Goodwill	100,000
Consolidated total assets	$1,450,000

   Answer (A) is incorrect. The unadjusted sum of the assets of Pater and Subito is $1,740,000. Answer (C) is incorrect. The amount of $1,350,000 excludes goodwill. Answer (D) is incorrect. The parent's total assets equal $1,325,000.

39. In the December 31 consolidated financial statements of Pater and its subsidiary, total retained earnings should be

   A. $985,000

   B. $825,000

   C. $795,000

   D. $755,000

Answer (D) is correct. *(CPA, adapted)*
   REQUIRED: The total retained earnings.
   DISCUSSION: Pater acquired Subito in a business combination and properly accounts for the investment in its separate statements using the equity method. Subito's separate net income for the year is reflected in full in consolidated net income and in Pater's retained earnings. It is given that the consolidation did not affect Subito's separate net income. Thus, consolidated retained earnings consist only of Pater's $755,000 of retained earnings.
   Answer (A) is incorrect. The amount of $985,000 includes the subsidiary's retained earnings. Answer (B) is incorrect. The figure of $825,000 includes the subsidiary's net income, an amount already reflected in the parent's retained earnings under the equity method. Answer (C) is incorrect. The figure of $795,000 includes the subsidiary's net income minus the dividends paid, an amount already accounted for using the equity method.

40. Rowe, Inc., owns 80% of Cowan Co.'s outstanding capital stock. On November 1, Rowe advanced $100,000 in cash to Cowan. What amount should be reported related to the advance in Rowe's consolidated balance sheet as of December 31?

   A. $0

   B. $20,000

   C. $80,000

   D. $100,000

Answer (A) is correct. *(CPA, adapted)*
   REQUIRED: The amount of an advance by a parent to a subsidiary reported in consolidated statements.
   DISCUSSION: Because consolidated statements present amounts for the parent and subsidiary as if they were one economic entity, the effects of intraentity transactions must be eliminated. Thus, reciprocal balances, e.g., a receivable and a payable for an advance, between the parent and subsidiary are eliminated in full. This procedure is followed even if a noncontrolling interest exists. Accordingly, no amount for the advance is reported in the consolidated statements.
   Answer (B) is incorrect. The amount of $20,000 is based on the assumption that a portion of the transaction is allocated to the noncontrolling interest. Answer (C) is incorrect. The amount of $80,000 is based on the assumption that only the portion of the transaction allocated to the noncontrolling interest is eliminated. Answer (D) is incorrect. The amount of $100,000 is based on the assumption that the transaction was with an external party.

Questions 41 and 42 are based on the following information. On January 1, Pathan Corp. purchased 80% of Samoa Corp.'s $10 par common stock for $975,000. Pathan had no prior equity interest in Samoa. The remaining 20% of this stock is held by NCI Co., an unrelated party. On the acquisition date for this business combination, the carrying amount of Samoa's net assets was $1 million. The fair values of the assets acquired and liabilities assumed were the same as their carrying amounts on Samoa's balance sheet except for plant assets (net), the fair value of which was $100,000 in excess of the carrying amount. The fair value of the noncontrolling interest (NCI) is 20% of the implied fair value of the acquiree's net assets at the acquisition date. (No exceptions to the recognition or measurement principles apply.) For the year ended December 31, Samoa's net income included in consolidated net income was $190,000, and Samoa paid cash dividends totaling $125,000.

41. The goodwill recognized by Pathan at the date of the business combination is

A. $0

B. $98,750

C. $118,750

D. $243,750

Answer (C) is correct. *(CPA, adapted)*
REQUIRED: The initial goodwill recognized.
DISCUSSION: Goodwill is the excess of (1) the sum of the acquisition-date fair values of (a) the consideration transferred, (b) any NCI in the acquiree, and (c) the acquirer's previously held equity interest in the acquiree over (2) the net of the acquisition-date fair values of the identifiable assets acquired and liabilities assumed.

Consideration transferred		$ 975,000
NCI [($975,000 ÷ 80%) × 20%]		243,750
Acquisition-date fair value of net assets acquired:		
Carrying amount:	$1,000,000	
Understatement of plant assets:	100,000	(1,100,000)
Goodwill		$ 118,750

Answer (A) is incorrect. The sum of the acquisition-date fair values of the consideration transferred and the NCI (the acquirer had no previously held equity interest in the acquiree) exceeds the net of the acquisition-date fair values of the identifiable assets acquired and liabilities assumed (no exceptions to the recognition and measurement principles apply). Answer (B) is incorrect. The amount of $98,750 equals $118,750 minus 20% of $100,000. Answer (D) is incorrect. The amount of $243,750 is the acquisition-date fair value of the NCI.

42. In the December 31 consolidated balance sheet, the NCI is reported at

A. $200,000

B. $213,000

C. $243,750

D. $256,750

Answer (D) is correct. *(CPA, adapted)*
REQUIRED: The amount of the NCI at year end.
DISCUSSION: An NCI is the equity of a subsidiary not directly or indirectly attributable to the parent. Thus, the NCI is equal to the 20% (100% – 80%) interest in Samoa not held by Pathan. The fair value of the NCI at the acquisition date was $243,750 [($975,000 ÷ 80%) implied fair value of acquiree × 20%]. The NCI to be reported in the year-end balance sheet equals its fair value at the beginning of the year, plus 20% of the net income, minus 20% of the dividends. Thus, the NCI is reported at $256,750.

Fair value on 1/1	$243,750
NCI in subsidiary's net income included in consolidated net income ($190,000 × 20%)	38,000
NCI in subsidiary's dividends paid ($125,000 × 20%)	(25,000)
Noncontrolling interest at 12/31	$256,750

Answer (A) is incorrect. The amount of $200,000 equals 20% of the carrying amount of Samoa's net assets on 1/1. Answer (B) is incorrect. The amount of $213,000 equals 20% of the carrying amount of the net assets on 1/1, plus 20% of net income, minus 20% of dividends. Answer (C) is incorrect. The NCI measured at fair value at 1/1 was $243,750.

24.7 Consolidated Reporting -- Net Income and Retained Earnings

43. To effect a business combination, Proper Co. acquired all the outstanding common shares of Scapula Co., a business entity, for cash equal to the carrying amount of Scapula's net assets. The carrying amounts of Scapula's assets and liabilities approximated their fair values at the acquisition date, except that the carrying amount of its building was more than fair value. In preparing Proper's year-end consolidated income statement, what is the effect of recording the assets acquired and liabilities assumed at fair value, and should goodwill amortization be recognized?

	Depreciation Expense	Goodwill Amortization
A.	Lower	Yes
B.	Higher	Yes
C.	Lower	No
D.	Higher	No

Answer (C) is correct. *(CPA, adapted)*
REQUIRED: The effect of the combination on depreciation and goodwill amortization.
DISCUSSION: A business combination is accounted for as an acquisition. Accordingly, the identifiable assets acquired and liabilities assumed ordinarily are recorded at their acquisition-date fair values. The differences between those fair values and carrying amounts will affect net income when related expenses are incurred. The effect of recording the building at fair value in the consolidated balance sheet instead of its higher carrying amount on Scapula's books will be to decrease future depreciation. Goodwill is the excess of (1) the sum of the acquisition-date fair values (with some exceptions) of (a) the consideration transferred, (b) any noncontrolling interest in the acquiree, and (c) the acquirer's previously held equity interest in the acquiree over (2) the net of the acquisition-date fair values (with some exceptions) of the identifiable assets acquired and liabilities assumed. Thus, Proper recognizes goodwill for the excess of the cash paid over the fair value of the net assets acquired (given an acquisition of 100% of Scapula's common shares). This amount will be tested for impairment, not amortized.
Answer (A) is incorrect. Goodwill will be recognized but not amortized. Answer (B) is incorrect. Depreciation will decrease, and goodwill will be recognized but not amortized. Answer (D) is incorrect. Depreciation will decrease.

44. A 70%-owned subsidiary declares and pays a cash dividend. What effect does the dividend have on the retained earnings and noncontrolling interest balances in the consolidated balance sheet?

A. No effect on either retained earnings or the noncontrolling interest.

B. No effect on retained earnings and a decrease in the noncontrolling interest.

C. Decreases in both retained earnings and the noncontrolling interest.

D. A decrease in retained earnings and no effect on the noncontrolling interest.

Answer (B) is correct. *(CPA, adapted)*
REQUIRED: The effect of payment of a cash dividend by a subsidiary.
DISCUSSION: The parent's investment in subsidiary, intraentity dividends, and the subsidiary's equity accounts, which include retained earnings, are among the eliminations in a consolidation. The equity (net assets) of the subsidiary not directly or indirectly attributable to the parent is reported separately in consolidated equity as the noncontrolling interest. Consolidated retained earnings equals the accumulated earnings of the consolidated group not distributed to the owners of, or capitalized by, the parent. Thus, it equals the parent's retained earnings. Accordingly, the subsidiary's cash dividend (debit subsidiary retained earnings, credit cash) reduces its retained earnings balance and the noncontrolling interest but not the consolidated retained earnings. When a 70%-owned entity pays cash dividends, 70% remains in the consolidated group.
Answer (A) is incorrect. Cash dividends from a subsidiary decrease the noncontrolling interest. Answer (C) is incorrect. Cash dividends from a subsidiary have no effect on consolidated retained earnings but decrease the noncontrolling interest. Answer (D) is incorrect. Cash dividends from a subsidiary have no effect on consolidated retained earnings.

45. Jane Co. owns 90% of the common stock of Dun Corp. and 100% of the common stock of Beech Corp. On December 30, Dun and Beech each declared a cash dividend of $100,000 for the current year. What is the total amount of dividends that should be reported in the December 31 consolidated financial statements of Jane and its subsidiaries, Dun and Beech?

A. $10,000

B. $100,000

C. $190,000

D. $200,000

Answer (A) is correct. *(CPA, adapted)*
REQUIRED: The dividends reported in consolidated financial statements.
DISCUSSION: The only dividends declared by the subsidiaries that are reported are those paid to noncontrolling interests. Beech has no NCIs because the parent (Jane) owns 100% of its shares. Accordingly, the dividends reported equal $10,000 ($100,000 declared by Dun × 10% noncontrolling ownership interest in Dun).
Answer (B) is incorrect. The amount declared by Dun or Beech is $100,000. Answer (C) is incorrect. The amount eliminated in the consolidation is $190,000. Answer (D) is incorrect. The amount of $200,000 is the total declared by Dun and Beech.

46. On January 1, Year 4, Pane Corp. exchanged 150,000 shares of its $20 par value common stock for all of Sky Corp.'s common stock. At that date, the fair value of Pane's common stock issued was equal to the fair value of the identifiable assets acquired and liabilities assumed. Both corporations continued to operate as separate businesses, maintaining accounting records with years ending December 31. In its separate statements, Pane accounts for the investment using the equity method. Information from separate company operations follows:

	Pane	Sky
Retained earnings – 12/31/Yr 3	$3,200,000	$925,000
Dividends paid – 3/25/Yr 4	750,000	200,000

If consolidated net income since the acquisition date was $800,000, what amount of retained earnings should Pane report in its June 30, Year 4, consolidated balance sheet?

A. $4,925,000

B. $4,125,000

C. $3,050,000

D. $3,250,000

Answer (D) is correct. *(CPA, adapted)*
REQUIRED: The consolidated retained earnings.
DISCUSSION: Retained earnings of the consolidated entity at the acquisition date consist solely of the retained earnings of the parent (if no gain on bargain purchase was recognized). The consolidated entry does not report any equity amounts of the subsidiary. Retained earnings of the consolidated entity at the reporting date consist of the parent's acquisition-date retained earnings, plus consolidated net income (no NCI exists), minus consolidated dividends paid. Sky's dividends, if any, are paid solely to Pane. Thus, consolidated dividends (those paid outside the entity) consist entirely of those paid by Pane.

Acquisition-date retained earnings of Pane	$3,200,000
Consolidated net income since acquisition date	800,000
Consolidated dividends paid since acquisition date	(750,000)
Consolidated retained earnings at reporting date	$3,250,000

Answer (A) is incorrect. The amount of $4,925,000 includes Sky's retained earnings at 12/31/Yr 4 and does not reflect an adjustment for the dividends paid. Answer (B) is incorrect. The amount of $4,125,000 is the sum of the retained earnings of Pane and Sky at 12/31/Yr 3. Answer (C) is incorrect. The amount of $3,050,000 results from treating Sky's dividends as consolidated dividends.

47. On January 2 of the current year, Peace Co. paid $310,000 to purchase 75% of the voting shares of Surge Co. Peace reported retained earnings of $80,000, and Surge reported contributed capital of $300,000 and retained earnings of $100,000. The purchase differential was attributed to depreciable assets with a remaining useful life of 10 years. Peace used the equity method in accounting for its investment in Surge. Surge reported net income of $20,000 and paid dividends of $8,000 during the current year. Peace reported income, exclusive of its income from Surge, of $30,000 and paid dividends of $15,000 during the current year. What amount will Peace report as dividends declared and paid in its current year's consolidated statement of retained earnings?

A. $8,000

B. $15,000

C. $17,000

D. $23,000

Answer (C) is correct. *(CPA, adapted)*
REQUIRED: The consolidated dividends declared and paid.
DISCUSSION: Peace acquired a greater than 50% share of the voting interests in Surge. Accordingly, Peace must consolidate Surge unless it does not have control. The facts given do not indicate that Peace lacks control of Surge. Moreover, under the equity method, the investor reduces its investment in the investee by the amount of dividends received. However, the equity method is not appropriate when the investor controls the investee except in parent-only statements. Consolidated statements are the general-purpose (GAAP-based) statements of a parent. In these statements, Peace should report only dividends paid to parties outside the consolidated entity. Assuming that Peace did not pay dividends to Surge, dividends reported as declared and paid in the consolidated statement of retained earnings equal $17,000.

Dividends declared and paid by Peace	$15,000
Dividends declared and paid by Surge	8,000
Intraentity dividends ($8,000 × 75%)	(6,000)
Consolidated dividends declared and paid	$17,000

Answer (A) is incorrect. The amount of dividends paid by Surge is $8,000. Answer (B) is incorrect. The amount paid by Peace is $15,000. Answer (D) is incorrect. The amount of $23,000 includes $6,000 of intraentity dividends.

Question 48 is based on the following information. The separate condensed balance sheets and income statements of Pater Corp. and its wholly owned subsidiary, Subito Corp., are as follows:

BALANCE SHEETS
As of December 31

Assets	Pater	Subito
Current assets		
Cash	$ 80,000	$ 60,000
Accounts receivable (net)	140,000	25,000
Inventories	90,000	50,000
Total current assets	$ 310,000	$135,000
Property, plant, and equipment (net)	515,000	280,000
Intangible assets	100,000	--
Investment in Subito (equity method)	400,000	--
Total assets	$1,325,000	$415,000
Liabilities and Equity		
Current liabilities		
Accounts payable	$ 160,000	$ 95,000
Accrued liabilities	110,000	30,000
Total current liabilities	$ 270,000	$125,000
Equity		
Common stock ($10 par)	$ 300,000	$ 50,000
Additional paid-in capital		10,000
Retained earnings	755,000	230,000
Total equity	$1,055,000	$290,000
Total liabilities and equity	$1,325,000	$415,000

INCOME STATEMENTS
For the Year Ended December 31

	Pater	Subito
Sales	$2,000,000	$750,000
Cost of goods sold	1,540,000	500,000
Gross margin	$ 460,000	$250,000
Operating expenses	260,000	150,000
Operating income	$ 200,000	$100,000
Equity in earnings of Subito	70,000	--
Income before income taxes	$ 270,000	$100,000
Provision for income taxes	70,000	30,000
Net income	$ 200,000	$ 70,000

Additional Information:

- On January 1, Pater purchased for $360,000 all of Subito's $10 par, voting common stock. On January 1, the fair value of Subito's assets and liabilities equaled their carrying amounts of $410,000 and $160,000, respectively. Pater amortizes intangible assets over a 10-year period.

- During the year, Pater and Subito paid cash dividends of $100,000 and $30,000, respectively. For tax purposes, Pater receives the 100% exclusion for dividends received from Subito.

- There were no intraentity transactions, except for Pater's receipt of dividends from Subito and Pater's recording of its share of Subito's earnings.

- No transactions affected other comprehensive income.

- Both Pater and Subito paid income taxes at the rate of 30%.

- Pater treats Subito as a reporting unit, and all goodwill acquired in the business combination is assigned to Subito for the purpose of testing impairment. However, goodwill was not impaired on December 31.

- Assume that no eliminations or adjustments in the consolidation procedure affect the amount of Pater's or Subito's net income included in consolidated net income.

48. In the December 31 consolidated financial statements of Pater and its subsidiary, net income should be

A. $270,000

B. $200,000

C. $190,000

D. $170,000

Answer (B) is correct. *(CPA, adapted)*
REQUIRED: The consolidated net income.
DISCUSSION: Because Pater owns 100% of Subito, all of Subito's net income for the period since acquisition is included in Pater's separate net income. Also, given that no eliminations or adjustments affect the separate net income of Pater and Subito, consolidated net income for the year is $200,000.
Answer (A) is incorrect. The sum of the net incomes of Pater and Subito equals $270,000. Answer (C) is incorrect. Pater's net income minus goodwill amortization ($100,000 ÷ 10 years) equals $190,000. However, goodwill is tested for impairment but not amortized. Goodwill was not impaired at December 31. Answer (D) is incorrect. Pater's net income minus the dividend payment, which does not affect equity-based net income, equals $170,000.

49. Purvis Company acquired a 100% interest in Smith Company on January 1, Year 1, at a price $200,000 in excess of its carrying amount. Of this excess, $40,000 was attributable to inventory (FIFO) and $70,000 to equipment with a 5-year remaining useful life that was depreciated on the straight-line basis. The remainder was attributable to goodwill. Condensed income statements for the year for Purvis and Smith are presented below:

	Purvis	Smith
Sales	$530,000	$440,000
COGS	(80,000)	(60,000)
Depreciation	(140,000)	(80,000)
Other expenses	(156,000)	(100,000)
Investment income	146,000	-0-
Net income	$300,000	$200,000

No intraentity transactions occurred during the year, and no other eliminations or adjustments were required in the consolidation procedure. Assuming Purvis applied the equity method in its parent-only statements, at what amount should net income be included in the December 31, Year 1, consolidated income statement?

A. $200,000

B. $300,000

C. $446,000

D. $500,000

Answer (B) is correct. *(Publisher, adapted)*
REQUIRED: The consolidated net income.
DISCUSSION: Equity in the earnings of a subsidiary is recorded on the parent-only income statement in accordance with the equity method. Purvis has a 100% interest in Smith. Hence, it recognizes $146,000 of investment income, consisting of 100% of Smith's net income ($200,000), minus the $40,000 increase in cost of goods sold (the FIFO inventory is presumed to have been sold) and additional depreciation of $14,000 ($70,000 ÷ 5 years). Consolidated net income thus equals the parent's separate net income of $300,000.
Answer (A) is incorrect. Smith's net income is $200,000. Answer (C) is incorrect. The amount of $446,000 results from double counting investment income. Answer (D) is incorrect. The total of Purvis's net income and Smith's net income is $500,000.

50. Parr Company acquired 80% of Syd Co. for $800,000. On the date of acquisition, September 1 of the current year, the fair value of the consideration transferred equaled 80% of the fair value and the carrying amount of the acquired net assets of Syd. Syd earned $600,000 of net income evenly throughout the calendar year and paid dividends of $90,000 on December 30. At what amount will the preacquisition earnings of Syd be included in consolidated net income for the calendar year of the acquisition?

A. $400,000

B. $320,000

C. $160,000

D. $0

Answer (D) is correct. *(Publisher, adapted)*
REQUIRED: The amount at which the preacquisition earnings will be included in consolidated net income.
DISCUSSION: When a subsidiary is initially consolidated during the year, its revenues, expenses, gains, and losses are included in the consolidated statements only from the initial consolidation date. Thus, Syd's earnings prior to September 1 are excluded from consolidated net income of the year of acquisition.
Answer (A) is incorrect. The amount of income Syd earned before the acquisition is $400,000. Answer (B) is incorrect. This amount is 80% of the amount of income that Syd earned before the acquisition. Answer (C) is incorrect. This amount is 80% of the amount of income that Syd earned after the acquisition.

24.8 Consolidated Reporting -- Intraentity Transactions

51. Shep Co. has a receivable from its parent, Pep Co. Should this receivable be separately reported in Shep's balance sheet and in Pep's consolidated balance sheet?

	Shep's Balance Sheet	Pep's Consolidated Balance Sheet
A.	Yes	No
B.	Yes	Yes
C.	No	No
D.	No	Yes

Answer (A) is correct. *(CPA, adapted)*
REQUIRED: The reporting of a subsidiary's receivable from its parent.
DISCUSSION: In a consolidated balance sheet, reciprocal balances, such as receivables and payables, between a parent and a consolidated subsidiary are eliminated in their entirety, regardless of the portion of the subsidiary's stock held by the parent. However, intraentity transactions should not be eliminated from the separate financial statements of the entities.
Answer (B) is incorrect. The receivable should be eliminated from the consolidated statements. Answer (C) is incorrect. The receivable should be reported on the subsidiary's balance sheet. Answer (D) is incorrect. The receivable should be eliminated from the consolidated statements but not from the subsidiary's balance sheet.

52. Wright Corp. has several subsidiaries that are included in its consolidated financial statements. In its December 31 trial balance, Wright had the following intraentity balances before eliminations:

	Debit	Credit
Current receivable due from Main Co.	$ 32,000	
Noncurrent receivable from Main Co.	114,000	
Cash advance to Corn Corp.	6,000	
Cash advance from King Co.		$ 15,000
Payable to King Co.		101,000

In its December 31 consolidated balance sheet, what amount should Wright report as intraentity receivables?

A. $152,000

B. $146,000

C. $36,000

D. $0

Answer (D) is correct. *(CPA, adapted)*
REQUIRED: The amount reported as intraentity receivables.
DISCUSSION: In a consolidated balance sheet, reciprocal balances, such as receivables and payables, between a parent and a consolidated subsidiary are eliminated in their entirety, regardless of the portion of the subsidiary's stock held by the parent. Thus, Wright should report $0 as intraentity receivables.
Answer (A) is incorrect. The amount of $152,000 includes intraentity transactions in the consolidated financial statements. Answer (B) is incorrect. The effects of intraentity transactions should be completely eliminated in consolidated financial statements. Answer (C) is incorrect. Intraentity transactions should not be netted out in the consolidated financial statements.

53. At December 31, Grey, Inc., owned 90% of Winn Corp., a consolidated subsidiary, and 20% of Carr Corp., an investee over which Grey cannot exercise significant influence. On the same date, Grey had receivables of $300,000 from Winn and $200,000 from Carr. In its December 31 consolidated balance sheet, Grey should report accounts receivable from affiliates of

A. $500,000

B. $340,000

C. $230,000

D. $200,000

Answer (D) is correct. *(CPA, adapted)*
REQUIRED: The accounts receivable from a consolidated subsidiary and an investee over which significant influence cannot be exercised.
DISCUSSION: In a consolidated balance sheet, reciprocal balances, such as receivables and payables, between a parent and a consolidated subsidiary are eliminated in their entirety, regardless of the portion of the subsidiary's stock held by the parent. Hence, the $300,000 receivable from Winn is eliminated. Because Grey cannot exercise significant influence over Carr, this investment should be accounted for on the fair-value basis. Receivables from an investee over which significant influence cannot be exercised are reported on the consolidated balance sheet. Grey should therefore report $200,000 in accounts receivable from affiliates.
Answer (A) is incorrect. The $300,000 receivable from Winn should be eliminated. Answer (B) is incorrect. The amount of $340,000 includes the receivable from Winn and 20% of the receivable from Carr. Answer (C) is incorrect. The amount of $230,000 includes 10% of the receivable from the consolidated subsidiary.

54. Perez, Inc., owns 80% of Senior, Inc. During the year just ended, Perez sold goods with a 40% gross profit to Senior. Senior sold all of these goods during the year. In its consolidated financial statements for the year, how should the summation of Perez and Senior income statement items be adjusted?

A. Sales and cost of goods sold should be reduced by the intraentity sales.

B. Sales and cost of goods sold should be reduced by 80% of the intraentity sales.

C. Net income should be reduced by 80% of the gross profit on intraentity sales.

D. No adjustment is necessary.

Answer (A) is correct. *(CPA, adapted)*
REQUIRED: The adjustment for intraentity inventory sales.
DISCUSSION: Given that all of the goods were sold, no adjustment is necessary for intraentity profit in ending inventory. Accordingly, the parent's cost should be included in consolidated cost of goods sold, and the price received by the subsidiary should be included in consolidated sales. The required adjustment is to eliminate the sale recorded by the parent and the cost of goods sold recorded by the subsidiary.
Answer (B) is incorrect. The elimination is made without regard to the noncontrolling interest. Answer (C) is incorrect. No profit should be eliminated. All of the goods sold to Senior have been resold. Answer (D) is incorrect. Sales and cost of sales should be reduced.

55. Parker Corp. owns 80% of Stith, Inc.'s common stock. During the year just ended, Parker sold Stith $250,000 of inventory on the same terms as sales made to third parties. Stith sold all of the inventory purchased from Parker during the year. The following information pertains to Stith and Parker's sales for the year:

	Parker	Stith
Sales	$1,000,000	$700,000
Cost of sales	(400,000)	(350,000)
Gross Profit	$ 600,000	$350,000

What amount should Parker report as cost of sales in its consolidated income statement for the year?

- A. $750,000
- B. $680,000
- C. $500,000
- D. $430,000

Answer (C) is correct. *(CPA, adapted)*
REQUIRED: The consolidated cost of sales.
DISCUSSION: Given that Stith purchased inventory from Parker for $250,000 and sold all of it during the year, $250,000 must be eliminated from consolidated cost of goods sold. Hence, the cost of sales in the consolidated income statement is $500,000 [($400,000 + $350,000) – $250,000].
Answer (A) is incorrect. The total of the amounts reported separately by Parker and Stith is $750,000. Answer (B) is incorrect. Parker's COGS plus 80% of Stith's equals $680,000. Answer (D) is incorrect. Parker's COGS plus 80% of Stith's, minus $250,000, equals $430,000.

56. Clark Co. had the following transactions with affiliated parties during the year just ended:

- Sales of $50,000 to Dean, Inc., with $20,000 gross profit. Dean had $15,000 of this inventory on hand at year end. Clark owns a 15% interest in Dean and does not exert significant influence.
- Purchases of inventories totaling $240,000 from Kent Corp., a wholly owned subsidiary. Kent's gross profit on the sale was $48,000. Clark had $60,000 of this inventory remaining on December 31.

Before eliminating entries, Clark had consolidated current assets of $320,000. What amount should Clark report in its December 31 consolidated balance sheet for current assets?

- A. $320,000
- B. $314,000
- C. $308,000
- D. $302,000

Answer (C) is correct. *(CPA, adapted)*
REQUIRED: The amount reported on the consolidated balance sheet for current assets.
DISCUSSION: When an investor buys inventory from an investee that is neither a consolidated subsidiary nor an equity-method investee, no adjustment for intraentity profit is made. Thus, no adjustment is made to the inventory purchased from Dean. When a parent buys inventory from a subsidiary, the inventory on the consolidated balance sheet must be adjusted to remove any intraentity profit. Hence, the inventory must be reduced by the pro rata share of intraentity profit made on the sale by Kent. The reduction is $12,000 [$48,000 gross profit × ($60,000 EI ÷ $240,000 purchases)]. Thus, current assets equal $308,000 ($320,000 – $12,000).
Answer (A) is incorrect. The amount of $320,000 does not eliminate intraentity transactions. Answer (B) is incorrect. The amount of $314,000 does not eliminate the effect of the transactions with Kent but subtracts the gross profit included in the inventory held by Dean. Answer (D) is incorrect. The amount of $302,000 treats the sales between Clark and Dean as an intraentity transaction.

57. Power Co. is a manufacturer and Slack Co., its 100%-owned subsidiary, is a retailer. The companies are vertically integrated. Thus, Slack purchases all of its inventory from Power. On January 1, Slack's inventory was $30,000. For the year ended December 31, its purchases were $150,000, and its cost of sales was $166,500. Power's sales to Slack reflect a 50% markup on cost. Slack then resells the goods to outside entities at a 100% markup on cost. At what amount should the intraentity inventory purchase be reported in the consolidated balance sheet at December 31?

- A. $16,500
- B. $9,000
- C. $13,500
- D. $6,750

Answer (B) is correct. *(E. Milacek)*
REQUIRED: The amount to report as intraentity inventory on the consolidated balance sheet.
DISCUSSION: Based on beginning inventory and purchases, Slack had $180,000 in inventory that was available to sell. If cost of goods sold is $166,500, $13,500 ($180,000 – $166,500) is still in Slack's inventory. As shown below, after the elimination of intraentity profit, Slack's inventory has a balance of $9,000 at the end of the year.

$$EI + 0.50EI = \$13,500$$
$$1.50EI = \underline{\quad 13,500}$$
$$EI = \underline{\underline{\$ 9,000}}$$

Answer (A) is incorrect. The difference between $166,500 and $150,000 is $16,500. Answer (C) is incorrect. Slack's ending inventory before the elimination of intraentity profits is $13,500. Answer (D) is incorrect. The amount of $6,750 is 50% of Slack's ending inventory before the elimination of intraentity profits.

Questions 58 and 59 are based on the following information. Scroll, Inc., a wholly owned subsidiary of Pirn, Inc., began operations on January 1, Year 4. The following information is from the condensed Year 4 income statements:

	Pirn	Scroll
Sales to Scroll	$100,000	$ --
Sales to others	400,000	300,000
	$500,000	$300,000
Cost of goods sold:		
Acquired from Pirn	--	80,000
Acquired from others	350,000	190,000
Gross profit	$150,000	$ 30,000
Depreciation	40,000	10,000
Other expenses	60,000	15,000
Income from operations	$ 50,000	$ 5,000
Gain on sale of equipment to Scroll	12,000	--
Income before income taxes	$ 38,000	$ 5,000

Additional Information

- Sales by Pirn to Scroll are made on the same terms as those made to third parties.
- Equipment purchased by Scroll from Pirn for $36,000 on January 1, Year 4, is depreciated using the straight-line method over 4 years.

58. Sales by Pirn to Scroll are made on the same terms as those made to third parties. In Pirn's December 31 consolidating worksheet, how much intraentity profit should be eliminated from Scroll's inventory?

A. $30,000

B. $20,000

C. $10,000

D. $6,000

Answer (D) is correct. *(CPA, adapted)*
REQUIRED: The intraentity profit to be eliminated from Scroll's inventory.
DISCUSSION: Sales by Pirn to Scroll totaled $100,000, and Scroll reported related COGS of $80,000. Thus, the remaining inventory of these items must have been $20,000. Because Pirn's gross profit rate was 30% ($150,000 gross profit ÷ $500,000 sales), the intraentity profit eliminated from Scroll's inventory should be $6,000 ($20,000 × 30%).
Answer (A) is incorrect. Scroll's total gross profit is $30,000. Answer (B) is incorrect. The intraentity inventory is $20,000. Answer (C) is incorrect. The total gross profit minus the intraentity inventory obtained from Pirn equals $10,000.

59. What amount should be reported as depreciation expense in Pirn's consolidated income statement?

A. $50,000

B. $47,000

C. $44,000

D. $41,000

Answer (B) is correct. *(CPA, adapted)*
REQUIRED: The depreciation expense in the consolidated income statement.
DISCUSSION: The depreciation attributable to the gain on sale of equipment to Scroll should be eliminated. Thus, the depreciation expense in the consolidated income statement should be $47,000 [$40,000 Pirn depreciation + $10,000 Scroll depreciation – ($12,000 gain ÷ 4 years)].
Answer (A) is incorrect. The amount of $50,000 does not eliminate the effect of the gain. Answer (C) is incorrect. Total depreciation minus the inventory profit equals $44,000. Answer (D) is incorrect. Total depreciation minus the inventory profit and the effect of the gain equals $41,000.

60. During the year just ended, Pard Corp. sold goods to its 80%-owned subsidiary, Seed Corp. At December 31, one-half of these goods were included in Seed's ending inventory. Reported selling expenses were $1.1 million and $400,000 for Pard and Seed, respectively. Pard's selling expenses properly included $50,000 in freight-out costs for goods sold to Seed. What amount of selling expenses should be reported in Pard's consolidated income statement?

A. $1,500,000

B. $1,480,000

C. $1,475,000

D. $1,450,000

Answer (D) is correct. *(CPA, adapted)*
REQUIRED: The consolidated selling expenses.
DISCUSSION: The effects of intraentity transactions are eliminated from consolidated financial statements in their entirety, regardless of the parent's percentage of ownership. Consequently, consolidated selling expense is $1,450,000 ($1,100,000 + $400,000 − $50,000 of freight-out incurred on a sale by Pard to Seed). These costs are not selling expenses because they are not necessary to bring the inventory to its existing condition and location (its salable condition).
Answer (A) is incorrect. The amount of $1,500,000 assumes no elimination of the effects of the intraentity transaction. Answer (B) is incorrect. The amount of $1,480,000 assumes that the selling expense eliminated is related to the inventory held by Seed and that a noncontrolling interest in the remainder ($25,000 × 20%) is also not eliminated. Answer (C) is incorrect. The amount of $1,475,000 assumes that the selling expense eliminated is related to the inventory held by Seed.

61. Pelota Co. owns 80% of Saginaw Co.'s outstanding common stock. Saginaw, in turn, owns 10% of Pelota's outstanding common stock. What percentage of the common stock cash dividends declared by the individual companies should be reported as dividends declared in the consolidated financial statements?

	Dividends Declared by Pelota	Dividends Declared by Saginaw
A.	90%	0%
B.	90%	20%
C.	100%	0%
D.	100%	20%

Answer (A) is correct. *(CPA, adapted)*
REQUIRED: The dividends declared by a parent and its subsidiary reported in the consolidated statements.
DISCUSSION: Because the parent owns 80% of the subsidiary and the subsidiary owns 10% of the parent, 80% of the dividends declared by the subsidiary and 10% of the dividends declared by the parent are not transferred outside of the consolidated group. These amounts are eliminated as intraentity transactions. Consequently, 90% of the parent's and 20% of the subsidiary's dividend payments are to third parties. Only the 90% declared by the parent will be reported as dividends declared. The 20% declared by the subsidiary is treated as a reduction of noncontrolling interest.
Answer (B) is incorrect. Zero percent of the subsidiary's dividends are treated as consolidated dividends declared. Answer (C) is incorrect. Ninety percent of the parent's dividends are treated as consolidated dividends declared. Answer (D) is incorrect. Ninety percent of the parent's dividends and 0% of the subsidiary's are treated as consolidated dividends declared.

62. Port, Inc., owns 100% of Salem, Inc. On January 1, Port sold Salem delivery equipment at a gain. Port had owned the equipment for 2 years and used a 5-year straight-line depreciation rate with no residual value. Salem is using a 3-year straight-line depreciation rate with no residual value for the equipment. In the consolidated income statement, Salem's recorded depreciation expense on the equipment for the year will be decreased by

A. 20% of the gain on sale.

B. 33 1/3% of the gain on sale.

C. 50% of the gain on sale.

D. 100% of the gain on sale.

Answer (B) is correct. *(CPA, adapted)*
REQUIRED: The consolidated depreciation expense on equipment sold by a parent to a subsidiary.
DISCUSSION: The effects of intraentity transactions are eliminated. Consequently, the equipment and the related depreciation expense are reported at amounts that exclude the gain on the sale to Salem. Given that the equipment was held by Port for 2 of its 5 years of estimated useful life, that it has no salvage value, and that Salem is depreciating it over 3 years, Salem recognizes as depreciation expense in its separate statements 33 1/3% of the acquisition cost, which equals the gain recognized by Port plus Port's carrying amount. Thus, 33 1/3% of the gain is included in the depreciation expense recorded on the equipment and are eliminated.
Answer (A) is incorrect. A percentage of 20% of the gain on sale assumes a 5-year life. Answer (C) is incorrect. A percentage of 50% of the gain on sale assumes a 2-year life. Answer (D) is incorrect. A percentage of 100% of the gain on sale assumes a 1-year life.

63. Moss Corp. owns 20% of Dobro Corp.'s preferred stock and 80% of its common stock. Dobro's stock outstanding at December 31, Year 1, is as follows:

10% cumulative preferred stock	$100,000
Common stock	700,000

Dobro reported net income of $60,000 for the year ended December 31, Year 1. What amount should Moss record as equity in earnings of Dobro for the year ended December 31, Year 1?

A. $50,000

B. $48,400

C. $48,000

D. $42,000

Answer (D) is correct. *(CPA, adapted)*
REQUIRED: The parent's equity in earnings of a subsidiary that has issued cumulative preferred stock.
DISCUSSION: Moss must consolidate Dobro because it holds more than 50% of its outstanding voting interests. Thus, the parent's financial statements for external financial reporting purposes must be consolidated statements. Dobro (the subsidiary) also has issued cumulative preferred stock, 20% of which is held by Moss. Accordingly, the earnings of the subsidiary included in consolidated earnings must include adjustments for (1) preferred dividends and (2) the noncontrolling interest's share of earnings available to common shareholders. Because the preferred stock is cumulative, the adjustments include dividends whether or not declared.

Earnings		$60,000
NCI's share of earnings available		
to common shareholders		
Earnings	$60,000	
Preferred dividends ($100,000 × 10%)	(10,000)	
	$50,000	
	× 20%	(10,000)
Earnings after elimination of NCI's share		$50,000
Preferred dividends payable		
outside the consolidated entity		
[$10,000 × (100% – 20% intraentity		
elimination)]		(8,000)
Earnings of subsidiary included		
in consolidated earnings		$42,000

Answer (A) is incorrect. The amount of $50,000 equals Dobro's net income minus the preferred dividends. Answer (B) is incorrect. The amount of $48,400 equals 80% of Dobro's net income plus 20% of a 20% share of the preferred dividends. Answer (C) is incorrect. The amount of $48,000 equals 80% of Dobro's net income.

64. On January 1, Pan Corp. sold a machine for $900,000 to Sarge Corp., its wholly owned subsidiary. Pan paid $1.1 million for this machine, which had accumulated depreciation of $250,000. Pan estimated a $100,000 salvage value and depreciated the machine on the straight-line method over 20 years, a policy that Sarge continued. In Pan's December 31 consolidated balance sheet, this machine should be included in cost and accumulated depreciation as

	Cost	Accumulated Depreciation
A.	$1,100,000	$300,000
B.	$1,100,000	$290,000
C.	$900,000	$40,000
D.	$850,000	$42,500

Answer (A) is correct. *(CPA, adapted)*
REQUIRED: The cost and accumulated depreciation in the consolidated balance sheet.
DISCUSSION: The effect of the intraentity transaction should be eliminated. Thus, the machine should be carried at cost ($1,100,000) minus accumulated depreciation of $300,000 {$250,000 + [($1,100,0000 – $100,000) ÷ 20]}.
Answer (B) is incorrect. The amount of $290,000 assumes that Year 1 depreciation is based on a $900,000 cost, $100,000 salvage value, and a remaining 20-year life. Answer (C) is incorrect. The sales price is $900,000, and $40,000 is the depreciation based on a $900,000 cost, $100,000 salvage value, and a remaining 20-year life. Answer (D) is incorrect. The carrying amount at the time of sale was $850,000, and $42,500 would be the depreciation in Sarge's separate financial statements assuming the $850,000 cost, a 20-year life, and no salvage value.

65. Wagner, a holder of a $1 million Palmer, Inc., bond, collected the interest due on March 31, and then sold the bond to Seal, Inc., for $975,000. On that date, Palmer, a 75% owner of Seal, had a $1,075,000 carrying amount for this bond. What was the effect of Seal's purchase of Palmer's bond on the retained earnings and noncontrolling interest amounts reported in Palmer's March 31 consolidated balance sheet?

	Retained Earnings	Noncontrolling Interest
A.	$100,000 increase	$0
B.	$75,000 increase	$25,000 increase
C.	$0	$25,000 increase
D.	$0	$100,000 increase

Answer (A) is correct. *(CPA, adapted)*
REQUIRED: The effect of the purchase by the subsidiary of the parent's debt.
DISCUSSION: The purchase was in substance a retirement of debt by the consolidated entity for less than its carrying amount. The transaction resulted in a constructive gain of $100,000 ($1,075,000 carrying amount – $975,000 price) and therefore a $100,000 increase in consolidated retained earnings. The noncontrolling interest was unaffected. The noncontrolling interest is the equity in a subsidiary not attributable to the parent. This transaction did not result in gain or loss for Seal.
Answer (B) is incorrect. The gain is not allocated. Answer (C) is incorrect. The noncontrolling interest is not affected. Answer (D) is incorrect. Retained earnings is increased by $100,000.

24.9 Combined Financial Statements

66. Combined statements may be used to present the results of operations of

	Entities under Common Management	Commonly Controlled Entities
A.	No	Yes
B.	Yes	No
C.	No	No
D.	Yes	Yes

Answer (D) is correct. *(CPA, adapted)*
REQUIRED: The condition(s) in which combined financial statements are appropriate.
DISCUSSION: Combined (as distinguished from consolidated) statements of commonly controlled entities may be more meaningful than separate statements. For example, combined statements may be used to combine the statements of (1) several entities with related operations when one individual owns a controlling interest in them or (2) entities under common management.
Answer (A) is incorrect. Common management justifies use of combined statements. Answer (B) is incorrect. Common control justifies use of combined statements. Answer (C) is incorrect. Management or common control justifies use of combined statements.

67. Ahm Corp. owns 90% of Bee Corp.'s common stock and 80% of Cee Corp.'s common stock. The remaining common shares of Bee and Cee are owned by their respective employees. Bee sells exclusively to Cee, Cee buys exclusively from Bee, and Cee sells exclusively to unrelated companies. Selected information for Bee and Cee for the year follows:

	Bee Corp.	Cee Corp.
Sales	$130,000	$91,000
Cost of sales	100,000	65,000
Beginning inventory	None	None
Ending inventory	None	65,000

What amount should be reported as gross profit in Bee and Cee's combined income statement for the year ended December 31?

A. $26,000

B. $41,000

C. $47,800

D. $56,000

Answer (B) is correct. *(CPA, adapted)*
REQUIRED: The gross profit in the combined income statement.
DISCUSSION: Cee buys exclusively from Bee. Thus, Cee's cost of sales equals the sales price charged by Bee, which represented a 30% [($130,000 – $100,000) ÷ $100,000] markup on the cost to the combined entity. Consequently, the gross profit of the combined entity on sales to unrelated companies should include Bee's markup as well as Cee's gross profit. Because Bee's sales were 130% of its cost, the cost to the entity of Cee's sales was $50,000 ($65,000 cost of sales ÷ 130%). The gross profit in the combined income statement was therefore $41,000 ($91,000 – $50,000).
Answer (A) is incorrect. Cee's gross profit was $26,000. Answer (C) is incorrect. The amount of $47,800 is the sum of 90% of Bee's and 80% of Cee's gross profits. Answer (D) is incorrect. The sum of Bee's and Cee's gross profits is $56,000.

68. At December 31, S Corp. owned 80% of J Corp.'s common stock and 90% of C Corp.'s common stock. J's net income for the year was $200,000, and C's net income was $400,000. C and J had no interentity ownership or transactions during the year. Combined financial statements are being prepared for C and J in contemplation of their sale to an outside party. In the combined income statement, combined net income should be reported at

A. $420,000

B. $520,000

C. $560,000

D. $600,000

Answer (D) is correct. *(CPA, adapted)*
REQUIRED: The combined net income.
DISCUSSION: Combined financial statements are appropriate when common management or common control exists for two or more entities not subject to consolidation. The calculation of combined net income is similar to the calculation for consolidated net income. Thus, combined net income should be recorded at the total of the net income reported by the combined entities, adjusted for any profits or losses from transactions between the combined entities. In the combined income statement issued for J Corp. and C Corp., net income should be reported at $600,000 ($200,000 + $400,000).
Answer (A) is incorrect. The amount of $420,000 is 70% of the combined net income. Answer (B) is incorrect. The amount of $520,000 equals 80% of the net income of J and 90% of the net income of C. Answer (C) is incorrect. The amount of $560,000 equals 80% of J's net income and 100% of C's net income.

69. Selected data for two subsidiaries of Dunn Corp. taken from December 31 preclosing trial balances are as follows:

	Banks Co. Debit	Lamm Co. Credit
Shipments to Banks	--	$150,000
Shipments from Lamm	$200,000	--
Intraentity inventory profit on total shipments	--	50,000

Additional data relating to the December 31 inventory are as follows:

Inventory acquired from outside parties	$175,000	$250,000
Inventory acquired from Lamm	60,000	--

At December 31, the inventory reported on the combined balance sheet of the two subsidiaries should be

A. $425,000

B. $435,000

C. $470,000

D. $485,000

Answer (C) is correct. *(CPA, adapted)*
REQUIRED: The inventory to be reported on the combined balance sheet of two subsidiaries.
DISCUSSION: When combined financial statements are prepared for unconsolidated subsidiaries, intraentity profits should be eliminated. The $60,000 of ending inventory acquired by Banks from Lamm is equal to 30% ($60,000 inventory remaining ÷ $200,000 shipments) of the total received from Lamm. Accordingly, $15,000 ($50,000 inventory profit on total shipments × 30%) should be eliminated. Given that $425,000 ($175,000 + $250,000) of the ending inventory held by Banks and Lamm was obtained from outside parties, the combined balance sheet of the two subsidiaries should report inventory of $470,000 ($425,000 + $60,000 – $15,000).
Answer (A) is incorrect. The total inventory acquired from outside parties is $425,000. Answer (B) is incorrect. The amount of $435,000 excludes the profit on inventory acquired from Lamm and subsequently sold. Answer (D) is incorrect. The amount of $485,000 does not exclude the intraentity inventory profit.

70. Mr. Cord owns four corporations. Combined financial statements are being prepared for these corporations, which have intraentity loans of $200,000 and intraentity profits of $500,000. What amount of these loans and profits should be included in the combined financial statements?

	Intraentity Loans	Profits
A.	$200,000	$0
B.	$200,000	$500,000
C.	$0	$0
D.	$0	$500,000

Answer (C) is correct. *(CPA, adapted)*
REQUIRED: The amount of intraentity loans and profits that should be included in combined financial statements.
DISCUSSION: Combined financial statements are appropriately issued when two or more entities are under common control or common management. When combined financial statements are issued, intraentity loans and profits should be eliminated in their entirety. Consequently, $200,000 in loans and $500,000 in profits should not be included in the combined financial statements.
Answer (A) is incorrect. The loans equaling $200,000 should not be included in the combined financial statements. Answer (B) is incorrect. When combined financial statements are issued, intraentity loans and profits should be eliminated in their entirety. Answer (D) is incorrect. The profits of $500,000 should not be included in the combined financial statements.

STUDY UNIT TWENTY-FIVE
INTERIM FINANCIAL REPORTING

Basic Concepts

The relevant guidance on interim reporting applies whenever entities issue interim financial information. Thus, when publicly traded companies elect to present **summarized interim financial information**, they must disclose certain minimum items. Moreover, because interim periods are **integral parts of an annual period**, their results ordinarily must be based on the accounting principles and practices used in the most recent annual statements. But certain principles and practices used for annual reporting may require modification in interim periods so that the interim report may relate more closely to the results of operations for the annual period.

Costs and Expenses

Revenues and costs associated directly with **revenues** (product costs) must be treated similarly for interim and annual reporting. However, certain exceptions are made in accounting for **inventory**: (1) An **estimated gross profit rate** may be used to determine cost of sales during an interim period; (2) a **LIFO liquidation** at an interim period must not be recognized if the inventory is expected to be replaced by year end, and interim cost of sales must include the expected replacement cost; (3) **market declines** reasonably expected to be restored by year end need not be recognized; and (4) in a **standard cost accounting system**, purchase price variances or volume or capacity cost variances that are planned and expected to be absorbed by year end ordinarily are deferred in interim periods.

Other costs and expenses must be recognized in interim periods as incurred or allocated among interim periods. Arbitrary allocations are not permitted. If costs and expenses cannot be readily identified with another interim period, they are recognized as incurred. Gains and losses similar to those that would not be deferred at year end are recognized immediately.

An entity subject to seasonal fluctuations must disclose the nature of the seasonality.

Accounting Changes

A change in an **accounting principle** made in an interim period is reported by **retrospective application** unless it is **impracticable** to do so. When application to prechange interim periods is impracticable, the change is made at the beginning of the next annual period. Information reported for each post-change interim period must **disclose** the effect of the change on (1) income from continuing operations, (2) net income (or other appropriate captions), and (3) related per-share amounts.

A **change in an accounting estimate** is accounted for on a prospective basis. The effect of the change is therefore recognized in the interim period in which the change in estimate is made and in future periods. Prior-period financial information is not restated.

Adjustments Related to Prior Interim Periods of the Current Year

Error corrections are accounted for in the same way in annual and interim statements. An adjustment related to prior interim periods of the current year is an adjustment or settlement of (1) litigation, (2) income taxes (except for the effects of retroactive tax legislation), (3) renegotiation proceedings, or (4) utility revenue under rate-making processes. If (1) all or part of the adjustment or settlement relates specifically to a prior interim period of the current year, (2) the effect is material, and (3) the amount became reasonably estimable in the current interim period, the financial information for prior interim periods affected is restated for the applicable amounts. In addition, any portion of the adjustment or settlement that is directly related to prior fiscal years is included in the determination of income of the first interim period of the current year. However, these adjustments affect only interim reporting. In annual statements, these items are reported in current income.

Interim Income Taxes

Interim income tax expense (benefit) is based on taxes calculated for (1) ordinary income (loss) and (2) taxes for all other items. **Ordinary income (loss)** is income (loss) from pre-tax continuing operations. (The term is not used in the tax law context of ordinary income versus capital gain.) The tax (benefit) related to interim ordinary income must be calculated using an **estimated annual effective tax rate**. This rate is estimated at the end of each interim period. The tax (benefit) for all other items (e.g., discontinued items and extraordinary items) is individually calculated and recognized when the items occur. The estimated tax rate must be applied to year-to-date ordinary income (loss) at the end of each interim period. The interim-period tax (benefit) related to ordinary income (loss) equals (1) year-to-date tax (benefit) minus (2) amounts reported in prior interim periods.

Differences between GAAP and IFRS

Under IFRS:

- An interim financial report must include, at a minimum, condensed financial statements (financial position, comprehensive income, changes in equity, and cash flows) and notes.
- If the interim financial report contains a complete set of statements, their form and content must conform to those required for annual statements. If the interim financial report contains condensed statements, they must include, at a minimum, all headings and subtotals included in the most recent annual statements.
- An interim financial report must include explanations of significant events and transactions.
- For an interim period, an inventory loss from a market decline must be recognized even if no loss is reasonably expected for the year.
- Each interim period is viewed as a discrete reporting period.
- LIFO liquidation is not an issue in interim or annual periods because LIFO is not a permitted accounting policy.

QUESTIONS

25.1 Basic Concepts

1. In considering interim financial reporting, how should such reporting be viewed?

    A. As a "special" type of reporting that need not follow generally accepted accounting principles.

    B. As useful only if activity is evenly spread throughout the year so that estimates are unnecessary.

    C. As reporting for a basic accounting period.

    D. As reporting for an integral part of an annual period.

Answer (D) is correct. *(CPA, adapted)*
    REQUIRED: The perspective of interim financial reporting.
    DISCUSSION: Each interim period is viewed primarily as an integral part of an annual period. Ordinarily, the results for an interim period should be based on the same accounting principles the enterprise uses in preparing annual statements. Certain principles and practices used for annual reporting, however, may require modification at interim dates so that interim reports may relate more closely to the results of operations for the annual period.
    Answer (A) is incorrect. Interim reporting is not a "special" type of reporting, and GAAP should be followed. Answer (B) is incorrect. Interim reports may be useful for seasonal and unevenly spread activities. Answer (C) is incorrect. The view that the interim period is a discrete accounting period is not generally accepted.

2. The Hoity-Toity Country Club offers membership privileges for a 3-year period under the following arrangements:

1) The applicant pays the entire $200,000 membership fee in eight quarterly installments during the first 2 years of the contract period.
2) The applicant is entitled to unlimited use of the facilities during the 3-year contract period.

Based on experience, Hoity-Toity is able to reasonably estimate uncollectible receivables. It prepares quarterly financial statements. In which accounting period(s) should Hoity-Toity recognize the membership fee as revenue for financial statement reporting?

    A. In the quarter that the membership contract is signed.

    B. Evenly over the eight quarters in which the installment payments are to be received.

    C. In the quarter that the membership period terminates.

    D. Evenly over the 12-quarter membership period.

Answer (D) is correct. *(CIA, adapted)*
    REQUIRED: The accounting period in which revenue should be recognized.
    DISCUSSION: In general, the results for an interim period should be based on the same accounting principles that the entity uses in preparing annual statements. SFAC 5 states that revenue should be recognized when it is realized or realizable and earned. For revenue associated with membership privileges, the earning process is completed in proportion to the amount of the membership period elapsed. This principle is applicable in both annual and interim periods. Thus, the membership fee should be allocated evenly over the 12-quarter membership period.
    Answer (A) is incorrect. Only one-twelfth of the fee should be accrued in the quarter that the membership contract is signed. Answer (B) is incorrect. The membership revenue should be prorated evenly over the membership period. Answer (C) is incorrect. Only one-twelfth of the fee should be accrued in the quarter that the membership period terminates.

3. How should material seasonal variations in revenue be reflected in interim financial statements?

    A. The seasonal variation should be disclosed by showing pro forma financial statements for subsequent interim periods within the fiscal year.

    B. Because the total revenue pattern of the current annual period is not known with certainty, any statements about seasonal patterns may be misleading and must be omitted from interim statements.

    C. Disclosures should warn the statement reader that revenues are subject to seasonal variation, but no supplemental schedules of past seasonality should be shown.

    D. The seasonal nature should be disclosed. Revenue information for 12-month periods ended at the interim date may be disclosed.

Answer (D) is correct. *(Publisher, adapted)*
    REQUIRED: The proper method of reflecting material seasonal variations in revenue in interim financial statements.
    DISCUSSION: If businesses issue interim information, certain disclosures are mandatory if they have material seasonal fluctuations. Such disclosures safeguard the user of the statements from being misled into believing that interim results from such businesses are fairly representative of annual results. Businesses must disclose the seasonal nature of their activities and should consider supplementing interim reports with information for the 12-month period that ended at the interim date for the current and preceding years.
    Answer (A) is incorrect. The disclosure requirement may be met by providing financial data for prior, not subsequent, interim periods within the fiscal year. Answer (B) is incorrect. Businesses must disclose the seasonal nature of their activities. Answer (C) is incorrect. Supplemental schedules with information for the 12-month period ending at the interim date for the current and preceding years are proper disclosures.

4. Which of the following is not a required disclosure when a publicly traded company elects to issue a financial summary of interim operations?

A. Basic and diluted earnings per share.

B. Significant changes in estimates or provisions for income tax.

C. Changes in accounting principles or estimates.

D. Changes in investment policy.

Answer (D) is correct.   *(CMA, adapted)*
REQUIRED: The interim financial reporting disclosures not required.
DISCUSSION: Presentation of interim income statements, statements of financial position, statements of cash flows, and disclosure of changes in investment policy are not required. However, when a publicly traded company elects to issue a financial summary of interim operations, minimum required disclosures include

1) Sales or gross revenues, provision for income taxes, extraordinary items, net income, and comprehensive income
2) Basic and diluted EPS
3) Seasonal revenues, costs, or expenses
4) Significant changes in estimates or provisions for income taxes
5) Disposal of a component of an entity and unusual or infrequent items
6) Contingent items
7) Changes in accounting principles or estimates
8) Significant changes in financial position (disclosure of balance sheet and cash flow data is encouraged)
9) Certain information about reportable operating segments
10) Certain information about defined benefit postretirement benefit plans
11) Certain information about fair value measurement of assets and liabilities

A change in investment policy is not required to be disclosed because it is not an accounting change.
Answer (A) is incorrect. Required interim disclosures include BEPS and DEPS. Answer (B) is incorrect. Required interim disclosures include estimates or provisions for income tax. Answer (C) is incorrect. Required interim disclosures include changes in estimates and principles.

5. On June 30, Tun Corp. incurred a $200,000 net loss from disposal of a component. Also on June 30, Tun paid $80,000 for property taxes assessed for the calendar year. What amount of the foregoing items should be included in the determination of Tun's net income or loss for the 6-month interim period ended June 30?

A. $280,000

B. $240,000

C. $180,000

D. $140,000

Answer (B) is correct.   *(CPA, adapted)*
REQUIRED: The amount of property taxes and loss from disposal of a component that should be included in the determination of net income or loss for the interim period.
DISCUSSION: Costs other than product costs, such as rent, interest, or property taxes, that will clearly benefit two or more interim periods should be allocated among those periods based on estimates of time expired, the benefit received, or the activity associated with each period. Thus, Tun should allocate $40,000 [$80,000 × (6 ÷ 12)] of the property taxes to the 6-month interim period ended June 30. Gains and losses that arise in an interim period that are similar to gains and losses that would not be deferred at year end should not be deferred to later interim periods within the same fiscal year. Consequently, gains or losses from disposal of a component should not be prorated over the balance of the fiscal year, so the loss on disposal ($200,000) should be recognized in full for the interim period ended June 30. The total included in the interim income statement for the two items is therefore $240,000 ($40,000 + $200,000).
Answer (A) is incorrect. The amount of $280,000 reflects a failure to prorate the property taxes. Answer (C) is incorrect. The amount of $180,000 reflects proration of the loss on disposal of a segment and the full amount of the property taxes. Answer (D) is incorrect. The amount of $140,000 reflects proration of the loss on disposal of a component.

6. For interim financial reporting, an extraordinary gain occurring in the second quarter should be

A. Recognized ratably over the last three quarters.

B. Recognized ratably over all four quarters, with the first quarter being restated.

C. Recognized in the second quarter.

D. Disclosed by note only in the second quarter.

Answer (C) is correct. *(CPA, adapted)*
REQUIRED: The appropriate recognition of an extraordinary gain in an interim report.
DISCUSSION: Extraordinary items are material gains or losses that are unusual in nature and infrequent in occurrence within the environment in which the business operates. Extraordinary items must be disclosed separately and included in the determination of net income for the interim period in which they occur. Gains and losses similar to those that would not be deferred at year end should not be deferred to later interim periods of the same year. Hence, the extraordinary gain should not be prorated.
Answer (A) is incorrect. The gain is not recognized in proportion to the passage of time within the annual accounting period. Answer (B) is incorrect. The gain should be recognized in the quarter in which it occurs. Answer (D) is incorrect. The gain should be recognized in income. Disclosure in notes is not sufficient.

7. Direct response advertising costs are capitalized (deferred) to provide an appropriate expense in each period for

	Interim Financial Reporting	Year-End Financial Reporting
A.	Yes	No
B.	Yes	Yes
C.	No	No
D.	No	Yes

Answer (B) is correct. *(CPA, adapted)*
REQUIRED: The type(s) of reporting in which direct response advertising costs may be deferred.
DISCUSSION: Direct response advertising costs are capitalized (deferred) for annual reporting purposes if (1) the primary objective is to make sales to customers who respond specifically to the advertising, and (2) probable future economic benefits result. An entity that capitalizes these costs must document that customers have specifically responded to the advertising. It also must document the benefits from prior direct response advertising. Moreover, the deferral of advertising costs is appropriate for interim financial reporting if their benefits clearly apply to more than one interim period. Thus, if a cost that would be fully expensed in an annual report benefits more than one interim period, it may be allocated to those interim periods.
Answer (A) is incorrect. Direct response advertising costs may be deferred for year-end financial reporting. Answer (C) is incorrect. Direct response advertising costs may be deferred for interim or year-end financial reporting. Answer (D) is incorrect. Direct response advertising costs may be deferred for interim financial reporting.

8. On March 15 of the current year, Chen Company paid property taxes of $120,000 on its factory building for the current calendar year. On April 1, Chen made $240,000 in unanticipated repairs to its plant equipment. The repairs will benefit operations for the remainder of the calendar year. What total amount of these expenses should be included in Chen's quarterly income statement for the 3 months ended June 30?

A. $60,000

B. $110,000

C. $150,000

D. $270,000

Answer (B) is correct. *(CPA, adapted)*
REQUIRED: The proper accounting for payments of property taxes and major repair costs in a quarterly income statement.
DISCUSSION: The benefit from the payment of the property taxes relates to all four quarters of the current year and should be prorated at $30,000 ($120,000 ÷ 4) per quarter. The benefit from the unanticipated repairs to plant equipment relates to the second, third, and fourth quarters. It should be spread evenly over these quarters at $80,000 ($240,000 ÷ 3) per quarter. The total amount of expenses that should be included in the quarterly income statement for the 3 months ended June 30 is therefore $110,000.
Answer (A) is incorrect. The amount of $60,000 results from not prorating the property taxes and from prorating the repair cost over all four quarters. Answer (C) is incorrect. The amount of $150,000 assumes that the entire repair cost is allocated to the first two quarters. Answer (D) is incorrect. The amount of $270,000 results from not allocating the repair expense.

9. Napier Corp. has estimated that total depreciation expense for the year ending December 31 will amount to $120,000 and that year-end bonuses to employees will total $240,000. In Napier's interim income statement for the 6 months ended June 30, what is the total amount of expense relating to these two items that should be reported?

- A. $0
- B. $60,000
- C. $180,000
- D. $360,000

Answer (C) is correct. *(CPA, adapted)*
REQUIRED: The amount of expenses related to depreciation and year-end bonuses that should be reported in the 6-month income statement.
DISCUSSION: Costs and expenses other than product costs should be either charged to income in interim periods as incurred or allocated among interim periods based on the benefits received. The depreciation and the bonuses to employees clearly provide benefits throughout the year, and they should be allocated ratably to all interim periods. In the interim income statement for the 6 months ended June 30, the total amount of expense that should be recorded is $180,000 [($360,000 ÷ 12 months) × 6 months].
Answer (A) is incorrect. Depreciation and bonus expenses should be allocated ratably. Answer (B) is incorrect. The amount of $60,000 excludes the allocation of bonuses. Answer (D) is incorrect. The amount of $360,000 allocates the expenses entirely to the 6-month interim period ending June 30.

10. In October Year 3, Snow Company spent $300,000 on an advertising campaign for subscriptions to the magazine it publishes concerning preparing for the winter sports season. The only two issues appear in October and in November. The magazine is sold only on a subscription basis, and the subscriptions started in October Year 3. Assuming Snow's fiscal year ends on March 31, Year 4, what amount of expense should be included in Snow's quarterly income statement for the 3 months ended December 31, Year 3, as a result of this expenditure?

- A. $75,000
- B. $100,000
- C. $150,000
- D. $300,000

Answer (D) is correct. *(CPA, adapted)*
REQUIRED: The amount of advertising expense included in the third quarter's income statement.
DISCUSSION: Advertising costs should be expensed, either as incurred or when advertising first occurs. Because the magazine is published only during October and November, and the expenses were incurred in October, recognition of subscription revenue and related expenses is appropriate only during that quarter. Accordingly, the entire advertising expense of $300,000 should be recognized in that period.
Answer (A) is incorrect. The amount of $75,000 results from allocating the $300,000 expense ratably to four quarters. Answer (B) is incorrect. The amount of $100,000 results from allocating 33 1/3% of the $300,000 expense. Answer (C) is incorrect. The amount of $150,000 results from allocating 50% of the $300,000 expense.

11. How are discontinued operations and extraordinary items that occur at midyear initially reported?

- A. Disclosed only in the notes to the year-end financial statements.
- B. Included in net income and disclosed in the notes to the year-end financial statements.
- C. Included in net income and disclosed in the notes to interim financial statements.
- D. Disclosed only in the notes to interim financial statements.

Answer (C) is correct. *(CPA, adapted)*
REQUIRED: The interim reporting of discontinued operations and extraordinary items.
DISCUSSION: Extraordinary items, material unusual or infrequent items, and gains or losses from disposal of a component of an entity are (1) separately reported in the interim statements, (2) included in interim-period net income, and (3) not prorated over the year.
Answer (A) is incorrect. Extraordinary items and gains or losses from disposal of a component of an entity are separately reported in the interim-period financial statements and included in interim-period net income. Answer (B) is incorrect. Extraordinary items and gains or losses from disposal of a component of an entity are separately reported in the interim statements. Answer (D) is incorrect. Discontinued operations and extraordinary items also are reported in interim-period net income.

25.2 Costs and Expenses

12. Which of the following reporting practices is permissible for interim financial reporting?

    A. Use of the gross profit method for interim inventory pricing.

    B. Use of the direct costing method for determining manufacturing inventories.

    C. Deferral of unplanned variances under a standard cost system until year end.

    D. Deferral of inventory market declines until year end.

Answer (A) is correct. *(CPA, adapted)*
    REQUIRED: The inventory reporting practice permissible in interim financial reporting.
    DISCUSSION: Certain accounting principles and practices followed for annual reporting purposes may be modified for interim reporting. For example, the gross profit method may be used for estimating cost of goods sold and inventory because a physical inventory count at the interim date may not be feasible.
    Answer (B) is incorrect. The direct costing method is never permissible for external financial reporting. Answer (C) is incorrect. Only variances that are planned and expected to be absorbed by the end of the annual period may be deferred. Answer (D) is incorrect. Only market declines that can reasonably be expected to be restored within the fiscal year may be deferred.

13. A store uses the gross profit method to estimate inventory and cost of goods sold for interim reporting purposes. Past experience indicates that the average gross profit rate is 25% of sales. The following data relate to the month of June:

Inventory cost, June 1	$25,000
Purchases during the month at cost	67,000
Sales	84,000
Sales returns	3,000

Based on the data above, what is the estimated ending inventory at June 30?

    A. $20,250

    B. $21,000

    C. $29,000

    D. $31,250

Answer (D) is correct. *(CIA, adapted)*
    REQUIRED: The estimated ending inventory under the gross profit method.
    DISCUSSION: In accordance with the gross profit method, cost of goods sold is estimated by multiplying the net sales figure by one minus the gross profit rate. In this example, the estimate of cost of goods sold is $60,750 [($84,000 sales – $3,000 sales returns) × (1.0 – .25)]. As indicated below, subtracting the estimated cost of goods sold from the goods available for sale results in an estimated ending inventory at June 30 of $31,250.

Beginning inventory	$25,000
June purchases	67,000
Goods available for sale	$92,000
Estimated COGS	(60,750)
Estimated ending inventory	$31,250

    Answer (A) is incorrect. The gross profit is $20,250. Answer (B) is incorrect. Purchases are subtracted from beginning inventory, and cost of goods sold ($84,000 × 75% = $63,000) is not adjusted for sales returns and is added to beginning inventory ($25,000 – $67,000 + $63,000 = $21,000). Answer (C) is incorrect. Cost of goods sold is not adjusted for sales returns.

14. An inventory loss from a market price decline occurred in the first quarter. The loss was not expected to be restored in the fiscal year. However, in the third quarter the inventory had a market price recovery that exceeded the market decline that occurred in the first quarter. For interim financial reporting, net inventory should

    A. Decrease in the first quarter by the amount of the market price decline and increase in the third quarter by the amount of the market price recovery.

    B. Decrease in the first quarter by the amount of the market price decline and increase in the third quarter by the amount of decrease in the first quarter.

    C. Decrease in the first quarter by the amount of the market price decline and not be affected in the third quarter.

    D. Not be affected in either the first quarter or the third quarter.

Answer (B) is correct. *(CPA, adapted)*
    REQUIRED: The proper interim financial reporting of a market decline and a market price recovery.
    DISCUSSION: A market price decline in inventory must be recognized in the interim period in which it occurs unless it is expected to be temporary, i.e., unless the decline is expected to be restored by the end of the fiscal year. This loss was not expected to be restored in the fiscal year, and the company should report the dollar amount of the market price decline as a loss in the first quarter. When a market price recovery occurs in an interim period, it should be treated as a change in estimate. The market price recovery recognized in the third quarter is limited, however, to the extent of losses previously recognized, whether in a prior interim or annual period. Accordingly, the inventory should never be written up to an amount above its original cost.
    Answer (A) is incorrect. The recovery recognized in the third quarter is limited to the amount of the losses previously recognized. Answer (C) is incorrect. Assuming no market price decline had been recognized prior to the current year, the first quarter loss and the third quarter recovery would be offsetting. The recognized third quarter gain is limited to the amount of the first quarter loss, and the year-end results would not be affected. Answer (D) is incorrect. The inventory amount is affected in both the first and third quarters.

15. When a standard cost system of accounting is used to determine costs for valuation of inventory in interim financial statements,

A. Unanticipated variances should be spread prospectively to the remaining interim periods in the current annual reporting period.

B. Unplanned variances should be recognized in the interim period in which they are incurred.

C. Unplanned volume variances should be retroactively allocated to prior interim periods in the current annual reporting period if they occur after the first quarter.

D. Unplanned variances should be deferred to the fourth quarter and recognized as a component of year-end adjustments.

Answer (B) is correct. *(Publisher, adapted)*
REQUIRED: The true statement about interim reporting of unplanned variances when using standard costs.
DISCUSSION: Planned standard cost variances may be deferred if they are expected to be absorbed in subsequent interim periods of a year. Unplanned or unanticipated variances, however, should be recognized in the interim period in which they are incurred.
Answer (A) is incorrect. Unanticipated variances should be expensed in the interim period in which they are incurred. Answer (C) is incorrect. An unplanned volume variance is not a basis for a retroactive restatement. Answer (D) is incorrect. Unplanned variances are not deferred.

25.3 Accounting Changes

16. Andrews Corp.'s $190,000 net income for the quarter ended September 30 included the following after-tax items:

- A $120,000 extraordinary gain, realized on April 30, was allocated equally to the second, third, and fourth quarters of the current year.

- A $32,000 loss (a period-specific effect of a change in accounting principle during the quarter) was recognized on September 30. Although the cumulative effect of the change at July 1 could be determined, it was not practicable to determine the period-specific effects of the change on prechange interim periods of the current year.

In addition, Andrews paid $96,000 on February 1 for current calendar-year property taxes. Of this amount, $24,000 was allocated to the third quarter of the year. For the quarter ended September 30, Andrews should report net income of

A. $222,000

B. $206,000

C. $182,000

D. $150,000

Answer (C) is correct. *(CPA, adapted)*
REQUIRED: The net income reported for the quarter.
DISCUSSION: Extraordinary items must be disclosed separately and included in the determination of net income for the interim period in which they occur. Gains and losses similar to those that would not be deferred at year end should not be deferred to later interim periods of the same year. Hence, the $120,000 extraordinary gain should be recognized in net income for the second quarter. No effect is permitted in third quarter income. A voluntary change in accounting principle is not permitted to take effect in an interim period if it is impracticable to apply the change retrospectively to prechange interim periods. Thus, Andrews is not permitted to change this accounting principle until January 1 of the following year. Accordingly, the $32,000 loss should not be included in third quarter income. Because property taxes were proportionally allocated among the four quarters, the $24,000 is properly included in third quarter income. As a result, Andrews should report third quarter net income of $182,000 [$190,000 – ($120,000 ÷ 3) + $32,000].
Answer (A) is incorrect. The amount of $222,000 does not include the adjustment for the proportionate extraordinary gain. Answer (B) is incorrect. The amount of $206,000 includes an adjustment for the $24,000 allocation of property taxes. Answer (D) is incorrect. The amount of $150,000 does not include an adjustment for the $32,000 period-specific effects of the accounting change.

17. In the third quarter of calendar Year 6, Li Co. documented justification for a change in accounting principle. Li also determined the cumulative effects of applying the new principle at January 1, Year 3, and the period-specific effects of applying it to the current quarter and the previously reported quarterly interim periods of the current and previous 3 fiscal years. If Li makes this change in the third quarter, the cumulative effect of applying the change to periods prior to the periods presented should be

A. Included in net income in the first quarter of calendar Year 6.

B. Included in net income in the third quarter of calendar Year 6.

C. Included in net income in the first period presented.

D. Reflected in the balance sheet at the beginning of the first period presented.

Answer (D) is correct. *(Publisher, adapted)*
   REQUIRED: The proper treatment of the cumulative effect of applying the change to periods prior to the periods presented.
   DISCUSSION: Retrospective application is generally required when it is practicable to determine the cumulative effect and the period-specific effects of a change in accounting principle in an interim period. Retrospective application results in changing previously issued financial statements to reflect the effects of the newly adopted accounting principle as if the new principle had always been used. Retrospective application requires that (1) the carrying amounts of assets, liabilities, and retained earnings as of the beginning of the first period reported be adjusted for the cumulative effect of the new principle on periods prior to the first period reported, and (2) each period reported be adjusted for the period-specific effects of applying the new principle.
   Answer (A) is incorrect. The cumulative effect is not included in net income directly. Answer (B) is incorrect. The amount will not be reported in the third quarter. Answer (C) is incorrect. The cumulative effect must be reflected in the carrying amounts of assets and liabilities at the beginning of the first period reported.

18. The following information is applicable to a change in accounting principle made in the second quarter of the year from FIFO to LIFO. The firm is able to apply the new principle retrospectively. For all relevant periods, prices have risen. The effect of the change is limited to the effects on the inventory balance and income tax provisions (a 40% tax rate).

Period	Net Income on the Basis of FIFO	Gross Effect of Change	Gross Effect Minus Income Taxes
Prior to 1st Qtr	$6,262,000	$300,000	$180,000
1st Qtr	1,032,400	60,000	36,000
2nd Qtr	1,282,400	60,000	36,000
3rd Qtr	1,298,600	90,000	54,000
4th Qtr	1,164,800	120,000	72,000

Net income for the first quarter should be restated as

A. $1,068,400

B. $1,032,400

C. $816,400

D. $996,400

Answer (D) is correct. *(Publisher, adapted)*
   REQUIRED: The restated net income for the first quarter resulting from a change in principle in the second quarter.
   DISCUSSION: The change in accounting principle should be effected by retrospective application unless determination of the cumulative effect or the period-specific effects is impracticable. The period-specific effects are adjustments made to the individual periods reported. Beginning balances of the first period reported are adjusted to reflect the cumulative effects of the change on all prior periods. Accordingly, given the period-specific effects for the first quarter, restated net income based on retrospective application is $996,400 ($1,032,400 − $36,000 gross after-tax effect of applying the new principle). Changing to LIFO when prices are rising decreases net income.
   Answer (A) is incorrect. The amount of $1,068,400 results from adding, not subtracting, the gross effect minus income taxes. Given rising prices, the change to LIFO lowers after-tax income. Answer (B) is incorrect. First quarter net income must be adjusted. Answer (C) is incorrect. The amount of $816,400 results from subtracting the cumulative after-tax effect on prior periods as well as the adjustment for the first quarter.

25.4 Adjustments Related to Prior Interim Periods of the Current Year

19. During the third quarter of Year 10, the accountant at the Laurie Company discovered that a machine purchased January 2, Year 8, for $120,000 had been erroneously charged against first quarter net income in Year 8. The machine should have been depreciated at a rate of $2,000 per month. If Laurie issues interim statements, the correction of this error should include

A. A charge of $66,000 to income before taxes of the third quarter of Year 10.

B. An adjustment of $48,000 to the previously declared income before taxes of the first quarter of Year 10.

C. An adjustment of $54,000 to the previously declared income before taxes of the first quarter of Year 10.

D. An adjustment of $6,000 to the previously declared income before taxes of the first quarter of Year 10.

Answer (D) is correct. *(Publisher, adapted)*
REQUIRED: The treatment of an accounting error.
DISCUSSION: An error was committed when the full cost of the asset was expensed in the period of acquisition. Instead, the cost should have been capitalized and the asset depreciated over its useful life. The correction of this error should be accounted for by restatement. Ignoring tax effects, this requires an entry to beginning retained earnings for the year to correct the understatement of income (and of retained earnings) that resulted from the error. If comparative statements are issued, a restatement of prior-period financial statements is also necessary. The previously reported income of the first quarter of Year 10 (as well as that for the second quarter) should be restated to reflect the $6,000 ($2,000 × 3 months) depreciation that should have been taken on the asset during that period.
Answer (A) is incorrect. The adjustment must be recorded in the first quarter of Year 10. Answer (B) is incorrect. The adjustment should be $6,000. Answer (C) is incorrect. The adjustment should only be for Year 10, not the entire life of the machine.

20. On June 15, Year 6, a court of law found the Panther Corporation, a calendar-year company, guilty of patent infringement and awarded damages of $5,000,000 to the plaintiff. Of this amount, $2,000,000 related to Year 4 and $2,000,000 to Year 5, and $500,000 related to each of the first two quarters of Year 6. No provision for loss had been recorded previously. If the applicable tax rate is 40%, this event should result in a

A. Charge of $3,000,000 to income reported for the second quarter of Year 6.

B. Restatement of the previously reported net income for the first quarter of Year 6 to include a charge of $300,000.

C. Restatement of the previously reported net income for the first quarter of Year 6 to include a charge of $2,700,000.

D. Restatement of the previously reported net income for the first quarter of Year 6 to include a charge of $3,000,000.

Answer (C) is correct. *(Publisher, adapted)*
REQUIRED: The proper treatment of the settlement of litigation related to a prior interim period and prior fiscal years.
DISCUSSION: The judgment is an item of profit or loss that relates to settlement of litigation occurring in other than the first interim period of the fiscal year. Moreover, all or a part of the item meets the criteria for an adjustment related to prior interim periods of that fiscal year. Thus, the financial statements for the prior interim periods should be restated to include their allocable portions of the adjustment. The portion of the adjustment directly related to prior fiscal years also should be included in the determination of net income of the first interim period of the current fiscal year. The settlement in this case occurred in the second quarter, so the first quarter should be restated for the $500,000 directly related to first-quarter operations and the $4,000,000 directly related to prior years' operations. The restated net income for the first quarter of Year 6 should therefore include a $2,700,000 adjustment ($4,500,000 – the tax savings of $1,800,000).
Answer (A) is incorrect. An after-tax loss of $300,000 is reported in the second quarter. Answer (B) is incorrect. The amount of the restatement is $2,700,000. Answer (D) is incorrect. The sum of the restatements for the first two quarters equals $3,000,000.

21. On June 1, Year 5, the Adipose Corporation, a calendar-year company, settled a patent infringement lawsuit. The court awarded Adipose $3,000,000 in damages. Of this amount, $1,000,000 related to each of Year 3 and Year 4, and $500,000 related to each of the first two quarters in Year 5. The applicable tax rate is 40%. What effect does the settlement have on the net income of the second quarter of Year 5?

A. $200,000

B. $300,000

C. $600,000

D. $1,800,000

Answer (B) is correct. *(Publisher, adapted)*
REQUIRED: The effect of a patent lawsuit settlement on second quarter net income.
DISCUSSION: If an item of profit related to settlement of litigation occurs in other than the first interim period of the fiscal year (here, the second quarter of a calendar-year company), and all or part of the item of profit meets the criteria for an adjustment related to a prior interim period of the current fiscal year, the portion of the item allocable to the current interim period should be included in the determination of net income for that period. Prior interim periods should be restated to include their allocable portions of the adjustment. Accordingly, $500,000 of the settlement should be included in the determination of net income for the second quarter. Given a tax rate of 40%, the settlement increases net income of the second quarter by $300,000.
Answer (A) is incorrect. The amount of the income tax is $200,000. Answer (C) is incorrect. The adjustment to be made to each year (Year 4 and Year 3) is $600,000. Answer (D) is incorrect. The income should not be recognized entirely in Year 5.

22. On September 30, Year 3, the Cantata Corporation, a calendar-year company, reached an agreement with the Internal Revenue Service. The company agreed to pay additional income taxes of $2,000,000 that directly related to a loss claimed in the third quarter of Year 1. In accordance with current authoritative guidance, this transaction should be recorded as a

A. Component of the net income reported for the third quarter of Year 3.

B. Restatement of the net income previously reported for the first quarter of Year 3.

C. Restatement of the beginning retained earnings previously reported for the third quarter of Year 3.

D. Restatement of the beginning retained earnings previously reported for the first quarter of Year 3.

Answer (A) is correct. *(Publisher, adapted)*
REQUIRED: The proper recording of an income tax settlement reached in the third quarter of the current year relating to the third quarter of a prior year.
DISCUSSION: A prior interim period adjustment may be required for (1) an adjustment or settlement of litigation, (2) income taxes (except for the effects of retroactive tax legislation), (3) renegotiation proceedings, and (4) utility revenue under rate-making processes. All or part of the adjustment or settlement must relate specifically to a prior interim period of the current year, its effect must be material, and the amount must have become reasonably estimable only in the current interim period. XYZ's transaction does not qualify as a prior interim period adjustment because no portion of the item is related to prior interim periods of the current fiscal year. Thus, the tax settlement liability should be included in net income in the third quarter of Year 3.
Answer (B) is incorrect. The item does not qualify for treatment as a prior interim period adjustment in the current fiscal year. Answer (C) is incorrect. The item should be a component of net income in the current fiscal year. Answer (D) is incorrect. A tax settlement related to a prior fiscal year is not treated as a prior-period adjustment.

25.5 Interim Income Taxes

23. For interim financial reporting, a company's income tax provision for the second quarter should be determined using the

A. Statutory tax rate for the year.

B. Effective tax rate expected to be applicable for the full year as estimated at the end of the first quarter.

C. Effective tax rate expected to be applicable for the full year as estimated at the end of the second quarter.

D. Effective tax rate expected to be applicable for the second quarter.

Answer (C) is correct. *(CPA, adapted)*
REQUIRED: The tax rate used to determine the interim income tax provision.
DISCUSSION: At the end of each interim period, an entity must make its best estimate of the effective tax rate expected to be applicable for the full fiscal year. That rate should be used in providing for income taxes on a current year-to-date basis.
Answer (A) is incorrect. The quarterly tax provision should be based on the rate expected, not the statutory rate.
Answer (B) is incorrect. The quarterly tax provision should be based on the rate expected to be applicable for the full year as determined at the end of the quarter, not the previous quarter. Answer (D) is incorrect. The quarterly tax provision should be based on the rate expected to be applicable for the full year, not just one quarter.

24. For interim financial reporting, the computation of a company's second quarter provision for income taxes uses an effective tax rate expected to be applicable for the full fiscal year. The effective tax rate should reflect anticipated

	Foreign Tax Rates	Available Tax Planning Alternatives
A.	No	Yes
B.	No	No
C.	Yes	No
D.	Yes	Yes

Answer (D) is correct. *(CPA, adapted)*
REQUIRED: The factors used to estimate the annual effective tax rate for interim statements.
DISCUSSION: The estimated effective annual tax rate should be based upon the statutory rate adjusted for the current year's expected conditions. These conditions include anticipated investment tax credits, foreign tax rates, percentage depletion, capital gain rates, and other tax planning alternatives.
Answer (A) is incorrect. The effective tax rate should reflect anticipated foreign tax rates. Answer (B) is incorrect. The effective tax rate should reflect anticipated foreign tax rates and available tax planning alternatives. Answer (C) is incorrect. The effective tax rate should reflect anticipated available tax planning alternatives.

25. The computation of a company's third quarter provision for income taxes should be based upon "ordinary" income (loss)

A. For the quarter at an expected annual effective income tax rate.

B. For the quarter at the statutory rate.

C. To date at an expected annual effective income tax rate, minus prior quarters' provisions.

D. To date at the statutory rate, minus prior quarters' provisions.

Answer (C) is correct. *(CPA, adapted)*
REQUIRED: The correct computation of a third quarter provision for income taxes.
DISCUSSION: The income tax provision for an interim period should be calculated by applying the estimated annual effective tax rate to the "ordinary" income (loss) for the year to date and then deducting the prior interim periods' income tax provisions. "Ordinary" in this context means excluding unusual or infrequent items, extraordinary items, discontinued operations, and cumulative effects of changes in accounting principles.
Answer (A) is incorrect. The calculation must apply the expected annual effective income tax rate to the cumulative "ordinary" income (loss) for the year to date and then subtract prior quarters' tax provisions. Answer (B) is incorrect. The company must use an expected annual effective income tax rate. Answer (D) is incorrect. The company must use an estimated tax rate.

26. During the first quarter of Year 3, Lipid Co. had income before taxes of $200,000, and its effective income tax rate was 15%. Lipid's Year 2 effective annual income tax rate was 30%, but Lipid expects its Year 3 effective annual income tax rate to be 25%. In its first quarter interim income statement, what amount of income tax expense should Lipid report?

A. $0

B. $30,000

C. $50,000

D. $60,000

Answer (C) is correct. *(CPA, adapted)*
REQUIRED: The amount of income taxes for the first interim period.
DISCUSSION: At the end of each interim period, the entity should make its best estimate of the effective tax rate expected to apply for the full fiscal year. This rate should be used in providing for income taxes on a current year-to-date basis. The ordinary income before taxes for the first quarter is $200,000, and the estimated annual effective tax rate for Year 3 is 25%. The income tax expense for the first interim period is therefore $50,000 ($200,000 × 25%).
Answer (A) is incorrect. Zero excludes any income tax expense. Answer (B) is incorrect. The amount of $30,000 is based on the quarterly effective income tax rate. Answer (D) is incorrect. The amount of $60,000 is based on the Year 2 effective annual income tax rate.

27. Bard Co., a calendar-year corporation, reported income before income tax expense of $10,000 and income tax expense of $1,500 in its interim income statement for the first quarter of the year. Bard had income before income tax expense of $20,000 for the second quarter and an estimated effective annual rate of 25%. What amount should Bard report as income tax expense in its interim income statement for the second quarter?

A. $3,500

B. $5,000

C. $6,000

D. $7,500

Answer (C) is correct. *(CPA, adapted)*
REQUIRED: The interim income tax expense for the second quarter.
DISCUSSION: Interim period tax expense equals the estimated annual effective tax rate, times year-to-date ordinary income, minus the tax expense recognized in previous interim periods. Accordingly, the income tax expense reported in the interim income statement for the second quarter is calculated as follows:

First quarter pre-tax income	$10,000
Second quarter pre-tax income	20,000
Total year-to-date income	$30,000
Times: estimated effective annual tax rate	25%
Total tax expense	$ 7,500
Minus: income tax expense for first quarter	(1,500)
Income tax expense for second quarter	$ 6,000

Answer (A) is incorrect. The amount of $3,500 equals the second quarter pre-tax income, times the estimated annual tax rate, minus the income tax expense for the first quarter. Answer (B) is incorrect. The amount of $5,000 equals the second quarter pre-tax income times the estimated annual tax rate. Answer (D) is incorrect. The amount of $7,500 is the total tax expense for the first two quarters.

28. The following information was used in preparing Nocturne Company's quarterly income statements during the first half of the current year:

Quarter	Income before Income Taxes	Estimated Effective Annual Income Tax Rate
1	$80,000	45%
2	70,000	45%

For the third quarter of the current year, income before income taxes was $50,000, and the estimated effective annual income tax rate was 40%. The income statement for the third quarter of the current year should include a provision for income taxes of

A. $12,500

B. $17,500

C. $20,000

D. $22,500

Answer (A) is correct. *(CIA, adapted)*
REQUIRED: The income taxes reported in the interim income statement for the third quarter.
DISCUSSION: The reported tax for the third quarter is calculated by multiplying the estimated annual effective tax rate determined at the end of the third quarter times the cumulative year-to-date ordinary income (loss). The cumulative tax reported for the first two quarters is then subtracted. At the end of the third quarter, the year-to-date ordinary income is $200,000 ($80,000 + $70,000 + $50,000), and the cumulative tax provision is $80,000 ($200,000 × 40%). Because the cumulative tax provision at the end of the second quarter was $67,500 [($80,000 + $70,000) × 45%], $12,500 ($80,000 – $67,500) should be reported as a provision for income taxes in the income statement for the third quarter.
Answer (B) is incorrect. The amount of $17,500 adds the estimated income tax of $50,000 at 40% to the cumulative tax provision and then subtracts $150,000 (80,000 + 70,000) × 40%. Answer (C) is incorrect. The amount of $20,000 is the third-quarter effective annual income tax rate multiplied by income before taxes ($50,000 × 40%). Answer (D) is incorrect. The amount of $22,500 is the second-quarter effective annual income tax rate multiplied by income before taxes ($50,000 × 45%).

25.6 IFRS

29. Wilson Corp. experienced a decline in the net realizable value (NRV) of its inventory to an amount $50,000 below cost. The loss occurred in the first quarter of its fiscal year. Wilson had expected this decline to reverse in the third quarter, and, in fact, the third quarter recovery exceeded the previous decline by $10,000. Wilson's inventory did not experience any other changes in NRV during the fiscal year. What amounts of loss or gain should Wilson report in its interim financial statements for the first and third quarters?

	First Quarter	Third Quarter
A.	$0	$0
B.	$0	$10,000 gain
C.	$50,000 loss	$50,000 gain
D.	$0	$60,000 gain

Answer (C) is correct. *(CPA, adapted)*
REQUIRED: The loss or gain reported for changes in the NRV of inventory in interim statements.
DISCUSSION: A decline in NRV below cost expected to be restored within the fiscal year may not be deferred at an interim reporting date even if no loss is anticipated for the year. If the loss is recovered later during the fiscal year (in another quarter), it should be treated as a change in estimate. The price recovery recognized is limited to the extent of the losses previously recognized because inventory may be written up only to the lower of cost or NRV as a result of a new assessment of NRV each period.
Answer (A) is incorrect. The first quarter decline and the third quarter recovery (limited to lower of cost or revised NRV) must be recognized when they occurred. Answer (B) is incorrect. A first quarter loss of $50,000 and a third quarter gain of $50,000 must be recognized. Answer (D) is incorrect. A first quarter loss of $50,000 must be recognized. The third quarter gain is limited to the increase in the revised NRV that is not above cost.

30. An inventory loss from a temporary market decline of $360,000 occurred in May. Richter Co. recorded this loss in May after its March 31 quarterly report was issued. What amount of inventory loss should be reported in Richter's quarterly income statement prepared under IFRS for the 3 months ended June 30?

A. $0

B. $90,000

C. $180,000

D. $360,000

Answer (D) is correct. *(CPA, adapted)*
REQUIRED: The temporary inventory loss from a market decline reported in a quarterly income statement under IFRS.
DISCUSSION: Under IFRS, an inventory loss from a writedown to NRV, restructuring, or impairment in an interim period is not deferred, regardless of whether it is expected to be recovered within the fiscal year. The $360,000 market decline occurring in the quarter ended June 30 is not considered temporary. Hence, it should be recognized in full in that quarter.
Answer (A) is incorrect. The decline should be recognized in full in the quarter ended June 30. Answer (B) is incorrect. The amount of $90,000 assumes proration over four quarters. Answer (C) is incorrect. The amount of $180,000 assumes proration over two quarters.

31. A company determined the following amounts for its inventory as of the end of the interim period on July 31, Year 2:

Historical cost	$80,000
Net realizable value (NRV)	77,000
Current replacement cost	76,000
Normal profit margin	2,000

The company expects that on December 31, Year 2, the inventory's NRV reduced by a normal profit margin will be at least $81,000. What amount of inventory should the company report in its interim financial statements under IFRS and under U.S. GAAP on July 31, Year 2?

	IFRS	U.S. GAAP
A.	$77,000	$80,000
B.	$77,000	$76,000
C.	$80,000	$80,000
D.	$80,000	$81,000

Answer (A) is correct. *(Publisher, adapted)*
REQUIRED: The inventory reported in interim financial statements under IFRS and under U.S. GAAP.
DISCUSSION: Under U.S. GAAP, the inventory is reported at its historical cost of $80,000 because no write-down of inventory is reasonably anticipated for the year. Under IFRS, the inventory is measured at the end of each interim period at the lower of cost ($80,000) and NRV ($77,000). Thus, the inventory is reported at its NRV of $77,000.
Answer (B) is incorrect. Under U.S. GAAP, the inventory loss from a market decline is deferred if no loss is reasonably anticipated for the year. Answer (C) is incorrect. Under IFRS, the inventory is measured at the lower of cost and NRV, regardless of whether the write-down is expected to be reversed at year end. Answer (D) is incorrect. Under U.S. GAAP, the inventory cannot be reported above its historical cost. Under IFRS, the inventory must not be reported at its historical cost when its NRV is lower.

Use Gleim **EQE Test Prep** Software Download for interactive study and performance analysis.

STUDY UNIT TWENTY-SIX
FOREIGN CURRENCY
TRANSLATION AND TRANSACTIONS

Foreign Currency Translation

Foreign currency translation expresses in the reporting currency amounts stated in a different currency. The reporting currency is the currency used by the reporting entity to prepare its financial statements. Translation is necessary when the financial statements of separate entities within a reporting entity are stated in different currencies. Consequently, translation into the reporting currency should reflect in the consolidated statements the financial results of the consolidated entities measured in their functional currencies. For example, the statements of a French subsidiary might be changed from euro to dollar amounts to be reported in the consolidated statements of a U.S. parent. The **functional currency** is the currency of the primary economic environment in which an entity operates, which usually is where it primarily generates and expends cash. For a foreign entity that is a direct and integral component or extension of a U.S. parent, the functional currency ordinarily is the U.S. dollar. For a foreign entity whose operations are relatively self-contained and integrated within a foreign country, the functional currency is most often the currency of that country. However, determining the functional currency ultimately is a matter of the economic facts and circumstances.

Translation requires (1) identifying a foreign entity's functional currency, (2) **remeasuring** the entity's financial statements into the functional currency if they are stated in another currency, and (3) **translating** the entity's financial statements into the reporting currency if it differs from the functional currency. Current exchange rates must be used to **remeasure monetary items**, and historical exchange rates must be used to **remeasure nonmonetary items**. The following items are remeasured at historical rates: (1) property, plant, equipment, and accumulated depreciation; (2) inventory at cost; (3) prepaid expenses; (4) marketable securities at cost, including debt not classified as held-to-maturity; (5) intangible assets; (6) goodwill; (7) deferred charges, credits, and income; (8) common stock; (9) preferred stock; and (10) revenues and expenses related to nonmonetary items (e.g., depreciation, amortization, and cost of goods sold). A current exchange rate is used to **translate** all items from the functional currency to the reporting currency.

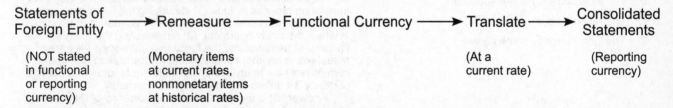

Statements of Foreign Entity ——→ Remeasure ——→ Functional Currency ——→ Translate ——→ Consolidated Statements

(NOT stated in functional or reporting currency)   (Monetary items at current rates, nonmonetary items at historical rates)   (At a current rate)   (Reporting currency)

Translation also provides information consistent with the expected economic effects of exchange rate changes on consolidated cash flows and equity. Changes involving foreign operations that are a direct extension of the parent are considered to affect parent cash flows directly. Thus, exchange rate gains and losses arising from **remeasurement of monetary assets and liabilities** are included in **current earnings**. This accounting is the same as for foreign currency transactions. Exchange rate changes involving foreign operations that are self-contained are considered to relate to the net investment in that operation and not to affect parent cash flows directly. Accordingly, exchange rate gains and losses arising from **translation** are included in **other comprehensive income (OCI)**, not earnings.

Foreign Currency Transactions

The terms of a foreign currency transaction are stated in a currency different from the entity's functional currency. For example, an entity whose functional currency is the U.S. dollar purchases inventory on credit from a German entity, and payment is to be in euros. The initial measurement of the transaction must be in the reporting entity's functional currency. The exchange rate used is the rate in effect on that date. A foreign currency **transaction gain or loss** results from a change in the exchange rate between the functional currency and the currency in which a foreign currency transaction is stated. This gain or loss is included in earnings in the period the exchange rate changes. However, if the transaction is (1) effective as a hedge of a **net investment in a foreign entity** or (2) an **intraentity transaction** that is effectively a **noncurrent investment**, the gain or loss is reported in the same manner as translation adjustments.

QUESTIONS

26.1 Foreign Currency Translation

1. The financial results of three foreign subsidiaries are included along with those of a U.S. parent in consolidated financial statements. The subsidiaries are distinct and separable from the parent and from each other. If the four operations are conducted in four different economic environments, how many different functional currencies most likely are necessary to measure these operations?

A. One.

B. Two.

C. Three.

D. Four.

Answer (D) is correct. *(Publisher, adapted)*
REQUIRED: The number of functional currencies involved in measuring the financial activities of a parent and three distinct subsidiaries operating in different environments.
DISCUSSION: The activities of an entity must be measured in terms of the currency of the primary economic environment in which the entity operates, that is, the functional currency. Because the four operations (parent and three subsidiaries) are distinct and separable from each other and are conducted in four different economic environments, each entity's assets, liabilities, and operations are measured using a different functional currency.
Answer (A) is incorrect. The operations are not all reported using the parent's functional currency. Answer (B) is incorrect. Each of the four operations (most likely) has its own functional currency. Answer (C) is incorrect. Each of the four operations (most likely) has its own functional currency.

2. The assets, liabilities, and operations of a foreign subsidiary are presented in the consolidated financial statements of a U.S.-based parent. They must be measured in

A. The functional currency of the subsidiary.

B. The local currency of the subsidiary.

C. The reporting currency.

D. The local currency of the parent.

Answer (A) is correct. *(Publisher, adapted)*
REQUIRED: The conversion of foreign subsidiary financial statements for consolidation purposes.
DISCUSSION: The assets, liabilities, and operations of a foreign entity must be measured using its functional currency. Thus, translation into the reporting currency should reflect in the consolidated statements the financial results of the consolidated entities measured in their functional currencies. The steps in the translation process include (1) identifying the functional currency of the entity (the currency of the primary economic environment in which the entity operates), (2) remeasuring the entity's financial statements into the functional currency if they are measured in another currency, and (3) translating (using a current rate) the entity's financial statements into the reporting currency if it differs from the functional currency.
Answer (B) is incorrect. The local currency of the subsidiary may not be its functional currency. Answer (C) is incorrect. The subsidiary's financial statement amounts are measured (or remeasured) in its functional currency. They are then translated into the reporting currency (if different). Translation is not measurement. Answer (D) is incorrect. The local currency of the parent may not be the functional currency of the subsidiary.

3. GAAP provide specific guidelines for translating foreign currency financial statements. The translation process begins with a determination of whether a foreign affiliate's functional currency is also its local reporting currency. Which one of the following factors indicates that a foreign affiliate's functional currency is the U.S. dollar?

A. Cash flows are primarily in foreign currency and do not affect parent's cash flows.

B. Financing is primarily obtained from local foreign sources and from the affiliate's operations.

C. Sales prices are responsive to short-term changes in exchange rates and worldwide competition.

D. Labor, materials, and other costs consist primarily of local costs to the foreign affiliate.

Answer (C) is correct. *(CMA, adapted)*
REQUIRED: The factor indicating that a foreign affiliate's functional currency is the U.S. dollar.
DISCUSSION: The functional currency is the currency of the primary economic environment in which an entity operates. It is normally the currency of the environment in which an entity primarily generates and expends cash. If a U.S. entity's foreign affiliate's sales prices respond to short-term changes in exchange rates and worldwide competition, its functional currency is likely to be the U.S. dollar.
Answer (A) is incorrect. Cash flows that are primarily in a foreign currency indicate that the foreign currency is the functional currency. Answer (B) is incorrect. When financing is obtained primarily from foreign sources and operations, the foreign currency is likely to be the functional currency. Answer (D) is incorrect. When costs are primarily paid in the foreign country, the foreign currency is likely to be the functional currency.

4. A wholly owned subsidiary of Ward, Inc., has certain expense accounts for the year ended December 31, Year 3, stated in local currency units (LCUs) as follows:

	LCU
Depreciation of equipment (related assets purchased Jan. 1, Year 1)	120,000
Provision for doubtful accounts	80,000
Rent	200,000

The exchange rates at various dates are as follows:

	Dollar Equivalent of 1 LCU
December 31, Year 3	$.40
Average for year ended 12/31/Year 3	.44
January 1, Year 1	.50

Assume that the LCU is the subsidiary's functional currency and that the charges to the expense accounts occurred approximately evenly during the year. What total dollar amount should be included in Ward's Year 3 consolidated income statement to reflect these expenses?

A. $160,000

B. $168,000

C. $176,000

D. $200,000

Answer (C) is correct. *(CPA, adapted)*
REQUIRED: The amount of expenses in the consolidated income statement.
DISCUSSION: When the local currency of the subsidiary is the functional currency, translation into the reporting currency is necessary. Assets and liabilities are translated at the exchange rate at the balance sheet date, and revenues, expenses, gains, and losses are usually translated at average rates for the period. Thus, the 400,000 LCU in total expenses should be translated at the average exchange rate of $.44, resulting in expenses reflected in the consolidated income statement of $176,000 (400,000 LCU × $.44).
Answer (A) is incorrect. The amount of $160,000 is based on the rate at December 31, Year 3. Answer (B) is incorrect. The amount of $168,000 is based on the average of the December 31, Year 3, rate and the average rate for Year 3. Answer (D) is incorrect. The amount of $200,000 is based on the rate at January 1, Year 1.

5. Which of the following is not part of foreign currency translation?

A. The functional currency of each foreign operation must be identified.

B. All elements of the financial statements of a foreign operation must be measured in the functional currency.

C. If the functional currency of a foreign operation differs from the reporting currency, translation using the current exchange rate method is required.

D. The gain or loss arising from translation must be included in earnings of the current period.

Answer (D) is correct. *(Publisher, adapted)*
REQUIRED: The item that is not part of foreign currency translation.
DISCUSSION: A gain or loss arising from translation from the functional currency into the reporting currency is not included in the current period's earnings. Translation adjustments are reported in OCI.
Answer (A) is incorrect. One step in the process is identifying the functional currency of each operation. Answer (B) is incorrect. One step in the process is measuring the elements of the financial statements of a foreign operation in the functional currency. Answer (C) is incorrect. One step in the process is translating functional currency amounts into the reporting currency using the current exchange rate method.

6. In preparing consolidated financial statements of a U.S. parent company with a foreign subsidiary, the foreign subsidiary's functional currency is the currency

    A. In which the subsidiary maintains its accounting records.

    B. Of the country in which the subsidiary is located.

    C. Of the country in which the parent is located.

    D. Of the environment in which the subsidiary primarily generates and expends cash.

Answer (D) is correct. *(CPA, adapted)*
    REQUIRED: The foreign subsidiary's functional currency.
    DISCUSSION: Translation converts foreign currency amounts into units of the reporting currency. The steps in the process include (1) identifying the functional currency of the entity (the currency of the primary economic environment in which the entity operates), (2) remeasuring the entity's financial statements into the functional currency if they are measured in another currency, and (3) translating (using a current rate) the entity's financial statements into the reporting currency if it differs from the functional currency.
    Answer (A) is incorrect. The currency in which the subsidiary maintains its accounting records may not be the functional currency indicated by the economic facts and circumstances. Answer (B) is incorrect. The currency of the country in which the subsidiary is located may not be the functional currency indicated by the economic facts and circumstances. Answer (C) is incorrect. The currency of the country in which the parent is located may not be the functional currency indicated by the economic facts and circumstances.

7. A wholly owned foreign subsidiary of Union Corporation has certain expense accounts for the year ended December 31, Year 10, stated in local currency units (LCUs) as follows:

	LCU
Amortization of patent (related patent acquired Jan. 1, Year 8)	40,000
Provision for doubtful accounts	60,000
Rent	100,000

The exchange rates at various dates are as follows:

	Dollar Equivalent of 1 LCU
December 31, Year 10	$.20
Average for year ended 12/31/Year 10	.22
January 1, Year 8	.25

The subsidiary's operations were an extension of the parent company's operations. What total dollar amount should be included in Union's income statement to reflect the above expenses for the year ended December 31, Year 10?

    A. $40,000

    B. $42,000

    C. $44,000

    D. $45,200

Answer (D) is correct. *(CPA, adapted)*
    REQUIRED: The dollar amount of remeasured expenses of a foreign subsidiary whose operations are an extension of the parent's.
    DISCUSSION: Given that the foreign subsidiary's operations are an extension of the parent's, the functional currency of the subsidiary is considered to be the U.S. dollar. Thus, remeasurement from the local currency to the U.S. dollar is required for financial statement purposes.
    Nonmonetary balance sheet items and related revenues and expenses (e.g., cost of sales, depreciation, and amortization) must be remeasured using historical rates to produce the same results as if those items had been initially recorded in the functional currency (U.S. dollar). Accordingly, the amortization of patent expense (LCUs = 40,000) must be remeasured at the rate of exchange in effect at the date the patent was acquired, $.25. Monetary and current value items must be remeasured at a current rate. Hence, provision for doubtful accounts and rent must be remeasured at the average Year 10 exchange rate of $.22. This is the customary approximation of the current rate used to remeasure expenses not related to nonmonetary items.

Patent amortization	40,000 × $.25 =	$10,000
Provision for doubtful accounts	60,000 × $.22 =	13,200
Rent	100,000 × $.22 =	22,000
Total remeasured expenses		$45,200

    Answer (A) is incorrect. The amount of $40,000 results from applying the year-end exchange rate to the total expenses. Answer (B) is incorrect. The amount of $42,000 results from applying the average rate to the patent and the year-end rate to the rent. Answer (C) is incorrect. The amount of $44,000 results from applying the average rate to the total expenses.

8. If an entity's books of account are not maintained in its functional currency, GAAP require remeasurement into the functional currency prior to the translation process. An item that should be remeasured by use of the current exchange rate is

    A. An investment in bonds to be held until maturity.

    B. A plant asset and the associated accumulated depreciation.

    C. A patent and the associated accumulated amortization.

    D. The revenue from a long-term construction contract.

Answer (A) is correct. *(CMA, adapted)*
    REQUIRED: The item that should be remeasured into the functional currency using the current exchange rate.
    DISCUSSION: Common nonmonetary balance sheet items and their related revenues, expenses, gains, and losses are remeasured at historical rates. All others are remeasured using the current rate. Thus, most monetary items, such as an investment in bonds, are remeasured at the current exchange rate.
    Answer (B) is incorrect. Plant assets are remeasured at historical rates. Answer (C) is incorrect. A patent is remeasured at historical rates. Answer (D) is incorrect. The revenue from a long-term construction contract is one of the exceptions for which the current rate is not to be used.

9. Certain balance sheet accounts of a foreign subsidiary of Rowan, Inc., have been translated into U.S. dollars on December 31 as follows:

| | Translated at | |
	Current Rates	Historical Rates
Note receivable, long-term	$240,000	$200,000
Prepaid rent	85,000	80,000
Patent	150,000	170,000
	$475,000	$450,000

The subsidiary's functional currency is the currency of the country in which it is located. What total amount should be included in Rowan's December 31 consolidated balance sheet for the above accounts?

- A. $450,000
- B. $455,000
- C. $475,000
- D. $495,000

Answer (C) is correct. *(CPA, adapted)*
REQUIRED: The total translated amount to be included in the consolidated balance sheet.
DISCUSSION: When the currency used to prepare a foreign entity's financial statements is its functional currency, the current rate method must be used to translate the foreign entity's financial statements into the reporting currency. The translation gains and losses arising from applying this method are included in OCI. Accumulated OCI is reported in the equity section of the consolidated balance sheet. Thus, the listed assets translated at current rates should be included in the consolidated balance sheet at $475,000.
Answer (A) is incorrect. The amount of $450,000 reflects translation at historical rates. Answer (B) is incorrect. The note and patent are translated at historical rates. Answer (D) is incorrect. The patent is translated at historical rates.

10. Which of the following is included in other comprehensive income?

- A. Unrealized holding gains and losses on trading securities.
- B. Unrealized holding gains and losses that result from a debt security being transferred into the held-to-maturity category from the available-for-sale category.
- C. Foreign currency translation adjustments.
- D. The difference between the accumulated benefit obligation and the fair value of pension plan assets.

Answer (C) is correct. *(CPA, adapted)*
REQUIRED: The inclusion in OCI.
DISCUSSION: Other comprehensive income (OCI) includes all items of comprehensive income not included in net income. Foreign currency translation adjustments for a foreign operation that is relatively self-contained and integrated within its environment do not affect cash flows of the reporting entity. Thus, they are excluded from earnings and reported in OCI.
Answer (A) is incorrect. Unrealized holding gains and losses on available-for-sale (not trading) securities are included in OCI. Answer (B) is incorrect. When a debt security is transferred to the held-to-maturity category from the available-for sale category, amounts previously recognized in OCI are not reversed. However, they are amortized to earnings in the same way as premium or discount. Moreover, the transfer does not result in recognition of any new amounts in OCI. If the transfer is to available-for-sale from held-to-maturity, any unrealized gains or losses that were previously unrecognized are recognized in OCI. Answer (D) is incorrect. The difference between the projected benefit obligation and the fair value of pension plan assets is the amount by which a defined benefit pension plan is over- or underfunded. It is reported as an asset or a liability. The excess of the ABO over the fair value of plan assets was the measure of the liability required to be recognized according to prior guidance.

11. A foreign subsidiary's functional currency is its local currency, which has not experienced significant inflation. The weighted-average exchange rate for the current year is the appropriate exchange rate for translating

	Wages Expense	Sales to Customers
A.	Yes	No
B.	Yes	Yes
C.	No	Yes
D.	No	No

Answer (B) is correct. *(CPA, adapted)*
REQUIRED: The item(s) translated at the weighted-average exchange rate for the current year.
DISCUSSION: When an entity's local currency is the functional currency and this currency has not experienced significant inflation, translation into the reporting currency of all elements of the financial statements must be at a current exchange rate. Assets and liabilities are translated at the exchange rate at the balance sheet date. Revenues (e.g., sales), expenses (e.g., wages), gains, and losses should be translated at the rates in effect when they were recognized. However, translation of income statement items at a weighted-average rate for the period is permitted.
Answer (A) is incorrect. Sales to customers are translated using the weighted-average exchange rate for the current year. Answer (C) is incorrect. Wages expense is translated using the weighted-average exchange rate for the current year. Answer (D) is incorrect. Wages expense and sales to customers are translated using the weighted-average exchange rate for the current year.

12. If all assets and liabilities of a firm's foreign subsidiary are translated into the parent's currency at the current exchange rate (the rate in effect at the date of the balance sheet), the extent of the parent firm's translation adjustment is based on the subsidiary's

A. Current assets minus current liabilities.

B. Total assets minus total liabilities.

C. Monetary assets minus monetary liabilities.

D. Operating cash flows.

Answer (B) is correct. *(CIA, adapted)*
REQUIRED: The basis for the parent's translation gain or loss if all assets and liabilities of the foreign subsidiary are translated at the current exchange rate.
DISCUSSION: When the functional currency of a foreign subsidiary is the local (foreign) currency, translation of all assets and liabilities into the reporting currency is required at the current rate as of the balance sheet date.
Answer (A) is incorrect. Translation of net assets (total assets – total liabilities), not just current net assets, is required. Answer (C) is incorrect. Translation of all assets, not just monetary holdings, is required. Answer (D) is incorrect. Translation is required for assets, not just for incoming cash.

13. The economic effects of a change in foreign exchange rates on a relatively self-contained and integrated operation within a foreign country relate to the net investment by the reporting entity in that operation. Consequently, translation adjustments that arise from the consolidation of that operation

A. Directly affect the reporting entity's cash flows but must not be included in earnings.

B. Directly affect the reporting entity's cash flows and must be included in earnings.

C. Do not directly affect the reporting entity's cash flows and must not be included in earnings.

D. Do not directly affect the reporting entity's cash flows but must be included in earnings.

Answer (C) is correct. *(Publisher, adapted)*
REQUIRED: The true statement about translation adjustments arising from consolidation of a self-contained foreign operation.
DISCUSSION: Foreign currency translation adjustments for a foreign operation that is relatively self-contained and integrated within its environment do not affect cash flows of the reporting entity and must be excluded from earnings. When an operation is relatively self-contained, the cash generated and expended by the entity is normally in the currency of the foreign country, and that currency is deemed to be the operation's functional currency.
Answer (A) is incorrect. When an operation is relatively self-contained, the assumption is that translation adjustments do not affect cash flows. Answer (B) is incorrect. When an operation is relatively self-contained, the assumption is that translation adjustments do not affect cash flows, and translation adjustments must be included in other comprehensive income, not earnings. Answer (D) is incorrect. Translation adjustments must be included in OCI, not earnings.

14. The current rate of exchange must be used for remeasuring certain balance sheet items and the historical rate of exchange for other balance sheet items. An item that must be remeasured using the historical exchange rate is

A. Accounts and notes receivable.

B. Accounts and notes payable.

C. Taxes payable.

D. Prepaid expenses.

Answer (D) is correct. *(CMA, adapted)*
REQUIRED: The item that should be remeasured using the historical exchange rate.
DISCUSSION: Financial statements are remeasured using current rates for monetary items and historical rates for nonmonetary items. Prepaid expenses, a nonmonetary item, must be remeasured using the historical rate.
Answer (A) is incorrect. Accounts and notes receivable are monetary items. Thus, they must be remeasured using the current rate of exchange. Answer (B) is incorrect. Accounts and notes payable are monetary items. Thus, they must be remeasured using the current rate of exchange. Answer (C) is incorrect. Taxes payable is a monetary item. Thus, it must be remeasured using the current rate of exchange.

15. Park Co.'s wholly owned subsidiary, Schnell Corp., maintains its accounting records in euros. Because all of Schnell's branch offices are in Switzerland, its functional currency is the Swiss franc. Remeasurement of Schnell's current-year financial statements resulted in a $7,600 gain, and translation of its financial statements resulted in an $8,100 gain. What amount should Park report as a gain in its income statement for the current year ended December 31?

A. $0

B. $7,600

C. $8,100

D. $15,700

Answer (B) is correct. *(CPA, adapted)*
REQUIRED: The gain reported as a result of translation and remeasurement.
DISCUSSION: The financial statements must be remeasured into the functional currency (Swiss francs) and then translated into the reporting currency (U.S. dollar). The $7,600 gain arising from remeasurement must be reported in current income. The $8,100 translation gain must be reported in OCI. Translation gains are not reflected in net income.
Answer (A) is incorrect. The gain on remeasurement must be reported in the income statement. Answer (C) is incorrect. The $8,100 translation gain is not reported in the income statement. Answer (D) is incorrect. The $8,100 translation gain is not added to the remeasurement gain.

16. When remeasuring foreign currency financial statements into the functional currency, which of the following items is remeasured using historical exchange rates?

    A. Inventories carried at cost.

    B. Equity securities reported at fair values.

    C. Bonds payable.

    D. Accrued liabilities.

Answer (A) is correct. *(CPA, adapted)*

REQUIRED: The item that is remeasured using historical exchange rates.

DISCUSSION: The current rate of exchange must be used for remeasuring certain balance sheet items and the historical rate of exchange for other balance sheet items. Nonmonetary balance sheet items and related revenue, expense, gain, and loss amounts are remeasured at the historical rate. Monetary items are remeasured at the current rate. Inventories carried at cost are nonmonetary items and are remeasured at historical rates.

Answer (B) is incorrect. Equity securities reported at fair values is a monetary item remeasured at the current rate. Answer (C) is incorrect. Bonds payable is a monetary item remeasured at the current rate. Answer (D) is incorrect. Accrued liabilities is a monetary item remeasured at the current rate.

17. The Brinjac Company owns a foreign subsidiary. Included among the subsidiary's liabilities for the year just ended are 400,000 LCUs of revenue received in advance, recorded when $.50 was the dollar equivalent per LCU, and a deferred tax liability for 187,500 LCU, recognized when $.40 was the dollar equivalent per LCUs. The rate of exchange in effect at year end was $.35 per LCU. If the dollar is the functional currency, what total should be included for these two liabilities on Brinjac's consolidated balance sheet at year end?

    A. $205,625

    B. $215,000

    C. $265,625

    D. $275,000

Answer (D) is correct. *(C.J. Skender)*

REQUIRED: The total of two liabilities of a foreign subsidiary in the consolidated statements if the functional currency is the U.S. dollar.

DISCUSSION: When a foreign entity's functional currency is the U.S. dollar, the financial statements of the entity recorded in a foreign currency must be remeasured in terms of the U.S. dollar. Revenue received in advance (deferred income) is considered a nonmonetary balance sheet item and is remeasured at the applicable historical rate (400,000 LCUs × $.50 per LCU = $200,000). Deferred charges and credits (except policy acquisition costs for life insurance companies) also are remeasured at historical exchange rates. Consequently, the deferred tax liability (a deferred credit) is remeasured at the historical rate (187,500 LCUs × $.40 per LCU) = $75,000). The total for these liabilities is therefore $275,000 ($200,000 + $75,000).

Answer (A) is incorrect. The amount of $205,625 results from applying the year-end rate to the total liabilities. Answer (B) is incorrect. The historical, not current, rate must be used to remeasure the deferred income. Answer (C) is incorrect. The historical rate is used to remeasure nonmonetary balance sheet items, including deferred tax assets and liabilities.

18. The Dease Company owns a foreign subsidiary with 3,600,000 local currency units (LCUs) of property, plant, and equipment before accumulated depreciation on December 31, Year 7. The subsidiary's functional currency is the U.S. dollar. Of this amount, 2,400,000 LCUs were acquired in Year 0 when the rate of exchange was 1.6 LCUs to $1, and 1,200,000 LCUs were acquired in Year 3 when the rate of exchange was 1.8 LCUs to $1. The rate of exchange in effect at December 31, Year 7, was 2 LCUs to $1. The weighted average of exchange rates in effect during Year 7 was 1.92 LCUs to $1. Assuming that the property, plant, and equipment are depreciated using the straight-line method over a 10-year period with no salvage value, how much depreciation expense relating to the foreign subsidiary's property, plant, and equipment should be charged in Dease's income statement for Year 7?

    A. $180,000

    B. $187,500

    C. $200,000

    D. $216,667

Answer (D) is correct. *(CPA, adapted)*

REQUIRED: The amount of remeasured depreciation expense recognized in consolidating a foreign subsidiary whose functional currency is the U.S. dollar.

DISCUSSION: Given that the subsidiary's functional currency is the U.S. dollar, the financial statements of the subsidiary must be remeasured in terms of the dollar. Nonmonetary assets and the related revenues and expenses are remeasured based on the historical rates in effect at the dates of the transactions. Depreciation expense relates to the property, plant, and equipment (nonmonetary assets), so the rate of exchange in effect when these fixed assets were acquired is used in remeasuring depreciation expense for the period.

Because 2,400,000 LCUs of fixed assets were acquired when the rate of exchange was 1.6, depreciation expense can be remeasured by multiplying the LCU depreciation by $1 ÷ 1.6, resulting in $150,000 of remeasured depreciation expense [(2,400,000 ÷ 10) × ($1 ÷ 1.6)]. Depreciation related to the asset that cost 1,200,000 LCUs is $66,667 in remeasured terms [(1,200,000 ÷ 10) × ($1 ÷ 1.8)]. Total depreciation expense equals $216,667 ($150,000 + $66,667).

Answer (A) is incorrect. The amount of $180,000 results from applying the current (year-end) rate to the total depreciation expense. Answer (B) is incorrect. The amount of $187,500 results from applying the average rate to the total depreciation expense. Answer (C) is incorrect. The rate prevailing at the time the assets were acquired should be used for each group of assets.

19. A foreign subsidiary of a U.S. parent reports its financial statements in its local currency although its functional currency is the U.S. dollar. In the consolidated financial statements, all of the following accounts of the subsidiary are remeasured into the functional currency at the historical rate except

    A. Marketable securities carried at cost.

    B. Inventories carried at market.

    C. Property, plant, and equipment.

    D. Goodwill.

Answer (B) is correct. *(J.W. Mantooth)*

    REQUIRED: The account that is not remeasured at the historical rate.

    DISCUSSION: When a foreign subsidiary's functional currency is the U.S. dollar, all elements of its financial statements reported in a foreign currency must be remeasured as if they had been recorded in the U.S. dollar. Nonmonetary balance sheet items and related revenue, expense, gain, and loss amounts are remeasured at the historical rate. Monetary items are remeasured at the current rate. Inventories carried at market are classified as monetary assets and must be remeasured at the current rate.

    Answer (A) is incorrect. Marketable securities carried at cost are remeasured using historical exchange rates. Answer (C) is incorrect. Property, plant, and equipment are remeasured using historical exchange rates. Answer (D) is incorrect. Goodwill is remeasured using historical exchange rates.

26.2 Foreign Currency Transactions

20. On October 1, Year 5, Mild Co., a U.S. company, purchased machinery from Grund, a German company, with payment due on April 1, Year 6. If Mild's Year 5 operating income included no foreign currency transaction gain or loss, the transaction could have

    A. Resulted in an extraordinary gain.

    B. Been denominated in U.S. dollars.

    C. Caused a foreign currency transaction gain to be reported as a contra account against machinery.

    D. Caused a foreign currency translation gain to be reported in OCI.

Answer (B) is correct. *(CPA, adapted)*

    REQUIRED: The reason no foreign currency transaction gain or loss occurred when a U.S. company purchased machinery from a German company.

    DISCUSSION: A foreign currency transaction results in a receivable or a payable fixed in terms of the amount of foreign currency. A change in the exchange rate between the functional currency and the currency in which the transaction is stated is a gain or loss that ordinarily should be included as a component of income from continuing operations in the period in which the exchange rate changes. If Mild Co.'s functional currency is the U.S. dollar and the transaction was stated in U.S. dollars, the transaction is a foreign transaction, not a foreign currency transaction. Thus, no foreign currency transaction gain or loss occurred.

    Answer (A) is incorrect. Foreign currency transaction gains and losses are ordinarily treated as operating items. Answer (C) is incorrect. Foreign currency transaction gains and losses are included in earnings. Answer (D) is incorrect. Foreign currency translation gains and losses result from translating functional currency amounts into the reporting currency. If the transaction was stated in U.S. dollars, no translation was needed.

21. Ball Corp. had the following foreign currency transactions during Year 4:

- Merchandise was purchased from a foreign supplier on January 20, Year 4, for the U.S. dollar equivalent of $90,000. The invoice was paid on March 20, Year 4, at the U.S. dollar equivalent of $96,000.

- On July 1, Year 4, Ball borrowed the U.S. dollar equivalent of $500,000 evidenced by a note that was payable in the lender's local currency on July 1, Year 6. On December 31, Year 4, the U.S. dollar equivalents of the principal amount and accrued interest were $520,000 and $26,000, respectively. Interest on the note is 10% per annum.

In Ball's Year 4 income statement, what amount should be included as foreign currency transaction loss?

    A. $0

    B. $6,000

    C. $21,000

    D. $27,000

Answer (D) is correct. *(CPA, adapted)*

    REQUIRED: The amount to be included as foreign currency transaction loss.

    DISCUSSION: When a foreign currency transaction gives rise to a receivable or a payable that is fixed in terms of the foreign currency, a change in the exchange rate between the functional currency and the currency in which the transaction is stated is a gain or loss that ordinarily should be included as a component of income from continuing operations in the period in which the exchange rate changes. In the Year 4 income statement, the foreign currency transaction loss should include the $6,000 difference between the $90,000 initially recorded as a payable and the $96,000 payment amount, the $20,000 difference between the $500,000 equivalent amount of the principal of the note on December 31 and its $520,000 equivalent on July 1, and the $1,000 difference between the $26,000 equivalent of the interest accrued and the $25,000 [$500,000 × 10% × (6 months ÷ 12 months)] interest on the initially recorded amount of the loan. The foreign currency transaction loss therefore equals $27,000 ($6,000 + $20,000 + $1,000).

    Answer (A) is incorrect. The loss must be recognized. Answer (B) is incorrect. The differences in principal and interest on the $500,000 note are excluded. Answer (C) is incorrect. The amount of $21,000 excludes the $6,000 difference in the recording and payment for the foreign purchase.

22. Shore Co. records its transactions in U.S. dollars. A sale of goods resulted in a receivable denominated in Japanese yen, and a purchase of goods resulted in a payable denominated in euros. Shore recorded a foreign currency transaction gain on collection of the receivable and a transaction loss on settlement of the payable. The exchange rates are expressed as so many units of foreign currency to one dollar. Did the number of foreign currency units exchangeable for a dollar increase or decrease between the contract and settlement dates?

	Yen Exchangeable for $1	Euros Exchangeable for $1
A.	Increase	Increase
B.	Decrease	Decrease
C.	Decrease	Increase
D.	Increase	Decrease

Answer (B) is correct. *(CPA, adapted)*
REQUIRED: The movements in exchange rates.
DISCUSSION: A gain on a receivable fixed in terms of a foreign currency results when the fixed amount of the foreign currency can be exchanged for a greater number of dollars at the date of collection, that is, when the number of foreign currency units exchangeable for a dollar decreases. A loss on a payable stated in a foreign currency results when the number of dollars needed to purchase the fixed amount of the foreign currency increases, that is, when the number of foreign currency units exchangeable for a dollar decreases.
Answer (A) is incorrect. A gain on a foreign currency receivable and a loss on a foreign currency payable result when the dollar weakens. Answer (C) is incorrect. A loss on a foreign currency payable results when the dollar weakens. Answer (D) is incorrect. A gain on a foreign currency receivable results when the dollar weakens.

23. On October 1, Velec Co., a U.S. company, contracted to purchase foreign goods requiring payment in local currency units (LCUs) 1 month after the receipt of the goods at Velec's factory. Title to the goods passed on December 15. The goods were still in transit on December 31. Exchange rates were one dollar to 22 LCUs, 20 LCUs, and 21 LCUs on October 1, December 15, and December 31, respectively. Velec should account for the exchange rate fluctuation in the year as

A. A loss included in net income before extraordinary items.

B. A gain included in net income before extraordinary items.

C. An extraordinary gain.

D. An extraordinary loss.

Answer (B) is correct. *(CPA, adapted)*
REQUIRED: The classification of a gain or loss due to exchange rate fluctuations.
DISCUSSION: A receivable or payable fixed in terms of a foreign currency is adjusted to its current exchange rate at each balance sheet date. The transaction gain or loss arising from this adjustment should ordinarily be reflected in earnings. Because title passed on December 15, the liability fixed in LCUs should have been recorded on that date at the 20-LCU exchange rate. The increase to 21 LCUs per dollar at year end decreases the dollar value of the liability and results in a foreign currency transaction gain. Such a gain is ordinarily treated as a component of income from continuing operations.
Answer (A) is incorrect. The strengthening of the dollar resulted in a gain. Answer (C) is incorrect. An extraordinary item is infrequent and unusual in nature. Exchange rates change frequently. Answer (D) is incorrect. Extraordinary items do not occur nearly as frequently as exchange rates change.

24. Toigo Co. purchased merchandise from a vendor in England on November 20 for 500,000 British pounds. Payment was due in British pounds on January 20. The spot rates to purchase 1 pound were as follows:

November 20	$1.25
December 31	1.20
January 20	1.17

How should the foreign currency transaction gain be reported on Toigo's financial statements at December 31?

A. A gain of $40,000 as a separate component of stockholders' equity.

B. A gain of $40,000 in the income statement.

C. A gain of $25,000 as a separate component of stockholders' equity.

D. A gain of $25,000 in the income statement.

Answer (D) is correct. *(CPA, adapted)*
REQUIRED: The foreign currency transaction gain.
DISCUSSION: Foreign currency transactions are recorded at the spot rate in effect at the transaction date. Transaction gains and losses ordinarily are recorded in earnings. On November 20, the entity made the following entry:

Inventory (500,000 pounds × $1.25)	$625,000	
Accounts payable (pounds)		$625,000

On December 31, the entity made the following entry:

Accounts payable [500,000 pounds × ($1.25 – $1.20)]	$25,000	
Transaction gain		$25,000

Answer (A) is incorrect. The entity recognizes a gain in earnings of $15,000 [500,000 pounds × ($1.20 – $1.17)] on January 20. Answer (B) is incorrect. The only effect of the change in the spot rate during the period is recognized at the balance sheet date. Answer (C) is incorrect. The gain is recognized in earnings. Translation adjustments are recognized in OCI.

25. Transaction gains and losses have direct cash flow effects when foreign-denominated monetary assets are settled in amounts greater or less than the functional currency equivalent of the original transactions. These transaction gains and losses should be reflected in income

A. At the date the transaction originated.

B. On a retroactive basis.

C. In the period the exchange rate changes.

D. Only at the year-end balance sheet date.

Answer (C) is correct. *(CMA, adapted)*
REQUIRED: The time when foreign currency transaction gains and losses should be reflected in income.
DISCUSSION: When a foreign currency transaction gives rise to a receivable or a payable that is fixed in terms of the amount of foreign currency to be received or paid, a change in the exchange rate between the functional currency and the currency in which the transaction is stated results in a gain or loss that ordinarily should be included as a component of income from continuing operations in the period in which the exchange rate changes.
Answer (A) is incorrect. The extent of any gain or loss cannot be known at the date of the original transaction. Answer (B) is incorrect. Retroactive recognition is not permitted. Answer (D) is incorrect. Gains and losses are to be recognized in the period of the rate change.

26. On September 1, Year 2, Cano & Co., a U.S. corporation, sold merchandise to a foreign firm for 250,000 local currency units (LCUs). Terms of the sale require payment in LCUs on February 1, Year 3. On September 1, Year 2, the spot exchange rate was $0.20 per LCU. On December 31, Year 2, Cano's year end, the spot rate was $0.19, but the rate increased to $0.22 by February 1, Year 3, when payment was received. How much should Cano report as foreign currency transaction gain or loss in its Year 3 income statement?

A. $0.

B. $2,500 loss.

C. $5,000 gain.

D. $7,500 gain.

Answer (D) is correct. *(CPA, adapted)*
REQUIRED: The foreign currency transaction gain or loss in the Year 3 income statement.
DISCUSSION: A receivable or payable fixed in terms of a foreign currency should be recorded at the current exchange rate and then adjusted to the current exchange rate at each balance sheet date. That adjustment is a foreign currency transaction gain or loss that is ordinarily included in earnings for the period of change. Furthermore, a gain or loss measured from the transaction date or the most recent intervening balance sheet date is recognized when the transaction is settled. Accordingly, Cano should recognize a foreign currency transaction gain of $7,500 [250,000 LCUs receivable × ($0.22 – $0.19)] in Year 3.
Answer (A) is incorrect. The exchange rate changed between the balance sheet date and the settlement date. Answer (B) is incorrect. A $2,500 loss was incurred in Year 2. Answer (C) is incorrect. The net transaction gain is $5,000.

27. Fay Corp. had a realized foreign currency transaction loss of $15,000 for the year ended December 31, Year 5, and must also determine whether the following items will require year-end adjustment:

- Fay had an $8,000 loss resulting from the translation of the accounts of its wholly owned foreign subsidiary for the year ended December 31, Year 5.

- Fay had an account payable to an unrelated foreign supplier payable in the supplier's local currency. The U.S. dollar equivalent of the payable was $64,000 on the October 31, Year 5, invoice date and $60,000 on December 31, Year 5. The invoice is payable on January 30, Year 6.

In Fay's Year 5 consolidated income statement, what amount should be included as foreign currency transaction loss?

A. $11,000

B. $15,000

C. $19,000

D. $23,000

Answer (A) is correct. *(CPA, adapted)*
REQUIRED: The amount to be included as foreign currency transaction loss.
DISCUSSION: Translation adjustments are reported in OCI. Translation adjustments are therefore not included in earnings. Furthermore, a receivable or payable fixed in terms of a foreign currency is recorded at the date of the transaction at the current rate of exchange. This receivable or payable must then be adjusted to the current rate at each balance sheet date. The gain or loss from this adjustment is included in earnings. Accordingly, the $4,000 ($64,000 – $60,000) gain adjustment arising from the foreign currency transaction should be included along with the realized foreign currency transaction loss of $15,000 in the Year 5 consolidated income statement. The amount to be reported is an $11,000 ($15,000 loss – $4,000 gain) foreign currency transaction loss.
Answer (B) is incorrect. The amount of $15,000 excludes the $4,000 gain. Answer (C) is incorrect. The gain was added to, rather than subtracted from, the loss. Answer (D) is incorrect. The translation loss is added to the loss, and the transaction gain is not included.

STUDY UNIT TWENTY-SEVEN
STATE AND LOCAL GOVERNMENTS

Objective

The **Governmental Accounting Standards Board (GASB)** determines the accounting and reporting requirements for state and local governments. Such accounting and reporting is used in making economic, social, and political decisions and in assessing accountability. The primary objective of governmental financial reporting is accountability, both fiscal and operational. **Fiscal accountability** is the responsibility of governments to justify that their actions in the current period have complied with public decisions concerning the raising and spending of public moneys in the short term. **Operational accountability** is governments' responsibility to report the extent to which they have met their accounting objectives efficiently and effectively, using all resources available for that purpose, and whether they can continue to meet their objectives for the foreseeable future. The financial statements of governmental funds emphasize fiscal accountability. The financial statements of proprietary funds and fiduciary funds provide information about the operational accountability of those funds. **Government-wide financial statements** provide information about the operational accountability of the governmental activities and business-type activities of the government as a whole.

Interperiod equity is a component of accountability. Financial resources received during a period should suffice to pay for the services provided during that period. Moreover, debt should be repaid during the probable period of usefulness of the assets acquired.

Fund Accounting

An accounting system should permit governments to (1) present fairly and with full disclosure their funds and activities in conformity with GAAP and (2) demonstrate compliance with finance-related legal and contractual provisions. A **fund** is an independent fiscal and accounting entity with a self-balancing set of accounts, which records (1) financial resources, (2) liabilities, (3) residual equities or balances, and (4) changes in them. Items in a fund are separated because they relate to specific activities or certain objectives. State and local governments should prepare an annual budget that covers all funds.

Funds used in governmental accounting include governmental funds, proprietary funds, and fiduciary funds. **Governmental funds** account for the nonbusiness activities of a government and its current, expendable resources (most often generated with tax revenue). The primary fund is the **general fund**, which accounts for all financial resources except those accounted for in other funds. **Special revenue funds** account for restricted or committed proceeds of specific revenue sources. Expenditure must be for a specified purpose (but not debt service or a capital project). Thus, the basis of the fund is a substantial inflow from restricted or committed revenue sources. **Capital project funds** account for financial resources restricted, committed, or assigned to be expended for capital purposes. These resources include general obligation bond proceeds to be used to construct major capital facilities, such as schools or bridges. But the capital assets themselves are not accounted for in these funds. Other capital facilities may be financed through proprietary funds or certain trust funds. **Debt service funds** do not account for debt but for resources restricted, committed, or assigned to paying principal and interest. They also account for resources being accumulated for future principal and interest payments. **Permanent funds** account for resources legally restricted so that only the earnings may be expended for the benefit of the government or its citizens. State and local governments are responsible for making sure the funds comply with their legal and operating requirements.

Proprietary funds account for the business-type activities of a government. They serve defined customer groups and are generally financed through fees. **Enterprise funds** may be used for any activities for which fees are charged to external users. They need not be used for insignificant activities. Examples are public utilities, public transit systems, and state-run lotteries. They are the funds most similar to private businesses. **Internal service funds** may be used for activities that provide goods and services to other subunits of the primary government and its component units or to other governments on a cost-reimbursement basis. However, if the reporting government is not the predominant participant, the activity should be reported as an enterprise fund. Examples are a decentralized information technology function or motor pool.

Fiduciary funds account for resources held by the government in trust or as an agent for specific individuals, private organizations, or other governments. These funds cannot be used for the reporting entity's purposes. For a trust fund, the trust agreement determines how long resources are held and the degree of management involvement. The government serves as a fiduciary of the trust. **Pension (and other employee benefit) trust funds** account for employee benefit programs. **Investment trust funds** account for resources held for investment on behalf of other governments in an investment pool. **Private-purpose trust funds** account for all other trust arrangements that benefit individuals, private organizations, or other governments. **Agency funds** account for resources held temporarily in a purely custodial capacity, such as tolls that will be remitted to a private business.

Measurement Focus and Basis of Accounting

The measurement focus of a set of financial statements is what is being measured or tracked by the information provided. The basis of accounting selected determines the timing of the recognition in the financial records of economic events or transactions. The **current financial resources measurement focus** and the modified accrual basis of accounting are used to report the **governmental funds**. This approach emphasizes short-term fiscal accountability for expendable available financial resources. The reporting elements are sources, uses, and balances of current financial resources.

Under the **modified accrual basis of accounting**, revenue or another increase in financial resources (such as bond issue proceeds) is recognized when it is measurable and available to finance expenditures of the current period. **Available** means collectible within the current period or soon enough thereafter to be used to pay liabilities of the current period. For property tax revenue, the phrase "soon enough thereafter" means not more than 60 days after the end of the year. But in unusual cases, a longer period may be justified. Property tax revenues are measurable when assessed property values can be multiplied by the tax rate to obtain the total tax to be levied. Operating **expenditures** (not expenses) are recognized when goods or services are acquired. Thus, expenditures are usually measurable and should be recognized when the related liability is incurred. However, expenditures for principal and interest on general long-term debt are usually recognized only when those amounts are due. The amount of an expenditure is what is normally paid with expendable available financial resources.

Inventory (e.g., materials or supplies) may be debited to expenditures when purchased (the **purchases method**) or used (the **consumption method**). The purchases method is used with a periodic system and the consumption method with a periodic or perpetual system. Under either method, the year-end inventory must be reported in the balance sheet. Under the purchases method, the unassigned fund balance of the general fund should be debited and the nonspendable fund balance credited to indicate the unavailability of resources (inventory) for other expenditures. **Prepayments** also may be accounted for using the purchases method or the consumption method.

The **economic resources measurement focus** and the accrual basis of accounting are used to report all other financial statements. This approach provides longer-term operational accountability information. It measures revenues and expenses in the same way as in for-profit accounting and emphasizes a longer-range measure of revenues earned or levied (and accrued immediately if measurable). Furthermore, this approach focuses on cost of services.

Under the **accrual basis** of accounting, most measurable transactions and events are recognized without regard to cash flows. Moreover, an operating expense is recognized when goods or services are used or consumed instead of an expenditure when they are acquired. Acquired but unused goods and services are treated as assets. Thus, revenues, expenses, gains, losses, assets, and liabilities from **exchange transactions** are accrued when the exchange occurs. (For nonexchange transactions, see "Sources of Financing" on page 626.)

General Capital Assets and Long-Term Liabilities

General capital assets are all capital assets not reported in the proprietary funds or the fiduciary funds. Thus, they usually result from expenditure of governmental fund resources. They are reported at historical cost, including other charges (freight-in, site preparation, etc.), only in the governmental activities column of the government-wide statement of net assets. Capital assets (but not land and inexhaustible art and historic objects) must be **depreciated** (except in governmental funds.) However, infrastructure assets (e.g., roads and bridges) need not be depreciated if they are maintained at an established condition level. In governmental funds, the full cost of a capital asset is debited as an expenditure when acquired. General long-term liabilities are all unmatured long-term liabilities not directly related to and expected to be paid from proprietary funds and fiduciary funds. They should be reported only in the governmental activities column of the government-wide statement of net assets.

In **proprietary funds**, capital assets and long-term liabilities related to proprietary fund activities are accounted for in the same way as in for-profit accounting. They are reported in those funds and in the government-wide statements. **Fiduciary funds** contain resources held in a trustee or custodial capacity. These resources cannot be used to finance the operations of the government. Thus, capital assets and long-term liabilities related to fiduciary funds are reported in the fund statements but not in the government-wide statements.

A **lease** is capitalized by a lessee or lessor if it meets the criteria used in for-profit accounting. Except in governmental fund statements, capital leases are initially and subsequently accounted for in the same way as in for-profit accounting. In the **governmental funds**, a **lessee** may need to account for a capital lease representing the acquisition or construction of a general capital asset. Thus, the lessee recognizes an expenditure and another financing source in accordance with the accounting for general obligation debt. A **lessor** recognizes a lease receivable to the extent it is another financing source that is measurable and available. The remainder is deferred. Furthermore, the noncurrent receivable is **not** a general capital asset.

	Governmental Funds Financial Statements	Proprietary Funds Financial Statements	Fiduciary Funds Financial Statements	Government-Wide Financial Statements
Measurement Focus	Current financial resources	Economic resources	Economic resources	Economic resources
Basis of Accounting	Modified accrual	Accrual	Accrual	Accrual
Capital Assets	No	Yes	Trust funds only	Yes
Long-Term Liabilities	No	Yes	Trust funds only	Yes

Budgetary Accounting

Annual budgets are often legally adopted by state and local governments. These budgets are legally binding to the administration. As a means of control, the budget is recorded as an integral part of the accounting system. A comparison of the budgetary accounts to actual revenues and expenditures is done throughout the year to ensure compliance with the budget. However, budgetary amounts are not reported in the financial statements. **Estimated revenues** is an anticipatory asset (a debit). It is the amount expected to be collected from a government's revenues, such as taxes, fees, and fines. **Estimated other financing sources** is an anticipatory asset that includes the sources of financing other than revenues. Examples are the face amount of long-term debt, issuance premium, and interfund transfers. **Estimated other financing uses** is an anticipatory liability (a credit) used to record an expected flow of resources to another fund. Issuance discount and interfund transfers for debt service are examples. **Appropriations** is an anticipatory liability reflecting the total amount authorized to be expended by the government for the fiscal period.

Fund balance or budgetary fund balance also is recorded (generally as a credit) in the budgetary entry. Fund balance is a real account. It is the difference (fund equity) between assets and liabilities. Some accountants use **budgetary fund balance**, a nominal account, to record the budgeted change in fund equity for the year.

EXAMPLE: A state adopts its budget for the year. The following entry records the budget for the general fund:

General fund:		
Estimated revenues -- sales taxes	$2,400,000,000	
Estimated other financing sources		
-- face amount of bonds	400,000,000	
Appropriations		$2,100,000,000
Estimated other financing uses		
-- transfer to debt service fund		600,000,000
Budgetary fund balance		100,000,000

Fund balance is classified according to the limits on the specific purposes for which resources may be spent. The following is the hierarchy of classifications:

- **Nonspendable.** These amounts (1) are in a form (e.g., inventory, prepayments, or long-term loans) that is not spendable or (2) must be kept intact (e.g., the principal of a permanent fund).

- **Restricted.** These amounts may be spent only for specific purposes established by (1) a constitutional mandate, (2) enabling legislation, or (3) an external provider.

- **Committed.** These amounts may be spent only for specific purposes established by a formal act of the entity's highest decision maker. This decision maker may redirect the resources by following the necessary due process.

- **Assigned.** These remaining amounts are not properly classifiable as nonspendable, restricted, or committed in a governmental fund other than the general fund. In the **general fund**, assigned fund balance includes amounts to be used for a specific purpose that are not restricted or committed. Expenditure is limited only by the entity's intent to use such amounts for specific purposes. An example of an assignment is an appropriation of fund balance to offset a budget deficit expected in the next year.

- **Unassigned.** The general fund is the only fund that reports a positive balance (the sum of the amounts not classified elsewhere). In other governmental funds, this classification is used only for a deficit balance.

EXAMPLE:

General Fund
Balance Sheet

Assets	$X,XXX,XXX
Liabilities	$X,XXX,XXX
Fund balance	
Nonspendable:	
Inventory	XX,XXX
Prepayments	XX,XXX
Principal of permanent fund	XXX,XXX
Restricted:	
Federal social services mandate	XXX,XXX
Committed	XXX,XXX
Assigned	XXX,XXX
Unassigned	X,XXX,XXX
Total fund balance	$X,XXX,XXX
Total liabilities and fund balance	$X,XXX,XXX

Encumbrance accounting may be used only for internal purposes and only in governmental funds. A government makes a commitment to expend resources when a contract is signed or a purchase order is approved. The amount may then be recorded as an encumbrance. The entry is to debit encumbrances and credit reserve for encumbrances. When the good is delivered or the service performed, **two entries are made**. The encumbrance entry is reversed, and the legal obligation to pay is recognized. Significant encumbrances are disclosed in the notes. If resources have been encumbered and classified as restricted, committed, or assigned, no separate display is needed in those classifications. If an encumbered amount has not been restricted, etc., it is not classified as unassigned. Instead, it is included in committed or assigned fund balance.

At year-end closing, the budgetary entries are reviewed, and encumbrances are removed from the books.

Sources of Financing

Most governmental revenue is from four types of **nonexchange transactions**. **Derived tax revenues** are assessments on exchange transactions. Examples are income taxes and sales taxes. Income is earned or a sale is completed and a tax is levied based on the amount of money transferred. **Imposed nonexchange revenues** are assessments on nongovernmental entities, for example, property taxes or fines. Payment is imposed on an act or omission of an act that is not an exchange. Examples are taxes on the ownership of property (e.g., real estate, motor vehicles, or stock) or the failure to obey a law (e.g., a traffic or environmental violation). **Government-mandated nonexchange transactions** occur when one government provides resources to another government and requires that they be used for a specific purpose. An example is a federal grant required to be used for primary education. Fulfillment of eligibility requirements is essential. **Voluntary nonexchange transactions** are legislative or contractual agreements that are not exchanges. They are entered into willingly by the parties. Examples are certain (1) grants, (2) entitlements, or (3) private donations. Fulfillment of eligibility requirements also is essential for government-imposed and voluntary nonexchange transactions. These requirements include (1) characteristics of recipients (e.g., school districts), (2) time of use (e.g., time when use is first allowed or time resources must be kept intact), (3) incurrence of allowed costs to be reimbursed, or (4) contingencies (e.g., resources to be raised by a recipient). Examples are a federal public transit grant applied for by a local government and a donation of an art collection to a city museum.

The timing of recognition of assets, liabilities, and expenses or expenditures arising from nonexchange transactions is not affected by the basis of accounting. However, revenue recognition on the modified accrual basis (i.e., in governmental funds) requires that (1) revenue be susceptible to accrual (measurable and available) and (2) the criteria below be met.

Category	Timing of Recognition
Derived tax revenues	**Assets** – Earlier of when underlying exchange has occurred or resources are received. **Revenues** – When underlying exchange has occurred (advance receipts are credited to deferred revenues). Resources also should be **available** if resources are accounted for in a governmental fund.
Imposed nonexchange revenues	**Assets** – Earlier of when an enforceable legal claim has arisen or resources are received. **Revenues** – When resources are required to be used or use is first allowed (for property taxes, the period for which levied). Resources also should be **available** if resources are accounted for in a governmental fund. Absent time requirements, asset and revenue recognition are at the same time.
Government-mandated and voluntary nonexchange transactions	**Assets and liabilities** – Earlier of when all eligibility requirements have been met or (for assets) resources are received. **Revenues and expenses or expenditures** – When all eligibility requirements have been met (advance receipts or payments are recorded as deferred revenues or advances, respectively). Given **time requirements**, revenues and expenses or expenditures are recorded when the resources are, respectively, received or paid. The resulting net assets, equity, or fund balance is restricted. Resources also should be **available** if resources are accounted for in a governmental fund.

Governments also obtain financing by issuing debt, such as bonds. The proceeds of such long-term debt are not revenues but are a major source of funding for governments. The **government-wide financial statements** report all resources and obligations, regardless of whether they are current or noncurrent. The receipt of cash and the related obligation are recognized. The inflow from a financing source is not. Any **premium received or discount paid** upon issuance is not recognized. Premium and discount do not affect the amount of long-term resources that must be spent to retire the bonds. In the **governmental fund financial statements**, the treatment is different because they have a short-term focus, and bonds are not repaid with current financial resources. The fund that will expend the resources recognizes the receipt of cash and the related other financing sources. Thus, the entry is to (1) debit cash for the amount received, (2) credit other financing sources for the face amount of the debt, and (3) credit other financing sources or debit other financing uses for issuance premium or discount, respectively.

Bonds may be issued to finance a **construction project**. Payments for the project are made from the proceeds. In the government-wide financial statements, the finished project (or construction-in-progress) is reported as a general capital asset. In the governmental fund financial statements, payments to the contractor are debited to expenditures in the capital projects fund. The capital asset itself is not capitalized in the governmental fund statements.

When the bonds are **retired**, the entries reflect the same differences in recognition as in the issuance. The government-wide financial statements recognize the reduction in assets (credit) and liabilities (debit) and interest expense (debit). Just as the receipt of the bond proceeds was not a revenue in the government-wide statements, so the retirement of the principal is not an expenditure. The accounting in the **governmental funds** requires multiple entries.

General fund resources are earmarked for debt service.

General fund:
Other financing uses -- interfund transfer to debt service fund
    Due to debt service fund

Debt service fund:
Due from general fund
    Other financing sources -- interfund transfer from general fund

The resources are transferred.

General fund:
Due to debt service fund
    Cash

Debt service fund:
Cash
    Due from general fund

Expenditures are debited when principal and interest are legally due.

Debt service fund:
Expenditure -- bond principal
Expenditure -- bond interest
    Bonds payable
    Interest payable

The current portion of the debt is repaid.

Debt service fund:
Bonds payable
Interest payable
    Cash

Governments may agree to construct physical improvements that will benefit one or more property owners. The government issues debt, pays for the improvements with the proceeds, and repays the debt with **special assessments** on the property owners.

Interfund transfers also are a source of financing for governmental funds.

Reporting Entity and the CAFR

The financial reporting entity consists of the primary government and its component units. The financial statements should include data from all component units. The **primary government** is financially accountable for the entities in its legal entity and certain others. Any state or general-purpose local government is a primary government.

Component units are legally separate entities (1) for which the primary government is financially accountable or (2) the omission of which would cause the financial statements to be **misleading**. **Blended component units** are, in substance, the same as the primary government and should be reported as a part of it. Blending is appropriate only if the component unit's governing body is substantively the same as the primary government's, or the component unit almost exclusively benefits the primary government. Blended component-unit **balances and transactions** are reported in the same way as those of the primary government. However, the primary government's **general fund** is the only general fund reported. The general fund of the blended component unit is reported as a **special revenue fund** of the primary government. The financial statements of the reporting entity should distinguish between the primary government and its component units. Thus, the government-wide financial statements report information about most **discretely (separately) presented** component units (DPCUs) in separate rows and columns. The **equity interest** in a DPCU must be reported as an asset. Information about a DPCU that is **fiduciary** is reported only in the fiduciary fund statements of the primary government. No other DPCU is reported in the fund financial statements.

Special-purpose governments (SPGs) are legally separate entities. If they have governmental and business-type activities or are engaged in two or more governmental programs, they should be reported as general-purpose governments. If an SPG is engaged in one governmental program (e.g., an assessment or drainage district), it may combine the government-wide and fund statements. If an SPG is engaged only in **business-type activities**, it presents the statements for **enterprise funds**. If it is engaged only in fiduciary activities, it reports the statements for fiduciary funds. **Public colleges and universities** must apply the guidance for SPGs.

State and local governments must present, as a matter of public record, a **comprehensive annual financial report (CAFR)**. The CAFR includes all funds of the primary government (and blended component units) and DPCUs. The **financial section** contains (1) the independent auditor's report, (2) management's discussion and analysis (MD&A), and (3) basic financial statements. MD&A is part of required supplementary information (RSI). It precedes the basic financial statements. It should contain an objective and easily readable analysis of financial activities based on **currently known** facts, decisions, or conditions. It also should emphasize the current year while providing comparisons with prior years. The **basic financial statements** include (1) government-wide financial statements; (2) fund financial statements; and (3) notes to the financial statements, including a summary of significant accounting policies. Notes are an integral part of the basic statements. They disclose information essential to fair presentation not reported on the face of the statements. The financial section also includes (1) RSI other than MD&A (e.g., budgetary comparison schedules for the general fund and each major special revenue fund), (2) combining statements, and (3) individual fund statements and schedules.

Government-Wide Reporting

Government-wide financial statements report information about the reporting government as a whole (other than fiduciary activities). They include a **statement of net assets** and a **statement of activities**. The statement of net assets displays three components: (1) invested in capital assets, net of related debt; (2) restricted net assets; and (3) unrestricted net assets. Capital assets to be reported include infrastructure assets. Separate rows and columns should be used to distinguish between (1) governmental and business-type activities of the primary government and (2) the primary government and its discretely presented component units.

The **statement of activities** presents operations in a format that displays **net (expense) revenue** for each governmental or business-type function. This amount equals expenses (at a minimum, the **direct expenses** of the function) minus program revenues. The minimum levels of detail for activities accounted for in governmental funds and in enterprise funds are by **function** and by **different identifiable activities**, respectively. **Direct expenses** must be reported by function. **Indirect expenses** may or may not be allocated. If indirect expenses are allocated, direct and indirect expenses are displayed in separate columns. **Program revenues** include (1) charges for services, (2) program-specific operating grants and contributions, and (3) program-specific capital grants and contributions. **General revenues** are not required to be reported as program revenues. They are reported separately after total net (expense) revenue for all functions. All taxes, including those levied for a special purpose, are general revenues. The following are reported separately at the bottom of the statement: (1) contributions to endowments, (2) contributions to permanent fund principal, (3) transfers between governmental and business-type activities, and (4) special and extraordinary items. **Special items** are significant transactions or other events that are either unusual or infrequent and are controllable by management.

Government-wide financial statements should reflect the economic resources measurement focus and the accrual basis of accounting also used by nongovernmental entities.

Governmental Funds Reporting

Fund financial statements report additional and detailed information about the primary government and must be reconciled to the government-wide statements. The focus of governmental and enterprise fund financial statements is on **major funds**. Major funds always include the general fund. They also include any governmental or enterprise fund with total assets, liabilities, revenues, or expenditures/ expenses that are (1) at least 10% of the corresponding element total for all funds of that category or type (i.e., total governmental or total enterprise funds) and (2) at least 5% of the corresponding element total for all governmental and enterprise funds combined. Separate columns should be used to present financial information for (1) each major fund and (2) nonmajor funds in total.

Required financial statements for governmental funds are (1) a balance sheet and (2) a statement of revenues, expenditures, and changes in fund balances. The **balance sheet** should be in balance sheet format (assets = liabilities + fund balances) with a total column. Fund balances should be classified as nonspendable, restricted, committed, assigned, or unassigned. A **summary reconciliation** of total governmental fund balances to net assets of governmental activities in the government-wide statement of net assets must be prepared. For example, general capital assets and general long-term liabilities not currently due are reconciling items because they are not reported on the balance sheet. The statement of revenues, expenditures, and changes in fund balances reports inflows, outflows, and balances of current financial resources. **Revenues** are classified in this statement by major source and **expenditures** by, at a minimum, function. The **other financing sources and uses** section includes (1) the face amount of long-term debt, (2) issuance premium or discount, (3) some payments to escrow agents for bond refundings, (4) interfund transfers, and (5) sales of capital assets (unless the sale is a special item).

Special and extraordinary items are reported separately after other financing sources and uses. A transaction or event meeting the definition of a special item is separately identified in a revenue or expenditure category if it is within management's control or disclosed in the notes if it cannot be controlled by management. **Debt refundings** in governmental funds are reported as other financing sources or uses, not gains or losses. A **summary reconciliation** of the net change in governmental fund balances to the change in net assets of governmental activities in the government-wide statement of activities must be prepared.

Proprietary Funds Reporting

Proprietary fund financial statements emphasize operating income, changes in net assets (or cost recovery), financial position, and cash flows. Moreover, these funds customarily do not record a budget and encumbrances. Required financial statements for **proprietary funds** are (1) a balance sheet or statement of net assets; (2) a statement of revenues, expenses, and changes in fund equity or net assets; and (3) a statement of cash flows. The **statement of net assets or balance sheet** classifies assets and liabilities as current or noncurrent. Net assets are reported in three components: (1) invested in capital assets, net of related debt; (2) restricted; and (3) unrestricted. Capital contributions (e.g., grants by developers) are not separately displayed. **Restricted assets** are subject to use restrictions imposed by external entities or by law. **Capital assets and long-term liabilities** of proprietary funds are reported in the government-wide statement of net assets and in the proprietary fund statement of net assets.

In the **statement of revenues, expenses, and changes in fund net assets (or fund equity)**, revenues are reported by major source either net, with disclosure of discounts and allowances, or gross, with discounts and allowances reported beneath the revenue amounts. The sequence of items in the all-inclusive format shown below must be followed in each column of the statement:

	Operating revenues (detailed)
+	Total operating revenues
	Operating expenses (detailed)
–	Total operating expenses
=	**Operating income (loss)**
+/–	Nonoperating revenues and expenses (detailed)
=	Income before other revenues, expenses, gains, losses, and transfers
+/–	Capital contributions, additions to endowments, special and extraordinary items, and interfund transfers
=	**Change in net assets**
+	Net assets – beginning
=	**Net assets – ending**

Net assets and changes in net assets are reported for total enterprise funds. They ordinarily are the same as the corresponding amounts for business-type activities in the government-wide statements. Any differences should be **reconciled**. For example, although internal service funds are proprietary funds, the activities they account for generally are governmental. Thus, they should be included in the governmental activities column in the government-wide statement of activities.

A **statement of cash flows** is required for (1) proprietary funds and (2) entities engaged in business-type activities, e.g., governmental utilities, healthcare providers, and colleges and universities. The guidance for preparing the statement is similar to that for nongovernmental entities. A government should (1) have a policy that defines operating items, (2) disclose that policy in the summary of significant accounting policies, and (3) apply it consistently. How transactions are categorized in a statement of cash flows is a consideration in defining operating items for proprietary funds. For example, if cash flows ordinarily are classified as being from capital and related financing activities, noncapital financing activities, and investing activities, then they are not included in operating income.

Fiduciary Funds Reporting

Fiduciary fund financial statements emphasize net assets and changes in net assets. They include information about all fiduciary funds and similar component units. Required statements are (1) a statement of fiduciary net assets and (2) a statement of changes in fiduciary net assets. Separate columns are provided for fund types but not for major funds.

A **statement of fiduciary net assets** reports assets, liabilities, and net assets for each fund type. However, it does not present the three components of net assets reported in the government-wide statement of net assets or in the proprietary fund statement of net assets. The statement reports capital assets and long-term liabilities related to fiduciary funds. They are not reported in the government-wide statements. **Agency fund** assets should equal liabilities in the statement of fiduciary net assets. Agency funds are **not** reported in the statement of changes in fiduciary net assets. A **statement of changes in fiduciary net assets** reports additions to, subtractions from, and the annual net change in net assets for each fiduciary fund type.

Interfund Activity

Interfund activity involves **internal events**. (A transaction is an external event.) **Reciprocal** interfund activities are comparable to exchange and exchange-like transactions. They include interfund loans and interfund services. **Interfund loans** result in interfund receivables and payables. Any amount not expected to be repaid reduces the interfund balances; it is reported as a transfer. Liabilities arising from interfund activity are not general long-term liabilities. Thus, they may be reported in governmental funds. **Interfund services** involve sales and purchases at prices equivalent to external exchange values. They result in revenues to seller funds and expenditures or expenses to buyer funds. Unpaid amounts are interfund receivables or payables. However, when the general fund accounts for risk-financing activity, charges to other funds are treated as reimbursements. In the fund financial statements, all transactions (those between activities and those within activities) are recognized. In the government-wide financial statements, however, only the transactions affecting the enterprise fund are recorded.

Interfund transfers are one-way (nonreciprocal) asset flows with no repayment required. They must be reported in the basic financial statements separately from revenues and expenditures or expenses. The reporting of transfers is different in the government-wide and the fund financial statements. Transfers **within the governmental activities section** are not reported in the government-wide statements. These transfers result in no overall change in governmental activities. Transfers **between governmental activities and business-type activities** are reported in both the government-wide statements and the fund statements.

QUESTIONS

27.1 Objective

1. King City Council will be establishing a library fund. Library fees are expected to cover 55% of the library's annual resource requirements. King has decided that an annual determination of net income is desirable in order to maintain management control and accountability over the library. What type of fund should King establish in order to meet its measurement objectives?

    A. Special revenue fund.

    B. General fund.

    C. Internal service fund.

    D. Enterprise fund.

Answer (D) is correct. *(CPA, adapted)*
REQUIRED: The fund used to account for library operations.
DISCUSSION: Enterprise funds may be used for any activities for which fees are charged to external users. Moreover, an enterprise fund (a proprietary fund) reports using the economic resources measurement focus and the accrual basis of accounting. This approach provides longer-term operational accountability information about economic activity. It measures revenues and expenses in the same way as in for-profit accounting. Thus, the enterprise fund's statement of revenues, expenses, and changes in fund net assets presents amounts for (1) operating income (loss); (2) income before other revenues, expenses, etc.; and (3) change in net assets. Because the library fund will charge fees and report on the accrual basis, King should account for it using an enterprise fund.
NOTE: No fund used in governmental accounting reports net income. The change in net assets includes such items as interfund transfers, capital contributions, and additions to endowments. These items do not correspond to amounts included in the net income of a for-profit entity.
Answer (A) is incorrect. A special revenue fund (a governmental fund) is reported using the modified accrual basis of accounting. However, measures of income are based on the accrual basis of accounting. Thus, a governmental fund is not appropriate for the library fund. Answer (B) is incorrect. The general fund (a governmental fund) reported using the modified accrual basis of accounting. However, measures of income are based on the accrual basis of accounting. Thus, a governmental fund is not appropriate for the library fund. Answer (C) is incorrect. An internal service fund (a proprietary fund) is used for activities that provide goods and services to other subunits of the primary government and its component units or to other governments on a cost-reimbursement basis. It is not used for activities for which fees are charged to external users.

2. Roy City received a gift, the principal of which is to be invested in perpetuity with the income to be used to support the local library. In which fund should this gift be recorded?

    A. Permanent fund.

    B. Investment trust fund.

    C. Private-purpose trust fund.

    D. Special revenue fund.

Answer (A) is correct. *(CPA, adapted)*
REQUIRED: The fund that records a gift to be invested in perpetuity.
DISCUSSION: Permanent funds are governmental funds. They account for resources restricted to the use of earnings for the benefit of the government or its citizens. An example is a perpetual-care fund for a public cemetery. Permanent funds are not private-purpose trust funds, which benefit individuals, private organizations, or other governments. Private-purpose trust funds are fiduciary funds.
Answer (B) is incorrect. An investment trust fund is a fiduciary fund that accounts for investments on behalf of other governments in an investment pool. Answer (C) is incorrect. A private-purpose trust fund is a fiduciary fund that accounts for trust arrangements other than investments held for other governments. These arrangements benefit individuals, private individuals, and other governments. Answer (D) is incorrect. A special revenue fund is a governmental fund that accounts for restricted or committed resources of specific revenue sources.

3. What body primarily determines the measurement focus and basis of accounting standards for governmental financial statements?

    A. Governmental Accounting Standards Board.

    B. National Council on Governmental Accounting.

    C. Governmental Accounting and Auditing Committee of the AICPA.

    D. Financial Accounting Standards Board.

Answer (A) is correct. *(CPA, adapted)*
REQUIRED: The authoritative body that issues pronouncements on GAAP for state and local governments.
DISCUSSION: The GASB is currently the primary standard-setting body for state and local governments.
Answer (B) is incorrect. The NCGA was a predecessor of the GASB. Answer (C) is incorrect. The GAAC is not currently an active and functioning committee of the AICPA. Answer (D) is incorrect. The FASB is the primary accounting standard setter for nongovernmental entities.

4. Governmental financial reporting should provide information to assist users in which situation(s)?

I. Making social and political decisions

II. Assessing whether current-year citizens received services but shifted part of the payment burden to future-year citizens

    A. I only.

    B. II only.

    C. Both I and II.

    D. Neither I nor II.

Answer (C) is correct. *(CPA, adapted)*
REQUIRED: The use(s) of governmental reporting.
DISCUSSION: GASB Concepts Statement 1 states, "Financial reporting by state and local governments is used in making economic, social, and political decisions and in assessing accountability." It also states that "interperiod equity is a significant part of accountability and is fundamental to public administration." Thus, "financial reporting should help users assess whether current-year revenues are sufficient to pay for the services provided that year and whether future taxpayers will be required to assume burdens for services previously provided."
Answer (A) is incorrect. Governmental financial reporting also provides information for assessing whether current-year citizens received services but shifted part of the payment burden to future-year citizens. Answer (B) is incorrect. Governmental financial reporting also provides information for making social and political decisions. Answer (D) is incorrect. Governmental financial reporting also provides information for making social and political decisions and assessing whether current-year citizens received services but shifted part of the payment burden to future-year citizens.

5. The statement of activities of the government-wide financial statements is designed primarily to provide information to assess which of the following?

    A. Operational accountability.

    B. Financial accountability.

    C. Fiscal accountability.

    D. Functional accountability.

Answer (A) is correct. *(CPA, adapted)*
REQUIRED: The primary form of accountability provided by government-wide financial statements.
DISCUSSION: Fiscal accountability is the responsibility of governments to justify that their actions currently comply with public decisions concerning the raising and spending of public resources in the short term. Operational accountability is a government's responsibility to report the extent to which it has met accounting objectives efficiently and effectively, using all resources available, and whether it can continue to do so in the near future. The governmental funds financial statements focus on the fiscal accountability of governmental activities. However, government-wide financial statements focus on the operational accountability of the governmental and business-type activities of the government as a whole. The financial statements of fiduciary funds and proprietary funds provide information about operational accountability.
Answer (B) is incorrect. The government-wide statements focus on operational accountability. Moreover, financial accountability is not as accurate a phrase as fiscal accountability. The term "fiscal" is preferable because it means having to do with the public treasury or revenues. Answer (C) is incorrect. Fiscal accountability is the main focus of governmental funds financial statements. Answer (D) is incorrect. Operational accountability includes but is not limited to functional accountability.

27.2 Fund Accounting

6. State and local governments report various funds to the extent their activities meet the fund criteria. Governmental funds include

    A. Internal service funds.

    B. Nonexpendable trust funds.

    C. Enterprise funds.

    D. Permanent funds.

Answer (D) is correct. *(Publisher, adapted)*
REQUIRED: The governmental funds.
DISCUSSION: Governmental funds (the general fund, special revenue funds, capital projects funds, debt service funds, and permanent funds) emphasize sources, uses, and balances of current financial resources, often with use of budgetary accounts. Expendable assets are assigned to funds based on their intended use, liabilities are assigned to the funds from which they will be paid, and the difference (fund equity) is the fund balance. Permanent funds report resources legally restricted so that earnings only, not principal, may be expended for the benefit of the government or its citizenry, that is, to support the government's programs. An example is a perpetual-care fund for a public cemetery. Permanent funds should be distinguished from private-purpose trust funds.
Answer (A) is incorrect. Internal service funds are proprietary funds. Answer (B) is incorrect. The expendable and nonexpendable trust fund types are no longer permitted. Answer (C) is incorrect. Enterprise funds are proprietary funds.

7. The accounting systems of state and local governmental entities should be organized and operated using which structure?

A. Proprietary fund.

B. Fiduciary fund.

C. Governmental fund.

D. Fund.

Answer (D) is correct. *(Publisher, adapted)*
REQUIRED: The structure of governmental accounting systems of state and local governments.
DISCUSSION: An accounting system should permit state and local governments to (1) present fairly and with full disclosure the funds and activities of state and local governments in conformity with GAAP and (2) demonstrate compliance with finance-related legal and contractual provisions. To satisfy these objectives, state and local government accounting systems use funds. A fund is a fiscal and accounting entity with a self-balancing set of accounts. It records (1) financial resources (including cash), (2) related liabilities, (3) residual equities or balances, and (4) changes in all of the above. Items in a fund are separated because they relate to specific activities or certain objectives that are subject to special regulations or limitations. The three categories of funds used by state and local governments are governmental, proprietary, and fiduciary.
Answer (A) is incorrect. Proprietary funds are only one of the categories of funds used by state and local governments. Answer (B) is incorrect. Fiduciary funds are only one of the categories of funds used by state and local governments. Answer (C) is incorrect. Governmental funds are only one of the categories of funds used by state and local governments.

8. A state or local government may report which fiduciary funds?

A. Private-purpose trust funds.

B. Expendable trust funds.

C. Nonexpendable trust funds.

D. Permanent funds.

Answer (A) is correct. *(Publisher, adapted)*
REQUIRED: The fiduciary funds.
DISCUSSION: Fiduciary funds include pension (and other employee benefit) trust funds, investment trust funds, private-purpose trust funds, and agency funds. Pension (and other employee benefit) trust funds report resources held for (1) members and beneficiaries of pension plans (defined benefit or contribution), (2) other postemployment benefit plans, or (3) other employee benefit plans. Investment trust funds are used by a sponsoring government to report the external portions of external investment pools. Private-purpose trust funds are used for all other trust arrangements, whether the beneficiaries are individuals, private entities, or other governments.
Answer (B) is incorrect. Expendable trust funds are no longer permitted. Answer (C) is incorrect. Nonexpendable trust funds are no longer permitted. Answer (D) is incorrect. Permanent funds are governmental funds.

9. A local governmental unit may use which of the following types of funds?

	Fiduciary	Proprietary
A.	Yes	No
B.	Yes	Yes
C.	No	Yes
D.	No	No

Answer (B) is correct. *(CPA, adapted)*
REQUIRED: The types of funds that may be used by a local governmental unit.
DISCUSSION: Three broad categories of funds may be used by a state or local governmental unit for general purpose financial statements.

1) Governmental – general, special revenue, debt service, capital projects, and permanent funds

2) Proprietary – enterprise and internal service funds

3) Fiduciary – pension (and other employee benefit) trust, investment trust, private-purpose trust, and agency funds

10. Cal City maintains several major fund types. The following were among Cal's cash receipts during the current year:

Unrestricted state grant	$1,000,000
Interest on bank accounts held for employees' pension plan	200,000

What amount of these cash receipts should be accounted for in Cal's general fund?

A. $1,200,000

B. $1,000,000

C. $200,000

D. $0

Answer (B) is correct. *(CPA, adapted)*

REQUIRED: The amount of cash receipts to be accounted for in the general fund.

DISCUSSION: The general fund is used to account for all transactions of a governmental unit that are not accounted for in another fund. The interest is accounted for in a pension trust fund. Thus, the general fund accounts for only the $1,000,000 grant.

Answer (A) is incorrect. The amount of $1,200,000 incorrectly includes the interest. Answer (C) is incorrect. The amount of $200,000 incorrectly includes the interest and excludes the unrestricted state grant. Answer (D) is incorrect. The amount of $0 excludes the unrestricted state grant.

11. Revenues that are legally restricted to expenditures for specified purposes should be accounted for in special revenue funds, including

A. Resources accumulated for payment of general long-term debt principal and interest.

B. Pension trust fund revenues.

C. Gasoline taxes to finance road repairs.

D. Proprietary fund revenues.

Answer (C) is correct. *(CPA, adapted)*

REQUIRED: The revenues legally restricted to expenditures for specified purposes that should be accounted for in special revenue funds.

DISCUSSION: Special revenue funds account for restricted or committed proceeds of specific revenue sources. Expenditures must be for a specified purpose (but not debt service or a capital project). Thus, the basis of the fund is a substantial inflow from restricted or committed revenue sources. Gasoline taxes levied to finance road repair are revenues legally restricted to expenditures for specified purposes that should be accounted for in special revenue funds.

Answer (A) is incorrect. Resources accumulated for payment of general long-term debt principal and interest are accounted for in the debt service fund. Answer (B) is incorrect. Pension trust fund revenues are accounted for in the pension trust fund. Answer (D) is incorrect. Proprietary fund revenues are accounted for in either enterprise or internal service funds.

12. Bay Creek's municipal motor pool maintains all city-owned vehicles and charges the various departments for the cost of rendering the maintenance services. In which of the following funds should Bay account for the cost of such maintenance?

A. General fund.

B. Internal service fund.

C. Special revenue fund.

D. Special assessment fund.

Answer (B) is correct. *(CPA, adapted)*

REQUIRED: The fund in which to account for the cost of vehicle maintenance provided by the motor pool to other departments.

DISCUSSION: An internal service fund is used when one governmental entity provides goods or services to other subunits of the primary government and its component units or to other governments on a cost-reimbursement basis. However, if the reporting government is not the predominant participant, the activity should be reported as an enterprise fund.

Answer (A) is incorrect. The general fund is used to account for transactions not accounted for in other governmental funds. Answer (C) is incorrect. The special revenue fund is used to account for certain restricted categories of revenue. Answer (D) is incorrect. The special assessment fund type is not used in general-purpose financial statements.

13. The following equity balances are among those maintained by Cole City:

Enterprise funds	$1,000,000
Internal service funds	400,000

Cole's proprietary equity balances amount to

A. $1,400,000

B. $1,000,000

C. $400,000

D. $0

Answer (A) is correct. *(CPA, adapted)*

REQUIRED: The amount of proprietary equity balances.

DISCUSSION: Proprietary funds include enterprise funds and internal service funds. Thus, the proprietary equity balances equal $1,400,000 ($1,000,000 + $400,000).

Answer (B) is incorrect. The amount of $1,000,000 excludes the equity balance of the internal service funds. Answer (C) is incorrect. The amount of $400,000 excludes the equity balance of the enterprise funds. Answer (D) is incorrect. The amount of $0 excludes the equity balances of the enterprise funds and the internal service funds.

14. Kew City received a $15,000,000 federal grant to finance the construction of a center for rehabilitation of drug addicts. The proceeds of this grant should be accounted for in the

A. Special revenue funds.

B. General fund.

C. Capital projects funds.

D. Trust funds.

Answer (C) is correct. *(CPA, adapted)*

REQUIRED: The fund used to account for a federal grant required to be used for construction of a specific capital asset.

DISCUSSION: The capital projects fund accounts for resources restricted, committed or assigned to be expended for capital purposes. These resources include general obligation bond proceeds dedicated to the construction of major capital facilities such as schools, bridges, or tunnels. But other capital facilities may be financed through proprietary funds or certain trust funds.

Answer (A) is incorrect. Special revenue funds account for restricted or committed proceeds of specific revenue sources. Expenditure must be for a specified purpose (but not debt service or a capital project). Thus, the basis of the fund is a substantial inflow from restricted or committed revenue sources. Answer (B) is incorrect. A general fund accounts for all resources of the governmental unit not otherwise restricted for special purposes or accounted for in another fund. Answer (D) is incorrect. A grant for a drug rehabilitation center is not accounted for in a trust fund. A trust fund accounts for assets held by a governmental entity in the capacity of a trustee for individuals, private entities, or other governments.

15. A state government had the following activities:

I.   State-operated lottery
II. State-operated hospital

Which of the above activities may be accounted for in an enterprise fund?

A. Neither I nor II.

B. I only.

C. II only.

D. Both I and II.

Answer (D) is correct. *(CPA, adapted)*

REQUIRED: The activities to be accounted for in the enterprise fund.

DISCUSSION: Enterprise funds may be used to account for any activity of a state or local government that provides goods or services to external users for a fee. Both a state-operated hospital and a state-operated lottery are typical enterprise fund activities.

Answer (A) is incorrect. A state-run hospital and a state-run lottery provide services to external users for a fee. Answer (B) is incorrect. A state-run hospital provides services to external users for a fee. Answer (C) is incorrect. A state-run lottery provides services to external users for a fee.

16. An activity that provides goods to other subunits of the primary government on a cost reimbursement basis should be reported as a(n)

A. Fiduciary fund.

B. Agency fund.

C. Enterprise fund in some cases.

D. Internal service fund in all cases.

Answer (C) is correct. *(Publisher, adapted)*

REQUIRED: The fund used to report an activity providing goods to other subunits of the primary government on a cost reimbursement basis.

DISCUSSION: Internal service funds may be used for activities that provide goods and services to other subunits of the primary government and its component units or to other governments on a cost-reimbursement basis. However, if the reporting government is not the predominant participant, the activity should be reported as an enterprise fund.

Answer (A) is incorrect. Fiduciary funds emphasize net assets and changes in net assets. They report assets that cannot be used to support the government's own programs because they are held in trust or in an agency capacity. Answer (B) is incorrect. An agency fund is a fiduciary fund used by a government that holds resources for specific individuals, private entities, or other governments on a purely custodial basis and not as a trustee. Answer (D) is incorrect. Use of an internal service fund is inappropriate if the reporting government is not the predominant participant.

17. Grants that are to be transferred to secondary recipients by a local government should be accounted for in which fund if the government has no administrative or direct involvement in the program?

A. Investment trust fund.

B. Private-purpose trust fund.

C. Agency fund.

D. Special assessment fund.

Answer (C) is correct. *(Publisher, adapted)*
REQUIRED: The funds that account for grants to be transferred to secondary recipients.
DISCUSSION: Agency funds may account for certain grants and other financial assistance to be transferred to, or spent on behalf of, secondary recipients (individuals, private entities, or other governments). The agency fund acts purely as a custodian. It receives the grants and passes them through to the ultimate recipients. However, if the recipient government has administrative or direct financial involvement in the program, the pass-through grant is accounted for in an appropriate governmental, proprietary, or trust fund.
Answer (A) is incorrect. An investment trust fund is used to report the external portion of an external investment pool. Answer (B) is incorrect. A private-purpose trust fund is a trust arrangement used for purposes not served by pension (and other employee benefit) trust funds or by investment trust funds. Answer (D) is incorrect. A special assessment fund is not permitted for general-purpose external reporting purposes.

27.3 Measurement Focus and Basis of Accounting

18. In which of the following fund types of a city government are revenues and expenditures recognized on the same basis of accounting as the general fund?

A. Private-purpose trust.

B. Internal service.

C. Enterprise.

D. Debt service.

Answer (D) is correct. *(CPA, adapted)*
REQUIRED: The fund that recognizes revenues and expenditures on the same basis as the general fund.
DISCUSSION: The debt service fund is the only fund listed that is classified as a governmental fund. The other funds are proprietary or fiduciary. Governmental funds use the modified accrual basis, and proprietary and fiduciary funds use the accrual basis.
Answer (A) is incorrect. A private-purpose trust fund is a fiduciary fund. It is accounted for in a manner similar to that of proprietary funds. Answer (B) is incorrect. The internal service fund is a proprietary fund. It uses the accrual basis of accounting. Answer (C) is incorrect. The enterprise fund is a proprietary fund. It uses the accrual basis of accounting.

19. A major exception to the general rule of expenditure accrual for governmental funds of a state or local government relates to unmatured

	Principal of General Long-Term Debt	Interest on General Long-Term Debt
A.	Yes	Yes
B.	Yes	No
C.	No	Yes
D.	No	No

Answer (A) is correct. *(CPA, adapted)*
REQUIRED: The major exception to the general rule of expenditure accrual for governmental units.
DISCUSSION: According to the modified accrual basis of accounting, expenditures are recognized when liabilities are incurred. For general long-term debt, however, principal and interest expenditures ordinarily are recognized when payments on the debt are due.
Answer (B) is incorrect. The interest on general long-term debt is recognized when due, not when incurred. Answer (C) is incorrect. The principal of general long-term debt is recognized when due. Answer (D) is incorrect. The principal and interest of general long-term debt are recognized when due, not when incurred.

20. When a snowplow purchased by a governmental unit is received, it should be recorded in the general fund as a(n)

A. Encumbrance.

B. Expenditure.

C. General capital asset.

D. Appropriation.

Answer (B) is correct. *(CPA, adapted)*
REQUIRED: The effect of receipt of equipment.
DISCUSSION: Governmental funds are accounted for on the modified accrual basis. Accordingly, a general fund normally recognizes an expenditure (a use of financial resources) when the liability is incurred, if measurable. When previously ordered goods are received, the entry in the general fund includes a debit to expenditures for the actual amount to be paid. Thus, an expenditure is recognized when the liability is incurred, that is, when performance of a contract is complete or virtually complete.
Answer (A) is incorrect. An encumbrance is recorded for the purchase commitment. Answer (C) is incorrect. General capital assets are reported only in the government-wide statement of net assets. Answer (D) is incorrect. Appropriations are accounted for when recording the budget. They are amounts authorized to be spent during a period.

21. Governmental expenditures for insurance extending over more than one accounting period

  A. Must be accounted for as expenditures of the period of acquisition.

  B. Must be accounted for as expenditures of the periods subsequent to acquisition.

  C. Must be allocated between or among accounting periods.

  D. May be allocated between or among accounting periods or may be accounted for as expenditures of the period of acquisition.

Answer (D) is correct. *(CPA, adapted)*
  REQUIRED: The proper treatment of expenditures extending over more than one period.
  DISCUSSION: Prepaid insurance may be reported by either the purchases method or the consumption method. Under the purchases method, an expenditure is reported when the policy is purchased. Under the consumption method, an expenditure is reported as the asset is consumed.
  Answer (A) is incorrect. Prepaid insurance also may be allocated between or among accounting periods. Answer (B) is incorrect. Prepaid insurance should be recognized by either the purchase method or the consumption method in the period of acquisition. Answer (C) is incorrect. Prepaid insurance may be accounted for as expenditures of the period of acquisition.

22. Government-wide financial statements are prepared using the

	Economic Resources Measurement Focus	Current Financial Resources Measurement Focus	Accrual Basis	Modified Accrual Basis
A.	Yes	No	Yes	No
B.	No	Yes	No	Yes
C.	Yes	No	No	Yes
D.	No	Yes	Yes	No

Answer (A) is correct. *(Publisher, adapted)*
  REQUIRED: The measurement focus and basis of accounting used in government-wide financial statements.
  DISCUSSION: Government-wide financial statements are prepared using the economic resources measurement focus and the accrual basis of accounting and should report all of the government's assets, liabilities, revenues, expenses, gains, and losses. The economic resources measurement focus differs from the shorter-term flow-of-current-financial-resources approach used in governmental funds. It measures revenues and expenses in the same way as in proprietary funds or commercial accounting but does not necessarily emphasize net income. Instead, the emphasis is on a longer-range measure of revenues earned or levied (and accrued immediately if measurable). Moreover, the economic resources model focuses on cost of services. The accrual basis of accounting recognizes most transactions when they occur, regardless of when cash is received or paid.
  Answer (B) is incorrect. Government-wide financial statements use the economic resources measurement focus and the accrual basis of accounting. Only governmental fund financial statements use the current financial resources measurement focus and the modified accrual basis of accounting. Answer (C) is incorrect. Government-wide financial statements use the accrual basis of accounting. Answer (D) is incorrect. Government-wide financial statements use the economic resources measurement focus.

23. Proprietary fund financial statements are prepared using the

	Economic Resources Measurement Focus	Current Financial Resources Measurement Focus	Accrual Basis	Modified Accrual Basis
A.	Yes	No	Yes	No
B.	No	Yes	No	Yes
C.	Yes	No	No	Yes
D.	No	Yes	Yes	No

Answer (A) is correct. *(Publisher, adapted)*
  REQUIRED: The measurement focus and basis of accounting used in proprietary fund financial statements.
  DISCUSSION: The economic resources measurement focus and the accrual basis of accounting are required in the proprietary fund financial statements. The economic resources measurement focus differs from the shorter-term flow-of-current-financial-resources approach used in governmental funds. It measures revenues and expenses in the same way as in commercial accounting but does not necessarily emphasize net income. Instead, the emphasis is on a longer-range measure of revenues earned or levied (and accrued immediately if measurable). Moreover, the economic resources model focuses on cost of services. The accrual basis of accounting recognizes most transactions when they occur, regardless of when cash is received or paid.
  Answer (B) is incorrect. Proprietary fund financial statements use the economic resources measurement focus and the accrual basis of accounting. Only governmental fund financial statements use the current financial resources measurement focus and the modified accrual basis of accounting. Answer (C) is incorrect. Proprietary fund financial statements use the accrual basis of accounting. Answer (D) is incorrect. Proprietary fund financial statements use the economic resources measurement focus.

24. Liabilities of a defined benefit pension plan for benefits and refunds are reported in a state or local government's fiduciary fund financial statements using the

	Economic Resources Measurement Focus	Current Financial Resources Measurement Focus	Accrual Basis	Modified Accrual Basis
A.	Yes	No	Yes	No
B.	No	Yes	No	Yes
C.	Yes	No	No	Yes
D.	No	Yes	Yes	No

Answer (A) is correct. *(Publisher, adapted)*
REQUIRED: The measurement focus and basis of accounting used in fiduciary fund financial statements.
DISCUSSION: The economic resources measurement focus and the accrual basis of accounting are required in the fiduciary fund financial statements. Liabilities of defined benefit pension plans and of postemployment benefit plans other than pensions are recognized on the accrual basis, that is, when the transaction or event occurs. For plan liabilities for benefits and refunds, the transaction occurs when the benefits and refunds become due and payable under the plan's terms.
Answer (B) is incorrect. Fiduciary fund financial statements ordinarily use the economic resources measurement focus and the accrual basis of accounting. Only governmental fund financial statements use the current financial resources measurement focus and the modified accrual basis of accounting. Answer (C) is incorrect. Fiduciary fund financial statements ordinarily use the accrual basis of accounting. Answer (D) is incorrect. Fiduciary fund financial statements ordinarily use the economic resources measurement focus.

25. Which of the following fund types used by a government most likely would have a fund balance designated as nonspendable because of an increase in an inventory of supplies?

A. General.

B. Internal service.

C. Private-purpose trust.

D. Capital projects.

Answer (A) is correct. *(CPA, adapted)*
REQUIRED: The fund type most likely to have a fund balance reserved for inventory of supplies.
DISCUSSION: Governmental units normally record the purchases of supplies inventory in an internal service fund or in the general fund. However, an internal service fund is a proprietary fund for which an amount for net assets, not fund balance, is reported. A fund balance is reported for the general fund. In accounting for supplies, the expenditure account may be debited when the materials and supplies are purchased or when they are consumed. Under either method, the inventory of supplies remaining at year end must be reported on the balance sheet as an asset. Under the purchases method, resources have already been deemed to be expended to acquire these supplies. Thus, part of the unassigned fund balance should be reclassified as nonspendable because of an increase in an inventory of supplies. This nonspendable classification must be established (credited) to indicate the unavailability of resources in this amount for other expenditures.
Answer (B) is incorrect. An internal service fund is a proprietary fund. Thus, net assets, not fund balance, is reported for an internal service fund. Answer (C) is incorrect. A private-purpose trust is a fiduciary fund. Thus, net assets, not fund balance, is reported for a private-purpose trust fund. Answer (D) is incorrect. Supplies are not generally recognized as an asset of a capital projects fund.

26. Which of the following funds of a governmental unit recognizes revenues in the accounting period in which they become available and measurable?

	General Fund	Enterprise Fund
A.	Yes	No
B.	No	Yes
C.	Yes	Yes
D.	No	No

Answer (A) is correct. *(CPA, adapted)*
REQUIRED: The criteria for revenue recognition for general and enterprise funds.
DISCUSSION: The general fund is accounted for on the modified accrual basis. This basis of accounting recognizes revenues in the period in which they are susceptible to accrual (measurable and available). The enterprise fund is a proprietary fund that is accounted for on the accrual basis. This basis of accounting recognizes revenues in the accounting period in which the exchange occurs.
Answer (B) is incorrect. The availability criterion applies to the general fund, not the enterprise fund. Answer (C) is incorrect. The enterprise fund recognizes revenues when the exchange occurs. However, the availability criterion applies only to funds accounted for on the modified accrual basis. Answer (D) is incorrect. The general fund recognizes revenues when they are available and measurable.

27. In which situation(s) are property taxes due to a governmental unit recorded as deferred revenue?

I.   Property taxes receivable are recognized in advance of the year for which they are levied.

II. Property taxes receivable are collected in advance of the year in which they are levied.

    A. I only.

    B. Both I and II.

    C. II only.

    D. Neither I nor II.

Answer (B) is correct. *(CPA, adapted)*
    REQUIRED: The situation(s) when taxes due are recorded as deferred revenue.
    DISCUSSION: Property taxes are recognized on the modified accrual basis in the governmental funds. A property tax assessment is made to finance the budget of a specific period. Hence, the revenue produced should be recognized in the period for which the assessment was levied, provided it meets the criterion of being susceptible to accrual (available and measurable). When property taxes are recognized or collected in advance, they should be recorded as deferred revenue in a governmental fund. They are not recognized as revenue until the year for which they are levied. A property tax assessment is classified as an imposed nonexchange revenue transaction. In such a transaction, assets (not revenues) should be recognized when an enforceable legal claim arises or when resources are received, whichever is earlier. Thus, recognition of a receivable in a year prior to that for which the property taxes were levied implies that, under the enabling statute, the enforceable legal claim arose in that prior year.
    Answer (A) is incorrect. Property taxes collected in advance should be initially recorded as deferred revenue. Answer (C) is incorrect. Property taxes recognized in advance should be initially recorded as deferred revenue. Answer (D) is incorrect. Property taxes recognized or collected in advance should be initially recorded as deferred revenue.

28. A public school district should recognize revenue from property taxes levied for its debt service fund when

    A. Bonds to be retired by the levy are due and payable.

    B. Assessed valuations of property subject to the levy are known.

    C. Funds from the levy are measurable and available to the district.

    D. Proceeds from collection of the levy are deposited in the district's bank account.

Answer (C) is correct. *(CPA, adapted)*
    REQUIRED: The timing of property tax recognition.
    DISCUSSION: Debt service funds apply the modified accrual basis of accounting. Thus, revenues are recognized when they are susceptible to accrual (measurable and available). Moreover, assets from imposed nonexchange revenue transactions, such as property tax levies, should be recognized when an enforceable legal claim arises or the resources are received, whichever is earlier. If the legal claim arises in the period after that for which the property taxes are levied, a receivable is recognized when revenues are recognized. Revenues are recognized in the period for which the taxes are levied if the availability criterion is met. For property taxes, this criterion is met if the taxes are collected within the current period or soon enough afterward (not exceeding 60 days) to pay current liabilities.
    Answer (A) is incorrect. Revenues are recognized in the period for which property taxes are levied. Answer (B) is incorrect. The assessed valuations are necessary for calculating the amount of tax but do not make the tax revenue available. Answer (D) is incorrect. Revenues are recognized in the period for which property taxes are levied.

29. Governmental fund financial statements are prepared using the

	Economic Resources Measurement Focus	Current Financial Resources Measurement Focus	Accrual Basis	Modified Accrual Basis
A.	Yes	No	Yes	No
B.	No	Yes	No	Yes
C.	Yes	No	No	Yes
D.	No	Yes	Yes	No

Answer (B) is correct. *(Publisher, adapted)*
REQUIRED: The measurement focus and basis of accounting used in governmental fund financial statements.
DISCUSSION: The current financial resources measurement focus and the modified accrual basis of accounting are required in the financial statements of governmental funds. The emphasis is on determination of financial position and changes therein (sources, uses, and balances of financial resources). Revenues should be recognized when they become available and measurable; expenditures should be recognized when the fund liability is incurred, if measurable. However, unmatured interest on general noncurrent liabilities is recognized when due.
Answer (A) is incorrect. The economic resources measurement focus and the accrual basis are used in the (1) government-wide statements; (2) fund statements for proprietary funds; and (3), with certain exceptions, fund statements for fiduciary funds. Answer (C) is incorrect. The economic resources measurement focus is used in the government-wide statements and in most other funds. Answer (D) is incorrect. The accrual basis is used in the government-wide statements and in most other funds.

27.4 General Capital Assets and Long-Term Liabilities

30. Which of the following capital assets are least likely to be considered infrastructure assets of a state or local government?

A. Buildings.

B. Sewer systems.

C. Roads.

D. Lighting systems.

Answer (A) is correct. *(Publisher, adapted)*
REQUIRED: The capital assets least likely to be considered infrastructure assets.
DISCUSSION: Infrastructure assets are capital assets that normally are stationary and can be preserved for a longer time than most capital assets, e.g., roads, bridges, water and sewer systems, drainage systems, and lighting systems. However, buildings, other than those that are ancillary parts of a network of infrastructure assets, are not deemed to be infrastructure assets.
Answer (B) is incorrect. Sewer systems are considered infrastructure assets. Answer (C) is incorrect. Roads are considered infrastructure assets. Answer (D) is incorrect. Lighting systems are considered infrastructure assets.

31. If a capital asset is donated to a governmental unit, the asset is accounted for in an enterprise fund, and eligibility requirements are met, it should be recorded

A. At the donor's carrying amount as revenue.

B. At estimated fair value as revenue.

C. At the lower of the donor's carrying amount or estimated fair value as deferred revenues.

D. As a memorandum entry only.

Answer (B) is correct. *(CPA, adapted)*
REQUIRED: The method of recording capital assets donated to a governmental unit.
DISCUSSION: The amount to be reported for a capital asset ordinarily is its cost. However, if a capital asset is donated to a governmental unit, it should be recorded at its estimated fair value at the time of acquisition plus any ancillary charges. If the capital asset is accounted for in a proprietary fund, it should be reported in the government-wide statement of net assets and in the proprietary funds statement of net assets. For a voluntary nonexchange transaction, such as a contribution, assets are recognized when all eligibility requirements are met or the resources are provided, whichever is earlier. Revenue is recognized in the government-wide statement of activities and the proprietary funds statement of revenues, expenses, and changes in fund net assets (or fund equity) when eligibility requirements are met. Because an enterprise fund uses the accrual basis of accounting, the resources need not be "available."
Answer (A) is incorrect. The donor's carrying amount may not reflect the asset's fair value at the time of the governmental unit's receipt of the asset. Answer (C) is incorrect. The enterprise fund should recognize revenue. Answer (D) is incorrect. The fair value of the donated asset should be recognized.

32. The government-wide financial statements report capital assets

A. In the general fixed assets account group.

B. At historical cost, including ancillary charges.

C. Only in the notes if they are donated.

D. At estimated fair value.

Answer (B) is correct. *(Publisher, adapted)*
REQUIRED: The reporting of capital assets in the government-wide financial statements.
DISCUSSION: Capital assets include land, land improvements, easements, buildings, vehicles, machinery, equipment, works of art, historical treasures, infrastructure, and other tangible and intangible operating assets with useful lives greater than one reporting period. They are reported at historical cost, including ancillary charges necessary to put them in their intended location and condition for use. Ancillary charges, e.g., freight, site preparation, and professional fees, are directly attributable to acquisition of the assets.
Answer (A) is incorrect. Presentation of government-wide financial statements eliminates the need for the general fixed assets account group and the general long-term debt account group. Answer (C) is incorrect. Capital assets are reported at historical cost, including ancillary charges, in the statements. Answer (D) is incorrect. Only donated capital assets are reported at estimated fair value at the time of acquisition plus ancillary charges.

33. Tree City reported a $1,500 net increase in fund balance for governmental funds for the current year. During the year, Tree purchased general capital assets of $9,000 and recorded depreciation expense of $3,000. What amount should Tree report as the change in net assets for governmental activities?

A. ($4,500)

B. $1,500

C. $7,500

D. $10,500

Answer (C) is correct. *(CPA, adapted)*
REQUIRED: The change in net assets for governmental activities.
DISCUSSION: General capital assets are not specifically related to activities reported in nongovernmental funds, usually result from expenditure of governmental fund financial resources, and should be reported at historical cost in the governmental activities column of the government-wide statement of net assets. They are not reported as assets in the fund financial statements. Moreover, capital assets must be depreciated unless they are infrastructure assets that meet certain requirements. The modified accrual basis of accounting is required in the financial statements of governmental funds, and the accrual basis of accounting is required in the government-wide statements. Thus, the calculation of the $1,500 net increase in the fund balance for governmental funds most likely reflects a $9,000 expenditure (modified accrual basis) to acquire the general capital assets. The effect of the expenditure is a decrease in current financial resources of $9,000. However the government-wide statements report an expense of $3,000 (accrual basis) for depreciation and a depreciated asset with a carrying amount of $6,000 ($9,000 cost – $3,000 depreciation). The effect of recognizing depreciation expense is a decrease in economic resources of $3,000. Reconciling the net increase in fund balance for governmental funds to the change in net assets for governmental activities therefore requires adding $6,000 ($9,000 modified accrual basis expenditure – $3,000 accrual basis expense). The change in net assets for governmental activities is $7,500 ($1,500 + $6,000 reconciling item).
Answer (A) is incorrect. The excess of the expenditure over the sum of the expense and the increase in fund balance is ($4,500). Answer (B) is incorrect. The amount of $1,500 is the increase in fund balance. Answer (D) is incorrect. The amount of $10,500 assumes depreciation is not recognized.

643

34. Which capital assets must be depreciated in the government-wide financial statements?

   A. All capitalized collections of works of art.

   B. All infrastructure assets.

   C. All noncapitalized collections of historical treasures.

   D. All capitalized collections that are exhaustible.

Answer (D) is correct. *(Publisher, adapted)*
REQUIRED: The capital assets that must be depreciated.
DISCUSSION: Individual items or collections of works of art, historical treasures, and similar assets ordinarily must be capitalized. However, if a collection is held in furtherance of public service and not for gain; protected, preserved, cared for, and kept unencumbered; and subject to a policy that sale proceeds are to be used to obtain other collection items, capitalization is not required. If capitalized collections or individual items are exhaustible, for example, because their useful lives are reduced by display, educational, or research uses, they must be depreciated.
Answer (A) is incorrect. Capitalized collections or individual items that are inexhaustible need not be depreciated.
Answer (B) is incorrect. Infrastructure assets that are part of a network or a subsystem of a network need not be depreciated if the assets are managed using a system with certain characteristics and if the government documents preservation of the assets at an established and disclosed condition. Answer (C) is incorrect. Capitalization is needed for depreciation.

35. General capital assets and general noncurrent liabilities must be reported in the

   A. Governmental funds financial statements.

   B. General account groups.

   C. General fund's balance sheet.

   D. Governmental activities column of the government-wide statement of net assets.

Answer (D) is correct. *(Publisher, adapted)*
REQUIRED: The reporting of general capital assets and general noncurrent liabilities.
DISCUSSION: General capital assets are not specifically related to activities reported in nongovernmental funds, usually result from expenditure of governmental fund financial resources, and should be reported in the governmental activities column of the government-wide statement of net assets. They are not reported as assets in governmental funds or in a general fixed assets account group. General noncurrent liabilities are not reported as liabilities in governmental funds or in a general noncurrent debt account group. They should be reported in the governmental activities column of the government-wide statement of net assets. General noncurrent liabilities include the unmatured principal amounts of general obligation indebtedness (such as bonds, warrants, and notes); lease-purchase agreements and other commitments not recorded as current liabilities in governmental funds; and the noncurrent portions of liabilities for capital leases, operating leases with scheduled rent increases, compensated absences, claims and judgments, pensions, special termination benefits, and landfill closure and postclosure care.
Answer (A) is incorrect. General capital assets and general noncurrent liabilities do not meet the criteria for recognition in governmental funds, which have a current financial resources measurement focus. Answer (B) is incorrect. The general fixed assets and general noncurrent debt account groups have been eliminated. Answer (C) is incorrect. General capital assets and general noncurrent liabilities traditionally have not been reported in any given fund or funds. The reason is that they apply to all governmental activities. Moreover, general capital assets are not financial, and general noncurrent liabilities are not current. Thus, they do not meet the criteria for recognition in the general fund, which has a current financial resources measurement focus.

36. If a state or local government reports eligible infrastructure assets using the modified approach,

A. Complete condition assessments must be performed annually.

B. Expenditures for the assets are capitalized.

C. No depreciation expense is required to be recognized.

D. The assets are not being preserved at or above the established and disclosed condition level.

Answer (C) is correct. *(Publisher, adapted)*
REQUIRED: The implication of reporting eligible infrastructure assets using the modified approach.
DISCUSSION: Under the modified approach, infrastructure assets that are part of a network or subsystem of a network (eligible infrastructure assets) need not be depreciated if the government uses an asset management system with certain characteristics and documents that the assets are being preserved approximately at (or above) a condition level established and disclosed by the government. An asset management system should include an updated inventory of eligible infrastructure assets, perform condition assessments and summarize results using a measurement scale, and make annual estimates of the annual amounts needed to maintain the assets at the established condition level.
Answer (A) is incorrect. A government using the modified approach must document that complete condition assessments are performed in a consistent manner every 3 years and that the three most recent assessments provide reasonable assurance that the assets are being preserved at or above the established and disclosed condition level. Answer (B) is incorrect. Under the modified approach, expenditures (except those for additions and improvements) are expensed when incurred. Answer (D) is incorrect. If the assets are not being preserved at or above the established and disclosed condition level, the modified approach must be abandoned, and depreciation must be recognized.

37. Jonn City entered into a capital lease for equipment during the year. How should the asset obtained through the lease be reported in Jonn City's government-wide statement of net assets?

A. General capital asset.

B. Other financing use.

C. Expenditure.

D. Not reported.

Answer (A) is correct. *(CPA, adapted)*
REQUIRED: The reporting of a capital lease in the government-wide statement of net assets.
DISCUSSION: In the government-wide financial statements, a capital lease obligation associated with general governmental activities is recorded as a general capital asset and a liability under the accrual basis of accounting. In governmental fund financial statements, the asset financed by a capital lease is debited to an expenditure, and the lease financing is credited to an other financing source under the modified accrual basis of accounting.
Answer (B) is incorrect. The leased asset is debited to an asset and credited to a liability in the government-wide statements. It is debited to an expenditure and credited to an other financing source in the governmental funds statements. Answer (C) is incorrect. Expenditures are recognized only in the governmental funds statements. Answer (D) is incorrect. The acquisition of a leased asset must be reported.

38. In Soan County's general fund statement of revenues, expenditures, and changes in fund balances, which of the following has an effect on the excess of revenues over expenditures?

A. Purchase of fixed assets.

B. Payment to a debt-service fund.

C. Special items.

D. Proceeds from the sale of capital assets.

Answer (A) is correct. *(CPA, adapted)*
REQUIRED: The item affecting the excess of revenues over expenditures of the general fund.
DISCUSSION: The general fund is a governmental fund. Governmental funds report capital outlays as expenditures. Thus, the purchase of fixed assets affects the excess of revenues over expenditures.
Answer (B) is incorrect. In the general fund, the entry to record the earmarking of resources for debt service is to debit other financing uses--interfund transfer to debt service fund and to credit due-to-debt service fund. The transfer is recorded by a debit to due-to-debt service fund and a credit to cash. These entries do not affect revenues or expenditures. Answer (C) is incorrect. Special items are significant transactions or other events that are (1) unusual or infrequent and (2) within the control of management. They are reported separately after other financing sources and uses and do not affect revenues or expenditures. Answer (D) is incorrect. Proceeds from the sale of capital assets are recorded by a debit to cash and a credit to other financing sources (unless the sale is a special item). The sale does not affect revenues or expenditures.

27.5 Budgetary Accounting

39. Assuming no outstanding encumbrances at year end, closing entries for which of the following situations would increase the fund balance at year end?

A. Actual revenues were less than estimated revenues.

B. Estimated revenues exceed actual appropriations.

C. Actual expenditures exceed appropriations.

D. Appropriations exceed actual expenditures.

Answer (D) is correct. *(CPA, adapted)*
REQUIRED: The situation that increases fund balance at year end.
DISCUSSION: Fund balance is a real account. It is the difference between the assets and liabilities of a governmental fund. Appropriations (public funds set aside for a specific purpose) are recognized in the budgetary entry at the beginning of the fiscal period. If they exceed the government's actual expenditures for the year, fund balance increases unless sufficient encumbrances are carried over to offset the excess.
Answer (A) is incorrect. If actual revenues were less than estimated revenues, the effect would be to decrease fund balance. Answer (B) is incorrect. Appropriations is a budgetary amount credited at the beginning of the period and reversed at the end of the period. However, actual appropriations is not an account used in governmental accounting. Answer (C) is incorrect. If actual expenditures exceed appropriations, the effect is to decrease fund balance.

40. Park City uses encumbrance accounting and formally integrates its budget into the general fund's accounting records. For the year ending July 31, the following budget was adopted:

Estimated revenues	$30,000,000
Appropriations	27,000,000
Estimated transfer to debt service fund	900,000

When Park's budget is adopted and recorded, Park's budgetary fund balance should have a

A. $3,000,000 credit balance.

B. $3,000,000 debit balance.

C. $2,100,000 credit balance.

D. $2,100,000 debit balance.

Answer (C) is correct. *(CPA, adapted)*
REQUIRED: The budgetary fund balance when a budget is adopted and recorded.
DISCUSSION: The initial entry to record the budget consists of a $30,000,000 debit to estimated revenues, a $27,000,000 credit to appropriations, and a $900,000 credit to estimated transfer to debt service fund (an estimated other financing use). The $2,100,000 difference between the debit and the sum of the credits is credited to budgetary fund balance. Some accountants prefer to use budgetary fund balance in the budgetary entry rather than fund balance. Budgetary fund balance is a nominal account that is eliminated at the end of the period. Fund balance is a real (balance sheet) account.
Answer (A) is incorrect. The $900,000 estimated transfer to the debt service fund must be credited. Answer (B) is incorrect. The budgetary fund balance should have a credit balance. The budgetary fund balance and the estimated transfer must be credited. Answer (D) is incorrect. Estimated revenues should be debited.

41. For the budgetary year ending December 31, Maple City's general fund expects the following inflows of resources:

Property taxes, licenses, and fines	$9,000,000
Proceeds of debt issue	5,000,000
Interfund transfers for debt service	1,000,000

In the budgetary entry, what amount should Maple record for estimated revenues?

A. $9,000,000

B. $10,000,000

C. $14,000,000

D. $15,000,000

Answer (A) is correct. *(CPA, adapted)*
REQUIRED: The amount to be recorded as estimated revenues.
DISCUSSION: Revenues are recognized in governmental funds when they are susceptible to accrual (measurable and available). They are increases in (sources of) fund financial resources other than from interfund transfers, debt issue proceeds, and redemptions of demand bonds. Interfund transfers-in are classified as other financing sources. Proceeds of long-term debt not recorded as fund liabilities also are classified as other financing sources. The major source classifications are (1) taxes, (2) licenses and permits, (3) intergovernmental revenues, (4) charges for services, (5) fines and forfeits, and (6) miscellaneous revenues. Hence, Maple's revenues include taxes, licenses, and fines equal to $9 million.
Answer (B) is incorrect. The amount of $10,000,000 incorrectly includes the interfund transfers. Answer (C) is incorrect. The amount of $14,000,000 incorrectly includes the debt issue proceeds. Answer (D) is incorrect. The amount of $15,000,000 incorrectly includes the debt issue proceeds and interfund transfers.

42. In the current year, New City issued purchase orders and contracts of $850,000 that were chargeable against the current year's budgeted appropriations of $1,000,000. The journal entry to record the issuance of the purchase orders and contracts should include a

A. Credit to vouchers payable of $1,000,000.

B. Debit to encumbrances of $850,000.

C. Debit to expenditures of $1,000,000.

D. Credit to appropriations of $850,000.

Answer (B) is correct. *(CPA, adapted)*
REQUIRED: The entry for issuance of purchase orders and contracts.
DISCUSSION: When a purchase order is approved or a contract is signed, an estimated liability is recorded in the encumbrances account for the amount of the purchase order. The entry is a debit to encumbrances and a credit to the appropriate fund balance classification.
Answer (A) is incorrect. Expenditures will be debited and vouchers payable credited for $850,000 when the liability has been incurred. Answer (C) is incorrect. Expenditures will be debited and vouchers payable credited for $850,000 when the liability has been incurred. Answer (D) is incorrect. Appropriations is a budgetary account that is credited when the budget is adopted and debited when the budgetary accounts are closed.

43. Which of the following amounts are included in a general fund's encumbrances account?

I.   Outstanding vouchers payable amounts

II. Outstanding purchase order amounts

III. Excess of the amount of a purchase order over the actual expenditure for that order

A. I only.

B. Both I and III.

C. II only.

D. Both II and III.

Answer (C) is correct. *(CPA, adapted)*
REQUIRED: The amounts included in a general fund's encumbrances account.
DISCUSSION: The encumbrances account is debited when goods are approved to be purchased, and a purchase order is prepared. When the goods are actually received, it is credited. Thus, the encumbrances account includes only those amounts that represent outstanding purchase orders.
Answer (A) is incorrect. Vouchers payable amounts are liabilities. When the criteria for liability recognition are met, the encumbrance is reversed. Answer (B) is incorrect. The encumbrances account does not include vouchers payable amounts, only outstanding purchase order amounts. Answer (D) is incorrect. The excess of the actual expenditure over the purchase order are recorded in the expenditures control account.

44. Gold County received goods that had been approved for purchase but for which payment had not yet been made. Should the accounts listed below be increased?

	Encumbrances	Expenditures
A.	No	No
B.	No	Yes
C.	Yes	No
D.	Yes	Yes

Answer (B) is correct. *(CPA, adapted)*
REQUIRED: The effect of receipt of previously ordered goods on the encumbrances and expenditures accounts.
DISCUSSION: The encumbrances account will be decreased when previously ordered goods have been received. Expenditures and vouchers payable will be increased for the actual amount to be paid for the goods.
Answer (A) is incorrect. The expenditures control account is increased upon receipt of goods previously ordered. Answer (C) is incorrect. The encumbrances account is decreased and the expenditures account is increased at the time goods are received. Answer (D) is incorrect. The encumbrances account is decreased when the goods are received.

45. During its fiscal year ended June 30, Cliff City issued purchase orders totaling $5,000,000, which were properly charged to encumbrances at that time. Cliff received goods and related invoices at the encumbered amounts totaling $4,500,000 before year end. The remaining goods of $500,000 were not received until after year end. Cliff paid $4,200,000 of the invoices received during the year. What amount of Cliff's encumbrances were outstanding at June 30?

A. $0

B. $300,000

C. $500,000

D. $800,000

Answer (C) is correct. *(CPA, adapted)*
REQUIRED: The amount of encumbrances outstanding.
DISCUSSION: In fund accounting, when a commitment is made to expend monies, the encumbrances account is debited and fund balance-committed (or assigned) is credited. When the goods are received, this entry is reversed. Because goods totaling $500,000 were not received at year end, encumbrances outstanding total $500,000 ($5,000,000 – $4,500,000). Assuming that encumbrances outstanding at year end do not lapse, they should be reported in the appropriate classification of fund balance.
Answer (A) is incorrect. Not all of the goods related to the encumbrance amounts were received during the year. Answer (B) is incorrect. The amount of $300,000 is the excess of goods received over amount actually paid on the invoices during the year. Answer (D) is incorrect. The amount of $800,000 is the excess of total encumbrances over the amount paid on the invoices.

46. Elm City issued a purchase order for supplies with an estimated cost of $5,000. When the supplies were received, the accompanying invoice indicated an actual price of $4,950. Elm accounts for supplies in its general fund using the purchase method. What amount should Elm have debited (credited) to encumbrances after the supplies and invoice were received?

A. $(50)

B. $50

C. $4,950

D. ($5,000)

Answer (D) is correct. *(CPA, adapted)*
REQUIRED: The debit (credit) to encumbrances after the supplies and invoice were received.
DISCUSSION: Expenditures are actual decreases in net financial resources. They are recognized in the governmental funds when fund liabilities are incurred, if measurable. When goods are received by, or services are rendered to, a governmental unit, a journal entry is made to debit expenditures control and to credit vouchers payable. In addition, a previously recorded encumbrance must be reversed. This entry involves crediting encumbrances and debiting the appropriate classification of fund balance for $5,000.
Answer (A) is incorrect. Encumbrances is credited for the original estimated cost. Answer (B) is incorrect. The amount of $50 is the difference between the estimated and actual price. Answer (C) is incorrect. The amount of $4,950 is the actual, not the estimated, price.

47. When Rolan County adopted its budget for the year ending June 30, $20,000,000 was recorded for estimated revenues control. Actual revenues for the year ended June 30 amounted to $17,000,000. In closing the budgetary accounts at June 30,

A. Revenues control should be debited for $3,000,000.

B. Estimated revenues control should be debited for $3,000,000.

C. Revenues control should be credited for $20,000,000.

D. Estimated revenues control should be credited for $20,000,000.

Answer (D) is correct. *(CPA, adapted)*
REQUIRED: The journal entry to close estimated revenues control and revenues control.
DISCUSSION: Estimated revenues control is a budgetary account recognized upon the adoption of the budget. Revenues control is a nominal account in which revenues are recorded when they meet the criteria of being available and measurable. At year end, both accounts are closed to budgetary fund balance. The journal entry to close estimated revenues control and actual revenues to fund balance is

Revenues control	$17,000,000	
Budgetary fund balance	3,000,000	
Estimated revenues control		$20,000,000

Answer (A) is incorrect. Revenues control should be debited for $17,000,000. Answer (B) is incorrect. Estimated revenues control should be credited for $20,000,000. Answer (C) is incorrect. Revenues control should be debited in the closing entry.

48. Should a special revenue fund with a legally adopted budget maintain its accounts on an accrual basis and integrate budgetary accounts into its accounting system?

	Maintain on Accrual Basis	Integrate Budgetary Accounts
A.	Yes	Yes
B.	Yes	No
C.	No	Yes
D.	No	No

Answer (C) is correct. *(CPA, adapted)*
REQUIRED: The accounting by a special revenue fund with a legally adopted budget.
DISCUSSION: The current financial resources measurement focus and the modified accrual basis of accounting are required in the financial statements of governmental funds. Because a special revenue fund is a governmental fund, it should maintain its accounts on the modified accrual basis. The integration of budgetary accounts into the formal accounting system is a management control technique used to assist in controlling expenditures and enforcing revenue provisions. The extent to which the budgetary accounts should be integrated varies among governmental fund types and according to the nature of fund transactions. However, integration is considered essential in the general fund, special revenue funds, and other annually budgeted governmental funds with numerous types of revenues, expenditures, and transfers. Thus, a special revenue fund with a legally adopted budget should integrate its budgetary accounts into its accounting system.
Answer (A) is incorrect. Special revenue funds are maintained on the modified accrual basis. Answer (B) is incorrect. Special revenue funds are maintained on the modified accrual basis. Moreover, a special revenue fund with a legally adopted budget should integrate its budgetary accounts into its accounting system. Answer (D) is incorrect. A special revenue fund with a legally adopted budget should integrate its budgetary accounts into its accounting system.

49. The following information pertains to Park Township's general fund at December 31:

Total assets, including $200,000 of cash $1,000,000
Total liabilities   600,000
Fund balance – committed   100,000

At December 31, what amount should Park report as unassigned fund balance for the general fund in its governmental funds balance sheet?

A. $200,000

B. $300,000

C. $400,000

D. $500,000

Answer (B) is correct. *(CPA, adapted)*
REQUIRED: The amount to be reported as unassigned fund balance.
DISCUSSION: The amount in the unassigned fund balance is equal to the amount of assets available to finance expenditures of the current and succeeding years that is not nonspendable, restricted, committed, or assigned. Unassigned fund balance is the residual classification of the general fund. The fund balance is $400,000 ($1,000,000 assets – $600,000 liabilities). Given that $100,000 is committed, the unassigned fund balance is $300,000 ($400,000 – $100,000). Fund balance is committed to the extent it can only be used for specific purposes determined by formal action of the government's highest decision maker.
Answer (A) is incorrect. The amount of cash available is $200,000. Answer (C) is incorrect. The amount of $400,000 incorrectly includes the committed fund balance. Answer (D) is incorrect. The amount of $500,000 is net assets (assets minus liabilities) plus the committed fund balance.

50. A budgetary fund balance encumbered for an amount in excess of a balance of encumbrances indicates

A. An excess of vouchers payable over encumbrances.

B. An excess of appropriations over encumbrances.

C. An excess of purchase orders over invoices received.

D. A recording error.

Answer (D) is correct. *(CPA, adapted)*
REQUIRED: The reason the encumbrances of budgetary fund balance exceeds the encumbrance balance.
DISCUSSION: The entry to record an encumbrance is a debit to encumbrances and a credit to the appropriate classification of fund balance. Thus, the amount by which budgetary fund balance is encumbered should never exceed encumbrances. If it does, a recording error must exist.
Answer (A) is incorrect. An expenditure and a payable are recorded when the encumbrance is reversed or when no encumbrance is recorded. The vouchers payable may exceed the encumbrances, but the amount by which budgetary fund balance is encumbered should never exceed encumbrances. Answer (B) is incorrect. The amount by which budgetary fund balance is encumbered should never exceed encumbrances. Answer (C) is incorrect. An excess of purchase orders over invoices received signifies that not all amounts appropriated have been encumbered.

51. Encumbrances would not appear in which fund?

A. Capital projects.

B. Special revenue.

C. General.

D. Enterprise.

Answer (D) is correct. *(CPA, adapted)*
REQUIRED: The fund in which encumbrances do not appear.
DISCUSSION: Encumbrances are budgetary control accounts. They are used only for internal purposes in governmental funds, especially general and special revenue funds. An enterprise fund is a proprietary fund. The accounts and reports of proprietary funds are maintained and prepared in essentially the same way as in for-profit accounting. Thus, budgetary control accounts are not used in enterprise funds.
Answer (A) is incorrect. The capital projects fund is a governmental fund. Answer (B) is incorrect. The special revenue fund is a governmental fund. Answer (C) is incorrect. The general fund is a governmental fund.

27.6 Sources of Financing

52. State University received two contributions during the current year that must be used to provide scholarships. Contribution A for $10,000 was collected during the year, and $8,000 was spent on scholarships. Contribution B is a pledge for $30,000 to be received next fiscal year. What amount of contribution revenue should the university report in its statement of activities?

A. $8,000

B. $10,000

C. $38,000

D. $40,000

Answer (D) is correct. *(CPA, adapted)*
REQUIRED: The contribution revenue reported in the statement of activities of a public university.
DISCUSSION: The contributions are voluntary nonexchange transactions (legislative or contractual agreements, other than exchanges, entered into willingly by the parties). No eligibility requirements (such as types of recipients) must be met, so the donee recognizes cash and revenue in the amount of $10,000 when Contribution A is received. However, Contribution B was announced 1 fiscal year in advance. Nevertheless, if the promise is verifiable, the resources are measurable, and collection is deemed to be probable, State University should debit a receivable and credit contribution revenue in the amount of $30,000 at the time of the announcement. Total contribution revenue is therefore $40,000 ($10,000 + $30,000).
Answer (A) is incorrect. This amount may be reclassified as unrestricted net assets (or fund balance) as a result of its use for the purpose to which it was restricted. Answer (B) is incorrect. The pledge may be recognized as revenue if its collection is probable. Answer (C) is incorrect. The full amount of Contribution A may be reported although part was not spent.

53. Chase City imposes a 2% tax on hotel charges. Revenues from this tax will be used to promote tourism in the city. Chase should record this tax as what type of nonexchange transaction?

A. Derived tax revenue.

B. Imposed nonexchange revenue.

C. Government-mandated transaction.

D. Voluntary nonexchange transaction.

Answer (A) is correct. *(CPA, adapted)*
REQUIRED: The type of nonexchange transaction.
DISCUSSION: Derived tax revenues are assessments on exchange transactions, for example, income, sales, and, in this case, hotel room rentals. The government recognizes assets when the underlying exchange occurs (or when resources are received, if earlier). Revenues (net of estimated refunds) are recognized when the underlying exchange occurs. The requirements to use the proceeds for promotion of tourism is a purpose restriction, and the resulting net assets, equity, or fund balance is restricted until used.
Answer (B) is incorrect. Imposed nonexchange revenues (e.g., property taxes and fines) are assessments on nongovernmental entities, including individuals, that are not based on exchange transactions. Answer (C) is incorrect. Government-mandated nonexchange transactions occur when one government provides resources to a government at another level and requires that they be used for a specific purpose (e.g., federal programs that state or local governments are required to implement). Answer (D) is incorrect. Voluntary nonexchange transactions arise from legislative or contractual agreements, other than exchanges, entered into willingly by the parties (e.g., certain grants and private donations).

54. Resources received as a result of revenue-generating activities, such as interest and rents, are recognized as revenues in a governmental fund when they are measurable and available. Revenues received as a result of an imposed nonexchange transaction, such as property taxes or fines, are recognized when the

A. Resources to be received are measurable and available.

B. Governmental body has a legally enforceable right to the resources.

C. Time period in which the resources can be used begins.

D. Resources are received.

Answer (C) is correct. *(Publisher, adapted)*
REQUIRED: The timing of revenue recognition for an imposed nonexchange transaction.
DISCUSSION: A governmental fund is accounted for on the modified accrued basis. Thus, revenues are recognized when the resources to be received are susceptible to accrual (measurable and available). Furthermore, imposed nonexchange revenues also cannot be recognized until (1) the period in which the resources must be used or (2) the first period in which use is permitted. But a receivable may be accrued when the governmental body has a legally enforceable right to the resources.
Answer (A) is incorrect. For an imposed nonexchange transaction, additional criteria apply. Answer (B) is incorrect. The receivable, not the revenue, for an imposed nonexchange transaction is recognized when the governmental body has a legally enforceable right to it. Answer (D) is incorrect. An asset is recognized at the earlier of when the legally enforceable claim arises or when resources are received.

55. During the year just ended, Todd City received two state grants: one to buy a bus and one for bus operation. During the year, 90% of the capital grant was used for the bus purchase, but 100% of the operating grant was disbursed. Todd accounts for its bus operations in an enterprise fund. Todd is liable for general obligation bonds issued for the water and sewer fund, which will service the debt, and for revenue bonds to be repaid from admission fees collected from users of the municipal recreation center. Both issues are expected to be paid from enterprise funds and to be secured by Todd's full faith and credit, as well as its taxing power. In reporting the state grants for the bus purchase and operation, what should Todd include as grant revenues for the year ended December 31?

	90% of the Capital Grant	100% of the Capital Grant	Operating Grant
A.	Yes	No	No
B.	No	Yes	No
C.	No	Yes	Yes
D.	Yes	No	Yes

Answer (C) is correct. *(CPA, adapted)*
REQUIRED: The grant revenues for the year.
DISCUSSION: The grants for bus purchase and operation are voluntary nonexchange transactions. Revenues are recognized in such transactions when all eligibility requirements, including time requirements, are met. If the modified accrual method is used to account for the transaction, resources also should be "available," Todd has apparently met the eligibility requirements because it has what are presumably the characteristics of a recipient (it is a local government with a bus operation), and the period when the resources are required to be used or when use is first permitted has begun. Other eligibility requirements are not relevant based on the stated facts. The availability criterion has been met but is not relevant because the bus operation is accounted for in an enterprise fund, which uses the accrual method. The requirement to use the grants for bus purchase and operation is a purpose restriction and has no bearing on revenue recognition. Its effect is to cause the recipient to classify the unused resources as restricted. Thus, 100% of both grants should be recognized as revenues.
Answer (A) is incorrect. One hundred percent of both grants should be recognized. Answer (B) is incorrect. One hundred percent of the operating grant should be recognized. Answer (D) is incorrect. One hundred percent of the capital grant should be recognized.

56. A capital projects fund for a new city courthouse recorded a receivable of $300,000 for a state grant and a $450,000 transfer from the general fund. What amount should be reported as revenue by the capital projects fund?

A. $0

B. $300,000

C. $450,000

D. $750,000

Answer (B) is correct. *(CPA, adapted)*
REQUIRED: The revenue reported by a capital projects fund that received a state grant and an interfund transfer.
DISCUSSION: Governmental fund revenues are increases in fund financial resources other than from interfund transfers, debt issue proceeds, and redemptions of demand bonds. Thus, revenues of a capital projects fund include grants. The grant (a voluntary nonexchange transaction) is recognized when all eligibility requirements, including time requirements, have been met. When modified accrual accounting is used, as in a capital projects fund, the grant must also be "available." Other financing sources include proceeds from bonds and interfund transfers.
Answer (A) is incorrect. The grant is a revenue. Answer (C) is incorrect. The interfund transfer is an other financing source. Answer (D) is incorrect. The interfund transfer is an other financing source.

57. The renovation of Fir City's municipal park was accounted for in a capital projects fund. Financing for the renovation, which was begun and completed in the same year, came from the following sources:

Grant from state government	$400,000
Proceeds from general obligation bond issue	500,000
Transfer from Fir's general fund	100,000

In its governmental funds statement of revenues, expenditures, and changes in fund balances for the year, Fir should report these amounts as

	Revenues	Other Financing Sources
A.	$1,000,000	$0
B.	$900,000	$100,000
C.	$400,000	$600,000
D.	$0	$1,000,000

Answer (C) is correct. *(CPA, adapted)*
REQUIRED: The amounts to be reported in the governmental funds statement of revenues, expenditures, and changes in fund balances.
DISCUSSION: Governmental fund revenues are increases in fund financial resources other than from interfund transfers, debt issue proceeds, and redemptions of demand bonds. Thus, revenues of a capital projects fund include grants. The grant (a voluntary nonexchange transaction) is recognized when all eligibility requirements, including time requirements, have been met. When modified accrual accounting is used, as in a capital projects fund, the grant also must be "available." Other financing sources include proceeds from bonds and interfund transfers. Thus, Fir reports revenues of $400,000 and other financing sources of $600,000 ($500,000 + $100,000) in its governmental fund statement of revenues, expenditures, and changes in fund balances.
Answer (A) is incorrect. The proceeds from the bond issue and the transfer from the general fund should be reported under other financing sources. Answer (B) is incorrect. The proceeds from bond issue should be reported under other financing sources. Answer (D) is incorrect. The grant should be reported under revenues.

58. In Year 1, Menton City received $5,000,000 of bond proceeds to be used for capital projects. Of this amount, $1,000,000 was expended in Year 1 with the balance expected to be incurred in Year 2. When should the bond proceeds be recorded in a capital projects fund?

A. $5,000,000 in Year 1.

B. $5,000,000 in Year 2.

C. $1,000,000 in Year 1 and $4,000,000 in Year 2.

D. $1,000,000 in Year 1 and in the general fund for $4,000,000 in Year 1.

Answer (A) is correct. *(CPA, adapted)*
REQUIRED: The date(s) bond proceeds should be recorded in a capital projects fund.
DISCUSSION: The general obligation debt will be reported as a general noncurrent liability in the governmental activities column of the government-wide statements of net assets, and expenditures will be recorded in Year 1 and Year 2. The face amount of long-term debt, issuance premium or discount, certain payments to escrow agents for bond refundings, transfers, and sales of capital assets not qualifying as special items are reported as other financing sources and uses in the governmental funds statement of revenues, expenditures, and changes in fund balances. Thus, the entry in the capital projects fund in Year 1, the year of receipt, to record the bond proceeds is a debit to cash and a credit to other financing sources – bond issue proceeds for $5,000,000.
Answer (B) is incorrect. The $5,000,000 in bond proceeds should have been recognized in Year 1 when the proceeds were received. Answer (C) is incorrect. The amount of $1,000,000 is the expenditure in Year 1, and $4,000,000 is the expenditure in Year 2. But cash is debited in the fund in Year 1. Answer (D) is incorrect. No amount is recognized in the general fund.

59. Grove Township issued $50,000 of bond anticipation notes at face amount and placed the proceeds in its capital projects fund. All legal steps were taken to refinance the notes, but Grove was unable to consummate refinancing. In the capital projects fund, which account should be credited to record the $50,000 proceeds?

A. Other financing sources control.

B. Revenues control.

C. Deferred revenues.

D. Bond anticipation notes payable.

Answer (D) is correct. *(CPA, adapted)*
REQUIRED: The account to be credited to record the proceeds from bond anticipation notes.
DISCUSSION: Bond anticipation notes of governmental funds should be reported as general noncurrent liabilities in the governmental activities column of the government-wide statement of net assets if (1) all legal steps have been taken to refinance them and (2) the intent is supported by an ability to consummate the refinancing on a long-term basis. If both criteria are not met, the bond anticipation notes should be reported as a liability in the governmental fund in which the proceeds are recorded and in the government-wide statement of net assets. Thus, because Grove was unable to consummate the refinancing, the proceeds should be recorded as a bond anticipation note payable in the capital projects fund.
Answer (A) is incorrect. Other financing sources control would be credited if Grove had been able to consummate refinancing. Answer (B) is incorrect. The notes should be recorded in the capital projects fund by a debit to cash and a credit to bond anticipation notes payable. Answer (C) is incorrect. No revenues or deferred revenues should be recognized.

60. What is the major difference between an exchange transaction and a nonexchange transaction for governmental units?

A. The relationship between the amount of value given and received.

B. Time requirements and whether the transaction is required by law.

C. Purpose restrictions placed upon fund balances.

D. Whether resources acquired can be further exchanged.

Answer (A) is correct. *(CPA, adapted)*
REQUIRED: The major difference between an exchange transaction and a nonexchange transaction.
DISCUSSION: In a nonexchange transaction, a government either gives or receives value without directly receiving or giving equal value in return.
Answer (B) is incorrect. Time requirements affect the timing of recognition. Also, the effect on the timing of recognition depends on whether the nonexchange transaction is imposed, government-mandated, or voluntary. Answer (C) is incorrect. Purpose restrictions on fund balances affect the classification of those funds as unrestricted, temporarily restricted, or permanently restricted. They determine how those amounts are to be used. Answer (D) is incorrect. Whether resources acquired can be further exchanged relates to time requirements and purpose restrictions.

61. During the year, Public College received the following:

● An unrestricted $50,000 pledge to be paid the following year

● A $25,000 cash gift restricted for scholarships

● A notice from a recent graduate that the college is named as a beneficiary of $10,000 in that graduate's will

What amount of contribution revenue should Public College report in its statement of activities?

A. $25,000

B. $35,000

C. $75,000

D. $85,000

Answer (C) is correct.   *(CPA, adapted)*
   REQUIRED: The contribution revenue reported by a public college.
   DISCUSSION: The private donations are voluntary nonexchange transactions. These arise from legislative or contractual agreements, other than exchanges, entered into willingly by the parties (e.g., certain grants and private donations). Revenues are recognized by recipients when all eligibility requirements are met. Thus, a recipient debits an asset or a liability and credits revenue. Eligibility requirements are that (1) the recipient has certain characteristics (e.g., it is a public college); (2) any time requirements are satisfied (e.g., use in a given period); (3) the donation is on an expenditure-driven basis, and the recipient has incurred costs; and (4) a contingent recipient action required by the provider has occurred. In the case of the contributions to Public College, only the first requirement applies, and it has been satisfied. The promise of $50,000 in cash to be paid the following year is recognizable as a receivable and a revenue in the current year if, in addition to meeting eligibility requirements, (1) the promise is verifiable and (2) the resources are measurable and probable of collection. The $25,000 of restricted cash already received also should be treated as revenue. The testamentary gift is not recognized as revenue because of verifiability and collectibility issues. For example, the gift may not be received for many years if the recent graduate is young, and the will may be changed.
   Answer (A) is incorrect. The $50,000 pledge should be recognized. Answer (B) is incorrect. The $50,000 pledge should be recognized, but the testamentary gift should not. Answer (D) is incorrect. The testamentary gift should not be recognized.

27.7 Reporting Entity and the CAFR

62. Financial reporting by general-purpose governments includes presentation of MD&A as

A. Required supplementary information after the notes to the financial statements.

B. Part of the basic financial statements.

C. A description of currently known facts, decisions, or conditions expected to have significant effects on financial activities.

D. Information that may be limited to highlighting the amounts and percentages of change from the prior to the current year.

Answer (C) is correct.   *(Publisher, adapted)*
   REQUIRED: The nature of MD&A.
   DISCUSSION: Management's discussion and analysis (MD&A) is required supplementary information (RSI) that precedes the basic financial statements and provides an analytical overview of financial activities. It is based on currently known facts, decisions, or conditions and includes comparisons of the current and prior years, with an emphasis on the current year, based on government-wide information. Currently known facts are those of which management is aware at the audit report date.
   Answer (A) is incorrect. MD&A precedes the basic financial statements. Answer (B) is incorrect. The basic financial statements are limited to the government-wide financial statements, fund statements, and notes. Answer (D) is incorrect. MD&A should state the reasons for change from the prior year, not merely the amounts or percentages of change.

63. What approach to presentation of the notes to the financial statements has been adopted for financial reporting by state and local governments?

A. The notes are essential for fair presentation of the statements.

B. The notes are required supplementary information (RSI).

C. The notes have the same status as MD&A.

D. The notes give equal focus to the primary government and its discretely presented component units.

Answer (A) is correct.   *(Publisher, adapted)*
   REQUIRED: The approach to presentation of the notes to the financial statements.
   DISCUSSION: Notes to the financial statements are an integral part of the basic financial statements. They disclose information essential to fair presentation that is not reported on the face of the statements. The focus is on the primary government's governmental activities, business-type activities, major funds, and nonmajor funds in the aggregate.
   Answer (B) is incorrect. Notes are part of the basic statements, not RSI. Answer (C) is incorrect. RSI includes MD&A, budgetary comparison schedules for governmental funds, and information about infrastructure assets reported using the modified approach, not the notes. Answer (D) is incorrect. The notes focus on the primary government.

64. Budgetary comparison schedules presented by a state or local government must

    A. Be reported for the general fund and each major special revenue fund with a legally adopted budget.

    B. Be presented instead of budgetary comparison statements included in the basic statements.

    C. Convert the appropriated budget information to the GAAP basis for comparison with actual amounts reported on that basis.

    D. Compare only the final appropriated budget with actual amounts.

Answer (A) is correct. *(Publisher, adapted)*
    REQUIRED: The true statement about budgetary comparison schedules.
    DISCUSSION: Certain information must be presented as RSI in addition to MD&A. Budgetary comparison schedules must be reported for the general fund and each major special revenue fund with a legally adopted annual budget. A schedule includes the original budgets, that is, the first complete appropriated budgets; the final appropriated budgets; and the actual inflows, outflows, and balances stated on the budgetary basis of accounting. Thus, budgetary comparison schedules are not required for proprietary funds, fiduciary funds, and governmental funds other than the general fund and major special revenue funds.
    Answer (B) is incorrect. A government may elect to report budgetary comparison information in a statement as part of the basic statements. Answer (C) is incorrect. The budgetary comparison schedules compare the budgets with actual inflows, outflows, and balances stated on the government's budgetary basis. However, a reconciliation to GAAP is required. Answer (D) is incorrect. The original and final appropriated budgets are compared with the actual inflows, outflows, and balances.

65. Users of a government's financial statements should be able to distinguish between the primary government and its component units. Furthermore, an overview of the discretely presented component units should be provided. Accordingly,

    A. The government-wide statements provide discrete presentation of component unit data, including data for fiduciary component units.

    B. Condensed financial statements for major component units must be presented in the notes to the basic statements.

    C. Information about each major component unit must be provided in the reporting entity's basic statements.

    D. Major component unit information must be provided in the form of combining statements.

Answer (C) is correct. *(Publisher, adapted)*
    REQUIRED: The appropriate presentation of component unit data.
    DISCUSSION: To provide an overview of component units, discrete presentation of component unit data is required in the government-wide statements, but fiduciary component units are included only in the fund statements. Blended component units are reported in accordance with GASB guidance. Each major component unit should be reported in the basic statements by presentation (1) in a separate column in the government-wide statements, (2) in combining statements of major component units after the fund statements, or (3) of condensed statements (a statement of net assets and a statement of activities) in the notes. The aggregated total component unit information should be the entity totals derived from the component units' statements of net assets and activities. However, major component unit information is not required for fiduciary component units.
    Answer (A) is incorrect. Information for fiduciary component units is presented only in the fund financial statements with information for the primary government's fiduciary funds. Answer (B) is incorrect. Major component units may be presented in combining statements after the fund statements, in separate columns in the government-wide statements, or in condensed statements in the notes. Answer (D) is incorrect. Major component units may be presented in combining statements after the fund statements, in separate columns in the government-wide statements, or in condensed statements in the notes.

66. How should state appropriations to a state university choosing to report as engaged only in business-type activities be reported in its statement of revenues, expenses, and changes in net assets?

- A. Operating revenues.
- B. Nonoperating revenues.
- C. Capital contributions.
- D. Other financing sources.

Answer (B) is correct. *(CPA, adapted)*
REQUIRED: The reporting of state appropriations to a state university in a statement of revenues, expenses, and changes in net assets.
DISCUSSION: Public colleges and universities are special-purpose governments (SPGs). A state university engaged only in business-type activities is an SPG that reports the statements for enterprise funds. Thus, it reports all revenues, including capital contributions, in a proprietary fund statement of revenues, expenses, and changes in fund net assets. This statement separately displays operating revenues, nonoperating revenues, capital contributions, and other items. The government should have a policy defining operating revenues. One consideration is how items are classified in the statement of cash flows. Thus, an item classified as a financing or investing activity is not an operating cash flow. Accordingly, grants (appropriations) made for operating purposes are generally classified as nonoperating revenues. (They are reported as cash flows from noncapital financing activities in the cash flow statement.) Grants made for capital purposes (e.g., to acquire capital assets) are classified as capital contributions. (They are reported as cash flows from capital and related financing activities in the cash flow statement.) If the appropriations are not for capital purposes, they should be reported as nonoperating revenues.
Answer (A) is incorrect. Revenues from providing educational services, not operating grants, are reported as operating revenues. Answer (C) is incorrect. The state appropriations are not reported as capital contributions if they are operating grants. Answer (D) is incorrect. Other financing sources are recognized in governmental, not proprietary, funds.

67. Which of the following statements are required to be presented for special-purpose governments engaged only in business-type activities (such as utilities)?

- A. Statement of net assets only.
- B. Management's discussion and analysis (MD&A) and required supplementary information (RSI) only.
- C. The financial statements required for governmental funds, including MD&A.
- D. The financial statements required for enterprise funds, including MD&A and RSI.

Answer (D) is correct. *(CPA, adapted)*
REQUIRED: The statements presented for special-purpose governments engaged only in business-type activities.
DISCUSSION: SPGs are legally separate entities that are component units or other stand-alone governments. If an SPG is engaged only in business-type activities, it presents only the financial statements for enterprise funds. These are the statements presented by all proprietary funds. For an SPG, the basic financial statements and required supplementary information (RSI) include (1) management's discussion and analysis (MD&A), (2) enterprise (proprietary) fund statements (statement of net assets; statement of revenues, expenses, and changes in fund net assets; and statement of cash flows), (3) notes, and (4) RSI other than MD&A.
Answer (A) is incorrect. The SPG also must present MD&A, RSI other than MD&A, and the other statements presented by enterprise funds (statement of revenues, expenses, and changes in fund net assets and statements of cash flows). Answer (B) is incorrect. An SPG engaged only in business-type activities also must present (1) a statement of net assets; (2) a statement of revenues, expenses, and changes in fund net assets; and (3) a statement of cash flows. Answer (C) is incorrect. The SPG presents the statements for enterprise funds, not governmental funds.

68. If a city government is the primary reporting entity, which of the following is an acceptable method to present component units in its combined financial statements?

    A. Consolidation.

    B. Cost method.

    C. Discrete presentation.

    D. Government-wide presentation.

Answer (C) is correct. *(CPA, adapted)*
    REQUIRED: The acceptable method of presenting component units in the combined financial statements of the primary reporting entity.
    DISCUSSION: The financial reporting entity of a state or local government consists of the primary government and its component units. A component unit is a legally separate entity for which the primary government is financially accountable. A component unit must be blended or discretely presented. A blended component unit is in effect the same as the primary government. It is blended by reporting it as part of the primary government. Discrete presentation reports component unit information in columns and rows separate from the information of the primary government.
    Answer (A) is incorrect. Consolidation accounts for a combination in which a nongovernmental acquirer obtains control of a nongovernmental acquiree. Blending is not the same as consolidation. For example, the general fund of a blended component unit is presented as a special revenue fund of the primary government. Answer (B) is incorrect. The cost method is an accounting principle. Answer (D) is incorrect. Government-wide financial statements report information for the government as a whole. They do not display funds or fund types.

27.8 Government-Wide Reporting

69. Which of the following would be reported as program revenues on a local government's government-wide statement of activities?

    A. Charges for services.

    B. Taxes levied for a specific function.

    C. Proceeds from the sale of a capital asset used for a specific function.

    D. Interest revenues.

Answer (A) is correct. *(CPA, adapted)*
    REQUIRED: The program revenue reported on a government-wide statement of activities.
    DISCUSSION: The statement of activities presents operations in a format that displays net (expense) revenue for each function. The purpose is to report the relative financial burden to the taxpayers for that function. The net (expense) revenue for each governmental or business-type function equals expenses (at a minimum, the direct expenses of the function) minus program revenues. Charges for services constitute a category of program revenues resulting from charges to customers, applicants, or others who directly benefit from what is provided (goods, services, or privileges) or who are otherwise directly affected. Thus, fines and forfeitures are treated as charges for services because they are paid by persons directly affected by a program or service.
    Answer (B) is incorrect. General revenues are revenues that are not required to be reported as program revenues. They are reported separately after total net (expense) revenue for all functions. All taxes, including those levied for a special purpose, are general revenues. Answer (C) is incorrect. Proceeds from the sale of a capital asset used for a specific function are not revenues. Answer (D) is incorrect. Interest revenues are general revenues.

70. Government-wide financial statements

    A. Display individual funds.

    B. Display aggregated information about fund types.

    C. Exclude information about discretely presented component units.

    D. Use separate columns to distinguish between governmental and business-type activities.

Answer (D) is correct. *(Publisher, adapted)*
    REQUIRED: The information reported in government-wide financial statements.
    DISCUSSION: The basic financial statements include government-wide financial statements, fund financial statements, and the notes to the financial statements. Government-wide financial statements do not display funds or fund types but instead report information about the overall government. They distinguish between the primary government and its discretely presented component units and between the governmental activities and business-type activities of the primary government by reporting such information in separate rows and columns.
    Answer (A) is incorrect. Fund information is reported in the fund financial statements. Answer (B) is incorrect. Government-wide financial statements do not display funds or fund types. Answer (C) is incorrect. Separate rows and columns report information about discretely presented component units.

71. During the year just ended, Todd City received two state grants: one to buy a bus and one for bus operation. During the year, 90% of the capital grant was used for the bus purchase, but 100% of the operating grant was disbursed. Todd accounts for its bus operations in an enterprise fund. Todd is liable for general obligation bonds issued for the water and sewer fund, which will service the debt, and for revenue bonds to be repaid from admission fees collected from users of the municipal recreation center. Both issues are expected to be paid from enterprise funds and to be secured by Todd's full faith and credit, as well as its taxing power. Which of Todd's noncurrent obligations should be accounted for only in the government-wide financial statements?

	General Obligation Bonds	Revenue Bonds
A.	Yes	Yes
B.	Yes	No
C.	No	Yes
D.	No	No

Answer (D) is correct. *(CPA, adapted)*
REQUIRED: The bonds reported in the government-wide financial statements.
DISCUSSION: Noncurrent liabilities directly related to and expected to be paid from a proprietary fund, such as an enterprise fund, are not general noncurrent liabilities. They should be reported in the proprietary fund statement of net assets as well as the government-wide statement of net assets. They are specific fund liabilities even though they are backed by the full faith and credit of the governmental unit. The water and sewer fund and the municipal recreation center fund are both enterprise funds.
Answer (A) is incorrect. The bond issues are not general noncurrent liabilities and should be reported in the government-wide statement of net assets and in the proprietary fund statement of net assets. Answer (B) is incorrect. The general obligation bonds are reported in the government-wide statement of net assets and in the proprietary fund statement of net assets. Answer (C) is incorrect. The revenue bonds are reported in the government-wide statement of net assets and in the proprietary fund statement of net assets.

72. The government-wide statement of net assets must

A. Be presented in a classified format.

B. Present assets and liabilities in order of liquidity.

C. Use the balance sheet format.

D. Display net assets in three components.

Answer (D) is correct. *(Publisher, adapted)*
REQUIRED: The required presentation of the government-wide statement of net assets.
DISCUSSION: The GASB requires that the government-wide statement of net assets display net assets in three components: invested in capital assets, net of related debt; restricted net assets; and unrestricted net assets.
Answer (A) is incorrect. A classified format is acceptable but not required. Answer (B) is incorrect. The GASB encourages but does not require governments to present assets and liabilities in order of liquidity. Answer (C) is incorrect. The GASB permits governments to use the balance sheet format, although it prefers the net asset format.

73. In the government-wide statement of net assets, restricted capital assets should be included in the

A. Expendable component of restricted net assets.

B. Nonexpendable component of restricted net assets.

C. Invested in capital assets, net of related debt, component of net assets.

D. Designated component of net assets.

Answer (C) is correct. *(Publisher, adapted)*
REQUIRED: The classification of restricted capital assets in the statement of net assets.
DISCUSSION: Net assets has three components: (1) invested in capital assets, net of related debt; (2) restricted net assets; and (3) unrestricted net assets. Invested in capital assets, net of related debt, includes unrestricted and restricted capital assets, net of accumulated depreciation and related liabilities for borrowings. However, debt related to significant unspent proceeds is classified in the same net assets component as those proceeds.
Answer (A) is incorrect. Restricted net assets are subject to constraints imposed by external entities (creditors, grantors, or other governments) or by law (constitutional provisions or enabling legislation). If permanent endowments or permanent fund principal amounts are included, restricted net assets should be displayed as expendable and nonexpendable. Nonexpendable means that the net assets are retained in perpetuity. However, capital assets must be included in the invested in capital assets, net of related debt, component of net assets, even if they are restricted and expendable. Answer (B) is incorrect. Capital assets must be included in the invested in capital assets, net of related debt, component of net assets, even if they are restricted and nonexpendable. Answer (D) is incorrect. Designations of net assets are not reported on the face of the statement.

74. The government-wide statement of activities reports

    A. Activities accounted for in governmental funds by segment.

    B. Activities accounted for in enterprise funds at the fund level of detail.

    C. Net (expense) revenue for each function equal to expenses minus program revenues.

    D. Net (expense) revenue for each function equal to expenses minus general revenues.

Answer (C) is correct. *(Publisher, adapted)*
    REQUIRED: The reporting in the government-wide statement of activities.
    DISCUSSION: The statement of activities presents operations in a format that displays net (expense) revenue for each function, thereby reporting the relative financial burden to the taxpayers for that function. The net (expense) revenue for each governmental or business-type function equals expenses (at a minimum, the direct expenses of the function) minus program revenues, i.e., charges or fees and fines deriving directly from the function or program, and contributions that are restricted to the function or program.
    Answer (A) is incorrect. The minimum levels of detail for activities accounted for in governmental funds are by function. Answer (B) is incorrect. The minimum levels of detail for activities accounted for in enterprise funds are by different identifiable activities. Answer (D) is incorrect. General revenues are reported separately after total net (expense) revenue for all functions.

75. How are expenses reported in the government-wide statement of activities?

    A. Interest on general noncurrent liabilities is ordinarily treated as a direct expense.

    B. At a minimum, direct expenses should be reported for each function.

    C. If indirect expenses are allocated, a full-cost approach must be used.

    D. Direct and allocated indirect expenses are aggregated in a single column.

Answer (B) is correct. *(Publisher, adapted)*
    REQUIRED: The reporting of expenses in the statement of activities.
    DISCUSSION: Direct expenses are specifically associated with a service, program, or department. Hence, they are clearly identifiable with a given function. The net (expense) revenue for each function equals expenses (at a minimum, the direct expenses of the function) minus program revenues. However, indirect expenses need not be allocated and included in the determination of net (expense) revenue for each function.
    Answer (A) is incorrect. Interest on general noncurrent liabilities is a direct expense only in unusual circumstances, that is, when the borrowing is essential to establishing or maintaining a program and when omitting the interest from the program's direct expenses would be misleading. Answer (C) is incorrect. Direct expenses must be reported by function, but indirect expenses may or may not be allocated. A government may choose to allocate some indirect expenses, to adopt a full-cost allocation approach, or not to allocate. Answer (D) is incorrect. If indirect expenses are allocated, direct and indirect expenses should be displayed in separate columns.

76. The government-wide statement of activities should report which of the following categories of program revenues?

    I.   Charges for services

    II. Earnings of permanent funds that finance general fund programs

    III. Program-specific capital grants and contributions

    A. I only.

    B. I and III only.

    C. II and III only.

    D. I, II, and III.

Answer (B) is correct. *(Publisher, adapted)*
    REQUIRED: The categories of program revenues.
    DISCUSSION: Program revenues include (1) charges for services (fees for specific services, licenses and permits; operating special assessments; other amounts charged to service recipients; and fines and forfeitures) and (2) program-specific grants and contributions, both operating and capital. They may also include earnings on endowments, permanent fund investments, or other investments restricted to a given program. Earnings of endowments or permanent funds that finance general fund programs or general operating expenses are not program revenues. However, when earnings on a program's invested accumulated resources are legally restricted for use by the program, those earnings are program revenues.
    Answer (A) is incorrect. Program revenues also include program-specific grants and contributions, both operating and capital. Answer (C) is incorrect. Earnings of endowments or permanent funds that finance general fund programs or general operating expenses are not program revenues. However, program revenues also include program-specific grants and contributions, both operating and capital. Answer (D) is incorrect. Earnings of permanent funds that finance general fund programs are not program revenues.

77. General revenues reported in the government-wide statement of activities

    A. Include all taxes.

    B. Exclude taxes levied for a specific purpose.

    C. Are aggregated with contributions, special and extraordinary items, and transfers in a line item.

    D. Exclude interest and grants.

Answer (A) is correct. *(Publisher, adapted)*
    REQUIRED: The true statement about general revenues.
    DISCUSSION: General revenues are revenues not required to be reported as program revenues. They are reported separately after total net (expense) revenue for all functions in the government-wide statement of activities. All taxes, including those levied for a special purpose, are general revenues.
    Answer (B) is incorrect. All taxes are general revenues but should be reported by type of tax, e.g., income, sales, or property. Answer (C) is incorrect. Contributions to endowments, contributions to permanent fund principal, transfers between governmental and business-type activities, and special and extraordinary items are reported separately in the same manner as general revenues (at the bottom of the statement of activities to determine the change in net assets for the period). Answer (D) is incorrect. General revenues are all revenues not required to be reported as program revenues.

78. Preparation of government-wide financial statements requires elimination of

    A. Receivables from fiduciary funds from the statement of net assets.

    B. The effects on the statement of activities of interfund services provided and used between functions.

    C. Internal balances from the total primary government column in the statement of net assets.

    D. Net residual amounts due between governmental and business-type activities from those columns in the statement of net assets.

Answer (C) is correct. *(Publisher, adapted)*
    REQUIRED: The elimination necessary in the preparation of government-wide financial statements.
    DISCUSSION: Numerous eliminations and reclassifications are necessary in preparing the government-wide statements. Thus, interfund receivables and payables are eliminated in the governmental and business-type activities columns of the statement of net assets, except for net residual amounts due (presented as internal balances). However, the total primary government column excludes internal balances.
    Answer (A) is incorrect. Fund receivables from, or payables to, fiduciary funds are treated in the statement of net assets as arising from transactions with external parties, not as internal balances. Answer (B) is incorrect. Eliminations are not made in the statement of activities for the effects of interfund services provided and used between functions (e.g., the sale of power by a utility to the general government). Answer (D) is incorrect. Net residual amounts due between governmental and business-type activities are presented as interfund balances in the appropriate columns but are eliminated in the total primary government column.

79. In the government-wide statement of activities, special items are transactions or other events that are

    A. Unusual in nature and infrequent in occurrence.

    B. Unusual in nature or infrequent in occurrence, but not within management's control.

    C. Unusual in nature and infrequent in occurrence, and within management's control.

    D. Unusual in nature or infrequent in occurrence, and within management's control.

Answer (D) is correct. *(Publisher, adapted)*
    REQUIRED: The characteristics of special items.
    DISCUSSION: Extraordinary items are unusual in nature and infrequent in occurrence. Special items are significant transactions or other events within the control of management that are either unusual or infrequent. They are reported separately after extraordinary items.
    Answer (A) is incorrect. Extraordinary items are unusual in nature and infrequent in occurrence. Answer (B) is incorrect. Special items are within management's control. Answer (C) is incorrect. Extraordinary items are not within management's control.

80. A summary reconciliation of the government-wide and fund financial statements

    A. Must be presented at the bottom of the fund statements or in an accompanying schedule.

    B. Must be presented as required supplementary information.

    C. Must be presented in the notes.

    D. Is recommended but not required.

Answer (A) is correct. *(Publisher, adapted)*
    REQUIRED: The presentation of a summary reconciliation of the government-wide and fund financial statements.
    DISCUSSION: A government must provide a summary reconciliation to the government-wide statements at the bottom of the fund statements or in a schedule. Brief explanations on the face of the statements may suffice, but a more detailed explanation in the notes may be necessary.
    Answer (B) is incorrect. RSI consists of MD&A, budgetary comparison schedules, and information about infrastructure assets reported using the modified approach. Answer (C) is incorrect. The summary reconciliation must be presented at the bottom of the fund statements or in an accompanying schedule. Additional detail may need to be given in the notes. Answer (D) is incorrect. The summary reconciliation is required.

81. Which of the following activities should be excluded when fund financial statements are converted to government-wide financial statements?

    A. Proprietary activities.

    B. Fiduciary activities.

    C. Government activities.

    D. Enterprise activities.

Answer (B) is correct. *(CPA, adapted)*
    REQUIRED: The activities excluded from government-wide financial statements.
    DISCUSSION: Fiduciary funds account for resources held by the government in trust or as an agent for (1) specific individuals, (2) private organizations, or (3) other governments. These resources are not available to finance the government's programs. Consequently, they are reported only in the fund statements (statements of fiduciary net assets and changes in fiduciary net assets). Moreover, fund receivables from, or payables to, fiduciary funds are treated in the government-wide statement of net assets as amounts arising from transactions with external parties, not as internal balances. Thus, they are reclassified, not eliminated in the preparation of the government-wide statements.
    Answer (A) is incorrect. The government-wide statement of activities displays columns for governmental activities and business-type activities. Proprietary activities presumably include activities of proprietary funds (enterprise funds and internal service funds). The balances of internal service funds that are not eliminated are usually reported in the governmental activities column. The balances of enterprise funds that are not eliminated are reported in the business-type activities column. Answer (C) is incorrect. The government-wide statement of activities displays columns for governmental activities and business-type activities. Governmental activities are usually reported in the governmental funds and in internal service funds. Internal service funds are proprietary funds. Answer (D) is incorrect. The government-wide statement of activities displays columns for governmental activities and business-type activities. Business-type activities are usually reported in enterprise funds. Enterprise funds are proprietary.

82. In preparing Chase City's reconciliation of the statement of revenues, expenditures, and changes in fund balances to the government-wide statement of activities, which of the following items should be subtracted from changes in fund balances?

    A. Capital assets purchases.

    B. Payment of long-term debt principal.

    C. Internal service fund increase in net assets.

    D. Book value of capital assets sold during the year.

Answer (D) is correct. *(CPA, adapted)*
    REQUIRED: The item(s) subtracted from changes in fund balances in the reconciliation of the governmental funds statements to the government-wide statements.
    DISCUSSION: In the statement of activities, only the gain or loss on the sale of a capital asset is reported. (The acquisition was recorded in the governmental funds as an expenditure for its full amount.) But in the governmental funds' statement of revenues, expenditures, and changes in fund balances, the proceeds are recorded as an increase in resources. Consequently, the change in net assets (statement of activities) differs from the change in fund balances by the carrying amount of the capital assets sold. This item requires a reconciling subtraction from the change in fund balance.
    Answer (A) is incorrect. Governmental funds report capital purchases as expenditures (decreases in the fund balance). The reconciling item is the amount by which these expenditures exceeded the depreciation recognized in the statement of activities for the current period. This item is added to the net change in fund balances. Answer (B) is incorrect. The payment of long-term debt principal is an expenditure in the governmental funds (debt service fund). This transaction does not affect the change in net assets reported in the statement of activities. Thus, this item is added to the net change in fund balances. Answer (C) is incorrect. Internal service funds are proprietary funds that account for activities that provide goods or services to other subunits of the primary government and its component units or to other governments on a cost reimbursement basis. In the preparation of the statement of activities, the effects of internal service activities must be eliminated to avoid double counting. The purpose is to prevent recognition of both the activities of the internal service fund and the charges made to the participating funds or functions. Thus, the preparation of the statement of activities essentially involves reducing (through an intraentity elimination) the balance of the internal service fund to zero. The effect on the reconciliation is an addition to the net change in fund balances because of the elimination of charges to governmental funds by a proprietary fund.

27.9 Governmental Funds Reporting

83. Tott City's serial bonds are serviced through a debt service fund with cash provided by the general fund. In the financial statements of the governmental funds, how are cash receipts and cash payments reported?

	Cash Receipts	Cash Payments
A.	Revenues	Expenditures
B.	Revenues	Interfund transfers
C.	Interfund transfers	Expenditures
D.	Interfund transfers	Interfund transfers

Answer (C) is correct. *(CPA, adapted)*
REQUIRED: The reporting of cash receipts and payments in the governmental fund financial statements.
DISCUSSION: Cash receipts of a debt service fund provided by the general fund are interfund transfers (other financing sources), not revenues. The cash receipts are interfund transfers because they are nonreciprocal activities with no repayment required. Cash payments made to retire principal and interest payments of serial bonds are recorded as expenditures of the governmental unit's resources. An expenditure is recognized in a governmental fund when the liability is incurred, if measurable, except for the unmatured principal and interest on general long-term debt (e.g., the serial bonds), which are recognized when due.
Answer (A) is incorrect. Transfers to a debt service fund are not considered revenues. Answer (B) is incorrect. Transfers to a debt service fund are not revenues, and cash payments from a debt service fund to retire principal and pay interest are expenditures. Answer (D) is incorrect. Cash payments from a debt service fund to retire principal and pay interest are expenditures.

84. Wood City, which is legally obligated to maintain a debt service fund, issued the following general obligation bonds on July 1:

Term of bonds	10 years
Face amount	$1,000,000
Issue price	101
Stated interest rate	6%

Interest is payable January 1 and July 1. What amount of bond issuance premium should be amortized in Wood's debt service fund for the year ended December 31 of the year of issue?

A. $1,000

B. $500

C. $250

D. $0

Answer (D) is correct. *(CPA, adapted)*
REQUIRED: The amount of bond premium amortized in the debt service fund.
DISCUSSION: The debt service fund of a governmental unit is a governmental fund that accounts for resources restricted, committed, or assigned to paying principal and interest. But these funds do not account for the debt itself. They also account for resources being accumulated for future principal and interest payments. Bond issuance premium may be recorded as an other financing source in the debt service fund. However, because this fund has a current financial resources measurement focus, that is, a focus on fiscal accountability for current spendable resources, premium is not amortized in the debt service fund.
Answer (A) is incorrect. The amount of $1,000 is the annual straight-line amortization. Answer (B) is incorrect. The amount of $500 is the straight-line amortization for 6 months. Answer (C) is incorrect. The amount of $250 is the straight-line amortization for 3 months.

85. In connection with Albury Township's long-term debt, the following cash accumulations are available to cover payment of principal and interest on

Bonds for financing of water treatment plant construction	$1,000,000
General long-term obligations	400,000

The amount of these cash accumulations that should be accounted for in Albury's debt service funds is

A. $0

B. $400,000

C. $1,000,000

D. $1,400,000

Answer (B) is correct. *(CPA, adapted)*
REQUIRED: The amount of cash accumulations to be accounted for in debt service funds.
DISCUSSION: A debt service fund is used to account for resources restricted, committed, or assigned to paying principal and interest. But these funds do not account for the debt itself. They also account for resources being accumulated for future principal and interest payments. Water treatment plants and other utilities are customarily accounted for in enterprise funds because they tend to be financed and operated in the same manner as private businesses. Cash accumulations to cover payment of principal and interest on enterprise fund obligations are accounted for in the enterprise fund itself. Hence, only the $400,000 of proceeds from general long-term obligations should be accounted for in the debt service funds.
Answer (A) is incorrect. The amount accumulated for payment of the general long-term obligations is properly accounted for in the debt service fund. Answer (C) is incorrect. The amount accumulated for the bonds should be accounted for in the water-utility enterprise fund. Answer (D) is incorrect. The amount of $1,400,000 includes the bonds for the water-utility fund project.

86. Dale City is accumulating financial resources that are legally restricted to payments of general long-term debt principal and interest maturing in future years. At December 31 of the current year, $5,000,000 has been accumulated for principal payments, and $300,000 has been accumulated for interest payments. These restricted funds should be accounted for in the

	Debt Service Fund	General Fund
A.	$0	$5,300,000
B.	$300,000	$5,000,000
C.	$5,000,000	$300,000
D.	$5,300,000	$0

Answer (D) is correct. *(CPA, adapted)*
REQUIRED: The funds in which to account for financial resources reserved for principal and interest.
DISCUSSION: Debt service funds account for resources restricted, committed, or assigned to paying principal and interest. But these funds do not account for the debt itself. They also account for resources being accumulated for future principal and interest payments. The general fund does not account for these transactions, except to record transfers to the debt service fund.
Answer (A) is incorrect. The debt service fund, not the general fund, accounts for resources restricted, committed, or assigned to paying principal and interest. But these funds do not account for the debt itself. They also account for resources being accumulated for future principal and interest payments. Answer (B) is incorrect. The debt service fund also accounts for the accumulation of principal. Answer (C) is incorrect. The debt service fund also accounts for the accumulation of interest.

87. The focus of certain fund financial statements is on major funds. Accordingly,

A. Major internal service funds must be presented separately in the statement of net assets for proprietary funds.

B. The main operating fund is always reported as a major fund.

C. Combining statements for nonmajor funds are required.

D. Enterprise funds not meeting the quantitative criteria are not eligible for presentation as major funds.

Answer (B) is correct. *(Publisher, adapted)*
REQUIRED: The true statement about major fund reporting.
DISCUSSION: The focus of governmental and enterprise fund financial statements is on major funds. Major fund reporting is not required for internal service funds. Each major fund is presented in a separate column and nonmajor funds in one column. Combining statements are not required for nonmajor funds. The main operating fund (e.g., the general fund) is always reported as a major fund, and any governmental or enterprise fund believed to be particularly important to users may also be reported in this way. Other individual governmental or enterprise funds must be reported as major if they meet the quantitative thresholds.
Answer (A) is incorrect. Major fund reporting requirements apply to governmental and enterprise funds but not to internal service funds. Answer (C) is incorrect. Combining statements for nonmajor funds are not required but may be reported as supplementary information. Answer (D) is incorrect. A government may report any governmental or enterprise individual fund as major if it is believed to be particularly important to users.

88. A fund must be reported as major if

A. Total assets of that fund are at least 10% of the total assets of all governmental funds.

B. Total expenditures of that fund are at least 10% of the total expenditures of all governmental funds and enterprise funds combined.

C. Total liabilities of that fund are 10% of the total liabilities of all governmental funds and 5% of the total liabilities of all governmental and enterprise funds combined.

D. Total revenues of that fund are 10% of the total revenues of all governmental funds and 3% of the total revenues of all enterprise funds.

Answer (C) is correct. *(Publisher, adapted)*
REQUIRED: The criteria for requiring major fund reporting.
DISCUSSION: The main operating fund (e.g., the general fund) is always reported as a major fund, and any governmental or enterprise fund believed to be particularly important to users also may be reported as a major fund. Moreover, any fund must be reported as major if revenues, expenditures/expenses, assets, or liabilities (excluding revenues and expenditures/expenses reported as extraordinary items) of the fund are (1) at least 10% of the corresponding element total for all funds of the same category or type, that is, for all governmental or all enterprise funds, and (2) the same element that met the 10% criterion is at least 5% of the corresponding element total for all governmental and enterprise funds combined.
Answer (A) is incorrect. A capital projects fund is major if total assets of that fund are at least 10% of the total assets of all governmental funds and 5% of the corresponding element total for governmental funds and enterprise funds combined. Answer (B) is incorrect. To be classified as major, a capital projects fund also must have total expenditures of at least 10% of the total expenditures of all governmental funds. Answer (D) is incorrect. Total revenues also must be at least 5% of the corresponding element total for governmental funds and enterprise funds combined.

89. Which financial statement must be presented for governmental funds?

A. A statement of activities.

B. A statement of cash flows.

C. A statement of revenues, expenses, and changes in fund net assets.

D. A financial statement in balance sheet format.

Answer (D) is correct. *(Publisher, adapted)*
REQUIRED: The governmental fund financial statement.
DISCUSSION: A balance sheet is required for governmental funds. It should be in balance sheet format (assets = liabilities + fund balances) with a total column and segregation of fund balances into reserved and unreserved amounts.
Answer (A) is incorrect. A statement of activities is a required government-wide statement. Answer (B) is incorrect. A statement of cash flows is required for proprietary funds. Answer (C) is incorrect. A statement of revenues, expenses, and changes in fund net assets is required for proprietary funds.

90. A statement of revenues, expenditures, and changes in fund balances must be reported for governmental funds. In that statement,

A. Debt refundings are treated as extraordinary items.

B. Revenues are classified, at a minimum, by function.

C. Proceeds of long-term debt should be reported in the other financing sources and uses classification.

D. Expenditures are classified by major expenditure source.

Answer (C) is correct. *(Publisher, adapted)*
REQUIRED: The appropriate reporting in the statement of revenues, expenditures, and changes in fund balances.
DISCUSSION: A statement of revenues, expenditures, and changes in fund balances is required for governmental funds. It reports inflows, outflows, and balances of current financial resources for each major fund, for nonmajor funds in the aggregate, and in a total column. In this statement, the other financing sources and uses classification appears after excess (deficiency) of revenues over expenditures. Other financing sources and uses include the face amount of long-term debt, issuance premium or discount, some payments to escrow agents for bond refundings, transfers, and sales of most capital assets.
Answer (A) is incorrect. Debt refundings in governmental funds are not extraordinary items. They result in other financing sources or uses, not gains or losses. Answer (B) is incorrect. Revenues are classified in this statement by major source. Answer (D) is incorrect. Expenditures are classified in this statement by, at a minimum, function.

91. Brandon County's general fund had the following transactions during the year:

Transfer to a debt service fund	$100,000
Payment to a pension trust fund	500,000
Purchase of equipment	300,000

What amount should Brandon County report for the general fund as other financing uses in its governmental funds statement of revenues, expenditures, and changes in fund balances?

A. $100,000

B. $400,000

C. $800,000

D. $900,000

Answer (A) is correct. *(CPA, adapted)*
REQUIRED: The amount reported in the general fund as other financing uses.
DISCUSSION: Other financing sources and uses are reported in the governmental funds statement of revenues, expenditures, and changes in fund balances. They include (1) the face amount of long-term debt, (2) issuance premium or discount, (3) some payments to escrow agents for bond refundings, (4) interfund transfers, and (5) sales of capital assets. Accordingly, the only item reported in the general fund as other financing uses is the $100,000 transfer to a debt service fund.
Answer (B) is incorrect. The amount of $400,000 includes the purchase of equipment. It should be reported as an expenditure for a capital asset in the statement of revenues, expenditures, and changes in fund balances. Answer (C) is incorrect. The amount of $800,000 omits the transfer. It includes the purchase of equipment. This purchase should be reported as an expenditure for a capital asset in the statement of revenues, expenditures, and changes in fund balances. The payment to the pension trust fund also is reported as an expenditure. Answer (D) is incorrect. The amount of $900,000 includes the purchase of equipment. It should be reported as an expenditure for a capital asset in the statement of revenues, expenditures, and changes in fund balances. The payment to a pension trust fund also is reported as an expenditure.

27.10 Proprietary Funds Reporting

92. An interfund transfer

   A. Is the internal counterpart to an exchange or an exchange-like transaction.

   B. Results in a receivable and a payable.

   C. Is reported in a proprietary fund's statements after nonoperating revenues and expenses.

   D. Is reported in a proprietary fund as an other financing source or use.

Answer (C) is correct. *(Publisher, adapted)*
REQUIRED: The treatment of an interfund transfer.
DISCUSSION: Interfund transfers are one-way asset flows with no repayment required. In a governmental fund, a transfer is an other financing use (source) in the transferor (transferee) fund. In a proprietary fund's statement of revenues, expenses, and changes in fund net assets, transfers should be reported separately after nonoperating revenues and expenses in the same component as capital contributions, additions to endowments, and special and extraordinary items.
    Answer (A) is incorrect. Nonreciprocal interfund activity is analogous to nonexchange transactions. Answer (B) is incorrect. Reciprocal interfund activity results in a receivable and a payable. Answer (D) is incorrect. In a governmental fund, a transfer is an other financing use (source) in the transferor (transferee) fund.

93. Nox City reported a $25,000 net increase in the fund balances for total governmental funds. Nox also reported an increase in net assets for the following funds:

Motor pool internal service fund	$ 9,000
Water enterprise fund	12,000
Employee pension fund	7,000

The motor pool internal service fund provides service to the general fund departments. What amount should Nox report as the change in net assets for governmental activities?

   A. $25,000

   B. $34,000

   C. $41,000

   D. $46,000

Answer (B) is correct. *(CPA, adapted)*
REQUIRED: The change in net assets for governmental activities.
DISCUSSION: Separate rows and columns are used in the government-wide financial statements to distinguish between governmental and business-type activities of the primary government. Governmental activities are normally reported in governmental funds and internal service funds. Proprietary funds consist of enterprise and internal service funds. Business-type activities are usually reported in enterprise funds. Thus, the change in net assets for governmental activities is $34,000 ($25,000 net increase for all governmental funds + $9,000 net increase for the internal service funds). Fiduciary activities, such as those of an employee pension fund, are reported only in the fiduciary fund financial statements because their resources are not available for the government's programs.
    Answer (A) is incorrect. The amount of $25,000 omits the internal service fund's increase in net assets. Answer (C) is incorrect. The amount of $41,000 includes the pension fund's increase in net assets. Answer (D) is incorrect. The amount of $46,000 includes the enterprise fund's increase in net assets.

94. The following transactions were among those reported by Corfe City's electric utility enterprise fund for the year just ended:

Capital contributed by subdividers	$ 900,000
Cash received from customer households	2,700,000
Proceeds from sale of revenue bonds	4,500,000

In the electric utility enterprise fund's statement of cash flows for the year ended December 31, what amount should be reported as cash flows from capital and related financing activities?

   A. $4,500,000

   B. $5,400,000

   C. $7,200,000

   D. $8,100,000

Answer (B) is correct. *(CPA, adapted)*
REQUIRED: The amount reported as cash flows from capital and related financing activities.
DISCUSSION: The statement of cash flows of a for-profit business classifies items as operating, financing, and investing. The cash flows of a proprietary fund uses four classifications: operating, noncapital financing, capital and related financing, and investing. Operating activities include producing and delivering goods and providing services. Thus, cash from customer households is a revenue item reported under cash flows from operating activities. Capital and related financing activities include (1) acquiring and disposing of capital assets used to provide goods or services; (2) borrowings and repayments of debt related to acquiring, constructing, or improving capital assets; and (3) paying for capital assets obtained on credit. Assuming the sale of revenue bonds and the capital contributions by subdividers are for the acquisition or improvement of capital assets, the amount to report under capital and related financing activities is $5,400,000 ($900,000 + $4,500,000).
    Answer (A) is incorrect. The amount of $4,500,000 omits the capital contributed by subdividers. Answer (C) is incorrect. The amount of $7,200,000 includes customer fees revenue and omits capital contributed by subdividers. Answer (D) is incorrect. The amount of $8,100,000 includes customer fees.

95. The statement of revenues, expenses, and changes in fund net assets for proprietary funds

    A. Combines special and extraordinary items in a subtotal presented before nonoperating revenues and expenses.

    B. Must report revenues at gross amounts, with discounts and allowances disclosed parenthetically.

    C. Distinguishes between operating and nonoperating revenues and expenses.

    D. Must define operating items in the same way as in the statement of cash flows.

Answer (C) is correct. *(Publisher, adapted)*
    REQUIRED: The true statement about the statement of revenues, expenses, and changes in fund net assets.
    DISCUSSION: A statement of revenues, expenses, and changes in fund net assets or fund equity (either label may be used) is the required operating statement for proprietary funds. Operating and nonoperating revenues and expenses should be distinguished, with separate subtotals for operating revenues, operating expenses, and operating income.
    Answer (A) is incorrect. Nonoperating revenues and expenses are presented immediately after operating income (loss). Moreover, special and extraordinary items are reported separately. Answer (B) is incorrect. Revenues are reported by major source either net with disclosure of discounts and allowances or gross with discounts and allowances reported beneath the revenue amounts. Answer (D) is incorrect. A government should consistently follow appropriate definitions of operating items. The GASB provides general guidelines and mandates consistent use of definitions, but it does not require that the categorization of items in the statement of cash flows control the definitions of operating items in the statement of revenues, expenses, and changes in fund net assets.

96. Dogwood City's water enterprise fund received interest of $10,000 on long-term investments. How should this amount be reported on the statement of cash flows?

    A. Operating activities.

    B. Noncapital financing activities.

    C. Capital and related financing activities.

    D. Investing activities.

Answer (D) is correct. *(CPA, adapted)*
    REQUIRED: The classification of interest received on long-term investments in the statement of cash flows of a governmental utility.
    DISCUSSION: The GASB requires reporting of cash flows of proprietary funds and entities engaged in business-type activities, e.g., public benefit corporations and authorities, governmental utilities, governmental healthcare providers, and public colleges and universities. Cash flows should be classified as operating, financing, and investing. Investing activities include making and collecting loans (other than program loans) and acquiring and disposing of debt and equity instruments. Cash inflows from investing include interest and dividends received as returns on loans (not program loans), debt of other entities, equity securities, and each management or investment pools. Thus, interest on investments is a cash inflow from an investing activity.
    Answer (A) is incorrect. Operating activities are all transactions and other events that are not classified as either financing or investing activities. In general, operating activities involve transactions and other events, the effects of which are included in the determination of operating income. Answer (B) is incorrect. Noncapital financing activities include borrowings for purposes other than acquiring, constructing, or improving capital assets and debt. Cash flows may include grants and subsidies received or paid, tax receipts, debt proceeds, and cash received from or paid to other funds (excluding flows from interfund services provided or used). Answer (C) is incorrect. Capital and related financing activities include borrowings and repayments of debt related to acquiring, constructing, or improving capital assets; acquiring and disposing of capital assets used to provide goods or services; and paying for capital assets obtained on credit.

97. A state or local government must present which financial statements for proprietary funds?

I.   A statement of activities
II. A statement in net assets or balance sheet format
III. A statement of cash flows

   A. I only.

   B. I and III only.

   C. II and III only.

   D. I, II, and III.

Answer (C) is correct. *(Publisher, adapted)*
REQUIRED: The statement(s) required for proprietary funds.
DISCUSSION: Proprietary funds emphasize determination of operating income, changes in net assets (or cost recovery), financial position, and cash flows. A statement of net assets or balance sheet is required for proprietary funds, with assets and liabilities classified as current or noncurrent. Either a net assets format (assets – liabilities = net assets) or a balance sheet format (assets = liabilities + net assets) may be used. A statement of revenues, expenses, and changes in fund net assets or fund equity (either label may be used) is the required operating statement for proprietary funds. A statement of cash flows also is required for proprietary funds. However, the direct method (including a reconciliation of operating cash flows to operating income) must be used. The direct method reports major classes of gross operating cash receipts and payments and their sum (net cash flow from operating activities). The minimum classes to be reported are cash receipts from customers, cash receipts from interfund services provided, other operating cash receipts, cash payments to employees for services, cash payments to other suppliers, cash payments for interfund services used, and other operating cash payments.
Answer (A) is incorrect. A statement of activities is a government-wide statement. Answer (B) is incorrect. Proprietary funds also must report a statement in net assets or balance sheet format. Answer (D) is incorrect. Proprietary funds report a statement in net assets or balance sheet format; a statement of revenues, expenses, and changes in fund net assets or fund equity; and a statement of cash flows. However, a statement of activities is a government-wide statement.

98. In a statement of net assets or balance sheet for proprietary funds,

   A. Net assets must be reported in two components: restricted or unrestricted.

   B. Capital contributions must be reported in a separate component of net assets.

   C. Designations must be shown on the face of the statement.

   D. Assets and liabilities must be classified.

Answer (D) is correct. *(Publisher, adapted)*
REQUIRED: The appropriate display in the statement of net assets or balance sheet for proprietary funds.
DISCUSSION: A statement of net assets or balance sheet is required for proprietary funds, and assets and liabilities must be classified as current or noncurrent. Either a net assets format (assets – liabilities = net assets) or a balance sheet format (assets = liabilities + net assets) may be used. Furthermore, net assets should be reported in three components (invested in capital assets, net of related debt; restricted; and unrestricted), capital contributions should not be displayed as a separate component, and designations should not be shown on the face of the statements.
Answer (A) is incorrect. Net assets should be reported in three components, including invested in capital assets, net of related debt. Answer (B) is incorrect. One of the three components of net assets is not capital contributions. Answer (C) is incorrect. Designations are removable at the discretion of the reporting government and should not be reported in the statement.

99. A statement of cash flows for proprietary funds

   A. Is optional.

   B. Must be prepared using either the direct method or the indirect method.

   C. Must be prepared using the direct method.

   D. Need not reconcile operating cash flows to operating income if the direct method is used.

Answer (C) is correct. *(Publisher, adapted)*
REQUIRED: The true statement about the statement of cash flows for proprietary funds.
DISCUSSION: A statement of cash flows is required for proprietary funds. However, the direct method (including a reconciliation of operating cash flows to operating income) must be used. The direct method reports major classes of gross operating cash receipts and payments and their sum (net cash flow from operating activities). The minimum classes to be reported are cash receipts from customers, cash receipts from interfund services provided, other operating cash receipts, cash payments to employees for services, cash payments to other suppliers, cash payments for interfund services used, and other operating cash payments.
Answer (A) is incorrect. A statement of cash flows for proprietary funds is required. Answer (B) is incorrect. The direct method is required. Answer (D) is incorrect. The reconciliation is required.

100. The summary of significant accounting policies must make which of the following general disclosures?

A. The policy for applying FASB pronouncements issued before November 30, 1989, to business-type activities.

B. The policy for defining operating and nonoperating revenues of proprietary funds.

C. The measurement focus and basis of accounting of the fund financial statements.

D. The capital acquisitions for the period presented by major classes.

Answer (B) is correct. *(Publisher, adapted)*
REQUIRED: The general disclosure required to be made in the summary of significant accounting policies.
DISCUSSION: A government should have a policy that defines operating items in a way that is consistent with the nature of the activity, disclose that policy in the summary of significant accounting policies, and apply it consistently. How transactions are categorized in a statement of cash flows is a consideration in defining operating items for proprietary funds. For example, cash flows classified as from capital and related financing activities, noncapital financing activities, and investing activities ordinarily are not included in operating income.
Answer (A) is incorrect. A government must apply all nonconflicting FASB Statements and Interpretations, APB Opinions, and ARBs issued on or before November 30, 1989. It must disclose its election regarding whether to apply nonconflicting FASB guidance issued after November 30, 1989, that were developed for business entities. Answer (C) is incorrect. A government must disclose in the summary of significant accounting policies the measurement focus and basis of accounting used in the government-wide financial statements. Answer (D) is incorrect. The capital acquisitions for the period presented by major classes are details required to be disclosed in a note but not in the summary of significant accounting policies.

27.11 Fiduciary Funds Reporting

101. The debt service transactions of a special assessment bond issue for which the government is not obligated in any manner should be reported in a(n)

A. Agency fund.

B. Enterprise fund.

C. Special revenue fund.

D. Debt service fund.

Answer (A) is correct. *(CPA, adapted)*
REQUIRED: The reporting of debt service transactions of a special assessment bond issue for which the government is not obligated.
DISCUSSION: The debt service transactions of a special assessment issue for which the government is not obligated in any manner should be reported in an agency fund rather than a debt service fund. This treatment reflects the limitation of the government's duty to act as an agent for the assessed property owners and the bondholders.
Answer (B) is incorrect. An enterprise fund is a proprietary fund used to account for activities for which fees are charged to external users. Answer (C) is incorrect. A special revenue fund is a governmental fund used to account for the proceeds of specific revenue sources that are legally restricted and expended for a specific purpose. Answer (D) is incorrect. The government is not obligated for this special assessment bond issue.

102. Glen County uses governmental fund accounting and is the administrator of a multiple-jurisdiction deferred compensation plan covering both its own employees and those of other governments participating in the plan. This plan is an eligible deferred compensation plan under the U.S. Internal Revenue Code and Income Tax Regulations, and it meets the criteria for a pension (and other employee benefit) trust fund. Glen has legal access to the plan's $40 million in assets, of which $2 million pertain to Glen and $38 million to the other participating governments. In Glen's balance sheet, what amount should be reported in an agency fund for plan assets and as a corresponding liability?

A. $0

B. $2,000,000

C. $38,000,000

D. $40,000,000

Answer (A) is correct. *(CPA, adapted)*
REQUIRED: The deferred compensation plan assets and liability to record in an agency fund.
DISCUSSION: The plan should be reported in a pension (and other employee benefit) trust fund in the statements of fiduciary net assets and changes in fiduciary net assets if it meets the criteria for that fund type. This treatment is in accordance with Internal Revenue Code. It requires all assets and income of the plan to be held in trust for the exclusive benefit of participants and their beneficiaries. Consequently, no amounts should be reported in an agency fund.
Answer (B) is incorrect. The plan must be reported as a pension (and other employee benefit) trust fund. Answer (C) is incorrect. The government is a trustee, not a mere agent. Hence, no amount is reported in an agency fund. Answer (D) is incorrect. All amounts are held in trust.

103. Which of the following is a required financial statement for an investment trust fund?

A. Statement of revenues, expenditures, and changes in fiduciary net assets.

B. Statement of activities.

C. Statement of revenues, expenses, and changes in fiduciary net assets.

D. Statement of changes in fiduciary net assets.

104. Items reported only in the fund financial statements of a general-purpose government are those arising from

A. Proprietary activities.

B. Fiduciary activities.

C. Exchange-like transactions.

D. Nonexchange-like transactions.

105. Which financial statements must be reported for fiduciary funds?

I. Statement of fiduciary net assets

II. Statement of changes in fiduciary net assets

III. Statement of revenues, expenditures, and changes in fund balances

IV. Statement of cash flows

A. I and II only.

B. I, II, and III only.

C. II, III, and IV only.

D. I, II, III, and IV.

Answer (D) is correct. *(CPA, adapted)*
REQUIRED: The required financial statement for an investment trust fund.
DISCUSSION: A sponsoring governmental entity should report the external portion of each of its external investment pools as an investment trust fund. Separate statements of fiduciary net assets and changes in fiduciary net assets should be presented for each such fund. The external portion belongs to legally separate entities not included in the reporting entity.
Answer (A) is incorrect. Fiduciary funds emphasize net assets and changes in net assets, not revenues and expenditures. Answer (B) is incorrect. A statement of activities is presented in the government-wide financial statements. Answer (C) is incorrect. Fiduciary funds emphasize net assets and changes in net assets, not revenues and expenses.

Answer (B) is correct. *(Publisher, adapted)*
REQUIRED: The items reported only in the fund financial statements.
DISCUSSION: The resources of fiduciary activities are not available to finance the government's programs. Thus, they are reported only in the fund financial statements. Fiduciary activities are reported in or with the fiduciary funds of the primary government. Fiduciary component units are reported with the primary government's fiduciary funds only in the fund financial statements.
Answer (A) is incorrect. Government-wide statements report governmental and business-type (proprietary) activities. Answer (C) is incorrect. Government-wide statements recognize exchange or exchange-like transactions when the exchange occurs. Answer (D) is incorrect. Government-wide statements recognize nonexchange-like transactions.

Answer (A) is correct. *(Publisher, adapted)*
REQUIRED: The financial statements reported by fiduciary funds.
DISCUSSION: Fiduciary fund financial statements include information about all fiduciary funds and similar component units. The statements report information in a separate column for each fund type but not by major fund. The notes present financial statements for individual pension plans and postemployment healthcare plans unless separate GAAP reports have been issued. A statement of fiduciary net assets (equivalent to the statement of plan net assets required for defined benefit pension plans) is required for fiduciary funds. It reports assets, liabilities, and net assets for each fiduciary fund type but does not present the three components of net assets reported in the government-wide statement of net assets or in the proprietary fund statement of net assets. A statement of changes in fiduciary net assets (equivalent to the statement of changes in plan net assets required for defined benefit pension plans) is required for fiduciary funds. It reports additions to, subtractions from, and the annual net change in net assets for each fiduciary fund type.
Answer (B) is incorrect. The statement of revenues, expenditures, and changes in fund balances is required for governmental funds. Answer (C) is incorrect. The statement of revenues, expenditures, and changes in fund balances is required for governmental funds; the statement of cash flows is required for proprietary funds; and the statement of fiduciary net assets and the statement of changes in fiduciary net assets are required for fiduciary funds. Answer (D) is incorrect. The statement of revenues, expenditures, and changes in fund balances is required for governmental funds, and the statement of cash flows is required for proprietary funds.

106. River City has a defined contribution pension plan. How should River report the pension plan in its financial statements?

A. Amortize any transition asset over the estimated number of years of current employees' service.

B. Disclose in the notes to the financial statements the amount of the pension benefit obligation and the net assets available for benefits.

C. Disclose in the notes to the financial statements the classes of employees covered and the employer's and employees' obligations to contribute to the fund.

D. Accrue a liability for benefits earned but not paid to fund participants.

Answer (C) is correct. *(CPA, adapted)*
REQUIRED: The method for reporting a defined contribution pension plan.
DISCUSSION: A defined contribution pension plan must report a plan description, a summary of significant accounting policies, and information about investment concentrations. The plan description should identify the plan as a defined contribution plan and disclose the number of participating employers and other contributing entities. The description also should include (1) classes of employees covered, (2) the total current membership, (3) a brief description of plan provisions, (4) the authority under which they are established (or may be amended), and (5) contribution requirements.
Answer (A) is incorrect. No transition asset arises under a defined contribution plan. Answer (B) is incorrect. A pension benefit obligation arises under a defined benefit pension plan. Answer (D) is incorrect. Under a defined contribution plan, the governmental employer's obligation is for contributions, not benefits.

107. Which of the following is a reporting requirement for agency funds?

A. They should be reported in a statement of fiduciary net assets and a statement of changes in fiduciary net assets.

B. Agency fund assets should equal liabilities in the statement of fiduciary net assets.

C. An agency fund used as a clearing account should report as assets the amounts pertaining to the other funds.

D. An agency fund should not be used as a clearing account.

Answer (B) is correct. *(Publisher, adapted)*
REQUIRED: The reporting requirement for agency funds.
DISCUSSION: Agency fund assets should equal liabilities in the statement of fiduciary net assets, but agency funds are not reported in the statement of changes in fiduciary net assets.
Answer (A) is incorrect. Agency funds are not reported in the statement of changes in fiduciary net assets. Answer (C) is incorrect. An agency fund used as a clearing account distributes resources to other funds as well as to other entities. For example, a county tax collector may distribute taxes to other funds and other governments. Assets pertaining to other funds are reported in those funds, not in the agency fund. Answer (D) is incorrect. An agency fund may be used as a clearing account to distribute resources to other funds as well as to other entities.

108. Fiduciary fund financial statements report

A. Information by major fund.

B. Three components of net assets.

C. A separate column for each fund type.

D. No separate statements for individual pension plans.

Answer (C) is correct. *(Publisher, adapted)*
REQUIRED: The reporting in fiduciary fund financial statements.
DISCUSSION: Fiduciary fund financial statements include information about all fiduciary funds and similar component units. The statements report information in a separate column for each fund type but not by major fund. The notes present financial statements for individual pension plans and postemployment healthcare plans unless separate GAAP reports have been issued. A statement of fiduciary net assets is required for fiduciary funds. It reports assets, liabilities, and net assets for each fiduciary fund type but does not present the three components of net assets reported in the government-wide statement of net assets or in the proprietary fund statement of net assets.
Answer (A) is incorrect. Major funds are reported only in governmental and enterprise fund statements. Answer (B) is incorrect. Three components of net assets are reported only in the government-wide statement of net assets and in the proprietary fund statement of net assets. Answer (D) is incorrect. Separate financial statements for individual pension plans and postemployment healthcare plans are reported in the notes. However, if separate GAAP financial statements have been issued for such plans, information is given in the notes about how those statements may be obtained.

27.12 Interfund Activity

109. On December 31 of the current year, Elm Village paid a contractor $4,500,000 for the total cost of a new Village Hall built during the current year on Village-owned land. Financing for the capital project was provided by a $3,000,000 general obligation bond issue sold at face amount on December 31 of the current year, with the remaining $1,500,000 transferred from the general fund. What account and amount should be reported in Elm's current-year financial statements for the general fund?

   A. Other financing sources control $4,500,000

   B. Expenditures control $4,500,000

   C. Other financing sources control $3,000,000

   D. Other financing uses control $1,500,000

Answer (D) is correct. *(CPA, adapted)*
REQUIRED: The account and amount to be reported in the financial statements for the general fund.
DISCUSSION: Accounting for state and local governments requires that transfers be reported as other financing sources by the governmental fund receiving the transfer and other financing uses by the governmental fund making the transfer. However, the bond issue proceeds and the cost of construction will be accounted for in the capital projects fund. Accordingly, the general fund should record only the interfund transfer out. The appropriate entry is to debit other financing uses control – interfund transfer for $1,500,000 and to credit a liability. The capital projects fund should credit other financing sources – interfund transfer for $1,500,000 and debit a receivable.
    Answer (A) is incorrect. Other financing uses control is debited to record transfers out of a fund. Furthermore, the $3,000,000 from the bond issue was not transferred in or out of the general fund. Answer (B) is incorrect. The sum paid to the contractor is reflected in the capital projects fund. Answer (C) is incorrect. The capital projects fund credits other financing sources control – bond issue proceeds for $3,000,000.

110. During the current year, a city's electric utility, which is operated as an enterprise fund, rendered billings for electricity supplied to the general fund. Which of the following accounts should be debited by the general fund?

   A. Appropriations.

   B. Expenditures.

   C. Due to electric utility enterprise fund.

   D. Other financing uses – interfund transfer-out.

Answer (B) is correct. *(CPA, adapted)*
REQUIRED: The account debited by the general fund for receipt of services supplied by an enterprise fund.
DISCUSSION: Enterprise funds are used to account for operations similar to those of private businesses. This rendition of services by the enterprise fund to the general fund is presumably at prices equivalent to external exchange values. Thus, it is classified as an interfund service provided and used. The result is revenue to the seller (the enterprise fund) and an expenditure to the buyer (the general fund). Unpaid amounts are interfund receivables or payables. The entry is to debit expenditures control and credit due to enterprise fund.
    Answer (A) is incorrect. Appropriations is debited when the budgetary accounts are closed. Answer (C) is incorrect. Due to enterprise fund should be credited. Answer (D) is incorrect. The provision of electricity is an interfund service provided and used, not an interfund transfer.

111. The following pertains to Grove City's interfund receivables and payables at December 31:

Due to special revenue
  fund from general fund $10,000
Due to agency fund from
  special revenue fund   4,000

How should Grove report these interfund amounts for the special revenue fund in its governmental fund balance sheet at December 31?

   A. As an asset of $6,000.

   B. As a liability of $6,000.

   C. As an asset of $4,000 and a liability of $10,000.

   D. As an asset of $10,000 and a liability of $4,000.

Answer (D) is correct. *(CPA, adapted)*
REQUIRED: The reporting of interfund amounts in the special revenue fund.
DISCUSSION: In a special revenue fund, funds due to the special revenue fund are receivables (assets), and funds due to another fund from the special revenue fund are payables (liabilities). Thus, Grove should report a $10,000 asset and a $4,000 liability in the special revenue fund.
    Answer (A) is incorrect. In a special revenue fund, assets are not reported net of liabilities. Answer (B) is incorrect. The amount of $6,000 is the amount of net assets. Answer (C) is incorrect. "Due to special revenue fund" is a receivable (asset), and "due from special revenue fund" is a payable (liability).

112. Interfund activity is classified as

A. Operating transfers and residual equity transfers.

B. Operating transfers, residual equity transfers, and reimbursements.

C. Quasi-external transfers and residual equity transfers.

D. Reciprocal and nonreciprocal.

Answer (D) is correct. *(Publisher, adapted)*
REQUIRED: The classification of interfund activity.
DISCUSSION: Interfund activity may be reciprocal or nonreciprocal. Reciprocal interfund activity is analogous to exchange and exchange-like transactions, for example, interfund loans and services provided and used. Nonreciprocal interfund activity is analogous to nonexchange transactions, for example, interfund transfers and reimbursements.
Answer (A) is incorrect. Authoritative guidance that has been superseded classified transfers as operating transfers and residual equity transfers. Answer (B) is incorrect. Authoritative guidance that has been superseded classified "interfund transactions" as (1) loans or advances, (2) quasi-external transactions, (3) reimbursements, and (4) transfers (operating and residual equity). Answer (C) is incorrect. Authoritative guidance that has been superseded recognized quasi-external transactions (not transfers), operating transfers, and residual equity transfers. Interfund activity is now classified as reciprocal and nonreciprocal.

113. An internal service provided and used

A. Is the internal counterpart to a nonexchange transaction.

B. Results in expenditures or expenses to buyer funds and revenues to seller funds.

C. Normally is accounted for as a reimbursement.

D. Requires recognition of an other financing source by the transferee fund and an other financing use by the transferor fund.

Answer (B) is correct. *(Publisher, adapted)*
REQUIRED: The treatment of an internal service provided and used.
DISCUSSION: Interfund services provided and used are transactions at prices equivalent to external exchange values. They result in revenues to seller funds and expenditures or expenses to buyer funds. Unpaid amounts are interfund receivables or payables.
Answer (A) is incorrect. An internal service provided and used is a reciprocal interfund activity, which is analogous to an exchange or an exchange-like transaction. Answer (C) is incorrect. Interfund services provided and used normally result in revenues to sellers and expenditures or expenses to buyers. Reimbursements are not displayed in the statements.
Answer (D) is incorrect. A transfer (nonreciprocal interfund activity) is an other financing source (use) in a transferee (transferor) governmental fund. An internal service provided and used is reciprocal interfund activity.

114. Through an internal service fund, New County operates a centralized data processing center to provide services to New's other governmental units. This internal service fund billed New's parks and recreation fund $150,000 for data processing services. What account should New's internal service fund credit to record this $150,000 billing to the parks and recreation fund?

A. Data processing department expenses.

B. Interfund transfers.

C. Interfund reimbursements.

D. Operating revenues control.

Answer (D) is correct. *(CPA, adapted)*
REQUIRED: The account to be credited by an internal service fund to record a billing to other governmental units.
DISCUSSION: Interfund services provided and used are sales and purchases of goods and services at prices equivalent to external exchange values. They result in revenues to seller funds and expenditures or expenses to buyer funds. Unpaid amounts are interfund receivables or payables. Thus, billings issued for services rendered by an internal service data processing center to other governmental units should be recorded as a debit to a receivable and a credit to operating revenues control.
Answer (A) is incorrect. The services provided should be recorded as a revenue, not a decrease in an expense.
Answer (B) is incorrect. Interfund services provided and used are reciprocal interfund activities. Interfund transfers are nonreciprocal interfund activities. Answer (C) is incorrect. Interfund services provided and used are reciprocal interfund activities. Interfund reimbursements are nonreciprocal interfund activities.

STUDY UNIT TWENTY-EIGHT
NOT-FOR-PROFIT ENTITIES

Introduction

Nongovernmental not-for-profit entities (NFPs) have three characteristics. They (1) have transactions that are infrequent in businesses, such as grants and contributions; (2) have no single indicator of performance, such as net income; and (3) report net assets rather than equity. They include, among other possibilities, private institutions of higher learning, healthcare entities, and voluntary health and welfare entities (VHWEs).

External financial reporting by NFPs should help external users assess (1) the **services** an entity provides and its ability to continue to provide those services and (2) how managers discharge their **stewardship** responsibilities and other aspects of their performance.

Other objectives are to provide information about (1) the liquidity of the entity, (2) economic resources, (3) obligations, (4) net resources, and (5) changes in items (1) through (4). Financial accounting and reporting as of the end of the reporting period is based on a **net assets model**. Net assets equals the residual interest in the assets of an NFP that remains after subtracting its liabilities. Net assets is divided into the following classes based on the presence or absence of donor restrictions: (1) permanently restricted, (2) temporarily restricted, and (3) unrestricted. Changes in the classes of net assets, including the effects of reclassification, also must be reported. The net assets model emphasizes combined information for the entity as a whole, not individual funds. **Fund accounting** is not required for external reporting, but it may be used for internal purposes. Separate fund information may be disclosed in external financial reports if the required combined information is reported.

Financial Statements

A complete set of financial statements for an NFP includes a statement of financial position as of the end of the reporting period, a statement of activities and a statement of cash flows for the reporting period (see Study Unit 19), and accompanying notes. The presentation of accounts is similar to that required or permitted for businesses.

A **statement of financial position** reports total amounts of assets, liabilities, and net assets. Assets and liabilities are combined into reasonably homogeneous groups. Information about liquidity is provided by (1) sequencing assets according to their nearness of conversion to cash and liabilities according to their nearness to their maturity and resulting use of cash, (2) classifying assets and liabilities as current and noncurrent, or (3) disclosing relevant information in notes to the financial statements. Amounts of net assets are classified and reported as (1) unrestricted, (2) temporarily restricted, and (3) permanently restricted. These classifications are based on the existence or absence of donor-imposed restrictions. **Unrestricted net assets** result from providing goods and services and from receipts of contributions and dividends or interest, minus expenses. The only limits are the nature of the organization, its environment, its specified purposes, and contractual agreements. These assets may be **board-designated** (internally restricted). **Temporarily restricted net assets** result from restrictions removable by the passage of time (time restrictions) or by the actions of the NFP (purpose restrictions). Temporary restrictions may be for support of operating activities, investment for a specified term (term endowments), use in a specified future period, or acquisition of long-lived assets. **Permanently restricted net assets** result from asset increases and decreases subject to restrictions not removable by passage of time or by the NFP's actions. They may result from reclassifications within the classes of net assets created by donor stipulations.

A **statement of activities** reports the amount of changes in the categories of net assets for the period. It uses descriptive terminology, such as "change in net assets" or "change in equity." Events that simultaneously increase one class of net assets and decrease another (reclassifications) are reported separately. **Revenues** are reported at their gross amounts as increases in unrestricted net assets unless the use of the assets received is subject to a donor-imposed restriction. **Expenses** are reported at their gross amounts as decreases in unrestricted net assets. Information about expenses is reported by their **functional classification** in the statement of activities or in notes. Primary functional classifications are program services and supporting activities. **Program services** result in goods and services being distributed to beneficiaries, customers, or members to fulfill the purposes of the entity. Those services are the major purpose and output of the entity. They often relate to several major programs. **Supporting activities** include management and general, fund-raising, and membership-development activities. VHWEs must report a statement of functional expenses. They also must report expenses by their natural classification.

	Non-VHWE NFPs	VHWEs
Statement of financial position	×	×
Statement of activities	×	×
Statement of cash flows	×	×
Statement of functional expenses		×

Contributions

The accounting for contributions received and contributions made applies to all entities. A **contribution** is an unconditional transfer of cash or other assets to an entity or a settlement or cancelation of its liabilities. It is a voluntary nonreciprocal transfer by another entity not acting as an owner. For this purpose, assets include cash, securities, land, buildings, use of facilities or utilities, materials and supplies, intangible assets, services, and unconditional promises to give those items in the future. A promise is unconditional if the probability that the promise will not be kept is remote. An unconditional promise to give is a written or oral agreement to contribute assets to another entity. Sufficient verifiable documentation must exist before the promise may be recognized (debit a receivable and credit revenue).

Contributions received ordinarily are accounted for when received at **fair value** as credits to revenues or gains. Debits are to assets, liabilities, or expenses. If present value is used to measure the fair value of an unconditional promise to give cash, later interest accruals are recorded as contribution income (expense) by donees (donors). But an **unconditional promise to give** expected to be collected in less than 1 year may be recognized at **net realizable value**. **Contributions of services** are recognized if they (1) create or enhance nonfinancial assets, or (2) require special skills, are provided by those having such skills, and would usually be purchased if not obtained by donations. **Collections** are works of art, historical treasures, etc. that are (1) held for public exhibition, education, or research in furtherance of public service; (2) protected, kept unencumbered, cared for, and preserved; and (3) subject to a policy that requires the proceeds of their sale to be used to acquire other collection items. An NFP may choose to capitalize or not capitalize collections. Capitalization of part of the collections is not permitted. If an NFP **capitalizes collections**, items acquired in exchange transactions are recognized as assets and measured at cost. Contributed items are recognized as assets and as contributions in the appropriate net asset class and measured at fair value. If an NFP does **not capitalize collections**, no assets or contributions are recognized.

However, GAAP do not apply to transfers of assets from, or tax benefits provided by, a government to a business. Nevertheless, GAAP do not prohibit accounting for such contributions as revenues or gains. Indeed, such treatment is consistent with the accounting for most contributions.

Unrestricted contributions are reported as unrestricted revenues and increases in unrestricted net assets. **Permanently** restricted contributions are reported as restricted support and as increases in permanently restricted net assets. **Temporarily** restricted contributions are reported as restricted support and as increases in temporarily restricted net assets. However, restricted contributions may be recognized as unrestricted support when the restrictions are met in the period the contribution is received, and the entity consistently applies and discloses this policy. **Expiration** of a restriction on a contribution is recognized when the restriction expires. A restriction expires when its purpose has been fulfilled or the stipulated time has elapsed. Expirations are reported as increases in one class of net assets and decreases in another. These expirations are reclassifications that are reported as separate items.

Receipt of an **unconditional promise to give** with payment due in future periods usually is reported as restricted support and an increase in temporarily restricted net assets. However, if the donor intended to support current activities, the promise is reported as unrestricted revenue and an increase in unrestricted net assets. Contributions of **long-lived assets** received without donor restrictions may be reported as restricted support if **implying a time restriction** on their use is an established accounting policy of the recipient. Because a time restriction expires, it is temporary. **Conditional promises to give** are recognized when the conditions on which they depend are substantially met.

Contributions made by a not-for-profit entity are measured at their fair values. The donor entity recognizes them as expenses in the period made.

A donor may make a contribution to an NFP that agrees to use it on behalf of a **third party beneficiary**. A recipient NFP that accepts **cash** or other **financial assets** recognizes the **fair value** of the assets as a **liability** to the specified beneficiary when it recognizes the assets received from the donor. If the assets are **nonfinancial**, such as materials or supplies, the recipient need not recognize the assets and the liability. The recipient must disclose this accounting policy and apply it consistently. If the donor explicitly grants the recipient **variance power**, the recipient recognizes the fair value of any assets received as a contribution. Variance power is the unilateral power to redirect the use of the assets to another beneficiary.

Investments

Equity securities with readily determinable fair values and **all debt securities** are to be measured at fair value in the statement of financial position. The total change in fair value includes the change in unpaid interest on debt securities (or unpaid dividends on equity securities until the ex-dividend date) and the holding gain or loss (realized or unrealized). Purchased investments are initially recorded at cost. Those received as contributions are recorded at fair value. **Gains and losses** are reported when they occur. They are changes in unrestricted net assets unless restricted. If unrealized gains and losses were recognized in prior periods, gains and losses recognized for a current disposition of the same investments exclude the amounts previously recognized. **Investment income** is reported when earned as increases in unrestricted net assets unless restricted. Revenues and expenses ordinarily are reported at gross amounts. But investment revenues may be reported net of related expenses if the amount of expenses is disclosed. Realized and unrealized losses may be **netted** against realized and unrealized gains. Gains and income that are donor-restricted to certain uses may be reported as increases in unrestricted net assets if the **restrictions expire** in the period the gains and income are recognized. If the entity adopts this policy, it must apply the same policy to contributions, report consistently, and disclose the accounting policy.

A donor may require a gift to be invested permanently or for a specified term. The result is a **donor-restricted endowment fund**. However, under GAAP, gains and losses on the investments are changes in unrestricted net assets. If a **specific security** is to be held permanently, the gains and losses on that security are assumed to be changes in permanently restricted net assets. If the donee may **choose investments**, the **gains** are not permanently restricted. Thus, the gains (the net appreciation of the fund investments) are unrestricted or temporarily restricted if the income is unrestricted or temporarily restricted, respectively. **Losses** reduce temporarily restricted net assets. This reduction is to the extent that a donor's temporary restriction on net appreciation of the fund has not expired prior to the losses. Any remaining losses reduce unrestricted net assets. If losses reduce the fund's assets below the level required by the law or by the donor, gains restoring the fair value to the required level are increases in unrestricted net assets.

NOTE: The foregoing treatment of gains and losses assumes no legal or donor requirement to the contrary.

Healthcare Entities (HCEs)

HCEs include such entities as hospitals, nursing homes, clinics, and medical practices. They may be in the form of (1) private for-profit businesses, (2) private not-for-profit entities, or (3) governmental bodies. The typical basic **financial statements** reported by a nongovernmental HCE are the (1) statement of financial position, (2) statement of operations (may be combined with the statement of changes), (3) statement of changes in net assets (or equity if for-profit), and (4) statement of cash flows. **Revenues** of an HCE are recognized at the time a service is provided. The three principal sources of HCE revenue are patient service revenue, premium revenue, and other revenues.

Patient service revenues are recorded on an accrual basis at the provider's established rates, that is, at their **gross amount**. In the statement of operations, a provision for bad debts must be presented on a separate line as a subtraction from patient service revenue. This guidance applies to entities that recognize significant patient service revenue when services are rendered without assessing ability to pay. A substantial amount of healthcare is paid for by third-party payors, such as insurance companies and the federal government. Because the collection practices for the two types of payors are so different, the receivables are recorded separately in the accounting records. Certain patients will not pay the amounts they have been billed. Thus, an HCE establishes an allowance account. HCEs also acknowledge that certain patients cannot be expected to pay. **Charity care** amounts cannot justifiably be treated as receivables because, at the time the service is rendered, they are not expected to be paid. Accordingly, they are reductions of revenue and receivables. Moreover, HCEs do not expect to collect the full amount billed to **third-party payors**. However, the accounting treatment is not the same. These reductions are the result of contracts between the HCE and the payor. The HCE can make a reasonable estimate of these write-offs because the terms of the contract are known.

Premium revenues result from agreements to provide healthcare rather than by actually providing services. For example, an integrated delivery system may contract to provide all health-related services for a certain group within its primary service area for a specified amount per member per month.

Other revenues may be in the form of donated medicine or supplies. Occasionally, a supplier may cancel an invoice billed to an HCE. Not-for-profit HCEs also can recognize revenue from volunteer services if they either (1) create or enhance nonfinancial assets or (2) require special skills, are provided by those having such skills, and would usually be purchased if not obtained by donations. Furthermore, other revenues result from (1) providing educational programs, (2) proceeds from the sale of cafeteria meals, and (3) gifts and grants whether or not restricted to a specific purpose.

Revenues are **reported** on the statement of operations at their net amounts. **Expense** recognition by for-profit HCEs generally is the same as for other business entities. A governmental HCE's treatment of expenses resulting from nonexchange transactions depends on the type of transaction (see Study Unit 27). Not-for-profit HCEs must report three categories of **net assets** and the changes in them during the reporting period.

QUESTIONS

28.1 Introduction

1. Which of the following is ordinarily not considered one of the major distinguishing characteristics of nonbusiness entities?

A. Significant amounts of resources are provided by donors in nonreciprocal transactions.

B. There is an absence of defined, transferable ownership interests.

C. Performance indicators similar to a business enterprise's profit are readily available.

D. The primary operating purpose is not to provide goods or services at a profit.

Answer (C) is correct. *(Publisher, adapted)*
REQUIRED: The statement not ordinarily considered a major characteristic of nonbusiness entities.
DISCUSSION: SFAC 4, *Objectives of Financial Reporting by Nonbusiness Organizations*, states that the objectives of financial reporting are derived from the common interests of those who provide the resources to nonbusiness entities. Such entities ordinarily have no single indicator of performance comparable to a business entity's profit. Thus, nonbusiness entity performance is usually evaluated in terms of management stewardship.
Answer (A) is incorrect. SFAC 4 specifically gives significant amounts of resources provided by donors in nonreciprocal transactions as a distinguishing characteristic of nonbusiness entities. Answer (B) is incorrect. SFAC 4 specifically gives an absence of defined, transferable ownership interests as a distinguishing characteristic of nonbusiness entities. Answer (D) is incorrect. SFAC 4 specifically gives the primary operating purpose is not to provide goods or services at a profit as a distinguishing characteristic of nonbusiness entities.

2. Which of the following is a characteristic of nonbusiness entities?

A. Noneconomic reasons seldom underlie the decision to provide resources to nonbusiness enterprises.

B. Business and nonbusiness entities usually obtain resources in the same way.

C. Both nonbusiness and business entities use scarce resources in the production and distribution of goods and services.

D. The operating environment of nonbusiness entities ordinarily differs from that of business entities.

Answer (C) is correct. *(Publisher, adapted)*
REQUIRED: The characteristic of nonbusiness entities.
DISCUSSION: The operating environments of nonbusiness and business entities are similar in many ways. Both produce and distribute goods and services using scarce resources.
Answer (A) is incorrect. Many noneconomic factors affect decisions to provide resources to nonbusiness enterprises. Answer (B) is incorrect. Business entities obtain resources by providing goods and services. Many nonbusiness entities obtain resources from contributors and are accountable to the providers of those resources or to their representatives. Answer (D) is incorrect. The operating environments of nonbusiness and business entities are similar.

3. Net assets is an element of the financial statements of not-for-profit entities (NFPs). It

A. Is the residual interest in the assets of an NFP after subtracting its liabilities.

B. Is the change in equity during a period from transactions and other events and circumstances not involving resource providers.

C. Differs from equity in business enterprises because it is not a residual interest.

D. Consists of the probable future economic benefits obtained or controlled by a particular entity as a result of past transactions or events.

Answer (A) is correct. *(Publisher, adapted)*
REQUIRED: The definition of the net assets element of the financial statements of not-for-profit entities.
DISCUSSION: Net assets equal the residual interest in the assets of an entity that remains after subtracting its liabilities. For a business enterprise, equity (the ownership interest) is the analogue of net assets. In an NFP, which has no ownership interest in the same sense as a business enterprise, the net assets element is divided into three classes based on the presence or absence of donor-imposed restrictions.
Answer (B) is incorrect. Comprehensive income is the change in equity of a business enterprise during a period from transactions and other events and circumstances from nonowner sources. Answer (C) is incorrect. Equity and net assets are residuals. Answer (D) is incorrect. Assets, not net assets, are probable future economic benefits obtained or controlled by a particular entity as a result of past transactions or events.

4. For external reporting purposes, the not-for-profit reporting model requires information about

    A. Individual funds of the entity but not about the entity as a whole.

    B. The entity as a whole but not about individual funds.

    C. Individual funds of the entity and the entity as a whole.

    D. The entity and precludes reporting individual fund information.

Answer (B) is correct. *(Publisher, adapted)*
    REQUIRED: The information required by the not-for-profit reporting model.
    DISCUSSION: The not-for-profit reporting model emphasizes information about the entity as a whole, not individual funds. Consequently, fund accounting is no longer required for external reporting but is not precluded.

28.2 Financial Statements

5. GAAP applying to financial statements of not-for-profit entities focus on

    A. Basic information for the entity as a whole.

    B. Standardization of funds nomenclature.

    C. Inherent differences of not-for-profit entities that affect reporting presentations.

    D. Distinctions between current fund and noncurrent fund presentations.

Answer (A) is correct. *(CPA, adapted)*
    REQUIRED: The focus of GAAP applying to the statements of NFPs.
    DISCUSSION: The applicable guidance is intended to promote the relevance, understandability, and comparability of financial statements issued by NFPs by requiring that certain basic information be reported. The focus of the required financial statements is on the NFP as a whole and on (1) reporting assets, liabilities, and net assets; (2) changes in net assets; (3) flows of economic resources; (4) cash flows, borrowing and repayment of borrowing, and other factors affecting liquidity; and (5) service efforts.
    Answer (B) is incorrect. GAAP do not focus on technical vocabulary but on the financial and economic status of the entity. Answer (C) is incorrect. GAAP do not focus on inherent differences in reporting but on the economic and financial status of the entity. Answer (D) is incorrect. GAAP do not focus on differences between current and noncurrent presentations but on presenting the economic and financial status of the firm.

6. Forkin Manor, a nongovernmental not-for-profit entity, is interested in having its financial statements reformatted using terminology that is more readily associated with for-profit entities. The director believes that the term "operating profit" and the practice of separating recurring and nonrecurring items more accurately depict the entity's activities. Under what condition will Forkin be allowed to use "operating profit" and to separate its recurring items from its nonrecurring items in its statement of activities?

    A. The entity reports the change in unrestricted net assets for the period.

    B. A parenthetical disclosure in the notes implies that the not-for-profit entity is seeking for-profit entity status.

    C. Forkin receives special authorization from the Internal Revenue Service that this wording is appropriate.

    D. At a minimum, the entity reports the change in permanently restricted net assets for the period.

Answer (A) is correct. *(CPA, adapted)*
    REQUIRED: The condition allowing an NFP to use the term operating profit and to separate recurring and nonrecurring items in its statement of activities.
    DISCUSSION: In its statement of activities, an NFP classifies revenues, expenses, gains, and losses within the three classes of changes in net assets (permanently restricted, temporarily restricted, and unrestricted). Within a class or classes, other classifications are permitted, for example, operating and nonoperating, expendable and nonexpendable, earned and unearned, and recurring and nonrecurring. Furthermore, a term such as operating income or operating profit is permitted when an intermediate measure of operations is reported. However, this measure must be in a financial statement that reports the change in unrestricted net assets for the period.
    Answer (B) is incorrect. The NFP need not seek for-profit status to report in the described manner. Answer (C) is incorrect. The NFP need not obtain IRS authorization to report in the described manner. Answer (D) is incorrect. The NFP should report the changes in all three classes of net assets regardless of whether additional classifications are included in the statement of activities.

7. In a statement of financial position, a not-for-profit entity should report amounts for which of the following classes of net assets?

I.   Unrestricted
II. Temporarily restricted
III. Permanently restricted

A.   I, II, and III.

B.   I and II only.

C.   I and III only.

D.   II and III only.

Answer (A) is correct. *(Publisher, adapted)*
REQUIRED: The classes of net assets reported in a statement of financial position of an NFP.
DISCUSSION: An NFP must report amounts for all three classes: permanently restricted net assets, temporarily restricted net assets, and unrestricted net assets. Information regarding the nature and amounts of permanently or temporarily restricted net assets should be provided by reporting amounts on the face of the statement or by including details in the notes to financial statements.
Answer (B) is incorrect. A not-for-profit entity should also report amounts for permanently restricted assets. Answer (C) is incorrect. A not-for-profit entity should also report amounts for temporarily restricted assets. Answer (D) is incorrect. A not-for-profit entity should also report amounts for unrestricted assets.

8. In Year 1, Gamma, a not-for-profit entity, deposited at a bank $1 million given to it by a donor to purchase endowment securities. The securities were purchased January 2, Year 2. At December 31, Year 1, the bank recorded $2,000 interest on the deposit. In accordance with the bequest, this $2,000 was used to finance ongoing program expenses in March Year 2. At December 31, Year 1, what amount of the bank balance should be included as current assets in Gamma's classified balance sheet?

A. $0

B. $2,000

C. $1,000,000

D. $1,002,000

Answer (B) is correct. *(CPA, adapted)*
REQUIRED: The amount of the bank balance classified as current assets.
DISCUSSION: An NFP may classify its assets and liabilities as current or noncurrent. Current assets are those reasonably expected to be realized in cash, sold, or consumed during the operating cycle or within 1 year, whichever is longer. Accordingly, the $2,000 of interest recorded at December 31, Year 1, should be classified as current because the bequest stipulated that it be used for ongoing program expenses. However, the $1 million restricted to the purchase of endowment securities is not classified as current. Assets received with a donor-imposed restriction limiting their use to long-term purposes should not be classified with assets available for current use.
Answer (A) is incorrect. The interest should be included in current assets. Answer (C) is incorrect. The interest, not the principal, should be included in current assets. Answer (D) is incorrect. Only the interest should be included in current assets.

9. In its statement of activities, a not-for-profit entity may report expenses as decreases in which of the following classes of net assets?

	Unrestricted	Permanently Restricted	Temporarily Restricted
A.	Yes	Yes	No
B.	Yes	No	Yes
C.	Yes	No	No
D.	Yes	Yes	Yes

Answer (C) is correct. *(Publisher, adapted)*
REQUIRED: The reporting of expenses in an NFP's statement of activities.
DISCUSSION: In a statement of activities, revenues and expenses ordinarily should be reported as gross amounts. Revenues may be reported as increases in either unrestricted or restricted (temporarily or permanently) net assets. Expenses ordinarily should be reported as decreases in unrestricted net assets. However, investment revenues, reported as increases in unrestricted or restricted net assets, may be reported net of related fees such as custodial fees and investment advisory fees provided that these fees are disclosed either on the face of the statement or in the related notes.
Answer (A) is incorrect. NFPs should report expenses as decreases in unrestricted net assets. Expenses do not decrease permanently restricted net assets. Answer (B) is incorrect. NFPs should report expenses as decreases in unrestricted net assets. Expenses do not decrease temporarily restricted net assets. Answer (D) is incorrect. NFPs should report expenses as decreases in unrestricted net assets. Expenses do not decrease permanently and temporarily restricted net assets.

10. Pharm, a nongovernmental not-for-profit entity, is preparing its year-end financial statements. Which of the following statements is required?

- A. Statement of changes in financial position.
- B. Statement of cash flows.
- C. Statement of changes in fund balance.
- D. Statement of revenue, expenses, and changes in fund balance.

Answer (B) is correct. *(CPA, adapted)*
REQUIRED: The statements required in a complete set of financial statements of not-for-profit entities.
DISCUSSION: A complete set of financial statements of an NFP includes (1) a statement of financial position as of the end of the reporting period, (2) a statement of activities, (3) a statement of cash flows for the reporting period, and (4) accompanying notes.
Answer (A) is incorrect. A statement of changes in financial position is not required for nongovernmental NFPs. Answer (C) is incorrect. A statement of changes in fund balance is not required for nongovernmental NFPs. Answer (D) is incorrect. A statement of revenue, expenses, and changes in fund balance is not required for nongovernmental NFPs.

11. For which of the following assets held by a religious entity should depreciation be recognized in the entity's general purpose external financial statements?

- A. The house of worship.
- B. A priceless painting.
- C. A nationally recognized historical treasure.
- D. Land used for a building site.

Answer (A) is correct. *(Publisher, adapted)*
REQUIRED: The asset held by an NFP for which depreciation should be recognized.
DISCUSSION: All NFPs must recognize the cost of using up long-lived tangible assets (depreciation) in their general purpose external financial statements. Hence, a building used for religious activity is ordinarily depreciable.
Answer (B) is incorrect. Depreciation does not have to be recognized for certain works of art whose economic benefit or service potential is used up so slowly that their estimated useful lives are extraordinarily long. Answer (C) is incorrect. Depreciation does not have to be recognized for historical treasures whose economic benefit or service potential is used up so slowly that their estimated useful lives are extraordinarily long. Answer (D) is incorrect. Land is normally not depreciated by any entity.

12. Health Policy Foundation (HPF), a voluntary health and welfare entity supported by contributions from the general public, included the following costs in its statement of functional expenses for the year:

Fund-raising	$1,000,000
Administrative (including data processing)	600,000
Research	200,000

HPF's functional expenses for program services included

- A. $1,800,000
- B. $1,000,000
- C. $600,000
- D. $200,000

Answer (D) is correct. *(CPA, adapted)*
REQUIRED: The amount of functional expenses for program services incurred by a VHWE.
DISCUSSION: An NFP's statement of activities or notes thereto should classify expenses by function. The major functional classes include program services and supporting services. Management and general expenses, along with fund-raising expenses, are classified in the supporting services category. Program services expenses are those directly related to the administration of programs. Of the costs given, only the research costs ($200,000) are program services expenses.
Answer (A) is incorrect. The amount of $1,800,000 includes $1,000,000 of fund-raising expenses and $600,000 of administrative expenses that should be included in supporting services expenses. Answer (B) is incorrect. The amount of $1,000,000 of fund-raising expenses should be classified as supporting services expenses. Answer (C) is incorrect. The amount of $600,000 of administrative expenses should be classified as supporting services expenses.

13. Functional expenses recorded in the general ledger of ABC, a nongovernmental not-for-profit entity, are as follows:

Soliciting prospective members	$45,000
Printing membership benefits brochures	30,000
Soliciting membership dues	25,000
Maintaining donor list	10,000

What amount should ABC report as fund-raising expenses?

- A. $10,000
- B. $35,000
- C. $70,000
- D. $110,000

Answer (A) is correct. *(CPA, adapted)*
REQUIRED: The fund-raising expenses.
DISCUSSION: The major functional classes of expenses for an NFP are program services and supporting activities. The latter include management and general, fund-raising, and membership development activities. Fund-raising expenses include maintaining donor lists ($10,000). Soliciting members and dues and printing membership benefits brochures are membership-development activities.
Answer (B) is incorrect. The amount of $35,000 includes the cost of soliciting dues, a membership-development activity. Answer (C) is incorrect. The amount of $70,000 is the cost of soliciting members and dues. Answer (D) is incorrect. Only the cost of the donor list is an expense of fund-raising.

14. For the fall semester of the current year, Micanopy University, a private not-for-profit institution, assessed its students $3,000,000 for tuition and fees. The net amount realized was only $2,500,000 because scholarships of $400,000 were granted to students and tuition remissions of $100,000 were allowed to faculty members' children attending Micanopy. What amount should Micanopy report for the period as revenues for tuition and fees?

A. $2,500,000

B. $2,600,000

C. $2,900,000

D. $3,000,000

Answer (D) is correct. *(CPA, adapted)*
REQUIRED: The amount reported as revenues for tuition and fees.
DISCUSSION: Revenues from exchange transactions are recognized in accordance with GAAP. Tuition and fees for private, not-for-profit colleges and universities are received in an exchange transaction. Thus, the full amount of the tuition assessed is reported as revenue. Tuition waivers, scholarships, and like items are recorded as expenses if given in exchange transactions. Refunds are handled by merely debiting revenues and crediting cash, so tuition is automatically reported net of refunds.
Answer (A) is incorrect. The amount of $2,500,000 assumes that only net tuition is recorded. Answer (B) is incorrect. The amount of $2,600,000 assumes that scholarships are deducted before recording tuition revenues. Answer (C) is incorrect. The amount of $2,900,000 assumes that tuition remissions are deducted before recording tuition revenues.

15. Cancer Educators, a not-for-profit entity, incurred costs of $10,000 in its combined program services and fund-raising activities. Which of the following cost allocations might Cancer report in its statement of activities?

	Program Services	Fund-Raising	General Services
A.	$0	$0	$10,000
B.	$0	$6,000	$4,000
C.	$6,000	$4,000	$0
D.	$10,000	$0	$0

Answer (C) is correct. *(CPA, adapted)*
REQUIRED: The allocation of costs for combined functions.
DISCUSSION: NFPs must provide information about expenses reported by functional classification. The $10,000 of costs should therefore be divided between program services and fund-raising.
Answer (A) is incorrect. None of the costs resulted from general services. Answer (B) is incorrect. The costs resulted from program services and fund-raising. The entire $10,000 should be allocated between those classifications. Answer (D) is incorrect. The costs resulted from both program services and fund-raising. Therefore, $10,000 should be allocated between those classifications.

16. Environs, a community foundation, incurred $10,000 in management and general expenses during the current year. In Environs' statement of activities for the current year ended December 31, the $10,000 should be reported as

A. A direct reduction of fund balance.

B. Part of supporting services.

C. Part of program services.

D. A contra account to offset revenue.

Answer (B) is correct. *(CPA, adapted)*
REQUIRED: The expense classification for management and general expenses in the statement of activities.
DISCUSSION: Two functional categories of expenses for an NFP are program services expenses and supporting services expenses. Supporting services expenses, which do not relate to the primary mission of the entity, may be further subdivided into (1) management and general expenses, (2) fund-raising expenses, and (3) membership development costs.
Answer (A) is incorrect. A direct reduction of fund balance would be the result of a transfer or a refund to a donor. Moreover, fund accounting information is not required to be externally reported. Answer (C) is incorrect. Program services expenses relate directly to the primary mission of the NFP. Answer (D) is incorrect. Only costs directly related to a certain source of support, such as a special event or estimated uncollectible pledges, may be offset against revenue.

17. The following expenditures were made by Green Services, a society for the protection of the environment:

Printing of the annual report	$12,000
Unsolicited merchandise sent to encourage contributions	25,000
Cost of an audit performed by a CPA firm	3,000

What amount should be classified as fund-raising costs in the society's statement of activities?

A. $37,000

B. $28,000

C. $25,000

D. $0

Answer (C) is correct. *(CPA, adapted)*
REQUIRED: The amount to be reported as fund-raising costs in the activity statement.
DISCUSSION: The two major classifications of expenses for an NFP are (1) program service expenses and (2) supporting services expenses. Program service expenses relate directly to the primary purpose or mission of the entity. Supporting services expenses are further classified as management and general expenses, fund-raising expenses, and membership development costs. The only cost here that is related to fund-raising is the unsolicited merchandise sent to encourage contributions.
Answer (A) is incorrect. The amount of $37,000 classifies all of the expenses as fund-raising expenses when only the unsolicited merchandise is related to fund-raising. Answer (B) is incorrect. The cost of an audit is a management-related expense. Answer (D) is incorrect. This answer assumes that none of the expenses listed are related to fund-raising when the unsolicited merchandise is a fund-raising expense.

18. On January 2 of the current year, a nonprofit botanical society received a gift of an exhaustible fixed asset with an estimated useful life of 10 years and no salvage value. The donor's cost of this asset was $20,000, and its fair value at the date of the gift was $30,000. What amount of depreciation of this asset should the society recognize in its current year financial statements?

A. $3,000

B. $2,500

C. $2,000

D. $0

Answer (A) is correct. *(CPA, adapted)*
REQUIRED: The amount of depreciation to be recognized in the financial statements.
DISCUSSION: NFPs must recognize depreciation in the statement of activities. Moreover, contributions are recorded at their fair value when received. Assuming the straight-line method is used, the amount of depreciation that the nonprofit botanical society should recognize is $3,000 [($30,000 fair value – $0 salvage value) ÷ 10 years].
Answer (B) is incorrect. Depreciation on a straight-line basis for this asset is not the average of cost and fair value. Answer (C) is incorrect. Depreciation on a straight-line basis for this asset is not based on the donor's cost. Answer (D) is incorrect. Depreciation on a straight-line basis for this asset would result in a $3,000 per year charge to depreciation. All NFPs must recognize depreciation in their statements of activity.

19. In Year 1, a nonprofit trade association enrolled five new member companies, each of which was obligated to pay nonrefundable initiation fees of $1,000. These fees were receivable by the association in Year 2. Three of the new members paid the initiation fees in Year 2, and the other two new members paid their initiation fees in Year 3. Annual dues (excluding initiation fees) received by the association from all of its members have always covered the entity's costs of services provided to its members. It can be reasonably expected that future dues will cover all costs of the entity's future services to members. Average membership duration is 10 years because of mergers, attrition, and economic factors. What amount of initiation fees from these five new members should the association recognize as revenue in Year 2?

A. $5,000

B. $3,000

C. $500

D. $0

Answer (A) is correct. *(CPA, adapted)*
REQUIRED: The amount of initiation fees to be reported as revenue.
DISCUSSION: Membership dues received or receivable in exchange transactions that relate to several accounting periods should be allocated and recognized as revenue in those periods. Nonrefundable initiation and life membership fees are recognized as revenue when they are receivable if future dues and fees can be reasonably expected to cover the costs of the entity's services. Otherwise, they are amortized to future periods. Hence, given that future dues are expected to cover the entity's costs, the $5,000 in nonrefundable initiation fees should be recognized as revenue when assessed and reported as such in the Year 2 statement of activities.
Answer (B) is incorrect. The full amount of nonrefundable initiation fees that are receivable in Year 2 are also recognized as revenue, provided that future dues and fees can be reasonably expected to cover costs of the entity's services. Answer (C) is incorrect. The full amount of nonrefundable initiation fees are not recognized by being allocated across the average membership duration. Answer (D) is incorrect. The full amount of all nonrefundable initiation fees is recognized as revenue, provided that future dues and fees can be reasonably expected to cover costs of the entity's services.

Questions 20 through 22 are based on the following information. United Together, a labor union, had the following receipts and expenses for the current year ended December 31:

Receipts:		Expenses:	
Per capita dues	$680,000	Labor negotiations	$500,000
Initiation fees	90,000	Fund-raising	100,000
Sales of organizational supplies	60,000	Membership development	50,000
Gift restricted by donor for loan		Administrative and general	200,000
purposes for 10 years	30,000		
Gift restricted by donor for loan		Additional information: The union's constitution provides that 10% of the per capita dues are designated for the Strike Insurance Fund to be distributed for strike relief at the discretion of the union's executive board.	
purposes in perpetuity	25,000		

20. In United Together's statement of activities for the current year ended December 31, what amount should be reported as revenue?

A. $795,000

B. $830,000

C. $825,000

D. $885,000

Answer (D) is correct. *(CPA, adapted)*
REQUIRED: The amount classified as revenue.
DISCUSSION: NFPs generate resources through contributions, exchange transactions, and agency transactions. Revenues are recognized on contributions and exchange transactions. Contributions of resources by donors result from nonreciprocal transactions. Thus, revenue includes the resources provided by (1) membership dues, (2) initiation fees, (3) sales revenue, (4) investment income, (5) gains and losses on the disposal of fixed assets and investments, (6) fees for services rendered, and (7) the contributions received as restricted support. United Together should recognize $885,000 ($680,000 dues + $90,000 initiation fees + $60,000 sales + $30,000 gift + $25,000 gift) of revenue in the current year.
Answer (A) is incorrect. The initiation fees of $90,000 should be included as revenue. Answer (B) is incorrect. The revenue should include the amounts for gifts. Answer (C) is incorrect. The amount for sales of organizational supplies should be included as revenue.

21. In United Together's statement of activities for the current year ended December 31, what amount should be reported under the classification of program services expenses?

A. $850,000

B. $600,000

C. $550,000

D. $500,000

Answer (D) is correct. *(CPA, adapted)*
REQUIRED: The amount to be reported.
DISCUSSION: Program services include the expenses that relate directly to the primary missions of the NFP. These expenses include both the direct expenses clearly identified with the program and a systematic and rational allocation of indirect costs. Because the $500,000 labor negotiation expenses are the only expenses that relate directly to the primary mission of the labor union, $500,000 should be reported in the statement of activities.
Answer (A) is incorrect. Fund-raising, membership development, and administrative costs relate to supporting services. Answer (B) is incorrect. The fund-raising amount should be supporting services expenses. Answer (C) is incorrect. The expenses for membership development are supporting services expenses.

22. In United Together's statement of activities for the current year ended December 31, what amount should be reported under the classification of restricted support?

A. $55,000

B. $30,000

C. $25,000

D. $0

Answer (A) is correct. *(CPA, adapted)*
REQUIRED: The amount of restricted support.
DISCUSSION: Contributions with donor-imposed restrictions, whether temporary or permanent, are reported as restricted support. Restricted support increases temporarily or permanently restricted net assets. Thus, $55,000 ($30,000 temporarily restricted gift + $25,000 permanently restricted gift) should be reported.
Answer (B) is incorrect. The amount of $30,000 omits the nonexpendable gift in perpetuity. Answer (C) is incorrect. The amount of $25,000 omits the nonexpendable gift for loan purposes that is donor-restricted for 10 years. Answer (D) is incorrect. Both donor-restricted gifts are capital additions.

23. During the current year, Mill Foundation, a nongovernmental not-for-profit entity, received $100,000 in unrestricted contributions from the general public. Mill's board of directors stipulated that $75,000 of these contributions would be used to create an endowment. At the end of the current year, how should Mill report the $75,000 in the net assets section of the statement of financial position?

A. Permanently restricted.

B. Unrestricted.

C. Temporarily restricted.

D. Donor restricted.

Answer (B) is correct. *(CPA, adapted)*
REQUIRED: The reporting of unrestricted contributions designated as an endowment.
DISCUSSION: An internal decision to classify a portion of unrestricted net assets as a board-designated endowment (a quasi-endowment) is not a restriction. If the contributions had been restricted by the donor, the classification of the assets would have been either permanently restricted or temporarily restricted.
Answer (A) is incorrect. The contributions were not restricted by the donors. Answer (C) is incorrect. The contributions were unrestricted because the endowment was designated by the board. Answer (D) is incorrect. The board of directors, not the donors, designated a portion of the contributions as an endowment.

24. A large not-for-profit entity's statement of activities should report the net change for net assets that are

	Unrestricted	Permanently Restricted
A.	Yes	Yes
B.	Yes	No
C.	No	No
D.	No	Yes

Answer (A) is correct. *(CPA, adapted)*
REQUIRED: The changes in net assets reported in a large NFP's statement of activities.
DISCUSSION: The statement of financial position should report the amounts of permanently restricted, temporarily restricted, and unrestricted net assets. The statement of activities should report the changes in each category.

25. In the preparation of the statement of activities for a nongovernmental NFP, all expenses are reported as decreases in which of the following net asset classes?

A. Total net assets.

B. Unrestricted net assets.

C. Temporarily restricted net assets.

D. Permanently restricted net assets.

Answer (B) is correct. *(CPA, adapted)*
REQUIRED: The net asset class in which expenses are recorded by a nongovernmental NFP.
DISCUSSION: All expenses of an NFP must be reported at gross amounts as decreases in unrestricted net assets. They may be classified as operating and nonoperating, recurring and nonrecurring, or in other ways. The statement of activities or notes reported by most NFPs also must provide information about expenses reported by their functional classification.
Answer (A) is incorrect. Total net assets is not a category of net assets. Answer (C) is incorrect. Revenues, gains, and losses, not expenses, are reported in temporarily restricted net assets in appropriate cases. Answer (D) is incorrect. Permanently restricted net assets is decreased only by losses.

26. At the beginning of the year, the Baker Fund, a nongovernmental not-for-profit corporation, received a $125,000 contribution restricted to youth activity programs. During the year, youth activities generated revenues of $89,000 and had program expenses of $95,000. What amount should Baker report as net assets released from restrictions for the current year?

A. $0

B. $6,000

C. $95,000

D. $125,000

Answer (C) is correct. *(CPA, adapted)*
REQUIRED: The net assets released from restrictions for the current year.
DISCUSSION: At the time the contribution was made, net restricted assets increased by $125,000. The restriction stated that the funds were to be used for youth activity programs. The amount of actual program expenses for the year is reported under net assets released from restrictions.
Answer (A) is incorrect. The incurrence of program expenses reduced restricted net assets by fulfilling the purpose of the restriction to the extent the resources were used. Answer (B) is incorrect. The amount of $6,000 is the excess of program expenses over revenues generated by youth activities. Answer (D) is incorrect. The purpose of the restriction was fulfilled only to the extent the contribution was used for the stated purpose.

27. A nongovernmental not-for-profit entity borrowed $5,000, which it used to purchase a truck. In which section of the entity's statement of cash flows should the transaction be reported?

    A. In cash inflow and cash outflow from investing activities.

    B. In cash inflow and cash outflow from financing activities.

    C. In cash inflow from financing activities and cash outflow from investing activities.

    D. In cash inflow from operating activities and cash outflow from investing activities.

Answer (C) is correct. *(CPA, adapted)*
    REQUIRED: The section of the statement of cash flows in which the purchase of a truck is reported by a nongovernmental NFP.
    DISCUSSION: The borrowing is a cash inflow from a financing activity because it arises from issuing debt. The purchase of the truck is a cash outflow from an investing activity because it involves the acquisition of property, plant, or equipment or other productive assets.
    Answer (A) is incorrect. The cash inflow is from a financing activity. Answer (B) is incorrect. The cash outflow is from an investing activity. Answer (D) is incorrect. Although the cash outflow is from an investing activity, the cash inflow is from a financing activity.

28. Which of the following assets of a nongovernmental not-for-profit charitable entity must be depreciated?

    A. A freezer costing $150,000 for storing food for the soup kitchen.

    B. Building costs of $500,000 for construction in progress for senior citizen housing.

    C. Land valued at $1 million being used as the site of the new senior citizen home.

    D. A bulk purchase of $20,000 of linens for its nursing home.

Answer (A) is correct. *(CPA, adapted)*
    REQUIRED: The asset of a nongovernmental not-for-profit charity that must be depreciated.
    DISCUSSION: NFPs recognize depreciation for most property and equipment. Exceptions are land used as a building site and certain individual works of art and historical treasures with extremely long useful lives. A freezer is a long-lived tangible asset that is depreciable equipment.
    Answer (B) is incorrect. Construction in progress is inventory. Inventory is not depreciated. Answer (C) is incorrect. Land is not depreciated. Answer (D) is incorrect. Linens are inventory. Inventory is not depreciated.

29. In a not-for-profit entity, which of the following should be included in total expenses?

	Grants to other organizations	Depreciation
A.	Yes	Yes
B.	Yes	No
C.	No	No
D.	No	Yes

Answer (A) is correct. *(CPA, adapted)*
    REQUIRED: The item(s), if any, included in total expenses by an NFP.
    DISCUSSION: Depreciation expense is recognized for most property and equipment. Other types of expenses recognized by NFPs may include (1) salaries, (2) rent, (3) electricity, (4) interest, (5) awards to others, (6) grants to subrecipients, and (7) professional fees. These are natural classifications of expense. But NFPs must report expenses by functional classification (major classes of program services and supporting activities).
    Answer (B) is incorrect. An NFP recognizes depreciation expense. Answer (C) is incorrect. An NFP recognizes depreciation and grants to other organizations as expenses. Answer (D) is incorrect. An NFP recognizes expenses for grants to other organizations.

30. How should operating expenses for a nongovernmental not-for-profit organization be reported?

    A. Change in temporarily restricted net assets.

    B. Change in unrestricted net assets.

    C. Change in permanently restricted net assets.

    D. Contra-account to associated revenues.

Answer (B) is correct. *(CPA, adapted)*
    REQUIRED: The reporting of operating expenses for an NFP.
    DISCUSSION: Revenues are reported as increases in unrestricted net assets unless the use of the assets received is restricted. All expenses are reported as decreases in unrestricted net assets.
    Answer (A) is incorrect. Operating expenses are never reported as changes in temporarily restricted net assets. But revenues may be temporarily or permanently restricted. Answer (C) is incorrect. Operating expenses are never reported as changes in permanently restricted net assets. Answer (D) is incorrect. Operating expenses are never reported as a contra-account to associated revenues. But the entity may report an amount for excess or deficit of operating revenues over expenses if the statement reports the changes in unrestricted net assets.

31. Fenn Museum, a nongovernmental not-for-profit organization, had the following balances in its statement of functional expenses:

Education	$300,000
Fundraising	250,000
Management and general	200,000
Research	50,000

What amount should Fenn report as expenses for support services?

A. $350,000

B. $450,000

C. $500,000

D. $800,000

Answer (B) is correct. *(CPA, adapted)*
REQUIRED: The amount of expenses for support services.
DISCUSSION: The expenses of not-for-profit entities (NFPs) are classified by function: program services or support services. Program services relate to the NFP's mission or service delivery objectives. Support services are all other activities of an NFP: management and general, fundraising, and membership development. Thus, the amount of expenses for support services is $450,000 ($250,000 fundraising + $200,000 management and general). Education and research are most likely program services of the Fenn Museum.
Answer (A) is incorrect. The amount of $350,000 is the sum of education and research expenses. Answer (C) is incorrect. The amount of $500,000 is the sum of either (1) education and management and general expenses or (2) management and general, fundraising, and research expenses. Education and research are program services. Answer (D) is incorrect. The amount of $800,000 includes the expenses incurred for the program services (education and research).

32. Nongovernmental not-for-profit organizations are required to provide which of the following external financial statements?

A. Statement of financial position, statement of activities, statement of cash flows.

B. Statement of financial position, statement of comprehensive income, statement of cash flows.

C. Statement of comprehensive income, statement of cash flows, statement of gains and losses.

D. Statement of cash flows, statement of comprehensive income, statement of unrelated business income.

Answer (A) is correct. *(CPA, adapted)*
REQUIRED: The external financial statements provided by nongovernmental NFPs.
DISCUSSION: Nongovernmental NFPs must provide external financial statements that include a statement of financial position based on a net assets model. Changes in the classes of net assets, including the effects of reclassification, must be reported in a statement of activities. A statement of cash flows also must be presented. It must follow the same guidance as that applicable to cash flow statements of for-profit entities. Furthermore, a statement of activities or the notes should provide information about expenses reported by functional classification, e.g., by major classes of program services and supporting services. However, only voluntary health and welfare entities (VHWEs) are required to report a statement of functional expenses.
Answer (B) is incorrect. A statement of comprehensive income presented as one continuous statement or as two separate but consecutive statements must be presented by for-profit entities. NFPs and for-profit entities that do not have items of other comprehensive income are not subject to the requirement. Answer (C) is incorrect. An NFP does not present a statement of comprehensive income or a statement of gains and losses. It presents a statement of net assets and a statement of activities. Answer (D) is incorrect. An NFP does not present a statement of comprehensive income or a statement of unrelated business income. It presents a statement of net assets and a statement of activities.

28.3 Contributions

33. VHWE is a voluntary welfare entity funded by contributions from the general public. During Year 4, unrestricted pledges of $600,000 were received, of which it was estimated that $72,000 would be uncollectible. By the end of Year 4, $480,000 of the pledges had been collected, and it was expected that an additional $48,000 of these pledges would be collected in Year 5, with the balance to be written off as uncollectible. Donors did not specify any periods during which the donations were to be used. Also during Year 4, VHWE sold a computer for $18,000. Its cost was $21,000, and its book value was $15,000. VHWE made the correct entry to record the gain on the sale. What amount should VHWE include as unrestricted support in Year 4 for contributions?

A. $480,000

B. $528,000

C. $531,000

D. $600,000

Answer (B) is correct. *(CPA, adapted)*
REQUIRED: The net contributions.
DISCUSSION: Because donors placed no restrictions on the pledges, they are not restricted support. Moreover, the pledge receivables are expected to be collected within 1 year and should be reported at their net realizable value. Amounts estimated as uncollectible should be subtracted from pledges received, and an allowance for uncollectible pledges account should be established. Accordingly, unrestricted support from contributions equaled the net realizable value of $528,000 ($480,000 + $48,000).
Answer (A) is incorrect. The amount of $480,000 assumes that unrestricted support is recorded on a cash basis. Answer (C) is incorrect. The amount of $531,000 assumes that the gain from the sale of the computer is added to unrestricted support. The gain is considered separately under the revenue category in the statement of activities. Answer (D) is incorrect. The amount of $600,000 assumes that pledge receivables are reported on a gross basis.

34. United Donees, a not-for-profit entity, received the following pledges:

Unrestricted $400,000
Restricted for capital additions   300,000

All pledges are legally enforceable and are expected to be received in the upcoming year. The experience of United Donees indicates that 10% of all pledges prove to be uncollectible. What amount may United Donees report as a reasonable estimate of the fair value of pledges receivable?

A. $270,000

B. $360,000

C. $630,000

D. $700,000

Answer (C) is correct. *(CPA, adapted)*
REQUIRED: The amount to report as a reasonable estimate of the fair value of pledges receivable.
DISCUSSION: NFPs must recognize unconditional promises to give at fair value. The present value of estimated future cash flows is an appropriate measure of fair value. However, unconditional promises to give expected to be collected in less than 1 year may be recognized at net realizable value. United Donees may therefore report net pledges receivable of $630,000 [($400,000 + $300,000) × (1.0 − .10)].
Answer (A) is incorrect. The amount of $270,000 is based on the assumption that only the pledges "restricted for capital additions" are reported as receivables, net of 10% of the amount. Answer (B) is incorrect. The amount of $360,000 is based on the assumption that only the unrestricted pledges are reported, net of 10% of that amount. Answer (D) is incorrect. Pledges receivable expected to be collected in less than 1 year may be reported at net realizable value.

35. On December 31, Year 3, Dahlia, a nongovernmental not-for-profit entity, purchased a vehicle with $15,000 unrestricted cash and received a donated second vehicle having a fair value of $12,000. Dahlia expects each vehicle to provide it with equal service value over each of the next 5 years and then to have no residual value. Dahlia has an accounting policy implying a time restriction on gifts of long-lived assets. In Dahlia's Year 4 statement of activities, what depreciation expense should be included under changes in unrestricted net assets?

A. $0

B. $2,400

C. $3,000

D. $5,400

Answer (D) is correct. *(CPA, adapted)*
REQUIRED: The depreciation expense included under changes in unrestricted net assets.
DISCUSSION: The expiration of a restriction is recognized when it expires. Expiration occurs when the stipulated time has elapsed, the purpose of the restriction has been fulfilled, or both. It is reported separately as a reclassification in the statement of activities as net assets released from restrictions. The effect is to increase one class of net assets and decrease another. For example, an implied time restriction on a long-lived depreciable asset expires as the economic benefits are used. Depreciation expense is reported as a decrease in unrestricted net assets. Consequently, Dahlia should record a decrease in unrestricted net assets related to depreciation of $5,400 [($15,000 + $12,000) ÷ 5-year useful life], assuming no residual value.
Answer (A) is incorrect. The expiration of a restriction is recognized when it expires. Consequently, Dahlia should record a decrease in both unrestricted net assets related to depreciation. Answer (B) is incorrect. The expiration of a restriction is recognized when it expires. Consequently, Dahlia should also record a decrease in unrestricted net assets related to depreciation of the vehicle purchased with unrestricted cash. Answer (C) is incorrect. The expiration of a restriction is recognized when it expires. Consequently, Dahlia should also record a decrease in unrestricted net assets related to depreciation of the donated vehicle.

36. Pica, a nongovernmental not-for-profit entity, received unconditional promises of $100,000 expected to be collected within 1 year. Pica received $10,000 prior to year end. Pica anticipates collecting 90% of the contributions and has a June 30 fiscal year end. What amount should Pica record as contribution revenue as of June 30?

    A. $10,000

    B. $80,000

    C. $90,000

    D. $100,000

Answer (C) is correct. *(CPA, adapted)*
    REQUIRED: The contribution revenue recorded at fiscal year end.
    DISCUSSION: An unconditional promise to give may be recognized as a contribution given sufficient verifiable documentation. Contributions received ordinarily are accounted for at fair value as credits to revenues or gains and as debits to assets, liabilities, or expenses. For an unconditional promise to give, the present value of estimated future cash flows is an appropriate measure of fair value. However, unconditional promises to give expected to be collected in less than 1 year may be recognized at net realizable value. The latter amount equals $90,000 ($100,000 unconditionally promised × 90% collection percentage).
    Answer (A) is incorrect. The amount collected is $10,000. Answer (B) is incorrect. The amount collected also should be recognized as revenue. Answer (D) is incorrect. Revenue equals the net realizable value, not the gross amount promised.

37. During Year 7, Jones Foundation received the following support:

- A cash contribution of $875,000 to be used at the board of directors' discretion
- A promise to contribute $500,000 in Year 8 from a supporter who has made similar contributions in prior periods
- Contributed legal services with a value of $100,000, which Jones would have otherwise purchased

At what amounts should Jones classify and record these transactions?

	Unrestricted Revenue	Temporarily Restricted Revenue
A.	$1,375,000	$0
B.	$875,000	$500,000
C.	$975,000	$0
D.	$975,000	$500,000

Answer (D) is correct. *(CPA, adapted)*
    REQUIRED: The amounts recorded for unrestricted and temporarily restricted revenues from contributions.
    DISCUSSION: The cash contribution ($875,000) was a revenue received in Year 7 that was without restrictions. Thus, it is classified as unrestricted support and increases unrestricted net assets. The unconditional promise to give ($500,000) with the amount due in Year 8 meets the definition of a contribution, assuming sufficient evidence in the form of verifiable documentation exists to recognize a promise to give. The promisee should recognize an asset and contribution revenue. However, the unconditional promise to give is reported ordinarily as restricted support unless the circumstances clearly indicate that the donor intended support for current activities. Thus, unconditional promises of future cash amounts usually increase temporarily restricted net assets. Contributions of services are recognized as revenues at fair value ($100,000) if they require special skills (e.g., legal training), are provided by those having such special skills, and would usually be purchased if not obtained by donations. They are classified as unrestricted support because the services presumably have been rendered, and any purpose for which the resource was restricted has been fulfilled. Consequently, Jones should recognize unrestricted revenue of $975,000 ($875,000 + $100,000) and restricted revenue of $500,000.
    Answer (A) is incorrect. The promise to contribute is temporarily restricted until actually received, and the contribution of legal services should be reported as an unrestricted contribution. Answer (B) is incorrect. Contributions of services are recognized as revenues at fair value if they require special skills, are provided by those having such special skills, and would usually be purchased if not obtained by donations. Answer (C) is incorrect. The promise to contribute is temporarily restricted revenue.

38. A family lost its home in a fire. On December 25, Year 3, a philanthropist sent money to the Benevolent Society to purchase furniture for the family. The resource provider did not explicitly grant the Society the unilateral power to redirect the use of the assets. During January Year 4, the Society purchased this furniture for the Addams family. The Society, a not-for-profit entity, should report the receipt of the money in its Year 3 financial statements as a(n)

A. Unrestricted contribution.

B. Temporarily restricted contribution.

C. Permanently restricted contribution.

D. Liability.

Answer (D) is correct. *(CPA, adapted)*
REQUIRED: The reporting of a transfer to an NFP with a direction that the assets be used to aid a specific beneficiary.
DISCUSSION: Assets may be transferred to an NFP or a charitable trust that raises or holds contributions for others. The relevant guidance applies when a donor makes a contribution to a recipient entity that agrees either to use the assets for the benefit of another entity designated by the donor or to transfer the assets to the beneficiary. The recipient entity should recognize the receipt of the assets as a contribution if the donor explicitly grants the entity variance power to redirect the use of the assets or if the recipient and the beneficiary are financially interrelated. However, if neither of these conditions applies, the recipient entity should recognize the fair value of the assets as a liability.
Answer (A) is incorrect. Reporting it as an unrestricted contribution is required when the recipient has been granted variance power, or the recipient and beneficiary are financially interrelated entities. Answer (B) is incorrect. Reporting it as a temporarily restricted contribution is required when the recipient has been granted variance power, or the recipient and beneficiary are financially interrelated entities. Answer (C) is incorrect. Recording it as a permanently restricted contribution is required when the recipient has been granted variance power, or the recipient and beneficiary are financially interrelated entities.

39. In Bow Co.'s current year annual report, Bow described its social awareness expenditures during the year as follows:

The Company contributed $250,000 in cash to youth and educational programs. The Company also gave $140,000 to health and human-service entities, of which $80,000 was contributed by employees through payroll deductions. In addition, consistent with the Company's commitment to the environment, the Company spent $100,000 to redesign product packaging.

What amount of the above should be included in Bow's income statement as charitable contributions expense?

A. $310,000

B. $390,000

C. $410,000

D. $490,000

Answer (A) is correct. *(CPA, adapted)*
REQUIRED: The amount of charitable contribution expense included in the income statement.
DISCUSSION: The guidance for contributions applies to for-profit entities as well as NFPs. Bow, a for-profit entity, cannot recognize an expense for contributions by employees. In addition, the redesign of a product's package cannot be considered a contribution. A contribution is (1) an unconditional transfer of cash or other assets to an entity or (2) a settlement of its liabilities in a voluntary nonreciprocal transfer by another entity not acting as an owner. Accordingly, the charitable contribution expense is $310,000 ($250,000 + $140,000 – $80,000).
Answer (B) is incorrect. The amount of $390,000 includes the employees' charitable contribution. Answer (C) is incorrect. The amount of $410,000 includes the redesign costs.
Answer (D) is incorrect. The amount of $490,000 includes the employees' charitable contribution and the redesign costs.

40. On December 30 of the current year, the Geology Museum, a not-for-profit entity, received a $14,000,000 donation of Knight Co. shares with donor-stipulated requirements as follows:

- Shares valued at $10,000,000 are to be sold with the proceeds used to erect a public viewing building
- Shares valued at $4,000,000 are to be retained, with the dividends used to support current operations

As a consequence of the receipt of the Knight shares, how much should the museum report as temporarily restricted net assets on its current year statement of financial position?

A. $0

B. $4,000,000

C. $10,000,000

D. $14,000,000

Answer (C) is correct. *(CPA, adapted)*
REQUIRED: The amount to report as temporarily restricted net assets.
DISCUSSION: A temporary restriction permits the donee entity to expend the donated assets as stipulated. It is satisfied either by the passage of time or by actions of the entity. The shares valued at $10,000,000 meet this definition because they are to be sold and used for a specified project. A permanent restriction requires that the resources be maintained permanently. However, the entity may use up or expend part or all of the income derived. The $4,000,000 stock donation meets this definition and should be reported as permanently restricted net assets. The museum should report $10,000,000 as temporarily restricted net assets.
Answer (A) is incorrect. The shares valued at $10,000,000 are temporarily restricted. Answer (B) is incorrect. The shares valued at $4,000,000 are permanently restricted, and the shares valued at $10,000,000 have temporary restrictions. Answer (D) is incorrect. Only the shares valued at $10,000,000 have temporary restrictions.

41. The Art Museum, a not-for-profit entity, received a contribution of historical artifacts. It need not recognize the contribution if the artifacts are to be sold and the proceeds used to

A. Support general museum activities.

B. Acquire other items for collections.

C. Repair existing collections.

D. Purchase buildings to house collections.

Answer (B) is correct. *(CPA, adapted)*
REQUIRED: The circumstance under which a contribution of artifacts to be sold need not be recognized.
DISCUSSION: Contributions of such items as art works and historical treasures need not be capitalized and recognized as revenues if they are added to collections that are (1) subject to a policy that requires the proceeds of sale of collection items to be used to acquire other collection items; (2) protected, kept unencumbered, cared for, and preserved; and (3) held for public exhibition, education, or research for public service purposes rather than financial gain.
Answer (A) is incorrect. If the proceeds are used to support general museum activities, the contribution must be recognized. Answer (C) is incorrect. If the proceeds are used to repair existing collections, the contribution must be recognized. Answer (D) is incorrect. If the proceeds are used to purchase buildings to house collections, the contribution must be recognized.

42. According to GAAP applying to accounting for contributions received and contributions made, what classification(s), if any, should be used by not-for-profit entities to report receipts of contributions?

	Unrestricted Support	Restricted Support
A.	No	No
B.	No	Yes
C.	Yes	No
D.	Yes	Yes

Answer (D) is correct. *(Publisher, adapted)*
REQUIRED: The classification(s), if any, of contributions received by NFPs.
DISCUSSION: Contributions received by NFPs must be reported as restricted support or unrestricted support. Contributions with donor-imposed restrictions are reported as restricted support. Restricted support increases permanently restricted net assets or temporarily restricted net assets. Contributions without donor-imposed restrictions are reported as unrestricted support.
Answer (A) is incorrect. NFPs must record contributions as unrestricted support or restricted support. Answer (B) is incorrect. NFPs also must record contributions as unrestricted support when applicable. Answer (C) is incorrect. NFPs also must record contributions as restricted support when applicable.

Questions 43 through 45 are based on the following information. On June 30 of the current year, Older Relatives Community Assistance (ORCA), a not-for-profit entity, received a building and the land on which it was constructed as a gift from Sapient Corporation. The building is intended to support the entity's education and training mission or any other purpose consistent with the entity's mission. Immediately prior to the contribution, the fair values of the building and land had been appraised as $700,000 and $300,000, respectively. Carrying amounts on Sapient's books at June 30 of the current year were $580,000 and $150,000, respectively.

43. If ORCA does not have a policy of implying time restrictions on gifts of long-lived assets, the gift should be recorded by the entity as

	Unrestricted Support	Restricted Support
A.	$300,000	$700,000
B.	$1,000,000	$0
C.	$0	$1,000,000
D.	$150,000	$580,000

Answer (B) is correct. *(Publisher, adapted)*
REQUIRED: The amount at which a contribution of long-lived assets should be recorded by the donee.
DISCUSSION: The terms of this contribution allow the long-lived assets to be used for any purpose consistent with the NFP's mission. It does not have a policy of implying time restrictions on gifts of long-lived assets. Thus, the building and land on which it was constructed should be recorded at fair value as assets and unrestricted support.
Answer (A) is incorrect. The building also should be recorded as unrestricted support. Answer (C) is incorrect. Both the building and land should be recorded as unrestricted support. Answer (D) is incorrect. Both the building and land should be recorded at fair value as unrestricted support.

44. If ORCA has a policy of implying time restrictions on gifts of long-lived assets, the gift should be recorded by the entity as

	Unrestricted Support	Restricted Support
A.	$300,000	$700,000
B.	$1,000,000	$0
C.	$0	$1,000,000
D.	$150,000	$580,000

Answer (C) is correct. *(Publisher, adapted)*
REQUIRED: The amount at which a contribution of long-lived assets should be recorded by the donee.
DISCUSSION: The terms of this gift allow the long-lived assets to be used for any purpose consistent with the NFP's mission. In the absence of a policy implying time restrictions on gifts of long-lived assets, the contribution should be recorded as unrestricted support. However, given that ORCA has a policy of implying a time restriction, the building and land on which it was constructed should be recorded at fair value as assets and restricted support. The restriction will expire over the expected useful life of the building.
Answer (A) is incorrect. The land also should be recorded as restricted support. Answer (B) is incorrect. Both the building and the land should be recorded as restricted support. Answer (D) is incorrect. Both the building and the land should be recorded at fair value as restricted support.

45. Sapient Corporation should record its contribution of the building and land as a

A. $730,000 reduction in contributed capital.

B. $1,000,000 reduction in contributed capital.

C. $730,000 expense.

D. $1,000,000 expense.

Answer (D) is correct. *(Publisher, adapted)*
REQUIRED: The amount at which a contribution of long-lived assets should be recorded by the donor.
DISCUSSION: Contributions made should be recognized as expenses in the period made. They should be measured at the fair value of the assets contributed.
Answer (A) is incorrect. The contribution should be recorded as an expense and measured at the fair value of the assets contributed. Answer (B) is incorrect. The contribution should be recorded as an expense. Answer (C) is incorrect. The contribution should be measured at the fair value of the assets contributed.

46. Not-for-profit entities must recognize a conditional promise to give when

A. The promise is received.

B. The promise is received in writing.

C. The conditions are met.

D. It is reasonably possible that the conditions will be met.

Answer (C) is correct. *(Publisher, adapted)*
REQUIRED: The timing of recognition of a conditional promise to give.
DISCUSSION: A conditional promise to give is one that depends on the occurrence of a specified future, uncertain event to establish the promisor's obligation. It is recognized when the conditions are substantially met, i.e., when the conditional promise becomes unconditional. If the possibility is remote that the condition will not be met, the recognition criterion is satisfied.
Answer (A) is incorrect. Receipt of the promise is not sufficient for recognition of a contribution. Answer (B) is incorrect. Receipt of the written promise is not sufficient for recognition of a contribution. Answer (D) is incorrect. The possibility that the condition will not be met must be remote before a contribution is recognized.

47. Napro Charities, a not-for-profit agency, receives free electricity on a continuous basis from a local utility company. The utility company's contribution is made subject to cancelation by the donor. Napro should account for this contribution as a(n)

A. Unrestricted revenue only.

B. Restricted revenue only.

C. Unrestricted revenue and an expense.

D. Restricted revenue and an expense.

Answer (C) is correct. *(Publisher, adapted)*
REQUIRED: The amount at which a contribution of electricity should be recorded by the donee.
DISCUSSION: A contribution of utilities, such as electricity, is a contribution of other assets, not a contribution of services. A simultaneous receipt and use of utilities should be recognized as both an unrestricted revenue and an expense in the period of receipt and use. The revenue and expense should be measured at estimated fair value. This estimate can be obtained from the rate schedule used by the utility company to determine rates charged to a similar customer.
Answer (A) is incorrect. The simultaneous receipt and use of electricity should be recorded as an expense in the period of receipt and use. Answer (B) is incorrect. The simultaneous receipt and use of electricity should be recorded as an unrestricted revenue and as an expense in the period of receipt and use. Answer (D) is incorrect. The simultaneous receipt and use of electricity should be recorded as an unrestricted revenue in the period of receipt and use.

48. Oz, a nongovernmental not-for-profit entity, received $50,000 from Ame Company to sponsor a play given by Oz at the local theater. Oz gave Ame 25 tickets, which generally cost $100 each. Ame received no other benefits. What amount of ticket sales revenue should Oz record?

A. $0

B. $2,500

C. $47,500

D. $50,000

Answer (B) is correct. *(CPA, adapted)*
REQUIRED: The amount of ticket sales revenue.
DISCUSSION: This transaction involves both a contribution and an exchange. In an exchange, the parties receive and sacrifice something of approximately equal value. Hence, Oz should recognize $2,500 of ticket revenue (25 tickets × $100), the fair value of the exchange element of the transaction. The fair value of the contribution element ($50,000 – $2,500) is recorded as contribution revenue in the period received. It is classified as temporarily restricted support until it is expended in fulfillment of the donor restriction.
Answer (A) is incorrect. Ticket sales revenue is recorded to account for the exchange element of the transaction. Answer (C) is incorrect. The amount of $47,500 is the contribution revenue. Answer (D) is incorrect. The amount of $50,000 is the ticket sales revenue plus the contribution revenue.

49. Following the destruction of its house of worship by fire, a religious entity held a rebuilding party. Part of the labor was donated by professional carpenters. The remainder was donated by members of the entity. Capitalization is required for the value of the services provided by

A. The professional carpenters only.

B. The members only.

C. The professional carpenters and the members.

D. Neither the professional carpenters nor the members.

Answer (C) is correct. *(Publisher, adapted)*
REQUIRED: The contributed services to be capitalized.
DISCUSSION: Contributions of services by the professional carpenters should be capitalized. The contributions of services requiring specialized skills, such as those of carpenters and electricians, should be recognized if they are provided by individuals possessing those skills and would typically need to be purchased if not provided by donation. Furthermore, donated services creating or enhancing nonfinancial assets must be recognized even though specialized skills are not involved. Because the members' labor helped rebuild the church, their contributions of services also should be capitalized.
Answer (A) is incorrect. The church members' donated labor also should be capitalized. Answer (B) is incorrect. The services of the professional carpenters also should be capitalized. Answer (D) is incorrect. The church members' donated labor and the services of the professional carpenters should be capitalized.

50. In July Year 1, Ross irrevocably donated $200,000 cash to be invested and held in trust by a church. Ross stipulated that the revenue generated from this gift be paid to Ross during Ross's lifetime. After Ross dies, the principal is to be used by the church for any purpose chosen by its governing body. The church received interest of $16,000 on the $200,000 for the year ended June 30, Year 2, and the interest was remitted to Ross. In the church's June 30, Year 2, annual financial statements,

A. $200,000 should be reported as revenue.

B. $184,000 should be reported as revenue.

C. $16,000 should be reported as revenue.

D. The gift and its terms should be disclosed only in notes to the financial statements.

Answer (A) is correct. *(CPA, adapted)*
REQUIRED: The proper accounting for a split-interest agreement.
DISCUSSION: An NFP should report an irrevocable split-interest agreement. Assets under the control of the NFP are recorded at fair value at the time of initial recognition, and the contribution is recognized as revenue. Because the NFP has a remainder interest, it should not recognize revenue from receipt of the income of the trust. Thus, the NFP should recognize revenue of $200,000 (the presumed fair value of the contributed cash).
Answer (B) is incorrect. The contribution is not reduced by the income paid to the donor. Answer (C) is incorrect. The income paid to the donor is not revenue of the NFP. Answer (D) is incorrect. The contribution should be recognized at fair value.

51. A nongovernmental not-for-profit entity (NFP) required an audit. The fair value of the service was $60,000, but the auditor accepted only $10,000, effectively donating $50,000 worth of services. The journal entry made by the NFP after completion of the audit and payment of the reduced fee is

A. Expense $60,000
       Revenue $50,000
       Cash   10,000

B. Expense $10,000
       Cash $10,000

C. Expenditure $60,000
       Revenue $50,000
       Cash   10,000

D. Expenditure $10,000
       Cash $10,000

Answer (A) is correct. *(K. Putnam)*
REQUIRED: The entry to record donated accounting services.
DISCUSSION: Contributions of services that require specialized skills and would have to be paid for if not donated are recognized. Contributions received are recognized as (1) revenues or gains when received and (2) assets, decreases in liabilities, or expenses given the form of the benefits. Thus, the donated audit services, which do not result in capitalization of an asset, are recognized as an expense because their benefits are used up as they are provided. The entry is to debit expense and credit cash and contribution revenue.
Answer (B) is incorrect. The donated services are recognized as an expense and a revenue. Answer (C) is incorrect. NFPs are required to use full accrual accounting. These entities use the term expense rather than expenditure. Expenditures are recognized in the governmental funds of state and local governments. These funds use the modified accrual basis of accounting. Answer (D) is incorrect. An expense and revenue are recognized for donated professional services that otherwise would have to be paid for.

52. In its fiscal year ended June 30, Year 4, Barr College, a large private institution, received $100,000 designated by the donor for scholarships for superior students. On July 26, Year 4, Barr selected the students and awarded the scholarships. How should the July 26 transaction be reported in Barr's statement of activities for the year ended June 30, Year 5?

A. As both an increase and a decrease of $100,000 in unrestricted net assets.

B. As a decrease only in unrestricted net assets.

C. By footnote disclosure only.

D. Not reported.

Answer (A) is correct. *(CPA, adapted)*
REQUIRED: The treatment by a private not-for-profit entity of funds received and used for a designated purpose.
DISCUSSION: When Barr College received the contribution, it should have been classified as temporarily restricted because it was to be used for a specified purpose. Once the purpose has been fulfilled, the temporary restriction expires, and the amount should be reclassified as a decrease in temporarily restricted net assets and an increase in unrestricted net assets. When the scholarships are awarded, unrestricted net assets are decreased.
Answer (B) is incorrect. Unrestricted net assets also must be increased. Answer (C) is incorrect. A donation must be reported on the face of the statement of activities. Answer (D) is incorrect. This donation must be reported as (1) an increase and a decrease in unrestricted net assets and (2) a decrease in temporarily restricted net assets when its purpose is fulfilled and the scholarships are awarded.

53. During the current year, a voluntary health and welfare entity receives $300,000 in unrestricted pledges. Of this amount, $100,000 has been designated by donors for use next year to support operations. If 15% of the unrestricted pledges are expected to be uncollectible, what amount of unrestricted support should the entity recognize in its current-year financial statements?

    A. $300,000

    B. $270,000

    C. $200,000

    D. $170,000

Answer (D) is correct. *(CPA, adapted)*
    REQUIRED: The current-year unrestricted support to be recognized.
    DISCUSSION: Only $200,000 of the pledged total constitutes unrestricted support. These pledges may be recognized at net realizable value (NRV) if their collection is expected in less than one year. The NRV of these pledges is $170,000 [$200,000 × (1.0 – .15 estimated uncollectible)].
    Answer (A) is incorrect. This figure is the total amount of pledges. Answer (B) is incorrect. The amount of $100,000 of the pledges is restricted until the next year. Answer (C) is incorrect. The amount of $200,000 does not reflect the estimated uncollectible pledges.

54. Stanton College, a not-for-profit entity, received a building with no donor stipulations as to its use. Stanton does not have an accounting policy implying a time restriction on donated assets. What type of net assets should be increased when the building was received?

I.   Unrestricted
II. Temporarily restricted
III. Permanently restricted

    A. I only.

    B. II only.

    C. III only.

    D. II or III.

Answer (A) is correct. *(CPA, adapted)*
    REQUIRED: The classification of net assets affected by a contribution of a building.
    DISCUSSION: Contributions without donor-imposed restrictions are reported as unrestricted support, which increases unrestricted net assets. If Stanton had an accounting policy to imply a time restriction on gifts of long-lived assets, the gift of the building would be reported as temporarily restricted support even though no donor restrictions were imposed.
    Answer (B) is incorrect. Temporarily restricted net assets are increased by contributions classified as restricted support. Answer (C) is incorrect. Permanently restricted net assets are increased by contributions classified as restricted support. Answer (D) is incorrect. Temporarily and permanently restricted net assets are increased by contributions classified as restricted support.

55. A storm damaged the roof of a new building owned by K-9 Shelters, a not-for-profit entity. A supporter of K-9, a professional roofer, repaired the roof at no charge. In K-9's statement of activities, the damage and repair of the roof should

    A. Be reported by note disclosure only.

    B. Be reported as an increase in both expenses and contributions.

    C. Be reported as an increase in both net assets and contributions.

    D. Not be reported.

Answer (B) is correct. *(CPA, adapted)*
    REQUIRED: The treatment of services received at no charge by a not-for-profit entity.
    DISCUSSION: Contributions of services at fair value are recognized if they require special skills, are provided by individuals having those skills, and would have to be purchased if not received by donation. Hence, K-9 should report an expense and contribution revenue for the services received.

56. The Turtle Society, a nongovernmental not-for-profit entity (NFP), receives numerous contributed hours from volunteers during its busy season. Chris, a clerk at the local tax collector's office, volunteered 10 hours per week for 24 weeks transferring turtle food from the port to the turtle shelter. His rate of pay at the tax office is $10 per hour, and the prevailing wage rate for laborers is $6.50 per hour. What amount of contribution revenue should Turtle Society record for this service?

    A. $0

    B. $840

    C. $1,560

    D. $2,400

Answer (A) is correct. *(CPA, adapted)*
    REQUIRED: The amount of contribution revenue recorded for a volunteer's service.
    DISCUSSION: Contributions of services are recognized if they (1) create or enhance nonfinancial assets, or (2) require special skills, are provided by those having such skills, and would usually be purchased if not obtained by donations. The volunteer's efforts meet neither of these criteria. Thus, no contribution revenue is recognized.
    Answer (B) is incorrect. The amount of $840 equals 24 weeks, times 10 hours per week, times $3.50 per hour ($10 – $6.50). Answer (C) is incorrect. The amount of $1,560 equals 24 weeks, times 10 hours per week, times $6.50 per hour. Answer (D) is incorrect. The amount of $2,400 equals 24 weeks, times 10 hours per week, times $10 per hour.

57. Janna Association, a nongovernmental not-for-profit entity, received a cash gift with the stipulation that the principal be held for at least 20 years. How should the cash gift be recorded?

    A. A temporarily restricted asset.

    B. A permanently restricted asset.

    C. An unrestricted asset.

    D. A temporary liability.

Answer (A) is correct. *(CPA, adapted)*
    REQUIRED: The classification of a cash gift with a time restriction.
    DISCUSSION: Temporarily restricted net assets result from restrictions removable by the passage of time (time restrictions) or by the actions of the NFP (purpose restrictions). A stipulation that the principal be held for at least 20 years is a temporary time restriction.
    Answer (B) is incorrect. Once 20 years pass, the asset is no longer restricted. Answer (C) is incorrect. The asset cash gift is restricted for at least 20 years. Answer (D) is incorrect. Cash is an asset.

58. In July Year 3, Katie irrevocably donated $200,000 cash to be invested and held in trust by a church. Katie stipulated that the revenue generated from this gift be paid to her during her lifetime. After Katie dies, the principal is to be used by the church for any purpose chosen by its governing body. The church received interest of $16,000 on the $200,000 for the year ended June 30, Year 4, and the interest was remitted to Katie. In the church's June 30, Year 4, annual financial statements,

    A. $200,000 should be reported as revenue.

    B. $184,000 should be reported as revenue.

    C. $16,000 should be reported as revenue.

    D. The gift and its terms should be disclosed only in notes to the financial statements.

Answer (A) is correct. *(CPA, adapted)*
    REQUIRED: The proper accounting for a split-interest agreement.
    DISCUSSION: An NFP should report an irrevocable split-interest agreement. Assets under the control of the NFP are recorded at fair value at the time of initial recognition, and the contribution is recognized as revenue. Because the NFP has a remainder interest, it should not recognize revenue from receipt of the income of the trust. Thus, the NFP should recognize revenue of $200,000 (the presumed fair value of the contributed cash).
    Answer (B) is incorrect. The contribution is not reduced by the income paid to the donor. Answer (C) is incorrect. The income paid to the donor is not revenue of the NFP. Answer (D) is incorrect. The contribution should be recognized at fair value.

59. Pann, a nongovernmental not-for-profit organization, provides food and shelter to the homeless. Pann received a $15,000 gift with the stipulation that the funds be used to buy beds. In which net asset class should Pann report the contribution?

    A. Endowment.

    B. Temporarily restricted.

    C. Permanently restricted.

    D. Unrestricted.

Answer (B) is correct. *(CPA, adapted)*
    REQUIRED: The net asset class in which a gift with a stipulation is reported.
    DISCUSSION: A temporary restriction is donor-imposed. It permits the donee to use up or expend the donation as specified. It is satisfied by the passage of time or by actions of the donee. A statement of financial position of an NFP reports net assets in three classes: (1) unrestricted, (2) temporarily restricted, and (3) permanently restricted. The cash gift is reported in temporarily restricted net assets because it will be expended for the stated purpose.
    Answer (A) is incorrect. A permanent endowment requires resources to be maintained permanently. Moreover, an endowment is not a net asset class. Answer (C) is incorrect. Permanently restricted net assets are subject to restrictions not removable by the passage of time or the NFP's actions. Answer (D) is incorrect. The cash gift is restricted support.

60. Whitestone, a nongovernmental not-for-profit organization, received a contribution in December, Year 1. The donor restricted use of the contribution until March, Year 2. How should Whitestone record the contribution?

    A. Footnote the contribution in Year 1 and record as income when it becomes available in Year 2.

    B. No entry required in Year 1 and record as income in Year 2 when it becomes available.

    C. Report as income in Year 1.

    D. Report as deferred income in Year 1.

Answer (C) is correct. *(CPA, adapted)*
    REQUIRED: The recording of a time-restricted contribution.
    DISCUSSION: A nongovernmental NFP recognizes contributions received as revenues or gains in its statement of activities. A contribution by definition is unconditional, voluntary, and not reciprocal, and the donor does not act as an owner. Thus, it does not arise from an exchange transaction. A donor-imposed restriction does not preclude recognition of contribution revenue or gain (income). It merely limits the use of contributed assets.
    Answer (A) is incorrect. The contribution should be recognized. A donor-imposed restriction merely limits the use of contributed assets. Answer (B) is incorrect. The contribution should be recognized when received if it is unconditional, voluntary, and nonreciprocal, and the donor does not act as an owner. Answer (D) is incorrect. By definition, a contribution does not result in deferred revenue (income). Deferred revenue arises from exchange transactions with service beneficiaries for specific activities that have not yet occurred.

61. A nongovernmental not-for-profit animal shelter receives contributed services from the following individuals valued at their normal billing rate:

Veterinarian provides volunteer animal care	$8,000
Board members volunteer to prepare books for audit	4,500
Registered nurse volunteers as receptionist	3,000
Teacher provides volunteer dog walking	2,000

What amount should the shelter record as contribution revenue?

A. $8,000

B. $11,000

C. $12,500

D. $14,500

Answer (C) is correct. *(CPA, adapted)*
REQUIRED: The contribution revenue recognized for contributed services.
DISCUSSION: Contributions of services are recognized if they (1) create or enhance nonfinancial assets or (2) (a) require special skills, (b) are provided by those having such skills, and (c) would usually be purchased if not obtained by donations. The services provided by the veterinarian and the board members are recognized as contribution revenue. The services provided by the registered nurse and the teacher are not. Veterinary services and bookkeeping require special skills, are provided by persons with such skills (assuming the board members have accounting experience or training), and otherwise would be paid for by an animal shelter. Thus, the animal shelter should record $12,500 ($8,000 + $4,500) as contribution revenue.
Answer (A) is incorrect. The amount of $8,000 includes only the value of services provided by the veterinarian. Answer (B) is incorrect. The amount of $11,000 includes the value of services provided by the registered nurse and excludes the value of the services provided by the board members. Answer (D) is incorrect. The amount of $14,500 includes the value of the services provided by the teacher.

28.4 Investments

62. Eleemosynary Institution (EI) received a donation of equity securities with readily determinable fair values. The securities had appreciated in value after they were purchased by the donor, and they continued to appreciate through the end of EI's fiscal year. At what amount should EI report its investment in donated securities in its year-end balance sheet?

A. Donor's cost.

B. Fair value at the date of receipt.

C. Fair value at the balance sheet date.

D. Fair value at either the date of receipt or the balance sheet date.

Answer (C) is correct. *(CPA, adapted)*
REQUIRED: The valuation of donated equity securities.
DISCUSSION: In its statement of financial position, a not-for-profit entity should measure the following investments at fair value: (1) equity securities with readily determinable fair values and (2) debt securities. Thus, the total change in the fair value of the donated securities from the date of receipt to the balance sheet date must be reported in the statement of activities.
Answer (A) is incorrect. All investments to which the relevant GAAP apply are reported at fair value. Answer (B) is incorrect. All investments to which the relevant GAAP apply are reported at fair value at the balance sheet date. Answer (D) is incorrect. All investments to which the relevant GAAP apply are reported at fair value only at the balance sheet date.

63. On December 31 of the current year, Communities Organized for Social Improvement (COSI), a not-for-profit entity, holds an investment in common stock of one publicly traded entity and an investment in debt securities of another. The not-for-profit entity holds the common stock as a long-term investment and has the intent and the ability to hold the debt securities until maturity.

	Investment in Common Stock	Investment in Debt Securities
Original cost	$50,000	$35,000
Amortized cost		$28,000
Fair value	$63,000	$40,000

In the December 31 statement of financial position for the current year, COSI should value these investments as

	Investment in Common Stock	Investment in Debt Securities
A.	$50,000	$28,000
B.	$50,000	$40,000
C.	$63,000	$28,000
D.	$63,000	$40,000

Answer (D) is correct. *(Publisher, adapted)*
REQUIRED: The amount to be recorded by an NFP for investments in equity and debt securities.
DISCUSSION: GAAP applying to accounting for certain investments held by NFPs require them to measure investments in equity securities with readily determinable fair values and all investments in debt securities at fair value in the statement of financial position.
Answer (A) is incorrect. This investment should not be measured at original or amortized cost. Answer (B) is incorrect. This investment should not be measured at original cost. Answer (C) is incorrect. This investment should not be measured at amortized cost.

Questions 64 through 68 are based on the following information. Early in Year 2, a not-for-profit entity (NFP) received a $2,000,000 gift from a wealthy benefactor. This benefactor specified that the gift be invested in perpetuity with income restricted to provide speaker fees for a lecture series named for the benefactor. The NFP is permitted to choose suitable investments and is responsible for all other costs associated with initiating and administering this series. Neither the donor's stipulation nor the law addresses gains and losses on this permanent endowment. In Year 2, the investments purchased with the gift earned $50,000 in dividend income. The fair value of the investments increased by $120,000.

64. The $2,000,000 gift should be recorded in the Year 2 statement of activity as an increase in

- A. Unrestricted net assets.
- B. Temporarily restricted net assets.
- C. Permanently restricted net assets.
- D. Either unrestricted or temporarily restricted net assets.

Answer (C) is correct. *(Publisher, adapted)*
REQUIRED: The classification of a gift to be invested in perpetuity.
DISCUSSION: A donor-imposed restriction limits the use of contributed assets. This gift is unconditional in the sense that no condition is imposed on the transfer, but it includes a permanent restriction on the use of the assets. The gift should therefore be classified as an increase in permanently restricted net assets.
Answer (A) is incorrect. Recording the gift as unrestricted net assets would conflict with the donor's stipulation that the gift be invested in perpetuity, a permanent restriction. Answer (B) is incorrect. Recording the gift as temporarily restricted net assets would conflict with the donor's stipulation that the gift be invested in perpetuity, a permanent restriction. Answer (D) is incorrect. Recording the gift as either unrestricted or temporarily restricted net assets would conflict with the donor's stipulation that the gift be invested in perpetuity, a permanent restriction.

65. Three presentations in the lecture series were held in Year 2. The speaker fees for the three presentations amounted to $90,000. The not-for-profit entity used the $50,000 dividend income to cover part of the total fees. Because the board of directors did not wish to sell part of the investments, the entity used $40,000 in unrestricted resources to pay the remainder of the speaker fees. In the Year 2 statement of activity, the $50,000 of dividend income should be recorded as an increase in

- A. Unrestricted net assets.
- B. Temporarily restricted net assets.
- C. Permanently restricted net assets.
- D. Either unrestricted or temporarily restricted net assets.

Answer (D) is correct. *(Publisher, adapted)*
REQUIRED: The classification of expended dividend income generated from investments held in perpetuity.
DISCUSSION: Income from donor-restricted permanent endowments must be classified as an increase in temporarily restricted or permanently restricted net assets if the donor restricts its use. However, if the donor-imposed restrictions are met in the same reporting period as the gains and investment income are recognized, the gains and income may be reported as increases in unrestricted net assets. This accounting is permitted if the entity (1) has a similar policy for reporting contributions received, (2) reports on a consistent basis from period to period, and (3) adequately discloses its accounting policy. The temporary restriction on the $50,000 of investment income was met by expenditure in Year 2, the year the gain and income were recognized. Thus, the dividend revenue may be classified as an increase in either unrestricted or temporarily restricted net assets, depending on the NFP's accounting policy.
Answer (A) is incorrect. Investment income in these circumstances may also be reported as an increase in temporarily restricted net assets. Answer (B) is incorrect. Investment income in these circumstances may also be reported as an increase in unrestricted net assets. Answer (C) is incorrect. Investment income in these circumstances may be reported as an increase in either unrestricted or temporarily restricted net assets.

66. The NFP's accounting policy is to record gains and investment income, for which a donor-imposed restriction is met in the same accounting period as the gains and investment income are recognized, as increases in unrestricted net assets. In the Year 2 statement of activity, the $120,000 unrealized gain should be recorded as

A. A $40,000 increase in unrestricted net assets and an $80,000 increase in temporarily restricted net assets.

B. A $120,000 increase in unrestricted net assets.

C. A $120,000 increase in temporarily restricted net assets.

D. A $120,000 increase in permanently restricted net assets.

Answer (B) is correct. *(Publisher, adapted)*
REQUIRED: The classification of unrealized gain from investments held in perpetuity.
DISCUSSION: Recognition of gains and investment income as increases in unrestricted net assets is permitted if the donor-imposed restrictions are met in the same reporting period as the gains and investment income are recognized. However, the entity must (1) have a similar policy for reporting contributions received, (2) report on a consistent basis from period to period, and (3) adequately disclose its accounting policy. The temporary restriction on the income was met by expenditure in Year 1, the year the income and the gain were recognized. Thus, consistent with its policy, the NFP should treat the gain as an increase in unrestricted net assets. Given that the donor of the endowment allows the NFP to choose suitable investments and that no permanent restriction is imposed on the gain by the donor or by the law, the classification of the gain is the same as that of the income.
Answer (A) is incorrect. The entire unrealized gain, not just $40,000, should be recorded as an increase in unrestricted net assets. Answer (C) is incorrect. The unrealized gain should be recorded as unrestricted net assets, not temporarily restricted net assets. Answer (D) is incorrect. The unrealized gain should be recorded as unrestricted net assets, not permanently restricted net assets.

67. If the lecture series were not scheduled to begin until Year 3, the $50,000 dividend income would be recorded in the Year 2 statement of activity as an increase in

A. Unrestricted net assets.

B. Temporarily restricted net assets.

C. Permanently restricted net assets.

D. Either unrestricted or temporarily restricted net assets.

Answer (B) is correct. *(Publisher, adapted)*
REQUIRED: The classification of unexpended dividend income generated from investments held in perpetuity.
DISCUSSION: Gains and investment income from donor-restricted permanent endowments must be classified as increases in temporarily restricted net assets if the donor restricts the use of these resources to a specific purpose that either expires with the passage of time or can be met by actions of the entity. The restriction is temporary because it will expire when the income is expended in a future period. Moreover, the income cannot be classified as unrestricted because recognition and the expiration of the restriction do not occur in the same period.
Answer (A) is incorrect. The income cannot be classified as unrestricted because recognition and the expiration of the restriction do not occur in the same period. Answer (C) is incorrect. The restriction will expire when the income is expended in a future period. Thus, the restricted income is not classified as an increase in permanently restricted net assets. Answer (D) is incorrect. The income cannot be classified as unrestricted because recognition and the expiration of the restriction do not occur in the same period.

68. If the lecture series were not scheduled to begin until Year 3, the $120,000 unrealized gain should be recorded in the Year 3 statement of activity as an increase in

A. Unrestricted net assets.

B. Temporarily restricted net assets.

C. Permanently restricted net assets.

D. Either unrestricted or temporarily restricted net assets.

Answer (B) is correct. *(Publisher, adapted)*
REQUIRED: The classification of an unrealized gain on investments held in perpetuity.
DISCUSSION: Given that the NFP has the discretion to choose suitable investments (as opposed to holding specific securities in perpetuity), the gain is not permanently restricted absent a donor stipulation or a legal requirement. Rather, the gain has the same classification as the income. The latter is temporarily restricted because it is to be expended in a future period. Hence, the gain is also temporarily restricted.
Answer (A) is incorrect. The gain has the same classification as the income, which is temporarily restricted, not unrestricted. Answer (C) is incorrect. The gain has the same classification as the income, which is temporarily restricted, not permanently restricted. Answer (D) is incorrect. The gain has the same classification as the income, which is temporarily restricted, neither unrestricted nor temporarily restricted.

69. A not-for-profit voluntary health and welfare entity received a $500,000 permanent endowment. The donor stipulated that the income be used for a mental health program. The endowment fund reported $60,000 net decrease in fair value and $30,000 investment income. The entity spent $45,000 on the mental health program during the year. What amount of change in temporarily restricted net assets should the entity report?

    A. $75,000 decrease.

    B. $15,000 decrease.

    C. $0.

    D. $425,000 increase.

Answer (C) is correct. *(CPA, adapted)*
REQUIRED: The change in temporarily restricted net assets.
DISCUSSION: The contribution of $500,000 to be maintained in an endowment as a permanent source of income is classified as an increase in permanently restricted net assets. The income is restricted to use for a mental health program. Income from donor-restricted permanent endowments must be classified as an increase in temporarily restricted or permanently restricted net assets if the donor restricts its use. However, if the donor-imposed restrictions are met in the same reporting period as the investment income is recognized, it may be reported as an increase in unrestricted net assets, provided that the entity has a similar policy for reporting contributions received, reports on a consistent basis from period to period, and adequately discloses its accounting policy. The restriction on the use of the $30,000 of income expired when it was spent (along with the additional $15,000, presumably from other sources). Absent donor stipulations or contrary legal requirements, losses on investments of a permanent endowment reduce temporarily restricted net assets to the extent that a donor's temporary restriction on net appreciation of the fund has not expired prior to the losses. Any remaining losses are reductions of unrestricted net assets. Accordingly, in the absence of any such donor restriction, the $60,000 decrease in the fair value of the endowment's investments reduced unrestricted net assets. The effect on temporarily restricted net assets of (1) creation of the endowment, (2) the receipt and expenditure in the same period of investment income, and (3) the decline in the fair value of the principal of the endowment (absent a donor restriction) is therefore $0.
Answer (A) is incorrect. The amount of $75,000 is the sum of the fair value decrease and the excess of expenditures over income. Answer (B) is incorrect. The figure of $15,000 is the excess of the amount spent over the income. Answer (D) is incorrect. The amount of $425,000 equals the contribution minus the sum of the fair value decrease and the excess of expenditures over income.

70. Lane Foundation received a permanent endowment of $500,000 in Year 7 from Gant Enterprises. The endowment assets were invested in publicly traded securities, and Lane is permitted to choose suitable investments. Gant did not specify how gains and losses from dispositions of endowment assets were to be treated. No restrictions were placed on the use of dividends received and interest earned on fund resources. In Year 8, Lane realized gains of $50,000 on sales of fund investments and received total interest and dividends of $40,000 on fund securities. What amount of these capital gains, interest, and dividends increases unrestricted net assets?

    A. $0

    B. $40,000

    C. $50,000

    D. $90,000

Answer (D) is correct. *(CPA, adapted)*
REQUIRED: The amount of capital gains, interest, and dividends that increases unrestricted net assets.
DISCUSSION: Without an explicit donor stipulation or law to the contrary, assuming the donee is allowed to choose suitable investments, income and gains or losses on a donor-restricted endowment fund's assets are changes in unrestricted net assets. Thus, the increase in unrestricted net assets is $90,000 ($50,000 gains + $40,000 interest and dividends).
Answer (A) is incorrect. The amount of $0 assumes the income and gains are restricted. Answer (B) is incorrect. The amount of $40,000 assumes the gains are restricted. Answer (C) is incorrect. The amount of $50,000 assumes the income is restricted.

71. Maple Church has cash available for investments from contributions with different restrictions. Maple's policy is to maximize its financial resources. How may Maple pool its investments?

A. Maple may not pool its investments.

B. Maple may pool all investments but must equitably allocate realized and unrealized gains and losses among participants.

C. Maple may pool only unrestricted investments but must equitably allocate realized and unrealized gains and losses among participating funds.

D. Maple may pool only restricted investments but must equitably allocate realized and unrealized gains and losses among participating funds.

Answer (B) is correct. *(CPA, adapted)*
   REQUIRED: The true statement about pooling of investments by an NFP.
   DISCUSSION: Investment pools, including investments from contributions with different restrictions, are created for portfolio management. Ownership interests are assigned (ordinarily in terms of units) to the pool categories (participants) based on the market value of the cash and securities obtained from each participant. Current market value also determines the units allocated to additional assets placed in the pool and to value withdrawals. Investment income, realized gains and losses, and recognized unrealized gains and losses are allocated based on the units assigned.
   Answer (A) is incorrect. Pooling of investments is allowed to obtain investment flexibility and reduce risk. Answer (C) is incorrect. No prohibition exists as to the types of investments that may be pooled. Answer (D) is incorrect. All types of investments may be pooled.

72. RST Charities received equity securities valued at $100,000 as an unrestricted gift. During the year, RST received $5,000 in dividends from these securities; at year end, the securities had a fair market value of $110,000. By what amount did these transactions increase RST's net assets?

A. $100,000

B. $105,000

C. $110,000

D. $115,000

Answer (D) is correct. *(CPA, adapted)*
   REQUIRED: The increase in an NFP's net assets from an unrestricted contribution of securities that paid dividends and appreciated after receipt.
   DISCUSSION: Not-for-profit entities must measure investments in equity securities with readily determinable fair values and all investments in debt securities at fair value in the statement of financial position. Unrealized holding gains or losses (changes in fair value) are reported in the statement of activities as changes in unrestricted net assets (barring a legal or donor restriction). Investment income (e.g., dividends) is reported when earned as increases in unrestricted net assets (barring a legal or donor restriction). Accordingly, the donee's unrestricted net assets increased by $115,000 [$100,000 fair value of contribution + $5,000 in dividends + $10,000 ($110,000 – $100,000) unrealized holding gain in fair value].
   Answer (A) is incorrect. The amount of $100,000 excludes the dividends and the unrealized holding gain. Answer (B) is incorrect. The amount of $105,000 excludes the unrealized holding gain. Answer (C) is incorrect. The amount of $110,000 excludes the dividends.

73. During the current year, the local humane society, a nongovernmental not-for-profit organization, received a $100,000 permanent endowment from Cobb. Cobb stipulated that the income must be used to care for older horses that can no longer race. The endowment reported income of $8,000 in the current year. What amount of unrestricted contribution revenue should the humane society report for the current year?

A. $108,000

B. $100,000

C. $8,000

D. $0

Answer (D) is correct. *(CPA, adapted)*
   REQUIRED: The unrestricted contribution revenue from a permanent endowment.
   DISCUSSION: Without explicit or implicit restrictions, contributions are unrestricted revenues or gains (restricted support). Donor-restricted contributions are restricted revenues or gains. Cobb required that the income from the donor-restricted endowment fund be used to care for older horses. Thus, the $100,000 contribution is reported as permanently restricted, not unrestricted, contribution revenue. The income from the donor-restricted endowment fund is investment income, not contribution revenue.
   Answer (A) is incorrect. The amount of $108,000 is the sum of the permanently restricted contribution and the income. Answer (B) is incorrect. The amount of $100,000 equals the permanently restricted contribution. Answer (C) is incorrect. The amount of $8,000 equals the income from the endowment.

74. During the current year, the Finn Foundation, a nongovernmental not-for-profit organization, received a $1,000,000 permanent endowment from Chris. Chris stipulated that the income must be used to provide recreational activities for the elderly. The endowment reported income of $80,000 in the current year. What amount of permanently restricted contribution revenue should Finn report at the end of the current year?

A. $1,080,000

B. $1,000,000

C. $80,000

D. $0

Answer (B) is correct. *(CPA, adapted)*
REQUIRED: The permanently restricted contribution revenue reported given a permanent endowment and endowment income.
DISCUSSION: A permanent endowment is a donation restricted by the donor to generate investment income in perpetuity. Thus, the $1,000,000 contribution is an addition to permanently restricted net assets. Moreover, a contribution to an NFP is recognized as a revenue or a gain. Assuming that Finn's ongoing major or central operations include soliciting contributions, the donation is classified as a revenue. Because it is a permanent endowment, it is also classified as restricted support. However, the income is temporarily restricted. The restriction on the income is satisfied by the actions of the donee (use of recreational activities for the elderly).
Answer (A) is incorrect. The amount of $1,080,000 includes temporarily restricted income. Answer (C) is incorrect. The amount of $80,000 includes temporarily restricted income but not the permanently restricted contribution. Answer (D) is incorrect. The amount of $0 does not include the permanently restricted contribution.

75. A nongovernmental, not-for-profit organization received the following donations of corporate stock during the year:

	Donation 1	Donation 2
Number of shares	2,000	3,000
Adjusted basis	$ 8,000	$5,500
Fair market value at time of donation	8,500	6,000
Fair market value at year end	10,000	4,000

What net value of investments will the organization report at the end of the year?

A. $12,000

B. $13,500

C. $14,000

D. $14,500

Answer (C) is correct. *(CPA, adapted)*
REQUIRED: The net value of investments.
DISCUSSION: Investments in equity securities (corporate stock) with readily determinable fair values are measured at fair value in the statement of financial position. Accordingly, the net value of the investments at the end of the year is $14,000 ($10,000 FV at year end + $4,000 FV at year end).
Answer (A) is incorrect. The amount of $12,000 equals the sum of the adjusted basis of Donation 1 and the fair value of Donation 2 at year end. Answer (B) is incorrect. The amount of $13,500 equals the sum of the adjusted bases of Donations 1 and 2. Answer (D) is incorrect. The amount of $14,500 equals the sum of the fair values of Donations 1 and 2 at the time of the donation.

76. A nongovernmental not-for-profit organization received a $2 million gift from a donor who specified it be used to create an endowment fund that would be invested in perpetuity. The income from the fund is to be used to support a specific program in the second year and beyond. An investment purchased with the gift earned $40,000 during the first year. At the end of the first year, the fair value of the investment was $2,010,000. What is the net effect on temporarily restricted net assets at year end?

A. $0

B. $10,000 increase.

C. $40,000 increase.

D. $50,000 increase.

Answer (D) is correct. *(CPA, adapted)*
REQUIRED: The net effect on temporarily restricted net assets of receipt of a permanent endowment, investment income, and appreciation of the investments.
DISCUSSION: The donor made a cash gift. Thus, the donor did not specify that a specific security be held permanently, and the donee may choose investments. In these circumstances, the gains (net appreciation of the fund investments) are temporarily restricted if the income is temporarily restricted. Given that the income is to be used up or expended as specified by the donor, the income is temporarily restricted. Accordingly, the $10,000 gain on the permanent endowment and the $40,000 of income increase temporarily restricted net assets by $50,000.
Answer (A) is incorrect. The gain and the income are temporarily restricted. Answer (B) is incorrect. The income also is temporarily restricted. Answer (C) is incorrect. The gain also is temporarily restricted.

28.5 Healthcare Entities (HCEs)

77. Monies from educational programs of a hospital normally are included in

    A. Premium revenue.

    B. Patient service revenue.

    C. Nonoperating gains.

    D. Other revenue.

Answer (D) is correct. *(CPA, adapted)*
    REQUIRED: The classification of monies derived from educational programs of a hospital.
    DISCUSSION: Revenues of an HCE include patient service revenue, premium revenue, resident service revenue, and other revenue. Other revenue, gains, or losses derive from services other than providing healthcare services or coverage to patients, enrollees, or residents. One source of other revenue is student tuition and fees. Thus, the monies received from an educational program conducted by a hospital should be classified as other revenue.
    Answer (A) is incorrect. Premium revenue is derived from a capitation arrangement, that is, from a contract under which a prepaid healthcare plan pays a per-individual fee to a provider. Answer (B) is incorrect. Educational program revenue is not directly related to patient care and is therefore not includible in patient service revenues. Answer (C) is incorrect. Nonoperating gains typically arise from activities such as sales of investments or fixed assets.

78. Which of the following should normally be considered ongoing or central transactions for a not-for-profit hospital?

I.   Room and board fees from patients
II. Recovery room fees

    A. Neither I nor II.

    B. Both I and II.

    C. II only.

    D. I only.

Answer (B) is correct. *(CPA, adapted)*
    REQUIRED: The item(s), if any, that are ongoing or central transactions for a not-for-profit hospital.
    DISCUSSION: Revenues arise from an entity's ongoing major or central operations. Revenue from healthcare services includes inpatient and outpatient services provided directly to patients for their medical care. The resulting revenues derive from furnishing room and board and nursing services. Healthcare service revenues are also earned by the operating room, recovery room, labor and delivery room, and other ancillary departments that provide patient care.
    Answer (A) is incorrect. Both room and board fees from patients and recovery room fees are ongoing or central transactions. Answer (C) is incorrect. Room and board fees from patients are also ongoing or central transactions. Answer (D) is incorrect. Recovery room fees are also ongoing or central transactions.

79. Valley's community hospital normally includes proceeds from the sale of cafeteria meals in

    A. Deductions from dietary service expenses.

    B. Ancillary service revenues.

    C. Patient service revenues.

    D. Other revenues.

Answer (D) is correct. *(CPA, adapted)*
    REQUIRED: The classification of revenue from cafeteria meals.
    DISCUSSION: Other revenues are derived from services other than providing healthcare services or coverage to patients, residents, or enrollees. This category includes proceeds from sale of cafeteria meals and guest trays to employees, medical staff, and visitors.
    Answer (A) is incorrect. Revenues from cafeteria sales are accounted for separately and not as a component of any related expenses. Answer (B) is incorrect. "Ancillary service revenues" is not a proper classification for hospital revenues. Answer (C) is incorrect. Patient service revenues are healthcare services revenues.

80. Under Cura Hospital's established rate structure, healthcare services revenues of $9,000,000 would have been earned for the current year ended December 31. However, only $6,750,000 was collected because of charity allowances of $1,500,000 and discounts of $750,000 to third-party payors. For the current year ended December 31, what amount should Cura report as net healthcare services revenues in the statement of operations?

A. $6,750,000

B. $7,500,000

C. $8,250,000

D. $9,000,000

Answer (A) is correct. *(CPA, adapted)*
   REQUIRED: The healthcare services revenues reported in the statement of operations.
   DISCUSSION: Gross healthcare services revenues do not include charity care, which is disclosed separately in the notes to the financial statements. Moreover, such revenues are reported in the financial statements net of contractual and other adjustments. Thus, healthcare services revenues are recorded in the accounting records at the gross amount (excluding charity care) of $7,500,000 but reported in the financial statements at the net realizable value of $6,750,000.
   Answer (B) is incorrect. The amount of $7,500,000 equals gross revenues. Answer (C) is incorrect. The amount of $8,250,000 assumes that charity allowances are included in gross and net revenues. Answer (D) is incorrect. Charity care is excluded from gross revenue, and contractual adjustments are subtracted to arrive at net revenue.

81. In healthcare accounting, restricted net assets are

A. Not available unless the directors remove the restrictions.

B. Restricted as to use only for board-designated purposes.

C. Not available for current operating use; however, the income generated is available for current operating use.

D. Restricted as to use by the donor, grantor, or other source of the resources.

Answer (D) is correct. *(CPA, adapted)*
   REQUIRED: The definition of restricted net assets.
   DISCUSSION: In healthcare entity accounting, the term "restricted" is used to describe resources that have been restricted as to their use by the donors or grantors of those resources. Temporarily restricted net assets are those donor-restricted net assets that can be used by the not-for-profit entity for their specified purpose once the donor's restriction is met. Permanently restricted net assets are those with donor restrictions that do not expire with the passage of time and cannot be removed by any actions taken by the entity.
   Answer (A) is incorrect. Donor restrictions are not removable by the board. Temporary restrictions expire by passage of time or by actions by the entity consistent with the donor's restrictions. Answer (B) is incorrect. Board-designated restrictions are board-removable. Answer (C) is incorrect. Income generated by restricted net assets can be restricted for specific purposes.

82. Palma Hospital's patient service revenue for services provided in the current year at established rates amounted to $8,000,000 on the accrual basis. For internal reporting, Palma uses the discharge method. Under this method, patient service revenue is recognized only when patients are discharged, with no recognition given to revenue accruing for services to patients not yet discharged. Patient service revenue at established rates using the discharge method amounted to $7,000,000 for the current year. According to generally accepted accounting principles, Palma should report patient service revenue for the current year of

A. Either $8,000,000 or $7,000,000, at the option of the hospital.

B. $8,000,000.

C. $7,500,000.

D. $7,000,000.

Answer (B) is correct. *(CPA, adapted)*
   REQUIRED: The amount of patient service revenue to be reported.
   DISCUSSION: The general principle is that gross service revenue is recorded on the accrual basis at the healthcare entity's established rates, regardless of whether it expects to collect the full amount. Contractual and other adjustments are also recorded on the accrual basis and subtracted from gross service revenue to arrive at net service revenue. Charity care is excluded from service revenue for financial reporting purposes. Thus, the discharge method currently used by Palma Hospital for internal reporting is not acceptable under GAAP. In its general purpose external financial statements, Palma should report $8,000,000 of patient service revenue based on established rates.
   Answer (A) is incorrect. The $7,000,000 resulting from the discharge method is not acceptable under GAAP. Answer (C) is incorrect. The amount of $7,500,000 is the average of the $8,000,000 accrual basis amount and the $7,000,000 discharge method amount. Answer (D) is incorrect. The $7,000,000 resulting from the discharge method is not acceptable under GAAP.

83. In April of the current year, Delta Hospital purchased medicines from Field Pharmaceutical Co. at a cost of $5,000. However, Field notified Delta that the invoice was being canceled and that the medicines were being donated to Delta. Delta should record this donation of medicines as

A. A memorandum entry only.

B. A $5,000 credit to nonoperating expenses.

C. A $5,000 credit to operating expenses.

D. Other operating revenue of $5,000.

Answer (D) is correct. *(CPA, adapted)*
REQUIRED: The accounting for a donation of medicine.
DISCUSSION: Contributions of noncash assets that are not long-lived are reported at fair value in the statement of operations. Donated medicines, office supplies, and other materials that normally would be purchased by a hospital should be credited at fair value as other revenue because they directly relate to ongoing major operations but are not derived from services directly provided to patients, residents, or enrollees.
Answer (A) is incorrect. Donated assets should be recorded at their fair value when received. Answer (B) is incorrect. This donation should be credited to another revenue account or a gain account. It is not a nonoperating expense. Answer (C) is incorrect. This donation should be credited to another revenue account or a gain account. It is not an operating expense.

84. Which of the following normally is included in the other revenue, gains, or losses of a hospital?

	Fees from Educational Programs	Unrestricted Gifts
A.	No	No
B.	No	Yes
C.	Yes	No
D.	Yes	Yes

Answer (D) is correct. *(CPA, adapted)*
REQUIRED: The items(s), if any, included in other revenue, gains, or losses of a hospital.
DISCUSSION: Other revenue, gains, or losses may appropriately be recognized by a hospital for services other than healthcare or coverage provided to patients, residents, or enrollees. Other revenue, gains, or losses may include cafeteria sales, fees from educational programs, sales of medical supplies, and office space rentals. Revenue or expense results from an entity's ongoing major or central operations. Gains or losses result from peripheral or incidental transactions and from all transactions and other events and circumstances that do not generate revenue or expense (SFAC 6). Thus, contributions, either unrestricted or for a specific purpose, should be treated as gains unless fundraising is an ongoing major activity of the hospital. They are recognized at fair value.
Answer (A) is incorrect. A hospital normally recognizes fees from its educational programs and unrestricted gifts as other revenue, gains, or losses. Answer (B) is incorrect. A hospital normally recognizes fees from its educational programs as other revenue, gains, or losses. Answer (C) is incorrect. Unrestricted gifts are usually classified as other revenue, gains, or losses unless fundraising is an ongoing major activity of the hospital.

85. An organization of high school seniors performs services for patients at Leer Hospital. These students are volunteers and perform services that the hospital would not otherwise provide, such as wheeling patients in the park and reading to patients. They donated 5,000 hours of service to Leer in the current year. At a minimum wage rate, these services would amount to $18,750, while it is estimated that the fair value of these services was $25,000. In Leer's current year statement of activities, what amount should be reported as nonoperating revenue?

A. $25,000

B. $18,750

C. $6,250

D. $0

Answer (D) is correct. *(CPA, adapted)*
REQUIRED: The nonoperating revenue to record for services by volunteers.
DISCUSSION: Contributed services are recognized if they (1) create or enhance nonfinancial assets or (2) require special skills, are provided by persons possessing those skills, and would ordinarily be purchased if not provided by donation. Hence, the hospital should report no revenue. Nonfinancial assets are not involved, and no special skills, such as those of professionals or craftsmen, are required.
Answer (A) is incorrect. The volunteered services do not meet the criteria for revenue recognition of contributions. The fair value amount should not be recorded. Answer (B) is incorrect. The volunteered services do not meet the criteria for revenue recognition of contributions. The estimated hourly wage should not be recorded. Answer (C) is incorrect. The volunteered services do not meet the criteria for revenue recognition of contributions. No amount should be recorded.

86. General purpose external financial reporting by a healthcare entity requires presentation of

A. Fund group information by a not-for-profit entity.

B. A statement of operations.

C. A separate statement of changes in equity, net assets, or fund balance.

D. A performance indicator only by for-profit entities.

Answer (B) is correct.   *(Publisher, adapted)*
REQUIRED: The true statement about external reporting by a healthcare entity.
DISCUSSION: The basic financial statements of a healthcare entity include a balance sheet; a statement of operations; a statement of changes in equity, net assets, or fund balance; and a statement of cash flows.
Answer (A) is incorrect. Fund accounting may be used for internal purposes but is not required or encouraged for external reporting. Answer (C) is incorrect. The statement of changes in equity, net assets, or fund balance may be combined with the statement of operations. Answer (D) is incorrect. The statement of operations of all HCEs, including NFPs, should report a performance indicator and other changes in net assets.

Use Gleim **EQE Test Prep** Software Download for interactive study and performance analysis.

APPENDIX A
SUBUNIT CROSS-REFERENCES TO INTERMEDIATE AND ADVANCED FINANCIAL ACCOUNTING TEXTBOOKS

This section contains the tables of contents of current intermediate and advanced financial accounting textbooks with cross-references to the related subunits or study units in this study manual. The texts are listed in alphabetical order by the first author. As you study a particular chapter in your intermediate or advanced textbook, you can easily determine which subunit(s) to study in your Gleim EQE material.

Professors and students should note that, even though new editions of the texts listed below may be published as you use this study material, the new tables of contents usually will be very similar, if not the same. Thus, this edition of *Financial Accounting Exam Questions and Explanations* will remain current and useful.

If you are using a textbook that is not included in this list or if you have any suggestions on how we can improve these cross-references to make them more relevant/useful, please submit your request/feedback at www.gleim.com/crossreferences/FIN or email them to FINcrossreferences@gleim.com.

INTERMEDIATE ACCOUNTING TEXTBOOKS

Horngren, Harrison Jr., and Oliver, *Accounting: The Financial Chapters*, Ninth Edition, Prentice Hall, 2012.

Kieso, Weygandt, and Warfield, *Intermediate Accounting*, Fourteenth Edition, John Wiley & Sons, Inc., 2012.

Needles and Powers, *Financial Accounting*, Eleventh Edition, South-Western College Publishing Co., 2012.

Nikolai, Bazley, and Jones, *Intermediate Accounting Update*, Eleventh Edition, South-Western College Publishing Co., 2010.

Spiceland, Sepe, and Nelson, *Intermediate Accounting*, Seventh Edition, McGraw-Hill, Inc., 2013.

Stice and Stice, *Intermediate Accounting*, Eighteenth Edition, South-Western College Publishing Co., 2012.

Warren, Reeve, and Duchac, *Corporate Financial Accounting*, Eleventh Edition, South-Western College Publishing Co., 2012.

ADVANCED ACCOUNTING TEXTBOOKS

Baker, Christensen, and Cottrell, *Advanced Financial Accounting*, Ninth Edition, McGraw-Hill, Inc., 2011.

Beams, Anthony, Bettinghaus, and Smith, *Advanced Accounting*, Eleventh Edition, Prentice Hall, Inc., 2012.

Fischer, Taylor, and Cheng, *Advanced Accounting*, Eleventh Edition, South-Western College Publishing Co., 2011.

Halsey and Hopkins, *Advanced Accounting*, First Edition, Cambridge Business Publishers, 2012.

Hamlen, Huefner, and Largay, *Advanced Accounting*, Second Edition, Cambridge Business Publishers, 2013.

Hoyle, Schaefer, and Doupnik, *Advanced Accounting*, Tenth Edition, McGraw-Hill, Inc., 2011.

Jeter and Chaney, *Advanced Accounting*, Fifth Edition, John Wiley & Sons, Inc., 2012.

INTERMEDIATE ACCOUNTING TEXTBOOKS

Horngren, Harrison Jr., and Oliver, *Accounting: The Financial Chapters,* **Ninth Edition, Prentice Hall, 2012.**

Chapter   1 - Accounting and the Business Environment - SU 1
Chapter   2 - Recording Business Transactions - SU 2
Chapter   3 - The Adjusting Process - SU 2
Chapter   4 - Completing the Accounting Cycle - SU 2
Chapter   5 - Merchandising Operations - 6.1
Chapter   6 - Merchandise Inventory - SU 6
Chapter   7 - Internal Control and Cash - 5.2
Chapter   8 - Receivables - 5.3-5.5
Chapter   9 - Plant Assets and Intangibles - SU 7, SU 9
Chapter 10 - Current Liabilities and Payroll - SU 11
Chapter 11 - Long-Term Liabilities, Bonds Payable, and Classification of Liabilities on the Balance Sheet - SU 12
Chapter 12 - Corporations, Paid-In Capital, and the Balance Sheet - N/A
Chapter 13 - Corporations: Effects on Retained Earnings and the Income Statement - SU 3
Chapter 14 - Statement of Cash Flows - SU 19
Chapter 15 - Financial Statement Analysis - SU 22

Kieso, Weygandt, and Warfield, *Intermediate Accounting,* **Fourteenth Edition, John Wiley & Sons, Inc., 2012.**

Chapter   1 - Financial Accounting and Accounting Standards - 1.7-1.9
Chapter   2 - Conceptual Framework Underlying Financial Accounting - 1.1-1.5
Chapter   3 - The Accounting Information System - 2.1-2.4
Chapter   4 - Income Statement and Related Information - SU 3
Chapter   5 - Balance Sheet and Statement of Cash Flows - SU 19
Chapter   6 - Accounting and the Time Value of Money - SU 4
Chapter   7 - Cash and Receivables - 5.2-5.6
Chapter   8 - Valuation of Inventories: A Cost Basis Approach - 6.1-6.4
Chapter   9 - Inventories: Additional Valuation Issues - 6.5-6.7
Chapter 10 - Acquisition and Disposition of Property, Plant, and Equipment - SU 7
Chapter 11 - Depreciation, Impairments, and Depletion - 7.5, SU 8
Chapter 12 - Intangible Assets - SU 9
Chapter 13 - Current Liabilities and Contingencies - SU 11
Chapter 14 - Long-Term Liabilities - SU 12
Chapter 15 - Stockholders' Equity - SU 15
Chapter 16 - Dilutive Securities and Earnings Per Share - 16.1-16.2
Chapter 17 - Investments - SU 10
Chapter 18 - Revenue Recognition - 1.5, SU 21
Chapter 19 - Accounting for Income Taxes - SU 17
Chapter 20 - Accounting for Pensions and Postretirement Benefits - 11.4, SU 13
Chapter 21 - Accounting for Leases - SU 14
Chapter 22 - Accounting Changes and Error Analysis - SU 18
Chapter 23 - Statement of Cash Flows - SU 19
Chapter 24 - Full Disclosure in Financial Reporting - 10.7, SU 20

Needles and Powers, *Financial Accounting,* **Eleventh Edition, South-Western College Publishing Co., 2012.**

Chapter   1 - Uses of Accounting Information and the Financial Statements - 1.7-1.8, 2.1
Chapter   2 - Analyzing Business Transactions - 2.1, 2.3
Chapter   3 - Measuring Business Income - SU 3
Chapter   4 - Financial Reporting and Analysis - SU 20, SU 22
Chapter   5 - The Operating Cycle and Merchandising Operations - 6.1
Chapter   6 - Inventories - SU 6
Chapter   7 - Cash and Receivables - 5.2-5.6
Chapter   8 - Current Liabilities and Fair Value Accounting - SU 4, SU 11
Chapter   9 - Long-Term Assets - SUs 7-9
Chapter 10 - Long-Term Liabilities - SU 12
Chapter 11 - Stockholders' Equity - SU 15
Chapter 12 - The Statement of Cash Flows - SU 19
Chapter 13 - Financial Performance Measurement - SU 22
Chapter 14 - Investments - SU 10

Nikolai, Bazley, and Jones, *Intermediate Accounting Update,* **Eleventh Edition, South-Western College Publishing Co., 2010.**

Spiceland, Sepe, and Nelson, *Intermediate Accounting,* **Seventh Edition, McGraw-Hill, Inc., 2013.**

Stice and Stice, *Intermediate Accounting*, Eighteenth Edition, South-Western College Publishing Co., 2012.

Warren, Reeve, and Duchac, *Corporate Financial Accounting*, Eleventh Edition, South-Western College Publishing Co., 2012.

ADVANCED ACCOUNTING TEXTBOOKS

Baker, Christensen, and Cottrell, *Advanced Financial Accounting*, **Ninth Edition, McGraw-Hill, Inc., 2011.**

Chapter   1 - Intercorporate Acquisitions and Investments in Other Entities - 24.1
Chapter   2 - Reporting Intercorporate Investments - 24.2-24.4
Chapter   3 - The Reporting Entity and Consolidated Financial Statements - 24.2-24.4
Chapter   4 - Consolidation of Wholly Owned Subsidiaries - 24.1, 24.2
Chapter   5 - Consolidation of Less-than-Wholly-Owned Subsidiaries - 24.1, 24.2
Chapter   6 - Intercompany Inventory Transactions - 24.5, 24.8
Chapter   7 - Intercompany Transfers of Services and Noncurrent Assets - 25.5, 24.8
Chapter   8 - Intercompany Indebtedness - 24.5, 24.8
Chapter   9 - Consolidation Ownership Issues - 24.1-24.5
Chapter 10 - Additional Consolidation Reporting Issues - 24.6-24.8
Chapter 11 - Multinational Accounting: Foreign Currency Transactions and Financial Instruments - 26.2
Chapter 12 - Multinational Accounting: Translation of Foreign Entity Statements - 26.1
Chapter 13 - Segment and Interim Reporting - 20.4, SU 25
Chapter 14 - SEC Reporting - N/A
Chapter 15 - Partnerships: Formation, Operation, and Changes in Membership - SU 23
Chapter 16 - Partnerships: Liquidation - 23.5
Chapter 17 - Governmental Entities: Introduction and General Fund Accounting - 27.1-27.3
Chapter 18 - Governmental Entities: Special Funds and Government-wide Financial Statements - SU 27
Chapter 19 - Not-for-Profit Entities - SU 28
Chapter 20 - Corporations in Financial Difficulty - N/A

Beams, Anthony, Bettinghaus, and Smith, *Advanced Accounting*, **Eleventh Edition, Prentice Hall, Inc., 2012.**

Chapter   1 - Business Combinations - 24.1-24.5
Chapter   2 - Stock Investments – Investor Accounting and Reporting - 10.1-10.3
Chapter   3 - An Introduction to Consolidated Financial Statements - 24.5-24.8
Chapter   4 - Consolidation Techniques and Procedures - 24.5-24.8
Chapter   5 - Intercompany Profit Transactions – Inventories - 24.5, 24.8
Chapter   6 - Intercompany Profit Transactions – Plant Assets - 24.5, 24.8
Chapter   7 - Intercompany Profit Transactions – Bonds - 24.5, 24.8
Chapter   8 - Consolidations – Changes in Ownership Interests - N/A
Chapter   9 - Indirect and Mutual Holdings - N/A
Chapter 10 - Subsidiary Preferred Stock, Consolidated Earnings per Share, and Consolidated Income Taxation - N/A
Chapter 11 - Consolidation Theories, Push-Down Accounting, and Corporate Joint Ventures - 24.1, 24.3-24.5
Chapter 12 - Derivatives and Foreign Currency: Concepts and Common Transactions - SU 26
Chapter 13 - Accounting for Derivatives and Hedging Activities - SU 26
Chapter 14 - Foreign Currency Financial Statements - SU 26
Chapter 15 - Segment and Interim Financial Reporting - 20.4, SU 25
Chapter 16 - Partnerships – Formation, Operations, and Changes in Ownership Interests - SU 23
Chapter 17 - Partnership Liquidation - 23.5
Chapter 18 - Corporate Liquidations and Reorganizations - N/A
Chapter 19 - An Introduction to Accounting for State and Local Governmental Units - 27.1-27.3
Chapter 20 - Accounting for State and Local Governmental Units – Governmental Funds - 27.4-27.9
Chapter 21 - Accounting for State and Local Governmental Units – Proprietary and Fiduciary Funds - 27.10, 27.11
Chapter 22 - Accounting for Not-for-Profit Organizations - SU 28
Chapter 23 - Estates and Trusts - N/A

Fischer, Taylor, and Cheng, *Advanced Accounting*, Eleventh Edition, South-Western College Publishing Co., 2011.

Chapter   1 - Business Combinations: New Rules for a Long-Standing Business Practice - 24.1
Chapter   2 - Consolidated Statements: Date of Acquisition - 24.2
Chapter   3 - Consolidated Statements: Subsequent to Acquisition - 24.2-24.5
Chapter   4 - Intercompany Transactions: Merchandise, Plant Assets, and Notes - 24.5, 24.8
Chapter   5 - Intercompany Transactions: Bonds and Leases - 24.5, 24.8
Chapter   6 - Cash Flows, EPS, Taxation - N/A
Chapter   7 - Special Issues in Accounting for an Investment in a Subsidiary - 24.5-24.8
Chapter   8 - Subsidiary Equity Transactions, Indirect Subsidiary Ownership, and Subsidiary Ownership of Parent Shares - 24.5
Chapter   9 - The International Accounting Environment - SU 26
Chapter 10 - Foreign Currency Transactions - 26.2
Chapter 11 - Translation of Foreign Financial Statements - 26.1
Chapter 12 - Interim Reporting and Disclosures about Segments of an Enterprise - 20.4, SU 25
Chapter 13 - Partnerships: Characteristics, Formation, and Accounting for Activities - 23.1, 23.2
Chapter 14 - Partnerships: Ownership Changes and Liquidations - 23.3-23.5
Chapter 15 - Governmental Accounting: The General Fund and the Account Groups - 27.1, 27.2
Chapter 16 - Governmental Accounting: Other Governmental Funds, Proprietary Funds, and Fiduciary Funds - 27.3-27.11
Chapter 17 - Financial Reporting Issues - N/A
Chapter 18 - Accounting for Private Not-for-Profit Organizations - 28.1-28.4
Chapter 19 - Accounting for Not-for-Profit Colleges and Universities and Health Care Organizations - 28.5
Chapter 20 - Estates and Trusts: Their Nature and the Accountant's Role - N/A
Chapter 21 - Debt Restructuring, Corporate Reorganizations, and Liquidations - 12.6

Halsey and Hopkins, *Advanced Accounting*, First Edition, Cambridge Business Publishers, 2012.

Chapter   1 - Accounting for Intercorporate Investments - SU 24
Chapter   2 - Introduction to the Consolidation Process - 24.1-24.5
Chapter   3 - Consolidated Financial Statements Subsequent to the Date of Acquisition - 24.5-24.8
Chapter   4 - Consolidated Financial Statements and Intercompany Transactions - 24.5, 24.8
Chapter   5 - Consolidated Financial Statements with Less than 100% Ownership - 24.1-24.5
Chapter   6 - Accounting for Foreign Currency Transactions and Derivatives - SU 26
Chapter   7 - Consolidation of Foreign Subsidiaries - 26.1, 26.2
Chapter   8 - Government Accounting: Fund-Based Financial Statements - SU 27
Chapter   9 - Government Accounting: Government-Wide Financial Statements - 27.7, 27.8
Chapter 10 - Accounting for Not-for-Profit Organizations - SU 28
Chapter 11 - Segment Disclosures and Interim Financial Reporting - 20.4, SU 25
Chapter 12 - Accounting for Partnerships - SU 23

Hamlen, Huefner, and Largay, *Advanced Accounting*, Second Edition, Cambridge Business Publishers, 2013.

Chapter   1 - Intercorporate Investments: An Overview - SU 24
Chapter   2 - Mergers and Acquisitions - SU 24
Chapter   3 - Consolidated Financial Statements: Date of Acquisition - 24.2-24.5
Chapter   4 - Consolidated Financial Statements Subsequent to Acquisition - 24.5-24.8
Chapter   5 - Consolidated Financial Statements: Outside Interests - 24.5-24.8
Chapter   6 - Consolidated Financial Statements: Intercompany Transactions - 24.5, 24.8
Chapter   7 - Consolidating Foreign Currency Financial Statements - SU 26
Chapter   8 - Foreign Currency Transactions and Hedging - SU 26
Chapter   9 - Futures, Options and Interest Rate Swaps - 10.6
Chapter 10 - State and Local Governments: Introduction and General Fund Transactions - SU 27
Chapter 11 - State and Local Governments: Other Transactions - SU 27
Chapter 12 - State and Local Governments: External Financial Reporting - SU 27
Chapter 13 - Private Not-For-Profit Organizations - SU 28
Chapter 14 - Partnership Accounting and Reporting - SU 23
Chapter 15 - Bankruptcy and Reorganization - N/A
Chapter 16 - The SEC and Financial Reporting - N/A

Hoyle, Schaefer, and Doupnik, *Advanced Accounting*, Tenth Edition, McGraw-Hill, Inc., 2011.

Jeter and Chaney, *Advanced Accounting*, Fifth Edition, John Wiley & Sons, Inc., 2012.

INDEX

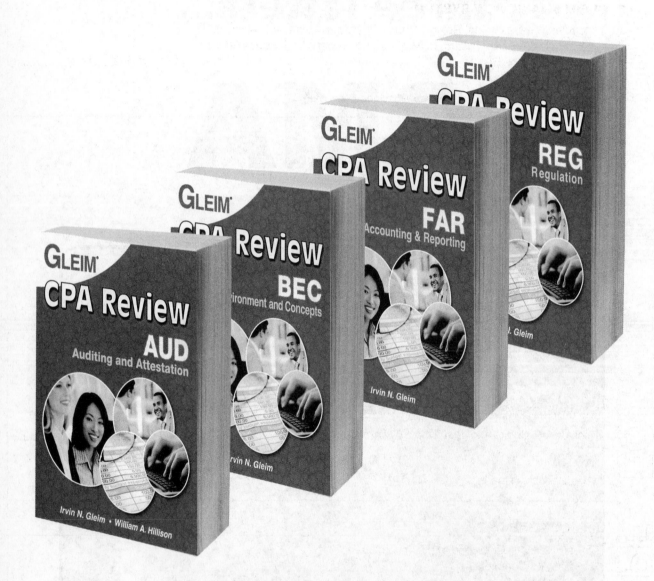

GLEIM CPA REVIEW SYSTEM

All 4 sections, including Gleim Online, Review Books, *Test Prep Software Download*, *Simulation Wizard*, Audio Review, *CPA Review: A System for Success* Booklet, plus bonus Book Bag.

$989.95 x _____ = $_____

Also available by exam section (does not include Book Bag).

GLEIM CMA REVIEW SYSTEM

Includes: Gleim Online, Review Books, *Test Prep Software Download*, Audio Review, *Essay Wizard*, *CMA Review: A System for Success* Booklet, plus bonus Book Bag.

$739.95 x _____ = $_____

Also available by exam part (does not include Book Bag).

GLEIM CIA REVIEW SYSTEM

Includes: Gleim Online, Review Books, *Test Prep Software Download*, Audio Review, *CIA Review: A System for Success* Booklet, plus bonus Book Bag.

$824.95 x _____ = $_____

Also available by exam part (does not include Book Bag).

GLEIM EA REVIEW SYSTEM

Includes: Gleim Online, Review Books, *Test Prep Software Download*, Audio Review, *EA Review: A System for Success* Booklet, plus bonus Book Bag.

$629.95 x _____ = $_____

Also available by exam part (does not include Book Bag).

"THE GLEIM EQE SERIES" EXAM QUESTIONS AND EXPLANATIONS

Includes: 5 Books and *Test Prep Software Download*.

$112.25 x _____ = $_____

Also available by part.

GLEIM ONLINE CPE

Try a FREE 4-hour course at gleim.com/cpe
- Easy-to-Complete
- Informative
- Effective

Contact
GLEIM PUBLICATIONS
for further assistance:

gleim.com
800.874.5346
sales@gleim.com

SUBTOTAL $_____

Complete your order on the next page

GLEIM® PUBLICATIONS, INC.

P. O. Box 12848   Gainesville, FL 32604

TOLL FREE:	800.874.5346	Customer service is available (Eastern Time):
LOCAL:	352.375.0772	8:00 a.m. - 7:00 p.m., Mon. - Fri.
FAX:	352.375.6940	9:00 a.m. - 2:00 p.m., Saturday
INTERNET:	gleim.com	Please have your credit card ready,
EMAIL:	sales@gleim.com	or save time by ordering online!

SUBTOTAL (from previous page) $_____

Add applicable sales tax for shipments within Florida. _____

Shipping (nonrefundable) 14.00

TOTAL $_____

Email us for prices/instructions on shipments outside the 48 contiguous states, or simply order online.

NAME (please print) _____

ADDRESS _____ Apt. _____

(street address required for UPS/Federal Express)

CITY _____ STATE _____ ZIP _____

_____ MC/VISA/DISC/AMEX _____ Check/M.O. Daytime Telephone (_____)

Credit Card No. _____ - _____ - _____ - _____

Exp. _____ / _____ Signature _____
   Month / Year

Email address _____

1. We process and ship orders daily, within one business day over 98.8% of the time. Call by 3:00 pm for same day service.
2. Gleim Publications, Inc. guarantees the immediate refund of all resalable texts, unopened and un-downloaded Test Prep Software, and unopened and un-downloaded audios returned within 30 days. Accounting and Academic Test Prep online courses may be canceled within 30 days if no more than the first study unit or lesson has been accessed. In addition, Online CPE courses may be canceled within 30 days if no more than the Introductory Study Questions have been accessed. Accounting Practice Exams may be canceled within 30 days of purchase if the Practice Exam has not been started. Aviation online courses may be canceled within 30 days if no more than two study units have been accessed. This policy applies only to products that are purchased directly from Gleim Publications, Inc. No refunds will be provided on opened or downloaded Test Prep Software or audios, partial returns of package sets, or shipping and handling charges. Any freight charges incurred for returned or refused packages will be the purchaser's responsibility.
3. Please PHOTOCOPY this order form for others.
4. No CODs. Orders from individuals must be prepaid.

Subject to change without notice. 07/12

For updates and other important information, visit our website.

GLEIM
KNOWLEDGE
TRANSFER
SYSTEMS®